VARIETY Film Reviews 1907-1980

A SIXTEEN-VOLUME SET,

Including an Index to Titles

Garland Publishing, Inc.
New York and London
1985

Contents

OF THE SIXTEEN-VOLUME SET

VOLUME SIXTEEN

Edited by Debra Handy

Garland Publishing, Inc.
New York and London
1985

Library of Congress Cataloging in Publication Data
Main entry under title:

Variety film reviews, 1907–1980

   Contents: v. 1. 1907–1920—v. 2.—1921–1925—
[etc.]—v. 16. Index to titles.

   1. Moving-pictures—Reviews.   I. Daily variety.
PN1995.V34   1983   791.43′75   82-15691
ISBN 0-8240-5200-5 (v. 1)
ISBN 0-8240-5215-3 (v. 16)

Manufactured in the United States of America

Printed on acid-free,
250-year-life paper

Preface

The reviews contained in these volumes are complete and comprehensive reproductions of the original reviews printed in *Variety*, which first took note of the film branch of show business in 1907. Coverage of film was spasmodic in the early years and was, in fact, discontinued between March 1911 and January 1913, when reviews became a more regular, permanent feature of the publication.

It should be noted that even though *Variety* did not list running times until March 1923, it was not until July 1927 that they distinguished feature length from short subjects. This compilation, therefore, reproduces all films reviewed until July 1927, after which time only feature length films are included.

User's Guide

The Variety Title Index has been created as a companion index to the fifteen-volume Garland Publication, *Variety Film Reviews 1907-1980*. It is an alphabetical index of the over 40,000 film reviews published by *Variety* from January 19, 1907 to December 31, 1980. Insofar as all titles listed are as published in *Variety*, some may, on occasion, differ from the actual full title of the film as released. Spelling is identical to that used in the *Variety* review.

In order to find a review, locate the title in question in the Index, i.e. Fame 4/30/80. The date(s) which follows indicates the date of the issue(s) in which the review appeared. If there is more than one date listed, then *Variety* reviewed the film on each of those dates. Then turn to the correct volume of *Variety Film Reviews* in which the reviews are reproduced in chronological order. The date of each issue will appear at the top of the column where the reviews for that issue begin.

In a case where *Variety* lists a foreign title with an English translation or an *English* title with a foreign translation, the sub-title listing will have no date but will be followed by a cross reference in parenthesis referring to *Variety's* main title.

In alphabetizing, the following standard practices have been used:

All titles are alphabetized word by word rather than letter by letter.

Hyphenated words are treated as though two separate words.

All standard abbreviations such as Mr. and Col. are listed as though spelled out (Mister and Colonel), with the exception of Mrs. which is listed as such.

Single letter abbreviations, for example, G. I. Blues, are listed at the beginning of each letter, with such exceptions as M.A.S.H. which is recognized as a word and alphabetized as such.

Roman or Arabic numerals are listed as they would be spelled in English. Zero, however, has been listed as the letter O, as it is thought to be less confusing.

Articles at the beginning of a title, whether foreign or English, are disregarded and alphabetized by the next word found in the title, such as:

Sprung von der Bruecke, Der

Caine Mutiny, The

INDEX

A

ABC Del Amor 4-12-67
ABC of Love (See: ABC Del Amor)
A Belles Dents 8-17-66
A Bor 10-03-33
A Bout de Souffle 1-27-60
A Brivele der Mamen 9-20-39
A Cama ao Alcance de Todos 8-27-69
A Casa Assassinada 9-04-74
A Cause, A Cause d'une Femme 5-22-63
A Cavallo della Tigre 3-07-62
A Chacun Son Enfer 2-16-77
A Ciascuno il Suo 5-03-67
A Coeur Joie 7-26-67
A Compadecida 4-09-69
A Confederacao--O Pove e Que Faz a Historia 10-10-79
A Cruz de Ferro 4-09-69
A Csunya Lany 9-11-35
A Culpa 10-15-80
A Dama Do Lotacao 5-31-78
A Derrota 8-09-67
A Donto Pillanat 4-27-38
A Double Tour 9-09-59
A Falecida 9-01-65
A Falu Rossza 2-16-38
A Ferfi Mind Orult 10-27-37
A Flor Da Pele 9-29-76
A Grande Cidade 9-14-66
A-Haunting We Will Go 7-08-42
A Holgy Kisse Bogaras 11-09-38
A Hora et Vez de Augusto Matraga 5-25-66
A Idade Da Terra 9-17-80
A.K.A. Cassius Clay 11-04-70
A Kedves Somszed 2-28-79
A Kiralylany Zsamolya 3-02-77
A Kiralyno Huszarja 1-15-36
A Kis Valentino 2-28-79
A L'Aube Du Troisieme Jour 11-06-63
A La Guerre Comme a la Guerre 8-09-72
A Lenda de Ubirajara 4-07-76
A Los Cuatro Vientos 8-03-55
A L'Ouest Rien de Nouveau 12-24-30
A Megfagyott Gyermek 10-20-37
A Mezzanotte Va La Ronda Del Piacere 3-26-75
A Miniszter Baratja 12-13-39
A Morte Comanda Cangaco 7-12-61
A Mulher de Todos 4-01-70
A Navalha Na Carne 4-29-70
A Noite do Espantalho 10-02-74
A Noite Do Meu Bem 5-14-69
A Noszty Fiu Este Toth Marival 2-23-38
A Nous Deux 6-06-79
A Nous Deux la France 5-27-70
A Nous la Liberte 1-05-32:23 and 5-31-32
A Nous les Petites Anglaises 1-14-76
A 009 Missione Hong Kong (See: Red-Dragon)
A Paty Jezdec Je Strach 7-27-66
A Penultima Donzela 1-14-70
A Piros Bugyellaris 9-21-38
A Pozdravuji Vlastovsky 8-09-72
A Primeira Missa 5-24-61
A Promessa 5-23-73
A Queda 4-05-78
A Quelques Jours Pres (See: Matter of Days, A)
A Repulo Arany 12-27-32
A Sangre Fria 8-06-47
A Santa Alianca 6-28-78
A Sori Sdesi Tihje 9-06-72
A Tizedes Meg a Tobbiek 9-14-66
A Toda Maquina 11-21-51
A Toi de Faire Mignonne 10-23-63
A Tout Casser 10-30-68
A Tout Prendre 8-28-63
A Trombitas 2-28-79
A Un Dios Desconocido 9-28-77
A Ven Gazember 1-17-33
A Vereb Is Madar 6-11-69
A Vida Provisoria 5-14-69
Aarohi 8-04-65
Aaron Loves Angela 12-24-75

Aaron Slick from Punkin Crick 2-20-52
Aarti 10-02-63
Aashirwaa 8-05-70
Aasman Mahal 7-27-66
Abajo El Telon 12-28-55
Abandoned 10-05-49
Abarembo Kaido 7-31-57
ABBA--The Movie 12-14-77
Abbott & Costello Go to Mars 3-25-53
Abbott & Costello in Hollywood 8-22-45
Abbott & Costello in Society 8-09-44
Abbott & Costello in the Foreign Legion 7-12-50
Abbott & Costello Meet Captain Kidd 11-26-52
Abbott & Costello Meet Dr. Jekyll & Mr. Hyde 7-29-53
Abbott & Costello Meet Frankenstein 6-30-48
Abbott & Costello Meet the Keystone Kops 2-09-55
Abbott & Costello Meet the Invisible Man 3-07-51
Abbott & Costello Meet the Killer, Boris Karloff 8-03-49
Abbott & Costello Meet the Mummy 5-11-55
Abby 1-01-75
Abdication, The 9-18-74
Abduct Me (See: Enlevez-Moi)
Abduction 10-15
Abduction, The (See: Entfuehrung, Die)
Abductors, The 2-02-72
Abdul the Damned 3-13-35 and 5-13-36
Abdulla the Great 4-04-56
Abe Lincoln in Illinois 1-24-40
Abel Twoj Brat 7-15-70
Abel, Your Brother (See: Abel Twoj Brat)
Abelha Na Chuva, Uma 8-02-72
Abenteuer Des Werner Holt, Die 3-03-65
Abenteuer in Engadine 12-23-36
Abenteuer in Wien 10-29-52
Abenteuerin von Tunis 11-03-31
Abfahrer, Die 5-23-79
Abicinema 8-27-75
Abie's Irish Rose 4-25-28 and 12-26-28
Abie's Irish Rose 11-27-46:14
Abilene Town 1-09-46
Abilene Trail 3-14-51
Abismos de Pasion 8-14-63
Able-Minded Lady 3-03-22
Abnae el Samte 8-16-75
Abominable Doctor Phibes, The 5-26-71
Abominable Snowman 10-30-57
About Face 4-15-42
About Face 4-16-52
About Love (See: De L'Amour)
About Mrs. Leslie 5-05-54
About Seven Girls (See: Om 7 Flickor)
About Something Else (See: O Necem Jinem)
About Supernatural Things (See: O Vecoch Nadprirozonych)
Above and Beyond 11-19-52
Above Suspicion 4-28-43
Above the Clouds 1-09-34
Above Us the Waves 4-06-55
Abraham Lincoln 1-24-24
Abraham Lincoln 8-27-30
Abraham Lincoln's Clemency 11-12-10
Abroad With Two Yanks 7-26-44
Abschied (See: Farewell)
Abschied 10-29-69
Abschied von den Wolken 12-23-59
Abschied von Gestern 9-14-66
Absences Repetees 9-06-72
Absent Minded (See: Distrait, Le)
Absent Minded Professor, The 2-22-61
Absentee, The (See: Ausente, La)
Absentee, The 5-14-15
Absolute Quiet 5-06-36
Absturz, Der 8-09-23
Abu El Banat 10-24-73
Abu Raihan Beruni 6-18-80
Abuele Automovil, El 9-11-57
Abuna Messias 1-03-40
Abus de Confiance 12-24-38
Abuse of Authority (See: Katachrissis Exoussias)
Abused Confidence (See: Abus de Confiance)
Abusuan 8-29-73
Abwege 11-14-28
Abysses, Les 1-16-63
Abyssinia 7-22-36 and 12-16-36
AC/DC: Let There Be Rock 10-01-80
Acadie, L'Acadie, L' 6-09-71
Accattone 9-06-61
Accent on Youth 8-14-35

Accident 2-15-67
Accidental Honeymoon, The 5-17-18
Accidental Life, An (See: Slucajni Zivot)
Accidents Don't Happen (See: Nincsenek Veletlenek)
Accidents Will Happen 4-27-38
Accomplice 9-25-46
Accomplished Mrs. Thompson, The 6-19-14
According to Advice 3-21-13
According to Hoyle 6-16-22
According to Law 3-17-16
According to Mrs. Hoyle 6-20-51
According to St. John 2-18-16
According to the Code 7-21-16
Accursed, The (See: Maudits, Les)
Accusation (See: Atto di Accusa)
Accused 8-12-36:19 and 12-30-36
Accused, The 11-17-48
Accused of Murder 1-30-57
Accused--Stand Up (See: Accusee--Levez Vous)
Accusee--Levez Vous 10-01-30
Accuser, The (See: Imprecateur, L')
Accusing Finger 11-18-36
Accusing Voice, The 5-22-14
Ace Eli and Rodger of the Skies 4-25-73
Ace High 6-28-18
Ace in the Hole 5-09-51
Ace of Aces 11-14-33
Ace of Cards 10-20-26
Ace of Hearts 10-28-21
Aces and Eights 8-12-36
Aces High 10-01-69
Aces High 5-26-76
Aces of the Turf (See: As du Turf, Les)
Aces Wild 1-27-37
Achalta Ota 5-28-80
Achilles Heel Is My Weapon, The (See: Achilleshaelen er Mit
   Vaaben)
Achilleshaelen er Mit Vaaben 3-28-79
Acht Maedels Im Boot 11-15-32
Acht Tage Gluck 7-28-31
48 Stunden Bis Acapulco 2-07-68
Acid Mantra, or Rebirth of a Nation 10-09-68
Acosada 5-13-64
Acquittal, The 12-20-23
Acquitted 1-28-16
Acquitted 12-11-29
Acrobate, L' 3-24-76
Across 110th Street 12-27-72
Across the Badlands 9-20-50
Across the Bridge 8-28-57
Across the Continent 4-28-22
Across the Deadline 1-20-22
Across the Deadline 4-08-25
Across the Divide 10-02-09
Across the Island of Ceylon 11-06-09
Across the Isthmus 11-20-09
Across the Ocean on the Lusitania 11-02-07
Across the Pacific 11-10-26
Across the Pacific 8-19-42
Across the Plains 6-07-39
Across the Rio Grande 8-31-49
Across the River 9-09-64
Across the Sierras 4-16-41
Across the Unknown (See: Wycieczka W Nieznane)
Across the Wide Missouri 9-19-51
Across the World 1-22-30
Across to Singapore 5-02-28
Act of Love 12-16-53
Act of Murder 1-20-65
Act of Murder, An 8-25-48
Act of the Heart 9-30-70
Act of Vengeance 6-12-74
Act of Violence (See: Ato de Violencia)
Act of Violence 12-22-48
Act One 12-18-63
Actas de Marusia 5-19-76
Acteon 8-04-65
Action 2-20-80
Action for Slander 8-04-37
Action Immediate 5-22-57
Action in Arabia 2-16-44
Action in the North Atlantic 5-19-43
Action of the Tiger 8-21-57 and 8-28-57
Action: The October Crisis of 1970 2-26-75
Activist, The 12-03-69
Acto da Primavera 8-04-65
Actors and Sin 5-28-52
Actors and the Savages, The (See: Actorul Si Salbaticii)
Actors' Fund Field Day 10-15-10

Actorul Si Salbaticii 7-30-75
Actress, The 7-11-28
Actress, The 8-05-53
Ad Ogni Costo (See: Grand Slam)
Ada 7-26-61
Adalen Riots, The (See: Adalen 31)
Adalen 31 5-21-69
Adam and Eva 2-15-23
Adam and Eve (See: Adamo ed Eva)
Adam and Eve (See: Adan y Eva)
Adam and Evelyne 6-08-49
Adam and Evil 8-10-27
Adam at 6 A.M. 9-23-70
Adam Becomes a Man 9-14-60
Adam 11 2-12-10
Adam Had Four Sons 2-19-41
Adam 2 10-22-69
Adamo ed Eva 1-25-50
Adam's Apple 9-26-28
Adam's Pajamas (See: Piyama de Adan, El)
Adam's Rib 3-01-23
Adam's Rib 11-02-49
Adam's Tree (See: Alberio di Adamo, L')
Adam's Woman 4-08-70
Adan y Eva 11-28-56
Adding Machine, The 9-24-69
Addio, Alexandra (See: Love Me--Love My Wife)
Addio, Fratello Crudele 2-23-72
Addio Mia Bella Napoli (See: Farewell, My Beautiful Naples)
Address Unknown 4-19-44
Adela Jeste Nevecerela 6-21-78
Adelaide 5-01-68
Adelantados, Los 7-17-74
Adele 1-31-19
Adele Hasn't Had Her Supper Yet (See: Adela Jeste Nevecerela)
Adieu Cherie 1-01-47
Adieu l'Ami 8-28-68
Adieu Les Beaux Jours 5-01-34
Adieu Mascotte 9-18-29
Adieu Philippine 11-22-61
Adieu Poulet 12-24-75
Adios Alicia 12-28-77
Adios, Amigo 1-14-76
Adios, Ciguena, Adios 11-17-71
Adios Gringo 1-31-68
Adios Juventud 10-11-44
Adios Sabata 9-01-71
Adjutant des Zaren, Der 3-06-29
Adjutant of the Czar, The (See: Adjutant des Zaren, Der)
Admirable Crichton, The 6-19-57
Admiral Nakhimov 8-13-47
Admiral Was a Lady, The 5-10-50
Admirals All 7-03-35
Adolescence of Cain (See: Cain Adolescente)
Adolescent, The (See: Adolescente, L')
Adolescente, L' 1-31-79
Adolescentes, Los 2-11-76
Adolescents, The (See: Fleur de l'Age ou Les Adolescentes, Las)
Adolf & Marlene 6-01-77
Adolf the Slacker (See: Samvetsomma Adolf)
Adolf's Military Adventures (See: Samvetsomma Adolf)
Adolphe, or the Awkward Age (See: Adolphe, ou L'Age Tendre)
Adolphe, ou L'Age Tendre 7-24-68
Adonis Is Robbed of His Clothes 11-27-09
Adopted Parents, The 10-01-10
Adopted Son, The 11-02-17
Adoption, L' 12-13-78
Adoption, The (See: Orokbefogadas or Adoption, L')
Adorable 5-23-33
Adorable Cheat, The 4-18-28
Adorable Creatures 1-18-56
Adorable Deceiver, The 12-22-26
Adorable Julia 5-23-62
Adorable Liar (See: Adorable Menteuse)
Adorable Menteuse 3-07-62
Adorable Outcast 2-13-29
Adorables Creatures 10-15-52
Adoration 1-16-29
Adoring an Ad 1-29-10
Adrienne Lecouvreur 11-09-38
Adrien's Story (See: Histoire d'Adrien)
Adrift 5-26-71
Adua and Her Colleagues (See: Adua e le Compagne)
Adua e le Compagne 9-14-60
Adult Fun 12-06-72
Adulterio a Brasileira 12-31-69
Adulterous Wife, The (See: Yoru No Tsuzani)
Adultery--Brazilian Style (See: Adulterio a Brasileira)

4

Adults, The (See: Grandes Personnes, Les)
Advantage, The (See; Avantazh)
Adventure 4-22-25
Adventure 12-19-45
Adventure, The (See: Avventura, L')
Adventure at the Door (See: Pustolov Pred Vratima)
Adventure Girl 8-14-34
Adventure in Baltimore 3-23-49
Adventure in Blackmail 8-18-43
Adventure in Bokhara 8-23-44
Adventure in Diamonds 1-24-40
Adventure in Manhattan 10-28-36
Adventure in Sahara 12-21-38
Adventure in Warsaw 11-02-55
Adventure in Washington 8-06-41
Adventure Is Adventure (See: Aventure C'Est L'Aventure, L')
Adventure Island 8-13-47
Adventure Limited 3-20-29
Adventure Mad 5-09-28
Adventure of Fifine 7-24-09
Adventure of Natsuko 2-18-53
Adventure of Salvador Rosa, An 9-25-40
Adventure of Sherlock Holmes' Smarter Brother, The 12-03-75
Adventure of the Strange Stone Castle, The (See: Kiganjo no Boken)
Adventure Shop, The 1-03-19
Adventure Starts Here (See: Har Borjar Aventyret)
Adventure Starts Tomorrow (See: Aventure Commence Demain, L')
Adventurer, The 10-26-17
Adventurer, The 9-26-28
Adventurers, The 3-21-51
Adventurers, The 3-25-70
Adventures, The 1-15-10
Adventure's End 11-17-37
Adventures in Iraq 9-22-43
Adventures in Pygmy Land 3-07-28
Adventures in the Far North 9-13-23
Adventures in Vienna (See: Abenteuer in Wien)
Adventures of a Beggar 2-22-08
Adventures of a Dentist 7-05-78
Adventures of a Rookie 8-18-43
Adventures of a Young Man 6-20-62
Adventures of Baron Muenchhausen, The (See: Muenchhausen)
Adventures of Barry McKenzie 10-25-72
Adventures of Bullwhip Griffin, The 3-01-67
Adventures of Captain Fabian 9-26-51
Adventures of Captain Kettle, The 11-17-22
Adventures of Captain Marvel 3-05-41
Adventures of Carol, The 11-02-17
Adventures of Casanova 2-18-48
Adventures of Chico 2-23-38
Adventures of Don Coyote 4-30-47
Adventures of Don Juan 12-29-48
Adventures of Gallant Bess 7-28-48
Adventures of Garel Hama 2-19-15
Adventures of Giacomo Casanova, The (See: Avventure di Giacomo
    Casanova, Le)
Adventures of Goopy and Bagha, The (See: Goopy Gyne Bagha Byne)
Adventures of Hajji Baba 10-13-54
Adventures of Huckleberry Finn 5-11-60
Adventures of I-Have-Come, The 4-30-75
Adventures of Ichabod and Mr. Toad, The 8-24-49
Adventures of Jane Arden 4-05-39
Adventures of Janne Wangman, The (See: Janne Wangmans Bravader)
Adventures of Joselito and Tom Thumb (See: Aventuras de Joselito
    y Pulgarcito)
Adventures of Kitty Cobb, The 10-31-14
Adventures of Kitty O'Day 11-29-44
Adventures of Marco Polo 2-16-38
Adventures of Mark Twain 5-03-44
Adventures of Martin Eden, The 2-25-42
Adventures of Maya 4-24-29
Adventures of Nils Holgerssons 8-07-63
Adventures of Picasso, The (See: Picassos Aeventyr)
Adventures of Rabbi Jacob, The (See: Aventures de Rabbi Jacob,
    Les)
Adventures of Robinson Crusoe, The 6-02-54
Adventures of Rusty 8-15-45
Adventures of Salavin, The (See: Aventures de Salavin, Les)
Adventures of Sherlock Holmes, The 9-06-39
Adventures of the Flying Cadets 9-22-43
Adventures of the Wilderness Family, The 1-14-76
Adventures of Werner Holt (See: Abenteuer des Werner Holt, Die)
Adventuress of Tunis (See: Abenteuerin von Tunis)
Adventurous Blonde 12-01-37
Adventurous Sex, The 6-17-25

Adventurous Soul, The 12-07-27
Adversary, The 4-01-70
Adversary, The (See: Pratidwandi)
Advice to Lovelorn 12-19-33
Advise and Consent 5-23-62
Advokatka 8-02-78
Aegean Tragedy (See: Tragodie tou Aegaeou)
Aegget Ar Lost 4-16-75
Aerial Acrobatics 1-29-10
Aerial Gunner 3-24-43
Aerial Revenge, An 5-14-15
Aerograd 1-01-36
Aerograd 8-07-68
Aeroplane Contest at Rheims 9-25-09
Af Mila le Morgenstein 4-03-63
Affaeren I Moelleby 1-12-77
Affair at Akitsu (See: Akitsu Onsen)
Affair Blum, The 9-21-49
Affair in Havana 12-04-57
Affair in Reno 2-27-57
Affair in Trinidad 7-30-52
Affair LaFont, The 10-11-39
Affair Nina B, The (See: Affaire Nina B)
Affair of an Egg, The 9-10-10
Affair of Honor (See: Lovagias Ugy)
Affair of Susan 11-06-35
Affair of the Follies 3-02-27
Affair of the Heart or Tragedy of a Postal Worker (See: Ljubavni
    Slucaj ou Tragedija Sluzbenice P.T.T.)
Affair to Remember, An 7-17-56
Affair With a Stranger 6-10-53
Affaire Blaireau, L' 3-29-32
Affaire Coffin, L' 6-04-80
Affaire Crazy Capo, L' 10-24-73
Affaire des Poisons, L' 12-28-55
Affaire Dominici, L' 3-21-73
Affaire D'Une Nuit, L' 10-05-60
Affaire du Collier de la Reine, L' 10-16-46
Affaire Maurizius, L' 7-07-54
Affaire Nina B 7-12-61
Affaire Suisse, L' 12-20-78
Affairs 8-22-79
Affairs of a Gentleman 6-26-34
Affairs of a Model 7-30-52
Affairs of a Rogue, The 2-16-49
Affairs of Adelaide (See: Britannia Mews)
Affairs of Anatol 8-26-21
Affairs of Annabel 8-10-38
Affairs of Cappy Ricks 6-30-37
Affairs of Cellini 9-11-34
Affairs of Dobie Gillis 6-03-53
Affairs of Geraldine 11-27-46
Affairs of Maupassant 2-09-38
Affairs of Susan 3-28-45
Affairs Within Walls (See: Kabe No Nakano Himegoto)
Affection 11-14-73
Affectionately Yours 5-07-41
Affiche Rouge, L' 4-28-76
Affinita Elettive 10-04-78
Afghanistan 10-02-29
Afincaos, Los 11-19-41
Aflame in the Skies 11-02-27
Afraid of Love 4-08-25
Afraid to Fight 6-30-22
Afraid to Love 4-13-27
Afraid to Talk 12-20-32
Africa, Addio! 3-09-66
Africa Adventure 9-29-54
Africa Ama 12-01-71
Africa, Farewell! (See: Africa, Addio!)
Africa Loves (See: Africa Ama)
Africa Screams 5-04-49
Africa Speaks 9-24-30
Africa--Texas Style 5-17-67
African Diamond Conspiracy 5-29-14
African Elephant, The 10-20-71
African Holiday 6-09-37
African Lion 8-10-55
African Queen, The 12-26-51
African Treasure 5-14-52
Africanus Sexualis (See: Black Is Beautiful)
Afskedens Time 11-28-73
Aftenlandet 3-02-77
After a Million 5-14-24
After a Night of Love (See: Dopo una Notte d'Amore)
After All (See: Vegul)
After Business Hours 6-17-25 and 4-21-26
After Dark 1-07-25

After Five 2-05-15
After Goya (See: Goyescas)
After His Own Heart 5-02-19
After Mein Kampf? 9-18-40
After Mein Kampf 8-02-61
After Midnight 9-30-21
After Midnight 8-17-27
After Office Hours 3-13-35
After Shadows, Light (See: Gheroub Wa Cherouk)
After the Ball 3-26-24
After the Ball 12-13-32 and 3-21-33
After the Ball 8-21-57
After the Dance 8-21-35
After the Deluge (See: Despues del Diluvio)
After the Fog 1-29-30
After the Fox 10-12-66
After the Last Move (See: Nach Meinem Letzten Umzug)
After the Rain (See: Fah Larng Fon)
After the Show 10-07-21
After the Storm 5-16-28
After the Storm (See: Despues de la Tormenta or Nach dem Sturm)
After the Thin Man 12-30-36
After Tomorrow 3-08-32
After Tonight 11-07-33
After You, Comrade 4-05-67
Aftermath 6-08-27 and 12-07-27
Afternoon of the Bulls (See: Tardes de Toros)
Against a Crooked Sky 12-24-75
Against All Flags 11-26-52
Against All Odds 8-13-24
Against Reason and by Force (See: Contra la Razon y Por la
    Fuerza)
Against the Law 12-18-34
Against the Wind 2-25-48
Agatha 2-14-79
Agaton Sax and the Bykoebing Village Festival (See: Agaton Sax
    Och Bykoebings Gaestabud)
Agaton Sax Och Bykoebings Gaestabud 12-08-76
Age d'Or, L' 9-23-64
Age of Love, The (See: Eta Dell'Amore, L')
Age for Love 11-17-31
Age Ingrat, L' 1-20-65
Age of Assassins, The (See: Satsujinkyo Jidai)
Age of Christ, The (See: Kristore Roky)
Age of Consent 9-06-32
Age of Consent 5-14-69
Age of Illusions (See: Almodozasok Kora)
Age of Indiscretion 5-23-35
Age of Innocence 10-23-34
Age of the Earth, The (See: A Idade da Terra)
Agee 9-24-80
Agence Matrimoniale 6-18-52
Agent 69 Jensen I Skorpionens Tegn 7-27-77
Agent 69 Jensen I Skyttens Tegn 8-02-78
Agent 69 Jensen in the Sign of Sagittarius (See: Agent 69 Jensen
    I Skyttens Tegn)
Agent 69 Jensen in the Sign of Scorpio (See: Agent 69 Jensen I
    Skorpionens Tegn)
Agent X-25 Reports (See: Spijun X-25 Javlja)
Agenzia Riccardo Finzi ... Praticamente Detective 2-20-80
Aggie Appleby 10-24-33
Agilok und Blubbo 3-26-69
Agit 9-06-72
Agitator, The 8-24-49
Agnoula 11-05-41
Agnus Dei (See: Egi Barany)
Agonas 10-29-75
Agony and the Ecstasy, The 9-15-65
Agony of Fear, The 10-08-15
Agony of Mr. Boroka, The (See: Forro Vizet A Kopaszra)
Agony of the Eagles 5-12-22
Agostino 12-26-62
Agosto '68 9-10-69
Agraharathil Kazhuthai 1-31-79
Agression, L' 4-23-75
Agua en el Suelo, El 5-01-34
Aguas Bajan Turbias, Las 2-18-53
Aguila 6-25-80
Aguila Blanca 5-07-41
Aguirre: The Wrath of God (See: Aquirre, Der Zorn Gottes)
Agustina de Aragon 11-01-50
Agustina of Aragon (See: Agustina de Aragon)
Ah! Afti I Guineka Mou 10-25-67
Ah, Love Is Beautiful (See: Que Bonito Amor)
Ah! Nomugi Toge 7-30-80
Ah, Wilderness 1-01-36
Ahi Viene Martin Corona 7-02-52
Ahora Seremos Felices 6-28-39
Ai Kruie 2-23-77

Ai Kwai Legg 8-24-77
Ai No Borei 5-24-78
Ai No Corrida 2-25-76
Ai No Kawaki 8-10-66 and 3-15-67
Aida 10-13-54
Aido (Slave of Love) 7-09-69
Aigle et la Colombe, L' 3-23-77
Aiguille Rouge, L' 8-15-51
Aika Hyva Ihmiseksi 8-09-78
Aile et la Cuisse, L' 11-10-76
Aililia 9-03-75
Aimez-Vous les Femmes? 5-13-64
Aimless Bullet, The 11-13-63
Aine des Ferchaux, L' 10-02-63
Ainsi Finit la Nuit 1-25-50
Ain't Love Funny 7-06-27
Ain't Misbehavin' 5-25-55
Air Cadet 2-21-51
Air Circus 9-05-28
Air de Paris, L' 9-22-54
Air Devils 5-11-38
Air Eagles 1-26-32
Air Force 2-03-43
Air Hawks 6-12-35
Air Heroes (See: Heroes del Aire)
Air Hostess 1-24-33
Air Hostess 7-06-46
Air Legion 11-14-28
Air Mail 11-08-32
Air Mail, The 3-25-25
Air Mail Pilot 5-02-28
Air Patrol, The 1-18-28
Air Police 4-29-31
Air Strike 7-13-55
Airborne 6-13-62
Airplane! 7-02-80
Airport 2-18-70
Airport 1975 10-16-74
Airport '77 3-23-77
Ajandek Ez A Nap 2-27-80
Ajuricaba 8-31-77
Akahige 9-08-65
Akai Satsui 11-18-64
Akai Tenshi 11-02-66
Akamegumo 10-18-67
Akasen Chitai 7-25-56
Akasen Tamanoi Nekeraremasu 5-28-75
Akce Kalimantan 7-04-62
Akcija Stadion 8-17-77
Akee Bororo 7-25-73
Akenfield 1-29-75
Akhras Al-Hob 11-20-68
Akibiori 7-26-78
Akiket a Pas Cirta Elkisert 9-16-59
Akitsu Onsen 11-19-80
Akjica 8-10-60
Akramana 2-06-80
Akran 12-03-69
Aktenskapsleken 12-25-35
Aktorzy Prowincjonalni 5-21-80
Al Aswar 7-25-79
Al Boustagui 11-20-68
Al Capone 2-11-59
Al Chet 9-15-37
Al Diablo Con Este Cura 5-31-67
Al Diavolo Con Celebrita 2-08-50
Al Fahd 8-16-72
Al-Haress 11-06-68
Al Hayatt Al Yawmiyah Fi Qariah Suriyah 7-07-76
Al Jennings of Oklahoma 1-17-51
Al Kautsar 12-14-77
Al Moutmarred 11-13-68
Al Raas 2-06-80
Al Servicio de la Mujer Espanola 10-04-78
Al Son de la Marimba 8-25-43
Al Tarik 8-04-65
Al Tariq 2-12-75
Al Tejruba 2-06-80
Al Tish' Ali Im Ani Ohev 4-18-79
Al Toque de Clarin 8-13-41
Al-Yemen 1-14-31
Al Zouga Talattshar 7-04-62
Aladdin 9-28-17
Aladdin and His Lamp 2-06-52
Aladdin from Broadway 3-23-17
Aladdin's Other Lamp 7-13-17
Alakazam the Great 7-12-61
Alakdang Gubat 6-23-76

Alambrista 5-24-78
Alamo, The 10-26-60
Alarm Clock Andy 3-19-20
Alaska Highway 6-23-43 and 10-27-43
Alaska Passage 2-04-59
Alaska Patrol 1-19-49
Alaska Seas 1-27-54
Alaskan, The 9-17-24
Alaskan Adventures 3-02-27
Alat 10-15-75
Alaztosan Jeletem 9-07-60
Alba Regia 11-22-61
Albaniles, Los 7-06-77
Albany Night Boat 9-26-28
Albatros, L' 9-22-71
Albatross, The (See: Albatros, L')
Albeniz 8-13-47
Alberio di Adamo, L' 1-20-37
Albero Degli Zoccoli, L' 5-24-78
Albert, R.N. 10-21-53
Albert Schweitzer 2-06-57
Albert--Warum? 1-17-79
Albert--Why? (See: Albert--Warum?)
Albuquerque 1-21-48
Alcatraz Island 10-13-37
Alcohol (See: Alcool)
Alcoholiday--The Story of a Thirst, An 6-04-24
Alcool 9-24-80
Alder King, The (See: Erlkoenig, Der)
Alderman's Picnic, The 1-15-10
Aldevaran 11-05-75
Alejandra 9-08-43
Aleko 1-12-55
Aleksa Dundic 8-20-58
Aleluia, Gretchen 6-15-77
Alert in the Mediterranean (See: Alerte En Mediterranee)
Alert in the South (See: Alerte Au Sud)
Alerte Au Sud 2-10-54
Alerte En Mediterranee 11-02-38
Alex and the Gypsy 9-29-76
Alex in Wonderland 12-23-70
Alex the Great 3-21-28
Alexander Graham Bell 4-05-39
Alexander Hamilton 9-22-31
Alexander Nevsky 3-29-39
Alexander the Great (See: O Megalexandros)
Alexander the Great 4-04-56
Alexanderplatz (See: Sur le Pave de Berlin)
Alexander's Ragtime Band 6-01-38
Alexandre le Bienheureux 2-28-68
Alexandria ... Why? (See: Iskindiria ... Leh?)
Alfie 3-30-66
Alfie Darling 3-19-75
Alfred the Great 7-23-69
Alfredo, Alfredo 12-19-73
Alf's Button 4-09-30
Algerian War, The (See: Guerre D'Algerie, La)
Algiers 6-29-38
Algo Flota Sobre El Agua 9-29-48
Ali-Baba 1-19-55
Ali Baba and the Forty Thieves 3-21-08
Ali Baba and the Forty Thieves 1-17-19
Ali Baba and the Forty Thieves 1-12-44
Ali Baba Goes to Town 10-20-37
Ali the Man: Ali the Fighter 7-30-75
Alias a Gentleman 1-28-48
Alias Bad Man 7-28-31
Alias Big Shot (See: Alias Gardelito)
Alias Bulldog Drummond 9-11-35
Alias French Gertie 4-16-30
Alias Gardelito 5-30-62
Alias Jesse James 3-18-59
Alias Jimmy Valentine 4-23-20
Alias Julius Caesar 11-10-22
Alias Mary Brown 8-09-18
Alias Mary Dow 7-03-35
Alias Mary Smith 8-30-32
Alias Mike Moran 3-28-19
Alias Miss Dobbs 6-25-20
Alias Mrs. Jessop 12-14-17
Alias Nick Beal 1-19-49
Alias Night Wind 10-11-23
Alias the Champ 10-25-49
Alias the Deacon 6-22-27
Alias the Deacon 5-15-40
Alias the Doctor 3-08-32
Alias the Lone Wolf 10-05-27
Alibi 4-10-29

Alibi 5-13-31
Alibi, L' (See: Alibi, The)
Alibi, The 4-19-39
Alibi, The 3-31-43
Alibi for Murder 10-07-36
Alice Adams 6-28-23
Alice Adams 8-21-35
Alice Doesn't Live Here Anymore 12-11-74
Alice in der Stadten 10-19-74
Alice in Spanish Wonderland (See: Alicia en la Espana de las Maravillas)
Alice in the Cities (See: Alice in der Stadten)
Alice in Wonderland 1-22-15
Alice in Wonderland 12-26-33
Alice in Wonderland 7-04-51
Alice in Wonderland 8-01-51
Alice in Wonderland 9-08-76
Alice or the Last Escapade (See: Alice Ou la Derniere Fugue)
Alice Ou la Derniere Fugue 1-12-77
Alice's Adventures in Wonderland 9-17-10
Alice's Adventures in Wonderland 11-15-72
Alice's Restaurant 8-13-69
Alicia 10-16-74
Alicia en la Espana de las Maravillas 5-24-78
Alien (See: In Der Fremde)
Alien 5-23-79
Alien, The 6-04-15
Alien, The 3-26-80
Alien Enemy, An 4-19-18
Alien Souls 5-05-16
Aliens, The (See: O Alienista)
Alieskine Liubov 10-11-61
Aliki--My Love 12-18-63
Alimony 6-15-49
Alimony Madness 5-09-33
Alise et Chloe 11-18-70
Alive and Kicking 6-24-59
Alkeste--Die Bedeutung, Protektion Zu Haben 4-22-70
Alkeste--The Importance of Having Protection (See: Alkeste--Die Bedeutung, Protektion Zu Haben)
Alksande Par 5-26-65
All Aboard 5-11-27
All About Alice 5-10-72
All About Eve 9-13-50
All-American, The 10-04-32
All-American, The 7-22-53
All-American Boy, The 11-07-73
All American Chump 11-04-36
All-American Co-Ed 10-08-41
All-American Sweetheart 12-08-37
All-Around Reduced Personality--Outtakes, The (See: Allseitig Reduzierte Persoenlichkeit Redupers, Die)
All Ashore 2-11-53
All at Sea 12-25-57
All by Myself 6-02-43
All Dolled Up 3-25-21
All Fall Down 3-28-62
All for a Girl 6-25-15
All for a Nickle 10-02-09
All for a Woman 12-09-21
All for Mary 1-11-56
All for Old Ireland 7-16-15
All Hands on Deck 4-05-61
All Her Life (See: Toute Sa Vie)
All I Desire 6-24-53
All in a Night's Work 3-22-61
All Is Love (See: Vsichko e Lyubov)
All Is Well (See: Tout Va Bien)
All Mad About Him (See: Toutes Folles De Lui)
All Man 11-24-16
All Man 8-02-18
All Men Are Apes 11-24-65
All Men Are Enemies 5-29-34
All Men Are Mad (See: A Ferfi Mind Orult)
All Mine to Give 11-06-57
All Mixed Up 11-11-64
All My Sons 2-25-48
All Neat in Black Stockings 4-09-69
All Night 12-06-18
All Night Long 2-14-62
All Night Through (See: Unruhige Nacht)
All Nudity Will Be Punished (See: Toda Nudez Sera Castigada)
All of a Sudden Norma 12-20-18
All of Me 2-06-34
All on Account of a Letter 9-25-09
All on Account of a Lie 10-08-10
All on Account of the Milk 1-22-10
All on Account of the Milk 7-31-14

All Over the Town 3-09-49
All Over Town 9-22-37
All People Will Be Brothers (See: Alle Menschen Werden Brueder)
All Quiet on the Western Front 5-07-30
All Roads Lead to Rome (See: Tous Les Chemins Menent a Rome)
All Soul's Day (See: Zaduszki)
All Soul's Eve 2-18-21
All Stars (See: Tous Vedettes)
All That Heaven Allows 10-26-55
All That Jazz 12-12-79
All the Advantages 5-24-72
All the Brothers Were Valiant (See: Brothers Were Valiant)
All the Brothers Were Valiant 10-21-53
All the Fine Young Cannibals 7-20-60
All the King's Horses 3-13-35
All the King's Men 11-09-49
All the Loving Couples 4-09-69
All the Night Hides (See: Ossa Krivi I Nichta)
All the Other Girls Do 11-02-66
All the President's Men 3-31-76
All the Right Noises 10-27-71
All the Way Home 9-18-63
All the Way Up 6-17-70
All the World for Nothing 11-22-18
All the Young Men (See: Kazdy Mlady Muz)
All the Young Men 8-03-60
All This and Heaven Too 6-12-40
All This and World War II 11-17-76
All Through the Night 12-03-41
All Woman 5-24-18
All Women Have Secrets 11-22-39
All Wrong 5-16-19 and 6-06-19
Alla en el Rancho Grande 10-21-36 and 12-02-36
Alla en el Rancho Grande 2-16-49
Alle Jahre Wieder 7-12-67
Alle Menschen Werden Brueder 4-11-73
Allegations (See: Rumeurs)
Allegheny Uprising 11-08-39
Allegri Masnadieri 10-20-37
Allegro Cantante, L' 4-27-38
Allegro Non Troppo 12-08-76
Alleman 1-15-64
Aller Retour 8-16-78
Aller Simple, Un 6-30-71
Allergic to Love 5-03-44
Alles Um Eine Frau 1-01-36
Allez France 11-18-64
Alliance, L' 9-16-70
Alligator 11-19-80
Alligator Named Daisy 12-28-55
Alligator People, The 7-15-59
Alljon Meg a Menet! 7-03-74
Allo, Allo, Carnaval 2-12-36
Allonsanfan 10-22-75
Allotment Wives, Inc. 1-02-46
Allotria 7-22-36
All's Fair in Love 11-06-09
All's Fair in Love 1-14-11
All's Quiet on the Western Front (See: A l'Ouest Rien de Nouveau)
Allseitig Reduzierte Persoenlichkeit Redupers, Die 6-28-78
Alluring Goal, The 5-07-30
Allvarsamme Leken, Den 8-31-77
Almafuerte 2-08-50
Almatlan Evek 9-16-59
Almighty Dollar, The 8-25-16
Almodo Ifjusag 10-09-74
Almodozasok Kora 8-04-65
Almost a Divorce 9-01-31
Almost a Dream (See: Casi un Sueno)
Almost a Gentleman 3-22-39
Almost a Honeymoon 10-08-30 and 1-14-31
Almost a Husband 10-17-19
Almost a Lady 9-29-26
Almost a Love Story (See: Pochti Lyubovna Istorya)
Almost a Man (See: Uomo a Meta, Un)
Almost Angels 8-29-62
Almost Human 3-14-28
Almost Human 7-30-80
Almost Married 6-06-19
Almost Married 7-26-32
Almost Perfect Affair, An 4-11-79
Almost Summer 4-26-78
Almost Transparent Blue (See: Kagirinaku Tomei Ni Chikai Buruu)
Aloha 4-29-31
Aloha, Bobby and Rose 4-16-75
Aloha Oe 11-12-15
Aloise 4-16-75
Aloma of the South Seas 5-19-26

Aloma of the South Seas 8-27-41
Alone (See: Sam or Sola)
Alone at Daybreak (See: Solos En La Madrugada)
Alone in London 6-25-15
Alone in New York 1-08-15
Alone in Paris (See: Seul a Paris)
Alone in the World (See: Seuls au Monde)
Alone or With Others (See: Seul ou Avec Les Autres)
Along Came a Soldier ... (See: Kom en Soldat, Der),
Along Came Jones 6-13-45
Along Came Love 1-13-37
Along Came Ruth 7-30-24
Along Came Sally 6-19-34
Along Came Youth 1-14-31
Along the Fango River (See: Au Long de la Riviere Fango)
Along the Great Divide 5-02-51
Along the Navajo Trail 12-12-45
Along the Oregon Trail 9-10-47
Along the Rio Grande 1-29-41
Along the Sidewalks (See: Long des Trottoirs, Le)
Alpagueur, L' 3-31-76
Alpenbaringen 1-10-79
Alpha Beta 11-21-73
Alphabet Murders, The 3-16-66
Alphaville, a Strange Adventure of Lemmy Caution (See: Alphaville,
    une Etrange Aventure de Lemmy Caution)
Alphaville, Une Etrange Aventure du Lemmy Caution 5-05-65
Alpine Echo, An 9-18-09
Alpine Love (See: Scarpo al Sole, Le)
Alpine Retreat, An 11-19-10
Alraune 5-02-28 and 12-24-30
Alraune 12-10-52
Als Twee Druppels Water 5-08-63
Alskarinnan 7-10-63
Also Es War So ... 6-01-77
Alster Case, The 12-10-15
Alt Paa et Braet 3-02-77
Alta Infedelta 2-26-64
Altar Stairs 12-08-22
Altarpiece Maker (See: Iconostasis)
Altars of Desire 4-27-27
Altars of the World 1-21-76
Altas Variedades 8-10-60
Alte Burscherherlichkeit 6-21-32
Alte Fritz, Der 5-02-28
Alte Lied, Das 9-15-31
Alte und Junge Kaiser 12-11-35
Altered States 12-10-80
Alternative 10-02-68
Alternative Miss World, The 11-26-80
Altitude 3,200 8-24-38
Altri Tempi 9-17-52
Alupihang Dagat 9-10-75
Alvarez Kelly 10-05-66
Alvin Purple 1-02-74
Alvin Rides Again 12-25-74
Alvorada 5-29-63
Always a Bride 11-27-40
Always a Bride 8-26-53
Always a Bridesmaid 9-29-43
Always a New Beginning 3-20-74
Always Another Dawn 10-06-48
Always Audacious 11-12-20
Always for Pleasure 1-17-79
Always Further On (See: Tarahumara)
Always Goodbye 5-27-31
Always Goodbye 6-29-38
Always in My Heart 3-04-42
Always in Trouble 11-09-38
Always Leave Them Laughing 11-23-49
Always the Woman 7-14-22
Always Together 12-17-47
Always Tomorrow 11-13-34
Always Trouble With the Teachers (See: Immer Aerger Mit Den
    Paukern)
Always with Me 12-01-76
Alyam Alyam 5-31-78
Alzire Oder der Neue Kontinent 4-11-79
Alzire or the New Continent (See: Alzire Oder der Neue Kontinent)
Am Galgen Haengt Die Liebe 4-19-61 and 8-22-62
Am I Guilty? 10-02-40
Am Rande der Welt 12-21-27
Amada Amante 3-28-79
Amador 5-19-65
Amanecer en Puerta Oscura 7-24-57
Amangeldy 6-28-39
Amanita Pestilens 7-14-65

Amant de Cinq Jours, L' 4-05-61
Amant de Lady Chatterley, L' 2-08-56
Amant de Poche, L' 2-15-78
Amantes, Los 11-28-56
Amantes del Desierto, Los 2-12-58
Amantes Del Diablo, Los 10-27-71
Amanti, Gli (See: Place for Lovers, A)
Amanti di Gramigna, L' 2-12-69
Amanti Senza Amore 5-05-48
Amants, Les 9-17-58
Amants de Brasmart, Les 6-27-51
Amants de Minuit, Les 5-13-53
Amants de Teruel, Les 5-23-62
Amants de Tolede, Les 3-11-53
Amants du Tage, Les 6-08-55
Amants Maudits, Les 8-20-52
Amants Terribles, Les 10-14-36
Amarcord 1-16-74
Amarga Verdad 3-14-45
Amarilly of Clothesline Alley 3-08-18
Amateur Acrobat 4-04-08
Amateur Adventuress, The 5-09-19
Amateur Billiards 4-09-10
Amateur Crook 1-12-38
Amateur Daddy 4-26-32
Amateur Devil, An 2-04-21
Amateur Gentleman, The 8-18-26
Amateur Gentleman, The 2-05-36 and 4-29-36
Amateur Widow, An 5-16-19
Amateur Wife 4-30-20
Amator 9-05-79
Amazing Colossal Man, The 9-04-57
Amazing Dobermans, The 12-01-76
Amazing Dr. Clitterhouse, The 6-22-38
Amazing Grace 7-17-74
Amazing Imposter, The 1-25-19
Amazing Lovers 10-14-21
Amazing Mr. Forrest 6-28-44
Amazing Mr. Williams 1-03-40
Amazing Monsieur Fabre 9-03-52
Amazing Mrs. Holliday 2-10-43
Amazing Quest 8-19-36
Amazing Vagabond 7-24-29
Amazing Wife 3-07-19
Amazon, The 10-29-10
Amazon Head Hunters 11-15-32
Amazon Quest 5-11-49
Amazon Symphony (See: Sinfonia Amazonica)
Amazon Trader, The 8-15-56
Amazons, The 8-17-17
Ambassadeurs, Les 4-28-76
Ambassador Bill 11-17-31
Ambassadors, The (See: Ambassadeurs, Les)
Ambassador's Daughter, The 8-01-56
Ambitieuse, L' 8-05-59
Ambition 6-30-16
Ambitious One, The (See: Ambitieuse, L')
Ambush (See: Zaseda)
Ambush 2-15-39
Ambush 12-21-49
Ambush at Cimarron Pass 2-19-58
Ambush at Tomahawk Gap 5-06-53
Ambush Bay 8-31-66
Ambush Trail 2-06-46
Ambushers, The 12-20-67
Amelie or the Time to Love (See: Amelie ou le Temps D'Aimer)
Amelie ou le Temps D'Aimer 7-05-61
Amelie's Trip (See: Voyage d'Amelie, Le)
Amendment to the Law for the Defence of the State (See:
     Dopalnenie K Zakona Za Zaschitita Na Darjavata)
Amere Victoire (See: Bitter Victory)
America 10-10-14
America 2-28-24
America, America 12-18-63
America at the Movies 7-14-76
America Lost and Found 11-07-79
America Seen by a Frenchman (See: Amerique Vue Par un Francais,
     L')
America Under Fire 2-17-37
Americain, L' 10-08-69
American, The (See: Americain, L')
American Aristocracy 10-27-16
American Beauty 10-12-27
American Beauty, The 7-07-16
American Buds 4-05-18
American Citizen, An 1-09-14
American Consul, The 2-16-17

American Dream, An 8-31-66
American Dream, The (See: Droemmen Om Amerika)
American Dreamer, The 4-14-71
American Empire 12-09-42
American Farmers Visit Russia and Indonesia Today 11-16-55
American Fleet in French Waters, The 1-07-11
American Friend, The (See: Amerikanische Freund, Der)
American Game, The 4-18-79
American Game Trails 10-22-15
American Gang Busters 3-27-40
American Gigolo 1-30-80
American Girl, An 5-07-58
American Graffiti 6-20-73
American Guerrilla in the Philippines 11-08-50
American Hot Wax 3-15-78
American in Paris, An 8-29-51
American in Vacanza, Un (See: Week's Leave, A)
American Invasion, An 3-28-13
American Live Wire 3-15-18
American Love (See: Amour a l'Americaine)
American Madness 8-09-32
American Maid 12-07-17
American Manners 10-15-24
American Methods 4-27-17
American Nitro 3-28-79
American Odyssey 11-05-80
American Prisoner 10-02-29
American Revolution 2 9-10-69
American Romance, An 6-28-44
American Sexual Revolution 6-23-71
American Soldier, The (See: Amerikanische Soldat, Der)
American Success Company, The 11-28-79
American Surplus, The (See: Kao Nok Na)
American Torso (See: Amerikai Anzix)
American Tragedy, An 8-11-31
American Venus 1-27-26
American Way, The 7-04-19
American Widow, An 12-21-17
American Wife, An (See: Moglie Americana, Una)
American Wilderness 2-02-72
Americanization of Emily, The 10-28-64
Americano 12-29-54
Americano, The 12-29-16
America's Answer 8-02-18
America's Fat (See: Gordo de America, El)
Americathon 8-15-79
Amerikai Anzix 3-02-77
Amerikanische Freund, Der 6-08-77
Amerikanische Soldat, Der 10-28-70
Amerique Vue Par un Francais, L' 4-20-60
Ami de la Famille, L' 7-24-57
Ami Viendra Ce Soir, Un 5-08-46 (Also see: Friend Will Come
     Tonight, A)
Amiche, L' 9-28-55
Amiche: Andiano Alla Festa 9-06-72
Amici Miei 12-17-75
Amici Per la Pelle 9-28-55
Amico, Un 10-09-68
Amis, Les 6-09-71
Amities Particulieres, Les 9-09-64
Amityville Horror, The 8-01-79
Amlash Enchanted Forest, The 6-05-74
Amo Non Amo 3-07-79
Amo Te Sola 7-22-36
Amok 10-23-46
Among Human Wolves 11-27-40
Among People (See: Sredi Ludei)
Among the Cannibal Isles 7-26-18
Among the Living 9-03-41
Among the Missing 11-06-34
Among Vultures (See: Unter Geiern)
Amor Brujo, El 7-26-67
Amor, Carnaval E Sonho 2-28-73
Amor del Captain Brando, El 7-03-74
Amor Der Perdicao 10-15-80
Amor en el Aire 10-02-68
Amor Solfeando, El 12-08-31
Amor Ultimo Modelo 1-20-43
Amore 2-20-74
Amore Amaro 12-04-74
Amore Che Canta, L' 4-07-34
Amore Difficile, L' 1-16-63
Amore e Chiacchere 2-26-58
Amore e Morte 10-04-32
Amore e Rabbia 7-23-69
Amore in Citta 3-10-54

9

Amore in 4 Dimensioni 4-15-64
Amore Mio Aiutami 12-17-69
Amori e Veleni 4-26-50
Amorous Adventures of Don Quixote and Sancho Panza 4-21-76
Amorous Adventures of Moll Flanders, The 5-26-65
Amorous Ones, The (See: As Amorosas)
Amorous Prawn, The 11-21-62
Amos 'n' Andy (See: Check and Double Check)
Amour 8-19-70
Amour, L' 7-22-70
Amour, L' 8-23-72
Amour a l'Americaine 1-26-32
Amour a la Bouche, L' (See: Mannequin)
Amour a la Mer, L' 8-04-65
Amour a Vingt Ans, L' 5-30-62
Amour, Amour 10-11-32
Amour Autour de la Maison, L' (See: Love Locked Out)
Amour C'Est Gai, l'Amour C'est Triste, L' 11-26-69
Amour Chante, L' 12-03-30
Amour de la Vie: Artur Rubinstein, L' 6-04-69
Amour de Pluie, Un 4-24-74
Amour de Poche 3-26-58
Amour D'Une Femme, L' 6-30-54
Amour en Fuite, L' 1-24-79
Amour en Herbe, L' 7-27-77
Amour en Question, L' 11-01-78
Amour Est En Jeu, L' 10-09-57
Amour Fou, L' 8-07-68
Amour Humain, L' 6-09-71
Amour, L'Apres-Midi, L' 8-30-72
Amour, Madame, L' 4-02-52
Amour Toujours L'Amour, L' 9-03-52
Amour Viole, L' 12-28-77
Amoureuse, L' 11-01-72
Amoureux du France, Les 6-03-64
Amours Celebres, Les 11-08-61
Amours de Paris, Les 3-08-61
Amours de Toni, Les 11-18-36
Ampelopede, L' 3-06-74
Amphibious Man, The 7-24-63
Amphitheatre, The (See: Renidero, El)
Amphytrion 3-31-37
Amsterdam Affair 6-12-68
Amsterdam Kill 5-11-77
Amulet of Ogum, The (See: O Amuleto de Ogum)
An 01, L' 3-21-73
Ana y Los Lobos 5-28-73
Anacoreta, El 1-12-77
Analfabeto, El 10-11-61
Anaparastasis 11-11-70 and 12-12-73
Anastasia 12-19-56
Anastasia Passed By (See: Duios Anastasia Trecea)
Anatahan 7-15-53 (Also see: Devil's Pitchfork, The)
Anatoliki Periferia 11-28-79
Anatomie d'un Rapport 9-29-76
Anatomie des Liebesakts 2-25-70
Anatomy of a Murder 7-01-59
Anatomy of a Relationship (See: Anatomie d'un Rapport)
Anatomy of the Act of Love (See: Anatomie des Liebesakts)
Anatra All'Arancia, L' 1-14-76
Anchorite, The (See: Ancoreta, El)
Anchors Aweigh 7-18-45
Ancient Highway 11-11-25
Ancient Mariner, The 1-20-26
Ancines Woods, The (See: Bosque de Ancines, El)
And a Man Came ... (See: E Venne Un Uomo)
And a Still Small Voice 12-13-18
And Adventure in Hearts 1-09-20
And Baby Makes Three 11-30-49
And Baby Makes Three 12-06-72
And Death Is Dead (See: Et, Morte la Mort)
And Die of Pleasure (See: Et, Mourir de Plaisir)
And God Created Woman (See: Et Dieu Crea la Femme)
And Hope to Die (See: Course du Lievre a Travers les Champs, La)
And Jimmy Went to the Rainbow's Foot (See: und Jimmy Ging Zum Regenbogen)
... And Justice for All 9-19-79
And Long Live Liberty (See: Et Vive La Liberte)
And Love Has Vanished (See: Dvoje)
And Love Laughs At It (See: Und die Liebe Lacht Dazu)
... And My Love to the Swallows (See: A Pozdravuji Vlastovsky)
And Now for Something Completely Different 10-31-71 and 8-16-72
And Now, Miguel 5-18-66
And Now the Screaming Starts 5-09-73
And Now Tomorrow 10-18-44
And One Was Beautiful 4-03-40
And Quiet Flows the Don (Tichy Don) 6-01-60
... And My Love to the Swallows (See: A Pozdravuji Vlastovsky)
And Quiet Rolls the Day (See: Ekdin Pratidin)
And Satan Calls the Turns (See: Et Satan Conduit le Bal)

... And Saucy At That! (See: Und Noch Frech Dazu!)
And So It Is (See: Ukamau)
And So They Were Married 5-20-36
And Soon the Darkness 7-22-70
And Sudden Death 7-22-36
And That on Monday Morning (See: Und Das Am Montagmorgen)
And the Angels Sing 4-26-44
And the Pussta Shines (See: Und Es Leuchtet die Pussta)
And the Rain Blots Out All Traces (See: Und Der Regen Verwischt Jede Spur)
And the Son (See: Et Du Fils)
And the Third Year, He Resuscitated (See: ... Y Al Tercer Ano Resucito)
And the Villainess Still Pursued Him 11-13-09
And Then There Were None 7-11-45
And They Lived Happily Ever After (See: Colorin, Colorado)
And Who Kisses Me? (See: Und Wer Kuesst Mich?)
Andalousie 5-02-51
Andalusian Nights (See: Andalusische Naechte)
Andalusische Naechte 7-20-38
Andere, Der 1-19-32 (Also see: Other, The)
Andere Laechein, Das 6-21-78
Anderson Tapes, The 5-12-71
Andersson Family, The (See: Familjen Andersson)
Andes Odyssey, The (See: Odisea de los Andes, La)
Andre Gide 4-09-52
Andrei Roublov 6-04-69
Androcles and the Lion 10-29-52
Andromeda Strain, The 3-10-71
Andy 1-20-65
Andy Hardy Comes Home 7-30-58
Andy Hardy Gets Spring Fever 7-12-39
Andy Hardy Meets a Debutante 7-03-40
Andy Hardy's Blonde Trouble 4-05-44
Andy Hardy's Double Life 12-02-42
Andy Hardy's Private Secretary 2-26-41
Andy Warhol's Women 1-12-72
Anemone 5-01-68
Ang Boyfriend Kung Badoy 4-01-76
Ang Leon at Ang Daga 5-05-76
Ang Nobya Kong Sexy 3-12-75
Ang Pinakamagandang Hayop Sa Balat Ng Lupa 12-12-75
Angaaende Lone 7-08-70
Ange et la Femme, L' 2-01-78
Ange Gardien, L' 1-31-79
Ange Rouge, L' (See: Red Angel)
Angel 9-15-37
Angel and Sinner 2-26-47
Angel and the Badman 2-12-47
Angel and Woman (See: Ange et La Femme, L')
Angel, Angel, Down We Go 8-13-69
Angel Babe (See: Engelchen)
Angel Baby 5-10-61
Angel Came Down from Heaven, An (See: Bajo un Angel del Cielo)
Angel Child 9-13-18
Angel Comes to Brooklyn, An 12-05-45
Angel Exterminador, El 5-23-62
Angel Face 12-03-52
Angel from Texas, An 5-08-40
Angel in Exile 12-29-48
Angel in My Pocket 12-04-68
Angel Levine, The 7-15-70
Angel Mine 1-10-79
Angel Number 9 11-27-74
Angel of Broadway, The 11-02-27
Angel of Crooked Street 5-26-22
Angel of Dawson's Camp, The 4-30-10
Angel of the House 1-30-14
Angel on My Shoulder 9-18-46
Angel on the Amazon 12-22-48
Angel Paso Sobre Brooklyn 9-25-57
Angel Passed over Brooklyn, An (See: Angel Paso Sobre Brooklyn)
Angel Unchained 8-19-70
Angel Who Pawned Her Harp 9-15-54
Angel with the Trumpet, The (See: Engel Mit der Posaune, Der)
Angel with the Trumpet 2-22-50
Angel Wore Red 8-31-60
Angela 5-11-55
Angela 7-04-73
Angela Davis, L'Enchainement 12-28-77
Angela Davis: Portrait of a Revolutionary 1-26-72
Angela Davis, The Sequence of Events (See: Angela Davis, L'Enchainement)
Angele 11-13-34
Angeles y Querubines 8-16-72
Angeli del Quartiere, Gli 9-03-52
Angelika 10-06-54
Angelina 4-07-48

Anton, The Terrible 9-29-16
Antonia: A Portrait of the Woman 9-04-74
Antonio das Mortes 5-21-69
Antonio di Padova 7-20-49
Antonio Gaudi: An Unfinished Vision 6-05-74
Antonio Gramsci--I Grorni del Carcere 8-31-77
Antonio Gramsci--The Days of Prison (See: Antonio Gramsci--I
    Grorni del Carcere)
Ants in His Pants 3-06-40
Ants' Nest (See: Hongyboly)
Antti Puuhaara 7-27-77
Antti the Treebranch (See: Antti Puuhaara)
Antwort Kennt Nur der Wind, Die 7-30-75
Anugraham 1-31-79
Anuradha 7-05-61
Anxiety (See: Ansiedad)
Anxious to Return (See: Gui Xin Shi Jian)
Any Gun Can Play 9-18-68
Any Man's Wife 6-16-37
Any Number Can Play 6-08-49
Any Wednesday 10-19-66
Any Which Way You Can 12-17-80
Any Wife 2-10-22
Any Woman 5-27-25
Anybody's Blonde 11-24-31
Anybody's War 7-16-30
Anybody's Woman 8-20-30
Anyone Can Kill Me (See: Tous Peuvent Me Tuer)
Anyone Can Play 2-07-68
Anything Can Happen (See: Tout Peut Arriver)
Anything Can Happen 2-27-52
Anything for a Song 8-06-47
Anything for a Thrill 7-21-37
Anything Goes 2-12-36
Anything Goes 1-25-56
Anything Once 10-12-17
Anything Once 6-17-25
Anzio 6-19-68
Aoi Yaju (See: Blue Beast, The)
Aoom 7-22-70
Apa 7-26-67
Apa ca un Bivol Negru 9-08-71
Apache 6-30-54
Apache, L' 12-19-19
Apache, The 2-06-29
Apache Ambush 8-10-55
Apache Chief 10-19-49
Apache Country 5-21-52
Apache Drums 4-25-51
Apache Kid, The 9-24-41
Apache Rider, The 9-26-28
Apache Rifles 11-04-64
Apache Rose 3-26-47
Apache Territory 9-03-58
Apache Trail 6-24-42
Apache Uprising 1-12-66
Apache War Smoke 9-24-52
Apache Warrior 7-24-57
Apache Woman 10-12-55
Apaches of Paris 7-18-28
Apam Nehany Boldog Eve 3-29-78
Apando, El 8-25-76
Aparajito 9-18-57 and 11-19-58
Apart From Life (See: Chi No Mure)
Apartment, The 5-18-60
Apartment for Peggy 9-15-48
Apartment 29 4-13-17
Apasionadamente 6-21-44
Apasionata (See: Apasionadamente)
Ape 12-15-76
Ape, The 5-02-28
Ape, The 11-06-40
Ape and Superape 3-28-73
Ape Regina, L' 1-30-63
Ape Woman, The (See: Donna Scimmia, La)
Apeman, The 3-17-43
Apfel Ist Ab, Der 1-26-49
Aphonya 8-25-76
Apocalypse, L' 6-03-70
Apocalypse Now 5-16-79
Apoi S-A Nascut Legenda 6-24-70
Apokal 5-26-71
Apollo Goes on Holiday 3-06-68
Apology for Murder 10-03-45
Apostle of Vengeance, The 6-16-16
Appaloosa, The 9-14-66
Appartement des Filles, L' 1-01-64
Appassionata 3-20-29 and 7-10-29
Appassionata 11-20-46

Appassionata 8-21-74
Appeal of the Prairie, The 9-17-10
Appeal on a Cross 1-30-57
Appearance of Evil, The 9-27-18
Appearances 6-24-21
Appelkriget 4-19-72
Appelez-Moi Mathilde 1-14-70
Applause 10-09-29
Apple, The (See: Pomme, La)
Apple, The 5-28-80
Apple Dumpling Gang, The 6-25-75
Apple Dumpling Gang Rides Again 6-20-79
Apple Fell, The (See: Apfel Ist Ab, Der)
Apple of Discord, The (See: Manzana de la Discordia, La)
Apple Pie 9-24-75
Apple, the Stem and the Seeds, The (See: Pomme, la Queue et les
    Pepins, La)
Apple War, The (See: Appelkriget)
Appointment, The 5-28-69
Appointment for Love 10-29-41
Appointment for Murder 3-17-54
Appointment in Berlin 7-21-43
Appointment in Honduras 10-28-53
Appointment in London 2-25-53
Appointment in Tokyo 11-28-45
Appointment with a Shadow 9-03-58
Appointment with Crime 5-29-46
Appointment with Danger 4-18-51
Appointment with Life (See: Rendez-Vous de Juillet)
Appointment with Murder 10-13-48
Appointment with Venus 10-24-51
Appollon An Occupied Factory (See: Appollon una Fabbria Occupata)
Appollon una Fabbria Occupata 10-08-69
Apprenti Salaud, L' 2-02-77
Apprentice, The (See: Fleur Bleue)
Apprentice Heel, The (See: Apprenti Salaud, L')
Apprentice Sorcerers, The (See: Apprentis Sorciers, Les)
Apprentices, The (See: Apprentis, Les)
Apprenticeship of Duddy Kravitz, The 4-10-74
Apprentis, Les 8-12-64
Apprentis Sorciers, Les 2-09-77
Apres L'Amour 1-12-32
Apres L'Amour 3-17-48
Apres Mein Kampf Mes Crimes 4-24-40
April Blossoms 2-03-37
April 1, 2000 5-20-53
April Fool 11-03-26
April Fools, The 5-28-69
April Has 30 Days (See: April Hat 30 Tage, Ein)
April Hat 30 Tage, Ein 7-30-80
April in Paris 11-19-52
April in Portugal (See: Gran Senora, La)
April Love 11-20-57
April Showers 11-22-23
April Showers 3-10-48
Apur Sanshar 9-23-59
Aquella Casa En Las Afueras 11-19-80
Aquella Larga Noche 9-26-79
Aquellos Anos Locos 9-30-70
Aquirre, Der Zorn Gottes 5-30-73
Arab, The 6-18-15
Arab, The 7-16-24
Arabella 9-03-69
Arabesque 5-04-66
Arabian Adventure 5-30-79
Arabian Knight, An 8-13-20
Arabian Love 5-19-22
Arabian Nights 12-23-42
Arabian Nights (See: Arabische Naechte)
Arabian Nights (See: Fiore Delle Mille e Una Notte, Il)
Arabische Naechte 6-04-80
Araignee D'Eau, L' 3-17-71
Aran 9-05-79
Aranyer Din Ratri 7-08-70
Arashi 7-31-57
Araya 5-20-59
Arbored Colony (See: Laubenkolonie)
Arbre de Guernica, L' 12-10-75
Arc 8-12-70
Arcadians, The 12-14-27
Arch, The 11-13-68
Arch of Triumph 2-18-48
Arche de Noe, L' 2-26-47
Archie's Archery 10-29-10
Archimede le Clochard 5-13-59
Archimede the Tramp (See: Archimede le Clochard)
Arctic Flight 7-30-52

Arctic Fury 5-11-49
Arctic Manhunt 8-24-49
Ard, El 5-13-70
Arde 9-08-71
Ardent Love (See: Faja Lobbi)
Ardent Room, The (See: Chambre Ardente, La)
Ardoise, L' 1-28-71
Ardour Aflame (See: Jo-En)
Are All Men Alike? 1-21-21
Are Husbands Necessary? 6-17-42
Are Passions Inherited 3-02-17
Are the Children to Blame 12-01-22
Are These Our Children 11-17-31
Are These Our Parents 8-30-44
Are They Born or Made? 12-25-14
Are We Civilized 6-19-34
Are You a Failure? 4-26-23
Are You a Mason? 3-26-15
Are You a Mason? 11-06-34
Are You Afraid? (See: Er I Bange?)
Are You Engaged to a Greek Sailor or an Airline Pilot? (See:
     Etes Vous Fiancee A Un Marin Grec Ou A Un Pilote De Ligne?)
Are You Interested in the Thing? (See: Vous Interessez-Vous
     a la Chose?)
Are You Legally Married? 7-18-19
Are You Listening? 4-26-32
Are You There? 7-14-31
Are You With It? 3-17-48
Arena 6-24-53
Aren't Men Beasts? 2-03-37
Aren't We All? 7-05-32
Aren't We Wonderful (See: Wir Wunderkinder)
Argent de Poche, L' 3-24-76
Argent des Autres, L' 9-06-78
Argentine Love 12-24-24
Argentine Nights 9-04-40
Argentine Symphony (See: Sinfonia Argentina)
Argine, L' 10-26-38
Argonauts, The 1-07-11
Argyle Case, The 2-09-17
Argyle Case, The 9-04-29
Argyle Secrets, The 4-21-48
Ari No Machi No Maria 8-12-59
Aria Dia Atlety 6-25-80
Aria for an Athlete (See: Aria Dia Atlety)
Ariane 3-18-31
Ariane, Jeune Fille Russe 3-15-32
Ariane, Russian Maid (See: Ariane, Jeune Fille Russe)
Arid Land (See: Welikatara)
Arise, My Love 10-23-40
Aristocats, The 11-25-70
Aristocracy 11-21-14
Aristocrates, Les 11-23-55
Arizona 12-20-18
Arizona 11-20-40
Arizona Bound 4-13-27
Arizona Bound 9-10-41
Arizona Bushwhackers 2-14-68
Arizona Cat Claw, The 11-21-19
Arizona Cowboy 4-26-50
Arizona Cyclone 5-09-28
Arizona Cyclone 3-11-42
Arizona Days 5-08-29
Arizona Days 4-14-37
Arizona Express 4-23-24
Arizona Gunfighter 9-29-37
Arizona Kid, The 5-21-30
Arizona Kid, The 10-11-39
Arizona Legion 7-05-39
Arizona Mahoney 2-24-37
Arizona Manhunt 9-19-51
Arizona Raiders 7-21-65
Arizona Raiders, The 9-16-36
Arizona Ranger, The 3-24-48
Arizona Romeo 5-13-25
Arizona Sweepstakes 1-20-26
Arizona Territory 10-04-50
Arizona Terror 9-29-31
Arizona Terrors 4-01-42
Arizona to Broadway 7-25-33
Arizona Trail 5-03-44
Arizona Whirlwind 4-05-44
Arizona Wildcat 1-25-28
Arizona Wildcat 11-09-38
Arizonian, The 7-31-35
Arkadas 8-02-78
Arkansas Judge 7-23-41
Arkansas Traveler 10-05-38

Arm at the Left (See: Arme a Gauche, L')
Arm Chair, The (See: Karosszek, A)
Arm in Arm, Down the Street (See: Del Brazo y Por la Calle)
Arm of the Law 7-05-32
Arma, L' 8-09-78
Armaguedon 3-23-77
Armata Brancaleone, L' 6-01-66
Arme a Gauche, L' 7-21-65
Armee der Liebenden Oder Aufstand der Perversen 3-21-79
Armee des Ombres, L' 9-24-69
Armino Negro 10-14-53
Armored Car 7-28-37
Armored Car Robbery 6-14-50
Armored Command 8-02-61
Armored Vault 11-14-28
Armorer's Daughter 10-15-10
Arms and the Girl 10-12-17 and 10-19-17
Arms and the Woman 12-03-10
Arms and the Woman 11-10-16
Arms of Night, The (See: Bras de la Nuit, Les)
Armstrong-Ambers Fight 8-30-39
Armstrong-Jenkins Fight 7-24-40
Armstrong's Wife 12-03-15
Army Bound 10-29-52
Army Girl 7-20-38
Army Nakano School, The (See: Rikugun Nakano Gakko)
Army of Lovers Or Revolt of the Perverts (See: Armee der
     Liebenden Oder Aufstand der Perversen)
Army Surgeon 11-11-42
Army Wives 11-22-44
Arnelo Affair 2-12-47
Arnold 10-24-73
Around Peking 10-22-10
Around the World 11-24-43
Around the World in 80 Days 10-24-56
Around the World in 80 Minutes 11-24-31
Around the World Under the Sea 4-06-66
Around the World Via Graf Zeppelin 11-06-29
Aroused 8-28-68
Arp Statue, The 9-15-71
Arpenteurs, Les 5-10-72
Arpete, L' 4-17-29
Arrangement, The 11-19-69
Arrangiatevi! 11-11-59
Arrebato 10-15-80
Arrest Bulldog Drummond 11-23-38
Arrest of the Duchess de Berry 3-19-10
Arretez les Tambours 2-22-61
Arriba Hazana 6-21-78
Arrival of Josie, The 7-31-14
Arrival of Perpetua, The 3-26-15
Arrival of the Lusitania 10-12-07
Arrive Before Daybreak (See: Stici Pre Svitanja)
Arrivederci, Baby 12-21-66
Arrivederci, Papa 7-20-49
Arriviste, L' 2-09-77
Arrivistes, Les 5-04-60
Arrow in the Dust 4-21-54
Arrowhead 6-17-53
Arrowsmith 12-15-31
Arroz Con Leche 12-13-50
Arruza 6-16-71
Arsenal 11-13-29
Arsene Lupin 2-16-17
Arsene Lupin 3-01-32
Arsene Lupin Against Arsene Lupin (See: Arsene Lupin Contre
     Arsene Lupin)
Arsene Lupin Contre Arsene Lupin 10-03-62
Arsene Lupin Returns 2-23-38
Arsenic and Old Lace 9-06-44
Arshin Mal Alan 3-10-37
Arshin Takes a·Wife 8-02-50
Arson for Hire 3-18-59
Arson Gang Busters 6-01-38
Arson, Inc. 5-04-49
Arson Squad 9-26-45
Art of Getting Along, The (See: Arte di Arrangiarsi, L')
Art of Killing 11-22-78
Art of Living, The (See: Arte de Vivir, El)
Art of Love, The 5-12-65
Art of Loving, The (See: Jak Byc Kochana)
Arte de Vivir, El 8-04-65
Arte di Arrangiarsi, L' 4-06-55
Arthur 1-21-31 and 6-09-31
Arthur Miller on Home Ground 9-05-79
Arthur Penn, 1922--Themes and Variants 5-27-70
Arthur Takes Over 4-07-48

Art. 519, Codice Penale 7-08-53
Article 519, Penal Code (See: Art. 519, Codice Penale)
Artie, the Millionaire Kid 4-14-16
Artificial Sons (See: Hijos Artificiales, Los)
Artillery Sergeant Kalen 4-11-62
Artisten in der Zirkuskuppel: Ratlos, Die 9-11-68
Artists and Models 8-04-37
Artists and Models 11-09-55
Artists and Models Abroad 11-02-38
Artists' Entrance (See: Entree des Artists)
Artists' Pay Day 1-07-11
Artists Under the Big Top: Perplexed, The (See: Artisten in
    der Zirkuskuppel: Ratlos, Die)
Artless One, The (See: Ingenu, L')
Arturo Toscanini 5-03-44
Arvacska 5-26-76
Arven 5-23-79
Aryan, The 3-24-16
Arzt Stellt Fest ..., Der 5-18-66
Arzt Von St. Pauli, Der 6-11-69
Arzt Von Stalingrad, Der 8-27-58
As a Man Lives 12-15-22
As a Man Thinks 4-25-19
As a Turtle On Its Back (See: Tortue Sur Le Dos, La)
As a Woman Sows 1-28-16
As Amorosas 7-02-69
As Armas 2-18-70
As Deusas 3-07-73
As Du Turf, Les 4-19-32 and 5-22-35
As Easy As Pie (See: Comme Sur Des Roullettes)
As Far As Love Can Go (See: Aussi Loin Que L'Amour)
As Far As the Eye Sees (See: So Weit Das Auge Reicht)
As For All These Women (See: For Att Inte Tala Om Alla Dessa
    Kvinnor)
As Good as Married 5-26-37
As Horas de Maria 10-10-79
As Husbands Go 1-30-34
As in a Looking Glass 3-03-16
As Long As I Live (See: Si Lange Leben In Mirist)
As Long as One Is Intoxicated (See: Pourvu Qu'On Ait L'Ivresse)
As Long as They're Happy 4-06-55
As Long as You Are Healthy (See: Tant Qu'On A La Sante)
As Long as You Live (See: Solange du Lebst)
As Man Desires 2-11-25
As Man Made Her 3-16-17
As Men Love 5-11-17
As the Devil Commands 10-17-33
As the Earth Turns 4-17-34
As the Moon (See: Comme la Lune)
As the Sea Rages 8-24-60
As the Sun Went Down 2-21-19
As Time Goes By 7-31-74
As Ye Sow 12-19-14
As You Desire Me 6-07-32
As You Like It 9-16-36 and 11-11-36
As Young as You Feel 6-06-51
As Young as We Are 9-24-58
Asa-Hanna 5-15-46
Asa-Nisse I Kronans Kläder 1-14-59
Asa-Nisse in Military Uniform (See: Asa-Nisse I Kronans Kläder)
Asayake No Uta 7-10-74
Ascenseur Pour L'Echafaud 5-07-58
Ascent (See: Aarohi)
Ascent, The (See: Voshojdenie or Kodiyettom)
Asesino de Pedralbes, El 10-11-78
Ash Wednesday (See: Miercoles de Ceniza)
Ash Wednesday 11-21-73
Ashani Sanket 8-01-73
Ashanti 2-07-79
Ashes and Diamonds (See: Popiol i Diament)
Ashes of Embers 9-29-16
Ashes of Hope 10-05-17
Ashes of Memory (See: Ceneri Della Memoria)
Ashes of Vengeance 8-30-23
Ashes to the Wind (See: Ceniza al Viento)
Ashwathama 2-13-80
Asi Era Pancho Villa 8-05-59
Asi Se Quierre en Jalisco 8-18-43
Asia's Desert 7-03-29
Asignatura Pendiente 8-17-77
Ask a Policeman 4-26-39
Ask Any Girl 5-13-59
Aspects of France (See: Visages de France, Les)
Asphalt 4-10-29 and 5-07-30
Asphalt Fever, The (See: Pyretos Stin Asphalto)
Asphalt Jungle, The 5-10-50
Asphalt Night (See: Asphaltnacht)
Asphalte 8-19-59

Asphaltnacht 10-08-80
Asphyx, The 9-20-72
Assasinat du Pere Noel, L' (See: Who Killed Santa Claus?)
Assasins De L'Ordre 6-16-71
Assassin Connait la Musique, L' 10-30-63
Assassin Est Dans L'Annuaire, L' 4-18-62
Assassin Musicien, L' 5-14-75
Assassin N'Est Pas Coupable, L' 11-06-46
Assassin of Rome, The (See: Girolimoni, Il Mostro di Roma)
Assassination, The (See: Attentat, L')
Assassination Bureau, The 3-05-69
Assassination in Sarajevo (See: Atentat U Sarajevu)
Assassination of Matteotti, The (See: Delitto Matteotti, Il)
Assassination of Ryoma 11-13-74
Assassination of Trotsky, The 4-12-72
Assassins et Voleurs 6-19-57
Assassins of Order, The (See: Assasins de L'Ordre)
Assault 2-24-71
Assault, The 7-21-65
Assault and Battery (See: Misshandlingen)
Assault on a Queen 6-22-66
Assault on Agathon 10-13-76
Assault on Precinct 13 11-17-76
Assigned to Danger 5-05-48
Assignment, The 5-25-77
Assignment K 6-12-68
Assignment in Brittany 3-10-43
Assignment in Korea (See: Uppdrag I Korea)
Assignment--Paris 9-10-52
Assignment to Kill 12-11-68
Associate, The (See: Associe, L')
Association, The 7-09-75
Associe, L' 10-03-79
Assunta Spina 5-05-48
Asterix et Cleopatra 1-15-69
Astonished Heart 2-15-50
Astragale, L' 1-01-69
Astrologer, The 7-25-08
Astrologer, The 12-17-75
Astro-Zombies, The 5-07-69
Asya's Happiness (See: Istoriya Asi Klyachimol)
Asylum 8-02-72
At Dere Tor 11-19-80
At First Sight 7-06-17
At Green Cockatoo By Night (See: Nachts Im Gruenen Kakadu)
At Gunpoint 12-07-55
At Home Among Strangers (See: Svoi Sriedi Chougikh)
At Home at Last 3-20-09
At Long Last Love 3-05-75
At Night All Cats Are Gray (See: Nuit Tous Les Chats Sont
    Gris, La)
At Piney Ridge 5-12-16
At Risk of Life (See: Dorogoi Tsenoi)
At Sword's Point 1-23-52
At the Bar of Justice 3-19-10
At the Beginning of Summer (See: Ne Fillim Te Veres)
At the Brink of the Brink of the Bench (See: Au Bout du Bout
    du Banc)
At the Circus 10-18-39
At the Earth's Core 6-23-76
At the Edge of the World (See: Am Rande der Welt)
At the Edge of the World 6-20-28 and 6-19-29
At the Eleventh Hour 3-12-10
At the End of the World 8-19-21
At the Front in No. Africa 3-03-43
At the Grey House 11-23-27
At the Hour of Dawn 5-08-14
At the Meeting With Joyous Death (See: Au Rendez-Vous de la Mort
    Joyeuse)
At the Mercy of Men 4-26-18
At the Monkey House 2-16-07
At the Old Crossroads 10-10-14
At the Order of the Czar (See: Par Ordre Du Tsar)
At the Rink 12-15-16
At the Sea Shore 4-20-07
At the Service of Spanish Womanhood (See: Al Servicio de la Mujer
    Espanola)
At the Sound of the Bugle (See: Al Toque de Clarin)
At the South Pole 2-27-29
At the Stage Door 12-16-21
At the Terminus (See: Tam Na Konecne)
At 12 O'Clock 3-21-13
At War with the Army 12-13-50
At Yale 8-01-28
At Your Doorstep 10-21-64
At Your Own Request (See: Na Wlasna Prosbe)
At Zije Republika 3-23-66
At Ziji Duchove! 2-28-79

Ate a ultima Gota 5-28-80
Atentat U Sarajevu 8-18-76
Athena 11-03-54
Atithi 9-21-66
Atlantic 11-20-29/12-04-29 and 10-08-30
Atlantic Adventure 9-04-35
Atlantic City 8-02-44
Atlantic City, U.S.A. 9-03-80
Atlantic Convoy 7-08-42
Atlantic Ferry 7-23-41
Atlantic Flight (See: Stormo Atlantico, Lo)
Atlantic Flight 9-22-37
Atlantic Swimmers, The (See: Atlantikschwinner, Die)
Atlantic Wall, The (See: Mur De L'Atlantique, Le)
Atlantide, L' 6-21-32
Atlantikschwinner, Die 7-07-76
Atlantis, The Lost Continent 4-19-61
Ato de Violencia 12-24-80
Atoll K 11-21-51
Atom, The 9-20-18
Atomic City, The 4-09-52
Atomic Kid, The 12-08-54
Atomic Physics 12-31-47
Atomic Submarine 2-17-60
Atonement (See: Suehne)
Atonement 5-18-17
Atout Coeur 10-20-31
Atout Coeur A Tokyo Pour OSS 117 11-23-66
Atracadores, Los 7-11-62
Atragon 3-17-65
Atras de las Nubes 10-31-62
Att Alska 9-09-64
Atta Boy! 12-29-26
Atta Boy's Last Race 10-20-16
Attack! 6-14-44
Attack! 9-12-56
Attack of the Crab Monsters 3-20-57
Attack of the 50-Foot Woman 5-14-58
Attack of the Killer Tomatoes 1-31-79
Attack of the Puppet People 8-20-58
Attack on the Iron Coast 3-20-68
Attanasio, Cavallo Vanesio 5-13-53
Attanasio, The Vain Horse (See: Attanasio, Cavallo Vanesio)
Attempt, The (See: Zamach)
Attempt at a Crime (See: Ensayo de un Crimes)
Attempted Suicide 2-09-07
Attentat 9-10-80
Attentat, L' 10-18-72
Attenti Al Buffone 12-31-75
Attention, les Enfants Regardent 4-26-78
Attention les Yeux 3-03-76
Attention, the Kids Are Watching (See: Attention, les Enfants
    Regardent)
Attica 3-06-74
Attico, L' 5-08-63
Attila 3-16-55
Attila 74 11-19-75
Atto di Accusa 3-21-51
Attonde Dagen, Den 8-15-79
Attorney for the Defense 5-31-32
Au Bonheur Des Dames (See: Shop Girls of Paris)
Au Bout du Bout du Banc 7-11-79
Au Coeur de la Vie 9-18-63
Au-Dela de la Peur 10-29-75
Au Dela des Grilles 10-19-49
Au Dela des Sables 5-15-74
Au Grand Terrace 5-09-51
Au Hasard Balthazar 5-11-66
Au Long de la Riviere Fango 2-05-75
Au Nom de la Loi 5-10-32
Au Nom de la Race 3-12-75
Au Nom du Fuhrer 3-07-79
Au Pan Coupe 3-06-68
Au Petit Bonheur 6-05-46
Au Petit Zouave 8-09-50
Au Pied, Au Cheval et Par Sputnik 10-01-58
Au Rendez-Vous de la Mort Joyeuse 1-16-73
Au Revoir ... A Lundi 9-05-79
Au Revoir Monsieur Grock 9-06-50
Au Royaume des Cieux 10-26-49
Auandar Anapu 8-28-74
Aube D'Islam, L' 5-05-71
Aube N'est Pas Encore Levee, L' 7-18-73
Auberge du Peche, L' 3-29-50
Auberge Rouge, L' 11-28-51
Auch Zwerge Haben Klein Angefangen 7-01-70
Auction Block, The 2-22-18
Auction Block, The 2-17-26

Auctioneer, The 2-02-27
Audacious Mr. Square 11-01-23
Audience, The (See: Udienza, L')
Audrey 3-31-16
Audrey Rose 4-06-77
Auf Biegen Oder Brechen 9-01-76
Auf Der Insel 6-01-77
Auf Der Reeperbahn Nachts Um Halb Eins (See: Hamburg at 12:30)
Auf Der Reeperbahn Nachts Um Halb Eins 12-03-69
Aufrechte Gang, Der 6-30-76
Aufstand, Der 7-02-80
Aufwind 5-23-79
Augh, Augh! 10-01-80
August and July 4-11-73
August der Starke 2-03-37
August 14 8-18-48
August '68 (See: Agosto '68)
August Star, The (See: Sao Thang Tam)
August Weekend 7-22-36
Auguste 11-15-61
Aulad El Rih 9-10-80
Auld Robin Gray 10-22-10
Aunt Clara (See: Doda Clara)
Aunt Green, Aunt Brown and Aunt Lilac (See: Tant Gron, Tant Brun
    Och Tant Gredelin)
Aunt Isabel (See: Iza Neni)
Aunt Tula (See: Tia Tula, La)
Aunt Zita (See: Tante Zita)
Auntie Mame 11-26-58
Auntie Takes the Children to the Country 11-07-08
Aus der Ferne Sehe Ich Dieses Land 10-11-78
Auschwitz Street (See: Lagerstrasse Auschwitz)
Ausente, La 7-30-52
Ausleiferung, Die 8-28-74
Aussi Loin Que L'Amour 11-03-71
Aussi Longue Absence, Une 3-08-61
Austerlitz 6-29-60
Australia After Dark 12-17-75
Australia's Wild Nor-West 9-30-21
Austro-German Fronts, The 2-02-17
Autant en Emporte L'Histoire 2-08-50
Authentic Trial of Carl-Emmanuel Jung, The (See: Authentique
    Proces de Carl-Emmanuel Jung, L')
Authentique Proces de Carl-Emmanuel Jung, L' 8-07-68
Authorized Instructor (See: Educatore Autorizzato)
Auto and No Money, An (See: Auto und Kein Geld, Ein)
Auto Hero, The 11-21-08
Auto und Kein Geld, Ein 8-12-36
Autobiography of a Flea 2-09-77
Autobiography of a Princess 10-08-75
Autopsie d'un Complot 8-02-78
Autopsy 11-28-73
Autopsy 10-04-78
Autopsy of a Conspiracy (See: Autopsie d'un Complot)
Autre Homme, Une Autre Chance, Un (See: Another Man, Another
    Chance)
Autres, Les 5-22-74
Autumn Afternoon, An (See: Samma No Aji)
Autumn Crocus 11-06-34
Autumn Leaves 4-18-56
Autumn Love 10-31-28
Autumn Marathon (See: Osenny Maraphon)
Autumn Marriage (See: Osennie Svadjby)
Autumn Sonata 9-13-78
Aux Deux Masques 6-07-23
Aux Jardins de Murcie (See: Heritage)
Aux Jardins de Murcie 4-26-23
Aux Urnes, Citoyens 4-12-32
Aux Urnes, Citoyens 10-11-72
Aux Yeux du Souvenir 12-15-48
Avalanche 12-12-28
Avalanche 7-10-46
Avalanche 9-06-78
Avalanche, The 7-04-19
Avalanche Express 7-25-79
Avant le Deluge 4-07-54
Avantazh 2-22-78
Avanti 12-27-72
Avare, L' 3-26-80
Ave Maria 8-14-14
Ave Maria 9-16-36
Avec Des Si 11-27-63
Avec l'Assurance 6-28-32
Avec le Peau des Autres 9-21-66
Avec le Sourire 2-08-39
Avenged by the Sea 3-14-08
Avenger 4-22-31
Avenger, The 10-10-33

Avengers, The   11-04-42
Avengers, The   6-14-50
Avenging Conscience, The   8-07-14
Avenging Dentist, The   1-08-10
Avenging Fangs   6-01-27
Avenging Rider   11-14-28
Avenging Rider, The   9-29-43
Avenging Shadow   6-13-28
Avenging Trail, The   1-11-18
Aventuras de Joselito y Pulgarcito   10-26-60
Aventure C'est L'Aventure, L'   5-17-72
Aventure Commence Demain, L'   3-24-48
Aventure de Billy le Kid, Une   3-17-71
Aventures d'Arsene Lupin, Les   5-22-57
Aventures de Rabbi Jacob, Les   11-14-73
Aventures de Salavin, Les   12-30-64
Aventures de Till L'Espiegle, Les   1-16-57
Aventurier de Seville, L'   6-09-54
Aventuriers, Les   3-29-67
Average Man, An (See: Borghese Piccolo Piccolo, Un)
Average Woman   4-02-24
Aveu, L'   5-06-70
Aveux les Plus Doux, Les   6-30-71
Aviateur, L'   2-18-31
Aviation at L.A.   2-26-10
Aviation Contests at Rheims   9-25-09
Aviation Craze, The   10-22-10
Aviator, The   1-15-30 (Also see: Aviateur, L')
Avivato   11-30-49
Avocate D'Amour   9-14-38
Avodah   2-19-36
Avoir 20 Ans Dans les Aures   5-10-72
Avventura, L'   5-25-60
Avventure di Giacomo Casanova, Le   3-16-55
Avventura di Salvator Rosa, Un' (See: Adventure of Salvator
    Rosa, An)
Awakening   1-09-29
Awakening, The (See: Amour Humain, L')
Awakening, The   10-09-09
Awakening, The   11-23-17
Awakening, The   9-17-80
Awakening Giant--China, The   5-30-73
Awakening of Jim Burke   5-22-35
Awans   8-25-76
Awara   4-11-56
Away All Boats   5-16-56
Away Goes Prudence   7-09-20
Awful Manners, The (See: Vilaines Manieres, Les)
Awful Truth, The   7-08-25
Awful Truth, The   10-20-37
A.W.O.L. (See: Desertoren)
Axe, The (See: Baltagul)
Axel Munthe, Der Arzt von San Michele   10-24-62
Axel Munthe, Doctor of San Michele (See: Axel Munthe, Der Arzt
    Von San Michele)
Ay, Jalisco No te Rajes   12-31-41
Ay, Pena, Penita, Pena   12-02-53
Ay-Rab, The (See: Bougnoul, Le)
Ayudeme Ud, Compadra   11-20-68
Az Angyalek Foldje (See: Land of Angels)
Az Aranyember   2-10-37
Az Elcserelt Ember   5-04-38
Az Ember Neha Teved   2-23-38
Az En Lanyom Nem Olyan   5-04-38
Az Erod   2-28-79
Az Okos Mama   4-01-36
Az Otodik Pecset   3-02-77
Az Prijde Kocour   5-22-63
Az Uj Foldesur   1-29-36
Azahares Rojos   3-15-61
Azais   8-25-31 and 8-30-32
Aziza   6-25-80
Azonositas   7-14-76
Azure Express   11-09-38

B

B.F.'s Daughter   2-18-48
B.S., I Love You   3-03-71
Baara   8-23-78 and 2-07-79
Baba Yaga   7-25-73
Babae, Hindi Ka Dapat Nilalang   4-23-75
Babatu   5-26-76

Babbitt   7-16-24
Babbitt   12-18-34
Babbling Tongues   8-17-17
Babe Comes Home   6-01-27
Babe Ruth Story, The   7-21-48
Babek   7-02-80
Babes in Arms   9-20-39
Babes in Bagdad   12-10-52
Babes in Toyland   12-18-34
Babes in Toyland   12-06-61
Babes on Broadway   12-03-41
Babes on Swing Street   9-20-44
Babette Goes to War (See: Babette S'en Va-T-En Guerre)
Babette S'en Va-T-En Guerre   9-09-59
Babies for Sale   6-12-40
Baboona   1-29-35
Bab's Burglar   11-02-17
Bab's Candidate   7-09-20
Bab's Diary   9-28-17
Baby and the Battleship, The   8-01-56
Baby Blue Marine   4-28-76
Baby Carriage, The (See: Ubagaruma)
Baby Carriage, The (See: Barnvagnen)
Baby Cyclone, The   10-17-28
Baby Doctor Engel (See: Kinderarzt Dr. Engel)
Baby Doll   12-05-56
Baby Face   6-27-33
Baby Face Harrington   6-26-35
Baby Face Morgan   10-21-42
Baby Face Nelson   11-06-57
Baby Love   3-12-69
Baby Maker, The   9-30-70
Baby Mine   9-28-17
Baby Mine   1-11-28
Baby Rosemary   8-11-76
Baby Sitter, La   11-05-75
Baby Snakes   12-26-79
Baby Swallows a Nickel   12-04-09
Baby Take a Bow   7-03-34
Baby The Rain Must Fall   1-13-65
Baby Vickie   3-05-69
Babylon   5-14-80
Babylone-XX   9-03-80
Baby's Bodyguard (See: Mue Phuen Po Look On)
Babysitter, The   10-08-69
Baccara   2-19-36
Bacchanale   7-01-70
Bach: B-Minor Mass (See: Bach: H-Moll Messe)
Bach: H-Moll Messe   4-25-79
Bachelor, The (See: Scapolo, Lo)
Bachelor, The   11-12-10
Bachelor and the Bobby Soxer, The   6-04-47
Bachelor Apartment   5-20-31
Bachelor Bait   12-25-34
Bachelor Brides   5-19-26
Bachelor Daddy   4-28-22
Bachelor Daddy   7-02-41
Bachelor Father   2-04-31
Bachelor Flat   11-29-61
Bachelor Girl, The   7-24-29
Bachelor in Paradise   11-01-61
Bachelor Mother   2-21-33
Bachelor Mother   7-05-39
Bachelor of Arts   4-17-35
Bachelor of Hearts   12-24-58
Bachelor Party, The   3-06-57
Bachelor's Affairs   6-28-32
Bachelor's Baby   10-08-10
Bachelor's Baby   5-11-27
Bachelor's Baby, A   7-07-22
Bachelors' Club   9-04-29
Bachelor's Daughters, The   9-11-46
Bachelor's Love, A   11-06-09
Bachelors' Paradise   7-18-28
Bachelor's Romance, The   4-02-15
Bachelor's Visit   9-25-09
Bachelor's Wife, A   5-16-19
Bacio di una Morta, Il   11-30-49
Back Among the Old Folks   3-05-10
Back at the Front   10-01-52
Back Door to Heaven   4-12-39
Back Door Users (See: Vi Som Gar Koksvagen)
Back from Eternity   8-29-56
Back from Shanghai   3-26-30
Back from the Dead   8-14-57
Back Home and Broke   1-05-23
Back in Circulation   7-28-37
Back in the Saddle   3-26-41

Back of the Man 3-02-17
Back of the Store (See: Trastienda, La)
Back Pay 2-17-22
Back Pay 6-04-30
Back Row, The 2-21-73
Back Stage 10-03-19
Back Street 8-30-32
Back Street 2-12-41
Back Street 10-11-61
Back to Bataan 5-30-45
Back to God's Country 1-03-20
Back to God's Country 10-26-27
Back to God's Country 9-23-53
Back to Liberty 1-25-28
Back to Life Again (See: Zycie Raz Jeszcze)
Back to Nature 9-02-36
Back to the Door (See: De Espaldas a la Puerta)
Back to the Wall (See: Dos Au Mur, Le)
Back to the Woods 8-02-18
Back to Yellow Jacket 9-08-22
Back Trail 10-13-48
Back Trail, The 8-06-24
Backbone (See: Kicma)
Backbone 5-03-23
Backfire 1-18-50
Background 10-14-53
Background to Danger 6-09-43
Backlash 3-26-47
Backlash 3-07-56
Backstage 6-29-27
Backstage 6-30-37
Backstairs 6-09-26 and 12-14-27
Backtrack 6-04-69
Backward, Turn Backward, O Time in Your Flight 9-11-09
Bad 3-30-77
Bad and the Beautiful, The 11-19-52
Bad Bascomb 2-06-46
Bad Birds, Good Birds (See: Uccellacci e Uccellini)
Bad Blonde 5-06-53
Bad Boy 10-30-35
Bad Boy 12-20-39
Bad Boy 1-26-49
Bad Boy, The 3-09-17
Bad Boys (See: Furyo Syonen)
Bad Case of Grippe, A 12-18-09
Bad Charleston Charlie 5-16-73
Bad Company 3-25-25
Bad Company 11-10-31
Bad Company 10-04-72
Bad Day at Black Rock 12-15-54
Bad Eyes (See: Onda Ogon)
Bad for Each Other 12-09-53
Bad Girl 8-18-31
Bad Guy 9-01-37
Bad Guys, The (See: Rosszemberek)
Bad Lands 8-16-39
Bad Liaisons, The (See: Mauvaises Rencontres, Les)
Bad Little Angel 12-06-39
Bad Lord Byron 3-30-49
Bad Man, The 4-27-07
Bad Man, The 10-11-23
Bad Man, The 10-01-30
Bad Man, The 4-02-41
Bad Man from Red Butte, The 6-12-40
Bad Man of Brimstone 1-19-38
Bad Man of Deadwood 9-17-41
Bad Man's Money 5-22-29
Bad Men of Missouri 8-06-41
Bad Men of the Hills 10-28-42
Bad Men of Tombstone 3-09-49
Bad News Bears, The 4-07-76
Bad News Bears Go to Japan, The 6-14-78
Bad News Bears in Breaking Training, The 7-27-77
Bad One, The 6-18-30
Bad Seed, The 7-25-56
Bad Sister 4-01-31
Bad Sleep Well, The 7-05-61
Bad Son, A (See: Mauvais Fils, Un)
Bad Sorts (See: Warui Yatsura)
Bad Spirits of the Euphrates, The (See: Firatin Cinleri)
Bad Starters, The (See: Mal Partis, Les)
Bad Time for Squealers (See: Sales Temps Pour Les Mouches)
Bad Timing 2-20-80
Badarna 5-29-68
Badge of Honor 5-29-34
Badge of Marshall Brennan, The 8-14-57
Badge 373 7-18-73

Badi Blagoslovena 5-31-78
Badjao 7-26-61 and 10-04-61
Badlanders, The 7-16-58
Badlands 10-10-73
Badlands of Dakota 9-10-41
Badlands of Montana 5-15-57
Badman's Country 5-28-58
Badman's Gold 10-24-51
Badman's Territory 4-17-46
Baer-Galento Bout 7-10-40
Bag and Baggage 3-05-24
Bag of Marbles, A (See: Sac de Billes, Un)
Bag Race, A 2-19-10
Bagdad 11-23-49
Baghe Sangui 7-14-76
Bagnostraefling, Der 3-15-50
Bahama Passage 12-10-41
Baie des Anges, La 3-20-63
Bailarin y Trabajador 7-01-36
Bailiff of Griefensee, The (See: Landvogt von Griefensee, Der)
Bailout at 43,000 5-15-57
Baisers Voles 9-18-68
Baishey Stravana 9-14-60
Bait 2-17-54
Bait, The 1-07-21
Bajecni Muzi s Klikou 2-07-79
Bajo un Angel del Cielo 9-16-42
Bakaruhaban 7-31-57
Baker of Valorgue, The (See: Boulanger de Valorgue, Le)
Baker's Bread, The (See: Brot Des Baeckers, Das)
Baker's Hawk 1-12-77
Baker's Wife, The (See: Femme du Boulanger, La)
Bako; L'Autre Rive 8-23-78
Bako, The Other Shore (See: Bako, L'Autre Rive)
Bakuso 3-29-67
Bal, Le 11-10-31 and 10-04-32
Bal Cupidon, Le 6-22-49
Bal de Nuit 8-19-59
Bal de Samedi Soir, Le 6-19-68
Bal des Voyous, Le 8-21-68
Bal du Comte D'Orgel, Le 5-13-70
Bal Tabarin 6-18-52
Balaclava 4-30-30
Balada O Trubi I Oblaku 8-09-61
Balalaika 12-20-39
Balaoo or the Demon Ape 10-03-14
Balarrasa 5-09-51
Balcony, The 3-20-63
Bald-Headed Betty 9-10-75
Baleine Qui Avait Mal Aux Dents, Une 4-17-74
Baleydier 2-02-32
Bali 1-13-71
Balinese Love 12-08-31
Balint Fabian Meets God (See: Fabian Balint Talalkozasa Istennel)
Ball, The (See: Bal, Le)
Ball, The (See: Bal, Le)
Ball at Savoy 1-29-36
Ball at the Castle (See: Ballo al Castello)
Ball of Count Orgel, The (See: Bal du Comte d'Orgel, Le)
Ballad for a Dog (See: Ballade Pour un Chien)
Ballad for a Hoodlum (See: Ballade Pour un Vovou)
Ball of Fire 12-03-41
Ballad About a Trumpet and a Cloud (See: Balada O Trubi I Oblaku)
Ballad in Blue 3-03-65
Ballad of a Hussar 7-31-63
Ballad of Cable Hogue 3-11-70
Ballad of Carl-Henning, The (See: Balladem Om Carl-Henning)
Ballad of Cossack Golota 3-09-38
Ballad of Josie, The 12-27-67
Ballad of Tara 5-28-80
Ballad of the Daltons, The (See: Ballade des Daltons, La)
Ballad of the Silk Tree (See: Nemu No Ki No Uta)
Ballada O Soldatie 5-18-60
Ballade des Daltons, La 9-27-78
Ballade Pour un Chien 3-27-68
Ballade Pour un Vovou 3-20-63
Balladem Om Carl-Henning 5-07-69
Balle Au Coeur, Une 3-16-66
Balle Suffit ..., Une 2-09-55
Ballerina 10-04-50
Ballerina a Buon Dio 10-01-58
Ballerina and God, The (See: Ballerina a Buon Dio)
Ballet Gayane 12-27-78
Ballet Girl, The 1-28-16
Ballo Al Castello 11-01-39
Ballon Rouge, Le 5-16-56
Ballongen 12-04-46

Balloon, The (See: Ballongen)
Balloon Man (See: Globero, El)
Balloon of Cantella, The (See: Globo de Cantolla, El)
Baltagul 9-17-69
Baltic Deputy 9-08-37
Baltic Tragedy, A (See: Baltutlaminingen)
Baltimore Bullet, The 2-27-80
Baltutlaminingen 11-25-70
Bambi 5-27-42
Bambole, Le 2-03-65
Bambolona, La 1-15-69
Bamboo Blonde, The 6-19-46
Bamboo Gods and Iron Men 1-23-74
Bamboo Prison 12-15-54
Bamboo Saucer, The 11-06-68
Bamse 2-11-70
Banana Skin (See: Peau de Banane)
Bananas 4-28-71
Banco a Bangkok 7-22-64
Band of Angels 7-10-57
Band of Ninja, A (See: Ninja Bugelijo)
Band Plays On, The 12-25-34
Band Wagon, The 7-08-53
Banda J. & S. Cronaca Criminale Del Far West (See: Sonny & Jed)
Bandbox, The 12-05-19
Bande a Bonnot, La 11-13-68
Bande a Bouboule, La 1-12-32
Bande a Part 4-29-64
Bandera, La 10-02-35
Bandera Rota 9-05-79
Bandida, La 9-05-62
Bandido 8-15-56
Bandidos de Rio Frio 3-28-56
Bandini 8-12-64
Bandit, The 2-12-10
Bandit, The 6-01-49
Bandit, The (See: Amanti Di Gramigna, L')
Bandit King of Texas 10-05-49
Bandit of Sherwood Forest, The 2-20-46
Bandit of Tacca Del Lupo, The (See: Brigante Di Tacca Del Lupo, Il)
Bandit of Zhobe, The 3-11-59
Bandit Queen 11-29-50
Bandit Trail, The 9-10-41
Banditen der Autobahn 12-28-55
Banditi a Milano 5-22-68
Banditi a Orgosolo 8-30-61
Bandits at Orgosolo (See: Banditi a Orgosolo)
Bandit's Baby, The 6-17-25
Bandits in Milan (See: Banditi a Milano)
Bandits of Cold River, The (See: Bandidos de Rio Frio)
Bandits of Corsica, The 3-18-53
Bandits of Dark Canyon 12-10-47
Bandits of Death Valley, The 2-12-15
Bandits of El Dorado 6-27-51
Bandits of Highway (See: Banditen der Autobahn)
Bandits of the West 8-19-53
Bandits on the Wind 9-26-62
Bandit's Son, The 2-08-28
Bandolero 6-05-68
Bandolero, The 10-29-24
Bang 5-25-77
Bang Bang 8-25-71
Bang Bang Gang, The 8-26-70
Bang Bang Kid, The 6-26-68
Bang, Bang, You're Dead 8-24-66
Bang the Drum Slowly 8-15-73
Bang! You're Dead 3-24-54
Bangkok No Yoru 4-13-66
Banished 11-01-78
Banished from Paradise 7-14-65
Banjo 4-16-47
Banjo on My Knee 12-16-36
Banjoman 11-26-75
Bank, The (See: Chaplin in "The Bank")
Bank Alarm 6-23-37
Bank Dick, The 12-04-40
Bank Holiday 2-09-38
Bank Shot, The 7-10-74
Banked Fires (See: Ukroschenie Ognia)
Banker's Daughter, The 10-29-10
Banker's Daughter, The 4-24-14
Banks of the Ganges, The 4-02-10
Bannerline 9-19-51
Banning 7-05-67
Banquero 5-20-70
Banquiere, La 9-03-80
Banshun (See: Late Spring)

Bantam Cowboy 8-15-28
Bao Feng Chou Yu 1-17-79
Baptism (See: Keresztelo)
Baquet des Fraudeurs, Le 7-30-52
Bar at the Crossing, The (See: Bar de la Fourche, Le)
Bar de la Fourche, Le 7-12-72
Bar du Sud 5-04-38
Bar du Telephone, Le 9-17-80
Bar L Ranch 9-24-30 and 12-24-30
Bar Mitzvah 6-12-57
Bar Nothin' 11-25-21
Bar Sinister 8-24-55
Bar Sinister, The 4-20-17
Bar 20 7-21-43
Bar 20 Justice 9-21-38
Bar 20 Rides Again 7-08-36
Bara en Mor 3-08-50
Barabbas 6-13-62
Baranski 4-02-80
Baratsagos Arczot Kerek 3-04-36
Barbacka 2-05-47
Barbagia 10-22-69
Barbara 8-19-70
Barbara Frietchie 10-01-24
Barbarella 10-09-68
Barbarian, The 5-16-33
Barbarian and the Geisha, The 10-01-58
Barbarians of the North (See: Barbaros del Norte, Los)
Barbaros del Norte, Los 3-28-62
Barbary Coast 10-16-35
Barbary Coast Gent 8-02-44
Barbary Pirate 8-03-49
Barbary Sheep 9-14-17
Barbe-Bleue 9-19-51
Barbed Wire 8-10-27
Barbed Wire 7-02-52
Barber of Seville 7-27-49
Barber of Seville, The 4-16-47
Barber of Seville, The 11-28-73
Barber of Stanford Hill 2-20-63
Barberina 11-01-32
Barcarole 3-27-35 and 10-21-36
Bardelys the Magnificent 10-13-26
Bare en Tagsten 1-18-67
Bare Fists 5-09-19
Bare Knees 1-25-28
Bare Knuckles 2-08-78
Bareback Rider, The 1-29-10
Baree, Son of Kazan 5-24-18
Baree, Son of Kazan 5-20-25
Barefoot Battalion 6-09-54
Barefoot Boy 11-15-23
Barefoot Boy 8-31-38
Barefoot Contessa, The 9-29-54
Barefoot Executive, The 2-24-71
Barefoot in the Park 5-24-67
Barefoot Mailman, The 11-07-51
Barefooted Gen (See: Hadashi No Gen)
Bargain, The 11-14-14
Bargain, The 9-08-31
Barge-Keeper's Daughter 9-12-45
Bargee, The 4-29-64
Bari Trekey Paliye 9-09-59
Bariera 12-21-66
Barierata 7-18-79
Barker, The 12-12-28
Barkleys of Broadway, The 4-13-49
Barna fran Blasjofjaellet 12-24-80
Barnabe 6-01-38
Barnacle Bill 7-02-41
Barnen Fran Frostmofjallet (See: Children, The)
Barney 1-12-77
Barnfoerbjudet 1-02-80
Barnstormer, The 5-26-22
Barnum Was Right 10-30-29
Barnvagnen 5-15-63
Barnyard Cavalier, A 3-24-22
Barnyard Follies 12-04-40
Barocco 12-01-76
Baron Blood 10-25-72
Baron de L'Ecluse, Le 4-27-60
Baron Munchhausen (See: Baron Prasil)
Baron of Arizona 2-15-50
Baron of the Locks, The (See: Baron de L'Ecluse, Le)
Baron Prasil 7-18-62
Baroness and the Butler 2-16-38
Baroud 12-13-32
Barquero 5-20-70

Barra Pesada 11-16-77
Barranco 7-12-32
Barravento 7-04-62
Barren Lives (See: Vidas Secas)
Barretts of Wimpole Street, The 10-02-34
Barretts of Wimpole Street, The 1-16-57
Barricade 12-13-39
Barricade 3-08-50
Barricade, The 3-09-17
Barricade at Point du Jour, The (See: Barricade du Point du
    Jour, La)
Barricade du Point du Jour, La 3-08-78
Barrier (See: Bariera or Barierata)
Barrier, The 1-19-17
Barrier, The 3-24-26
Barrier, The 11-03-37
Barriers Burned Away 3-11-25
Barriers of Folly 12-15-22
Barriers of the Law 4-01-25
Barrow Race, A 11-06-09
Barry 9-21-49
Barry Lyndon 12-17-75
Barry McKenzie Holds His Own 1-01-75
Bars of Hate 11-11-36
Bartered Bride (See: Verkaufte Braut)
Bartleby 3-24-71
Barwy Orchronne 5-18-77
Bas Ya Bahar 9-13-72
Base of the Air Is Red, The (See: Fond de l'Air Est Rouge, Le)
Baseball Fan, The 8-29-08
Basement Melody (See: Melodie En Sous-Sol)
Bashful Bachelor, The 3-18-42
Bashful Buccaneer, The 1-20-26
Bashful Elephant, The 2-14-62
Bashful Young Man, The 7-18-08
Basilischi, I 7-31-63
Basket of Mexican Tales (See: Canasta de Cuentos Mexicanos)
Basketball Fix, The 9-19-51
Basketball Stars 9-18-74
Basseinut 8-03-77
Bastien, Bastienne 9-19-79
Bastyasetany 3-12-75
Bat, The (See: Fledermaus, Die)
Bat, The 3-17-26
Bat, The 8-12-59
Bat Whispers, The 1-21-31
Bataan 5-26-43
Bataille de France, La 7-08-64
Bataille de L'Eau Lourde, La 3-17-48
Bataille du Rail (See: Battle of the Rails)
Bataille du Rail 3-27-46
Bataillon du Ciel, Le 1-01-47
Batalla de Chile, II: El Golpe de Estada, La 7-14-76
Batalla de Chile III, La 5-07-80
Bateau D'Emile, Le 3-21-62
Bateau Sur L'Herbe, Le 4-28-71
Bath House Blunder 4-21-16
Bath Tub Perils 6-16-16
Bathers, The (See: Badarna)
Bathing Beauty 5-31-44
Bathing Suit Salesman, A 1-07-16
Batingaw 4-03-74
Batman 7-20-66
Batmanova, Singing Slave 1-22-64
Batouk 5-17-67
Battaglia di Algeri, La 9-07-66
Battements de Coeur 3-20-40
Battle, The (See: Kampf, Der)
Battle, The 4-24-34
Battle, The 11-27-34
Battle at Apache Pass 4-02-52
Battle at Bloody Beach 7-12-61
Battle Beneath the Earth 5-15-68
Battle Beyond the Stars 7-30-80
Battle Circus 1-28-53
Battle Cry 2-02-55
Battle Cry of Peace, The 8-13-15
Battle Flame 5-13-59
Battle for Kiev 1-08-36
Battle for New Britain, The (See: Attack!)
Battle for Paris 9-18-29
Battle for Russia 10-06-43
Battle for the Planet of the Apes 5-23-73
Battle for the Railway (See: Dvoboj Za Juznu Prugu)
Battle Hymn 12-19-56
Battle in Outer Space 6-15-60
Battle in the Clouds, The 1-08-10

Battle of Algiers (See: Battaglia di Algeri, La)
Battle of Bademuende (See: Schlacht von Bademuende)
Battle of Blood Island 5-18-60
Battle of Britain 9-15-43
Battle of Britain 9-17-69
Battle of Broadway 4-27-38
Battle of Chile, II: Coup d'Etat, The (See: Batalla de Chile,
    II: El Golpe de Estado, La)
Battle of Chile, Part III: The Power of the People, The (See:
    Batalla de Chile, III, La)
Battle of France, The (See: Bataille de France, La)
Battle of Gallipoli 12-08-31
Battle of Gettysburg 6-27-13
Battle of Greed 5-18-38
Battle of Hearts 5-26-16
Battle of Life, The 12-15-16
Battle of Love, The 8-06-15
Battle of Love's Return 6-23-71
Battle of Mons 3-20-29
Battle of Paris 2-12-30
Battle of Przemysl 8-06-15
Battle of River Plate 11-14-56
Battle of Rogue River 3-03-54
Battle of Somme 12-05-28
Battle of the Amazons 12-05-73
Battle of the Bulge 12-22-65
Battle of the Bulge--The Brave Rifles, The 2-09-66
Battle of the Coral Sea 10-14-59
Battle of the Neretva, The (See: Bitka Na Neretvi)
Battle of the Rails 12-14-49
Battle of the Sexes 4-17-14
Battle of the Sexes, The 10-17-28
Battle of the Sexes, The 12-30-59
Battle of the Somme, The 10-06-16
Battle of the Waltzes (See: Walzerkrug)
Battle of Torreon 5-15-14
Battle of the Villa Florita, The 5-26-65
Battle Stations 2-01-56
Battle Taxi 1-12-55
Battle Zone 10-15-52
Battleflag (See: Standarte, Die)
Battleground 9-28-49
Battles of a Nation 11-26-15
Battles of Chief Pontiac 12-17-52
Battles of Coronel and Falkland Islands, The 2-15-28
Battles of Falkland Island 2-29-28
Battling Bunyan 3-25-25
Battling Butler 8-25-26
Battling Fool, The 7-16-24
Battling Jane 10-04-18
Battling Mason 3-04-25
Battling Orioles, The 11-05-24
Batu-Bato Sa Langit 11-05-75
Bavu 5-17-23
Bawbs O' Blue Ridge 11-17-16
Bawdy Adventures of Tom Jones, The 9-08-76
Baxter 1-31-73
Baxter, Vera Baxter 6-22-77
Bay of the Angels, The (See: Baie des Anges, La)
Bayou 6-05-57
Bbicot 7-31-57
Be a Little Sport 7-04-19
Be Blessed (See: Badi Blagoslovena)
Be Careful Ladies (See: Mefiez-Vous Mesdames)
Be Dear to Me (See: Ingen Tid Til Kaertegn)
Be Good Unto Death (See: Legy Jo Mindhalalig)
Be Mine Tonight 4-18-33
Be My Guest 4-21-65
Be Reasonable 3-17-22
Be Seeing You, Father (See: Arrivederci, Papa)
Be Sick ... It's Free (See: Medico Della Mutua, Il)
Be So Till Death (See: Legy Mindhalalig)
Be Yourself 3-12-30
Beach Ball 9-29-65
Beach Blanket Bingo 4-07-65
Beach Girls and the Monster 9-22-65
Beach Guard in Winter, The (See: Cuvar Plaze U Zimskom Periodu)
Beach Hotel, The (See: Hotel De La Plage, L')
Beach House, The (See: Casotto, Il)
Beach of Dreams 6-03-21
Beach Party 7-17-63
Beach Red 8-02-67
Beach Umbrella, The (See: Ombrellone, L')
Beachcomber, The 11-30-38 (Also see: Vessel of Wrath)
Beachcomber, The 8-18-54
Beachhead 2-03-54
Beads of One Rosary, The (See: Paciorki Jednego Rozanca)
Beans 9-27-18
Bear, The (See: Ours, L' or Lokis)
Bear and the Doll, The (See: Ours et la Poupee, L')

Bear Cage, The (See: Cage Aux Ours, La)
Bear Cat 3-31-22
Bear Country 1-28-53
Bear Hunt in Russia, A 12-18-09
Bear Hunt in the Rockies 1-15-10
Bear Island 1-23-80
Bearded General (See: Chang Kun Ui Su Yum)
Bears and I, The 10-16-74
Bear's Wedding, The 8-01-28
Beast, The (See: Duvad or Bestione, Il)
Beast, The (See: Bete, La)
Beast, The 1-16-20
Beast, The 12-24-80
Beast at Bay (See: Bete a L'Affut, La)
Beast from Haunted Cave 3-23-60
Beast from 20,000 Fathoms, The 6-17-53
Beast Is Loose, The (See: Fauve Est Lache, Le)
Beast Must Die, The 4-24-74
Beast of Budapest 2-12-58
Beast of Hollow Mountain, The 8-29-56
Beast of the City 3-15-32
Beast of Yucca Flats, The 5-24-61
Beast with Five Fingers, The 12-25-46
Beast with 1,000,000 Eyes 12-14-55
Beasts (See: Bestije)
Beasts of Berlin 11-22-39
Beat Generation, The 7-01-59
Beat Girl 11-16-60
Beat the Band 2-26-47
Beat the Devil 12-02-53
Beate's Mystery (See: Ratsel Um Beate)
Beating the Game 9-23-21
Beating the Odds 5-16-19
Beatrice Fairfax 8-11-16 and 8-25-16
Beau Bandit 6-18-30
Beau Broadway 8-01-28
Beau Brummell 4-04-24
Beau Brummell 10-06-54
Beau Geste 9-01-26
Beau Geste 7-26-39
Beau Geste 7-20-66
Beau Ideal 1-21-31
Beau James 6-12-57
Beau Masque 12-27-72
Beau Monstre, Un 2-24-71
Beau Revel 3-18-21
Beau Sabreur 1-25-28
Beau Serge, Le 6-04-58
Beau Voyage, Le 2-18-48
Beaujolais Nouveau Est Arrive, Le 4-26-78
Beaute du Diable, La 4-19-50
Beauties of the Night (See: Belles de Nuit, Les)
Beautiful Adventure 9-27-32
Beautiful Adventure, The (See: Schoene Abenteuer, Das)
Beautiful Adventure, The 10-26-17
Beautiful American, The (See: Belle Americaine, La)
Beautiful and Beloved Mexico (See: Mexico Lindo y Querido)
Beautiful and the Damned, The 12-15-22
Beautiful Blonde from Bashful Bend, The 5-25-49
Beautiful Blue Danube 2-27-29
Beautiful but Broke 3-01-44
Beautiful but Dumb 9-12-28
Beautiful Cheat, The 4-21-26
Beautiful Cheat, The 7-18-45
Beautiful City, The 11-25-25
Beautiful Galathea, The (See: Wunderschoene Galathee, Die)
Beautiful Gambler, The 8-12-21
Beautiful Image, The (See: Belle Image, La)
Beautiful Ippolita, The (See: Bellezza Ippolita, La)
Beautiful Liar 12-16-21
Beautiful Lie, The 6-02-17
Beautiful Love (See: Bel Amour)
Beautiful Maneuver Time (See: Schoen Ist Die Manoeverzeit)
Beautiful Michoacan (See: Que Lindo Es Michoacan)
Beautiful Miller's Wife, The (See: Bella Mugnaia, La)
Beautiful Mrs. Reynolds, The 1-11-18
Beautiful People 11-27-74
Beautiful Stranger 7-21-54
Beautiful Swindlers, The 11-01-67
Beautiful Trip, The (See: Beau Voyage, Le)
Beautifully Trimmed 12-10-20
Beauty and Bullets 1-23-29
Beauty and the Bad Man 6-24-25
Beauty and the Beast 12-24-47 (Also see: Belle et la Bete, La)
Beauty and the Beast 2-07-79
Beauty and the Boss 4-05-32
Beauty and the Rogue 2-08-18
Beauty and the Thieves (See: Bizyo to Tozoku)

Beauty for Sale 9-19-33
Beauty for the Asking 2-15-39
Beauty in Chains 3-08-18
Beauty Jungle, The 9-02-64
Beauty Market 1-24-20
Beauty of the Day (See: Belle de Jour)
Beauty of the Devil, The (See: Beaute du Diable, La)
Beauty on Parade 7-26-50
Beauty Parlor (See: Peluqueria de Senoras)
Beauty Parlor 10-04-32
Beauty Prize, The 12-31-24
Beauty Proof 7-25-19
Beauty Shop 5-12-22
Beauty Shoppers 7-13-27
Beauty Spot (See: Grain de Beaute)
Beauty Up His Sleeve (See: Manche et La Belle, Une)
Beauty's Worth 3-31-22
Beaux Dimanches, Les 10-30-74
Beaux Jours, Les 10-23-35
Beaver Valley 7-05-50
Bebert and the Train (See: Bebert et L'Omnibus)
Bebert et L'Omnibus 12-25-63
Bebo's Girl (See: Ragazza di Bube, La)
Because, Because of a Woman (See: A Cause, A Cause d'une Femme)
Because He Loved Her 1-21-16
Because I Love You 9-11-29
Because I Loved You 1-29-30
Because of Eve 12-15-48
Because of Him 1-09-46
Because of the Cats (See: Niet Voor de Poesen)
Because of You 10-08-52
Because They're Young 3-09-60
Because You're Mine 9-03-52
Becket 3-04-64
Beckoning Flame, The 12-17-15
Beckoning Trail, The 8-04-16
Becky 10-26-27
Becky Sharp 6-19-35
Becquer's Great Love (See: Gran Amour de Becquer, El)
Bed, The (See: Cama, La)
Bed and Board (See: Domicile Conjugal)
Bed and Breakfast 1-07-31
Bed of Roses 7-04-33
Bed Sitting Room, The 7-16-69
Bedazzled 12-13-67
Bedelia 6-05-46
Bedeviled Gold (See: Demonio Del Oro, El)
Bedevilled 4-13-55
Bedford Incident, The 10-13-65
Bedknobs and Broomsticks 10-13-71
Bedlam 4-24-46
Bedniyat Louka 7-18-79
Bedroom, The (See: O Quarto)
Bedroom Blunder, A 9-28-17
Bedroom Window 6-11-24
Bedside 3-13-34
Bedside Dentist (See: Tandlaege Pa Sengekanten)
Bedside Head (See: Rektor Paa Sengekanten)
Bedside Highway (See: Motorvej Paa Sengekanten)
Bedside Manner 6-13-45
Bedside Mazurka (See: Mazurka Paa Sengekanten)
Bedside Romance (See: Romantik Paa Sengekanten)
Bedside Sailors (See: Soemaend Paa Sengekanten)
Bedtime for Bonzo 1-17-51
Bedtime Story 12-10-41
Bedtime Story 6-03-64
Bedtime Story, A 4-25-33
Bedzie Lepiej 4-07-37
Bee in the Rain (See: Abelha na Chuva, Uma)
Been Down So Long It Looks Like Up To Me 9-08-71
Beer Chase (See: Bierkampf)
Beer Festival (See: Bockbierfest)
Bees, The 11-15-78
Beethoven Concerto 3-31-37
Beethoven--Days in a Life (See: Beethoven--Tage aus Einem Leben)
Beethoven 'Fidelio' 3-21-79
Beethoven--Tage Aus Einem Leben 12-15-76
Beetle, The 1-02-20
Before and After 2-19-10
Before Dan (See: Pratyusha)
Before Dawn 10-24-33
Before God and Man (See: Isten Es Ember Elott)
Before Him All Rome Trembled 2-09-47
Before Hindsight 11-16-77
Before I Hang 10-02-40
Before Midnight (See: Eifelkor)
Before Midnight 8-26-25
Before Midnight 1-16-34

Before Morning 11-21-33
Before Silence Came 2-28-79
Before Sundown (See: Vor Sonnenuntergang)
Before the Battle (See: Veille d'Armes)
Before the Dawn 8-28-09
Before the Day Breaks (See: Zanim Nadejdzie Dzien)
Before the Deluge (See: Avant le Deluge)
Before the Fact--The Ecology of a Crime (See: Antefatto)
Before the Mountain Was Moved 3-11-70
Before the Revolution (See: Prima Della Rivoluzione)
Before the Truth (See: Pre Istine)
Before This Night Is Over (See: Kym Sa Skonci Tato Noc)
Before Winter Comes 1-15-69
Beg, Borrow or Steal 12-01-37
Begar 12-18-46
Beggar of Cawnpore, The 4-28-16
Beggar on Horseback 6-10-25
Beggar Student, The (See: Bettelstudent, Der)
Beggar Woman, The 3-01-18
Beggars, The 8-07-63
Beggars and Proud Ones (See: Mendiants Et Orgueilleux)
Beggars in Ermine 5-01-34
Beggars of Life 9-26-28
Beggar's Opera (See: Drei Groschenoper)
Beggar's Opera, The 6-17-53
Begging the Ring 3-21-79
Beginning of the End 7-03-57
Beginning or the End 2-19-47
Beguiled, The 3-10-71
Beguin de la Garnison, Le 5-09-33
Behave Yourself 9-12-51
Behemoth, Sea Monster 11-04-59
Behind a Mask 12-03-10
Behind City Lights 9-19-45
Behind Closed Doors 1-28-16
Behind Closed Doors 4-24-29
Behind Closed Shutters 6-11-52
Behind Green Lights 4-24-35
Behind Green Lights 1-16-46
Behind Jury Doors 3-28-33
Behind Locked Doors 9-08-48
Behind Office Doors 3-25-31
Behind Prison Gates 8-23-39
Behind Prison Walls 5-26-43
Behind Show-Window 4-24-57
Behind Stone Walls 4-19-32
Behind That Curtain 7-03-29
Behind the Altar 2-06-29
Behind the Barriers (See: Au Dela des Grilles)
Behind the Clouds (See: Atras de las Nubes)
Behind the Curtain 7-23-24
Behind the Door 1-31-20
Behind the Eight Ball 12-09-42
Behind the Enemy Lines 4-11-45
Behind the Evidence 2-05-35
Behind the Facade (See: Derriere la Facade)
Behind the Front 2-10-36
Behind the German Lines 12-05-28
Behind the Great Wall 12-16-59
Behind the Green Door 8-16-72
Behind the Headlines 6-09-37
Behind the High Wall 6-13-56
Behind the Lines 9-15-16
Behind the Makeup 1-15-30
Behind the Mask 5-03-32
Behind the Mask 4-03-46
Behind the Mask 11-12-58
Behind the Mike 11-03-37
Behind the News 12-25-40
Behind the Rising Sun 7-14-43
Behind the Scenes 10-31-14
Behind the Wall (See: Za Sciana)
Behinderte Liebe 5-30-79
Behold a Pale Horse 8-19-64
Behold Homolka Man (See: Ecce Homo Homolka)
Behold My Wife 10-15-20
Behold My Wife 2-20-35
Behold the Man! 1-28-20
Beiderseits der Rollbahn 8-12-53
Being Respectable 8-06-24
Being There 12-19-79
Being Two Isn't Easy 11-20-63
Beiss Mich, Liebling 10-14-70
Bejleren 8-20-75
Bekenntnisse des Hochstaplers Felix Krull, Die 6-12-57
Bekotott Szemmel 3-12-75
Bel Age, Le 10-28-59
Bel Ami 3-19-47

Bel Ami 4-09-58
Bel Ami 2000--Oder Wie Verfuehrt Man Einen Playboy 12-07-66
Bel Amour 7-18-51
Bel Ordure 5-23-73
Bela Lugosi Meets a Brooklyn Gorilla 9-10-52
Belated Flowers 11-29-72
Belated Meal 5-01-09
Belated Weddings, The 10-23-09
Belfer 1-10-79
Belgian, The 11-02-17
Belgian Army, The 9-17-10
Belgian War Pictures 12-04-14
Beli Bim--Chornoye Ukho 7-05-78
Believe in God (See: Creo en Dios)
Believe in Me 9-08-71
Believe It or Not (See: O Impossivel Acontece)
Believe Me, Xantippe 6-07-18
Beliye Nochi 10-11-61
Bell, The (See: Campana Del Infierno, La)
Bell, The 5-03-67
Bell' Antonio, Il 4-20-60
Bell, Book and Candle 10-22-58
Bell Boy 3-39-23
Bell Boy, The 3-22-18
Bell for Adano, A 6-20-45
Bell Jar, The 3-21-79
Bella Donna 11-19-15
Bella Donna 4-19-23
Bella Donna 8-14-34 and 3-06-35
Bella Grinta, Una 7-14-65
Bella Mugnaia, La 12-28-55
Belladonna 7-04-73
Bellamy Trial 1-30-29
Bellboy, The 7-13-60
Belle 5-30-73
Belle Americaine, La 10-18-61
Belle de Jour 4-19-67
Belle Equipe, La 10-07-36
Belle et la Bete, La 12-04-46
Belle Fille Comme Moi, Une 9-27-72
Belle Image, La 7-18-51
Belle le Grand 2-28-51
Belle Ma Povere 3-19-58
Belle Mentalite 11-04-53
Belle Meuniere, La 1-05-49
Belle O Brutte Si Spasen Tutte (See: Pretty or Plain, They All
    Get Married)
Belle of Broadway 12-01-26
Belle of New York, The 2-28-19
Belle of New York, The 2-20-52
Belle of Old Mexico 2-08-50
Belle of the Harvest 11-27-09
Belle of the 90's 9-25-34
Belle of the Season, The 8-01-19
Belle of the Yukon 11-29-44
Belle Otero, La 12-22-54
Belle Que Voila, La 5-10-50
Belle Russe, La 7-10-14
Belle Starr 8-27-41
Belle Starr's Daughter 10-27-48
Belle Trave 8-25-76
Belle Vie, La 9-04-63
Belles and Ballets 7-27-60
Belles de Nuit, Les 10-15-52
Belles Manieres, Les 5-16-79
Belles of St. Trinians, The 10-13-54
Belles on Their Toes 4-09-52
Bellezza Ippolita, La 7-18-62
Bellissima 4-09-52
Bellissima Novembre, Un (See: That Splendid November)
Bellman, The 4-09-47
Bello Onesto Emigrato Australia Sposerebbe Compaesan Illibata
    1-19-72
Bells, The 9-20-18
Bells Are Ringing 6-08-60
Bells Go Down, The 5-12-43
Bells in Old Town, The (See: Klockorna I Gambia Sta'n)
Bells of Autumn 3-26-80
Bells of Capistrano 9-16-42
Bells of Coronado, The 1-18-50
Bells of Old Town 1-22-47
Bells of Rosarita 5-16-45
Bells of St. Mary's, The 11-28-45
Bells of San ANgelo, The 5-28-47
Bells of San Fernando 4-02-47
Bells Without Joy (See: Carillons Sans Joie)
Beloved 1-30-34
Beloved Adventuress, The 7-06-17

Beloved Bachelor, The 1-20-31
Beloved Blackmailer, The 8-02-18
Beloved Brat 1-12-38
Beloved Brute, The 11-12-24
Beloved Cheater, The 3-19-20
Beloved Corinna (See: Geliebte Corinna)
Beloved Electra (See: Szerelem, Elektra)
Beloved Enemy, The 12-30-36
Beloved Imposter, The 12-13-19
Beloved Infidel 11-18-59
Beloved Jim 12-14-17
Beloved Love (See: Ljubavni Zivot Budmira Trajkovica)
Beloved Lover (See: Amada Amante)
Beloved of the World (See: Liebling der Welt)
Beloved Rogue, The 3-16-27
Beloved Traitor, The 3-01-18
Beloved Vagabond, The 11-08-23
Beloved Vagabond, The 9-09-36 and 2-10-37
Below the Belt 12-17-80
Below the Border 2-25-42
Below the Deadline 6-10-36
Below the Deadline 10-02-46
Below the Hill 9-01-65
Below the Line 9-23-25
Below the Rio 10-18-23
Below the Sahara 6-03-53
Below the Sea 6-06-33
Below the Surface 6-11-20
Beloy and the Kid 6-23-76
Belphegor 5-13-21
Belstone Fox, The 11-28-73
Belyazani Atomi 7-25-79
Belyi Parohod 7-14-76
Ben 6-14-72
Ben Blair 3-03-16
Ben et Benedict 4-27-77
Ben-Gurion Remembers 12-13-72
Ben-Hur 1-06-26
Ben-Hur 11-18-59
Bend of the River 1-23-52
Beneath the Czar 5-08-14
Beneath the Planet of the Apes 5-06-70
Beneath the Sea 11-29-32
Beneath the 12-Mile Reef 12-16-53
Beneath the Valley of the Ultravixens 4-18-79
Beneath Western Skies 5-17-44
Benedict Arnold and Major Andre 11-20-09
Benefactor, El 6-06-73
Benefactor, The (See: Benefactor, El)
Beneficiary, The 3-12-80
Benefit of the Doubt, The 10-04-67
Bengal Brigade 10-20-54
Bengal Tiger 8-05-36
Bengal Tiger 8-02-72
Bengazi 9-21-55
Bengelchen Liebt Kruze und Quer 3-05-69
Benito Cereno 8-27-69
Benitou 3-31-22
Benjamin 1-10-73
Benjamin or The Memories of a Virgin (See: Benjamin ou Les
    Memoires d'Un Puceau)
Benjamin ou les Memoires d'Un Puceau 1-24-68
Benji 11-13-74
Benny Goodman Story, The 12-21-55
Benson Murder Case, The 4-16-30
Benvenuto, Reverendo! 6-28-50
Beregis Automobilyi (See: Uncommon Thief, An)
Bereketli Topraklar Uzerinde 9-03-80
Berenice 4-05-67
Berg Ruft, Der 2-16-38
Bergado 5-05-76
Berge in Flammen 10-13-31
Bergere et le Ramoneur, La 10-08-52
Bergslagsfolk 3-23-38
Berkeley Square 9-19-33
Berlin 12-21-27
Berlin 6-13-28
Berlin After Dark 5-29-29
Berlin Alexander Platz 10-27-31
Berlin Alexanderplatz 5-16-33
Berlin Alexanderplatz 9-17-80
Berlin Correspondent 8-12-42
Berlin--Dein Filmgesicht 8-20-80
Berlin Express 4-07-48
Berlin Is Worth a Sin (See: Berlin Ist Eine Suende Wert)
Berlin Ist Eine Suende Wert 4-13-66
Berlin Via America 8-02-18
Berlin--Your Film Profile (See: Berlin--Dein Filmgesicht)
Berliner Ballade 9-28-49

Berliner Bettwurst 2-16-77
Berlinger 7-14-76
Bermuda Mystery 4-19-44
Bermuda Triangle, The 1-17-79
Bernardine 7-03-57
Beroringen (See: Touch, The)
Berserk 12-27-67
Bertha (the Sewing Machine Girl) 1-05-27
Bertie's Elopement 9-24-10
Beru and Those Women (See: Beru et Ces Dames)
Beru et Ces Dames 11-20-68
Beschreibung Einer Insel 8-15-79
Besieged (See: Stato d'Assedio, Lo)
Besieged House, The (See: O Sobrado)
Besserer Herr, Ein 11-14-28
Best Bad Man, The 12-02-25
Best Boy 9-19-79
Best Foot Forward 6-30-43
Best Friends (See: Koo Hoo)
Best Friends 11-19-75
Best House in London, The 7-30-69
Best Man, The 5-02-19
Best Man, The 4-01-64
Best Man Wins 1-08-35
Best Man Wins 5-19-48
Best of Benny Hill 4-02-75
Best of Cinerama, The 12-25-63
Best of Enemies 7-18-33
Best of Enemies, The 12-20-61
Best of Everything, The 10-14-59
Best of Luck, The 7-09-20
Best of the Badman 5-02-51
Best of Walt Disney's True-Life Adventures, The 10-15-75
Best Part, The (See: Meilleure Part, La)
Best People, The 10-21-25
Best Things in Life Are Free, The 9-25-56
Best Way to Get Along, The (See: Meilleure Facon de Marcher, La)
Best Years of Our Lives, The 11-27-46
Bestiaire D'Amour, Le 1-12-66
Bestije 8-17-77
Bestione, Il 10-16-74
Beszallasolas 12-14-38
Bet, The (See: Opklada)
Bete, La 8-27-75
Bete a L'Affut, La 7-01-59
Bete Errante, La 9-06-32
Bete Humaine, La 2-15-39
Bete Mais Discipline 9-26-79
Bethsabee 11-21-51
Betia, La 1-12-72
Betrayal 8-31-17
Betrayal 5-08-29
Betrayal 9-20-39
Betrayal, The 5-08-29
Betrayal, The 6-30-48
Betrayal from the East 4-25-45
Betrayed 7-21-54
Betrayed Women 2-01-56
Betrogen Bis Zum Juengsten Tag 5-15-57
Betsy, The 2-15-78
Betsy Ross 9-07-17
Betsy's Burglar 3-09-17
Bettelstudent, Der 12-16-36 and 12-30-36
Better a Widow (See: Meglio Vedova)
Better Man, The 8-14-14
Better 'Ole, The 2-28-19
Better 'Ole, The 10-13-26
Better Than Gold 2-26-10
Better Times 7-11-19
Better Way, The 7-13-27
Better Wife 7-11-19
Better Woman, The 10-29-15
Bettie's Choice 10-09-09
Bettina Loved a Soldier 8-04-16
Betty Blokk-Buster Follies 8-18-76
Betty Co-Ed 11-27-46
Betty Is Punished 10-15-10
Betty Is Still at Her Old Tricks 10-08-10
Betty of Graystone 3-24-16
Betty Takes a Hand 1-04-18
Betty to the Rescue 3-02-17
Between 11 o'Clock and Midnight (See: Entre Onze Heures et
    Minuit)
Between Fear and Duty (See: Med Strahom In Dolznostjo)
Between Fighting Men 2-14-33
Between Friends 5-14-24
Between Heaven and Hell (See: Nasa Lupa Ang Langit At Impiyerno)

Between Heaven and Hell   10-10-56
Between Men   12-03-15
Between Men   1-29-36
Between Men   5-23-79
Between Midnight and Dawn   9-27-50
Between Night and Day (See: Zwischen Nacht Und Tag)
Between Sweet and Salt Water (See: Entre la Mer et l'Eau Douce)
Between Tears and Smiles   10-28-64
Between the Lines   4-20-77
Between Two Husbands   8-20-24
Between Two Women   8-11-37
Between Two Women   12-20-44
Between Two Worlds   5-10-44
Between Us (See: Oss Emellan)
Between Us Girls   9-02-42
Between Wars   12-18-74
Between Worlds   7-09-24
Beulah   5-14-15
Beverly Hills Call Boys, The   11-11-70
Beverly of Graustark   4-21-26
Beware   6-19-46
Beware, My Lovely   7-30-52
Beware of a Saintly Whore (See: Warnung Vor Einer Heiligen Nutte)
Beware of Bachelors   2-06-29
Beware of Blondes   8-22-28
Beware of Blondes   12-16-36
Beware of Blondie   4-05-50
Beware of Ladies   1-13-37
Beware of Married Men   4-11-28
Beware of Pity   6-26-46
Beware of Widows   5-25-27
Beware Spooks!   10-25-39
Beware the Blob   6-07-72
Beware: When a Widow Falls in Love (See: Mag-Ingat: Kapag Biyda
   Ang Umbig)
Bewitched   6-20-45
Bewitched (See: Embrujo)
Beyond   9-09-21
Beyond a Reasonable Doubt   9-12-56
Beyond and Back   2-08-78
Beyond Bengal   5-22-34
Beyond Evil   5-07-80
Beyond Fear (See: Au-Dela De La Peur)
Beyond Glory   6-16-48
Beyond Good and Evil (See: Oltre il Bene e il Male)
Beyond London's Lights   4-11-28
Beyond Love and Evil   3-17-71
Beyond Mombasa   10-17-56
Beyond Our Own   11-05-47
Beyond Price   6-24-21
Beyond Reasonable Doubt   10-01-80
Beyond the Blue Horizon   5-06-42
Beyond the Bridge (See: Dincolo de Pod)
Beyond the Crossroads   1-27-22
Beyond the Door   8-06-75
Beyond the Forest   10-19-49
Beyond the Last Frontier   11-03-43
Beyond the Law   4-11-19
Beyond the Law   11-06-34
Beyond the Law   10-02-68
Beyond the Oder and Neisse--Today (See: Jenseits von Oder und
   Neisse--Heute)
Beyond the Poseidon Adventure   5-30-79
Beyond the Purple Hills   7-19-50
Beyond the Rainbow   3-03-22
Beyond the Rio Grande   5-28-30
Beyond the Rockies   9-20-32
Beyond the Rocks   5-12-22
Beyond the Sacramento   5-07-41
Beyond the Sands (See: Au Dela Des Sables)
Beyond the Shadows   8-09-18
Beyond the Sierras   12-12-28
Beyond the Sun (See: Mas Alla Del Sol)
Beyond the Time Barrier   9-14-60
Beyond the Valley of the Dolls   6-24-70
Beyond Thirteen Rivers (See: Tero Nodim Parey)
Beyond Time (See: Nincs Ido)
Beyond This Place   5-06-59
Beyond Tomorrow   4-03-40
Beyond Victory   4-08-31
Bez Milosci   10-01-80
Bez Znieczulenia   2-07-79
Bharat Mata   8-27-58
Bhowani Junction   5-09-56
Bhumika   11-15-78
Bhuvan Shome   9-03-69
Bialata Staia   7-01-70
Biancaneve e i Sette Lavri   1-25-50
Bianco, Il Giallo, Il Nero, Il   2-05-75

Bianco, Rosso e ... (See: White Sister, The)
Biassoli Embers, The (See: Brace Dei Biassoli, La)
Bible   3-20-74
Bible, The   9-28-66
Bible Pictures   12-22-22
Bice Skoro Propast Sveta   5-14-69
Biches, Les   4-10-68
Biciklisti   8-12-70
Bicycle Thief, The   12-15-48 and 12-07-49
Bicycle Thieves (See: Ladri di Biciclette)
Bicycling to the Moon   3-06-63
Bidasses en Folie, Les   1-12-72
Bidasses S'En Vont En Guerre, Les   1-01-75
Bidone, Il   11-02-55
Bielaya Ptitsa S Tchornem Piatnom   11-10-71
Bienvenido Mr. Marshall   7-29-53
Bierkampf   7-13-77
Big and Little (See: Gross und Klein)
Big and the Small, The (See: Veliki i Mali)
Big Attraction, The (See: Grosse Attraktion, Die)
Big Baby Doll (See: Bambolona, La)
Big Bad Mama   9-04-74
Big Bad Sis   10-27-76
Big Banana Feet   12-08-76
Big Beat, The   2-05-58
Big Bird Cage, The   7-12-72
Big Blockade, The   2-18-42
Big Blond Guy With One Black Shoe, The (See: Grand Blond avec une
   Chassure Noire, Le)
Big Bluff   7-13-55
Big Bluff, The   10-24-31
Big Bonanza, The   2-28-45
Big Boodle, The   1-30-57
Big Boss, A (See: Grand Patron, Un)
Big Boss, The (See: Fists of Fury)
Big Boss, The   5-21-41
Big Bounce, The   2-12-69
Big Boy   9-17-30
Big Brain, The   8-08-33
Big Brawl, The   8-27-80
Big Broadcast, The   10-18-32
Big Broadcast of 1936, The   9-18-35
Big Broadcast of 1937, The   10-28-36
Big Broadcast of 1938, The   2-09-38
Big Brother   12-27-23
Big Brother Cheng   8-27-75
Big Brown Eyes   5-06-36
Big Bus, The   6-23-76
Big Business   6-02-37
Big Business Girl   6-16-31
Big Cage, The   5-16-33
Big Caper, The   4-03-57
Big Cat, The   4-27-49
Big Chamorro Circus, The (See: Gran Circo Chamorro, El)
Big Chance, The   9-05-33
Big Chief, The (See: Grand Chef, Le)
Big Circus, The   7-08-59
Big City, The (See: A Grande Cidade)
Big City, The   3-28-28
Big City, The   9-15-37
Big City, The   3-24-48
Big City Blues   9-13-32
Big Clock, The   2-18-48
Big Combo   2-16-55
Big Country, The   8-13-58
Big Cube, The   3-12-69
Big Dan   12-20-23
Big Delirium, The (See: Grand Delire, Le)
Big Departure, The (See: Grand Depart, Le)
Big Dig, The (See: Taalat Blamilch)
Big Duel in the North Sea (See: Nankai No Dai Ketto)
Big Executive   10-03-33
Big Families, The (See: Grandes Familles, Les)
Big Family, A   6-08-55
Big Fella   7-07-37
Big Fisherman, The   7-01-59
Big Fix, The   10-04-78
Big Flag, The (See: Grand Pavois, Le)
Big Frame, The   3-18-53
Big Gamble, The   9-22-31
Big Gamble, The   8-16-61
Big Game   8-26-21
Big Game, The (See: Grand Jeu, Le)
Big Grasshopper, The (See: Grande Sauterelle, La)
Big Grey-Blue Bird, A (See: Grosser Graublauer Vogel, Ein)
Big Gundown, The   8-14-68
Big Guns, The   9-26-73

Big Gusher, The 7-18-51
Big Guy, The 11-29-39
Big Hand for the Little Lady, A 4-27-66
Big Hangover 3-15-50
Big Happiness 9-03-20
Big Hearted Herbert 11-20-34
Big Heat, The 9-23-53
Big Heat, The 2-05-58
Big Highway, The (See: Gran Ruta, La)
Big Holdup 11-05-75
Big Hop, The 1-09-29
Big House, The 7-02-30
Big House, U.S.A. 3-02-55
Big Jack 4-13-49
Big Jake 5-26-71
Big Jim Garrity 4-21-16
Big Jim McLain 8-27-52
Big Job, The 10-13-65
Big Killing, The 7-04-28
Big Knife, The 9-21-55
Big Land, The 1-30-57
Big Leaguer, The 7-15-53
Big Lift, The 4-12-50
Big Love Game, The (See: Grosse Liebespiel, Das)
Big Mamma (See: Mammasantissima, Il)
Big Maneuvers, The (See: Grandes Manoeuvres, Les)
Big Medicine 9-24-10
Big Mess, The (See: Grosse Verhau, Der)
Big Meeting, The (See: Grand Rendezvous, Le)
Big Money 11-26-30
Big Money 6-18-58
Big Mouth, The 6-28-67
Big News 10-09-29
Big Night, The (See: Grand Soir, Le)
Big Night, The 11-07-51
Big Noise, The 5-09-28
Big Noise, The 7-08-36
Big Noise, The 9-20-44
Big Operator, The (See: Grand Escogriffe, Le)
Big Operator, The 8-05-59
Big Pal, The 2-03-26
Big Parade, The 11-11-25 and 12-02-25
Big Parade of Comedy, The 8-26-64
Big Party, The 4-16-30
Big Payoff, The 1-24-33
Big Pond, The 5-21-30 (Also see: Grande Mare, La)
Big Punch, The 3-25-21
Big Punch, The 5-26-48
Big Race, The 3-06-34
Big Red 4-18-62
Big Red One, The 5-14-80
Big Request Concert 8-02-61
Big Roads, The (See: Grands Chemins, Les)
Big Runaround, The (See: Grande Vadrouille, La)
Big Scare, The (See: Grande Frousse, La or Grande Trouille, La)
Big Sentiments Make for Good Sports (See: Grands Sentiments
     Font Les Bons Gueuletons, Les)
Big Shot, The 1-05-32
Big Shot, The 8-11-37
Big Shot, The 6-03-42
Big Shots, The (See: Grandes Gueules, Les or Caids, Les)
Big Show, The (See: Altas Variedades)
Big Show, The 7-14-26
Big Show, The 3-03-37
Big Show, The 5-10-61
Big Show-Off, The 5-16-45
Big Sister, The 9-15-16
Big Sky, The (See: Sara Akash)
Big Sky, The 7-09-52
Big Sleep, The 8-14-46
Big Sleep, The 3-15-78
Big Softie, The (See: Grand Dadais, Le)
Big Sombrero, The 2-02-49 and 4-13-49
Big Steal, The 6-15-49
Big Store, The (See: Grand Bazar, Le)
Big Store, The 6-18-41
Big Street, The 8-05-42
Big Swag, The (See: Grosse Caisse, La)
Big T-N-T Show, The 1-19-66
Big Thumbs 8-17-77
Big Timber 6-22-17
Big Timber 10-25-50
Big Time 9-11-29
Big Time or Bust 1-16-34
Big Tip Off 4-27-55
Big Town 12-27-32
Big Town 2-19-47
Big Town After Dark 11-19-47

Big Town Czar 4-26-39
Big Town Girl 11-10-37
Big Town Ideas 6-10-21
Big Town Scandal 5-26-48
Big Trail, The 10-29-30 (Also see: Grosse Fahrt, Die)
Big Trees, The 2-06-52
Big Tremaine 12-01-16
Big Trail, The (See: Grande Epreuve, La)
Big Vacation, The (See: Grands Vacances, Les)
Big Wash!, The (See: Grande Lessive!, La)
Big Wednesday 5-24-78
Big Wheel, The 11-09-49
Bigamist, The 12-04-09
Bigamist 9-09-21
Bigamist, The 3-31-22
Bigamist, The 10-28-53
Bigger Man, The 10-08-15
Bigger Splash, A 5-15-74
Bigger Than Barnum's 7-14-26
Bigger Than Life 8-15-56
Biggest Bundle of Them All, The 1-17-68
Biggest Game, The (See: Det Stoerste Spillet)
Biggest Show on Earth, The 5-03-18
Bigorne, Caporal de France, La 9-03-58
Bij de Besten Af (See: Ape and Superape)
Bijou 10-18-72
Bijoutiers du Clair de Lune, Les 5-07-58
Bijoux de Famille, Les 3-19-75
Bijutaril de Familie 8-06-58
Bike Boy 10-11-67
Bikini Beach 7-08-64
Biladi, une Revolution 10-14-70
Bilans Kwartalny 7-09-75
Bilbao 5-24-78
Bilder Aus Einem Fremden Land 6-21-72
Bildnis Einer Trinkerin 3-12-80
Bilitis 4-06-77
Bill 12-13-23
Bill and Coo 12-24-27
Bill Apperson's Boy 7-18-19
Bill Cracks Down 5-19-37
Bill Henry 8-22-19
Bill of Divorcement, A 9-01-22 and 4-19-23
Bill of Divorcement, A 10-04-32
Bill of Divorcement, A 3-13-40
Bill Peters' Kid 1-28-16
Bill, the Billposter 11-13-09
Billet de Logement, Le 10-18-32
Billeting (See: Beszallasolas)
Billeting Order (See: Billet de Logement, Le)
Billie 9-08-65
Billiken 10-09-09
Billion Dollar Brain 11-22-67
Billion Dollar Hobo 6-21-78
Billion Dollar Scandal 1-10-33
Billionaire, The 5-29-14
Billions 12-10-20
Billposter's Trials 9-04-09
Billy Budd 8-29-62
Billy in the Lowlands 1-17-79
Billy Jack 5-05-71
Billy Jack Goes to Washington 4-20-77
Billy Jim 2-03-22
Billy Liar 8-21-63
Billy Rose's Jumbo 12-05-62
Billy the Kid 10-22-30
Billy the Kid 5-28-41
Billy the Kid in Texas 11-20-40
Billy the Kid Returns 9-21-38
Billy the Kid Trapped 4-22-42
Billy the Kid Wanted 11-26-41
Billy the Kid's Fighting Pals 6-25-41
Billy the Kid's Range War 3-12-41
Billy the Kid's Roundup 1-07-42
Billy Two Hats 11-07-73
Bim 3-31-76
Bimbo the Great 5-03-61
Binding Ties (See: Holdudvar)
Binge (See: Parranda)
Bingo Long Traveling All-Stars and Motor Kings, The 5-19-76
Bio-Graphia 11-05-75
Biography of a Bachelor Girl 3-06-35
Biotaxia 6-26-68
Birch Forest (See: Brzezina)
Birch Interval 3-24-76
Birch Tree, The (See: Breza)
Bird of Paradise 9-13-32

25

Black Magic 8-24-49
Black Magic 2 12-14-77
Black Mama, White Mama 1-31-73
Black Marble, The 2-27-80
Black Market Babies 4-03-46
Black Market Rustlers 9-01-43
Black Midnight 11-09-49
Black Monocle, The (See: Monocle Noir, Le)
Black Moon 7-03-34
Black Moon 9-24-75
Black Narcissus 5-07-47
Black Natchez 9-27-67
Black Nissen 6-12-14
Black Oak Conspiracy, The 4-13-77
Black On White (See: Mustaa Valkoisella)
Black on White 10-15-69
Black Orchid, The 1-28-59
Black Orchids 12-29-16
Black-Out 10-21-70
Black Oxen 1-03-24 and 1-10-24
Black Palm Trees (See: Svarta Palmkronor)
Black Panther, The 12-21-77
Black Panther's Cub 6-03-21
Black Parachute, The 5-24-44
Black Paradise 6-23-26
Black Patch 9-11-57
Black Pearl 3-20-29
Black Pearls (See: Crni Biseri)
Black Peter (See: Cerny Petr)
Black Pirate (See: Corsaro Nero, Il)
Black Pirate, The 3-10-26
Black Rain of Sayama, The (See: Sayama No Kuroi Ame)
Black Raven, The 6-30-43
Black Ridinghood 3-20-29
Black River (See: Rio Negro)
Black Rodeo 6-28-72
Black Room, The 8-21-35
Black Rose 8-09-50
Black Roses (See: Schwarze Rosen)
Black Roses 5-13-21
Black Samson 8-07-74
Black Scorpion, The 9-25-57
Black Sea Fighters 8-18-43
Black Sea Mutiny 6-23-31
Black Seed (See: Upho Ceme)
Black Shadows 3-19-20
Black Shadows 6-21-23
Black Shadows 10-05-49
Black Shampoo 6-02-76
Black Sheep 7-03-35
Black Sheep, A 10-18-15
Black Sheep, The (See: Pecora Nera, La or Mouton Noir, Le)
Black Sheep of Whitehall 2-18-42
Black Shield of Falworth 8-04-54
Black Silk 7-12-61
Black Six 3-20-74
Black Skins (See: Peaux Noires)
Black Sleep, The 6-13-56
Black Spurs 5-05-65
Black Stallion, The 10-17-79
Black Stork, The 3-02-17
Black Sun (See: Soleil Noir)
Black Sun 5-31-78
Black Sunday 2-22-61
Black Sunday 3-30-77
Black Swan, The 10-21-42
Black Tent, The 3-28-56 and 6-12-57
Black 13 11-24-54
Black Thursday (See: Guichets Du Louvre, Les)
Black Torment, The 10-21-64
Black Triangle, The 10-10-14
Black Tuesday 12-22-54
Black Tulip, The (See: Tulipe Noire, La)
Black Veil for Lisa, A 7-16-69
Black Victory (See: Victoire en Chantant, La)
Black Watch, The 5-15-29
Black Waters 7-10-29
Black Whale, The (See: Schwarze Walfisch)
Black Whip, The 1-02-57
Black-White-Red Four Poster (See: Schwarz-Weiss-Rote Himmelbett,
    Das)
Black Widow 10-27-54
Black Wind (See: Viento Negro)
Black Windmill, The 5-08-74
Black Wings 8-07-63
Black Zoo 5-08-63
Blackbeard, the Pirate 12-03-52
Blackbeard's Ghost 1-17-68

Blackbird, The 2-03-26
Blackbirds 10-22-15
Blackbirds 12-10-20
Blackboard Jungle, The 3-02-55
Blackguard, The 5-27-25
Blackhawk 8-13-52
Blackie's Redemption 4-25-19
Blackjack Ketchum, Desperado 4-04-56
Blacklist, The 2-18-16
Blackmail 10-22-20
Blackmail 7-10-29 and 10-09-29
Blackmail 9-13-39
Blackmail 8-06-47
Blackmailed 2-07-51
Blackmailer 7-29-36
Blackout 5-05-54
Blackout 5-31-78
Blacks Britannica 3-28-79
Blackwell's Island 3-08-39
Blacula 8-02-72
Blade 12-05-73
Blades of Musketeers 9-02-53
Blaireau Case, The (See: Affaire Blaireau, L')
Blaise Pascal 3-26-75
Blajackor 3-27-46
Blame the Woman 11-01-32
Blanc et le Noir, Le 6-02-31
Blanche 6-30-71
Blanche Fury 3-03-48
Blank Check, A 10-16-09
Blarney 10-20-26
Blarney Kiss 8-22-33
Blarney Stone, The 3-28-33
Blast of Silence 4-12-61
Blaue Licht, Das 4-29-32
Blaze O'Glory 1-01-30 and 1-15-30 (Also see: Sombras de Gloria)
Blaze of Noon 3-05-47
Blazing Air Way to India 4-26-23
Blazing Arrows 10-27-22
Blazing Barriers 11-17-37
Blazing Days 6-08-27
Blazing Forest, The 10-01-52
Blazing Frontier 4-19-44
Blazing Guns 10-20-43
Blazing Love 5-05-16
Blazing Saddles 2-13-74
Blazing Sand (See: Brennender Sand)
Blazing Six Shooters 3-13-40
Blazing Sixes 8-04-37
Blazing Sun, The 11-08-50
Blazing Trail, The 5-13-21
Blazing Trail, The 11-16-49
Ble en Herbe, Le 3-24-54
Bleak Moments 8-23-72
Blechtrommel, Die 5-16-79
Bled, Le 7-17-29
Bless the Beasts and Children 7-14-71
Blessed Event 9-06-32
Blessed Miracle, The 4-16-15
Blessed Rose, The (Rosal Bendito, El)
Blessing, The (See: Aashirwaa)
Blessings of the Land 11-24-65
Blessington's Bonnie Babies 10-23-09
Blight of Sin 9-11-09
Blind Adventure 11-07-33
Blind Adventure, The 1-18-18
Blind Alibi 5-25-38
Blind-Alley (See: Al Tarik)
Blind Alley 4-26-39
Blind Alleys 3-02-27
Blind Bargain, A 12-08-22
Blind Beast, The 4-23-69
Blind Bird, The 4-28-65
Blind Circumstances 9-15-22
Blind Date 9-04-34
Blind Date 8-26-59
Blind Desire 6-09-48
Blind Girl of Sorrento (See: Cieca di Sorrento, La)
Blind Goddess, The 4-07-26
Blind Goddess, The 9-29-48
Blind Hearts 10-14-21
Blind Husbands 12-12-19
Blind Is Beautiful (See: Blind Makker)
Blind Justice 9-22-16
Blind Makker 9-15-76
Blind Man's Eyes 3-14-19
Blind Youth 6-25-20

Blinde Passagiere 3-24-37
Blinders (See: Kara Kafa)
Blindfold (See: Bekotott Szemmel)
Blindfold 2-20-29
Blindfold 5-18-66
Blindfolded 5-03-18
Blindfolded Eyes (See: Ojos Vendados, Los)
Blinding Trail, The 4-11-19
Blindman 4-12-72
Blindness of Courage, The 8-20-15
Blindness of Devotion, The 11-12-15
Blindness of Divorce, The 5-31-18
Blindness of Love, The 3-17-16
Blindness of Virtue, The 8-27-15
Blinky 8-30-23
Bliss of Mrs. Blossom, The 10-09-68
Bliss on Earth 1-30-57
Blithe Spirit 4-25-45
Blizna 2-02-77
Blizzard, The 3-19-24
Blob, The 9-10-58
Block Busters 8-16-44
Block File, The (See: Dossier Noir, Le)
Block Signal, The 9-29-26 and 10-27-26
Blockade 6-08-38
Blockade 10-20-65
Blockade, The 5-22-29 and 7-31-29
Block-Heads 8-31-38
Blockhead Fair, The (See: Foire Aux Cancres, La)
Blockhouse, The 7-04-73
Bloko 5-11-66
Blomkvist, Master Detective (See: Master Detectiven Blomkvist)
Blomstrande Tider 2-20-80
Blonde Alibi 3-20-46
Blonde Bait 10-10-56
Blonde Bandit 1-11-50
Blonde by Choice 5-09-28
Blonde Captive 3-01-32
Blonde Comet 12-31-41
Blonde Comme Ca!, Une 2-27-63
Blonde Crazy 12-08-31
Blonde de Pekin, La 1-31-68
Blonde Dream, A (See: Blonder Traum, Ein)
Blonde Dynamite 3-01-50
Blonde Fever 11-22-44
Blonde for a Day 7-31-46
Blonde for a Night 11-14-28
Blonde from Brooklyn 6-27-45
Blonde from Peking, The (See: Blonde de Pekin, La)
Blonde from Singapore 9-03-41
Blonde Gypsy, The (See: Caraque Blonde, La)
Blonde Ice 7-28-48
Blonde Inspiration 2-19-41
Blonde Like That, A (See: Blonde Comme Ca!, Une)
Blonde Nachtigall 8-25-31
Blonde Nightingale (See: Blonde Nachtigall)
Blonde or Brunette 1-12-27
Blonde Ransom 5-30-45
Blonde Saint, The 11-24-26
Blonde Savage 10-08-47
Blonde Trouble 8-04-37
Blonde Vampire 9-15-22
Blonde Venus 9-27-32
Blonder Traum, Ein 10-18-32
Blondes Are Dangerous 11-10-37
Blondes at Work 3-16-38
Blondes for Danger 3-16-38
Blondie 11-02-38
Blondie Brings Up Baby 11-08-39
Blondie for Victory 10-14-42
Blondie Goes Latin 2-19-41
Blondie Goes to College 2-11-42
Blondie Has Servant Trouble 8-07-40
Blondie Hits the Jackpot 9-14-49
Blondie in Society 7-02-41
Blondie Johnson 2-28-33
Blondie Knows Best 9-18-46
Blondie Meets the Boss 3-08-39
Blondie of the Follies 9-13-32
Blondie on a Budget 2-28-40
Blondie Plays Cupid 10-30-40
Blondie Takes a Vacation 7-19-39
Blondie's Big Deal 3-16-49
Blondie's Holiday 3-05-47
Blondie's Lucky Day 4-24-46
Blondie's Number One 6-23-71
Blondie's Reward 8-18-48
Blondie's Secret 1-26-49

Blondy 1-28-76
Blood Alley 9-21-55
Blood and Black Lace 6-23-65
Blood and Fire (See: Blood Och Eld)
Blood and Guts 9-20-78
Blood and Lace 3-17-71
Blood and Light (See: Sang et Lumieres)
Blood and Sand 8-11-22
Blood and Sand 5-21-41
Blood and Steel 3-11-25
Blood and Steel 12-16-59
Blood Arrow 5-07-58
Blood Bath 3-09-66
Blood Beast from Outer Space 11-08-67
Blood Bonds (See: Stimme des Blutes)
Blood Brothers 2-25-53
Blood Condor (See: Yawar Mallku)
Blood Feast 5-06-64
Blood for Dracula 2-20-74
Blood from the Mummy's Tomb 10-27-71
Blood in the Streets 1-14-76
Blood Kin (See: Last of the Mobile Hot Shots, The)
Blood Letting, The (See: Saignee, La)
Blood Money 11-21-33)
Blood Och Eld 3-27-46
Blood of a Poet (See: Sang D'Un Poete)
Blood of Dracula 1-08-58
Blood of Hussain, The 5-14-80
Blood of the Condor (See: Yawar Mallku)
Blood of the Railroad Workers (See: Rallarblod)
Blood of the Vampire 9-03-58
Blood on the Land (See: To Homa Vaftike Kokkino)
Blood on the Moon 11-10-48
Blood on the Sun 5-02-45
Blood Relatives (See: Liens De Sang, Les)
Blood Ship, The 7-20-27
Blood Stains in a New Car (See: Manchas de Sangre en un Coche Nuevo)
Blood to the Head, The (See: Sang a la Tete, Le)
Blood Will Tell 5-29-14
Blood Will Tell 3-09-17
Blood Will Tell 1-25-28
Bloodbrothers 9-20-78
Bloodeaters 10-29-80
Bloodhounds of Broadway 10-29-52
Bloodless Duel, A 9-04-08
Bloodline 7-04-79
Bloodshed at the Wedding (See: Makedonska Krava Svadba)
Bloody Brood, The 11-04-59
Bloody Hands, The (See: Maos Sangrentas)
Bloody Life (See: Ai Kruie)
Bloody Mama 3-18-70
Bloody Nitrate (See: Caliche Sangriento)
Bloody Twilight (See: Matomeno Heliovasilema)
Bloomfield 7-07-71
Blooming Angel 2-13-20
Blossom Time 7-24-34
Blossoms in the Dust 6-25-41
Blossoms on Broadway 11-17-37
Blot, The 8-19-21
Bloudeni 8-03-66
Blow for Blow (See: Coup pour Coup)
Blow-Up 12-21-66
Blow Your Own Horn 1-10-24
Blowdry 11-10-76
Blowing Wild 9-16-53
Bludgeon, The 10-15-15
Blue 4-24-68
Blue and the Grey, or the Days of '61, The 6-20-08
Blue Angel, The 4-30-30 and 12-10-30
Blue Angel, The 8-26-59
Blue Bandanna, The 11-28-19
Blue Beard 12-04-09
Blue Beast, The 2-03-65
Blue Bird, The 4-05-18
Blue Bird, The 1-24-40
Blue Bird, The 5-12-76
Blue Blazes 1-13-22
Blue Blazes 4-21-26
Blue Blazes Rawden 2-22-18
Blue Blood 6-21-18
Blue Blood 1-27-26
Blue Blood 1-17-51
Blue Blood and Red 4-07-16
Blue Bonnet, The 10-31-19
Blue Collar 2-08-78
Blue Country, The (See: Pays Bleu, Le)
Blue Dahlia, The 1-30-46

Blue Danube, The 5-02-28
Blue Danube, The 11-20-34
Blue Denim 7-29-59
Blue Envelope Mystery, The 10-13-16
Blue Ferns, The (See: Fougeres Bleues, Les)
Blue Fin 11-15-78
Blue Fire Lady 5-10-78
Blue Gardenia, The 3-18-53
Blue Grass of Kentucky 1-18-50
Blue Hawaii 11-29-61
Blue Idol, The 10-13-31
Blue Jeans 3-22-18
Blue Lagoon, The 4-26-23
Blue Lagoon, The 3-09-49
Blue Lagoon, The 6-11-80
Blue Lamp, The 1-25-50
Blue Light, The (See: Blaue Licht, Das)
Blue Max, The 6-22-66
Blue Montana Skies 5-03-39
Blue Movie, or "F**ck" 6-25-69
Blue Movie 10-13-71
Blue Murder at St. Trinian's 1-08-58
Blue Pearl 3-05-20
Blue Sextet 5-24-72
Blue Sierra 5-08-46
Blue Skies 7-17-29
Blue Skies 9-25-46
Blue Steel 7-17-34
Blue Streak, The 3-30-17
Blue Streak, The 3-03-26
Blue Streak M'Coy 9-03-20
Blue Suede Shoes 2-13-80
Blue Summer 11-21-73
Blue Veil, The 10-22-47
Blue Veil, The 9-12-51
Blue Velvet 4-29-70
Blue Water, White Death 5-12-71
Blue, White and Perfect 12-24-41
Bluebeard 1-31-45
Bluebeard (See: Barbe-Bleue)
Bluebeard 8-23-72
Bluebeard, Jr. 6-16-22
Bluebeard's Eighth Wife 8-09-23
Bluebeard's Eighth Wife 3-23-38
Bluebeard's Seven Wives 1-13-26
Bluebeard's Six Mothers-in-Law (See: Seis Suegras De Barba Azul,
    Las)
Bluebeard's Ten Honeymoons 3-30-60
Blueprint for Murder, A 7-29-53
Blueprint for Robbery 1-18-61
Blues Brothers, The 6-18-80
Blues Buster 10-25-50
Blues in the Night 11-05-41
Blues Under the Skin 2-21-73
Bluff 10-20-16
Bluff 4-30-24
Bluff Stop 3-29-78
Bluffer, The 1-10-19
Blum 8-26-70
Blume in Love 5-23-73
Blume von Hawaii, Die 4-25-33
Blumenfrau, Die 7-12-32
Blumenfrau von Lindenau, Die 5-13-31
Blushing Brides 8-06-30
Blushing Charlie (See: Lyckliga Skitar)
Boarder, The (See: Pensionnaire, La)
Boarders, The (See: Wspolny Pokoj)
Boarding School, The (See: Residencia, La)
Boardwalk 11-14-79
Boat on the Grass, The (See: Bateau Sur L'Herbe, Le)
Boatniks, The 5-27-70
Bob & Carol & Ted & Alice 7-02-69
Bob & Daryl & Ted & Alex 6-21-72
Bob Hampton of Placer 5-06-21
Bob le Flambeur 11-07-56
Bob Mathias Story, The 10-06-54
Bob, Son of Battle 6-11-47
Bobbed Hair 3-31-22
Bobbed Hair 11-04-25
Bobbie Jo and the Outlaw 4-07-76
Bobbie of the Ballet 6-02-16
Bobbikins 8-05-59
Bobby Deerfield 9-14-77
Bobby Geht Los 12-22-31
Bobby Starts Off (See: Bobby Geht Los)
Bobby, The Gasoline Boy 10-02-29
Bobby's Krig 7-03-74
Bobby's War (See: Bobby's Krig)

Bobo, The 5-31-67
Bobo, Jacco 11-21-79
Bobosse 4-08-59
Bob's Electric Theatre 10-23-09
Boccaccio 9-16-36
Boccaccio '70 5-16-62
Bockbierfest 4-08-31
Body, The (See: Ratai)
Body, The 11-11-70
Body and Soul 11-05-20
Body and Soul 11-09-27
Body and Soul 3-18-31
Body and Soul 8-13-47
Body and the Blood, The (See: Cuerpo y la Sangre, El)
Body Disappears, The 12-03-41
Body of Love (See: Corpo d'Amore)
Body of My Enemy, The (See: Corps de Mon Ennemi, Le)
Body Punch, The 9-05-28
Body Snatcher, The 2-21-45
Body to Heart (See: Corps a Coeur)
Bodyguard, The (See: Yojimbo)
Bodyguard 9-01-48
Bodyguard, The 7-30-80
Bodyhold 12-14-49
Boeing, Boeing 12-01-65
Bof ... Anatomie D'Un Livreur 4-07-71
Bofors Gun 8-21-68
Bogeyman (See: Kummatty)
Boglio Vivere Con Letizia 2-16-38
Bogus Uncle 1-18-18
Boheme, La 3-03-26
Boheme, La 10-13-65
Bohemian Dancer 12-12-28
Bohemian Girl, The 2-08-23
Bohemian Girl, The 2-19-36
Bohemian Rapture 2-04-48
Bohoc a Falon 1-31-68
Bohrloch Oder Bayern Ist Nicht Texas, Das 4-13-66
Boiling Point, The 11-08-32
Boiling Pot, The (See: Pot-Bouille)
Boina Blanca 11-19-41
Bois des Amants, Le 8-31-60
Bois Sacre, Le 12-27-39
Boite de Nuit 8-08-51
Bokyo 7-09-75
Bold and the Brave, The 3-21-56
Bold Caballero, The 3-17-37
Bold Dragoon, The (See: Freche Husar, Der)
Bold Emmet, Ireland's Martyr 8-30-15
Bold Frontiersman, The 4-28-48
Bold Impersonation, A 8-27-15
Bolek and Lolek 12-16-36
Bolero 2-20-34
Bolibar 8-29-28
Boliche 7-31-34
Bolshaia Doroga 9-11-63
Bolshevism on Trial 5-02-19
Bolshoi Ballet, The 10-30-57
Bolshoi Ballet 67 9-28-66
Bolted Door, The 9-11-14
Bolted Door, The 4-05-23
Bom the Soldier (See: Soldat Bom)
Bomb Has Been Stolen, A (See: S-A Furat O Bomba)
Bomb Throwers, The 5-14-15
Bomba and the Hidden City 10-18-50
Bomba on Panther Island 1-11-50
Bomba, The Jungle Boy 3-02-49
Bombardier 5-12-43
Bombay Buddha, The 7-02-15
Bombay Clipper, The 1-14-42
Bombay Mail 1-09-34
Bombay Talkie 11-25-70
Bomben Auf Monte Carlo 9-15-31
Bomber and Paganini (See: Bomber und Paganini)
Bomber und Paganini 2-02-77
Bomber's Moon 7-14-43
Bombers B-52 10-30-57
Bombs over Burma 8-12-42
Bombs over Monte Carlo (See: Bomben auf Monte Carlo)
Bombshell 10-24-33
Bomsalva 3-27-78
Bon Baisers A Lundi 12-11-74
Bon Baisers de Hong Kong 12-31-75
Bon Bast 7-27-77
Bon Dieu Sans Confession, Le 10-14-53
Bon et Les Mechants, Le 2-04-76
Bon Voyage 5-09-62
Bon Voyage, Charlie Brown (And Don't Come Back!) 5-28-80

Bonanza Town 7-18-51
Bonaparte and the Revolution (See: Bonaparte et la Revolution)
Bonaparte et la Revolution 9-22-71
Bond Between, The 4-06-17
Bond Boy 10-13-22
Bond of Fear, The 9-21-17
Bond Street 6-02-48
Bondage (See: Kotolek)
Bondage 10-19-17
Bondage 11-07-28
Bondage 4-25-33
Bondage of Fear 1-12-17
Bonded Woman, The 8-04-22
Bonditis 5-10-67
Bondman, The 3-24-16
Bondman, The 6-05-29
Bonds of Honor 1-31-19
Bonds of Love 11-07-19
Bonds of Passion, The 9-17-15
Bondwomen 12-17-15
Bone 8-02-72
Bonheur, Le 3-06-35 and 3-04-36
Bonheur, Le 3-03-65
Bonheur Dans 20 Ans, Le 12-15-71
Bonheur Est Pour Demain, Le 10-10-62
Bonitas Las Tapatias 1-03-62
Bonjour Paris 12-02-53
Bonjour Toubib 5-15-57
Bonjour Tristesse 1-15-58
Bonne Annee, La 5-09-73
Bonne Aventure, La 8-02-32
Bonne Chance 10-30-35
Bonne Chance Charlie! 8-01-62
Bonne Occase, La 4-07-65
Bonne Soupe, La 2-12-64
Bonne Tisane, La 4-16-58
Bonnes A Tuer 2-09-55
Bonnes Causes, Les 5-08-63
Bonnes Femmes, Les 5-04-60
Bonnie and Clyde 8-09-67
Bonnie Annie Laurie 10-11-18
Bonnie Bonnie Lassie 10-31-19
Bonnie Brier Bush 12-02-21
Bonnie Parker Story, The 7-09-58
Bonnie Prince Charlie 11-03-48
Bonnie Scotland 8-28-35
Bonnot's Gang (See: Bande A Bonnot, La)
Bons Debarras, Les 3-05-80
Bons Vivants, Les 11-24-65
Bonsoir Paris, Bonjour L'Amour 5-01-57
Bonus, The (See: Premia)
Bonzo Goes to College 9-03-52
Boob, The 6-02-26
Boob Weekly, The 5-12-16
Boogey Man, The 11-19-80
Boogie Man Will Get You, The 10-14-42
Book Agent, The 6-02-17
Book of Good Love, The (See: Libro de Buen Amor, El)
Book of Nature, The 11-14-14
Book of Numbers 4-11-73
Book That Should Turn (See: Yakilacak Kitap)
Booloo 8-03-38
Boom 5-29-68
Boom 11-15-72
Boom, Il 10-16-63
Boom, The (See: Boom, Il)
Boom Town 8-07-40
Boomerang (See: Bumerang)
Boomerang 1-29-47
Boomerang 2-07-79
Boomerang, The 5-02-19
Boomerang, The 7-08-25
Boomerang Bill 2-10-22
Boon, The (See: Anugraham)
Boot Polish 9-03-58
Boothill Brigade 9-29-37
Bootleggers 6-12-74
Bootles' Baby 5-28-15
Boots 3-14-19
Boots and Saddle 10-13-37
Boots and Saddles 11-03-16
Boots Malone 12-26-51
Boots of Destiny 7-28-37
Bop Girl Goes Calypso, The 7-17-57
Boquitas Pintadas 6-26-74
Bora Bora 12-04-68
Borcs Amerikaban 9-21-38
Borcs in America (See: Borcs Amerikaban)

Bordee, En 10-27-31
Bordellet--En Glaedespigess Erindringer 5-24-72
Bordello (See: Freudenhaus, Das)
Bordello--Memoirs of a Pleasure Girl, The (See: Bordellet--En Glaedespigess Erindringer)
Border 10-23-35
Border Badmen 11-21-45
Border Bandits 4-03-46
Border Blackbirds 10-05-27
Border Brigands 6-26-35
Border Buckeroo 8-04-43
Border Caballero 7-22-36
Border Cafe 6-09-37
Border Cavalier 10-12-27
Border Crossing, The (See: Uebergang, Der)
Border Devils 5-17-32
Border Feud 5-21-47
Border Flight 6-24-36
Border G-Man 7-20-38
Border Incident 8-31-49
Border Intrigue 5-13-25
Border Law 9-15-31
Border Legion, The 8-02-18
Border Legion, The 10-22-24
Border Legion, The 7-02-30
Border Legion, The 11-27-40
Border of Sin, The (See: Suendige Grenze, Die)
Border Outlaws 11-29-50
Border Patrol 1-27-43
Border Patrolman 7-01-36
Border Phantom 2-17-37
Border Raiders, The 10-04-18
Border Rangers 9-27-50
Border River 1-06-54
Border Romance 5-28-30
Border Saddlemates 4-30-52
Border Sheriff, The 4-21-26
Border Street 4-05-50
Border Tale, A 12-03-10
Border Treasure 8-30-50
Border Vengeance 8-12-25
Border Vigilantes 4-02-41
Border Wildcat 4-24-29
Border Wireless, The 10-11-18
Border Wolves 3-02-38
Border Women 8-27-24
Borderland 7-28-22
Borderland 4-14-37
Borderline 1-11-50
Borderline 7-23-80
Bordertown 1-29-35
Bordertown Gun Fighters 10-06-43
Borghese Piccolo Piccolo, Un 5-25-77
Boris Godunov 1-25-56
Born Again 10-23-14
Born Again 9-06-78
Born for Glory 10-23-35
Born Free 3-23-66
Born Losers 7-12-67
Born of Fire (See: Im Feuer Bestanden)
Born of Unknown Father (See: Ne De Pere Inconnu)
Born Reckless 6-11-30
Born Reckless 7-21-37
Born Reckless 4-01-59
Born to Be Bad 6-05-34
Born to Be Bad 8-23-50
Born to Be Loved 6-10-59
Born to Be Wild 2-23-38
Born to Boogie 12-20-72
Born to Dance 12-09-36
Born to Fight 5-25-38
Born to Gamble 10-09-35
Born to Kill 4-16-47
Born to Kill 6-04-75
Born to Love (See: Nacida Para Amar)
Born to Love 4-29-31
Born to Raise Hell 10-15-75
Born to Sing 1-21-42
Born to Speed 1-22-47
Born to the West 6-30-26
Born to the West 3-16-38
Born to Win 10-13-71
Born Yesterday 11-22-50
Borneo 9-08-37
Borrowed Chateau (See: Kolcsonkert Kastely)
Borrowed Clothes 8-28-09
Borrowed Clothes 11-22-18
Borrowed Finery 1-20-26

Borrowed Hero 12-17-41
Borrowed Plumage 7-06-17
Borrowed Trouble 11-17-48
Borrowed Wives 10-29-30
Borrowing Trouble 10-27-37 and 11-17-37
Borsalino 4-01-70
Borsalino & Co. 11-06-74
Boscop Diagram, The (See: Graphique de Boscop, Le)
Bosko Buha 8-15-79
Bosque de Ancines, El 5-06-70
Boss, The (See: Jefe, El or Caid, Le)
Boss, The 5-14-15
Boss, The 8-22-56
Boss and the Worker, The (See: Padrone e l'Operaio, Il)
Boss of Big Town 1-13-43
Boss of Camp Four 1-05-23
Boss of Hangtown Mesa 9-16-42
Boss of Lone Valley 12-22-37
Boss of the Lazy Y 4-12-18
Boss of the Rawhide 9-13-44
Boss Rider of Gun Creek 12-16-36
Boss' Son, The 9-20-78
Bossu, Le 3-02-60
Boston Blackie and the Law 11-20-46
Boston Blackie's Little Pal 9-06-18
Boston Blackie's Rendezvous 8-22-45
Boston Strangler, The 10-16-68
Boszka Ema 7-23-80
Botany Bay 9-30-53
Botschaft der Goetter 5-26-76
Botta e Risposta 4-26-50
Bottle, The 6-11-15
Bottleneck (See: Ingorgo, L')
Bottom of the Bottle 2-01-56
Bottom of the World, The 7-16-30
Bottoms Up 3-27-34
Bottoms Up 3-03-60
Bou Posleden 11-17-76
Bouboule's Gang (See: Bande a Bouboule, La)
Boucher, Le 3-11-70
Boucher, la Star et L'Orpheline, Le 3-12-75
Boudoir Diplomat, The 12-10-30 (Also see: Don Juan Diplomatico)
Boudu Sauve des Eaux (See: Boudu Saved from Drowning)
Boudu Saved from Drowning 3-01-67
Bouffon, Le 5-15-09
Bought 8-18-31
Bought and Paid for 11-03-16
Bought and Paid for 3-17-22
Bougnoul, Le 5-14-75
Boulanger de Valorgue, Le 3-25-53
Boulder Dam 4-01-36
Boule de Suif 12-12-45
Boulevard 12-14-60
Boulevard du Rhum 10-27-71
Boulevard Nights 3-21-79
Boum Sur Paris 4-07-54
Bound for Glory 10-27-76
Bound in Morocco 8-02-18
Bound on the Wheel 7-30-15
Boundary Fire (See: Grenzfeuer)
Boundary Rider, The 9-11-14
Bountiful Summer 12-26-51
Bounty Hunter 8-25-54
Bounty Killer, The 6-23-65
Bouquet, The 10-29-10
Bourgeois Gentilhomme, Le 9-17-58
Bourlive Vino 7-28-76
Bowery, The 10-10-33
Bowery at Midnight 11-11-42
Bowery Batallion 2-14-51
Bowery Blitzkrieg 10-08-41
Bowery Bombshell 7-24-46
Bowery Boy 1-01-41
Bowery Boys Meet the Monsters 7-07-54
Bowery Buckaroos 10-15-47
Bowery Champs 11-08-44
Bowery Cinderella, A 1-25-28 and 2-22-28
Bowery to Broadway 10-25-44
Box, The 8-20-75
Boxcar Bertha 5-31-72
Boxer 8-16-67
Boxer, The 11-13-63
Boxer, The 11-16-77
Boy (See: Shonen)
Boy 12-11-40
Boy ... A Girl, A 5-14-69
Boy, A Girl, and a Bike, A 6-01-49
Boy, A Girl, and a Dog, A 6-26-46

Boy Across the Street, The 8-10-66
Boy and a Camel, A 8-07-68
Boy and His Dog, A 3-26-75
Boy and the Ball and the Hole in the Wall, The (See: Nino y el Muro, El)
Boy and the Bridge, The 8-05-59
Boy and the Law, A 4-03-14
Boy and the Pirates 4-06-60
Boy Detectives, The (See: Emil to Tantei Tachi)
Boy, Did I Get a Wrong Number 6-08-66
Boy Friend 6-21-39
Boy Friend, The 8-25-26
Boy Friend, The 12-22-71
Boy from Indiana 3-29-50
Boy from Oklahoma 1-20-54
Boy Girl, The 2-23-17
Boy in the Tree (See: Pojken I Tradet)
Boy Kumasenu, The 7-15-53
Boy Like Me, A (See: Muchacho Como Yo, Un)
Boy Meets Girl 8-31-38
Boy Named Charlie Brown, A 12-03-69
Boy of Flanders, A 4-16-24
Boy of Mine 12-27-23
Boy of the Plantation (See: Menino de Engheno)
Boy of the Streets 11-30-27
Boy of the Streets 12-01-37
Boy on a Dolphin 4-17-57
Boy Rider, The 11-02-27
Boy Slaves 1-18-39
Boy Trouble 4-05-39
Boy! What a Girl 2-05-47
Boy Who Caught a Crook 10-18-61
Boy Who Cried Werewolf, The 8-01-73
Boy Who Cried Wolf, The 5-25-17
Boy Who Stole a Million, The 9-21-60 and 7-05-61
Boy with Green Hair, The 11-17-48
Boy Woodburn 5-19-22
Boys (See: Drenge)
Boys, The 10-03-62
Boys, The 7-24-63
Boys and Girls (See: Des Garcons et des Filles)
Boys and Girls 7-23-69
Boys from Brazil, The 9-27-78
Boys from Syracuse 7-17-40
Boys from the Streets 3-15-50
Boys in Company C., The 1-25-78
Boys in the Band, The 3-18-70
Boys in the Sand 12-22-71
Boys' Night Out 6-13-62
Boys of Paul Street, The 3-19-69
Boys of the City 8-21-40
Boys of the Prater (See: Praterbuben)
Boys' Ranch 5-01-46
Boys' Reformatory 5-10-39
Boys' Town (See: Ciudad de los Ninos, La)
Boys Town 9-07-38
Boys Will Be Boys 5-20-21
Brabanconne, La 2-23-32
Brace Dei Biassoli, La 9-24-80
Brace Up 3-15-18
Braddock-Farr Fight 1-26-38
Braddock-Lewis Fight 6-30-37
Braggarts, The (See: Fanfarrones, Los)
Brain, The (See: Cerveau, Le)
Brain Eaters 11-05-58
Brain from Planet Arous, The 1-08-58
Brainstorm 5-12-65
Brainwashed 7-05-61
Bramble Bush, The 8-22-19
Bramble Bush, The 1-20-60
Brancaleone Alle Crociate 8-04-71
Brancaleone at the Crusades (See: Brancaleone Alle Crociate)
Brand, The 2-28-19
Brand-Boerge Rykker Ud 3-03-76
Brand in der Oper 11-12-30
Brand in the Opera (See: Brand in der Oper)
Brand of Cowardice 7-29-25
Brand of Cowardice, The 11-03-16
Brand of Satan, The 6-29-17
Brand X 6-03-70
Branded 11-10-31
Branded 11-15-50
Branded a Coward 10-23-35
Branded a Thief 3-25-25
Branded Man 6-06-28
Branded Men 12-15-31
Branded Sombrero 3-21-28

Branded Woman 9-10-20
Brandenburg Arch 7-03-29
Branding Broadway 11-29-18
Branding Iron 11-12-20
Brandstellen 6-28-78
Brandy for the Parson 6-04-52
Brannen 8-22-73
Brannigan 3-19-75
Branquinol 1-18-50
Bras de la Nuit, Les 12-20-61
Brasher Doubloon 2-05-47
Brasil Ano 2000 6-03-70
Brass 3-15-23
Brass Bottle, The 2-12-64
Brass Buttons 3-14-19
Brass Check, The 3-15-18
Brass Knuckles 12-21-27 and 2-22-28
Brass Legend, The 12-26-56
Brass Target 12-13-78
Brassie, The 8-11-31
Brat, The 11-07-19
Brat, The 6-18-30
Brat, The 8-25-31
Bratya Karamazovy 7-30-69
Bravados, The 6-04-58
Brave and Bold 5-24-18
Brave Boy (See: Nino Valiente)
Brave Bulls, The 4-18-51
Brave Don't Cry, The 8-27-52
Brave Don't Die, The (See: Valientes No Mueren, Los)
Brave One, The 9-19-56
Brave Pigeon (See: Paloma Brava)
Brave Seaman (See: Mutige Seefahrer, Der)
Brave Sinner, The (See: Brave Suender, Der)
Brave Soldat Schwejk, Der 1-18-61
Brave Suender, Der 11-10-31 and 4-04-33
Brave Warrior 5-14-52
Brave Warrior, The (See: O Bravo Guerreiro)
Brave Women of '76 11-06-09
Bravest Way, The 6-07-18
Bravo Maestro 6-07-78
Bravo of the 1900's, A (See: Guapo Del 900, Un)
Brawl Among the Men (See: Du Rififi Chez les Hommes)
Brawn of the North 4-05-23
Brazen Beauty, The 9-20-18
Brazen Women of Balzac, The 7-21-71
Brazil 10-25-44
Brazil 3-06-74
Brazil Year 2000 (See: Brasil Ano 2000)
Brazo Fuerte, El 8-02-61
Breach of Promise 10-02-09
Breach of Promise 11-22-32
Bread 8-09-18
Bread 7-23-24
Bread and Chocolate (See: Pane e Cioccolata)
Bread and Games (See: Brot und Spiele)
Bread and Roses (See: Brot und Rosen)
Bread-Carrier, The (See: Laporteuse de Pain)
Bread, Love and Imagination (See: Pane, Amore, E Fantasia)
Bread, Love and Jealousy (See: Pane, Amore, E Gelosia)
Bread of Love, The (See: Karlekans Brad)
Bread of the Young Years, The (See: Brot der Fruehen Jahre, Das)
Break Away (See: Przed Odlotem)
Break in the Circle 5-08-57
Break of Day 1-12-77
Break of Hearts 5-22-35
Break the News 1-08-41
Break the News to Mother 5-30-19
Break Up (See: Eutanasia Di Un Amore)
Break-Up, The (See: Razlom)
Break Up, The 8-06-30
Breakdown (See: Kvar)
Breakdown 7-16-52
Breaker, The 12-01-16
Breaker, Breaker 4-27-77
Breaker Morant 4-23-80
Breakfast at Sunrise 11-16-27
Breakfast at Tiffany's 10-11-61
Breakfast for Two 11-24-37
Breakfast in Bed 4-12-78
Breakfast in Hollywood 1-16-46
Breakfast with the Devil (See: Dorucak Sa Davalom)
Breakheart Pass 2-04-76
Breaking Away 7-11-79
Breaking Chains 3-30-27
Breaking Glass 5-28-80
Breaking Home Ties 5-17-23

Breaking into Society 10-03-08
Breaking into Society 12-20-23
Breaking It Up (See: A Tout Casser)
Breaking Point, The 2-04-21
Breaking Point, The 4-09-24
Breaking Point, The 9-13-50
Breaking Point, The 6-02-76
Breaking the Bank 10-09-09
Breaking the Ice 9-07-38
Breaking with Old Ideas 7-07-76
Breakout (See: Kitores)
Breakout 11-01-50
Breakout 5-07-75
Breakthrough 11-01-50
Breakthrough 3-21-79
Breakup, The (See: Rupture, La)
Breath of Scandal 11-26-24
Breath of Scandal, A 10-26-60
Breath of the Gods 10-29-20
Breathing Together: Revolution of the Electric Family 5-19-71
Bred in Old Kentucky 1-12-27
Bred in the Bone 10-22-15
Breed of Courage 11-02-27
Breed of Men 2-07-19
Breed of the Border 5-16-33
Breed of the Sunset 6-13-28
Breezing Home 3-24-37
Breezy 11-07-73
Breezy Jim 2-14-19
Brelan D'As 10-29-52
Brenn, Hexe, Brenn 5-20-70
Brennende Geheimnis 4-25-33
Brennende Herz, Das (See: Burning Heart, The)
Brennender Sand 6-01-60
Brent Jord 7-30-69
Breve Cielo 4-02-69
Breve Vacanza, Una 8-22-73
Brevet Fra Afdode 3-19-47
Brewster McCloud 11-18-70 and 12-09-70
Brewster's Millions 5-01-14
Brewster's Millions 1-28-21
Brewster's Millions 2-05-35 and 4-10-35
Brewster's Millions 3-14-45
Breza 8-16-67
Briarcliff Auto Races 5-02-08
Bribe, The 2-09-49
Bricklayers, The (See: Albaniles, Los)
Bridal Couple Dodging Cameras 5-09-08
Bridal Path, The 8-05-59
Bridal Suite 5-24-39
Bridal Wreath, The (See: Morsiusseppele)
Bride, The (See: Nevesta)
Bride, The 8-08-73
Bride and Groom's Visit to the New York Zoological Gardens, A
   11-13-09
Bride and the Beast 2-12-58
Bride by Mistake 8-02-44
Bride Came C.O.D., The 7-02-41
Bride Comes Home 1-01-36
Bride for a Night (See: Moglie Per Una Notte)
Bride for a Night, A 10-08-24
Bride for Henry, A 9-29-37
Bride for Sale 10-19-49
Bride Goes Wild, The 2-25-48
Bride in Trouble, A (See: Novia en Apuros, Una)
Bride Is Too Beautiful, The (See: Mariee Est Trop Belle, La)
Bride of Buddha 4-16-41
Bride of Fear, The 4-19-18
Bride of Frankenstein 5-15-35
Bride of Hate, The 12-29-16
Bride of the Andes 9-14-66
Bride of the Atom 6-01-55
Bride of the Desert 11-20-29
Bride of the Gorilla 11-07-51
Bride of the Lake 9-25-34
Bride of the Regiment 5-28-30
Bride of the Storm 4-07-26
Bride of Torocko (See: Torockoi Menyasszony)
Bride of Vengeance 3-30-49
Bride 68 4-16-30
Bride Sur le Cou, La 5-10-61
Bride To Be (See: Pepita Jimenez)
Bride Walks Out 7-15-36
Bride with a Dowry 9-01-54
Bride Wore Black, The (See: Mariee Etait en Noire, La)
Bride Wore Boots, The 3-20-46
Bride Wore Crutches, The 7-24-40

Bride Wore Red, The 9-29-37
Bride's Awakening, The 5-03-18
Bride's Awakening, The 9-29-37
Bride's Silence, The 9-21-17
Bridegroom for Two 3-08-32
Bridegroom's Joke, The 12-04-09
Brides Are Like That 3-25-36
Brides of Dracula 5-18-60
Brides of Fu Manchu 12-14-66
Bridge, The (See: Bruecke, Die)
Bridge at Remagen, The 6-25-69
Bridge in the Jungle, The 11-04-70
Bridge of San Luis Rey, The 5-22-29
Bridge of San Luis Rey, The 2-02-44
Bridge of Shadows 10-17-13
Bridge of Sighs, The 5-28-15
Bridge of Sighs, The 11-17-22
Bridge of Sighs, The 3-25-25
Bridge of Sighs, The 5-06-36
Bridge of Time, The 10-22-15
Bridge on the River Kwai, The 11-20-57
Bridge That Failed, The 1-29-15
Bridge to the Sun 8-16-61
Bridge Too Far, A 6-08-77
Bridges at Toko-Ri, The 12-29-54
Bridges Burned 2-02-17
Brief, Der 12-07-66
Brief Encounter 11-28-45
Brief Heaven (See: Breve Cielo)
Brief Intermission, A (See: Syntomo Dialima)
Brief Moment 10-03-33
Brief Rapture 3-05-52
Brief Story of a Brief Meeting (See: Sjuget Dlja Nebolsciovo
    Rasskaza)
Brieftraeger Mueller 11-11-53
Brig, The 9-09-64
Brigade, La 8-28-74
Brigade Anti-Gangs 10-19-66
Brigade Mondaine 9-20-78
Brigadista, El 3-15-78
Brigadoon 8-11-54
Brigand, The (See: Brigante, Il)
Brigand, The 6-04-52
Brigand of Kandahar, The 8-18-65
Brigante, Il 9-06-61
Brigante di Tacca del Lupo, Il 10-29-52
Brigante Musolino, Il 6-06-51
Brigham Young 8-28-40
Bright College Years 6-02-71
Bright Eyes 7-02-30
Bright Eyes 12-25-34
Bright Leaf 5-24-50
Bright Lights 11-18-25
Bright Lights 8-21-35
Bright Lights, The 3-03-16
Bright Lights of Broadway 10-18-23
Bright Road 4-08-53
Bright Shawl 4-26-23
Bright Skies 4-30-20
Bright Sunny Skies (See: Yan Yang Tian)
Bright Victory 7-25-51
Brighton Rock 2-04-48
Brighton Strangler, The 5-02-45
Brigitte et Brigitte 5-04-66
Brilliant Marriage 9-23-36
Brimstone 8-17-49
Bring 'Em Back Alive 6-21-32
Bring Him In 10-28-21
Bring Me the Head of Alfredo Garcia 8-07-74
Bring On the Girls 2-21-45
Bring Your Smile Along 6-22-55
Bringing Home Father 6-02-17
Bringing Up Baby 2-16-38
Bringing Up Betty 7-25-19
Bringing Up Father 3-21-28
Bringing Up Father 11-27-46
Brink of Life (See: Nara Livet)
Brink's Job, The 12-13-78
Britain's Far Flung Battle Line 8-09-18
Britannia Mews 3-09-49
British Agent 9-25-34
British Intelligence 2-14-40
British War Doc. 6-11-41
British War Pictures 5-18-17 and 8-17-17
Brittany Lassies 3-12-10
Britton of the Seventh 5-05-16
Broad Coalition, The 1-26-72
Broad Daylight (See: Plein Soleil)

Broadminded 7-07-31
Broadway 5-29-29
Broadway 5-06-42
Broadway After Dark 5-21-24
Broadway and Home 1-21-21
Broadway, Arizona 9-28-17
Broadway Babies 6-26-29
Broadway Bad 3-07-33
Broadway Big Shot 1-14-42
Broadway Bill 2-15-18
Broadway Bill 12-04-34
Broadway Broke 12-27-23
Broadway Bubble 11-19-20
Broadway Butterfly 5-20-25
Broadway Cowboy, A 7-02-20
Broadway Daddies 6-06-28
Broadway Drifter, The 6-29-27
Broadway Fever 2-20-29
Broadway Gallant, The 6-16-26
Broadway Gold 8-02-23
Broadway Gondolier 7-24-35
Broadway Hoofer, The 12-18-29
Broadway Hostess 12-18-35
Broadway Jones 3-23-17
Broadway Light 10-27-22
Broadway Limited 6-18-41
Broadway Love 1-18-18
Broadway Madness 1-18-28
Broadway Melody, The 2-13-29
Broadway Melody of 1936, The 9-25-35
Broadway Melody of 1938, The 8-18-37
Broadway Melody of 1940, The 2-07-40
Broadway Musketeers 10-19-38
Broadway Nights 6-29-27
Broadway or Bust 7-16-24
Broadway Peacock 3-24-22
Broadway Rhythm 1-19-44
Broadway Rose 9-22-22
Broadway Saint, A 7-25-19
Broadway Scandal, A 5-31-18
Broadway Scandals 10-30-29
Broadway Serenade 4-05-39
Broadway Sport, The 7-06-17
Broadway Thru a Keyhole 11-07-33
Broadway to Cheyenne 9-27-32
Broadway to Hollywood 9-05-33
Broder Carl 5-19-71
Broederna Lejonhjaerta 10-05-77
Broken Arrow 6-14-50
Broken Barriers 2-13-29
Broken Blossoms 5-16-19
Broken Blossoms 6-10-36 and 1-20-37
Broken Chains 12-01-16
Broken Chains 12-15-22
Broken Comedy (See: Comedia Rota)
Broken Commandments 10-24-19
Broken Doll, A 7-22-21
Broken Doll, The 10-22-10
Broken Dreams 11-28-33
Broken Fetters 6-23-16
Broken Flag (See: Bandera Rota)
Broken Gate, The 3-30-27
Broken Hearts 3-10-26
Broken Hearts of Broadway 7-19-23
Broken Hearts of Hollywood 10-20-26
Broken Journey 4-21-48
Broken Jug, The (See: Zerbrochene Krug, Der)
Broken Lance 7-28-54
Broken Law, The 12-03-15
Broken Laws 2-04-25
Broken Locket 9-25-09
Broken Love 10-23-46
Broken Mask 3-21-28
Broken Melody 7-20-38
Broken Melody, A 10-30-09
Broken Road 7-22-21
Broken Rose, The 6-05-14
Broken Shoes 4-03-34
Broken Spell, A 4-02-10
Broken Star, The 2-01-56
Broken Talisman, The (See: Telesme Schekaste)
Broken Ties 8-28-09
Broken Ties 2-22-18
Broken Toys (See: Juguetes Rotos)
Broken Treaty at Battle Mountain 1-22-75
Broken Violin 7-04-23
Broken Wing 10-11-23
Broken Wing, The 3-29-32

Broken Wings, The 4-03-68
Brokiga Blad 12-08-31
Brollopet Pa Solo 11-13-46
Brollopsbesvar 9-30-64
Brollopsnatten 4-23-47
Bronco Billy 6-11-80
Bronco Bullfrog 10-28-70
Bronco Buster 4-16-52
Bronco Twister 3-30-27 and 5-18-27
Bronte 7-12-72
Bronte Sisters, The (See: Soeurs Bronte, Les)
Bronze Bell 7-08-21
Bronze Bracelet, The 7-24-74
Bronzes, Les 12-06-78
Brood, The 6-06-79
Brooding Eyes 4-28-26
Brooklyn Orchid 1-28-26
Brot der Fruehen Jahre, Das 5-30-62
Brot des Baeckers, Das 4-27-77
Brot und Rosen 8-09-67
Brot und Spiele 8-19-64
Brother, Can You Spare a Dime? 3-19-75
Brother Carl (See: Broder Carl)
Brother Devil (See: Fra Diavolo)
Brother Joe (See: Hermano Jose, El)
Brother John 3-24-71
Brother Man 10-15-10
Brother Officers 3-05-15
Brother Orchid 5-29-40
Brother Rat 10-19-38
Brother Rat and a Baby 1-10-40
Brother Sun, Sister Moon 3-21-73
Brotherhood 8-18-76
Brotherhood, The 11-20-68
Brotherhood of Satan, The 4-28-71
Brotherly Love 4-01-70
Brothers 4-17-29
Brothers 7-24-29
Brothers 11-19-30
Brothers 3-23-77
Brothers, The (See: Brueder, Die)
Brothers, The (See: Kesyttomat Veljekset)
Brothers, The 10-09-09
Brothers, The 5-14-47
Brother's Devotion, A 3-19-10
Brothers and Sisters 9-17-80
Brothers in Law 3-13-57
Brothers in the Saddle 2-09-49
Brothers Karamazov (See: Fratelli Karamazov, I)
Brothers Karamazov (See: Bratya Karamazovy)
Brothers Karamazov, The 2-19-58
Brothers Lionheart, The (See: Broederna Lejonhjaerta)
Brothers of Iron (See: Hermanos de Hierro, Los)
Brothers of the West 12-07-38
Brothers Rico, The 8-21-57
Brothers Were Valiant 1-19-23
Brother's Wrong, A 10-30-09
Brott I Sol 2-04-48
Brought to Terms 12-04-09
Brown Derby, The 5-26-26
Brown of Harvard 2-01-18
Brown of Harvard 5-05-26
Brown on Resolution 5-29-35
Browning Version, The 3-21-51
Brubaker 6-18-80
Bruce Lee and I 1-28-76
Bruce Lee--True Story 12-08-76
Bruecke, Die 2-03-60
Brueder, Die 12-15-76
Brune Que Voila, La 6-15-60
Bruno--Der Schwarze, es Blies ein Jager Wohl in Sein Horn
   11-03-71
Bruno--The Black One, A Hunter Blows His Horn (See: Bruno--Der
   Schwarze, es Blies ein Jager Wohl in Sein Horn)
Brushfire 2-07-62
Brussels-Transit 12-17-80
Brutality (See: Flucht Ins Schilf)
Brutalization of Franz Blum, The (See: Verrohung Des Franz Blum,
   Der)
Brute, The (See: Bruto, El)
Brute, The 5-08-14
Brute, The 4-20-27
Brute and the Beast, The 12-04-68
Brute Breaker, The 11-07-19
Brute Force 6-18-47
Brute Man, The 10-23-46
Brute Master, The 12-17-20
Brutes and Savages 11-22-78
Brutalization of Franz Blum, The (See: Verrohung Des Franz Blum,
   Der)

Bruto, El 9-02-53
Brutti, Sporchi e Cattivi 6-02-76
Brutus 5-26-76
Brzezina 2-16-72
Bubasinter 8-25-71
Bubble, The (See: Bulle, La)
Bubble, The 12-28-66
Bubbles 6-18-20
Bube U Glavi 8-19-70
Buccaneer, The 1-12-38
Buccaneer, The 12-17-58
Buccaneer's Girl, The 3-01-50
Buchanan Rides Alone 8-06-58
Buck 2-28-79
Buck and the Preacher 4-19-72
Buck Benny Rides Again 4-17-40
Buck Privates 2-01-28
Buck Privates 2-05-41
Buck Privates Come Home 3-12-47
Buck Rogers 4-04-79
Buckaroo from Powder River 4-07-48
Buckaroo Kid, The 11-24-26
Buckaroo Sheriff of Texas 12-27-50
Bucket of Blood, A 10-28-59
Bucking Broadway 12-07-17
Bucking Society 5-05-16
Bucking the Barrier 6-14-23
Bucking the Tiger 5-06-21
Bucking the Truth 8-25-26
Bucklige von Soho, Der 12-07-66
Buckshot John 1-29-15
Buckskin 4-03-68
Buckskin Frontier 3-17-43
Buckskin Lady, The 7-03-57
Bucktown 7-09-75
Budai Cukraszda 1-15-36
Budapest Candy Store (See: Budai Cukraszda)
Budapest Fairy Tale (See: Pesti Mese)
Budapest Tales (See: Budapesti Mesek)
Budapesti Mesek 3-02-77
Buddha 7-03-63
Buddies (See: Polare)
Budding Love (See: Amour En Herbe, L')
Buddy Holly Story, The 5-17-78
Buddy, The Little Guardian 1-21-11
Budjenje Pacova 7-12-67
Buebchen 10-16-68
Buechse der Pandora 3-06-29
Buehne Frei Fuer Marika 1-14-59
Buen Amor, El 5-22-63
Buffalo Bill 3-15-44
Buffalo Bill and the Indians, or Sitting Bull's History Lesson
   6-30-76
Buffalo Bill in Tomahawk Territory 1-30-52
Buffalo Bill Rides Again 4-02-47
Buffalo Fight 11-05-10
Buffalo Racing in Madeira 11-06-09
Buffet Froid 1-02-80
Bug 6-11-75
Bugkiller, The (See: Bubasinter)
Bugle Call, The 5-05-16
Bugle Call, The 10-05-27
Bugle Sounds, The 12-17-41
Bugler of Algiers, The 11-24-16
Bugles in the Afternoon 2-06-52
Bugles of Fear, The (See: Clarines del Miedo, Los)
Bugsy Malone 6-09-76
Buhay at Pag-Ibig Ni Boy Zapanta 8-25-76
Build a House, Plant a Tree (See: Postav Dom, Zasad Strca)
Builder of Bridges, The 6-11-15
Builders of Castles 4-13-17
Builders of Socialism 1-29-36
Building a Nation 6-28-39
Building a Railroad in Africa 9-28-07
Bulgarian Night, The (See: Nuit Des Bulgares, La)
Bull Fight in Mexico, A 3-26-10
Bulldog Breed, The 12-21-60
Bulldog Courage 9-08-22
Bulldog Drummond 12-15-22 and 12-22-22
Bulldog Drummond 5-08-29
Bulldog Drummond 8-21-34
Bulldog Drummond Comes Back 9-08-37
Bulldog Drummond in Africa 8-31-38
Bulldog Drummond's Secret Police 4-05-39
Bulldog Edition 10-14-36
Bulldog Jack 5-22-35
Bulldog Pluck 9-21-27 and 10-26-27

Bulldogs of the Trail, The 4-30-15
Bulle, La 4-28-76
Bullenkoster, Das (See: Miner's Wife, The)
Bullet Code 2-28-40
Bullet for a Badman 7-01-64
Bullet for Joey, A 4-06-55
Bullet for Pretty Boy, A 7-15-70
Bullet for Sandoval, A 6-03-70
Bullet for Stefano, A 11-01-50
Bullet in the Heart, A (See: Balle Au Coeur, Une)
Bullet Is Waiting, A 9-01-54
Bullet Proof 4-30-20
Bullet Scars 3-04-42
Bullet Train 7-30-75
Bullets and Ballots 6-03-36
Bullets and Brown Eyes 2-25-16
Bullets Don't Turn Back (See: I Spheres Den Guyrizoun Pisso)
Bullets for O'Hara 7-30-41
Bullets for Rustlers 2-14-40
Bullfight 7-11-56
Bullfight, The (See: Course des Taureaux, La)
Bullfighter and the Lady 5-02-51
Bullfighters, The 4-11-45
Bullin' the Bullsheviki 10-24-19
Bullitt 10-16-68
Bulls, Love and Glory (See: Toros, Amor y Gloria)
Bullwhip 6-04-58
Bully 10-04-78
Bully, The 4-23-10
Bumerang 5-04-60
Bump on the Head, A (See: Bare en Tagsten)
Bumptious as a Fireman 9-24-10
Buna Seara, Irina 7-23-80
Bunco Squad 8-16-50
Bundle of Joy 12-12-56
Bungalow Bungle, The (See: J. Rufus Wallingford)
Bungalow 13 11-24-48
Bungalowing 6-08-17
Bunker Bean 7-01-36
Bunny Lake Is Missing 10-06-65
Bunny O'Hare 6-30-71
Bunty Pulls the Strings 1-07-21
Buona Sera, Mrs. Campbell 12-18-68
Buone Notizie 12-19-79
Buongiorno, Elefante! 8-20-52
Buono, Il Brutto, Il Cattivo, Il (See: Good, the Bad, and the
    Ugly, The)
Buque Maldito, El 9-25-74
Buraikan 5-27-70
Burden of Proof 9-13-18
Burdush 8-19-70
Bureaucrats, The (See: Messieurs les Ronds de Cuir)
Burg Theatre 12-02-36
Burglar, The 10-05-17
Burglar, The 5-01-57
Burglar and the Lady, The 12-31-15
Burglar by Proxy 8-29-19 and 10-17-19
Burglar for a Night, A 9-06-18
Burglar in the Trunk 11-06-09
Burglars (See: Einbrecher)
Burglars, The (See: Casse, Le)
Burgos Trial, The (See: Proceso de Burgos, El)
Buried Alive 11-06-09
Buried Alive 1-10-40
Buried Alive 1-17-51 (Also see: Sepolta Viva, La)
Buried Treasure 2-18-21
Burma Convoy 10-01-41
Burma Victory 12-19-45
Burn 10-21-70
Burn 'Em Up Barnes 8-26-21
Burn 'Em Up Barnes 4-03-35
Burn 'Em Up O'Connor 3-01-39
Burn, Samar, Burn (See: Sunugin Ang Samar!)
Burned Barns, The (See: Granges Brulees, Les)
Burned Bridge (See: Verbrande Brug)
Burned City, The (See: Ciudad Cremada, La)
Burning (See: Usijanje)
Burning Body (See: O Corpo Ardente)
Burning Cross, The 8-13-47
Burning Daylight 7-02-20
Burning Daylight 4-25-28
Burning Fuse, The (See: Feu Aux Poudres, Le)
Burning Gold 2-23-27
Burning Gold 5-27-36
Burning Heart, The 5-14-30
Burning Hills, The 8-08-56
Burning Sands 9-08-22
Burning Secret, The (See: Brennende Geheimnis)

Burning the Candle 3-30-17
Burning Trail, The 4-29-25
Burning Up 2-12-30
Burning Up Broadway 2-29-28
Burning Words 6-07-23
Burning Wind 10-31-28
Burning Years, The (See: Anni Struggenti, Gli)
Burns and Allen 5-21-30
Burns-Moir Fight 12-21-07
Burns-Palmer Fight 2-29-08
Burnt Fingers 3-30-27
Burnt Land (See: Tierra Quemada)
Burnt Offerings 8-25-76
Burnt Wings 3-26-20
Burschenlied aus Heidelberg, Ein 9-15-31
Bury Me Dead 9-24-47
Bus, The 4-14-65
Bus, The 8-25-76
Bus Did Not Stop, The (See: Nem Alt Meg Az Autobusz)
Bus Is Coming, The 7-21-71
Bus Riley's Back in Town 3-17-65
Bus Stop 8-15-56
Busca, La 9-07-66
Busca de la Muerte, En 7-26-61
Bush Christmas 6-04-47 and 11-26-47
Bush Leaguer, The 8-31-27
Bushbaby, The 10-21-70
Busher, The 5-30-19
Bushido 7-03-63
Bushkhugin Ulger 7-30-80
Bushman 10-20-71
Bushman, The 6-01-27
Bushranger 2-06-29
Bushwhackers, The 12-19-51
Business and Pleasure 2-16-32
Business Is Business 9-10-15
Business of Life, The 4-05-18
Busman's Honeymoon 8-07-40
Busses Roar 8-19-42
Buster, The 5-17-23
Buster and Billie 6-12-74
Buster Keaton Story, The 4-17-57
Busting 1-30-74
Busy Body, The 2-01-67
Busy Body, The (See: Tracassin, Le or Mor(d)skab)
Busy Inn, The 4-12-18
But Aren't You Ever Going to Change Margarita? (See: Pero No Vas a
    Cambiar Nunca Margarita?)
But Do Not Deliver Us From Evil (See: Mais Ne Nous Deliverez Pas
    du Mal)
But It Isn't Serious (See: Ma Non e Una Cosa Seria)
But Not for Me 8-19-59
But the Flesh Is Weak 4-19-32
But What Do They Want? (See: Mais Qu'Est-Ce Qu'Elles Veulent?)
But Where Is Daniel Vax? 4-10-74
Butasagom Tortenete 4-13-66
Butch and Sundance--The Early Years 6-06-79
Butch Cassidy and the Sundance Kid 9-10-69
Butch Minds the Baby 3-25-42
Butcher, The (See: Boucher, Le)
Butcher Boy, The 4-20-17
Butcher, the Star and the Orphan, The (See: Boucher, la Star et
    l'Orpheline, Le)
Butley 1-23-74
Butt, The (See: Fimpen)
Butter and Egg Man 8-29-28
Buttercup Chain, The 10-07-70
Butterfield 8 10-26-60
Butterflies 3-14-13
Butterflies Are Free 7-05-72
Butterflies in the Rain 12-29-26
Butterfly 1-21-25
Butterfly Cloud (See: Leptirov Oblak)
Butterfly Girl, The 6-03-21
Butterfly Man, The 5-21-20
Butterfly Murders, The 8-01-79
Butterfly on the Shoulder, A (See: Papillon Sur L'Epaule, Un)
Butterfly on the Wheel, A 11-19-15
Butterfly Ranch 12-22-22
Buttons 2-22-28
Buy Me That Town 7-30-41
Buying an Automobile 12-05-08
Bwana Devil 12-03-52
Bwana Toshi No Uta 9-08-65
By a Nose (See: Courte Tete)
By Appointment Only 11-21-33
By Candlelight 1-09-34
By Chance Balthazar (See: Au Hasard Balthazar)

By Divine Right 4-02-24
By Foot, By Horse and By Car (See: Pied, A Cheval et en Voiture)
By Hook or By Crook (See: Auf Biegen Oder Brechen)
By Hook or Crook 9-20-18
By Love Possessed 6-14-61
By Love Redeemed 1-28-16
By Power of Attorney; or, The Mystery of Jack Hilton 5-08-14
By Proxy 7-26-18
By Right of Possession 8-17-17
By Right of Purchase 3-22-18
By Rocket to the Moon 2-11-31
By the Lake (See: U Ozera)
By the Light of a Star (See: En la Luz de Una Estrella)
By the Light of the Silvery Moon 3-25-53
By the Skin of His Teeth (See: Um Eine Nasenlaenge)
By the Tennis Courts (See: Du Cote des Tennis)
By the World Forgot 10-04-18
By Whose Hand? 4-14-16
By Whose Hand? 11-23-27
By Whose Hand? 8-16-32
By Your Leave 1-01-35
Bye Bye Barbara 4-09-69
Bye-Bye Bavaria! (See: Servus Bayern!)
Bye, Bye Birdie 4-10-63
Bye-Bye Brasil 12-19-79 (Also see: Bye-Bye Brazil)
Bye Bye Braverman 2-07-68
Bye-Bye Brazil 5-21-80 (Also see: Bye-Bye Brasil)
Bye-Bye Monkey 5-24-78
Byelorussian Station, The (See: Bjelorusski Voksal)
Byugai, Obicham Te 7-25-79
Byways (See: Abwege)
Bzlet 9-05-79

C

C.C. and Company 10-21-70
'C'-Man 4-20-49
C.S. Blues 5-02-79
Ca Ira--Il Fiume Della Rivolta 9-16-64
Ca N'Arrive Qu'Aux Autres 7-28-71
Ca N'Arrive Qu'Aux Vivants 8-19-59
Ca Va Barder 6-15-55
Ca Va, Ca Vient 4-14-71
Ca Va Etre Ta Fete 3-01-61
Cab No. 13 (See: Fiacre N. 13, Il)
Cabalgata del Circo, La 7-04-45
Caballito Criollo 4-07-54
Caballo Blanco, El 6-13-62
Cabaret 5-04-27
Cabaret 6-09-54
Cabaret 2-16-72
Cabaret, The 5-31-18
Cabaret Girl, The 1-10-19
Cabaret Mineiro 10-22-80
Cabezas Cortadas 7-15-70
Cabin in the Cotton 10-04-32
Cabin in the Sky 2-10-43
Cabin of Old Lunen 12-11-35
Cabinet of Caligari, The 5-16-62
Cabinet of Dr. Caligari, The 4-08-21
Cabinet of Dr. Larifari (See: Kabinet des Dr. Larifari, Das)
Cabiria (See: D'Annunzio's Cabiria)
Cabo de Hornos 4-11-56
Caccia Tragica 4-14-48
Cachorros, Los 10-08-75
Cackling Hen (See: Gallina Clueca, La)
Cactus Crandall 8-30-18
Cactus Flower 9-03-69
Cactus in the Snow 1-19-72
Cada Feria un Amor, En 7-19-61
Cada Quien Su Vida 4-20-60
Cadaveri Eccellenti 3-31-76
Caddie 4-14-76
Caddy, The 8-05-53
Caddyshack 7-23-80
Cadet Girl 11-19-41
Cadet-Rousselle 12-22-54
Cadets (See: Kadetten)
Caesar and Cleopatra 1-02-46
Cafe Colette 2-03-37
Cafe Concordia 8-04-43
Cafe de Paris 11-09-38

Cafe du Cadran, Le 4-23-47
Cafe Express 9-10-80
Cafe Hostess 1-10-40
Cafe in Cairo, A 3-25-25
Cafe Metropole 5-05-37
Cafe Moscow 3-04-36
Cafe Odeon 4-15-59
Cafe on Plyushicha Street (See: Tri Topolia Na Pliushiche)
Cafe Society 2-08-39
Cage, La 6-12-63
Cage, La 6-18-75
Cage, The (See: Cage, La)
Cage Aux Filles, La 2-08-50
Cage Aux Folles, La 11-01-78
Cage Aux Folles II, La 12-31-80
Cage Aux Ours, La 10-02-74
Cage Aux Rossignols, La (See: Cage of Nightingales, A)
Cage de Verre, La 5-19-65
Cage of Evil 6-29-60
Cage of Gold 10-04-50
Cage of Nightingales, A 3-05-47
Cage of Women (See: Cage Aux Filles, La)
Caged 5-03-50
Caged Fury 2-18-48
Cagliostro 5-08-29
Cagliostro 3-19-75
Cahill, United States Marshal 6-20-73
Caid, Le 12-07-60
Caida, La 7-08-59
Caidos en el Infierno 9-29-54
Caids, Les 11-22-72
Caifanes, Los 11-08-67
Caillaux Case, The 11-15-18
Cain 1-07-31
Cain Adolescente 8-12-59
Cain and Artem 6-11-30
Cain and Mabel 10-21-36
Cain de Nulle Part 9-23-70
Cain From Nowhere (See: Cain de Nulle Part)
Caine Mutiny, The 6-09-54
Cairo 8-12-42
Cairo 1-30-63
Cairo Road 6-28-50
Cakes of Pont Aven, The (See: Galettes de Pont Aven, Les)
Calaboose 8-04-43
Calabuch 9-12-56
Calamity (See: Urgia)
Calamity Jane 10-21-53
Calamity Jane and Sam Bass 6-08-49
Calcutta 4-16-47
Calcutta 5-14-69
Calcutta 71 9-06-72
Calda Vita, La 4-22-64
Caleb Piper's Girl 5-09-19
Caleb Powers Trials 3-28-08
Calendar, The 11-10-31
Calendar, The 6-02-48
Calendar Girl 2-12-47
Calibre .38 3-28-19
Caliche Sangriento 11-05-69
Califfa, La 3-17-71
California 6-29-27
California 12-18-46
California Conquest 6-11-52
California Dreaming 4-04-79
California Firebrand 4-21-48
California Frontier 12-14-38
California in '49 3-30-27
California Joe 3-15-44
California Mail 5-08-29
California Mail 1-27-37
California or Bust 6-01-27
California Passage 12-27-50
California Reich, The 3-31-76
California Romance, A 5-17-23
California Split 8-07-74
California Straight Ahead 7-14-37
California Suite 12-13-78
California Trail, The 8-01-33
Californian, The 7-07-37
Caligula 11-21-79
Call, The (See: Weswanie)
Call, The 1-29-10
Call, The 3-30-38
Call a Messenger 11-15-39
Call At Midnight, A 5-22-29
Call from the Wild 8-12-21
Call Her Savage 11-29-32

Call Him Mr. Shatter 1-14-76
Call It a Day 5-12-37
Call It Luck 7-17-34
Call Me Bwana 4-10-63
Call Me From Afar (See: Posowi Mnja W Dal Swjet Luju)
Call Me Madam 3-04-53
Call Me Mathilde (See: Appellez-Moi Mathilde)
Call Me Mister 1-24-51
Call Northside 777 1-21-48
Call of Courage 11-11-25
Call of Her People 6-02-17
Call of Spring, The (See: Praznovanje Pomladi)
Call of the Blood 3-07-13
Call of the Blood 2-25-48
Call of the Canyon 12-20-23
Call of the Canyon 8-19-42
Call of the Circus 1-29-30
Call of the Cumberlands, The 2-04-16
Call of the Dance, The 9-24-15
Call of the East 11-17-22
Call of the Flesh 9-17-30 (Also see: Chanteur de Seville, Le)
Call of the Front, The (See: Tieng Goi, Phiatruoc)
Call of the Gods (See: Ruf der Goetter)
Call of the Heart 4-23-10
Call of the Heart 1-25-28
Call of the Heart, The (See: Richiamo del Cuore)
Call of the Jungle 8-30-44
Call of the Klondike 12-20-50
Call of the Mate 8-06-24
Call of the North 12-02-21
Call of the North, The 8-14-14
Call of the Prairie 12-02-36
Call of the Rockies 6-15-38
Call of the Soul, The 2-07-19
Call of the South Seas 7-19-44
Call of the Wild 9-27-23
Call of the Wild 8-21-35
Call of the Wild 3-07-73
Call of the Yukon 4-27-38
Call of Youth, The 12-17-20
Call Out the Marines 1-14-42
Call the Mesquiteers 3-02-38
Call-Up, The (See: Repmanad)
Callahans and Murphys 7-13-27
Callaway Went Thataway 11-14-51
Calle Corrientes 8-18-43
Calle Grita, La (See: Street Calls, The)
Calle Mayor 9-12-56 and 10-03-56
Called Back 1-22-15
Called to the Front 11-28-14
Calling All Husbands 11-06-40
Calling All Marines 9-27-39
Calling All Stars 3-17-37
Calling Bulldog Drummond 7-11-51
Calling Dr. Death 12-15-43
Calling Dr. Gillespie 6-17-42
Calling Dr. Kildare 5-17-39
Calling Homicide 10-17-56
Calling Philo Vance 2-14-40
Calliope 11-24-71
Calm, The 11-04-64
Calm Yourself 7-31-35
Calmos 2-11-76
Calypso 5-27-59
Calypso Heat Wave 6-05-57
Calypso Joe 5-15-57
Calzonzin Inspector 6-12-74
Cama, La 10-30-68
Camada Negra 5-11-77
Camarades 5-06-70
Cambio, El 5-23-73
Cambio de Sexo 6-01-77
Camelot 10-25-67
Cameo Kirby 1-01-15
Cameo Kirby 2-12-30
Camera Buff (See: Amator)
Cameraman, The 9-19-28
Cameriera Bella Presenza Offresi 11-28-51
Cameron of the Royal Mounted 2-17-22
Camicie Rosse 11-12-52
Camille (See: Dame Aux Camelias, La)
Camille 1-22-10
Camille 1-07-16
Camille 10-12-17
Camille 9-16-21
Camille 4-27-27

Camille 1-27-37
Camille 2000 7-16-69
Camino de la Vida, El 7-25-56
Camino de las Llamas, El 5-20-42
Camino de los Gatos, El 2-07-45
Camion, Le 5-18-77
Camisards, Les 3-01-72
Cammino Della Speranza, Il 1-10-51
Camouflage (See: Barwy Orchronne)
Camouflage Kiss, The 4-12-18
Camp Followers, The (See: Soldatesse, Le)
Camp on Blood Island 4-23-58
Campanada, La 4-16-80
Campana Del Infierno, La 9-26-73
Campanadas a Medianoche 5-18-66
Campane a Martello 1-25-50
Campbell's Kingdom 9-11-57
Campbells Are Coming, The 10-01-15
Campo di Maggio 9-16-36
Campo Mamula 8-19-59
Campus Confessions 9-14-38
Campus Flirt, The 9-22-26
Campus Honeymoon 1-28-48
Campus Knights 9-11-29
Campus Rhythm 10-06-43
Campus Sleuth 5-12-48
Can a Woman Love Twice? 4-05-23
Can-Can 3-09-60
Can-Cannes 10-01-80
Can Heironymus Merkin Ever Forget Mercy Humppe and Find True
    Happiness? 3-12-69
Can I Do It ... Till I Need Glasses? 11-14-79
Can This Be Dixie? 11-18-36
Canadian, The 12-01-26
Canadian Pacific 3-09-49
Canadians, The 3-08-61
Canal, The (See: Kanal)
Canal Zone 4-01-42
Canal Zone 12-07-77
Cananea Prison (See: Carcel de Cananea, La)
Canaries Sometimes Sing 9-24-30
Canaris 3-02-55
Canary Murder Case, The 3-13-29
Canasta de Cuentos Mexicanos 12-19-56
Cancel My Reservation 9-20-72
Cancelled Debt 10-26-27
Cancer (See: Rak)
Cancion de Cuna 11-05-41
Cancion de Los Barrios 4-02-41
Cancion Para Recordar, Una 10-05-60
Canciones Para Despues de Una Guerra 6-23-71
Candida la Mujer Del Ano 4-14-43
Candida Millionaires (See: Candida Millionaria)
Candida Millionaria 10-08-41
Candida, Woman of the Year (See: Candida la Mujer del Ano)
Candidate, The (See: Kandidat, Der)
Candidate, The 6-21-72
Candidate for Murder 9-25-68
Candidates for Marriage (See: Heiratskandidaten)
Candide 2-01-61
Candlelight in Algeria 3-22-44
Candles at 9 6-14-44
Candleshoe 12-21-77
Candy 12-18-68
Candy Girl, The 6-08-17
Candytuft--I Mean Veronica 7-22-21
Caniche 5-16-79
Canillita y la Dama, El 8-03-38
Canker of Jealousy, The 3-19-15
Cannabis 9-30-70
Cannibal Attack 11-10-54
Cannibal Girls 4-18-73
Cannibali, I 9-30-70
Cannibals, The (See: Cannibali, I)
Cannon and the Nightingale, The 10-22-69
Cannon for Cordoba 9-30-70
Cannonball 7-21-76
Cannonball Express 3-15-32
Canoa 7-14-76
Canon City 6-23-48
Canonity 6-23-78
Can't Help Singing 12-20-44
Can't Stop the Music 6-04-80
Cantata (See: Oldas es Kotes)
Cantata de Chile 7-28-76
Canterbury Tale, A 5-31-44
Canterbury Tales, The 7-12-72
Canterville Ghost, The 5-31-44

Canticle (See: Cantico)
Cantico 8-05-70
Cantiga da Rua 3-29-50
Canto del Cisne, El 7-04-45
Cantor, El 8-09-78
Cantor's Son, The 12-29-37
Canvas Kisser, The 6-17-25
Canyon City 12-15-43
Canyon Crossroads 3-16-55
Canyon Hawks 10-15-30
Canyon of Adventure 3-21-38
Canyon of Fools 3-15-23
Canyon of Light 1-26-27
Canyon of Missing Men 3-26-30
Canyon Passage 7-24-46
Canyon River 8-22-56
Canzone del Sole, La 5-13-36
Canzone del l'Amore, La 3-18-31
Canzoni di Mezzo Secolo 11-03-54
Cap de L'Esperance, Le 1-02-52
Cape Fear 3-07-62
Cape Forlorn (See: Menschen im Kaefig)
Cape Forlorn 1-28-31
Cape Horn (See: Cabo de Hornos)
Cape of Hope, The (See: Cap de l'Esperance, Le)
Caper of the Golden Bulls 5-17-67
Caperucita Roja, La 6-15-60
Caperucita y Sus Tres Amigos 6-28-61
Capitaine Ardant 8-20-52
Capitaine Fracasse, Le 3-20-52
Capitaine Fracasse, Le 6-07-61
Capital Punishment 9-03-15
Capital Punishment 2-04-25
Capitan, Le 4-17-46
Capitan, Le 11-09-60
Capitan Veneno 5-12-43
Capitol 1-31-20
Capitu 10-30-68
Capone 4-16-75
Caporal Epingle, Le 5-30-62
Cappello a Tre Punte, Il 9-30-36
Cappotto, Il 6-04-52
Cappotto di Astrakan, Il 8-06-80
Cappy Ricks 8-26-21
Cappy Ricks Returns 12-04-35
Caprice 5-17-67
Caprice de Caroline Cherie, Un 5-13-53
Caprice of the Mountains 7-14-16
Caprices de Marie, Les 3-11-70
Caprices of Kitty, The 2-26-15
Capricious Summer (See: Rozmarne Leto)
Capricorn One 6-07-78
Captain, The (See: Kapitaen, Der)
Captain and His Hero, The (See: Hauptmann und Sein Held, Der)
Captain Apache 10-20-71
Captain Blood 9-10-24
Captain Blood 1-01-36
Captain Boycott 9-10-47
Captain Calamity 12-23-36
Captain Careless 10-17-28
Captain Carey U.S.A. 2-22-50
Captain Caution 8-07-40
Captain China 11-02-49
Captain Courtesy 4-16-15
Captain Eddie 6-20-45
Captain Fly-by-Night 2-08-23
Captain Fracasse (See: Capitaine Fracasse, Le)
Captain from Castile 11-26-47
Captain from Cologne, The (See: Hauptmann Von Koln, Der)
Captain Fury 5-10-39
Captain Grant's Children 1-25-39
Captain Hates the Sea, The 12-04-34
Captain Horatio Hornblower 4-18-51
Captain Hurricane 7-03-35
Captain Is a Lady, The 6-26-40
Captain January 7-09-24
Captain January 4-29-36
Captain John Smith and Pocahontas 11-18-53
Captain Kidd 8-01-45
Captain Kidd, Jr. 4-25-19
Captain Kreutzer (See: Hauptmann Kreutzer)
Captain Kronos: Vampire Hunter 6-26-74
Captain Lash 2-06-29
Captain Leshi (See: Kapetan Lesi)
Captain Lightfoot 2-16-55
Captain Lust 3-30-77
Captain Mikula, The Kid (See: Kapetan Mikula Mali)
Captain Milkshake 12-09-70
Captain Moonlight 5-15-40
Captain Nemo and the Underwater City 12-17-69

Captain Newman, M.D. 10-23-63
Captain of Grey Horse Troop 5-18-17
Captain of His Soul, The 2-08-18
Captain of Koepenick, The (See: Hauptmann von Koepenick, Der)
Captain of the Guard 4-02-30
Captain of the Koepenick (See: Hauptmann von Koepenick, Der)
Captain Pirate 7-23-52
Captain Poison (See: Capitan Veneno)
Captain Salvation 6-29-27
Captain Scarlett 9-23-53
Capt. Scott 6-27-13
Captain Sinbad 6-26-63
Captain Swagger 12-26-28
Captain Swift 9-26-14
Captain Thunder 5-13-31
Captain Tugboat Annie 3-06-46
Captain's Captain, The 1-03-19
Captain's Courage, A 2-02-27
Captains Courageous 5-19-37
Captain's Daughter, The (See: Kapitanskaia Dotschka)
Captain's Kid, The 1-20-37
Captains of the Clouds 1-21-42
Captain's Paradise, The 6-24-53
Captain's Table, The 1-14-59
Captivation 6-02-31 and 9-29-31
Captive, The 3-26-10
Captive, The 4-30-15
Captive City, The (See: Citta' Prigioniera, La)
Captive City, The 3-26-52
Captive Flock (See: Pleneno Yato)
Captive Girl 4-19-50
Captive God, The 7-07-16
Captive Heart, The 4-10-46
Captive of Billy the Kid 1-16-52
Captive of Nazi Germany 8-05-36
Captive Wild Woman 4-28-43
Captive Women 10-01-52
Capture, The 4-05-50
Capture That Capsule 5-24-61
Captured 8-22-33
Car, The 5-11-77
Car 99 2-27-35
Car of Dreams 9-18-35
Car Wash 9-01-76
Cara a Cara 10-30-68
Cara Sposa 10-12-77
Carabiniers, Les 6-19-63
Carambolages 5-22-63
Carapate, La 11-01-78
Caraque Blonde, La 4-07-54
Caravan 10-02-34
Caravan 4-17-46
Caravan to Russia 10-28-59
Caravan to Vaccares 8-21-74
Caravan Trail, The 3-27-46
Caravans 11-08-78
Carbine Williams 4-16-52
Carcel de Cananea, La 1-25-61 and 8-02-61
Card, The 3-05-52
Cardboard Cavalier 4-06-49
Cardboard Lover 9-05-28
Cardena Perpetu 7-30-80
Cardigan 2-24-22
Cardillac 9-10-69
Cardinal, The 4-08-36
Cardinal, The 10-16-63
Cardinal Messias (See: Abuna Messias)
Career 7-12-39
Career 9-30-59
Career Girl 3-08-44
Career of Katherine Bush, The 8-08-19
Career Woman 12-16-36
Careers 6-12-29
Carefree 8-31-38
Careful, Soft Shoulders 8-12-42
Careless Age 9-25-29
Careless Lady 4-19-32
Careless Tramp 10-02-09
Careless Years, The 9-04-57
Caretaker, The 7-03-63
Caretakers, The 8-21-63
Carevo Novo Ruho 8-09-61
Carey Treatment, The 3-29-72
Cargaison Blanche 3-17-37
Cargaison Blanche 5-07-58
Cargo to Capetown 4-05-50
Caribbean 8-06-52
Caribbean Mystery, The 7-18-45

Cariboo Trail 7-05-50
Carica Eroica 12-24-52
Carillons Sans Joie 5-16-62
Carl Hagenbeck's Menagerie at Hamburg 1-11-08
Carlos and Elisabeth 4-16-24
Carlota 7-21-71
Carlton-Browne of the F.O. 3-18-59
Carmela 5-18-49
Carmen (See: Chaplin's Carmen)
Carmen 11-05-15
Carmen 6-15-17
Carmen 12-01-43
Carmen 12-04-46
Carmen 12-28-49
Carmen 8-05-70
Carmen, Baby 10-11-67
Carmen Comes Home 1-13-60
Carmen Jones 10-06-54
Carmen de la Ronda 10-07-59
Carmen of Granada (See: Carmen de la Ronda)
Carmen of the Klondike 3-08-18
Carmen of the North 5-14-20
Carnal Knowledge 6-30-71
Carnation Kid 2-27-29
Carnaval 10-21-53
Carne 12-04-68
Carnegie Hall 3-05-47
Carnet du Bal, Un 10-20-37 (Also see: Life Dances On)
Carnets du Major Thompson, Les 1-11-56
Carnival 7-01-21 and 8-05-21
Carnival 11-17-31
Carnival 2-20-35
Carnival 10-30-46
Carnival and Love (See: Karneval und Liebe)
Carnival Boat 3-22-32
Carnival Evening (See: Marknadsafton)
Carnival Girl, The 12-29-26
Carnival in Ceylon 3-21-14
Carnival in Costa Rica 3-26-47
Carnival Is Here Again (See: E' Tornato Carnevale)
Carnival King 2-20-29
Carnival Lady 12-05-33
Carnival Night 10-23-57
Carnival of Crime 7-10-29
Carnival of Japanese Firemen in Tokyo 1-07-11
Carnival of Sinners 4-02-47
Carnival of Souls 10-03-62
Carnival Queen 11-03-37
Carnival Rock 10-09-57
Carnival Story 3-24-54
Carnival's End (See: Rosenmontag)
Carny 5-21-80
Caro Michele 7-14-76
Caro Papa 5-23-79
Carolina 2-20-34
Carolina Blues 12-13-44
Carolina Cannonball 1-26-55
Carolina Moon 7-17-40
Caroline Cherie 3-21-51
Caroline Cherie 2-28-68
Carolyn of the Corners 2-21-19
Carom Shots (See: Carambolages)
Carosello Napoletano 5-05-54
Carousel 2-22-56
Carpet from Bagdad, The 5-14-15
Carpetbaggers, The 4-15-64
Carrefour 11-30-38
Carriage to Vienna (See: Kocar Do Vidne)
Carrie 6-11-52
Carrie 11-03-76
Carrington V.C. 12-15-54
Carrosse D'Or, Le 3-11-53
Carrot Queen, The (See: Reina Zanahoria)
Carrot Top (See: Poil de Carotte)
Carry It On 7-29-70
Carry On! 12-28-27
Carry On Admiral 5-22-57
Carry On Again, Doctor 12-10-69
Carry On Cabby 8-28-63
Carry On Camping 6-04-69
Carry On Cleo 12-16-64
Carry On Constable 3-02-60
Carry On Cowboy 4-06-66
Carry On Cruising 4-18-62
Carry On Doctor 3-27-68
Carry On Emmanuelle 12-06-78

Carry On England 11-03-76
Carry On Jack 2-26-64
Carry On Loving 11-11-70
Carry On Nurse 3-18-59
Carry On Regardless 4-12-61
Carry On Screaming 8-24-66
Carry On, Sergeant 12-05-28
Carry On, Sergeant 9-24-58
Carry On Spying 7-22-64
Carry On Teacher 9-02-59
Carry On Up the Jungle 4-22-70
Carry On, Up the Khyber 12-25-68
Cars That Ate Paris, The 6-26-74
Carson City 5-07-52
Carson City Cyclone 5-26-43
Carson City Kid 7-24-40
Carson City Raiders 6-02-48
Carta de Amor, Una 7-26-44
Carter Case, The 2-25-42
Carthage in Flames 1-25-61
Cartouche 5-09-62
Carve Her Name with Pride 2-26-58
Caryl of the Mountains 9-30-36
Cas du Dr. Laurent, Le 4-17-57
Casa Chica, La 5-10-50
Casa de la Troya, La 11-04-59
Casa de la Zorra, La 9-03-47
Casa de las Palomas, La 3-01-72
Casa de los Cuervos, La 5-28-41
Casa de Munecas 11-17-43
Casa del Angel, La 5-15-57
Casa del Sur, La 7-30-75
Casa en Que Vivimos, La 8-12-70
Casa Esta Vacia, La 7-25-45
Casa Grande, La 7-16-75
Casa Manana 7-11-51
Casa Ricordi 1-19-55
Casa Sin Fronteras, La 5-03-72
Casablan 12-09-64
Casablanca 12-02-42
Casanova 12-21-27
Casanova 12-22-76
Casanova and Co. 3-09-77
Casanova Brown 8-02-44
Casanova in Burlesque 1-26-44
Casanova '70 7-21-65
Casanova's Big Night 3-03-54
Casbah 3-10-48
Cascabel 8-31-77
Cascarrabias 10-22-30
Case Against Brooklyn, The 5-14-58
Case Against Mrs. Ames, The 6-03-36
Case Against X, The (See: Ouvert Contre X)
Case at Law, A 11-16-17
Case for a Young Hangman, A (See: Pripad Pro Zacinajiciho Kata)
Case for the Defence, The 7-25-19
Case of Becky, The 10-14-21
Case of Clara Deane, The 5-10-32
Case of Colonel Redl (See: Fall des Oberst Redl, Der)
Case of the Curious Bride, The 4-10-35
Case of Dr. Laurent, The 7-02-58
Case of Jonathan Drew, The 6-13-28
Case of Lena Smith, The 1-16-29
Case of Patty Smith, The 6-06-62
Case of the Lucky Legs, The 11-13-35
Case of Sergeant Grischa, The 3-12-30
Case of the Baby Sitter, The 9-17-47
Case of the Black Cat, The 12-30-36
Case of the Black Parrot, The 1-15-41
Case of the 44's, The 9-09-64
Case of the Frightened Lady, The 7-10-40
Case of the Full Moon Murders, The 11-28-73
Case of the General Staff Colonel Redl, The (See: Fall des
    General-Stabs-Oberst Redl, Der)
Case of the Howling Dog, The 10-23-34
Case of the Missing Man, The 11-27-35
Case of the Naves Brothers, The (See: O Caso Dos Irmaos Naves)
Case of the Queen's Necklace, The (See: Affaire du Collier de
    la Reine, L')
Case of the Red Monkey, The 8-17-55
Case of the Stuttering Bishop, The 6-02-37
Case of the Velvet Claws 9-02-36
Case of Tomatoes, A 9-18-09
Case Van Geldern 9-27-32
Casey at the Bat 6-23-16
Casey at the Bat 4-06-27
Casey Jones 12-28-27
Casey's Shadow 3-08-78

Cash? Cash! 6-11-69
Cash McCall 12-09-59
Cash on Delivery 2-01-56
Casi Casados 10-18-61
Casi un Sueno 5-19-43
Casino de Paris 11-27-57
Casino Murder Case 4-17-35
Casino Royale 4-19-67
Casino to Korea 9-27-50
Caso Mattei, Il 2-16-72
Casotto, Il 10-22-80
Casque D'Or 5-28-52
Cass Timberlane 11-05-47
Cassandra Crossing, The 2-02-77
Casse, Le 11-03-71
Cassidy 10-19-17
Cassidy of Bar 20 3-30-38
Cast a Dark Shadow 9-28-55
Cast a Giant Shadow 3-30-66
Cast into the Flames 11-26-10
Cast-Off, The 2-15-18
Casta Diva 5-22-35
Casta Susana, La 12-06-44
Castagne Sono Buone, Le 2-17-71
Castaway Cowboy, The 7-24-74
Castaways of Turtle Island, The (See: Naufrages de L'Ile de
    la Tortue, Les)
Caste 7-20-17
Castelul Condamnatilor 8-05-70
Castiglione, La 8-17-55
Castiglioni Brothers, The (See: Fratelli Castiglioni, I)
Castigo Al Traidor 3-23-66
Castillo de la Pureza, El 4-24-74
Castle, The (See: Slottet or Schloss, Das)
Castle in Flanders (See: Schloss in Flandern, Das)
Castle in Sweden (See: Chateau en Suede)
Castle in the Desert 2-04-42
Castle Is Swinging, The (See: Svanger Pa Slottet, Det)
Castle Keep 7-23-69
Castle of Crimes 4-04-45
Castle of Evil 10-11-67
Castle of Purity (See: Castillo de la Pureza, El)
Castle of the Doomed (See: Castelul Condamnatilor)
Castle of the Rose, The (See: Jangmeae Sung)
Castle on the Hudson 2-28-40
Castle Vogeloed (See: Schloss Vogeloed)
Castles for Two 4-13-17
Castles in Spain (See: Chateaux En Espagne)
Castles in the Air 5-16-19
Castles in the Air 7-16-52
Castrati, I (See: Voci Bianche, Le)
Cat, The (See: Chat, Le or Gatto, Il)
Cat, The (See: Gata, La or Gato, El)
Cat, The 7-06-66
Cat and Mouse (See: Chat et la Souris, Le)
Cat and Mouse (See: Katz und Maus)
Cat and the Canary, The 9-14-17
Cat and the Canary, The 11-01-39
Cat and the Canary, The 11-22-78
Cat and the Fiddle 2-20-34
Cat Ate the Parakeet, The 1-26-72
Cat Ballou 5-12-65
Cat Creeps, The 11-12-30
Cat Creeps, The 4-10-46
Cat from Outer Space, The 6-21-78
Cat Girl 9-04-57
Cat Has Nine Lives, The (See: Neun Leben Hat Die Katze)
Cat in the Bag, The (See: Chat Dans le Sac, Le)
Cat Murkil and the Silks 6-16-76
Cat O' Nine Tails 6-09-71
Cat on a Hot Tin Roof 8-13-58
Cat People, The 11-18-42
Cat Shows Its Claws, The (See: Chatte Sort Ses Griffes, La)
Cat-Women of the Moon 12-16-53
Catalan Cuckold (See: Salut I Forca Al Canut)
Catalan, The Minstrel 1-07-11
Catalina Caper, The 12-20-67
Catamount Killing, The 12-18-74
Catch As Catch Can 7-13-27
Catch As Catch Can 1-31-68
Catch Me a Spy 9-22-71
Catch My Soul 3-27-74
Catch-22 6-10-70
Catcher, The (See: Greifer, Der)
Catching Up 8-27-75
Catered Affair, The 4-25-56
Catherina and Her Daughters (See: Katerina A Jeji Deti)
Catherine et Cie 10-29-75

Catherine, il Suffit D'Un Amour 6-04-69
Catherine Inc. (See: Catherine et Cie)
Catherine, One Love Is Enough (See: Catherine, Il Suffit D'Un
    Amour)
Catherine the Great 1-30-34 and 2-20-34
Cathy's Child 5-02-79
Catlow 10-13-71
Catman of Paris, The 2-20-46
Cats, The 12-25-69
Cat's Pajamas, The 9-01-26
Cat's Paw, The 8-21-34
Cats' Play (See: Macskajatek)
Catskill Honeymoon 2-01-50
Catspaw, The 1-14-16
Cattle Drive 7-18-51
Cattle Empire 2-12-58
Cattle King 6-19-63
Cattle Queen 10-10-51
Cattle Queen of Montana 11-17-54
Cattle Raiders 5-04-38
Cattle Stampede 12-29-43
Cattle Thief, The 5-27-36
Cattle Thieves 11-13-09
Cattle Town 11-26-52
Cattleman's Daughter, The 3-04-11
Caucasian Customs 10-02-09
Cauchemars 5-14-80
Caudillo 7-06-77
Caught 4-04-08
Caught 10-06-31
Caught 2-23-49
Caught Cheating 3-11-31
Caught in the Act 2-12-41
Caught in the Draft 5-28-41
Caught in the Fog 12-05-28
Caught Plastered 9-15-31
Caught Red-Handed (See: Flagrant Delit)
Caught Short 6-25-30
Causa Kralik 5-28-80
Cause for Alarm 1-31-51
Cause for Divorce 1-31-24
Cause Toujours Mon Lapin 12-20-61
Caution to the Wind (See: Con el Culo Al Aire)
Cavalcade 1-10-33
Cavalcade d'Amour 2-14-40
Cavalcade des Heures, La (See: Love Around the Clock)
Cavalcade of Academy Awards 4-17-40
Cavalcade of the West 9-30-36
Cavale, La 10-27-71
Cavaleur, Le 1-24-79
Cavalier, The 11-07-28
Cavalier of the West 2-09-32
Cavaliere Inesistente, Il 11-18-70 and 9-01-71
Cavalieri della Montagna 1-25-50
Cavalleria Rusticana 12-24-47
Cavalliers of the Navy (See: Flottans Kavaljerer)
Cavalry-Captain Wronski (See: Rittmeister Wronski)
Cavalry Scout 4-18-51
Cavalrymen, The (See: Hussards, Les)
Cavanaugh of Rangers 2-22-18
Cave, Un 7-12-72
Cave Man, The 12-03-15
Cave Man, The 3-03-26
Cave of Outlaws 10-31-51
Cave Se Rebiffe, Le 10-18-61
Cavern, The 11-10-65
Cavern of Death, The (See: Neal of the Navy: Part VI)
Caves du Majestic, Les 11-21-45
Cayman Triangle, The 12-07-77
Caza, La 7-06-66
Ce Cher Victor 5-14-75
Ce Corps Tant Desire 6-10-59
Ce Joli Monde 12-04-57
Ce Repondeur Ne Prend Pas De Message 7-25-79
Ce Sacre Grand-Pere 5-15-68
Ce Siecle a 50 Ans 4-26-50
Ce Soir les Jupons Volent 7-11-56
Ce Soir ou Jamais 10-25-61
Cease Fire 11-25-53
Cecilia 11-19-75
Cecilia of the Pink Roses 6-07-18
Ceddo 6-01-77
Ceiling Zero 1-22-36
Cela S'Appelle L'Aurore 5-16-56
Celebrated Case, A 5-08-14
Celebration at Big Sur 4-07-71
Celebrity 12-12-28
Celebrul 702 6-27-62

Celeste 12-23-70
Celestial Brothers, The 7-24-63
Celestina, La 7-30-69
Celestina 8-11-76
Celine and Julie Go Boating (See: Celine et Julie Vont en
    Bateau)
Celine et Julie Vont en Bateau 8-21-74
Cell, The (See: Zelle, Die)
Cell 2455, Death Row 4-13-55
Cell Zero, The (See: To Kelli Miden)
Cellar, The (See: Hamartef)
Celui Qui Doit Mourir 5-15-57
Cena Grada 8-12-70
Cenerentola 6-01-49
Ceneri Della Memoria 9-14-60
Ceniza Al Viento 10-28-42
120 Rue de la Gare 4-17-46
122 Rue de Provence 5-10-78
125 Rue Montmartre 10-28-59
Centennial Summer 5-29-46
Cento Piccoloe Mamme 7-30-52
Central Airport 5-09-33
Centroforward Murio Al Amanecer, El 5-24-61
C'eravama Tanti Amati 1-15-75
Cercle Rouge, Le 11-11-70
Ceremony, The (See: Gishiki)
Ceremony, The 12-18-63
Cerf-Volant du Bout du Monde, Le 5-07-58
Cerniti Angueli 8-05-70
Cerny Petr 8-12-64
Cerny Prador 9-03-58
Cerromaior 10-15-80
Certain Major, A (See: Alaztosan Jeletem)
Certain Mr. Gran, A (See: Gewisser Herr Gran)
Certain Rich Man, A 2-03-22
Certain Smile, A 7-30-58
Certain, Very Certain, As a Matter of Fact ... Probable (See:
    Certo, Certissimo, Anzi ... Probabile)
Certain Young Man 6-13-28
Certo, Certissimo, Anzi ... Probabile 7-22-70
Certo Giorno, Un 10-08-69
Cerveau, Le 3-19-69
Ces Dames Preferent le Mambo 3-12-58
Cesar 11-25-36
Cesar et Rosalie 11-15-72
Cest a Slava 7-16-69
C'est Arrive a Oden 12-05-56
C'est Arrive a Paris 3-11-53
C'est Arrive a Trente-Six Chandelles 12-04-57
C'est Dur Pour Tout le Monde 7-09-75
C'est la Faute d'Adam 5-07-58
C'est la Vie! 9-03-80
C'est la Vie Parisienne (See: It's the Paris Life)
C'est la Vie Rrose 3-02-77
C'est Pas Moi, C'est Lui 2-27-80
Cesta Duga Godinu Dana 8-06-58 and 8-20-58
Cesty Muzu 8-16-72
Cet Age Sans Pitie 5-14-80
Cet Homme Est Dangereux 3-17-54
Cet Obscure Objet du Desir 8-31-77
Cetiri Dana Do Smrti 8-25-76
Cette Nuit La 10-01-58
Cette Sacree Gamine 4-18-56
Cette Vielle Canaille 12-12-33
Cetvrti Sputnik 8-16-67
Ceux du 'Viking' 3-15-32
Cha-Cha-Cha Boom 9-26-59
Chac 3-12-75
Chacal de Nahueltoro, El 6-10-70
Chacun Sa Chance 1-07-31
Chad Hanna 12-18-40
Chafed Elbows 3-15-67
Chagrin and Pity (See: Chagrin et la Pitie, Le)
Chagrin et la Pitie, Le 6-16-71
Chaika 11-28-73
Chain, The (See: Retez)
Chain Gang 10-04-50
Chain Lightning 9-08-22
Chain Lightning 2-08-50
Chain of Circumstance 8-15-51
Chain of Evidence 5-08-57
Chain of Islands, A (See: Nihon Retto)
Chain of Love (See: Chamloey Sawat)
Chain Reaction 4-23-80
Chained 10-26-27
Chained 9-04-34

Chains of the Past 8-07-14
Chair de L'Orchidee, La 2-19-75
Chair de Poule 11-27-63
Chair et le Diable, La 8-04-54
Chairman, The 6-18-69
Chaise Vide, La 1-01-75
Chajrchan Ondor Chaana Bajna 8-16-78
Chaleur du Sien 11-30-38
Chalice of Courage, The 7-30-15
Chalice of Sorrow, The 9-29-16
Chalk Garden, The 4-08-64
Challenge, The (See: Sfida, La)
Challenge, The 12-29-16
Challenge, The 10-04-39
Challenge, The 2-18-48
Challenge, The 5-25-60
Challenge Accepted, The 12-13-18
Challenge for Robin Hood, A 7-31-68
Challenge of Chance, The 6-27-19
Challenge of Greatness 9-15-76
Challenge of the Law, The 12-17-20
Challenge of the Range 6-22-49
Challenge the Wild 6-09-54
Challenge to Be Free 1-15-75
Challenge to Lassie 11-02-49
Challenge to Live 3-07-62
Challenges (See: Desafios, Los)
Chalutzim 4-10-34
Chamade, La 11-20-68
Chamber of Horrors 8-31-66
Chambre Ardente, La 4-25-62
Chambre Blanche, La 5-20-70
Chambre Rouge, La 2-21-73
Chambre Verte, La 3-29-78
Chameleon 9-20-78
Chamloey Sawat 4-30-75
Champ, The 11-17-31
Champ, The 3-28-79
Champ for a Day 9-16-53
Champagne 9-05-28
Champagne 7-03-29
Champagne Charlie 5-13-36
Champagne Charlie 9-13-44
Champagne for Breakfast 7-10-35
Champagne for Caesar 2-08-50
Champagne Waltz 2-10-37
Champagner (See: Champagne)
Champignon, Le 4-22-70
Champion 3-16-49
Champion Cook, The (See: Cordon Bleu, Le)
Champion du Regiment 9-27-32
Champion Gate Crasher (See: Roi des Resquilleurs, Le)
Champion of Lost Causes 4-29-25
Champion of Pontresina, The (See: Springer von Pontresina, Der)
Champion Shot, The (See: Shuetzen Koenig, Der)
Chan at Monte Carlo 12-22-37
Chan at the Olympics 5-26-37
Chan at Treasure Island 8-23-39
Chan on Broadway 9-22-37
Chance (See: Szansa)
Chance, La 1-12-32 and 5-31-32
Chance and Violence (See: Hasard et la Violence, Le)
Chance at Heaven 12-26-33
Chance Glory (See: Hasards de la Gloire, Les)
Chance Meeting on the Ocean (See: Spotkanie Na Atlantyku)
Chance of a Lifetime, The 12-22-43
Chance of a Lifetime 5-03-50
Chance of a Night-Time 6-02-31
Chances 6-16-31
Chandler 12-08-71
Chandu the Magician 10-04-32
Chang 5-04-27
Chang Kun Ui Su Yum 7-02-69
Change, The (See: Cambio, El)
Change of Habit 10-22-69
Change of Heart 5-15-34
Change of Heart 1-05-38
Change of Heart, A 10-23-09
Change of Heart, A 10-03-14
Change of Heart, A 1-25-28
Change of Mind 10-08-69
Change of Seasons, A 12-24-80
Change One's Life (See: Mudar De Vida)
Change Pas de Main 7-09-75
Changeling, The 2-20-80
Changes 2-05-69
Changing Husbands 6-25-24
Changing Woman, The 8-16-18

Cheaters, The 7-04-45
Cheaters at Play 3-01-32
Cheating Blondes 5-23-33
Cheating Cheaters 1-25-19
Cheating Cheaters 12-07-27
Cheating Cheaters 12-11-34
Cheating Herself 8-15-19
Cheating the Public 1-25-18
Cheats, The (See: Tricheurs, Les)
Chechahcos, The 5-07-24
Check and Double Check 10-08-30
Check to the Queen (See: Jaque a la Dama)
Check Your Guns 11-19-47
Checker Player, The (See: Joueur d'Echecs, Le)
Checkered Coat, The 7-21-48
Checkered Flag, The 1-27-26
Checkered Flag, The 6-19-63
Checkers 11-21-13
Checkers 12-08-37
Checkmate 12-26-73
Checkpoint 1-02-57
Cheech and Chong's Next Movie 7-23-80
Cheer Leader, The 1-25-28
Cheer Up and Smile 8-06-30
Cheer Up Boys (See: Hardi Les Gars)
Cheerful Fraud 1-05-27
Cheerful Givers 4-20-17
Cheerleaders, The 6-13-73
Cheers for Miss Bishop 1-15-41
Cheers of the Crowd 4-08-36
Chelovek Ukhodit Za Ptitsami 1-26-77
Chelsea Girls, The 1-18-67
Chelsea My Love 9-22-76
Chelsea 7750 4-03-14
Chelyuskin 5-29-35
Chemin de la Mauvaise Route, Le 10-23-63
Chemin de Paradis 12-03-30
Chemin des Ecoliers, Le 2-03-60
Chemin Perdu, Le 8-20-80 and 8-27-80
Chemineau, Le (See: Open Road, The)
Chemins de Katmandou, Les 10-22-69
Chemins de L'Exil, ou les Dernieres Annees de Jean-Jacques
    Rousseau, Les 12-27-78
Chemmeen 7-02-69
Cherchez L'Idole 4-01-64
Chere Inconnue 5-21-80
Chere Louise 5-24-72
Chereshovata Gradina 7-25-79
Cheri 5-31-50
Cheri-Bibi 5-25-38
Cheri-Bibi 6-29-55
Cheri, Fais Moi Peur 9-03-58
Cherie 1-14-31 and 6-16-31
Cherokee Uprising 11-22-50
Cherokee Strip 6-02-37
Cherokee Strip 10-02-40
Cherry, Harry & Raquel 9-24-69
Cherry Orchard, The (See: Chereshovata Gradina)
Chess Board of Fate 5-22-14
Chess Player, The 5-21-30
Chess Players, The (See: Shatranj Ke Khilari)
Chetan, Indian Boy (See: Tschetan, Der Indianerjunge)
Chetniks 1-13-43
Cheval d'Orgeuil, Le 9-17-80
Cheval Pour Deux, Un 2-28-62
Chevalier de la Nuit, Le 3-31-54
Chevalier de Pardaillan, Le 11-14-62
Cheyenne 3-20-29
Cheyenne 4-23-47
Cheyenne Autumn 10-07-64
Cheyenne Kid, The 3-13-40
Cheyenne Rides Again 5-18-38
Cheyenne Roundup 4-14-43
Cheyenne Social Club, The 6-10-70
Cheyenne Takes Over 12-10-47
Chez Maxim's Doorman (See: Chasseur de Chez Maxim's, Le)
Chez Nous 9-20-78
Chhatrabhang 7-14-76
Chi E' Piu Felice di Me? 2-23-38
Chi No Hate Ni Ikuru Mono 1-25-61
Chi No Mure 7-15-70
Chiameremo Andrea, Lo 11-15-72
Chicago 12-28-27
Chicago After Midnight 3-07-28
Chicago Calling 12-05-51
Chicago Confidential 8-21-57

Chicago Deadline 8-31-49
Chicago Herald Movies 7-10-14
Chicago, Kid, The 2-14-45
Chicago Maternity Center Story, The 5-02-79
Chicago 70 6-10-70
Chicago Syndicate 6-29-55
Chick 9-26-28
Chicken a la King 6-13-28
Chicken Casey 1-26-17
Chicken Chronicles, The 10-19-77
Chicken Every Sunday 12-08-48
Chicken in the Case 2-04-21
Chicken Wagon Family 9-27-39
Chickens 3-11-21
Chickie 4-29-25
Chicos Crecen, Los 9-16-42
Chiedo Asilo 1-16-80
Chief, The 12-05-33
Chief Cook, The 9-21-17
Chief Crazy Horse 2-23-55
Chieko-Sho (See: Portrait of Chieko)
Chien de Pique, Le 2-08-61
Chien Fou, Le 9-28-66
Chien Jaune, Le 7-19-32
Chienne, La 1-12-32
Chiens, Les 5-02-79
Chiens Perdus Sans Colliers 11-02-55
Chiffonniers D'Emmaus, Les 4-13-55
Chikamatsu Monogatari 5-11-55
Chikita 1-24-62
Chikuzan Hitori Tabi 7-27-77
Child for Sale 3-26-20
Child in Judgement, A 12-10-15
Child in the Crowd, A (See: Enfant Dans la Foule, Un)
Child in the House 8-22-56
Child Is a Wild Thing, A 9-15-76
Child Is Born, A 1-17-40
Child Is Ours, The (See: Nino Es Nuestro, El)
Child Is Waiting, A 1-16-63
Child of Danube (See: Kind der Donau, Das)
Child of Divorce 10-16-46
Child of Manhattan 2-14-33
Child of M'Sieu 2-14-19
Child of Mystery, A 12-29-16
Child of Paris Secrets, A 5-19-16
Child of the Night (See: Enfant de la Nuit, L')
Child of the West, A 3-10-16
Child of the Wild, A 2-23-17
Child Shall Lead Them, A 9-08-22
Child Thou Gavest Me, The 1-13-22
Child Woman, The (See: Femme-Enfant, La)
Childhood of Ivan, The (See: Detstvo Ivana)
Childhood of Maxim Gorky 9-28-28
Childhood II 5-24-72
Childish Things 7-02-69
Children, The 12-28-49
Children, The 7-09-80
Children from Blue Lake Mountain, The (See: Barna fran
    Blasjofjaellet)
Children from No. 67, The (See: Kinder aus No. 67, Die)
Children in the House, The 4-21-16
Children, Mothers and a General (See: Kinder, Mutter und ein
    General)
Children Must Laugh 4-06-38
Children of Agony (See: Smertens Boern)
Children of Babylon 10-08-80
Children of Banishment 3-07-19
Children of Chance (See: Campane a Martello)
Children of Chance 12-03-30 and 1-28-31
Children of Chaos 4-26-50
Children of Destiny 9-03-20
Children of Divorce 4-20-27
Children of Dreams 7-21-31
Children of Dust 8-30-23
Children of Eve 11-12-15
Children of Fortune (See: Glueckskinder)
Children of Jazz 7-12-23
Children of Labor 9-28-77
Children of Love, The (See: Enfants de l'Amour, Les)
Children of Metropolis 7-03-29
Children of No Importance 4-04-28
Children of Oblivion, The (See: Enfants de l'Oubil, Les)
Children of Paradise (See: Enfants du Paradis, Les)
Children of Pleasure 8-06-30
Children of Rage 1-22-75

City That Stopped Hitler--Heroic Stalingrad, The (See: City That
    Stopped, The)
City's Child, A 7-21-71
Ciudad Cremada, La 10-27-76
Ciudad de los Ninos, La 9-11-57
Ciulinii Baraganului 5-21-58
Civil War 2-12-10
Civilian Clothes 9-10-20
Civilization 6-09-16
Civilization's Child 4-21-16
Claim, The 3-22-18
Clair de Femme 9-26-79
Clair de Terre 4-01-70
Claire's Knee (See: Genou de Claire, Le)
Clairette's 28 Days (See: 28 Jours de Clairette)
Clairvoyant 6-12-35
Clambake 10-18-67
Clan Des Siciliens, Le 12-10-69
Clan of the White Lotus 6-11-80
Clancy 1-07-11
Clancy in Wall St. 5-07-30
Clancy Street Boys 5-05-43
Clancy's Kosher Wedding 9-07-27
Clandestine 6-02-48
Clandestines, Les 4-20-55
Clandestins, Les 5-22-46 (Also see: Clandestine)
Clans of Intrigue 4-20-77
Clara de Montargis 7-04-51
Clarence 10-20-22
Clarence 3-10-37
Clarence and Angel 8-20-80
Clarence, the Cross-Eyed Lion 2-10-65
Clarines del Miedo, Los 9-17-58
Clarion, The 3-10-61
Clark 9-21-77
Clash by Night 5-14-52
Class of '44 4-04-73
Class of Miss MacMichael 9-13-78
Classe Operaia Va in Paradiso, La 2-09-72
Classe Tous Risques 7-27-60
Classified 11-11-25
Classmates 2-27-14
Classmates 12-31-24
Claude Duval 5-07-24
Claude Francois: Le Film de Sa Vie 5-30-79
Claude Francois: The Film of His Life (See: Claude Francois: Le
    Film de Sa Vie)
Claudelle Inglish 8-30-61
Claudia 8-18-43
Claudia and David 7-24-46
Claudia Case, The (See: O Caso Claudia)
Claudine 4-03-40
Claudine 4-10-74
Clavo, El 6-22-49
Claw, The 6-14-18
Claw, The 5-11-27
Claws of the Hun, The 7-05-18
Clay 12-23-64 and 5-26-65
Clay Dollars 10-28-21
Clay Pigeon 7-21-71
Clay Pigeon, The 2-09-49
Cle Sur la Porte, La 12-13-78
Clean Heart, The 9-17-24
Clean Up, The 8-10-17
Clean Up 10-04-23
Clean-Up Man, The 3-21-28
Clear All Wires 3-07-33
Clear Horizons (See: Horizonte Te Hapura)
Clear Skies 7-26-61
Clear the Decks 4-03-29
Clearing the Range 5-27-31
Clearing the Trail 9-26-28
Clemenceau Case, The 4-23-15
Cleo de 5 a 7 12-20-61
Cleo from 5 to 7 (See: Cleo de 5 a 7)
Cleopatra 8-21-34
Cleopatra 6-19-63
Cleopatra Jones 7-04-73
Cleopatra Jones and the Casino of Gold 6-18-75
Cleopatra, Queen of Sex 5-10-72
Clerambard 10-22-69
Clerk Vanished, A (See: Forsvundne Fuldmaegtig, Den)
Clever Mrs. Carfax, The 11-09-17
Clickety-Clack (See: Dodeska-Den)
Client de la Morte Saison, La 2-04-70
Cliff of Sin, The 11-26-52
Climax (See: Klimaks)
Climax 9-01-71
Climax, The 2-26-30

Climax, The 9-27-44
Climber, The (See: Sticenik)
Climbers, The 8-27-15
Climbers, The 10-31-19
Climbers, The 5-04-27
Climbing High 12-14-38
Climbing Mount Everest 10-11-23
Clinch (See: Klincz)
Clinging Vine, The 7-21-26
Clipa 9-05-79
Clipped Wings 5-04-38
Clipped Wings 11-25-53
Clive of India 1-22-35
Cloak and Dagger 9-11-46
Clock, The 3-30-17
Clock, The 3-28-45
Clockface Cafe (See: Cafe Du Cadran, Le)
Clockwork Orange, A 12-15-71
Clodhopper, The 6-29-17
Cloister Touch, The 2-05-10
Cloistered 5-27-36
Clonus Horror, The (See: Parts the Clonus Horror)
Close Call for Boston Blackie, A 2-20-46
Close Call for Ellery Queen, A 3-11-42
Close Encounters of the Third Kind 11-09-77
Close Harmony 5-01-29
Close Shave, A 9-24-10
Close to My Heart 10-10-51
Closed Gate, The 6-01-27
Closed Pages (See: Pagine Chiuse)
Closed Road, The 4-21-16
Closed Shutters, The (See: Volets Clos, Les)
Closed Ward (See: Lukket Avd)
Close-Up 4-07-48
Closet Children, The (See: Enfants Du Placard, Les)
Closin' In 6-28-18
Closing Net, The 10-22-15
Clothes 3-13-14
Clothes Make the Man 10-29-10
Clothes Make the Pirate 12-02-25
Clothes Make the Woman 6-06-28
Cloud, The 3-09-17
Cloud Dancer 6-11-80
Cloud Dodger 11-28-28
Cloud in the Teeth, A (See: Nuage Entre les Dents, Un)
Cloudburst 1-30-52
Clouded Yellow, The 11-29-50
Clouds over Europe 6-21-39
Clown, The (See: Ansichten Eines Clowns)
Clown, The 6-16-16
Clown, The 9-21-27
Clown, The 12-24-52
Clown Ferdinand and the Rocket (See: Klaun Ferdinand A Raketa)
Clown George 9-13-32
Clown King, The (See: Re Burlone, Il)
Clown Murders, The 10-06-76
Clowns, I 9-16-70
Clowns, The (See: Clowns, I)
Clowns on the Wall (See: Bohoc A Falon)
Club, The 10-08-80
Club de Femmes 7-01-36 and 10-13-37
Club de Femmes 1-23-57
Club Havana 1-23-46
Clue, The 7-16-15
Clue of the Twisted Candle 11-27-68
Cluny Brown 5-01-46
Cma 10-01-80
C'mon, Let's Live a Little 3-15-67
Coach 3-08-78
Coach, The (See: Trener)
Coal Miner's Daughter 2-20-80
Coast Guard 8-30-39
Coast of Folly, The 9-02-25
Coast of Opportunity 12-24-20
Coast of Skeletons 11-10-65
Coast Patrol, The 3-25-25
Coast to Coast 10-08-80
Coastal Command 4-19-44
Coax Me 8-01-19
Cobbler and the Millionaire 8-21-09
Cobra, The 4-10-68
Cobra Strikes, The 5-19-48
Cobra Woman, The 4-26-44
Cobweb, The 6-08-55
Cocaine 5-19-22
Cocaine Traffic, or The Drug Terror, The 2-27-14
Cocco di Mamma, Il 3-19-58
Cochecito, El 9-07-60

Cock o' the Walk 4-16-30
Cock of the Air 1-26-32
Cockeyed Cavaliers 7-31-34
Cockeyed Cowboys of Calico County 4-15-70
Cockeyed Happiness (See: Zesowate Szczescie)
Cockeyed Miracle, The 7-17-46
Cockeyed World, The 8-07-29
Cockleshell Heroes 11-23-55
Cocktail Hour 6-06-33
Cocktail Molotov 2-27-80
Cocktails 12-26-28
Coco la Fleur, Candidat 2-28-79
Coco-the-Flower, Candidate (See: Coco la Fleur, Candidat)
Cocoanut (See: Noix de Coco)
Cocoanut Grove 5-18-38
Cocoanuts, The 5-29-29
Code of Honor, The 12-17-30
Code of Marcia Gray, The 3-10-16
Code of Scotland Yard 9-01-48
Code of the Air 12-19-28
Code of the Cow Country 6-15-27
Code of the Outlaw 2-18-42
Code of the Range 5-11-27
Code of the Range 2-03-37
Code of the Rangers 4-13-38
Code of the Scarlet 7-11-28
Code of the Sea 5-28-24
Code of the Secret Service 5-17-39
Code of the Silver Sage 4-12-50
Code of the Streets 4-19-39
Code of the West 4-15-25
Code of the West 2-26-47
Code of the Wilderness 7-02-24
Code of the Yukon 12-20-18
Code 7, Victim 5 11-18-64
Code 2 3-11-53
Codine 5-22-63
Coeur a l'Envers, Le 11-05-80
Coeur de Lilas 3-01-32
Coeur Ebloui, Le 6-15-38
Coeur Fou, Le 4-01-70
Coeur Froid, Le 5-04-77
Coeur Gros Comme Ca!, Un 1-24-62
Coeur Vert, Le 4-27-66
Coffee Culture 2-05-10
Coffey-Flynn Fight Picture 6-11-15
Coffret de Laque, Le 8-02-32
Coffy 5-16-73
Cognasse 9-13-32
Cohabitation 6-11-75
Cohens and the Kellys, The 2-24-26
Cohens and the Kellys in Africa, The 12-24-30
Cohens and the Kellys in Atlantic City, The 3-20-29
Cohens and the Kellys in Hollywood, The 4-26-32
Cohens and the Kellys in Paris, The 2-08-28
Cohens and the Kellys in Scotland, The 3-12-30
Cohens and the Kellys in Trouble, The 4-18-33
Coiffeur Des Dames 11-08-32 (Also see: Coiffeur pour Dames)
Coiffeur pour Dames (See: French Touch)
Coiffeur pour Dames 6-07-32 (Also see: Coiffeur des Dames)
Coin, The (See: Fric, Le)
Coincidence 7-22-21
Cold Cuts (See: Buffet Froid)
Cold Days (See: Hideg Napok)
Cold Deck, The 11-09-17
Cold Heart, The (See: Coeur Froid, Le)
Cold Homeland (See: Kalte Heimat)
Cold Journey 6-04-75
Cold Soup, The (See: Soupe Froide, La)
Cold Storage Romance, A 10-08-10
Cold Tracks 7-24-63
Cold Turkey 2-03-71
Cold Wind in August, A 8-02-61
Colder Than Death (See: Kaelter Als Der Tod)
Colditz Story, The 2-09-55
Cole Younger, Gunfighter 4-02-58
Colera Del Viento, La 4-14-71
Colleagues 4-03-63
Collectionneuse, La 3-08-67
Collections Privees 7-11-79
Collective Marriage 7-21-71
Collector, The (See: Collectionneuse, La)
Collector, The 5-26-65
Colleen 3-11-36
Colleen Bawn, The 2-07-24
College 9-14-27
College Boarding House (See: Casa de la Troya, La)
College Chums 2-29-08

College Coach 11-14-33
College Coquette 8-28-29
College Days 10-27-26
College Girl, The (See: Sextanerin, Die)
College Girls (See: Muchachas Que Estudian)
College Hero 11-23-27
College Holiday 12-30-36
College Humor 6-27-33
College Love 8-07-29
College Lovers 12-03-30
College Orphan, The 10-22-15
College Rhythm 11-27-34
College Scandal 7-17-35
College Sweethearts 1-21-42
College Swing 4-27-38
College Widow, The 11-09-27
Collegiate 1-29-36
Collier de Chanvre, Le 6-04-41
Collier de la Reine, Le 2-11-31
Collision (See: Karambol)
Colombes, Les 9-27-72
Colombo and Its Environs 10-01-10
Colonel and the Werewolf, The (See: O Coronel e O Lobisomem)
Colonel Bontemps 5-28-15
Colonel Bridau 7-04-19
Colonel Chabert 6-11-47
Colonel Effingham's Raid 10-03-45
Colonel Wolodyjowski 7-02-69
Colonel's Wife, The 1-22-15
Color Me Dead 1-14-70
Color Sergeant's Horse, The 12-24-10
Colorado 11-05-15
Colorado 3-11-21
Colorado 9-04-40
Colorado Ambush 5-09-51
Colorado Kid 1-12-38
Colorado Ranger 6-07-50
Colorado Serenade 6-12-46
Colorado Sundown 2-13-52
Colorado Sunset 8-02-39
Colorado Territory 5-18-49
Colorado Trail 11-02-38
Colorin, Colorado 9-29-76
Colossus of New York 6-25-58
Colossus of Rhodes, The 12-13-61
Colours of the Rainbow, The (See: Ta Chromata Tis Iridos)
Colt Comrades 6-23-43
Colt .45 5-03-50
Coltelli Dei Vendicatori, I (See: Knives of the Avenger)
Columbia Revolt, The 11-06-68
Columbus Discovers Kraehwinkel (See: Columbus Entdeckt Kraehwinkel)
Columbus Entdeckt Kraehwinkel 9-15-54
Columbus of Sex 5-13-70
Column, The 11-06-68
Column South 5-13-53
Coma 1-25-78
Comanche 3-07-56
Comanche, Der 9-19-79
Comanche, The (See: Comanche, Der)
Comanche Station 2-24-60
Comanche Territory 4-05-50
Comancheros, The 11-01-61
Combat, The 9-22-16
Combat Dans L'Ile, Le 9-26-62
Combat Squad 9-30-53
Come Across 7-17-29 and 7-31-29
Come and Get It 11-18-36
Come Back, The 4-21-16
Come Back Africa 9-16-59
Come Back, All Is Forgiven 10-02-29
Come Back Baby 6-19-68
Come Back Charleston Blue 7-05-72
Come Back, Little Sheba 12-03-52
Come Back Peter 2-17-71
Come Blow Your Horn 5-22-63
Come Closer, Folks 11-25-36
Come Fill the Cup 9-26-51
Come Fly with Me 4-03-63
Come Home and Meet My Wife (See: Romanzo Popolare)
Come L'Amore 7-03-68
Come Live with Me 1-22-41
Come Next Spring 2-08-56
Come On, The 2-15-56
Come On Children 4-11-73
Come On, Cowboys 6-16-37
Come On Danger 12-31-41
Come On In 9-27-18
Come On, Leathernecks 8-24-38

Come On, Marines 3-27-34
Come On, My Dear Little Birdie (See: Komm Nur, Mein Liebstes
    Voegelein)
Come On Now, Panciano (See: 'Ora Panciano)
Come On Over 3-17-22
Come On, Rangers 1-04-39
Come on Tarzan 1-17-33
Come One, Come All 10-28-70
Come Out Fighting 9-05-45
Come Out of the Kitchen 5-16-19
Come Out of the Pantry 12-11-35
Come Perdere Una Moglie e Trovare Un' Amante 12-13-78
Come Persi la Guerra 2-04-48
Come, Quando, Con Chi 12-31-69
Come September 6-28-61
Come Spy with Me 1-18-67
Come Through 6-22-17
Come to My House 1-18-28
Come to the Stable 6-22-49
Come to Your Senses 10-20-71
Comeback--Artur Rubinstein in Poland, The 11-19-75
Comedia Rota 10-10-79
Comedians, The 11-01-67
Comedie Fantastica 8-06-75
Comedien Harmonists, Die 4-27-77
Comedy and Tragedy 11-06-09
Comedy-Graph, The 2-26-10
Comedy Harmonists, The (See: Comedien Harmonists, Die)
Comedy Man, The 9-09-64
Comedy of Terrors, The 1-29-64
Comes a Horseman 10-11-78
Comet over Broadway 12-21-38
Cometogether 9-29-71
Comeuppance, The (See: Ardoise, L')
Comic, The 11-12-69
Comin' Round the Mountain 4-29-36
Comin' Round the Mountain 8-14-40
Comin' Round the Mountain 6-20-51
Comin' Thro' the Rye 12-31-24
Comin' Thro' the Rye 11-12-47
Coming Apart 10-08-69
Coming Home 2-15-78
Coming of Amos 9-16-25
Coming of the Law, The 5-30-19
Coming Out Party 3-20-34
Coming Through 2-11-25
Comisar Acuza, Un 7-17-74
Comizi D'Amore 8-05-64
Command, The 1-20-54
Command Decision 12-29-48
Command Performance 3-18-31
Command Performance 9-08-37
Command to Love (See: Liebe auf Befehl or Liebeskommando)
Commanding Officer, The 4-02-15
Commandos Strike at Dawn, The 12-16-42
Commare Secca, La 9-05-62
Comme la Lune 9-14-77
Comme Sur des Roullettes 4-20-77
Comme un Boomerang 9-01-76
Comme un Pot des Fraises 9-16-74
Comment Qu'elle Est! 10-12-60
Comment Reussir en Amour 11-28-62
Comment Reussir Quand on Est Con et Pleurnichard 7-03-74
Comment Trouvez-Vous Ma Soeur? 3-18-64
Comment Yukong Deplace les Montagnes 3-17-76
Commissario, Il 5-30-62
Commissario Pepe, Il 10-22-69
Commitment, The 2-04-76
Committee, The 1-01-69
Common Clay 3-07-19
Common Clay 8-06-30
Common Fascism, The 12-01-65
Common Ground 7-28-16
Common Law 11-01-23
Common Law, The 9-29-16
Common Law, The 7-21-31
Common Level, A 7-16-20
Common Man, The (See: Dupont Lajoie)
Common Property 11-14-19
Common Sense 6-11-20
Communale, La 11-03-65
Commune 18 (See: Realengo 18)
Communion 9-21-77
Communion Solennelle, La 2-09-77
Commuter Kind of Love, A (See: Kjaerleikens Ferjreiser)
Commuting 6-22-17
Como Era Gostoso O Meu Frances 7-14-71

Como Todos las Madres (See: Like All Mothers)
Como Vai, Vai Bem 6-11-69
Compagni, I 11-20-63
Compagno Don Camillo, Il 10-27-65
Compagnons de la Marguerite, Les 2-15-67
Companeras and Companeros 10-28-70
Companero 10-08-75
Companero de Viaje 9-05-79
Companion Wanted (See: On Demande Compagnon)
Company Limited (See: Simbaddha)
Company She Keeps, The 12-20-50
Companys, Catalonia On Trial (See: Companys, Proces a Catalunya)
Companys, Proces a Catalunya 5-16-79
Compartment Tueurs 12-01-65
Competition 1-31-68
Competition, The 12-03-80
Complessi, I 10-27-65
Complexes (See: Complessi, I)
Complicated Man, A (See: Fuzuzatsu No Kare)
Compliments of Mr. Flow 2-19-41
Complot, Le 6-13-73
Compromise 10-28-25
Compromise 9-11-68
Compromised 1-21-31
Compromised 11-10-31
Compromising Daphne 11-12-30
Comptes A Rebours 2-17-71
Compulsion 2-04-59
Compulsory Husband 3-19-30
Computer Superman, The (See: Yod Manoot Computer)
Computer Wore Tennis Shoes, The 12-24-69
Comrade John 11-12-15
Comrade Nikanorova Awaits You (See: Was Oshidajet Grashdanka
    Nikanorova)
Comrade President Centre-Forward (See: Drug Pretsednik Centafor)
Comrade X 12-11-40
Comrades 2-29-28
Comrades of 1918 2-25-31
Comradeship (See: Kameradschaft)
Comte de Monte-Cristo 3-09-55
Comte de Monte Cristo, Le 1-17-62
Con El Culo Al Aire 10-29-80
Con el Viento Solano 5-18-66
Con-Fusion (See: Con-Fusione)
Con-Fusione 9-17-80
Con las Alas Rotas 7-27-38
Con Mucho Carino 9-12-79
Concentratin' Kid 1-26-30
Concentration, La 1-01-69
Concentration Camp 3-22-39
Concerning Lone (See: Angaaende Lone)
Concert 12-16-21
Concert, The (See: Konzert, Das)
Concert, The 3-04-21
Concert at the End of Summer (See: Koncert Na Konci Leta)
Concert for Bangladesh 3-29-72
Concert for Mourners (See: Koncert Pre Pozostalych)
Concert in the Tyrol (See: Konzert in Tirol)
Concert Magic 10-20-48
Concert of Stars 3-04-53
Concorde--Airport '79, The 8-01-79
Concubines, The 6-25-69
Condamne a Mort S'Est Echappe, Un 12-12-56
Conde, Un 9-30-70
Conde de Monte Cristo, El 11-17-43
Condemned (See: Skazany)
Condemned 9-24-24
Condemned 11-06-29
Condemned, The (See: Totstellen)
Condemned Man Escaped, A (See: Condamne a Mort S'Est Eschappe, Un)
Condemned of Altona, The 9-11-63
Condemned to Death 2-16-32 and 7-19-32
Condemned to Live 10-09-35
Condemned to Sin (See: Verdammt zur Suende)
Condemned Women 3-09-38
Condottieri 7-14-37
Conduct Unbecoming 9-17-75
Conductor 1492 3-19-24
Cone of Silence 5-18-60
Coney Island 2-15-28
Coney Island 5-19-43
Confession Al Amanecer (See: Confession at Dawn)
Confession 7-21-37
Confession 8-19-42
Confession, The (See: Aveu, L')

Counterfeit Bill, The (See: Falscher Fuffziger, Ein)
Counterfeit Killer, The 5-22-68
Counterfeit Lady 1-13-37
Counterfeit Plan, The 3-27-57
Counterfeit Traitor, The 4-04-62
Counterfeiters, The 6-02-48
Counterfeiters, The 5-13-53
Counterplot 10-07-59
Counterpoint 12-27-67
Counterspy Meets Scotland Yard 11-15-50
Countess Charming, The 9-21-17
Countess for a Night (See: Ole Kreivitar, En)
Countess from Hong Kong, A 1-11-67
Countess of Monte Christo (See: Graefin von Monte Christo)
Countess of Mont Cristo, The 4-03-34
Countess of Monte Cristo, The 11-03-48
Country Beyond 11-24-26
Country Beyond 5-06-36
Country Boy, The 2-19-15
Country Bride 6-15-38
Country Called Chile, A (See: Pais Llamado Chile, Un)
Country Cousin, The 12-19-19
Country Doctor, The 3-18-36
Country Doctor, The 7-03-63
Country Fair 5-14-41
Country Flapper 8-04-22
Country Gentlemen 1-27-37
Country Girl, The 12-01-54
Country Girl's Peril 7-10-09
Country God Forgot, The 9-29-16
Country I Come From, The (See: Pays D'Ou Je Viens, Le)
Country Idyl 12-05-08
Country, Inc. (See: Pais S.A.)
Country Is Calm, The (See: Es Herrscht Ruhe Im Land)
Country Kid, The 11-01-23
Country, Love and Duty (See: Patria, Amore, e Dovere)
Country Mouse, The 11-14-14
Country Music Holiday 6-18-58
Country Parson, The 10-29-15
Country Priest, The (See: Odemarksprasten)
Country School, The (See: Ecole Buissonniere, L')
Country Schoolmaster, A 3-26-10
Count's Wooing, The 11-20-09
County Chairman 10-23-14
County Chairman 1-22-35
County Fair 11-24-37
County Fair 8-09-50
County Fair, The 5-31-32
Coup de Feu a L'Aube 9-06-32
Coup de Grace (See: Tiro de Gracia or Fangschuss, Der)
Coup de Grace, Le 3-24-65
Coup de Roulis 6-07-32
Coup de Sirocco, Le 5-02-79
Coup de Tete 3-07-79
Coup D'Etat (See: Kaigenrei or Zamach Stanu)
Coup du Parapluie, Le 11-05-80
Coup Pour Coup 3-01-72
Coupe a Dix Francs, La 2-26-75
Couple (See: Futari)
Couple, A (See: Couple, Un)
Couple, Un 12-07-60
Couple Ideal, Le 6-19-46
Couple Temoin, Le 4-06-77
Coups de Feu 5-17-39
Courage 11-18-21
Courage 6-11-30
Courage for Every Day (See: Kazdy Den Odvahu)
Courage for Two 2-07-19
Courage, Fuyons 10-24-79
Courage, Let's Run for It (See: Courage, Fuyons)
Courage of Black Beauty 7-17-57
Courage of Marge O'Doone, The 6-04-20
Courage of Silence, The 2-02-17
Courage of the People, The (See: Corajo del Pueblo, El)
Courage of the West 12-08-37
Courageous Coward, The 4-25-19
Courageous Dr. Christian 4-03-40
Courageous Mr. Penn 1-05-44
Courier of Lyons 6-15-38
Courrier Sud 2-24-37
Cours Apres Moi Que Je T'Attrape 9-15-76
Course a L'Echalote, La 10-22-75
Course des Taureaux, La 10-24-51
Course du Lievre a Travers les Champs, La 9-20-72
Course en Tete, La 4-03-74
Court Concert (See: Hofkonzert)
Court Jester, The 2-01-56
Court Martial (See: Prijeki Sud)

Court Martial 10-31-28
Court Martialed 8-20-15
Courte Tete 4-03-57
Courtesan, The 5-26-16
Courtesan, The 11-13-63
Courtin' Trouble 5-04-49
Courtin' Wildcats 12-25-29
Courting of the Merry Widow, The 3-26-10
Court-Martial of Billy Mitchell, The 12-14-55
Courtney's of Curzon Street 4-23-47
Courtship of Andy Hardy, The 2-11-42
Courtship of Eddie's Father, The 3-13-63
Courtship of Miles Standish, The 1-29-10
Courtship of O'San 3-06-14
Cousin Angelica (See: Prima Angelica, La)
Cousin, Cousine 11-26-75
Cousin Jim 7-14-16
Cousin Jules, Le 8-22-73
Cousin Betty 11-07-28
Cousines, Les (See: From Ear to Ear)
Cousins, Les 3-04-59
Couteau dans la Plaie, Le 1-16-63
Couteau Sous La Gorge, Le 4-11-56
Couturiere de Ces Dames, Le 5-02-56
Couturiere de Luneville 5-10-32 and 10-25-32
Covek Nije Tica 5-11-66
Covenant with Death, A 1-11-67
Cover Girl 3-08-44
Cover Me, Babe 10-07-70
Covered Tracks (See: Verwehte Spuren)
Covered Trail, The 5-21-24
Covered Trailer, The 11-15-39
Covered Wagon, The 3-22-23
Covered Wagon Days 5-08-40
Covered Wagon Raid 7-12-50
Covered Wagon Trails 5-08-40
Cover-Up 2-23-49
Covert Action (See: Sono Stato Un Agente Cia)
Covjek Koga Treba Ubiti 8-15-79
Cow, The (See: Gav)
Cow and the Prisoner, The (See: Vache et le Prisonnier, La)
Cow Country 5-20-53
Cow Gift, The (See: Go-Daan)
Cow Girl of St. Catherine (See: Sennerin von St. Kathrein, Die)
Cow Town 5-10-50
Coward, The (See: Kapurush)
Coward, The 10-08-15
Coward, The 8-24-27
Cowardice Court 6-27-19
Cowardly Way, The 11-12-15
Cowards 4-22-70
Cowards Live on Hope (See: Laches Vivent d'Espoir, Les)
Cowboy 2-12-58
Cowboy, The 1-20-54
Cowboy and the Blonde, The 4-23-41
Cowboy and the Countess, The 3-17-26
Cowboy and the Flapper, The 12-10-24
Cowboy and the Indians, The 11-02-49
Cowboy and the Kid, The 7-29-36
Cowboy and the Lady, The 11-17-22
Cowboy and the Lady, The 11-09-38
Cowboy and the Prizefighter, The 2-22-50
Cowboy and the Senorita, The 4-05-44
Cowboy Commandos 7-14-43
Cowboy Counsellor 2-07-33
Cowboy from Brooklyn 6-15-38
Cowboy from Sundown 8-07-40
Cowboy in Manhattan 4-07-43
Cowboy in the Clouds 1-26-44
Cowboy Millionaire 6-05-35
Cowboy Quarterback 8-09-39
Cowboy Serenade 4-01-42
Cowboys, The 1-12-72
Cowboys and the Bachelor Girls, The 12-03-10
Cowboys from Texas 12-06-39
Cowboy's Vindication, A 12-24-10
Cows (See: Vrane)
Coyote Fangs 9-17-24
Crab, The 2-16-17
Crab Basket, The (See: Panier a Crabes, Le)
Crab Drum, The (See: Crabe Tambour, Le)
Crabe Tambour, Le 11-16-77
Crack in the Mirror 5-11-60
Crack in the World 2-10-65
Crack o' Dawn 10-21-35
Cracked Nuts 4-08-31
Crackerjack, The 5-13-25
Cracker's Bride 3-27-09

Cracking Up 7-27-77
Cracks, Les 3-20-68
Cracksman, The 8-07-63
Crack-Up 1-13-37
Crack-Up 6-19-46
Cradle, The 3-24-22
Cradle Buster 6-09-22
Cradle of Courage 9-24-20
Cradle Snatchers 6-01-27
Cradle Song (See: Cancion de Cuna)
Cradle Song 11-21-33
Craig's Wife 12-05-28
Craig's Wife 10-07-36
Crainquebille 8-04-54
Crammer, The (See: Pauker, Der)
Cramp (See: Krc)
Cran D'Arret 1-28-70
Crash, The 11-07-28
Crash, The 9-13-32
Crash Dive 4-21-43
Crash Donovan 8-12-36
Crash Landing 2-05-58
Crashin' Thru Danger 10-05-38
Crashing Hollywood 12-29-37
Crashing Through to Berlin 8-16-18
Crashing Thru 4-19-23
Crashing Thru 12-27-39
Crashout 5-18-55
Cravache, La 5-10-72
Craving, The 9-27-18
Crawling Hand, The 11-25-64
Craze 6-12-74
Crazies, The 1-24-73
Crazy Days (See: Ludi Dani)
Crazy-Horse Paris-France 11-02-77
Crazy House 10-20-43
Crazy Joe 2-06-74
Crazy Lola (See: Tolle Lola, Die)
Crazy Mama 7-16-75
Crazy Night, A (See: Egy Oeruelt Ejszaka)
Crazy over Horses 11-28-51
Crazy Paradise 8-11-65
Crazy Pete (See: Pierrot le Fou)
Crazy Quilt, The 10-27-65
Crazy Sea (See: Mare Matto)
Crazy Sex 8-04-76
Crazy Show (See: Branquinol)
Crazy That Way 4-30-30
Crazy to Marry 8-05-21
Crazy Women (See: Locas, Las)
Crazy World of Julius Vrooder, The 9-25-74
Crazy World of Laurel and Hardy, The 12-27-67
Crazylegs, All-American 9-30-53
Creation 9-08-22
Creation du Monde, La 1-16-63
Creation of the World (See: Creation du Monde, La)
Creature, The (See: Criatura, La)
Creature from the Black Lagoon 2-10-54
Creature Walks Among Us, The 3-14-56
Creature with the Atom Brain 6-22-55
Creatures, Les 9-07-66
Creatures the World Forgot 4-07-71
Crecer de Golpe 9-28-77
Creeper, The 10-06-48
Creeping Flesh, The 3-14-73
Creeping Unknown, The 6-27-56
Creo en Dios 8-04-43
Crescendo 11-01-72
Crest of the Wave 7-21-54
Cresus 10-05-60
Crew, The (See: Equipage, L' or Eqipaj)
Crew Cut 11-26-80
Cri du Coeur, Le 9-04-74
Cri du Cormoran le Soir Au-Dessus des Jonques, Le 3-03-71
Cria Cuervos 2-04-76
Criatura, La 2-01-78
Cricket, The 11-16-17
Cricket in the Ear (See: Shtourets V Ouhoto)
Cricket on the Hearth 3-12-24
Cries and Whispers 12-20-72
Criez-le Sur les Toits 8-20-32
Crime Afloat 8-25-37
Crime Against Joe 3-14-56
Crime and Passion 2-25-76
Crime and Punishment (See: Crime et Chatinaut)
Crime and Punishment (See: Prestuplenie I Nakazanie)
Crime and Punishment 2-09-17
Crime and Punishment 7-20-27

Crime and Punishment 11-20-35
Crime and Punishment 11-27-35
Crime and Punishment 3-03-48
Crime and Punishment, U.S.A. 4-01-59
Crime at Porta Romana (See: Delitto A Porta Romana)
Crime by Night 7-26-44
Crime de David Levinstein, Le 5-08-68
Crime des Justes, Le 2-08-50
Crime Doctor, The 5-15-34
Crime Doctor, The 7-07-43
Crime Doctor's Courage, The 3-07-45
Crime Doctor's Diary, The 3-23-49
Crime Doctor's Gamble, The 11-26-47
Crime Doctor's Manhunt, The 9-18-46
Crime Doctor's Strangest Case, The 12-15-43
Crime Doctor's Warning, The 12-19-45
Crime Does Not Pay (See: Crime Ne Paie Pas, Le)
Crime et Chatiment 6-12-35
Crime et Chatinaut 1-23-57
Crime in the Streets 4-11-56
Crime in the Sun (See: Brott I Sol)
Crime, Inc. 6-27-45
Crime Ne Paie Pas, Le 5-30-62
Crime Nobody Saw, The 4-07-37
Crime of David Levinstein, The (See: Crime de David Levinstein, Le)
Crime of Dr. Crespi, The 1-15-36
Crime of Dr. Forbes 7-08-36
Crime of Dr. Hallet 3-16-38
Crime of Helen Stanley 8-21-34
Crime of Mastrovanni, The (See: Delitto di Mastrovanni, El)
Crime of Passion 1-16-57
Crime of the Century, The 2-21-33
Crime of the Century, The 6-12-46
Crime of the Just, The (See: Crime des Justes, Le)
Crime over London 11-11-36
Crime Patrol, The 5-13-36
Crime Ring 7-27-38
Crime School 5-04-38
Crime Takes a Holiday 12-07-38
Crime Thief, The (See: Voleur de Crimes, Le)
Crime Wave 1-13-54
Crime Without Passion 9-04-34
Crimen de Cuenca, El 1-23-80
Crimenes de Petiot, Los 10-25-72
Crimes of Petiot, The (See: Crimenes de Petiot, Los)
Criminal, The 7-09-15
Criminal, The 10-27-16
Criminal, The 9-21-60
Criminal at Large 12-26-33
Criminal Code 1-07-31
Criminal Conversation 10-29-80
Criminal Court 8-14-46
Criminal Lawyer 2-03-37
Criminal Lawyer 8-29-51
Criminal Records (See: Zapis Zbrodni)
Criminali Della Galassia, I (See: Wild, Wild Planet)
Criminals of the Air 8-18-37
Criminals Within 8-20-41
Crimson Blade, The 4-01-64
Crimson Canary 11-07-45
Crimson Canyon 12-12-28
Crimson Challenge 4-14-22
Crimson Circle 10-27-22
Crimson Circle, The 4-24-29 and 2-12-30
Crimson Circle, The 4-08-36 and 12-30-36
Crimson Circle, The 4-08-36 and 12-30-36
Crimson City 4-18-28
Crimson Clue, The 3-19-15
Crimson Cross 4-21-22
Crimson Cult, The 4-29-70
Crimson Dove, The 5-25-17
Crimson Gardenia, The 6-20-19
Crimson Key, The 7-02-47
Crimson Kimono, The 9-09-59
Crimson Pirate, The 8-27-52
Crimson Romance 10-16-34
Crimson Runner 5-27-25
Crimson Stain Mystery, The 8-18-16
Crimson Trail, The 3-20-35
Crimson Wing, The 10-29-15
Crinoline and Romance 2-15-23
Cripple Creek 6-25-52
Crippled Hand, The 4-21-16
Criqui-Kilbane Fight 6-07-23
Crise Est Finie, La 3-20-35
Crisis 3-15-39
Crisis 6-21-50

Crisis, The 10-06-16
Criss Cross 1-12-49
Cristo Del Oceano, El 5-05-71
Cristo Proibito 6-27-51
Cristo Si e Fermato a Eboli 3-21-79
Cristobal's Gold (See: Or du Cristobal, L')
Critical Age 8-09-23
Critical Situation, The 2-12-10
Critic's Choice 4-03-63
Crni Biseri 8-20-58
Croix de Bois, Les 4-12-32
Croix des Vivants, La 8-22-62
Croix du Sud 6-07-32
Croix et la Banniere, La 6-21-61
Cromwell 7-22-70
Cronaca di Poveri Amanti 5-05-54
Cronaca Familiare 9-12-62
Cronica de um Industrial 5-30-79
Cronica de un Subversivo Latino Americano 11-17-76
Cronica de una Senora 7-21-71
Crook of Dreams 2-21-49
Crooked Alley 11-15-23
Crooked Circle 10-04-32
Crooked Love (See: Luci Sommerse)
Crooked Path 9-25-09
Crooked Path, The 7-30-15
Crooked River 2-14-51
Crooked Road, The 6-12-40
Crooked Straight 10-24-19
Crooked Streets 7-30-20
Crooked Way, The 4-27-49
Crooked Web 11-23-55
Crooks and Coronets 4-09-69
Crooks Can't Win 5-30-28
Crook's Honor (See: Ganovenehre)
Crooks in Cloisters 8-26-64
Crooks Tour 9-25-40
Crooner 8-23-32
Croquemitoufle 6-10-59
Crosby Case, The 4-03-34
Cross and the Banner, The (See: Croix et la Banniere, La)
Cross and the Switchblade, The 5-27-70
Cross Bearer, The 1-11-18
Cross Breed, The 12-07-27
Cross-Country (See: Kros Kontri)
Cross Country Cruise 1-23-34
Cross Country Romance 6-26-40
Cross Currents 12-03-15
Cross Examination 3-01-32
Cross-Eyed Saint, The (See: Per Grazia Ricevuta)
Cross Investigation (See: Contre-Enquete)
Cross My Heart 11-20-46
Cross of Iron 2-09-77
Cross of Lorraine, The 11-10-43
Cross of St. Anne (See: Anna na Shee)
Cross of the Living (See: Croix des Vivants, La)
Cross Streets 7-10-34
Cross-Up 2-26-58
Crossed Swords 7-28-54
Crossed Tails 4-16-24
Crossed Trails 4-28-48
Crossed Wires 5-30-23
Crossfire 10-24-33
Crossfire 6-25-47
Crossing of the Rhine, The (See: Passage du Rhin, Le)
Crossing the Andes 11-05-10
Crossing the Sahara 2-07-24
Crossing Trails 2-17-22
Crossplot 12-03-69
Crossroad, The (See: Encrucijada, La)
Crossroad of Love 10-17-28
Crossroads (See: Carrefour)
Crossroads 6-24-42
Crossroads of New York 5-26-22
Crossroads of Passion 2-28-51
Crosswinds 8-08-51
Crouching Beast, The 9-11-35 and 9-02-36
Crowd, The 2-22-28
Crowd Inside, The 6-02-71
Crowd Roars, The (See: Foule Hurle, La)
Crowd Roars, The 3-29-32
Crowd Roars, The 8-03-38
Crowded Hour, The 4-29-25
Crowded Paradise 5-09-56
Crowded Sky, The 8-24-60
Crown Jewels 12-20-18
Crown of Lies, The 4-07-26
Crown of Sonnets 8-31-77

Crown Prince (See: Kronprinsen)
Crown Prince's Double, The 1-07-16
Crowning Experience 10-26-60
Crow's Nest 11-17-22
Crucial Moment, The (See: A Donto Pillanat)
Crucial Test, The 6-30-16
Crucible, The 12-25-14
Crucible of Life, The 2-08-18
Crucified Woman, The (See: Uwasa No Onna)
Cruel Girl Friend, The (See: Grausame Freundin, Die)
Cruel Love (See: Kruta Lubost)
Cruel Sea (See: Bas Ya Bahar)
Cruel Sea, The 4-01-53
Cruel Tower, The 12-12-56
Crueldade Mortal 2-02-77
Crueles, Las 3-03-71
Cruise, The (See: Rejs)
Cruise of the Hellion 9-14-27
Cruise of the Make Believes, The 8-23-18
Cruise of the Speejacks 5-02-28
Cruiser Emden 9-13-32
Cruiser Potemkin 6-16-26
Cruisin' Down the River 7-22-53
Cruisin' 57 11-05-75
Cruising 2-13-80
Cruiskeen Lawn 2-04-25
Crusade Against Rackets 8-04-37
Crusader, The 10-11-32
Crusades, The 8-28-35
Crush Proof 7-12-72
Crvena Zemlja 8-20-75
Crveno Klasje 7-14-71
Cry, The (See: Grido, Il or Urlo, L')
Cry and the Silence, The (See: Csend es Kialttas)
Cry Baby Killer, The 6-18-58
Cry Danger 2-07-51
Cry Dr. Chicago 7-21-71
Cry for Cindy 5-26-76
Cry for Happy 1-11-61
Cry Freedom 5-03-61
Cry from the Streets, A 8-13-58
Cry Havoc 11-10-43
Cry in the Night, A 5-08-14
Cry in the Night, A 8-15-56
Cry in the Wind 10-04-67
Cry Murder 2-01-50
Cry of Battle 10-16-63
Cry of the Banshee 8-05-70
Cry of the Black Wolves, The (See: Schrei der Schwarzen Woelfe, Der)
Cry of the City 9-15-48
Cry of the Cormoran at Night Over the Junks (See: Cri du Cormorant le Soir Au-Dessus des Jonques, Le)
Cry of the Earth, The (See: Grido Della Terra, Il)
Cry of the Heart (See: Cri du Coeur, Le)
Cry of the Hunted 3-11-53
Cry of the Weak 4-25-19
Cry of the Werewolf 8-16-44
Cry of the World 5-10-32
Cry Terror 4-16-58
Cry, the Beloved Country 1-23-52
Cry Tough 7-29-59
Cry Uncle 7-29-71
Cry Vengeance 11-24-56
Cry Wolf 7-02-47
Crying Woman, The (See: Femme Qui Pleure, La)
Crystal Ball, The 1-20-43
Crystal Cup, The 10-26-27
Crystal Gazer, The 8-03-17
Crystal Submarine, The 7-25-28
Csaladi Potlek 1-19-38
Csampeszek 8-06-58
Csardasfurstin, Die 5-01-35
Csend es Kialttas 1-31-68
Cseplo Gyuri 8-23-78
Csillagosok, Katonak 11-22-67
Csipetke 12-26-33
Csokolj Meg Edes 4-12-32 and 11-29-32
Csunay Lany 10-23-35
Cu Minile Curate 6-14-78
Cuando Canta el Corazon 9-03-41
Cuando Canta la Ley 5-31-39
Cuando el Amor Rie 4-22-31
Cuando Estallo la Paz 9-05-62
Cuando Florezca el Naranjo 5-12-43
Cuando Los Hijos Se Van 5-26-43
Cuando Regree Mama 3-22-61
Cuanto Vale Tu Hijo 1-31-62

Cub, The 7-23-15
Cub Reporter 9-22-22
Cuba 12-19-79
Cuba Baila 8-09-61
Cuba-Crossing 2-13-80
Cuba Dances (See: Cuba Baila)
Cuba My Love (See: Cuba No Koibito)
Cuba No Koibito 10-22-69
Cuba Va 9-29-71
Cuban Fight Against Demons (See: Pelea Cubana Contra Los
    Demonios, Una)
Cuban Fireball 3-14-51
Cuban Love Song 12-08-31
Cuban Pete 7-24-46
Cubs, The (See: Cachorros, Los)
Cucaracha, La 5-27-59
Cuccagna, La 11-14-62
Cuckoo Clock, The 12-14-38
Cuckoos, The 4-30-30
Cuckoo's Egg (See: Kuckucksei, Das)
Cudna Devojka 8-08-62
Cuenca Crime, The (See: Crimen de Cuenca, El)
Cuerpo y la Sangre, El 7-04-62
Cuidado Con El Amor 1-19-55
Cuisine Au Beurre, La 1-29-64
Cul-De-Sac 6-08-66
Culottes Rouges, Les 1-16-63
Culpable 8-03-60
Culpepper Cattle Company, The 4-12-72
Cult of the Cobra 3-30-55
Culte Vaudou au Dahomey, Le 11-22-72
Cumberland Romance 8-13-20
Cumbite 6-29-66
Cumparsita, La 10-01-47
Cunning vs. Cunning 5-28-15
Cuore di Cane 3-17-76
Cuore di Mamma 2-26-69
Cuore Infranto (See: Broken Love)
Cuore Semplice, Un 10-25-78
Cuori Solitari 1-28-70
Cup of Life 10-28-21
Cupid by Proxy 7-12-18
Cupid Club, The (See: Bal Cupidon, Le)
Cupid, Cowpuncher 7-30-20
Cupidity (See: Fettowa, El)
Cupid's Fireman 4-30-24
Cupid's Round Up 2-01-18
Cupid's Understudy 7-25-19
Cupola 5-23-62
Cura Gaucho, El 7-23-41
Cure de Village, Le 11-30-49
Cure for Love, The 1-11-50
Cure for Rheumatism, A 3-27-09
Curee, La 7-27-66
Curing a Masher 10-01-10
Curio Lake, The (See: Jezioro Osbloiwosei)
Curly Top 8-07-35
Curlytop 4-22-25
Cursa 6-14-78
Curse of Creed, The 5-08-14
Curse of Drink 9-15-22
Curse of Frankenstein, The 5-15-57
Curse of Iku 3-22-18
Curse of the Cat People, The 2-23-44
Curse of the Demon 2-26-58
Curse of the Faceless Man 8-20-58
Curse of the Mummy's Tomb, The 9-02-64
Curse of the Undead 7-01-59
Curse of the Voodoo 12-22-65
Curse of the Werewolf 5-03-61
Cursed Money (See: Zie Pare)
Cursed Mountain (See: Sierra Maldita)
Curso En Que Amamos A Kim Novak, El 2-20-80
Curtain 10-08-20
Curtain at Eight 2-13-34
Curtain Call 4-10-40
Curtain Call at Cactus Creek 5-24-50
Curtain Falls, The 5-22-35
Curtain Up 5-14-52
Curtains for Mrs. Knudsen (See: Det Er Nat Med Fru Knudsen)
Curucu, Beast of the Amazon 10-31-56
Custard Cup 4-26-23
Custer of the West 11-15-67
Customer of the Off Season, The (See: Client de la Morte Saison,
    Le)
Customs Agent 4-19-50
Cutting Heads (See: Cabezas Cortadas)

Cuvar Plaze u Zimskom Periodu 7-07-76
Cycle of Adversity 1-16-14
Cycle Savages 5-06-70
Cycles South 5-12-71
Cyclists, The (See: Biciklisti)
Cyclo-Homo 6-27-08
Cyclone 2-27-20
Cyclone Fury 8-15-51
Cyclone Kid 11-24-31
Cyclone Kid, The 8-12-42
Cyclone of the Rouge 5-04-27
Cyclone on Horseback 6-18-41
Cyclone Ranger 5-22-35
Cyclops 8-21-57
Cyclops 11-10-76
Cynara 1-03-33
Cynthia 5-14-47
Cynthia of the Minute 7-16-20
Cyprus 10-27-76
Cyrano de Bergerac 7-08-25
Cyrano de Bergerac 11-15-50
Cyrano and D'Artagnan (See: Cyrano et D'Artagnan)
Cyrano et D'Artagnan 6-03-64
Cytherea 5-28-24
Czar and the Carpenter, The (See: Zar und Zimmermann)
Czar and the Shepherd, The 5-29-35
Czar I General 7-20-66
Czar Ivan, the Terrible 3-14-28
Czar of Broadway, The 7-02-30
Czar Wants to Sleep, The 12-18-34
Czardas Princess (See: Csardasfurstin, Die)
Czar's Courier, The (See: Kurier des Zaren)
Czas Przeszly 11-14-62
Czerwone I Zlote 12-31-69
Czifra Nyomorusag 10-26-38
Czikos Baroness 4-12-32
Czlowiek z Marmuru 6-01-77
Czontvary 2-27-80
Czudaki 12-18-74

D

Daag 2-20-77
D'Day the Sixth of June 5-30-56
DM-Killer 2-24-65
D.I., The 5-29-57
D.O.A. 12-28-49
D.T.'s, The (See: Myten)
D-Zug 13 Hat Verspaetung 6-02-31
Da Bancarella a Bancarotta (See: Peddlin' in Society)
Da Lang Tao Sha 1-10-79
Da Svante Forsvandt 1-14-76
Daag 2-20-77
Dablova Past 7-04-62
Dad and Dave Come to Town 11-2-38
Dad Rudd, M.P. 8-21-40
Dadathes, I 10-31-79
Daddies 2-14-24
Daddy 4-19-23
Daddy Long Legs (See: Vadertje Langbeen)
Daddy Long Legs 5-16-19
Daddy Long Legs 6-09-31
Daddy Long Legs 5-04-55
Daddy's Gone A-Hunting 2-25-25
Daddy's Gone A-Hunting 5-28-69
Daddy's War (See: Guerra de Papa, La)
Dad's Army 3-24-71
Dage I Min Fars Hus 4-24-68
Dagfin 3-23-27
Dagmar Is Where It's At (See: Nu Gaar Den Paa Dagmar)
Dagmar's Hot Pants, Inc. 10-27-71
Dagny 6-01-77
Dahana-Aranja 7-28-76
Dai Kyoju Gappa 4-19-67
Dai Majin Gyakushu 1-25-67
Dai Tatsumaki (See: Whirlwind)
Daibosatsu Toge (See: Sword of Doom, The)
Daisies (See: Sedmikrasky)
Daisy Kenyon 11-26-47
Daisy Miller 5-22-74
Daj Sto Das 8-27-80
Dakota 11-07-45
Dakota 10-16-74

Dakota Incident 7-25-56
Dakota Kid, The 7-04-51
Dakota Lil 2-01-50
Dal Sabato Al Lunedi 4-03-63
Daleks Invade Earth 2150 A.D. 8-10-66
Dalia and the Sailors 9-16-64
Dallas 11-22-50
Dalle Ardenne All'Inferno (See: Dirty Heroes)
Dalton Gang, The 11-30-49
Dalton Girls, The 12-11-57
Daltons Ride Again, The 11-21-45
Daluyong at Habagat 6-23-76
Dam, The (See: Damm, Der)
Dam Busters 6-01-55
Dama de Beirut, La 11-24-65
Dama de la Muerte, La 9-11-46
Dama de las Camelias, La 10-04-44
Dama Duende, La 6-27-45
Dama Na Kolejich 8-03-66
Dama s Sobatchkoi 5-25-60
Dama Spathi 1-11-67
Damaged Goods 9-26-14
Damaged Goods 10-01-15
Damaged Goods 6-23-37
Damaged Hearts 2-28-24
Damaged Lives 6-16-37
Damaged Love 1-28-31
Dame aux Camelias, La 12-04-34 and 3-27-35
Dame aux Camelias, La 12-30-53
Dame Care (See: Frau Sorge)
Dame Chance 10-27-26
Dame Dans l'Auto Avec des Lunettes et un Fusil, La 11-11-70
Dame de Chez Maxim 4-25-33
Dame de Pique, La 8-25-37
Dame de Pique, La 2-16-66
Dame in Schwarz, Die (See: Lady in Black)
Dame Mit der Maske, Die 11-14-28
Damernes Ven 9-10-69
Dames 8-21-34
Dames Ahoy 4-02-30
Dames du Bois du Boulogne, Les 3-11-64
Dames Get Along (See: Femmes S'en Balancent, Les)
Damien--Omen II 6-07-78
Damm, Der 10-28-64
Damn Citizen 1-22-58
Damn Yankees 9-17-58
Damnation Alley 10-26-77
Damned, The 6-25-69
Damned Be Those Who Cry 9-05-79
Damned Don't Cry, The 4-12-50
Damned Lovers, The (See: Amants Maudits, Les)
Damon and Pythias 12-11-14
Damon and Pythias 9-12-62
D'Amore Si Muore 2-14-73
Damsel in Distress 11-24-37
Damsel in Distress, A 10-17-19
Damsel of Bard (See: Destino, Il)
Dan 9-04-14
Dan Cetrnaesti 5-17-61 and 8-09-61
Dan Matthews 1-29-36
Dance, The (See: Gamberge, La or Salto)
Dance Band 6-12-35 and 1-08-36
Dance, Charlie, Dance 9-01-37
Dance Fever 9-26-28
Dance, Fools, Dance 3-25-31
Dance, Girl, Dance 10-31-33
Dance, Girl, Dance 8-28-40
Dance Goes On, The (See: Tanz Geht Weiter, Der)
Dance Hall 12-18-29
Dance Hall 7-23-41
Dance Hall 6-14-50
Dance Into Happiness (See: Tanz ins Gluck)
Dance Little Lady 7-28-54
Dance Madness 1-27-26
Dance Magic 7-13-27
Dance Music 9-04-35
Dance of Death (See: Paarunger)
Dance of Death, The 9-29-71
Dance of Fire (See: Danza de Fuego)
Dance of Life, The 8-21-29
Dance of the Herons (See: De Dans Van de Reiger)
Dance Program, A (See: Carnet de Bal, Un)
Dance Team 1-19-32
Dance with Me, Henry 12-12-56
Dance with Me into the Morning (See: Tanze Mit Mir in Den Morgen)
Dancer and the King, The 11-21-14
Dancer and the Worker, The (See: Bailarin y Trabajador)

Dancer of Barcelona 11-27-29
Dancer of Paris, The 3-31-26
Dancer of Sanssouci (See: Taenzerin von Sanssouci)
Dancers, The 1-07-25
Dancers, The 11-19-30
Dancers in the Dark 3-22-32
Dancer's Peril 3-02-17
Dances of the Various Nations 8-28-09
Dancin' Fool 5-07-20
Dancing at Hitler's Quarters (See: Dancing W Kwaterze Hitlera)
Dancing Cheat, The 4-16-24
Dancing Co-Ed 9-27-39
Dancing Days 12-29-26
Dancing Dynamite 8-25-31
Dancing Feet 4-01-36
Dancing Girl, The 1-22-15
Dancing Girl of Butte, The 1-15-10
Dancing Hawk, The (See: Tanczacy Jastrzab)
Dancing Heart, The 12-28-55
Dancing Hussar, The (See: Tanzhusar, Der)
Dancing in Manhattan 1-24-45
Dancing in the Dark 11-09-49
Dancing in the Rain (See: Ples U Kisi)
Dancing Lady 12-05-33
Dancing Man 7-24-34
Dancing Masters, The 10-27-43
Dancing Mothers 2-17-26
Dancing on a Dime 10-16-40
Dancing Pirate 6-24-36
Dancing Sweeties 8-20-30
Dancing the Sirtaki (See: Diplopenies)
Dancing W Kwaterze Hitlera 6-19-68
Dancing with Crime 7-02-47
Dancing Years, The 4-26-50
Dandy Dick 3-06-35
Dandy in Aspic, A 4-03-68
Dandy, The All American Girl 5-26-76
Danger Ahead 8-05-21
Danger Ahead 3-20-40
Danger: Diabolik 5-15-68
Danger Flight 12-06-39
Danger Game, The 4-26-18
Danger! Go Slow! 12-13-18
Danger in the Pacific 8-05-42
Danger Is a Woman 4-23-52
Danger Lights 11-19-30
Danger--Love at Work 12-01-37
Danger Mark, The 7-12-18
Danger of Escape (See: Fluchtgefahr)
Danger on the Air 7-20-38
Danger on Wheels 4-17-40
Danger Patrol 6-20-28
Danger Patrol 11-24-37
Danger Points 12-22-22
Danger Quest, The 4-07-26
Danger Rider 12-12-28
Danger Route 1-31-68
Danger Signal, The 11-19-15
Danger Signal, The 7-22-25
Danger Signal, The 11-14-45
Danger Street 9-26-28
Danger Street 2-26-47
Danger Trail, The 5-04-17
Danger Valley 6-03-21
Danger Valley 2-23-38
Danger Within 2-25-59
Danger Woman 7-10-46
Danger Zone 6-13-51
Danger Zone, The 1-17-19
Dangerous 1-01-36
Dangerous Adventure, A 9-15-37
Dangerous Affair, A 12-01-31
Dangerous Age 2-08-23
Dangerous Blonde 5-21-24
Dangerous Blondes 10-13-43
Dangerous Business 12-03-20
Dangerous Charter 9-26-62
Dangerous Corner 2-05-35
Dangerous Coward 10-08-24
Dangerous Crossing 7-22-53
Dangerous Crossing (See: Gleisdreick)
Dangerous Curve Ahead 10-07-21
Dangerous Curves 7-17-29
Dangerous Days 3-19-20
Dangerous Dude, A 8-25-26
Dangerous Exile 11-27-57
Dangerous Flirt 12-17-24
Dangerous Friends 11-10-26

Dangerous Game, A 12-22-22
Dangerous Game, A 3-05-41
Dangerous Girl (See: I Sao Untarai)
Dangerous Guests (See: Gefaehrliche Gaeste)
Dangerous Holiday 7-07-37
Dangerous Hour 12-20-23
Dangerous Hours 2-06-20
Dangerous Innocence 6-10-25
Dangerous Intrigue 1-22-36
Dangerous Intruder 11-21-45
Dangerous Journey 8-09-44
Dangerous Kisses (See: Farlige Kys)
Dangerous Lady 10-29-41
Dangerous Little Demon 3-24-22
Dangerous Love 8-25-22
Dangerous Maid 12-13-23
Dangerous Medicine 8-17-38
Dangerous Meetings, The (See: Liaisons Dangereuses, Les)
Dangerous Millions 12-04-46
Dangerous Mission 2-24-54
Dangerous Money 10-15-24
Dangerous Moonlight 7-30-41
Dangerous Nan McGrew 6-25-30
Dangerous Number 3-10-37
Dangerous Pair, A 9-11-09
Dangerous Paradise 11-12-20
Dangerous Paradise 2-19-30
Dangerous Partners 8-08-45
Dangerous Passage 12-20-44
Dangerous Paths 9-30-21
Dangerous Profession, A 10-26-49
Dangerous Secrets 10-26-38
Dangerous Summer (See: Farlig Sommer)
Dangerous Talent 3-05-20
Dangerous to Know 3-16-38
Dangerous to Men 6-11-20
Dangerous Toys 6-17-21
Dangerous Trails 3-26-24
Dangerous Venture 2-19-31
Dangerous Virtue 11-03-26
Dangerous Waters 1-29-36
Dangerous When Wet 5-13-53
Dangerous Woman 5-22-29
Dangerous Years 12-17-47
Dangerous Youth 6-11-58
Dangerously They Live 4-15-42
Dangerously Yours 2-28-33
Dangerously Yours 10-20-37
Dangers of the Arctic 7-12-32
Dangers of Youth (See: Peligros de Juventud)
Dani 6-30-65
Dani Od Snova 5-28-80
Daniel Boone 10-28-36
Daniel Boone, Trail Blazer 2-13-57
Danmark Er Lukket 10-15-80
D'Annunzio's Cabiria 5-15-14
Danny Boy 5-28-41
Danny Boy 3-27-46
Dans L'Ombre du Harem 4-25-28
Dans les Rues 8-30-39
Dans une Ile Perdue 2-18-31
Danse Macabre 8-06-58
Dante, Akta're Fore Hajen 1-10-79
Dante, Mind the Shark (See: Dante, Akta're Fore Hajen)
Dante's Inferno 10-01-24
Dante's Inferno 8-07-35
Danton 6-17-21
Danton 2-18-31 and 9-01-31
Danube Flows On, The (See: Valurile Dunarii)
Danza de Fuego 3-01-50
Dao Ruang 5-23-79
Daosawan Chan Rak Ter 4-09-75
Daosawan I Love You (See: Daosawan Chan Rak Ter)
Daphne, The (See: Jinchoge)
Daphne and the Pirate 2-18-16
Daphnis and Chloe '66 (See: Daphnis Ke Chloe '66)
Daphnis Ke Chloe '66 11-02-66
Daraku Suru Onna 8-02-67
Darby O'Gill and the Little People 4-29-59
Darby's Rangers 1-22-58
Darclee 5-24-61
Dare, The (See: O Desafio)
Dare Devil Circus Queen, The 7-02-15
Dare-Devil's Time (See: Hajducka Vremena)
Daredevil Drivers 3-02-38
Daredevil in the Castle 3-05-69
Daredevil Kate 8-25-16
Daredevil Rodman Law 5-22-14

Daredevils of Earth 1-22-36
Daredevils of the Clouds 7-21-48
Daredevils of the Red Circle 7-05-39
Daredevil's Reward 1-25-28
Daring Caballero, The 6-29-49 and 7-27-49
Daring Chances 9-03-24
Daring Chap in Crooked Tour, A (See: Toller Hecht auf Krummer
   Tour)
Daring Danger 6-28-32
Daring Daughters 3-28-33
Daring Deeds 1-25-28
Daring Game 5-01-68
Daring Love 9-17-24
Daring of Diana, The 7-21-16
Daring Years, The 3-19-24
Daring Young Man, The 7-24-35
Daring Youth 5-28-24
Dark, The 5-02-79
Dark Alleys 10-11-23
Dark Angel 9-11-35
Dark Angel, The 10-14-25
Dark at the Top of the Stairs, The 9-14-60
Dark Avenger 5-11-55
Dark City 8-09-50
Dark Command, The 4-10-40
Dark Corner, The 4-03-46
Dark Delusion 4-09-47
Dark Dreams 6-02-71
Dark Eyes 4-27-38
Dark Hazard 2-27-34
Dark Horse, The 6-14-32
Dark Horse, The 7-17-46
Dark Hour, The 8-05-36
Dark Intruder 7-28-65
Dark Is the Night 3-20-46
Dark Journey 2-17-37
Dark Lady (See: Satri Ti Lok Leum)
Dark Lantern, A 8-13-20
Dark Man, The 1-31-51
Dark Manhattan 3-17-37
Dark Mirror 5-14-20
Dark Mirror, The 10-02-46
Dark Mountain, The 9-06-44
Dark of the Sun (See: Mercenaries, The)
Dark Passage 9-03-47
Dark Past, The 12-29-48
Dark Places 5-22-74
Dark Purpose 1-29-64
Dark Rapture 10-12-38
Dark Red Roses 3-05-30
Dark River (See: Ciemna Rzeka)
Dark River 3-07-56
Dark Road, The 3-23-17
Dark Room of Damocles, The (See: Als Twee Druppels Water)
Dark Sands 8-24-38
Dark Secrets 1-25-23
Dark Side of Tomorrow 7-08-70
Dark Silence, The 9-22-16
Dark Skies 12-25-29
Dark Spring 10-21-70
Dark Stairways 7-16-24
Dark Star 5-01-74
Dark Star, The (See: Dunkle Stern, Der)
Dark Star 5-01-74
Dark Streets 10-09-29
Dark Streets of Cairo 12-04-40
Dark Sun (See: Temne Slunce)
Dark Swan, The 11-26-24
Dark Tower, The 6-23-43
Dark Valley (See: Valle Negro)
Dark-Veiled Bride, The (See: Kara Carsafli Gelin)
Dark Victory 3-15-39
Dark Waters 11-01-44
Darkened Rooms 12-18-29
Darkening Trail, The 6-11-15
Darker Than Amber 8-19-70
Darkest Russia 4-13-17
Darkness at Daytime (See: Nappali Sotetseg)
Darkness at Midday (See: Mahiru No Ankoku)
Darkness Fell on Gotenhafen (See: Nacht Fiel Ueber Gotenhafen)
Darkness to Dawn 5-01-14
Darktown Strutters 10-15-75
Darlin' Mine 9-03-20
Darling 7-21-65
Darling (See: Rakas)
Darling, How Could You 8-08-51
Darling Lili 6-24-70
Darling of New York 1-24-24
Darling of Paris, The 1-26-17

Darling of the Gods (See: Liebling der Goetter)
Darling of the Rich 1-12-23
Darned Loot (See: Maudite Galette, Une)
Daro' un Milione 4-07-37
Darshan 5-08-74
D'Artagnan 2-04-16
Darwin Adventure, The 10-11-72
Das Hab' Ich von Papa Gelernt 11-18-64
Dash of Courage, A 5-26-16
Dash to Death, A 9-04-09
Date by the Danube (See: Dunaparti Randevu)
Date with Judy, A 6-23-48
Date with the Falcon, A 11-12-41
Dateline Diamonds 4-06-66
Daughter Angele 8-30-18
Daughter-In-Law, The (See: Nevestka or Snaha)
Daughter of Darkness 2-04-48
Daughter of Destiny 1-04-18
Daughter of Destiny, A 7-18-28
Daughter of Devil Dan 7-22-21
Daughter of Dr. Jekyll 8-28-57
Daughter of Eve 10-03-19
Daughter of Israel 5-23-28
Daughter of Luxury 12-08-22
Daughter of MacGregor, The 9-22-16
Daughter of Maryland, A 11-09-17
Daughter of Mine 5-02-19
Daughter of Minister (See: Hija del Ministro, La)
Daughter of Rosie O'Grady 3-29-50
Daughter of Russia, A 4-09-15
Daughter of Shanghai 12-29-37
Daughter of the City, A 12-31-15
Daughter of the Day 9-01-16
Daughter of the Dragon 8-25-31
Daughter of the Gods, A 10-20-16
Daughter of the Hills 4-03-14
Daughter of the Jungle 3-16-49
Daughter of the Poor, A 3-23-17
Daughter of the Railroad Crossing Guard, The (See: Fille du
    Garde Barriere, La)
Daughter of the Regiment, The (See: Fille du Regiment, La)
Daughter of the Regiment, The 7-10-29
Daughter of the Sands 2-20-52
Daughter of the Sea, A 12-03-15
Daughter of the Sioux, A 1-08-10
Daughter of the South, A 10-18-18
Daughter of the Tong 8-16-39
Daughter of the West 3-30-49
Daughter of the Wolf, A 7-11-19
Daughter of Two Fathers 3-20-29
Daughter of Two Worlds 1-09-20
Daughter; Or, I, a Woman, Part III, The 9-23-70
Daughter Pays, The 12-24-20
Daughters Courageous 6-21-39
Daughters, Daughters (See: Abu el Banat)
Daughters of Darkness 5-26-71
Daughters of Desire 5-22-29
Daughters of Men 4-24-14
Daughters of Pleasure 7-23-24
Daughters of Poverty 12-18-09
Daughters of Satan 10-04-72
Daughters of the Rich 6-21-23
Daughters of Today 10-11-23 and 3-05-24
Daughters Who Pay 5-13-25
Dauphins, The (See: Delfini, I)
David 2-06-52
David 3-07-79
David and Bathsheba 8-15-51
David and Goliath 5-17-61
David and Lisa 9-05-62
David and the Ice Age (See: Wintermaerchen)
David Copperfield 11-08-23
David Copperfield 1-22-35
David Copperfield 1-14-70
David Garrick 8-14-14
David Garrick 5-05-16
David Golder 10-25-32
David Harding, Counterspy 5-24-50
David Harum 2-26-15
David Harum 3-06-34
David Holzman's Diary 11-01-67
Davy 1-22-58
Davy Crockett 8-04-16
Davy Crockett and the River Pirates 7-18-56
Davy Crockett, Indian Scout 1-11-50
Davy Crockett--King of the Wild Frontier 5-18-55
Dawn (See: Morgenrot)
Dawn 12-05-19

Dawn 3-14-28 and 6-06-28
Dawn 4-25-79
Dawn, The 7-26-67
Dawn at Socorro 7-14-54
Dawn Devils (See: Demons de L'Aube, Les)
Dawn Has Not Broken Yet (See: Aube N'Est Pas Encore Levee, L')
Dawn Maker, The 9-08-16
Dawn of a Tomorrow, The 3-26-24
Dawn of Freedom, The 3-19-10
Dawn of Islam, The (See: Aube d'Islam, L')
Dawn of Love, The 10-06-16
Dawn of Revenge 12-15-22
Dawn of the Dead 4-18-79
Dawn of the East 10-28-21
Dawn of Tomorrow, The 6-11-15
Dawn of Understanding, The 11-29-18
Dawn of Victory, The (See: I Haravgui Tis Nikis)
Dawn on the Great Divide 12-16-42
Dawn on the Third Day (See: A L'Aube Du Troisieme Jour)
Dawn over Ireland 2-23-38
Dawn Patrol 12-14-38
Dawn Patrol, The 7-16-30
Dawn Rider 10-16-35
Dawn to Dawn 1-09-34
Dawn Trail, The 1-07-31
Dawning Nation (See: Yowake No Kuni)
Day After Day 11-10-43
Day and the Hour, The (See: Jour et L'Heure, Le)
Day at the Beach, A 5-13-70
Day at the Races, A 6-23-37
Day at the Sea Shore, A 2-15-08
Day by Day, Desperately (See: Giorno per Giorno, Disperatamente)
Day Does Not Die (See: Ktory Neumrie, Den)
Day Dream (See: Hakujitsumu)
Day Dreams 1-17-19
Day Elvis Came to Bremerhaven, The (See: Tag, An Dem Elvis Nach
    Bremerhaven Kam, Der)
Day for My Love (See: Pro Mou Lasku, Den)
Day for Night (See: Nuit Americaine, La)
Day in a Solar, A (See: Dia en el Solar, Un)
Day in Congress, A 5-31-50
Day in Moscow, A 12-25-57
Day in Soviet Russia, A 9-03-41 and 10-29-41
Day in the Death of Joe Egg, A 5-17-72
Day of Anger 11-05-69
Day of Days, The 1-30-14
Day of Faith 11-29-23
Day of Fear 6-12-57
Day of Fury, A 4-11-56
Day of Glory, The (See: Jour de Gloire, Le)
Day of Happiness, A (See: Den Stchastia)
Day of Reckoning, A 6-25-15
Day of Reckoning 11-07-33
Day of the Animals 6-08-77
Day of the Badman 1-15-58
Day of the Dolphin, The 12-19-73
Day of the Evil Gun 3-06-68
Day of the Jackal, The 5-16-73
Day of the Locust, The 4-30-75
Day of the Outlaw 9-16-59
Day of the Owl (See: Giorno della Civetta, Il)
Day of the Triffids, The 5-01-73
Day of the Vistula, The (See: Dzien Wisly)
Day of the Woman 11-22-78
Day of Triumph 12-01-54
Day of Wind (See: Tuulinen Paiva)
Day of Wrath 4-28-48
Day Shall Dawn (See: Jago Hua Savera)
Day Star (See: Dnevnye Zvezdy 9-03-69)
Day the Bookies Wept, The 9-20-39
Day the Earth Caught Fire, The 11-22-61
Day the Earth Stood Still, The 9-05-51
Day the Fish Came Out, The 10-04-67
Day the Tree Blooms, The (See: Kde Reky Maji Slunce)
Day the World Ended, The 1-11-56
Day They Robbed the Bank of England, The 5-25-60
Day Time Ended, The 11-19-80
Day to Remember, A 11-18-53
Day Will Dawn, The 6-03-42
Day You Love Me, The (See: Dia Que Me Quieras, El)
Daybreak 1-11-18
Daybreak 6-02-31
Daybreak (See: Jour Se Leve, Le)
Daybreak 6-02-48
Daybreak in Udi 6-07-50
Daydreamer, The 7-13-66
Dayereh Cycle 11-16-77
Days and Nights 5-01-46

Days and Nights in the Forest (See: Aranyer Din Ratri)
Days Are Numbered, The (See: Giorni Contati, I)
Days Are Passing, The (See: Zemaljski Dani Teku)
Days in My Father's House (See: Dage I Min Fars Hus)
Days of Betrayal (See: Dny Zrady)
Days of Dreams (See: Dani Od Snova)
Days of Freedom 1-29-36
Days of Glory 5-03-44
Days of Heaven 9-13-78
Days of Jesse James 12-27-39
Days of Love (See: Giorni d'Amore or Dias Del Amor, Los)
Days of Old Cheyenne 6-23-43
Days of St. Patrick 1-14-21
Days of the Past (See: Dias del Pasado, Los)
Days of 36 (See: Imeres Tou 36)
Days of Thrills and Laughter 3-15-61
Days of Water, The (See: Dias del Agua, Los)
Days of Wine and Roses 12-05-62
Day's Pleasure, A 12-12-19
Daytime Assailant (See: Hakuchi No Torima)
Day-Time Wife 11-15-39
Daytime Wives 8-30-23
Dayton's Devils 10-09-68
De Blanke Slavin 12-24-69
De Dans Van de Reiger 2-16-66
De Espaldas a la Puerta 12-02-59
De 5 Og Spionerne 10-29-69
De Fresa, Limon y Menta 9-25-77
De L'Amour 3-10-65
De la Part des Copains 1-31-71
De la Sierra al Valle 2-01-39
De Loteling 1-30-74
De Luxe Annie 5-24-18
De Man die Zijin Haar Kort Liet Knippen 9-28-66
De Mayerling A Serajevo 5-22-40
De 141 Dage 9-14-77
De Plaats van de Vreemdeling (See: Alien, The)
De Roede Heste 1-01-69
De Sade 10-01-69
De Tal Palo, Tal Astilla 11-16-60
De Utjentes Marked 10-15-69
De Verloedering Van de Swieps 10-25-67
De Witte Van Sichem 6-25-80
De Yongs, The 9-22-76
Deacon's Daughter, The 1-15-10
Dead and the Alive, The (See: Juk Un Ja San Ja)
Dead Are Alive, The 7-12-72
Dead Birds 3-03-65
Dead Don't Dream, The 8-18-48
Dead End 8-04-37
Dead End, A (See: Peruvaziambalan)
Dead End, The (See: Bon Bast)
Dead Game 5-17-23
Dead Heat on a Merry-Go-Round 10-12-66
Dead Landscape (See: Holt Videk)
Dead Line 5-07-20
Dead Man's Curve 4-18-28
Dead Man's Eyes 9-13-44
Dead Man's Float 8-20-80
Dead Man's Gulch 3-17-43
Dead Man's Shoes 7-26-39
Dead March, The 8-25-37
Dead Men Tell 3-26-41
Dead Men Tell No Tales 7-26-39
Dead Men Walk 4-07-43
Dead of Night 9-19-45 and 7-03-46
Dead of Summer (See: Ondata Di Calore)
Dead One, The (See: Muerto, El)
Dead One in the Thames River, The (See: Tote Aus der Themse, Die)
Dead One of Beverly Hills, The (See: Tote von Beverly Hills, Die)
Dead or Alive (See: Elve Vagy Halva)
Dead Pay the Price for Death, The (See: Tsenu Smerti Sprosi u Miortvykh)
Dead Pigeon on Beethoven Street 11-29-72
Dead Reckoning 1-29-47
Dead Ringer 1-29-64
Dead Run 5-14-69
Dead Season of Loves, The (See: Morte-Saison des Amours, La)
Dead Shot Baker 10-12-17
Dead Times (See: Temps Morts)
Dead Woman's Hand, The (See: Mano Della Morta, La)
Deadfall 9-11-68
Deadlier Sex 3-19-20
Deadlier Than the Male 1-25-67
Deadliest Sin, The 10-17-56
Deadline, The 1-26-32

Deadline at Dawn 2-13-46
Deadline at 11 3-12-20
Deadline for Murder 6-19-46
Deadline--USA 3-12-52
Deadlock (See: Sikator)
Deadlock 10-21-70
Deadly Affair, The 2-01-67
Deadly Bees, The 1-25-67
Deadly Companions, The 6-07-61
Deadly Cruelty (See: Crueldade Mortal)
Deadly Duo 1-31-62
Deadly Fathoms 5-23-73
Deadly Females, The 12-01-76
Deadly Hero 8-11-76
Deadly Is the Female 11-02-49
Deadly Mantis, The 3-27-57
Deadly Shots on Broadway (See: Todesschuesse Am Broadway)
Deadly Spring (See: Halalos Tavasz)
Deadly Trackers, The 11-28-73
Deadwood Coach, The 1-21-25
Deaf Smith and Johnny Ears 6-06-73
Deal 2-01-78
Dealers in Death 12-18-34
Dealing: Or the Berkeley-to-Boston Forty-Brick Lost-Bag Blues 1-26-72
Dear Augustin, The (See: Liebe Augustin, Der)
Dear Boys 5-28-80
Dear Brat 4-25-51
Dear Brigitte 2-03-65
Dear Caroline (See: Caroline Cherie)
Dear Comrades (See: Queridos Companeros)
Dear Family (See: Liebe Familie, Die)
Dear Family, The 7-24-63
Dear Fatherland, Be at Peace (See: Lieb Vaterland, Magst Ruhig Sein)
Dear Friends (See: Queridas Amigas)
Dear Heart 12-02-64
Dear Irene (See: Draga Irena or Kaere Irene)
Dear John (See: Kare John)
Dear Louise (See: Chere Louise)
Dear Michael (See: Caro Michele)
Dear Mr. Prohack 9-21-49
Dear Mother, I'm All Right (See: Liebe Mutter, Mir Geht Gut)
Dear Murderer 6-04-47
Dear Octopus 9-15-43
Dear Papa (See: Caro Papa)
Dear Ruth 5-28-47
Dear Summer Sister (See: Natsu No Omoto)
Dear Wife (See: Cara Sposa)
Dear Wife 11-09-49
Dearest Executioners (See: Queridisimos Verdugos)
Dearie 7-06-27
Death, The (See: A Falecida)
Death and Homicide (See: Mord Und Totschlag)
Death at a Broadcast 10-22-41
Death at an Old Mansion (See: Honjin Satsujin Jiken)
Death at Dawn (See: Muerte Al Amanecer)
Death at Work (See: Morte al Lavoro, La)
Death Called Engelchen 7-24-63
Death Collector 2-02-77
Death Comes at High Noon (See: Doeden Kommer Til Middag)
Death Dance, The 8-02-18
Death Disturbs (See: Mort Trouble, La)
Death Duel 7-27-77
Death Flies East 3-06-35
Death From a Distance 1-08-36
Death Game 4-27-77
Death Goes North 7-26-39
Death Has No Friends 11-18-70
Death Has No Mercy 7-25-79
Death in Small Doses 8-28-57
Death in the Saddle (See: Smrt V Sedle)
Death in the Sky 2-17-37
Death in This Garden (See: Mort En Ce Jardin, La)
Death in Venice 4-07-71
Death Is My Trade 7-27-77
Death Kiss 1-31-33
Death Leap 5-10-23
Death Magazine or How to Become a Flowerpot (See: Todesmagazin oder Wie Werde Ich ein Blumentopf?)
Death of a Beauty (See: Mort de Belle, La)
Death of a Bureaucrat (See: Muerte de un Burocrata, La)
Death of a Cameraman (See: Morte di un Operatore)
Death of a Champion 8-30-39
Death of a Corrupt Man (See: Mort d'un Pourri)
Death of a Cyclist (See: Muerte de un Ciclista)
Death of a Dream 7-19-50
Death of a Friend (See: Morte di un Amico)

Death of a Guide (See: Mort D'Un Guide)
Death of a Gunfighter 4-30-69
Death of a Jew (See: Sabra)
Death of a Killer (See: Mort D'un Tueur, La)
Death of a Lumberjack, The (See: Mort d'un Bucheron, La)
Death of a Nun (See: Dood Van Efn Non)
Death of a Salesman 12-12-51
Death of a Scoundrel 10-31-56
Death of Alexandros, The (See: O Thanatos Tou Alexandrou)
Death of Ipu, The (See: Moartea Lui Ipu)
Death of Tarzan, The 7-10-68
Death of the Fisherman Marc Leblanc, The (See: Tod des Fischers
    Marc Leblanc, Der)
Death of the Flea Circus Owner or Ottocaro Weiss Modifies His
    Signature, The (See: Tod des Flohzirkusdirektors Oder
    Ottocaro Weiss Reformiert Seine Firma, Der)
Death of the President (See: Zmierc Prezydenta)
Death of the Water Carrier (See: Essakamat)
Death on the Diamond 9-25-34
Death on the Nile 9-27-78
Death on the Set 9-16-36
Death or Freedom (See: Tod Oder Freiheit)
Death Play 9-08-76
Death Race 2000 5-07-75
Death Rides a Horse 7-16-69
Death Rides the Plains 1-12-44
Death Rides the Range 1-17-40
Death Ship 4-16-80
Death Takes a Holiday 2-27-34
Death Took Place Last Night (See: Morte Risale a Leri Sera, La
Death Valley 7-27-27
Death Valley Gunfighter 4-20-49
Death Valley Manhunt 11-17-43
Death Valley Outlaws 10-01-41
Death Valley Rangers 2-02-44
Death Weekend 10-06-76
Death, Where Is Your Victory? (See: Mort, Ou Est Ta Victoire?)
Death Wish 7-24-74
Deathcheaters 12-22-76
Deathsport 4-26-78
Deathstyles 11-24-71
Deathwatch 3-23-66
Deathwatch 2-06-80
Debt, The 4-27-17
Debut, The (See: Naciala)
Debutantes en el Amor, Los 10-01-69
Decade Prodigieuse, La 12-15-71
Decameron, The (See: Decamerone, Il)
Decameron Nights 9-17-24 and 5-30-28
Decameron Nights 1-21-53
Decamerone, Il 7-07-71
Deceived Women (See: Mujeres Enganadas)
Deceiver, The 11-24-31
Deceivers, The (See: Zozos, Les)
Decent Life, A (See: Ett Anstaendigt Liv)
Deception 4-22-21
Deception 1-17-33
Deception 10-23-46
Decima Vittima, La (See: Tenth Victim, The)
Decision Against Time 7-10-57
Decision at Sundown 11-06-57
Decision Before Dawn 12-19-51
Decision of Christopher Blake, The 12-01-48
Decks Ran Red, The 9-24-58
Declasse 3-25-25
Decline and Fall 7-17-68
Decorated by the Emperor 1-22-10
Decoy 11-06-46
Decoy, The 7-21-16
Dedee 4-13-49
Dedee D'Anvers (See: Dedee)
Dedicated To ... (See: Dedicatoria)
Dedicatoria 5-28-80
Dee Kraft Phun Leben 5-04-38
Deemster, The 2-16-17
Deep, The 6-22-77
Deep Blue Sea, The 8-31-55
Deep End 9-16-70
Deep in My Heart 12-01-54
Deep in the Heart of Texas 9-09-42
Deep Jaws 5-05-76
Deep Purple, The 1-08-15
Deep Purple 5-07-20
Deep Red 6-23-76
Deep Six 1-01-58
Deep Sleep 12-26-73
Deep Throat 6-28-72

Deep Throat--Part II 2-13-74
Deep Thrust--The Hand of Death 5-23-73
Deep Valley 7-30-47
Deep Waters 6-30-48
Deer, The (See: Gavaznha)
Deer Hunter, The 11-29-78
Deer Hunting in the Celebos Islands 9-10-10
Deerslayer 11-10-43
Deerslayer, The 9-18-57
Deewar 1-19-77
Defeat, The (See: A Derrota)
Defeated Victor, The (See: Uomo Facile, Un)
Defector, The 11-16-66
Defendant (See: Obzalovany)
Defenders of the Law 5-27-31
Defense de Savoir 11-28-73
Defense or Tribute 1-28-16
Defense Rests, The 8-21-34
Defense Takes the Floor, The (See: Slovo Dlia Zaschity)
Defiance 11-27-74
Defiance 3-12-80
Defiant Delta (See: Prkosna Delta)
Defiant Ones, The 8-06-58
Defroque, Le 3-17-54
Defying Destiny 1-10-24
Defying the Law 6-11-24
Degree of Murder, A (See: Mord und Totschlag)
Dein Kind, Das Unbekannte Wesen 10-14-70
Deine Frau--Das Unbekannte Wesen 3-12-69
Deja Que los Perros Ladren 9-27-61
Deja S'Envole la Fleur Maigre 5-15-63
Dejeuner Sur L'Herbe, Le 12-02-59
Del Amor y Otras Soledades 9-03-69
Del Brazo y Por la Calle 9-14-66
Del Rosa ... Al Amarillo 4-28-65
Delay in Marienborn 7-03-63
Delfini, I 9-07-60
Delia's Secret 5-22-29
Delicate Balance, A 10-31-73
Delicate Delinquent, The 5-29-57
Deliciosamente Amoral 3-19-69
Delicious 12-29-31
Delicious Little Devil, The 4-18-19 and 4-25-19
Deliciously Amoral (See: Deliciosamente Amoral)
Delightful Rogue, The 10-23-29
Delightfully Dangerous 2-28-45
Delije 8-14-68
Delinquent Daughters 11-08-44
Delinquent Parents 7-06-38
Delinquents, The (See: Golfos, Los)
Delinquents, The 2-27-57
Delirium 7-25-79
Delit de Fuite 4-29-59
Delitto A Porta Romana 12-17-80
Delitto D'Amore 5-29-74
Delitto di Giovanni Episcopo, Il (See: Flesh Will Surrender, The)
Delitto di Mastrovanni, El 7-31-35
Delitto Matteotti, Il 9-05-73
Deliver Us From Evil (See: Szabadits Meg A Gonosztol)
Deliverance 8-22-19
Deliverance 7-19-72
Delka Polibku Devadesat 4-13-66
Delphine 3-05-69
Deluge 10-10-33
Deluge, The (See: Potop)
Delusions of Grandeur (See: Folie des Grandeurs, La)
Demain, la Chine 10-12-66
Demain les Momes 11-10-76
Demanty Noci 8-05-64
Dementia 12-28-55
Demetrius and the Gladiators 6-02-54
Demi-Bride, The 3-23-27
Demi-Paradise, The 12-08-43
Demise of Herman Durer, The 3-26-80
Democracy 9-03-20
Demoiselles de Rochefort, Les 3-01-67
Demolition Squad, The (See: Diverzanti)
Demon, The (See: Demonio, Il or Onibaba)
Demon Barber of Fleet Street, The 10-11-39
Demon in the Blood (See: Demonio en la Sangre, El)
Demon Lover Diary 2-13-80
Demon of Steppes 1-22-30
Demon Pond 3-26-80
Demon Seed 3-70-77
Demoniaque, Le 2-14-68
Demonic One, The (See: Demoniaque, Le)
Demonio, Il 9-04-63
Demonio del Oro, El 12-30-42

Demonio en la Sangre, El 4-22-64
Demons (See: Shura)
Demons de L'Aube, Les 5-08-46
Demons de Minuit, Les 2-07-62
Demons du Midi 2-06-80
Demons of the South (See: Demons du Midi)
Demonstrator 10-20-71
Dempsey-Firpo Fight 9-20-23
Dempsey-Sharkey Fight 7-27-27
Den Dobbelte Mand 4-07-76
Den'en Ni Shisu 5-14-75
Den Enes Doed... 6-04-80
Den Stchastia 8-05-64
Dendang Perantau 7-25-79
Denial, The 3-11-25
Denize Inen Sokak 8-10-60
Denmark Closed Down (See: Danmark Er Lukket)
Denonciation, La 5-02-62
Dente Per Dente 1-02-52
Dentelliere, La 5-25-77
Dentist in the Chair 8-24-60
Denunciation, The (See: Denonciation, La)
Denver and the Rio Grande 3-26-52
Denver Dude, The 5-04-27
Deo Gratias 7-10-63
Depart, Le 5-17-67
Department Store (See: Grandi Magazzini)
Departure (See: Partire or Depart, Le)
Departure from the Clouds (See: Abschied Von Den Wolken)
Dependent, The (See: Dependiente, El)
Dependiente, El 7-31-68
Deported 10-18-50
Deps 8-21-74
Depth of the Furrow 6-23-22
Depths, The (See: Abysses, Les)
Depths of Passion (See: Abismos de Pasion)
Deputy from the Baltic 4-07-37
Deputy Marshal 10-12-49
Deranged 2-27-74
Derby 11-04-70
Derby Day 6-18-52
Derby Race 9-14-07
Derecho de Nacer 5-19-71
Derecho de Nacer, El 9-17-52
Derelict 11-26-19 (Also See: Desempare)
Derelict, The 4-27-17
Derive, Le 10-23-63
Dernier Amant Romantique, Le 5-10-78
Dernier Baiser, Le 6-15-77
Dernier Choc, Le 5-31-32
Dernier Domicile Connu 3-04-70
Dernier Homme, Le 4-09-69
Dernier Melodrame, Le 12-17-80
Dernier Metro, Le 9-17-80
Dernier Milliardaire 11-06-34 and 11-06-35
Dernier Saut, Le 5-06-70
Dernier Tournant, Le 6-14-39
Derniere Berceuse, La 6-30-31
Derniere Femme, La 4-07-76
Derniere Jeunesse 12-13-39
Derniere Sortie avant Roissy 9-07-77
Derniers Jours de Pompei, Les 5-03-50
Derobade, Le 12-12-79
Derriere la Facade 5-03-39
Dersu Uzala 8-13-75
Dervis I Smrt 8-21-74
Dervish and Death, The (See: Dervis I Smrt)
Deryne, Hol Van? 5-26-76
Des Enfants Gates 9-14-77
Des Femmes Disparaissent 8-19-59
Des Garcons et des Filles 10-18-67
Des Gens Sans Importance 2-29-56
Des Journees Entieres dans les Arbres 10-20-76
Des Morts 2-07-79
Des Pissenlits Par la Racine 6-17-64
Desafios, Los 6-10-70
Desarraigados, Los 9-23-59 and 3-09-60
Desarroi 1-15-47
Descent into Hell (See: Caidos en el Infierno)
Description D'Un Combat 6-28-61
Description of an Island (See: Beschreibung Einer Insel)
Desde El Abismo 4-23-80
Dese Nise 7-28-76
Desempare 4-29-31
Desencanto, El 10-20-76
Desert Bandit 5-28-41
Desert Blossoms 12-16-21
Desert Bride, The 5-23-28
Desert de Pigalle, Le 6-18-58

Desert des Tartares, Le 12-29-76
Desert Desperadoes 7-22-59
Desert Driven 6-14-23
Desert Flower, The 6-03-25
Desert Fox, The 10-03-51
Desert Fury 7-30-47
Desert Gold 11-07-19
Desert Gold 3-24-26
Desert Gold 5-13-36
Desert Hawk 8-09-50
Desert Hell 6-18-58
Desert Island (See: Dans Une Ile Perdue)
Desert Law 9-27-18
Desert Legion 3-18-53
Desert Love 5-28-20
Desert Lovers (See: Amantes del Desierto, Los)
Desert Man, The 4-20-17
Desert Mice 1-13-60
Desert Nights 5-08-29
Desert of Lost Men 12-12-51
Desert of the Tartars, The (See: Desert des Tartares, Le)
Desert Outlaw, The 11-05-24
Desert Passage 5-14-52
Desert People 9-13-67
Desert Phantom 8-18-37
Desert Pirate, The 1-25-28
Desert Pursuit 7-09-52
Desert Rats, The 5-13-53
Desert Rider 7-10-29
Desert Sands 8-10-55
Desert Song, The 4-10-29
Desert Song, The 12-15-43
Desert Song, The 4-29-53
Desert Tigers (See: Tigres Del Desierto, Los)
Desert Trail 8-21-35
Desert Valley 12-29-26
Desert Vengeance 3-11-31
Desert Victory 3-31-43
Desert Vigilante 8-24-49
Desert Wooing, A 7-05-18
Deserted at the Altar 9-29-22
Deserted Piazza, The (See: Piazza Vuota, La)
Deserter, The (See: Deserteur, Le or Zbehove)
Deserter, The 6-23-16
Deserter, The 4-07-71
Deserter USA 5-14-69
Deserters and the Nomads, The (See: Zbehove a Tulaci)
Deserteur, Le 5-03-39
Deserto Rosso, Il 9-16-64
Desertoren 5-12-71
Desert's Price, The 2-03-26
Deshonra 7-30-52
Desideria, La Vita Interiore 10-15-80
Desiderio 5-08-46
Desiderium (See: Sutedelan)
Design for Death 1-28-48
Design for Living 11-28-33
Design for Murder 12-04-40
Design for Scandal 11-12-41
Designing Woman 3-13-57
Desir et L'Amour, Le 7-30-52
Desirable 9-18-34
Desire (See: Touha; Desiderio or Begar)
Desire 10-11-23
Desire 4-15-36
Desire for Love (See: Ai No Kawaki)
Desire in the Dust 9-14-60
Desire Me 10-01-47
Desire of the Moth, The 10-26-17
Desire, the Interior Life (See: Desideria, La Vita Interiore)
Desire Under the Elms 3-12-58
Desired Woman, The 3-08-18
Desired Woman, The 8-31-27
Desiree 11-17-54
Desk Set 5-15-57
Desordre a Vingt Ans, Le 10-04-67
Desordre et la Nuit, Le 7-16-58
Despair 5-24-78
Despatch Bearer, The 12-07-07
Desperado, El (See: Dirty Outlaws, The)
Desperado, The 6-23-54
Desperado of Panama, The 11-28-14
Desperadoes, The 3-17-43
Desperadoes Are in Town, The 11-14-56
Desperadoes of Dodge City 9-08-48
Desperadoes Outpost 10-08-52
Desperados, The 4-30-69

Desperate 5-14-47
Desperate Adventure, A 8-10-38
Desperate Cargo 10-08-41
Desperate Chance 4-11-28
Desperate Characters 7-14-71
Desperate Game 4-14-26
Desperate Hero, The 6-18-20
Desperate Hours 9-14-55
Desperate Journey 8-19-42
Desperate Living 10-26-77
Desperate Moment 3-25-53
Desperate Moment, A 1-27-26
Desperate Ones, The 4-03-68
Desperate Search 11-26-52
Desperate Trails 6-24-21
Desperate Trails 8-16-39
Desperate Women, The 4-14-54
Despinia Eton 39 (See: Mademoiselle--Age 39)
Despoiler, The 12-31-15
Despoiler, The 3-10-16
Despues de la Tormenta 9-14-55 and 12-28-55
Despues del Diluvio 9-18-68
Destination Big House 6-14-50
Destination Gobi 2-18-53
Destination Inner Space 6-22-66
Destination Moon 6-28-50
Destination Murder 6-07-50
Destination 60,000 7-10-57
Destination Tokyo 12-22-43
Destination Unknown 4-11-33
Destination Unknown 10-07-42
Destinees 2-10-54
Destinies (See: Sudbine)
Destino, Il 2-16-38
Destiny 4-09-15
Destiny 12-13-44
Destiny (See: Rekava or Elokuu)
Destiny (See: Taqdeer)
Destiny in Trouble (See: O Destino Em Apuros)
Destiny of a Man (See: Sudba Czelovieka)
Destiny of Russia 5-11-27
Destiny, or The Soul of a Woman (See: Soul of a Woman, The)
Destiny's Isle 9-01-22
Destiny's Skein 8-06-15
Destiny's Toy 6-30-16
Destitute Mary (See: Marie La Misere)
Destroy All Monsters 6-04-69
Destroy, She Said 10-04-69
Destroyed Youths (See: Tuhottu Nuoruns)
Destroyer 8-18-43
Destroyers, The 6-09-16
Destroying Angel, The 12-10-15
Destruction 12-31-15
Destructors, The 2-14-68
Destructors, The 7-31-74
Destry 12-08-54
Destry Rides Again 6-21-32
Destry Rides Again 12-06-39
Det Andre Skiftet 11-12-80
Det Ar Min Modell 10-30-46
Det Brinner en Eld 5-30-45
Det Er Ikke Appelsiner, Det Er Heste 7-26-67
Det er Nat Med Fru Knudsen 2-24-71
Det Glada Kalaset 10-30-46
Det Gode Og det Onde 4-09-75
Det Kom en Gest 11-26-47
Det Regnar Pa Var Karlek 1-08-47
Det Sista Aventyret 10-08-75
Det Stoerste Spillet 10-16-68
Det Stora Aventyret 4-14-54
Det Tossede Paradis (See: Crazy Paradise)
Det Vackraste Pa Jorden 10-22-47
Detective, The 5-29-68
Detective, Un (See: Detective Belli)
Detective Belli 12-23-70
Detective Craig's Coup 8-07-14
Detective Kitty O'Day 5-24-44
Detective Riccardo Finizi (See: Agenzia Riccardo Finzi ... Prac-
   ticamente Detective
Detective Story 9-26-51
Detective Swift 1-29-15
Detectives 7-25-28
Detenuto in Attesa di Giudizio 12-01-71
Determination 3-10-22
Detour (See: Nachts Auf Den Strassen)
Detour 1-23-46
Detour, The 7-19-67

Detras De Esa Puerta (See: Political Asylum)
Detroit 9000 8-22-73
Detroit-Pittsburgh Baseball Series 10-23-09
Detruire, Dit-Elle (See: Destroy, She Said)
Detstvo Ivana 7-04-62
Dette Menneskebarn 3-05-47
Deuce Duncan 11-22-18
Deuce of Spades 7-28-22
Deus e o Diabo Na Terr Do Sol 5-20-64
Deutscher Fruehling 4-09-80
Deutschland, Bleiche Mutter 3-05-80
Deutschland Dada 10-29-69
Deutschland Gruesst Kennedy 10-07-64
Deutschland im Herbst 3-29-78
Deux Amis Silencieux 6-09-71
Deux Anglaises et le Continent, Les 12-15-71
Deux Crimes D'Amour 3-25-53
Deux Femmes en Or 6-09-71
Deux Heures a Tuer 2-02-66
Deux Hommes Dans la Ville 11-14-73
Deux Hommes Dans Manhattan 11-04-59
Deux Lions Au Soleil 9-03-80
Deux Memoires, Les 3-06-74
Deux Orphelines, Les 3-28-33 and 2-13-34
Deux ou Trois Choses Que Je Sais d'Elle 4-05-67
Deux Saisons de la Vie, Les 9-06-72
Deux Sous de Violettes 12-05-51
Deux Super Flics 2-08-78
Deux Verites, Les 7-30-52
Deuxieme Bureau 10-23-35
Deuxieme Souffle, Le 11-09-66
Devastation (See: Pimeanpirtin Havitys)
Devdas 8-01-56
Deveti Krug 5-18-60
Devi 5-23-62
Deviations on Gratifications 3-24-71
Devil, The (See: Diavolo, Il)
Devil, The 1-21-21
Devil and Dan'l Webster, The (See: Here Is a Man)
Devil and Miss Jones, The 4-09-41
Devil and Mr. Jones, The 3-19-75
Devil and the Deep, The 8-23-32
Devil and the Pulpit, The (See: Chair et le Diable, La)
Devil and the Ten Commandments, The (See: Diable et les Dix
   Commandments, Le)
Devil at 4 O'Clock 9-27-61
Devil Bat, The 1-22-41
Devil Bat's Daughter 4-10-46
Devil by the Tail, The (See: Diable Par le Queue, Le)
Devil Commands, The 2-19-41
Devil Dancer, The 11-09-27
Devil Dodger, The 10-05-17
Devil Dogs 8-29-28
Devil Dogs of the Air 2-12-35
Devil Doll, The 8-12-36
Devil Doll, The 6-24-64
Devil Goddess 8-31-55
Devil Horse, The 6-09-26
Devil in Love, The 5-22-68
Devil in Miss Jones, The 2-21-73
Devil in Silk (See: Teufel in Seide)
Devil in the Box, The (See: Diable Dans la Boite, Le)
Devil in the Heart, The (See: Diable au Coeur, Le)
Devil Is a Sissy 10-21-36
Devil Is a Woman, The 5-08-35
Devil Is Beating His Wife, The (See: Veri Az Ordog A Feleseget)
Devil Is Driving, The 12-20-32
Devil Is Driving, The 7-07-37
Devil Makes Three, The 8-13-52
Devil May Care 12-25-29
Devil May Well Laugh, The (See: Teufel Hat Gut Lachen, Der)
Devil of a Woman, A (See: Weibsteufel, Der)
Devil on Horseback, The 3-23-54
Devil Pays, The 4-05-32
Devil Played the Balalaika, The (See: Teufel Spielte Balalaika,
   Der)
Devil Probably, The (See: Diable Probablement, Le)
Devil Queen, The (See: Rainha Diaba, A)
Devil Riders, The 2-09-44
Devil Rides Out, The 6-12-68
Devil Ship 12-10-47
Devil-Ship Pirates, The 3-25-64
Devil Stone, The 12-21-17
Devil, the Servant, and the Man, The 2-05-10
Devil Thumbs a Ride, The 2-26-47
Devil Tiger 2-13-34
Devil to Pay, The 12-10-20
Devil to Pay, The 12-24-30
Devil with Hitler, The 10-21-42
Devil with Women, A 10-22-30

Diavolo Bianco, Il 2-18-48
Diavolo Innamorato (See: Devil in Love, The)
Dice of Destiny 12-17-20
Dice of Fate 9-18-29
Diciottenni, Le 4-11-56
Dick Tracy 12-19-45
Dick Tracy Meets Gruesome 10-01-47
Dick Tracy Returns 8-03-38
Dick Tracy vs. Cueball 11-06-46
Dick Tracy's Dilemma 5-14-47
Dick Turpin 9-29-22
Dick Turpin 1-28-25
Dick Turpin 12-05-33
Dictator, The 6-25-15
Dictator, The 7-07-22
Dictator, The 2-12-35
Did It Ever Happen to You? 1-12-17
Did Somebody Laugh? (See: Hoer, Var Der Ikke En, Som Lo?)
Did You Hear the One About the Traveling Saleslady? 2-21-68
Die, Die, My Darling 4-28-65
Die in Madrid (See: Mourir A Madrid)
Die Laughing 3-26-80
Die, Monster, Die 11-24-65
Die of Love (See: Mourir d'Aimer)
Die ... We'll Do the Rest (See: Mourez ... Nous Ferons le Reste)
Diego Corrientes 10-21-59
Diener Lassen Bitten 9-09-36
Dieppe Automobile Race 9-28-07
Dieu a Besoin des Hommes 10-11-50
Dieu a Choisi Paris 7-16-69
Dieu le Veut 12-15-76
Diez Fusiles Esperan 6-24-59 and 7-15-59
16 Anos 6-16-43
Difendo il Mio Amore 10-03-56
Different Moralities (See: Zweierlei Moral)
Different Roads (See: Var Sin Vag)
Different Story, A 4-19-78
Different Trades in Bombay 10-08-10
Difficult Bachelor, A (See: Soltero Dificil, Un)
Difficult Life, A (See: Vita Difficile, Una)
Difficult Love (See: Amore Difficile, L')
Difficult Transport, A (See: Nje Udhetimi I Veshtire)
Difficult Years 8-23-50
Dig That Uranium 2-22-56
Digan Lo Que Digan 8-21-68
Digby, the Biggest Dog in the World 6-19-74
Diggers 12-22-31
Diggers in Blighty 5-16-33
Dikaia Okhota Korolia Stakha 8-27-80
Dilemma 12-19-62
Diligin Mo Ng Hamog Ang Uhaw Na Lupa 11-19-75
Dilizansa Snova 8-10-60
Dillinger 3-14-45
Dillinger 6-13-73
Dillinger e Morto 2-05-69
Dillinger Is Dead (See: Dillinger e Morto)
Dimanche 8-08-56
Dimanche de la Vie, Le 3-09-66
Dimanches de Ville d'Avary, Les 9-12-62
Dimboola 5-16-79
Dime with a Halo 3-20-63
Dimenticare Venezia (See: To Forget Venice)
Diminetile Unui Baiat Cuminte 6-19-68
Dimitri Gorin's Career 9-13-61
Dimples 2-11-16
Dimples 10-14-36
Dimri i Fundit 1-17-79
Dinah East 12-30-70
Dincolo de Pod 6-02-76
Dindon, Le 1-02-52
Diner Lassen Bitten 9-09-36
Dinero ed Amore 3-24-37
Ding Dong Williams 4-17-46
Dingaka 5-19-65
Dingen die Niet Voorbijgaan 10-28-70
Dinky 7-03-35
Dinner at Eight 8-29-33
Dinner at the Ritz 11-10-37
Dinner for Savages (See: Repas des Fauves, La)
Dinner Is Served (See: Diener Lassen Bitten)
Dinner on the Grass (See: Dejeuner Sur l'Herbe, Le)
Dino 6-12-57
Dinosaurus 6-15-60
Dinty 11-26-20
Dio Mio, Come Sono Caduta In Basso 12-11-74
Dio Perdona ... Io No (See: God Forgives, I Don't)
Dionysus in '69 3-11-70

Dios Bendiga Cada Rincon de Esta Casa 9-28-77
Dip of Death, The 1-14-11
Diplomacy 3-03-16
Diplomacy 9-15-26
Diplomaniacs 5-04-33
Diplomatic Courier 6-11-52
Diplopenies 7-20-66
Diputado, El 2-07-79
Directed by John Ford 9-15-71
Directoire Gown 7-25-08
Dirigible 4-08-31
Dirigible Balloons at St. Louis 12-04-09
Dirt 3-21-79
Dirty Dingus Magee 7-29-70 and 11-04-70
Dirty Dozen, The 6-21-67
Dirty Dreamer (See: Sale Reveur)
Dirty Harry 12-22-71
Dirty Heroes 11-24-71
Dirty Little Billy 5-17-72
Dirty Mary, Crazy Larry 5-15-74
Dirty O'Neil 6-26-74
Dirty Outlaws, The 6-30-71
Dirty Seven, The (See: Neung Toh Jet)
Dirty Story, A (See: Sale Histoire, Une)
Dirty Weekend, The (See: Mordi E Fuggi)
Dirty Western, A 5-07-75
Dirty Work 12-25-34
Dirtymouth 6-17-70
Dis-Moi Que Tu M'Aimes 12-25-74
Dis-Moi Qui Tuer 12-29-65
Disappearance 9-28-77
Disaster 10-20-48
Disastrous Flirtation, A 8-29-08
Disbanded, The (See: Sbandati)
Disbarred 1-11-39
Disc Jockey 9-05-51
Discard, The 3-24-16
Discarded Lovers 2-09-32
Disciple, The 10-22-15
Disco of Love, The (See: Discoteca del Amor, La)
Disco Volante, Il 2-10-65
Discoteca Del Amor, La 8-27-80
Discontented Husbands 3-12-24
Discord 7-18-28
Discover Turquoise Mountain (See: Chajrchan Ondor Chaana Bajna)
Discovery 6-25-47
Discovery of America, The 6-17-70
Discreet Charm of the Bourgeoisie, The (See: Charme Discret de la Bourgeoisie, Le)
Discretion Wanted (See: Diskret Ophold)
Discretion--Word of Honor (See: Diskretion--Ehrensache)
Disembodied, The 8-28-57
Disenchantment, The (See: Desencanto, El)
Disgrace of the Village, The (See: A Falu Rossza)
Disgraced 7-18-33
Dishoner Bright 10-07-36
Dishonest Profit, The (See: Unanstaendige Profit, Der)
Dishonest Steward, The 10-08-10
Dishonored 3-11-31
Dishonored 12-13-50
Dishonored Lady 4-23-47
Dishonored Medal, The 5-08-14
Dishonour (See: Deshonra)
Disillusion 11-02-49
Diskret Ophold 11-27-46
Diskretion--Ehrensache 3-15-39
Dismissed on His Wedding Night (See: Sissignore)
Disorder (See: Disordine, Il)
Disorder and Early Torment (See: Unordnung und Fruehes Leid)
Disorder and Night (See: Desordre et la Nuit, Le)
Disorder Is 20 Years Old (See: Desordre a Vingt Ans, Le)
Disorderly Conduct 4-12-32
Disorderly Orderly, The 12-16-64
Disordine, Il 5-16-62
Disparus de Saint-Agil, Les 5-25-38
Dispatch from Reuters, A 9-25-40
Disputed Passage 10-18-39
Disque 413 8-19-36
Disraeli 8-26-21
Disraeli 10-09-29
Dissolution of Parliament 7-03-09
Distance (See: Dooratwa)
Distance 9-24-75
Distant Cry from Spring, A (See: Harukanaru Yama No Yobigoe)
Distant Drums 12-05-51
Distant Thunder (See: Ashani Sanket)
Distant Trumpet, A 5-27-64
Distant Wind, The (See: Viente Distante, El)

Distinto Amanecer 6-28-44
Distrait, Le 12-23-70
Distress (See: Desarroi)
District Attorney, The 3-05-10 and 9-03-15
Disturbance (See: Poloh)
Dit Vindarna Bar 11-24-48
Dita Saxova 7-24-68
Dites--le Avec des Fleurs 9-11-74
Dites Lui Que Je L'Aime 10-05-77
Ditte Menneskebarn 3-05-47
Dive Bomber 8-13-41
Diver's Honor, A 10-08-10
Diver's Remorse, The 10-23-09
Diverse World: The Test and Bare Conscience, A (See: Sharen Sviat
    (Izpit & Gola Savest))
Diversion 11-07-13
Diversions 3-17-76
Diverzanti 8-16-67
Divided Heart 11-24-54
Divided Sky, The (See: Geteilte Himmel, Der)
Dividend, The 6-16-16
Divina Creatura 7-14-76
Divine 6-25-75
Divine Creature (See: Divina Creatura)
Divine Cruise, The 5-22-29
Divine Ema (See: Boszka Ema)
Divine Jette, The (See: Goettliche Jette, Die)
Divine Lady 3-27-29
Divine Madness 9-17-80
Divine Obsession, The 11-05-75
Divine Plan, The (See: Chhatrabhang)
Divine Sacrifice, The 1-28-18
Divine Sinner, The 9-26-28
Divine Woman, The 1-18-28
Division Brandenberg 12-28-60 and 1-18-61
Divka's Trema Velbloudy (See: Girl with Three Camels)
Divorce 6-28-23
Divorce 10-17-45
Divorce American Style 6-07-67
Divorce Among Friends 4-08-31
Divorce and the Daughter 11-17-16
Divorce Game, The 6-15-17
Divorce Heureux, Un 5-14-75
Divorce in the Family 11-01-32
Divorce Italian Style (See: Divorzio All'Italiana)
Divorce of Lady X, The 1-19-38
Divorce Surprises (See: Surprises du Divorce)
Divorce Trap, The 5-30-19
Divorced 10-29-15
Divorcee 5-14-30
Divorcee, The 1-24-19
Divorcement, Le 8-22-79
Divorzio All'Italiana 12-27-61
Divota Prasine 8-20-75
Dixiana 9-10-30
Dixie 6-30-43
Dixie Dugan 3-10-43
Dixie Flyer, The 10-06-26
Dixie Handicap 12-31-24
Dixie Jamboree 1-10-45
Dixieme Symphonie, La 10-04-67
17e Parallele le Vietnam en Guerre 3-13-68
17eme Ciel, Le 5-11-66
Dizengoff 99 6-13-79
Dizziness (See: Vertigo)
Dizzy Dames 7-22-36
Dizzy Heights 12-31-15
Django DeBastardo (See: Stranger's Gundown, The)
Djavulens Oga 11-09-60
Djevojka I Hrast 8-10-55
Djungelaeventyret Campa-Campa 6-09-76
Djungelsaga, En 5-21-58
Djurgardskvallar 4-02-47
Dnevnye Zvezdy 9-03-69
Dny Zrady 6-19-74
Do and Dare 10-27-22
Do Ankhen Barah Haath 9-03-58
Do It Now 11-28-08
Do Not Disturb 12-22-65
Do Not Mention the Cause of Death (See: Uzrok Smrti Ne
    Prominjati)
Do Not Throw Cushions into the Ring 6-17-70
Do That to Me (See: Me Faire Ca A Moi)
Do We Start Off With a Dance (See: Skal Vi Danse Foerst)
Do You Hear the Dogs Barking? (See: No Oyes Ladrar Los Perros?)
Do You Keep a Lion at Home? (See: Mate Doma Liva?)
Do You Know Pavla Plesa (See: Poznajete Li Pavla Plesa)
Do You Know 'Sunday Monday'? (See: Ismeri a Szandi-Mandit?)

Do You Like Women? (See: Aimez-Vous Les Femmes?)
Do You Love Me? 4-17-46
Do You Want to Remain a Virgin Forever? (See: Wilst Du Ewig Jung-
    frau Bleiben?)
Do Your Duty 11-07-28
Dobri Stari Pianino 8-19-59
Dobro Morje 8-06-58
Dobro Poshalovat 7-05-78
Doc 8-11-71
Doc Savage ... The Man of Bronze 5-07-75
Dock Brief, The 10-03-62
Docks of Hamburg 7-09-30
Docks of New Orleans 3-17-48
Docks of New York 9-19-28
Docks of New York 2-28-45
Docks of San Francisco 3-15-32
Docteur Francois Gailland 12-31-75
Docteur Laennec 7-13-49
Docteur Popoul 10-04-72
Doctor and the Girl, The 9-14-49
Doctor and the Healer, The (See: Medico e lo Stregone, Il)
Doctor and the Woman, The 4-26-18
Dr. Antonio (See: Dottor Antonio, Il)
Doctor at Large 4-03-57
Doctor at Sea 8-03-55
Doctor Beware 5-02-51
Dr. Black, Mr. Hyde 1-21-76
Dr. Blood's Coffin 5-03-61
Dr. Broadway 5-06-42
Dr. Bull 10-10-33
Dr. Christian Meets the Women 6-26-40
Dr. Coppelius 4-10-68
Dr. Crippen 8-21-63
Dr. Cyclops 3-06-40
Doctor Death: Seeker of Souls 11-14-73
Doctor Doolittle 12-20-67
Dr. Ehrlich's Magic Bullet 2-07-40
Dr. Epameinondas 4-06-38
Dr. Fabian--Lachen Ist Die Best Medizin 11-19-69
Dr. Fabian--Laughing Is the Best Medicine (See: Dr. Fabian--
    Lachen Ist Die Best Medizin)
Doctor Faustus 10-25-67
Dr. Fu Manchu 7-24-29 and 5-07-30
Dr. Gillespie's Criminal Case 5-05-43
Dr. Gillespie's New Assistant 11-11-42
Dr. Goldfoot and the Bikini Machine 11-10-65
Dr. Goldfoot and the Girl Bombs 11-16-66
Dr. Heckyl & Mr. Hype 7-02-80
Doctor in Clover 3-16-66
Doctor in Distress 8-07-63
Doctor in Love 7-20-60
Doctor in the House 4-07-54
Doctor in Trouble 6-24-70
Dr. Jack 1-05-23
Dr. Jekyll and Mr. Hyde 4-02-20
Dr. Jekyll and Mr. Hyde 7-23-41
Dr. Jekyll and Sister Hyde 10-27-71
Dr. Jim 12-02-21
Doctor Judym 7-28-76
Dr. Kildare Goes Home 9-04-40
Dr. Kildare's Crisis 12-04-40
Dr. Kildare's Strange Case 4-17-40
Dr. Kildare's Victory 12-03-41
Dr. Kildare's Wedding Day 8-20-41
Dr. Knock 5-05-37
Dr. Laurent's Case (See: Cas du Dr. Laurent, Le)
Dr. Mabuse 8-10-27
Dr. Mabuse, The Gambler 6-02-22
Dr. Mabuse's Will (See: Testament du Dr. Mabuse)
Dr. Med. Hiob Praetorius 1-27-65
Dr. Med. Sommer II 10-14-70
Doctor Monica 6-26-34
Dr. No 10-17-62
Dr. Norman Bethune 6-06-79
Dr. O'Dowd 2-14-40
Doctor of St. Paul, The (See: Arzt von St. Pauli, Der)
Doctor of Stalingrad, The (See: Arzt von Stalingrad, Der)
Dr. Phibes Rises Again 7-19-72
Dr. Plern (See: Plern)
Doctor Poenaru 6-14-78
Dr. Rameau 7-23-15
Dr. Renault's Secret 10-21-42
Dr. Rhythm 4-27-38
Dr. Socrates 10-09-35
Dr. Strangelove; or, How I Learned to Stop Worrying and Love the
    Bomb 1-22-64
Doctor Syn 9-08-37
Doctor Takes a Wife 5-01-40

Dr. Terror's House of Horrors 3-03-65
Doctor Vlimmen 3-22-78 and 8-09-78
Dr. Who and the Daleks 7-07-65
Doctor X 8-09-32
Doctor, You've Got to Be Kidding 3-08-67
Doctor Zhivago 12-29-65
Doctora Quiere Tangos, La 8-24-49
Doctor's Bride 9-04-09
Doctor's Diagnosis, The (See: Arzt Stellt Fest ..., Der)
Doctor's Diary, A 2-24-37
Doctor's Dilemma 12-03-58
Doctor's Lunch 7-25-08
Doctor's Secret 2-06-29
Doctor's Secret, The (See: Secret du Docteur, Le)
Doctor's Secretary 1-07-11
Doctor's Wives 4-29-31
Doctor's Wives 1-27-71
Doctor's Women 6-05-29
Doctress Wants Tangos, The (See: Doctora Quiere Tangos, La)
Doda Clara 8-31-77
Dodeska-Den 12-09-70
Dodge City 4-12-39
Dodge City Trail 5-26-37
Dodging (See: Seitenspruenge)
Dodging a Million 2-01-18
Dodsworth 9-30-36
Doeden Kommer Til Middag 10-14-64
Does, The (See: Biches, Les)
Does a Man Want Much Land? (See: Skarabea)
Does It Pay? 12-13-23
Does One Ever Know (See: Sait-On Jamais)
Dog, The (See: Perro, El)
Dog Catcher's Love, A 6-29-17
Dog Circus Rehearsal 8-28-09
Dog Day Afternoon 8-27-75
Dog Law 10-10-28
Dog of Flanders, A 9-25-35
Dog of Flanders, A 12-23-59
Dog of the Regiment 11-02-27
Dog on Business, A 9-10-10
Dog Pickpocket 10-16-09
Dog That Liked Trains, The (See: Pas Koji Je Voleo Vozove)
Dogadaj 8-20-69
Dogora 8-04-65
Dogs, The (See: Chiens, Les)
Dog's Best Friend 1-20-60
Dog's Heart (See: Cuore Di Cane)
Dog's Life, A 4-19-18
Dogs of War, The 12-10-80
Dog's World, A (See: Mondo Cane)
Doigts dans la Tete, Les 12-25-74
Doing Their Bit 8-23-19
Dok Jinnung Nurguni 12-31-69
Dokter Pulder Zaait Papavers 7-07-76
Doktor Glas 6-19-68
Dokuritsu Kikanjutai Imada Shagekichu 10-07-64
Dolce Corpo di Deborah, Il (See: Sweet Body of Deborah, The)
Dolce Vita, La 2-17-60
Dolci Notti, Le 11-14-62
Dolci Signore, Le (See: Anyone Can Play)
Dolemite 8-06-75
Doll, The (See: Poupee, La; Lalka; Pupa, La; or Vaxdockan)
Doll Face 12-19-45
Doll Merchant 8-17-55
Dollar and the Law, The 11-24-16
Dollar Devils 4-19-23
Dollar Down 8-12-25
Dollar Mark, The 9-11-14
Dollars ($) 12-15-71
Dollars Tra i Dente, Un (See: Stranger in Town, A)
Dollars and Sense 6-25-20
Dollars and the Woman 3-24-16
Dolls, The (See: Bambole, Le)
Doll's House, A 6-15-17
Doll's House, A 5-31-18
Doll's House, A 2-17-22
Doll's House, A 5-09-73
Doll's House, A 5-23-73
Doll's House, The (See: Casa de Munecas)
Dolly 12-12-28
Dolly Gets Ahead (See: Dolly Macht Karriere)
Dolly Kaput (See: Puppe Kaputt)
Dolly Macht Karriere 11-12-30 and 7-21-31
Dolly Sisters 9-26-45
Dolly's Career (See: Dolly Macht Karriere)
Dolly's Vacation 12-20-18

Dolores 11-16-49
Dolores de Arada 4-24-14
Dolphin 7-04-79
Dolyna Miru 5-15-57
Dom Bez Okien 5-23-62
Dom Kallar Oss Mods 4-17-68
Dom S Mezzanimon (See: House with an Attic)
Dom V A Kotorom la Jivou 7-02-58
Domani e Troppo Tardi 11-01-50
Domani e un Altro Giorno 2-28-51
Domaren 5-17-61
Dombey and Sons 7-11-19
Dome (See: Cupola)
Domenica 4-02-52
Domenica D'Agosto 5-03-50
Domenica d'Estate, Una 6-06-62
Domenica e Sempre Domenica 7-02-58
Domestic Meddlers 12-05-28
Domestic Relations 6-09-22
Domestic Trouble 6-20-28
Domicile Conjugal 8-26-70
Dominant Sex, The 2-10-37
Domingo a Tarde 9-08-65
Domino Kid 8-21-57
Domino Principle, The 3-23-77
Don Camillo 5-28-52
Don Camillo and Hon. Peppone (See: Don Camillo e L'on. Peppone)
Don Camillo e L'on. Peppone 12-07-55
Don Camillo in Moscow (See: Compagno Don Camillo, Il)
Don Desperado 5-11-27
Don Giovanni 9-16-70
Don Giovanni 10-24-79
Don Giovanni in Sicilia 7-26-67
Don Is Dead, The 11-14-73
Don Juan (See: Don Giovanni)
Don Juan 8-11-26
Don Juan 12-18-34
Don Juan 3-14-56
Don Juan 7-18-56
Don Juan Diplomatico 4-22-31
Don Juan in Sicily (See: Don Giovanni in Sicilia)
Don Juan 1973 ou Si Don Juan Etait une Femme 3-07-73
Don Juan (or, If Don Juan Were a Woman) (See: Don Juan 1973 ou
    Si Don Juan Etait une Femme)
Don Juan Quilligan 6-06-45
Don Juan's 3 Nights 9-08-26
Don Mike 2-23-27
Don of Japan--Big Schemes, The (See: Nippon no Don--Yabohen)
Don Q, Son of Zorro 6-17-25
Don Quichotte 10-17-28
Don Quichotte 4-11-33
Don Quintin el Amargao 10-30-35
Don Quintin, the Bitter (See: Don Quintin el Amargao)
Don Quixote 11-06-09
Don Quixote 6-06-33
Don Quixote 1-08-35
Don Quixote 5-29-57
Don Quixote 8-01-73
Don Quixote de la Mancha 5-11-49
Don Ramiro (See: Habla Mudita)
Don Segundo Sombra 9-17-69
Don Simon de Lira 1-01-47
Don Winslow of the Coast Guard 3-31-43
Dona Barbara 2-21-45
Dona Flor and Her 2 Husbands (See: Dona Flor e Seurs Dois
    Maridos)
Dona Flor e Seurs Dois Maridos 9-14-77
Dona Mentiras 1-14-31
Dona Perfecta 11-09-77
Donatella 10-24-56
Donde Estas Corazon? 9-06-61
Donde Mueren las Palabras 6-05-46 (Also see: Where Words Fail)
Dondi 8-23-61
Donkey in a Brahmin Village (See: Agraharathil Kazhuthai)
Donkey Skin (See: Peau D'Ane)
Donna del Fiume, La 11-16-55
Donna del Lago, La 8-04-65
Donna Della Domenica, La 1-28-76
Donna D'Una Notte, La 3-14-33
Donna e Bello 11-20-74
Donna e una Cosa Meravigliosa, La 9-16-64
Donna Juana 5-02-28
Donna Nel Mondo, La 2-27-63
Donna Scimmia, La 5-06-64
Donne del Giorno 7-31-57
Donne e Briganti 7-04-51
Donne Sole 7-11-56
Donnez-Moi Dix Hommes Desesperes 5-09-62

Donnez-Moi Ma Chance 2-12-58
Donogoo Tonka 4-22-36 and 7-29-36
Donovan Affair, The 5-01-29
Donovan's Brain 10-07-53
Donovan's Reef 6-19-63
Don's Party 10-06-76
Don't 2-17-26
Don't Answer the Phone 4-16-80
Don't Be a Sucker 5-08-46
Don't Be Offended, Beatrice (See: No Te Ofendas, Beatriz)
Don't Be Weak With Life (See: No Hay Que Aflojarle a la Vida)
Don't Bet on Blondes 7-24-35
Don't Bet on Love 8-01-33
Don't Bet on Women 3-11-31
Don't Bite, We Love You (See: Mords Pas On T'Aime)
Don't Bother to Knock 7-16-52
Don't Bother to Knock 6-07-61
Don't Call Me Little Girl 6-24-21
Don't Change Hands (See: Change Pas de Main)
Don't Change Your Husband 2-07-19
Don't Count On Us (See: Non Contate Su Di Noi)
Don't Cry (See: Ne Pleure Pas)
Don't Cry Mother (See: Ne Sirj Edesanyam)
Don't Cry with Your Mouth Full (See: Pleure Pas la Bouche
    Pleine)
Don't Doubt Your Wife 3-24-22
Don't Drink the Water 11-12-69
Don't Ever Ask Me If I Love (See: Al Tish' Ali Im Ani Ohev)
Don't Ever Die, Mother (See: Kaachan Shiguno Iyada)
Don't Ever Leave Me 7-27-49
Don't Ever Marry 4-16-20
Don't Fence Me In 10-24-45
Don't Fumble, Darling! (See: Nicht Fummelin, Liebling!)
Don't Gamble with Love 3-04-36
Don't Gamble with Strangers 5-29-46
Don't Get Personal 1-20-22
Don't Get Personal 2-26-36
Don't Get Personal 12-31-41
Don't Give Up (See: Tappa Inte Sugen)
Don't Give Up the Ship 6-03-59
Don't Go Away! (See: Ne Si Otivai)
Don't Go in the House 6-11-80
Don't Go Near the Water 11-13-57
Don't Just Lay There 5-13-70
Don't Just Stand There 3-27-68
Don't Knock the Rock 12-26-56
Don't Knock the Twist 4-11-62
Don't Know Anything But I'll Tell You All (See: Je Sais Rien Mais
    Je Dirai Tout)
Don't Lean Out the Window (See: Ne Naginji Se Van or Kihajolni
    Veszelyes)
Don't Let It Get You 11-23-66
Don't Let the Angels Fall 5-14-69
Don't Look Back 6-14-67
Don't Look Now 10-24-73
Don't Lose Your Head 3-08-67
Don't Make Waves 6-21-67
Don't Marry 5-23-28
Don't Marry for Money 8-30-23
Don't Meddle with Fortune (See: Ne Diraj U Srecu)
Don't Neglect Your Wife 7-29-21
Don't Panic Chaps! 12-30-59
Don't Play With Martians (See: Ne Jouez Pas Avec Les Martians)
Don't Raise the Bridge, Lower the River 6-05-68
Don't Shoot 8-25-22
Don't Take It to Heart 11-15-44
Don't Tell Everything 12-16-21
Don't Tell Me Any Stories (See: Erzaehl Mir Nichts)
Don't Tell the Wife 2-23-27
Don't Tell the Wife 2-24-37
Don't Touch the Coin (See: Touchez Pas Au Grisbi)
Don't Touch White Women! (See: Touche Pas A La Femme Blanche!)
Don't Trifle with Women (See: Non Scherzare Con Le Donne)
Don't Turn 'em Loose 9-30-36
Don't Turn the Other Cheek 10-09-74
Don't Worry (See: Ne Goryuy)
Don't Worry, We'll Think of a Title 5-18-66
Don't Write Letters 5-19-22
Dood Van Efn Non 10-08-75
Dooley's Thanksgiving 12-04-09
Doolins of Oklahoma, The 6-01-49
Doom, The (See: Osinda)
Doom of Darkness, The 8-15-13
Doomed at Sundown 11-10-37
Doomed Battalion, The 6-14-32
Doomed Caravan 1-08-41
Doomed Souls (See: Ossudeni Doushi)
Doomed to Die 8-29-13

Doomed to Die 8-07-40
Doomsday 4-04-28
Doomsday Voyage 2-16-72
Door, The 3-12-10
Door Between, The 11-23-17
Door Opens, A (See: Tuer Geht Auf, Eine)
Door Remains Open, The (See: Vrata Ostaiu Otvorena)
Door That Had No Key 8-25-22
Door That Has No Key 4-22-21
Door-to-Door Maniac 11-23-66
Door with 7 Locks 7-10-40
Dooratwa 1-31-79
Doors of Night, The (See: Portes de la Nuit, Les)
Doorway to Hell 11-05-30
Dopalnenie K Zakona Za Zaschitita Na Darjavata 11-10-76
Dope (See: Rauschgift)
Dope 4-03-14
Dopo una Notte D'Amore 11-06-35
Doppio a Meta, Un 9-06-72
Doppio Delitto 1-11-78
Dora and the Magic Lantern (See: Dora et la Lanterne Magique)
Dora et la Lanterne Magique 3-01-78
Dorado de Pancho Villa, Un 7-19-67
Doramundo 10-25-78
Dorian Gray 11-18-70
Dormant Power, The 10-12-17
Dorothea's Rache 3-06-74
Dorothea's Revenge (See: Dorothea's Rache)
Dorogoi Tsenoi 4-29-59
Dorothy and the Scarecrow of Oz 4-23-10
Dorothy Vernon of Haddon Hall 5-07-24
Dorp Aan de Rivier 7-22-59 and 12-09-59
Dos Angeles y un Pecador 8-22-45
Dos Au Mur, Le 4-16-58
Dos Corazones y un Cielo 11-25-59
Dos Hijos Desobedientes 4-13-60
Dos Huerianas, Las 10-18-44
Dos Rivales, Los 5-17-44
Dos Tipos de Cuidado 4-07-54
Dos y Media ... Veneno, Las 1-13-60
Dosango 8-06-58
Dossier 51, Le 5-31-78
Dossier Noir, Le 6-01-55
Dossier Prostitution 4-29-70
Dost Dobri Chlai 8-16-72
Dosti 7-21-65
Dot Dot Dot 12-08-71
Dottor Antonio, Il 12-22-37
D'Ou Viens-Tu Johnny? 3-04-64
Douaumont 9-01-31
Double, The (See: Kagemusha or Dvoynikat)
Double Alibi 3-13-40
Double-Barreled Detective Story 9-08-65
Double Bed, The (See: Lit a Deux Places, Le)
Double Bunk 4-19-61
Double by Half (See: Doppio a Meta, Un)
Double Chase, The 11-07-13
Double Confession 5-13-53
Double Crime in the Maginot Line 4-19-39
Double Cross 8-13-41
Double Cross Roads 4-30-30
Double Crossbones 11-22-50
Double Crossed 9-21-17
Double Crossers 9-29-76
Double Danger 2-16-38
Double Date 3-12-41
Double Deal 12-27-50
Double Destiny (See: Zweite Leben, Das)
Double Door 5-08-34
Double Dyed Deceiver 6-11-20
Double Dynamite 11-07-51
Double Elopement, A 11-12-10
Double Exposure 12-20-44
Double Exposure of Holly, The 10-13-76
Double Face (See: Gesicht Im Dunkeln, Das)
Double Harness 7-25-33
Double Haul, A 1-15-15
Double Indemnity 4-26-44
Double Initiation 4-22-70
Double Life, A 12-31-47
Double McGuffin, The 6-13-79
Double Man, The (See: Den Dobbelte Mand)
Double Man, The 4-26-67
Double Murder (See: Doppio Delitto)
Double Negative 5-28-80
Double Nickels 5-25-77
Double or Nothing 8-18-37

Double Pisces, Scorpio Rising 9-16-70
Double Speed 2-06-20
Double Standard, The 8-03-17
Double-Stop 5-08-68
Double Suicide, A 6-27-08
Double Suicide at Amijima (See: Shinju Ten No Amijima)
Double Suicide of Sonezaki 9-06-78
Double Trouble 4-05-67
Double Twist (See: A Double Tour)
Double Wedding 9-22-37
Doubles 3-22-78
Doubling for Romeo 10-28-21
Doubling with Danger 9-29-26
Doubt, The (See: Duda, La)
Doubting Thomas 7-17-35
Douce 7-13-49
Douce Violence 4-18-62
Doucement les Basses! 4-21-71
Douceur D'Aimer, La 11-12-30 and 12-22-31
Douceur du Village, La 5-13-64
Dough, The (See: Guita, La)
Dough Boys 9-24-30 (Also see: Frente Marchen!, Die)
Doughboys in Ireland 12-15-43
Doughgirls, The 8-23-44
Doughnuts and Society 6-24-36
Douglas 11-18-70
Doulos, Le 4-03-63
Douze Heures D'Horloge 5-13-59
12 Travaux d'Asterix, Les 11-17-76
Dove, The 1-11-28
Dove, The 5-22-74
Dove Vai in Vacanza? 1-10-79
Doverie 1-19-77
Doves, The (See: Colombes, Les)
Down Among the Sheltering Palms 4-01-53
Down Argentine Way 10-09-40
Down by the Rio Grande 6-18-24
Down Dakota Way 9-07-49
Down Home 10-29-20
Down in Arkansaw 10-12-38
Down in San Diego 7-30-41
Down Laredo Way 8-12-53
Down Memory Lane 9-14-49
Down Mexico Way 10-29-41
Down Missouri Way 8-14-46
Down on the Farm 4-30-20
Down on the Farm 10-12-38
Down Rio Grande Way 7-29-42
Down Texas Way 8-12-42
Down the Ancient Staircase (See: Per le Antiche Scale)
Down the Grade 8-17-27
Down the Stretch 5-04-27
Down the Stretch 11-11-36
Down the Wyoming Trail 6-14-39
Down Three Dark Streets 9-08-54
Down to Earth 8-10-17
Down to Earth 9-06-32
Down to Earth 7-30-47
Down to the Sea 8-12-36
Down to the Sea in Ships 12-08-22 and 1-25-23
Down to the Sea in Ships 2-16-49
Down to Their Last Yacht 9-25-34
Down Town 2-05-58
Downfall, The (See: Absturz, Der)
Downhill Racer 10-29-69
Downpour 12-06-72
Downstairs 10-11-32
Downstream From the Sun (See: Nizvodno Od Sunca)
Dowry, The (See: Wiano)
Dozhivem do Polnidelnika 6-25-69
Dracos 9-19-56
Dracula 2-18-31
Dracula 7-04-79
Dracula A.D. 1972 10-25-72
Dracula and the 7 Golden Vampires 6-04-75
Dracula Contra Frankenstein 10-25-72
Dracula Father and Son (See: Dracula Pere et Fils)
Dracula Has Risen from the Grave 11-20-68
Dracula Pere et Fils 9-29-76
Dracula--Prince of Darkness 1-19-66
Dracula Versus Frankenstein (See: Dracula Contra Frankenstein)
Dracula's Daughter 5-20-36
Dracula's Dog 6-21-78
Draegerman Courage 5-26-37
Draft 258 2-08-18
Drag 6-26-29
Drag Harlan 12-17-20
Draga Irena 8-12-70

Dragees au Poivre 9-11-63
Drageurs, Les 4-15-59
Drag Net, The 6-06-28
Dragnet 7-02-47
Dragnet 8-25-54
Dragnet Night (See: Soir de Rafle, Un)
Dragnet Patrol 2-23-32
Dragon, The 1-14-16
Dragon Inn (See: Lung Mun Kar Chuan)
Dragon Lives, The 10-04-78
Dragon Murder Case, The 8-28-34
Dragon Painter, The 10-03-19
Dragon Reincarnate 10-08-75
Dragon Seed 7-19-44
Dragon Squad 7-23-75
Dragonfly 7-13-55
Dragonfly 2-18-76
Dragonfly Squadron 2-03-54
Dragon's Claw 3-10-22
Dragon's Gold 1-27-54
Dragonwyck 2-20-46
Dragoon Wells Massacre 5-08-57
Dragstrip Girl 5-01-57
Dragstrip Riot 4-23-58
Drake Case, The 9-18-29
Drake of England 5-29-35
Drama of Shanghai, The (See: Drame de Shanghai, Le)
Drama of the Rich (See: Fatti di Gente Perbene)
Dramatic School 12-07-38
Drame de Shanghai, Le 11-16-38
Dramma Borghese, Un 9-12-79
Drango 1-16-57
Drapeau Noir Flotte Sur la Marmite, Le 11-10-71
Dream, The (See: San or Moemoea)
Dream, The (See: Reve, Le)
Dream Cheater 4-09-20
Dream Fair, The (See: Foire aux Chimeres, La)
Dream Girl 5-05-48
Dream Girl, The 7-14-16
Dream, It Costs Nothing (See: Sonar, No Cuesta Nada)
Dream Lady, The 8-09-18
Dream Melody, The 5-22-29
Dream No More 1-11-50
Dream of a Cossack 2-20-52
Dream of a Father (See: Fadern)
Dream of a World 10-21-70
Dream of Butterfly, The (See: Sogno di Butterfly, Il)
Dream of Freedom, A (See: Droem om Frihet, En)
Dream of Kings, A 12-17-69
Dream of Lieschen Mueller, THe (See: Traum von Lieschen Mueller,
    Der)
Dream of Love 12-26-28
Dream of Passion, A 5-24-78
Dream of Schonbrunn (See: Traum von Schonbrunn)
Dream of the Rhine (See: Traum von Rhein, Der)
Dream Road of the World (See: Traumstrasse der Welt)
Dream Spectres 5-08-09
Dream Street 4-15-21
Dream Town (See: Traumstadt)
Dream Wife 3-11-53
Dream World (See: Traeumende Mund, Der)
Dreamboat 7-23-52
Dreamed Life, The (See: Vie Revee, La)
Dreamer 4-25-79
Dreamer, The (See: Reveur, La)
Dreamer, The 4-09-10
Dreamer, The (See: Traumulus)
Dreamer, The 4-08-70
Dreamers, The (See: Fantasterne)
Dreaming Lips 2-10-37 and 5-26-37
Dreaming Out Loud 9-18-40
Dreaming Youth (See: Almodo Ifjusag)
Dreamland of Desire 7-05-61
Dreams 7-23-69
Dreams Came by Coach (See: Dilizansa Snova)
Dreams Come True 11-11-36
Dreams Die at Dawn (See: Sogni Muoiono all'Alba, I)
Dreams in a Drawer (See: Sogni nel Cassetto, I)
Dreams, Life, the Death of Filip Filipovic (See: Snovi, Zivot,
    Smrt Filipa Filipovic)
Dreams Make No Noise When They Die (See: Droemme Stoejer Ikke,
    Naar De Doer)
Dreams of Glass 9-25-68
Dreams of Love (See: Szerelmi Almok)
Dreams That Money Can Buy 4-28-48
Drei Blaue Jungs und ein Blondes Maedel 1-13-37
Drei Groschenoper 5-20-31 and 7-13-60
Drei Maederl um Schubert 9-16-36

Drei Maenner im Schnee 7-27-55
Drei Tage Liebe 3-25-31
Drei Tage Mitelarest 5-23-33
Drei um Christine, Die 7-15-36
Drei Von der Tankstelle, Die (See: From the Gas Station)
Drei Wenschen 12-29-37
Dreigroschenoper, Die (See: Threepenny Opera, The or Drei
   Groschenoper
Dreiklang 8-03-38
Dreimaederlhaus, Das 1-21-59
Drenge 3-09-77
Dress, The (See: Klanningen)
Dress Parade 11-02-27
Dressed to Kill 3-14-28
Dressed to Kill 7-23-41
Dressed to Kill 5-22-46
Dressed to Kill 7-23-80
Dressed to Thrill 11-27-35
Dressmaker from Paris 3-18-25
Dressmaker of Luneville (See: Couturiere de Luneville)
Drevo Jelania 6-21-78
Dreyfus 4-29-31
Dreyfus Case, The 9-01-31
Dreyfus or the Unbearable Truth (See: Dreyfus ou L'Intolerable
   Verite)
Dreyfus ou L'Intolerable Verite 2-05-75
Drift Fence 3-11-36
Drifter 9-24-75
Drifter, The 2-11-16
Drifter, The 3-20-29
Drifter, The 3-15-32
Drifter, The 5-24-44
Drifter, The 9-07-66
Drifters, The 12-27-18
Drifting 8-23-23
Drifting 8-02-32
Drifting, The (See: Derive, Le)
Drifting Along 2-20-46
Drifting Thru 5-05-26
Drifting Westward 2-15-39
Driftwood 3-24-16
Driftwood 12-12-28
Driftwood 11-05-47
Driller Killer 7-04-79
Drilling-Hole or Bavaria Isn't Texas (See: Bohrloch Oder Bayern
   Ist Nicht Texas, Das)
Drink 10-30-09
Dritte, Der 8-16-72
Dritte Generation, Die 5-23-79
Dritte Geschiecht, Das 9-11-57
Drive a Crooked Road 3-17-54
Drive, He Said 6-02-71
Drive-In 5-28-76
Driven 12-01-22
Driven by Fate 8-20-15
Driven from Home 5-25-27
Driven to Steal 4-09-10
Driver, The 7-26-78
Driver Dagg Faller Regn 3-19-47
Driver's Seat, The (See: Identikit)
Drivin' Fool 11-01-23
Droem om Frihet, En 11-11-70
Droemme Stoejer Ikke, Naar De Doer 5-16-79
Droemmen Om Amerika 12-08-76
Droit D'Aimer, Le 8-30-72
Drole de Colonel, Un 5-15-68
Drole de Dimanche, Un 12-31-58
Drole de Jeu 3-13-68
Drolesse, La 5-09-79
Drop Dead, My Love (See: Marito E Mio E L'Amazzo Quando Mi Pare)
Drop Kick, The 9-21-27
Drop the Curtain (See: Abajo el Telon)
Dropped from Heaven (See: Tombe du Ciel)
Dropped from the Clouds 9-25-09
Drowning Pool, The 6-18-75
Drug Connection 3-24-76
Drug Moi, Kol'ka 11-15-61
Drug Pretsednik Centafor 8-10-60
Drug Traffic, The 4-26-23
Druga Mlodosc 10-18-39
Drugarcine 8-15-79
Drum 8-04-76
Drum, The 4-20-38
Drum Beat 11-03-54
Drum Taps 5-02-33
Drummer of Tacuari, The (See: Tambor de Tacuari, El)
Drummond at Bay 8-04-37
Drummond Escapes 2-24-37
Drummond's Bride 7-05-39

Drummond's Peril 3-23-38
Drummond's Revenge 12-22-37
Drums Across the River 5-19-54
Drums Along the Mohawk 11-08-39
Drums in the Deep South 10-03-51
Drums o' Voodoo 5-15-34
Drums of Africa 4-24-63
Drums of Destiny 11-10-37
Drums of Fate 1-19-23
Drums of Fu Manchu 2-14-40 and 11-10-43
Drums of Jeopardy 3-19-24
Drums of Jeopardy 4-15-31
Drums of Love 2-01-28
Drums of Tabu, The 6-07-67
Drums of Tahiti 1-13-54
Drums of the Congo 7-22-42
Drums of the Desert 8-10-27
Drums of the Desert 11-06-40
Drumsticks, A Thanksgiving Story 11-26-10
Drunkard, The (See: Pocharde, La)
Drunkard's Fate 10-09-09
Drunken Angel 2-03-60
Drunken Monkey in a Tiger's Eye 11-29-78
Drunter und Drieber 12-20-32
Drusilla with a Million 5-27-25
Drvo Bez Koren 7-31-74
Dry Martini 11-07-28
Drylanders 10-02-63
Drzwi w Murze 9-25-74
Du 1-15-69
Du aer inte Klok, Madicken 1-02-80
Du Barry Was a Lady 5-05-43
Du Barry, Woman of Passion 11-05-43
Du Bist die Welt Fuer Mich 1-27-54
Du Bist Mein Glueck 11-18-36
Du Bist Min--Ein Deutsches Tagebuch 7-30-69
Du Bout des Levres 1-28-76
Du Cote D'Orouet 9-01-71
Du Cote des Tennis 11-10-76
Du er Ikke Alene 3-08-78
Du Gamia, Du Fria 9-13-72
Du Grabage Chez les Veuves 5-13-64
Du Mouron Pour les Petits Oiseaux 2-27-63
Du Rififi a Paname 4-06-66
Du Rififi Chez les Femmes 6-10-59
Du Rififi Chez les Hommes 6-08-55
Du Soleil Plein les Yeux 6-10-70
Dual Alibi 6-18-47
Dub, The 1-17-19
Dubrovsky 4-01-36
Dubrovsky 8-12-59
Duchess and the Dirtwater Fox, The 3-17-76
Duchess of Benameji, The (See: Duquesa de Benameji, La)
Duchess of Buffalo 8-18-26
Duchess of Doubt 6-08-17
Duchess of Idaho 6-14-50
Duchess of Parma, The (See: Contessa di Parma, La)
Duck in Orange Sauce (See: Anatra All'Arancia, L')
Duck Rings at Half Past Seven (See: Ente Klingelt Um 1/2 7, Die)
Duck Soup 11-28-33
Duck, You Sucker 6-21-72
Ducks and Drakes 4-01-21
Dud, The 3-19-20
Duda, La 7-26-72
Dude Bandit, The 6-27-33
Dude Cowboy 9-10-41
Dude Goes West, The 4-28-48
Dude Ranch 4-29-31
Dude Ranger, The 10-02-34
Dude Wrangler, The 7-23-30
Dudes Are Pretty People 4-15-42
Due Colonelli, I 1-16-63
Due Kennedy, I 10-29-69
Due Madri, Le 5-22-40
Due Misantropi, I 10-29-69
Due Pezzi di Pane 3-28-79
Due Soldi di Speranza 6-04-52
Duel, The (See: Poedino or Plokhoy Khoroshyi Chelovek)
Duel, The 7-04-62
Duel at Apache Wells 2-20-57
Duel at Diablo 5-18-66
Duel at Silver Creek 7-16-52
Duel in Mid Air, A 11-13-09
Duel in the Jungle 7-07-54
Duel in the Sun 1-01-47
Duel of the Titans 3-27-63
Duel on the Mississippi 9-21-55
Duel Without Honor (See: Duello Senza Onore)

Duelle 6-02-76
Duellists, The 6-01-77
Duello Senza Onore 4-26-50
Duerme, Duerme, Mi Amor 2-19-75
Duet for Cannibals (See: Duett fur Kannibaler)
Duett fur Kannibaler 5-21-69
Duffy 9-18-68
Duffy of San Quentin 2-17-54
Duffy's Tavern 8-22-45
Dugan of the Bad Lands 9-15-31
Duggan of the Dugouts 8-22-28
Dugun 8-02-78
Duios Anastasia Trecea 7-30-80
Duke Comes Back 12-08-37
Duke Is Tops, The 7-20-38
Duke of Chicago 3-30-49
Duke of the Navy 2-11-42
Duke of West Point 12-21-38
Duke Steps Out, The 4-17-29
Duke Wore Jeans, The 4-02-58
Duke's Plan, The 2-19-10
Dulcie's Adventure 10-06-16
Dulcima 7-07-71
Dulcinea 9-12-62
Dulcy 9-20-23
Dulcy 10-02-40
Dull Razor, The 11-26-10
Dulscy 4-21-76
Dumb-bells in Ermine 7-30-30
Dumb But Disciplined (See: Bete Mais Discipline)
Dumb Girl of Portici, The 4-07-16
Dumbo 10-01-41
Duminica la Ora 6 7-20-66
Dummy, The 3-23-17
Dummy, The 3-06-29
Dummy in Disguise 9-24-10
Dunaparti Randevu 2-03-37 and 3-31-37
Dunce Cap, The 10-15-10
Dunce Class on Vacation, The (See: Hababam Sinifi Tatilde)
Dunderklumpen 10-16-74
Dunkirk 3-26-58
Dunkle Gassen (See: Dark Alleys)
Dunkle Stern, Der 8-10-55
Dunwich Horror, The 1-12-70
Dupe, The 6-30-16
Duped 2-26-10
Duped Till the Last (See: Betrogen Bis Zum Juengsten Tag)
Dupes, The 6-28-72
Dupont-Barbes 3-05-52
Dupont Lajoie 2-26-75
Duquesa de Benameji, La 4-26-75
Durango Kid, The 8-28-40
Durango Valley Raiders 11-02-38
Durante L'Estate 9-08-71
Duration of the Day (See: Regne Du Jour, Le)
Duraton Family, The (See: Famille Duraton, La)
Durchdreher, Der 5-23-79
Durchs Brandenburger Tor (See: Brandenburg Arch)
During Night and Morning (See: Zwischen Nacht und Morgen)
Durs a Cuire, Les 6-24-64
Dusk to Dawn 9-08-22
Dusman 3-19-80
Dust 7-28-16
Dust Be My Destiny 8-16-39
Dust Flower 7-07-22
Dust From Underground (See: Poussiere Sur la Ville)
Dust of Desire 7-11-19
Dusty and Sweets McGee 6-16-71
Dusty Ermine 9-23-36
Dutch Kids 1-07-11
Dutch Types 11-19-10
Dutchman 12-28-66
Duty's Reward 6-15-27
Duvad 5-24-61
Duvidha 11-19-75
Dva Musketyri (See: Jester's Tale, A)
Dvenatets 11-24-71
Dvoboj Za Juznu Prugu 8-16-78
Dvoje 8-23-61
Dvorianckoe Gnezdo 7-23-69
Dvoynikat 7-30-80
Dybbuk, The 2-02-38
Dybbuk, The 11-20-68
Dying Swan, The (See: Mort du Cygne, La)
Dyke, The (See: Argine, L')
Dym Bramborove Nate 3-09-77
Dymky 5-25-66
Dyn Amo 7-12-72

Dynamit 4-30-47
Dynamite (See: Dynamit)
Dynamite 1-01-30
Dynamite 11-17-48
Dynamite 8-16-72
Dynamite Brothers, The (See: Fratelli Dinamite, I)
Dynamite Dan 10-08-24
Dynamite Delaney 1-26-38
Dynamite Denny 9-20-32
Dynamite Jack 11-22-61
Dynamite Pass 3-22-50
Dynamite Ranch 12-27-32
Dynamiters, The 6-27-56
Dynasty 9-07-77
Dyrlaegens Plejeboern 1-15-69
Dyrygent 9-10-80
Dyspeptic and His Double, The 9-04-09
Dzieje Grzechu 5-28-75
Dzien Wisly 10-01-80
Dziura W Zlemi 8-05-70

E

E Atit de Aproape Fericirea 8-09-78
E Comincio il Viaggio Nella Vertigini 1-26-77
E Poi lo Chiamarono il Magnifico 10-11-72
E Primavera 3-15-50
E Simonal 8-19-70
E' Tornato Carnevale 1-13-37
E Venne un Uomo 9-08-65
Each Dawn I Die 7-19-39
Each Day I Cry 7-24-63
Each One's Luck (See: Chacun Sa Chance)
Each Pearl a Tear 9-08-16
Each to His Kind 2-09-17
Eadie Was a Lady 3-07-45
Eadweard Muybridge, Zoopraxographer 9-22-76
Eager Lips 8-17-27
Eager to Live (See: Febbre Di Vivere)
Eagle (See: Aguila)
Eagle, The 6-28-18
Eagle, The 11-11-25
Eagle and the Dove, The (See: Aigle et la Colombe, L')
Eagle and the Hawk, The 5-16-33
Eagle and the Hawk, The 2-08-50
Eagle Has Landed, The 12-22-76
Eagle in a Cage 12-22-71
Eagle of the Sea 11-17-26
Eagle Squadron 6-17-42
Eagle with Two Heads 9-29-48
Eagles Attack at Dawn (See: Ha'pritza Ha'gdola)
Eagle's Brood, The 1-29-36
Eagle's Feather 10-11-23
Eagle's Mate, The 7-10-14
Eagle's Wing 8-01-79
Eagle's Wings, The 11-24-16
Eakins 11-28-73
Earl Carroll Sketchbook 8-14-46
Earl Carroll's Vanities 3-07-45
Earl of Chicago, The 1-03-40
Earl of Pawtucket, The 7-16-15
Earl of Puddlestone 8-14-40
Early Bird, The 12-17-24
Early Bird, The 12-08-65
Early Cranes 6-25-80
Early Mornings (See: Petits Matins, Le)
Early to Bed 7-22-36
Early to Wed 6-23-26
Early Works (See: Rani Radovi)
Earrings of Madame De ..., The 7-21-54
Earth (See: Zimlia)
Earth, The (See: Ard, El)
Earth and the Sky, The (See: Tierra y el Cielo, La)
Earth Is a Sinful Song (See: Maa On Syntinen Laulu)
Earth Is Flat, The (See: Jorden Er Flad)
Earth Light (See: Clair de Terre)
Earth Trembles, The (See: Terra Trema, La)
Earth vs. the Flying Saucers 6-06-56
Earth Woman, The 6-23-26
Earthbound 8-13-20
Earthbound 6-05-40
Earthling, The 7-30-80

Eight Days of Happiness (See: Acht Tage Gluck)
Eight Following One (See: Shmonah Be'ikvot Ekhad)
Eight Girls in a Boat (See: Acht Maedels im Boot)
8 Girls in a Boat 1-16-34
813 1-28-21
800 Heroes 11-20-76
800 Leagues on the Amazon (See: 800 Legues Por el Amazonas)
800 Leguas Por el Amazonas 8-12-59
Eight Iron Men 10-22-52
Eight Kilos of Happiness (See: Osam Kila Srece)
Eight O'Clock Walk 3-24-54
Eight on the Lam 4-26-67
8 x 8 3-20-57
Eighteen and Anxious 11-13-57
Eighteen Minutes 4-24-35
1812 9-13-44
Eighteen Year Olds (See: Diciottenni, Le)
Eighth, The (See: Osmiat)
Eighth Commandment, The 6-25-15
Eighth Day, The (See: Huitieme Jour, Le or Attonde Dagen, Den)
Eighth Day of the Week 9-03-58
Eighth Door, The (See: Osma Vrata)
Eighty Blocks from Tiffany's 3-26-80
80 Hussars (See: 80 Huszar)
80 Huszar 5-24-78
80-Mile Speed (See: 120-As Tempo)
80 Steps to Jonah 10-22-69
80,000 Suspects 8-21-63
81st Blow, The 4-30-75
81st Street 12-26-28
Eika Katappa 10-29-69
Ein Jahr 5-21-69
Einbrecher 1-07-31
Eine Von Uns 11-29-32
Einer Von Uns Beiden 1-24-79
Einmaleins der Liebe, Das 1-06-37
Eins 12-08-71
Einstein Theory 2-08-23
Eiszeit 8-06-75
Ekdin Pratidin 2-06-80
Ekdromi 11-23-66
Ekel, Das 6-23-31 and 2-16-32
Ekino To Kalokeri 11-17-71
Ekko af et Skud 4-01-70
El 5-13-53
El Alamein 12-16-53
El Cid 12-06-61
El Condor 6-24-70
El Dorado 12-18-63
El Dorado 6-14-67
El Dorado Pass 5-04-49
El Greco 10-19-66
El Haram 5-26-65
El Hayat Kifar 11-20-68
El Leila El Akhira 5-20-64
El Less Wal Kilab 7-10-63
El 113 1-22-36
El Paso 3-02-49
El Paso Stampede 10-14-53
El Paso Wrecking Corp. 1-25-78
El Shaytan El Saheir 8-12-64
Elastic Transformation 8-28-09
Eldfagein 8-27-52
Eldridge Cleaver 9-02-70
Eleanor Roosevelt Story, The 10-20-65
Elective Affinities (See: Wahlverwandschaften, Die or Affinita
    Elettive)
Electra 5-30-62 and 9-05-62
Electra Glide in Blue 5-23-73
Electric Horseman, The 12-05-79
Electric Insoles 1-22-10
Electronic Monster, The 5-25-60
Eleftherios Venizelos 1910-1927 4-02-80
Elegido, El 2-23-77
Elena and the Men (See: Elena et les Hommes)
Elena et les Hommes 10-03-56
Elephant Boy 2-24-37 and 4-07-37
Elephant Ca Trompe Enormement, Un 10-06-76
Elephant Can Be Extremely Deceptive, An (See: Elephant Ca Trompe
    Enormement, Un)
Elephant God, The (See: Joi Baba Felunath)
Elephant Man, The 10-01-80
Elephant Stampede 10-24-51
Elephant Story (See: Zo Monogatari)
Elephant Walk 3-31-54
Eletbetancoltatott Lany 5-26-65
Elevator to the Gallows (See: Ascenseur Pour l'Echafaud)
11 Harrowhouse 6-26-74
11,000 Series, The (See: Onze Mille Verges, Les)

11 x 14 5-25-77
Eleven Years and One Day (See: Elf Jahre und ein Tag
11 Who Were Loyal 5-22-29
Eleventh Command, The (See: Jedanaesta Zapovest)
Eleventh Commandment 10-22-24
Eleventh Hour, The (See: Godzina Szczytu)
Eleventh Hour, The 7-26-23
Eleventh Hour Guest, The (See: Invite de la 11me Heure, L')
Eleventh Hour Redemption, An 12-03-10
Elf Jahre und ein Tag 10-02-63
Eli Eli 10-09-40
Elinor Norton 3-06-35
Elisa 5-15-57
Elisa, My Love (See: Elisa, Vida Mia)
Elisa, Vida Mia 5-11-77
Elisabeth Von Oesterreich 8-11-31 and 12-15-31
Elise, or Real Life (See: Elise ou la Vraie Vie)
Elise ou la Vraie Vie 5-20-70
"Elite" Group, The (See: Race des "Seigneurs," La)
Elixier des Teufels, Die 7-27-77
Elixir of Dreams 3-27-09
Elixir of Love 10-29-47
Elixir of Strength 3-21-08
Elixir of the Devil, The (See: Elixier des Teufels, Die)
Eliza Comes to Stay 4-22-36
Eliza Fraser 12-29-76
Elizabeth and Essex 10-04-39
Elizabeth of Austria (See: Elisabeth Von Oesterreich)
Elizabeth of Ladymead 1-05-49
Eliza's Horoscope 10-01-75
Ella Cinders 6-09-26
Elle Boit Pas, Elle Fume Pas, Elle Drague Pas, Mais ... Elle
    Cause! 5-13-70
Elle Ne Cause Plus Elle Flingue 9-20-72
Elle Court, Elle Court la Banlieue 5-02-73
Ellery Queen and the Murder Ring 9-24-41
Ellery Queen and the Perfect Crime 8-13-41
Ellery Queen, Master Detective 12-25-40
Ellery Queen's Penthouse Mystery 3-12-41
Elles Etaient Douze Femmes 6-05-40
Elmer and Elsie 8-07-34
Elmer Gantry 6-29-60
Elmer the Great 5-30-33
Elokuu 7-24-57
Elope, If You Can 4-14-22
Elopement 11-07-51
Eloy 3-12-69
Elstree Calling 2-26-30
Elstree Story, The 2-25-53
Eltavozott Nap 1-31-68
Elusive Isabel 5-05-16
Elusive Pimpernel, The 11-15-50
Elve Vagy Halva 2-27-80
Elveszett Paradicsom 7-15-64
Elvira Fernandez 7-29-42
Elvira Madigan 5-10-67
Elvis! Elvis! 7-27-77
Elvis on Tour 11-08-72
Elyazerly 8-28-74
Embarrassing Moments 3-12-30
Embarrassing Moments 11-20-34
Embarrassment of Riches, The 9-27-18
Embassy 7-29-36
Embassy 3-08-72
Ember a Hid Alatt 5-06-36 and 12-02-36
Embers (See: Sholay)
Embezzled Heaven, The (See: Veruntreute Himmel, Der)
Embrace, The (See: Etreinte, L')
Embrace of Fate (See: Orm Ok Savan)
Embraceable You 7-28-48
Embrasement, L' 6-07-23
Embrassez-Moi 11-15-32
Embrujo 7-23-41
Embryo 1-17-68
Embryo 5-26-76
Emden Geht Nach USA: Wir Koennen So Viel 9-15-76
Emden Goes to the U.S.A.: We Can Do So Much (See: Emden Geht
    Nach USA: Wir Koennen So Viel)
Emergency Call 6-27-33
Emergency Call 5-28-52
Emergency Exit (See: Sortie De Secours)
Emergency Hospital 3-21-56
Emergency Landing 6-18-41
Emergency Squad 4-17-40
Emergency Ward (See: Sala de Guardia)
Emergency Wedding 11-15-50
Emigrantes 1-26-49

Emigrants, The (See: Utvandrarna)
Emil 4-27-38
Emil and the Detective (See: Emil und die Detektive)
Emil and the Detectives 2-27-35
Emil and the Detectives 10-14-64
Emil to Tantei Tachi 9-12-56
Emil und die Detektive 12-22-31
Emile's Boat (See: Bateau d'Emile, Le)
Emilienne 6-25-75
Emily 12-15-76
Emitai 7-12-72
Emma 2-09-32
Emma Mae 12-29-76
Emmanuelle 7-31-74
Emmanuelle 2 1-21-76
Emmenez-Moi Au Ritz 10-12-77
Emmerdeur, L' 9-12-73
Emmy of Stork's Nest 10-08-15
Emperor, The (See: Kejsaren)
Emperor and a General, The (See: Nippon No Ichiban Nagai Hi)
Emperor and the Golem, The 1-12-55
Emperor Chien Lung and the Beauty 4-02-80
Emperor Jones, The 9-26-33
Emperor Lee 2-21-68
Emperor Meiji and the Great Russo-Japanese War 1-29-58
Emperor of California (See: Kaiser von Kalifornien)
Emperor of Capri, The (See: Imperatore di Capri, L')
Emperor of the North Pole, The 5-23-73
Emperor Waltz, The 5-05-48
Emperor's Candlesticks 6-30-37
Emperors, Citizens and Comrades (See: Kaiser, Buerger und
    Genossen)
Emperor's Nightingale 5-16-51
Emperor's Waltz (See: Kaiserwalzer)
Empire de la Nuit, L' 1-16-63
Empire of the Ants 7-06-77
Empire of the Night, The (See: Empire de la Nuit, L')
Empire of the Sun (See: Impero del Sole, L')
Empire Strikes Back, The 5-14-80
Employee's Entrance 1-24-33
Empreinte des Geants, L' 4-23-80
Empresa Perdona un Momento de Locura, La 5-30-79
Empress and I, The (See: Ich und die Kaiserin)
Empress Dowager, The 4-02-75
Empty Canvas, The 3-18-64
Empty Chair, The (See: Chaise Vide, La)
Empty Cradle 7-26-23
Empty Hands 8-20-24
Empty Holsters 10-20-37
Empty Saddles 2-03-37
Empty Star, The (See: Estrella Vacia, La)
En Cas de Malheur 9-17-58
En Compagnie de Max Linder 9-11-63
En Dias Come Estos 8-12-64
En Effeuillant la Marguerite 10-31-56
El El Balcon Vacio 8-08-62
En Este Pueblo No Hay Ladrones 8-04-65
En la Ardiente Obscuriadad 9-02-59
En la Luz de Una Estrella 6-18-41
En Moremita Clara 6-28-44
En Och En 3-22-78
Enamorada 2-05-47
Enamorada 12-07-49
Encercles, Les 4-24-68
Enchanted April 3-13-35
Enchanted Barn, The 1-17-19
Enchanted Cottage, The 4-16-24
Enchanted Cottage, The 2-14-45
Enchanted Forest, The 9-19-45
Enchanted Forest, The 7-26-67
Enchanted Hill, The 1-20-26
Enchanted Island 11-05-58
Enchanted Mirror, The 7-22-59
Enchanted Valley, The 3-24-48
Enchanting Shadow, The (See: Tchien Gnu You Houn)
Enchanting Shadow, The (See: Chin Nu Yu Hun)
Enchantment 11-04-21
Enchantment 12-08-48
Enclos, L' 3-15-61
Enclosure, The (See: Enclos, L' or In Kluis)
Encore 11-21-51
Encore 10-29-80
Encounter (See: Imbarco a Mezzanotte)
Encounter in Salzburg 10-28-64
Encrucijada, La 9-16-59
Encrucyada Para Una Monja (See: Nun at the Crossroads, A)
End, The 5-03-78
End of a Priest (See: Fararuv Konec)
End of August at the Hotel Ozone, The 7-05-67
End of Autumn (See: Akibiori)

End of Day, The (See: Smultronstallet)
End of Innocence 9-07-60
End of Mrs. Cheney, The (See: Frau Cheney's Ende)
End of Night (See: Nishant)
End of Pyrenees, The (See: Fin des Pyrenees, La)
End of St. Petersburg, The 4-25-28 and 6-06-28
End of the Affair 3-02-55
End of the Cangaceiros, The (See: A Morte Comanda o Cangaco)
End of the Day, The (See: Fin du Jour, La)
End of the Game, The (See: Fin Del Juego, El)
End of the Game, The 3-21-19
End of the Night (See: Fin de la Noche, El)
End of the Party (See: Fin de Fiesta)
End of the Rainbow, The (See: Ende des Regenbogens, Das)
End of the Rainbow, The 11-03-16
End of the River 11-12-47
End of the Road 11-11-36
End of the Road 11-15-44
End of the Road 11-24-54
End of the Road 1-28-70
End of the Road, The 11-19-15
End of the Tour, The 2-09-17
End of the Trail 11-04-36
End of the Trail, The 8-11-16
End of the World, The (See: Fin du Monde, La)
End of the World in Our Usual Bed on a Night Full of Rain, The
    2-01-78
End Play 12-24-75
Ende des Regenbogens, Das 10-31-79
Endless Horizons (See: Horizons Sans Fin)
Endless Night, The (See: Endlose Nacht, Die)
Endless Summer, The 6-22-66
Endless Trail, The (See: Golapi Ekhon Trainey)
Endlose Nacht, Die 5-22-63
Endstation 7-03-35
Enemies, The (See: Ennemis, Les)
Enemies of Children 12-20-23
Enemies of Progress 1-16-34
Enemies of the Law 7-14-31
Enemies of Youth 6-24-25
Enemy, The (See: Nemica, La or Dusman)
Enemy, The 1-11-28
Enemy Agent 4-24-40
Enemy Agents Meet Ellery Queen 8-26-52
Enemy Below, The 11-27-57
Enemy from Space 9-04-57
Enemy General, The 8-17-60
Enemy of Men 6-16-26
Enemy of the People, An 8-30-78
Enemy of Women 8-30-44
Enemy the Sea, The 11-20-63
Enemy to the King, An 11-17-16
Enfance Nue, L' 9-04-68
Enfant dans la Foule, Un 6-02-76
Enfant de L'Amour, L' 9-10-30
Enfant de la Nuit, L' 11-22-78
Enfant du Miracle, L' 6-21-32
Enfant Sauvage, L' 2-18-70
Enfants de L'Amour, Les 12-09-53
Enfants de L'Oubli, Les 2-21-79
Enfants du Paradis, Les 2-26-47
Enfants du Placard, Les 5-18-77
Enfants du Soleil, Les 5-23-62
Enfants Terribles, Les 5-24-50
Enforcer, The 1-24-51
Enforcer, The 12-22-76
Engel Mit der Posaune, Der 11-24-48
Engel Mit Kleinen Fehlern 4-29-36
Engelchen 3-27-68
Engineer's Romance, The 1-15-10
England Made Me 6-06-73
English Derby, The 6-19-09
English Program 12-27-23
English Without Tears 8-16-44
Englishman and the Girl, The 2-26-10
Englishman's Home, An 10-18-39
Enigma, The (See: Szyfry)
Enigmatic Mr. Parkes, The (See: Enigmatique Monsieur Parkes, L')
Enigmatique Monsieur Parkes, L' 9-03-30 and 11-12-30
Enjeu de la Vie 9-19-56
Enjo 9-16-59
Enkel Melodi, En 9-04-74
Enlevement des Sabines, L' 1-03-62
Enlevez-Moi 11-15-32
Enlighten Thy Daughter 12-29-16
Enlighten Thy Daughter 2-20-34
Ennemi Public No. 1, L' 1-20-54
Ennemis, Les 2-21-62

Ennemis, Les 5-22-68
Enough Praying (See: Ya Basta Con Rezar)
Enraged Sheep, The (See: Mouton Enrage, Le)
Enredos de Papa, Los 8-09-39
Enrico Caruso, Legend of a Voice (See: Enrico Caruso, Leggenda
    di una Voce)
Enrico Caruso, Leggenda di una Voce 11-21-51
Enrico Mattei Affair, The (See: Caso Mattei, Il)
Ensayo de un Crimes 11-07-56
Ensign Pulver 2-26-64
Enslaved, The 2-20-29
Entanglement (See: Tetetoria)
Ente Klingelt Um 1/2 7, Die 1-15-69
Entente Cordiale 5-17-39
Enter Arsene Lupin 11-15-44
Enter Laughing 8-02-67
Enter Madame 12-22-22
Enter Madame 1-15-35
Enter the Dragon 8-22-73
Enterprising Clerk, An 2-19-10
Entertainer, The 8-03-60
Entertainer, The 12-31-75
Entertaining Mr. Sloane 4-18-70
Entfuehrung, Die 7-01-36 and 6-15-38
Entfuehrung Ins Gluck 5-09-51
Enticement 3-25-25
Enticing Goal, The 5-21-30
Entire Days in the Trees (See: Des Journees Entieres dans les
    Arbres)
Entourloupe, L' 7-23-80
Entraineuse, L' 3-20-40
Entre la Mer et L'Eau Douce 7-10-68
Entre Onze Heures et Minuit 6-22-49
Entre Tu et Vous 5-20-70
Entree des Artists 11-23-38
Entrega Immediata 1-01-64
Envers du Paradis, L' 1-13-54
Environment 3-01-23
Envoi des Fleurs 6-14-50
Envy 1-19-17
Eolomea 8-01-73
Epic Mt. Everest 2-18-25
Epic of Everest, The 12-24-24
Epidemic, The (See: Zaraza)
Epihirissis Dourios Ippos 11-09-66
Epilogue 10-14-64 (See: Hvad Med Os?)
Episode 5-19-37
Eqipaj 6-18-80
Equine Hero, An 2-19-10
Equinox 10-21-70
Equipage, L' 4-18-28
Equipage, L' 11-13-36 and 10-26-38
Equus 10-19-77
Er I Bange? 4-14-71
Er Oder Ich 12-17-30
Era e Lisi 8-15-79
Era Lui ... Si! Si! 1-23-52
Era Notte a Roma 11-02-60
Eraserhead 3-23-77
Eravamo Sette Sorelle 2-23-38
Erbe Von Bjoerndal, Das 12-07-60
Erbinka 5-10-67
Ercole e la Regina di Lidia 5-27-59
Eredita Dello Zio, L' 7-03-35
Eredita' Ferramonti 6-09-76
Eresz El A Szakallamat 8-27-75
Erfinder, Der 11-19-80
Erik a Buzakalasz 5-17-39
Erika's Passions 11-08-78
Erinnerungen An die Zukunft 5-13-70
Erlkoenig, Der 7-14-31
Ermine and Rhinestones 9-01-26
Ernest Must Be Married (See: Hay Que Casar a Ernesto)
Ernesto 3-07-79
Eroberung der Zitadelle, Die 7-13-77
Eroe Dei Nostri Tempi, Un 10-21-59
Eroica 11-07-51
Eroica 5-20-59
Eroica 8-22-62
Eroina 10-15-80
Eros et Gyakusatsu 10-29-69
Eros Plus Massacre (See: Eros et Gyakusatsu)
Erotic Adventures of Zorro, The 9-20-72
Erotic Films of Peter de Rome, The 3-07-73
Erotic Memoirs of a Male Chauvinist Pig, The 9-05-73
Erotic Stories (See: Contos Eroticos)
Eroticism 7-17-29
Eroticon 11-24-71
Erotikon (See: Seduction)

Erotikus 8-08-73
Erotissimo 6-25-69
Errand Boy, The 12-06-61
Erste Polka, Die 3-14-79
Erste Walzer, Der 1-17-79
Erstwhile Susan 12-12-19
Erzaehl Mir Nichts 1-27-65
Es 1-26-66
Es Dach Ueberem Chopf 5-09-62
Es Flustert die Liebe 2-05-36
Es Geschah Am Hellichten Tag 7-23-58
Es Geschah Am 20 Juli 7-13-55
Es Geschehen Noch Wunder 4-09-52
Es Gibt Nur Eine Liebe 12-26-33 and 2-03-37
Es Herrscht Ruhe Im Land 6-30-76
Es Ist Alte Geschichte 8-30-72
Es Leuchten Die Sterne 4-13-38
Escadrille de la Chance, L' 7-20-38
Escadrille of Chance (See: Escadrille de la Chance, L')
Escalation 3-13-68
Escalier de Service 12-01-54
Escalofrio Diabolico 10-27-71
Escandalo en la Familia 8-02-67
Escapade (See: Seitensprung)
Escapade 5-31-32
Escapade 7-10-35
Escapade 8-10-55
Escapade, L' 3-13-74
Escapade in Japan 9-11-57
Escape 9-10-30
Escape 10-30-40
Escape 3-31-48
Escape, The (See: Fuga, La; Flugten; or Flucht, Die)
Escape, The 6-05-14
Escape, The 5-09-28
Escape, The 11-08-39
Escape by Night 9-29-37
Escape by Night 3-03-65
Escape from Alcatraz 6-20-79
Escape from Crime 6-03-42
Escape from Devil's Island 11-27-35
Escape from East Berlin 10-24-62
Escape from Fort Bravo 11-11-53
Escape from Hong Kong 5-13-42
Escape from Red Rock 1-15-58
Escape from San Quentin 10-30-57
Escape from the Dark 6-16-76
Escape from the Planet of the Apes 5-26-71
Escape from Zahrain 5-30-62
Escape in the Desert 4-25-45
Escape Me Never 4-17-35 and 5-29-35
Escape Me Never 11-05-47
Escape of the Ape, The 8-29-08
Escape to Athena 1-24-79
Escape to Berlin (See: Flucht Nach Berlin)
Escape to Burma 4-06-55
Escape to Danger 8-18-43
Escape to Glory 11-20-40
Escape to Paradise 12-06-39
Escape to the Sun (See: Habricha el Hashemesh)
Escape to Witch Mountain 3-19-75
Escaped, The (See: Evadidos, Los)
Escaped from Dartmoor 4-16-30
Escaped from Hell 2-06-29
Escapement 3-12-58
Escardon Volapuk, L' 3-03-71
Escargot Dans la Tete, Un 11-19-80
Esclave Blanche, L' 3-22-39
Escondida, La 10-03-56
Escondites, Los 12-09-70
Escopeta Nacional, La 5-10-78
Escort West 1-21-59
Escuela de Musica 3-28-56
Escuela de Vagabudos 4-13-55
Eshet Ha'Gibor 12-18-63
Eskimo 11-21-33
Esmeralda 9-17-15
Esos Hombres 8-25-37
Espana Otra Vez 5-28-69
Espejo, El 7-14-43
Espejo de la Bruja, El 8-22-62
Esperando a Papa 7-30-80
Espionage 3-17-37
Espionage Agent 9-27-39
Espionne, L' 4-17-46
Espions, Les 5-07-58
Espiritu de la Colmena, El 10-03-73

Espontaneo, El 7-29-64
Espy 2-05-75
Esqueleto de la Senora Morales, El 6-22-60
Essakamat 9-19-79
Estate Violenta 1-20-60
Esthappan 10-22-80
Esther and the King 11-23-60
Esther Waters 10-06-48
Esto es Alegria 4-12-67
Estouffade a la Caraibe 11-08-67
Estoy Casada, Ja Ja 5-30-62
Estrella Vacia, La 6-29-60
Et Dieu ... Crea la Femme 1-23-57
Et du Fils 11-01-72
Et la Tendresse? ... Bordel! 4-11-79
Et, Morte la Mort 8-08-62
Et Mourir de Plaisir 9-28-60
Et Satan Conduit le Bal 11-14-62
Et Vive la Liberte 2-15-78
Eta Dell'Amore, L' 3-03-54
Eta Della Pace, L' 5-14-75
Etalon, L' 3-11-70
Etat de Siege 2-14-73
Etat Sauvage, L' 5-03-78
Ete, L' 12-18-68
Ete Sauvage, Un 7-22-70
Eternal City, The 1-01-15
Eternal City, The 1-24-24
Eternal Flame 9-22-22
Eternal Gift, The 11-05-41
Eternal Grind, The 4-14-16
Eternal Links (See: Evig a Lankar)
Eternal Love 5-04-17
Eternal Love 5-15-29
Eternal Magdalene, The 4-25-19
Eternal Mask 1-20-37
Eternal Mask, The (See: Ewige Maske, Die)
Eternal Melodies 2-18-48
Eternal Prayer 10-30-29
Eternal Question, The 6-30-16
Eternal Return, The 12-17-47
Eternal Sappho, The 5-12-16
Eternal Sea 4-06-55
Eternal Secret (See: Orok Titok or Secreto Eterno)
Eternal Sin, The 3-23-17
Eternal Struggle 10-18-23
Eternal Temptress, The 12-14-17
Eternal Three 10-04-23
Eternal Times (See: Vetchni Vremena)
Eternal Woman 5-22-29
Eternally Yours 10-04-39
Eternel Retour, L' (See: Eternal Return, The)
Etes Vous Fiancee a un Marin Grec ou a un Pilote de Ligne?
     11-25-70
Ethel's Luncheon 9-11-09
Ethiopians, The 10-06-71
Etoile Disparait, Une 9-06-32 and 2-20-35
Etoile du Sud, L' 3-05-69
Etoile Sans Lumiere 4-24-46
Etoiles de Midi, Les 7-13-60
Etoiles Ne Meurent Jamais, Les 6-12-57
Etrange Desir de Monsieur Bard, L' 4-07-54
Etrange Destin 6-19-46
Etrange Madame X, L' 7-04-51
Etrange Monsieur Steve, L' 7-10-57
Etrange Monsieur Victor, L' 6-01-38
Etrangere, L' 2-18-31
Etrangere, L' 2-14-68
Etrangers, Les 7-16-69
Etrangleur, L' 3-17-71
Etre Libre 12-04-68
Etreinte, L' 5-20-70
Etrusco Uccidi Encore, L' (See: Dead Are Alive, The)
Ett Anstaendigt Liv 4-18-79
Eucharistic Congress 11-10-26
Eugen Heisst Wohlgeboren 9-18-68
Eugene Aram 7-16-15
Eugene Aram 4-16-24
Eugene Means Well-Born (See: Eugen Heisst Wohlgeboren)
Eugenie Grandet 11-06-46
Eugenie--The Story of Her Journey into Perversion 8-12-70
Eugenio 11-19-80
Eunuch, The 5-10-72
Eureka Stockade 2-02-49
Europa di Notte 4-29-59

Europe by Night (See: Europa di Notte)
Europe '51 9-24-52
Europeans, The 5-16-79
Eutanasia di un Amore 10-25-78
Eva (See: Halbzarte, Die)
Eva 1-12-38
Eva 2-02-49
Eva 10-17-62
Eva a 5116 7-15-64
Eva and the Grasshopper 11-28-28
Eva Erbt das Paradies 10-17-51
Eva Inherits Paradise (See: Eva Erbt das Paradies)
Eva Peron Story, The 9-10-52
Evades, Les 7-13-55
Evadidos, Los 7-08-64
Evangeline 1-30-14
Evangeline 8-15-19 and 8-22-19
Evangeline 7-31-29
Eve and the Handyman 5-10-61
Eve Knew Her Apples 4-25-45
Eve of St. Mark, The 5-17-44
Eve Wants to Sleep Also 11-05-58 (Also see: Ewa Chce Spac)
Evel Knievel 7-07-71
Evelyn Prentice 11-13-34
Even as You and I 4-06-17
Even Break, An 7-27-14
Even If You Are Mud, Still You Return to Dust (See: Putik Ka Man ...
     Sa Alabok Magbabalik)
Even unto Death 2-05-15
Evenement le Plus Important Depuis Que L'Homme a Marche Sur la
     Lune, L' 10-17-73
Evening at the Djurgarden (See: Djurgardskvallar)
Evening Clothes 3-23-27
Evening Land (See: Aftenlandet)
Evening Sun's War Pictures 1-08-15
Evening with the Royal Ballet, An 11-11-64
Evenings for Sale 11-15-32
Evensong 9-25-34 and 11-20-34
Event, The (See: Dogadaj)
Events 6-03-70
Ever in My Heart 10-17-33
Ever Since Eve 10-28-21
Ever Since Eve 4-03-34
Ever Since Eve 6-30-37
Ever Since Venus 11-01-44
Everest Symphony 7-21-71
Evergreen 5-08-34 and 1-15-35
Evergreen, The (See: Sang Nok Soo)
Everlasting Glory, The 8-20-75
Everlasting Whisper, The 10-14-25
Every Bastard a King 7-31-68
Every Day Has Its Secret (See: Chaque Jour a Son Secret)
Every Day Is a Holiday 7-06-66
Every Day's a Holiday 12-22-37
Every Day's a Holiday 12-02-64
Every Girl Should Be Married 11-10-48
Every Girl's Dream 9-07-17
Every Home Should Have One 3-11-70
Every Inch a Gentleman (See: Todo un Caballero)
Every Inch a Lady 9-10-75
Every Little Crook and Nanny 6-14-72
Every Man for Himself and God Against All (See: Jeder Fuer
     Sich und Gott Gegen Alle)
Every Night at Eight 8-07-35
Every Saturday Night 3-18-36
Every Sunday Morning (See: Tutte Le Domeniche Mattina)
Every Wednesday (See: Minden Szerdan)
Every Which Way but Loose 12-20-78
Every Woman Has a Secret (See: Jede Frau Hat ein Geheimnis)
Every Year Again (See: Alle Jahre Wieder)
Everybody Does It 8-31-49
Everybody Go Home 11-21-62
Everybody He Is Nice, Everybody He Is Beautiful (See: Tout Le
     Monde Il Est Beau, Tout Le Monde Il Est Gentil)
Everybody Sing 1-26-38
Everybody's Acting 11-10-26
Everybody's Baby 11-30-38
Everybody's Dancin' 4-12-50
Everybody's Doing It 1-12-38
Everybody's Girl 10-18-18
Everybody's Hobby 9-27-39
Everybody's Old Man 4-01-36
Everybody's Sweetheart 10-08-20
Everybody's Woman (See: Signora di Tutti, La)
Everyday Life in a Syrian Village (See: Al Hayatt Al Yawmiyah Fi
     Qariah Suriyah)
Everyman (See: Jedermann)

Eyes Full of Sun (See: Du Soleil Plein Les Yeux)
Eyes in the Night 9-09-42
Eyes of Envy 8-31-17
Eyes of Julia Deep, The 8-09-18
Eyes of Laura Mars 8-02-78
Eyes of Love, The (See: Yeux de L'Amour, Les)
Eyes of Mystery, The 1-24-18
Eyes of Texas 7-21-48
Eyes of the Forest 3-26-24
Eyes of the Heart 11-05-20
Eyes of the Mummy 8-18-22
Eyes of the Soul 4-25-19
Eyes of the Underworld 10-07-42 and 1-06-43
Eyes of the World, The 7-05-18
Eyes of the World, The 8-20-30
Eyes of Youth 11-07-19
Eyes without a Face (See: Yeux Sans Visage, Les)
Eyewitness 8-22-56
Eyewitness 9-16-70
Eyewitness ... North Vietnam 11-23-66
Ez a Villa Elado 5-08-35

F

FBI Code 98 4-08-64
FBI Girl 11-14-51
FBI Story, The 8-19-59
F Comme Fairbanks 5-05-76
F for Fairbanks (See: F Comme Fairbanks)
F.J. Holden, The 5-04-77
FM 3-03-78
F Man 5-06-36
F.P.1 9-19-33
F.P.1 Antwortet Nicht 1-17-33
F.P.1 Doesn't Answer (See: F.P.1 Antwortet Nicht)
F.T.A. 7-12-72
Faaroedokument 1-14-70
Fabian 10-29-80
Fabian Balint Talalkozasa Istennel 7-23-80
Fabiola 2-08-23
Fabiola 6-22-49
Fable, A 5-19-71
Fabuleuse Aventure de Marco Polo, La 9-01-65
Fabuleuses Aventures du Legendaire Baron du Munchhausen, Les
    5-23-79
Fabulous Adventure of Marco Polo (See: Fabuleuse Aventure
    de Marco Polo, La)
Fabulous Adventures of the Legendary Baron Munchhausen, The (See:
    Fabuleuses Aventures du Legendaire Baron du Munchhausen, Les)
Fabulous Bastard from Chicago 7-02-69
Fabulous Dorseys, The 2-26-47
Fabulous Senorita 3-26-52
Fabulous South Seas, The (See: Geisterland Der Suedsee)
Fabulous Suzanne, The 12-18-46
Fabulous Texan, The 11-12-47
Fabulous World of Jules Verne, The 5-03-61
Face, The (See: Ansiket or Arc)
Face Behind the Mask 2-12-41
Face Behind the Scar 3-06-40
Face Between 5-26-22
Face in the Crowd, A 5-29-57
Face in the Dark, The 4-19-18
Face in the Fog 10-13-22
Face in the Moonlight, The 7-09-15
Face in the Rain, A 3-20-63
Face in the Sky 2-21-33
Face of a Fugitive 4-29-59
Face of Another, The (See: Tanin No Kao)
Face of Fire 7-29-59
Face of Fu Manchu, The 10-06-65
Face of Marble, The 2-13-46
Face of Medusa, The 7-12-67
Face of the World 11-11-21
Face of War, A 3-06-68
Face on the Barroom Floor 6-28-23
Face on the Barroom Floor 10-18-32
Face to Face (See: Licem U Lice; Prossopo Me Prossopo; Cara a
    Cara; or Frau Sucht Liebe, Eine)
Face to Face 10-06-22
Face to Face 11-19-52
Face to Face 4-07-76
Face to the Sun (See: Soleil en Face, Le)

Face Value 1-04-18
Faces 6-26-68
Faces in the Dark 11-30-60
Faces in the Fog 10-18-44
Facing the Footlights 5-29-14
Facing the Gatling Guns 7-03-14
Facing the Music 6-27-33
Facori Family, The 11-12-10
Facteur S'en Va-T-En Guerre, Le 9-28-66
Factory B (See: Pogon B)
Factory Magdalen, A 3-19-15
Factory Outing, The (See: Firmaskovturen)
Facts of Life, The 11-16-60
Facts of Love 11-02-49
Facundo, el Tigre de Los Llanos 10-01-52
Facundo, Tiger of the Plains (See: Facundo, el Tigre de Los
    Llanos)
Fad, Jal 6-06-79
Faddija 2-08-50
Fade to Black 10-15-80
Faded Flower, The 7-14-16
Faded Lilies 6-26-09
Fadern 9-10-69
Faetrene Paa Torndal 10-17-73
Fagyongyok 8-22-79
Fah Larng Fon 6-28-78
Faham, El 5-16-73
Fahrenheit 451 9-14-66
Fahrt Ins Abenteuer, Die 6-16-66
Fai Lui Ching Chuen 6-11-69
Faible Femme, Une 4-04-33
Faibles Femmes 3-11-59
Fail Safe 9-16-64
Faille, La 6-11-75
Failure (See: Rotagg)
Failure, The (See: Neal of the Navy: Part III)
Faint Heart and Fair Lady 11-02-17
Fair, The (See: Kirmes)
Fair and Warmer (See: Mustergatte, Der)
Fair and Warmer 11-28-19
Fair Barbarian, The 12-21-17
Fair Cheat 11-15-23
Fair Co-Ed, The 10-26-27
Fair Enough 12-20-18
Fair Exchange, A 9-25-09
Fair in the Rain (See: Kermis In de Regen)
Fair Lady 3-24-22
Fair of the Dove (See: Verbena de la Paloma, La)
Fair People 9-03-30
Fair Play 7-15-25
Fair Pretender, The 5-31-18
Fair Warning 2-11-31
Fair Warning 3-24-37
Fair Week 6-04-24
Fair Wind to Java 4-29-53
Fairy Dance (See: Samodivsko Horo)
Fairy of Happiness (See: Maerchen vom Glueck)
Fairy Tale Auto (See: Meseauto)
Faites Sauter la Banque 4-01-64
Faith 2-07-19
Faith 3-05-20
Faith Endurin' 3-22-18
Faith Healer, The 3-18-21
Faith, Hope and Witchcraft 7-27-60
Faith of a Child, The 6-25-15
Faith of the Strong 10-03-19
Faithful City 4-02-52
Faithful Heart 9-01-22
Faithful Heart 8-22-33
Faithful in My Fashion 6-12-46
Faithful Soldier of Pancho Villa, A (See: Dorado de Pancho
    Villa, Un)
Faithful until Death 6-12-14
Faithful Wives 2-23-27
Faithful Woman, A (See: Femme Fidele, Une)
Faithfulness (See: Fedelta')
Faithless 11-22-32
Faithless Lover 3-14-28
Faits Divers a Paris 8-09-50
Faja Lobbi 7-06-60
Fake, The 10-12-27
Fake, The 6-24-53 and 10-28-53
Faking of the President 1974 5-19-76
Falak 1-31-68
Falcon and the Co-eds, The 11-10-43
Falcon in Danger, The 7-14-43
Falcon in Hollywood, The 12-13-44

Falcon in Mexico, The 7-26-44 and 8-09-44
Falcon in San Francisco, The 7-25-45
Falcon Out West, The 3-08-44
Falcon Strikes Back, The 3-17-43
Falcon Takes Over, The 5-06-42
Falcons, The (See: Magasiskola)
Falcon's Adventure, The 12-11-46
Falcon's Alibi, The 4-17-46
Falcon's Brother, The 9-30-42
Fall, Der 5-03-72
Fall, The (See: Fall, Der; A Queda; or Sturz, Der)
Fall, The 10-29-69
Fall des General-Stabs-Oberst Redl, Der 3-18-31
Fall des Oberst Redl, Der 8-30-32
Fall Guy, The 5-28-30
Fall In 5-19-43
Fall of a Body (See: Chute d'un Corps, La)
Fall of a Nation, The 6-09-16
Fall of a Saint 9-24-20
Fall of an Empress 4-23-24
Fall of Babylon, The 4-02-10
Fall of Babylon, The 7-25-19
Fall of Berlin, The 9-12-45 and 6-18-52
Fall of Constantinople, The 1-29-15
Fall of Eve, The 6-19-29
Fall of the House of Usher 5-21-52
Fall of the Roman Empire, The 3-25-64
Fall of the Romanoffs, The 9-14-17
Fall Roberts, Der 5-23-33
Fallen Angel 10-24-45
Fallen Idol, The 5-22-14
Fallen Idol, The 5-23-19
Fallen Idol, The 10-06-48
Fallen Sparrow, The 8-18-43
Fallen Woman, A (See: Daraku Suru Onna)
Falling for You 7-04-33
Falling in Love (See: Trouble Ahead)
Falling in Love 9-25-34
Falling in Love Again 11-19-80
Falling Point (See: Point de Chute)
Falsche Bewegung 7-30-75
Falsche Dimitry, Der 2-08-23
Falsche Ehemann, Der 4-15-31 and 10-25-32
Falsche Gewicht, Das 11-10-71
Falscher Feldmarschall 7-12-32
Falscher Fuffziger, Ein 2-17-37
False Alarm, The 12-01-26
False Ambitions 7-26-18
False Brands 3-10-22
False Colors 12-18-14
False Colors 11-03-43
False Dimitry, The (See: Falsche Dimitry, Der)
False Evidence 4-25-19
False Face 12-15-76
False Faces 11-29-32
False Faces 7-07-43
False Faces, The 2-21-19
False Fathers 5-08-29
False Field Marshall (See: Falscher Feldmarschall)
False Friend, The 9-24-10
False Friend, The 6-02-17
False Fronts 6-09-22
False Gods 5-16-19
False Husband (See: Falsche Ehemann, Der)
False Kisses 11-25-21
False Madonna 1-26-32
False Magistrate, The 7-17-14
False Passport, The (See: Viza Zla)
False Policeman (See: Nissei Keiji)
False Pretenses 10-30-35
False Rapture 5-07-41
False Road 5-07-20
False Student, The (See: Nise Daigakusi)
False Uniforms 11-29-32
Fame 3-25-36
Fame 4-30-80
Fame and Fortune 12-13-18
Fame Is the Spur 10-08-47
Fame Street 4-12-32
Familia, Bien, Gracias, La 1-23-80
Familia Unida Esperando la Llegada de Hallewyn, La 8-30-72
Familiaridades 4-08-70
Familiarities (See: Familiaridades)
Familie Schimek 6-12-57
Familien Gyldenkaal 12-31-75
Familien Gyldenkaal Spraenger Banken 12-29-76
Familien Gyldenkaal Vinder Valget 10-26-77

Familien Med De 100 Boern 10-25-72
Familien Swedenhielm 4-02-47
Familienglueck 9-03-75
Familienparade 3-24-37
Familjen Andersson 2-15-39
Famille Duraton, La 5-08-40
Famille Fenouillard, La 4-26-61
Family, The (See: Abusuan)
Family, The 12-25-74
Family Adventure (See: Viva Lo Imposible)
Family Affair, A 4-21-37
Family Bonus (See: Csaladi Potlek)
Family Chronicle (See: Cronaca Familiare)
Family Cupboard, The 10-22-15
Family Doctor 3-05-58
Family, Fine, Thanks, The (See: Familia, Bien, Gracias, La)
Family Honeymoon 12-08-48
Family Honor, The 3-30-17
Family Honor, The 1-26-77
Family Jewels, The (See: Bijutaril de Familie or Bijoux de Famille, Les)
Family Jewels, The 6-23-65
Family Life (See: Zycie Rodzinne)
Family Life (See: Prapanch)
Family Life 12-08-71
Family Nest (See: Gsaladi Tuzfezek)
Family on Parade (See: Familienparade)
Family Plot 3-24-76
Family Portrait (See: Retrato de Familia)
Family Schimek (See: Familie Schimek)
Family Secret, The 9-17-24
Family Secret, The 10-24-51
Family Skeleton, The 3-08-18
Family Stain, The 10-29-15
Family Upstairs 7-21-26
Family Way, The 12-28-66
Family With 100 Children, The (See: Familien Med De 100 Boern)
Famous Ferguson Case, The 4-26-32
Famous Love Affairs (See: Amours Celebres, Les)
Famous Mrs. Fair, The 4-26-23
Famous 702, The (See: Celebrul 702)
Fan, The 4-06-49
Fanatics, The (See: Mordus, Les)
Fanatiques, Les 3-19-58
Fanchon the Cricket 5-14-15
Fancy Baggage 3-20-29
Fancy Pants 7-19-50
Fando and Lis (See: Fando y Lis)
Fando y Lis 7-02-69
Fanfan la Tulipe 4-30-52
Fanfare 12-17-58
Fanfarrones, Los 11-30-60
Fang and Claw (See: Griffe et la Dent, La)
Fang and Claw 1-01-36
Fangelse 3-25-59
Fangs of Destiny 4-04-28
Fangs of Justice 1-19-27
Fangs of the Wild 1-25-28
Fangs of the Wild 3-24-54
Fangschuss, Der 8-25-76
Fanny 1-21-48
Fanny 6-21-61
Fanny by Gaslight 6-07-44
Fanny Elssler 12-08-37
Fanny Foley Herself 10-27-31
Fanny Hawthorn 11-13-29
Fanny Hill 10-08-69
Fanny Hill: Memoirs of a Woman of Pleasure 3-17-65
Fan's Notes, A 5-31-72
Fantabulous Inc. 10-30-68
Fantasia 11-13-40
Fantasia Among the Squares (See: Fantasia Chez les Ploucs)
Fantasia Chez les Ploucs 2-10-71
Fantasies Behind the Pearly Curtain 11-26-75
Fantasm 8-04-76
Fantasm Comes Again 5-10-78
Fantasma de la Opereta, El 2-21-61
Fantasmas en Buenos Aires 8-12-42
Fantasmi a Roma 8-09-61
Fantasterne 12-20-67
Fantastic Balloon Trip, The (See: Viaje Fantastico En Globo)
Fantastic Comedy (See: Comedie Fantastica)
Fantastic Night 10-12-49
Fantastic Plastic Machine, The 4-02-69
Fantastic Voyage 7-27-66
Fantastica 5-14-80
Fantastico Mundo del Dr. Coppelius, El (See: Dr. Coppelius)
Fantine 10-02-09

Fantomas 3-27-14 (Also see: False Magistrate, The)
Fantomas 3-20-34
Fantomas 12-02-64
Fantomas Against Scotland Yard (See: Fantomas Contre Scotland
     Yard)
Fantomas Contre Scotland Yard 4-12-67
Fantome de la Liberte, Le 8-28-74
Fantozzi 6-18-75
Fantozzi Against the World (See: Fantozzi Contro Tutti)
Fantozzi Contro Tutti 12-17-80
Far Away and Close (See: Langt Borta Och Naera)
Far Country, The 1-26-55
Far Cry, The 4-07-26
Far from Dallas 12-20-72
Far from Moscow 7-04-51
Far from the Madding Crowd 6-30-16
Far from the Madding Crowd 9-27-67
Far from the Trees (See: Lejos De los Arbores)
Far from Vietnam 10-04-67
Far Frontier, The 1-19-49
Far Horizons 5-25-55
Far Jag Lana Din Fru? 7-15-59
Far Jag Lov, Magistern! 3-24-48
Far Out, Star Route 12-08-71
Far Road, The (See: Toi Ippon No Michi)
Far Shore, The 8-18-76
Far Til Fire I Hoejt Humoer 8-25-71
Far-West, Le 5-30-73
Fararuv Konec 5-21-69
Faraway Tomorrow (See: Toi Ashita)
Farbe des Himmels, Die 6-13-79
Farceur, Le 8-10-60
Farewell (See: Abschied)
Farewell 9-24-30
Farewell Again 5-19-37
Farewell, Doves! 8-15-62
Farewell From Yesterday (See: Abschied von Gestern)
Farewell, My Beautiful Naples 10-08-47
Farewell, My Lovely 8-13-75
Farewell, Scarlett 2-04-76
Farewell to Arms, A 12-13-32
Farewell to Arms, A 12-25-57
Farewell to Yesterday 9-13-50
Farewell to Youth (See: Adios Juventud)
Farewells, The (See: Pozegnania or Het Afscheid)
Fargo Express 3-07-33
Fargo Kid 2-12-41
Farlig Sommer 4-23-69
Farlige Kys 1-10-73
Farmer, The 3-02-77
Farmer in the Dell, The 3-11-36
Farmer Takes a Wife, The 8-14-35
Farmer Takes a Wife 4-22-53
Farmer's Daughter, The 11-14-28
Farmer's Daughter, The 2-14-40
Farmer's Daughter, The 2-19-47
Farmer's Treasure 9-25-09
Farmer's Wife, The 3-21-28 and 1-22-30
Farmer's Wife, The 2-19-41
Farming in a Flat 10-30-09
Faro da Padre, Le 7-31-74
Faro Document 1979 (See: Farodokument 1979)
Faroan 5-25-66
Farodokument 1979 11-05-80
Farrebique 1-15-47
Fascinating Youth 3-17-26
Fascination 4-21-22
Fascination 7-28-31
Fascist, The 6-23-65
Fascist Jew, The (See: Ebreo Fascista, L')
Fashion Madness 2-22-28
Fashion Model 4-04-45
Fashion Row 1-31-24
Fashions for Women 3-30-27
Fashions in Love 7-03-29
Fashions of 1934 1-23-34
Fast and Furious 7-06-27
Fast and Furious 10-18-39
Fast and Loose 12-03-30
Fast and Loose 2-15-39
Fast and Sexy 8-31-60
Fast and the Furious, The 11-03-54
Fast Anstaendiges Maedchen, Ein 11-06-63
Fast Break 2-21-79
Fast Bullets 3-04-36
Fast Charlie--The Moonbeam Rider 5-30-79

Fast Companions 9-13-32
Fast Company 3-22-18
Fast Company 10-09-29
Fast Company 6-29-38
Fast Company 4-08-53
Fast Company 5-23-79
Fast Lady, The 1-16-63
Fast Life 8-21-29
Fast Life 12-27-32
Fast Mail 7-14-22
Fast on the Draw 10-11-50
Fast Set, The 11-19-24
Fast Train 12-05-08
Fast Worker, The 1-07-25
Fast Workers, The 3-21-33
Faster, Pussycat, Kill! Kill! 2-09-66
Fastest Guitar Alive, The 5-17-67
Fastest Gun Alive 6-20-56
Fat Angels 10-29-80
Fat Baby 7-04-08
Fat City 5-24-72
Fat Man, The 4-04-51
Fat Man's Worries (See: Martyre de l'Obese, Le)
Fat Spy 5-18-66
Fata Morgana 5-11-66
Fata Morgana 10-13-71
Fatal Card, The 10-08-15
Fatal Comma, The (See: Fatalnata Zapetaya)
Fatal Hour, The 12-24-20
Fatal Hour, The 1-17-40
Fatal Introduction, The 3-24-16
Fatal Lady 7-15-36
Fatal Love 9-18-09
Fatal Marriage 6-09-22
Fatal Mistake, The 1-28-25
Fatal Night, The 6-02-48
Fatal Shot, The (See: Fejloves)
Fatal Wedding, The 1-23-14
Fatal Witness, The 9-05-45
Fatal Woman, The (See: Fata Morgana)
Fatalnata Zapetaya 7-25-79
Fate, La (See: Queens, The)
Fate Is the Hunter 9-16-64
Fate of a Flirt 5-12-26
Fate of an Innocent, The 10-20-65
Fate of Lee Kahn 11-13-74
Fated Hour, The 3-30-17
Fate's Boomerang 5-26-16
Father (See: Apa)
Father and Son 8-04-16
Father and Son 6-05-29
Father Brown 6-16-54
Father Brown, Detective 1-22-35
Father by Force (See: Silom Otac)
Father Came Too 2-12-64
Father Damian Story (See: Molokai)
Father Goose 11-18-64
Father Heart Wants to Get Married (See: Papa Corazon Se Quiere
     Casar)
Father Is a Bachelor 2-15-50
Father Is a Prince 11-06-40
Father Love (See: Arashi)
Father Master (See: Padre, Padrone)
Father of a Soldier 7-14-65
Father of Four in a Sunny Mood (See: Far Til Fire I Hoejt Humoer)
Father of the Bride 5-10-50
Father of the Girl, The (See: Pere De Mademoiselle)
Father of the Godfathers (See: Corleone)
Father O'Flynn 12-28-38
Father Serge (See: Otietz Sergii)
Father Takes a Wife 7-16-41
Father Takes the Air 6-20-51
Father Unawares (See: Papa Sans le Savoir)
Father Was a Full-Back 8-17-49
Fathers and Sons (See: Padri e Figli)
Father's Choice 3-28-13
Father's Dilemma 10-01-52
Father's First Half Holiday 4-10-09
Father's Little Dividend 2-21-51
Father's Son 2-25-31
Father's Son 2-19-41
Father's Trip, The (See: Voyage du Pere, Le)
Fathom 7-26-67
Fatiche di Ercole, La 7-02-58
Fatso 1-30-80
Fatti di Gente Perbene 2-05-75
Fatty and Mabel Adrift 2-04-16
Fatty and the Broadway Stars 12-10-15

Fatty Finn 7-23-80
Faubourg Montmartre 10-13-31
Fault, The (See: A Culpa)
Fault of Abbot Mouret, The (See: Faute de L'Abbe Mouret, La)
Faust 11-17-26 and 12-08-26
Faust 11-23-60
Faust 7-15-64
Faust and the Devil 4-26-50
Faust in der Tasche, Die 5-23-79
Faust XX 8-03-66
Faustina 5-22-57
Faustina 11-20-68
Faustine and the Beautiful Summer (See: Faustine et le Bel Ete)
Faustine et le Bel Ete 1-19-72
Faustrecht der Freiheit 5-28-75
Faut Aller Parmi le Monde Pour le Savoir 6-09-71
Faut-il les Marier? 7-19-32
Faut Pas Prendre les Enfantes du Bon Dieu Pour des Canards
    Sauvages 9-25-68
Faute de L'Abbe Mouret, La 11-11-70
Fauve Est Lache, Le 3-11-59
Faux-Cul, Le 10-29-75
Faux Pas de Deux 10-20-76
Favor to a Friend, A 8-15-19
Favorite Fool, A 10-08-15
Favorite of Schonbrunn, The 12-11-29
Fazil 6-06-28
Fear (See: Angst; Paura, La; or O Fovos Strah)
Fear 9-26-28
Fear 4-03-46
Fear and Desire 4-01-53
Fear Eats Out the Soul (See: Angst Essen Seele Auf)
Fear Fighter, The 9-30-25
Fear in the Night 2-19-47
Fear Is the Key 1-17-73
Fear Market 1-09-20
Fear No Evil 4-06-49
Fear Not 12-07-17
Fear of Fear 10-20-76
Fear of Power 7-09-58
Fear on the City (See: Peur Sur La Ville)
Fear Strikes Out 2-06-57
Fear Woman, The 7-11-19
Fearless Fagan 7-09-52
Fearless Lover 7-15-25
Fearless Rider, The 2-08-28
Fearless Vampire Killers (or, Pardon Me, but Your Teeth Are in
    My Neck), The 11-15-67
Fearmakers, The 9-24-58
Fears (See: Miedos, Los)
Feast, The (See: Fraznik)
Feast of Friends 10-08-69
Feast of Life, The 4-28-16
Feather, The 12-11-29
Feather in Her Hat 10-30-35
Feathertop 4-14-16
Febbre Di Vivere 7-29-53
Fecundity 7-17-29
Fed One, The (See: Hranjenik)
Fed Up (See: Ras Le Bol)
Fedelta' 9-08-65
Federal Agent 5-14-36
Federal Agent at Large 3-22-50
Federal Bullets 10-27-37
Federal Fugitives 5-07-41
Federal Man 6-28-50
Federal Man-Hunt 1-11-39
Federale, Il (See: Fascist, The)
Fedora 3-12-15
Fedora 8-09-18
Fedora 2-06-46
Fedora 8-23-78
Feedback (See: Obratnaya Sviaz)
Feedback 3-28-79
Feel My Pulse 3-07-28
Feelings 8-17-77
Feerie du Jazz 1-07-31
Feet First 11-05-30
Feet of Clay 9-24-24
Fegefeuer 4-21-71 and 10-27-71
Fehlschuss 2-16-77
Fejloves 2-26-69
Fekete Gyemantok 5-13-38
Fekete Gyemantok 3-23-77
Feldherrnhuegel, Der 11-04-53

Feldobott Ko 2-26-69
Felices 60, Los (See: Happy Sixties, The)
Felicidad 7-24-57 and 9-30-59
Felicite 5-23-79
Felines, Les 3-17-76
Felines, The (See: Felins, Les)
Felins, Les 6-24-64
Felix and Otilia 9-06-72
Felix O'Day 9-17-20
Felmegyek a Ministerhez 6-27-62
Fem Ar--Som Vi Saa Dem 11-26-47
Female 11-07-33
Female, The 9-03-24
Female Animal 1-28-70
Female Animal, The 1-15-58
Female Fugitive 4-13-38
Female Hamlet 7-27-77
Female Jungle 6-27-56
Female of the Species, The 12-15-16
Female on the Beach 7-13-55
Female Prisoner, The (See: Prisonniere, La)
Female Response, The 12-27-72
Female Sleuth 10-09-09
Female Soldier, The (See: Soldadera, La)
Female Spy 2-02-07
Female Three Times (See: Femmine Tre Volte)
Female Trouble 2-05-75
Femina Ridens 10-22-69
Feminin-Feminin 3-28-73
Feminine Regime (See: Weiberregiment)
Feminine Touch, The 9-17-41
Feminine Touch, The 4-04-56
Feminine Wiles (See: Cosas de Mujer)
Femme a Sa Fenetre, Une 10-27-76
Femme au Couteau, La 10-29-69
Femme Aux Bottes Rouges, La 10-23-74
Femme dans le Train 10-18-32
Femme de Jean, La 3-20-74
Femme de Mes Reves, La 3-15-32
Femme Douce, Une 6-25-69
Femme du Boulanger, La 10-12-38
Femme Ecarlate, La 6-11-69
Femme en Bleu, La 1-17-73
Femme en Homme, La 5-31-32
Femme-Enfant, La 5-28-80
Femme Est une Femme, Une 9-20-61
Femme et le Pantin, La 4-08-59
Femme Fatale, Une 7-23-75
Femme Fidele, Une 9-15-76
Femme Flic, La 1-23-80
Femme Infidele, La 11-27-68
Femme Mariee, La 9-16-64
Femme Nue, La 8-29-33
Femme Qui Pleure, La 12-06-78
Femme, un Jour, Une 2-02-77
Femmes, Les 11-19-69
Femmes au Soleil 7-10-74
Femmes d'Abord, Les 5-01-63
Femmes de Paris 1-06-54
Femmes de Sade 5-05-76
Femmes, Femmes 11-20-74
Femmes Sans Nom 7-12-50
Femmes S'en Balancent, Les 6-09-54
Femmine Tre Volte 11-27-57
Fen 4-25-79
Fence Riders 5-10-50
Fengelset 4-06-49
Fenouillard Family, The (See: Famille Fenouillard, La)
Fenyes Szelek 2-26-69
Fernand 4-09-80
Ferocious One, The (See: Lyutyi)
Ferocious Pal 4-24-34
Ferroviere, Il 6-13-56
Ferry Across the Mersey 12-09-64
Ferry to Hong Kong 7-15-59
Festa, Flour and ... (See: Feste, Farina E ...)
Feste, Farina E ... 9-24-80
Festival 9-13-67
Festival of Riflemen in Schilda (See: Schuetzenfest in Schilda)
Festival Panafricain 7-14-71
Fete a Henriette, La 2-18-53
Fete Espagnole, La 9-20-61
Fete Sauvage, La 2-18-76
Fetes Galantes, Les 4-20-66
Fettered Woman, The 11-02-17
Fettowa, El 7-24-57
Feu a Volonte 5-26-65
Feu aux Levres, Le 8-22-73
Feu aux Poudres, Le 4-03-57

Feu de Paille, Le 5-22-40 (Also see: Fire in the Straw)
Feu Follet, Le 9-11-63
Feu Matthias Pascal 11-24-37
Feu Sacre, Le 5-26-71
Feud, The 2-19-10
Feud Girl, The 5-19-16
Feud Maker 7-20-38
Feud of the Range 7-19-39
Feud of the Trail 6-22-38
Feud of the West 5-27-36
Feudin' Fussin' and a-Fightin' 6-09-48
Feuer um Mitternacht 3-29-78
Feuerschiff, Das 5-15-63
Feuerwerk 12-15-54
Feuerzangenbowle, Die 10-14-70
Feux de la Chandeleur, Les 5-31-72
Fever (See: Fiebre)
Fever 6-30-71
Fever Heat 5-15-68
Fever in the Blood, A 1-11-61
Fever Rises in El Pao, The (See: Fievre Monte a El Pao, La)
Few Days in the Life of I.I. Oblomov, A 5-28-80
ffolkes 4-23-80
Fiaca, La 4-02-69
Fiaca, The (See: Fiaca, La)
Fiacre N. 13, Il 7-07-48
Fiammata, La 2-18-53
Fiancee, The (See: Verlobte, Die)
Fiancee du Pirate, La 9-17-69
Fiancees (See: Fidanzati, I)
Fiat Voluntas Dei 7-15-36
Fibbers, The 10-26-17
Fickle Finger of Fate, The 6-14-67
Fickle Women 8-20-20
Fico d'India 11-19-80
Fidanzati, I 5-29-63
Fiddle and the Fan 9-18-09
Fiddler on the Roof 11-03-71
Fiddlin' Buckaroo 1-09-34
Fidele Bauer, Der 10-17-51
Fidelio 7-29-70 and 4-14-71
Fidlovacka 7-07-31
Fiebre 10-13-76
Field Lilies (See: Lalie Polne)
Fields of Honor 1-18-18
Fiend Who Walked the West 8-06-58
Fiend Without a Face 5-28-58
Fiendish Plot of Dr. Fu Manchu, The 8-13-80
Fiercest Heart, The 3-29-61
Fiesta 12-31-41
Fiesta 6-18-47
Fietsen Naar de Maan (See: Bicycling to the Moon)
Fietsen Naar de Maan 2-27-63
Fievre Monte a El Pao, La 2-03-60
Fifi la Plume 6-02-65
Fifi the Feather (See: Fifi la Plume)
15 Maiden Lane 10-14-36
15 Wives 9-25-34
15 Yok Yok 2-15-78
Fifth Avenue Girl 8-23-39
Fifth Avenue Models 5-06-25
Fifth Commandment, The (See: Fuenfte Gebot, Das)
Fifth Floor, The 3-12-80
Fifth Musketeer, The 4-11-79
Fifth Rider Is Fear, The (See: A Paty Jezdec Je Strach)
Fifth Seal, The (See: Az Otodik Pecset)
Fifty Candles 1-06-22
Fifty Fathoms Deep (See: Mon Ami Tim)
Fifty Fathoms Deep 9-22-31
Fifty-Fifty (See: Hetzi-Hetzi or Halbe-Halbe)
Fifty-Fifty 10-20-16
Fifty-Fifty Girl, The 5-16-28
55 Days at Peking 5-01-63
50 Million Frenchmen 4-01-31
51 File, The (See: Dossier 51, Le)
50 Roads to Town 6-09-37
52nd Street 10-06-37
$50,000 Climax Show, The 6-04-75
50 Years Before Your Eyes 6-21-50
Fig Leaf (See: Fugefalevel)
Fig Leaves 7-07-26
Figaro 4-03-29 and 11-27-29
Figaro Gran Giornata 11-07-33
Figaro's Great Day (See: Figaro Gran Giornata)
Fight, The 1-22-15
Fight, The 3-17-71
Fight Film in France 8-12-21

Fight for a Million, A 4-16-15
Fight for Freedom (See: Ija Ominira)
Fight for Life, A 5-15-14
Fight for Life, The 3-06-40
Fight for Love, A 2-22-08
Fight for Love, A 3-21-19
Fight for Matterhorn 7-31-29
Fight for Peace, The 5-18-38
Fight for Rome--Part 1 (See: Kampf Um Rom (Part I))
Fight for Your Lady 10-20-37
Fight for Your Life 12-21-77
Fight of the Age 5-20-21
Fight of the Tertia (See: Kampf Der Tertia)
Fight to the Death (See: Metralleta Stein)
Fight to the Finish, A 7-07-37
Fight to the Last 12-28-38
Fighter, The 8-19-21
Fighter, The 5-07-52
Fighter Attack 11-25-53
Fighter Squadron 11-24-48
Fighters, The 1-23-74
Fighters' Paradise 9-24-24
Fightin' Mad 11-25-21
Fightin' Strain 9-27-23
Fighting American 6-04-24
Fighting Back 8-04-48
Fighting Bill Fargo 5-20-42
Fighting Blade 10-18-23
Fighting Blood 10-18-23
Fighting Bob 6-04-15
Fighting Boob, The 6-23-26
Fighting Buckaroo, The 4-07-43
Fighting Caravans 1-28-31
Fighting Champ 3-14-33
Fighting Chance 7-23-20
Fighting Coast Guard 5-20-51
Fighting Cock, The (See: Coqueluche, La)
Fighting Code, The 1-16-34
Fighting Colleen, A 11-28-19
Fighting Coward 3-19-24
Fighting Cub, The 7-29-25
Fighting Demon 7-29-25
Fighting Destiny 3-21-19
Fighting Devil Dogs 5-11-38
Fighting Eagle, The 8-17-27
Fighting Edge 4-21-26
Fighting Failure 3-16-27
Fighting Father Dunne 5-12-48
Fighting Flames 8-19-25
Fighting Fool 3-29-32
Fighting Fools 4-27-49
Fighting for Fatherland 4-16-30
Fighting for France 11-26-15
Fighting for Gold 4-04-19
Fighting for Justice 8-06-24
Fighting for Love 1-05-17
Fighting for Verdun 10-13-16
Fighting Frontier 2-10-43
Fighting Fury 10-08-24
Fighting Gentleman 11-15-32
Fighting Grin, The 1-18-18
Fighting Gringo, The 11-29-39
Fighting Guardsman, The 10-10-45
Fighting Guerrillas, The (See: Chetniks)
Fighting Guide 9-29-22
Fighting Heart 10-22-24
Fighting Hero 10-09-34
Fighting Hombre, The 7-27-27
Fighting Hope, The 7-23-15
Fighting in France 11-26-15
Fighting Kentuckian, The 9-14-49
Fighting Lady, The 12-20-44
Fighting Legion 4-09-30
Fighting Love 5-25-27
Fighting Lover 6-10-21
Fighting Mad 12-13-39
Fighting Mad 1-28-48
Fighting Mad 4-28-76
Fighting Man of the Plains 10-12-49
Fighting Marshall 4-12-32
Fighting O'Flynn, The 1-05-49
Fighting Odds 10-05-17
Fighting Parson, The 8-08-33
Fighting Pioneers 5-29-35
Fighting Playboy, The 6-02-37
Fighting President, The 4-11-33
Fighting Prince of Donegal, The 8-24-66
Fighting Ranger, The 4-17-34

Fighting Red Head, The 7-18-28
Fighting Redhead, The 1-18-50
Fighting Renegade 9-06-39
Fighting Roosevelts, The 1-25-19
Fighting Sap, The 11-02-27
Fighting Sea Monsters 3-17-43
Fighting Seabees, The 1-19-44
Fighting Shepherdess, The 4-02-20
Fighting Sheriff 5-13-25
Fighting Sheriff, The 5-27-31
Fighting 69th, The 1-10-40
Fighting Stallion 5-03-50
Fighting Stock 4-24-35
Fighting Stranger 9-23-21
Fighting Streak 6-09-22
Fighting Texan 8-18-37
Fighting Texans 8-01-33
Fighting the Flames 12-09-25
Fighting Thoroughbred 8-25-26
Fighting Thoroughbreds 1-18-39
Fighting Three, The 10-19-27
Fighting Through 2-21-19
Fighting Thru 1-28-31
Fighting Trooper, The 1-08-35
Fighting Valley 12-08-43
Fighting Vigilantes, The 11-26-47
Fighting Youth 9-30-25
Fighting Youth 11-06-35
Figlio di D'Artagnan, Il 5-03-50
Figurehead, The 6-18-20
Figures Don't Lie 1-18-28
Figures in a Landscape 7-29-70
Fil a la Patte, Un 3-02-55
File of the Golden Goose, The 6-04-69
File 113 2-23-32
Filip Cel Bun 6-14-78
Filip the Good (See: Filip Cel Bun)
Fill 'Er Up With Super (See: Plein De Super, Le)
Fille a Croquer, Une 6-27-51
Fille au Fouet, La 11-05-52
Fille au Violoncelle, La 10-24-73
Fille aux Yeux d'Or, La 8-30-61
Fille aux Yeux Gris, La 12-19-45
Fille Cousue de Fil Blanc, Une 1-12-77
Fille D'en Face, La 2-28-68
Fille de Hambourg, La 9-03-58
Fille du Diable, La 5-15-46
Fille du Garde Barriere, La 10-01-75
Fille du Puisatier, La 5-28-41
Fille du Regiment, La 6-27-33
Fille et Des Fusils, Une 2-10-65
Fille Nomme Amour, Une 4-16-69
Fille Pour L'Ete, Une 7-20-60
Fille Unique, Une 5-19-76
Filles de la Nuit 8-26-59
Fillmore 5-24-72
Film, The (See: Pelicula, La)
Film d'Amore e d'Anarchia 5-30-73
Film Detective, The 9-04-14
Film Parade, The 12-26-33
Film Portrait 7-12-72
Film Without a Name 10-25-50
Filming of Golden Eagle, The 4-03-29
Filming "Othello" 6-28-78
Fils, Le 2-28-73
Fils d'Amerique, Un 6-21-32
Fils d'Amr Est Mort, Le 8-27-75
Fils de Caroline Cherie, Le 4-20-55
Fils de France 4-17-46
Fils de l'Autre, Le 3-22-32
Fils de L'Eau, Les 11-26-58
Fils Improvist, Le 12-13-32
Fils Unique, Un 12-10-69
Filthiest Show in Town, The 3-21-73
Filumena Marturano 3-05-52
Fimpen 3-27-74
Fin de Fiesta 3-30-60
Fin de la Noche, El 2-09-44
Fin Del Juego, El 7-15-70
Fin des Pyrenees, La 10-28-70
Fin du Jour, La 5-03-39
Fin du Monde, La 2-11-31
Final Accord (See: Schlussakkord)
Final Assignment 11-12-80
Final Battle, The (See: Lutte Finale, La)
Final Chapter--Walking Tall 6-22-77
Final Close Up, The 6-06-19
Final Comedown, The 5-03-72

Final Countdown, The 7-16-80
Final Curtain, The 2-11-16
Final Cut 7-30-80
Final Edition 3-01-32
Final Hour, The 8-05-36
Final Judgment, The 10-29-15
Final Test 4-15-53
Finance Director, The (See: Herr Finanzdirektor, Der)
Finche C'e Guerra C'e Speranza 1-15-75
Find the Blackmailer 10-20-43
Find the Idol (See: Cherchez L'Idole)
Find the Witness 2-24-37
Find the Woman 6-07-18
Find Your Man 10-08-24
Finders Keepers 2-18-21
Finders Keepers 3-07-28
Finders Keepers 12-19-51
Finders Keepers 12-14-66
Finders Keepers, Lovers Weepers 5-15-68
Findling, Der 4-30-69
Fine Clothes 10-21-25
Fine Feathers 6-18-15
Fine Feathers 7-08-21
Fine Madness, A 5-04-66
Fine Manners (See: Belles Manieres, Les)
Fine Manners 9-08-26
Fine Pair, A 5-07-69
Finest Hours, The 5-06-64
Finestra Sul Lunapark, La 9-04-57
Finger Man 6-15-55
Finger of God, The (See: Palec Bozy)
Finger of Guilt 11-14-56
Finger Points, The 4-08-31
Finger Prints 1-26-27
Finger Prints 1-19-46
Fingerprints Don't Lie 4-11-51
Fingers 2-01-78
Fingers at the Window 3-18-42
Fingers in the Head (See: Doigts Dans la Tete, Les)
Finian's Rainbow 10-09-68
Finishing School 5-01-34
Finn and Hattie 2-04-31
Finnegan's Ball 10-28-27
Finnegans Wake 5-19-65
Finney 10-29-69
Fiore Delle Mille e Una Notte, Il 5-29-74
Firatin Cinleri 8-02-78
Fire (See: Fuoco)
Fire 7-23-69
Fire and Steel 7-06-27
Fire and Sword 2-27-14
Fire At Will (See: Feu a Volonte)
Fire Bride 3-17-22
Fire Brigade, The 12-22-26
Fire Cat, The 2-25-21
Fire Department of New York City, The 1-14-11
Fire Down Below 5-29-57
Fire Flingers, The 3-28-19
Fire in the Middle 5-31-78
Fire in the Opera (See: Brand in der Oper)
Fire in the Straw 7-07-43
Fire of Girdlestone, The 9-29-16
Fire on the Plains (See: Nobi)
Fire over Africa 10-06-54
Fire over England 1-27-37 and 3-10-37
Fire Patrol, The 5-21-24
Fire Sale 6-08-77
Fire to the Lips (See: Feu aux Levres, Le)
Fire-Tongue Bowl, The (See: Feuerzangenbowle, Die)
Fire Woman 10-27-71
Fireball 8-16-50
Fireball 500 6-15-66
Firebird, The 11-20-34
Firebrand, The (See: Eldfagein)
Firebrand Johnson 9-10-30
Firecreek 1-24-68
Firefly, The 7-28-37
Firefly of France, The 6-14-18
Firefly of Tough Luck, The 10-19-17
Fireman (See: Chaplin's Fireman)
Fireman, Save My Child 8-31-27
Fireman, Save My Child 2-23-32
Fireman, Save My Child 4-28-54
Firemen of Viggen, The (See: Pompieri Di Viggiu, I)
Firepower 4-11-79
Fires of Conscience 9-29-16
Fires of Faith 5-09-19
Fires of Fate 8-09-23
Fires of Fate 4-04-33

Fires of Innocence 9-29-22
Fires of Youth, The 8-30-18
Fire's Share, The (See: Part Du Feu, La)
Fireworks (See: Fuochi d'Artificio or Feuerwerk)
Fireworks Woman 8-06-75
Firing Line, The 7-11-79
Firing Squad, The (See: Fusilacion, La or Peloton d'Execution)
Firm in Love, The (See: Verliebte Firma, Die)
Firm Man, The 4-23-75
Firm Weds, The (See: Firma Heiratet, Die)
Firma Heiratet, Die 7-12-32
Firmaskovturen 3-01-78
Firpo-Brennan Fight 3-29-23
First a Girl 11-20-35 and 1-08-36
First Aid 10-13-31
First Airship Crossing the English Channel 9-11-09
First Auto, The 6-29-27
First Baby, The 5-27-36
First Born, The 2-04-21
First Charge of the Machetes (See: Primera Carga Al Machete, La)
First Chronicle (See: Primera Cronica)
First Circle, The 1-17-73
First Comes Courage 9-08-43
First Communion (See: Prima Communione)
First Cry (See: Krik)
First Day of Liberty (See: Pierwszy Dzieri Wolnosci)
First Day of Peace, The (See: Pervy Den Mira)
First Deadly Sin 10-22-80
First Degree 2-01-23
First Effort (See: Opera Prima)
First Error Step, The 7-25-79
First Family 12-31-80
First Film Concert 11-15-39
First Fires, The (See: Uzavreli Grad)
First Forty Days 10-04-50
First Front, The 11-16-49
First Gentleman, The 3-31-48
First Gray Hair, The 10-29-10
First Great Train Robbery, The 1-17-79
First 100 Years, The 3-16-38
First Kiss, The 8-22-28
First Lady 9-01-37
First Law, The 7-26-18
First Law of Nature, The 4-23-15
First Legion, The 4-11-51
First Lesson, The (See: Parvi Urok)
First Love (See: Primo Amore or Moi Tinh Dau)
First Love 1-06-22
First Love 11-08-39
First Love 7-22-70
First Love 11-02-77
First Man into Space 2-18-59
First Mass, The (See: A Primeira Missa)
First Men in the Moon 8-05-64
First Night 2-09-27
First Nudie Musical, The 3-10-76
First of the Few, The 9-02-42
First Offenders 5-17-39
First Opera Film Festival 6-02-48
First Polka, The (See: Erste Polka, Die)
First Position 11-08-72
First Spaceship on Venus 12-19-62
First Start 2-18-53
First Step, The 12-17-75
First Sunshine Comedy 11-16-17
First Teacher, The (See: Piervij Utchitelh)
First Texan, The 6-13-56
First Time, The (See: Premiere Fois, La)
First Time, The 1-30-52
First Time, The 4-02-69
First Time, On the Grass, The (See: Prima Volta Sull'Erba, La)
First Time Round 8-16-72
First to Fight 1-25-67
First to Fight, The 8-18-31
First Traveling Saleslady, The 8-15-56
First Voyage (See: Premier Voyage)
First Waltz, The (See: Erste Walzer, Der)
First Weapons, The (See: Premieres Armes, Les)
First Woman 4-21-22
First World War, The 11-13-34
First Yank into Tokyo 9-05-45
First Year, The 3-10-26
First Year, The 8-23-32
Fischio Al Naso, Il 7-12-67
Fish, Football and Girls (See: Hashechuna Shelanu)
Fish Hawk 9-05-79

Fish-Kettle John (See: O Psarovannos)
Fish That Saved Pittsburgh, The 11-07-79
Fisherman, The 9-11-09
Fisherman's Bride 11-27-09
Fisherman's Granddaughter, The 2-26-10
Fisherman's Wharf 2-08-39
Fishing Boats on the Ocean 8-08-08
Fishing Smack, The 11-12-10
F.I.S.T. 4-19-78
Fist in the Pocket (See: Faust in der Tasche, Die)
Fist of Fear Touch of Death 9-24-80
Fist of Fury 11-01-72
Fists in the Pockets (See: Pugni In Tasca, I)
Fists of Fury 6-27-73
Fit for a King 9-01-37
Fitzwilly 12-20-67
Five 4-25-51
Five Accursed Gentlemen, The (See: Cinq Gentlemen Maudits, Les)
Five Against the House 5-18-55
Five and Ten 7-14-31
5 and 10 Cent Annie 9-12-28
Five and the Spies (See: De 5 Og Spionerne)
Five Ashore for Singapore (See: Cinq Gars Pour Singapour)
Five Branded Women 4-06-60
Five Came Back 6-21-39
Five Card Stud 7-17-68
Five Cents of Lavarede, The (See: Cinq Sous de Lavarede, Les)
Five Days--Five Nights (See: Fuenf Tage--Fuenf Naechte)
Five Days from Home 4-19-78
Five Days to Live 1-13-22
Five Dollar Baby, The 6-30-22
Five Easy Pieces 9-16-70
Five Evenings (See: Pyat' Vecherov)
Five Finger Exercise 4-18-62
5 Fingers 2-13-52
Five Fingers of Death 3-21-73
Five Forks (See: Cinco Tenedores)
Five-Forty (See: Ot Ora Negyven)
Five from Barska Street 3-16-55
Five Gates to Hell 9-23-59
Five Gents' Trick Book 12-29-65
Five Girls Around the Neck (See: Pet Holek Na Krku)
Five Golden Hours 3-08-61
Five Graves to Cairo 5-05-43
Five Guns to Tombstone 3-08-61
Five Guns West 4-20-55
Five in a Million (See: Pet Z Milionu)
Five-Leaf Clover, The (See: Trefle a Cinq Feuilles, Le)
Five-Legged Sheep, The (See: Mouton A Cinq Pattes, Le)
Five Little Peppers 9-06-39
Five Little Peppers at Home 3-06-40
Five Little Peppers in Trouble 9-18-40
Five-Man Army 3-04-70
$5,000,000 Counterfeit Plot 8-14-14
Five Million Years to Earth 1-31-68
Five Minutes of Paradise (See: Pet Minuta Raja)
Five Minutes to Twelve 1-29-10
Five of a Kind 10-12-38
Five on the Black Hand Side 10-24-73
Five out of a Million 11-18-59
Five Paupers in an Automobile (See: Cinque Poveri in Automobile)
Five Pennies, The 5-06-59
5% de Risque 7-30-80
5% Risk (See: 5% de Risque)
5 + 5 4-02-80
Five Star Final 9-15-31
Five Steps to Danger 1-23-57
Five the Hard Way 4-16-69
$5,000 an Hour 12-06-18
$5,000 Reward 5-10-18
5,000 Fingers of Dr. T., The 6-17-53
Five Times Five 7-26-39
Five Weeks in a Balloon 8-15-62
Five-Year Plan, The 6-02-31
Five Years--As We Saw Them (See: Fem Ar--Som Vi Saa Dem)
Fixed Bayonets 11-21-51
Fixer, The 9-17-15
Fixer, The 11-20-68
Fixer Dugan 5-10-39
Fizessen Nagysad 4-14-37
Flaaden's Friske Fyre 9-22-65
Flag Lieutenant, The 7-06-27
Flag Lieutenant, The 11-08-32
Flagermusen 11-06-68
Flagrant Delit 4-01-31
Flame 2-19-75
Flame, The (See: Fiammata, La)
Flame, The 1-14-48

Flame and the Arrow, The 6-21-50
Flame and the Fire 3-09-66
Flame and the Flesh 4-28-54
Flame in the Streets 6-28-61
Flame of Araby 11-21-51
Flame of Calcutta 6-24-53
Flame of Life, The 2-15-23
Flame of Love (See: Phairak Soom Suang)
Flame of Love, The 11-05-30
Flame of New Orleans 4-30-41
Flame of Passion 11-05-15
Flame of Stamboul 2-28-51
Flame of the Argentine 7-21-26
Flame of the Barbary Coast 4-18-45
Flame of the Desert 10-31-19
Flame of the Islands 12-28-55
Flame of the West 9-26-45
Flame of the Yukon 7-13-17
Flame of Torment (See: Enjo)
Flame of Youth 1-21-21
Flame of Youth 1-28-21
Flame of Youth 9-28-49
Flame Over Vietnam 6-28-67
Flame Within, The 6-05-35
Flamenco 5-26-54
Flames 11-17-26
Flames 8-30-32
Flames of Chance 1-18-18
Flames of Desire 6-17-25
Flames of Johannis, The 4-14-16
Flames of Justice 5-01-14
Flames of Passion 12-15-22
Flames of the Flesh 2-13-20
Flames Over the Adriatic (See: Flammes Sur L'Adriatique)
Flamin' Fire-Chief (See: Brand-Boerge Rykker Ud)
Flaming Barriers 1-31-24
Flaming Feather 12-19-51
Flaming Forest 11-24-26
Flaming Forties 3-11-25
Flaming Frontier 2-14-68
Flaming Frontier, The 4-07-26
Flaming Fury 6-15-49
Flaming Gold 2-20-34
Flaming Hearts (See: Flammende Herzen)
Flaming Hearts 3-01-23
Flaming Hour 12-15-22
Flaming Lead 11-15-39
Flaming Love 1-21-25
Flaming Omen, The 10-26-17
Flaming Star 12-21-60
Flaming Sun (See: Sol en Llamas)
Flaming Teen-Age, The 10-17-56
Flaming Waters 1-27-26
Flamingo Road 4-06-49
Flamme Empor 6-06-79
Flammende Herzen 3-29-78
Flammes Sur L'Adriatique 8-28-68
Flanagan 4-07-76
Flanders and Alcott Report on Sex Response, The 3-17-71
Flap 10-28-70
Flapper, The 5-21-20
Flareup 11-12-69
Flare-Up Sal 2-01-18
Flash, The 1-25-23
Flash Gordon 3-11-36
Flash Gordon 12-03-80
Flash Gordon's Trip to Mars 2-16-38
Flash of an Emerald, The 10-15-15
Flashback 6-04-69
Flashbacks 10-12-38
Flashing Fangs 12-01-26
Flashing Guns 8-27-47
Flashlight, The 5-18-17
Flat Next Door, The 12-03-10
Flat Top 11-19-52
Flattery 12-31-24
Flavor of Green Tea over Rice, The 1-17-73
Flaxy Martin 1-19-49
Flea in Her Ear, A 10-23-68
Fledermaus, Die (See: Flagermusen or Waltz Time)
Fledermaus, Die 1-19-32
Fledermaus, Die 11-24-37
Fledermaus, Die 3-17-48
Fleet's In, The 10-03-28
Fleet's In, The 1-21-42
Fleetwing 7-25-28
Fleisch 12-05-79

Flemish Farm, The 8-25-43
Flesh 12-13-32
Flesh 10-02-68
Flesh and Blood 3-21-51
Flesh and Fantasy 9-22-43
Flesh and Fury 3-12-52
Flesh and the Devil 1-12-27
Flesh and the Fiends 2-10-60
Flesh and the Spur 2-20-57
Flesh for Frankenstein 2-27-74
Flesh Gordon 7-31-74
Flesh Is Weak, The 8-14-57
Flesh of the Orchid, The (See: Chair de L'Orchidee, La)
Flesh Will Surrender, The 11-01-50
Fleshpot on 42nd Street 7-12-72
Fleur Bleue 6-09-71
Fleur D'Oranger, La 11-08-32
Fleur D'Oseille 10-25-67
Fleur de L'age ou les Adolescentes, La 9-09-64
Fleurs du Miel, Les 3-17-76
Flic, Un 2-04-48
Flic, Un 11-15-72
Flic Ou Voyou 6-27-79
Flic Story 10-08-75
Flick 4-22-70
Flicka Och Hyacinter 2-03-71
Flickan Fran Fjellbyn 4-06-49
Flickan Fran Tredje Raden 11-16-49
Flickan I Frack 7-24-57
Flickorna 10-02-68
Flickorna I Smaland 10-22-47
Flickornas Alfred 9-18-35
Fliegende Schatten 5-10-32
Fliers 5-29-35
Fliers of the Open Skies (See: Letaci Velikog Neba)
Flight 9-18-29
Flight 11-02-60
Flight, The (See: Flucht, Die)
Flight, The 5-26-71
Flight Angels 5-15-40
Flight at Midnight 8-30-39
Flight Command 12-18-40
Flight Commander, The 10-12-27 and 5-09-28
Flight for Freedom 2-03-43
Flight from Ashiya 4-01-64
Flight from Destiny 1-01-41
Flight from Glory 8-11-37
Flight into Darkness (See: Equipage, L')
Flight into France (See: Fuga in Francia)
Flight into Nowhere 5-04-38
Flight Level 450 (See: Flygniva 450)
Flight Lieutenant 8-05-42
Flight Nurse 11-04-53
Flight of Monsieur Valette, The 11-13-09
Flight of the Doves 3-31-71
Flight of the Duchess, The 3-10-16
Flight of the Lost Balloon 11-01-61
Flight of the Phoenix 12-15-65
Flight of the White Heron 5-26-54
Flight That Disappeared, The 9-20-61
Flight to Fame 12-14-38
Flight to Hong Kong 10-03-56
Flight to Mars 11-07-51
Flight to Tangier 10-14-53
Flim-Flam Man, The 7-12-67
Flipper 5-01-63
Flipper's New Adventure 5-27-64
Flirt, The 3-31-16
Flirt, The 1-05-23
Flirtation Walk 12-04-34
Flirting Widow, The 8-06-30
Flirting with Danger 3-06-35
Flirting with Death 9-28-17
Flirting with Fate 6-30-16
Flirting with Fate 12-14-38
Flirting with Love 9-03-24
Flirto-Maniac, The 2-05-10
Flirty Affliction, A 9-24-10
Flitterwochen 7-01-36
Flivvering 3-09-17
Floating College 12-12-28
Floating Mine, The 3-19-15
Floch 9-20-72
Flock, The (See: Suru)
Floetenkonzert 1-07-31
Floetenkonzert Von Sanssouci, Das 10-20-31
Flood, The 4-29-31
Flood Area, The (See: Inundados, Los)

Flood Tide 1-22-58
Floodgates 3-26-24
Floods of Fear 11-26-58
Floodtide 3-30-49
Floor Above, The 4-10-14
Floor Below, The 3-08-18
Floor Show 11-08-78
Floorwalker, The 5-19-16
Flor de Durazno 12-12-45
Flor de Mayo 7-15-59
Flor de Santidad 4-18-73
Flor Sylvestre 1-24-45
Flora Four Flush 10-31-14
Floradora Girl 6-04-30
Florence Nightingale 4-09-15
Florentine Dagger, The 5-01-35
Flores de Papel 3-15-78
Florian 4-03-40
Florida Enchantment, A 8-14-14
Florida Special 6-03-36
Flottans Kavaljerer 4-13-49
Flourishing Times (See: Blomstrande Tider)
Flower Drum Song 11-08-61
Flower Lady (See: Blumenfrau, Die)
Flower Market, The 7-21-65
Flower of Faith, The 12-18-14
Flower of Faith, The 9-22-16
Flower of Holiness (See: Flor de Santidad)
Flower of No Man's Land, The 6-23-16
Flower of the Night 10-21-25
Flower of the North 1-20-22
Flower of Youth 2-15-08
Flower Parade of Pasadena 1-29-10
Flower Seller of Lindenau, The (See: Blumenfrau von Lindenau,
    Die)
Flower Thief 6-04-69
Flowering Wheat, The (See: Ble En Herbe, Le)
Flowing Gold 3-12-24
Flowing Gold 8-28-40
Flucht, Die 6-28-78 and 7-02-80
Flucht Ins Schilf 3-25-53
Flucht Nach Berlin 3-15-61
Fluchtgefahr 8-27-75
Fluechtling Aus Chicago, Der 3-18-36
Fluffy 4-07-65
Fluga Ger Ingen Sommar, En 11-26-47
Flugten 5-02-73
Flunking Out (See: Asignatura Pendiente)
Flurry, The (See: Memetih)
Flute Concert (See: Floetenkonzert)
Flute Concert of Sanssouci, The (See: Floetenkonzert von
    Sanssouci, Das)
Fly, The 7-16-58
Fly by Night 1-21-42
Fly Cop, The 9-21-17
Fly God, The 7-05-18
Fly in the Ointment, A (See: Fil a la Patte, Un)
Fly-Away Baby 7-14-37
Flygniva 450 4-30-80
Flyin' Cowboy, The 5-16-28
Flying Blind 8-20-41
Flying Cadets 10-15-41
Flying Colors 9-14-17
Flying Cranes (See: Letiat Jouravly)
Flying Deuces, The 10-11-39
Flying Devils 8-29-33
Flying Doctor, The 10-21-36
Flying Down to Rio 12-26-33
Flying Dutchman, The (See: Vliegende Hollander, De)
Flying Fists 8-27-24
Flying Fists 3-02-38
Flying Fleet 2-13-29
Flying Fontaines, The 12-23-59
Flying Fool 8-28-29
Flying Fool 10-20-31
Flying Fortress 7-15-42
Flying G-Men 3-22-39
Flying Gold (See: A Repulo Arany)
Flying Guillotine 3-19-75
Flying High 2-23-27
Flying High 12-15-31
Flying Hoofs 3-04-25
Flying Horseman, The 9-22-26
Flying Hostess 12-16-36
Flying Irishman, The 3-08-39
Flying Leathernecks 7-25-51
Flying Luck 3-21-28

Flying Mail, The 6-29-27
Flying Marine, The 8-07-29
Flying Matchmaker, The 11-01-67
Flying Missile, The 12-27-50
Flying Pat 12-17-20
Flying Romeos 4-04-28
Flying Saucer 1-11-50
Flying Serpent, The 1-23-46
Flying Shadows (See: Fliegende Schatten or Ombres Fuyantes)
Flying Squad 8-02-32
Flying Tigers 9-23-42
Flying Torpedo, The 3-17-16
Flying "U" Ranch, The 11-02-27
Flying Wild 4-16-41
Flying with the Marines 6-28-18
Flying Wonders, The (See: Wunder des Fliegens)
Focal Point (See: Point de Mire, Le)
Foersterchristl, Die 3-04-31 and 4-29-31
Foersterchristl, Die 10-29-52
Fog 1-09-34
Fog 11-24-65
Fog, The 7-26-23
Fog, The 1-16-80
Fog Bound 5-30-23
Fog Island 4-11-45
Fog over Frisco 6-12-34
Foggy Quay (See: Quai des Brumes, Le)
Fogo Morto 7-14-76
Foiled 11-27-09
Foiled by a Cigarette, or The Stolen Plans of the Fortress
    10-15-10
Foire aux Cancres, La 11-27-63
Foire aux Chimeres, La 10-09-46
Folie des Grandeurs, La 12-22-71
Folies Bergere 2-27-35 and 4-22-36
Folies-Bergere 3-06-57
Folies Bourgeoises 7-21-76
Folk Tales of River Bend (See: Hansuli Banker Upakatha)
Folket I Simlangsdalen 6-16-48
Folks at Red Wolf Inn, The 11-22-72
Folks from Way Down East, The 4-24-14
Folle a Tuer 9-03-75
Folle de Toujane, La 5-01-74
Folle Nuit, La 5-03-32
Follie per l'Opera (See: Mad About Opera)
Follies Girl, The 4-25-19
Follies Girl 8-25-43
Follies of Barbara, The (See: Locuras de Barbara, Las)
Follow a Star 12-23-59
Follow Me 5-07-69
Follow Me, Boys 10-12-66
Follow Me Quietly 7-13-49
Follow That Camel 12-20-67
Follow That Dream 3-28-62
Follow That Horse 7-20-60
Follow That Man (See: Suivez Cet Homme)
Follow That Woman 8-22-45
Follow the Band 4-28-43
Follow the Boys 2-27-63
Follow the Boys 3-29-44
Follow the Fleet 2-26-36
Follow the Girl 8-03-17
Follow the Leader 12-10-30
Follow the Leader 6-07-44
Follow the Star 3-01-78
Follow the Sun 3-21-51
Follow Thru 9-17-30
Follow Your Heart 10-28-36
Following in Father's Footsteps 4-13-07
Following the Flag to France 6-28-18
Folly of Revenge, The 7-28-16
Folly of Vanity 1-28-25
Folly to Be Wise 12-10-52
Foma Gordeev 8-03-60
Fome de Amor 6-16-68
Fond de l'Air Est Rouge, Le 11-16-77
Fonissa, I 10-30-74
Fontamara 9-03-80
Food for Scandal 11-05-20
Food Gamblers, The 8-10-17
Food of the Gods, The 6-09-76
Fool, The 4-15-25
Fool and His Money, A 4-16-20
Fool and His Money, A 7-15-25
Fool Killer, The 4-28-65
Fool of Love 9-18-29
Fool There Was, A 3-12-15

Fool There Was, A 7-21-22
Foolin' Around 4-23-80
Foolish Age, The 11-11-21
Foolish Happiness 5-08-29
Foolish Husbands 10-20-48
Foolish Maiden 1-16-29
Foolish Matrons 8-26-21
Foolish Parents 11-08-23
Foolish Virgin (See: Vierge Folle)
Foolish Virgin 12-10-24
Foolish Wives 1-20-22
Foolish Years (See: Lude Godina)
Fools 12-23-70
Fools and Riches 5-30-23
Fools and Their Money 6-20-19
Fool's Awakening 3-19-24
Fools First 8-04-22
Fools for Luck 9-28-17
Fools for Luck 6-13-28
Fools for Scandal 3-30-38
Fool's Gold 5-09-19
Fool's Gold 10-09-46
Fool's Highway 4-02-24
Fools in the Dark 8-20-24
Fools of Baragan (See: Ciulinii Baraganului)
Fools of Desire 3-26-41
Fools of Fashion 10-20-26
Fools of Fate 10-16-09
Fools of Fortune 12-22-22
Fool's Parade 6-23-71
Fool's Paradise 12-16-21
Fool's Revenge, The 2-18-16
Fools Rush In 5-25-49
Football Daft 7-07-22
Footfalls 9-16-21
Foothills of Savoy, The 3-26-10
Footlight Fever 3-26-41
Footlight Glamour 11-10-43
Footlight Parade 10-10-33
Footlight Ranger 4-05-23
Footlight Serenade 7-08-42
Footlight Varieties 3-28-51
Footlights 10-07-21
Footlights and Fools 11-13-29
Footlights and Shadows 2-13-20
Footlights of Fate, The 8-25-16
Footlights or the Farm 10-01-10
Footloose Heiress 10-13-37
Footloose Widows 6-23-26
Footsteps (See: Pasos)
Footsteps in the Dark 3-05-41
Footsteps in the Fog 8-24-55
Footsteps in the Night 5-16-33
Footsteps in the Night 7-24-57
Footsteps of Aztecs 6-16-26
For a Few Dollars More (See: Per Qualche Dollaro in Piu)
For a Fistful of Dollars (See: Per Un Pugno di Dollari)
For a Price (See: Intoccabili, Gli)
For a Woman's Fair Name 3-10-16
For a Woman's Honor 10-03-19 and 11-14-19
For Alimony Only 9-22-26
For an Unimportant Reason (See: Thi Asimanton Aformin)
For Another Woman 6-24-25
For Att Inte Tala Om Alla Dessa Kvinnor 7-01-64
For Beauty's Sake 6-25-41
For Better, For Worse 5-02-19
For Better For Worse 10-13-54
For Better or Worse (See: Pour Le Meilleur Et Pour Le Pire)
For Big Stakes 6-30-22
For Clemence (See: Pour Clemence)
For France 9-28-17
For Freedom and Love (See: Um Freiheit und Liebe)
For Heaven's Sake 4-07-26
For Heaven's Sake 12-06-50
For Hennes Skull (See: For Her Sake)
For Her Country's Sake 10-15-10
For Her Sake 8-27-30 and 11-12-30
For Home and Country 11-28-14
For Husbands Only 9-06-18
For King and Country 11-07-14
For King or Kaiser 2-05-15
For Ladies Only 10-26-27
For Love and Gold (See: Armata Brancaleone, L')
For Love of Ivy 7-10-68
For Love One Dies (See: D'Amore Si Muore)
For Love or Money 7-31-34
For Love or Money 6-21-39
For Love or Money 6-26-63

For Me and My Gal 9-09-42
For Men Only 1-16-52
For Men Only (See: Per Uomini Soli)
For Napoleon and France (See: Napoleon and France)
For One Cent's Worth of Love (See: Pour un Sou D'Amour)
For Pete's Sake 6-26-74
For Sale 7-16-24
For Sale, A Baby 11-06-09
For Singles Only 6-19-68
For the Beast (See: Ape and Superape)
For the Continuance of the World (See: Pour la Suite du Monde)
For the Defense 3-10-16
For the Defense 7-23-30
For the First Time 8-19-59
For the Freedom of the World 9-14-17
For the King 4-02-10
For the Love o' Lil 12-17-30
For the Love of Benji 6-15-77
For the Love of Mariastella (See: Malacarne)
For the Love of Mary 9-01-48
For the Love of Mike 8-24-27
For the Love of Mike 1-03-33
For the Love of Mike 8-03-60
For the Love of Rusty 7-02-47
For the Service 6-03-36
For the Soul of Rafael 10-08-20
For the Term of His Natural Life 6-12-29
For Them That Trespass 5-18-49
For Those Two in Peril 5-10-44
For Those We Love 12-02-21
For Those Who Think Young 5-20-64
For Valor 4-07-37
For Valour 11-23-17
For Whom the Bell Tolls 7-21-43
For Whom the Larks Sing (See: Akiket a Pas Cirta Elkisert)
For Whom to Be Murdered 12-20-78
For Wives Only 12-08-26
For Woman's Favor 10-22-24
For You I Die 12-24-47
For You, My Boy 4-26-23
For You Only (See: Solo Per Te)
Foraarsdag I Helvede, En 3-09-77
Forbid Them Not 9-27-61
Forbidden (See: Proibito)
Forbidden 1-12-32
Forbidden 11-25-53
Forbidden Adventure 6-30-37
Forbidden Adventure, The 12-03-15
Forbidden Cargo 5-13-25
Forbidden Cargo 5-12-54
Forbidden Cargoes 9-23-25
Forbidden Christ (See: Cristo Proibito)
Forbidden City, The 10-11-18
Forbidden Company 7-12-32
Forbidden Desert 12-25-57
Forbidden Fruit (See: Fruit Defendu, Le)
Forbidden Fruit 12-17-15
Forbidden Fruit 1-28-21
Forbidden Games (See: Jeux Interdits)
Forbidden Ground (See: Tiltott Terulet)
Forbidden Heaven 9-09-36
Forbidden Hours 7-25-28
Forbidden Island 2-11-59
Forbidden Journey 9-27-50
Forbidden Jungle 6-21-50
Forbidden Love 1-16-29
Forbidden Paradise 11-19-24
Forbidden Paths 7-20-17
Forbidden Planet 3-14-56
Forbidden Priests (See: Pretres Interdits)
Forbidden Room, The (See: Anima Persa)
Forbidden Room, The 3-21-19
Forbidden Sands (See: Kindan No Suna)
Forbidden Territory 11-06-34
Forbidden Thing 12-03-20
Forbidden Things Are In Fashion (See: Prohibido Esta, Lo)
Forbidden to Know (See: Defense de Savoir)
Forbidden to Step on Clouds (See: Prohibido Pisar las Numbes)
Forbidden to the Public (See: Interdit au Public)
Forbidden Trail 11-04-36
Forbidden Trails 5-21-20
Forbidden Trails 12-31-41
Forbidden Under the Censorship of the King 8-16-72
Forbidden Valley 10-15-20
Forbidden Valley 3-30-38
Forbidden Woman 2-27-20
Forbidden Woman 11-02-27
Forbidden Zone 3-26-80

Forbin Project, The 4-01-70
Force of Arms 8-15-51
Force of Evil 12-29-48
Force of One, A 7-04-79
Force 10 from Navarone 11-29-78
Forced Landing 1-01-36
Forced Landing 7-09-41
Foreign Affair, A 6-16-48
Foreign Affairs 12-04-35
Foreign Agent 10-28-42
Foreign Correspondent 8-28-40
Foreign Devils 4-11-28
Foreign Intrigue 5-23-56
Foreign Legion 6-27-28
Foreigner, The (See: Pardesi or Etrangere, L')
Foreigner, The 1-18-78
Foreigners (See: Kocksgatan 48)
Foreman, The 10-22-10
Foreman Went to France 5-13-42
Foreplay 3-12-75
Forest Havoc 6-08-27
Forest King 3-17-22
Forest of Farewell, The (See: Foret d'Adieu, Le)
Forest of the Hanged (See: Padurea Spinzuratilor)
Forest People of Siberia 10-09-29
Forest Rangers, The 9-30-42
Forester's Daughter, The (See: Foersterchristl, Die)
Forester's Little Daughter, The (See: Foersterchristl, Die)
Foret D'Adieu, Le 9-17-52
Foretold by Fate (See: Roy Likit)
Forever After 11-10-26
Forever Amber 10-15-47
Forever and a Day 1-20-43
Forever Darling 2-08-56
Forever Female 6-03-53
Forever My Love (See: Itsu Itsu Made Mo)
Forever My Love 3-28-62
Forever Young, Forever Free 12-15-76
Forever Yours 6-09-37
Forever Yours 9-26-45
Forfeit, The 3-07-19
Forged Passport 2-22-39
Forget-Me-Not 4-06-17
Forget Me Not 7-28-22
Forget Me Not 4-22-36
Forgiven 4-24-14
Forgiven, or the Jack O'Diamonds 6-26-14
Forgotten 9-05-28
Forgotten 6-06-33
Forgotten Commandments 6-07-32
Forgotten Faces 8-08-28
Forgotten Faces 7-08-36
Forgotten Girls 3-20-40
Forgotten Island of Santosha 6-19-74
Forgotten Men 5-16-33
Forgotten Ones, The (See: Olvidados, Los)
Forgotten Village, The 8-27-41
Forgotten Woman 8-09-39
Forgotten Women 3-15-32
Forgotten Women 7-06-49
Forlorn River 9-29-26
Forlorn River 10-06-37
Formula, The 12-10-80
Formynderne 10-29-80
Forro Vizet a Kopaszra 8-29-73
Forsaking All Others 1-01-35
Forsaking Others 12-22-22
Forsummad Av Sin Fru 12-10-47
Forsvundne Fuldmaegtig, Den 11-10-71
Fort Algiers 7-22-53
Fort Apache 3-10-48
Fort Bowie 2-05-58
Fort Defiance 10-31-51
Fort Dobbs 1-22-58
Fort Dodge Stampede 9-05-51
Fort du Fou 2-27-63
Fort Massacre 4-30-58
Fort of the Mad (See: Fort du Fou)
Fort Osage 1-23-52
Fort Savage Raiders 3-14-51
Fort Ti 5-13-53
Fort Utah 6-07-67
Fort Vengeance 4-01-53
Fort Worth 5-16-51
Fort Yuma 9-28-55
Forteresse, La 5-07-47
40th Door, The 8-20-24
Fortress, The (See: Az Erod or Forteresse, La)

Fortress of Silence, The (See: Citadelle du Silence, La)
Fortress on the Volga 1-06-43
Fortunat 11-30-60
Fortunata and Jacinta (See: Fortunata y Jacinta)
Fortunata y Jacinta 4-08-70
Fortunate Misfortunate, A 11-05-10
Fortunate Youth, The 3-24-16
Fortune, The 5-21-75
Fortune and Men's Eyes 6-09-71
Fortune Carree 4-27-55
Fortune Cookie, The 10-19-66
Fortune Follows the Brave 12-04-09
Fortune Hunter (2 reviews) 1-18-28
Fortune Hunter, The 10-10-14
Fortune Hunters 9-25-09
Fortune Is a Woman 3-20-57
Fortune Teller 5-14-20
Fortune's Child 1-31-19
Fortune's Fool 8-22-28
Fortune's Mask 10-06-22
Fortunes of Captain Blood 5-17-50
Fortunes of Fifi, The 3-02-17
40 Anos Sin Sexo 2-21-79
40 Carats 6-27-73
48 Hours of Love (See: Quarante-Huit Heures d'Amour)
48 Hours to Acapulco (See: 48 Stunden Bis Acapulco)
Forty First, The (See: Sorok Pervyi)
45 Fathers 12-15-37
Forty-Five Minutes from Broadway 10-22-10
45 Minutes from Broadway 9-03-20
Forty Four (See: Styridsatstyri)
Forty Guns 9-18-57
Forty-Horse Hawkins 7-02-24
40 Little Mothers (See: Mioche, Le)
40 Little Mothers 4-17-40
40 Naughty Girls 9-08-37
Forty-Niners 12-20-32
Fortyniners 4-28-54
49th Man, The 5-13-53
49th Parallel 11-05-41
40 Pounds of Trouble 12-12-62
42nd Heaven, The (See: 42 Himmel, Der)
42nd Street 3-14-33
Forty Thieves 7-12-44
40,000 Horsemen 2-05-41
Forty Winks 2-04-25
Forty Years (See: Veertig Jaren)
40 Years Without Sex (See: 40 Anos Sin Sexo)
Forvandlingen 10-08-75
Forward Center Dies at Dawn, The (See: Centroforward Murio Al
    Amanecer, El)
Forward Pass 12-04-29
Forza del Destino, La 7-05-50
Fossa Degli Angeli, La 12-29-37
Fossil (See: Kaseki)
Foto Haber 7-15-64
Fotografia 4-24-74
Fou, Le 10-14-70
Fou du Labo 4, Le 1-17-68
Fougeres Bleues, Les 6-15-77
Foul Play (See: Mauvais Coups, Les)
Foul Play (See: Przepraszam, Czy Tu Bija?)
Foul Play 7-12-78
Foule Hurle, La 10-25-32
Found Alive 4-17-34
Foundling (See: Guacho or Findling, Der)
Foundling, The 1-14-16
Fountain, The 9-04-34
Fountain of Life (See: Lebensborn)
Fountain of Love, The 10-22-69
Fountainhead, The 6-29-49
Four Aces 1-17-33
4 Boys and a Gun 1-30-57
4 Charlots Mousquetaires, Les 3-06-74
Four Charlots Musketeers, The (See: 4 Charlots Mousquetaires,
    Les)
Four Clowns 7-01-70
4D Man 10-07-59
Four Daughters 8-17-38
Four Days in November 10-07-64
Four Days of Naples, The 11-28-62
Four Days to Death (See: Cetiri Dana Do Smrti)
Four Days Wonder 12-23-36
Four Devils, The 10-10-28 and 6-19-29
4 Faces West 5-12-48
Four Fast Guns 11-25-59
Four Feathers 5-28-15
Four Feathers, The 6-19-29

Four Feathers, The 4-26-39
Four Flies in Gray Velvet (See: Quattro Mosche Di Velluto Grigio)
4 Flights to Love 4-15-42
Four Flusher, The 1-18-28
Four for Texas 12-25-63
4 Frightened People 1-30-34
Four Girls in Town 12-05-56
Four Girls in White 1-25-39
Four Guns to the Border 9-22-54
Four Hearts 2-27-46
Four Horsemen of the Apocalypse, The 2-18-21
Four Horsemen of the Apocalypse, The 2-14-62
Four Hours to Kill 4-17-35
400 Blows, The (See: Quatre Cents Coups, Les)
400 Million, The 3-15-39
413 9-11-14
Four in a Jeep 4-11-51
Four in the Morning 8-04-65
Four Infantry Men (See: Quatre de l'Infanterie)
Four Infantry Men 6-18-30
Four Jacks and a Jill 11-12-41
Four Jills in a Jeep 3-15-44
Four Just Men, The 6-21-39
Four Leaved Clover, The 7-09-15
Four Men and a Prayer 4-27-38
Four Moods (See: Hsi, Nou, Ai, Lueh)
Four Moods 10-25-72
Four Mothers 1-15-41
Four Musketeers, The 3-12-75
Four Nights of a Dreamer (See: Quatre Nuits d'un Reveur)
491 1-22-64
Four of the Moana, The (See: Quatre du Moana, Les)
Four of Them (See: Quatre d'Entre Elles)
Four Poster, The 10-08-52
Four Seasons, The (See: Godisnja Doba)
Four-Sided Triangle 5-20-53
Four Skulls of Jonathan Drake, The 5-13-59
Four Sons 2-15-28
Four Sons 5-29-40
Four Stars 12-27-67
4 Steps in the Clouds 11-03-48
4 x 4 7-21-65
Four Truths, The (See: Quatres Verites, Les)
4 Walls 8-22-28
Four Ways Out 12-08-54
Four Winds of Heaven (See: Na Semi Vetrach)
Four Wives 11-22-39
Fourchambault 8-28-29
Fourfooted Ranger 4-04-28
Four's a Crowd 8-17-38
14, The 7-11-73
Fourteen Days, The (See: Dan Cetrnaesti)
14-18 4-03-63
Fourteen Hours 2-28-51
14,000 Witnesses 7-12-61
14th Day, The (See: Dan Cetrnaesti)
14th Lover, The 2-17-22
XIVth Olympiad--The Glory of Sport 9-08-48
Fourth Alarm, The 12-17-30
Fourth Commandment, The 4-06-27
Fourth Companion, The (See: Cetvrti Sputnik)
Fourth Estate, The 1-21-16
Fourth from the Right, The (See: Vierte von Rechts, Die)
Fourth Horseman, The 1-31-33
Fourth Musketeer 4-05-23
Fous du Stade, Les 11-01-72
Fox, The 12-23-21
Fox, The 12-13-67
Fox Farm 8-11-22
Fox in the Chicken Coop, The 6-28-78
Fox Movietone Follies of 1929 5-29-29
Fox of Paris, The (See: Fuchs Von Paris, Der)
Fox Woman, The 7-16-15
Foxbat 12-21-77
Foxes 2-27-80
Foxes of Harrow, The 9-24-47
Foxfire 6-15-55
Foxhole in Cairo 10-12-60
Foxtrot 3-31-76
Foxy Brown 4-17-74
Foxy Ernest 4-02-10
Foxy Hoboes 2-09-07
Foxy Lady (See: Sao Rang Sung)
Foxy Lady 10-06-71
Fra Diavolo 11-24-31
Fragment of an Empire 2-05-30
Fragment of Fear 9-09-70

Fragments 8-05-21
Fraiche 4-21-76
Frail Flowers Are Disappearing, The (See: Deja S'Envole La Fleur Maigre)
Fram for Lilla Marta 3-27-46
Frame of Mind (See: Sposob Bycia)
Frame Up, The 11-05-15
Framed 6-22-27
Framed 4-02-30
Framed 5-22-40
Framed 3-05-47
Framed 8-20-75
Frame-Up, The 6-22-17
Frame-Up, The 8-11-37
Framing Framers 1-04-18
Francais Si Vous Saviez 3-07-73
Francaise et L'Amour, La 10-05-60
France in Arms 11-02-17
France Incorporated (See: France Societe Anonyme)
France Societe Anonyme 4-10-74
Francesca di Rimini 2-22-08
Franchise Affair, The 2-28-51
Francis 12-14-49
Francis Covers the Big Town 6-10-53
Francis, God's Fool 9-27-50
Francis Goes to the Races 5-23-51
Francis Goes to West Point 6-18-52
Francis in the Haunted House 7-04-56
Francis in the Navy 6-29-55
Francis Joins the Wacs 7-07-54
Francis of Assisi 7-12-61
Francis the First 4-23-47
Franciscain de Bourges, Le 4-24-68
Francois Villon 10-19-49
Francoise or Conjugal Life (See: Francoise ou la Vie Conjugale)
Francoise ou la Vie Conjugale 2-12-64
Frank and Eva--Living Apart Together 12-26-73
Frankenstein 12-08-31
Frankenstein and the Monster from Hell 6-26-74
Frankenstein Conquers the World 7-13-66
Frankenstein Created Woman 3-15-67
Frankenstein--Italian Style 11-23-77
Frankenstein Meets the Space Monster 8-04-65
Frankenstein Meets the Wolf Man 2-24-43
Frankenstein Must Be Destroyed 6-11-69
Frankenstein--1970 7-16-58
Frankie and Johnnie 5-27-36
Frankie and Johnny 3-30-66
Frank's Greatest Adventure 5-03-67
Franz 2-16-72
Frasier, the Sensuous Lion 6-27-73
Frasquita 1-22-36
Fratelli Castiglioni, I 10-13-37
Fratelli Dinamite, I 9-28-49
Fratelli Karamazov, I 4-14-48
Fraternal Amazon (See: Fraternelle Amazonie)
Fraternelle Amazonie 8-04-65
Fraternity Row 2-23-77
Frau Cheney's Ende 10-02-63
Frau, Die Weiss, Was Sie Will, Eine 7-22-36
Frau Gegenuber, Die 5-24-78
Frau Genuegt Nicht?, Eine 8-31-55
Frau Mit Verantwortung, Eine 3-14-79
Frau Nach der Man Sich Sehnt, Die (See: Woman Longed For)
Frau Ohne Bedeutung, Eine 11-18-36
Frau Sorge 5-02-28
Frau Sucht Liebe, Eine 2-05-69
Frau Von der Man Spricht 5-02-33
Frau Warren's Gewerbe 4-20-60
Frau Wirtin Blaest Auch Gern Trompete 5-13-70
Frau Wirtin Hat Auch Eine Nichte 6-11-69
Frau Wirtin Hat Auch Einen Grafen 1-15-69
Frau Wirtin Treibt es Jetzt Noch Toller 11-18-70
Frauds and Frenzies 11-01-18
Fraudulent Death (See: Mort En Fraude)
Frauen um den Sonnen Koenig (See: Private Life of Louix XIV, The)
Frauendiplomat, Der 4-12-32
Frauenparadies, Das 11-25-36
Fraulein 5-07-58
Fraulein Doktor 4-09-69
Fraulein Else (See: Miss Else)
Fraulein Faehnrich 4-03-29
Fraznik 8-16-67
Freak, The 12-03-10
Freaks 7-12-32
Freaky Friday 12-22-76
Freche Husar, Der 11-14-28
Freckled Rascal 7-24-29
Freckles (See: Sommersprossen)

Freckles 6-08-17
Freckles 1-25-28
Freckles 10-30-35
Freckles 9-28-60
Freckles Comes Home 4-08-42
Free 3-14-73
Free Air 6-16-22
Free and Easy 4-23-30 (Also see: Metteur en Scene, Le)
Free and Easy 3-19-41
Free and Equal 4-22-25
Free, Blonde and 21 4-10-40
Free Booters 9-18-09
Free Escape (See: Echappement Libre)
Free for All (See: Piedra Libre)
Free for All 11-02-49
Free Lips 1-16-29
Free Love 7-07-26
Free Love 12-17-30
Free Man, A (See: Homme Libre, Un)
Free Soul, A 6-09-31
Freebie and the Bean 11-13-74
Freedom 1-14-31
Freedom 7-24-57
Freedom for Ghana 7-24-57
Freedom for Us (See: A Nous La Liberte)
Freedom of the Press 9-26-28
Freedom Radio 2-05-41
Freedom to Love 6-17-70
Freewheelin' 11-17-76
Freeze-Out, The 4-29-21
Freezing Point (See: Hoyten)
Freight Elevator, The (See: Monte-Charge, Le)
Freighters of Destiny 4-12-32
Freiheit Fur Die Liebe (See: Freedom to Love)
Fremd Bin Ich Eigezogah 5-16-79
Fremde Stadt 5-31-72
Fremmande Hamn 11-17-48
Fremmed Banker Paa, En 11-02-60
French Blue 12-18-74
French Calvinists, The (See: Camisards, Les)
French Can-Can 6-01-55
French Cigarettes, The (See: Gauloises Bleues, Les)
French Connection, The 10-06-71
French Connection II 5-14-75
French Doll 9-06-23
French Dressing 12-14-27
French Dressing 5-27-64
French Heels 3-03-22
French Key, The 5-22-46
French Leave (See: Poudre D'Escampette, La)
French Leave 9-03-30 and 12-08-31
French Leave 4-21-48
French Line, The 1-06-54
French Mistress 9-14-60
French People, If You Only Knew (See: Francais Si Vous Saviez)
French Postcards 9-12-79
French Touch 9-08-54
French Way, The 9-10-52
French Without Tears 11-15-39
French Woman and Love, The (See: Francaise et L'Amour, La)
Frenchie 11-29-50
Frenchman's Creek 9-20-44
Frenesia D'Estate 4-15-64
Frente Marchen!, Die 4-22-31
Frenzied Flames 12-08-26
Frenzy 7-24-46
Frenzy 5-31-72
Freshie, The 12-22-22
Freshman, The 7-15-25
Freshman Love 1-29-36
Freshman Year 9-21-38
Freud 12-19-62
Freudenhaus, Das 3-17-71
Freundin So Goldig Wie Du, Eine 10-27-31
Fric, Le 8-05-59
Fric Frac 8-02-39
Frida's Songs (See: Frida's Visor)
Frida's Visor 10-20-31
Friday Foster 12-31-75
Friday on My Mind 9-30-70
Friday the 13th 9-08-16
Friday the 13th 12-05-33 and 5-22-34
Friday the 13th 5-14-80
Friday the 13th ... The Orphan 12-12-79
Fridericus 3-24-37
Frieda 6-25-47 and 8-20-47
Friederike 2-28-33
Friend, A (See: Amico, Un)
Friend, The (See: Arkadas)

Friend from India 1-25-28
Friend Husband 8-09-18
Friend of the Family, The (See: Ami de la Famille, L')
Friend Will Come This Evening, A (See: Ami Viendra Ce Soir, Un)
Friend Will Come Tonight, A 7-14-48
Friendly Enemies 5-06-25
Friendly Enemies 6-24-42
Friendly Expression, Please (See: Baratsagos Arczot Kerek)
Friendly Husband, A 6-14-23
Friendly Neighbors 11-13-40
Friendly Persuasion, The 9-26-56
Friends 3-24-71
Friends, The (See: Amis, Les)
Friends and Lovers 11-10-31
Friends Are As Friends Go 7-14-65
Friends for Life (See: Amici Per la Pelle)
Friends: Let's Go to the Party (See: Amiche: Andiano Alla Festa)
Friends of Eddie Coyle, The 6-13-73
Friends of Mr. Sweeney 7-31-34
Friends Through Thick and Thin (See: Compagnons de la Marguerite, Les)
Friendship (See: Dosti)
Friendship in Full Bloom 1-15-75
Friesennot 10-28-36
Fright 10-27-71
Frightened City, The 9-20-61
Frightened Lady 11-12-41
Frihetens Murar 4-11-79
Fringe Benefits 2-20-74
Fringe of Society, The 10-05-17
Frisco Jenny 1-10-33
Frisco Kid, The 11-27-35
Frisco Kid, The 7-04-79
Frisco Lil 2-18-42
Frisco Sal 2-14-45
Frisco Sally Levy 4-13-27
Frisco Tornado 9-13-50
Frisco Waterfront 12-25-35
Fritz the Cat 4-05-72
Frivolous Sal (See: Flaming Love)
Frock Coat 8-28-09
Froeken April 3-11-59
Frog, The 4-07-37
Frogmen, The 6-13-51
Frogs 3-29-72
Froken Julie 5-16-51
From Beyond the Seas 3-12-10
From Cabin Boy to King 11-13-09
From Czar to Stalin (See: Vom Zar Bis Stalin)
From Ear to Ear 1-20-71
From Headquarters 7-17-29
From Headquarters 11-21-33
From Hell It Came 9-04-57
From Hell to Heaven 3-21-33
From Hell to Texas 5-14-58
From Hell to Victory 9-12-79
From Here to Eternity 7-29-53
From Hong Kong With Love (See: Bon Baisers De Hong Kong)
From Lumiere to Langlois 9-23-70
From Mayerling to Serajevo (See: De Mayerling A Serajevo)
From Noon Till Three 8-04-76
From Now On 10-22-20
From Out of the Big Snows 8-13-15
From Pink to Yellow (See: Del Rosa ... Al Amarillo)
From Russia with Love 10-16-63
From Saturday to Monday (See: Dal Sabato al Lunedi)
From Shop Girl to Duchess 3-26-15
From the Abyss (See: Desde El Abismo)
From the Arctics to the Tropics 9-24-10
From the Boys (See: De La Part Des Copains)
From the Earth to the Moon 11-12-58
From the Gas Station 10-15-30
From the Golden West 8-08-13
From the Ground Up 10-14-21
From the Highway (See: Lu Kur Yue Dau Kur)
From the Hills to the Valley (See: De la Sierra al Valle)
From the Life of the Marionettes 7-23-80
From the Mixed-Up Files of Mrs. Basil E. Frankweiler 10-03-73
From the Other Side (See: Onkraj)
From the Police, With Thanks (See: Polizia Ringrazia, La)
From the Terrace 6-28-60
From This Day Forward 2-27-46
From Two to Six 2-15-18
Front, The 9-15-76
Front Page, The 3-25-31
Front Page, The 12-11-74
Front Page Story 2-03-54
Front Page Story, A 5-17-23 and 8-30-23

87

G

G.I. Blues 10-19-60
G.I. Honeymoon 3-21-45
G.I. Jane 8-08-51
G.I. War Brides 8-07-46
G-Men 5-08-35
Ga Pa Vattnet Om du Kan 9-12-79
Gabbiano, Il 9-28-77
Gable and Lombard 2-18-76
Gabriel over the White House 4-04-33
Gabriela 5-03-50
Gab's Nur Einmal, Das 4-09-58
Gaby 3-28-56
Gade Uden Ende 8-05-64
Gadfly, The 9-19-56
Gaesschen Zum Paradies 11-25-36
Gaestearbejdere 5-22-74
Gafe, El 1-20-60
Gai Savoir, Le 7-09-69
Gaietes de L'Escadron 10-04-32
Gaiety George 4-24-46
Gaiety Girl, The 8-06-24
Gaiety Girls 3-02-38
Gaijin--Caminos Da Liberdade 5-14-80
Gaily, Gaily 12-03-69
Gaki Zoshi 5-16-73
Gal Who Took the West 9-14-49
Gal Young Un 11-07-79
Galapagos 7-11-62
Galaxina 8-27-80
Gale Dansker, Den 12-03-69
Galeries Levy Et Cie 2-16-32
Galets D'Etreta, Les 4-05-72
Galettes de Pont Aven, Les 9-03-75
Galgenvoegel 4-01-31
Galia 2-16-66
Galileo 9-11-68
Galileo 1-15-75
Gallant Bess 9-04-46
Gallant Blade, The 10-13-48
Gallant Defender 4-22-36
Gallant Fool 3-16-27
Gallant Hours, The 5-18-60
Gallant Hussar 10-03-28
Gallant Journey 9-11-46
Gallant Lady 1-23-34
Gallant Legion, The 5-26-48
Gallant Sons 11-13-40
Galley Slave 9-11-09
Galley Slave, The 12-03-15
Gallina Clueca, La 1-19-44
Gallo en Corral Ajeno, Un 9-03-52
Galloper, The 9-17-15
Galloping Age 4-16-24
Galloping Devil 5-27-21
Galloping Dynamite 4-07-37
Galloping Fish 7-30-30
Galloping Fury 11-30-27
Galloping Gallagher 5-07-24
Galloping Kid 9-15-22
Galloping Major, The 5-16-51
Galloping Romeo 10-31-33
Galloping Thru 3-08-32
Galloping Thunder 10-12-27 and 10-26-27
Gallos de la Madrugada, Los 7-28-71
Gals, Incorporated 7-07-43
Gam-Peralia 8-07-63
Gaman 1-31-79
Gambara Tai Barugon 4-27-66
Gamberge, La 3-28-62
Gambier's Advocate 6-23-16
Gambit 11-16-66
Gamble in Lives, A 12-17-20
Gamble in Souls, A 12-01-16
Gambler, The (See: Joueur, Le or Irgok)
Gambler, The 5-23-08
Gambler, The 10-30-09
Gambler, The 10-02-74
Gambler from Natchez 8-11-54
Gamblers, The 10-03-19
Gamblers, The 8-28-29
Gamblers, The 11-26-69

Gambler's Choice 4-26-44
Gambler's Doom, The 2-19-10
Gambler's End, A 11-19-10
Gambler's Wife, The 9-10-10
Gambling 12-11-34
Gambling Daughters 9-10-41
Gambling House 12-27-50
Gambling in Souls 3-21-19
Gambling Lady 4-10-34
Gambling on the High Seas 7-31-40
Gambling Passion 10-09-09
Gambling Sex 12-27-32
Gambling Ship 7-18-33
Gambling Ship 1-25-39
Gambling Terror 3-10-57
Gambling with Death 12-18-09
Gambling Wives 4-16-24
Game, The 11-13-09
Game Chicken, A 3-10-22
Game Is Set, The (See: Jeux Sont Faits, Les)
Game Is Sex, The 7-30-69
Game of Death, A 11-28-45
Game of Death, The 6-13-79
Game of Life, The 7-23-24
Game of Love, A 2-20-74
Game of Poker, A 3-28-13
Game of Solitaire, The (See: Jeu de Solitaire, Le)
Game of the Apple (See: Uvadi Hra O Jablo)
Game of Truth, The (See: Jeu de la Verite, Le)
Game Old Knight, A 10-22-15
Game Pass (See: Wildwechsel)
Game That Kills 9-22-37
Game with Fate, A 6-14-18
Gamekeeper, The 9-24-80
Gamera Tai Gyaos 4-19-67
Gamera Tai Uchu Kaiju Bairusu 5-22-68
Gamera vs. Gyaos (See: Gamera Tai Gyaos)
Gamera vs. Outer Space Monster Virus (See: Gamera Tai Uchu Kaiju
    Bairusu)
Games 9-20-67
Games, The 4-08-70
Games of Love (See: Jeux de L'Amour, Les)
Games of the XXI Olympiad Montreal 1976 6-08-77
Games That Lovers Play 2-17-71
Gamesters, The 11-05-20
Gamin 10-03-79
Gamin de Paris 9-20-32
Gamma People, The 9-12-56
Gammera the Invincible 12-27-67
Gang, Le 2-09-77
Gang, The 12-28-38
Gang Bullets 12-28-38
Gang Buster 1-28-31
Gang Busters 3-23-55
Gang des Otages, Le 3-07-73
Gang Leader, The (See: Pandillero, El)
Gang of Outsiders (See: Bande A Part)
Gang That Couldn't Shoot Straight, The 12-15-71
Gang War 11-21-28
Gang War 4-03-40
Gang War 4-30-58
Ganga 9-13-61
Ganga Zumba 1-26-72
Ganges at Benares, The 3-14-13
Gang's All Here, The 3-15-39
Gang's All Here, The 6-25-41
Gang's All Here, The 12-01-43
Gangs of Chicago 5-22-40
Gangs of New York 5-25-38
Gangs of Sonora 7-16-41
Gangs of the Waterfront 8-08-45
Gangster, The 10-01-47
Gangster Movie, The (See: Gangsterfilmen)
Gangsterens Laerling 8-04-76
Gangsterfilmen 12-04-74
Gangstergirl, A (See: Het Gangstermeisje)
Gangsters, The 3-13-14
Gangster's Apprentice, The (See: Gangsterens Laerling)
Gangster's Boy 11-09-38
Gangway 8-18-37
Gangway for Tomorrow 11-03-43 and 12-22-43
Ganja and Hess 4-18-73
Ganovenehre 4-27-66
Gans-Herman Fight 1-26-07
Gans-Nelson Fight 9-26-08
Gants Blancs du Diable, Les 5-23-73
Ganzer Kerl, Ein 4-29-36
Gappa-Triphibian Monster (See: Dai Kyoju Gappa)

Garage, The (See: Garaget)
Garage, The 1-16-20
Garage Sale 12-08-76
Garaget 10-08-75
Garakuta (See: Rabble, The)
Garbage of Paris, The 10-09-09
Garcon Sauvage, Le 9-19-51
Garconne, La 6-19-57
Garden, The 6-01-77
Garden Murder Case, The 3-04-36
Garden of Allah, The 9-07-27
Garden of Allah, The 11-14-28
Garden of Allah, The 11-25-36
Garden of Allie, The 1-18-18
Garden of Delights, The (See: Jardin De Las Delicias, El)
Garden of Eden 3-21-28
Garden of Eden 9-01-54
Garden of Evil 6-30-54
Garden of Knowledge, The 1-12-17
Garden of Lies, The 7-23-15
Garden of Paradise, The (See: Paradiesgarten, Der)
Garden of Stones, The (See: Baghe Sangui)
Garden of the Finzi-Continis, The (See: Giardino del Finzi-
    Continis, Il)
Garden of the Moon 8-17-38 and 9-21-38
Garden of Torture, The (See: Jardin des Supplices, Le)
Garden of Weeds 11-05-24
Garden That Tilts, The (See: Jardin Qui Bascule, Le)
Gardener of Argenteuil, The (See: Jardinier d'Argenteuil, Le)
Garm Hava 6-19-76
Garment Jungle, The 4-24-57
Garofano Rosso, Il 9-29-76
Garrincha--Allegria Do Povo 7-03-63
Garrincha--Hero of the People (See: Garrincha--Allegria Do Povo)
Garrison's Finish 5-30-23
Garrison's Paramour (See: Beguin de la Garnison, Le)
Garter Girl, The 5-14-20
Gas House Kids Go West, The 7-23-47
Gas Lamps (See: Petrolejove Lampy)
Gas, Oil and Water 7-07-22
Gas Pump Girls 12-19-79
Gas-s-s-s 8-26-70
Gaslight 7-10-40
Gaslight 5-10-44
Gaslight Follies 10-03-45
Gasoline Alley 1-17-51
Gasoline Station (See: Tankstelle)
Gaspards, Les 1-30-74
Gasparone 1-19-38
Gata, La 8-01-56
Gatan 4-13-49
Gate Crasher 12-19-28
Gate of Hell (See: Jigokumen)
Gatefold Girl, The (See: Rapportpigen)
Gates of Brass 7-18-19
Gates of Doom, The 3-02-17
Gates of Eden, The 11-03-16
Gates of Fire, The (See: Portes de Feu, Les)
Gates of Gladness 1-18-18
Gates of Heaven 10-04-78
Gates of the Night 3-22-50
Gates to Paradise 7-03-68
Gateway 8-10-38
Gateway of the Caucasus 1-21-31
Gateway of the Moon 1-11-28
Gathering of Eagles, A 6-05-63
Gato, El 3-01-61
Gato Con Botas, El 11-22-61
Gator 5-12-76
Gatti Rossi in Un Labirinto di Vetro (See: Eyeball)
Gatto, Il 1-18-78
Gatto a Nove Code, Il (See: Cat o' Nine Tails)
Gatto Selvaggio, Il 10-23-68
Gattopardo, Il (See: Leopard, The)
Gaucho, The (See: Goucho, Il)
Gaucho, The 11-09-27
Gaucho-Priest, The (See: Cura Gaucho, El)
Gaucho Serenade 5-15-40
Gaucho War, The (See: Guerra Gaucha, La)
Gauchos of El Dorado 12-17-41
Gauloises Bleues, Les 5-15-68
Gauner und der Liebe Gott, Der 2-01-61
Gauntlet, The 7-23-20
Gauntlet, The 12-21-77
Gav 9-08-71

Gavaznha 12-18-74
Gay Adventure, The 7-29-36
Gay Adventure, The 10-14-53
Gay Adventurer, The 8-22-28
Gay Amigo, The 5-18-49
Gay and Devilish 5-19-22
Gay Blades 4-03-46
Gay Bride, The 12-18-34
Gay Buckaroo, The 1-19-32
Gay Caballero, The 3-29-32
Gay Caballero, The 9-25-40
Gay Deceiver, The 10-06-26
Gay Deceivers, The 6-11-69
Gay Deception, The 10-16-35
Gay Defender, The 12-28-27
Gay Desperado, The 10-14-36
Gay Diplomat, The 10-13-31
Gay Divorcee, The 11-20-34
Gay Falcon, The 9-17-41
Gay Intruders, The 6-02-48
Gay Knowledge, The (See: Gai Savoir, Le)
Gay Lord Waring, The 4-14-16
Gay Love 9-11-34
Gay Misery (See: Czifra Nyomorusag)
Gay Old Bird, The 4-27-27
Gay Old Dog, The 11-07-19
Gay Old Time (See: Saltstaenk Och Krutgubbar)
Gay Party, The (See: Det Glada Kalaset)
Gay Purr-ee 10-17-62
Gay Ranchero, The 1-14-48
Gay Retreat, The 10-12-27
Gay Sisters, The 6-03-42
Gay Vagabond, The 5-21-41
Gazebo, The (See: Jo)
Gazebo, The 12-16-59
Gazoros, Serres 10-30-74
Gebissen Wird Nur Nachts--Happening Der Vampire 8-04-71
Gefaehrliche Gaeste 3-01-50
Gefahren der Liebe (See: Woman Branded, A)
Gefangene der Liebe 9-22-54
Gefrorene Herz, Das 2-20-80
Gefundenes Fressen 4-27-77
Geheime Reichssache 11-21-79
Geheimnis der Drei Dschunken, Das 11-24-65
Geheimnis der Gelden Narzizzen, Das (See: Devil's Daffodil, The)
Geheimnis der Gruenen Stecknadel, Das 5-03-72
Gehulfe, Der 5-19-76
Geisha Boy, The 11-19-58
Geisha Girl 5-21-52
Geisterland der Suedsee 8-10-60
Gelbe Flagge, Die 1-12-38
Gelbe Haus am Pinnasberg, Das 4-01-70
Gelbe Haus des King Fu, Das 5-06-31
Gelbe Stern, Der 12-10-80
Geld, Geld, Geld (See: Money, Money, Money)
Geld und Geist 12-30-64
Gelegenhietsarbeit einer Sklavin 5-29-74
Geliebte Corinna 7-24-57
Gelobt Sei Was Hart Macht 6-07-72
Gelosia 5-05-48
Gelosia 12-16-53
Gendarme a New York, Le 11-10-65
Gendarme and the Creatures from Outer Space, The (See: Gendarme
    et les Extra-Terrestres, Le)
Gendarme de Champignol, Le 6-24-59
Gendarme de Saint-Tropez, Le 8-25-65
Gendarme en Balade, Le 11-11-70
Gendarme et les Extra-Terrestres, Le 4-04-79
Gendarme Gets Married, The (See: Gendarme Se Marie, Le)
Gendarme Se Marie, Le 11-20-68
Gendarme Takes Off, The (See: Gendarme en Balade, Le)
Gene Autry and the Mounties 1-24-51
Gene Krupa Story, The 12-23-59
General, The 2-09-27
General Crack 12-11-29
General Della Rovere (See: Generale Della Rovere, Il)
General Died at Dawn, The 9-09-36
General Film Show 5-01-14
General House Cleaning (See: Grosse Reinemachen, Das)
General Idi Amin Dada 6-26-74
General John Regan 10-24-33
General Massacre 4-04-73
General Spanky 3-03-37
General Suvorov 9-24-41
General Yamashita (See: Tomoyuki Yamashita)
Generale Della Rovere, Il 9-09-59
General's Birthday, The 11-06-09
Generals Without Buttons 1-26-38
Generation (See: Pokelanie)

Generation 12-10-69
Genese D'un Repas 3-14-79
Genesis, Chapter X 9-05-79
Genesis II 11-26-69
Genesis III 12-09-70
Genesis 4 10-06-71
Genesis Children, The 8-16-72
Genevieve 7-08-53
Genghis Khan 9-17-52 and 7-08-53
Genghis Khan 4-21-65
Genii 9-17-69
Genio, due Compari, un Pollo, Un 1-28-76
Genius, The (See: Genio, due Compari, un Pollo, Un)
Genius at Work 8-07-46
Genji Monogatari 5-14-52
Genou de Claire, Le 12-02-70
Gens du Voyage, Les 4-06-38
Gente Conmigo 8-11-65
Gente en Buenos Aires 11-06-74
Gente Fina e Otra Coisa 11-23-77
Gentle Annie 12-20-44
Gentle Cyclone, The 8-25-26
Gentle Gangster, A 6-23-43
Gentle Giant 10-11-67
Gentle Gunman, The 10-29-52
Gentle Gunmen, The (See: Tontons Flingueurs, Les)
Gentle Julia 4-02-24
Gentle Julia 4-15-36
Gentle People, The 10-11-72
Gentle People and the Quiet Land, The 1-12-76
Gentle Rain, The 2-16-66
Gentle Sex, The 5-19-43
Gentle Woman, A (See: Femme Douce, Une)
Gentleman After Dark, A 3-18-42
Gentleman at Heart, A 1-07-42
Gentleman D'Epsom, Le 10-17-62
Gentleman from America 3-15-23
Gentleman from Arizona 1-31-40
Gentleman from Dixie 11-05-41
Gentleman from L.A. 9-26-36
Gentleman from Maxim, The (See: Herren vom Maxim, Die)
Gentleman from Mississippi 9-26-14
Gentleman from Nowhere, The 9-15-48
Gentleman Gunfighter, The 12-19-19
Gentleman Jim 11-04-42
Gentleman of Leisure, A 3-05-15
Gentleman of Leisure, A 7-19-23
Gentleman of Paris 10-05-27
Gentleman of Paris, A 12-29-31
Gentleman of Quality, A 3-07-19
Gentleman of Quality, A 11-03-26
Gentleman Preferred, A 6-13-28
Gentleman Tramp, The 3-12-75
Gentleman's Agreement 11-12-47
Gentleman's Fate 6-30-31
Gentleman's Gentleman, A (See: Besserer Herr, Ein)
Gentlemen Are Born 11-27-34
Gentlemen in White Vests (See: Herren Mit Der Weissen Weste, Die)
Gentlemen Marry Brunettes 9-14-55
Gentlemen of the Press 5-15-29
Gentlemen Prefer Blondes 1-18-28
Gentlemen Prefer Blondes 7-01-53
Gentlemen with Guns 3-13-46
Gentlemen's Agreement, A 8-02-18
Geordie 9-28-55
Georg 9-25-68
Georg Hauser's Happy Minutes (See: Gluecklichen Minuten des Georg Hauser, Die)
George and Margaret 4-17-40
George Raft Story, The 12-06-61
George VI Coronation 7-21-37
George Washington Carver 4-17-40
George Washington Cohen 5-22-29
George Washington, Jr. 3-26-24
George Washington Slept Here 9-23-42
George White's 1935 Scandals 5-01-35
George White's Scandals 8-01-45 and 10-17-45
Georges Qui? 4-11-73
Georges Who? (See: Georges Qui?)
Georgia, Georgia 3-08-72
Georgia 'Possum Hunt, A 2-05-10
Georgy Girl 7-13-66
Gerald Cramson's Lady 3-11-25
Geraldine 3-06-29
Geraldine 12-30-53
German Diary, A (See: Du Bist Min--Ein Deutsches Tagebuch)
German Side of the War, The 10-08-15

German Spring (See: Deutscher Fruehling)
Germania 7-03-14
Germania Anno Zero 6-09-48
Germans Strike Again, The 5-18-49
Germany at War 12-31-15
Germany in Autumn (See: Deutschland im Herbst)
Germany Meets Kennedy (See: Deutschland Gruesst Kennedy)
Germany, Pale Mother (See: Deutschland, Bleiche Mutter)
Germany the Year Naught (See: Germania Anno Zero)
Germany's Side of the War 9-26-28
Germinal 10-16-63
Geronimo 11-22-39
Geronimo 4-25-62
Gertie 12-18-14
Gertrud 1-13-65
Gervaise 9-19-56
Geschichten aus dem Wienerwald 7-07-37
Geschichten aus dem Wienerwald 11-21-79
Geschichtsunterricht 10-03-73
Geschminkte Jugend (See: Painted Youth)
Gesicht im Dunkeln, Das 8-20-69
Gestaendnis Unter Vier Augen 10-13-54
Gestandnis der Drei, Das 3-06-29
Gestapo 6-05-40
Gestohlene Gesicht, Das 12-03-30
Gesuzza la Sposa Garibaldina 11-18-36
Get Back 7-04-73
Get Carter 1-20-71
Get Charlie Tully 7-28-76
Get Going 6-23-43
Get Hep to Love 9-30-42
Get On with It 4-03-69
Get Outta Town 3-30-60
Get Rich Quick 12-24-10
Get That Girl 6-14-32
Get to Know Your Rabbit 6-21-72
Get Your Diploma First (See: Passe Ton Bac D'Abord)
Get Your Handkerchiefs Ready (See: Preparez Vos Mouchoirs)
Get Your Man 6-03-21
Get Your Man 12-07-27
Get Yourself a College Girl 11-25-65
Getaway, The (See: Derobade, La)
Get-Away, The 6-18-41
Getaway, The 12-13-72
Getaway Kate 9-06-18
Geteilte Himmel, Der 8-12-64
Gettin' Back 10-02-74
Getting Even 9-18-09
Getting Even with Everybody 8-28-09
Getting Gertie's Garter 2-09-27
Getting Gertie's Garter 11-28-45
Getting Mary Married 4-11-19
Getting of Wisdom, The 8-31-77
Getting Straight 4-29-70
Getting Together 11-24-76
Gewisser Herr Gran 10-03-33
Gewitter im Mai 3-09-38
Gharibeh-Va-Meh 7-02-75
Gheroub Wa Cherouk 8-05-70
Ghetto Terezin 2-27-52
Ghidrah, the Three-Headed Monster 10-06-65
Ghorba, El 11-24-71
Ghost, The (See: Revenant, Le)
Ghost, The 2-19-10
Ghost and Mr. Chicken, The 1-12-66
Ghost and Mrs. Muir, The 5-21-47
Ghost and the Guest, The 5-12-43
Ghost Breaker 9-15-22
Ghost Breaker, The 12-11-14
Ghost Breakers, The 6-12-40
Ghost Catchers 5-31-44
Ghost Chasers 5-30-51
Ghost City 3-22-32
Ghost Club, The 5-29-14
Ghost Comes Home, The 2-28-40
Ghost Diver 10-30-57
Ghost Flower, The 8-23-18
Ghost Galleon, The (See: Buque Maldito, El)
Ghost Goes West, The 1-15-36
Ghost House, The 10-12-17
Ghost in the Garret 4-01-21
Ghost in the Invisible Bikini 4-06-66
Ghost Lady, The (See: Dama Duende, La)
Ghost of Dragstrip Hollow 8-12-59
Ghost of Frankenstein, The 3-04-42
Ghost of Hidden Valley 7-24-46
Ghost of Rosy Taylor, The 7-26-18

Ghost of Slumber Mountain 4-18-19
Ghost of the China Sea 8-27-58
Ghost of the Oven 10-29-10
Ghost of the Rancho, The 8-02-18
Ghost Patrol 2-01-23
Ghost Patrol 9-16-36
Ghost Ship, The 12-29-43
Ghost Ship, The 7-22-53
Ghost Stories (See: Kwaidan)
Ghost Talks 2-27-29
Ghost Town 1-06-37 and 1-27-37
Ghost Town 12-21-55
Ghost Town Gold 2-10-37
Ghost Town Law 5-13-42
Ghost Town Renegades 7-30-47
Ghost Train (See: Spoegelsestoget)
Ghost Train, The 10-12-27
Ghost Train, The 10-31-31; 2-21-33; and 5-02-33
Ghost Valley 8-30-32
Ghost Valley Raiders 4-03-40
Ghost Wagon, The 10-08-15
Ghost Walks, The 4-03-35
Ghosts 6-11-15
Ghosts in Buenos Aires (See: Fantasmas en Buenos Aires)
Ghosts in Rome (See: Fantasmi A Roma)
Ghosts--Italian Style 1-29-59
Ghosts of Berkeley Square 11-12-47
Ghosts on the Loose 7-07-43
Ghoul, The 1-30-34
Ghoul, The 6-11-75
Giacca Verde, La 8-29-79
Giacomo Casanova 12-21-38
Giacomo Casanova: Childhood and Adolescence (See: Infanzia,
     Vocazione e Prime Esperienze di Giacomo Casanova Veneziano)
Giant 10-10-56
Giant Behemoth, The 3-18-59
Giant from the Unknown 3-19-58
Giant Gila Monster, The 7-15-59
Giant of Marathon 5-18-60
Giants-White Sox 4-17-14
Giardino del Finzi-Continis, Il 12-23-70
Gibbi West Germany 5-28-80
Gibraltar 2-08-39
Gideon's Day 4-02-58
Gidget 3-18-59
Gidget Goes Hawaiian 5-31-61
Gidget Goes to Rome 7-31-63
Gifle, La 10-23-74
Gift 11-16-66
Gift Girl, The 3-09-17
Gift Horse 7-23-52
Gift of Gab 10-02-34
Gift of Love 2-12-58
Gift Supreme 4-16-20
Gifts of an Eagle 12-24-75
Gigantis 5-27-59
Gigi 11-02-49
Gigi 5-21-58
Gigolette 5-15-35
Gigolettes of Paris 10-17-33
Gigolo 10-13-26
Gigot 6-20-62
Gilda 3-20-46
Gilda Live 3-26-80
Gilded Butterfly, The 3-03-26
Gilded Cage, The 9-29-16
Gilded Dream, The 11-12-20
Gilded Fool, A 8-29-08
Gilded Highway, The 3-31-26
Gilded Lily, The 3-11-21
Gilded Lily, The 2-12-35
Gilded Spider, The 4-28-16
Gilded Youth 12-31-15
Gildersleeve on Broadway 10-27-43
Gildersleeve's Bad Day 5-05-43
Gildersleeve's Ghost 6-21-44
Gili-Bili Starik So Staroukhoi 6-02-65
Giliap 12-24-75
Gimme 1-19-23
Gimme Shelter 11-25-70
Ginger 4-25-19
Ginger 7-24-35
Ginger 3-17-71
Gingerhead (See: Poil de Carotte)
Gingham Girl, The 7-20-27
Ginzberg the Great 1-25-28
Giordano Bruno 11-28-73
Giornata Balorda, La 2-22-61

Giornata Speciale, Una 5-18-77
Giorni Cantati, I 9-05-79
Giorni Contati, I 3-07-62
Giorni D'Amore 12-22-54
Giorni Dell'Ira, I (See: Day of Anger)
Giorno Della Civetta, Il 2-28-68
Giorno Per Giorno, Disperatamente 1-17-62
Giovane Attila, Il 8-25-71
Giovane Normale, Il 12-31-69
Giovani Mariti 5-07-58
Giovani Tigri, I 3-13-68
Giovanna D'Arco Al Rogo 11-03-54
Giovanni Lupo, King of the Blackhands 5-14-15
Gioventu Perduta 4-14-48
Giovinezza Giovinezza 1-14-70
Gipfelsturmer, Der 4-14-37
Gipsy Cavalier, A 10-27-22
Girl, The (See: Devojka)
Girl, A Guy and a Gob, A 3-05-41
Girl Across the Way, The (See: Fille D'En Face, La)
Girl Alaska, The 8-22-19
Girl and Guns, A (See: Fille et des Fusils, Une)
Girl and Press Photographer (See: Pigen og Pressefotografen)
Girl and the Bugler, The 10-18-67
Girl and the Dream Castle, The (See: Pigen Og Droemmeslottet)
Girl and the Echo, The (See: Paskutine Atostogu Diena)
Girl and the Gambler, The 6-07-39
Girl and the General, The (See: Ragazza e il Generale, La)
Girl and the Judge, The 2-05-10
Girl and the Millionaire, The (See: Pigen og Millionaeren)
Girl and the Oak, The (See: Dkevojka I Hrast)
Girl and the Palio, The (See: Ragazza del Palio, La)
Girl at Home, The 5-04-17
Girl at the Lock, The 10-17-14
Girl Called Love, A (See: Fille Nomme Amour, Une)
Girl Can't Help It, The 12-19-56
Girl Crazy 3-29-32
Girl Crazy 8-04-43
Girl Danced Into Life, The (See: Eletbetancoltatott Lany)
Girl Days of a Queen (See: Maedchenjahre Einer Koenigin)
Girl Dodger, The 2-28-19
Girl Downstairs, The 12-28-38
Girl Fit to Be Killed, A (See: Holka Na Zabiti)
Girl for the Summer, A (See: Fille Pour L'Ete, Une)
Girl Friend, The 10-02-35
Girl Friend As Sweet as You, A (See: Freundin So Goldig Wie Du,
     Eine)
Girl Friends, The (See: Amiche, L')
Girl from Alaska, The 4-29-42
Girl from Avenue A, The 10-16-40
Girl from Bohemia, The 8-16-18
Girl from Bohemian Forest, The (See: Jana)
Girl from Calgary, The 11-22-32
Girl from Chicago 12-21-27
Girl from Coney Island, The 12-15-26
Girl from Gay Paree 12-07-27
Girl from God's Country 11-18-21
Girl from God's Country 8-07-40
Girl from Hamburg, The (See: Fille de Hambourg, La)
Girl from Hanoi, The 8-06-75
Girl from Havana, The 9-04-29
Girl from Havana, The 9-11-40
Girl from His Town, The 8-13-15
Girl from Jones Beach, The 6-22-49
Girl from Jungfrusund (See: Jungfrun pa Jungfrusund)
Girl from Korfu, The (See: Protevousianikes Peripeties)
Girl from Leningrad, The 12-31-41
Girl from Mandalay, The 5-13-36
Girl from Manhattan, The 9-15-48
Girl from Maxim's (See: Dame de Chez Maxim)
Girl from Maxim's 9-23-36
Girl from Mellons, The 2-12-10
Girl from Mexico, The 5-24-39
Girl from Millelire Street, The (See: Ragazza di Via Millelire,
     La)
Girl from Missouri, The 8-07-34
Girl from Monterey, The 1-05-44
Girl from Montmartre, The 2-24-26
Girl from Outside, The 11-14-19
Girl from Paris, The 1-06-37
Girl from Parma, The (See: Parmigiana, La)
Girl from Petrovka, The 8-14-74
Girl from Poltava, The 2-17-37
Girl from Porcupine 11-24-22
Girl from Rio, The 10-12-27
Girl from Rio, The 9-06-39
Girl from Rocky Point 3-03-22
Girl from Salt Fields 5 (See: Ragazza Delle Saline, La)

Girl from San Lorenzo, The 3-08-50
Girl from Scotland Yard, The 6-02-37
Girl from 10th Avenue, The 5-29-35
Girl from the Chorus, A (See: Maedel vom Ballett, Ein)
Girl from the Dress Circle, The (See: Flickan fran Tredje Raden)
Girl from the Marchcroft, The (See: Tosen Fran Stormytorpet)
Girl from the Mountain Village (See: Flickan Fran Fjellbyn)
Girl from the Mountains (See: Devojka Sa Kosmaja)
Girl from the Reeperbahn, The (See: Maedel von der Reeperbahn,
    Das)
Girl from the Revue, The 9-05-28
Girl from Valladolid (See: Muchachita De Valladolid)
Girl from Woolworth's, The 12-25-29
Girl Habit 7-07-31
Girl Happy 1-27-65
Girl He Didn't Buy, The 6-20-28
Girl He Left Behind, The 10-31-56
Girl Hunters, The (See: Drageurs, Les)
Girl Hunters, The 6-12-63
Girl I Left Behind Me, The 1-29-15
Girl I Loved, The 3-29-23 and 5-24-23
Girl in a Million, A 6-05-46
Girl in Australia, The (See: Bello Onesto Emigrato Australia
    Sposerebbe Compaesan Illibata)
Girl in Black, The (See: To Koritsi Me Ta Mara)
Girl in Black Stockings 10-02-57
Girl in Bohemia, A 11-07-19
Girl in Danger 11-06-34
Girl in Every Port, A 2-22-28
Girl in Every Port, A 12-26-51
Girl in 419 5-23-33
Girl in Glass Cage 9-18-29
Girl in His House, The 6-21-18
Girl in His Room 6-16-22
Girl in Love (See: Enamorada)
Girl in Mourning, The (See: Nina de Luto, La)
Girl in No. 29, The 3-20-34
Girl in Possession 3-20-34
Girl in Tails (See: Flickan I Frack)
Girl in the Case 10-02-40
Girl in the Case 5-24-44
Girl in the Checkered Coat 4-06-17
Girl in the Dark, The 3-01-18
Girl in the Headlines 11-20-63
Girl in the Kremlin, The 4-24-57
Girl in the Limousine 10-08-24
Girl in the Mist, A 1-30-57
Girl in the Moon, The 8-06-30
Girl in the News 1-01-41
Girl in the Park, The (See: Visnja Ta Tasmajdanu)
Girl in the Pullman 11-02-27
Girl in the Rain, The 7-23-20
Girl in the Rain 3-02-27
Girl in the Red Velvet Swing 10-12-55
Girl in the Show 10-09-29
Girl in the Taxi 9-15-37
Girl in the Tuxedo 1-16-29
Girl in the Web, The 7-23-20
Girl in the Window (See: Ragazza In Vetrina, La)
Girl in the Woods 6-18-58
Girl in the Yellow Pajamas, The (See: Ragazza In Pigiama Giallo, La)
Girl in 313 6-19-40
Girl in White, The 3-19-52
Girl Is a Gun, A (See: Aventure de Billy le Kid, Une)
Girl Knew, A (See: Jeune Fille Savait, Une)
Girl Like That, A 3-09-17
Girl Loves Boy 4-28-37
Girl Merchants (See: Marchands de Filles)
Girl Missing 3-21-33
Girl Most Likely, The 12-18-57
Girl Must Live, A 5-10-39 and 10-08-41
Girl Named Mary, A 1-31-20
Girl Named Poo Lom, A (See: Poo Lom)
Girl Named Tamiko, A 12-05-62
Girl Next Door, The 5-13-53
Girl Nihilist 7-25-08
Girl No. 217 9-05-45
Girl of Finland (See: Lapualaismorsian)
Girl of Limberlost 5-14-24
Girl of Lost Lake, The 8-18-16
Girl of My Dreams 3-20-35
Girl of My Dreams, The 12-06-18
Girl of My Heart 2-18-21
Girl of Solbakken, The (See: Synnove Solbakken)
Girl of the Dance Hall, The 10-29-15
Girl of the Day, The (See: Donne del Giorno)
Girl of the Golden West, The 1-08-15
Girl of the Golden West 5-24-23

Girl of the Golden West 10-29-30
Girl of the Golden West 3-16-38
Girl of the Limberlost, The 11-13-34
Girl of the Limberlost, The 9-19-45
Girl of the Mountains (See: Golfo)
Girl of the Night 10-05-60
Girl of the Ozarks 8-12-36
Girl of the Port 7-16-30
Girl of the Rio 1-12-32
Girl of the Sea, The 7-09-20
Girl of the Streets (See: Maedel der Strasse)
Girl of the Timber Lands 1-26-17
Girl of Tin, The (See: Ragazza de Latte, La)
Girl of Yesterday, A 10-15-15
Girl on a Motorcycle, The (See: Motocyclette, La)
Girl on the Barge 2-27-29
Girl on the Bridge, The 12-12-51
Girl on the Front Page 11-11-36
Girl on the Stairs 3-04-25
Girl Overboard 8-14-29
Girl Overboard 3-03-37
Girl Passing Through, The (See: Ragazza Di Passaggio, La)
Girl Philippa, The 1-05-17
Girl Problem, The 2-21-19
Girl Refugee, The (See: Prosfygopoula)
Girl Rush 10-25-44
Girl Rush 8-10-55
Girl Said No, The 4-09-30
Girl Said No, The 6-23-37
Girl Scout, The 11-06-09
Girl Shy 4-02-24
Girl Spy Before Vicksburg, The 1-07-11
Girl Stroke Boy 8-18-71
Girl Thief 1-12-38
Girl Thief, The 3-12-10
Girl Trouble 9-23-42
Girl Watchers, The (See: Os Paqueras)
Girl Who Came Back, The 5-17-23
Girl Who Came Back, The 9-18-35
Girl Who Dared, The 8-13-20
Girl Who Didn't Think, The 2-02-17
Girl Who Doesn't Know, The 12-15-16
Girl Who Had Everything, The 3-04-53
Girl Who Knew Too Much, The 11-26-69
Girl Who Liked Purple Flowers, The (See: Lila Akac, A)
Girl Who Stayed at Home, The 3-28-19
Girl Who Wouldn't Quit, The 3-29-18
Girl Who Wouldn't Work, The 8-12-25
Girl with a Million 4-01-21
Girl with a Pistol, The (See: Ragazza Con la Pistola, La)
Girl with a Suitcase (See: Ragazza Con la Valigia, La)
Girl with Golden Hair, The (See: Chrissomaloussa)
Girl with Green Eyes, The 5-20-64
Girl with Grey Eyes (See: Fille Aux Yeux Gris, La)
Girl with Hyacinths--The Suicide (See: Flicka Och Hyacinter)
Girl with Ideas, A 11-03-37
Girl with No Regrets, The 1-31-19
Girl with the Cello, The (See: Fille au Violoncelle, La)
Girl with the Golden Eyes, The (See: Fille Aux Yeux D'Or, La)
Girl with the Golden Panties, The (See: Muchacha de las Bragas
    de Oro, La)
Girl with the Green Eyes, The 7-07-16
Girl with the Jazz Heart, The 1-07-21
Girl with the Long Hair, The 12-31-75
Girl with the Red Scarf, The (See: Selvi Boylum Al Yazmalim)
Girl with the Whip, The (See: Fille Au Fouet, La)
Girl with Three Camels 7-31-68
Girl Without a Room 12-12-33
Girl Without a Soul, The 8-24-17
Girl Woman, The 8-08-19
Girl Worth Having, A 3-14-13
Girlhood of a Queen (See: Maedchenjahre einer Koenigin)
Girlfriends 5-10-78
Girls (See: Devtchata)
Girls 7-04-19
Girls, The (See: Flickorna)
Girls About Town 11-03-31
Girls' Alfred, The (See: Flickornas Alfred)
Girls and Gynecologists (See: Maedchen Beim Frauenarzt)
Girls' Apartment (See: Appartement des Filles, L')
Girls Are for Loving 5-30-73
Girls at Arms (See: Piger I Troejen)
Girls at Arms, Part 2 (See: Piger I Troejen 2)
Girls at Sea (See: Piger Til Soes)
Girls at Sea 11-26-58
Girls Behind Bars 5-17-59
Girls' Boarding School (See: Internado Para Senoritas)
Girls Can Play 6-23-37

Girls' Club (See: Club de Femmes)
Girls Demand Excitement 2-11-31
Girl's Desire, A 9-08-22
Girls Don't Gamble 3-04-21
Girl's Dormitory (See: Maedchenpensionat)
Girl's Dormitory 9-02-36
Girl's Folly, A 2-16-17
Girl's Dormitory 9-02-36
Girls for Eilat (See: Havou Banot Le'Eilat)
Girls for Sale 10-27-76
Girls, Girls (See: Maedchen, Maedchen)
Girls, Girls, Girls! 11-07-62
Girls Gone Wild 4-24-29
Girls in Chains 9-01-43
Girls in Distress (See: Jeunes Filles en Detresse)
Girls in Prison 9-12-56
Girls in Smaland, The (See: Flickorna I Smaland)
Girls in the Night 1-14-53
Girls in Uniform (See: Maedchen in Uniform)
Girls in White (See: Maedchen in Weiss)
Girls Marked Danger 5-26-54
Girls Men Forget 11-26-24
Girls of Piazza di Spagna (See: Ragazze di Piazza di Spagna)
Girls of Pleasure Island 2-25-53
Girls of San Frediano, The (See: Ragazze di Sanfrediano, Le)
Girls of the Big House 11-14-45
Girls of the Night (See: Filles de la Nuit)
Girls of the Range 2-26-10
Girls of the Road 7-24-40
Girls on Probation 1-12-38
Girls on Probation 10-26-38
Girls on the Beach 5-19-65
Girls on the Loose 4-02-58
Girls Orchestra (See: Orquesta de Senoritas)
Girls' School 9-28-38
Girls School 2-08-50
Girl's Start, A (See: Egy Lany Elindul)
Girls' Town 4-15-42
Girls Town 9-30-59
Girls Under 21 11-13-40
Girls Who Dare 5-22-29 and 7-24-29
Girls Will Be Boys 10-02-34
Girolimoni, Il Mostro di Roma 1-10-73
Giron 6-19-74
Girovaghi, I 2-13-57
Giselle 5-03-78
Gishiki 7-14-71
Git Along, Little Dogie 12-08-37
Gitan, Le 12-31-75
Gitta Discovers Her Heart (See: Gitta Entdeckt Ihr Herz)
Gitta Entdeckt Ihr Herz 10-04-32
Giu La Testa (See: Duck, You Sucker)
Giudizio Universale, Il 9-13-61
Giulietta de Gli Spiriti 11-03-65
Giulietta e Romeo (See: Romeo and Juliet)
Giuseppe Verdi 11-30-38
Giv Gud en Chance Om Soendagen 5-13-70
Give a Girl a Break 12-02-53
Give and Take 1-09-29
Give Becky a Chance 7-27-17
Give 'Em Hell, Harry 9-03-75
Give God a Chance on a Sunday (See: Giv Gud en Chance Om Sonendagen)
Give Her a Ring 8-12-36
Give Her Anything 1-13-22
Give Me a Sailor 7-27-38
Give Me Back My Skin (See: Rendez-Moi Ma Peau)
Give Me Five (See: Qua La Mano)
Give Me My Chance (See: Donnez-Moi Ma Chance)
Give Me My Son 3-03-22
Give Me Ten Desperate Men (See: Donnez-Moi Dix Hommes Desesperes)
Give Me Your Heart 9-16-36
Give My Regards to Broadway 5-26-48
Give Out, Sisters 9-02-42
Give Us the Moon 8-02-44
Give Us This Day 10-19-49
Give Us This Night 4-08-36
Give Us Wings 11-13-40
Given Word, The (See: O Pagador de Promess)
Givoi Troup 7-23-69
Gizmo 7-27-77
Glacier Fox, The 1-31-79
Glad Rag Doll, The 6-05-29
Glada Paraden 6-16-48
Glade Skraddaren, Den 2-18-48
Gladiator, The 8-31-38
Gladiatorerna 6-04-69
Gladiators, The (See: Gladiatorerna)
Gladiators 7 4-29-64
Gladiola 10-22-15

Glaeserne Zelle, Die 6-21-78
Glaive et la Balance, La 2-13-63
Glamour 6-16-31
Glamour 5-15-34
Glamour Boy 9-10-41
Glamour for Sale 10-23-40
Glamour Girl 12-31-47
Glamourous Night 5-19-37
Glas Wasser, Das 7-13-60
Glass Alibi, The 5-01-46
Glass Bottom Boat, The 4-20-66
Glass Cage, The (See: Cage de Verre, La)
Glass Castle, The (See: Chateau de Verre, Le)
Glass Ceiling, The (See: Techo de Cristal, El)
Glass Cell, The (See: Glaeserne Zelle, Die)
Glass Houses 3-17-22
Glass Houses 4-29-70
Glass Key, The 6-19-35
Glass Key, The 9-02-42
Glass Menagerie, The 9-20-50
Glass Mountain, The 2-16-49
Glass of Water, A (See: Glass Wasser, Ein)
Glass of Water, A (See: Glas Wasser, Das)
Glass of Whiskey, A (See: Vaso de Whisky, Un)
Glass Slipper 2-16-55
Glass Wall, The 3-04-53
Glass Wasser, Ein 5-17-23
Glass Web, The 10-14-53
Gleam O'Dawn 5-19-22
Gleisdreick 2-24-37 and 6-22-38
Glen and Randa 6-02-71
Glenn Miller Story, The 1-06-54
Glenrowan Affair, The 8-01-51
Gliding Virgin, The (See: Schwebende Jungfrau, Die)
Glimpses of Paris 9-11-09
Glimpses of the Moon 4-05-23
Glissements Progressifs du Plaisir 3-27-74
Global Affair, A 2-05-64
Globero, El 4-05-61
Globe's War Films 1-21-16
Globo de Cantolla, El 7-12-44
Gloria 11-01-32
Gloria 10-05-77
Gloria 9-10-80
Gloria Mundi 12-03-75
Gloriana 11-03-16
Gloria's Romance (serial) episodes 1 & 2: 5-26-16; episodes 3 & 4: 6-02-16; episodes 5 & 6: 6-09-16
Glorifying the American Girl 1-15-30
Glorious Adventure, The 8-16-18
Glorious Betsy 5-02-28
Glorious Dust (See: Divota Prasine)
Glorious Fool, The 3-24-22
Glorious Lady, The 11-07-19
Glorious Nights (See: Noches de Gloria)
Glorious Times in the Spessarto (See: Herrliche Zeiten im Spessart)
Glorious Trail, The 10-17-28
Glory 4-21-16 and 1-26-17
Glory 1-11-56
Glory Alley 5-21-52
Glory Boy 6-30-71
Glory Brigade, The 5-13-53
Glory Guys, The 7-14-65
Glory of Clementina 6-23-22
Glory of Faith 11-30-38
Glory of Yolanda, The 3-02-17
Glory Sky (See: Ouranos)
Glory Stompers, The 12-06-67
Glory Trail 4-21-37
Glos Z Tamtego Swiata 4-03-63
Gluecklichen Jahre der Thorwalds, Die 11-28-62
Gluecklichen Minuten des Georg Hauser, Die 7-31-74
Glueckskinder 10-21-36 and 6-09-37
Gnezdo Na Vetru 7-23-80
Gnome-Mobile, The 5-31-67
Go and Get It 7-23-20
Go and Get It 2-20-29
Go-Between, The 6-02-71
Go Chase Yourself 4-20-38
Go-Daan 8-12-64
Go For Broke 3-28-51
Go For It 7-28-76
Go France (See: Allez France)
Go Get 'Em Garringer 3-07-19
Go-Getter, The 4-12-23
Go-Getter, The 6-09-37
Go-Go Bigbeat 5-19-65

Go, Go, Go World (See: Pelo Nel Mondo, Il)
Go Go Mania 5-26-65
Go into Your Dance 5-08-35
Go, Man, Go 1-20-54
Go Naked in the World 1-18-61
Go On, Little Martha (See: Fram for Lilla Marta)
Go On Mama (See: Vas Y Maman)
Go See Mother ... Father Is Working (See: Va Voir Maman ... Papa
    Travaille)
Go Straight 10-07-25
Go Tell the Spartans 6-14-78
Go to Blazes 4-11-62
Go West 10-28-25
Go West 12-18-40
Go West, Young Lady 11-26-41
Go West, Young Man 1-31-19
Go West, Young Man 11-25-36
Goal! World Cup 1966 10-19-66
Goalie's Anxiety at the Penalty Kick, The 3-29-72
Goat, The 10-04-18
Goat Getter, The 7-21-26
Goat Horn, The (See: Kozijat Rog)
Goat's Horn, The (See: Kozuu Pos)
Gobs and Gals 4-30-52
Gobsek 7-21-37
God and the Devil in Land of Sun (See: Deus e o Diabo Na Terr Do
    Sol)
God Bless Each Corner of This Home (See: Dios Bendiga Cada Rincon
    De Esta Casa)
God Chose Paris (See: Dieu a Choisi Paris)
God Forgives, I Don't 5-21-69
God Gave Me 20¢ 11-24-26
God Has Need of Men (See: Dieu A Besoin des Hommes)
God Is My Co-Pilot 2-21-45
God Is My Partner 7-03-57
God, Man and the Devil 1-25-50
God of Little Children 1-19-17
God Told Me To 12-01-76
God, Why Is There a Border in Love? (See: Kamisama Naze Ai Ni Mo
    Kokkyo Ga Aru No)
God Wills It So (See: Dieu Le Veut)
God With Us (See: Gott Mit Uns)
Goddess (See: Devi)
Goddess, The 4-23-58
Goddess of Lost Lake, The 10-18-18
Goddesses, The (See: As Deusas)
Godelureaux, Les 4-05-61
Godfather, The 3-08-72
Godfather, Part II, The 12-11-74
Godisnja Doba 9-05-79
Godless Girl 4-03-29
Godless Men 2-04-21
Gods, The (See: Emitai)
God's Angels Are Everywhere 5-05-48
God's Country 6-09-31
God's Country and the Law 7-07-22
God's Country and the Man 11-03-37
God's Country and the Woman 4-28-16
God's Country and the Woman 1-13-37
God's Crucible 1-19-17
God's Gift to Women 4-22-31
God's Gold 6-17-21
God's Good Man 8-29-19
God's Great Wilderness 9-07-27
God's Half Acre 8-18-16
God's Law and Man's 5-04-17
God's Little Acre 5-14-58
God's Man 4-06-17
Gods of Asia 6-16-22
Gods of Pestilence (See: Goetter der Pest)
God's Outlaw 7-11-19
God's Police Patrol (See: Funkstreife Gottes)
Godsend, The 1-16-80
Godspell 3-28-73
Godzilla, King of the Monsters 4-25-56
Godzilla vs. Megalon 6-16-76
Godzilla vs. the Thing 9-23-64
Godzina Szczytu 1-01-75
Goetter der Pest 4-22-70
Goettliche Jette, Die 4-07-37
Gog 6-09-54
Gogo 4-17-63
Goha 5-21-58
Gohaku Muika 1-25-67
Goin' Coconuts 10-11-78
Goin' Down the Road 7-22-70
Goin' Home 12-29-76

Goin' South 10-04-78
Goin' to Town 5-15-35
Goin' to Town 9-17-44
Going (See: Gaman)
Going Crooked 12-22-26
Going for Broke (See: Alt Paa Et Braet)
Going Highbrow 9-04-35
Going Hollywood 12-26-33
Going Home 11-24-71
Going Home 10-11-72
Going in Style 12-19-79
Going My Way 3-08-44
Going Places 1-11-39
Going Some 7-23-20
Going Steady (See: Yotz' Im Kavua)
Going Steady 2-05-58
Going Straight 5-26-16
Going the Limit 8-26-25
Going Up 10-11-23
Going Wild 1-28-41
Golapi Ekhon Trainey 9-05-79
Gold (See: Or, L')
Gold 10-11-32
Gold 10-02-74
Gold and Lead (See: Or et le Plomb, L')
Gold and the Girl 8-12-25
Gold and the Woman 3-17-16
Gold Chevrons 11-23-27
Gold Cure, The 1-10-19
Gold Diggers, The 9-13-23
Gold Diggers in Paris 5-25-38
Gold Diggers of Broadway 9-04-29
Gold Diggers of 1933 6-13-33
Gold Diggers of 1935 3-20-35
Gold Diggers of 1937 12-30-36
Gold Dust Gertie 6-02-31
Gold Fever 7-23-52
Gold for the Caesars 6-17-64
Gold for the Tough Guys of the Prairie (See: Guld Til Praeriens
    Skrappe Drenge)
Gold, Frankincense and Myrrh (See: Mirisi, Zlato I Tamjan)
Gold Grabbers 11-24-22
Gold in the Hand (See: Oro En La Mano)
Gold Is Where You Find It 2-16-38
Gold Madness 10-11-23
Gold Mine in the Sky 7-06-38
Gold Necklace, A 10-15-10
Gold of Naples, The (See: Oro Di Napoli, L')
Gold of Rome, The (See: Oro di Roma, L')
Gold of the 7 Saints 2-08-61
Gold Racket, The 8-04-37
Gold Raiders 6-18-52
Gold Rush, The 7-01-25; 8-19-25; and 3-04-42
Gold Rush Maisie 7-31-40
Goldbergs, The 11-22-50
Goldcabbage Family, The (See: Familien Gyldenkaal)
Goldcabbage Family Breaks the Bank, The (See: Familien Gyldenkaal
    Spraenger Banken)
Golden Age of Comedy, The 1-08-58
Golden Apples of the Sun 6-09-71
Golden Arrow, The 5-06-36
Golden Arrow, The 4-22-64
Golden Bed, The 1-21-25
Golden Blade, The 8-26-53
Golden Boy 8-16-39
Golden Breed 11-13-68
Golden Calf, The 4-30-30
Golden Chance, The 12-31-15
Golden Claw, The 11-05-15
Golden Clown, The 3-21-28
Golden Coach, The (See: Carrosse D'Or, Le)
Golden Cocoon, The 12-16-25
Golden Dawn 7-30-30
Golden Demon (See: Konjiki Yasha)
Golden Disk 3-12-58
Golden Dreams 6-16-22
Golden Earrings 8-27-47
Golden Eye, The 9-22-48
Golden Fern (See: Zlate Kapradi)
Golden Fetter, The 3-09-17
Golden Fleece, The 8-09-18
Golden Fleecing, The 8-21-40
Golden Fortress, The (See: Sonar Kella)
Golden Gallows 2-24-22
Golden Gate Girl 5-28-41
Golden Gift, The 3-03-22

Golden Girl 11-07-51
Golden Gloves 8-28-40
Golden Gloves Story 4-26-50
Golden Goal, The (See: Lockende Ziel, Das)
Golden Goal, The 5-31-18
Golden Harvest 11-07-33
Golden Hawk, The 10-29-52
Golden Head, The 4-14-65
Golden Heart, The 7-10-64
Golden Helmet (See: Casque d'Or)
Golden Hoofs 2-19-41
Golden Hope, The 2-11-21
Golden Horde, The 9-19-51
Golden Lady, The 2-07-79
Golden Lake 5-01-35
Golden Lies 2-18-16
Golden Light (See: Kultainen Kyntilanjalka)
Golden Lily, The 2-05-10
Golden Link, The 9-01-54
Golden Lotus, The 6-15-17
Golden Madonna, The 4-27-49 and 9-07-49
Golden Mask 3-10-54
Golden Mass, The (See: Messe Doree, La)
Golden Mistress 10-20-54
Golden Mountains (See: Guld Og Gronne Skove)
Golden Mountains 4-19-32
Golden Necklace, A 10-15-10
Golden Needles 7-17-74
Golden Night (See: Nuit D'Or)
Golden Ophelia 1-29-75
Golden Ox Inn (See: Zum Goldenen Ochsen)
Golden Partners (See: Ogon No Paatonaa)
Golden Pestilence, The (See: Goldene Pest, Die)
Golden Queen (See: Zlata Reneta)
Golden Rendezvous 12-14-77
Golden Salamander 2-08-50
Golden Silence 4-19-23
Golden Snare 7-15-21
Golden Stallion, The 10-26-49
Golden Swallow, The (See: Hsia Yu-Yen)
Golden Swan (See: Hong Thong)
Golden Taiga 8-14-35
Golden Thing, The (See: Goldene Ding, Das)
Golden Trail 10-08-20
Golden Trail 9-25-40
Golden Trumpet, The 11-22-61
Golden Twenties, The 3-22-50
Golden Venus (See: Venus de l'Or, La)
Golden Voyage of Sinbad, The 1-16-74
Golden Wall, The 7-12-18
Golden Web, The 9-29-26
Golden Widow, A (See: Veuve En Or, Une)
Golden Yukon 2-22-28
Goldencauliflower Family Gets the Vote, The (See: Familien
    Gyldenkaal Vinder Valget)
Goldene Ding, Das 2-02-72
Goldene Pest, Die 2-16-55
Goldengirl 6-20-79
Goldfinger 9-23-64
Goldfish, The 5-21-24
Goldie 6-30-31
Goldie Gets Along 6-06-33
Goldsmith's Embankment (See: Quai Des Orfevres)
Goldstein 5-06-64
Goldtown Ghost Riders 5-20-53
Goldwyn Follies, The 2-02-38
Golem 10-01-80
Golem, The 6-24-21
Golem, The 2-26-36 and 3-24-37
Golf Fiend, The 10-15-10
Golf Widows 7-04-28
Golfo 5-21-58
Golfos, Los 5-25-60
Golge 8-27-80
Golgotha 4-24-35 and 2-17-37
Goliath and the Barbarians 12-02-59
Goliath and the Dragon 1-25-61
Goliath and the Vampires 4-29-64
Golu Hadawatha 12-24-69
Gondola del Diavolo, La 2-18-48
Gone Are the Days 10-02-63
Gone in 60 Seconds 7-31-74
Gone to Earth 9-27-50
Gone to the Dogs 11-08-39
Gone with History (See: Autant En Emporte L'Histoire)
Gone with the Wind 12-20-39
Gong Show Movie, The 5-21-80
Good and Naughty 6-16-26

Good and the Bad, The (See: Det Gode Og Det Onde)
Good as Gold 6-08-27
Good Bad Girl, The 5-20-31
Good Bad Man, The 4-14-16
Good Bad Wife, The 1-21-21
Good-Bye Alicia (See: Adios Alicia)
Good Bye, Bill 1-31-19
Good-Bye Girls 5-03-23
Good-Bye Kiss 11-14-28
Good-Bye, My Lady 4-11-56
Good-Bye ... See You Monday (See: Au Revoir ... A Lundi)
Good Causes, The (See: Bonnes Causes, Les)
Good Companions, The 3-14-33 and 10-17-33
Good Companions, The 4-03-57
Good Crew, The (See: Belle Equipe, La)
Good Dame 3-20-34
Good Day for a Hanging, A 12-24-58
Good Deed (See: Upkar)
Good Die Young, The 3-17-54
Good Earth, The 2-10-37
Good Enough to Eat (See: Fille a Croquer, Une)
Good Evening, Irina (See: Buna Seara, Irina)
Good Evening to Everybody (See: Magandang Gabi Sa Inyong Lahat)
Good Fairy, The 2-05-35
Good Fellows, The 8-11-43
Good for Nothing, The 6-12-14
Good for Nothing, The 1-30-17
Good-for-Nothings (See: Taugenichts)
Good Girls, The (See: Bonnes Femmes, Les)
Good Girls Go to Paris 6-28-39
Good Glue, A 9-17-10
Good Gracious Annabelle 4-04-19
Good Guys and the Bad Guys, The (See: Bon et les Mechants, Le)
Good Guys and the Bad Guys, The 9-10-69
Good Guys Wear Black 6-28-78
Good Humor Man 5-31-50
Good Intentions 7-30-30
Good Life, The (See: Belle Vie, La)
Good Little Devil, A 3-13-14
Good Lord Without Confession (See: Bon Dieu Sans Confession, Le)
Good Loser, A 7-19-18
Good Love, The (See: Buen Amor, El)
Good Luck (See: Bonne Chance)
Good Luck Charlie (See: Bonne Chance Charlie!)
Good Luck for the Coming Year 6-05-09
Good Luck, Miss Wyckoff 5-09-79
Good Luck, Mr. Yates 7-21-43
Good Luck or The Marriage (See: Mazel Tov Ou Le Mariage)
Good Man, A (See: Hombre Bueno, Un)
Good Medicine (See: Bonne Tisane, La)
Good Morning and Goodbye 12-20-67
Good Morning Boys 2-24-37
Good Morning, Elephant! (See: Buongiorno, Elefante!)
Good Morning, Judge 6-27-28
Good Morning, Judge 4-21-43
Good Morning, Miss Dove 11-16-55
Good Neighbor Sam 6-17-64
Good News (See: Buone Notizie)
Good News 9-10-30
Good News 12-03-47
Good Night, Nurse 6-28-18
Good Night Paul 6-21-18
Good Old Days, The 6-28-39
Good Old Piano (See: Dobri Stari Pianino)
Good Old Soak, The 4-28-37
Good Provider 4-14-22
Good References 9-24-20
Good Riddance (See: Bons Debarras, Les)
Good Sam 7-28-48
Good Sea, The (See: Dobro Morje)
Good Sinner, The (See: Brave Suender, Der)
Good Soldier Schweik, The (See: Brave Soldat Schwejk, Der)
Good Soup (See: Bonne Soupe, La)
Good, the Bad, and the Ugly, The 12-27-67
Good Thief, The (See: Ladrone, Il)
Good Time Charley 11-23-27
Good Time Girl 5-05-48 and 5-24-50
Good Times 4-26-67
Good Times, Wonderful Times 9-01-65
Good Woman 5-20-21
Good Year, The (See: Bonne Annee, La)
Goodbye Again 9-05-33
Goodbye Again 7-05-61
Goodbye, Beautiful Days (See: Adieu Les Beaux Jours)
Goodbye Broadway 5-18-38
Goodbye, Charlie 11-11-64
Goodbye, Columbus 3-19-69
Goodbye Darling (See: Adieu Cherie)

Goodbye Dove (See: Proshaite Golubi)
Goodbye Emmanuelle 7-12-78
Goodbye Flickmania 12-19-79
Goodbye Gemini 8-12-70
Goodbye Girl, The 11-16-77
Goodbye in the Mirror 8-05-64
Goodbye Love 4-03-34
Goodbye, Mr. Chips 5-17-39
Goodbye, Mr. Chips 10-15-69
Goodbye, Mister Grock (See: Au Revoir Monsieur Grock)
Goodbye Moscow (See: Saraba Mosukowa Gurentai)
Goodbye, My Fancy 4-11-51
Goodbye, Norma Jean 1-28-76
Goodbye Singing, The (See: Chant Du Depart, Le)
Goodbye, Stork, Goodbye (See: Adios Ciguena, Adios)
Goodnight, Ladies and Gentlemen (See: Signore, Signori,
    Buonanotte)
Goodnight Sweetheart 6-14-44
Goona-Goona 9-20-32
Goopy Gyne Bagha Byne 7-02-69
Goose and the Gander, The 9-18-35
Goose Boy, The 10-17-51
Goose Game, The (See: Juego de la Oca, El)
Goose Girl, The 1-29-15 and 11-29-18
Goose Hangs High, The 3-11-25
Goose Woman, The 8-05-25
Gooseflesh (See: Chair de Poule)
Goransson's Boy (See: Goranssons Pojke)
Goranssons Pojke 5-16-45
Gorath 5-20-64
Gordo de America, El 9-15-76
Gordon's War 8-08-73
Gorechto Pladne 5-26-65
Gorgeous Hussy, The 9-09-36
Gorgo 1-25-61
Gorgon, The 8-26-64
Gori, Gori, Moja Zvezda 12-08-76
Gorilla, The 11-23-27
Gorilla, The 2-25-31
Gorilla, The 5-24-39
Gorilla at Large 5-05-54
Gorilla Greets You, The (See: Gorille Vous Salue Bien, Le)
Gorilla Hunt, The 11-24-26
Gorilla Man 12-09-42
Gorilla Ship, The 8-02-32
Gorilla von Soho, Der 10-25-72
Gorilla's Waltz (See: Valse du Gorille, La)
Gorille Vous Salue Bien, Le 10-08-58
Goroda I Gody 8-28-74
Gorp 5-07-80
Gosh 12-04-74
Gospel According to St. Matthew, The (See: Vangelo Secondo
    Matteo, Il)
Gospel Road, The 3-21-73
Gospodin Nuima 12-24-69
Gossip 5-17-23
Got It Made 10-09-74
Got What She Wanted 12-31-30
Gotch-Hackenschmidt Wrestling Match 5-30-08
Goto, Island of Love (See: Goto, L'Ile D'Amour)
Goto, L'Ile D'Amour 10-30-68
Gotoma the Buddha 7-24-57
Gott Mit Uns 8-05-70
Gotterdammerung (See: Damned, The)
Gottes Engels Sind Ueberall (See: God's Angels Are Everywhere)
Goualeuse, La 11-30-38
Goucho, Il 10-21-64
Goupi Mains Rogues (See: It Happened at the Inn)
Gout de la Violence, Le 9-20-61
Gouverneur, Der 6-14-39
Government Girl 11-10-43
Governor, The (See: Gouverneur, Der)
Governor's Boss, The 6-18-15
Governor's Daughter, The 12-04-09
Governor's Lady, The 3-19-15
Gow 12-05-33
Goya 2-03-71
Goyescas 6-28-44
Goyokin 9-03-69
Gozencho No Jikanwari 1-02-74
Grabbe's Last Summer (See: Grabbes Letzter Sommer)
Grabbes Letzter Sommer 12-17-80
Grace's Place 11-14-73
Gracie Allen Murder Case, The 5-17-39
Gradiva 10-21-70
Graduate, The 12-20-67
Graduation Year (See: Annee du Bac, L')
Graefin von Monte Christo 5-10-32

Graft 12-01-31
Grafter, The 2-02-07
Grafters 8-31-17
Grail, The 12-20-23
Grain de Beaute 3-22-32
Grain of Dust 9-26-28
Grain of Dust, The 1-25-18
Grajski Biki 11-01-67
Gramma Ston Nazim Hikmet 10-27-76
Gran Amour de Becquer, El 11-27-46
Gran Aventura, La 7-31-74
Gran Circo Chamorro, El 11-30-55
Gran Dia, El 9-11-57
Gran Mentiroso, El 12-30-53
Gran Ruta, La 12-15-71
Gran Senora, La 10-21-59
Gran Varieta 4-27-55
Grand Amour, Le 4-02-69
Grand Bazar, Le 9-26-73
Grand Blond Avec une Chaussure Noire, Le 12-27-72
Grand Bluff, Le 7-24-57
Grand Canary 7-24-34
Grand Canyon 12-07-49
Grand Canyon Trail 11-24-48
Grand Central Murder 4-22-42
Grand Central Power House Explosion 12-24-10
Grand Ceremonial, Le 4-02-69
Grand Chef, Le 4-08-59
Grand Concert, The 9-10-52
Grand Dadais, Le 8-16-67
Grand Delire, Le 4-23-75
Grand Depart, Le 12-20-72
Grand Duchess and the Waiter, The 2-10-26
Grand Escogriffe, Le 12-15-76
Grand Exit 11-13-35
Grand Guignol 6-07-23
Grand Hotel (See: Menschen Im Hotel)
Grand Hotel 4-19-32
Grand Illusion 9-14-38
Grand Jeu, Le 5-15-34
Grand Jeu, Le 5-26-54
Grand Jury 8-05-36
Grand Jury Secrets 7-05-39
Grand Larceny 3-03-22
Grand Maneuver, The 10-10-56
Grand Meaulnes, Le 10-18-67
Grand National Night 4-29-53
Grand Old Girl 3-06-35
Grand Ole Opry 7-03-40
Grand Parade, The 2-05-30
Grand Passion, The 1-04-18
Grand Patron, Un 1-02-52 (Also see: Perfectionist, The)
Grand Pavois, Le 9-01-54
Grand Piano, The (See: Royalut)
Grand Prix 12-28-66
Grand Rendezvous, Le 3-01-50
Grand Restaurant, Le 10-12-66
Grand Rock, Le 6-04-69
Grand Sabordage, Le 3-08-72
Grand Slam 2-28-33
Grand Slam 12-27-67
Grand Soir, Le 8-25-76
Grand Substitution, The 11-24-65
Grand Terrace, The (See: Au Grand Terrace)
Grand Theft Auto 6-15-77
Grandad Rudd 3-20-35
Grande Apello, Il 11-25-36
Grande Barriere de Corail, La 9-30-70
Grande Bouffe, La 5-16-73
Grande Colpo Dei Sette Uomini D'Oro, Il 11-23-66
Grande Epreuve, La 6-13-28 (Also see: Soul of France, The)
Grande Fille Toute Simple, Une (See: Just a Big, Simple Girl)
Grande Frousse, La 12-02-64
Grande Guerre, La 9-16-59
Grande Lessive!, La 12-11-68
Grande Maffia, La 10-06-71
Grande Mare, La 8-20-30
Grande Olimpiade, La 2-08-61
Grande Sauterelle, La 2-08-67
Grande Speranza, La 11-03-54
Grande Strada Azzurra, La 3-26-58
Grande Trouille, La 8-28-74
Grande Vadrouille, La 12-21-66
Grande Vie, La 8-31-60
Grandes Familles, Les 12-17-58
Grandes Gueules, Les 11-24-65
Grandes Manoeuvres, Les 11-16-55
Grandes Personnes, Les 2-22-61

Grandeur et Decadence 6-02-37
Grandeur Nature 6-05-74
Grandfather (See: Fad, Jal)
Grandfather Automobile, The (See: Abuele Automovil, El)
Grandfather's Pills 7-18-08
Grandi Magazzini 11-15-39
Grandma and the Eight Children in Town (See: Mormor og de Atte
    Ungene i Byen)
Grandma Sabella (See: Nonna Sabella, La)
Grandma's Boy 6-16-22
Grandmother, The (See: Nona, La)
Grandmother's Plot 10-22-10
Grandpa Goes to Town 4-24-40
Grandpa Schultz (See: Opa Schulz)
Grands Chemins, Les 7-31-63
Grands Moyens, Les 2-04-76
Grands Sentiments Font les Bons Gueuletons, Les 1-02-74
Grands Vacances, Les 12-20-67
Grandstand for General Staff (See: Feldherrnhuegel, Der)
Granges Brulees, Les 6-20-73
Granny Get Your Gun 1-10-40
Granny's Birthday 3-05-10
Grapedealer's Daughter, The 2-25-70
Grapes of Wrath, The 1-31-40
Graphique de Boscop, Le 12-29-76
Grasp of Greed, The 7-07-16
Grass Cutters, The (See: Kusa-O Karu Musume)
Grass Eater, The 8-30-61
Grass Is Greener, The 11-30-60
Grass Orphan, The 2-22-23
Grasshopper, The (See: Cicala, La)
Grasshopper, The 5-20-70
Grateful Dead, The 6-08-77
Gratitude 9-25-09
Grausame Freundin, Die 8-09-32
Graustark 9-09-25
Grauzone 8-22-79
Grave Disappointment, A 9-11-09
Gravitation (See: Gravitcija)
Gravitcija 8-14-68
Gravy Train, The 6-26-74
Gray Dawn 6-09-22
Gray Lady Down 3-08-78
Gray Parasol, The 10-04-18
Gray Sentinel, The 3-28-13
Gray Towers Mystery, The 10-17-19
Gray Wolf's Ghost, The 10-31-19
Grayeagle 12-28-77
Grazie, Tia 3-20-68
Grease 6-07-78
Grease Ball (See: Boule de Suif)
Greased Lightning 5-02-19
Greased Lightning 7-18-28
Greased Lightning 7-20-77
Greaser's Palace 7-26-72
Great Accident, The 6-25-20
Great Adventure, The (See: Det Stora Aventyret or Gran Aventura,
    La)
Great Adventure, The 2-22-18
Great Adventure, The 1-14-21
Great Adventure, The 4-28-22
Great Adventure, The 5-07-52
Great Air Robbery, The 2-20-20
Great Alone 7-07-22
Great American Broadcast, The 4-30-41
Great American Bugs Bunny-Road Runner Chase, The 8-01-79
Great American Cowboy, The 3-20-74
Great American Pastime, The 11-21-56
Great Armored Car Swindle, The 4-08-64
Great Bank Robbery, The 6-25-69
Great Bank Sensation, The 3-12-15
Great Barrier, The 2-17-37
Great Barrier Reef, The (See: Grande Barriere de Corail, La)
Great Battle, The 9-22-71
Great Beginning, The 11-27-40
Great Betrayal, The 5-21-47
Great Big Thing, A 7-03-68
Great Bradley Mystery, The 4-20-17
Great British Train Robbery, The 4-05-67
Great Bunch of Girls, A 9-26-79
Great Call, The (See: Grande Apello, Il)
Great Caruso, The 4-18-51
Great Catherine, The 11-06-68
Great Citizen, The 1-18-39
Great City, The (See: Mahanagar)
Great Commandment, The 10-21-42
Great Dan Patch, The 7-20-49
Great Dawn, The 8-13-47
Great Day, The (See: Gran Dia, El)

Great Day, The (See: Giornata Speciale, Una)
Great Day, The 12-17-20
Great Day, The 5-02-45
Great Day in the Morning 5-16-56
Great Deception 8-18-26
Great Defender, The 7-17-34
Great Diamond Mystery 10-22-24
Great Diamond Robbery, The 3-27-14 and 5-08-14
Great Diamond Robbery, The 4-24-29
Great Diamond Robbery, The 12-02-53
Great Dictator, The 10-16-40
Great Divide, The 2-05-10
Great Divide, The 1-17-16
Great Divide, The 2-11-25
Great Divide, The 2-19-30
Great Document, The (See: To Mega Docoumento)
Great Dream, The 7-31-63
Great Drive 12-27-32
Great Earthquake in Sicily 2-06-09
Great Ecstasy of the Woodcarver Steiner, The (See: Grosse Ekstase
    des Bildschnitzers Steiner, Die)
Great Elephant Kraal 10-27-22
Great Escape, The 4-17-63
Great Escape from Dien Bien Phu, The (See: Haek Kai Narok Dien
    Bien Phu)
Great Event at Podunk 9-04-09
Great Expectations 1-19-17
Great Expectations 3-08-23
Great Expectations 1-29-35
Great Expectations 12-25-46
Great Feed, The (See: Grande Bouffe, La)
Great Flamarion, The 1-17-45
Great Flirtation, The 6-26-34
Great Gabbo, The 9-18-29
Great Gambini, The 7-14-37
Great Gamble, The 6-27-19
Great Game, The 9-10-30
Great Garrick, The 9-29-37
Great Gatsby, The 11-24-26
Great Gatsby, The 4-27-49
Great Gatsby, The 3-27-74
Great Gildersleeve, The 11-11-42
Great Glinka, The 12-24-47
Great God Gold 5-08-35
Great Gundown, The 8-10-77
Great Guns 9-10-41
Great Guy 1-06-37
Great Hope, The (See: Grande Speranza, La)
Great Hospital Mystery, The 7-07-37
Great Hotel Murder, The 3-06-35
Great House, The (See: Casa Grande, La)
Great Impersonation 12-18-35
Great Impersonation, A 9-30-21
Great Imposter, The 11-23-60
Great Indian Film Bazaar, The 2-06-80
Great Is My Country 7-01-59
Great Jasper, The 2-21-33
Great Jesse James Raid, The 8-12-53
Great Jewel Robbery, The 6-14-50
Great John Ericsson, The 5-18-38
Great John L., The 6-06-45
Great K. & A. Train Robbery, The 10-27-26
Great Leap, The 5-15-14
Great Lie, The 4-09-41
Great Locomotive Chase, The 5-23-56
Great London Mystery, The 12-17-20
Great Love, The (See: Grand Amour, Le or Grosse Liebe, Die)
Great Love, The 8-16-18
Great Lover 8-25-31
Great Lover, The 11-26-20
Great Lover, The 9-14-49
Great MacArthy, The 8-13-75
Great McGinty, The 7-24-40
Great McGonagall, The 8-20-75
Great Mail Robbery, The 7-20-27
Great Man, The 11-28-56
Great Man Votes, The 1-11-39
Great Man's Lady, The 3-18-42
Great Meadow, The 3-18-31
Great Mike, The 12-27-44
Great Missouri Raid, The 12-06-50
Great Mr. Handel, The 10-14-42
Great Mr. Nobody, The 4-02-41
Great Moment, The 7-29-21
Great Moment, The 6-07-44
Great Night, The 1-25-23

Great Northfield, Minnesota Raid, The 4-12-72
Great Olympiad, The (See: Grande Olimpiade, La)
Great O'Malley, The 3-10-37
Great Passion, The (See: Grosse Sehnsucht, Die)
Great Patriotic War, The 12-01-65
Great Plane Robbery, The 11-20-40
Great Plane Robbery, The 3-08-50
Great Power, The 3-27-29
Great Prince Shan 5-28-24
Great Problem, The 4-07-16
Great Profile, The 8-21-40
Great Python Robbery, The 5-08-14
Great Race, The 6-30-65
Great Redeemer, The 10-29-20
Great Rock 'n' Roll Swindle, The 3-05-80
Great Rocky Mountain Jazz Party, The 4-26-78
Great Romance, The 3-28-19
Great Rupert, The 1-04-50
Great St. Louis Bank Robbery, The 2-25-59
Great St. Trinian's Train Robbery, The 3-16-66
Great Santini, The 10-31-79
Great Saturday, The (See: Sao 5)
Great Scoop, The 3-19-10
Great Scout and Cathouse Thursday, The 6-16-76
Great Scuttling, The (See: Grand Sabordage, Le)
Great Sensation, The 9-09-25
Great Shadow, The 5-21-20
Great Silence, The 4-09-15
Great Sinner, The 6-29-49
Great Sioux Massacre, The 9-22-65
Great Sioux Uprising, The 6-24-53
Great Swindle, The 5-14-41
Great Tenor, The (See: Grosse Tenor, Der)
Great Texas Dynamite Chase, The 8-18-76
Great Train Robbery, The 12-25-14
Great Train Robbery, The 3-05-41
Great Vacuum Robbery, The 11-26-15
Great Victor Herbert, The 11-29-39
Great Waldo Pepper, The 3-05-75
Great Wall, The 1-19-66
Great Wall of China, The 10-28-70
Great Waltz, The 11-02-38
Great Waltz, The 11-01-72
Great War, The (See: Grande Guerra, La)
Great Waves Purify the Sand (See: Da Lang Tao Sha)
Great Well, The 4-16-24
Great White Hope, The 10-14-70
Great White Tower, The (See: Shiroi Kyoto)
Great White Trail, The 6-08-17
Great White Way, The 1-10-24
Great Yearning, The 9-17-30
Great Ziegfeld, The 4-15-36
Greater Claim, The 3-11-21
Greater Glory, The 5-05-26
Greater Law, The 7-20-17
Greater Love Hath No Man 7-16-15
Greater Profit 8-19-21
Greater Than a Crown 8-26-25
Greater Than Fame 1-16-20
Greater Will, The 12-17-15
Greatest, The 5-25-77
Greatest Love, The 2-25-21
Greatest Love of All 11-12-24
Greatest Power, The 6-29-17
Greater Question, The 1-02-20
Greatest Show on Earth, The 1-02-52
Greatest Story Ever Told, The 2-17-65
Greatest Thing in Life, The 1-03-19
Greece on the March 4-09-41
Greece Without Ruins 10-20-65
Greed 2-02-17
Greed 12-10-24
Greedy People, The (See: Kilet Khon)
Greek Tycoon, The 5-10-78
Greeks Had a Word for Them 2-09-32
Green Berets, The 6-19-68
Green Caravan 12-22-22
Green Cloak, The 10-22-15
Green Cockatoo, The 7-30-47
Green Dolphin Street 10-22-47
Green Emperor, The (See: Gruene Kaiser, Der)
Green Eyes 8-16-18
Green Eyes 12-04-34
Green Fields (See: Gruner Felder)
Green Fingers 2-19-47
Green Fire 12-29-54
Green Flame, The 7-30-20
Green for Danger 12-11-46

Green Glove, The 1-30-52
Green Goddess 8-16-23
Green Goddess 2-19-30
Green Grass of Wyoming 4-21-48
Green Grow the Rushes 11-21-51
Green Harvest (See: Verte Moisson, La)
Green Heart, The (See: Coeur Vert, Le)
Green Hell 1-24-40
Green Helmut, The 6-28-61
Green Horizons (See: Zalene Obzory)
Green Is the Heath 10-16-35 (Also see: Gruen Ist die Heide)
Green Jacket, The (See: Giacca Verde, La)
Green Light 2-17-37
Green Magic 5-11-55
Green Man, The 9-26-56
Green Mansions 3-25-59
Green Mare, The 11-25-59
Green Pack, The 10-23-34
Green Parrot 1-09-29
Green Pastures, The (See: Verdes Praderas, Las)
Green Pastures 7-22-36
Green Promise, The 3-09-49
Green Room, The (See: Chambre Verte, La)
Green Scarf 9-08-54
Green Shadow (See: Sombra Verde)
Green Slime, The 5-28-69
Green Spook, The (See: Spectre Vert, Le)
Green Stockings 1-14-16
Green Swamp, The 1-07-16
Green Temptation 3-24-22
Green Wall, The (See: Muralla Verde, La)
Green Widow, The (See: Vihreae Leski)
Green Years, The (See: Os Verdes Anos or Zoldar)
Green Years, The 3-13-46
Greene Murder Case, The 8-14-29
Green-Eyed Blonde, The 12-11-57
Greengage Summer 4-12-61
Greenhorn and the Girl, The 10-01-10
Greenhorns, The 4-23-10
Greenland (See: Groenland)
Greenwich Village 8-09-44
Greenwich Village Story 9-04-63
Greenwood Tree, The 12-17-30
Greetings 12-25-68
Greetings and a Living (See: Salut en de Kost)
Greifer, Der (See: Copper, The)
Greifer, Der 9-03-58
Grell Mystery, The 11-23-17
Greluchon Delicat 10-23-34
Grenzfeuer 12-30-36
Gretchen, the Greenhorn 8-15-16
Grete Minde 5-25-77
Gretel und Liesel 1-28-31
Gretna Green 3-26-15
Greven Fran Granden 11-16-49
Grey Devil, The 7-20-27
Grey Gardens 10-01-75
Grey Horizon, The 8-22-19
Greyfriars Bobby 7-19-61
Greyhound, The 6-05-14
Greyhound Ltd. 3-27-29
Grhana 2-13-80
Gri-Gri 4-11-56
Gribouille (See: Heart of Paris)
Gridiron Flash 1-22-35
Grido, Il 9-25-57
Grido Della Terra, Il 6-08-49
Grieche Sucht Griechin 11-30-66
Griechische Feigen 6-01-77
Grief Street 10-13-31
Griffe et la Dent, La 5-26-76
Griffin and Phoenix 12-01-76
Grihapravesh 2-06-80
Grim Comedian 1-27-22
Grim Game, The 8-29-19
Grimaces 10-22-80
Grimm's Fairy Tales for Adults 1-27-71
Gringalet 10-02-46
Gringalet 10-21-59
Grinning Guns 8-03-27
Grip of Iron 5-22-14
Grip of Jealousy, The 2-18-16
Grip of the Strangler 10-15-58
Grip of the Yukon 7-11-28
Gripsholm Castle, The (See: Schloss Gripsholm)
Grissly's Millions 1-17-45
Grissom Gang, The 5-26-71
Grit 3-05-24

Grit Wins 3-20-29
Grito Sagrado, El 8-04-54
Grizzly 5-26-76
Grock 3-18-31
Groenland 5-14-52
Groom Wore Spurs, The 2-07-51
Groove Tube, The 5-15-74
Groper, The (See: Trouble-Fesses, Le)
Gros Bill, Le 10-19-49
Gross und Klein 7-02-80
Grosse Atlantik, Der 7-10-63
Grosse Attraktion, Die 9-15-31
Grosse Caisse, La 8-18-65
Grosse Ekstase des Bildschnitzers Steiner, Die 9-03-75
Grosse Fahrt, Die 4-22-31
Grosse Liebe, Die 2-23-32
Grosse Liebesspiel, Das 1-15-64
Grosse Reinemachen, Das 6-29-38
Grosse Sehnsucht, Die 10-13-31 (Also see: Great Yearning, The)
Grosse Tenor, Der 6-02-31
Grosse Tete, Une 7-25-62
Grosse Verhau, Der 9-22-71
Grosser Graublauer Vogal, Ein 7-14-71
Grosstadt Schmetterling (See: City Butterfly)
Grosstadtjugend (See: Children of Metropolis)
Grotze Farmer, The (See: Grotzepuur, De)
Grotzepuur, De 12-03-75
Grouch, The (See: Ekel, Das)
Grouch, The 11-29-18
Ground Floor to the Left (See: In Parterre Links)
Grounds for Marriage 12-13-50
Groundstar Conspiracy, The 5-10-72
Group, The 3-02-66
Group Portrait with Lady (See: Gruppenbild mit Dame)
Groupie Girl 10-07-70
Groupies 11-18-70
Growing Up Suddenly (See: Crecer De Golpe)
Growing Youth, The (See: Reifende Jugend)
Grown-Up Children 4-17-63
Growth of Soil 10-02-29
Grozny Vek 11-16-77
Grudge, The 6-04-15
Gruen Ist die Heide 1-03-33
Gruene Kaiser, Der 3-15-39
Gruesome Stories (See: Unheimliche Geschichten)
Grumpy 3-29-23
Grumpy 8-06-30 (Also see: Cascarrabias)
Gruner Felder 10-27-37
Gruppenbild mit Dame 5-18-77
Gruppo Di Famiglia In Un Interno (See: Conversation Piece)
Gruss und Kuss, Veronika 3-04-36
Grzeszny Zywot Franciszka Buly 9-24-80
Gsaladi Tuzfezek 2-28-79
Guacho 11-03-54
Guadalajara 6-16-43
Guadalcanal Diary 10-27-43
Guaglio 5-18-49
Guapo Del 900, Un 9-28-60
Guard, The (See: Hlidac)
Guard That Girl 11-13-35
Guarded Lips 5-26-22
Guardian, The 8-17-17
Guardian Angel, The (See: Ange Gardien, L')
Guardian of the Wilderness 3-02-77
Guardians, The (See: Formynderne)
Guardians of the West 10-24-28
Guardie e Ladri 3-05-52
Guardsman, The 9-07-27
Guardsman, The 9-15-31
Gudrun 12-04-63
Guendalina 5-22-57
Guepier, Le 3-17-76
Guerrillero, Ou Celui Qui N'Y Croyait Pas, Le 11-05-69
Guernica 7-12-72
Guerra Conjugal 6-04-75
Guerra de Los Pasteles, La 12-20-44
Guerra de Papa, La 9-28-77
Guerra Del Cerdo, La 8-27-75
Guerra Empieza en Cuba, La 1-22-58
Guerra Gaucha, La 12-16-42
Guerra la Gano Yo, La 1-12-44
Guerre D'Algerie, La 5-17-72
Guerre des Boutons, La 5-16-62
Guerre des Gosses, La 11-18-36
Guerre des Policiers, La 12-05-79
Guerre Est Finie, La 5-18-66
Guerre Secret 7-21-65
Guerrilla Brigade 4-15-42

Guerrilla Fighter, The (See: Padatik)
Guerrilla Girl 4-29-53
Guerrilla, or He Who Did Not Believe, The (See: Guerillero, Ou
     Celui Qui N'Y Croyait Pas, Le)
Guess What We Learned in School Today? 5-20-70
Guess Who's Coming to Dinner? 12-06-67
Guest, The (See: Ospite, L')
Guest at Steenkampskraal, The 3-09-77
Guest in the House 12-06-44
Guest Is Coming, A (See: Det Kom En Gest)
Guest Wife 7-25-45
Guest Workers (See: Gaestearbejdere)
Guests Are Coming 12-08-65
Gueule D'Amour 10-27-37
Gueule de l'Autre, La 2-13-80
Gueule Ouverte, La 5-15-74
Gueux au Paradis, Les 3-06-46
Guglielmo Tell 8-10-49
Gui Xin Shi Jian 8-27-80
Guichets du Louvre, Les 7-03-74
Guide, The 2-10-65
Guide for the Married Man, A 4-19-67
Guignolo, Le 6-11-80
Guignolo, The (See: Guignolo, Le)
Guile of Women 3-04-21
Guilt 11-22-67
Guilt Is My Shadow 3-29-50
Guilt of Janet Adams, The 3-05-47
Guilty (See: Schuldig)
Guilty? 4-09-30
Guilty As Hell 8-09-32
Guilty Bystander 2-15-50
Guilty Generation, The 11-24-31
Guilty Hands 9-01-31
Guilty Man, The 3-08-18
Guilty Melody 8-05-36
Guilty of Love 9-17-20
Guilty of Treason 1-04-50
Guilty One, The 6-18-24
Guilty Parents 4-10-34
Guilty Trails 10-26-38
Guilty Wife, The 8-16-18
Guinea Pig, The 11-10-48
Guinea Pig Couple, The (See: Couple Temoin, Le)
Guinguette 4-01-59
Guita, La 8-19-70
Guitare et le Jazz Band, La 11-01-23
Guitars of Love 1-18-56
Guld Og Gronne Skove 8-13-58
Guld Til Praeriens Skrappe Drenge 9-22-71
Gulliver's Travels 12-20-39
Gulliver's Travels 8-03-77
Gumball Rally, The 7-28-76
Gumshoe 12-29-71
Gun, The (See: Arma, L')
Gun Battle at Monterey 11-06-57
Gun Belt 7-08-53
Gun Brothers 9-05-56
Gun Code 10-16-40
Gun Duel in Durango 5-01-57
Gun Fever 1-15-58
Gun Fighter 9-13-23
Gun Fighter, The 2-23-17
Gun for a Coward 1-16-57
Gun Glory 7-24-57
Gun Gospel 12-28-27
Gun Hand Garrison 12-28-27
Gun Hawk, The 10-16-63
Gun Justice 4-03-34
Gun Law 3-20-29
Gun Law 6-29-38
Gun Man from Bodie 10-29-41
Gun Moll, The (See: Mome Vert De Gris, La)
Gun Packer 11-09-38
Gun Play 1-01-36
Gun Ranger 2-10-37
Gun Runner 1-09-29
Gun Runner 6-15-49
Gun Runners, The (See: Neal of the Navy: Part VII)
Gun Smoke 4-29-31
Gun Smoke 1-08-36
Gun Smugglers 12-29-48
Gun Street 2-14-62
Gun Talk 1-14-48
Gun That Won the West 7-20-55
Gun the Man Down 3-06-57
Gun Town 3-20-46
Gunby's Sojourn in the Country, The 2-26-10
Gunes Ne Zaman Dogacak 8-02-78

Gunesli Bataklik 8-16-78
Gunfight, A 5-26-71
Gunfight at Comanche Creek 3-04-64
Gunfight at Dodge City 5-13-59
Gunfight at the O.K. Corral 5-15-57
Gunfight in Abilene 5-03-67
Gunfighter, The 4-26-50
Gunfighters 6-11-47
Gunfighters of Abilene 1-13-60
Gunfighters of Casa Grande 9-01-65
Gunfire 7-19-50
Gung Ho 12-22-43
Gunga Din 1-25-39
Gunki Hatameku Motoni 8-16-72
Gunlords of Stirrup Basin 8-18-37
Gunman's Walk 6-18-58
Gunmen from Laredo 2-25-59
Gunmen of Abilene 2-15-50
Gunn 6-14-67
Gunplay 5-02-51
Gunpoint 3-23-66
Guns 9-10-80
Guns, The (See: Os Fuzis)
Guns and Guitars 1-13-37
Guns at Batasi 9-09-64
Guns at Loos 3-07-28
Guns for San Sebastian 3-27-68
Guns, Girls and Gangsters 12-31-58
Guns of August, The 12-09-64
Guns of Darkness 7-18-62
Guns of Fort Petticoat 3-13-57
Guns of Hate 5-12-48
Guns of Navarone, The 5-03-61
Guns of the Magnificent Seven 5-21-69
Guns of the Pecos 3-24-37
Guns of the Timberland 2-03-60
Guns of the Trees 1-22-64
Gunshot (See: Coups de Feu)
Gunsight Ridge 8-28-57
Gunslinger 8-01-56
Gunslingers 8-09-50
Gunsmoke 2-11-53
Gunsmoke in Tucson 7-30-58
Gunsmoke Mesa 6-14-44
Gunsmoke Ranch 1-12-38
Gunsmoke Trail 6-22-38
Guru, The 2-12-69
Gus 6-30-76
Gusanos, Los 2-13-80
Gusanos de Seda 9-29-76
Guts in the Sun (See: Tripes au Soleil, Les)
Gutter Magdalene, A 6-02-16
Guttersnipe 2-03-22
Guttersnipes (See: Rannstensungar)
Guv'nor, The 10-16-35
Guy, a Gal and a Pal, A 5-02-45
Guy and a Gal, A (See: Kille Och En Tjej, En)
Guy Could Change, A 1-23-46
Guy Fawkes 10-11-23
Guy Like Me Should Never Die, A (See: Type Comme Moi Ne Devrait
     Jamais Mourir, Un)
Guy Named Joe, A 12-29-43
Guy Who Came Back, The 5-23-51
Guyana: Cult of the Damned 1-30-80
Guys and Dolls 11-02-55
Gyerekbetegsegek 5-11-66
Gypsies 8-05-36
Gypsies Go to Heaven (See: Tabor Ollhodit Webo)
Gypsy 2-03-37
Gypsy 9-26-62
Gypsy, The (See: Gitan, Le)
Gypsy and the Gentleman 2-05-58
Gypsy Baron, The (See: Zigeunerbaron, Der)
Gypsy Baron, The 9-18-35
Gypsy Blood 5-13-21
Gypsy Colt 1-27-54
Gypsy Joe 3-24-16
Gypsy Law (See: Kriss Romani)
Gypsy Melody 8-19-36
Gypsy Moths, The 8-27-69
Gypsy of the North 5-02-28
Gypsy Passion 3-31-22
Gypsy Trail, The 12-20-18
Gypsy Violinist, The 4-24-29
Gypsy Wildcat 8-09-44
Gypsy's Vengeance, A 2-08-08
Gziekolwiek Jestes, Panie Prezydencie 2-07-79

H

H.C. Andersen I Italien 4-18-79
H8 8-20-58
H.M. Pulham, Esq. 11-19-41
H.M.S. Defiant 4-04-62
H-Man, The 6-03-59
Ha Megjon Jozsef 7-28-76
Hababam Sinifi Tatilde 8-02-78
Habanera, La 1-26-38
Haben Ha'oved 11-20-68
Haber's Photo Shop (See: Foto Haber)
Habibeti--Ya Habba Atoot 9-05-79
Habit 9-09-21
Habit of Happiness, The 3-24-16
Habla Mudita 7-04-73
Habricha el Hashemesh 8-16-72
Hackenschmidt-Rogers Wrestling Match 2-29-08
Hadaka No Shima 11-15-61
Hadaka No Taisho 9-09-59
Hadaka No Taiyo 7-15-59
Hadashi No Gen 7-28-76
Haek Kai Narok Dien Bien Phu 11-23-77
Haendeligt Uheld 2-10-71
Haendler der Vier Jahreszeiten, Der 4-12-72
Haervaerk 11-16-77
Haeschen in der Grube 1-01-69
Hagenbeck's Menagerie 10-29-10
Hagringen 8-03-60
Hai-Tang 10-08-30
Hail 5-24-72
Hail-Fellow Well-Met, A (See: Monsieur de Compagnie, Un)
Hail, Hero! 10-08-69
Hail! Mafia (See: Je Vous Salue, Mafia)
Hail the Artist (See: Salut L'Artiste)
Hail the Conquering Hero 6-07-44
Hail the Woman 1-20-22
Hail, Thieves (See: Salut, Voleurs)
Hail to the Rangers 12-01-43
Haine 2-06-80
Hair 3-14-79
Hair Trigger Baxter 12-01-26
Hairpins 8-06-20
Hairy Ape, The 5-17-44
Haiti--Papa Doc Is Dead, Baby Doc Lives 6-14-72
Hajducka Vremena 3-02-77
Hajduk 3-12-75
Hajka 8-17-77
Hakuchi No Torima 8-10-66
Hakujitsumu 9-09-64
Halalos Tavasz 1-17-40
Halbe-Halbe 3-29-78
Halbstarken, Die 11-07-56
Halbzarte, Die 5-13-59
Haldane of the Secret Service 11-01-23
Half a Century of Songs (See: Canzoni di Mezzo Secolo)
Half a Hero 7-29-53
Half a Sinner 6-26-34
Half a Sinner 6-05-40
Half a Sixpence 12-27-67
Half an Hour 1-28-21
Half Angel 6-03-36
Half Angel 4-11-51
Half Breed 7-21-22
Half Breed, The 7-14-16
Half-Breed, The 4-16-52
Half Dollar Bill 1-17-24
Half-Marriage 8-14-29
Half Million Bribe, The 4-21-16
Half Naked Truth, The 1-03-33
Half Past Midnight 2-11-48
Half Pint 8-24-60
Half Pint of Beer, A (See: Egy Pikolo Vilagos)
Half Price Honeymoon (See: Naszut Felaron)
Half Shot at Sunrise 10-15-30
Half-Strong Ones, The (See: Halbstarken, Die)
Half-Way Girl 7-29-25
Half-Way House 8-08-45
Half Way to Heaven 12-11-29
Half-Way to Hell 11-17-54
Half Way to Shanghai 9-09-42
Halfback, The 5-04-17

Halfway Up the Sky (See: Mi-Chemin du Ciel, A)
Halka 1-19-38
Hall Alla Doerrar Oeppna 11-21-73
Hall Room Boys, The 7-18-19
Hallelujah 8-28-29
Hallelujah, I'm a Bum 2-14-33
Hallelujah the Hills 5-15-63
Hallelujah Trail, The 6-16-65
Halliday Brand, The 1-16-57
Hallo, Amerika 11-24-65
Hallo, Baby 3-10-76
Hallo Budapest 11-13-35
Halloween 10-25-78
Halls of Anger 3-18-70
Halls of Montezuma 12-13-50
Hallucination Generation 12-21-66
Ham and Eggs at the Front 3-14-28
Ham from the Ardennes (See: Jambon D'Ardenne)
Hamartef 6-19-63
Hamburg at 12:30 5-08-29
Hamburg Syndrome, The (See: Hamburger Krankheit, Die)
Hamburg Uprising of 1923, The (See: Hamburger Aufstand Oktober
    1923, Der)
Hamburger Aufstand Oktober 1923, Der 11-10-71
Hamburger Krankheit, Die 10-31-79
Hamida 7-27-66
Hamido 5-11-55
Ha'Mil'Hama Le'Ahar Ha'Mil'Hama 7-23-69
Hamile 10-20-65
Hamiskhak Ha'Amiti 11-26-80
Hamlet (See: Hamile)
Hamlet 11-11-21
Hamlet 5-12-48
Hamlet 11-21-62
Hamlet 7-29-64
Hamlet 9-30-64
Hamlet 12-17-69
Hamlet 12-01-76
Hammer 9-20-72
Hammer for the Witches (See: Kladivo Na Carodejnice)
Hammerhead 7-24-68
Hammersmith Is Out 5-17-72
Hamnstad 11-24-48
Hampelmann, Der 9-15-31
Hampton 5-12-71
Hanare Goze Orin (See: Banished)
Hand, The (See: Main, La)
Hand at the Window, The 4-26-18
Hand in Hand 12-14-60
Hand in Hand 7-14-65
Hand in the Trap, The (See: Mano en la Trampa, La)
Hand Invisible, The 3-07-19
Hand-Me-Down Suit, A (See: Ubranie Prawie Nowe)
Hand of Death 8-25-76
Hand of Peril, The 3-24-16
Hand of Uncle Sam, The 4-02-10
Hand That Rocks the Cradle 5-18-17
Hand to Cut Off, A (See: Main a Couper, La)
Handcuffed 11-06-29
Handcuffs (See: Lisice)
Handcuffs or Kisses 10-14-21
Handful Love, A (See: Handfull Kaerlek, En)
Handfull Kaerlek, En 3-06-74
Handicapped Love (See: Behinderte Liebe)
Handle with Care 1-27-22
Handle with Care 12-27-32
Handle with Care 4-09-58
Handling of the Fleet 11-09-07
Hands, The 7-04-62
Hands Across the Border 6-30-26
Hands Across the Border 12-08-43
Hands Across the Table 11-06-35
Hands of a Stranger 9-26-62
Hands of Nara 9-22-22
Hands of Orlac, The (See: Mains d'Orlac, Les)
Hands of Orlac, The 6-20-28
Hands of the Ripper 10-13-71
Hands Off 7-27-27
Hands on the City (See: Mani Sulla Citta, La)
Hands Up 4-27-17
Hands Up 1-20-26
Hands Up (serial) 8-09-18; 9-13-18; and 9-20-18
Handsome Antonio (See: Bell' Antonio, Il)
Handsome Brute 7-07-26
Handsome Face (See: Beau Masque)
Handsome Serge, The (See: Beau Serge, Le)
Handy Andy 8-07-34
Handyman, The (See: Gehulfe, Der)

Hang On Doggy (See: Teci, Teci, Kuza Moj)
Hang Tuah 9-04-57
Hangar 18 7-30-80
Hanging, The (See: Koshikei)
Hanging of Jake Ellis, The 2-26-69
Hanging Tree, The 1-28-59
Hangman, The 4-29-59
Hangman's House 5-16-28
Hangman's Knot 10-29-52
Hangman's Noose (See: Collier de Chanvre, Le)
Hangmen Also Die 3-24-43
Hangover Square 1-17-45
Hank and Lank 10-01-10 and 10-15-10
Hank and Lank as the Sandwich Men 11-26-10
Hank and Lank: Life Savers 11-12-10
Hank and Lank Take a Rest 10-29-10
Hank and Lank--Uninvited Guests 10-22-10
Hanna I Societen 11-19-41
Hanna in Society (See: Hanna I Societen)
Hannah Lee 7-08-53
Hannibal 6-08-60
Hannibal 1-10-73
Hannibal Brooks 3-05-69
Hannibal Tanur Ur 9-04-57
Hannie Caulder 11-17-71
Hanno Cambiato Faccia 9-01-71
Hanover Street 5-16-79
Hans Andersen in Italy (See: H.C. Andersen I Italien)
Hans Christian Andersen 11-26-52
Hans le Marin 12-07-49
Hans the Sailor (See: Hans le Marin)
Hansel and Gretel 10-06-54
Hansuli Banker Upakatha 11-21-62
Happening, The 3-29-67
Happening of the Vampires (See: Gebissen Wird Nur Nachts--
    Happening der Vampire)
Happenings, The 5-07-80
Happiest Days of Your Life, The 3-15-50
Happiest Millionaire, The 6-28-67
Happiest of Men, The (See: Plus Heureux Des Hommes, Le)
Happiness (See: Bonheur, Le or Felicidad)
Happiness 5-04-17
Happiness 3-12-24
Happiness Ahead 6-20-28
Happiness Ahead 10-16-34
Happiness C.O.D. 12-25-35
Happiness Cage, The 7-12-72
Happiness in 20 Years (See: Bonheur Dans 20 Ans, Le)
Happiness Is for Tomorrow (See: Bonheur Est Pour Demain, Le)
Happiness Is So Near (See: E Atit De Aproape Fericiera)
Happiness Is within Us (See: Namonaku Mazushiku Utsukushiku)
Happiness of Three Women 2-23-17
Happiness of Three Women, The 11-10-54
Happy 1-09-34
Happy Alexandre (See: Alexandre Le Bienheureux)
Happy Anniversary 11-04-59
Happy As the Grass Was Green 12-12-73
Happy Birthday, Davy 4-01-70
Happy Birthday, Gemini 4-30-80
Happy Birthday, Wanda June 12-08-71
Happy Confusion (See: Chuen Chulamoon)
Happy Day 10-27-76
Happy Days (See: Beaux Jours, Les or Bedzie Lepiej)
Happy Days 2-19-30
Happy Days 5-08-74
Happy Divorce, A (See: Divorce Heureux, Un)
Happy End 6-12-68
Happy Ending, The 3-04-25
Happy Ending, The 11-19-69
Happy Ever After 11-29-32
Happy Ever After 7-07-54
Happy Family Life, A (See: Familienglueck)
Happy Games 7-21-65
Happy Go Lovely 3-07-51
Happy Go Lucky (See: Au Petit Bonheur)
Happy-Go-Lucky 2-10-37
Happy Go Lucky 12-30-42
Happy He, Who Like Ulysses (See: Heureux Qui Comme Ulysse ...)
Happy Hooker, The 5-14-75
Happy Hooker Goes Hollywood, The 6-04-80
Happy Hooker Goes to Washington, The 9-07-77
Happy Is the Bride 3-12-58
Happy Land 11-10-43
Happy Landing 8-28-34
Happy Landing 1-26-38
Happy Life of Leopold Z, The (See: Vie Heureuse de Leopold Z, La)

Happy Mother's Day ... Love, George 8-22-73
Happy New Year (See: Buck)
Happy Parade (See: Glada Paraden)
Happy Road, The 1-30-57
Happy Sixties, The 11-04-64
Happy Tailor, The (See: Glade Skraddaren, Den)
Happy Thieves, The 1-17-62
Happy Time, The 8-20-52
Happy Warrior, The 7-08-25
Happy Years, The 5-31-50
Happy Years of the Thorwalds (See: Gluecklichen Jahre der
    Thorwalds, Die)
Ha'pritza Ha'gdola 3-11-70
Haps and Mishaps 10-23-09
Har Borjar Aventyret 12-15-65
Har Har Du Ditt Liv 7-12-67
Hara-Kari 12-05-28
Hara-Kiri (See: Seppuku)
Harassed (See: Acosada)
Harald Hondfaste 4-23-47
Harbor City (See: Hamnstad)
Harbor Lights 8-30-23
Harbor of Missing Men 4-19-50
Harcmodor 2-27-80
Hard Boiled Canary 2-26-41
Hard Boiled Haggerty 8-27-27
Hard Boiled Ones (See: Durs A Cuire, Les)
Hard Cash 10-10-13
Hard Contract 4-16-69
Hard Day's Night, A 7-15-64
Hard, Fast and Beautiful 5-30-51
Hard Fists 6-01-27
Hard Guy, The 11-19-41
Hard Hombre, The 9-29-31
Hard Knocks 10-08-80
Hard Luck Corporal, The (See: Caporal Epingle, Le)
Hard Luck Marie (See: Pechmarie)
Hard Man, The 12-04-57
Hard Part Begins, The 11-14-73
Hard Ride, The 4-21-71
Hard Road, The 3-05-15
Hard Road, The 5-06-70
Hard Rock Breed, The 3-08-18
Hard Rock Harrigan 7-31-35
Hard Times 9-24-75
Hard to Get 10-02-29
Hard to Get 11-09-38
Hard to Handle 2-07-33
Hard Way, The 9-23-42
Hardboiled 3-20-29
Hardboiled Egg Time (See: Temps des Oeufs Durs, Les)
Hardcore 2-14-79
Harder They Come, The 9-06-72
Harder They Fall, The 3-28-56
Hardest Way, The 7-28-22
Hardi les Gars 11-17-31
Hardings' Heritage 4-24-14
Hardys Ride High, The 4-19-39
Harem 2-07-68
Harem Girl 1-16-52
Hari-Kari 5-15-14
Hark to the Cock (See: Chui Petela)
Harlan County, U.S.A. 10-20-76
Harlem Globetrotters, The 10-17-51
Harlem Is Heaven 6-07-32
Harlem on the Prairie 2-09-38
Harlequin 5-07-80
Harlis 2-07-73
Harlot 3-10-71
Harlow 5-19-65
Harlow 6-23-65
Harmon of Michigan 9-17-41
Harmony at Home 1-29-30
Harmony Lane 10-30-35
Harmony Row 5-16-33
Harnessing a Horse 5-01-14
Haro 3-01-78
Harold and Maude 12-15-71
Harold Lloyd's Funny Side of Life 11-23-66
Harold Lloyd's World of Comedy 4-04-62
Harold Teen 8-15-28
Harold Teen 6-05-34
Harom Sarkany 11-25-36 and 12-30-36
Harp in Hock, A 11-02-27
Harp of Burma 1-30-57
Harp of Burma, The (See: Biruma No Tategoto)
Harper 2-16-66
Harper Valley, P.T.A. 6-07-78

Harpoon 11-24-48
Harrad Experiment, The 5-16-73
Harrad Summer, The 8-14-74
Harriet and the Piper 10-22-20 and 1-28-21
Harriet Craig 11-01-50
Harrigan's Kid 3-10-43
Harry and His Valet (See: Harry of Kammertjener)
Harry and Tonto 7-31-74
Harry and Walter Go to New York 6-16-76
Harry Black 7-30-58
Harry Bros., The 3-05-10
Harry in Your Pocket 8-22-73
Harry Munter 1-14-70
Harry of Kammertjener 5-30-62
Harukanaru Yama No Yobigoe 5-28-80
Harum Scarum 10-27-65
Harvard, Here I Come 4-01-42
Harvest 10-11-39
Harvest, and So Ye Shall Reap 10-18-67
Harvest Is Plentiful (See: Mies Es Mucha, La)
Harvest Melody 12-08-43
Harvest of Hate 2-13-29
Harvest: 3,000 Years 4-07-76
Harvester, The 11-09-27
Harvester, The 7-08-36
Harvey 10-18-50
Harvey Girls, The 1-02-46
Harvey Middleman, Fireman 7-14-65
Has Anybody Seen My Gal 6-11-52
Has the World Gone Mad 4-19-23
Hasard et la Violence, Le 5-08-74
Hasards de la Gloire, Les 4-04-73
Haschish 10-23-68
Hasenklein 5-31-32
Hasereth Festival Hayeladim 8-06-80
Hashechuna Shelanu 1-01-69
Hashi No Nai Kawa 7-23-69
Hashimura Togo 8-17-17
Hashoter Azulai 7-28-71
Hassan Terro 11-06-68
Hassan, Terrorist (See: Hassan Terro)
Hasta Que El Matrimonio Nos Separe 3-23-77
Hasty Heart, The 9-21-49 and 12-07-49
Hat Check Girl 10-11-32
Hat Check Honey 3-08-44
Hat, Coat and Glove 7-31-34
Hat Juggler, The 8-28-09
Hatari 5-23-62
Hatarnegol 3-31-71
Hatbox Mystery, The 8-27-47
Hatchet Man, The 2-09-32
Hate (See: Haine)
Hate 6-22-17
Hate 6-30-22
Hate Ship, The 1-15-30 and 11-19-30
Hater of Men 6-22-17
Hatful of Rain, A 6-19-57
Hatred 1-29-41
Hats Off 1-06-37
Hatsukoi Jigokuhen 5-22-68
Hatter's Castle 12-24-41
Haunted Bedroom, The 6-27-19
Haunted Castle, The (See: Spukschloss Im Spessart, Das)
Haunted Gold 1-17-33
Haunted Hat 9-04-09
Haunted House 9-18-40
Haunted House, The 12-19-28
Haunted Pajamas, The 6-22-17
Haunted Range, The 10-05-27
Haunted Ship, The 2-01-28
Haunted Strangler, The 5-28-58
Haunting, The 8-21-63
Haunting Fear, The 6-18-15
Haunting of M, The 11-28-79
Haunts 7-20-77
Hauptdarsteller, Der 12-28-77
Hauptlehrer Hofer 2-09-77
Hauptmann Kreutzer 7-06-77
Hauptmann und Sein Held, Der 9-14-55
Hauptmann von Koepenick, Der 1-12-32 and 1-24-33
Hauptmann von Koepenick, Der 9-12-56
Hauptmann von Koln, Der 12-21-60
Hauptsache Ferien 9-27-72
Haus des Lebens 3-25-53
Haus in der Karpfengasse, Das 7-07-65
Hausfrauen-Report 8-25-71
Havana Rose 9-19-51
Havana Widows 11-28-33

Have a Heart 10-23-34
Have a Nice Weekend 9-24-75
Have Rocket, Will Travel 7-29-59
Have You Heard of the San Francisco Mime Troup? 7-03-68
Havi 200 Fix 10-21-36
Having a Wild Weekend 6-23-65
Having Wonderful Crime 2-21-45
Having Wonderful Time 6-15-38
Havoc (See: Unheil, Das or Haervaerk)
Havou Banot le'Eilat 6-30-65
Hawaii 10-05-66
Hawaii Calls 3-02-38
Hawaiian Buckaroo 2-02-38
Hawaiian Nights 8-23-39
Hawaiians, The 6-17-70
Hawk, The 5-11-17
Hawk of Powder River, The 3-03-48
Hawk of Wild River, The 2-13-52
Hawk the Slayer 12-24-80
Hawkin's Hat 10-29-10
Hawk's Nest, The 6-27-28
Hawley's of High Street 6-06-33
Hawmps 5-26-76
Hawthorne of the U.S.A. 11-21-19
Hay Foot, Straw Foot 6-27-19
Hay Que Caesar a Ernesto 9-17-41
Hay Que Romper la Rutina 10-09-74
Hay Tang 3-26-30
Hayam Ha'Acharon 5-07-80
Haz a Sziklak Alatt 9-17-58
Hazal 5-21-80
Hazard 3-17-48
Hazardous Valley 11-30-27
Hazel Kirke 2-04-16
Hazing, The 1-18-78
He 1-09-34 (Also see: Rosier de Mme. Husson, Le)
He and She 6-24-70
He Comes Up Smiling 9-13-18
He Couldn't Take It 3-27-34
He Couldn't Say No 4-06-38
He Did and He Didn't 2-04-16
He Died After the War (See: Tokyo Senso Sengo Hiwa)
He Fell in Love with His Wife 10-30-09
He Fell in Love with His Wife 3-10-16
He Found a Star 10-08-41
He Got Rid of the Moths 1-22-10
He Got There After All 2-09-17
He Hired the Boss 3-10-43
He Is Charming (See: Il Est Charmant)
He Is Heading to the Glory Again (See: Ke Xana Pros Ti Doxa Trava)
He Knew Women 4-23-30
He Knows You're Alone 8-27-80
He Laughed Last 7-25-56
He Loved an Actress 5-25-38
He Married His Wife 1-17-40
He Met the Champion 9-17-10
He Nacido en Buenos Aires 12-30-59
He Never Gives Up 7-25-79
He or I (See: Er Oder Ich)
He Ran All the Way 6-06-51
He Rides Tall 2-26-64
He Stayed for Breakfast 8-14-40
He Tried On Handcuffs 9-11-09
He Walked by Night 11-10-48
He Walked Through the Fields (See: Hou Halach Ba'Sadot)
He Wanted to Become King (See: Ithele Na Guini Vassilias)
He Was Her Man 5-22-34
He Was Mattia Pascal (See: Il Fu Mattia Pascal)
He Was 25¢ Short of His Salary 5-29-09
He Who Laughs Last Laughs Best 11-28-08
He Who Loves in a Glass House (See: Wer im Glashous Liebt (Der Graben)
He Who Rides a Tiger 1-26-66
Head 10-16-68 and 11-13-68
Head, The (See: Al Raas)
He Who Sings Thinks No Harm
Head 10-16-68 and 11-13-68
Head, The (See: Al Raas)
Head, The 10-18-61
Head Against the Walls (See: Tete Contre les Murs, La)
Head First into Fortune (See: Kopeueber Ins Glueck)
Head Man, The 9-26-28
Head of a Tyrant 5-11-60
Head of Normande St. Onge, The (See: Tete de Normande St.-Onge, La)
Head of the Family 12-19-28
Head of the Family 9-06-67

Head On 9-29-71
Head On 10-01-80
Head over Heels 10-24-79
Head over Heels in Love 2-17-37
Headhunters, The (See: Hovedjaegerne)
Headin' East 12-29-37
Headin' for God's Country 7-28-43
Headin' for the Rio Grande 2-24-37
Headin' for Trouble 10-06-31
Headin' Home 9-24-20
Headin' North 9-22-22
Headin' North 12-24-30
Headin' South 3-01-18
Headin' West 2-10-22
Headin' Westward 7-24-29
Heading for Heaven 12-24-47
Headless Ghost, The (See: Pi Hua Kad)
Headless Horseman, The 1-05-23
Headless Horseman, The 6-25-75
Headless Woman, The (See: Mujer Sin Cabeza, Una)
Headleys at Home, The 3-01-39
Headline 12-08-43
Headline Crasher 8-11-37
Headline Shooter 10-24-33
Headline Woman, The 6-26-35
Heads or Tails (See: Pile ou Face)
Heads Up 4-21-26
Heads Up 10-15-30
Heads We Go 9-12-33
Headstand, Madam (See: Kopfstand, Madam)
Headwaiter, The 7-03-29
Health 8-27-80
Hear Me Good 10-16-57
Hearse, The 9-24-80
Heart and Soul 5-25-17
Heart and Soul 6-28-50
Heart as Big as That!, A (See: Coeur Gros Comme Ca!, Un)
Heart Bandit, The 1-31-24
Heart Beat 12-05-79
Heart Buster, The 7-09-24
Heart in Pawn, A 2-28-19
Heart Is a Lonely Hunter, The 7-31-68
Heart Line, The 7-15-21
Heart of a Child, The 4-16-20
Heart of a Clown, The 12-04-09
Heart of a Coward, The 5-11-27
Heart of a Follies Girl 3-14-28
Heart of a Girl, The 6-21-18
Heart of a Gypsy, The 12-05-19
Heart of a Hero, The 11-03-16
Heart of a Lion, The 2-01-18
Heart of a Man, The 6-17-59
Heart of a Nation 3-17-43
Heart of a Painted Woman, The 4-23-15
Heart of a Race Trout 7-24-09
Heart of a Siren 4-08-25
Heart of a Texan 8-04-22
Heart of a Woman, The 10-08-20
Heart of Arizona 4-20-38
Heart of Broadway 4-04-28
Heart of Ezra Greer, The 10-26-17
Heart of Gold 1-17-19
Heart of Humanity, The 1-03-19
Heart of Juanita, The 12-05-19
Heart of Lincoln, The 3-05-15
Heart of Maryland, The 3-26-15
Heart of New York 3-08-32
Heart of Nora Flynn, The 4-21-16
Heart of Paris 1-18-39
Heart of Paula, The 4-07-16
Heart of Rachel, The 10-04-18
Heart of Romance, The 2-08-18
Heart of Salome, The 4-27-27 and 6-08-27
Heart of Tara, The 3-10-16
Heart of Texas Ryan, The 2-23-17
Heart of the Blue Ridge, The 10-29-15
Heart of the Forest (See: Corazon del Bosque, El)
Heart of the Golden West 11-18-42
Heart of the Hills 12-05-19
Heart of the Hills, The 10-13-16
Heart of the Matter 11-11-53
Heart of the North 9-30-21
Heart of the North 12-14-38
Heart of the Rio Grande 3-11-42
Heart of the Rockies 9-22-37
Heart of the Rockies 3-28-51
Heart of the Sunset 7-12-18
Heart of the West 2-17-37

Heart of the Wilds 8-23-18
Heart of the Yukon, The 5-18-27
Heart of 20 6-25-20
Heart of Virginia 5-05-48
Heart of Wetona, The 1-10-19
Heart Punch 12-13-32
Heart Raider 6-07-23
Heart Specialist, The 3-24-22
Heart-Stealer (See: Rubacuori)
Heart Strings 1-26-17
Heart Thief, The 4-27-27
Heart Throbs (See: Battements de Coeur)
Heart to Heart 9-12-28
Heart to Let, A 8-05-21
Heart Trouble 10-10-28
Heart Trump for OSS 117 in Tokyo (See: Atout Coeur A Tokyo Pour
  OSS 117)
Heartaches 7-02-47
Heartbeat 9-06-39
Heartbeat 4-24-46
Heartbreak 10-20-31
Heartbreak Kid, The 12-13-72
Heartbreak People (See: Huadjai Ti Jom Din)
Heartbreak Ridge 4-06-55
Heartbreaker (See: Rubacuori)
Heartbreakers, The 2-11-16
Hearth Fires (See: Feux de la Chandeleur, Les)
Heartland 3-12-80
Heartland Reggae 3-26-80
Heartless Husbands 8-25-26
Hearts Adrift 2-20-14
Hearts Aflame (See: Plomienne Serca)
Hearts Aflame 2-08-23
Hearts and Masks 7-01-21
Hearts and Minds 5-15-74
Hearts and Spangles 7-14-26
Hearts and Sparks 7-07-16
Hearts and Spurs 7-15-25
Hearts Are Trumps (See: Atout Coeur)
Hearts Are Trumps 1-28-21
Hearts Asleep 3-28-19
Heart's Desire 9-04-35 and 7-14-37
Hearts Divided 9-01-22
Hearts Divided 6-17-36
Heart's Foul Play, A (See: Herz Spielt Falsch, Ein)
Heart's Haven 11-24-22
Hearts High (See: Hjerter Er Trumf)
Hearts in Bondage 10-21-36
Hearts in Dixie 3-06-29
Hearts in Exile 4-09-15
Hearts in Exile 12-04-29
Hearts of Humanity 9-27-32
Hearts of Men 11-12-15
Hearts of Men 4-11-19 and 6-20-19
Hearts of Men 6-06-28
Hearts of Oak 5-15-14
Hearts of Oak 1-21-25
Hearts of the West 10-01-75
Hearts of the World 4-12-18
Hearts of Youth 5-20-21
Hearts That Are Human 11-19-15
Heartsease 8-29-19
Heartstrings 11-08-23
Heat (See: Zhoy)
Heat 6-21-72
Heat Lightning 3-13-34
Heat Wave 5-22-35
Heathens of Kummerow, The (See: Heiden von Kummerow, Die)
Heat's On, The 12-01-43
Heave Up (See: Hiev Up)
Heaven and Earth 9-12-13
Heaven and Hell (See: Yompaban Cha)
Heaven Can Wait 7-21-43
Heaven Can Wait 6-28-78
Heaven Is Round the Corner 3-08-44
Heaven Knows, Mr. Allison 3-20-57
Heaven on Earth 6-08-27
Heaven on Earth 12-22-31
Heaven on Earth 11-02-60
Heaven On One's Head (See: Ciel Sur la Tete, Le)
Heaven Only Knows 7-30-47
Heaven Over the Marshes (See: Cielo Sulla Palude)
Heaven with a Gun 4-02-69
Heaven with Barbed Wire Fence 12-06-39
Heaven Without Love (See: Pukotina Raja)
Heavenly Bodies, The (See: Corps Celestes, Les)
Heavenly Body, The 12-29-43
Heavenly Days 8-02-44

Heavenly Play, The (See: Himlaspelet)
Heaven's Above! 6-19-63
Heaven's Gate 11-26-80
Heavy Load 5-28-75
Heavy Traffic 7-25-73
Heavy Trouble (See: Barra Pesada)
Heavy Water Battle, The (See: Bataille de L'Eau Lourde, La)
Hecho Violento, Un 10-07-59
Hectic Days 5-29-35
Hedda 11-26-75
Hedelmaton Puu 7-02-47
Heedless Moths 6-10-21
Heels Go to Hell (See: Salauds Vont En Enfer, Les)
Hei Tiki 2-05-35
Heiden von Kummerow, Die 3-20-68
Heidi 11-10-37
Heidi 12-31-52
Heidi 4-03-68
Heidi and Peter 5-18-55
Heights of Hazard 11-12-15
Heilige Erbe, Das 5-01-57
Heiligen Wassern, An 1-18-61
Heimatland 10-05-55
Heimatsklange 2-18-31
Heimlich, Still und Leise 11-25-53
Heinrich 5-18-77
Heinrich Heine Revue 9-10-80
Heintje—A Heart Goes on a Journey (See: Heintje—Ein Herz Geht
  Auf Reisen)
Heintje—Ein Herz Geht Auf Reisen 12-03-69
Heintje—Einmal Wird die Sonne Wieder Scheinen 6-03-70
Heintje—Once the Sun Will Be Shining Again (See: Heintje—Einmal
  Wird die Sonne Wieder Scheinen)
Heir, The (See: Heritier, L')
Heir of Clavencourt Castle, The 12-18-09
Heir of the Ages 7-20-17
Heir of the Largarderes, The 4-02-15
Heir to the Hoorah, The 11-03-16
Heir to Trouble 2-12-36
Heiratskandidaten 5-07-58
Heiress, The 1-10-13
Heiress, The 7-16-15
Heiress, The 9-07-49
Heiress at "Coffee Dan's," The 12-15-16
Heiress for a Day 3-01-18
Heirs, The (See: Heritiers, Les or Os Herdeiros)
Heiser Sand auf Sylt (See: New Life Style, The)
Heisse Spur St. Pauli 12-29-71
Heisses Blut 6-24-36
Heist, The (See: Apando, El)
Hej, Stine! 1-31-71
Held by the Enemy 10-01-20
Held by the Law 2-09-27
Held for Ransom 8-22-08
Held for Ransom 7-20-38
Held in Trust 9-03-20
Held to Answer 11-15-23
Helden 1-28-59
Heldorado 12-25-46
Helen Morgan Story, The 9-18-57
Helen of Troy 2-04-25 and 12-14-27
Helen of Troy 12-21-55
Helena 4-16-24
Helena Ritchie 12-29-16
Helene 1-26-38
Helen's Babies 1-21-25
Helga 1-17-68
Helga and Michael (See: Helga und Michael)
Helga und Michael 10-30-68
Heliotrope 12-03-20
Hell and High Water 12-19-33
Hell and High Water 2-03-54
Hell Below 5-02-33
Hell Below Zero 6-30-31
Hell Below Zero 1-27-54
Hell Bent for Heaven 5-05-26
Hell Bent for Frisco 8-11-31
Hell Bent for Leather 1-13-60
Hell Bent for Love 7-31-34
Hell Bound 5-13-31
Hell Bound 10-02-57
Hell Cat, The 12-29-18
Hell Cat, The 7-10-34
Hell Diggers, The 8-26-21
Hell Divers 12-29-31
Hell Divers 8-14-57
Hell Fire Austin 8-02-32
Hell Harbor 4-09-30

Hell in the City (See: Nella Citta l'Inferno)
Hell in the Heavens 12-18-34
Hell in the Pacific 12-11-68
Hell Is a City 5-18-60
Hell Is for Heroes 5-30-62
Hell Morgan's Girl 3-02-17
Hell of a Life, A (See: Verdammt Gutes Leben, Ein)
Hell of Manitoba, The (See: Hoelle von Manitoba, Die)
Hell on Devil's Island 8-21-57
Hell on Earth 2-06-34 (Also see: Niemandsland)
Hell on Frisco Bay 12-28-55
Hell on Wheels 9-27-67
Hell Raiders of the Deep 6-09-54
Hell Roarin' Reform 2-21-19
Hell Ship, The 2-20-20
Hell Ship Bronson 6-20-28
Hell-Ship Morgan 3-11-36
Hell Squad 10-29-58
Hell to Eternity 8-03-60
Hell-to-Pay Austin 8-11-16
Hell Up in Harlem 1-02-74
Hell with Heroes, The 8-14-68
Hellbenders, The 9-06-67
Hellcats, The 6-18-69
Hellcats of the Navy 5-01-57
Helldorado 1-08-35
Helle 6-07-72
Helle for Lykke 7-23-69
Heller in Pink Tights 3-09-60
Hellfighters, The 11-27-68
Hellfire 6-01-49
Hellgate 9-10-52
Hellion, The 10-03-19
Hellions, The 11-15-61
Hellish Love (See: Hoellische Liebe)
Hello, America (See: Hallo, Amerika)
Hello, Baby (See: Hallo, Baby)
Hello Cheyenne! 6-20-28
Hello, Dolly 12-24-69
Hello Down There 3-26-69
Hello, Everybody 12-24-30
Hello, Everybody 1-31-33
Hello, Frisco, Hello 3-10-43
Hello-Goodbye 7-08-70
Hello Goodnight Goodbye 8-27-75
Hello, Hello, Japan (See: Moshi-Moshi, Hallo Japan)
Hello, It's Me (See: Zdrastovoui Eto Ia)
Hello, Jerusalem (See: Salut, Jerusalem)
Hello, Moscow 6-19-46
Hello Sister 3-05-30
Hello, Sister! 5-09-33
Hello Sucker 7-02-41
Hello Trouble 10-18-32
Hello, Vera (See: Szevasz; Vera)
Hell's Angels 6-04-30 and 1-17-40
Hell's Angels '69 7-30-69
Hell's Angels on Wheels 6-14-67
Hell's Belles 4-09-69
Hell's Cargo 11-29-39
Hell's Crossroads 5-22-57
Hell's End 7-19-18
Hell's Five Hours 3-26-58
Hell's Half Acre 2-10-54
Hell's Headquarters 5-31-32
Hell's Heroes 1-01-30 (Also see: Galgenvoegel)
Hell's Highroad 10-07-25
Hell's Highway 9-27-32
Hell's Hinges 2-11-16
Hell's Hole 11-22-23
Hell's Holiday 7-18-33
Hell's Horizon 11-23-55
Hell's House 2-16-32
Hell's Island 7-23-30
Hell's Island 5-05-55
Hell's Kitchen 7-05-39
Hell's Outpost 3-09-55
Hellstrom Chronicle, The 6-16-71
Hellzapoppin' 12-24-41
Help! 8-04-65
Help! De Doktor Verzuipt 7-31-74
Help! Help! Police 5-02-19
Help--I Love Twins! (See: Hilfe--Ich Liebe Zwillinge!)
Help, I'm an Heir (See: Segitseg Orokoltem)
Help Me, My Love (See: Amore Mio Aiutami)
Help, My Bride Steals (See: Hilfe, Meine Frau Klaut)
Help! The Doctor Is Drowning (See: Help! De Doktor Verzuipt)
Help Wanted 5-07-15
Help Wanted--Male! 8-20-20

Help Yourself 9-24-20
Helyet Az Oregeknek 1-08-35
Hem Hayu Asara 12-07-60
Hemat I Natten 5-25-77 and 9-28-77
Hempas Bar 10-19-77
Hemsoborna 8-01-56
Hen, The (See: Poule, La)
Hen-Pecked Husband (See: Papaucshos)
Hennes Melodi 2-18-42
Hennessy 7-23-75
Henriette's Holiday (See: Fete a Henriette, La)
Henry Aldrich, Boy Scout 1-05-44
Henry Aldrich, Editor 9-30-42
Henry Aldrich for President 7-30-41
Henry Aldrich Gets Glamour 12-30-42
Henry Aldrich Haunts a House 11-10-43
Henry Aldrich Plays Cupid 4-26-44
Henry Aldrich Swings It 6-30-43
Henry Aldrich's Little Secret 6-14-44
Henry and Dizzy 3-18-42
Henry VIII 10-17-33
Henry VIII and His Six Wives 8-02-72
Henry V 4-24-46
Henry IV 3-10-48
Henry Goes Arizona 12-13-39
Henry, King of Navarre 5-07-24
Henry Miller Odyssey, The 9-18-74
Henry, the Rainmaker 1-26-49
Her Accidental Husband 4-19-23
Her Adopted Parents 10-01-10
Her Adventurous Night 6-26-46
Her American Husband 1-25-18
Her Beloved Villain 12-03-20
Her Better Half 11-15-18
Her Better Self 5-25-17
Her Big Night 12-29-26
Her Body in Bond 6-21-18
Her Bodyguard 8-08-33
Her Boy 2-01-18
Her Broken Promise 5-05-16
Her Brother (See: Ototo)
Her Busy Day 9-18-09
Her Cardboard Lover 5-27-42
Her Code of Honor 3-07-19
Her Country First 11-01-18
Her Debt of Honor 2-04-16
Her Debt of Honor 3-29-18
Her Decision 5-17-18
Her Discretion 10-12-27
Her Double Life 9-29-16
Her Duplicate Husband 12-25-14
Her Elephant Man 2-20-20
Her Excellency, The Governor 7-06-17
Her Family Jewels 1-21-76
Her Fatal Millions 7-12-23
Her Fatal Sin 1-08-15
Her Father Said No 12-29-26
Her Father's Gold 5-12-16
Her Father's Keeper 3-23-17
Her Father's Son 10-20-16
Her Fiance and the Dog 10-08-10
Her Fighting Chance 5-18-17
Her Final Reckoning 6-28-18
Her First Affair 2-26-47
Her First Affaire 12-27-32
Her First Appearance 4-23-10
Her First Ball (See: Su Primer Baile)
Her First Beau 5-07-41
Her First Biscuits 6-26-09
Her First Elopement 1-21-21
Her First Kiss 8-22-19
Her First Love (See: Tu M'Ami--To T'Amo)
Her First Mate 9-05-33
Her First Romance 5-02-51
Her Five-Foot Highness 4-09-20
Her Forgotten Past 11-07-33
Her Generous Way 12-04-09
Her Gilded Cage 8-04-22
Her Good Name 1-26-17
Her Great Chance 10-18-18
Her Great Hour 1-07-16
Her Great Price 3-17-16
Her Greater Love 4-06-17
Her Guilty Secret 2-13-14
Her Half Brother 12-15-22
Her Highness and the Bellboy 7-11-45
Her Highness Commands (See: Ihre Hoheit Befiehlt)
Her Highness, the Laundress (See: Purpur Und Waschblau)

Her Honor the Governor 7-21-26
Her Hour 11-16-17
Her Husband Lies 3-24-37
Her Husband's Affairs 7-23-47
Her Husband's Friend 11-22-18
Her Husband's Secret 7-15-25
Her Husband's Secretary 3-24-37
Her Husband's Trademark 2-24-22
Her Jungle Love 3-23-38
Her Kind of Man 4-24-46
Her Kingdom of Dreams 9-26-19 and 10-17-19
Her Kommer Vi 11-26-47
Her Ladyship 5-01-14
Her Last Affaire 11-06-35
Her Last Part (See: Son Dernier Role)
Her Life and His 2-02-17
Her Lord and Master 4-01-21
Her Love Story 10-08-24
Her Mad Bargain 4-28-22
Her Mad Night 11-29-32
Her Majesty 8-18-22
Her Majesty Love (See: Ihre Majestaet die Liebe)
Her Majesty Love 12-01-31
Her Man 8-23-18
Her Man 1-21-25
Her Man 9-17-30
Her Man o' War 9-15-26
Her Martyrdom 2-26-15
Her Master's Voice 2-26-36
Her Maternal Right 5-05-16
Her Melody (See: Hennes Melodi)
Her Mistake 4-05-18
Her Moment 8-16-18
Her Most Beautiful Day (See: Ihr Schoenster Tag)
Her Mother's Secret 12-17-15
Her Naked Soul 4-28-16
Her New Beau 3-28-13
Her New York 1-26-17
Her Official Fathers 4-13-17
Her One Mistake 5-17-18
Her Only Son 5-28-15
Her Only Way 8-23-18
Her Own Free Will 9-10-24
Her Own Money 2-24-22
Her Own Way 6-11-15
Her Painted Hero 10-29-15
Her Panelled Door 8-29-51
Her Price 8-02-18
Her Primitive Man 4-05-44
Her Private Affair 1-15-30
Her Purchase Price 2-11-21
Her Reckoning 11-05-15
Her Reputation 9-13-23 and 9-27-23
Her Resale Value 6-27-33
Her Right to Live 1-12-17
Her Screen Idol 6-21-18
Her Second Chance 4-28-26
Her Second Husband 1-11-18
Her Silent Sacrifice 11-30-17
Her Sister 1-11-18
Her Sister from Paris 8-26-25
Her Sister's Rival 11-30-17
Her Sister's Secret 9-11-46
Her Sister's Sin 4-23-10
Her Social Value 2-17-22
Her Splendid Folly 11-14-33
Her Story 9-01-22
Her Strange Wedding 6-15-17
Her Sturdy Oak 8-12-21
Her Summer Hero 6-20-28
Her Sweet Revenge 4-30-10
Her Temporary Husband 1-03-24
Her Terrible Ordeal 1-15-10
Her Triumph 2-12-15
Her Twelve Men 6-30-54
Her Unwilling Husband 12-10-20
Her Vocation 7-23-15
Her Wedding Night 10-01-30
Her Wild Oat 2-08-28
Her Winning Way 9-23-21
Her Wonderful Lie 5-10-50
Her Younger Sister (See: Su Hermana Menor)
Herbie Goes Bananas 7-02-80
Herbie Goes to Monte Carlo 6-22-77
Herbie Rides Again 3-27-74
Herbst der Gammler 11-01-67
Hercule 4-13-38

Hercules 5-13-59
Hercules and Queen of Lydia (See: Ercole e la Regina di Lidia)
Hercules' Pills (See: Pillole di Ercole, Le)
Here, Beneath the North Star (See: Taala Pohjantahden Alla)
Here Come the Co-eds 1-31-45
Here Come the Girls 10-21-53
Here Come the Huggetts 12-08-48
Here Come the Jets 6-03-59
Here Come the Marines 5-28-52
Here Come the Nelsons 1-16-52
Here Come the Tigers 5-31-78
Here Come the Waves 12-20-44
Here Comes Carter 11-18-36
Here Comes Cookie 10-16-35
Here Comes Elmer 10-27-43
Here Comes Everybody 11-15-72
Here Comes Happiness 5-14-41
Here Comes Kelly 8-04-43
Here Comes Mr. Jordan 7-30-41
Here Comes the Band 9-25-35
Here Comes the Bride 1-24-19
Here Comes the Groom 6-19-34
Here Comes the Groom 7-11-51
Here Comes the Navy 7-24-34
Here Comes Trouble 4-08-36
Here Comes Trouble 4-14-48
Here I Am a Stranger 9-27-39
Here Is a Man 7-16-41
Here Is Ireland 10-09-40
Here Is My Heart 12-25-34
Here Is the Beauty (See: Belle Que Voila, La)
Here We Are Coming (See: Her Kommer Vi)
Here We Go Again 8-26-42
Here We Go Round the Mulberry Bush 1-24-68
Here You Have Your Life (See: Har Har Du Ditt Liv)
Hereafter of Terror, The (See: Mas Alla del Terror)
Herederos, Los 7-08-70
Hereditary Instinct 2-05-30
Heredity 7-26-18
Herencia, La 5-06-64
Here's Berlin (See: Hier Spricht Berlin)
Here's Flash Casey 10-20-37
Here's Looking at You, Kid 10-08-80
Here's to Romance 10-09-35
Herfra Min Verden Gaar 2-18-76
Heritage 10-01-20
Heritage 5-29-35
Heritage 11-06-40
Heritage, L' 8-27-75
Heritage, The (See: Arven or Orokseg)
Heritage, The (See: Heritage, L' or Slaegten)
Heritage of Bjoerndal (See: Erbe von Bjoerndal, Das)
Heritage of France, The 11-14-19
Heritage of the Desert 1-24-24
Heritage of the Desert 3-14-33
Heritage of the Desert 3-22-39
Heritier, L' 4-11-73
Heritier de Mondesir, L' 6-05-40
Heritiers, Les 3-30-60
Herkulesfurdoi Emlek 3-02-77
Hermana Blanca, La 12-28-60
Hermanas Karambazo, Las 7-06-60
Hermano Jose, El 11-19-41
Hermanos, Las 7-04-62
Hermanos del Hierro, Los 12-27-61
Hermine und die 7 Aufrechten 9-25-35
Hermine and 7 Righteous Men (See: Hermine und die 7 Aufrechten)
Hermit of Bird Island, The 3-12-15
Hero, The (See: Nayak)
Hero, The 3-08-23
Hero Ain't Nothin' but a Sandwich, A 12-14-77
Hero at Large 2-06-80
Hero for a Day 9-13-39
Hero for a Night, A 12-28-27
Hero of All Girls' Dreams, The 4-24-29
Hero of Our Times, A (See: Eroe Dei Nostri Tempi, Un)
Hero of Submarine D-2, The 3-10-16
Hero of the Circus 12-19-28
Hero on Horseback 7-13-27
Herod the Great 12-14-60
Heroes (See: Helden)
Heroes 11-02-77
Heroes All 11-17-31
Heroes and Husbands 9-01-22
Heroes Are Made 3-22-44
Heroes Are Not Wet Behind the Ears (See: Heros N'Ont Pas Froid Aux Oreilles, Les)
Heroes Are Tired (See: Heros Sont Fatigues, Les)

Heroes del Aire 9-11-57
Heroes for Sale 7-25-33
Heroes in Blue 2-08-28
Heroes in Blue 12-06-39
Heroes of Shipka 9-12-56
Heroes of Telemark, The 11-03-65
Heroes of the Alamo 4-06-38
Heroes of the Hills 8-03-38
Heroes of the Marne (See: Heros de la Marne)
Heroes of the Night 6-29-27
Heroes of the Range 8-19-36
Heroes of the Saddle 1-17-40
Heroes of the Sea 4-30-41
Heroes of the Street 12-22-22
Heroic Charge (See: Carica Eroica)
Heroic Fair (See: Kermesse Heroique, La)
Heroic Father, A 8-21-09
Heroic Somnambulist 5-22-09
Heroin (See: Eroina)
Heroina 9-06-72
Heroine (See: Heroina)
Heroines du Mal, Les 5-23-79
Heroines of Evil, The (See: Heroines du Mal, Les)
Heros de la Marne 1-11-39
Hero's Island 9-19-62
Heros N'Ont Pas Froid Aux Oreilles, Les 1-10-79
Heros Sont Fatigues, Les 9-28-55
Hero's Wife, The (See: Eshet Ha'Gibor)
Herostratus 1-17-68
Herr Buerovorsteher, Der 6-28-32
Herr der Welt, Der 12-18-35
Herr Finanzdirektor, Der 10-13-31
Herr Kobin Geht Auf Abenteuer 12-04-35
Herr Mit der Schwarzen Melone, Der 8-03-60
Herr Puntila and His Chauffeur Matti (See: Herr Puntila und Sein
    Knecht Matti)
Herr Puntila und Sein Knecht Matti 12-11-57
Herr Ueber Leben und Tod 6-22-25
Herren Machen Das Selber, Dass Ihnen Der Arme Mann Feydnt Wird,
    Die 3-26-80
Herren mit der Weissen Weste, Die 4-01-70
Herren Og Hans Tjenere 7-22-59
Herren vom Maxim, Die 4-07-37
Herrenpartie 7-15-64
Herrliche Zeiten im Spessart 11-08-67
Herrscher, Der 4-07-37
Hers to Hold 7-14-43
Hertha's Awakening (See: Hertha's Erwachen)
Hertha's Erwachen 3-14-33
Herz Aus Glas 12-01-76
Herz Spielt Falsch, Ein 7-15-53
Herzblatt--Wie Sag Ichs Meiner Tochter 10-22-69
He's a Cockeyed Wonder 10-25-50
He's My Guy 3-17-43
He's Quite a Man (See: Tozi Istinski Musch)
Hesper of the Mountains 8-04-16
Hester Street 5-14-75
Het Afscheid 9-14-66
Het Dwaallicht 5-30-73
Het Gangstermeisje 7-05-67
Het Mes 4-26-61
Het Verloren Paradise 9-27-78
Hetenkint Egyszer Lathatom 4-07-37
Hetzi-Hetzi 12-08-71
Heung 8-10-77
Heureux Qui Comme Ulysse ... 8-12-70
Heute Nacht Oder Nie 9-13-72
Hex 9-19-73
Hexer, Der 8-30-32
Hexer, Der 4-28-65
Hey Boy (See: Guaglio)
Hey Boy, Hey Girl 4-15-59
Hey Hey Cowboy 4-06-27
Hey! Hey! U.S.A. 10-05-38
Hey, Let's Twist 12-20-61
Hey Mister I Am Your Wife (See: Hoy Mister Ako Ang Misis Mo)
Hey, Rookie 4-12-44
Hey, Rube 3-20-29
Hey There, It's Yogi Bear 5-27-64
Heym Hayu Assara (See: They Were Ten)
Hi Beautiful 11-29-44
Hi, Buddy 2-17-43
Hi-De-Ho 5-14-47
Hi Diddle Diddle 8-04-43
Hi Doc (See: Bonjour Toubib)
Hi Gaucho 4-29-36
Hi Good-Lookin' 3-15-44

Hi, Mom 4-15-70
Hi, Nellie 2-06-34
Hi'Ya Chum 2-10-43
Hi'Ya, Sailor 10-06-43
Hi-Yo Silver 4-17-40
Hiawatha 10-30-09
Hiawatha 12-10-52
Hibernatus 9-24-69
Hickey and Boggs 8-30-72
Hidden Aces 8-31-27
Hidden Children, The 4-06-17
Hidden Code, The 7-23-20
Hidden Danger 3-02-49
Hidden Enemy 4-03-40
Hidden Eye, The 7-25-45
Hidden Fear 7-17-57
Hidden Fires 11-08-18
Hidden Fortress, The 7-08-59 and 11-25-59
Hidden Gold 3-28-33
Hidden Gold 5-22-40
Hidden Guns 3-07-56
Hidden Hand, The 9-23-42
Hidden in the Sunlight (See: Ukryty W Sloncu)
Hidden Light 11-19-20
Hidden Menace, The 4-10-40
Hidden One, The (See: Escondida, La)
Hidden Power 8-02-39
Hidden River 12-13-50
Hidden Scar, The 10-06-16
Hidden Spring, The 7-27-17
Hidden Truth, The 1-25-19
Hidden Valley 10-27-16
Hidden Way, The 12-08-26
Hide and Seek 6-24-64
Hide and Seek 9-15-76
Hide in Plain Sight 3-19-80
Hide n' Seek (See: Miskhak Makhbuim)
Hide-Out 8-28-30
Hide-Out, The 4-23-30
Hideaway 7-21-37
Hideaway Girls 1-20-37
Hideg Napok 7-27-66
Hideout 3-30-49
Hideout, The (See: Planque, La)
Hideout in the Alps 4-27-38
Hiding Place, The (See: Versteck, Das)
Hiding Place, The 5-14-75
Hiding Places, The (See: Escondites, Los)
Hidir 8-02-78
Hier Spricht Berlin 4-12-32
Hiev Up 6-28-78
Higgins Family, The 9-07-38
High 7-10-68
High and Handsome 9-02-25
High and Low (See: Tengoku To-Jigoku)
High and the Mighty, The 5-26-54
High Anxiety 12-21-77
High-Ballin' 6-07-78
High Barbaree 3-12-47
High Bright Sun, The 2-10-65
High Command 7-27-38
High Conquest 3-12-47
High Cost of Loving 3-12-58
High Explosive 3-24-43
High Finance 4-13-17
High Flier, The 10-20-26
High Flight 9-25-57 and 3-19-58
High Flyers 11-10-37
High Fury 11-03-48
High Gear 4-18-33
High Hand, The 9-15-26
High Hat 4-27-27
High Hat 3-16-38
High Heels 10-28-21
High Hell 4-02-58
High Infidelity (See: Alta Infedelta)
High Life, The (See: Grande Vie, La)
High Lifers, The (See: Bons Vivants, Les)
High Lonesome 8-16-50
High Noon 4-30-52
High Plains Drifter 3-28-73
High Powered 2-21-45
High-Powered Rifle, The 8-03-60
High Pressure 2-02-32
High Priestess of Sexual Witchcraft 6-20-73
High Princip, The (See: Vyssi Princip)
High Rise 1-17-73
High Rolling 7-06-77

High Royal Highness 3-01-18
High School 1-10-40
High School 5-21-69
High School Confidential 5-28-58
High School Girl 3-20-35
High School Hellcats 8-27-58
High School Hero 10-26-27
High School Hero 10-23-46
High Sierra 1-22-41
High Sign, The 3-24-22
High Society 5-11-55
High Society 7-18-56
High Society Blues 4-23-30
High Speed 7-27-17
High Speed 5-28-24
High Speed 4-12-32
High Speed Biker, A 10-08-10
High Stakes 5-31-18
High Street (See: Rue Haute)
High Tension 7-15-36
High Terrace 3-20-57
High Tide 8-30-18
High Tide 8-06-47
High Tide at Noon 5-15-57
High Time 9-21-60
High Treason 10-02-29
High Treason 11-21-51
High Up (See: Bbicot)
High Velocity 9-28-77
High Wall 12-17-47
High Wall, The (See: Vysoka Zed)
High, Wide and Handsome 7-28-37
High, Wild and Free 3-13-68
High Wind in Jamaica, A 5-26-65
Higher and Higher 12-15-43
Higher Command (See: Hoehere Befehl, Der)
Highest Bid, The 6-30-16
Highest Bidder, The 4-15-21
Highest Trump, The 1-25-19
Highlander's Defiance, The 1-15-10
Highly Dangerous 12-13-50
Highway Dragnet 1-27-54
Highway of Cats (See: Camino de los Gatos, El)
Highway of Hope, The 6-22-17
Highway Patrol 8-10-38
Highway Queen (See: Malkat Hakvish)
Highway 13 12-29-48
Highway 301 11-29-50
Highway West 8-06-41
Highwayman, The 8-22-51
Highways by Night 8-12-42
Hija del Ministro, La 4-07-43
Hi-Jacked 6-28-50
Hijo de Pistolero, El (See: Son of a Gunfighter)
Hijos Artificiales, Los 8-04-43
Hikinige 4-27-66
Hiko Shojo (See: Each Day I Cry)
Hilda Crane 5-02-56
Hilfe--Ich Liebe Zwillinge! 2-25-70
Hilfe, Meine Frau Klaut 8-26-64
Hill, The 6-09-65
Hill in Korea, A 10-10-56
Hill 24 Doesn't Answer 5-11-55
Hillbilly Blitzkrieg 9-16-42
Hillcrest Mystery, The 4-05-18
Hills Have Eyes, The 12-20-78
Hills of Home 10-06-48
Hills of Kentucky 2-23-27
Hills of Missing Men 3-31-22
Hills of Oklahoma, The 6-28-50
Hills of Old Wyoming 6-09-37
Hills of Peril 5-04-27
Hills of Utah 9-12-51
Hills Run Red, The 10-11-67
Hilton Hano 4-17-68
Him (See: El)
Himiko 5-29-74
Himlaspelet 10-11-44
Hindenburg, The 12-24-75
Hindle Wakes 10-13-31
Hindu, The 5-27-53
Hinotori 10-22-80
Hinton's Double, The 4-20-17
Hints on Horsemanship 11-12-24
Hippie Revolt, The 12-20-67
Hippocrates 11-15-72
Hippodrome 12-26-28

Hippolyt, the Lackey 1-05-32
Hips, Hips, Hooray 2-27-34
Hired Gun, The 9-11-57
Hired Hand, The 7-07-71
Hired Killer, The 3-01-67
Hired Man, The 3-22-18
Hired Wife 3-13-34
Hired Wife 9-11-40
Hireling, The 5-23-73
Hiring a Gem 10-22-10
Hirok Rajar Deshe 12-17-80
Hiroshima 5-18-55
Hiroshima Mon Amour 5-13-59
Hiroshima My Love (See: Hiroshima Mon Amour)
Hirourzi 5-31-78
Hirsekorn Butts In (See: Hirsekorn Grieft Ein)
Hirsekorn Does Something About It (See: Hirsekorn Grieft Ein)
Hirsekorn Grieft Ein 10-20-31 and 6-21-32
His and Hers 2-01-61
His Auto Ruination 3-17-16
His Best Pupil (See: Su Mejor Alumno)
His Birthright 9-20-18
His Breach of Discipline 10-29-10
His Bread and Butter 4-28-16
His Brother's Keeper 3-28-13
His Brother's Place 7-18-19
His Brother's Wife 6-16-16
His Brother's Wife 8-19-36
His Buddy's Wife 7-08-25
His Butler's Sister 11-10-43
His Captive Woman 4-10-29
His Children's Children 11-08-23
His Crucible 9-17-15
His Darker Self 3-26-24
His Daughter Is Peter (See: Seine Tochter Ist Peter)
His Day of Glory (See: Giornata di Gloria, La)
His Divorce Grounds (See: Sein Scheidungsgrund)
His Divorce Reason (See: Sein Scheidungsgrund)
His Divorced Wife 11-28-19
His Dog 8-17-27
His Double Life 12-19-33
His Enemy, the Law 6-21-18
His Excellency 1-23-52
His Exciting Night 12-07-38
His Family Tree 2-12-36
His Father's Portrait (See: Portrait de Son Pere, Le)
His Father's Rifle 6-25-15
His Father's Son 3-23-17
His Fears Confirmed 2-26-10
His Fight (See: Sein Kampf)
His First Command 12-25-29
His First Flame 5-11-27
His First Girl 5-01-09
His First Valentine 3-19-10
His Flesh and Blood 6-19-14
His Forgotten Wife 6-25-24
His Girl Friday 1-10-40
His Glorious Night 10-09-29
His Grace Gives Notice 8-01-33
His Great Triumph 6-16-16
His Greatest Gamble 7-24-34
His Highness, Love (See: Son Altesse l'Amour)
His Hour 10-08-24
His House in Order 3-12-20
His House in Order 3-21-28
His Jazz Bride 10-27-26
His Just Deserts 2-12-10
His Kind of Woman 7-18-51
His Last Burglary 2-26-10
His Last Cartridge 2-08-08
His Last Dollar 11-07-14
His Last Game 12-18-09
His Last Haul 3-20-29
His Last Parade 1-14-11
His Last Race 9-27-23
His Last 12 Hours 11-18-53
His Late Excellency 6-12-29
His Lordship 11-18-36
His Love Song (See: Sein Liebeslied)
His Lucky Day 10-02-29
His Majesty Bunker Bean 4-12-18
His Majesty O'Keefe 12-30-53
His Majesty the American 10-31-19
His Masterpiece 11-20-09
His Master's Eye (See: Oeil du Maitre, L')
His Master's Voice 10-21-25
His Mother's Boy 1-04-18
His Mother's House (See: Mors Hus)

His Mother's Thanksgiving 12-03-10
His Mystery Girl 1-31-24
His New Lid 12-03-10
His New York Wife 11-10-26
His Night Out 11-20-35
His Official Fiancee 10-10-19
His Official Wife (See: Seine Offizielle Frau)
His Own Blood 4-22-64
His Own Home Town 5-24-18
His Own People 1-04-18
His Own Son 11-07-08
His Pajama Girl 9-03-20
His Parisian Wife 1-25-19
His Picture in the Papers 2-04-16
His Private Life 11-14-28
His Private Secretary 8-08-33
His Rise to Fame 6-29-27
His Robe of Honor 1-18-18
His Royal Highness (See: Koenigliche Hoheit)
His Royal Highness 10-18-32
His Second Chance 4-28-26
His Secretary 12-23-25
His Supreme Moment 4-15-25
His Sweetheart 2-02-17
His Tiger Lady 5-30-28
His Wife 11-05-15
His Wife's Good Name 9-22-16
His Wife's Husband 5-12-22
His Wife's Lover (See: Zein Weib's Lubovnick)
His Wife's Money 2-27-20
His Wife's Mother 12-08-16
His Wild Oats 7-21-16
His Woman 12-08-31
His Young Wife 3-23-49
Histoire d'Adele H., L' 9-24-75
Histoire d'Adrien 5-21-80
Histoire d'Amour, Une 12-05-51
Histoire d'O., L' 9-03-75
Histoire d'un Poisson Rouge 5-13-59
Histoire de Paul 11-05-75
Histoire Immortelle, Une 7-17-68
Histoire Simple, Une 11-15-78
Histoire Tres Bonne et Tres Joyeuse de Colinot Trousse Chemise,
    L' 11-21-73
Histoires Extraordinaires 3-15-50
Histoires Extraordinaires 6-05-68
Historia de Amor, Una 6-28-67
Historia de Crimenes 12-23-42
Historia de un Gran Amor 10-13-43
Historia de una Chica Sola 9-10-69
Historia de una Mala Mujer 7-07-48
Historia de una Noche 4-30-41
Historia del 900 8-24-49
Historia Zoltej Cizemki 8-29-62
Historien Om Barbara 5-10-67
Historien Om En Moder 10-31-79
History Is Made at Night 3-31-37
History Lessons (See: Geschichtsunterricht)
History of Mr. Polly, The 2-16-49
History of Postwar Japan as Told by a Bar Hostess (See: Nippon
    Sengoshi-Madam Onboro No Seikatsu)
History of the Blue Movie, The 11-11-70
Hit 9-26-73
Hit and Miss 3-14-19
Hit and Run (See: Delit de Fuite or Hikinige)
Hit and Run 3-20-57
Hit Man 12-27-72
Hit of the Show 7-11-28
Hit Parade (See: Schlagerparade)
Hit Parade, The 6-02-37
Hit Parade of 1941 10-23-40
Hit Parade of 1943 3-10-43
Hit Parade of 1947 4-30-47
Hit Parade of 1951 10-25-50
Hit 'Romemont 7-01-70
Hit Song (See: Schlager)
Hit the Deck 1-22-30
Hit the Deck 3-09-55
Hit the Ice 6-30-43
Hit the Road 7-09-41
Hit the Saddle 8-04-37
Hit the Trail Holliday 6-14-18
Hitch Hike Lady 1-22-36
Hitch Hike to Heaven 3-18-36
Hitchhike to Happiness 4-18-45
Hitch-Hiker, The 1-21-53
Hitch Of It, The (See: Zoff)
Hitchhiker, The (See: Stopar)

Hitchhikers, The 2-09-72
Hitler 2-28-62
Hitler, A Career (See: Hitler, eine Karriere)
Hitler, a Film from Germany 11-30-77
Hitler Around the Corner (See: Hitler Iz Naseg Sokaka)
Hitler? Connais Pas! 5-22-63
Hitler--Dead or Alive 11-18-42
Hitler, eine Karriere 6-29-77
Hitler Gang, The 4-26-44
Hitler Iz Naseg Sokaka 8-20-75
Hitlerjunge Quex 7-17-34
Hitler? Never Heard of Him! (See: Hitler? Connais Pas!)
Hitler: The Last Ten Days 5-09-73
Hitler's Children 12-30-42
Hitler's Hangman 6-09-43
Hitler's Reign of Terror 5-01-34
Hittin' the Trail 9-29-37
Hitting a New High 12-01-37
Hitting the Trail 11-22-18
Hjartats Rost 6-30-31
Hjerter er Trumf 4-07-76
Hlidac 8-19-70
Ho 11-13-68
Ho Perduto Mio Marito 3-24-37
Ho Scelto L'Amore 5-13-53
Ho Sognato il Paradiso 7-12-50
Hoa-Binh 4-01-70
Hoarded Assets 12-20-18
Hoax (See: Schabernack)
Hoax, The 12-06-72
Hobbs in a Hurry 10-04-18
Hoboes' Christmas 12-24-10
Hoboes in Paradise 10-18-50
Hobson's Choice 10-13-31
Hobson's Choice 3-03-54
Hochzeitsreise, Die 10-15-69
Hochzeitsreise Zu Dritt 3-21-33
Hochzeitstraum, Ein 10-28-36
Hocuspocus 10-12-66
Hodina Pravdy 8-02-78
Hoedown 6-21-50
Hoehere Befehl, Der 4-15-36
Hoelle von Manitoba, Die 12-29-65
Hoellische Liebe 12-14-49
Hoer, Var der Ikke en, Som Lo? 9-20-78
Hoffman 7-22-70
Hofkonzert 4-07-37
Hofrat Geiger 2-18-48
Hog Wild 6-11-80
Hogan's Alley 11-25-25
Hogy Szaladnak a Fak 11-15-67
Hoito Rabu 3-05-80
Hokum (See: Allotria)
Hokuspokus 7-30-30
Hold Back the Dawn 7-30-41
Hold Back the Night 7-25-56
Hold Back Tomorrow 9-21-55
Hold 'Em Jail 8-23-32
Hold 'Em Navy! 11-10-37
Hold 'Em Yale 5-01-35
Hold Everything 3-26-30
Hold Me Tight 5-23-33
Hold On 3-16-66
Hold That Baby! 7-06-49
Hold That Blonde 11-14-45
Hold That Co-ed 9-28-38
Hold That Ghost 7-30-41
Hold That Girl 3-27-34
Hold That Kiss 5-11-38
Hold That Line 4-02-52
Hold That Lion 9-08-26
Hold That Woman 11-20-40
Hold the Press 12-05-33
Hold Your Horses 1-28-21
Hold Your Man 10-16-29
Hold Your Man 7-04-33
Holdudvar 2-26-69
Hold-Up in Calabria, A 2-29-08
Hole, The (See: Trou, Le)
Hole in the Ground, A (See: Dziura W Zlemi)
Hole in the Head, A 5-20-59
Hole in the Moon, A (See: Hor Balevana)
Hole in the Wall 1-06-22
Hole in the Wall 4-17-29
Hole in the Wall, A (See: Jarha Fi Lhaite or Trou dans le Mur, Un)
Hole in the Wall, A (See: Nar Rosorna Sla-Ut)
Holiday (See: Jour de Fete)

Homme Sans Visage, L'   6-26-74
Hommes, Les   4-04-73
Hommes en Blanc, Les   11-23-55
Hommes Ne Pensent Qu'a Ca, Les   8-11-54
Hommes Veulent Vivre, Les   1-30-63
Homo Eroticus   11-24-71
Homosexual Century, The (See: Race D'Ep)
Hon Dansade en Sommar   3-05-52
Hondo   11-25-53
Honest Hutch   9-17-20
Honest Interview, The (See: Ehrliche Interview, Das)
Honest Man, An   5-10-18
Honest Person Needed (See: Persona Honrada Se Necesita)
Honesty-Best Policy   8-25-26
Honey (See: Miel, La or Jede Frau Hat Etwas)
Honey   4-02-30 (Also see: Cherie)
Honey Flowers, The (See: Fleurs du Miel, Les)
Honey Pot, The   3-22-67
Honey, Scare Me (See: Cheri, Fais Moi Peur)
Honeybaby, Honeybaby   10-09-74
Honeychile   11-14-51
Honeycomb, The (See: Madriguera, La)
Honeyless Honeymoon, The   2-02-17
Honeymoon (See: Flitterwochen; Smekmanad; Honning Maane; or
   Taxidi Toy Melitos)
Honeymoon   4-03-29
Honeymoon   4-16-47
Honeymoon, The   12-07-17
Honeymoon at Niagara Falls   3-02-07
Honeymoon Deferred   2-21-40
Honeymoon Express, The   9-08-26 and 10-06-26
Honeymoon Flats   11-28-28
Honeymoon for Three   2-12-41
Honeymoon for Three, A   3-19-15
Honeymoon Hate   12-14-27
Honeymoon Hotel   6-03-64
Honeymoon in Bali   9-13-39
Honeymoon Killers, The   9-10-69
Honeymoon Lane   8-04-31
Honeymoon Limited   8-05-36
Honeymoon Lodge   7-28-43
Honeymoon Machine, The   7-05-61
Honeymoon Ranch   10-22-20
Honeymoon Trio, The (See: Voyage de Noces, Le)
Honeymoon's Over, The   12-20-39
Honeysuckle Rose   7-16-80
Hong Kong   11-14-51
Hong Kong Affair   4-16-58
Hong Kong Confidential   10-01-58
Hong Kong Emmanuelle   4-06-77
Hong Kong Tycoon, The   8-01-79
Hong Thong   9-14-77
Hongyboly   8-16-72
Honjin Satsujin Jiken   7-14-76
Honkers, The   3-01-72
Honky   11-17-71
Honky Tonk   6-12-29
Honky Tonk   9-17-41
Honneurs de la Guerre, Les   7-26-61
Honning Maane   8-30-78
Honningmane   11-05-80
Honno (See: Lost Sex)
Honolulu   2-01-39
Honolulu-Tokyo-Hong Kong   12-18-63
Honoo to Onna   5-01-68
Honor   9-11-29
Honor Among Lovers   3-04-31
Honor Among Men   12-10-24
Honor Among Thieves (See: Parola Di Ladro)
Honor and Glory (See: Cest A Slava)
Honor Bound   11-26-20
Honor Bound   5-09-28
Honor of His Family, The   1-29-10
Honor of Mary Blake, The   12-15-16
Honor of Old Glory   7-03-14
Honor of the Family   10-20-31
Honor of the Mounted   10-04-32
Honor of the Press   7-19-32
Honor of the Range   5-01-34
Honor of the West   7-26-39
Honor System, The   2-16-17
Honor Thy Name   8-04-16
Honorable Algy   11-03-16
Honorable Catherine, The   8-25-48
Honorable Friend, The   8-25-16
Honor's Altar   3-17-16
Honor's Cross   6-28-18
Honors Easy   8-14-35

Honors of War, The (See: Honneurs de la Guerre, Les)
Hoodlum, The (See: Voyou, Le)
Hoodlum, The   9-05-19
Hoodlum, The   6-06-51
Hoodlum Empire   2-20-52
Hoodlum Priest   2-22-61
Hoodlum Saint, The   2-06-46
Hoodlum's Ball, The (See: Bal Des Voyous, Le)
Hoodlums' Sun (See: Soleil Des Voyous, Le)
Hoodman Blind   3-26-24
Hoodoo, The   10-01-10
Hoodoo Ann   4-07-16
Hoofbeats of Vengeance   6-12-29
Hook, The   1-16-63
Hook and Ladder No. 9   12-21-27
Hook, Line and Sinker   12-31-30
Hook, Line and Sinker   3-26-69
Hooked Generation   4-16-69
Hooper   7-26-78
Hoopla   12-05-33
Hooray for Love   7-17-35
Hooray for the Blue Hussars (See: Hurra for de Blaa Husarer)
Hoosier Holiday   8-25-43
Hoosier Schoolboy   6-30-37
Hoosier Schoolmaster, The   11-14-14
Hoosier Schoolmaster, The   3-19-24
Hoosier Schoolmaster, The   9-25-35
Hootenanny Hoot   8-28-63
Hop Pickers, The (See: Starci Na Chmelu)
Hop, the Devil's Brew   2-04-16
Hopalong Cassidy   10-02-35
Hopalong Cassidy Returns   1-06-37
Hopalong Rides Again   11-17-37
Hope (See: Umut)
Hope   7-21-22
Hope, The (See: Nadeje)
Hope, The   9-24-20
Hope Chest, The   1-10-19
Hopeless Ones, The   2-23-66
Hopla Paa Sengekanten   2-04-76
Hopper, The   2-01-18
Hoppla, Jetzt Kommt Eddie   5-13-59
Hoppla, Now Comes Eddie (See: Hoppla, Jetzt Kommt Eddie)
Hoppy Serves a Writ   3-17-43 and 4-28-43
Hoppy's Holiday   5-07-47
Hopscotch   7-23-80
Hor Balevana   5-19-65
Hora de las Sorpresas, La   11-05-41
Hora de los Hornos, La   6-26-68
Hora de los Ninos, La   10-14-70
Hora de Maria y el Pajaro de Oro, La   4-07-76
Horace 62   2-14-62
Hordubal   10-29-80
Hori, Ma Panenko   12-06-67
Horizon (See: Horizont)
Horizon   5-16-33
Horizon, L'   5-03-67
Horizons Sans Fin   7-15-53
Horizons West   9-24-52
Horizont   11-22-32
Horizont   9-08-71
Horizontal Lieutenant, The   4-04-62
Horizonte Te Hapura   1-24-79
Horloger de Saint-Paul, L'   1-30-74
Horn Blows at Midnight, The   4-04-45
Hornet's Nest   9-02-70
Hornets' Nest, The (See: Guepier, Le)
Horoki (See: Lonely Lane)
Horoscope (See: Horoskop)
Horoscope of Family Hesselbach (See: Horoskop der Familie
   Hesselbach, Das)
Horoskop   8-20-69
Horoskop der Familie Hesselbach, Das   2-15-56
Horror Castle   4-21-65
Horror House   4-29-70
Horror Island   4-02-41
Horror of Dracula   7-05-58
Horror of Frankenstein   10-21-70
Horror of It All, The   9-16-64
Horror on Snape Island   4-26-72
Horrors of the Black Museum   4-22-59 and 5-06-59
Horrors of War   2-14-40
Horse, La   3-11-70
Horse and the Haystack, The   9-04-09
Horse Ate the Hat, The   9-08-31
Horse Boy, The (See: Abarembo Kaido)
Horse Feathers   8-16-32
Horse for Two, A (See: Cheval Pour Deux, Un)

Horse in the Gray Flannel Suit, The 10-16-68
Horse of Another Color, A 6-22-07
Horse of Pride (See: Cheval d'Orgeuil, Le)
Horse Play 3-13-34
Horse Shoes 5-25-27
Horse Soldiers, The 6-10-59
Horse with the Flying Tail, The 1-25-61
Horseman of the Plains 5-02-28
Horsemen, The 2-07-51
Horsemen, The 6-23-71
Horsemen of the Sierras 3-08-50
Horse's Mouth, The 9-17-58
Horseshoe, The 4-02-10
Hose, Die (See: Royal Scandal, The)
Hose, Die 12-21-27
Hosekraemmeren 12-29-71
Hoshizora No Marionette 8-23-78
Hospital, The 12-08-71
Hospital of the Transfiguration (See: Szpital Przemienienia)
Hospitality 11-08-23
Hospitals: The White Mafia (See: Bisturi: La Mafia Bianca)
Hostage, The (See: El Shaytan El Saheir)
Hostage, The 1-25-08
Hostage, The 9-14-17
Hostage, The 8-17-66
Hostage Gang, The (See: Gang Des Otages, Le)
Hostages 8-11-43
Hostages, The (See: Otages, Les)
Hosteria del Caballito Blanco, La 6-30-48
Hostess Also Has a Count, The (See: Frau Wirtin Hat Auch Einen
    Grafen)
Hostess Also Has a Niece, The (See: Frau Wirtin Hat Auch Eine
    Nichte)
Hostess Also Likes to Blow the Horn, The (See: Frau Wirtin
    Auch Gern Trompete)
Hostess Exceeds All Rounds, The (See: Frau Wirtin Treibt Es
    Jetzt Noch Toller)
Hostile Country 5-17-50
Hostile Guns 7-26-67
Hoszakadas 7-31-74
Hot Angel 12-10-58
Hot Blood (See: Heisses Blut)
Hot Blood 2-29-56
Hot-Blooded Paolo (See: Paolo Il Caldo)
Hot Car Girl 6-18-58
Hot Cargo 3-13-46
Hot Cars 8-08-56
Hot Cat? (See: Kuuma Kissa?)
Hot Channels 5-23-73
Hot Circuit 3-22-72
Hot Curves 7-09-30
Hot Days (See: Dias Calientes, Los)
Hot Enough for June 3-11-64
Hot for Paris 1-08-30
Hot-Head (See: Coup de Tete)
Hot Heels 5-23-28
Hot Heiress 3-18-31
Hot Lead 10-24-51
Hot Lead and Cold Feet 7-12-78
Hot Millions 9-04-68
Hot Money 7-29-36
Hot Month of August, The (See: O Zestos Minas Augoustos)
Hot News 7-25-28
Hot News 11-25-53
Hot Pepper 1-24-33
Hot Potato (See: Patata Bollente, La)
Hot Potato 4-07-76
Hot Rabbit, The (See: Chaud Lapin, Le)
Hot Rhythm 4-19-44
Hot Rock, The 1-26-72
Hot Rod 10-25-50
Hot Rod Gang 8-27-58
Hot Rod Girl 9-05-56
Hot Rod Rumble 5-15-57
Hot Rods to Hell 2-01-67
Hot Saturday 11-08-32
Hot Spell 5-14-58
Hot Spot 10-22-41
Hot Steel 6-26-40
Hot Stuff 5-15-29
Hot Stuff 6-06-79
Hot Summer Night 1-23-57
Hot Times 12-18-74
Hot Tip 10-23-35
Hot Tomorrows 5-03-78
Hot Traces of St. Pauli (See: Heisse Spur St. Pauli)
Hot Water 9-10-24
Hot Water 11-03-37

Hot Years (See: Tople Godine)
Hotel 1-18-67
Hotel Adieu 12-28-55
Hotel Alojamiento 4-27-66
Hotel Berlin 3-07-45
Hotel Continental 3-22-32
Hotel de la Plage, L' 2-08-78
Hotel de Verano 5-10-44
Hotel des Etudiants 10-04-32
Hotel Du Nord 2-01-39
Hotel for Strangers (See: Hotel Pro Cizince)
Hotel for Women 8-02-39
Hotel Haywire 6-16-37
Hotel Imperial 1-05-27
Hotel Imperial 5-10-39
Hotel Kikelet 9-22-37
Hotel Mysteries 4-10-29
Hotel Pacific 12-31-75
Hotel Paradiso 9-07-66
Hotel Pro Cizince 5-10-67
Hotel Reserve 6-28-44
Hotel Sahara 7-18-51
Hotel Springtime (See: Hotel Kikelet)
Hotel Variety 1-10-33
Hotelgeheimnisse (See: Hotel Mysteries)
Hotheads, The (See: Tetes Brulees, Les)
H.O.T.S. 9-12-79
Hotshots, The (See: Cracks, Les)
Hottentot, The 2-22-23
Hottentot, The 9-11-29
Hottest Girl, The (See: Sao Jom Tu)
Hottest Show in Town, The 11-20-74
Hou Halach Ba'Sadot 1-31-68
Houdini 5-20-53
Houkutuslintu 4-02-47
Hound-Dog Man 11-04-59
Hound of Silver Creek 9-05-28
Hound of the Baskervilles 9-15-22
Hound of the Baskervilles, The 10-02-29
Hound of the Baskervilles, The 4-19-32
Hound of the Baskervilles, The 3-29-39
Hound of the Baskervilles, The 4-01-59
Hound of the Baskervilles, The 11-08-78
Hound That Thought He Was a Raccoon, The 8-10-60
Hounds of Notre Dame, The 10-22-80
Houp-La 7-25-28
Hour Before Dawn 7-16-20
Hour Before the Dawn 3-08-44
Hour-Glass Sanatorium, The (See: Sanatorium Pod Klepsydra)
Hour of Liberation Has Sounded, The (See: Saat El Fahrir Daakat,
    Barra Ya Isti Mar)
Hour of Mary and the Bird of Gold, The (See: Hora de Maria y el
    Pajaro de Oro, La)
Hour of Parting, The (See: Afskedens Time)
Hour of Reckoning, The 11-30-27 and 1-25-28
Hour of the Blast Furnaces (See: Hora de los Hornos, La)
Hour of the Gun 10-04-67
Hour of the Wolf, The (See: Vergtimmen or I Ora Tou Lykou)
Hour of 13, The 10-01-52
Hour of Truth, The (See: Hodina Pravdy)
Hours of Love, The (See: Ore Dell'Amore, Le)
House 9-21-77
House, The (See: Maison, La or Kuca)
House Across the Bay 2-28-40
House Across the Street, The 8-17-49
House Built on Sand, A 12-29-16
House by the Lake, The 3-23-77
House by the River 3-29-50
House by the Sea, The (See: Huset Ved Havet)
House Calls 3-15-78
House Divided, A 6-06-19
House Divided, A 1-12-32
House I Live In, The (See: Dom V A Kotorom la Jivou)
House in Karp Lane, The (See: Haus in der Karpfengasse, Das)
House in Montevideo, The (See: Montevideo)
House in Naples 9-30-70
House in the Country, The (See: Maison de Campagne, La)
House in the South, The (See: Casa Del Sur, La)
House in the Sun 5-29-29
House Is Empty, The (See: Casa Esta Vacia, La)
House Is Not a Home, A 8-05-64
House Next Door, The 7-23-15
House of a Thousand Candles 4-08-36
House of 1,000 Dolls 11-08-67
House of Bamboo 7-06-55
House of Cards 10-23-68
House of Cards, The 12-18-09
House of Dances (See: Maison de Danse)

House of Dark Shadows 9-02-70
House of Death 8-16-32
House of Dracula 12-05-45
House of Fear 3-21-45
House of Fear, The 1-29-15
House of Fear, The 6-14-39
House of Frankenstein 12-20-44
House of Fright 5-17-61
House of Glass, The 3-01-18
House of Gold, The 6-28-18
House of Greed 8-14-34
House of Horror 6-19-29
House of Intrigue, The 11-18-59
House of Lies, The 9-22-16
House of Life (See: Haus Des Lebens)
House of Light, The (See: Chambre Blanche, La)
House of Mirrors, The 8-11-16
House of Mirth, The 8-16-18
House of Moliere (See: Maison de Moliere)
House of Mystery 6-04-41
House of Mystery, The 7-10-14
House of Numbers 6-26-57
House of Ricordi 12-28-55
House of Rothschild 3-20-34
House of Sand, A 6-13-62
House of Scandal, The 6-06-28
House of Secrets 10-23-29
House of Secrets 2-24-37
House of Secrets 10-31-56
House of Seven Hawks, The 11-11-59
House of Shame 8-29-28
House of Silence, The 4-26-18
House of Strangers 6-15-49
House of Tears, The 12-10-15
House of Temperley, The 5-15-14
House of the Angel, The (See: Casa del Angel, La)
House of the Bories, The (See: Maison des Bories, La)
House of the Crows, The (See: Casa de los Cuervos, La)
House of the Doves, The (See: Casa de las Palomas, La)
House of the Fox (See: Casa de la Zorra, La)
House of the Lost Court, The 5-14-15
House of the Lute 8-08-79
House of the Maltese (See: Maison du Maltais, La)
House of the Seven Gables 3-13-40
House of the Sleeping Virgins, The 5-08-68
House of the Three Girls (See: Dreimaederlhaus, Das)
House of Tolling Bells 9-17-20
House of Toys, The 5-28-20
House of Usher 6-29-60
House of Wax 4-15-53
House of Whispers 10-15-20
House of Women 4-11-62
House of Youth 12-03-24
House on Chelouche Street, The 11-14-73
House on 56th Street 12-05-33
House on Haunted Hill 12-03-58
House on 92nd Street, The 9-12-45
House on Skull Mountain, The 10-16-74
House on Telegraph Hill, The 3-07-51
House on the Dune, The (See: Maison Dans la Dune, La)
House on the Square, The 10-17-51
House That Dripped Blood, The 3-03-71
House Under the Rocks, The (See: Haz a Sziklak Alatt)
House Under the Rocks 11-12-58
House Under the Trees, The (See: Maison Sous les Arbres, La)
House We Live In, The (See: Casa En Que Vivimos, La)
House with an Attic 12-23-64
House with Golden Windows 8-04-16
House Without Boundaries, The (See: Casa Sin Fronteras, La)
House Without Children, The 8-15-19
House Without Love, The 3-07-28
Houseboat 9-10-58
Housekeeper of Circle C., The 3-21-14
Housekeeper's Daughter 9-13-39
Housemaid, Highly Presentable, Seeks Occupation (See: Cameriera
    Bella Presenza Offresi)
Housemaster 2-09-38
Houses in This Alley (See: Maisons Dans Cette Ruelle)
Housewarming, The (See: Grihapravesh)
Housewife 8-14-34
Housewife Report (See: Hausfrauen-Report)
Houston Story, The 1-11-56
Hovedjaegerne 1-12-72
How a Pretty Girl Sold Her Hair Restorer 11-07-08
How About Us? 11-13-63
How Are You? Well? (See: Como Vai, Vai Bem)
How Baxter Started In 6-24-25
How Binks Butted In 10-09-09

How Britain Prepared 6-02-16
How Brown Got Married 8-21-09
How Burke Was Captured 12-22-31
How Callahan Cleaned Up Little Hell 6-11-15
How Could You Caroline 5-24-18
How Could You Jean? 7-05-18
How Czar Peter the Great Married Off His Moor (See: Skas Pro To,
    Kar Zar Petr Arapa Shenil)
How Did a Nice Girl Like You Get Into This Business? (See: Wie
    Kommt Ein So Reizendes Maedchen Zu Diesem Gewerbe?)
How Do I Become Rich and Happy? 10-22-30
How Do I Love Thee? 9-30-70
How Do You Do 5-22-46
How Do You Like My Sister? (See: Comment Trouvez-Vous Ma Soeur?)
How French Perfumes Are Made 11-27-09
How Green Was My Valley 10-29-41
How He Earned His Medal 10-16-09
How He Lied to Her Husband 1-28-31
How Hubby Got a Raise 10-15-10
How Hubby Made Good 1-15-10
How I Became a Negro (See: Wie Ich Ein Neger Wurde)
How I Lost the War (See: Come Persi la Guerra)
How I Won the War 10-25-67
How Long Does a Man Live? (See: Meddig El Az Ember?)
How Low Can You Fall? (See: Dio Mio, Come Sono Caduta In Basso)
How Molly Made Good 10-15-15
How Rastus Got His Turkey 12-03-10
How She Won Him 9-17-10
How Short Is the Time for Love (See: Wie Kurz Ist Die Zeit Zum
    Lieben)
How Sweet It Is 6-26-68
How Tasty Was My Little Frenchman (See: Como Era Gostoso O Meu
    Frances)
How the Landlord Collected His Rents 9-25-09
How the West Was Won 11-07-62
How to Be Very, Very Popular 7-20-55
How to Beat the High Cost of Living 6-25-80
How to Behave in a Fourposter Bed (See: Takt Og Tone I Himmel-
    sengen)
How to Commit Marriage 5-28-69
How to Educate a Wife 6-04-24
How to Frame a Figg 2-17-71
How to Handle Women 6-20-28
How to Love (See: Konsten Att Elska)
How to Make a Monster 9-17-58
How to Make Good When One Is a Jerk and a Crybaby (See: Comment
    Reussir Quand On Est Con et Pleurnichard)
How to Marry a Millionaire 11-11-53
How to Murder a Rich Uncle 10-30-57
How to Murder Your Wife 1-20-65
How to Save a Marriage and Ruin Your Life 1-24-68
How to Seduce a Playboy (See: Bel Ami 2000--Oder--Wie Verfuehrt
    Man Einen Playboy)
How to Seduce a Woman 1-30-74
How to Steal a Million 7-13-66
How to Stuff a Wild Bikini 7-28-65
How to Succeed in Business Without Really Trying 2-15-67
How to Succeed in Love (See: Comment Reussir En Amour)
How to Succeed with Sex 3-18-70
How to Tame a Mother-in-Law 9-18-09
How Uncle Sam Prepares 4-20-17
How, When, With Whom (See: Come, Quando, Con Chi)
How Willingly You Sing 9-24-75
How Women Love 10-27-22
How Wonderful to Die Assassinated (See: Quanto E'Bello Lu Murire
    Accisco)
How Yukong Moved Mountains (See: Comment Yukong Deplace Les
    Montagnes)
Howards of Virginia, The 9-04-40
How's About It 2-03-43
Howzer 12-13-72
Hoy Mister Ako Ang Misis Mo 6-16-76
Hoyten 4-13-66
Hranjenik 8-12-70
Hry Lasky Salive 9-15-71
Hsi, Nou, Ai, Lueh 10-14-70
Hsia Yu-Yen 5-01-68
Hu-Man 10-22-75
Huadjai Ti Jom Din 4-25-79
Huck and Tom 3-08-18
Huckleberry Finn 2-27-20
Huckleberry Finn 8-11-31
Huckleberry Finn 2-15-39
Huckleberry Finn 4-03-74
Hucksters, The 7-02-47
Hud 5-08-63
Huddle 6-21-32

Hudson-Fulton Land Parade 10-09-09
Hudson-Fulton Military Parade 10-09-09
Hudson's Bay 12-25-40
Hue and Cry (See: Haro)
Hue and Cry 2-26-47
Huelga 10-04-67
Hugasan Mo Ang Aking Kasalaman 6-23-76
Hugo and Josefin (See: Hugo Och Josefin)
Hugo Och Josefin 3-06-68
Hugo the Hippo 7-14-76
Hugon the Mighty 11-29-18
Hugs and Kisses (See: Puss & Kram)
Huis Clos 2-09-55
Huitieme Jour, Le 7-20-60
Huk 8-08-56
Hula 8-31-27
Hulda from Holland 8-04-16
Hullabaloo 10-30-40
Hullabaloo over George and Bonnie's Pictures, The 10-24-79
Hum Dono 7-11-62
Human Adventure 10-21-36
Human Beast (See: Nikudan)
Human Beast, The (See: Bete Humaine, La)
Human Cargo 5-27-36
Human Comedy, The 3-03-43
Human Condition, The 12-30-59
Human Desire 8-11-54
Human Desires 1-28-25
Human Driftwood 4-07-16
Human Duplicators, The 5-19-65
Human Dutch, The (See: Alleman)
Human Experiments 2-13-80
Human Factor, The 11-05-75
Human Factor, The 12-19-79
Human Hearts 8-04-22
Human Jungle, The 9-15-54
Human Monster, The 3-27-40
Human Orchid, The 6-23-16
Human Pyramid (See: Pyramide Humaine, La)
Human Revolution, The 1-30-74
Human Side, The 9-18-34
Human Soul, The 8-14-14
Human Stuff 6-25-20
Human Targets 1-26-32
Human Torpedoes (See: Siluri Umani)
Human Vapor, The 5-27-64
Human Wolves 6-12-14
Human Wreckage 7-04-23
Humanity 4-25-33
Humanoids From the Deep 4-23-80
Humdrum Brown 4-12-18
Humeur Vagabonde, L' 9-22-71
Humming Bird 1-17-24
Humo en los Ojos 1-15-47
Humoresque 6-04-20
Humoresque 12-25-46
Humpback of Cedar Lodge, The 8-21-14
Humpbacked Horse, The (See: Konek Gorbunok)
Humphrey Takes a Chance 5-24-50
Hun Within, The 8-30-18
Hunch 12-23-21
Hunchback, The (See: Bossu, Le)
Hunchback, The 9-04-09
Hunchback, The 12-26-13
Hunchback of Notre Dame, The 9-06-23
Hunchback of Notre Dame, The 12-20-39
Hunchback of Notre Dame, The 11-06-57
Hunchback of Soho, The (See: Bucklige von Soho, Der)
Hunchback of the Morgue, The 5-16-73
Hunchback's Might 4-16-30
Hunchback's Night, The (See: Shabe Quzi)
Hunde, Wollts Ihr Ewig Leben 9-09-59
Hundred Days After Childhood, A (See: Sto Dnej Posle Detstwa)
Hundred Pound Window, The 12-08-43
Hungarian Nights 6-25-30
Hungarian Rhapsody 8-07-29
Hungarian Rhapsody and Allegro Barbaro (See: Magyar Rapszodia and Allegro Barbaro)
Hungarians, The (See: Magyarok)
Hunger (See: Sult or Pasi)
Hunger for Love (See: Fome de Amor)
Hunger Years (See: Hungerjahre)
Hungerjahre 3-05-80
Hungnam Story, The 3-21-51
Hungry Actor 8-21-09
Hungry Arms 8-25-26
Hungry Eyes 3-08-18
Hungry Heart, A 1-26-17

Hungry Heart, The 11-30-17
Hungry Hearts 12-01-22
Hungry Hill 1-15-47
Hungry Wives 4-18-73
Hunt, The 12-31-15
Hunt the Man Down 12-27-50
Hunted 3-05-52
Hunted, The 2-04-48
Hunted Men 5-18-38
Hunted People 10-17-28
Hunted Samurai, The 7-21-71
Hunted Woman, The 2-03-16
Hunter, The 7-30-80
Hunter of Fall, The (See: Jaeger von Fall, Der)
Hunters, The (See: Kynighi, I)
Hunters, The 8-06-58
Hunters of the Deep 12-15-54
Hunting Accident, A (See: Moi Laskoviy I Niejnie Zver)
Hunting Big Game 12-08-22 and 1-12-23
Hunting Flies (See: Polowanie Na Muchy)
Hunting Ground, The (See: Table Aux-Creves, La)
Hunting Jack Rabbits in Hungary 10-23-09
Hunting of the Hawk, The 4-06-17
Hunting Party 5-26-71
Hunting Scenes in Bavaria (See: Jagdszene aus Niederbayern)
Hunting Sea Lions in Tasmania 12-24-10
Hunting Shadows (See: Riskiton Varjossa)
Hunting the Lion with Bow and Arrow (See: Chasse au Lion a L'Arc, La)
Hunting the Panther 9-17-10
Hunting Tigers in India 12-11-29
Huntingtower 3-21-28
Huntress 10-11-23
Hurra, die Schule Brennt 3-11-70
Hurra--Ein Junge 11-10-31 and 6-28-32
Hurra for de Blaa Husarer 12-09-70
Hurra, Unsere Eltern Sind Nicht Da 9-30-70
Hurra, Wir Sind Mal Wieder Junggesellen 2-17-71
Hurrah--A Boy (See: Hurra--Ein Junge)
Hurrah, Our Parents Aren't There (See: Hurra, Unsere Eltern Sind Nicht Da)
Hurrah, the School Is Burning (See: Hurra, die Schule Brennt)
Hurray, a Boy (See: Hurra, Ein Junge)
Hurray, We Are Bachelors Again (See: Hurra, Wir Sind Mal Wieder Junggesellen)
Hurricane (See: Bao Feng Chou Yu)
Hurricane 5-12-26
Hurricane 10-30-29
Hurricane 4-04-79
Hurricane, The 11-10-37
Hurricane Horseman 11-17-31
Hurricane Hutch 4-16-24
Hurricane Island 7-11-51
Hurricane Kid, The 1-07-25
Hurricane Smith 2-04-42
Hurricane Smith 9-17-52
Hurricane's Gal 7-28-22
Hurry, Charlie, Hurry 7-09-41
Hurry Sundown 2-15-67
Hurry Tomorrow 12-03-75
Hurry Up, Or I'll Be 30 11-14-73
Husband and Wife (See: Marito E Moglie)
Husband and Wife 8-18-16
Husband by Proxy 6-13-28
Husband for Anna Zaccheo, A (See: Marito Per Anna Zaccheo, Un)
Husband-Hunter, The 11-12-20
Husband Hunters 2-23-27
Husbands 11-04-70
Husbands and Lovers 12-10-24
Husbands for Rent 7-04-28 and 7-25-28
Husband's Holiday 12-29-31
Husbands in the City (See: Mariti In Citta)
Husbands or Lovers 11-23-27
Husbands Vacationing (See: Maridos en Vacaciones)
Huset ved Havet 6-11-80
Hush 4-29-21
Hush ... Hush, Sweet Charlotte 12-23-64
Hush Money 11-25-21
Hush Money 7-14-31
Hussards, Les 2-08-56
Hussy, The (See: Drolesse, La)
Hussy 3-26-80
Hustle 12-24-75
Hustler, The 9-27-61
Hustler from Canton, The 9-29-76
Hustruer 8-27-75
Hutch of the U.S.A. 8-20-24
Hutch Stirs 'Em Up 8-30-23

Hvad Med Os? 10-21-64 (Also see: How About Us?)
Hvem Ska' Med Hvem? 6-23-71
Hvezda Putuje Na Jug 8-12-59
Hvor Er Liget, Moeller? 4-14-71
Hvorfor Goer De Det? 2-10-71
Hyah, Stine! (See: Hej, Stine!)
Hyde Park Corner 12-11-35
Hyena's Voyage, The (See: Touki-Bouki)
Hymn to a Tired Man (See: Nihon No Seishun)
Hypnotic Eye 1-20-60
Hypnotic Wife 9-04-09
Hypnotized 1-17-33
Hypnotizing Mother-in-Law 4-04-08
Hypochondriac, The (See: Malato Immaginario, Il)
Hypocrisy, The 6-16-16
Hypocrites, The 11-07-14
Hypothese du Tableau Vole, L' 3-07-79
Hypothesis of the Stolen Painting (See: Hypothese du Tableau
    Vole, L')
Hyppolit, A Lakaj 1-17-33
Hyppolite, the Lackey (See: Hyppolit, A Lakaj)
Hysteria 9-08-65

I

I, a Lover 1-31-68
I, a Man 8-30-67
I--a Woman (See: Jeg--En Kvinde)
I Accuse (See: J'Accuse)
I Accuse 10-14-21
I Accuse! 2-05-58
I Accuse My Parents 1-10-45
I Aim at the Stars 9-07-60
I Am a Camera 8-10-55
I Am a Criminal 3-01-39
I Am a Dancer 8-16-72
I Am a Delinquent (See: Soy Un Delincuente)
I Am a Fugitive from a Chain Gang 11-15-32
I Am a Thief 1-08-35
I Am an Elephant, Madame (See: Ich Bin einin Elefant, Madame)
I am Anna Magnani (See: Io Sono Anna Magnani)
I Am Curious--Tahiti 11-18-70
I Am Curious--Yellow (See: Jag Ar Nyfiken--Gul)
I Am from Siam 8-25-31
I Am Guilty 7-08-21
I Am Longing for You (See: Ich Sehne Mich Nach Dir)
I Am Looking for a Man (See: Ich Suche einen Mann)
I Am Looking for My Own (See: Isehu Cheloveka)
I Am Maria (See: Jag Ar Maria)
I Am Mexico (See: Soy Mexico)
I Am Not Afraid 4-05-39
I Am Pierre Riviere (See: Je Suis Pierre Riviere)
I Am Suzanne 1-23-34
I Am the Law 12-22-22
I Am the Law 8-31-38
I Am the Man 3-04-25
I Am What My Films Are (See: Was Ich Bin, Sind Meine Filme)
I Am With You (See: Jag Ar Med Eder)
I Am with You 3-02-49
I and My Wife (See: Ich und Meine Frau)
I and You (See: Ich und Du)
I Antarsia Ton Deka 11-11-70
I as in Icarus (See: I Comme Icare)
I Believe 6-29-17
I Believe in You (See: Tengo Fe en Ti)
I Believe in You 4-02-52
I Believed in You 4-17-34
I Belong to Me (See: Leg Er Sgu Min Egen or Io Sono Mia)
I Bombed Pearl Harbor 11-29-61
I Bury the Living 7-02-58
I By Day, You By Night (See: Ich Bei Tag, Du Bei Nacht)
I Came as a Stranger (See: Fremd Bin Ich Eigezogah)
I Can Explain 3-31-22
I Can Get It for You Wholesale 3-14-51
I Can't Escape 9-04-34
I Can't Give You Anything But Love, Baby 9-25-40
I Can't ... I Can't 10-01-69
I Care Not (See: Ich Will Nicht Wissen)
I Care Not Who You Are (See: Ich Will Nicht Wissen Wer Du Bist)
I Cheated the Law 1-12-49
I Chose Love (See: Ho Scelto L'Amore)
I Comme Icare 1-23-80

I Confess 2-11-53
I Conquer the Sea 1-29-36
I Corpi Presentano Tracce Di Violenza Carnale (See: Torso)
I Could Go On Singing 3-13-63
I Could Never Have Sex with Any Man Who Has So Little Regard
    for My Husband 7-25-73
I Cover Big Town 2-26-47
I Cover Chinatown 2-09-38
I Cover the Underworld 4-27-55
I Cover the War 7-07-37
I Cover the Waterfront 5-23-33
I Danced with Don Porfirio 9-22-43
I Deal in Danger 10-26-66
I Demand Payment 11-30-38
I Den Groenne Skov 4-10-68
I Den Store Pyramide 4-24-74
I Did It (See: Sono Stato Io)
I Did It (See: Voltam, En)
I Did It Three Times (See: Je L'Ai Ete Trois Fois)
I Did Kill Facundo (See: Yo Mate a Facundo)
I Died a Thousand Times 10-12-55
I Diki Ton Dikaston 11-06-74
I Din Fars Lomme 4-11-73
I Do 9-23-21
I Dodens Vantrum 7-31-46
I Don't Care Girl, The 12-24-52
I Don't Know You Any More (See: Non Ti Conosco Piu)
I Dood It 7-28-43
I Dream of Jeanie 6-11-52
I Dream Too Much 12-04-35
I Dreamt of Paradise (See: Ho Sognato il Paradiso)
I Escaped from Devil's Island 8-22-73
I Escaped from the Gestapo 4-21-43
I Even Met a Happy Gypsy (See: Sreo Sam Cak I Srecne Cigane)
I.F. 1 Doesn't Answer (See: I.F. 1 Ne Reponde Plus)
I.F. 1 Ne Reponde Plus 4-25-33
I Faresonen 7-12-61
I Fix America and Return (See: Sistemo L'America e Torno)
I Give My Heart 11-13-35 (Also see: Loves of Mme. Du Barry)
I Give My Love 7-24-34
I Go Out (See: Ich Geh' Aus)
I Go Out, You Stay Home (See: Ich Geh Aus, Du Bleibst Da)
I Had a Feeling I Was Dead (See: Ich Dachte, Ich Waere Tot)
I Had Seven Daughters (See: J'Avais Sept Filles)
I Haravgui Tis Nikis 11-03-71
I Hate My Body (See: Odio a Mi Cuerpo)
I Have Lived 9-12-33
I Have No Faith in Women 3-12-30
I Have Sinned (See: Al Chet)
I Have Two Mothers and Two Fathers (See: Imam Dvije Mame I Dva
    Tate)
I Hear Zato-Ichi Singing (See: Zato Ichi No Uta Ga Kikoeru)
I Huvet Paa en Gammal Gubbe 2-05-69
I, Jane Doe 5-19-48
I Jomfruens Tegn 8-01-73
I, Justice (See: Ja Spravedlnost)
I Katara Tis Manas 9-13-61
I Kill, You Kill (See: Io Uccido, Tu Uccidi)
I Killed Einstein, Gentlemen (See: Zabil Jsem Einsteina, Panove)
I Killed Geronimo 11-29-50
I Killed Rasputin (See: J'Ai Tue Rasputine)
I Killed That Man 2-18-42
I Killed the Count 5-17-39
I Killed Wild Bill Hickok 1-18-56
I Kiss Your Hand 8-30-32
I Knew Her Well (See: Io La Conoscevo Bene)
I Knew That Woman (See: Yo Conoci Esa Mujer)
I Know Where I'm Going 11-14-45 and 8-06-47
I Learned It from Father (See: Das Hab' Ich Von Papa Gelernt)
I Like It That Way 4-24-34
I Like Mike 1-18-61
I Like Your Nerve 9-15-31
I Live As I Please 1-29-47
I Live for Love 10-23-35
I Live for You 10-02-29
I Live in Danger 6-17-42
I Live in Fear (See: Ikimono No Kiroku)
I Live in Grosvenor Square 5-30-45
I Live My Life 10-16-35
I Lived with You 6-27-33
I Loevens Tegn 8-04-76
I Love a Bandleader 8-15-45
I Love a Mystery 2-28-45
I Love a Soldier 11-08-44
I Love Another (See: Jeg Elsker en Enden)
I Love Blue (See: Jeg Elsker Blat)
I Love Melvin 2-04-53
I Love My Country (See: Patrioten)

I Love My Home (See: Jesli Dorog Tebe Twoij Dom)
I Love My Wife 12-16-70
I Love That Man 7-11-33
I Love Trouble 12-24-47
I Love You (See: Je T'Aime or Jag Alskar Dig, Argbigga)
I Love You 1-11-18
I Love You Again 8-07-40
I Love You, Alice B. Toklas 8-28-68
I Love You ... But Why (See: Je T'Adore ... Mais Pourquoi)
I Love You, I Kill You (See: Ich Liebe Dich, Ich Toete Dich)
I Love You, I Love You (See: Je T'Aime, Je T'Aime)
I Love You I Love You Not (See: Amo Non Amo)
I Love You, Karlsson (See: Jag Elskar Dig, Karlsson)
I Love, You Love (See: Io Amo, Tu Ami or Jag Alskar, Du Alskar)
I Love You Me No Longer (See: Je T'Aime Moi Non Plus)
I Love You Only (See: Amo Te Sola)
I Love You Rosa (See: Ani Obev Otach Rosa)
I Loved a Woman 9-26-33
I Loved You Wednesday 6-20-33
I Married a Communist 9-21-49
I Married a Doctor 4-22-36
I Married a Monster from Outer Space 9-17-58
I Married a Spy 7-13-38
I Married a Witch 10-21-42
I Married a Woman 5-07-58
I Married Adventure 9-25-40
I Married an Angel 5-20-42
I Married for Love (See: Szerelembol Nosultem)
I, Maureen 9-20-78
I May See Her Once a Week (See: Hetenkint Egyszer Lathatom)
I Met a Murderer 3-15-39
I Met Him in Paris 6-09-37
I Met My Love Again 1-12-38
I Miss You, Hugs and Kisses 5-31-78
I, Mobster 1-14-59
I Morgen, Min Elskede 5-12-71
I Need a Mother (See: Necesito Una Madre)
I Need You So Much, Love (See: Te Necesito Tanto, Amor)
I Never Cried Like This Before (See: Kind Van De Zon)
I Never Promised You a Rose Garden 7-20-77
I Never Sang for My Father 10-21-70
I Only Asked 11-19-58
I Ora Tou Lykou 11-21-79
I Passed for White 3-02-60
I Promise to Pay 3-03-37
I Remember Mama 3-10-48
I Ring Doorbells 1-02-46
I-Ro-Ha-Ni-Ho-He-To 9-14-60
I Sao Untarai 1-19-77
I Saw Her First (See: Yo La Primero)
I Saw Jesus Die (See: Jeg Saa Jesus Doe)
I Saw What You Did 5-12-65
I See a Dark Stranger 7-10-46
I See Ice 2-23-38
I See This Land from Afar (See: Aus Der Ferne Sehe Ich Dieses
    Land)
I Sell Anything 1-01-35
I Sent a Letter to My Love (See: Chere Inconnue)
I Sette Dell' Orsa Maggiore 7-29-53
I Shot Billy the Kid 8-02-50
I Shot Jesse James 2-02-49
I Sing, I Cry 12-12-79
I, Sinner (See: Yo, Pecador)
I Slik en Natt 8-06-58
I Spheres Den Guyrizoun Pisso 11-01-67
I Spy 8-29-33
I Stand Accused 11-02-38
I Stand Condemned 7-08-36
I Start Counting 11-18-70
I Stole a Million 7-19-39
I Sua 5-11-77
I Surrender Dear 8-25-48
I Take This Oath 6-19-40
I Take This Woman 6-16-31
I Take This Woman 1-31-40
I Tembelides Tis Eforis Kiladas 8-23-78
I Thank a Fool 7-25-62
I Thank You 10-08-41
I, the Jury 7-22-53
I, Tintin (See: Moi, Tintin)
I, Too, Am Only a Woman (See: Ich Bin Auch Nur Eine Frau)
I Tvillingernes Tegn 7-30-75
I Tyrens Tegn 9-18-74
I Walk Alone 12-17-47
I Walk in Moscow 5-27-64
I Walk the Line 10-14-70
I Walked with a Zombie 3-17-43
I Wanna Hold Your Hand 4-19-78

I Want a Divorce 9-04-40
I Want a Solution (See: Orid Halla)
I Want My Man 4-08-25
I Want to Be a Chorus Girl (See: Yo Quiero Ser Bataclana)
I Want to Be a Mother 3-03-37
I Want to Be a Woman (See: Cambio De Sexo)
I Want to Die with You (See: Yo Quiero Morir Contigo)
I Want to Forget 12-20-18
I Want to Live (See: Ich Will Leben)
I Want to Live 10-29-58
I Want to Live with Joy (See: Boglio Vivere con Letizia)
I Want What I Want 3-01-72
I Want You 10-31-51
I Want You for Myself (See: Te Quiero Para Mi)
I Wanted Wings 3-26-41
I Was a Communist for the FBI 4-25-51
I Was a Convict 3-08-39
I Was a Male War Bride 8-10-49
I Was a Prisoner in Siberia 9-24-52
I Was a Prisoner on Devil's Island 7-30-41
I Was a Shoplifter 4-12-50
I Was a Spy 9-19-33 and 1-16-34
I Was a Teenage Frankenstein 1-01-58
I Was a Teenage Werewolf 7-10-57
I Was an Adventuress (See: J'Etais une Aventuriere)
I Was an Adventuress 5-01-40
I Was an American Spy 3-28-51
I Was Born in Buenos Aires (See: He Nacido en Buenos Aires)
I Was Born in Jerusalem (See: Ani Yerushalmi)
I Was Framed 4-08-42
I Was Happy Here 7-13-66
I Was Monty's Double 11-05-58
I Was 19 (See: Ich War 19)
I Will Give a Million (See: Daro' un Milione)
I Will Go Like a Wild Horse (See: J'Irai Comme un Cheval Fou)
I Will Go Spit on Your Graves (See: J'Irai Cracher Sur Vos
    Tombes)
I Will, I Will ... For Now 2-11-76
I Will Love You Always (See: Je Vous Aimerai Toujours)
I Will Repay 11-23-17
I Will Repay 3-12-24
I Win the War (See: Guerra la Gano Yo, La)
I Wonder Who's Kissing Her Now 6-11-47
I Wouldn't Be in Your Shoes 5-05-48
I, You, They (See: Je, Tu, Elles)
Ia Wa Kokyo O Koite 2-08-67
Ibis Rouge, L' 6-11-75
Ibo Kyodai 9-03-58
Ice 5-06-70
Ice-Age (See: Eiszeit)
Ice Castles 12-20-78
Ice Cold in Alex 7-09-58
Ice Continent, The (See: Continente Di Ghiaccio)
Ice Flood, The 10-27-26
Ice Follies of 1939 3-08-39
Ice Palace 6-15-60
Ice Station Zebra 10-23-68
Icebound 3-05-24
Ice-Capades 8-20-41
Ice-Capades Revue 12-16-42
Iced Bullet, The 1-05-17
Iceland 8-12-42
Iceland Fisherman (See: Pecheur d'Islande)
Iceman Cometh, The 10-24-73
Ich Bei Tag, Du Bei Nacht 1-03-33
Ich Bin Auch Nur eine Frau 1-02-63
Ich Bin ein Antistar 4-27-77
Ich Bin ein Elefant, Madame 4-09-69
Ich Dachte, Ich Waere Tot 7-02-75
Ich Geh' Aus 4-29-31
Ich Geh Aus, Du Bleibst Da 11-29-32
Ich Glaub Nie Mehr An eine Frau 10-24-33 (Also see: I Have No
    Faith in Women)
Ich Liebe Dich, Ich Toete Dich 5-19-71
Ich Sehne Mich Nach Dir 9-09-36
Ich Suche einen Mann 3-16-66
Ich und die Kaiserin 4-04-33
Ich und Du 3-10-54
Ich und Meine Frau 9-23-53
Ich War 19 6-19-68
Ich Werde Dich Auf Haenden Tragen 4-01-59
Ich Will Leben 7-27-77
Ich Will Nicht Wissen 10-18-32
Ich Will Nicht Wissen Wer Du Bist 2-21-23
Ich Zwing Dich Zu Leben 6-28-78
Ichijo Sayuri: Nureta Yokujo 1-16-74
Ichijo Sayuri: Wet Desire (See: Ichijo Sayuri: Nureta Yokujo)
Iconoclast, The 10-08-10

Iconoclast, The 3-14-13
Iconostasis 10-14-70
Icy Breasts (See: Seins de Glace, Les)
I'd Climb the Highest Mountain 1-17-51
I'd Give My Life 8-19-36
I'd Like to Have My Troubles (See: Meine Sorgen Moecht' Ich
    Haben)
I'd Rather Be Rich 7-29-64
Ida Regenye 4-24-34
Idaho 2-17-43
Idaho Kid 8-04-37
Idaho Red 4-24-29
Idaho Transfer 3-26-75
Idea Girl 2-06-46
Ideal Couple (See: Couple Ideal, Le)
Ideal Husband, An 11-26-47
Ideal Husband, The (See: Idealer Gatte, Ein)
Ideal Woman, The (See: Ideale Frau, Die)
Ideal Woman, The 6-12-29
Ideal Woman Sought (See: Ideale Frau Gesucht)
Ideale Frau, Die 9-23-59
Ideale Frau Gesucht 11-05-52
Idealer Gatte, Ein 1-13-37
Idealist 8-18-76
Identification Marks: None (See: Rysopis)
Identikit 5-29-74
Identite Judiciaire 5-09-51
Identity Unknown 4-04-45
Idi Amin Dada (See: General Idi Amin Dada)
Idiot, L' 6-26-46 and 2-04-48
Idiot, The (See: Makuchi)
Idiot, The 8-05-59
Idiot a Paris, Un 4-05-67
Idiot in Paris, An (See: Idiot a Paris, Un)
Idiot's Delight 1-25-39
Idle Class, The 9-30-21
Idle Hands 6-10-21
Idle on Parade 4-01-59
Idle Rich, The 2-17-22
Idle Rich, The 6-19-29
Idle Tongues 3-11-25
Idle Wives 9-22-16
Idler, The 1-01-15
Ido Zero Daisakusen 9-17-69
Idol, The (See: Pajarito Gomez)
Idol, The 11-05-15
Idol, The 8-03-66
Idol Dancer 3-26-20
Idol of Paris 3-10-48
Idol of the Crowds 12-08-37
Idol of the North 5-20-21
Idol of the Stage, The 2-11-16
Idol of Vienna, The (See: Liebling von Wien, Der)
Idolators 9-07-17
Idoles, Les 5-08-68
Idolmaker, The 11-05-80
Idols, The (See: Idoles, Les)
Idols of Clay 11-19-20
Idu Dani 8-12-70
Idyl in Cairo, An (See: Idylle Au Caire)
Idylle Au Caire 7-25-33
If ... 12-11-68
If a Man Answers 8-29-62
If All the Guys in the World (See: Si Tous Les Gars du Monde ...)
If Ever I See You Again 5-17-78
If He Hollers, Let Him Go 10-02-68
If I Had a Girl (See: Keby Som Mal Dievca)
If I Had a Gun (See: Keby Som Mal Puska)
If I Had a Million 12-06-32
If I Had a Million Rubles 4-24-74
If I Had Four Dromedaries (See: Si J'Avais Quatre Dromadaires)
If I Had My Way 5-01-40
If I Marry Again 1-14-25
If I Were a Millionaire (See: Si Yo Fuera Milleonario)
If I Were a Queen 11-17-22
If I Were a Spy or Breakdown (See: Si J'Etais un Espion ou
    Breakdown)
If I Were Free 1-09-34
If I Were King 7-30-15
If I Were King 7-02-20
If I Were King 9-21-38
If I Were Rich (See: Si Yo Fuera Rica)
If I Were Single 12-28-27 and 3-07-28
If I'm Lucky 8-28-46
If It Doesn't Come from Your Heart (See: Markers, Staakt Uw Wild
    Geraas)
If It Were To Do Over Again (See: Si C'Etait a Refaire)
If It's Tuesday, This Must Be Belgium 4-09-69
If Marriage Fails 6-03-25
If Moscow Strikes 5-07-52
If Music Be the Food of Love (See: Nedtur)
If Only Jim 3-18-21

If Paris Were Told to Us (See: Si Paris Nous Etait Conte)
If Pigs Had Wings (See: Porci Con Le Ali)
If the Emperor Only Knew (See: Si l'Empereur Savait Ca)
If the Emperor Only Knew That (See: Si l'Empereur Savait Ca)
If the Wind Frightens You (See: Si le Vent Te Fait Peur)
If This Be Sin 6-28-50
If Versailles Were Told to Me (See: Si Versailles M'Etait Conte)
If War Comes Tomorrow 7-20-38
If Winter Comes 3-08-23
If Winter Comes 12-24-47
If You Believe It It's So 7-14-22
If You Could Only Cook 1-01-36
If You Knew Susie 2-04-48
If You Play with Crazy Birds (See: Spielst Du Mit Schraegen
    Voegeln)
If You Wish It (See: Si Tu Veux)
If You Work Hard, You'll Eat Soup (See: Kung May Tiyaga, May
    Nilaga)
If Your Heart Can Feel (See: Jesli Msz Serce Bijace)
Igdenbu 12-17-30
Igen 7-15-64
Igloi Diakok 4-03-35
Igloo 7-26-32
Igy Joettem 8-31-66 and 11-30-66
Ihr Schoenster Tag 5-09-62
Ihre Hoheit Befiehlt 3-25-31 and 11-10-31
Ihre Majestaet die Liebe 1-28-31
Ija Ominira 9-05-79
Ikari No Koto 8-06-58
Ikarie XB 1 7-24-63
Ikaru 5-15-57
Ikarus 6-13-79
Ikimono No Kiroku 9-18-63
Il ... Bel Paese 1-18-78
Il Est Charmant 3-15-32 and 4-12-32
Il Est Minuit Dr. Schweitzer 12-10-52
Il Etait une Fois dans l'Est 5-15-74
Il Etait une Fois un Flic 3-01-72
Il Faut Vivre Dangereusement 9-10-75
Il Fu Mattia Pascal 3-31-37
Il Ne Faut Pas Mourir pour Ca 7-17-68
Il N'Y A Pas de Fumee 5-30-73
Il N'Y A Pas d'Oubli 8-25-76
Il Pleut sur Santiago 12-10-75
Il Pleut Toujours Ou C'Est Mouille 6-12-74
Il Sont Nus (See: We Are All Naked)
Il Suffit d'Aimer 9-14-60
Il Suffit d'une Fois 12-04-46
Il Y A Longtemps Que Je T'Aime 9-05-79
Il Y A un Train Toutes les Heures 7-04-62
Ile du Bout du Monde, L' 3-25-59
Ile Mysterieuse, L' 11-28-73
Ileksen 3-28-79
Iles Enchantees, Les 5-12-65
I'll Be Seeing You 12-20-44
I'll Be Your Sweetheart 7-11-45
I'll Be Yours 1-22-47
I'll Carry You On My Hands (See: Ich Werde Dich auf Haenden
    Tragen)
I'll Cry Tomorrow 12-21-55
I'll Find You Again (See: Ti Ritrovera)
I'll Fix It 11-20-34
I'll Force You to Live (See: Ich Zwing Dich Zu Leben)
I'll Get Back to Kandara (See: Je Reviendrai a Kandara)
I'll Get By 9-27-50
I'll Get Him Yet 5-23-19
I'll Get You 2-04-53
I'll Give a Million 7-13-38
I'll Go to the Minister (See: Felmegyek A Ministerhez)
I'll Love You Always 4-03-35
I'll Love You Tomorrow (See: Prong Nee Chan Ja Rak Koon)
Ill Met by Moonlight 3-20-57
I'll Never Believe in Women Again (See: Ich Glaub Nie Mehr an
    Eine Frau)
I'll Never Forget You 12-12-51
I'll Never Forget What's 'Is Name 12-27-67
I'll Remember April 4-18-45
I'll Say So 1-10-19
I'll See You in My Dreams 12-12-51
I'll Show You the Town 6-10-25
I'll Take Happiness (See: Helle For Lykke)
I'll Take Her Like a Father (See: Faro Da Padre, Le)
I'll Take Romance 12-22-37
I'll Take Sweden 6-02-65
I'll Tell the World 4-24-34
Ill-Tempered Minister, The 12-04-09
I'll Wait for You 5-14-41
Illegal 10-04-23
Illegal 8-31-55
Illegal, The (See: Alambrista)
Illegal Border (See: Suendige Grenze, Die
Illegal Entry 6-08-49

118

Illegal Traffic 11-23-38
Illegals, The 7-07-48
Illegitimate Child (See: Enfant de l'Amour, L')
Illiac Passion, The 1-17-68
Illicit 1-21-31
Illiterate One, The (See: Analfabeto, El)
Illuminacja 8-22-73
Illumination (See: Illuminacja)
Illuminations 6-16-76
Illusion (See: Iluzija or Iluzia)
Illusion 10-02-29
Illusion of Blood 3-09-66 (Also see: Yotsuya Kwaidan)
Illusions of a Lady 1-30-74
Illustrated Man, The 2-19-69
Illustrious Prince, The 11-21-19
Ils 12-23-70
Ils Etaient Neuf Celibataires 12-27-39
Ils Sont Fous Ces Sorciers 8-02-78
Ils Sont Grands Ces Petits 4-04-79
Ilse--Harem Keeper of the Oil Sheiks 2-18-76
Iluvia Roja 3-08-50
Iluzia 7-23-80
Iluzija 8-16-67
Ilya Mourometz 8-05-59
I'm a Real Mexican (See: Soy Puro Mexicano)
I'm a Stranger Here Myself 10-09-74
I'm a Woman Already (See: Ya Soy Mujer)
I'm All Right, Jack 8-19-59
I'm an Anti-Star (See: Ich Bin Ein Antistar)
Im Bann des Eulenspiegels 1-17-33
I'm Curious--Blue (See: Jag ar Nyfiken--Blaa)
I'm Expecting (See: Jag Aer Med Barn)
Im Feuer Bestanden 9-26-79
I'm from Missouri 3-22-39
I'm from the City 8-10-38
Im Geheimdienst 9-01-31 and 12-08-31
I'm Going to Get You ... Elliot Boy 10-06-71
Im Herzen des Hurrican 4-02-80
I'm in the Revue (See: Je Suis de la Revue)
Im Lauf der Zeit 3-17-76
I'm Married, Ha Ha (See: Estoy Casada, Ja Ja)
Im Namen des Volkes 7-10-74
I'm No Angel 10-17-33
I'm Nobody's Sweetheart Now 8-07-40
I'm Not Mata Hari (See: Yo No Soy La Mata Hari)
I'm Photogenic (See: Sono Fotogenico)
Im Pokoriaetsa Nebo 7-31-63
I'm Poor But Angry (See: Siroma Sam Al'Sam Besan)
Im Prater Blueh'n Wieder die Baeume 9-17-58
I'm Still Alive 10-02-40
I'm Timid But I'm Treating It (See: Je Suis Timide Mais Je Me
    Soigne)
I'm Twenty (See: Mne Dvatsat Let)
Image, L' 2-04-76
Image, Flesh and Voice 2-25-70
Image Maker, The 2-09-17
Image of Love 12-23-64
Images 5-10-72
Imagination (See: Kalpana)
Imago 9-30-70
Imam Dvije Mame I Dva Tate 8-14-68
Imbarco a Mezzanotte 5-28-52
Imeres Tou 36 11-15-72
Imi Hageneralit 6-20-79
Imitation General 6-26-58
Imitation of Christ 2-04-70
Imitation of Life 11-27-34
Imitation of Life 2-04-59
Immacolata and Concetta: The Other Jealousy (See: Immacolata e
    Concetta: L'Altra Gelosia)
Immacolata e Concetta: L'Altra Gelosia 5-21-80
Immaculate, The 12-13-50
Immediate Call (See: Rappel Immediat)
Immediate Lee 11-17-16
Immer Aerger mit den Paukern 1-15-69
Immigrant, The 12-31-15
Immigrant, The 6-22-17
Immigrants (See: Emigrantes)
Immoral Mr. Teas, The 1-27-60
Immoral Tales (See: Contes Immoraux)
Immorale, L' 5-17-67
Immoralist, The (See: Immorale, L')
Immortal, The (See: Immortelle, L')
Immortal Face 10-22-47
Immortal Flame, The 3-10-16
Immortal Garrison, The 4-03-57
Immortal Love (See: Eien No Hito)
Immortal Melodies (See: Unsterbliche Melodien or Melodie Immortali)

Immortal Sergeant 1-13-43
Immortal Story, An (See: Histoire Immortelle, Une)
Immortal Vagabond, The 3-26-30 and 8-04-31
Immortalita 9-17-69
Immortality (See: Immortalita)
Immortals of Scotland 12-21-27
Immortelle, L' 5-08-63
Imp of the Bottle, The 11-20-09
Impaciencia Del Corazon 3-09-60
Impact 3-16-49
Impasse (See: Honoo To Onna)
Impasse 2-12-69
Impatient Heart (See: Impaciencia Del Corazon)
Impatient Maiden 3-08-32
Impatient Years, The 8-23-44
Imperatore di Capri, L' 3-29-50
Imperfect Lady, The 3-12-47
Imperial Singing Pictures 5-15-14
Imperial Venus (See: Venere Imperiale)
Impero Del Sole, L' 9-12-56
Impersonator, The 4-17-14
Impersonator's Joke 11-07-08
Importance of Being Earnest, The 6-18-52
Important C'Est D'Aimer, L' 2-12-75
Important Witness, The 9-26-33
Impossible Catherine 10-10-19
Impossible Goodbye, The (See: Dom Bez Okien)
Impossible Is Not French (See: Impossible Pas Francais)
Impossible Mrs. Bellew 10-27-22
Impossible Object 5-23-73
Impossible on Saturday (See: Pas Question le Samedi)
Impossible Pas Francais 12-25-74
Impossible Years, The 11-27-68
Imposter, The (See: Impostor, El)
Imposter, The 9-10-15
Imposter, The 1-25-18
Imposter, The 2-09-44
Imposter, The 3-30-55
Imposters (See: Imposztorok)
Imposters 11-21-79
Impostor, El 8-31-60
Imposztorok 2-26-69
Impotence (See: Xala)
Imprecateur, L' 9-14-77
Impressionable Years, The 3-26-52
Imprevisto, L' 5-17-61
Imprint of Giants, The (See: Empreinte des Geants, L')
Improper Duchess, The 2-12-36
Improvised Son, The (See: Fils Improvist, Le)
Impures, Les 4-20-55
In a Lonely Place 5-17-50
In a Monastery Garden 3-20-35
In a Pinch 6-13-19
In a Wild Moment (See: Moment D'Egarement, Un)
In a Year of 13 Moons (See: In einem Jahr mit 13 Monden)
In Africa 4-23-10
In Again--Out Again 4-27-17
In All Intimacy (See: In Alle Stilte)
In Alle Stilte 5-03-78
In Amanullah's Land 7-03-29
In Ancient Greece 2-19-10
In Arabia 12-15-22
In Bad 2-01-18
In Bed--In Bad 9-21-17
In Berlin's Underworld 2-12-30
In Burning Darkness (See: En la Ardiente Obscuriadad)
In Caliente 7-03-35
In Calvert's Valley 1-12-23
In Capo Al Mondo 9-04-63
In Case of Accident (See: En Cas de Malheur)
In Celebration 1-22-75
In Cold Blood (See: A Sangre Fria)
In Cold Blood 12-13-67
In Defense of a Nation 6-25-15
In Defiance of the Law 8-07-14
In den Klauen des Goldenen Drachen 1-18-67
In der Fremde 7-16-75
In Disagreement (See: U Raskoraku)
In Early Arizona 12-28-38
In einem Jahr mit 13 Monden 3-07-79
In Enemy Country 5-22-68
In Extreme Blows of Fate The Just Milieu Brings Death (See: In
    Gefahr Groesster Not Bringt Der Mittelweg Den Tod)
In Face of the World (See: Urok Istoriji)
In Fast Company 6-11-24
In Fast Company 7-24-46
In Folly's Trail 9-03-20

In for 30 Days 1-31-19
In for Treatment 3-05-80
In Full Cry 1-07-11
In Gay Madrid 6-11-30
In Gefahr Groesster Not Bringt Der Mittelweg Den Tod 8-27-75
In God We Trust 10-01-80
In Harm's Way 3-31-65
In His Grip 7-22-21
In His Steps 11-04-36
In Hollywood 10-01-24
In Honor's Web 11-21-19
In Hot Pursuit 9-11-09
In Jenen Tagen (See: In Those Days)
In Judgment Of 8-30-18
In Kluis 2-01-78
In-Laws, The 6-13-79
In Life's Cycle 9-24-10
In Like Flint 3-15-67
In Love and War 10-29-58
In Love, But Doubly 7-06-60
In Love, Every Pleasure Has Its Pain (See: Betia, La)
In Love with Life 5-29-34
In MacArthur Park 4-06-77
In Memorium 9-21-77
In Missoura 10-17-19
In Moment of Temptation 10-12-27
In Morocco 4-04-08
In My Life (See: Honningmane)
In Name Only 8-09-39
In Nome Del Padre 10-20-71
In Nome Del Papa Re 3-22-78
In Nome Del Popolo Italiano 12-29-71
In Nome Della Legge 4-13-49
In Old Amarillo 5-23-51
In Old Arizona 1-23-29
In Old Caliente 7-12-39
In Old California 6-10-42
In Old Cheyenne 6-23-31
In Old Cheyenne 4-16-41
In Old Chicago 1-05-38
In Old Colorado 2-26-41
In Old Kentucky 9-25-09
In Old Kentucky 1-03-20
In Old Kentucky 11-23-27 and 12-14-27
In Old Kentucky 12-04-35
In Old Mexico 9-28-38
In Old Missouri 5-01-40
In Old Monterey 8-09-39
In Old New Mexico 8-08-45
In Old Oklahoma 10-27-43
In Old Sacramento 5-01-46
In Old Santa Fe 3-20-35
In Old Siberia 7-24-29
In Olden Days (See: Altri Tempi)
In Our Time 2-02-44
In Parterre Links 4-17-63
In Person 12-18-35
In Praise of Older Women 9-20-78
In Prison Awaiting Trial (See: Detenuto In Attesa Di Guidizio)
In Punto Di Morte 9-01-71
In Pursuit of Polly 9-06-18
In Search of a Sinner 3-12-20
In Search of a Thrill 11-22-23
In Search of Anna 5-31-78
In Search of Dracula 5-21-75
In Search of Gregory 5-13-70
In Search of Hidden River 7-21-26
In Search of Historic Jesus 1-30-80
In Search of Noah's Ark 2-09-77
In Search of the Castaways 5-15-14
In Search of the Castaways 11-21-62
In Secret Service (See: Im Geheimdienst)
In Slumberland 7-27-17
In Soldier's Uniform (See: Bakaruhaban)
In Spite of Danger 4-10-35
In Such Times as These (See: En Dias Come Estos)
In the Affirmative (See: Avec Des Si)
In the Balance 1-04-18
In the Claws of the Golden Dragon (See: In den Klauen des Goldenen Drachen)
In the Coney Island of Hamburg at 12:30 (See: Hamburg at 12:30)
In the Consomme 12-04-09
In the Cool of the Day 5-15-63
In the Course of Time (See: Im Lauf Der Zeit)
In the Current (See: Sodrasban)
In the Days of St. Patrick (See: Days of St. Patrick)
In the Days of the Thundering Herd (See: Thundering Herd, The)
In the Diplomatic Service 10-20-16

In the Doghouse 12-27-61
In the Driver's Seat (See: Sarten Por El Mango, La)
In the Far East 10-27-37
In the First Degree 11-23-27
In the French Style 9-18-63
In the Good Old Summertime 6-29-49
In the Gorge (See: Na Klancu)
In the Gray of the Dawn 10-15-10
In the Green of the Woods (See: I Den Groenne Skov)
In the Heart of a Fool 5-06-21
In the Heart of the Hurricane (See: Im Herzen des Hurrican)
In the Heat of the Night 6-21-67
In the Hollow of Her Hand 1-03-19
In the Kingdom of Heaven (See: Au Royaume des Cieux)
In the Land of Monkeys and Snakes 1-14-11
In the Land of the Gold Mines 5-02-08
In the Line of Duty 4-10-14
In the Line of Duty 2-09-32
In the Lion's Jaw 9-19-14
In the Lost City of Sarzana (See: Nella Citta' Perduta di Sarzana)
In the Meantime, Darling 9-20-44
In the Midst of Life (See: Au Coeur de la Vie)
In the Mission of the Shadow 9-24-10
In the Money 1-09-34
In the Morning at 7, the World Is Still in Order (See: Morgens um 7 Ist Die Welt Noch In Ordnung)
In the Mouth of the World (See: Na Boca do Mundo)
In the Name of Life 10-22-47
In the Name of Love 8-26-25
In the Name of the Father (See: In Nome del Padre)
In the Name of the Fuhrer (See: Au Nom Du Fuhrer)
In the Name of the Italian People (See: In Nome Del Popolo Italiano)
In the Name of the Law (See: In Nome Della Legge or Au Nom de la Loi)
In the Name of the Law 7-14-22
In the Name of the People (See: Im Namen Des Volkes)
In the Name of the Pope King (See: In Nome Del Papa Re)
In the Name of the Race (See: Au Nom de la Race)
In the Navy 6-04-41
In the Next Room 4-09-30
In the Nick 7-20-60
In the Nick of Time 1-22-10
In the Palace of the King 10-01-15
In the Serpent's Power 2-12-10
In the Shadow of Old Mount Shasta 2-19-10
In the Shadow of the Cliffs 3-19-10
In the Shadow of the Harem (See: Dans l'Ombre du Harem)
In the Shadow of the Past (See: Teni Zabytykh Predkov)
In the Sign of Gemini (See: I Tvillingernes Tegn)
In the Sign of the Lion (See: I Loevens Tegn)
In the Sign of the Taurus (See: I Tyrens Tegn)
In the Sign of the Virgin (See: I Jomfruens Tegn)
In the Soviet Union 6-01-55
In the Spreewald 10-29-10
In the Stretch 6-26-14
In the Summertime (See: Durante L'Estate)
In the Torrid Wind (See: Con El Viento Solano)
In the Town of "S" (See: Ionytch)
In the Wake of a Stranger 4-13-60
In the Wake of Bounty 5-02-33
In the West 2-21-24
In the Woods (See: Rasho Mon)
In the Year of the Lord (See: Nell'Anno Del Signore)
In the Year of the Pig 3-12-69
In the Years of Famine 6-11-15
In This Corner 9-01-48
In This Our Life 4-08-42
In Those Days 8-13-47
In Town Tonight 2-12-35
In Walked Mary 3-12-20
In Which We Serve 10-07-42
In Wrong 12-19-19
In Your Dad's Pocket (See: I Din Fars Lomme)
Inadmissible Evidence 7-03-68
Inbreaker, The 6-26-74
Incantesimo Tragico 1-23-52
Incendiary Blonde 6-13-45
Incident 12-29-48
Incident, The (See: Jiken)
Incident, The 11-08-67
Incident at Phantom Hill 6-08-66
Incognito (See: Inkognito)
Incognito 5-28-58
Incomparable Bellairs 2-19-15
Incompreso 5-10-67
Inconnu de Shandigor, L' 5-03-67
Inconnue d'Hong Kong, L' 8-21-63

121

Inspector Sergil (See: Inspecteur Sergil, L')
Inspiration 11-05-15
Inspiration 6-06-28
Inspiration 2-11-31
Institution, The (See: Anstalt, Die)
Insurance Investigator 3-21-51
Insurrection, The 7-30-15
Intelligence Man, The 4-21-65
Intelligence Service (See: Deuxieme Bureau)
Intent to Kill 7-23-58
Interdit au Public 1-25-50
Interference 11-21-28
Interior Mechanism (See: Mecanismo Interior)
Interior of a Convent (See: Interno D'Un Convento)
Interiors 8-02-78
Interloper, The 5-24-18
Interlude (See: Intermezzo)
Interlude 5-08-57
Interlude 6-26-68
Intermediate Landing in Paris (See: Zwischenlandung in Paris)
Intermezzo 11-25-36
Intermezzo 12-29-37
Intermezzo 10-04-39
Intermittent Alarm Clock 2-01-08 and 4-04-08
Internado Para Senoritas 5-10-44
International Burlesque 11-29-50
International Crime 5-18-38
International Forum 2-26-41
International House 5-30-33
International Lady 10-15-41
International Police 4-10-57
International Settlement 1-26-38
International Squadron 8-13-41
International Velvet 6-28-78
Internationalists (See: Csillagosok, Katonak)
Internecine Project, The 10-02-74
Internes Can't Take Money 5-12-37
Interno D'Un Convento 8-02-78
Interns, The 6-13-62
Interpol Calling Lima 3-19-69
Interrupted Honeymoon, An 3-19-10
Interrupted Journey, The 10-19-49
Interrupted Melody 3-30-55
Interval 6-20-73
Interview, The 8-16-72
Intill Helvetets Portar 12-15-48
Intimate Lighting (See: Intimi Osvetlani)
Intimate Relations 3-25-53
Intimi Osvetlani 8-03-66
Into Her Kingdom 8-11-26
Into No Man's Land 7-25-28
Into the Blue 1-10-51
Into the Primitive 5-26-16
Into the Shadow 11-13-09
Into the Straight 1-18-50
Intoarcerea Lui Voda Lupusneanu 10-15-80
Intoccabili, Gli 5-28-69
Intolerance 9-08-16
Intramuros 7-29-64
Intransigents, The (See: Neprimirimite)
Intrigantes, Les 5-19-54
Intrigue 12-24-47
Intrigue, An 1-14-11
Intrigue, The 10-13-16
Intrigue, The 4-07-22
Introduce Me 3-11-25
Introduction to Anthropology, An (See: Jinrui Gaku Nyumon)
Introduction to Life (See: Vstuplenjie)
Introduction to the Enemy 3-12-75
Intruder, The (See: Intruso, El)
Intruder, The 4-25-33
Intruder, The 11-04-53
Intruder, The 5-23-62
Intruder in the Dust 10-12-49
Intruders, The (See: Intrus, Les)
Intrus, Les 3-01-72
Intrusion of Isabel 4-04-19
Intruso, El 4-18-45
Inundados, Los 9-05-62
Invaders, The 11-20-29
Invaders From Mars 4-08-53
Invasion (See: Invasione)
Invasion, L' 11-18-70
Invasion of the Body Snatchers 2-29-56
Invasion of the Body Snatchers 12-20-78
Invasion of the Love Drones 12-07-77
Invasion of the Saucer Men 7-10-57
Invasion Quartet 8-30-61

Invasion U.S.A. 12-10-52
Invasione 10-29-69
Inventor, The (See: Erfinder, Der)
Invenzione di Morel, L' 9-25-74
Investigator and the Woods, The (See: Sledovateliat y Gozato)
Invisible Adversaries (See: Unsichtbare Gegner)
Invisible Agent 8-05-42
Invisible Army 6-28-50
Invisible Boy, The 10-16-57
Invisible Chain, The 4-21-16
Invisible Enemy 4-13-38
Invisible Enemy, The 4-14-16
Invisible Fear 3-31-22
Invisible Front, The (See: Unsichtbare Front)
Invisible Ghost 5-14-41
Invisible Informer 8-21-46
Invisible Invaders 5-13-59
Invisible Killer, The 2-07-40
Invisible Man, The 11-21-33
Invisible Man Returns 1-17-40
Invisible Man's Revenge 6-07-44
Invisible Menace 1-26-38
Invisible Power 9-30-21
Invisible Ray, The 1-15-36
Invisible Stripes 1-03-40
Invisible Wall 10-15-47
Invisible Web 8-05-21
Invisible Woman, The 1-01-41
Invitation 1-23-52
Invitation, L' 5-16-73
Invitation to a Gunfighter 10-21-64
Invitation to Happiness 5-10-39
Invitation to Monte Carlo 8-26-59
Invitation to the Dance 5-16-56
Invitation to the Waltz 10-30-35
Invite de la 11me Heure, L' 10-10-45
Invite du Mardi, L' 11-01-50
Invited One, The (See: Invitee, L')
Invited Out 5-11-17
Invitee, L' 11-26-69
Io Amo, Tu Ami 5-03-61
Io, Io, Io ... e Gli Altri 4-06-66
Io La Conoscevo Bene 2-06-66
Io Sono Anna Magnani 11-05-80
Io Sono Mia 3-15-78
Io Uccido, Tu Uccidi 6-09-65
Ioannis Ofvieos 11-28-73
Ionytch 6-19-68
Ipcress File, The 3-24-65
Iphighenia 5-25-77
Iracema 5-19-76
Ireland, A Nation 10-10-14
Ireland in Revolt 1-14-21
Ireland's Border Line 11-01-39
Irene 3-03-26
Irene 4-24-40
Irene in Need (See: Irene in Noeten)
Irene in Noeten 9-09-53
Irezumi Ichidai 1-02-74
Irgok 8-16-72
Iris 9-11-68
Iris Och Lojtnantshjarta 1-01-47
Irish and Proud of It 11-02-38
Irish Boy, The 3-26-10
Irish Destiny 4-13-27
Irish Eyes Are Smiling 10-04-44
Irish Hearts 5-18-27
Irish in Us, The 8-07-35
Irish Luck 11-25-25
Irish Luck 11-15-39
Irish Scenes and Types 1-18-08
Irishman, The 5-10-78
Irma La Douce 6-05-63
Iro (See: Spoils of the Night)
Iron Buffalo, The (See: Ai Kwai Legg)
Iron Cross, The (See: A Cruz De Ferro)
Iron Crown, The 6-15-49
Iron Curtain, The 5-12-48
Iron Duke, The 12-18-34 and 1-29-35
Iron Flower (See: Vasvirag)
Iron Glove 3-24-54
Iron Heart, The 6-11-20
Iron Horse, The 9-03-24
Iron Justice 7-09-15
Iron Maiden, The 12-26-62
Iron Major, The 10-20-43
Iron Man (See: Vasember)
Iron Man 4-22-31

Iron Man 7-04-51
Iron Mask 2-27-29
Iron Mask, The (See: Masque de Fer, Le)
Iron Master 2-07-33
Iron Mistress, The 10-22-52
Iron Mountain Trail 5-27-53
Iron Petticoat, The 7-11-56
Iron Prefect, The (See: Prefetto di Ferro, Il)
Iron Ring, The 7-27-17
Iron Sheriff, The 4-24-57
Iron Strain, The 10-01-15
Iron Trail 11-04-21
Iron Test, The 10-18-18
Iron Test, No. 3, The 10-25-18
Iron Woman, The 10-13-16
Ironie du Sort, L' 5-29-74
Ironmaster, The (See: Maitre de Forges, Le)
Irony of Chance (See: Ironie du Sort, L')
Iroquois Trail, The 6-07-50
Irreconcilable Memories (See: Unversoehnliche Errinnerungen)
Irrer Duft von Frischem Heu, Ein 6-28-78
Irresistible Lover, The 10-26-27
Irrwege dere Leidenschaft (See: Labyrinth of Passion, A)
Is Any Girl Safe? 9-08-16
Is Divorce a Failure? 5-30-23
Is Everybody Happy? 11-06-29
Is Everybody Happy? 11-24-43
Is It Love (See: Sei Tu L'Amore)
Is Love Everything 3-04-25
Is Matrimony a Failure? 4-21-22
Is Money Everything? 4-26-23
Is My Face Red? 6-14-32
Is Paris Burning? 10-26-66
Is That Nice 5-25-27
Is There Justice? 9-22-31
Is There Sex After Death? 11-03-71
Is This "Fate"? (See: Von Wegen "Schicksal")
Is Your Daughter Safe? 6-15-27
Is Your Honeymoon Really Necessary 9-30-52
Is Zat So? 5-18-27
Isabel 7-24-68
Isabelle A Peur des Hommes 12-04-57
Isabelle and Lust (See: Isabelle Devant le Desir)
Isabelle Devant le Desir 2-26-75
Isabelle Is Afraid of Men (See: Isabelle A Peur des Hommes)
Isadora 12-25-68
Isang Gabi Sa Buhay Ng Isang Babae 6-23-76
Isang Gabi, Tatlong Babae 2-12-75
Isehu Cheloveka 8-29-73
Iskanja 9-05-79
Iskindiria ... Leh? 3-21-79
Isla, La 4-03-63
Isla, La 9-12-79
Isla de la Muerte, La (See: Island of the Doomed)
Isla de Pasion, La (See: Passion Island)
Island, The (See: Hadaka No Shima; On; or Isla, La)
Island, The 6-04-80
Island at the End of the World (See: Ile du Bout du Monde, L')
Island at the Top of the World, The 11-27-74
Island Battle (See: Combat Dans L'Ile, Le)
Island Captives 7-28-37
Island Fisherman (See: Pecheur d'Islande)
Island in the Sky 3-16-38
Island in the Sky 8-12-53
Island in the Sun 6-19-57
Island of Desire, The 1-05-17
Island of Dr. Moreau, The 7-13-77
Island of Doom 7-18-33
Island of Doomed Men 6-05-40
Island of Intrigue, The 4-11-19
Island of Lost Men 8-23-39
Island of Lost Souls, The 1-17-33
Island of Lost Women 4-08-59
Island of Love 4-10-63
Island of Procida 3-19-52
Island of Regeneration, The 6-04-15
Island of Rhodes, The 2-19-15
Island of Silence, The (See: To Nhei the Equeh)
Island of Surprise, The 1-28-16
Island of Terror 3-22-67
Island of the Blue Dolphins 5-13-64
Island of the Doomed 1-31-68
Island of the Silver Herons, The (See: Ostrov Stribrnych Volavek)
Island on the Continent (See: Sziget A Szarasfoldon)
Islands in the Stream 3-09-77
Isle of Conquest, The 10-31-19
Isle of Content, The 8-06-15

Isle of Destiny 4-10-40
Isle of Escape 4-02-30
Isle of Forgotten Sins 10-20-43
Isle of Forgotten Women 12-07-27
Isle of Fury 11-18-36
Isle of Lost Men 12-12-28
Isle of Lost Ships 5-17-23
Isle of Lost Ships 10-30-29
Isle of Love, The 5-19-16
Isle of Love, The 4-11-28
Isle of Paradise 7-26-32
Isle of the Dead 9-12-45
Isle of Vanishing Men 11-08-23
Ismeri a Szandi-Mandit? 6-11-69
Isn't It Romantic? 8-18-48
Isn't Life Wonderful? 12-03-24
Isn't Life Wonderful! 11-11-53
Isn't Mama Fabulous? (See: Ist Mama Nicht Fabelhaft?)
Isn't My Husband Wonderful? (See: Ist Mein Mann Nicht Fabelhaft?)
Isobel, or The Trail's End 12-24-20
Isola di Arturo, L' 7-11-62
Ispravi Se, Delfina 8-17-77
Ist Mama Nicht Fabelhaft? 4-15-59
Ist Mein Mann Nicht Fabelhaft? 12-09-36
Istanbul 1-16-57
Isten Es Ember Elott 2-26-69
Isten Hozta, Oernagy Ur! 3-11-70
Istoriya Asi Klyachimol 7-05-78
Istvan Bors 5-24-39
It (See: Es)
It 2-09-27
It 9-20-67
It Ain't Easy 11-29-72
It Ain't Hay 3-17-43
It All Adds Up (See: Kassen Stemmer)
It All Came True 4-10-40
It All Depends on Girls (See: Tout Depend des Filles)
It Always Rains on Sunday 12-03-47
It Always Rains Where It Is Wet (See: Il Pleut Toujours Ou C'Est Mouille, Il)
It Came from Beneath the Sea 6-22-55
It Came from Outer Space 5-27-53
It Can Be Done 5-13-21
It Can Be Done 5-08-29
It Can Only Get Worse (See: Durchdreher, Der)
It Can't Last Forever 7-07-37
It Comes, It Goes (See: Ca Va, Ca Vient)
It Comes Up Love 1-27-43
It Conquered the World 9-12-56
It Could Happen to You 7-07-37
It Could Happen to You 6-14-39
It Couldn't Have Happened 9-16-36
It Goes Better with Raspberry-Juice (See: Mit Himbeergeist Geht Alles Besser)
It Grows on Trees 11-05-52
It Had to Be You 10-29-47
It Had to Happen 2-19-36
It Happened at the Inn 12-26-45
It Happened at the World's Fair 4-03-63
It Happened Here 10-28-64
It Happened in Athens 6-20-62
It Happened in Broad Daylight (See: Es Geschah Am Hellichten Tag)
It Happened in Brooklyn 3-05-47
It Happened in Canada 5-16-62
It Happened in Chicago 9-07-38
It Happened in Flatbush 6-03-42
It Happened in Gibraltar 11-24-43
It Happened in Havana (See: Sucedio en la Habana)
It Happened in Hollywood 10-06-37
It Happened in Hollywood 1-24-73
It Happened in New York 4-10-35
It Happened in Paris (See: C'Est Arrive a Paris)
It Happened in Rome (See: Roma, Ore 11)
It Happened in Spain (See: Traviesa Molinera, La)
It Happened on 5th Avenue 2-05-47
It Happened on July 20 (See: Es Geschah Am 20 Juli)
It Happened on the Thirty Six Candles (See: C'est Arrive a Trente-Six Chandelles)
It Happened One Night (See: I Slik en Natt)
It Happened One Night 2-27-34
It Happened One Sunday 8-09-44
It Happened Out West 2-01-23
It Happened Out West 6-09-37
It Happened to Jane 4-22-59
It Happened to One Man 2-26-41
It Happened Tomorrow 3-22-44
It Happens Every Spring 5-11-49
It Happens Every Thursday 4-15-53

It Is an Old Story (See: Es Ist Alte Geschichte)
It Is Easier for a Camel 9-20-50
It Is Enough to Love (See: Il Suffit d'Aimer)
It Is Midnight Dr. Schweitzer (See: Il Est Minuit Dr. Schweitzer)
It Is Necessary to Be Among the Peoples of the World to Know Them
    (See: Faut Aller Parmi le Monde Pour le Savoir)
It Is Not the Cowl That Makes the Friar 11-14-08
It Is Raining on Our Love (See: Det Regnar Pa Var Karlek)
It Is Raining on Santiago (See: Il Pleut Sur Santiago)
It Is the Law 9-24-24
It Isn't Done 3-31-37
It Lives Again 5-10-78
It Might Have Been 2-12-10
It Must Be Love 10-06-26
It Only Happens to Others (See: Ca N'Arrive Qu'Aux Autres)
It Only Happens to the Living (See: Ca N'Arrive Qu'Aux Vivants)
It Pays to Advertise 11-14-19
It Pays to Advertise 2-25-31
It Rains in My Village (See: Bice Skoro Propast Sveta)
It Seemed Like a Good Idea at the Time 5-14-75
It Should Happen to You 1-20-54
It Shouldn't Happen to a Dog 5-22-46
It Shouldn't Happen to a Vet 4-14-76
It Started in Naples 7-06-60
It Started in Paradise 11-12-52
It Started with a Kiss 8-19-59
It Started with Eve 10-01-41
It Takes All Kinds 8-13-69
It! The Terror from Beyond Space 8-06-58
It Was Him ... Yes! Yes! (See: Era Lui ... Si! Si!)
It Was Not in Vain (See: Nije Bilo Uzalud)
It Won't Do to Take God's Children for Wild Geese (See: Faut Pas
    Prendre les Enfants du Bon Dieu Pour des Canards Sauvages)
Italian, The 1-01-15
Italian-Austrian War Film 10-08-15
Italian Barber, The 1-21-11
Italian Battle Front, The 8-17-17
Italian Connection, The 10-31-73
Italian Graffiti 6-19-74
Italian in America, An 1-10-68
Italian Journey--Love Included (See: Italienreise--Liebe Inbegriffen)
Italian Job, The 6-11-69
Italian of the Roses, The (See: Italien des Roses, L')
Italian Secret Service 3-06-68
Italiani Brava Gente 10-14-64
Italians Good People (See: Italiani Brava Gente)
Italien des Roses, L' 9-13-72
Italienreise--Liebe Inbegriffen 5-07-58
Itching Palms 9-13-23
Itchy Fingers 2-21-79
Itchy Palm, The (See: Main Chaude, Le)
Itel a Balaton 3-28-33
Itelet 8-05-70
Ithele Na Guini Vassilias 10-25-67
Itim 3-21-79
It's a Bear 3-07-19
It's a Bet 3-13-35
It's a Big Country 11-28-51
It's a Boy 6-27-33 and 6-12-34
It's a Date 3-27-40
It's a Funny, Funny World 7-19-78
It's a Gift 1-08-35
It's a Great Feeling 7-27-49
It's a Great Life 9-03-20
It's a Great Life 1-22-30
It's a Great Life 2-05-36
It's a Great Life 6-16-43
It's a Joke, Son! 1-22-47
It's a King 1-17-33
It's a Long Time I've Loved You (See: Il y a Longtemps Que
    Je T'Aime)
It's a Mad, Mad, Mad, Mad World 11-06-63
It's a Pleasure 2-28-45
It's a Small World 6-26-35
It's a Small World 5-31-50
It's a Wise Child 5-20-31
It's a Wonderful Life 12-25-46
It's a Wonderful World 5-17-39
It's a Wonderful World 9-05-56
It's a World Full of Children (See: Verden er Fuld af Boern)
It's Adam's Fault (See: C'est la Faute d'Adam)
It's Alive 10-16-74
It's All Happening 6-19-63
It's All Yours 1-12-38
It's Always Fair Weather 8-24-55
It's Easy to Become a Father 7-03-29
It's Great to Be Alive 7-11-33
It's Great to Be Young 9-18-46
It's Great to Be Young 6-13-56

It's Hard to Be Good 11-24-48
It's in the Air 11-13-35
It's in the Air 12-11-40
It's in the Bag 2-14-45
It's Love Again 5-20-36 and 5-27-36
It's Love I'm After 7-21-37
It's Me 3-21-79
It's My Turn 10-22-80
It's Never Too Late (See: Nunca Es Tarde)
It's Never Too Late to Mend 1-10-13
It's Nifty in the Navy (See: Flaaden's Friske Fyre)
It's No Laughing Matter 1-22-15
It's Not Me, It's Him (See: C'Est Pas Moi, C'Est Lui)
It's Not the Size That Counts 4-04-79
It's Only Money 11-21-62
It's Showtime 4-07-76
It's Springtime (See: E Primavera)
It's the Law 12-02-42
It's the Old Army Game 7-07-26
It's the Paris Life 7-14-54
It's the Rich Man's Fault That the Poor Man Is His Enemy (See:
    Herren Machen Das Selber, Dass Ihnen Der Arme Mann Feyndt
    Wird, Die)
It's Tough for Everybody (See: C'Est Dur Pour Tout le Monde)
It's Trad, Dad! 5-02-62
It's Turned Out Nice Again 6-25-41
It's You I Want 10-21-36
It's Your Birthday (See: Ca Va Etre Ta Fete)
It's Your Thing 8-26-70
Itsu Itsu Made Mo 12-10-52
Itto 2-27-35
Ivan 11-29-32 and 3-07-33
Ivan Grozny (See: Ivan the Terrible, Pts. I & II)
Ivan Pavlov 2-15-50
Ivan the Great 7-04-23
Ivan the Terrible (See: Grozny Vek)
Ivan the Terrible 3-12-47
Ivan the Terrible, Part II 10-29-58 and 12-02-59
Ivanhoe 6-11-52
I've Always Loved You 9-04-46
I've Been Around 4-17-35
I've Defended a Woman (See: Megvedtem Egy Asszonyt)
I've Got You You've Got Me By the Hairs of My Chinny Chin Chin
    (See: Je Te Tiens Tu Me Tiens Par La Barbichette)
I've Got Your Number 2-06-34
I've Gotta Horse 4-21-65
I've Had It (See: J'ai Mon Voyage)
I've Lived Before 7-18-56
I've Lost My Husband (See: Ho Perduto Mio Marito)
I've Made a Love Match (See: Szerelembol Nosultem)
I've Never Stolen in My Life (See: Nem Loptam en Eletemben)
Ivory Handled Gun 1-22-36
Ivory Snuff Box, The 9-17-15
Ivy 6-11-47
Iza Neni 11-21-33
Izbavitelj 3-09-77
Izgubljena Olovka 8-10-60

J

J.A Martin Photographe 5-18-77
J.D.'s Revenge 6-30-76
JK Years--a Political Trajectory, The (See: Os Anos JK--uma
    Trajetoria Politica)
J. Rufus Wallingford 10-15-15 and 10-22-15
J.W. Coop 12-01-71
J'Accuse 4-26-39
J'Ai Mon Voyage 4-18-71
J'Ai Tue Rasputine 5-10-67
J'Avais Sept Filles 2-02-55
J'Etais Une Aventuriere 2-15-39
J'Irai Comme un Cheval Fou 11-28-73
J'Irai Cracher Sur Vos Tombes 7-15-59
J-Men Forever 2-13-80
J3, Les 5-08-46
Ja, Spravedlnost 7-24-68
Jabberwocky 4-06-77
Jacare 12-23-42
Jack 3-06-14
Jack 3-30-77
Jack Ahoy 2-12-35
Jack and Jenny 6-17-64
Jack and Jill 11-23-17

Jack and the Beanstalk 8-03-17
Jack and the Beanstalk 4-09-52
Jack Called 3 Times (See: Suerte Llama Tres Veces, La)
Jack, El Destripador De Londres 10-27-71
Jack Frost 10-19-66
Jack Johnson 11-10-71
Jack-Knife Man, The 8-06-20
Jack London 11-24-43
Jack London's 6-27-13
Jack London's Adventures in the South Sea Islands (See: Jack
   London's)
Jack McCall, Desperado 3-25-53
Jack of All Trades 3-04-36
Jack of Diamonds 10-25-67
Jack of Hearts 9-15-26
Jack of Spades, The (See: Chien de Pique, Le)
Jack Slade 10-21-53
Jack Spurlock, Prodigal 2-15-18
Jack Straw 4-02-20
Jack, the Ripper (See: Jack, El Destripador De Londres)
Jack the Ripper 7-01-59
Jackal of Nahueltoro, The (See: Chacal de Nahueltoro, El)
Jackass Mail 6-17-42
Jackie Robinson Story, The 5-17-50
Jackpot, The 10-04-50
Jack's Birthday 1-08-10
Jack's the Boy 7-05-32
Jackson County Jail 5-05-76
Jacob the Liar (See: Jakob der Luegner)
Jacob Two-Two Meets the Hooded Fang 3-14-79
Jacqueline 6-13-56
Jacques Brel Is Alive and Well and Living in Paris 1-29-75
Jacques of the Silver North 6-06-19
Jacques, the Wolf 9-26-13
Jad 8-20-75
Jade Casket, The 6-26-29
Jade Mask 1-24-45
Jadzia 2-03-37
Jaeger von Fall, Der 12-02-36
Jaffery 7-14-16
Jag Aer Med Barn 12-26-79
Jag Alskar Dig, Argbigga 1-22-47
Jag Alskar, Du Alskar 5-29-68
Jag ar Maria 5-28-80
Jag Ar Med Eder 2-18-48
Jag Ar Nyfiken-Blaa 3-20-68
Jag Ar Nyfiken--Gul 11-01-67
Jag Elskar Dig, Karlsson 11-26-47
Jagdszene Aus Niederbayern 5-14-69
Jago Hua Savera 9-16-59
Jagte Raho 9-04-57
Jaguar 4-25-56
Jaguar 9-13-67
Jaguar 5-21-80
Jaguar Lives 9-05-79
Jaguar's Claws, The 6-08-17
Jail Bait 5-19-54
Jailbird, The 10-01-20
Jailbreak 8-12-36
Jailhouse Rock 10-16-57
Jak Byc Kochana 5-29-63
Jake the Plumber 11-02-27
Jakob der Luegner 7-16-75
Jakobli and Meyeli (See: Jakobli und Meyeli)
Jakobli und Meyeli 4-26-61
Jakten 5-18-60
Jakten 7-06-66
Jakub 3-16-77
Jalisco, Don't Backslide (See: Ay, Jalisco No Te Rajes)
Jalisco Gals Are Beautiful (See: Bonitas Las Tapatias)
Jalma la Double 3-21-28
Jalna 9-18-35
Jalopy 3-25-53
Jalsaghar 12-07-60
Jam Session 5-03-44
Jamaica Inn 5-31-39
Jamaica Run 4-08-53
Jamais Plus Toujours 4-07-76
Jambon D'Ardenne 5-04-77
Jamboree 3-29-44
Jamboree 11-27-57
James Boys in Missouri 4-25-08
James Dean, the First American Teenager 10-01-75
James Or Not (See: James Ou Pas)
James Ou Pas 10-28-70
Jamilya 7-12-72
Jana 6-24-36
Jane Austen in Manhattan 7-30-80
Jane Bleibt Jane 4-26-78

Jane Eyre 2-17-22
Jane Eyre 2-20-35
Jane Eyre 2-02-44
Jane Eyre 3-24-71
Jane Goes A-Wooing 1-10-19
Jane Is Jane Forever (See: Jane Bleibt Jane)
Jane Is Unwilling to Work 10-09-09
Jane Shore 6-04-15
Jane Steps Out 5-25-38
Jangmeae Sung 10-01-69
Janice Meredith 8-13-24
Janie 7-26-44
Janie Gets Married 6-05-46
Janiksen Vuosi 3-28-79
Janis 10-23-74
Janken 8-05-70
Janne Wangmans Bravader 12-15-48
Janosik 12-18-74
Japan 9-19-13
Japanese-American Film 6-01-27
Japanese Demon, A (See: Satori)
Japanese Nightingale, A 8-23-18
Japanese War Bride 1-09-52
Jaque a la Dama 10-04-78
Jardin de las Delicias, El 9-16-70
Jardin des Supplices, Le 10-20-76
Jardin Qui Bascule, Le 5-21-75
Jardinier D'Argenteuil, Le 10-19-66
Jarha Fi Lhaite 5-24-78
Jaroslaw Dabrowski 7-28-76
Jason and the Argonauts 6-05-63
Jassy 8-20-47
Jaula de los Leones, La 2-25-31
Java Head 2-08-23
Java Head 8-07-35
Javoronok 5-26-65
Jaws 6-18-75
Jaws of Hell 1-07-31
Jaws of Steel 2-22-28
Jaws 2 6-07-78
Jayhawkers, The 10-21-59
Jazz Age, The 4-17-29
Jazz All Around (See: Midt I En Jazztid)
Jazz Boat 11-23-60
Jazz Boy, The (See: Jazzgossen)
Jazz Cinderella 10-01-30
Jazz Girl, The 6-15-27
Jazz Heaven 11-06-29
Jazz Mad 7-18-28
Jazz on a Summer's Day 9-16-59
Jazz Singer, The 10-12-27
Jazz Singer, The 12-31-52
Jazz Singer, The 12-10-80
Jazzgossen 11-05-58
Jazzland 3-20-29
Jazzmania 3-15-23
Je L'Ai Ete Trois Fois 11-12-52
Je Reviendrai a Kandara 4-03-57
Je Sais Rien Mais Je Dirai Tout 1-02-74
Je Suis de la Revue 7-04-51
Je Suis Pierre Riviere 2-18-76
Je Suis Timide; Mais Je Me Soigne 9-06-78
Je T'Adore ... Mais Pourquoi 9-17-30
Je T'Aime 3-13-74
Je T'Aime, Je T'Aime 5-15-68
Je T'Aime Moi Non Plus 3-17-76
Je Te Tiens Tu Me Tiens Par La Barbichette 6-27-79
Je, Tu, Elles 9-03-69
Je Vais Craquer 5-21-80
Je Vous Aimerai Toujours 6-27-33
Je Vous Salue, Mafia 10-13-65
Jealousy (See: Gelosia; Heung; or Rak Ri Sayar)
Jealousy 11-24-16
Jealousy 5-30-23
Jealousy 9-26-28 and 12-12-28
Jealousy 9-18-29
Jealousy 11-27-34
Jealousy 7-25-45
Jean de la Lune 4-01-31 and 3-14-32
Jean Goes Foraging 10-29-10
Jean-Marc or Conjugal Life (See: Jean-Marc ou la Vie Conjugale)
Jean-Marc ou la Vie Conjugale 2-12-64
Jean the Matchmaker 9-24-10
Jean Valjean 12-04-09
Jeanne Dore 1-11-39
Jeanne Eagels 7-24-57
Jeannie 8-27-41

Jean's Wife (See: Femme de Jean, La)
Jedanaesta Zapovest 4-22-70
Jedda 6-15-55
Jede Frau Hat ein Geheimnis 3-17-37
Jede Frau Hat Etwas 5-20-31
Jeden Stribrny 8-04-76
Jeder Fuer Sich und Gott Gegen Alle 5-14-75
Jeder Stirbt Fuer Sich Allein 2-04-76
Jedermann 1-17-62
Jeepers Creepers 11-01-39
Jefe, El 11-26-58
Jeff 6-11-69
Jeg Elsker Blat 7-03-68
Jeg Elsker en Enden 1-22-47
Jeg--En Kvinde 9-29-65
Jeg--En Kvinde, II 3-27-68
Jeg Saa Jesus Doe 2-26-75
Jekyll and Hyde 1-05-32
Jelenido 2-16-72
Jennie 3-19-41
Jennie Gerhardt 6-13-33
Jennifer 5-24-78
Jennifer on My Mind 10-13-71
Jenny (See: Jadzia)
Jenny 4-09-58
Jenny 12-24-69
Jenny Be Good 7-02-20
Jenny Lamour 1-14-48
Jens Mansson I Amerika 11-12-47
Jens Monson in America (See: Jens Mansson I Amerika)
Jenseits Von Oder Und Neisse--Heute 5-05-65
Jeopardy 1-21-53
Jeremiah Johnson 5-10-72
Jeremy 5-23-73
Jericho 9-08-37
Jericho 3-27-46
Jerk, The (See: Corniaud, Le)
Jerk, The 12-12-79
Jerusalem File, The 2-09-72
Jes' Call Me Jim 5-28-20
Jesli Msz Serce Bijace 10-01-80
Jesse James 10-19-27
Jesse James 1-11-39
Jesse James at Bay 10-15-41
Jesse James, Jr. 4-01-42
Jesse James vs. the Daltons 1-27-54
Jesse James' Women 9-15-54
Jessica 3-21-62
Jester, The (See: Purimspieler, Der)
Jester's Tale, A 10-28-64
Jesus 10-24-79
Jesus Christ, Superstar 6-27-73
Jesus Trip, The 9-01-71
Jet Attack 3-26-58
Jet Generation 5-07-69
Jet Job 3-26-52
Jet Pilot 9-25-57
Jet Storm 9-02-59
Jeu Avec Le Feu, Le 2-05-75
Jeu de la Verite, Le 12-20-61
Jeu de Massacre 5-03-67
Jeu de Solitaire, Le 6-19-76
Jeudi On Chantera Comme Dimanche 7-19-67
Jeune Couple, Un 7-09-69
Jeune Fille Assassinee, La 11-20-74
Jeune Fille Savait, Une 5-05-48
Jeune Folle, La 10-08-52
Jeunes Filles en Detresse 3-06-40
Jeunes Loups, Les 4-24-68
Jeux de Femmes 5-29-46
Jeux de L'Amour, Les 6-15-60 and 11-02-60
Jeux Interdits 5-28-52
Jeux Sont Faits, Les 2-04-48
Jew at War, A 7-28-31
Jewel 9-03-15
Jewel in Pawn, A 4-20-17
Jewel Robbery 7-26-32
Jewelers of Moonlight, The (See: Bijoutiers Du Clair De Lune, Les)
Jewels of Brandenburg 5-28-47
Jewels of Sin (See: Joyas Del Pecado, Las)
Jewish Daughter (See: Yidishe Tochter)
Jews in Poland 5-01-57
Jezebel 3-16-38
Jezioro Osobliwosei 2-13-74
Jhor 2-13-80
Jiggs and Maggie in Society 2-11-48

Jiggs and Maggie Out West 3-22-50
Jigokumen 11-25-53
Jigsaw 3-09-49
Jigsaw 9-05-62
Jigsaw 5-29-68
Jiken 7-25-79
Jill in the Box (See: Stehaufmaedchen)
Jilt, The 11-17-22
Jilted Janet 2-22-18
Jim Bludso 2-02-17
Jim Grimsby's Boy 10-20-16
Jim Hanvey, Detective 5-12-37
Jim the Conqueror 1-05-27
Jim the Penman 3-25-21
Jim the Rancher 9-17-10
Jim, the World's Greatest 1-21-76
Jim Thorpe--All American 6-20-51
Jimi Hendrix 10-03-73
Jimmy and Sally 12-19-33
Jimmy Orpheus 10-26-66
Jimmy the Gent 3-27-34
Jimmy Valentine 11-21-28
Jimmy Valentine 3-04-36
Jinchoge 11-02-66
Jinks Wants to Be an Acrobat 10-22-10
Jinrui Gaku Nyumon 4-13-66
Jinx, The (See: Gafe, El)
Jinx, The 12-19-19
Jinx Money 5-19-48
Jiouchi 6-28-67
Jitterbugs 5-26-43
Jivaro 1-20-54
Jive Junction 1-19-44
Jo 9-29-71
Jo-Bachi 3-01-78
Jo-En 6-28-67
Joan at the Stake (See: Giovanna D'Arco Al Rogo)
Joan of Arc 7-17-14
Joan of Arc 10-20-48
Joan of Ozark 7-22-42
Joan of Paris 1-07-42
Joan of Plattsburg 5-03-18
Joan of the Woods 7-12-18
Joan the Woman 12-29-16
Joanna 12-16-25
Joanna 11-20-68
Joao 7-12-72
Job, The (See: Posto, Il)
Jocelyn 11-24-22
Jocelyn 4-23-52
Jockey, The 2-19-10
Jockey of Death, The 4-16-15
Joe 7-15-70
Joe Albany--A Jazz Life 12-17-80
Joe and Ethel Turp Call on the President 12-06-39
Joe and Maxi 6-21-78
Joe Butterfly 4-24-57
Joe Caligula 2-12-69
Joe Cocker: Mad Dogs and Englishmen 2-03-71
Joe Dakota 6-05-57
Joe Frazier vs. Muhammad Ali (See: Fight, The)
Joe Hill 5-26-71
Joe Kidd 7-12-72
Joe Louis Story, The 9-30-53
Joe Macbeth 11-02-55
Joe Palooka, Champ 4-10-46
Joe Palooka in Humphrey Takes a Chance 6-28-50
Joe Palooka in the Big Fight 2-23-49
Joe Palooka in the Counterpunch 9-14-49
Joe Palooka in the Squared Circle 12-27-50
Joe Palooka in Triple Cross 9-12-51
Joe Palooka in Winner Take All 8-25-48
Joe Palooka Meets Humphrey 2-01-50
Joe Panther 11-03-76
Joe Smith, American 1-07-42
Joerg Ratgeb, Maler 3-29-78
Joerg Ratgeb, Painter (See: Joerg Ratgeb, Maler)
Joey Boy 3-31-65
Johan 7-21-76
Johann Orth 12-06-32
Johanna Enlists 9-13-18
Johansson and Vestman (See: Johansson Och Vestman)
Johansson Gets Scolded (See: Var Herr Luggar Johansson)
Johansson Och Vestman 10-16-46
Johansson-Patterson 7-01-59
John and Julie 8-03-55
John and Marsha 7-31-74
John and Mary 11-26-69

John Barleycorn 7-17-14
John Dough and the Cherub 12-24-10
John F. Kennedy: Years of Lightning, Day of Drums 6-23-65
John Forrest Finds Himself 12-03-20
John Glayde's Honor 10-22-15
John Glenn Story, The 2-27-63
John Glueckstadt 7-09-75
John Goldfarb, Please Come Home 11-18-64
John Halifax, Gentleman 7-16-15
John Heartfield, Fotomonteur 4-27-77
John Loves Mary 1-26-49
John Meade's Woman 2-24-37
John Needham's Double 3-31-16
John Paul Jones 6-17-59
John Petticoats 11-07-19
John Smith 6-16-22
John the Violent (See: Ioannis Ofvieos)
John Wesley 4-28-54
Johnny Allegro 6-01-49
Johnny Angel 8-01-45
Johnny Apollo 4-17-40
Johnny Belinda 9-15-48
Johnny Come Lately 9-01-43
Johnny Comes Flying Home 3-20-46
Johnny Concho 7-11-56
Johnny Cool 10-09-63
Johnny Dark 6-02-54
Johnny Doesn't Live Here Anymore 6-28-44
Johnny Doughboy 5-12-43
Johnny Eager 12-10-41
Johnny Frenchman 7-18-45
Johnny, Get Your Gun 3-21-19
Johnny Get Your Hair Cut 2-02-27
Johnny Got His Gun 5-19-71
Johnny Guitar 5-05-54
Johnny Hallyday Par Francois Reichenbach 6-28-72
Johnny Hamlet 5-10-72
Johnny Holiday 12-14-49
Johnny Larsen 10-10-79
Johnny Minotaur 4-21-71
Johnny Nobody 12-01-65
Johnny O'Clock 2-05-47
Johnny on the Spot 2-21-19
Johnny One-Eye 6-14-50
Johnny Reno 3-02-66
Johnny Rocco 11-19-58
Johnny Steals Europe (See: Jonny Stiehlt Europa)
Johnny Stool Pigeon 7-20-49
Johnny the Giant Killer 7-08-53
Johnny Tiger 4-13-66
Johnny Tremain 5-01-57
Johnny Trouble 9-11-57
Johnny Unser 11-05-80
Johnny Vik 8-29-73
Johnny West 3-29-78
Johnny Yuma 9-13-67
Johnny's Pictures of the Polar Regions 4-23-10
Johnson-Ketchel Fight 10-30-09
Johnstown Flood, The 3-17-26
Joi Baba Felunath 12-12-79
Join the Marines 2-17-37
Joke, The (See: Zert)
Joke They Played on Bumptious, The 12-24-10
Joker, The (See: Farceur, Le)
Joker Is Wild, The 8-28-57
Jokers, The 4-26-67
Jokyo 7-06-60
Joli Mai, Le 5-15-63
Jolly Bad Fellow, A 5-13-64
Jolly Pleasant, The 7-03-29
Jolly Pirates (See: Allegri Masnadieri)
Jolly Vineyard 2-22-28
Jolson Sings Again 8-17-49
Jolson Story, The 9-18-46
Jonas 11-27-57
Jonas--Qui Aura 25 Ans en l'An 2000 8-25-76
Jonas--Who Will be 25 in the Year 2000 (See: Jonas--Qui Aura 25 Ans en l'An 2000)
Jonathan 5-30-73
Jonathan Livingston Seagull 10-10-73
Jongara 10-09-74
Joni 10-29-80
Jonny Rettet Nebrador 12-09-53
Jonny Saves Nebrador (See: Jonny Rettet Nebrador)
Jonny Stiehlt Europa 8-02-32
Jordan Is a Hard Road 11-19-15
Jorden Er Flad 2-09-77
Josefa's Loot (See: Magot de Josefa, Le)

Josefine Mutzenbacher 9-30-70
Joseph Andrews 3-16-77
Joseph Schmidt Story 3-07-51
Joseph the Dreamer 5-16-62
Josephine and Men 11-30-55
Josette 6-01-38
Josselyn's Wife 5-09-19
Josselyn's Wife 11-17-26
Joszef Katus 5-03-67
Jouet, Le 12-22-76
Joueur, Le 12-31-58
Joueur d'Echecs, Le 1-11-39
Jouluksi Kotiin 8-27-75
Jour de Fete 5-25-49
Jour de Gloire, Le 12-29-76
Jour et l'Heure, Le 3-27-63
Jour Se Leve, Le 7-26-39
Journal d'un Cure de Campagne, Le 9-12-51
Journal d'un Fou, Le 12-04-63
Journal d'un Suicide, Le 4-12-72
Journal d'une Femme de Chambre, Le 3-18-64
Journal d'une Femme en Blanc 5-26-65
Journal of a Crime 5-01-34
Journalist (See: Novinar)
Journalist, The 7-26-67
Journee Bien Remplie, Une 3-07-73
Journey 10-18-72
Journey, The (See: Viaje, El)
Journey, The 2-04-59
Journey Among Women 7-27-77
Journey for Margaret 10-28-42
Journey into Fear 8-05-42
Journey into Light 8-29-51
Journey into Self 4-02-69
Journey into Spring, A (See: Udhetim Ne Pranvere)
Journey of the Actors, The (See: O Thiassos)
Journey Through Rosebud 3-01-72
Journey to Italy 11-03-54
Journey to Jerusalem 10-30-68
Journey to Love 10-14-53
Journey to Shiloh 5-15-68
Journey to the Center of the Earth 12-09-59
Journey to the Far Side of the Sun 8-13-69
Journey to the Lost City 11-09-60
Journey to the 7th Planet 2-21-62
Journey Together 10-17-45
Journey's End 5-03-18
Journey's End 6-24-21
Journey's End 4-16-30 and 4-30-30
Journeys from Berlin 1971 2-06-80
Joven Rebelde, El 7-04-62
Joven, Viuda y Estanciera 7-23-41
Jovenes, Los 7-12-61 and 11-08-61
Jovenes Viegos, Los (See: Old Young People, The)
Jovenes y Bellas 8-01-62
Joy 9-21-77
Joy and the Dragon 1-19-17
Joy Girl, The 9-07-27
Joy in the Morning 3-10-65
Joy of Letting Go, The 7-14-76
Joy of Living 3-23-38
Joy of Living, The (See: Che Gioia Vivere)
Joy Ride 10-08-58
Joyas Del Pecado, Las 6-07-50
Joyous Liar, The 11-14-19 and 12-19-19
Joyous Troublemakers, The 7-02-20
Joyride 6-01-77
Jua Arom 4-30-75
Juan Lamaglia y Sra 4-08-70
Juan Moreira 8-08-73
Juan Pedro, El Dallador 4-29-70
Juan Pedro, the Scyther (See: Juan Pedro, El Dallador)
Juan Perez Jolote 10-08-75 and 3-09-77
Juan Vicente Gomez and His Era (See: Juan Vicente Gomez y Su Epoca)
Juan Vicente Gomez y Su Epoca 10-08-75
Juana Gallo 8-02-61
Juarez 4-26-39
Jubal 4-04-56
Jubilee 2-28-45
Jubilee 2-01-78
Jubilee Trail 1-20-54
Jubilo 12-19-19
Jucklins, The 12-17-20
Jud 9-01-71
Judenrichter, Der 8-03-60
Judex 12-18-63

Judge, The (See: Domaren)
Judge, The 2-23-49
Judge and The Assassin, The (See: Juge et L'Assassin, Le)
Judge Fayard Called the Sheriff (See: Juge Fayard Dit le Sheriff, Le)
Judge for the Young, The (See: Judendrichter, Der)
Judge Hardy and Son 12-13-39
Judge Hardy's Children 4-06-38
Judge Not 3-05-15
Judge Not 3-26-15
Judge Not 10-01-15
Judge Not; or, The Woman of Mona Diggings (See: Judge Not)
Judge Not That Ye Be Judged 8-28-09
Judge Priest 10-16-34
Judge Steps Out, The 5-11-49
Judgement (See: Itelet)
Judge's Friend, The (See: Mijn Vriend)
Judge's Ward 10-09-09
Judge's Whiskers 8-21-09
Judge's Wife, The 10-23-14
Judgement 1-27-22
Judgment at Nuremberg 10-18-61
Judgment House, The 11-30-17 and 2-08-18
Judgment of an Assassin 12-14-77
Judgment of Lake Balaton (See: Itel a Balaton)
Judgment of the Hills 8-03-27
Judgment of the Jungle 2-20-14
Judgment of the Storm 1-31-24
Judith 1-12-66
Judith and Holophernes (See: Head of a Tyrant)
Judith of Bethulia 3-27-14
Judith of the Cumberlands 8-04-16
Judith Therpauve 10-18-78
Judo Showdown 8-21-68
Judoka Agent Secret, Le 3-22-67
Judy Forgot 8-20-15
Judy of Rogues' Harbor 2-13-20
Juego de la Oca, El 6-02-65
Jueves Milagro, Los 7-02-58
Juge et L'Assassin, Le 3-03-76
Juge Fayard Dit le Sheriff, Le 1-19-77
Jugement Dernier, Le 1-16-46
Jugend 6-01-38
Jugend der Welt 7-29-36
Jugend von Heute 11-09-38
Juggernaut 9-23-36 and 7-21-37
Juggernaut 9-18-74
Juggernaut, The 3-12-15
Juggler, The 2-19-10
Juggler, The 5-06-53
Juguemos en el Mundo 9-22-71
Juguetes Rotos 12-21-66
Juha 9-04-57
Juif Polonais, Le 9-29-37
Juk un Ja San Ja 6-29-66
Juke Box Rhythm 3-25-59
Juke Girl 4-08-42
Jukebox Jenny 3-25-42
Jukyu-Sai No Chizu 5-21-80
Jula Treekul 5-07-80
Jula Treekul River (See: Jula Treekul)
Julefrokosten 12-08-76
Jules and Jim (See: Jules et Jim)
Jules' Breadwinner (See: Pain Des Jules, Le)
Jules et Jim 2-07-62
Jules le Magnifique 3-09-77
Jules of the Strong Heart 1-18-18
Jules Starts with Jules (See: Julio Comienza En Julio)
Jules the Magnificent (See: Jules le Magnifique)
Julia (See: Lieberschuler, Der)
Julia 9-21-77
Julia Misbehaves 8-18-48
Juliana Do Amor Perdido 10-14-70
Julie 10-03-56
Julie de Carneilhan 5-24-50
Julie Glue Pot (See: Julie Pot de Colle)
Julie la Rousse 9-09-59
Juliet and the Feel of the Times (See: Juliette et L'Air du Temps)
Juliet of the Spirits (See: Giulietta de Gli Spiriti)
Julietta 11-18-53
Juliette de Sade 12-24-69
Juliette et Juliette 3-13-74
Juliette et L'Air du Temps 8-25-76
Juliette or Key of Dreams (See: Juliette Ou le Clef des Songes)
Juliette Ou le Clef des Songes 5-16-51
Julio Comienza en Julio 5-16-79
Julius Caesar 11-14-14
Julius Caesar 5-14-15

Julius Caesar 2-10-22
Julius Caesar 6-03-53
Julius Caesar 6-10-70
July 14 2-07-33 and 10-24-33
July 4, 1910 12-18-09
Jument Vapeur, La 4-05-78
Jump 7-14-71
Jump for Glory 3-24-37
Jump into Hell 3-30-55
Jumpin' at the Bedside (See: Hopla Paa Sengekanten)
Jumping Ash 9-15-76
Jumping for Joy 2-29-56
Jumping into the Abyss (See: Sprung in den Abgrund)
Jumping Jacks 6-04-52
Jumping Over Puddles Again (See: Uz Zase Skacu Kaluze)
Jun 5-16-79
Junction City 7-09-52
June Bride 10-20-48
June Friday 8-27-15
June Madness 9-29-22
June Moon 3-18-31
Junge Graf, Der 12-16-36
Junge Liebe 6-12-34
Junge Lord, Der 8-05-70
Junge Moench, Der 1-17-79
Junge Suenderin, Die 12-28-60
Junge Toerless, Der 4-27-66
Junges Blut 5-13-36
Jungfrukallan 2-24-60
Jungfrun Pa Jungfrusund 4-26-50
Jungle, The 6-26-14
Jungle, The 8-13-52
Jungle Adventure Campa Campa (See: Djungelaeventyret Campa-Campa)
Jungle Adventures 9-16-21
Jungle Belles 5-18-27
Jungle Book, The 3-25-42
Jungle Book, The 10-04-67
Jungle Bride 5-16-33
Jungle Captive 6-13-45
Jungle Cat 8-10-60
Jungle Cavalcade 7-09-41
Jungle Child, The 9-22-16
Jungle Flight 2-26-47
Jungle Girl 5-28-41
Jungle Goddess 11-03-48
Jungle Headhunters 5-02-51
Jungle Heat 7-31-57
Jungle in the City, The (See: Sa Kagubatan Ng Lunsod)
Jungle Jim 2-24-37
Jungle Jim 12-22-48
Jungle Jim in the Forbidden Land 3-05-52
Jungle Killer 11-29-32
Jungle Lovers, The 9-24-15
Jungle Man-Eaters 6-09-54
Jungle Manhunt 10-03-51
Jungle Menace 10-27-37
Jungle Moon-Men 3-30-55
Jungle of Chang 11-14-51
Jungle Patrol 9-22-48
Jungle Princess, The 12-30-36
Jungle Saga (See: Djungelsaga, En)
Jungle Stampede 8-02-50
Jungle Trail, The 6-06-19
Jungle Woman 5-24-44 and 7-19-44
Jungle Woman, The 6-23-26
Junior Army 4-28-43
Junior Bonner 6-14-72
Junior G-Men of the Air 5-27-42
Junior Miss 6-13-45
Junior Prom 2-27-46
Juno and the Paycock 1-22-30
Junoon 1-31-79
Jupiter 11-05-52
Jupiter 3-31-71
Jupiter's Darling 1-26-55
Jury of Fate, The 8-17-17
Jury's Evidence 1-22-36
Jury's Secret, The 2-02-38
Jusqu'au Bout du Monde 2-27-63
Jusqu'au Coeur 6-04-69
Jusqu'au Dernier 5-22-57
Just a Big Simple Girl 11-02-49
Just a Gigolo 6-16-31
Just a Gigolo 2-21-79
Just a Song at Twilight 12-29-16
Just a Woman 12-21-17
Just a Woman 5-27-25
Just Across the Street 5-28-52

K

Karneval und Liebe 4-22-36
Karol Lir (See: King Lear)
Karosszek, A 11-15-39
Karugtong Ng Kahapon 11-12-75
Kaseki 3-26-75
Kashi To Kodomo 9-12-62
Kashima Paradise 5-16-73
Kasper in de Onderwereld 2-07-79
Kasper in the Underworld (See: Kasper in de Onderwereld)
Kassbach 3-07-79
Kassen Stemmer 8-18-76
Katachrissis Exoussias 11-10-71
Katawang Lupa 6-04-75
Kate 8-21-14
Katerina a Jeji Deti 7-28-76
Katerina Izmailova 5-17-67
Kathleen 1-26-38
Kathleen 11-12-41
Kathleen Mavourneen 8-22-19
Kathy O 4-23-58
Katia 11-16-38
Katia 2-24-60
Katie Did It 4-11-51
Katrina 11-30-49
Kattorna (See: Cats, The)
Katu 12-16-64
Katz & Karasso 1-26-72
Katz und Maus 2-15-67
Katzelmacher 10-22-69
Katzensteg, Der 1-26-38
Kazablan 8-22-73
Kazan 10-28-21
Kazan 6-15-49
Kazdy Den Odvahu 5-11-66
Kazdy Mlady Muz 8-10-66
Kazoku 4-14-71
Kde Reky Maji Slunce 9-06-61
Kdo Chce Zabot Jessii? 8-03-66
Kdo Hleda Zlate Dno 7-16-75
Ke Ha See Dang 11-05-80
Ke Xana Pros Ti Doxa Trava 10-29-80
Kean--The Madness of Genius 5-21-24
Keby Som Mal Dievca 8-25-76
Keby Som Mal Puska 8-16-72
Keep All Doors Open (See: Hall Alla Doerrar Oeppna)
Keep 'Em Flying 11-26-41
Keep 'Em Rolling 6-26-34
Keep 'Em Slugging 3-03-43 and 4-21-43
Keep Moving 11-19-15
Keep Smiling 1-20-26
Keep Smiling 8-17-38
Keep Talking Baby (See: Cause Toujours Mon Lapin)
Keep to the Right 11-05-20
Keep Your Powder Dry 2-21-45
Keeper, The 5-26-76
Keeper of the Bees 10-28-25
Keeper of the Bees 8-21-35
Keeper of the Flame 12-16-42
Keepers of the Night (See: Nachtwache)
Keeping Company 1-01-41
Keeping Up with Lizzie 5-13-21
Keetje Tippel 5-14-75
Keiko 9-12-79
Keim Tag Ohme Dich 3-14-33
Keine Feier Ohne Meier 11-01-32
Keith of the Border 2-15-18
Kejsaren 3-07-79
Kelek 10-22-69
Kelly and Me 1-16-57
Kelly Gang, The 9-03-24
Kelly of U.S.A. 12-18-34
Kelly the Second 10-07-36
Kelly's Heroes 6-17-70
Kemek 9-16-70
Ken Murray Shooting Stars 7-25-79
Kenguru, A 7-28-76
Kennedy Square 3-10-16
Kennel Murder Case, The 10-31-33
Kenner 3-26-69
Kennwort: Reiher 8-12-64
Kenny & Co. 11-24-76
Kentuckian, The 7-13-55
Kentuckians, The 2-04-21
Kentucky 12-21-38
Kentucky Cinderella, A 6-22-17
Kentucky Courage 5-16-28
Kentucky Derby 12-08-22
Kentucky Fried Movie, The 8-03-77

Kentucky Handicap, The 5-11-27
Kentucky Jubilee 7-18-51
Kentucky Kernels 1-08-35
Kentucky Moonshine 5-04-38
Kentucky Pioneer, A 10-08-10
Keow 4-23-80
Kept Husbands 3-25-31
Keresztelo 1-31-68
Kerleken Segrar 5-03-50
Kermesse Heroique, La 12-18-35 and 9-30-36
Kermesse Rouge, La 12-04-46
Kermis in de Regen 4-11-62
Kertes Hazak Utcaja 5-22-63
Kes 4-08-70
Kesakapina 7-08-70
Kesalla Kello Viisi 7-08-64
Keshoku Ichadai-Onna 9-17-52
Kesyttomat Veljekset 8-12-70
Ket Elhatarozas 11-22-78
Ket Felido a Pokolban 5-30-62
Ket Fogoly 2-09-38
Ket Vallomas 5-29-57
Kettles in the Ozarks, The 3-07-56
Kettles on Old MacDonald's Farm, The 5-01-57
Ketto Ganryu Jima (See: Samurai, Part III)
Keusche Kokotte, Die (See: Virgin Cocotte, The)
Key, The (See: Kagi)
Key, The 6-05-34
Key, The 6-11-58
Key and the Ring, The (See: Nyckeln Och Ringen)
Key Is in the Door, The (See: Cle Sur La Porte, La)
Key Largo 7-07-48
Key That Should Not Be Handed On, The (See: Klujch Bez Prava Peredachi)
Key to Love, The (See: Koonche Rak)
Key to Paradise, The (See: Noeglen Til Paradis)
Key to the City 2-01-50
Key to Yesterday, The 10-23-14
Key Witness 8-06-47
Key Witness 9-28-60
Keyhole (See: Noeglehullet)
Keyhole, The 4-04-33
Keys of the Kingdom, The 12-13-44
Keys of the Righteous 2-15-18
Khan el Khalili 7-19-67
Khao Yod 5-25-77
Khartoum 6-15-66
Khon Krang Detr 6-27-79
Khon Pukao 7-25-79
Khun Koo Con Mai 12-24-75
Khyber Patrol 8-25-54
Kibitzer, The 12-25-29
Kick-Back, The 7-28-22
Kick In 2-02-17
Kick In 12-22-22
Kick In 5-27-31
Kick-Off, The 8-25-26
Kicking the Moon Around 4-06-38
Kicma 8-20-75
Kid, The 4-23-10
Kid, The 8-25-16
Kid, The 1-21-21
Kid Blue 4-18-73
Kid Boots 10-13-26
Kid Brother, The 1-26-27
Kid Comes Back 12-29-37
Kid Dynamite 2-24-43
Kid for Two Farthings 5-18-55
Kid from Amarillo 10-10-51
Kid from Arizona 5-06-31
Kid from Broken Gun 8-13-52
Kid from Brooklyn, The 3-20-46
Kid from Cleveland, The 9-07-49
Kid from Kansas, The 9-24-41
Kid from Kokomo 5-24-39
Kid from Left Field, The 7-22-53
Kid from Sante Fe, The 9-25-40
Kid from Spain, The 11-22-32
Kid from Texas, The 4-05-39
Kid from Texas, The 3-01-50
Kid Galahad 6-02-37
Kid Galahad 7-25-62
Kid Glove Killer 3-11-42
Kid Head (See: Pibe Cabeza, El)
Kid Is Clever, The 7-12-18
Kid Millions 11-13-34
Kid Monk Baroni 4-23-52
Kid Nightingale 11-22-39

Kid Rides Again, The 3-17-43
Kid Rodelo 1-19-66
Kid Sister, The 10-12-27
Kid Sister, The 3-21-45
Kidnapped 5-11-17
Kidnapped 5-25-38
Kidnapped 9-08-48
Kidnapped 2-17-60
Kidnapped 12-15-71
Kidnapped Ladies (See: Raub der Sabinerinnen)
Kidnapper, The (See: Secuestador, El)
Kidnappers, The 1-27-54
Kidnapping Gorillas 4-16-41
Kidnapping of the President, The 8-13-80
Kids Are Alright, The 5-23-79
Kid's Clever, The 5-15-29
Kids Grow Up, The (See: Chicos Crecen, Los)
Kid's Last Ride 3-26-41
Kids of the Movies 7-03-14
Kids' War (See: Guerre des Gosses, La)
Kierion 9-18-68
Kierion 10-30-74
Kif Tebbi 5-22-29
Kiganjo No Boken 5-25-66
Kihajolni Veszelyes 5-24-78
Kiki 4-07-26
Kiki 3-11-31
Kiku and Isamu 9-16-59
Kilas 8-30-80
Kilas, O Mau Da Fita 10-15-80
Kildare of Storm 9-27-18
Kilenc Honap 10-26-77
Kilet Khon 6-15-77
Kill (See: Kiru)
Kill 12-15-71
Kill, The (See: Curee, La)
Kill a Dragon 11-01-67
Kill, Baby, Kill 10-30-68
Kill Barbara with Panic (See: Patayin Mo Sa Sindak Si Barbara)
Kill for the Truth (See: Phai Kam Plerng)
Kill Her Gently 9-17-58
Kill or Be Killed 6-14-50
Kill or Be Killed 5-21-80
Kill or Cure 11-14-62
Kill the Black Sheep (See: Zabiocie Czarna Owee)
Kill the Umpire 5-03-50
Kill Yourself, My Love (See: Suicidate, Mi Amor)
Kille Och En Tjej, En 8-20-75
Killed the Family and Went to the Movies (See: Matou a Familia e
    Foi Ao Cinema)
Killer (See: Kilas)
Killer, The (See: Tueur, Le)
Killer, The 2-11-21
Killer Ape 11-25-53
Killer at Large 10-28-36
Killer at Large 6-04-47
Killer Clans 4-07-76
Killer Dill 5-14-47
Killer Elite, The 12-24-75
Killer Fish 10-24-79
Killer Force 12-24-75
Killer Inside Me, The 10-20-76
Killer Is Loose, The 2-01-56
Killer Man (See: Scoumoune, La)
Killer McCoy 10-29-47
Killer Shark 4-12-50
Killer Shrews, The 7-01-59
Killer That Stalked New York, The 12-06-50
Killers, The (See: Kilas, O Mau Da Fita)
Killers, The 8-07-46
Killers, The 5-27-64
Killers and Thieves (See: Assassins et Voleurs)
Killers from Space 1-27-54
Killer's Kiss 9-21-55
Killers of Kilimanjaro 4-13-60
Killers of the Sea 6-16-37
Killers of the Wild 4-03-40
Killers Three 11-20-68
Killing, The 5-23-56
Killing Game (See: Jeu De Massacre)
Killing Kind, The 6-13-73
Killing Me Softly (See: Mitgift)
Killing of a Chinese Bookie, The 2-18-76
Killing of Sister George, The 12-18-68
Killing the Devil (See: Vrazda Inzenyra Certa)

Killing to Live 12-22-31
Kilmeny 7-23-15
Kilroy Was Here 7-09-47
Kim 12-06-50
Kimberley Jim 5-05-65
Kimen 8-28-74
Kimiko 4-14-37
Kind der Donau, Das 9-06-50
Kind Hearts and Coronets 6-29-49
Kind Lady 1-01-36
Kind Lady 6-20-51
Kind of Loving, A 4-25-62
Kind Stepmother (See: Edes Mostoha)
Kind Van de Zon 5-14-75
Kindaichi Kosuke no Boken 6-04-80
Kindan No Suna 4-06-60
Kinder aus No. 67, Die 2-27-80
Kinder, Mutter und ein General 5-18-55
Kinder Vor Gericht 6-16-31
Kinderarzt Dr. Engel 9-29-37
Kindling 7-16-15
Kindling Courage 3-08-23
Kindred of the Dust 1-27-22 and 9-01-22
King, The (See: Roi, Le)
King, The 10-29-41
King: A Filmed Record ... Montgomery to Memphis 3-04-70
King and Country 9-16-64
King and Four Queens, The 12-19-56
King and I, The 7-04-56
King and the Chorus Girl, The 3-31-37
King and the Mockingbird, The (See: Roi et l'Oiseau, Le)
King August the Strong (See: August der Starke)
King Baggot 4-10-14
King Bee Comedies 5-25-17
King Checkmated, The (See: Echec Au Roi)
King Cowboy 12-26-28
King Creole 5-28-58
King Dinosaur 9-28-55
King for a Day (See: Melech Leyom Echad)
King for a Night 12-12-33
King in New York, A 9-18-57
King Kong 3-07-33
King Kong 12-15-76
King Kong Escapes 6-26-68
King Kong vs. Godzilla 6-12-63
King Lear 1-05-17
King Lear 2-17-71
King Lear 9-29-71
King Murder, The 11-01-32
King Murray 4-02-69
King of Alcatraz 10-05-38
King of Beggars 6-19-14
King of Bootblacks (See: Roi du Cirage)
King of Burlesque 1-22-36
King of Champs Elysees (See: Roi des Champs Elysees, Le)
King of Chinatown 3-22-39
King of Coral Sea 7-14-54
King of Diamonds, The 10-11-18
King of Dodge City 8-13-41
King of Gamblers 7-07-37
King of Gate Crashers (See: Roi des Resquilleurs, Le)
King of Hearts, The (See: Roi de Coeur, Le)
King of Hockey 12-09-36
King of Hotels (See: Roi des Palaces, Le)
King of Jazz 5-07-30 (Also see: Feerie du Jazz)
King of Kings, The 4-20-27
King of Kings 10-11-61
King of Marvin Gardens, The 10-11-72
King of Newsboys 3-30-38
King of Paris 5-08-35
King of Sweden, The (See: Shvedski Krale)
King of the Arena 8-29-33
King of the Bandits 1-07-48
King of the Bullwhip 12-13-50
King of the Campus 4-24-29
King of the Cowboys 4-07-43
King of the Damned 1-15-36 and 2-05-36
King of the Gamblers 5-26-48
King of the Grizzlies 1-28-70
King of the Gypsies 12-13-78
King of the Herd 9-18-29
King of the Joropo 3-26-80
King of the Jungle 2-28-33
King of the Khyber Rifles 12-23-53
King of the Lumberjacks 4-17-40
King of the Roaring 20's--The Story of Arnold Rothstein
    6-21-61

King of the Royal Mounted 9-30-36
King of the Sierras 11-09-38
King of the Street Cleaners, The (See: Copculer Krali)
King of the Turf 4-07-26
King of the Turf 2-15-39
King of the Underworld 1-11-39
King of the White Elephant, The 4-09-41
King of the Wild Horses 5-14-24
King of the Wild Stallions 5-20-59
King of the Wire, The 8-20-15
King of Wild Horses 3-27-34
King on Main Street, The 10-28-25
King, Queen and Slave (See: Sahib, Bibi aur Ghulam)
King, Queen, Knave 5-24-72
King Rat 10-27-65
King Richard and the Crusaders 7-07-54
King Smiles--Paris Laughs 11-24-37
King Solomon of Broadway 10-23-35
King Solomon's Mines 6-30-37
King Solomon's Mines 9-27-50
King Spruce 6-25-20
King Steps Out, The 6-03-36
King Without Distractions, A (See: Roi Sans Divertissement, Un)
Kingdom at Stake, A 7-03-14
Kingdom for a House, A (See: Een Koninkrijk Voor een Huis)
Kingdom of Diamonds, The (See: Hirok Rajar Deshe)
Kingdom of Love, The 1-11-18
Kingdom of Naples, The (See: Regno di Napoli, Il)
Kingdom of the Spiders 11-16-77
Kingdom of Youth, The 10-11-18
Kingdom Within, The 2-01-23
Kingfisher's Roast 4-28-22
King's Command 1-15-10
King's Creek Law 12-13-23
King's Game, The 1-14-16
Kings Go Forth 6-11-58
King's Jester 2-15-08
King's Jester, The 6-04-47
King's New Clothes, The (See: Carevo Novo Ruho)
Kings of the Olympics 1-28-48
Kings of the Ring 6-13-28
Kings of the Ring 2-16-44
Kings of the Sun 12-18-63
King's People, The 3-31-37 and 5-19-37
King's Pirate, The 7-12-67
King's Protegee 8-28-09
King's Rhapsody 11-02-55
King's Row 12-24-41
King's Story, A 5-12-65
King's Thief 7-20-55
King's Vacation, The 1-24-33
Kinkaid, Gambler 12-01-16
Kino Kawa 8-03-66
Kinsman, The 7-18-19
Kipps 4-23-41
Kiri-No-Hata 10-10-79
Kirik Canaklar 7-12-61
Kirkastuva Savel 5-23-47
Kirlian Witness, The 11-22-78
Kirmes 7-20-60
Kirov 2-20-35 and 1-08-36
Kiru 7-24-68
Kisertet Lublon 3-02-77
Kismet 10-29-20
Kismet 11-05-30
Kismet 8-23-44
Kismet 12-07-55
Kiss, The (See: O Beijo)
Kiss, The 10-20-16
Kiss, The 7-08-21
Kiss, The 11-20-29
Kiss and Make Up 7-03-34
Kiss and Tell 9-12-45
Kiss Barrier, The 6-24-25
Kiss Before Dying, A 6-06-56
Kiss Before the Mirror 5-16-33
Kiss for Cinderella, A 1-06-26
Kiss for Corliss, A 10-19-49
Kiss for Susie, A 8-10-17
Kiss in the Dark, A 4-08-25
Kiss in the Dark, A 3-02-49
Kiss in Time, A 6-17-21
Kiss Length 90 (See: Delka Polibku Devadesat)
Kiss Me (See: Embrassez-Moi)
Kiss Me 2-06-29
Kiss Me Again 8-05-25
Kiss Me Again 1-14-31
Kiss Me, Darling (See: Csokolj Meg Edes)

Kiss Me Deadly 4-20-55
Kiss Me, Kate 10-28-53
Kiss Me, Kiss Me, Kiss Me 10-25-67
Kiss Me, Stupid 12-16-64
Kiss of a Dead Woman (See: Bacio Di Una Morta, Il)
Kiss of Death 8-13-47
Kiss of Fire 8-31-55
Kiss of Fire, The 11-27-40
Kiss of Hate, The 4-14-16
Kiss of the Vampire 7-31-63
Kiss or Kill 11-29-18
Kiss the Blood Off My Hands 10-20-48
Kiss the Boys Goodbye 6-18-41
Kiss the Girls and Make Them Die 1-11-67
Kiss the Other Sheik 8-14-68
Kiss Them for Me 11-06-57
Kiss Tomorrow Goodbye 8-02-50
Kisses 5-19-22
Kisses for Breakfast 7-23-41
Kisses for My President 8-19-64
Kisses Right and Left (See: Kys Til Hoejre Og Venstre)
Kisses That Cannot Be Forgotten 3-20-29
Kisses Till Monday (See: Bon Baisers a Lundi)
Kissin' Cousins 3-04-64
Kissing Bandit, The 11-17-48
Kit Carson 9-26-28
Kit Carson 8-28-40
Kitchen, The 7-26-61
Kite from Across the World, The (See: Cerf-Volant Du Bout Du
     Monde, Le)
Kitores 10-20-71
Kitten with a Whip 10-28-64
Kitty 6-12-29
Kitty 10-10-45
Kitty Foyle 12-18-40
Kivalina of the Ice Lands 7-01-25
Kjaerleikens Ferjreiser 7-30-80
Klabautermanden 7-09-69
Kladivo Na Carodejnice 4-08-70
Klann Grand Guignol 7-01-70
Klanningen 7-14-65
Klansman, The 11-06-74
Klara Lust 3-08-72
Klart Till Drabbning 12-15-37
Klassenkeile 4-30-69
Klaun Ferdinand a Raketa 5-01-63
Klein Dorrit 10-23-35
Kleine Frieren Auch Im Sommer 8-23-78
Kleine Godard, Der 11-22-78
Kleine Melodie aus Wien (See: Little Melody from Vienna)
Kleine Mutti 5-29-35
Kleine Schwindlerin, Die 4-07-37
Kleine Seitensprung, Der 9-01-31 and 1-05-32
Kleine Stadt Will Schlafen Gehn, Die 9-01-54
Kleine Welt, Die 2-09-77
Kleiner Mann, Was Nun? 8-22-33
Kleiner Vorchuss auf die Seligweit, Ein (See: Marital Happiness)
Klimaks 6-14-67
Klincz 6-11-80
Kliou, the Killer 8-18-37
Klockan Pa Ronneberga 1-02-46
Klockorna I Gambia Sta'n 1-22-47
Kloden Rokker 3-29-78
Klondike 9-27-32
Klondike Annie 3-18-36
Klondike Fever 2-13-80
Klondike Fury 7-15-42
Klondike Kate 2-23-44
Klujch Bez Prava Peredachi 1-19-77
Klute 6-30-71
Knack, The 5-19-65
Kneeler Peak (See: A Kiralylany Zsamolya)
Kneuss 11-22-78
Knickerbocker Buckaroo, The 5-30-19
Knickerbocker Holiday 3-01-44
Knife, The (See: Het Mes)
Knife, The 2-15-18
Knife, The 5-29-29
Knife in the Head (See: Messer Im Kopf)
Knife in the Water (See: Noz W Wodzie)
Knife in the Wound, The (See: Couteau Dans la Plaie, Le)
Knife to the Throat, The (See: Couteau Sous La Gorge, Le)
Knight, The (See: Rycerz)
Knight for a Night, A 10-02-09
Knight from Pardaillan, The (See: Chevalier de Pardaillan, Le)
Knight of the Night, The (See: Chevalier de la Nuit, Le)
Knight of the Plains 3-29-39
Knight of the Range, A 1-28-16

L

Lady Killer (See: Gueule d'Amour)
Lady Killer 1-02-34
Lady L 12-01-65
Lady, Let's Dance 1-26-44
Lady Lies, The (See: Dona Mentiras)
Lady Lies, The 9-11-29
Lady Luck 7-17-46
Lady Luck 9-23-36
Lady Mackenzie's Pictures 6-11-15
Lady Objects, The 10-12-38
Lady of Burlesque 5-05-43
Lady of Chance 1-16-29
Lady of Death, The (See: Dama de la Muerte, La)
Lady of Monosreau 12-20-23
Lady of Monte Carlo (See: Signora di Montecarlo, La)
Lady of Quality 12-26-13
Lady of Quality, A 12-27-23
Lady of Scandal, The 6-18-30
Lady of Secrets 2-26-36
Lady of the Camelias (See: Dame aux Camelias, La)
Lady of the Dugout, The 8-08-19
Lady of the Harem, The 8-25-26
Lady of the Lake, The (See: Donna del Lago, La)
Lady of the Law 8-20-75
Lady of the Night (See: Donna D'Una Notte, La)
Lady of the Night 3-04-25
Lady of the Pavements 3-13-29
Lady of the Rails (See: Dama Na Kolejich)
Lady of the Tropics 8-09-39
Lady of Vengeance 8-07-57
Lady on a Train 8-08-45
Lady on the Bus, The (See: A Dama Do Lotacao)
Lady Oscar 12-19-79
Lady Paname 6-28-50
Lady Pays Off, The 10-24-51
Lady Possessed 2-20-52
Lady Robin Hood 8-26-25
Lady Rose's Daughter 9-03-20
Lady Says No, The 11-28-51
Lady Scarface 7-23-41
Lady Seeks Room (See: Urilany Szobat Keres)
Lady Sings the Blues 10-18-72
Lady Surrenders, A 10-08-30
Lady Surrenders, A 6-18-47
Lady Takes a Chance, A 8-18-43
Lady Takes a Flyer, The 1-15-58
Lady Takes a Sailor, The 11-30-49
Lady Tiger (See: I Sua)
Lady to Love, A 3-05-30
Lady Tubbs 7-24-35
Lady Vanishes, The 8-31-38
Lady Vanishes, The 5-16-79
Lady Wants Mink, The 3-25-53
Lady Who Dared, The 6-09-31
Lady Who Lied, The 7-08-25
Lady Who Likes Mustaches, A 7-25-08
Lady Windermere's Fan 6-06-19
Lady Windermere's Fan 1-13-26
Lady with a Past 2-23-32
Lady with Red Hair 11-13-40
Lady with the Lamp, The 10-03-51
Lady with the Mask, The (See: Dame mit der Maske, Die)
Lady Without a Passport, A 7-19-50
Ladybird 3-09-27
Ladybug, Ladybug 12-11-63
Ladyfingers 11-18-21
Ladykillers, The 12-28-55
Lady's from Kentucky, The 4-12-39
Lady's Morals, A 11-12-30
Lady's Name, A 12-20-18
Lady's Profession, A 3-28-33
Laemna Mig Inte Ensam 6-04-80
Lafayette Escadrille 2-05-58
Lafayette, We Come! 10-25-18
Laforet the Soldier (See: Soldat Laforet, Le)
Lagerstrasse Auschwitz 3-12-80
Lagoon of Desire 9-04-57
Laia 8-16-72
Laili (See: Saga, En)
Lair of Love, The (See: Bestiaire d'Amour, Le)
Laisse Aller, C'Est Une Valse 5-05-71
Laissez les Vivre 12-31-69
Lajwanti 5-13-59
Lake Placid Serenade 12-20-44
Lalai-Dreamtime and Floating-Thistime 11-05-75
Lalie Polne 8-16-72
Lalka 7-09-69
Lam Ah Chun 7-26-78

Lama Nel Corpo, La (See: Murder Clinic, The)
Lamb, The 10-01-15
Lamb and the Lion, The 4-18-19
Lambert Is Threatened (See: Lambert Fuehlt Sich Bedroht)
Lambert Fuehlt Sich Bedroht 4-13-49
Lambeth Walk 4-03-40
Lamiel 10-04-67
Lamore 11-28-79
Lamp in the Desert 7-04-23
Lamp Post Inspector, The 3-05-10
Lamp Still Burns, The 11-10-43
Lamplighter, The 4-15-21
Lancelot and Guinevere 5-01-63
Lancelot du Lac 6-12-74
Lancelot of the Lake (See: Lancelot du Lac)
Lancer Spy 10-06-37
Lancieri di Savoia 3-09-38
Land, The 4-15-42
Land, The 4-13-55
Land and Sons (See: Land Og Synir)
Land Beyond the Law 6-29-27
Land Beyond the Law 8-18-37
Land des Lachelns, Das 12-10-52
Land des Laechelns, Das 12-17-30
Land des Schweigens und der Dunkelheit 5-10-72
Land in a Trance (See: Terra Em Transe)
Land Just Over Yonder, The 10-27-16
Land O' Lizards, The 9-29-16
Land of Angels 4-03-63
Land of Fighting Men 5-18-38
Land of Hope and Glory 12-07-27
Land of Jazz, The 1-21-21
Land of Liberty 6-21-39 and 1-15-41
Land of Long Shadows 6-22-17
Land of Love, The (See: Pendin Heng Kuam Rak)
Land of Milk and Honey (See: Pays de Cocagne)
Land of Missing Men (See: Port of Missing Men)
Land of Our Fathers 4-26-33
Land of Promise (See: Ziemia Obiecana)
Land of Promise, The 12-14-17
Land of Promise, The 11-27-35
Land of Silence and Darkness (See: Land des Schweigens und der
    Dunkelheit)
Land of Smiles (See: Land des Lachelns)
Land of the Head Hunters 12-25-14
Land of the Midnight Sun 12-24-30
Land of the Open Range 12-24-41
Land of the Pharaohs 6-22-55
Land of the Silver Fox 12-26-28
Land of the Six Guns 5-29-40
Land of Wanted Men 2-23-32
Land Og Synir 10-29-80
Land Raiders 11-26-69
Land Shark, The 1-22-15
Land That Dies, The (See: Terre Qui Meurt, La)
Land That Time Forgot, The 4-09-75
Land Unknown, The 6-19-57
Land Without Music 10-21-36
Land Without Stars (See: Pays Sans Etoiles, Le)
Land Without Women 10-30-29
Landfall 5-13-53
Landloper, The 4-05-18
Landlord, The 5-27-70
Landowner's Daughter (See: Sinha Moca)
Landru 11-08-23
Landru 2-06-63
Landrush 9-18-46
Landscape After the Battle (See: Krajobraz Po Bitwie)
Landvogt von Griefensee, Der 8-29-79
Lane That Had No Turning, The 1-13-22
Lanfier Colony, The (See: Kolona Lanfier)
Lange Beine--Lange Finger 8-24-66
Lange Jammer, Der 1-26-77
Langen Ferien der Lotte H. Eisner, Die 12-19-79
Langit, Lupa 5-05-76
Langlois 9-23-70
Langt Borta Och Naera 12-29-76
Language of Love (See: Karlekens Sprak)
Languid Kisses, Wicked Caresses (See: Languidi Baci, Perfide
    Carezze)
Languidi Baci, Perfide Carezze 2-09-77
Lantern Festival Adventure 7-25-79
Laong Dao 12-03-80
La'os Vaere 2-26-75
Lapland Calendar (See: Same Jakki)
Laporteuse de Pain 7-08-36
Lapualaismorsian 6-19-68
Laramie 10-19-49
Laramie Mountains 4-09-52

Larceny 8-11-48
Larceny in Her Heart 5-15-46
Larceny, Inc. 3-04-42
Larceny on the Air 2-10-37
Larceny with Music 9-08-43
Largas Vacaciones Del 36, Las 4-21-76
Largo Retorno, Un 6-04-75
Largo Viaje 7-05-67 and 6-19-68
Lariat Kid, The 5-08-29
Lark, The (See: Pacsirta)
Larme dans L'Ocean, Une 5-03-72
Lars Hard 9-22-48
Lars Ole, 5C 5-29-74
Larsson I Andra Giftet 10-30-35
Larsson's Second Marriage (See: Larsson I Andra Giftet)
Las Vegas 500 Milliones 1-15-69
Las Vegas Lady 1-28-76
Las Vegas Nights 3-26-41
Las Vegas Shakedown 6-01-55
Las Vegas Story, The 1-09-52
Lasca 12-05-19
Lasciate Ogni Speranza 10-27-37
Laserblast 3-08-78
Lash, The 10-06-16
Lash, The 12-17-30
Lash of Power, The 11-09-17
Lash of the Czar 2-13-29
Laski Mezi Kapkami Deste 7-23-80
Lasky Jedne Plavovlasky 9-01-65
Lass of the Lumberlands, A 10-27-16
Lassatok Felein 1-31-68
Lasse and Geir (See: Lasse Og Geir)
Lasse-Maja 3-31-43
Lasse Og Geir 8-25-76
Lassie Come Home 8-18-43
Last Act, The (See: Letzte Akt, Der)
Last Act, The 3-31-16
Last Act But One--Brundibar (See: Vorletzte Akt--Brundibar, Der)
Last Act of Martin Weston, The 10-14-70
Last Adventure, The (See: Det Sista Aventyret)
Last Affair, The 10-20-76
Last Alarm, The 8-25-26
Last American Hero, The 6-13-73
Last Angry Man, The 10-14-59
Last Bandit, The 2-23-49
Last Battle, The (See: Bou Posleden)
Last Billionaire (See: Dernier Milliardaire)
Last Blitzkrieg 12-17-58
Last Blow, The (See: Dernier Choc, Le)
Last Bohemian, The 6-23-31
Last Bridge, The (See: Letzte Bruecke, Die)
Last Campaign, The 9-20-78
Last Card, The 6-10-21
Last Challenge, The 10-04-67
Last Challenge of the Dragon, The 2-15-78
Last Chance 2-24-22
Last Chance, The 12-01-37
Last Chance, The 11-21-45
Last Chapter, The 2-19-15
Last Chapter, The 2-09-66
Last Command, The 1-25-28
Last Command, The 7-27-55
Last Company, The 4-02-30
Last Coupon, The 8-09-32
Last Cradle Song, The (See: Derniere Berceuse, La)
Last Crooked Mile, The 8-14-46
Last Cry, The (See: Letzte Schrei, Der)
Last Curtain Call, The 2-12-15
Last Dance, The 11-28-14
Last Dance, The 4-02-30
Last Days of Boot Hill 3-31-48
Last Days of Dolwyn 5-18-49
Last Days of Man on Earth 10-29-75
Last Days of Mussolini (See: Mussolini: Ultimo Atto)
Last Days of Pompei, The (See: Derniers Jours de Pompei, Les)
Last Days of Pompeii, The (See: Pompeii)
Last Days of Pompeii, The 4-14-26
Last Days of Pompeii, The 10-23-35
Last Days of Pompeii, The 6-15-60
Last Deal, The 2-05-10
Last Detail, The 12-05-73
Last Dewdrop, The (See: Nam Karng Yod Deo)
Last Eagle, The 7-17-29
Last Edition, The 11-11-25
Last Egyptian, The 12-11-14
Last Embrace, The 5-02-79
Last Escape, The 7-01-70
Last Exit Before Roissy (See: Derniere Sortie Avant Roissy)

Last Exploits of the Olsen Gang, The (See: Olsen Bandens Sidste Bedrifter)
Last Express, The 10-19-38
Last Five Minutes, The (See: Ultimi Cinque Minuti, Gli)
Last Flight, The 6-19-29
Last Flight, The 8-25-31
Last Flight of Noah's Ark, The 6-11-80
Last Fort, The 9-18-29
Last Foxtrot in Burbank 10-31-73
Last Frontier, The 10-20-26
Last Frontier, The 12-14-55
Last Frontier Uprising 8-20-47
Last Gangster, The 11-10-37
Last Gentleman, The 10-23-34
Last Grave at Dimbaza 3-26-75
Last Grenade, The 4-08-70
Last Hard Men, The 4-21-76
Last Hill, The 6-27-45
Last Holiday, The 5-17-50
Last Horseman, The 10-25-44
Last Hour, The 2-15-23
Last Hour, The 7-09-30
Last Hunt, The 2-15-56
Last Hurrah, The 10-15-58
Last Hurrah for Chivalry 10-15-80
Last Illusion, The 3-14-51
Last Journey, The 10-30-35 and 7-01-36
Last Judgment, The (See: Giudizio Universale, Il or Jugement Dernier, Le)
Last Kiss, The (See: Dernier Baiser, Le)
Last Known Address (See: Dernier Domicile Connu)
Last Leap, The (See: Dernier Saut, Le)
Last Love (See: Letzte Liebe or Kuam Rak Krang Sutai)
Last Maiden But One, The (See: A Penultima Donzela)
Last Man, The (See: Letzte Mann, Der or Dernier Homme, Le)
Last Man, The 12-10-24
Last Man, The 9-20-32
Last Man on Earth 12-17-24
Last Man on Earth 9-09-64
Last Man Out, The 10-20-16
Last Man to Hang, The 11-14-56
Last Married Couple in America, The 2-06-80
Last Meeting (See: Ultimo Incontro or Ultimo Encuentro)
Last Melodrama, The (See: Dernier Melodrame, Le)
Last Mile, The 8-30-32
Last Mile, The 1-14-59
Last Mission, The 10-15-52
Last Mission of Demolition Man Cloud, The (See: Posljednji Podvig Diverzanta Oblaka)
Last Moment, The 5-30-23
Last Moment, The 3-14-28
Last Movie, The 9-08-71
Last Musketeer, The 3-12-52
Last Night, The (See: El Leila El Akhira)
Last Night, The 1-29-30
Last Night, The 5-12-37
Last Night of Childhood (See: Ultima Noapte a Copilariei)
Last Night of Love, The (See: Ultima Notte d'Amore, L')
Last of His People 1-09-20
Last of Mohicans 1-07-21
Last of Mrs. Cheyney, The 8-14-29
Last of Mrs. Cheyney, The 2-24-37
Last of Sheila, The 5-23-73
Last of the Badmen 3-20-57
Last of the Blue Devils, The 11-14-79
Last of the Buccaneers 10-18-50
Last of the Clintons 11-13-35
Last of the Comanches 12-24-52
Last of the Cowboys, The 9-21-77
Last of the Desperados 1-25-56
Last of the Duanes, The 9-19-19
Last of the Duanes, The 9-24-24
Last of the Duanes, The 9-17-30
Last of the Duanes, The 9-10-41
Last of the Fast Guns, The 6-25-58
Last of the Ingrahams, The 2-16-17
Last of the Lone Wolf 10-22-30
Last of the Mobile Hotshots, The 12-31-69
Last of the Mohicans, The 9-09-36
Last of the Pagans, The 1-15-36
Last of the Pony Riders, The 11-04-53
Last of the Red Hot Lovers 6-07-72
Last of the Redmen 7-16-47
Last of the Secret Agents?, The 5-18-66
Last of the Ski Bums 11-05-69
Last of the Warrens 7-08-46
Last of the Wild Horses 12-15-48
Last 100 Days of Napoleon 4-10-14

Last Ones Shall Be First, The (See: Letzten Werden die Ersten Sein, Die)
Last Outlaw, The 8-10-27
Last Outlaw, The 6-17-36
Last Outpost, The 10-09-35
Last Outpost, The 4-11-51
Last Parade, The 3-04-31
Last Paradise, The (See: Ultimo Paradiso, L')
Last Payment, The 1-20-22
Last Performance, The 11-06-29
Last Picture Show, The 10-06-71
Last Plantation, The (See: Fogo Morto)
Last Posse, The 6-10-53
Last Raid of Zeppelin L-21, The 5-10-18
Last Rebel, The 6-14-18
Last Rebel, The 8-11-71
Last Refuge (See: Ultimo Refugio)
Last Remake of Beau Geste, The 7-13-77
Last Ride, The 2-16-32
Last Ride, The 9-13-44
Last Rites 3-26-80
Last Romantic Lover, The (See: Dernier Amant Romantique, Le)
Last Rose (See: Letzte Rose)
Last Rose from Casanova (See: Posledni Ruze Od Casanovi)
Last Round, The 6-19-14
Last Round-Up, The 8-28-29
Last Round-Up, The 5-15-34
Last Round-Up, The 10-08-47
Last Run, The 7-07-71
Last Safari, The 11-01-67
Last Sea, The (See: Hayam Ha'Acharon)
Last Sentence, The 1-05-17
Last Shot You Hear, The 2-19-69
Last Stand, The 6-01-38
Last Steps, The (See: Pas Perdus, Les)
Last Stop, The 1-12-49
Last Straw, The 2-27-20
Last Subway, The (See: Dernier Metro, Le)
Last Summer 5-21-69
Last Summer, The (See: Posledno Liato)
Last Summer Won't Happen 10-02-68
Last Sunset, The 5-24-61
Last Supper, The (See: Ultima Cena, La)
Last Survivor, The 6-14-78
Last Tango in Paris 10-18-72
Last Tasmanian, The 10-31-79
Last Tempest, The 3-24-76
Last Three Days, The (See: Ultimi Tre Giorni, Gli)
Last Time I Saw Archie, The 5-31-61
Last Time I Saw Paris, The 11-03-54
Last Torch Song, The (See: Ultimo Cuple, El)
Last Trail, The 1-26-27
Last Trail, The 1-23-34
Last Train from Bombay 8-06-52
Last Train from Gun Hill 4-15-59
Last Train from Madrid 6-23-37
Last Turning, The (See: Dernier Tournant, Le)
Last Tycoon, The 11-17-76
Last Valley, The 1-20-71
Last Volunteer, The 3-05-15
Last Voyage, The 1-20-60
Last Wagon, The 8-29-56
Last Waltz, The (See: Letzte Walzer, Der)
Last Waltz, The 11-16-27
Last Waltz, The 4-12-78
Last Warning, The 1-09-29
Last Warning, The 12-07-38
Last Wave, The 11-16-77
Last Wilderness, The 7-24-35
Last Winter, The (See: Dimri I Fundit)
Last Winter, The 6-13-62
Last Witness, The (See: Letzte Zeuge, Der)
Last Woman, The (See: Derniere Femme, La)
Last Woman of Shang 12-16-64
Last Woman on Earth, The 11-09-60
Last Word, The 11-21-79
Last Word, The (See: Poslednata Douma)
Last Year at Marienbad (See: Annee Derniere a Marienbad, L')
Last Years of Childhood, The (See: Letzten Jahre der Kindheit, Die)
Lata Lena Och Bla Ogdo Per 10-22-47
Late Autumn 7-22-70
Late Blossom, The (See: Soleil Se Leve En Retard, Le)
Late for the Recital 11-27-09
Late George Apley, The 2-05-47
Late Great Planet Earth, The 2-14-79
Late Liz, The 9-22-71
Late Matthias Pascal (See: Feu Matthias Pascal)

Late Season (See: U Toszezon)
Late Show (See: Nachtvorstellungen)
Late Show, The 2-02-77
Late Spring 7-12-72
Late Summer (See: Kohayagawake No Aki)
Latest from Paris 2-29-28
Latest on Robber Hotzenplotz, The (See: Nues Vom Raeuber Hotzenplotz)
Latin Lovers 7-22-53
Latin Quarter 5-08-29
Latin Quarter 10-31-45
Latitude Zero (See: Ido Zero Daisakusen)
Latuko 1-16-52
Laubenkolonie 6-06-33
Laugh and Get Rich 4-01-31
Laugh, Clown, Laugh 5-30-28
Laugh-In (See: Aililia)
Laugh It Off 12-20-39
Laugh, Pagliacci 2-04-48
Laugh Your Blues Away 2-17-43
Laughing Anne 5-05-54
Laughing at Danger 1-28-25
Laughing at Danger 8-21-40
Laughing at Death 6-05-29
Laughing at Life 7-18-33
Laughing at Trouble 2-03-37
Laughing Bill Hyde 9-27-18
Laughing Boy 5-15-34
Laughing Gas 12-21-07
Laughing Irish Eyes 4-08-36
Laughing Lady 10-23-46
Laughing Lady, The 1-08-30
Laughing Policeman, The 11-28-73
Laughing Sinners 7-07-31
Laughter 10-08-30
Laughter in Hell 1-17-33
Laughter in Paradise 6-17-51
Laughter in the Dark 5-14-69
Laughter Is the Best Medicine (See: Lachdoktor, Der)
Laughter Through Tears 11-21-33
Launching of the Roma 11-14-08
Launching the Voltaire 9-11-09
Laura 10-11-44
Laura: Les Ombres de L'Ete 1-23-80
Laura: Shadows of Summer (See: Laura: Les Ombres de L'Ete)
Lauracha 11-27-46
Laurel and Hardy's Laughing 20's 8-11-65
Lausbubenges Chichten 2-10-65
Lautare 8-02-72
Lautars, The (See: Lautare)
Lavender Hill Mob, The 7-04-51
Law, The (See: Loi, La)
Law and Disorder 6-11-58
Law and Disorder 10-09-74
Law and Jake Wade 6-04-58
Law and Lead 4-21-37
Law and Order 3-01-32
Law and Order 11-27-40
Law and Order 10-21-42
Law and Order 4-08-53
Law and the Fist, The (See: Prawo I Piese)
Law and the Lady, The 7-18-51
Law and the Man, The 12-24-10
Law and the Man, The 2-08-28
Law and the Woman, The 1-20-22
Law Comes to Texas, The 5-17-39
Law Commands 8-17-38
Law Decides, The 4-21-16
Law for Tombstone 12-29-37
Law in Her Hands 7-29-36
Law Is the Law, The (See: Loi C'Est La Loi, La)
Law Men 6-28-44
Law of Compensation, The 4-20-17
Law of Fear, The 3-21-28
Law of Life, The 2-04-16
Law of Men, The (See: Loi des Hommes, La)
Law of Men, The 5-16-19
Law of Nature, The 10-03-19 and 10-31-19
Law of Survival (See: Loi du Survivant, La)
Law of the Badlands 12-27-50
Law of the Barbary Coast 3-16-49
Law of the Golden West 5-18-49
Law of the Great Northwest, The 4-19-18
Law of the Land, The 8-17-17
Law of the Lash 3-19-47
Law of the Lawless 6-21-23
Law of the Lawless 3-25-64
Law of the Mounted 7-03-29 and 8-14-29

Law of the North 8-30-32
Law of the North, The 9-06-18
Law of the Northwest 7-07-43
Law of the Pampas 10-25-39
Law of the Panhandle 10-18-50
Law of the Plains 7-27-38
Law of the Range 6-27-28 and 11-07-28
Law of the Range 7-16-41
Law of the Ranger 4-07-37
Law of the Rio Grande 8-11-31
Law of the Saddle 7-05-44
Law of the Sea 5-03-32
Law of the Siberian Taiga 7-30-30
Law of the Texan 10-26-38
Law of the Tong 12-22-31
Law of the Tropics 9-03-41
Law of the Underworld 5-04-38
Law of the West 6-01-49
Law of West Tombstone 11-30-38
Law Rides Again, The 8-11-43
Law That Divides, The 10-18-18
Law That Failed, The 3-30-17
Law unto Herself, A 9-20-18
Law vs. Billy the Kid, The 7-28-54
Lawful Cheater, The 4-07-26
Lawful Larceny 7-26-23
Lawful Larceny 7-16-30
Lawless 4-12-50
Lawless Breed, The 12-03-52
Lawless Cowboys 1-16-52
Lawless Empire 2-13-46
Lawless Frontier, The 1-22-35
Lawless Frontiers (See: Fronteras Sin Ley)
Lawless Land 4-07-37
Lawless Legion, The 4-03-29
Lawless Nineties, The 7-01-36
Lawless Plainsmen 6-10-42
Lawless Range 5-13-36
Lawless Rider 10-27-54
Lawless Riders 4-22-36
Lawless Street, A 11-23-55
Lawless Valley 6-07-39
Lawless Woman 6-09-31
Lawman 3-24-71
Lawman Is Born, A 7-07-37
Lawrence of Arabia 12-19-62
Law's Outlaw 1-25-18
Law's Outlaw, The 6-10-21
Lawton Story, The 4-06-49
Lawyer, The (See: Advokatka)
Lawyer, The 12-10-69
Lawyer Man 1-03-33
Lawyer's Secret 6-02-31
Lay Down Your Arms 9-04-14
Lay My Burden Down 9-27-67
Lay Off Blondes (See: Touchez Pas Aux Blondes)
Lay That Rifle Down 3-31-55
Lazarillo de Tormes, El 12-23-59 and 9-14-60
Lazy Lena and Blue-Eyed Per (See: Lata Lena Och Bla Ogdo Per)
Lazy Lightning 12-29-26
Lazy River 4-10-34
Lazybones 12-09-25
Lea, in Winter (See: Lea, L'Hiver)
Lea, L'Hiver 4-07-71
Lead Brigade, The (See: Olovna Brigada)
Leadbelly 3-03-76
Leadville Gunslingers 3-26-52
League of Frightened Men 6-16-37
League of Gentlemen 4-13-60
Leah, The Forsaken 10-10-08
Le'an Ne'elan Daniel Waks? (See: But Where Is Daniel Vax?)
Leap, The (See: O Salto)
Leap from the Bridge, The (See: Sprung von der Bruecke, Der)
Leap Into the Void (See: Salto Nel Vuoto)
Leap to Fame (See: Salto a la Gloria)
Leap to Fame 4-19-18
Leap Year 11-01-32
Learned About Sailors 7-31-34
Learnin' of Jim Benton, The 12-21-17
Learning to Love 2-25-25
Learning Tree, The 6-25-69
Lease of Life 11-03-54
Leather Boys, The 2-05-64
Leather Burners 4-07-43 and 7-14-43
Leather Gloves 11-03-48
Leather-Pushers, The 11-20-40
Leather Saint, The 5-30-56
Leather Stocking 10-02-09

Leatherneck, The 4-24-29
Leathernecking 9-17-30
Leathernecks Have Landed, The 3-25-36
Leathernose (See: Nez de Cuir)
Leave All Hope (See: Lasciate Ogni Speranza)
Leave Her to Heaven 1-02-46
Leave It to Blondie 4-11-45
Leave It to God (See: Oxala)
Leave It to Henry 5-25-49
Leave It to Me 5-07-20
Leave It to Me 5-02-33
Leave It to Smith 4-24-34
Leave It to Susan 5-30-19
Leave It to the Irish 9-13-44
Leave It to the Marines 11-14-51
Leave Me Alone (See: Nechci Nic Slyset)
Leave Me Not Alone (See: Laemna Mig Inte Ensam)
Leave Us Alone (See: La'Os Vaere)
Leavenworth Case 1-22-36
Leaves of Memory 1-22-15
Leaving It All (See: Campanada, La)
Lebanon ... Why? 7-26-78
Leben Beginnt Mit 17, Das 7-07-54
Leben Mit Uwe 5-11-77
Leben von Adolf Hitler, Das 7-18-62
Leben Zu Zweit 10-30-68
Lebensborn 2-01-61
Lecon Particuliere, La 1-15-69
Led by Little Hands 9-10-10
Leech, The 3-24-22
Leech Woman 5-18-60
Left Bank (See: Rive Gauche)
Left Hand of God, The 8-24-55
Left, Right and Centre 6-24-59
Left-Handed 6-07-72
Left Handed Gun, The 4-30-58
Left-Handed Law 5-12-37
Left-Handed Woman, The (See: Linkshaendige Frau, Die)
Left, Right, Sickness of the Body (See: Kaliwa't Kanen Sakit Ng Katawan)
Leftover Ladies 11-10-31
Leg Er Sgu Min Egen 8-02-67
Legacy 10-20-63
Legacy 8-27-75
Legacy, The 10-22-10
Legacy, The 10-03-79
Legacy of Blood 3-08-78
Legal Identity (See: Identite Judiciaire)
Legally Dead 8-02-23
Legato 5-24-78
Legend About the Death and Resurrection of Two Young Men (See: Meztelen Vagy)
Legend of a Bandit, The 3-07-45
Legend of a Ghost 5-23-08
Legend of Boggy Creek, The 12-06-72
Legend of Daphne, The 3-19-10
Legend of Gosta Berling, The 10-31-28
Legend of Hell House, The 5-30-73
Legend of Hollywood, The 12-03-24
Legend of Julian Makabayan, The 2-20-80
Legend of Lobo, The 10-24-62
Legend of Lylah Clare, The 7-24-68
Legend of Narayama, The (See: Narayama Bushi-Ko)
Legend of Nigger Charley, The 5-17-72
Legend of Orpheus, The 12-04-09
Legend of Sterling Keep, The 6-12-09
Legend of the Fox 12-24-80
Legend of the Lighthouse 9-25-09
Legend of the Lost 12-18-57
Legend of the Mountain, The 4-25-79
Legend of the Oasis (See: Ech Burdijn Domog)
Legend of Tom Dooley, The 6-17-59
Legend of Ubirajara, The (See: A Lenda de Ubirajara)
Legend of William Tell, The 10-02-35
Legendary Champions 11-06-68
Legends of Anika 4-25-56
Legion of Lost Flyers 11-01-39
Legion of Missing Men 9-22-37
Legion of Terror 11-04-36
Legion of the Condemned 3-21-28
Legion of the Lawless 2-28-40
Legion Saute Sur Kolwezi, La 2-27-80
Legionaires in Paris 12-28-27
Legions d'Honneur 4-06-38
Legions of Honor (See: Legions d'Honneur)
Legions of the Nile 11-09-60
Legong, Dance of Virgins 10-09-35

Legy Jo Mindhalalig 4-22-36 and 10-28-36
Legy Mindhalalig 9-14-60
Leibenszeichen 5-15-68
Leichte Kavallerie 2-26-36
Leiden Des Jungen Werther, Die 12-15-76
Leidenschaften 6-28-72
Leidenschaftliche Bluemchen 5-10-78
Lejonet & Jungfrun 2-26-75
Lejos de los Arbores 7-12-72
Lek Pa Regnbagen 10-01-58
Lekcja Martwego Jezyka 6-11-80
Lektion I Karlek, En 11-04-59
Lelejska Gora 8-21-68
Le Mans 6-16-75
Lemmy for These Girls (See: Lemmy Pour les Dames)
Lemmy Pour les Dames 4-11-62
Lemon Drop Kid, The 10-30-34
Lemon Drop Kid, The 3-07-51
Lemon Popsicle 3-29-78
Lemonade Joe (See: Limonadovy Joe)
Lena Rais 3-26-80
Lena Rivers 10-17-14
Lena Rivers 9-30-25
Lena Rivers 5-24-32
Lend Me Your Husband 11-12-24
Lend Me Your Wife (See: Far Jag Lana Din Fru?)
Lenin Din Gavtyv 3-15-72
Lenin in 1918 6-28-39
Lenin in October 4-06-38
Lenin in Poland (See: Lenin v Polche)
Lenin v Polche 5-25-66
Lenin, You Rascal, You (See: Lenin Din Gavtyv)
Leningrad Skies (See: Leningradsko Nebo)
Leningradsko Nebo 9-14-60
Lenny 3-22-67
Lenny Bruce 3-22-67
Lenny Bruce Performance Film 11-20-74
Lenny Bruce Without Tears 11-24-71
Lenz 5-26-71
Leo and Loree 5-07-80
Leo M. Frank 7-30-15
Leo M. Frank (Showing Life in Jail) and Gov. Slaton (See: Leo M. Frank)
Leo the Last 5-13-70
Leon and the Rat, The (See: Ang Leon At Ang Daga)
Leon Morin, Pretre 9-13-61
Leon Morin Priest (See: Leon Morin, Pretre)
Leonardo da Vinci 11-26-52
Leone Have Sept Cabecas, Der 9-02-70
Leonor 9-10-75
Leopard, The (See: Al Fahd)
Leopard, The 4-17-63
Leopard Lady, The 2-29-28
Leopard Man, The 5-05-43
Leopard Men of Africa 7-31-40
Leopard Woman 10-08-20
Leopardess 3-29-23 and 5-30-23
Leopard's Bride, The 4-21-16
Leper (See: Tredowata)
Lepke 5-14-75
Leptirov Oblak 3-09-77
Les Girls 10-02-57
Less Than Kin 7-26-18
Less Than the Dust 11-10-16
Lesson in Love, A (See: Lektion I Karlek, En)
Lesson in Palmistry, A 11-06-09
Lesson of a Dead Language (See: Lekcja Martwego Jezyka)
Lessons in Love (See: Einmaleins der Liebe, Das)
Lessons in Love 6-10-21
Lest We Forget 2-01-18
Lest We Forget 4-17-35
Let Bygones Be Bygones 11-13-09
Let 'Em Have It 6-05-35
Let 'Er Go Gallagher 1-18-28
Let Freedom Ring 2-22-39
Let George Do It 8-24-38
Let George Do It 10-16-40
Let Go of My Beard (See: Eresz El a Szakallamat)
Let It Be 5-20-70
Let It Rain 3-09-27
Let Joy Reign Supreme (See: Que La Fete Commence)
Let Kathy Do It 12-10-15
Let Me Explain, Dear 12-13-32
Let Me Live (See: Mujhe Jeene Do)
Let No Man Write My Epitaph 9-21-60
Let the Balloon Go 5-05-76
Let the Beast Die (See: Que la Bete Meure)

Let the Good Times Roll 5-30-73
Let the People Sing 4-22-42
Let Them Live (See: Laissez Les Vivre)
Let Them Live 6-09-37
Let Them Talk (See: Digan Lo Que Digan)
Let Us Be Gay 7-16-30
Let Us Live 2-22-39
Let Women Alone 1-28-25
Letaci Velikog Neba 8-17-77
Letiat Jouravly 5-21-58
Let's Be Famous 3-15-39
Let's Be Fashionable 6-18-20
Let's Be Happy 5-22-57
Let's Be Ritzy 7-10-34
Let's Dance 8-09-50
Let's Do It Again 6-17-53
Let's Do It Again 10-08-75
Let's Elope 5-23-19
Let's Face It 8-11-43
Let's Fall in Love 1-23-34
Let's Get a Divorce 4-26-18
Let's Get Married (See: Marions-Nous)
Let's Get Married 3-03-26
Let's Get Married 4-14-37
Let's Get Married 3-30-60
Let's Get Those English Girls (See: A Nous Les Petites Anglaises)
Let's Get Together Tonight (See: Kom Saam Vanaand)
Let's Go 12-13-23
Let's Go, Barbara (See: Vamonos, Barbara)
Let's Go Collegiate 11-12-41
Let's Go Native 9-03-30
Let's Go Navy 8-01-51
Let's Go Places 3-05-30
Let's Go Steady 3-14-45
Let's Go, Young Guy! (See: Retsu-Go Waka Daisho)
Let's Have a Riot (See: Contestazione Generale)
Let's Kill Uncle 9-21-66
Let's Leave the War in Peace (See: Tengamos La Guerra En Paz)
Let's Live a Little 10-27-48
Let's Live Tonight 3-20-35
Let's Love and Laugh 5-27-31
Let's Make a Million 1-27-37
Let's Make a Night of It 7-07-37
Let's Make It Legal 11-14-51
Let's Make Love 8-24-60
Let's Make Music 12-11-40
Let's Not Get Angry (See: Ne Nous Fachons Pas)
Let's Play Hide-and-Seek (See: Skal Vi Lege Skjul?)
Let's Play in the World (See: Juguemos en el Mundo)
Let's Rock 5-07-58
Let's Scare Jessica to Death 8-25-71
Let's Sing Again 5-13-36
Let's Talk About Women (See: Parliamo Di Donne)
Let's Talk It Over 6-19-34
Let's Touch Wood (See: Touchons Du Bois)
Let's Try Again 6-26-34
Letter, The (See: Brief, Der or Lettre, La)
Letter, The 3-13-29
Letter, The 11-20-40
Letter for Evie, A 12-05-45
Letter from an Unknown Woman 4-14-48
Letter from Home 10-08-41
Letter from the Dead (See: Brevet Fra Afdode)
Letter of Introduction 8-03-38
Letter of Love (See: Carta de Amor, Una)
Letter to Nazim Hikmet, A (See: Gramma Ston Nazim Hikmet)
Letter to Three Wives 12-08-48
Letters from Marusia (See: Actas De Marusia)
Letters from My Mill (See: Lettres de Mon Moulin)
Letting in the Sunshine 2-28-33
Lettre, La 12-03-30
Lettre de Siberie 11-26-58
Lettres de Mon Moulin 12-22-54
Lettres de Stalingrad 4-23-69
Letty Lynton 5-03-32
Letzte Akt, Der 5-18-55
Letzte Bruecke, Die 4-07-54
Letzte Liebe 4-03-35
Letzte Liebe 8-22-79
Letzte Mann, Der 2-08-56
Letzte Rose 10-21-36
Letzte Schrei, Der 2-02-77
Letzte Walzer, Der 4-21-37
Letzte Zeuge, Der 5-03-61
Letzen Jahre der Kindheit, Die 10-31-79
Letzten Werden die Ersten Sein, Die 9-04-57

Life of Mozart, The 9-16-70
Life of Mussolini 3-09-38
Life of O'haru, The (See: Keshoku Ichadai-Onna)
Life of Our Savior, The 4-03-14
Life of Peter Vinogardiv 7-03-35
Life of Richard Wagner, The (See: Richard Wagner)
Life of Riley 9-07-27
Life of the Country Doctor 8-28-63
Life of the Hortobagy 2-14-40
Life of the Party, The 11-26-20
Life of the Party, The 11-12-30
Life of the Party, The 8-25-37
Life of Verdi (See: Giuseppe Verdi)
Life of Vergie Winters 6-19-34
Life on the Hegns Farm (See: Livet Paa Hegnsgaard)
Life Returns 1-04-39
Life Size (See: Grandeur Nature)
Life Starts Now (See: Nu Borjar Livet)
Life Study 1-31-73
Life with Blondie 1-23-46
Life with Father 8-30-47
Life with Henry 1-22-41
Life with Uwe (See: Leben Mit Uwe)
Life Without Soul 11-26-15
Lifeboat 1-12-44
Lifeguard 5-26-76
Life's a Funny Proposition 1-25-19
Life's a Game of Cards 8-15-08
Life's Cross Roads 9-26-14
Life's Crossroads 12-19-28
Life's Darn Funny 8-12-21
Life's Greatest Game 10-08-24
Life's Greatest Problem 4-04-19
Life's Just Great (See: Livet Ar Stenkul)
Life's Mockery 8-01-28
Life's Pitfalls 12-10-15
Life's Shadows 10-20-16
Life's Shop Window 11-14-14
Life's Temptation 1-01-15
Life's Twist 7-23-20
Life's Whirlpool 1-07-16
Life's Whirlpool 10-12-17
Lifespan 9-24-75
Lifetime, A (See: Toute Une Vie)
Lift, The 10-20-65
Lifted Veil, The 9-14-17
Lifting Shadows 4-09-20
Lifting the Ban of Coventry 7-02-15
Ligabue 12-06-78
Light (See: Lumiere)
Light, The 9-22-16
Light, The 1-25-19
Light Across the Way, The (See: Lumiere D'En Face, La)
Light at Dusk, The 8-04-16
Light at the Edge of the World, The 7-07-71
Light Auf Dem Galgen, Das 6-01-77
Light Cavalry (See: Leichte Kavallerie)
Light Fingers 8-21-29
Light from the Second Story Window, The 9-05-73
Light in the Clearing, The 3-03-22
Light in the Dark 9-01-22
Light in the Forest 4-30-58
Light in the Piazza 1-17-62
Light in the Window, The 12-07-27
Light Melody (See: Kirkastuva Savel)
Light of Asia, The 5-16-28
Light of Happiness, The 9-22-16
Light of the Western Stars, The 6-24-25
Light of the Western Stars, The 4-30-30
Light of Victory, The 2-28-19
Light of Western Stars 4-24-40
Light on the Gallows, The (See: Light Auf Dem Galgen, Das)
Light That Failed, The 10-27-16
Light That Failed, The 11-29-23
Light That Failed, The 12-27-39
Light Touch, The 10-31-51
Light Up the Sky 7-13-60
Light Within, The 2-15-18
Light Woman, A 1-09-29
Light Woman, The 9-24-20
Lighthouse, The 1-29-58
Lighthouse by the Sea 12-31-24
Lighthouse by the Sea, The 11-05-15
Lightnin' 7-22-25
Lightnin' 12-03-30
Lightnin' Crandall 11-17-37
Lightnin' in the Forest 4-21-48
Lightning 10-12-27

Lightning Bill Carson 7-01-36
Lightning Bolt 5-31-67
Lightning Conductor, The 5-15-14
Lightning Conductor, The 11-16-38
Lightning Flyer 4-08-31
Lightning Guns 12-06-50
Lightning Lariats 8-03-27
Lightning Over Water 5-28-80
Lightning Raider, The 12-20-18
Lightning Raiders 12-26-45
Lightning Romance 4-08-25
Lightning Speed 11-07-28
Lightning Strikes Twice 5-01-35
Lightning Strikes Twice 2-21-51
Lightning Strikes West 6-19-40
Lightning Swords of Death 3-06-74
Lights in the Night (See: Nattens Ljus)
Lights of Buenos Aires (See: Luces de Buenos Aires)
Lights of London 10-11-23
Lights of My City (See: Lumieres de Ma Ville)
Lights of New York 7-11-28
Lights of New York, The 5-26-16
Lights of Old Broadway 11-04-25
Lights of Old Santa Fe 11-08-44
Lights of Paris (See: Lumieres de Paris)
Lights of Paris 8-01-28
Lights of the Desert 6-16-22
Lights on the Murderer (See: Pleins Feux Sur l'Assassin)
Lights Out 10-25-23
Lights Out in Europe 4-03-40
Lightship, The (See: Feuerschiff, Das)
Ligne de Demarcation, La 6-08-66
Like a Boomerang (See: Comme Un Boomerang)
Like a Pot of Strawberries (See: Comme Un Pot Des Fraises)
Like All Mothers 5-16-45
Like Father, Like Son 2-01-61
... Like Once Lili Marlene (See: ... Wie Einst Lili Marleen)
Like Two Merry Acronauts (See: Wie Zwei Froehliche Luftschiffer)
Like Wildfire 5-25-17
Likely Story, A 4-16-47
Li'l Abner 11-04-59
Lila 4-11-62
Lila Akac, A 9-25-34 and 3-11-36
Lila Akac, A 7-31-74
Lilac (See: Coeur de Lilas)
Lilac Domino, The 12-11-40
Lilac Sunbonnet 8-11-22
Lilac Time 8-08-28
Lilacs in the Spring 1-05-55
Lili 3-11-53
Lilies of the Field 3-19-24
Lilies of the Field 2-26-30
Lilies of the Field 8-14-34
Lilies of the Field 7-03-63
Lilika 8-12-70
Liliom 10-08-30
Liliom 5-15-34 and 3-20-35
Lilith 9-23-64
Lille Spejl 3-01-78
Lille Virgil og Orla Froesnapper 4-02-80
Lilli Marlene 8-01-51
Lillian Russell 5-22-40
Lilly Turner 6-20-33
Lily, The 10-20-26
Lily Aime-Moi 4-30-75
Lily and the Rose, The 11-12-15
Lily Christine 9-20-32
Lily, Love Me (See: Lily Aime-Moi)
Lily of the Dust 8-27-24
Limbo 11-08-72
Limbo Line, The 1-01-69
Limehouse Blues, The 12-18-34
Limelight 3-11-36
Limelight 10-08-52
Limited Mail, The 9-02-25
Limonadovy Joe 8-05-64
Limousine Life 2-01-18
Limping Man, The 11-18-36
Limping Man, The 12-30-53
Lin Tse-hsu 8-23-78
Lina Braake--Die Interessen der Bank Koennen Nicht Die
    Interessen Sein, Lina Braake Hat 7-09-75
Lina Braake--The Bank's Interests Can't Be the Interests Lina
    Braake Has (See: Lina Braake--Die Interessen der Bank Koennen
    Nicht Die Interessen Sein, Lina Braake Hat)
Linceul N'a Pas De Poches, Un 2-05-75
Lincoln Conspiracy, The 10-12-77
Lincoln Cycle, The 4-27-17

Lincoln in the White House 1-18-39
Linda 4-03-29
Linda Be Good 10-29-47
Linda Lovelace Meets Miss Jones 8-27-75
Lindenwirtin von Rhein, Die 9-29-31
Line 5-17-61
Line of Demarcation (See: Ligne de Demarcation, La)
Line-Up, The 5-22-14
Linea D'Ombra 9-24-80
Lineup, The 5-29-34
Lineup, The 5-07-58
Lingerie 8-22-28
Link That Held, The 1-21-11
Linkshaendige Frau, Die 11-16-77
Linus and the Mysterious Red Brick House (See: Linus Eller
    Tegelhusets Hemlighet)
Linus Eller Tegelhusets Hemlighet 9-19-79
Liola (See: Very Handy Man, A)
Lion, The 8-01-62
Lion and the Girl, The 5-19-16
Lion and the Horse, The 3-26-52
Lion and the Lamb 4-08-31
Lion and the Mouse, The 2-21-19
Lion and the Mouse, The 5-30-28 and 6-20-28
Lion & the Virgin, The (See: Lejonet & Jungfrun)
Lion Has Seven Heads, The (See: Leone Have Sept Cabecas, Der)
Lion Has Wings, The 1-24-10
Lion Hunters, The 4-04-51
Lion in Winter, The 10-23-68
Lion Is in the Streets, A 9-09-53
Lions Are Loose, The (See: Lions Sont Laches, Les)
Lion's Bride, The 8-29-08
Lion's Den, The 5-23-19
Lion's Den, The 9-02-36
Lion's Jaw, The (See: Jaula de los Leones, La)
Lions Love 9-24-69
Lions Share, The (See: Part des Lions, La)
Lions Sont Laches, Les 10-04-61
Lipstick 4-07-76
Lipstick, The (See: Rossetto, Il)
Liquid Electricity 11-23-07
Liquidator, The 8-31-66
Lisa 5-09-62
Lisbon 8-01-56
Lisbon Story, The 3-06-46
Liselotte von der Pfalz 1-11-67
Lisice 8-12-70
Lissy 7-31-57
List of Adrian Messenger, The 5-29-63
Listen, Darling 10-19-38
Listen Lester 6-18-24
Listen, Let's Make Love? (See: Scusi, Facciamo L'Amore?)
Lisztomania 10-15-75
Liszt's Rhapsody (See: Wenn die Musik Nicht Waer)
Lit a Deux Places, Le 8-25-65
Lit ... le Bawdy Bed, Le 1-14-76
Little, a Lot, Passionately, A (See: Peu, Beaucoup,
    Passionnement, Un)
Little Accident 8-06-30
Little Accident 11-01-39
Little Acrobat, The 10-08-10
Little Advance on Marital Happiness, A (See: Marital Happiness)
Little Adventuress 11-09-38
Little Adventuress, The 6-29-27
Little Affair, A (See: Chotisi Baat)
Little America 10-16-35
Little American, The 7-06-17
Little Angel of Canyon Creek 11-07-14
Little Angels of Luck 9-17-10
Little Annie Rooney 10-21-25
Little Archimedes, The (See: Piccolo Archimede, Il)
Little Ark, The 2-23-72
Little Australians, The 1-31-40
Little Ballerina, The 3-07-51
Little Bather, The (See: Petit Baigneur, Le)
Little Beggar, The 2-26-10
Little Big Horn 11-02-27
Little Big Horn 5-30-51
Little Big Man 12-16-70
Little Big Shot 10-09-35
Little Birdie (See: Madarkak)
Little Bit of Heaven, A 6-13-28
Little Bit of Heaven, A 10-16-40
Little Boss, The 6-13-19
Little Boy (See: Buebchen)
Little Boy 9-17-10
Little Boy Lost 7-08-53
Little Boy Scout, The 7-13-17

Little Brother, The 2-23-17
Little Brother of the Rich, A 6-27-19
Little Brunette, The (See: En Moremita Clara)
Little Buckaroo 3-28-28
Little by Little (See: Petit a Petit)
Little Caesar 1-14-31
Little Cafe (See: Petit Cafe, Le)
Little Cigars 5-30-73
Little Clown, The 4-08-21
Little Colonel, The 3-27-35
Little Comrade 5-30-19
Little Convict, A 4-23-80
Little Coquette, A 2-27-09
Little Cripple 2-29-08
Little Damozel, The 2-21-33
Little Darling 9-11-09
Little Darlings 3-19-80
Little Dorrit (See: Klein Dorrit)
Little Dragons, The 7-23-80
Little Drummer of 1872 8-21-09
Little Duchess, The 8-10-17
Little Dutch Girl, The 9-03-15
Little Egypt 8-01-51
Little Escapes (See: Petites Fugues, Les)
Little Eva Ascends 1-27-22
Little Eve Edgarton 8-11-16
Little Fairground (See: Kohrinta)
Little Father 9-18-09
Little Fauss and Big Halsy 10-21-70
Little Flower of Jesus 1-04-39
Little Fool, The 5-06-21
Little Foxes, The 8-13-41
Little 'Fraid Lady 1-28-21
Little French Girl 6-03-25
Little Friend 8-07-34 and 10-23-34
Little Fugitive, The 9-23-53
Little Giant 5-30-33
Little Giant 2-27-46
Little Girl in Blue Velvet, The (See: Petite Fille en Velours
    Bleu, La)
Little Girl Next Door, The 6-23-16
Little Girl Next Door, The 5-10-23
Little Girl, the Dog and the Seal, The (See: Tjorven, Batsman
    Och Moses)
Little Girl Who Lives Down the Lane, The 3-16-77
Little Godard, A (See: Kleine Godard, Der)
Little Gray Lady 7-17-14
Little Gray Mouse 12-24-20
Little Humpbacked Horse 10-10-62
Little Hut 5-15-57
Little Intruder, The 3-28-19
Little Iodine 9-11-46
Little Irish Girl, The 5-12-26
Little Italy 7-22-21
Little Jack's Letter 3-26-10
Little Joe, Wrangler 12-23-42
Little Johnny Jones 8-16-23
Little Johnny Jones 2-05-30
Little Journey, A 1-05-27
Little Lady Eileen 8-18-16
Little Lady in the Train, A (See: Femme Dans le Train)
Little Liar, The (See: Mentirosa, La)
Little Liar, The 9-01-16
Little Lord Fauntleroy (See: Lord Fauntleroy)
Little Lord Fauntleroy 6-26-14
Little Lord Fauntleroy 4-08-36
Little Love of My Life (See: Ahi Viene Martin Corona)
Little Mademoiselle 10-01-15
Little Malcolm 7-10-74
Little Man (See: Shraga Katan)
Little Man, What Now? (See: Kleiner Mann, Was Nun?)
Little Man, What Now? 6-05-34
Little Marcel (See: Petit Marcel, Le)
Little Martyr, The 4-30-47
Little Match Girl, The 7-18-28
Little Meena's Romance 4-07-16
Little Melody from Vienna 11-17-48
Little Men 2-20-35
Little Men 12-04-40
Little Mermaid, The (See: Rousalochka or Mala Morska Vila)
Little Mickey Grogan 2-29-28
Little Minister, The 3-05-15
Little Minister, The 1-01-35
Little Miss Big 9-04-46
Little Miss Broadway 7-06-38
Little Miss Brown 6-11-15
Little Miss Devil 12-12-51
Little Miss Fortune 5-11-17

Loaded Pistols 12-22-48
Loan Shark 4-30-52
Loba y la Paloma, La 9-18-74
Loca, La 7-30-52
Local Bad Man 3-29-32
Local Boy Makes Good 12-01-31
Local Color 4-26-78
Locandiera, La 12-03-80
Locas, Las 8-03-77
Location Hunting (See: Reperages)
Lock Up Your Daughters 4-09-69
Locked Door, The 10-17-14
Locked Door, The 1-22-30
Locked Doors 1-14-25
Locked Lips 5-28-20
Lockende Ziel, Das (See: Alluring Goal, or The Enticing Goal,
   The)
Lockende Ziel, Das 6-20-33
Locket, The 12-18-46
Locotaire, Le 6-02-76
Locura de Amor (See: Mad Queen, The)
Locuras de Barbara, Las 11-25-59
Lodge in the Wilderness 9-22-26
Lodger, The (See: Sublokator)
Lodger, The 9-20-32
Lodger, The 1-05-44
Loegneren 1-20-71
Loffe Pa Luffen 2-18-48
Loffe, the Tramp (See: Loffe Pa Luffen)
Logan's Run 6-16-76
Loi, La 2-18-59
Loi C'Est la Loi, La 11-12-58
Loi des Hommes, La 7-25-62
Loi du Survivant, La 5-24-67
Loin de Vietnam (See: Far From Vietnam)
Lokis 9-09-70
Lola 11-14-14
Lola 2-22-61
Lola Montes 1-25-56
Lola's Lolos (See: Lolos de Lola, Les)
Lolita 6-13-62
Lollipop Cover, The 11-17-65
Lollipop Girls in Hard Candy, The 10-20-76
Lolly-Madonna XXX 2-14-73
Lolos de Lola, Les 1-18-76
Lombardi, Ltd. 10-31-19
London 10-27-26
London After Midnight 12-14-27
London Belongs to Me 8-25-48
London Blackout Murders 12-23-42
London by Night 8-04-37
London Can Take It 10-30-40
London in the Raw 7-22-64
London Melody 2-17-37
London Town 9-04-46
Lone Avenger, The 7-04-33
Lone Cowboy 2-06-34
Lone Eagle, The 12-21-27
Lone Fighter, The 11-15-23
Lone Gun 4-07-54
Lone Hand 4-09-20
Lone Hand, The 4-01-53
Lone Hand Texan, The 3-05-47
Lone Horseman, The 2-26-30
Lone Ranger, The 2-02-38
Lone Ranger, The 1-11-56
Lone Ranger and the Lost City of Gold, The 6-04-58
Lone Ranger Rides Again, The 2-15-39
Lone Rider, The 7-23-30
Lone Rider Ambushed 9-17-41
Lone Rider Crosses the Rio, The 3-05-41
Lone Rider in Ghost Town, The 9-10-41
Lone She Wolf, The (See: Louve Solitaire, La)
Lone Star 12-19-51
Lone Star Law Men 1-07-42
Lone Star Pioneers 3-22-39
Lone Star Raiders 12-25-40
Lone Star Ranger 1-22-30
Lone Star Ranger 3-11-42
Lone Star Ranger, The 6-27-19
Lone Star Trail 9-08-43
Lone Star Vigilantes, The 9-24-41
Lone Texan 2-11-59
Lone Trail, The 3-15-32
Lone Wagon, The 3-12-24
Lone Wolf (See: Birjuk)
Lone Wolf, The 7-07-17
Lone Wolf, The 5-07-24

Lone Wolf and His Lady 3-23-49
Lone Wolf Keeps a Date, The 12-18-40
Lone Wolf in London, The 11-26-47
Lone Wolf in Paris, The 5-25-38
Lone Wolf Meets a Lady, The 6-12-40
Lone Wolf Returns, The 2-05-36
Lone Wolf Spy Hunt, The 1-25-39
Lone Wolf Strikes, The 1-24-40
Lone Wolf Takes a Chance, The 3-12-41
Lone Wolf's Daughter, The 1-23-20
Lone Wolf's Daughter, The 3-06-29
Loneliness of the Long Distance Runner, The 10-03-62
Lonely Are the Brave 5-02-62
Lonely Bachelor, The 11-06-09
Lonely Heart, The 9-09-21
Lonely Hearts (See: Cuori Solitari)
Lonely Hearts Bandits 8-30-50
Lonely Lane 10-20-63
Lonely Man, The 5-15-57
Lonely Night 4-07-54
Lonely Road 9-09-36
Lonely Road, The 5-24-23
Lonely Trail, The 1-06-22
Lonely Trail, The 10-28-36
Lonely White Sail 5-11-38
Lonely Wife, The (See: Charulata)
Lonely Wives 3-18-31
Lonely Woman, The 5-10-18
Lonelyhearts 12-03-58
Loner, The (See: Solitaire, Le)
Loners, The 4-26-72
Lonesome 10-10-28
Lonesome Chap, The 4-20-17
Lonesome Cowboys 11-13-68
Lonesome Ladies 8-03-27
Lonesome Trail 8-13-30
Long and the Short and the Tall, The 3-08-61
Long Arm, The 7-04-56
Long Arm of Mannister, The 10-24-19
Long Chance 10-06-22
Long Dark Hall, The 2-14-51
Long Day's Dying 5-29-68
Long Day's Journey Into Night 5-30-62
Long des Trottoirs, Le 7-11-56
Long Drive, The (See: Cursa)
Long Duel, The 8-02-67
Long Good Friday, The 5-28-80
Long Goodbye, The 3-07-73
Long Gray Line, The 2-09-55
Long Haul, The 9-04-57
Long, Hot Summer, The 3-05-58
Long Is the Road 11-10-48
Long John Silver 12-22-54
Long Journey, A (See: Largo Viaje)
Long Lament, The (See: Lange Jammer, Der)
Long Lane's Turning, The 2-21-19
Long Legs--Long Fingers (See: Lange Beine--Lange Finger)
Long Live ... (See: Zendabad)
Long Live Death (See: Vive La Mort ou Viva La Muerte)
Long Live France (See: Vive La France)
Long Live Ghosts! (See: At Ziji Duchove!)
Long Live Hazana (See: Arriba Hazana)
Long Live Henry the Fourth, Long Live Love (See: Vive Henri IV,
   Vive l'Amour)
Long Live Jalisco, My Natal Land (See: Viva Jalisco Que Es Mi
   Tierra)
Long Live Life! (See: Viva la Vida!)
Long Live Progress (See: Awans)
Long Live the Bride and Groom (See: Vivan Los Novios)
Long Live the Island Frogs (See: Sum Gaegooli Manse!)
Long Live the King 11-29-23 and 12-06-23
Long Live the Middle Class (See: Viva la Clase Media)
Long Live the Republic (See: At Zije Republika)
Long Live Trail 11-06-29
Long, Long Trailer, The 1-06-54
Long Lost Father, The 2-27-34
Long Memory, The 2-04-53
Long Night, The 5-28-47
Long Pants 3-30-27
Long Returning, A (See: Largo Retorno, Un)
Long Ride from Hell, A 3-11-70
Long Riders, The 5-07-80
Long Rope, The 2-08-61
Long Ships, The 3-11-64
Long Shot 11-29-78
Long Shot, The 1-11-39
Long Trail, The 8-03-17

Long Vacation of Lotte H. Eisner, The (See: Langen Ferien der Lotte H. Eisner, Die)
Long Vacations of '36, The (See: Largas Vacaciones Del 36, Las)
Long Voyage Home, The 10-09-40
Long Wait, The 5-05-54
Long Way, The (See: Welte Weg, Der)
Long Weekend 5-10-78
Long Weekend, The (See: Puente, La)
Longest Day, The 10-03-62
Longest Journey, The (See: Najdolgiot Pat)
Longest Night, The 10-21-36
Longest Night, The 11-08-67
Longest Yard, The 8-28-74
Longhorn, The 10-10-51
Longing 202 (See: Sehnsucht 202)
Longue Marche, La 5-11-66
Longues Annees, Les 6-24-64
Look After Amelie (See: Occupe-Toi d'Amelie)
Look After My Wife (See: Rad Bizom a Felesegem)
Look at Liv, A 12-07-77
Look at This City (See: Schaut Auf Diese Stadt)
Look Back in Anger 6-03-59
Look Before You Love 12-22-48
Look Chao Phya 11-30-77
Look for the Silver Lining 6-29-49
Look in Any Window 3-22-61
Look Lovely and Shut Up (See: Sois Belle et Tais Toi)
Look Out for Love 2-16-38
Look Out Girls (See: Mefiez-Vous Fillettes)
Look Out, Paint (See: Prenez Garde a la Peinture)
Look Out Sister 12-22-48
Look See (See: Ecoute Voir)
Look Up and Laugh 7-10-35
Look Who's Laughing 9-17-41
Looking Back (See: Ohlednuti)
Looking for Death (See: Busca de La Muerte, En)
Looking for Love 7-08-64
Looking for Mr. Goodbar 10-19-77
Looking for the Sea Serpent 12-05-08
Looking for Trouble 6-02-26
Looking for Trouble 4-17-34
Looking Forward 5-02-33
Looking Glass War, The 2-04-70
Looking Into the Eyes of the Sun (See: Pogled U Zjenicu Sunca)
Looking Up 3-16-77
Lookout Girl 11-07-28
Loop, The (See: Oese, Die)
Looped for Life 10-08-24
Loophole 2-24-54
Looping 8-27-75
Looping the Loop 11-14-28 and 2-13-29
Loose Ankles 2-26-30
Loose Ends 10-22-30
Loose Ends 6-04-75 and 9-15-76
Loose in London 7-08-53
Loot 1-31-71
Looters, The 4-13-55
Lord and Lady Algy 10-03-19
Lord Byron of Broadway 3-12-30
Lord Chamber's Ladies 11-15-32
Lord Fauntleroy 9-23-21
Lord From the Lane, The (See: Greven Fran Granden)
Lord Jeff 6-22-38
Lord Jim 11-18-25
Lord Jim 2-24-65
Lord Love a Duck 1-19-66
Lord Loves the Irish, The 12-19-19
Lord of the Flies 5-22-63
Lord of the Rings, The 11-08-78
Lord Richard in the Pantry 8-06-30
Lord Shango 2-26-75
Lord Takes a Bride, The 1-29-58
Lords of Flatbush, The 5-01-74
Lords of High Decision, The 2-25-16
Lorelei of the Sea 8-31-17
Lorenzino de Medici 4-15-36
Lorna 8-18-65
Lorna Doone 12-08-22
Lorna Doone 1-08-35
Lorna Doone 5-30-51
Lorraine of the Lions 9-23-25
Lorsque L'Enfant Parait 11-07-56
Loser, A (See: Cave, Un)
Loser Takes All 7-11-56
Loser Wins, The (See: Zweimal Zwei im Himmelbett)
Losers, The 11-27-68
Losers, The 5-20-70
Loser's End, The 1-21-25

Lost 2-08-56
Lost 12-23-70
Lost--A Wife 6-24-25
Lost and Found (See: Oggetti Smarriti)
Lost and Found 3-22-23
Lost and Found 6-27-79
Lost and Won 1-26-17
Lost Angel 4-12-44
Lost Angel, The (See: Verlorene Engel, Der)
Lost Army, The (See: Popioly)
Lost at Sea 11-07-14
Lost at Sea 8-25-26
Lost at the Front 6-15-27
Lost Boundaries 6-29-49
Lost Boy, The (See: Sovsem Propashtshiy)
Lost Bridegroom, The 3-24-16
Lost Bridge (See: Zerwany Most)
Lost Canyon 1-20-43
Lost Children, The (See: Ztracenci)
Lost Chord, The 4-29-25
Lost Chord, The 8-18-37
Lost City, The 3-06-35
Lost Command, The 5-25-66
Lost Continent (See: Continente Perduto)
Lost Continent 7-25-51
Lost Continent 7-03-68
Lost Dogs Without Collars (See: Chiens Perdus Sans Colliers)
Lost Empire, The 1-23-29
Lost Expedition, The 10-10-28
Lost Face, The (See: Ztracena Tvar)
Lost Gods 7-09-30 and 10-08-30
Lost Happiness 3-03-48
Lost Honeymoon 3-12-47
Lost Honor of Katharine Blum, The (See: Verlorene Ehre der Katharina Blum, Die)
Lost Horizon 3-10-37
Lost Horizon 3-07-73
Lost in a Big City 4-19-23
Lost in a Harem 8-30-44
Lost in Alaska 7-30-52
Lost in London 12-18-14
Lost in Mid-Ocean 7-10-14
Lost in Siberia 10-23-09
Lost in the Arctic 8-01-28
Lost in the Dark (See: Sperduti Nel Buio)
Lost in the Stars 2-06-74
Lost in the Stratosphere 3-06-35
Lost in Transit 9-14-17
Lost Jungle, The 6-19-34
Lost Lady, A 1-21-25
Lost Lady, A 10-09-34
Lost Lagoon 2-05-58
Lost Life, A (See: Verlorenes Leben)
Lost Limited, The 9-07-27
Lost, Lonely and Vicious 10-22-58
Lost Love Juliana (See: Juliana do Amor Perdido)
Lost Man, The 5-14-69
Lost Missile 12-03-58
Lost Moment, The 10-15-47
Lost Money 1-23-20
Lost One, The (See: Verlorene, Der)
Lost One, The 3-31-48
Lost Paradise (See: Elveszett Paradicsom or Het Verloren Paradise)
Lost Paradise, The 9-04-14
Lost Patrol, The 12-18-29
Lost Patrol, The 4-03-34
Lost Pencil, The (See: Izgubljena Olovka)
Lost People, The 9-07-49
Lost Princess, The 10-31-19
Lost Ranch, The 9-21-38
Lost Romance, The 5-13-21
Lost Sex 7-03-68
Lost Shadow, The 3-28-28
Lost Souls (See: Infierno de Almas)
Lost Souvenirs (See: Souvenirs Perdus)
Lost Spring (See: Sekishun)
Lost Squadron, The 3-15-32
Lost, Strayed or Stolen 2-08-08
Lost Trail, The 11-28-45
Lost Tribe 7-03-29
Lost Tribe, The 11-12-24
Lost Tribe, The 4-20-49
Lost Valley (See: Verlorene Tal, Das)
Lost Volcano, The 6-28-50
Lost Way, The (See: Chemin Perdu, Le)
Lost Weekend, The 8-15-45
Lost World, The 2-11-25

Love in the Dark 11-24-22
Love in the Desert 5-08-29 and 8-21-29
Love in the Ring (See: Liebe im Ring)
Love in the Rough 10-01-30
Love in Waltz Time (See: Liebe Im 3/4 Takt)
Love-Ins, The 8-02-67
Love-Intrigue-Passion 8-30-23
Love Is a Ball 3-06-63
Love Is a Headache 2-02-38
Love Is a Lie 7-04-28
Love Is a Many Splendored Thing 8-10-55
Love Is a Racket 6-14-32
Love Is an Awful Thing 9-08-22
Love Is at Stake (See: Amour Est en Jeu, L')
Love Is Better Than Ever 2-06-52
Love Is Blue (See: Kuam Rak See Dam)
Love Is Gay, Love Is Sad (See: Amour C'Est Gai, L'Amour C'Est
   Triste, L')
Love Is Like That 5-09-33
Love Is Love (See: Liebe Ist Liebe)
Love Is Love 8-15-19
Love Is News 3-10-37
Love Is on the Air 9-15-37
Love Is Only a Word (See: Liebe Ist Nur Ein Wort)
Love Is 20 Years Old (See: Amour A Vingt Ans, L')
Love Is War 7-14-71
Love Island 7-23-52
Love, Latest Model (See: Amor Ultimo Modelo)
Love Laughs at Andy Hardy 12-04-46
Love Lesson (See: Licao de Amor)
Love Letter, The 2-15-23
Love Letters 1-04-18
Love Letters 8-22-45
Love Letters of a Star 12-02-36
Love Liar, The 3-31-16
Love Lies 8-25-31
Love, Life and Laughter 6-07-23
Love Life of Adolf Hitler, The 3-03-48
Love Life of Mimi, The (See: Vie de Boheme, La)
Love Light, The 1-14-21
Love, Live and Laugh 11-06-29
Love Living, Live Loving (See: Liebe Das Leben--Lebe Das Lieben)
Love Locked Out 12-14-49
Love Lottery 2-10-54
Love, Lust & Violence 7-02-75
Love Machine, The 8-04-71
Love-Mad Baronesses, The (See: Liebestollen Baronessen, Die)
Love, Madame (See: Amour, Madame, L')
Love Madness 9-24-20
Love Makes 'Em Wild 3-09-27
Love Makes Us Blind 8-24-27 and 5-02-28
Love Maneuvers (See: Manewry Milosne)
Love Mart, The 12-28-27
Love Mask, The 4-14-16
Love Masquerade 5-08-29
Love Master, The 5-21-24
Love Mates 1-31-68
Love Me 3-22-18
Love Me and the World Is Mine 2-08-28
Love Me Forever 7-03-35
Love Me Like I Do 3-18-70
Love Me--Love My Wife 6-16-71
Love Me or Leave Me 5-25-55
Love Me Tender 11-21-56
Love Me Tonight 8-23-32
Love Nest (See: Casa Chica, La)
Love Nest 10-17-51
Love Net, The 12-13-18
Love Never Dies 10-13-16
Love Never Dies 12-16-21
Love of a Clown 2-08-50
Love of a Little Girl, The (See: Tirak Cong Norng Noo)
Love of a Woman, The (See: Amour d'Une Femme, L')
Love of Aliocha, The (See: Alieskine Liubov)
Love of Anuradha (See: Anuradha)
Love of Captain Brando, The (See: Amor Del Capitan Brando, El)
Love of Jeanne Ney 2-08-28
Love of Lady Irma, The 3-26-10
Love of Life: Artur Rubinstein (See: Amour de la Vie: Artur
   Rubinstein, L')
Love of Paquita 9-21-27
Love of Perdition (See: Amor der Perdicao)
Love of Sunya 3-16-27
Love of the Rott Bros., The 7-17-29
Love of the White Snake 8-23-78
Love of Women 7-23-24

Love on a Bet 3-11-36
Love on a Budget 1-12-38
Love on Skis 11-14-33
Love on the Dole 4-30-41
Love on the Gallows (See: Am Galgen Haengt Die Liebe)
Love on the Run (See: Amour en Fuite, L')
Love on the Run 12-02-36
Love on Toast 12-22-37
Love on Wheels 8-09-32
Love or a Kingdom 12-08-37
Love or Justice 6-22-17
Love Order (See: Liebeskommando)
Love Over Night 12-19-28
Love Parade, The 11-27-29
Love Past Thirty 3-13-34
Love Piker 7-19-23
Love Pirate, The 7-25-28
Love Powder (See: Goona-Goona)
Love Prelude (See: Preludio D'Amore)
Love Sings (See: Amour Chante, L')
Love 65 (See: Karlek 65)
Love Slave 8-04-22
Love Slaves of the Amazons 12-04-57
Love Song (See: Liebeslied)
Love Special, The 3-25-21
Love Storm, The 10-20-31
Love Story (See: Douce or Histoire d'Amour, Une)
Love Story 11-22-44 (Also see: Lady Surrenders, A)
Love Story 12-16-70
Love Story, A (See: Historia de Amor, Una)
Love Story Film (See: Szerelmesfilm)
Love Sublime, A 3-09-17
Love, Sunshine and Songs (See: Karlek, Solsken Och Sang)
Love, Swedish Style 8-30-72
Love Swindle, The 8-16-18
Love Swindlers, The 10-20-76
Love Takes Flight 8-18-37
Love Tales of Boccaccio (See: Liebesgeschichten von Boccaccio)
Love That Brute 5-10-50
Love That Dares 5-09-19
Love That Lives, The 7-13-17
Love, the Afternoon (See: Amour, L'Apres-Midi, L')
Love Thief, The 12-29-16
Love Thief, The 8-04-26
Love Thrill, The 5-11-27
Love Thy Neighbor (See: Kochajmy Sie)
Love Thy Neighbor 12-25-40
Love Time 11-06-34
Love to Music (See: Amor Solfeando, El)
Love Toy, The 4-07-26
Love Trader 11-26-30
Love Trap, The 10-11-23
Love Trap, The 9-04-29
Love Under Difficulties 1-14-11
Love Under Fire 8-11-31
Love Victorious, The 7-31-14
Love Wager, The 11-02-27
Love Waltz, The 3-12-30 and 8-06-30
Love Wanga 1-07-42
Love Watches 7-12-18
Love Whispers (See: Es Flustert die Liebe)
Love with the Proper Stranger 12-25-63
Love Without Question 4-30-20
Lovebound 5-17-23
Loved One, The 10-13-65
Lovejoy's Nuclear War 10-29-75
Loveland 5-09-73
Lovelorn, The 12-21-27
Lovely Monster, A (See: Beau Monstre, Un)
Lovely Sundays (See: Beaux Dimanches, Les)
Lovely Swine (See: Bel Ordure)
Lovely to Look At 5-28-52
Lovely Way to Die, A (See: Lovely Way to Go, A)
Lovely Way to Go, A 6-19-78
Lover, The (See: Amoureuse, L')
Lover Come Back 6-09-31
Lover Come Back 6-12-46
Lover Come Back 12-13-61
Lover for Five Days (See: Amant de Cinq Jours, L')
Lover of Camille 11-12-24
Lover, Wife (See: Mogliamante)
Lovers 4-20-27
Lovers, The (See: Amantes, Los; Vlubennye; or Koo Rak)
Lovers, The 2-23-49
Lovers and Lollipops 9-28-55
Lovers and Luggers 4-06-38
Lovers and Other Strangers 8-12-70

Lunatic at Large   2-02-27
Lunatic at Large, A   9-24-10
Lune Avec les Dents, La   8-09-67
Lunes 1° Domingo 7   10-16-68
Lung Mun Kar Chuan   9-11-68
Lunga Notte Del '43, La   9-07-60
Lupa, La   12-02-53
Lupeni 29   7-24-63
Lupi Nell'Abisso   7-08-59
Lupo Della Sila, Il   2-08-50
Lure, The   8-28-14
Lure of Alaska, The   8-04-16
Lure of Egypt, The   5-13-21
Lure of Millions, The   11-28-14
Lure of the Crooning Waters   2-18-21
Lure of the Gown   3-20-09
Lure of the Jade   12-16-21
Lure of the Swamp   5-29-57
Lure of the Wasteland   8-23-39
Lure of the West   8-22-28
Lure of the Wild   2-03-26
Lure of the Wilderness   7-30-52
Lure of the Yukon, The   10-03-14
Lure of the Yukon, The   7-23-24
Lured   7-16-47
Luring Lips   7-29-21
Lusitania Sinking   6-18-15
Lust   3-20-29
Lust for a Vampire   9-15-71
Lust for Gold   5-25-49
Lust for Life   9-05-56
Lust of Ages, The   8-24-17
Lustige Witwer, Der (See: Merry Widower, The)
Lustigen Welber von Wien, Die   7-14-31
Lustigen Weiber von Windsor, Die   4-07-65
Lusty Men, The   10-01-52
Luther   7-03-29
Luther   2-06-74
Lutte Finale, La   10-31-62
Luv   7-26-67
Luxury   10-07-21
Luxury Girls   3-04-53
Luxury Liner   2-07-33
Luxury Liner   8-18-48
Lycistrata   11-15-72
Lyckliga Skitar   7-14-71
Lydia   8-20-41
Lydia   12-23-64
Lydia   10-28-70
Lydia Bailey   5-28-52
Lydia Gilmore   12-31-15
Lyftet   3-29-78
Lying Lips   3-11-21
Lying Truth   4-21-22
Lying Wives   6-17-25
Lykke Paa Rejsen   2-26-47
Lysistrata (See: Triumph of Love)
Lyudi y Zvery   9-05-62
Lyutyi   6-12-74

M   6-02-31; 4-04-33; and 4-18-33
M   3-07-51
M as in Mathieu (See: M Comme Mathieu)
M Comme Mathieu   9-08-71
Ma and Pa Kettle   3-23-49
Ma and Pa Kettle at Home   3-10-54
Ma and Pa Kettle at the Fair   3-19-52
Ma and Pa Kettle at Waikiki   3-09-55
Ma and Pa Kettle Back on the Farm   3-28-51
Ma and Pa Kettle Go to Town   3-29-50
Ma and Pa Kettle on Vacation   3-04-53
Ma Bhoomi   2-06-80
Ma Cherie   4-02-80
Ma Femme Est Formidable   9-19-51
Ma Femme Homme d'Affaire   9-27-32
Ma, He's Making Eyes at Me   5-01-40
Ma Non e Una Cosa Seria   4-22-36
Ma Nuit Chez Maud   5-14-69
Ma Pomme   12-13-50
Ma Soeur de Lait   6-22-38

Maa On Syntinen Laulu   5-29-74
Maa Vaere en Sengekant, Der   3-05-75
Ma'Agalim   7-09-80
Maaret, Daughter of the Mountains (See: Maaret Tunturien Tytto)
Maaret Tunturien Tytto   5-05-48
Maaske Ku'vi   2-25-76
Mababangong Bangungot   12-10-80
Mabaroshi Nouma   5-16-56
Mabette   3-23-17
Mabu   7-05-61
Macabre   3-12-58
Macadam   12-04-46
Macao   3-19-52
Macario   5-25-60 and 3-22-61
MacArthur   6-29-77
Macbeth   6-09-16
Macbeth   10-13-48
Macbeth   10-30-63
Macbeth   12-15-71
McCabe and Mrs. Miller   6-30-71
Macchia Rosa   9-10-69
McConnell Story, The   8-17-55
McCullochs, The   6-04-75
Macedoine   2-17-71
McFadden's Flats   2-09-27
McFadden's Flats   3-13-35
McGuire of the Mounted   7-19-23
McHale's Navy   7-01-64
McHale's Navy Joins the Air Force   6-09-65
Machete   12-10-58
Machine, La   9-14-77
Machine Gun Kelly   7-09-58
Machine Gun Mama   9-20-44
Machine-Gun Man (See: Hombre de la Ametralladora, El)
Macho Callahan   8-19-70
Macht Der Maenner Ist Die Geduld Der Frauen, Die   9-17-80
Macintosh and T.J.   11-26-75
Maciste   8-20-15
Maciste in Hell   6-30-31
Mack, The   3-21-73
Mackan   3-29-78
McKenna of the Mounted   11-08-32
Mackenna's Gold   3-26-69
McKenzie Break, The   10-21-70
Mackintosh Man, The   8-01-73
McLintock   11-13-63
McMasters, The   6-17-70
Macomber Affair, The   1-22-47
Macon County Line   4-24-74
McQ   1-23-74
Macskajatek   5-22-74
Macumba Love   5-18-60
Macunaima   9-17-69
McVicar   4-30-80
Mad About Men   12-01-54
Mad About Money   12-07-38
Mad About Music   3-02-38
Mad About Opera   4-12-50
Mad Bomber, The   4-04-73
Mad Cage, The (See: Cage Aux Folles, La)
Mad Dancer, The   4-29-25
Mad Dane, The (See: Gale Dansker, Den)
Mad Doctor, The   3-05-41
Mad Doctor of Market Street, The   1-07-42
Mad Dog (See: Wsciekly)
Mad Dog   5-05-76
Mad Dog, The (See: Chien Fou, Le)
Mad Dog Coll   5-03-61
Mad Empress, The   2-21-40
Mad Enough to Kill (See: Folle a Tuer)
Mad Fox, The (See: Koiya Koi Nasuna Koi)
Mad Game, The   11-14-33
Mad Genius, The   10-27-31
Mad Ghoul, The   11-03-43
Mad Girl, The (See: Jeune Folle, La)
Mad Heart, The (See: Coeur Fou, Le)
Mad Holiday   12-02-36
Mad Hour   4-18-28
Mad Love (See: Amour Fou, L')
Mad Love   3-08-23
Mad Love   8-07-35
Mad Lover, The   7-27-17
Mad Magician, The   3-31-54
Mad Marriage, The   2-04-21
Mad Martindales   4-22-42
Mad Max   5-16-79
Mad Men of Europe   6-26-40
Mad Miner   4-10-09

Mad Miss Manton, The 10-12-38
Mad Monster, The 6-03-42
Mad Night, The (See: Folle Nuit, La)
Mad Parade, The 9-22-31
Mad Queen, The 11-01-50
Mad Room, The 3-12-69
Mad Whirl, The 7-08-25
Mad Woman (See: Loca, La)
Mad Years, The (See: Annees Folles, Les)
Mad Youth 5-22-40
Madalena 5-17-61
Madam Kitty 1-19-77
Madam Satan 5-22-14
Madam Spy 1-11-18
Madam White Snake 11-03-65
Madame Aki 11-27-63
Madame Bo-Peep 5-25-17
Madame Bovary 11-27-34
Madame Bovary 6-02-37
Madame Bovary 7-09-47
Madame Bovary 8-03-49
Madame Butterfly 11-12-15
Madame Butterfly 12-27-32
Madame Butterfly 4-27-55
Madame Claude 5-18-77
Madame Curie 11-24-43
Madame De 10-21-53
Mme. Du Barry 10-30-34
Madame Du Barry 11-10-54
Madame Guillotine 8-20-24
Madame Jealousy 2-08-18
Madame la Presidente 2-11-16
Mme. Ne Veux Pas d'Enfant 4-25-33
Madame Peacock 10-29-20
Mme. Pompadour 8-03-27
Madame Racketeer 7-26-32
Madame Sans Gene 4-22-25
Madame Sans Gene 4-18-45
Madame Sans-Gene 6-20-62
Madame Sphinx 6-14-18
Madame Spy 2-13-34
Madame Spy 12-09-42
Mme. Wants No Children 4-13-27
Madame Who? 1-18-18
Madame X 1-21-16
Madame X 10-01-20
Madame X 5-01-29
Madame X 9-29-37
Madame X 2-23-66
Madame Xenobia 12-12-73
Madamiegella di Maupin 3-16-66
Madarkak 11-10-71 and 8-30-72
Madcap Betty 6-18-15
Madcap Madge 6-22-17
Madcap of the House 12-13-50
Madchen Christine, Das (See: Christina)
Madchen in Uniform 7-16-58
Maddalena 8-17-55
Maddalena 11-17-71
Maddening Flame, The (See: Feu Follet, Le)
Made 9-13-72
Made for Each Other 2-01-39
Made for Each Other 12-15-71
Made in Heaven 4-22-21
Made in Heaven 11-26-52
Made in Italy 3-30-66 and 5-03-67
Made in Paris 2-02-66
Made in Sweden 7-09-69
Made in U.S.A. 12-14-66
Made on Broadway 7-11-33
Madeleine 2-22-50
Madeline Is 4-28-71
Madelon, La 1-25-56
Mademoiselle 5-18-66
Mademoiselle--Age 39 4-04-56
Mademoiselle de Maupin (See: Madamiegella di Maupin)
Mlle. Desiree 11-17-48
Mademoiselle Docteur 4-21-37
Mademoiselle Fifi 8-02-44
Mademoiselle from Armentieres 7-18-28
Mademoiselle Has Fun (See: Mademoiselle S'Amuse)
Mademoiselle Ma Mere 9-27-39
Mlle. Midnight 5-28-24
Mademoiselle Modiste 4-28-26
Mlle. Paulette 5-17-18
Mademoiselle S'Amuse 3-24-48
Maden 8-02-78
Madhouse 3-27-74

Madigan 3-27-68
Madigan's Millions 2-04-70
Madison Avenue 8-01-62
Madison Square Garden 10-18-32
Madly 12-30-70
Madman, The (See: Fou, Le)
Madman of Lab 4 (See: Fou du Labo 4, Le)
Madmen of Mandoras 1-29-64
Madness of Helen, The 11-10-16
Madness of the Heart 9-07-49
Madness Rules (See: Matto Regiert)
Madness, the Whole Life Is Madness (See: Wahnsinn, Das Ganze
    Leven Ist Wahnsinn)
Mado 11-17-76
Madonna of Avenue A 8-14-29
Madonna of the Desert 3-10-48
Madonna of the Seven Moons 1-17-45
Madonna of the Sleeping Cars 10-16-29
Madonna of the Streets 10-29-24
Madonna of the Streets 12-03-30
Madonna, Where Are You? (See: Madonna, Wo Bist Du?)
Madonna, Wo Bist Du? 4-01-36
Madonnas and Men 6-18-20
Madonna's Secret, The 2-20-46
Madrasta, La 5-07-75
Madre 4-25-28
Madre a la Fuerza 8-21-40
Madriguera, La 7-16-69
Madron 12-23-70
Madwoman of Chaillot, The 6-25-69
Madwoman of Toujane (See: Folle de Toujane, La)
Maedchen Aus Zweiter Hand, Ein 6-02-76
Maedchen Beim Frauenarzt 4-21-71
Maedchen in Uniform 9-27-32
Maedchen in Weiss 10-07-36
Maedchen Irene, Das 11-18-36
Maedchen, Maedchen 3-08-67
Maedchen mit Gewalt 4-01-70
Maedchen von Gestern Nacht, Das 6-22-38
Maedchenjahre einer Koenigin 4-08-36
Maedchenjahre Einer Koenigin 1-19-55
Maedchenkrieg, Der 9-14-77
Maedchenpensionat 11-04-36
Maedel der Strasse 4-11-33
Maedel vom Ballett, Ein 2-24-37
Maedel von der Reeperbahn, Das 2-18-31
Maenak America 1-14-76
Maenner Im Gefaehrlichen Alter 6-30-54
Maerchen vom Glueck 10-05-49
Maes 10-27-76
Maestrita de los Obreros 4-01-42
Maestro di Vigevano, Il 1-15-64
Maestro e Margherita, Il 9-13-72
Maeva 9-06-61
Maffia, La 8-30-72
Mafia, The (See: Maffia, La)
Mafiaen, Det er Osse Mig 10-02-74
Mafioso 11-21-62
Mafu Cage, The 5-24-78
Mag-ingat: Kapag Biyda Ang Umbig 7-30-75
Maga Lesz a Ferjem 3-16-38
Magandang Gabi Sa Inyong Lahat 6-23-76
Magasiskola 3-11-70
Magda 10-12-17
Magda Is Expelled (See: Magdat Kicsapjak)
Magdalene of the Hills, A 4-20-17
Magdat Kicsapjak 4-13-38
Maggie, The 3-17-54
Maggie Pepper 2-14-19
Magic 11-01-78
Magic Adventure 12-19-73
Magic Blade, The 8-04-76
Magic Bow, The 9-25-46
Magic Box, The 9-26-51
Magic Boy 8-09-61
Magic Carpet, The 9-26-51
Magic Christian, The 12-17-69
Magic Country (See: Tierra Magica)
Magic Face, The 8-08-51
Magic Fire 5-09-56
Magic Flame 9-21-27
Magic Flower, The 1-29-10
Magic Fountain, The 8-16-61
Magic Garden, The 2-16-27
Magic Garden, The 2-06-52
Magic Garden of Stanley Sweetheart, The 5-27-70
Magic Horse, The 6-22-49

Magic Melody 10-09-09
Magic Mountain 4-22-36
Magic Night 11-08-32
Magic of Lassie, The 8-09-78
Magic Skin, The 10-29-15
Magic Sword, The 4-11-62
Magic Town 8-20-47
Magician, The 10-27-26
Magician of Lubin, The 5-23-79
Magistrate, The (See: Magistrato, Il)
Magistrato, Il 11-18-59
Magliari, I 12-16-59
Magliari, The (See: Magliari, I)
Magnet, The 11-01-50
Magnet of Doom, A (See: Aine des Ferchaux, L')
Magnetic Monster, The 2-11-53
Magnetic Tide, The 11-29-50
Magnificent Ambersons, The 7-01-42
Magnificent Brute, The 4-22-21
Magnificent Brute 10-28-36
Magnificent Cuckold, The (See: Magnifico Cornuto, Il)
Magnificent Doll 11-20-46
Magnificent Dope, The 6-03-42
Magnificent Flirt, The 6-27-28
Magnificent Fraud, The 7-19-39
Magnificent Lie, The 7-28-31
Magnificent Matador, The 5-18-55
Magnificent Obsession 1-08-36
Magnificent Obsession 5-12-54
Magnificent One, The (See: Magnifique, Le)
Magnificent Rogue (See: Lorenzino de Medici)
Magnificent Roughnecks 8-08-56
Magnificent Seven, The 10-05-60
Magnificent Seven Ride, The 7-26-72
Magnificent Two, The 7-19-67
Magnificent Yankee, The 11-15-50
Magnifico Cornuto, Il 11-25-64
Magnifique, Le 1-02-74
Magnum Force 12-12-73
Magot de Josefa, Le 10-16-63
Magus, The 12-11-68
Magyar Rapszodia and Allegro Barbaro 2-28-79
Magyarok 5-24-78
Mahanagar 7-08-64
Mahapurush 11-24-65
Mahatma Gandhi--20th Century Prophet 5-13-53
Mahiru No Ankoku 8-01-56
Mahler 4-10-74
Mahlzeitn 4-19-67
Mahogany 10-08-75
Mai Lanyok 12-15-37
Mai 68 11-13-74
Maid o' the Storm 7-26-18
Maid of Belgium, A 10-19-17
Maid of Formosa 8-10-49
Maid of Salem 3-10-37
Maid of the Mountains, A 4-02-10
Maid of the West 8-05-21
Maid of the Wild, The 10-08-15
Maid Tine (See: Tine)
Maid to Order 5-12-32
Maiden's War, The (See: Maedchenkrieg, Der)
Maids, The 1-29-75
Maid's Last Day, The 5-09-08
Maid's Night Out 5-25-38
Maidstone 9-16-70
Maigret and the St. Fiacre Case (See: Maigret et L'Affaire St. Fiacre)
Maigret et L'Affaire St. Fiacre 9-23-59
Maigret Lays a Trap (See: Maigret Tend un Piege)
Maigret Sees Red (See: Maigret Voit Rouge)
Maigret Tend un Piege 3-26-58
Maigret Voit Rouge 10-02-63
Mail Order Bride 1-15-64
Mail Train 7-09-41
Mailman Mueller (See: Brieftraeger Mueller)
Main, La 12-31-69
Main a Couper, La 3-13-74
Main Actor, The (See: Hauptdarsteller, Der)
Main Attraction, The 10-31-62
Main Chance, The 6-22-66
Main Chaude, Le 3-16-60
Main Event, The 11-02-27
Main Event, The 6-22-38
Main Event, The 6-20-79
Main Street (See: Calle Mayor)
Main Street 5-03-23
Main Street After Dark 11-29-44

Main Street Kid, The 12-31-47
Main Street Lawyer 11-08-39
Main Street to Broadway 7-29-53
Main Thing Holidays (See: Hauptsache Ferien)
Main Thing Is to Love, The (See: Important C'Est D'Aimer, L')
Mains d'Orlac, Les 4-26-61
Mains Sales, Les 9-12-51
Mainspring, The 11-24-16
Mais Ne Nous Deliverez Pas Du Mal 5-26-71
Mais Ou Est Donc Passe la 7eme Compagnie? 1-02-74
Mais Ou et Donc Ornicar 3-14-79
Mais Qu'est-Ce Qu'elles Veulent? 3-08-78
Mais Qu'est Ce Que J'Ai Fait Au Bon Dieu Pour Avoir Une Femme
   Qui Boit Dans Les Cafes Avec Les Hommes? 9-17-80
Maisie 6-07-39
Maisie Gets Her Man 5-27-42
Maisie Goes to Reno 8-16-44
Maisie Was a Lady 1-15-41
Maison, La 8-26-70
Maison Bonnadieu, La 1-02-52
Maison Dans la Dune, La 3-26-52
Maison de Campagne, La 11-26-69
Maison de Danse 3-18-31
Maison de Moliere 3-20-35
Maison des Bories, La 8-05-70
Maison du Maltais, La 10-26-38
Maison Sous les Arbres, La 6-16-71
Maisons Dans Cette Ruelle 8-23-78
Maitre Apres Dieu 5-02-51
Maitre de Forges, Le 12-26-33
Maitresse 2-11-76
Maj Pa Malo 6-16-48
Maja de los Cantares, La 8-07-46
Majd Holnap 2-27-80
Majestic Hotel Cellars (See: Caves du Majestic, Les)
Majesty of the Law, The 8-27-15
Majin 8-14-68
Major and the Judge 10-23-09
Major and the Minor, The 9-02-42
Major and the Steers, The (See: Major und die Stiere, Der)
Major Barbara 5-07-41
Major Dundee 3-17-65
Major und die Stiere, Der 1-25-56
Majordome, Le 5-05-65
Majordomo, The (See: Majordome, Le)
Majority of One, A 11-15-61
Make a Face 8-25-71
Make a Million 11-13-35
Make a Wish 8-25-37
Make Believe Ballroom 4-20-49
Make-Believe Wife, The 11-22-18
Make Haste to Live 3-31-54
Make Like a Thief 2-09-66
Make Love Not War 6-26-68
Make Me a Star 7-05-32
Make Me an Offer 12-22-54
Make Mine a Million 3-04-59
Make Mine Laughs 8-10-49
Make Mine Mink 8-17-60
Make Mine Music 4-17-46
Make Up (See: Maquillage)
Make-Up 7-07-37
Make Way for a Lady 12-16-36
Make Way for Tomorrow 5-12-37
Make Your Own Bed 5-17-44
Makedonska Krava Svadba 8-21-68
Makers of Men 9-16-25
Makers of Men 12-22-31
Making a Man 12-22-22
Making Good 3-04-21
Making It 2-03-71
Making It Pleasant for Him 12-04-09
Making of a King (See: Alte und Junge Kaiser)
Making of Maddalena, The 6-16-16
Making of O'Malley, The 6-24-25
Making the Blue Film 5-26-71
Making the Grade 2-10-22
Making the Grade 5-08-29
Making the Headlines 3-23-38
Making the Varsity 10-17-28
Makuchi 9-25-63
Mal, El (See: Rage)
Mal Partis, Les 2-11-76
Mala Morska Vila 3-09-77
Mala Ordina, La (See: Italian Connection, The)
Malacarne 11-17-48
Malaga 7-07-54
Malaga 2-03-60

Malambo 11-18-42
Malatesta 5-13-70
Malato Immaginario, Il 1-23-80
Malay Nights 2-07-33
Malaya 12-07-49
Malcolm X 5-24-72
Maldone 3-21-28
Maldonne 6-11-69
Male and Female 11-28-19
Male Animal, The 3-04-42
Male Dramaty 5-20-59
Male du Siecle, Le 3-19-75
Male of the Century, The (See: Male du Siecle, Le)
Maledetti Vi Amero' 6-11-80
Maledetto Imbroglio, Un 2-03-60
Malefices 4-11-62
Males, Les 6-09-71
Malheurs d'Alfred, Les 3-15-72
Mali Letni Blues 11-06-68
Mali Vojnici 5-22-68
Malia 2-06-52
Mama Gloria 9-17-41
Malibu Beach 5-24-78
Malicious Rival 11-13-09
Malin Plaisir, Le 4-30-75
Malizia 7-04-73
Malkat Hakvish 4-07-71
Malpas Mystery, The 5-21-69
Malpertius 5-17-72
Malta Story, The 7-08-53 and 7-14-54
Maltese Bippy, The 6-11-69
Maltese Falcon, The 6-02-31
Maltese Falcon, The 10-01-41
Maltese House, The 6-20-28
Maluala 7-30-80
Malwa 10-02-57
Mam-Zelle Nitouche 12-22-31
Mam'Zelle Nitouche 6-09-54
Mama Cumple 100 Anos 10-03-79
Mama Gloria 9-17-41
Mama, Ich Lebe 3-23-77
Mama, I'm Alive (See: Mama, Ich Lebe)
Mama Loves Papa 7-25-33
Mama Loves Papa 8-01-45
Mama Runs Wild 1-05-38
Mama Steps Out 4-28-37
Mama's Birthday Present 9-17-10
Mamaia 6-14-67
Maman et la Putain, La 5-16-73
Mama's Boy (See: Cocco di Mamma, Il)
Mamba 3-19-30
Mambo 11-24-54
Mame 2-27-74
Mamele 1-11-39
Mamito 6-25-80
Mamma Dracula 12-03-80
Mamma Roma 8-29-62
Mammasantissima, Il 4-11-79
Mammy 4-02-30
Mammy 10-13-37
Mamula Camp (See: Campo Mamula)
Man, a Woman and a Bank, A (See: Very Big Withdrawal, A)
Man, The (See: Ningen)
Man, The 7-19-72
Man About the House, A 8-06-47
Man About Town 5-31-32
Man About Town 6-14-39
Man About Town 10-22-47
Man Above the Law, The 1-04-18
Man Afraid 4-03-57
Man Against Man (See: Mann Gegen Mann)
Man Against Woman 12-20-32
Man Alive 9-26-45
Man Alone, A 9-21-55
Man Alone, The 2-22-23
Man and a Woman, A (See: Homme et Une Femme, Un)
Man and Beast 7-13-17
Man and Beast (See: Mensch und Bestie)
Man and Boy 3-15-72
Man and His Mate, A 4-23-15
Man and His Money, A 4-18-19
Man and His Sin, A (See: Homme et Son Peche, Un)
Man and His Soul 2-14-16
Man and His Wife, A 3-29-39
Man and His Woman 7-16-20
Man and Maid 4-08-25
Man and the Child, The (See: Homme et l'Enfant, L')
Man and the Girl 10-23-09
Man and the Moment 1-05-23
Man and the Moment 8-07-29

Man and the Woman, A 3-23-17
Man and War--Part III (See: Senso To Ningen)
Man and Wife 6-28-23
Man and Woman 9-09-21
Man at Large 9-10-41
Man at Six, The 8-11-31
Man at the Gate 1-29-41
Man at the Top 11-28-73
Man-Bait 1-19-27
Man Bait 1-30-52
Man Beast 12-12-56
Man Behind the Curtain, The 6-16-16
Man Behind the Door, The 11-28-14
Man Behind the Gun, The 12-24-52
Man Beneath, The 7-11-19
Man Betrayed, A 2-03-37
Man Betrayed, A 3-12-41
Man Between 10-04-23
Man Between, The 9-30-53
Man Called Adam, A 6-29-66
Man Called Autumn Flower, A (See: Hombre Llamado Flor De Otono, Un)
Man Called Back, The 8-02-32
Man Called Dagger, A 12-20-67
Man Called Flintstone, A 8-10-66
Man Called Gannon, A 6-11-69
Man Called Horse, A 4-29-70
Man Called La Rocca, A (See: Homme La Rocca, Un)
Man Called Noon, The 8-01-73
Man Called Peter, A 3-23-55
Man Called Sledge, A 3-03-71
Man Could Get Killed, A 3-16-66
Man Crazy 12-21-27
Man Crazy 12-16-53
Man-Eater of Kumaon 6-23-48
Man for All Seasons, A 12-14-66
Man for Burning, A (See: Uomo da Bruciare, Un)
Man Friday 5-14-75
Man from Beyond 4-07-22
Man from Bitter Ridge, The 4-20-55
Man from Bitter Root, The 7-07-16
Man from Black Hills, The 5-14-52
Man from Blankley's, The 4-02-30
Man from Brodney 12-20-23
Man from Button Willow, The 1-27-65
Man from Cairo, The 12-02-53
Man from Cheyenne, The 1-28-42
Man from Chicago, The 11-05-30 and 1-21-31
Man from Colorado, The 11-24-48
Man from Dakota, The 2-21-40
Man from Death Valley, The 10-13-31
Man from Del Rio, The 10-03-56
Man from Down Under, The 8-04-43
Man from Downing Street, The 4-14-22
Man from Frisco, The 4-26-44
Man from Funeral Range, The 10-11-18
Man from Galveston, The 1-15-64
Man from Glengarry, The 4-05-23
Man from God's Country, The 10-22-24
Man from God's Country, The 2-26-58
Man from Gun Town, The 1-08-36
Man from Hardpan, The 4-13-27
Man from Headquarters, The 10-17-28
Man from Headquarters, The 3-25-42
Man from Hell, The 10-02-34
Man from Hell's Edges, The 8-02-32
Man from Hell's River, The 6-30-22
Man from Home, The 11-07-14
Man from Home, The 5-05-22
Man from Hong Kong, The 6-11-75
Man from Istanbul, The (See: Homme D'Istanbul, L')
Man from Laramie, The 6-29-55
Man from Lost River, The 1-20-22
Man from Marrakech, The (See: Homme de Marrakech, L')
Man from Mexico, The 11-21-14
Man from Montana, The 11-30-17
Man from Montana, The 12-17-41
Man from Monterey, The 8-22-33
Man from Montreal, The 2-28-40
Man from Morocco, The 2-21-45
Man from Music Mountain, The 8-17-38
Man from Music Mountain, The 9-22-43
Man from Nevada, The 9-18-29
Man from New Mexico, The 8-30-32
Man from Nowhere, The 4-09-30
Man from Oklahoma, The 8-01-45
Man from Oregon, The 9-24-15
Man from O.R.G.Y., The 4-08-70

Man from Painted Post, The 10-05-17
Man from Planet X, The 3-14-51
Man from Rainbow Valley, The 6-19-46
Man from Rio, The (See: Homme de Rio, L')
Man from Rio Grande, The 11-10-43
Man from Sundown, The 8-16-39
Man from Swan Farm, The (See: Manden Paa Svanegrden)
Man from Texas, The 8-02-39
Man from Texas, The 3-31-48
Man from the Alamo, The 7-15-53
Man from the Diner's Club, The 4-03-63
Man from the East, A (See: E Poi Lo Chiamarono Il Magnifico)
Man from the Golden West, The (See: From the Golden West)
Man from the Niger, The (See: Homme du Niger, L')
Man from the Restaurant, The 1-29-30
Man from Toronto, The 2-28-33
Man from Tumbleweeds, The 5-29-40
Man from Wyoming, The 2-21-24
Man from Yesterday, The 6-28-32
Man Goes Through the Wall, A (See: Mann Geht Durch die Wand, Ein)
Man Hater, The 10-26-17
Man Hunt 5-09-33
Man Hunt 2-12-36
Man Hunt 6-11-41
Man Hunt, The 6-07-18
Man Hunter, The 3-01-19
Man Hunter, The 4-09-30
Man I Killed, The 1-28-32 (Also see: Homme Que J'ai Tue, L')
Man I Love, The 5-29-29
Man I Love, The 12-25-46
Man I Married, The 7-17-40
Man I Marry, The 11-04-36
Man in a Hurry (See: Homme Presse, L')
Man in a Million 3-11-21
Man in Blue, The 7-28-37
Man in Exile (See: O Desterrado)
Man in Gray, The 8-18-43
Man in Half Moon Street, The 10-18-44
Man in Hiding, The (See: Hombre Oculto, El)
Man in Hobbles 2-20-29
Man in Possession, The 7-21-31
Man in Swallow Tails, A (See: Homme en Habit, Un)
Man in the Attic 12-23-53
Man in the Black Derby, The (See: Herr Mit der Schwarzen Melone, Der)
Man in the Dark 4-08-53
Man in the Dark 1-20-65
Man in the Dinghy 10-31-51
Man in the Glass Booth, The 1-22-75
Man in the Gray Flannel Suit, The 4-04-56
Man in the Hispano (See: Homme a L'Hispano, L')
Man in the Iron Mask, The 6-28-39
Man in the Middle 1-15-64
Man in the Mirror, The 10-28-36
Man in the Moon 11-16-60
Man in the Net (See: Menschen Im Netz)
Man in the Net, The 4-22-59
Man in the Open, A 2-07-19
Man in the Photograph, The 4-15-64
Man in the Raincoat, The (See: Homme a l'Impermeable, L')
Man in the Rough 7-18-28
Man in the Saddle 11-14-51
Man in the Shadow 11-27-57
Man in the Sky, The 1-23-57
Man in the Trunk, The 9-16-42
Man in the Vault 12-26-56
Man in the White Suit, The 8-22-51
Man in the Wilderness 11-24-71
Man Inside, The 9-10-58
Man Is Absent-Minded 10-01-10
Man Is Dead, A (See: Homme Est Mort, Un)
Man Is News, The 7-26-39
Man Is Not a Bird (See: Covek Nije Tica)
Man Ist Nur Zweimal Jung 5-07-58
Man Kan Inte Valtas 3-29-78
Man Life Passed By, The 2-21-24
Man Looking for His Murderer (See: Mann, Der Seinen Moerder Sucht, Der)
Man Made Monster 3-26-41
Man-Made Women 9-19-28
Man Must Live, A 1-28-25
Man Next Door, The 3-14-13
Man Next Door, The 5-30-23
Man of a Thousand Faces 7-17-57
Man of Action, A 6-07-23
Man of Affairs 2-24-37
Man of Africa 10-24-56

Man of Aran 5-29-34 and 10-23-34
Man of Bronze, The 11-29-18
Man of Conflict 10-21-53
Man of Conquest 4-12-39
Man of Courage 4-21-22
Man of Courage 11-20-34
Man of Courage 3-31-43
Man of Desire (See: Homme de Desir, L')
Man of Fashion (See: Hombre de Moda, El)
Man of Gold, The (See: Az Aranyember)
Man of Iron 12-11-35
Man of Iron 12-19-73
Man of Iron, A 6-24-25
Man of La Mancha 12-06-72
Man of Marble (See: Czlowiek z Marmuru)
Man of Music 5-13-53
Man of My Life (See: Homme de Ma Vie, L')
Man of Mystery, The 1-05-17
Man of Sentiment, A 11-14-33
Man of Shame, The 10-29-15
Man of Sorrow, A 4-28-16
Man of Stone 11-18-21
Man of Straw, A (See: Uomo di Paglia, L')
Man of the First Century (See: Muz Z Prvniho Stoleti)
Man of the Forest 8-26-21
Man of the Forest 10-31-33
Man of the Forest, The (See: Karl For Sin Hatt)
Man of the Hour 11-27-40
Man of the Hour, The 10-10-14
Man of the Moment 9-28-55
Man of the People 3-03-37
Man of the West 9-17-58
Man of the World 3-25-31
Man of Two Worlds 1-16-34
Man of Violence 6-17-70
Man on a String 4-13-60
Man on a Swing 2-27-74
Man on a Tightrope 4-01-53
Man on Fire 6-05-57
Man on the Box, The 7-24-14
Man on the Box, The 9-30-25
Man on the Bridge (See: Hombre del Puente)
Man on the Eiffel Tower, The 12-21-49
Man on the Flying Trapeze, The 8-07-35
Man on the Prowl 12-04-57
Man on the Road, A (See: Hombre Va por El Camino, Un)
Man on the Roof (See: Mannen Pa Taget)
Man on the Run 6-01-49
Man on the Run, A (See: Homme en Fuite, Un)
Man Outside 6-20-33
Man Outside 5-08-68
Man Power 7-27-27
Man-Proof 12-15-37
Man Rustlin' 4-21-26
Man She Brought Back, The 10-13-22
Man Sku Vaere Noget Ved Musikken 7-12-72
Man, Some Women, A (See: Sey Seyeti)
Man Spricht Ueber Jacqueline 5-19-37
Man Stolen (See: On a Vole un Homme)
Man Tamer, The 5-27-21
Man That Married His Own Wife, The 4-28-22
Man They Could Not Hang, The 9-27-39
Man They Couldn't Arrest, The 8-11-31; 3-14-33; and 10-31-33
Man to Kill, A (See: Homme A Abattre, Un or Covjek Koga Treba Ubiti)
Man to Man 3-31-22
Man to Man 1-07-31
Man to Men, The 11-24-48
Man to Remember, A 10-05-38 and 11-09-38
Man Trackers 8-12-21
Man Trail, The 9-17-15
Man Trailer 5-29-34
Man-Trap 11-01-61
Man Trap, The 11-02-17
Man Trouble 9-10-30
Man Unconquerable 7-21-22
Man Under Cover 4-07-22
Man Under the Bed, The 3-12-10
Man Under the Bridge (See: Ember a Hid Alatt)
Man Upstairs, The 10-08-58
Man Walks in the City, A (See: Homme Marche Dans La Ville, Un)
Man Wanted 4-19-32
Man Wants to Live (See: Hommes Veulent Vivre, Les)
Man Who, The 8-19-21
Man Who Betrayed the Mafia, The (See: Homme Qui Trahit la Mafia, L')
Man Who Bought the World, The (See: O Homem Que Comprou O Mundo)
Man Who Broke the Bank at Monte Carlo, The 11-20-35

Man Who Came Back, The 6-11-15
Man Who Came Back, The 9-03-24
Man Who Came Back, The 1-07-31
Man Who Came for Coffee, The (See: Venga A Prendero Il Caffe
  Da Noi)
Man Who Came to Dinner, The 1-07-42
Man Who Changed 3-20-24
Man Who Changed His Mind 3-20-34 and 9-23-36
Man Who Changed His Name (See: Man Who Changed)
Man Who Changed His Name, The 10-23-34
Man Who Cheated Himself, The 12-20-50
Man Who Cheated Life, The 2-13-29
Man Who Could Cheat Death, The 6-24-59
Man Who Could Not Lose, The 11-21-14
Man Who Could Work Miracles, The 8-12-36 and 2-24-37
Man Who Couldn't Beat God, The 10-22-15
Man Who Couldn't Walk, The 8-24-60 and 1-15-64
Man Who Cried Wolf, The 9-29-37
Man Who Dared, The 10-22-20
Man Who Dared, The 9-12-33
Man Who Died, The 9-10-10
Man Who Fell to Earth, The 3-24-76
Man Who Fights Alone, The 7-30-24
Man Who Forgot, The 1-05-17
Man Who Found Himself, The 8-26-25
Man Who Found Himself, The 4-14-37
Man Who Got His Hair Cut Short, The (See: De Man Die Zijin Haar
  Kort Liet Knippen)
Man Who Had Power over Women, The 10-28-70
Man Who Haunted Himself, The 7-29-70
Man Who Incinerated People, The (See: Spalovac Mrtvol)
Man Who Is Talked About (See: Mann, Von Dem Man Spricht, Der)
Man Who Knew Love, The (See: Hombre Que Supo Amar, El)
Man Who Knew Too Much, The 1-08-35 and 3-27-35
Man Who Knew Too Much, The 5-02-56
Man Who Laughs, The (See: Uomo Che Ride, L')
Man Who Laughs, The 5-02-28
Man Who Learned, The 9-10-10
Man Who Lies, The (See: Homme Qui Ment, L')
Man Who Lived Again, The 12-23-36
Man Who Lived Twice, The 10-14-36
Man Who Lost, The 2-05-10
Man Who Lost Himself, The 6-04-20
Man Who Lost Himself, The 3-26-41
Man Who Loved Cat Dancing, The 6-27-73
Man Who Loved Redheads, The 1-26-55
Man Who Loved Women, The (See: Homme Qui Aimait les Femmes, L')
Man Who Loves the Birds, The (See: Chelovek Ukhodit Za Ptitsami)
Man Who Made Good, The 5-04-17
Man Who Murdered, The (See: Mann Der Den Mord Beging, Der)
Man Who Never Was, The 2-15-56
Man Who Played God, The 10-06-22
Man Who Played God, The 2-16-32
Man Who Played Square, The 3-11-25
Man Who Pleases Me, A (See: Homme Qui Me Plait, Un)
Man Who Quit Smoking, The (See: Mannen Som Slutade Roeka)
Man Who Reclaimed His Head, The 1-15-35
Man Who Returned to Life, The 3-04-42
Man Who Returns from Afar (See: Homme Qui Revient de Loin, L')
Man Who Saw Tomorrow 11-03-22
Man Who Seeks the Truth, The 10-08-41 (Also see: Homme Qui
  Cherche la Verite, L')
Man Who Shot Liberty Valance, The 4-11-62
Man Who Sleeps, A (See: Homme Qui Dort, Un)
Man Who Smiles, The 2-03-38
Man Who Sold Himself, The (See: Mann, Der Sich Verkaufte, Der)
Man Who Stole Peaches, The (See: Kradezat Na Praskovi)
Man Who Stole the Sun, The (See: Taiyo o Nusunda Otoko)
Man Who Stood Still, The 10-20-16
Man Who Talked Too Much, The 7-03-40
Man Who Thought Things, The (See: Mandem Der Taenkte Ting)
Man Who Took a Chance, The 2-09-17
Man Who Turned to Stone, The 2-20-57
Man Who Turned White, The 6-13-19
Man Who Understood Women, The 9-23-59
Man Who Walked Alone, The 3-21-45
Man Who Walks on the Water 6-05-09
Man Who Was Afraid, The 7-06-17
Man Who Was Exchanged, The (See: Az Elcserelt Ember)
Man Who Was Sherlock Holmes, The (See: Mann, der Sherlock Holmes
  War, Der)
Man Who Was Worth Millions (See: Homme Qui Valait Des Milliards,
  L')
Man Who Watched Trains Go By, The 12-31-52
Man Who Won, The 7-18-19
Man Who Won, The 10-11-23
Man Who Won, The 2-28-33
Man Who Would Be King, The 12-10-75

Man Who Wouldn't Die, The 4-22-42
Man Who Wouldn't Talk, The 1-17-40
Man Who Wouldn't Talk, The 1-22-58
Man Who Wouldn't Tell, The 12-06-18
Man with a Cloak, The 10-03-51
Man with a Round Hat (See: Homme au Chapeau Rond, L')
Man with Bogart's Face, The 5-28-80
Man with Broken Ear (See: Homme a l'Oreille Cassee)
Man with Connections, The (See: Pistonne, Le)
Man with Golden Keys, The (See: Homme Aux Cles D'Or, L')
Man with Green Eyes, The 2-05-30
Man with My Face, The 5-16-51
Man with Nine Lives, The 5-01-40
Man with 100 Faces, The 11-02-38
Man with the Axe (See: Parasuram)
Man with the Balloons, The 7-03-68
Man with the Frog, The (See: Mann mit dem Laubfrosch, Der)
Man with the Glass Eye, The (See: Mann Mit dem Glasauge, Der)
Man with the Golden Arm, The 12-14-55
Man with the Golden Brush, The (See: Mann Mit Dem Goldenen
  Pinsel, Der)
Man with the Golden Gun, The 12-11-74
Man with the Grey Glove, The (See: Uomo Dal Guanto Grigio, L')
Man with the Gun, The 2-15-39
Man with the Gun, The 10-12-55
Man with the Iron Heart, The 9-10-15
Man with the Red Carnation, The (See: O Anthropos Me To
  Garyfallo)
Man with the Transplanted Brain, The (See: Homme Au Cerveau
  Greffe, L')
Man with the Whistling Nose, The (See: Fischio Al Naso, Il)
Man with Three Wives, A 11-20-09
Man with 2 Faces, The 7-17-34
Man with Two Lives, The 3-11-42
Man with Two Mothers, The 6-16-22
Man Within, The 4-09-47
Man Without a Country, The 9-14-17
Man Without a Country, The 2-18-25
Man Without a Face, The (See: Homme Sans Visage, L')
Man Without a Heart, The 1-21-25
Man Without a Name (See: Azonositas or Mensch Ohne Namen)
Man Without a Name, A (See: Homme Sans Nom, Un)
Man Without a Star, The 3-02-55
Man Without Desire, The 3-12-24
Man Without Name (See: Mensch Ohne Namen)
Man, Woman and Sin 12-07-27
Man--Woman--Marriage 4-01-21
Man Worth While 9-09-21
Man You Love to Hate, The 8-15-79
Management Forgives a Moment of Madness, The (See: Empresa
  Perdona Un Momento De Locura, La)
Manager of the B & A, The 9-29-16
Manana Me Suicido 10-28-42
Manana Sera Otro Dia 7-12-67
Manaos 2-13-80
Manchas de Sangre en un Coche Nuevo 3-05-75
Manche et la Belle, Une 2-12-58
Manchu Eagle Murder Caper Mystery, The 3-26-75
Manchurian Candidate, The 10-17-62
Mandabi 9-11-68
Mandagarna Med Fanny 5-25-77
Mandalay 2-20-34
Mandarin Mystery, The 6-23-37
Mandarine, La 4-05-72
Mandarin's Gold 1-31-19
Mandem Der Taenkte Ting 5-21-69
Manden Paa Svanegrden 1-10-73
Mandingo 5-07-75
Mandragola, La 3-09-66
Mandrake, The (See: Mandragola, La)
Mandrake the Magician 6-28-39
Mandrin 1-16-63
Mandy 8-20-52
Manege 2-08-28
Maneges 3-08-50
Manesgazda 2-28-79
Manewry Milosne 11-18-36
Manfish 2-15-56
Manganinnie 7-16-80
Mango Tree, The 12-21-77
Manha Submersa 10-15-80
Manhandled 7-30-24
Manhandled 4-13-49
Manhattan 10-29-24
Manhattan 4-25-79
Manhattan Angel 12-01-48
Manhattan Cocktail 11-28-28
Manhattan Cowboy, The 5-22-29

Manhattan Heartbeat 6-05-40
Manhattan Knight 3-19-20
Manhattan Knights 9-05-28
Manhattan Love Song 9-04-34
Manhattan Madness 9-22-16
Manhattan Melodrama 5-08-34
Manhattan Merry-Go-Round 11-10-37
Manhattan Moon 8-21-35
Manhattan Parade 12-29-31
Manhattan Shakedown 10-18-39
Manhattan Tower 12-20-32
Manhunt (See: Hajka)
Manhunt (See: Chasse a l'Homme, La or Jakten)
Manhunt in the Jungle 4-16-58
Manhunters (See: Naganiacz)
Manhunters of the Caribbean 1-19-38
Mani 11-05-75
Mani Di Velluto 2-20-80
Mani Sulla Citta, La 9-11-63
Maniac 10-23-63
Maniacs on Wheels 7-11-51
Manicure Girls, The 6-17-25
Manila Calling 9-16-42
Manitou, The 3-01-78
Manja Valewska 11-11-36
Manji (See: All Mixed Up)
Manlo, The Flower (See: Manlohua)
Manlohua 7-31-63
Manly Times (See: Muzhki Vremena)
Mann Der Den Mord Beging, Der 2-11-31
Mann, Der Seinen Moerder Sucht, Der 3-11-31
Mann, Der Sherlock Holmes War, Der 8-18-37
Mann, Der Sich Verkaufte, Der 6-24-59
Mann Gegen Mann 7-28-76
Mann Geht Durch die Wand, Ein 3-02-60
Mann mit dem Glasauge, Der 4-02-69
Mann mit dem Goldenen Pinsel, Der 7-16-69
Mann mit dem Laubfrosch, Der 3-06-29
Mann, Von Dem Man Spricht, Der 5-12-37
Mannen Pa Taget 10-27-76
Mannen Som Slutade Roeka 1-31-73
Mannequin 1-13-26
Mannequin 12-22-37
Mannequin 8-18-76
Mannequins de Paris 11-07-56
Mannerheim Line 12-25-40
Mano Della Morta, La 11-16-49
Mano Dello Strangiero 8-04-54
Mano en la Trampa, La 5-24-61
Mano Negra, La 9-03-80
Manoa 5-28-80
Manoeuvre 12-05-79
Manoever Zwilling 9-12-56
Manolescu 10-02-29
Manolette 5-31-50
Manomaniac, The 5-15-14
Manon 4-06-49
Manon des Sources 2-18-53
Manon Lescaut 6-19-14
Manon Lescaut 12-15-26
Manon 70 3-06-68
Manpower 7-09-41
Manrape (See: Man Kan Inte Valtas)
Man's Castle, A 1-02-34
Man's Country 8-03-38
Man's Desire 7-25-19
Man's Enemy 7-10-14
Man's Favorite Sport? 1-22-64
Man's Game, A 10-16-34
Man's Home, A 12-23-21
Man's Hope 1-22-47
Man's Hunger (See: Soif des Hommes, La)
Man's Hunger, A 8-19-59
Man's Land, A 1-03-33
Man's Making, A 1-07-16
Man's Man, A 1-18-18
Man's Man, A 6-05-29
Man's Mate, A 5-21-24
Man's Paradise (See: Paradiso Dell'Uomo)
Man's Past, A 10-05-27
Man's Plaything 7-09-20
Man's Prerogative, A 4-30-15
Man's Return (See: Uomo Ritorna, Un)
Man's Size 4-26-23
Man's Woman 3-23-17
Man's World, A 7-05-18
Mansion de la Locura, La 8-22-73
Mansion of Madness, The (See: Mansion de la Locura, La)

Manslaughter (See: Requisitoire, Le)
Manslaughter 9-22-22
Manslaughter 7-30-30
Manson 9-13-72
Manthan 1-26-77
Manti Senza Amore (See: Prelude to Madness)
Mantle of Charity, The 9-27-18 and 11-22-18
Mantrap 7-14-26
Mantrap 7-14-26
Mantrap 5-12-43
Manuela 8-14-57
Manufacturing Bamboo Hats 9-04-09
Manulescu 4-04-33
Manx-man, The 4-13-17
Manxman, The 2-20-29 and 12-18-29
Many a Slip 9-01-31
Many Happy Returns 6-12-34
Many Passed By (See: Viele Kamen Vorbei)
Many Rivers to Cross 2-02-55
Manzana de la Discordia, La 5-28-69
Maos Sangrentas 9-14-55
Maquillage 11-29-32
Mar de Rosas 9-24-80
Mara of the Wilderness 6-22-66
Maracaibo 5-14-58
Marathon Derby 4-10-09
Marathon Man 9-29-76
Marauders, The 7-16-47
Marauders, The 4-20-55
Maravilla del Toreo 7-07-43
Marble Heart 9-25-09
Marble Heart 3-10-16
Marble Quarrying in Tennessee 2-05-10
Marcelino Bread and Wine (See: Marcelino Pan y Vino)
Marcelino Pan y Vino 6-01-55
Marcella 10-27-37
Marcellini Millions, The 5-11-17
March Hare, The 5-09-56
March on Paris 1914 4-26-78
March on Rome, The (See: Marcia Su Roma, La)
March or Die 8-03-77
Marchand de Venise, Le 12-09-53
Marchands de Filles 12-04-57
Marche au Soleil, La 10-04-32
Marcia Nuziale, La 3-04-36
Marcia Su Roma, La 1-16-63
Marcia Trionfale 4-07-76
Marco 11-24-71
Marco 12-26-73
Marco of Rio 5-14-69
Marco Polo 2-04-76
Marco Polo Junior 1-26-73
Marco Visconti 9-24-47
Marco's Theme (See: Tema Di Marco)
Mardi Gras 11-19-58
Mare, Il 9-12-62
Mare Matto 9-11-63
Mare Nostrum 2-17-26
Marge, La 9-22-76
Margie 9-18-40
Margie 10-16-46
Margin, The (See: Marge, La)
Margin for Error 1-13-43
Marginal Ones, The (See: Oka Oorie Katha)
Marguerite de la Nuit 2-29-56
Marguerite Divided by Three (See: Marguerite Drei)
Marguerite Drei 6-28-39
Marguerite of the Night (See: Marguerite de la Nuit)
Maria 9-10-47
Maria 10-08-75
Maria Candelaria 9-27-44
Maria Chapdelaine 1-01-35 and 10-02-35
Maria de la "O" 9-30-42
Maria die Magd 11-11-36
Maria D'Oro und Bello Blue (See: Once Upon a Time)
Maria du Bout du Monde 5-02-51
Maria Marten (or The Murder in the Red Barn) 3-28-38
Maria Nover 3-24-37
Maria of End of World (See: Maria du Bout du Monde)
Maria Pentayotissa 5-13-36
Maria Rosa 4-28-16
Maria Stuart 2-15-28
Maria, the Servant (See: Maria die Magd)
Maria Theresia 1-09-52
Mariage 1-29-75
Mariage a la Mode, Le 10-17-23
Mariage de Figaro, Le 5-08-63
Mariage de Ramuntcho, Le 9-17-47
Marian 3-14-79

Marianne 10-23-29
Marianne de Ma Jeunesse 5-11-55
Marianne of My Youth (See: Marianne de Ma Jeunesse)
Maria's Hours (See: As Horas de Maria)
Maribel and the Strange Family (See: Maribel y la Extrana Familia)
Maribel y la Extrana Familia 9-14-60
Marice Est Trop Bella, La 1-23-57
Maridos en Vacaciones 7-23-75
Marie 2-28-33
Marie-Anne 8-02-78 and 9-20-78
Marie Antoinette 2-27-29
Marie Antoinette 7-13-38
Marie-Antoinette 5-16-56
Marie Chantal Against Dr. Kha (See: Marie Chantal Contre Dr. Kha)
Marie Chantal Contre Dr. Kha 10-06-65
Marie des Iles 3-09-60
Marie du Port, La 4-26-50
Marie for Memory (See: Marie Pour Memoire)
Marie Galante 11-27-34
Marie la Misere 10-17-45
Marie, Ltd. 4-04-19
Marie-Louise 11-14-45
Marie-Octobre 5-27-59
Marie of Pentagious (See: Maria Pentayotissa)
Marie of the Isles (See: Marie des Iles)
Marie of the Port (See: Marie du Port, La)
Marie-Poupee 9-15-76
Marie Pour Memoire 5-15-68
Marie Soleil 4-21-65
Marie-The Doll (See: Marie-Poupee)
Marie Tudor 10-04-67
Mariee Est Trop Belle, La 1-23-57
Mariee Etait en Noire, La 4-24-68
Maries de l'An Deux, Les 5-05-71
Marigolds in August 3-12-80
Marihuana 11-08-50
Marika 3-23-38
Mariken van Nieumeghen 5-14-75
Marilyn 6-12-63
Marilyn and the Senator 4-16-75
Marine Raiders 6-21-44
Marines Are Coming, The 2-27-35
Marines Are Here 7-06-38
Marines Come Through, The 7-14-43
Marines Fly High 3-06-40
Marines, Let's Go 8-16-61
Marion, Das Gehoert Sich Nicht 3-14-33
Marion, It Isn't Done (See: Marion, das Gehoert Sich Nicht)
Marionettes, The 2-08-18
Marions-Nous 3-25-31
Marisa la Civetta 3-26-58
Marital Fulfillment 5-13-70
Marital Happiness 5-09-29
Mariti In Citta 3-19-58
Marito e Mio e L'Amazzo Quando Mi Pare 3-13-68
Marito e Moglie 7-02-52
Marito Per Anna Zaccheo, Un 12-30-53
Marius 10-27-31; 4-25-33; and 6-02-48
Marja Pieni 8-16-72
Marjoe 5-10-72
Marjorie Morningstar 3-12-58
Mark, The (See: Strange Case of Mary Page, The: Part IV)
Mark, The 2-01-61
Mark It Paid 1-24-33
Mark of Cain, The 1-14-48
Mark of the Beast 11-15-23
Mark of the Chinese Temple (See: Khao Yod)
Mark of the Day, The (See: Point du Jour, Le)
Mark of the Devil (See: Brenn, Hexe, Brenn)
Mark of the Gorilla 2-22-50
Mark of the Hawk 2-12-58
Mark of the Renegade 7-25-51
Mark of the Vampire 5-08-35
Mark of the Whistler 11-15-44
Mark of Zorro, The 12-03-20
Mark of Zorro, The 11-06-40
Marked Cards 7-26-18
Marked Cards 7-13-49
Marked Eyes (See: Yeux Cernes, Les)
Marked Girls 7-13-49
Marked Man, The (See: Hombre Senalado, El)
Marked Men 9-11-40
Marked Money 4-17-29
Marked Trails 10-11-44
Marked Woman 4-14-37
Marked Woman, The 12-11-14
Markers, Staakt Uw Wild Geraas 7-12-61

Market of Souls, The 9-12-19
Market of the Unknowns (See: De Utjentes Marked)
Market of Vain Desire, The 5-19-16
Marketa Lazarova 11-06-68
Markia 9-19-14
Marknadsafton 10-06-48
Marksman, The (See: Skytten)
Marlowe 10-08-69
Marmalade Revolution, The (See: Marmeladupporet)
Marmeladupporet 3-12-80
Marnie 6-10-64
Maroc 7 3-29-67
Marooned 11-19-69
Marooned Hearts 10-08-20
Marquess of Pompadour, The (See: Marquise von Pompadour, Die)
Marquis Preferred 1-23-29
Marquise d'O, La 5-19-76
Marquise von Pompadour, Die 1-28-31
Marquise von Pompadour, Die 2-19-36
Marriage (See: Mariage)
Marriage 11-08-18
Marriage 5-18-27
Marriage 5-22-29
Marriage 2-28-45
Marriage, The (See: O Casamento)
Marriage a La Mode (See: Mariage A La Mode, Le)
Marriage Agency (See: Agence Matrimoniale)
Marriage by Aeroplane 1-30-14
Marriage by Contract 11-14-28
Marriage Chance 1-19-23
Marriage Cheat, The 6-04-24
Marriage Circle 7-24-63
Marriage Circle, The 2-07-24
Marriage Clause, The 9-29-26
Marriage Forbidden 7-20-38
Marriage Game, The (See: Aktenskapsleken)
Marriage-Go-Round, The 12-07-60
Marriage in Haste (See: Paprika)
Marriage in Name (See: Namensheirat)
Marriage in the Shadows 9-15-48
Marriage Is a Private Affair 8-16-44
Marriage--Italian Style 12-23-64
Marriage License 10-27-26
Marriage Maker 9-20-23
Marriage Market, The 8-31-17
Marriage Morals 8-16-23
Marriage of a Young Stockbroker, The 8-18-71
Marriage of Corbal 6-10-36
Marriage of Figaro, The (See: Mariage de Figaro, Le)
Marriage of Figaro, The 11-08-50
Marriage of Kitty, The 8-20-15
Marriage of Maria Braun, The (See: Ehe der Maria Braun, Die)
Marriage of Mr. Mississippi, The (See: Ehe des Herr Mississippi, Die)
Marriage of Mr. Mississippi, The 7-05-61
Marriage of Molly-O, The 7-21-16
Marriage of Ramuntcho, The (See: Mariage de Ramuntcho, Le)
Marriage of the Cook, The 1-08-10
Marriage of the Nephew of the Maharajah of Tagore 11-20-09
Marriage of William Ashe 2-25-21
Marriage on Approval 1-09-34
Marriage on the Rocks 9-22-65
Marriage Pit, The 10-29-20
Marriage Playground, The 12-18-29
Marriage Price, The 3-21-19
Marriage Revolution, The (See: Revolucion Matrimonial, La)
Marriage Ring, The 9-27-18
Marriage, Tel Aviv Style (See: Nissuim Nosach Tel Aviv)
Marriage with Limited Liability (See: Ehe mit Beschraenkter Haftung)
Marriage Whirl 7-15-25
Married 2-24-26 and 5-19-26
Married Alive 8-10-27
Married and in Love 2-07-40
Married Bachelor 9-10-41
Married Before Breakfast 7-28-37
Married Couple, A 11-12-69
Married Couple of Year Two, The (See: Maries de l'An Deux, Les)
Married Flirts 11-19-24
Married for the First Time (See: Vpervye Zamuzhem)
Married in Haste 4-18-19
Married in Hollywood 9-25-29
Married Life 6-25-20
Married People 9-22-22
Married Priest, The (See: Prete Sposato, Il)
Married Woman, The (See: Femme Mariee, La)
Marry in Haste 2-07-24

Marry Me 7-15-25
Marry Me 11-29-32
Marry Me! 6-15-49
Marry Me Again 9-23-53
Marry the Boss' Daughter 11-19-41
Marry the Girl 4-04-28
Marry the Girl 8-04-37
Marrying Kind, The 3-12-52
Marrying Widows 9-04-34
Mars Attacks the World 11-09-38
Marseillaise, La 3-16-38 and 11-15-39
Marshal of Amarillo 10-20-48
Marshal of Cedar Rock 2-25-53
Marshal of Cripple Creek 8-20-47
Marshal of Mesa City 12-27-39
Marshall of Heldorado 7-19-50
Marshal's Daughter, The 6-17-53
Marta 5-05-71
Marta of the Lowlands 10-10-14
Martes, Orquideas, Los 6-25-41
Martha 8-28-74
Martha's Vindication 3-24-16
Marthe Richard 5-12-37
Martians, The (See: Disco Volante, Il)
Martien de Noel, Le 6-09-71
Martin 1-10-79
Martin and Lea (See: Martin et Lea)
Martin et Lea 12-27-78
Martin Fierro 7-24-68
Martin in the Clouds (See: Martin U Oblacima)
Martin Luther 5-13-53
Martin Roumagnac 1-08-47
Martin Soldat 10-12-66
Martin U Oblacima 8-09-61
Martlet's Tale, The 11-04-70
Marty 3-23-55
Martyr, The (See: Martyrer, Der)
Martyr Sex, The 4-16-24
Martyr to His Duty, A 1-08-15
Martyrdom of Philip Strong 12-01-16
Martyre de L'Obese, Le 4-18-33
Martyred Love (See: Mucednici Lasky)
Martyrer, Der 8-28-74
Martyries 11-05-75
Martyrs of the Alamo, The 10-19-15
Martyrs of the War, The 6-30-16
Maru Maru 4-02-52
Marusia 12-21-38
Marvellous Visit, The (See: Merveilleuse Visite, La)
Marvelous Angelique (See: Merveilleuse Angelique)
Marvels of the Bull Ring (See: Maravilla del Toreo)
Mary, La 8-28-74
Mary Burns, Fugitive 11-20-35
Mary Ellen Comes to Town 3-26-20
Mary Had a Little 7-21-61
Mary Jane Visits Her Country Cousin 7-03-09
Mary Jane's Pa 6-19-35
Mary Lawson's Secret 3-16-17
Mary Lou 1-21-48
Mary, Mary 9-04-63
Mary, Mary, Bloody Mary 5-21-75
Mary of Scotland 8-05-36
Mary of the Movies 6-21-23
Mary Poppins 9-02-64
Mary, Queen of Scots 12-22-71
Mary Regan 5-09-19
Mary Ryan, Detective 11-09-49
Mary Stevens, M.D. 8-08-33
Mary Stuart 11-28-08
Mary's Lamb 12-03-15
Mary's Start in die Ehe 12-08-31
Mary's Start into Matrimony (See: Mary's Start in die Ehe)
Maryjane 2-21-68
Maryland 7-03-40
Mas Alla Del Sol 8-06-75
Mas Alla Del Terror 9-17-80
Mas Infeliz Del Pueblo, El 4-16-41
Mascara de la Muerta, La 4-19-61
Mascarade 10-16-34
Mascottchen 5-08-29
Masculin Feminin 5-04-66
M*A*S*H 1-21-70
Mashenka 11-25-42
Mask, The 9-06-18
Mask, The 6-17-21
Mask, The 11-01-61
Mask and Destiny, The (See: Shuzenji Monogatari)
Mask of Death, The (See: Mascara de la Muerta, La)

Mask of Diijon, The 1-30-46
Mask of Dimitrios, The 6-07-44
Mask of Fu Manchu, The 12-06-32
Mask of Korea 8-09-50
Mask of Lopez 11-15-23
Mask of Lopez 10-26-27
Mask of the Avenger 6-27-51
Mask of the Dragon 5-02-51
Masked Angel, The 3-21-28
Masked Bride, The 12-02-25
Masked Emotion 7-24-29
Masked Raiders 9-28-49
Masked Rider, The 10-08-41
Masked Woman 1-12-27
Maskerade 1-27-37
Maskmaker, The 4-23-10
Masks (See: Persona)
Masks and Faces 5-10-18
Masks of the Devil 11-28-28
Masoch 9-10-80
Mason of the Mounted 9-06-32
Masque de Fer, Le 11-21-62
Masque of Life, The 10-27-16
Masque of the Red Death 6-24-64
Masquerade 5-19-43
Masquerade 4-21-65
Masquerade, The 9-11-29
"Masquerade" Cop, The 11-12-10
Masquerade in Mexico 12-05-45
Masquerade in Vienna (See: Maskerade)
Masquerader, The 8-18-22
Masquerader, The 9-05-33
Masqueraders, The 11-05-15
Masquerader's Charity 12-18-09
Massacre 1-23-34
Massacre 6-06-56
Massacre at Central High 11-17-76
Massacre Canyon 4-14-54
Massacre en Dentelles 4-23-52
Massacre in Lace (See: Massacre en Dentelles)
Massacre in Rome 8-22-73
Massacre River 4-06-49
Massaggiatrici, Le 1-23-63
Masseuses, The (See: Massaggiatrici, Le)
Master and His Servants, The (See: Herren Og Hans Tjenere)
Master and Man 6-18-15
Master and Margherita, The (See: Maestro e Margherita, Il)
Master Cracksman, The 6-19-14
Master Detectiven Blomkvist 3-24-48
Master Gunfighter, The 10-08-75
Master Hand, The 8-20-15
Master Man, The 5-09-19
Master Mind, The 5-29-14
Master Mind, The 9-17-20
Master Minds 1-11-50
Master Mystery, The 11-15-18
Master of Ballantrae 7-22-53
Master of Bankdam 8-27-47
Master of His Home 8-03-17
Master of Men 12-05-33
Master of Merripit, The 4-02-15
Master of Nuremburg, The 8-17-27
Master of the House 10-08-15
Master of the World (See: Herr der Welt, Der)
Master of the World 5-03-61
Master Over Life and Death (See: Herr Ueber Leben Und Tod)
Master Race, The 9-27-44
Master Rogues of Europe, The 5-28-15
Master Shakespeare 4-21-16
Master Spy 8-26-64
Master Stroke, A 7-09-20
Master Touch, The 5-08-74
Masterpiece 10-09-09
Masters of Men 5-17-23
Masters of the Congo Jungle 12-16-59
Masters of the Forest (See: Seigneurs de la Foret, Les)
Masterson of Kansas 11-24-54
Mata-Hari 7-27-27 and 11-14-28
Mata Hari 1-05-32
Mata-Hari 2-17-65
Matatabi 12-12-73 and 12-26-73
Match King, The 12-13-32
Matchless 9-20-67
Matchless 10-09-74
Matchmaker, The 5-07-58
Matchmaking of Anna, The (See: To Proxenio Tis Annas)
Mate Doma Liva? 8-18-65
Mater Amatisima 6-11-80

Maternal One, The (See: Maternelle, La)
Maternal Spark, The 12-14-17
Maternale 4-19-78
Maternelle, La 9-26-33 and 10-23-35
Maternite 5-08-35 and 6-09-37
Maternity 5-18-17
Mathew's Days (See: Zywot Mateusza)
Mathias Sandorf 3-20-63
Matilda 6-21-78
Matilda's Winning Ways 9-17-10
Matinee Idol, The 4-25-28
Matinee Ladies 4-13-27
Mating, The 7-16-15
Mating, The 10-04-18
Mating Call 10-10-28
Mating Game, The 2-18-59
Mating of Millie, The 3-10-48
Mating Season, The 1-10-51
Matka Joanna Od Aniotow 5-17-61
Matomeno Heliovasilema 5-13-59
Matou a Familia e Foi Ao Cinema 4-22-70
Matriarca, La 1-15-69
Matriarch, The (See: Matriarca, La)
Matriarchy (See: Matriarhat)
Matriarhat 5-31-78
Matriculation Exam (See: Reifende Jugend)
Matrimaniac, The 12-08-16
Matrimonial Agency Aurora (See: Eheinstitut Aurora)
Matrimonial Bed, The 8-27-30
Matrimonial Martyr, A 7-07-16
Matrimonial War (See: Guerra Conjugal)
Matrimony 10-29-15
Matrimony, A (See: Ehe, Eine)
Matsuri No Junbi 10-11-78
Mattanza 9-18-68
Mattatore, Il (See: Love and Larceny)
Matter of Days, A 5-21-69
Matter of Dignity, A 1-20-60
Matter of Fat, A 10-07-70
Matter of Honor, A (See: Questione d'Onore, Una)
Matter of Life and Death, A 11-13-46
Matter of Morals, A 6-22-60
Matter of Time, A 10-06-76
Matter of Who, A 10-11-61
Matto Regiert 6-11-47
Matzor 5-28-69
Maude Muller 10-30-09
Maudite Galette, Une 5-10-72
Maudits, Les 11-12-47
Maudits Sauvages, Les 6-09-71
Maurie 7-25-73
Mauvais Coups, Les 5-24-61
Mauvais Fils, Un 11-19-80
Mauvaises Rencontres, Les 9-14-55
Maverick, The 8-27-20
Maverick, The 12-24-52
Maverick Queen, The 5-02-56
Mawas 5-28-30
Mawson's Antarctic 3-12-15
Max and the Junkmen (See: Max et les Ferrailleurs)
Max Comes Across 2-09-17
Max et les Ferrailleurs 2-24-71
Max Havelaar 10-06-76
Max in a Dilemma 11-12-10
Max in the Alps 11-05-10
Max Is Almost Married 1-21-11
Max Makes Music 3-04-11
Max Wants a Divorce 3-23-17
Maxime 12-10-58
Maximka 10-21-53
Maxim's Porter (See: Chasseur de Chez Maxims, Le)
Maxwell Archer, Detective 5-06-42
May (See: Maes)
May Blossom 4-30-15
May Blossom 3-23-17
May God Forgive Me (See: Que Dios Me Perdone)
May I Have the Floor (See: Proshu Slova)
Maya 12-21-49
Maya 4-13-66
Maya Darpan 8-29-73
Mayakovsky Laughs 6-16-76
Mayakovsky Smejotsja (See: Mayakovsky Laughs)
Maybe It's Love 10-22-30
Maybe It's Love 2-12-35
Maybe Tomorrow (See: Majd Holnap)
Mayerling 2-19-36 and 9-15-37
Mayerling 10-30-68
Mayfair Melody 3-17-37

Maynila, Sa Mga Kuko Ng Liwanag 8-06-75
Mayor of Filbert, The 5-16-19
Mayor of 44th Street, The 3-18-42
Mayor of Hell 7-04-33
Maytime 11-22-23 and 6-04-24
Maytime 3-24-37
Maytime in Mayfair 6-01-49
Maze, The 7-08-53
Mazel Tov ou le Mariage 10-02-68
Mazurka 1-01-36
Mazurka Paa Sengekanten 9-16-70
Mazzetta, La 5-10-78
Me 10-01-75
Me and Captain Kid 11-07-19
Me and Charly (See: Mig og Charly)
Me and Marlborough 8-14-35
Me and My Brother 9-11-68
Me and My Gal 9-22-22
Me and My Gal 12-13-32
Me and My Gal 9-09-42
Me and My Kid Brother and Doggie (See: Mig og Min Lillebror
   og Boelle)
Me and My Pal 2-02-17
Me and the Colonel 8-06-58
Me and the Empress (See: Moi et L'Imperatrice)
Me and the 40-Year Old Men (See: Moi et les Hommes de Quarante
   Ans)
Me and the Mafia (See: Mig og Mafiaen)
Me and You (See: Mig og Dig)
Me Faire Ca a Moi 8-16-61
Me First (See: Primero Yo)
Me, Gangster 10-24-28
Me, I Want to Have Dough (See: Moi Y'en a Vouloir Des Sous)
Me, Me, Me ... and the Others (See: Io, Io, Io ... e Gli Altri)
Me, Natalie 7-16-69
Me Ti Lampsi Sta Matia 11-16-66
Me, Too, I'm the Mafia (See: Mafiaen, Det Er Osse Mig)
Me Vang Nha 7-30-80
Meadow, The (See: Prato, Il)
Meal, The 10-29-75
Mealtimes (See: Mahlzeitn)
Mean Dog Blues 2-22-78
Mean Streets 10-03-73
Meanders (See: Meandre)
Meandre 8-03-66
Meanest Gal in Town, The 2-20-34
Meanest Man in the World, The 1-13-43
Measure for Measure (See: Dente Per Dente)
Measure of a Man 10-22-24
Measure of a Man, The 11-17-16
Measure of Leon Dubray, The 11-12-15
Meat (See: Fleisch)
Meat Rack 3-25-70
Meatballs 6-27-79
Mecanica Nacional 1-29-75
Mecanismo Interior 8-04-71
Mecava 8-17-77
Mechanic, The 11-01-72
Mechanical Statues 1-26-07
Mechanics of Brain 12-12-28
Mechanics of the Brain 5-22-35
Med Kaerlig Hilsen 8-25-71
Med Strahom In Dolznostjo 8-18-76
Medal, The (See: Signum Laudis)
Medal for Benny, A 4-11-45
Medal for the General, A 7-12-44
Medan Porten var Stangd 1-22-47
Meddig El Az Ember? 5-15-68
Meddler, The 5-27-25
Meddling Women 11-05-24
Medea 3-11-70
Medena Veza 8-19-70
Mediator, The 11-17-16
Medic, The (See: Toubib, Le)
Medical Doctor Sommer The Second (See: Dr. Med. Sommer II)
Medicine Ball Caravan 8-25-71
Medicine Bend 6-16-16
Medicine Man, The 11-09-17
Medicine Man, The 6-25-30
Medico Della Mutua, Il 10-30-68
Medico e lo Stregone, Il 3-19-58
Medico of Painted Springs, The 6-25-41
Mediterranean Cruise 11-26-30
Mediterranean Holiday 12-23-64
Medium, The 9-12-51
Medium Cool 7-30-69
Medusa Raft, The (See: Splav Meduze)
Medusa Touch, The 2-08-78

Meet Balujev 7-24-63
Meet Boston Blackie 3-05-41
Meet Danny Wilson 1-16-52
Meet Dr. Christian 10-18-39
Meet John Doe 3-19-41
Meet Me After the Show 8-08-51
Meet Me at Dawn 1-15-47
Meet Me at the Fair 12-10-52
Meet Me in Las Vegas 2-08-56
Meet Me in St. Louis 11-01-44
Meet Me on Broadway 2-27-46
Meet Me Tonight 9-17-52
Meet Miss Bobby Socks 11-15-44
Meet Miss Mozart 12-01-37
Meet Mr. Lucifer 12-09-53
Meet My Sister 8-08-33
Meet Nero Wolfe 7-22-36
Meet the Baron 10-31-33
Meet the Boy Friend 7-21-37
Meet the Chump 2-12-41
Meet the Girls 8-31-38
Meet the Mayor 10-12-38
Meet the Missus 7-07-37
Meet the Missus 12-18-40
Meet the Mob 5-13-42
Meet the Navy 5-29-46
Meet the People 4-05-44
Meet the Sister (See: Versuchen Sie Meine Schwester)
Meet the Stewarts 5-20-42
Meet the Wife 6-23-31
Meet the Wildcat 10-30-40
Meeting in Bray (See: Rendez-Vous A Bray)
Meeting in Night (See: Mote I Natten)
Meeting in Paris (See: Rencontre a Paris)
Meeting in the Forest (See: Rendez-Vous en Foret, Les)
Meetings (See: Rencontres)
Meetings of Anna, The (See: Rendez-Vous D'Anna, Les)
Meetings with Remarkable Men 3-14-79
Meetings with the Devil (See: Rendez-Vous du Diable, Les)
Mefiez-Vous Fillettes 12-04-57
Mefiez-Vous Mesdames 11-20-63
Meg Ker a Nep 5-24-72
Meg-O-Ruerda 7-30-69
Megalomaniac, The (See: Rai Saneh Ha)
Meglio Vedova 11-20-68
Megszallottak 9-12-62
Meguara 10-30-74
Megvedtem Egy Asszonyt 8-24-38
Mei (See: Lost)
Meilleure Facon de Marcher, La 2-18-76
Meilleure Part, La 4-18-56
Mein Freund der Millionaer 2-02-32
Mein Freund der Nicht Nein Sagen Kann 1-11-50
Mein Herz Ruft Dir 4-17-34
Mein Kampf 11-30-60
Mein Leopold 1-05-32 and 4-05-32
Mein Lieber Robinson 9-06-72
Mein Liebster Ist Ein Jaegersman 9-16-36
Mein Schulfreund 8-03-60
Mein Vater, Der Affe und Ich 8-18-71
Meine Frau, die Hochstaplerin 10-13-31 and 2-09-32
Meine Freundin Barbara 6-15-38
Meine Kusine aus Warschau 9-15-31
Meine Nicht Tut das Nicht 9-28-60
Meine Sorgen Moecht' Ich Haben 7-02-75
Meine Tochter Patricia 8-19-59
Meineid (See: Perjury)
Meistersinger 12-25-29
Meistersinger von Nuernberg, Die 7-22-70
Mejor Papa Del Mundo, El 4-16-41
Melancholic Stories (See: Zwaarmoedige Verhalen)
Melancholy Baby 10-31-79
Melancolicas, Las 5-24-72
Melba 6-24-53
Melbourne Rendezvous 10-16-57
Melech Leyom Echad 8-06-80
Melinda 8-16-72
Melo 11-08-32 and 2-06-34
Melodias de America 2-11-42
Melodie der Liebe 5-31-32
Melodie der Welt (See: Melody of the World)
Melodie en Sous-Sol 4-17-63
Melodie Immortali 3-11-53
Melodies des Herzens 9-03-30
Melodies of America (See: Melodias de America)
Melodies of Verliski District (See: Melodii Veriiskogo Kvartala)
Melodii Veriiskogo Kvartala 8-28-74
Melodrama? 8-20-80

Melodrama in a Bowery Theatre 5-11-07
Melodrame 5-19-76
Melody 3-17-71
Melody and Moonlight 10-16-40
Melody Cruise 6-27-33
Melody for Three 3-05-41
Melody for Two 5-26-37
Melody in Spring 4-03-34
Melody Lane 7-17-29
Melody Lingers On, The 11-13-35
Melody Man 2-26-30
Melody of Love (See: Melodie der Liebe)
Melody of Love 5-12-54
Melody of Love, The 10-17-28
Melody of the Heart (See: Melodies des Herzens)
Melody of the Plains 7-07-37
Melody of the World 4-10-29
Melody Parade 8-18-43
Melody Ranch 1-01-41
Melody Time 5-19-48
Melody Trail 12-11-35
Melting Millions 3-02-17
Melting Pot, The 6-04-15
Meltosagos Kiasasszony 2-24-37
Melvin and Howard 9-10-80
Mem Ja (My Lady) 3-19-75
Member of Tattersalls, A 11-28-19
Member of the Wedding 12-17-52
Memetih 4-21-65
Memoire Courte, La 2-27-63
Memoire Courte, La 6-13-79
Memoirs of a Gigolo (See: Memorias de Um Gigolo)
Memoirs of a Streetwalker (See: Wat Zien Ik)
Memoirs of Leticia Valle (See: Memorias de Leticia Valle)
Memorandum 10-04-67
Memoria de Helena 10-14-70
Memorias de Leticia Valle 9-26-79
Memorias de Um Gigolo 10-14-70
Memorias del Subdesarrollo 6-26-68
Memories (See: Spomen)
Memories of Helena (See: Memoria de Helena)
Memories of the Future (See: Erinnerungen An die Zukunft)
Memories of Underdevelopment (See: Memorias del Subdesarrollo)
Memories Within Miss Aggie 4-24-74
Memory Lane 2-03-26
Memory of Justice, The 6-09-76
Memory of Us 5-01-74
Memphis Belle 3-22-44
Men 5-24-18
Men 5-07-24
Men, The (See: Males, Les or Hommes, Les)
Men, The 5-24-50
Men Against the Sky 8-28-40
Men and Jobs 1-17-33
Men and the Beasts, The (See: Lyudi y Zvery)
Men and Wolves (See: Uomini e Lupi)
Men and Women 4-01-25
Men Are Like That 8-06-30
Men Are Like That 8-18-31
Men Are Not Gods 12-09-36 and 1-20-37
Men Are Such Fools 3-14-33
Men Are Such Fools 6-22-38
Men at Dangerous Age (See: Maenner Im Gefaehrlichen Alter)
Men Call It Love 6-23-31
Men from the Monastery 11-27-74
Men in Exile 5-05-37
Men in Her Diary 9-12-45
Men in Her Life 12-01-31
Men in Her Life, The 11-05-41
Men in the Raw 10-18-23
Men in War 1-23-57
Men in White (See: Hommes en Blanc, Les)
Men in White 5-01-34 and 6-12-34
Men Like These 11-17-31
Men Must Fight 3-14-33
Men of America 2-28-33
Men of Boys Town 4-09-41
Men of Bronze 9-28-77
Men of Chance 1-05-32
Men of Daring 5-04-27
Men of Ireland 10-05-38
Men of Purpose 10-20-26
Men of Rio 7-06-60
Men of San Quentin 8-26-42
Men of Steel 7-14-26
Men of Texas 7-08-42
Men of the Desert 9-28-17
Men of the Fighting Lady 5-12-54

Men of the Hour 5-15-35
Men of the Hour, The 5-10-18
Men of the Night 7-28-26
Men of the Night 12-04-34
Men of the North 12-17-30
Men of the Plains 9-30-36
Men of the Sea 6-22-38
Men of the Sky 7-21-31
Men of Tomorrow 10-18-32 and 4-17-35
Men of Two Worlds 7-24-46
Men on Call 2-25-31
Men on Her Mind 5-24-44
Men on Wings 6-12-35
Men Only (See: Samo Ljudi)
Men or Not Men (See: Uomini e No)
Men She Married, The 11-17-16
Men Think Only of That (See: Hommes Ne Pensent Qu'A Ca, Les)
Men Who Have Made Love to Me 2-01-18
Men Who Tread on the Tiger's Tail, The 1-27-60
Men with Steel Faces 5-01-40
Men with Wings 10-26-38
Men Without a Profession 9-18-29
Men Without Law 12-03-30
Men Without Names 7-03-35
Men Without Souls 5-15-40
Men Without Women 2-05-30
Menace 11-27-34
Menace, La 3-29-61
Menace, La 10-19-77
Menace, The 1-18-18
Menace, The 2-02-32
Menace in the Night 10-08-58
Menaces 2-24-40
Menage All'Italiana 3-16-66
Menage, Italian Style (See: Menage All'Italiana)
Mendel Beilis 12-05-13
Mendiants et Orgueilleux 5-03-72
Menino de Engheno 7-20-66
Mennelsyden Varjo 7-24-46
Mennesker Moedes Og Soed Musik Opstaar I Hjertet 12-27-67
Mensch Ohne Namen 7-19-32 and 11-15-32
Mensch und Bestie 7-10-63
Menschen Im Hotel 2-03-60
Menschen Im Kaefig 12-10-30
Menschen Im Netz 9-16-59
Menschenfrauen 11-05-80
Mensonge de Nina Petrovna, Le 12-29-37 and 4-06-38
Mentirosa, La 7-22-42
Mephisto of a Masquerade 4-23-10
Mephisto Waltz, The 2-03-71
Mepris, Le 1-01-64
Mer 8-19-59
Mercenaries, The 2-14-68
Mercenario, Il (See: Mercenary, The)
Mercenary, The 3-04-70
Merchant of Slaves 8-24-49
Merchant of Venice, The (See: Marchand de Venise, Le)
Mercy Island 10-15-41
Mercy Plane 10-30-40
Merely Mary Ann 2-11-16
Merely Mary Ann 10-15-20
Merely Mary Ann 9-15-31
Merely Players 8-09-18
Merlusse 1-01-36 and 3-23-38
Mermaid, The 2-02-66
Mermaids of Tiburon 6-20-62
Merrill's Marauders 5-09-62
Merrily We Go to Hell 6-14-32
Merrily We Live 3-02-38
Merry Andrew 3-19-58
Merry Chase, The 9-22-48
Merry Comes to Town 6-02-37
Merry Farmer, The (See: Fidele Bauer, Der)
Merry Frinks, The 6-19-34
Merry-Go-Round 10-31-19
Merry-Go-Round 7-04-23
Merry-Go-Round of 1938 10-27-37
Merry Life (See: Vie en Rose, La)
Merry Monahans, The 8-16-44
Merry Singer, The (See: Allegro Cantante, L')
Merry Widow, The 1-25-08
Merry Widow, The 9-02-25
Merry Widow, The 10-16-34
Merry Widow, The 7-09-52
Merry Widow Takes Another, The 4-23-10
Merry Widower, The 5-22-29
Merry Wives, The 11-13-40
Merry Wives of Reno, The 6-12-34

Merry Wives of Tobias Rouke, The 10-25-72
Merry Wives of Vienna (See: Lustigen Weiber von Wien, Die)
Merry Wives of Windsor, The (See: Lustigen Weiber von Windsor, Die)
Merry Wives of Windsor, The 3-20-29
Merry Wives of Windsor, The 10-01-52
Mersekelt Egov 10-21-70
Merton of the Movies 9-10-24
Merton of the Movies 7-23-47
Merveilleuse Angelique 8-18-65
Merveilleuse Journee, La 12-13-32
Merveilleuse Visite, La 12-18-74
Mes Petites Amoureuses 1-01-75
Mesa of Lost Women 10-17-56
Meseauto 1-08-35 and 11-18-36
Mesquite Buckaroo 10-25-39
Mess in the House, A (See: Luda Kuca)
Message, The (See: O Recado)
Message, The 8-18-76
Message from Mars, A 6-03-21
Message from Space 11-01-78
Message from the Past (See: Neal of the Navy: Part V)
Message of the Mouse, The 7-27-17
Message of the Violin, The 10-29-10
Message to Garcia, A 4-15-36
Messager, Le 9-29-37
Messalina 8-27-24
Messaline 3-05-52
Messe Doree, La 2-12-75
Messenger, The (See: Messager, Le)
Messenger of Peace 3-22-50
Messer Im Kopf 10-25-78
Messia, Il 5-10-78
Messiah, The (See: Messia, Il)
Messiah of Evil 4-30-75
Messieurs les Ronds de Cuir 8-05-59
Messieurs Ludovic 5-22-46
Messidor 2-28-79
Metaf, Le 7-04-73
Metamorphose des Cloportes, La 10-27-65
Metamorphoses 12-12-73
Metamorphoses 5-17-78
Metamorphosis (See: Forvandlingen)
Metamorphosis of Smalltimers (See: Metamorphose des Cloportes, La)
Metello 5-27-70
Meteor 10-17-79
Methods in His Madness 3-26-10
Metralleta Stein 2-26-75
Metropoles 11-05-75
Metropolis 2-23-27 and 3-16-27
Metropolis--1939 8-02-39
Metropolitan 10-23-35
Metteur en Scene, Le 1-28-31
Metti, Una Sera a Cena 5-28-69
Meurtre en 45 Tours 6-15-60
Meurtre Est un Meurtre, Un 9-20-72
Meurtres 1-10-51
Meurtrier, Le 2-20-63
Meus Amores No Rio 7-15-59
Mexicali Kid, The 9-07-38
Mexicali Rose 1-29-30
Mexicali Rose 6-21-39
Mexican, The 4-03-57
Mexican Eyes (See: Ojos Tapatios)
Mexican Hayride 12-01-48
Mexican Mine Fraud, The 2-26-15
Mexican Revolution, The (See: Revolucion Mexicana, La)
Mexican Sniper's Revenge, The 7-31-14
Mexican Spitfire 12-13-39
Mexican Spitfire at Sea 1-07-42
Mexican Spitfire Out West 10-30-40
Mexican Spitfire Sees a Ghost 5-13-42
Mexican Spitfire's Baby 9-10-41 and 7-21-43
Mexican Spitfire's Elephant 8-05-42
Mexicana 11-21-45
Mexico de Mis Recuerdos 6-14-44
Mexico, la Revolucion Congelada 9-01-71
Mexico Lindo y Querido 4-26-61
Mexico, The Frozen Revolution (See: Mexico, la Revolucion Congelada)
Mexico Today 6-14-18
Meztelen Vagy 7-26-72
Mi Amor Eres Tu 10-08-41
Mi Candidato 5-18-38
Mi-Chemin du Ciel, A 6-30-31
Mi Hija Hildegart 9-28-77
Mi Lesz Veled Estzterke? 2-26-69

160

Mi Madre es Culpable 7-27-60
Mi Novia El ... (Travesti) 6-18-75
Mi Primer Pecado 5-25-77
Mi Primera Novia 4-13-66
Mi Querida Senorita 3-01-72
Mi Viuda Alegre 3-18-42
Mia Canzone al Vento, La 11-15-39
Mia Gyneka Stin Antistassi 11-11-70
Mia Signora, La 11-25-64
Miami 6-04-24
Miami Expose 7-25-56
Miami Story, The 3-31-54
Mice and Men 1-14-16
Michael and Mary 11-17-31 and 3-08-32
Michael Kohlhaas 5-21-69
Michael Kohlhaas 6-13-79
Michael O'Halloran 10-25-23
Michael O'Halloran 6-16-48
Michael Shayne, Private Detective 12-25-40
Michael Sheli 5-07-75
Michael Strogoff 6-12-14
Michael Strogoff 12-08-26
Michael the Brave (See: Mihai Viteazul)
Miche 5-31-32 and 12-06-32
Michel Strogoff 2-06-57
Michetonneuse, La 8-30-72
Michigan Kid, The 7-04-28
Michigan Kid, The 2-12-47
Mickey 12-06-18
Mickey 6-16-48
Mickey One 9-08-65
Mickey, the Kid 6-28-39
Micro-Cinematography-Recurrent Fever 11-12-10
Microbe, The 7-25-19
Microscope Mystery, The 11-03-16
Mictlan 5-27-70
Mid-Channel 11-19-20
Midaregumo 10-11-67
Midareru 8-05-64
Midas Run 5-07-69
Midas Touch, The 2-14-40
Middle Age Crazy 5-28-80
Middle Age Spread 7-18-79
Middle of the Night 5-20-59
Middle of the World, The (See: Milieu du Monde, Le)
Middle Watch, The 11-05-30 and 12-23-30
Middleman, The 3-05-15
Middleman, The (See: Dahana-Aranja)
Middleton Family at the New York World's Fair, The 10-04-39
Midgets Also Began Small (See: Auch Zwerge Haben Klein
    Angefangen)
Midi Minuit 7-01-70
Midlanders 9-09-21
Midnight 3-13-34
Midnight 3-15-39
Midnight Adventure 6-13-28
Midnight Alarm 8-23-23
Midnight Alibi 7-10-34
Midnight Angel 12-10-41
Midnight at Maxim's 6-18-15
Midnight Bell, A 8-12-21
Midnight Club, The 8-01-33
Midnight Court 3-10-37
Midnight Cowboy 5-14-69
Midnight Daddies 10-16-29
Midnight Desires 4-21-76
Midnight Episode 6-20-51
Midnight Escape, The 4-09-10
Midnight Express 12-03-24
Midnight Express 5-24-78
Midnight Express, The 2-10-26
Midnight Flower 10-11-23
Midnight Folly (See: Demons de Minuit, Les)
Midnight Gambols 6-18-20
Midnight Guest 4-05-23
Midnight Happenings (See: Maedchen Von Gestern Nacht, Der)
Midnight in Paris 10-01-47
Midnight Intruder 2-23-38
Midnight Kiss, The 10-27-26
Midnight Lace 10-19-60
Midnight Lady 7-12-32
Midnight Life 9-12-28
Midnight Limited 3-20-40
Midnight Lovers 10-27-26
Midnight Madness 8-15-28
Midnight Madness 2-06-80
Midnight Madness, A 5-31-18
Midnight Madonna 7-21-37

Midnight Man, The (See: Monsieur de Minuit, Le)
Midnight Man, The 3-20-74
Midnight Mary 7-18-33
Midnight Mass (See: Polnocna Omsa)
Midnight Meeting (See: Rendez-Vous de Minuit, Le)
Midnight Menace 7-14-37
Midnight Message 11-24-26
Midnight Morals 9-13-32
Midnight Mystery 6-04-30
Midnight Patrol, The 12-27-18
Midnight Patrol, The 5-10-32
Midnight, Place Pigalle 9-05-28
Midnight Pleasures (See: A Mezzanotte Va La Ronda Del Piacere)
Midnight ... Quai De Bercy (See: Minuit ... Quai De Bercy)
Midnight Romance, A 3-14-19
Midnight Sons 9-04-09
Midnight Special 1-21-31
Midnight Story, The 6-12-57
Midnight Sun, The 4-28-26
Midnight Taxi 10-31-28
Midnight Taxi, The 4-10-29
Midnight Taxi, The 4-07-37
Midnight Tradition (See: Tradition de Minuit, La)
Midnight Warning 3-14-33
Midnight Watch 3-09-27
Midshipmaid, The 12-27-32
Midshipman, The 10-14-25
Midshipman Jack 11-21-33
Midstream 9-18-29
Midsummer Holiday, A (See: Domenica D'Agosto)
Midsummer Madness 12-10-20
Midsummer Night's Dream, A (See: Sen Noci Svatojanske)
Midsummer Night's Dream, A 5-27-25
Midsummer Night's Dream, A 10-16-35
Midsummer Night's Dream, A 11-23-66
Midsummer Night's Dream, A 2-05-69
Midt I en Jazztid 5-14-69
Midway 6-16-76
Miedos, Los 9-10-80
Miel, La 9-19-79
Miercoles de Ceniza 8-27-58
Miert Rosszak a Magyar Filmek 7-22-64
Mies es Mucha, La 6-01-49
Mig og Mafiaen 1-02-74
Mig Og Charly 3-29-78
Mig Og Dig 2-26-69
Mig og Min Lillebror og Boelle 1-14-70
Might and the Man 5-18-17
Might Makes Right (See: Faustrecht Der Freiheit)
Mighty, The 1-01-30
Mighty Barnum, The 12-25-34
Mighty Crusaders, The 9-27-61
Mighty Joe Young 5-25-49
Mighty Lak' a Rose 3-22-23
Mighty McGurk, The 11-20-46
Mighty Peking Man, The 8-31-77
Mighty Treve, The 4-07-37
Mignon 1-22-15
Migove u Kibritena Boutiyka 7-25-79
Miguelin 4-28-65
Mihai Viteazul 11-21-73
Mijn Vriend 4-18-79
Mijn Nachten Met Susan, Olga, Albert, Julie, Piet & Sandra
    5-21-75
Mikado, The 1-25-39
Mikado, The 2-22-67
Mike 1-13-26
Mike and Meyer 2-12-15
Mike Test (See: Proba de Microfon)
Mikey and Nicky 12-22-76
Mikkai 9-07-60
Milady 1-25-23
Milady 9-12-33
Milady o' the Beanstalk 11-15-18
Milanese Story, A (See: Storia Milanese, Una)
Milano Odia: La Polizia Non Puo Sparare (See: Almost Human)
Milarepa 4-17-74
Milczenie 9-04-63
Mildred Pierce 10-03-45
Mile-a-Minute Kendall 5-10-18
Mile a Minute Man 9-15-26 and 7-27-27
Mile-a-Minute Morgan 3-19-24
Mile a Minute Romeo 4-16-24
Milenci V Roce Jedna 8-07-74
Milestones 9-10-20
Milestones 5-14-75
Milieu du Monde, Le 8-21-74
Milionario and Ze Rico in The Highway of Life (See: Milionario e
    Ze Rico na Estrada da Vida)

Milionario e Ze Rico na Estrada da Vida 11-26-80
Military Academy 8-07-40
Military Academy 4-26-50
Military Cyclists of Belgium 12-03-10
Military Kite Flying at Rheims 9-10-10
Military Secret 8-08-45
Military Tournament 1-18-08
Militiaman Bruggler (See: Standschuetze Bruggler)
Milizia Territoriale 4-15-36
Milk War in Bavaria (See: Farbe des Himmels, Die)
Milkman, The 10-11-50
Milky Way, The (See: Voie Lactee, La)
Milky Way, The 4-01-36
Mill on the Floss, The 11-22-39
Mill on the Po, The (See: Mulino del Po, Il)
Mille et Deuxieme Nuit 5-30-33
Mille et Une Mains 2-20-74
Millhouse: A White Comedy 10-06-71
Milliard Dans un Billard, Un 1-12-66
Millie 2-11-31
Millieme Fenetre, La 6-15-60
Million, Le 4-29-31 and 5-27-31
Million, The (See: Million, Le)
Million, The 2-19-15
Million Bid, A 6-01-27 and 6-15-27
Million Dollar Baby 5-08-35
Million Dollar Baby 5-28-48
Million Dollar Collar 3-20-29
$1,000,000 Duck 6-16-71
Million Dollar Kid 2-23-44
Million Dollar Legs 7-12-32
Million Dollar Legs 7-19-39
Million Dollar Mermaid 11-05-52
Million Dollar Mystery 6-26-14 and 7-10-14
Million Dollar Pursuit 5-23-51
$1,000,000 Racket 11-17-37
Million Dollar Ransom 9-25-34
Million Dollar Robbery 6-05-14
Million Dollar Weekend 10-13-48
Million for Love, A 6-06-28
Million for Mary, A 8-18-16
Million in a Billiard Table, A (See: Milliard Dans un Billard, Un)
Million in Jewels, A 2-01-23
Million Pound Note, The 1-13-54
Million to Burn, A 11-01-23
Million to One, A 6-01-38
Millionaire, The 11-18-21
Millionaire, The 4-15-31
Millionaire for Christy, A 8-01-51
Millionaire in Trouble 7-19-78
Millionaire Orphan 1-25-28
Millionaire Playboy 3-06-40
Millionaire Policeman 7-14-26
Millionaire Vagrant, The 5-25-17
Millionaires 5-04-27
Millionaire's Double, The 5-11-17
Millionaires d'un Jour (See: Simple Case of Money, A)
Millionaires in Prison 7-17-40
Millionaire's Son, The 4-28-16
Millionairess, The 10-26-60
Millions in the Air 12-18-35
Millions Like Us 11-17-43
Mills of the Gods 1-22-35
Milord l'Arsouille 2-29-56
Mimi (See: Dramma Borghese, Un)
Mimi 4-17-35 and 6-05-35
Mimi Metallurgico Ferito Nell'Onore 4-19-72
Mimi Pinson 9-24-58
Mimi, the Metalworker (See: Mimi Metallurgico Ferito Nell'Onore)
Mimino 8-03-77
Min Aelskade 4-25-79
Min and Bill 11-26-30
Min Van Klock-Johan 9-17-41
Mina, La 3-19-58
Mina Cycle, The (See: Dayereh Cycle)
Mina Droemmars Stad 11-24-76
Mina, Viento de Libertad 9-28-77
Mina, Wind of Freedom (See: Mina, Viento de Libertad)
Minamata, the Victims of Their World 7-12-72
Mind Benders, The 2-27-63
Mind of Mr. Reeder 3-15-39
Mind of Mr. Soames, The 9-23-70
Mind Over Motor 7-26-23
Mind Reader, The 4-11-33
Mind the Paint Girl 11-28-19
Mind Your Back, Professor (See: Pas Paa Ryggen, Professor)

Mind Your Own Business 2-17-37
Minden Szerdan 7-23-80
Mine, The (See: Mina, La or Maden)
Mine Own Executioner 11-26-47
Mine Soestres Boern Naar de er Vaerst 10-27-71
Mine to Keep 8-30-23
Mine Warfare 3-27-74
Mine with the Iron Door, The 10-29-24
Mine with the Iron Door, The 7-15-36
Mineiro Cabaret (See: Cabaret Mineiro)
Miner and Camille, The 4-30-10
Miners of the Don 11-14-51
Miner's Wife, The 4-03-74
Mines of Decauville, The 12-28-07
Minesweeper 11-10-43
Mingus 5-15-68
Mini-Skirt Mob, The 5-29-68
Mini Weekend 5-31-67
Miniature, The 2-26-10
Minister and Me, The (See: Ministro y Yo, El)
Minister's Daughter, The 10-16-09
Minister's Friend, The (See: A Miniszter Baratja)
Ministro y Yo, El 8-04-76
Ministry of Fear 10-18-44
Miniver Story, The 8-30-50
Minne, l'Ingenue Libertine 6-28-50
Minne, the Simple Wanton (See: Minne, l'Ingenue Libertine)
Minnesota Clay 2-10-65
Minnie 3-01-23
Minnie and Moskowitz 12-22-71
Minotaur, The 5-03-61
Minstrel Man 7-19-44
Mint of Hell 5-16-19
Minuit ... Quai de Bercy 7-08-53
Minute de Verite, La 11-12-52
Minute to Pray, A Second to Die, A 5-01-68
Minx, The 8-13-69
Mio 2-02-72
Mio Figlio Nerone 9-26-56
Mio Fratello Anastasia 10-17-73
Mio Mao 7-29-70
Mio Nome e Nessuno, Il 1-16-74
Mioche, Le 1-04-39
Miquette 5-22-40
Miquette and Her Mother (See: Miquette et Sa Mere)
Miquette et Sa Mere 5-24-50
Mira 3-17-71
Miracle, The (See: Miracolo, Il)
Miracle, The 2-21-13
Miracle, The 11-11-59
Miracle Baby 8-30-23
Miracle Can Happen, A 2-04-48
Miracle Child, The (See: Enfant du Miracle, L')
Miracle des Loups, Le 9-27-61
Miracle in Harlem 8-11-48
Miracle in Milan (See: Miracolo a Milano)
Miracle in Our Town (See: Nes Ba'ayara)
Miracle in Soho 7-24-57
Miracle in the Rain 2-01-56
Miracle Kid, The 1-14-42
Miracle Makers 12-20-23
Miracle Man, The 8-29-19
Miracle Man, The 4-26-32
Miracle of Life, The 10-08-15
Miracle of Life, The 10-06-22
Miracle of Life, The 6-01-49
Miracle of Lourdes (See: Ne Sirj Edesanyam)
Miracle of Love 12-18-68
Miracle of Love, The 1-03-20
Miracle of Malachias 7-12-61
Miracle of Money 5-14-20
Miracle of Morgan's Creek, The 1-05-44
Miracle of Our Lady of Fatima, The 8-27-52
Miracle of the Bells, The 3-03-48
Miracle of the Hills, The 8-12-59
Miracle of the Reef, The 4-11-56
Miracle of the White Stallions 3-27-63
Miracle of the Wolves 2-25-25 and 7-30-30
Miracle on 34th Street 5-07-47
Miracle Roses, The (See: Rosas del Milagro, Las)
Miracle Tree, The (See: Drevo Jelania)
Miracle Woman 7-28-31
Miracle Worker, The 5-02-62
Miracles for Sale 8-16-39
Miracles N'ont Lieu Qu'une Fois, Les 7-18-51
Miracles of the Gods (See: Botschaft der Goetter)
Miracles of the Wolves, The (See: Miracle des Loups, Le)
Miracles of Thursday (See: Jueves Milagro, Los)

Miracles Only Happen Once (See: Miracles N'ont Lieu Qu'Une Fois, Les)
Miracles Still Happen (See: Es Geschehen Noch Wunder)
Miracolo, Il 12-15-48
Miracolo a Milano 2-28-51
Miraculous Journey 8-11-48
Miraculous Virgin (See: Panna Zazracnica)
Mirage 5-19-65
Mirage 11-29-72
Mirage, The (See: Hagringen)
Mirage, The 4-08-25
Mirages de Paris 1-09-34
Miranda 4-14-48
Mirandy Smiles 12-20-18
Mireille's Sincere Love 5-15-09
Mirele Efros 10-25-39
Miris Poljs Kog Cveca 5-31-78
Miris Zemlje 8-16-78
Mirisi, Zlato I Tamjan 8-18-71
Mirno Leto 8-23-61
Miroir a Deux Faces, Le 12-03-58
Mirror, The (See: Zerkalo or Espejo, El)
Mirror Crack'd, The 12-17-80
Mirror Has Two Faces, The (See: Miroir a Deux Faces, Le)
Mirror, Mirror (See: Lille Spejl)
Mirror of Illusion (See: Maya Darpan)
Mirth and Sorrow 10-08-10
Mis Dias con Veronica 4-23-80
Mis Dos Amores 8-17-38
Mis Hijos 6-14-44
Misadventures of Merlin Jones, The 1-15-64
Misbehaving Husbands 1-15-41
Mischief 12-29-31
Mischief Maker, The 12-01-16
Misdeal (See: Maldonne)
Mise a Sac 12-06-67
Miser, The (See: Avare, L')
Miserabili, I 4-14-48
Miserables, Les (See: Miserables, Los or Miserabili, I)
Miserables, Les 1-30-14
Miserables, Les 12-07-17
Miserables, Les 5-12-26; 6-30-26; and 8-24-27
Miserables, Les 2-20-34
Miserables, Les 4-24-35
Miserables, Les 11-04-36
Miserables, Les 1-01-47
Miserables, Les 1-30-52
Miserables, Les 7-23-52
Miserables, Les 4-02-58
Miserables, Los 11-01-44
Misery (See: Jad)
Misfire (See: Fehlschuss or Bomsalva)
Misfit Earl, A 11-21-19
Misfit Wife, The 9-17-20
Misfits, The 2-01-61
Mishpahat Simchon 4-22-64
Miskhak Makhbuim 6-25-80
Mislaid Baby, The 11-20-09
Misleading Lady, The 4-12-32
Misleading Widow, The 9-05-19
Misled Youth (See: Gioventu Perduta or Verirrte Jugend)
Mismarried, The 11-01-50
Mismates 7-28-26
Misplaced Petticoat, The 1-07-11
Miss Adventure 5-02-19
Miss Ambition 11-22-18
Miss Annie Rooney 5-27-42
Miss April (See: Froeken April)
Miss Arizona 10-31-19
Miss Bluebeard 1-28-25
Miss Brewster's Millions 3-10-26
Miss Crusoe 10-03-19
Miss Cuple 9-30-59
Miss Deception 7-27-17
Miss Dulcie from Dixie 3-14-19
Miss Else 4-10-29
Miss Europe 9-03-30
Miss Fane's Baby 1-23-34
Miss Fane's Baby Is Stolen (See: Miss Fane's Baby)
Miss George Washington 11-24-16
Miss Grant Takes Richmond 9-28-49
Miss Hobbs 6-18-20
Miss Innocence 8-02-18
Miss Italia 3-29-50
Miss Jackie of the Army 12-21-17
Miss Jackie of the Navy 12-15-16
Miss Julie (See: Froken Julie)

Miss Keow (See: Keow)
Miss Laong Dao (See: Laong Dao)
Miss Lulu Bett 12-23-21
Miss Maliwan (See: Nangsao Maliwan)
Miss Midshipman (See: Fraulein Faehnrich)
Miss Mink of 1949 2-16-49
Miss Nobody 9-08-26
Miss O'Gynie and the Flower Men (See: Miss O'Gynie et les Hommes Fleurs)
Miss O'Gynie et les Hommes Fleurs 5-08-74
Miss Pacific Fleet 12-11-35
Miss Paprika (See: Paprika Kisasszony)
Miss Petticoats 8-04-16
Miss Pilgrim's Progress 2-08-50
Miss Pinkerton 7-12-32
Miss Polly 11-05-41
Miss President 10-09-35
Miss Robinson Crusoe 8-10-17
Miss Sadie Thompson 12-23-53
Miss Salak Jitr (See: Salak Jitr)
Miss Stone 8-19-59
Miss Susie Slagle's 12-12-45
Miss Tatlock's Millions 9-15-48
Miss Trevelez (See: Senorita de Trevelez, La)
Miss V from Moscow 1-06-43
Misshandlingen 5-06-70
Missing 6-21-18
Missing Corpse, The 6-27-45
Missing Daughters 6-14-39
Missing Evidence 11-22-39
Missing from St. Agil (See: Disparus de Saint-Agil, Les)
Missing Girls 10-07-36
Missing Guest, The 9-14-38
Missing Husbands 5-19-22
Missing Juror, The 12-20-44
Missing Link, The 5-11-27
Missing Link, The 5-14-80
Missing Links, The 12-17-15
Missing Millions 9-22-22
Missing People, The 5-31-39
Missing Persons 9-12-33
Missing Prisoners (See: Prisoneros Desaparecidos)
Missing Rembrandt 3-29-32
Missing Ten Days 4-16-41
Missing Witness 12-15-37
Missing Women 2-28-51
Mission Batangas 11-13-68
Mission Mars 9-25-68
Mission Speciale 5-15-46
Mission Stardust 7-02-69
Mission to Moscow 5-05-43
Missionary, A (See: Missionnaire, Un)
Missionnaire, Un 1-25-56
Mississippi 4-24-35
Mississippi Gambler 10-30-29
Mississippi Gambler 4-15-42
Mississippi Gambler, The 1-14-53
Mississippi Mermaid (See: Sirene du Mississippi, La)
Mississippi Rhythm 7-27-49
Missouri Breaks, The 5-19-76
Missouri Outlaw, A 3-04-42
Missouri Traveler 1-15-58
Missourians, The 11-29-50
Mistakes Will Happen (See: Az Ember Neha Teved)
Mr. A. Jonah 4-23-10
Mr. Ace 8-28-46
Mr. and Mrs. Duff 11-20-09
Mr. and Mrs. Jollygood Go Tandeming 3-14-08
Mr. and Mrs. Juan Lamaglia (See: Juan Lamaglia y Sra)
Mr. and Mrs. Kabal's Theatre (See: Theatre de M. et Mme. Kabal)
Mr. and Mrs. North 12-17-41
Mr. and Mrs. Smith 1-22-41
Mister Antonio 12-11-29
Mr. Arkadin 9-19-62
Mr. Barnes of New York 4-17-14
Mr. Barnes of New York 6-02-22
Mr. Belvedere Goes to College 4-06-49
Mr. Belvedere Rings the Bell 7-25-51
Mr. Big 5-26-43
Mr. Bill and the Conqueror 7-12-32
Mr. Billings Spends a Dime 3-08-23
Mr. Billion 3-02-77
Mr. Bingles' Melodrama 6-19-14
Mr. Blandings Builds His Dreamhouse 3-31-48
Mr. Boggs Steps Out 1-05-38
Mr. Boozer Gets a Fright 7-04-08
Mr. Broadway 9-19-33

Mohn Ist Auch eine Blume 5-18-66
Moi et l'Imperatrice 5-30-33
Moi et les Hommes de Quarante Ans 4-07-65
Moi, Fleur Bleue 11-16-77
Moi Laskoviy I Niejnie Zver 5-24-78
Moi Tinh Dau 8-09-78
Moi, Tintin 11-24-76
Moi Y'en a Vouloir Des Sous 3-14-73
Moine, Le 7-11-73
Mois le Plus Beau, Le 7-24-68
Moja Strana Svijeta 8-20-69
Moja Wojna--Moja Milosc 6-02-76
Mojave Kid, The 7-27-27
Moju (See: Blind Beast, The)
Mokey 3-25-42
Mokhtar 10-23-68
Mole, The (See: Topo, El)
Mole People, The 10-31-56
Moliere 5-31-78
Molly and I 3-26-20
Molly and Lawless John 12-27-72
Molly and Me 6-19-29
Molly and Me 3-07-45
Molly Entangled 11-30-17
Molly Go-Get-Em 1-18-18
Molly Louvain 5-10-32
Molly Maguires, The 1-21-70
Molly Make Believe 4-21-16
Molly O 11-25-21
Molly of the Follies 1-31-19
Mollycoddle, The 6-18-20
Molo 7-02-69
Molokai 12-30-59
Molti Sogni Per le Strada (See: Woman Trouble)
Molucca Islands 10-08-10
Mome Vert de Gris, La 6-10-53
Moment (See: Clipa or Tren)
Moment, The (See: Oejeblikket)
Moment Before, The 5-05-16
Moment by Moment 12-20-78
Moment d'Egarement, Un 12-21-77
Moment of Danger (See: Malaga)
Moment of Truth, The (See: Minute de Verite, La)
Moment of Truth, The (See: Momento Della Verita, Il)
Moment to Moment 1-26-66
Momento Della Verita, Il 3-31-65
Moments 9-25-74
Moments 5-16-79
Moments in a Matchbox (See: Migove u Kibritena Boutiyka)
Mom's 100 Years Old (See: Mama Cumple 100 Anos)
Mon Ami Pierrette 12-09-70
Mon Ami Tim 7-12-32
Mon Ami Victor 1-21-31
Mon Amour, Mon Amour 5-17-67
Mon and Ino (See: Ani Imouto)
Mon Coeur Balance 11-08-32
Mon Coeur Est Rouge 3-09-77
Mon Coquin de Pere 9-03-58
Mon Gosse de Pere 5-21-30
Mon Gosse de Pere 8-05-53
Mon Mari Est Merveilleux 7-08-53
Mon Oncle 5-21-58
Mon Oncle Antoine 6-09-71
Mon Oncle Benjamin 11-12-69
Mon Oncle d'Amerique 5-21-80
Mon Phoque et Elles 5-02-51
Mon Premier Amour 9-27-78
Mona 2-24-71
Mona Lisa Has Been Stolen, The (See: On a Vole la Joconde)
Monaca Santa 8-03-49
Monache Di Sant'Archangelo, Le 3-14-73
Monarch 3-05-80
Monastery 2-02-38
Monday or Tuesday (See: Pondeljak Ili Utorak)
Monday to Sunday (See: Lunes 1° Domingo 7)
Monday's Child 5-10-67
Mondays with Fanny (See: Mandagarna Med Fanny)
Monde du Silence, Le 6-06-56
Monde Etait Plein de Couleurs, Le 10-24-73
Monde Nouveau, Un 4-06-66
Monde Sans Soleil, Le 11-04-64
Mondesir Heir, The (See: Heritier de Mondesir, L')
Mondo Balordo 1-17-68
Mondo Cane 5-09-62
Mondo Cane No. 2 1-22-64
Mondo di Notte, Il 5-18-60
Mondo di Notte No. 3, Il 12-11-63
Mondo Hollywood 8-02-67

Mondo Rocco 3-11-70
Mondo Trasho 2-11-70
Monelle 2-08-50
Money 2-13-29
Money, The 9-24-75
Money and Gold (See: Geld und Geist)
Money and the Woman 9-18-40
Money Corral, The 4-25-19
Money for Nothing 2-16-32
Money from Home 12-02-53
Money Isn't Everything 9-20-18
Money Jungle, The 11-06-68
Money Madness 3-31-48
Money Magic 1-26-17
Money Master, The 9-10-15
Money Means Nothing 7-24-34
Money-Money 10-23-68
Money, Money, Money 2-22-23
Money, Money, Money 4-10-29
Money Monster 12-22-22
Money Movers 10-18-78
Money Order, The (See: Mandabi)
Money Talks 5-12-26
Money Talks 11-29-32
Money Talks 8-02-72
Money to Burn 4-21-22
Money to Burn 11-24-26
Money to Burn 1-03-40
Money Trap, The 1-19-66
Money, Women and Guns 10-08-58
Mongols, The 12-26-73
Mongrel and Master 5-22-14
Monique 4-01-70
Monique's Fault 11-07-28
Monismaenien 1995 8-20-75
Monitors, The 10-15-69
Monk, The (See: Moine, Le)
Monkey Bridge, The (See: Pont de Singe, Le)
Monkey Business 10-13-31
Monkey Business 9-10-52
Monkey Hustle, The 12-29-76
Monkey in Winter, A (See: Singe En Hiver, Un)
Monkey into Man 4-17-40
Monkey on My Back 5-15-57
Monkey Talks, The 2-23-27
Monkeynuts 6-13-28
Monkeys, Go Home 1-25-67
Monkey's Paw, The 11-08-23
Monkey's Paw, The 6-06-33
Monkey's Uncle, The 5-26-65
Monna Vanna 2-08-23 and 9-27-23
Monnaie de Singe 3-30-66
Monocle Noir, Le 9-27-61
Monocle Rit Jaune, Le 9-30-64
Monocled Eye, The (See: Oeil du Monocle, L')
Monocle's Sour Laugh, The (See: Monocle Rit Jaune, Le)
Monolith Monsters, The 10-23-57
Monolog 6-06-73
Monomaniac 5-15-14
Monosabio, El 8-02-78
Monpti 10-23-57
Monseigneur 1-25-50
Monsieur 6-03-64
Monsieur Albert 7-12-32
Monsieur Albert 4-07-76
Monsieur Balboss 10-29-75
Monsieur Beaucaire 8-13-24
Monsieur Beaucaire 5-15-46
Monsieur Brotoneau 8-30-39
Monsieur de Compagnie, Un 11-18-64
Monsieur de Minuit, Le 9-01-31
Monsieur de Pourceaugnac 11-08-32
Monsieur Fabre 10-24-51
Monsieur Gregoire S'Evade 6-12-46
Monsieur Hawarden 10-23-68
Monsieur la Souris (See: Midnight in Paris)
Monsieur, Madame et Bibi 4-05-32
Monsieur Papa 9-14-77
Monsieur Ripois 5-05-54
Monsieur Taxi 10-01-52
Monsieur Verdoux 4-16-47
Monsieur Vincent 10-22-47
Monsoon 2-04-53
Monster, The (See: Mostri, I)
Monster, The 2-18-25
Monster and the Girl, The 3-26-41
Monster from the Ocean Floor 6-09-54
Monster Maker, The 5-17-44

Monster of London City, The 8-02-67
Monster on the Campus 10-15-58
Monster That Challenged the World, The 5-22-57
Monster Walks, The 5-31-32
Monsters of the Deep 5-20-31
Monstrosity 12-16-64
Monsu' Travet 4-17-46
Mont-Dragon 1-13-71
Montana 1-04-50
Montana Belle 10-29-52
Montana Desperado 11-14-51
Montana Kid, The 9-15-31
Montana Moon 4-16-30
Montana Schoolmarm, A 2-06-09
Montana Territory 6-04-52
Monte Carlo 4-21-26
Monte Carlo 9-03-30
Monte Carlo Madness 6-07-32
Monte Carlo Story, The 6-19-57
Monte Cassino 11-03-48
Monte-Charge, Le 6-20-62
Monte Cristo 8-18-22
Monte Cristo 7-10-29
Monte Walsh 10-07-70
Montecassino 10-30-46
Monterey Pop 9-18-68
Montevideo 2-05-64
Montmartre 7-09-24
Montmartre Rose 6-12-29
Montoneros, Los 7-29-70
Montparnasse Girl (See: Petite de Montparnasse)
Montparnasse 19 5-07-58
Montreal Flight 871 (See: YUL 871)
Montreal Main 2-27-74
Monty Python and the Holy Grail 3-19-75
Moods of Love 2-02-77
Mool-Dori Village 7-25-79
Moon and Midnight (See: Midi Minuit)
Moon and Sixpence, The 9-09-42
Moon and the Sledgehammer, The 12-01-71
Moon by One's Teeth, The (See: Lune Avec Les Dents, La)
Moon for Your Love 11-27-09
Moon in Taurus 9-10-80
Moon Is Blue, The 6-03-53
Moon Is Down, The 3-10-43
Moon Madness 9-03-20
Moon of Israel 2-04-25 and 6-29-27
Moon over Burma 10-16-40
Moon over Her Shoulder 10-22-41
Moon over Las Vegas 4-12-44
Moon over Miami 6-18-41
Moon over Morocco (See: Sous la Lune du Maroc)
Moon over the Alley 10-01-80
Moon Pilot 1-17-62
Moon-Spinners, The 6-24-64
Moon-Struck Jean (See: Jean de la Lune)
Moon Zero Two 10-29-69
Moon's Our Home 5-20-36
Moondreaming John (See: Jean de la Lune)
Moonfleet 5-11-55
Moonlight and Honeysuckle 8-05-21
Moonlight and Pretzels 8-29-33
Moonlight in Havana 10-14-42
Moonlight in Hawaii 10-15-41
Moonlight in Vermont 12-22-43
Moonlight Masquerade 6-24-42
Moonlight Murder 4-01-36
Moonlight on the Prairie 2-19-36
Moonlight on the Range 10-06-37
Moonlight Serenade (See: Serenata a la Luz de la Luna)
Moonlight Sonata 2-24-37
Moonlighters, The 9-09-53
Moonlighting Wives 9-28-66
Moonraker 6-27-79
Moonraker, The 5-28-58
Moonrise 9-15-48
Moonrunners 5-28-75
Moonshine County Express 6-08-77
Moonshine Trail, The 10-24-19
Moonshine Valley 10-13-22
Moonshine War, The 7-01-70
Moonshiners, The 6-09-16
Moonstone 6-19-09
Moonstone 6-11-15
Moonstone, The 9-18-34
Moonstone of Fez, The 7-10-14

Moonstruck 4-17-09
Moontide 4-22-42
Moonwalk One 11-15-72
Moos Auf den Steinen 10-09-68
Moral 9-09-36
Moral Courage 5-04-17
Moral Deadline, The 2-14-19
Moral der Banditen, Die 7-28-76
Moral der Ruth Holbfass, Die 5-03-72
Moral Fabric, The 3-10-16
Moral Fibre 11-11-21
Moral Law, The 3-08-18
Moral Sinners 4-09-24
Moral Suicide 3-22-18
Moralist, The (See: Moralista, Il)
Moralista, Il 10-28-59
Morality (See: Moral)
Morals 1-06-22
Morals for Men 11-18-25
Morals for Women 11-17-31
Morals of Marcus, The 1-22-15
Morals of Marcus, The 4-10-35 and 1-15-36
Morals of Ruth Halbfass, The (See: Moral der Ruth Halbfass, Die)
Moran of the Lady Letty 2-10-22
Moran of the Marines 10-17-28
Moranbong 5-25-60
Moravian Land, The (See: O Moravske Zemi)
Morbidness (See: Morbo)
Morbo 8-02-72
Mord und Totschlag 5-03-67
Mordi e Fuggi 3-28-73
Mordprozess Mary Dugan 3-04-31
Mords Pas On T'Aime 5-05-76
Mor(d)skab 9-10-69
Mordus, Les 7-06-60
More 5-14-69
More American Graffiti 7-25-79
More Dead Than Alive 12-18-68
More Deadly Than the Male 12-12-19
More Excellent Way, The 4-06-17
More It Goes the Less It Goes, The (See: Plus Ca Va, Moins Ca Va)
More Pitied Than Scorned 10-20-22
More Precious Than Gold 11-06-09
More Than a Miracle 11-01-67
More Than a Queen 12-11-14
More Than a Secretary 12-16-36
More Than His Duty 10-08-10
More the Merrier, The 4-07-43
More Trouble 5-31-18
Morel's Invention (See: Invenzione di Morel, L')
Morena Clara 7-01-36
Morgan (A Suitable Case for Treatment) 4-13-66
Morgan the Pirate 6-07-61
Morgane 6-26-29
Morgan's Last Raid 2-20-29
Morgan's Raiders 2-15-18
Morganson's Finish 7-21-26
Morgen Beginnt Leben 8-22-33
Morgen Gaat Het Beter 3-15-39
Morgenrot 2-28-33 and 5-23-33
Morgens Um 7 Ist die Welt Noch In Ordnung 1-15-69
Morgiana 8-09-72
Morianna--I, the Body 2-21-68
Morire Gratis 11-06-68
Morituri 7-28-65
Moritz, Dear Moritz (See: Moritz, Lieber Moritz)
Moritz, Lieber Moritz 3-29-78
Moritz Macht Sein Glueck 1-17-33
Moritz Makes His Fortune (See: Moritz Macht Sein Glueck)
Mormon Maid, A 2-16-17
Mormor og de Atte Ungene i Byen 11-19-80
Morning 7-23-69
Morning, The (See: Jutro)
Morning After, The 4-19-72
Morning Departure 3-01-50
Morning Glory 8-22-33
Morning Mist (See: Manha Submersa)
Morning, Noon and Night 12-21-75
Morning of Six Weeks, A (See: Printemps en Hollande/Een Ochtend Van Zes Weken)
Morning Schedule, The (See: Gozencho No Jikanwari)
Morning Star 8-22-62
Morning Star, The 7-02-80
Mornings of a Sensible Youth, The (See: Diminetile Unui Baiat Cuminte)
Moro Witch Doctor 12-02-64
Morocco 11-19-30

Morozko 1-28-31
Morris' War Film 12-10-15
Mors Aux Dents, Le 11-21-79
Mors Hus 8-28-74
Morsiusseppele 4-07-54
Mort de Belle, La 4-05-61
Mort du Cygne, La 4-05-61
Mort d'un Bucheron, La 2-21-73
Mort d'un Guide 10-22-75
Mort d'un Pourri 12-21-77
Mort d'un Tueur, La 4-22-64
Mort en Ce Jardin, La 11-07-56
Mort en Fraude 7-24-57
Mort, Ou Est Ta Victoire? 2-05-64
Mort Trouble, La 3-18-70
Mort Vienne a Cavaldo, La (See: Death Rides a Horse)
Mortadella, La 1-12-72
Mortal Sin (See: Pecado Mortal)
Mortal Sin, The 3-16-17
Mortal Storm, The 6-12-40
Morte Al Lavoro, La 8-23-78
Morte Di un Amico 12-30-59
Morte Di un Operatore 7-25-79
Morte Risale A Leri Sera, La 11-11-70
Morte-Saison Des Amours, La 9-27-61
Mortgaged Wife, The 6-28-18
Mortmain 9-03-15
Mosch 10-29-80
Moscow As It Laughs 9-05-28
Moscow Does Not Believe in Tears (See: Moskwa Sljesam Nje Jerit)
Moscow Kamerny Theatre 4-26-23
Moscow Laughs 3-27-35
Moscow Nights (See: Nuit Moscovites)
Moscow Nights 11-20-35
Moscow Nights (See: I Stand Condemned)
Moscow-Shanghai 10-28-36
Moscow Skies 1-24-45
Moscow Strikes Back 8-19-42
Moses 2-25-76
Moses and Aaron 10-08-75
Moshi-Moshi, Hallo Japan 8-08-62
Moskwa Sljesam Nje Jerit 3-05-80
Mosquito Squadron 7-08-70
Moss on the Stones (See: Moos Auf den Steinen)
Moss Rose 5-21-47
Most Beautiful Age, The (See: Nejkrasnejsi Vek)
Most Beautiful Animal in the World, The (See: Ang Pinakamagandang Hayop Sa Balat Ng Lupa)
Most Beautiful Girl in the World (See: Plus Belle Fille du Monde, La)
Most Beautiful Life, The (See: Plus Belles Des Vies, Le)
Most Beautiful Month, The (See: Mois Le Plus Beau, Le)
Most Beautiful on the Earth, The (See: Det Vackraste Pa Jorden)
Most Beautiful Wife, The (See: Moglie Piu Bella, La)
Most Dangerous Game, The 11-22-32
Most Dangerous Man Alive, The 6-14-61
Most Gentle Confessions, The (See: Aveux Les Plus Doux, Les)
Most Immoral Lady, The 10-23-29
Most Important Event Since Man First Set Foot on the Moon, The (See: Evenement Le Plus Important Depuis Que L'Homme a Marche Sur La Lune, L')
Most Precious Thing, The 12-04-34
Most Wonderful Evening of My Life, The (See: Piu Bella Serata Della Mia Vita, La)
Mostri, I 11-27-63
Motards, Les 4-15-59
Mote I Natten 11-13-46
Motel Hell 10-22-80
Moth, The (See: Cma)
Moth, The 4-17-34
Moth and the Flame, The 5-21-15
Mother (See: Okasan)
Mother 9-19-14
Mother 1-04-18
Mother 5-04-27
Mother, The 5-18-27 and 6-05-34
Mother and Daughter (See: Maternale)
Mother and Daughter 8-27-75
Mother and Son 9-01-31
Mother and Sons 9-21-38
Mother and the Law, The 10-13-19 and 10-31-19
Mother and the Whore, The (See: Maman et la Putain, La)
Mother by Compulsion (See: Madre a la Fuerza)
Mother Carey's Chickens 7-27-38
Mother Courage and Her Children (See: Mutter Courage und Ihre Kinder)
Mother, Dearly Beloved (See: Mater Amatisima)

Mother Didn't Tell Me 2-01-50
Mother Eternal 4-22-21
Mother Gloria (See: Mama Gloria)
Mother Heart, The 6-17-21
Mother India (See: Bharat Mata)
Mother Instinct, The 4-09-15
Mother Instinct, The 7-27-17
Mother Is a Freshman 3-02-49
Mother Jeanne and Angels (See: Matka Joanna Od Aniotow)
Mother, Jugs and Speed 5-19-76
Mother Kuster's Trip to Heaven (See: Mutter Kusters Fahrt Zum Himmel)
Mother Knows Best 9-19-28
Mother Love (See: Maternite; Chaleur du Sien; or Mutterliebe)
Mother Machree 3-07-28
Mother o' Mine 8-31-17
Mother o' Mine 8-05-21
Mother of His Children 5-21-20
Mother of Mine 12-26-28
Mother Song (See: Mutterlied)
Mother Wore Tights 8-20-47
Motherhood (See: Maternite)
Motherland (See: Watan or Terra Madre)
Mother's Atonement, A 10-22-15
Mother's Boy 4-17-29
Mother's Confession, A 8-27-15
Mother's Crime, A 5-16-08
Mother's Cry, A 12-10-30
Mother's Day 9-24-80
Mother's Devotion, A (See: Vernost Materi)
Mother's Heart, A (See: Cuore di Mamma)
Mother's Heart, A 4-26-67
Mothers-in-Law 9-13-23
Mothers of France 3-16-17
Mothers of Men 3-05-20
Mother's Roses 1-08-15
Mother's Sin, A (See: Pecado de Una Madre, El)
Mother's Sin, A 1-25-18
Mothra 5-16-62
Motive for Revenge 7-03-35
Motive Was Jealousy, The (See: Per Motivi di Gelosia)
Motocyclette, La 7-24-68
Motor Madness 5-05-37
Motor Patrol 5-10-50
Motor Psycho 8-18-65
Motor Races at Monaco 11-07-08
Motorboating 8-03-17
Motorcycle Cops, The (See: Motards, Les)
Motorcycle Gang 11-27-57
Motoring Around the World 7-18-08
Motorvej Paa Sengekanten 10-04-72
Moucharde, La 9-24-58
Mouchette 4-05-67
Moulin Rouge 4-11-28 and 7-03-29
Moulin Rouge 2-13-34
Moulin Rouge 11-29-44
Moulin Rouge 12-24-52
Mount Hakkoda 7-27-77
Mount of Lament (See: Lelejska Gora)
Mount of Venus, The 4-23-75
Mount Venus 4-22-64
Mountain, The 10-03-56
Mountain Blizzard, A 3-19-10
Mountain Calls, The (See: Berg Ruft, Der)
Mountain Climbing Through a Telescope 1-26-07
Mountain Conqueror, The (See: Gipfelsturmer, Der)
Mountain Dew 9-21-17
Mountain Family Robinson 10-24-79
Mountain Justice 5-19-37
Mountain Man (See: Un de la Montagne)
Mountain Man, The (See: Khon Pukao)
Mountain Men, The 7-23-80
Mountain Men, The 7-23-80
Mountain Music 6-30-37
Mountain Pass (See: Passe Montagne)
Mountain Rat, The 5-22-14
Mountain Rhythm 7-12-39
Mountain Road, The 3-23-60
Mountains in Flames (See: Berge in Flammen)
Mountains of Manhattan 5-11-27
Mountebank's Son 9-25-09
Mountebank's Watchcase 11-06-09
Mounted Fury 12-22-31
Mounted Stranger 2-12-30
Mourez ... Nous Ferons le Reste 11-17-54
Mourir a Madrid 3-20-63
Mourir a Tue-Tete 6-06-79

Mourir d'Aimer   12-23-70
Mourning Becomes Electra   11-19-47
Mourning Suit, The   9-03-75
Mouse and His Child, The   6-29-77
Mouse on the Moon, The   5-15-63
Mouse That Roared, The   8-05-59
Mousetrap, The (See: Souriciere, La)
Moutarde Me Monte Au Nez, La   11-06-74
Mouth Agape, The (See: Gueule Ouverte, La)
Mouth to Mouth   5-10-78
Mouth Waters, The (See: Eau a la Bouche, L')
Mouthpiece, The   4-26-32
Mouton a Cinq Pattes, Le   8-11-54
Mouton Enrage, Le   3-27-74
Mouton Noir, Le   10-10-74
Moutonnet   8-12-36
Moutons de Panurge, Les   7-19-61
Move   8-05-70
Move On (See: Circulez)
Move Over, Darling   12-11-63
Movie Crazy   9-20-32
Movie, Movie   11-15-78
Movie Star, American Style; or, LSD, I Hate You!   8-17-66
Movie Stuntmen   9-23-53
Movies March On, The   7-05-39
Movietone Follies of 1930   6-25-30
Moving   12-18-74
Moving Finger, The   11-20-63
Moving Pictures of the War (See: Evening Sun's War Pictures)
Moving Violation   7-28-76
Mozart   10-09-40
Mozart   1-25-56 and 5-16-56
Mozart--A Childhood Chronicle (See: Mozart--Auf Zeichnungen
    Einer Jugend)
Mozart--Auf Zeichnungen einer Jugend   7-14-76
Mozart Story, The   11-17-48
Mozart's Last Requiem   9-18-09
Mozo No. 13, El   3-19-41
Mrigayaa   1-26-77 and 7-27-77
Mrs. Abad, I Am Bing (See: Mrs. Teresa Abad Ako Po Si Bing)
Mrs. Barrington   5-15-74
Mrs. Black Is Back   12-18-14
Mrs. Brown, You've Got a Lovely Daughter   5-22-68
Mrs. Dane's Confession   3-12-24
Mrs. Dane's Defense   1-11-18
Mrs. Dery, Where Are You? (See: Deryne, Hol Van?)
Mrs. Fitzherbert   12-17-47
Mrs. Husson's Virginity Prize (See: Rosier de Mme. Husson, Le)
Mrs. Leffingwell's Boots   10-04-18
Mrs. Mike   12-21-49
Mrs. Miniver   5-13-42
Mrs. Musashino (See: Musashino Fujin)
Mrs. O'Malley and Mr. Malone   11-08-50
Mrs. Parkington   9-20-44
Mrs. Peres and Her Divorce (See: Senora de Perez Se Divorcia, La)
Mrs. Pollifax--Spy   3-03-71
Mrs. Rivington's Pride   9-24-10
Mrs. Slacker   3-29-18
Mrs. Temple's Telegram   5-14-20
Mrs. Teresa Abad Ako Po Si Bing   6-23-76
Mrs. Upton's Device   10-17-13
Mrs. Warren's Profession (See: Frau Warren's Gewerbe)
Mrs. Wiggs   2-21-19
Mrs. Wiggs of the Cabbage Patch   1-01-15
Mrs. Wiggs of the Cabbage Patch   10-30-34
Mrs. Wiggs of the Cabbage Patch   10-07-42
Msdhumati   8-19-59
Mucednici Lasky   8-09-67
Muchacha De Las Bragas De Oro, La   5-07-80
Muchachas Que Estudian   9-27-39
Muchachita de Valladolid   10-15-58
Muchacho   9-16-70
Muchacho Como Yo, Un   4-10-68
Muchachos de Antes No Usaban Gomina, Los   4-02-69
Mucker, The (See: Os Mucker)
Mudar de Vida   9-14-66
Mudlark, The   11-08-50
Muddy Waters (See: Aguas Bajan Turbias, Las)
Mue Peun Khia   1-19-77
Mue Phuen Po Look On   12-10-75
Mueda   6-18-80
Muede Theodor, Der   10-28-36
Muenchhausen   6-21-78
Muerte Al Amanecer   8-31-77
Muerte de un Burocrata, La   7-27-66
Muerte de un Ciclista   6-01-55
Muerto, El   9-17-75
Muerto Falta a la Cita, El   2-07-45

Muerto 4-3-2-1-0 (See: Mission Stardust)
Muerto Hace las Maletas, El   10-25-72
Mug Town   1-20-43
Mugger, The   10-29-58
Muggs Rides Again   6-27-45
Muhomatsu No Issho   9-17-58
Muhomatsu the Rickshaw Man (See: Muhomatsu No Issho)
Muj Bracha Ma Prima Brachu   7-30-75
Mujer, Una   12-03-75
Mujer de la Tierra Caliente, La   7-26-78
Mujer de las Camelias, La   4-01-53
Mujer de Otro, La   12-20-67
Mujer Sin Alma, La   1-17-45
Mujer Sin Cabeza, Una   7-02-47
Mujer Sin Importancia, Una   3-28-45
Mujer, Un Hombre, Une Ciudad, Una   8-02-78
Mujer y la Selva, La   1-07-42
Mujeres Enganadas   7-12-61
Mujeres Que Trabajan   8-17-38
Mujhe Jeene Do   5-20-64
Mujo   10-14-70
Muke Po Mati   8-20-75
Mulatto, Il   8-09-50
Mulatto, The (See: Mulatto, Il)
Mule Train   7-26-50
Mulino Del Po, Il   10-19-49
Mulungu   8-28-74
Mummy, The   1-10-33
Mummy, The   7-15-59
Mummy and the Humming Bird, The   11-19-15
Mummy's Boys   12-16-36
Mummy's Curse, The   12-20-44
Mummy's Ghost, The   7-05-44
Mummy's Hand, The   9-25-40
Mummy's Shroud, The   3-29-67
Mummy's Tomb, The   10-14-42
Mumsie   10-05-27
Mumsy, Nanny, Sonny and Girly   2-18-70
Mumu   6-07-61
Mundo de Amor, Un   8-20-75
Mundo, Demonio y Carne   10-12-60
Munster, Go Home   6-22-66
Muppet Movie, The   5-30-79
Mur, Le   3-08-67
Mur a Jerusalem, Un   12-11-68
Mur de l'Atlantique, Le   10-28-70
Muralla Verde, La   11-11-70
Murder   8-13-30 and 10-29-30
Murder a la Mod   5-01-68
Murder Ahoy   9-30-64
Murder Among Friends   3-05-41
Murder at Dawn   4-05-32
Murder at 45 RPMs (See: Meurtre en 45 Tours)
Murder at Glen Athol   3-04-36
Murder at Midnight   10-06-31
Murder at the Gallop   5-08-63
Murder at the Vanities   5-22-34
Murder by an Aristocrat   6-17-36
Murder by Contract   12-10-58
Murder by Death   6-23-76
Murder by Decree   1-24-79
Murder by Invitation   7-30-41
Murder by the Clock   7-21-31
Murder Clinic, The   1-10-68
Murder Committed in a Sly and Cruel Manner and from Low Motives
    (See: Ubistvo Na Svirep I Podmukao Nacin I Iz Nishkih
    Pobudaj)
Murder Game (See: Moerderspiel)
Murder Game, The   4-13-66
Murder Goes to College   3-31-37
Murder, He Says   4-11-45
Murder in Greenwich Village   11-03-37
Murder in Mississippi   10-06-65
Murder in Reverse   12-25-46
Murder in the Air   7-10-40
Murder in the Big House   4-08-42
Murder in the Blue Room   11-01-44
Murder in the Cathedral   4-02-52
Murder in the Clouds   1-01-35
Murder in the Fleet   6-05-35
Murder in the Music Hall   2-20-46
Murder in the Night   7-17-40
Murder in the Private Car   7-10-34
Murder in the Red Barn   9-02-36
Murder in Times Square   6-02-43
Murder in Trinidad   5-29-34
Murder, Inc.   6-28-60
Murder Is a Murder, A (See: Meurtre Est Un Meurtre, Un)

Murder Is My Beat 5-04-55
Murder Is My Business 3-06-46
Murder Is News 6-28-39
Murder Man, The 7-31-35
Murder Most Foul 8-19-64
Murder, My Sweet 3-14-45
Murder of Dr. Harrigan, The 1-22-36
Murder on a Bridle Path 4-15-36
Murder on a Honeymoon 3-06-35
Murder on Approval 5-23-56
Murder on Diamond Row 11-17-37
Murder on the Blackboard 6-26-34
Murder on the Bridge (See: Richter Und Sein Henker, Der)
Murder on the Campus 3-13-34
Murder on the Orient Express 11-20-74
Murder on the Roof 1-29-30
Murder on the Waterfront 7-28-43
Murder on the Yukon 4-17-40
Murder over New York 12-04-40
Murder Reported 11-05-58
Murder, She Said 10-18-61 and 1-17-62
Murder Will Out 5-07-30
Murder Will Out 4-08-53
Murder with Pictures 11-25-36
Murder Without Crime 2-14-51
Murder Without Tears 6-17-53
Murdered House, The (See: A Casa Assassinada)
Murdered Young Girl, The (See: Jeune Fille Assassinee, La)
Murderer, The (See: Moerderer, Der)
Murderer, The (See: Meurtrier, Le)
Murderer Is Not Guilty, The (See: Assassin N'Est Pas Coupable, L')
Murderer Knows the Score, The (See: Assassin Connait la Musique, L')
Murderer Left No Clue, The 8-29-28
Murderer Lives at Number 21, The 8-20-47
Murderers Among Us 8-18-48
Murderers' Row 12-14-66
Murderess, The (See: Fonissa, I)
Murders (See: Meurtres)
Murders in the Rue Morgue 2-16-32
Murders in the Rue Morgue 9-01-71
Murders in the Zoo 4-04-33
Muriel, or The Time of a Return (See: Muriel, Ou le Temps d'un Retour)
Muriel, ou le Temps d'un Retour 9-11-63
Murieta 8-25-65
Murmuring Heart (See: Souffle Au Coeur, Le)
Murph the Surf 9-04-74
Murphy's War 1-27-71
Musashino Fujin 9-11-57
Muscle Beach Party 3-25-64
Musee du Louvre, Le 6-06-79
Mushroom, The (See: Champignon, Le)
Mushroom Eater, The (See: Hombre de los Hongos, El)
Music and Shadows (See: Musik I Morker)
Music Box Kid, The 6-01-60
Music for Madame 9-15-37
Music for Millions 12-13-44
Music Goes Round, The 2-26-36
Music I Morker 4-14-48
Music in Darkness (See: Music I Morker)
Music in Manhattan 7-26-44
Music in My Heart 1-10-40
Music in the Air 12-18-34
Music in the Blood (See: Musik Im Blut)
Music Is Magic 11-20-35
Music Lesson 10-09-09
Music Lovers, The 1-27-71
Music Machine, The 6-20-79
Music Man, The 4-11-62
Music Master, The 1-19-27
Music Room, The (See: Jalsaghar)
Music School (See: Escuela De Musica)
Musica, La 3-01-67
Musical Story 11-05-41
Musician Killer, The (See: Assassin Musicien, L')
Musician's Love Story, The 3-06-09
Musicians of the Sky (See: Musiciens du Ciel)
Musiciens du Ciel 4-03-40
Musik I Morker 7-29-59
Musik Im Blut 2-15-56
Musketeers, The (See: Congehovdingen)
Musolino the Bandit (See: Brigante Musolino, Il)
Muss 'Em Up 2-05-36
Mussolini Speaks 3-14-33
Mussolini: Ultimo Atto 4-10-74
Mussorgsky 8-22-51

Must We Marry? 3-20-29
Mustaa Valkoisella 5-29-68
Mustang 3-18-59
Mustang Country 3-24-76
Mustang: The House That Joe Built 4-14-76
Mustard Is in My Nose, The (See: Moutarde Me Monte Au Nez, La)
Mustergatte, Der 11-17-37
Mutation, The 5-29-74
Mute, The (See: Stumme, Der)
Mute and Love, The (See: Akhras Al-Hob)
Mutige Seefahrer, Der 11-25-36
Mutineers, The 5-04-49
Mutiny 3-02-17
Mutiny 2-20-52
Mutiny in Outer Space 5-19-65
Mutiny in the Arctic 5-07-41
Mutiny in the Big House 11-01-39
Mutiny of Ten, The (See: I Antarsia Ton Deka)
Mutiny of the Elsinore, The 8-06-20
Mutiny on the Blackhawk 8-09-39
Mutiny on the Bounty 11-13-35
Mutiny on the Bounty 11-14-62
Mutiny on the Elsinore 9-22-37
Mutt and Jeff 3-24-16
Mutter Courage und Ihre Kinder 8-02-61
Mutter Kusters Fahrt Zum Himmel 5-12-76
Mutterliebe 2-18-31
Mutterlied 1-26-38
Muurahaispolku 7-08-70
Muz Z Prvniho Stoleti 5-16-62
Muzhki Vremena 5-31-78
My Ain Folk 11-20-74
My American Uncle (See: Mon Oncle d'Amerique)
My American Wife 1-05-23
My American Wife 8-26-36
My Apple (See: Ma Pomme)
My Asylum (See: Chiedo Asilo)
My Beloved (See: Min Aelskade)
My Best Gal 4-12-44
My Best Girl 6-18-15
My Best Girl 11-09-27
My Bill 6-15-38
My Blood Runs Cold 3-17-65
My Blue Heaven 8-23-50
My Bodyguard 6-18-80
My Boy 1-06-22
My Brilliant Career 5-23-79
My Brother Anastasia (See: Mio Fratello Anastasia)
My Brother Has a Cute Brother (See: Muj Bracha Ma Prima Brachu)
My Brother Jonathan 2-18-48
My Brother Talks to Horses 11-20-46
My Brother, the Outlaw 2-07-51
My Brother's Keeper 7-21-48
My Buddy 9-27-44
My Candidate (See: Mi Candidato)
My Chauffeur 9-26-28
My Childhood 9-13-72
My Childish Father (See: Mon Gosse De Pere)
My Children (See: Mis Hijos)
My Country, a Revolution (See: Biladi, Une Revolution)
My Country First 5-19-16
My Cousin 11-29-18
My Cousin from Warsaw (See: Meine Kusine aus Warschau)
My Cousin Rachel 12-24-52
My Crimes After Mein Kampf (See: Apres Mein Kampf Mes Crimes)
My Dad 9-08-22
My Darling Clementine 10-09-46
My Darned Father (See: Mon Coquin de Pere)
My Daughter Hildegart (See: Mi Hija Hildegart)
My Daughter Is Different (See: Az En Lanyom Nem Olyan)
My Daughter Joy 6-28-50
My Daughter Patricia (See: Meine Tochter Patricia)
My Days with Veronica (See: Mis Dias Con Veronica)
My Dear Friend (See: Phuen Rak)
My Dear Miss Aldrich 10-06-37
My Dear Robinson (See: Mein Lieber Robinson)
My Dear Secretary 9-08-48
My Dearest (See: Ma Cherie)
My Dearest Lady (See: Mi Querida Senorita)
My Dog, Buddy 5-18-60
My Dog Rusty 6-09-48
My Dream Is Yours 3-16-49
My Dream Woman (See: Femme de Mes Reves, La)
My Fabulous Girlfriends (See: Stupende Le Mie Amiche)
My Fair Baby 12-12-73
My Fair Lady 10-28-64
My Father, the Ape and I (See: Mein Vater, der Affe und Ich)
My Father's Happy Years (See: Apam Nehany Boldog Eve)

My Father's House 9-24-47
My Favorite Blonde 3-18-42
My Favorite Brunette 2-19-47
My Favorite Spy 5-06-42
My Favorite Spy 10-10-51
My Favorite Wife 5-01-40
My Fiancee, the Transvestite (See: Mi Novia el ... (Travesti))
My First Girl Friend (See: Mi Primera Novia)
My First Love (See: Mon Premier Amour)
My First Love 6-13-51
My First Sin (See: Mi Primer Pecado)
My Flag 11-29-18
My Foolish Heart 10-19-49
My Forbidden Past 3-28-51
My Foster Sister (See: Ma Soeur de Lait)
My Four Years in Germany 3-15-18
My Friend Clock-John (See: Min Van Klock-Johan)
My Friend Flicka 4-07-43
My Friend Irma 8-17-49
My Friend Irma Goes West 5-31-50
My Friend Pierrette (See: Mon Ami Pierrette)
My Friend, the Doctor 10-08-10
My Friend the Millionaire (See: Mein Freund der Millionaer)
My Friend Victor (See: Mon Ami Victor)
My Friend Who Can't Say No (See: Mein Freund der Nicht Nein
    Sagen Kann)
My Friends (See: Amici Miei)
My Gal Loves Music 11-22-44
My Gal Sal 4-22-42
My Geisha 1-31-62
My Girl Friend, Barbara (See: Meine Freundin Barbara)
My Girl Tisa 1-21-48
My Girlfriend's Wedding 5-14-69
My Good Fellowmen (See: Vsichni Dobri Rodaci)
My Gun Is Quick 8-07-57
My Hands Are Clay 7-21-48
My Heart Belongs to Daddy 11-04-42
My Heart Calls You (See: Mein Herz Ruft Dir)
My Heart Hesitates (See: Mon Coeur Balance)
My Heart Is Calling 4-17-35
My Heart Is Red (See: Mon Coeur Est Rouge)
My Heart Is Upside-Down (See: Coeur a l'Envers, Le)
My Hobo 8-07-63
My Home Is Copacabana (See: Mitt Hem Ar Copacabana)
My Home Town 5-02-28
My Husband Is Marvelous (See: Mon Mari Est Merveilleux)
My Husband's Wives 12-31-24
My Hustler 7-12-67
My Irish Molly 10-02-40
My Kingdom for a Cook 10-20-43
My Lady "Incog" 1-28-16
My Lady of Whims 6-30-26
My Lady's Garter 3-19-20
My Lady's Latchkey 3-18-21
My Lady's Lips 7-14-26
My Lady's Past 8-21-29
My Lady's Slipper 1-28-16
My Last Mistress 1-26-49
My Learned Friend 10-13-43
My Leopold (See: Mein Leopold)
My Life with Caroline 7-16-41
My Lips Betray 11-07-33
My Little Boy 12-07-17
My Little Chickadee 2-14-40
My Little Loves (See: Mes Petites Amoureuses)
My Love Came Back 6-26-40
My Love Has Been Burning (See: Waga Koi Wa Moenu)
My Love, My Love (See: Mon Amour, Mon Amour)
My Lover, My Son 3-11-70
My Lucky Star 9-14-38
My Madonna 11-05-15
My Man 2-14-24
My Man 12-26-28
My Man and I 8-20-52
My Man Godfrey 9-23-36
My Man Godfrey 9-04-57
My Mao (See: Mio Mao)
My Margo 5-07-69
My Marriage 2-26-36
My Memories of Mexico (See: Mexico de Mis Recuerdos)
My Merry Widow (See: Mi Viuda Alegre)
My Michael (See: Michael Sheli)
My Model (See: Det Ar Min Modell)
My Mother 2-21-33
My Mother and the Roomer (See: Sarang Bang Sonnim Omoni)
My Mother-in-Law Is an Angel 11-30-07
My Mother Is a Miss (See: Mademoiselle Ma Mere)
My Mother Is to Blame (See: Mi Madre Es Culpable)

My Mother, The General (See: Imi Hageneralit)
My Name Is Ivan 6-26-63
My Name Is Julia Ross 11-14-45
My Name Is Nobody (See: Mio Nome e Nessuno, Il)
My Native Land 3-28-33
My Niece Doesn't Do That (See: Meine Nicht Tut das Nicht)
My Neighbor's Wife 5-27-25
My Night at Maud's (See: Ma Nuit Chez Maud)
My Nights with Susan, Olga, Albert, Julie, Piet & Sandra (See:
    Mijn Nachten Met Susan, Olga, Albert, Julie, Piet & Sandra)
My Official Wife 7-17-14
My Old Dutch 7-16-15
My Old Dutch 6-23-26
My Old Dutch 9-25-34
My Old Kentucky Home 4-28-22
My Old Kentucky Home 2-09-38
My Own Pal 3-17-26
My Own True Love 12-08-48
My Own United States 1-25-18
My Pal Gus 11-12-52
My Pal the King 10-11-32
My Pal Trigger 6-19-46
My Pal, Wolf 9-20-44
My Part of the World (See: Moja Strana Svijeta)
My Partner 3-24-16
My Past 3-18-31
My Reputation 1-09-46
My School Chum (See: Mein Schulfreund)
My Seal and Them (See: Mon Phoque et Elles)
My Second Brother (See: Nianchan)
My Sexy Girl Friend (See: Ang Nobya Kong Sexy)
My Side of the Mountain 2-26-69
My Sin 9-15-31
My Sister and I 10-02-29
My Sister and I 6-16-48
My Sister Eileen 9-16-42
My Sister Eileen 9-14-55
My Sister, My Love (See: Syskonbadd)
My Sisters' Kids at Their Worst (See: Mine Soestres Boern Naar
    de er Vaerst)
My Six Convicts 3-12-52
My Six Loves 3-06-63
My Slave 7-13-60
My Son 4-22-25
My Son Is a Criminal 3-15-39
My Son Is Guilty 1-17-40
My Son John 3-26-52
My Son, My Son! 3-13-40
My Son, the Hero 4-28-43
My Son, the Hero 9-18-63
My Song for You 8-14-34 and 5-29-35
My Song Goes Around the World (See: Lied Geht Um die Welt, Ein)
My Song of Love (See: Amore che Canta, L')
My Song to the Wind (See: Mia Canzone al Vento, La)
My Teenage Daughter 6-27-56
My True Story 3-07-51
My Two Loves (See: Mis Dos Amores)
My Uncle (See: Mon Oncle)
My Uncle Antoine (See: Mon Oncle Antoine)
My Uncle Benjamin (See: Mon Oncle Benjamin)
My Unmarried Wife 12-14-17
My Valet 10-01-15
My War--My Love (See: Moja Wojna--Moja Milosc)
My Way (See: Igy Joettem)
My Way 2-20-74
My Way Home 11-15-78
My Weakness 9-26-33
My Widow and I 9-06-50
My Wife (See: Mia Signora, La)
My Wife and I 5-20-25
My Wife as a Business Man (See: Ma Femme Homme d'Affaire)
My Wife, the Adventuress (See: Meine Frau, die Hochstaplerin)
My Wife, the Swindler (See: Meine Frau, die Hochstaplerin)
My Wife's Best Friend 10-08-52
My Wife's Family 3-15-32
My Wife's Gone to the Country 9-04-09
My Wife's Relatives 4-19-39
My Wild Irish Rose 6-16-22
My Wild Irish Rose 12-10-47
My Woman 10-17-33
My World Dies Screaming 10-22-58
Myr Vodjaschemu 9-06-61
Myra Breckinridge 6-24-70
Myrt and Marge 1-23-34
Mystere de la Chambre Jaune, Le 2-18-31 and 5-27-31
Mystere de la Villa Rose 1-12-32
Mystere de Saint-Val, Le 10-17-45
Mystere Koumiko, Le 8-04-65

Mystere Picasso, Le 5-16-56
Mysteres de Paris, Les 2-03-37
Mysteres de Paris, Les 10-24-62
Mysterians, The 5-27-59
Mysteries 2-07-79
Mysteries of India 7-28-22
Mysteries of Myra, The (serial) 4-21-16; 5-12-16; and 5-26-16
Mysteries of Notre Dame 11-04-36
Mysteries of Paris (See: Mysteres de Paris, Les)
Mysteries of Rome (See: Misteri di Roma, I)
Mysteries of the Orient 11-14-28
Mysterious Avenger 4-08-36
Mysterious Case of Rygseck Murders (See: Komisario Palmun Erehdys)
Mysterious Crossing 2-03-37
Mysterious Desperado, The 8-17-49
Mysterious Doctor, The 2-24-43
Mysterious Dr. Satan, The 11-20-40
Mysterious House of Dr. C., The 11-03-76
Mysterious Intruder 3-27-46
Mysterious Island 12-25-29
Mysterious Island 12-13-61
Mysterious Island, The (See: Ile Mysterieuse, L')
Mysterious Lady 8-08-28
Mysterious Miss Terry, The 8-24-17
Mysterious Mr. Moto 6-01-38 and 9-21-38
Mysterious Mr. Reeder 5-08-40
Mysterious Mr. Tiller, The 9-21-17
Mysterious Mr. Wong 3-13-35
Mysterious Mr. X, The 1-25-39
Mysterious Monsters, The 8-04-76
Mysterious Mrs. M., The 1-26-17
Mysterious Pilot 12-22-37 and 1-26-38
Mysterious Rider, The 5-11-27
Mysterious Rider, The 6-06-33
Mysterious Rider, The 11-16-38
Mysterious Witness, The 8-16-23
Mystery at the Burlesque 4-19-50
Mystery Broadcast 10-20-43
Mystery Club, The 8-25-26
Mystery Girl, The 2-28-19
Mystery House 6-01-38
Mystery in Mexico 6-23-48
Mystery Lake 8-26-53
Mystery Liner 4-10-34
Mystery Man 5-31-44
Mystery Man, The 3-27-35
Mystery of Carter Breene, The 12-31-15
Mystery of Edwin Drood, The 3-27-35
Mystery of Life, The 7-07-31
Mystery of Lonely Gulch, The 10-29-10
Mystery of Marie Roget 4-08-42
Mystery of Mr. Wong, The 4-12-39
Mystery of Mr. X, The 2-27-34
Mystery of Oberwald, The (See: Mistero di Oberwald, Il)
Mystery of Silistria, The 3-19-15
Mystery of the Diamond Belt 6-11-15
Mystery of the Hooded Horseman 8-04-37
Mystery of the Locked Room 12-03-15
Mystery of the Mary Celeste, The 12-04-35
Mystery of the Pink Villa 2-05-30
Mystery of the Poison Pool 10-17-14
Mystery of the Rose Villa (See: Mystere de la Villa Rose)
Mystery of the 13th Guest 10-13-43
Mystery of the Villa Rose 6-04-30
Mystery of the Wax Museum, The 2-21-33
Mystery of the White Room 3-29-39
Mystery of the Yellow Room (See: Mystere de la Chambre Jaune, Le)
Mystery of the Yellow Room 10-24-19
Mystery of 13 Hill Street 4-24-14
Mystery Plane 3-29-39
Mystery Ranch 7-05-32
Mystery Road 7-29-21
Mystery Sea Raider 8-07-40
Mystery Ship 8-06-41
Mystery Street 5-17-50
Mystery Submarine 11-22-50
Mystery Submarine 5-08-63
Mystery Train 8-25-31
Mystery Woman 1-22-35
Mystic, The 9-02-25
Mystic Circle Murder 10-11-39
Mystic Faces 9-13-18
Mystic Hour, The 5-25-17
Mystic Melodies 11-06-09
Mystic Mirror, The 10-17-28
Myten 7-13-66

N

N.P. 8-04-71
Na ... 6-27-73
Na Avionima Od Papira 8-16-67
Na Bialym Szlaku 11-13-63
Na Boca Do Mundo 2-07-79
Na Cha, the Great 3-19-75
Na Dnie (See: Lower Depths, The)
Na Klancu 8-18-71
Na Komete 9-02-70
Na Malenkom Ostrove 7-04-62
Na Samote U Lesa 7-28-76
Na Semi Vetrach 7-04-62
Na Wlasna Prosbe 9-24-80
Na Wylot 5-15-74
Nabonga 2-23-44
Nach dem Sturm 12-15-48
Nach Meinem Letzten Umzug 7-26-72
Nacha Regules 5-24-50
Nachgestal-Ten 3-06-29
Nacht Bummler 3-11-31
Nacht der Grossen Liebe 8-22-33
Nacht der Verwandlung 7-03-35
Nacht Fiel Ueber Gotenhafen 7-27-60
Nacht Gehort Uns, Die 3-18-31
Nacht Im Grand Hotel, Eine 12-29-31
Nacht Im Paradies, Eine 2-28-33
Nacht Mit Chandler, Die 3-12-80
Nacht Mit dem Kaiser 2-03-37
Nachtigall Madel, Das 1-31-33
Nachts Auf den Strassen 5-28-52
Nachts Im Gruenen Kakadu 1-22-58
Nachts, Wenn der Teufel Kam 3-05-58
Nachtschatten 9-06-72
Nachtvorstellungen 6-28-78
Nachtwache 6-10-53
Naciala 9-15-71
Nacida Para Amar 10-07-59
Nacionalna Klasa Do 785 CM3 4-18-79
Nackte Mann Auf dem Sportplatz, Der 8-28-74
Nada 1-30-74
Nadeje 4-15-64
Naeste Stop Paradis 11-26-80
Nagana 2-21-33
Naganiacz 8-12-64
Nagbabagang Silangan 11-05-75
Nahla 9-05-79
Nahota 8-26-70
Naif Aux 40 Enfants, Le 7-09-58
Nail of Brightness, The (See: Maynila, Sa Mga Kuko Ng Liwanag)
Nais 12-12-45
Naisenkuvia 7-08-70
Najdolgiot Pat 8-25-76
Naked Alibi 8-25-54
Naked Among the Wolves 7-24-63
Naked and the Dead, The 7-09-58
Naked Angels 5-21-69
Naked Ape, The 8-15-73
Naked as a Worm (See: Nu Comme un Ver)
Naked Brigade, The 4-28-65
Naked Came the Stranger 6-04-75
Naked City, The 1-21-48
Naked Dawn, The 7-27-55
Naked Earth, The 2-12-58 and 6-25-58
Naked Edge, The 7-05-61
Naked Eye, The 3-20-57
Naked Heart, The 12-13-50
Naked Hearts 5-19-16
Naked Hills, The 7-18-56
Naked Hours, The 10-21-64
Naked Jungle, The 2-17-54
Naked Kiss, The 1-20-65
Naked Maja, The 3-25-59
Naked Man in the Stadium, The (See: Nackte Mann Auf Dem Sport-
   platz, Der)
Naked Night, The 2-08-56
Naked Paradise 3-13-57
Naked Passion (See: Pasion Desnuda, La)
Naked Prey, The 3-16-66
Naked Runner, The 7-05-67
Naked Sea, The 10-26-55
Naked Soul, A 6-02-17

Naked Spur, The 1-14-53
Naked Street, The 8-17-55
Naked Sun, The (See: Hadaka No Taiyo)
Naked Truth, The 6-12-14
Naked Truth, The 12-11-57
Naked Winds of the Sea, The (See: Som Havets Nakna Vind)
Naked Woman 1-25-50
Naked Woman, The (See: Femme Nue, La)
Naked Zodiac 2-25-70
Nam Karng Yod Deo 12-06-78
Namak Haram 7-17-74
Name of the Game Is Kill, The 4-03-68
Name of the Prince of Peace 4-30-15
Name the Man 1-17-24
Name the Woman 7-25-28
Name the Woman 12-04-34
Name Was S.N., The (See: Se Llamaba S.N.)
Nameless Men 3-21-28
Nameless Star (See: Steaua Fara Nume)
Namensheirat 1-17-33
Namida o Shishi no Tategami 10-29-80
Namonaku Mazushiku Utsukushiku 8-30-61
Namu, the Killer Whale 8-03-66
Nan of the Music Mountain 12-21-17
Nana 5-19-26
Nana 2-06-34
Nana 10-05-55
Nana 5-05-71
Nana, Mom and Me 1-15-75
Nancy Comes Home 3-29-18
Nancy Drew and the Hidden Staircase 11-08-39
Nancy Drew--Detective 12-07-38
Nancy Drew--Reporter 3-01-39
Nancy Drew, Trouble Shooter 9-20-39
Nancy from Nowhere 2-03-22
Nancy Goes to Rio 2-01-50
Nancy Steele Is Missing 3-10-37
Nancy's Birthright 6-02-16
Nanette of the Wilds 12-01-16
Nanga Parbat 3-11-36
Nangsao Maliwan 5-21-75
Nankai No Dai Ketto 1-25-67
Nanny, The 10-13-65
Nanook of the North 6-16-22 and 9-01-48
Nantes and Its Surroundings 12-03-10
Naomi 7-02-80
Naples and Sorrento (See: Napuli e Surrinto)
Naples Au Baiser de Feu 2-02-38
Naples Millionaire (See: Napoli Milionaria)
Naples of Former Days (See: Napoli d'Altri Tempi)
Naples That Never Dies (See: Napoli Che Non Muore)
Naples Under the Kiss of Fire (See: Naples au Baiser de Feu)
Napoleon 4-27-27 and 1-23-29
Napoleon 12-21-27
Napoleon 2-26-41
Napoleon 4-13-55
Napoleon and France 4-17-14
Napoleon and Josephine 11-12-24
Napoleon and Samantha 7-12-72
Napoleon Bonaparte 5-29-35 and 3-30-55
Napoleon on St. Helena 12-11-29
Napoleon's Barber 11-28-28
Napoletani a Milano 9-02-53
Napoli Che Non Muore 8-30-39
Napoli D'Altri Tempi 1-26-38
Napoli Milionaria 7-18-51
Nappali Sotetseg 8-05-64
Naprawde Wczoraj (See: Yesterday in Fact)
Napuli e Surrinto 9-29-31
Nar Rosorna Sla-Ut 2-18-31
Nara Livet 5-21-58
Narayama Bushi-Ko 9-17-58
Narco--A Film About Love (See: Narko--En Film Om Kaerlighed)
Narco Men, The 11-24-71
Narcotics Story, The 3-05-58
Narko--En Film Om Kaerlighed 9-01-71
Narrische Gluck, Das (See: Foolish Happiness)
Narrow Corner, The 7-18-33
Narrow Margin, The 4-02-52
Narrow Path, The 11-29-18
Narrow Street 1-07-25
Narrow Trail, The 1-11-18
Nasa Lupa Ang Langit At Impiyerno 5-05-76
Nashville 6-11-75
Nashville Rebel 11-30-66
Nasilje Na Trgu 8-23-61
Nasty Habits 10-27-76
Nasty Rabbit, The 12-09-64

Nasvidenje V. Naslednji Vojni 8-13-80
Naszut Felaron 11-25-36
Natale Al Campo 119 2-18-48
Natale Che Quasi Non Fu, Il (See: Christmas That Almost Wasn't, The)
Natalia 7-15-70
Natalka Poltavka 12-30-36 (Also see: Girl from Poltava, The)
Nathalie 1-08-58
Nathalie Agent Secret 1-20-60
Nathalie Granger 9-06-72
Nation Aflame 4-07-37
National Barn Dance 9-06-44
National Class (See: Nacionalna Klasa Do 785 CM3)
National Health, or Nurse Norton's Affair, The 3-14-73
National Lampoon's Animal House 6-28-78
National Mechanics (See: Mecanica Nacional)
National Shotgun, The (See: Escopeta Nacional, La)
National Velvet 12-06-44
Nation's Peril, The 11-19-15
Native House (See: Otchi Dom)
Native Land 5-13-42
Native Pony (See: Caballito Criollo)
Native Son 4-25-51
Natives of Planet Earth (See: Nativos del Planeta Tierra)
Nativos Del Planeta Tierra 12-12-73
Natsu No Omoto 9-06-72
Nattens Ljus 9-03-58
Nattlek 9-07-66
Nattvaktens Hustru 3-24-48
Nattvardsgaesterna 3-20-63
Natun Pata 10-29-69
Natural Boundaries (See: Priroda Granica)
Natural Enemies 10-31-79
Natural Law, The 11-02-17
Natural Voice Talking Pictures 5-16-08
Nature's Fairyland 5-07-24
Nature's Half Acre 7-11-51
Naufrages de l'Ile de la Tortue, Les 9-01-76
Naughty 10-12-27
Naughty Baby 2-06-29
Naughty but Nice 7-06-27
Naughty but Nice 6-28-39
Naughty Duchess 10-31-28
Naughty Flirt 4-15-31
Naughty Marietta 3-27-35
Naughty Martine 4-22-53
Naughty Nanette 4-20-27
Naughty, Naughty 3-22-18
Naughty Nineties, The 6-20-45
Naughty Ones, The (See: Nemirni)
Naughty Victorians, The 11-19-75
Naulahka, The 3-15-18
Navajo 1-30-52
Navajo Joe 11-01-67
Navajo Kid, The 1-30-46
Navajo Run 6-08-66
Navajo Trail Raiders 10-19-49
Naval Academy 5-28-41
Naval Review 10-02-09
Nave Delle Donne Maledette, La 12-09-53
Navidad de Los Pobres, La 10-01-47
Navigator, The 10-15-24
Navrat Ztraceneho Syna 8-09-67
Navy Blue and Gold 11-17-37
Navy Blues 1-15-30
Navy Blues 5-12-37
Navy Blues 8-10-41
Navy Born 6-24-36
Navy Bound 2-21-51
Navy Comes Through, The 10-14-42
Navy Lark, The 10-21-59
Navy Secrets 3-22-39
Navy Spy 3-24-37
Navy vs. the Night Monsters, The 11-23-66
Navy Way, The 3-01-44
Navy Wife 1-08-36
Navy Wife 6-13-56
Nayak 7-13-66
Nazar Stodolya 8-18-37
Nazarene Cross and the Wolf (See: Nazareno Cruz y el Lobo)
Nazareno Cruz y el Lobo 6-18-75
Nazarin 5-20-59
Nazi Spy Ring 6-10-42
N'Diangane 6-04-76
Ne Bolit Golowa U Djatla 9-08-76
Ne de Pere Inconnu 5-16-51
Ne Diraj U Srecu 8-23-61
Ne Dokantchence Pismo 6-21-61

Ne Fillim Te Veres 1-24-79
Ne Goryuy 4-08-70
Ne Jouez Pas Avec les Martians 4-10-68
Ne Men ... Alla 11-15-72
Ne Naginji Se Van 8-17-77
Ne Nous Fachons Pas 5-04-66
Ne Pleure Pas 4-05-78
Ne Si Otivai 11-17-76
Ne Sirj Edesanyam 11-25-36
Nea 9-01-76
Neal of the Navy (serial) 9-10-15; Part II: 9-17-15; Part III:
    9-24-15; Part IV: 10-01-15; Part V: 10-08-15; Part VI:
    10-15-15; Part VII: 10-22-15; Part VIII: 10-29-15; Part IX:
    11-05-15; Part X: 11-12-15
Neapolitan Carousel (See: Carosello Napoletano)
Neapolitan Turk, The (See: Turco Napoletano, Il)
Neapolitans in Milan (See: Napoletani a Milano)
Near, Far the Morning (See: Lumapit Lumayo Ang Umaga)
Near Lady 12-06-23
Near Orouet (See: Du Cote D'Orouet)
Near the Trail's End 11-24-31
Nearly a King 2-18-16
Nearly a Lady 8-13-15
Nearly a Nasty Accident 5-24-61
Nearly Decent Girl, A (See: Fast Anstaendiges Maedchen, Eines)
Nearly Eighteen 10-20-43
Nearly Married 11-30-17
Nearly Spliced 5-26-16
Neath the Arizona Skies 3-20-35
Neath the Lion's Paw 6-26-14
Nebraskan, The 11-04-53
Necesito Una Madre 6-29-66
Necessary Evil, The 7-08-25
Nechci Nic Slyset 2-28-79
Neck and Neck 11-17-31
Necromancy 10-11-72
Necronomicon--Dreamed Sins (See: Necronomicon--Getraeumtte
    Sueaden)
Necronomicon--Getraeumtte Sueaden 4-24-68
Necrophagus 10-27-71
Necropolis 12-09-70
Ned Kelly 6-17-70
Ned McCobb's Daughter 2-20-29
Nedeini Matchove 8-25-76
Nedelja 8-20-69
Nedtur 11-19-80
Neem Annapurna 2-20-80
Ne'er Do Well, The 2-18-16
Ne'er Do Well 5-03-23
Ne'er to Return Road 9-30-21
Negatives 10-16-68
Neglected by His Wife (See: Forsummad Av Sin Fru)
Neglected Wives 6-25-20
Negresco 2-28-68
Negro Orpheus (See: Orfeu Negro)
Negro Soldier, The 2-23-44
Negro Woman From ..., The (See: Noire De ..., La)
Neige a Fondu Sur la Manicouagan, La 8-18-65
Neige Etait Sale, La 4-07-54
Neighbors 7-19-18
Neighbors 1-04-39
Neighbor's Wives 10-17-33
Neither by Day Nor by Night 7-12-72
Neither Seen Nor Recognized (See: Ni Vu, Ni Connu)
Neither the Sea Nor the Sand 1-30-74
Nejkrasnejsi Vek 7-16-69
Nell Gwyn 1-27-26
Nell Gwyn 6-26-35
Nell Gwynne 9-11-14
Nell of the Circus 11-28-14
Nell of the Dance Hall 11-12-15
Nell'anno Del Signore 11-26-69
Nella Citta L'Inferno 3-11-59
Nella Citta' Perduta Di Sarzana 10-08-80
Nellie, Beautiful Cloak Model 4-16-24
Nelson 8-31-27
Nelson Affair, The 3-28-73
Nem Alt Meg Az Autobusz 11-13-63
Nem Loptam en Eletemben 7-26-39
Nemesio 11-12-69
Nemesis 11-23-27
Nemica, La 3-11-53
Nemirni 8-16-67
Nemu No Ki No Uta 7-24-74
Nene 12-14-77
Nenita Unit 3-21-54
Neola the Sioux 6-18-15
Neon Palace, The 11-11-70
Neopolitans in Milan (See: Napoletani a Milano)

Neprimirimite 10-14-64
Neptune Factor, The 5-23-73
Neptune's Daughter 4-10-14
Neptune's Daughter 5-18-49
Nero 5-26-22
Nero's Big Weekend (See: Mio Figlio Nerone)
Nervous Wreck, The 10-13-26
Nes Ba'ayara 9-18-68
Neskolko Interwju Po Litschnym Woprosam 2-28-79
Nest, The (See: Nido, El)
Nest, The 1-18-28
Nest Break (See: Nestbruch)
Nest in the Wind (See: Gnezdo Na Vetru)
Nest of Gentle Folk, A (See: Dvorianckoe Gnezdo)
Nest of Vipers 9-05-79
Nest of Virgins (See: Rincon de las Virgenes, El)
Nestbruch 12-31-80
Net, The (See: Red, La or Netz, Das)
Net, The 4-07-16
Net, The 2-18-53
Netepichnaja Istoria 7-26-78
Network 10-13-76
Netz, Das 4-07-76
Neun Leben Hat die Katze 10-30-68
Neung Toh Jet 4-27-77
Neutral Port 1-08-41
Nevada 8-10-27
Nevada 4-15-36
Nevada City 7-16-41
Nevada Smith 6-01-66
Nevadan, The 1-11-50
Never a Dull Moment 11-03-43
Never a Dull Moment 11-01-50
Never a Dull Moment 5-15-68
Never Again Always (See: Jamais Plus Toujours)
Never Again Love (See: Nie Wieder Liebe)
Never Eat Green Apples 10-09-09
Never Fear 1-04-50
Never Give a Sucker an Even Break 10-08-41
Never Let Go 6-15-60
Never Let Me Go 3-25-53
Never Love a Stranger 7-09-58
Never Love Again (See: Nie Wieder Liebe)
Never on Sunday 5-25-60
Never Put It in Writing 4-22-64
Never Say Die 9-24-24
Never Say Die 3-08-39
Never Say Goodbye 10-23-46
Never Say Goodbye 2-15-56
Never Say Quit 4-04-19
Never So Few 12-09-59
Never Steal Anything Small 3-04-59
Never Take No for an Answer 12-26-51
Never Take Sweets from a Stranger 3-09-60
Never the Twain Shall Meet 7-29-25
Never the Twain Shall Meet 6-09-31
Never Too Late 10-27-65
Never Trust a Gambler 7-18-51
Never Wave at a WAC 12-17-52
Nevesinjska Puska 10-02-63
Nevesta 9-30-70
Nevestka 8-30-72
Neveu Silencieux, Un 11-08-78
Nevinost Bez Zastite 7-17-68
New Adventures of Get-Rich-Quick Wallingford (See: Wallingford)
New Adventures of J. Rufus Wallingford, The (See: J. Rufus
    Wallingford)
New Adventures of Tarzan, The 10-16-35
New Angels, The (See: Nuovi Angeli, I)
New Aristocrats, The (See: Nouveaux Aristocrats, Les)
New Babylon, The 12-04-29
New Beaujolais Wine Has Arrived, The (See: Beaujolais Nouveau
    Est Arrive, Le)
New Beginning, A (See: Nuevo Amanecer, Un)
New Brooms 11-04-25
New Centurions, The 7-26-72
New Champion, The 3-31-26
New China, The 3-12-52
New Commandment 11-11-25
New Diary of a Woman in White (See: Nouveau Journal d'une Femme
    en Blanc)
New Disciple 12-23-21
New Divorce Cure, A 1-22-10
New Earth, The 3-03-37
New Englander, The 2-14-24
New Faces 2-24-54
New Faces of 1937 7-07-37
New Fatherland 11-06-35

New Fist of Fury 6-23-76
New Frontier, The 12-18-35
New Frontier, The 8-16-39
New Game of Death, The 9-24-75
New Generation 2-07-79
New Gilgames (See: Uj Gilgames)
New Gulliver, The 5-01-35 and 11-06-35
New Horizons 5-17-39
New Interns, The 5-06-64
New Israel 5-14-52
New Kind of Love, A 8-28-63
New Klondike, The 3-24-26
New Leaf, A 3-10-71
New Leaf, The (See: Natun Pata)
New Life, A 10-16-09
New Life Style, The 8-12-70
New Lives for Old 3-04-25
New Love for Old 2-08-18
New Love or la Revolucion de Las Flores 10-16-68
New Mail Carrier 9-04-09
New Marshal of Gila Creek, The 2-26-10
New Men 12-26-28
New Mexico 5-02-51
New Moon 12-31-30
New Moon 6-19-40
New Moon, The 5-16-19
New Morals for Old 6-28-32
New One, The (See: Nuevos, Los)
New Orleans 8-21-29
New Orleans 4-30-47
New Orleans Uncensored 2-16-55
New Parthenon, The (See: O Neos Parthenonas)
New South Wales Gold Mine, A 11-26-10
New Spaniards, The (See: Nuevos Espanoles, Los)
New Squire, The (See: Az Uj Foldesur)
New Stenographer, The 3-04-11
New Teacher, The (See: Khun Koo Con Mai)
New Teacher, The 8-04-22
New Teacher, The 4-16-41
New Testament (See: Nouveau Testament)
New Toy, The (See: Nyt Legetoej)
New Toys 2-18-32
New War Films 11-26-15
New Wine 7-30-41
New World, A (See: Monde Nouveau, Un)
New Year's Eve 4-17-29
New Year's Sacrifice 9-04-57
New York 8-15-08
New York 2-11-16
New York 2-02-27
New York City--The Most 6-12-68
New York Confidential 2-16-55
New York Idea, The 12-03-20
New York Luck 1-04-18
New York, New York 6-22-77
New York Nights 2-05-30
New York on the Sea (See: New York Sur-Mer)
New York Peacock, The 2-09-17
New York Sur-Mer 8-05-64
New York Town 7-30-41
Newcomer, The (See: Nouveau Venu, Le)
Newcomers, The 9-06-72
Newcomers, The 7-18-73
Newcomers to Love (See: Debutantes en el Amor, Los)
Newly Rich 7-07-31
Newman's Law 5-08-74
News from the Village (See: Kaddu Beykat)
News Hounds 6-18-47
News Is Made at Night 7-19-39
News Parade, The 5-30-28
Newsboys' Home 1-25-29
Newsfront 5-10-78
Newsreel Era--70 Years of Headlines, The 5-24-72
Newsvendor and the Lady, The (See: Canillita y la Dama, El)
Next 8-11-71
Next Corner, The 2-14-24
Next Man, The 11-03-76
Next of Kin, The 6-17-42
Next Stop, Greenwich Village 2-04-76
Next Stop Paradise (See: Naeste Stop Paradis)
Next Time I Marry 12-07-38
Next Time We Love 2-05-36
Next to No Time 8-20-58
Next Voice You Hear, The 6-07-50
Nez de Cuir 4-23-52
Nezabybaemaya Osen 7-27-77
Nezha Defeats the Dragon (See: Nezha Nao Hai)
Nezha Nao Hai 5-28-80

Nguyen Van Troy 7-26-67
Ni Liv 5-21-58
Ni Ljuger 2-25-70
Ni Vu, Ni Connu 7-02-58
Niagara 1-21-53
Niagara Falls 9-24-41
Niagara in Winter Dress 9-04-09
Nianchan 7-13-60 and 11-02-60
Nibelungen, The 4-16-24
Nibelungen (Part I: Siegfried), Die 4-12-67
Nice Adventure, The (See: Bonne Aventure, La)
Nice Girl? 2-26-41
Nice Girl Like Me, A 11-12-69
Nice Neighbor, The (See: A Kedves Somszed)
Nice People 8-18-22
Nice Woman 2-23-32
Nicholas and Alexandra 12-08-71
Nicholas Nickleby 3-26-47
Nicht Alles Was Fliegt Ist Ein Vogel 4-25-79
Nicht Fummeln, Liebling! 2-04-70
Nicht Versohnt 9-22-65
Nichts Als Aerger Mit der Liebe 12-19-56
Nick Carter and the Red Club (See: Nick Carter et le Trefle
    Rouge)
Nick Carter et le Trefle Rouge 12-22-65
Nick Carter, Master Detective 12-13-39
Nickel Queen 6-30-71
Nickel Ride, The 5-22-74
Nickelodeon 12-22-76
Nicole and Her Virtue (See: Nicole et Sa Vertu)
Nicole et Sa Vertu 1-19-32
Nidhanaya 9-20-72
Nido, El 10-08-80
Nie Ma Mocnych 12-25-74
Nie Wieder Liebe 8-18-30 and 1-19-32
Niedorajda 1-12-38
Niedzielne Dzieci 5-18-77
Niejnosti 8-09-67
Niemandsland 12-29-31 (Also see: Hell on Earth)
Niet Voor de Poesen 4-11-73
Niewinni Czarodzieje 5-31-61
Night, The (See: Notte, La)
Night After Night 11-01-32
Night Alarm 1-08-35
Night Alone 8-03-38
Night and Day 5-30-33
Night and Day 7-10-46
Night and Fog (See: Nuit et Brouillard)
Night and the City 5-24-50
Night Angel, The 6-16-31
Night at a Honeymoon, A (See: Nuit de Noces, Une)
Night at Earl Carroll's, A 11-20-40
Night at the Cross Roads (See: Nuit du Carrefour, La)
Night at the Grand Hotel, A (See: Nacht im Grand Hotel, Eine)
Night at the Hotel, The (See: Nuit a l'Hotel, La)
Night at the Opera, A 12-11-35
Night at the Ritz, A 5-22-35
Night Beat 1-19-32
Night Beat 2-04-48
Night Before, The 10-31-73
Night Before Christmas, The (See: Questo Si Che E'Amore)
Night Before the Divorce, The 2-11-42
Night Bird, The 10-03-28
Night Birds 10-29-30 and 1-07-31 (Also see: Nacht Bummler)
Night Boat to Dublin 1-23-46
Night Bride, The 3-30-27
Night Club 8-14-29
Night Club, The 5-06-25
Night Club Girl 12-06-44
Night Club Lady 8-30-32
Night Club Queen 4-03-34
Night Club Scandal 12-22-37
Night Court 5-31-32
Night Creature 10-03-79
Night Creatures 5-09-62
Night Cry, The 4-07-26
Night Dance Hall (See: Bal de Nuit)
Night Digger, The 5-19-71
Night Editor 4-03-46
Night Evelyn Came Out of the Grave, The 7-26-72
Night Fighters, The 9-14-60
Night Flight 10-10-33
Night Flowers 9-05-79
Night Flyer, The 3-14-28
Night for Crime 3-10-43
Night Freight 8-17-55
Night Games (See: Noite Vazia)
Night Games (See: Nattlek)

174

Night Games 1-30-80
Night Guest (See: Nocni Host)
Night Has a Thousand Eyes, The 7-14-48
Night Hawk 4-16-24
Night Hawk, The 10-05-38
Night Heaven Fell, The 7-16-58
Night Holds Terror, The 7-13-55
Night Horsemen, The 11-04-21
Night in Bangkok, A (See: Bangkok No Yoru)
Night in Casablanca, A 4-17-46
Night in Hell, A (See: Schab Neschini Dar Djahannam)
Night in Montmartre, A 8-04-31
Night in New Orleans, A 5-06-42
Night in Paradise, A (See: Nacht im Paradies, Eine)
Night in Paradise, A 4-10-46
Night in Rome (See: Era Notte a Roma)
Night into Morning 5-23-51
Night Is My Kingdom (See: Nuit Est Mon Royaume, La)
Night Is Ours, The 2-05-30 (Also see: Nacht Gehort Uns, Die
    and Nuit Est a Nous, La)
Night Is Young, The 1-15-35
Night Key 4-21-37
Night Life 12-21-27
Night Life in Hollywood 3-08-23
Night Life in Reno 12-01-31
Night Life of New York 7-15-25
Night Life of the Gods 2-27-35
Night Mayor 11-29-32
Night Message, The 3-26-24
Night Monster 10-21-42
Night Moves 3-26-75
Night Must Fall 5-05-37
Night Must Fall 3-18-64
Night My Number Came Up, The 3-30-55
Night Nurse 7-21-31
Night of a Great Love, The (See: Nacht der Grossen Liebe)
Night of Adventure, A 6-07-44
Night of Change, A (See: Nacht der Verwandlung)
Night of Cobra Women 3-13-74
Night of Counting the Years, The 9-09-70
Night of Dark Shadows 8-11-71
Night of January 16th, The 9-10-41
Night of June 13th, The 9-20-32
Night of Love 1-26-27
Night of Love, A (See: Liebesnacht, Eine)
Night of My Love, The (See: A Noite Do Meu Bem)
Night of Mystery 6-30-37
Night of Mystery, A 4-18-28
Night of Nights, The 11-29-39
Night of Orange Fires (See: Noc Oranzovych Ohnu)
Night of Romance 1-14-25
Night of Saint-Germain Des Pres, The (See: Nuit de Saint-Germain
    Des Pres, La)
Night of San Juan, The (See: Notte Di San Juan, La)
Night of Terror 6-27-33
Night of the Blood Beast, The 12-10-58
Night of the Bride (See: Noe Novesty)
Night of the Demon 12-25-57
Night of the Dub 2-06-20
Night of the Flowers 11-29-72
Night of the Following Day, The 1-15-69
Night of the Garter 4-25-33
Night of the Generals 2-01-67
Night of the Grizzly, The 4-20-66
Night of the Hunter 7-20-55
Night of the Iguana 7-01-64
Night of the Juggler 5-14-80
Night of the Lepus 7-05-72
Night of the Living Dead 10-16-68
Night of the Mayas (See: Noche de los Mayas, La)
Night of the Party 2-13-34
Night of the Prowler, The 11-15-78
Night of the Quarter Moon 2-11-59
Night of the Scarecrow, The (See: A Noite Do Espantalho)
Night of the Seagull, The 2-04-70
Night of the Thousand Cats, The (See: Noche de los Mil Gatos, La)
Night Out, A 1-07-16
Night Over Chile, A (See: Nochi Nad Chili)
Night Parade 11-13-29
Night Passage 5-15-57
Night Paths (See: Wege In Der Nacht)
Night Patrol, The 7-14-26
Night People 3-17-54
Night Plane from Chungking 12-30-42
Night Porter, The 4-03-74
Night Raid (See: Soir de Rafle, Un)
Night Raiders 5-28-32
Night Ride 1-22-30

Night Rider 7-19-32
Night Riders, The 4-05-39
Night Riders of Montana 3-14-51
Night Runner, The 1-16-57
Night Ship, The 4-08-25
Night Song 11-12-47
Night Spot (See: Boite de Nuit)
Night Spot 3-30-38
Night Stage to Galveston 3-19-52
Night the World Exploded, The 6-19-57
Night They Raided Minsky's, The 12-04-68
Night Tide 9-06-61
Night Time in Nevada 10-27-48
Night to Remember, A 1-06-43
Night to Remember, A 7-09-58
Night Train 10-30-40
Night Train to Memphis 7-17-46
Night Train to Mundo Fine 11-23-66
Night unto Night 4-20-49
Night Visitor, The 2-24-71
Night Waitress 12-23-36
Night Walker, The 12-23-64
Night Watch 8-08-73
Night Watch, The 5-12-26
Night Watch, The 10-10-28
Night Watchman, The (See: Al-Haress)
Night Watchman, The 3-21-08
Night Watchman's Wife, The (See: Nattvaktens Hustru)
Night We Dropped a Clanger, The 9-23-59
Night We Got the Bird, The 2-22-61
Night Whispers, The 10-02-29
Night Wind 8-25-48
Night with Chandler, The (See: Nacht Mit Chandler, Die)
Night with the Emperor (See: Nacht mit dem Kaiser)
Night Without Sleep 10-01-52
Night Without Stars 4-18-51
Night Work 8-09-39
Night Workers 5-25-17
Night World 5-31-32
Nightclub Hostess (See: Entraineuse, L')
Nightcomers, The 9-08-71
Nightfall 12-05-56
Nighthawks 11-29-78
Nightingale 11-11-36
Nightingale, The 10-03-14
Nightingale Girl (See: Nachtigall Madel, Das)
Nightmare 11-11-42
Nightmare 5-16-56
Nightmare 4-22-64
Nightmare Alley 10-15-47
Nightmare in Blood 7-26-78
Nightmare in the Sun 3-17-65
Nightmares (See: Zmory or Cauchemars)
Nights and Days (See: Noci i Jutra or Noce i Dnie)
Nights of Farewell (See: Nuit des Adieux, La)
Nights of Lucretia Borgia 7-27-60
Nightshade (See: Nachtschatten)
Nightwing 7-04-79
Nihon No Seishun 5-28-69
Nihon Retto 6-15-66
Nije Bilo Uzalud 7-24-57
Nije Nego 8-16-78
Nijinsky 3-12-80
Nijushi No Hitomi 8-03-60
Nikdo Se Nebuds Smat 7-27-66
Nikki, Wild Dog of the North 6-07-61
Nikto Ne Chotel Uymirat 7-20-66
Nikudan 11-26-80
Nikutai No Gakko (See: School for Sex)
Nina de Luto, La 5-13-64
Nina, The Flower Girl 1-12-17
Nincs Ido 7-31-74
Nincsenek Veletlenek 3-15-39
Nine Days a Queen 10-07-36
Nine Days of One Year (See: Devyat Dney Odnogo Goda)
Nine Girls 3-29-44
Nine Hours to Rama 2-20-63
Nine Letters to Bertha (See: Nueve Cartas a Berta)
Nine Lives (See: Ni Liv)
Nine Lives Are Not Enough 9-03-41
Nine Lives of Fritz the Cat, The 5-22-74
Nine Months (See: Kilenc Honap)
999--Aliza the Policeman 4-26-72
Nine O'Clock Town, A 8-02-18
Nine Seconds from Heaven 6-30-22
Nine-Tenths of the Law 4-26-18
9-30-55 8-31-77
Nine to Five 12-17-80

Nineteen and Phyllis 1-07-21
1900 6-02-76
1905 7-11-56
1914 2-11-31 and 9-06-32
1918--A Man and His Conscience 7-24-57
1941 12-19-79
1984 3-14-56
Nineteen Red Roses (See: Nitten Roede Roser)
90 Degrees in the Shade 7-07-65
90 Minuten Aufenthalt 10-14-36
90 Minutes Stop (See: 90 Minuten Aufenthalt)
99 6-11-20
99 and 44/100% Dead! 6-19-74
99 River Street 9-09-53
99 Women 2-05-69
91-An Karlsson 12-04-46
92 in the Shade 8-27-75
92 Minuter Af I Gaar 5-31-78
92 Minutes of Yesterday (See: 92 Minuter Af I Gaar)
Ningen 9-11-63
Ningen Kakumei (See: Human Revolution, The)
Nini Tirabuscio 1-20-71
Ninja Bugelijo 1-25-67
Ninjutsu (See: Secret Scrolls (Part II))
Nino Es Nuestro, El 5-30-73
Nino Valiente 10-15-75
Nino y el Muro, El 9-22-65
Ninotchka 10-11-39
9th Circle, The (See: Deveti Krug)
Ninth Configuration, The 2-06-80
Ninth Guest, The 3-06-34
Ninth Heart, The 10-22-80
Niobe 4-09-15
Nippon Chinbotsu 5-22-74
Nippon No Don--Yabohen 1-18-78
Nippon No Ichiban Nagai Hi 9-13-67
Nippon O Shikaru 6-22-66
Nippon Sengoshi--Madam Onboro No Seikatsu 7-03-74
Nirjan Saikate 6-23-65
Nise Daigakusi 9-13-61
Nishant 5-26-76
Niskavuoren Naiset 11-30-38
Nissei Keiji 5-10-67
Nissuim Nosach Tel Aviv 12-26-79
Nitakayama Nobore 2-21-68
Nitra Sayan 1-15-75
Nitten Roede Roser 8-28-74 and 12-18-74
Nittioettan Karlssons Permis 3-24-48
Nitwits, The 6-26-35
Nix on Dames 11-27-29
Nizvodno Od Sunca 8-20-69
Nje Udhetimi I Veshtire 6-13-79
No Babies Wanted 6-13-28
No Blade of Grass 11-04-70
No Ceremony Without Meyer (See: Keine Feier Ohne Meier)
No Children Wanted (See: Mme. Ne Veux Pas D'Enfant)
No Control 7-06-27
No Day Without You (See: Keim Tag Ohme Dich)
No Defense 1-27-22
No Defense 7-10-29
No Deposit, No Return 1-28-76
No Down Payment 10-02-57
No Drums, No Bugles 8-11-71
No Escape 12-16-36
No Escape 8-05-53
No Exit (See: Huis Clos)
No Exit 7-11-62
No Funny Business 7-04-33 and 3-13-34
No-Good Ones, The (See: Os Cafajestes)
No Good to Die for That (See: Il Ne Faut Pas Mourir Pour Ca)
No Greater Glory 5-08-34
No Greater Love 5-17-32
No Greater Love 3-01-44
No Greater Sin 9-03-41
No Gun Man, The 4-01-25
No Hands on the Clock 12-10-41
No Hay Que Aflojarle a la Vida 8-27-75
No Highway 7-04-51
No Ho Tempo 5-16-73
No Holds Barred 12-24-52
No, Il Caso e Felicemente Fisolto 9-05-73
No Kidding 12-21-60
No Lady 5-20-31
No Leave, No Love 8-28-46
No Limit 1-21-31
No Limit 11-13-35
No Living Witness 10-11-32
No Longer Alone 10-04-78

No Love for Johnnie 2-22-61
No Man Is an Island 8-08-62
No Man of Her Own 1-03-33
No Man of Her Own 2-22-50
No Man's Daughter (See: Arvacska)
No Man's Gold 9-15-26
No Man's Land (See: Niemandsland)
No Man's Land 7-19-18
No Man's Land 6-29-27
No Man's Land 8-04-65
No Maps on My Taps 3-21-79
No Marriage Ties 8-08-33
No Mataras 12-01-43
No Men ... Alla 11-15-72
No Minor Vices 10-13-48
No, Mr. Johnson 10-20-65
No Money--No Fun 1-18-18
No Monkey Business 12-04-35
No More Credit (See: To Telefteo Psemma)
No More Easy Going (See: Mo Hoozue Wa Tsukanai)
No More Excuses 5-29-68
No More Ladies 6-26-35
No More Orchids 1-03-33
No More Time (See: No Ho Tempo)
No More Vacation for the Good Lord (See: Plus Des Vacances Pour
     Le Bon Dieu)
No More Women 1-31-24
No More Women 3-06-34
No Mother to Guide Her 2-28-24
No, My Darling Daughter 9-13-61
No, No, Nanette 1-08-30
No, No, Nanette 12-25-40
No Nukes 7-16-80
No One Is Going to Laugh (See: Nikdo Se Nebuds Smat)
No One Man 1-26-32
No Orchids for Miss Blandish 4-21-48
No Other Woman 6-20-28
No Other Woman 1-31-33
No Oyes Ladrar Los Perros? 5-28-75
No Path Through the Fire (See: Wognie Broda Nyet)
No Peace Under the Olive Trees (See: Non C'e Pace Tra Gli Ulivi)
No Pity for Women (See: Pas de Pitie Pour les Femmes)
No Place for a Lady 5-26-43
No Place for Jennifer 1-25-50
No Place to Go 12-14-27
No Place to Go 12-06-39
No Place to Hide 10-10-56
No Pockets in a Shroud (See: Linceul N'A Pas De Poches, Un)
No Problem! (See: Pas De Probleme!)
No Questions Asked 6-13-51
No Ransom 2-12-35
No Resting Place 8-01-51
No Return (See: Dosango)
No Road Back (See: Ingen Vag Tillbaka)
No Road Back 2-13-57
No Room at the Inn 11-10-48
No Room for the Groom 5-07-52
No Roses for OSS 117 (See: Pas De Roses Pour OSS 117)
No Sad Songs for Me 4-12-50
No Shooting Time for Foxes (See: Schonzeit Fuer Fuechse)
No Somos de Piedra 7-31-67
No Stars in the Jungle 7-19-67
No Te Ofendas, Beatriz 7-08-53
No Tears for Ananse 10-23-68
No, the Case Is Happily Resolved (See: No, Il Caso e Felicemente
     Fisolto)
No Time for Comedy 9-11-40
No Time for Flowers 12-03-52
No Time for Love 11-10-43
No Time for Sergeants 5-07-58
No Time for Tears 8-14-57
No Time to Be Young 8-14-57
No Time to Die 5-07-58
No Time to Marry 2-23-38
No Trace 9-20-50
No Trees in the Street 3-11-59
No Trespassing (See: Pe Aici Nu Se Trece)
No Trespassing 5-26-22
No Vietnamese Ever Called Me Nigger 10-02-68
No Villains 11-04-21
No Way Back 6-30-54 (Also see: Weg Ohne Umkehr)
No Way Back 6-16-76
No Way Out 8-02-50
No Way Out 11-13-63
No Way to Treat a Lady 3-13-68
Noah's Ark (See: Arche de Noe, L')
Noah's Ark 11-07-28
Nob Hill 5-30-45

Nobi 4-19-61
Nobleman's Dogs, The 11-27-09
Nobody 7-29-21
Nobody Home 8-29-19
Nobody Lives Forever 9-25-46
Nobody Runs Forever 8-28-68
Nobody Wants to Die (See: Nikto Ne Chotel Uymirat)
Nobody Waved Goodbye 8-19-64
Nobody's Baby 5-26-37
Nobody's Boy (See: Sans Famille)
Nobody's Bride 4-05-23
Nobody's Children 12-11-40
Nobody's Fool 10-28-21
Nobody's Fool 6-10-36
Nobody's Kid 5-06-21
Nobody's Money 2-01-23
Nobody's Perfect 1-10-68
Nobody's Widow 1-12-27
Nobody's Wife 3-08-18
Noc Listopadowa 5-02-33
Noc Novesty 9-06-67
Noc Oranzovych Ohnu 9-24-75
Noce I Dnie 11-12-75
Noces de Porcelaine, Les 6-18-75
Noces de Sable, Les (See: Daughter of the Sands)
Noces Rouges, Les 5-23-73
Noces Venetiennes, Les 8-19-59
Noche de Bodas 4-29-42
Noche de Curas 7-19-78
Noche de los Mayas, La 11-01-39
Noche de los Mil Gatos, La 10-25-72
Noche Del Sabado, La 5-23-51
Noche Terrible, La 7-05-67
Noches de Gloria 3-09-38
Nochi Nad Chili 8-03-77
Noci i Jutra 8-12-59
Nocni Host 8-09-61
Nocturnal Uproar (See: Tapage Nocturne)
Nocturne 10-16-46
Nocturno 9-06-72
Noe Novesty 9-06-67
Noedebo Praestegaard 11-27-74
Noedebo Vicarage (See: Noedebo Praestegaard)
Noeglehullet 10-16-74
Noeglen Til Paradis 9-30-70
Nogiku No Gotoki Kimi Nariki 5-25-66
Noi Gio 7-27-66
Noire De ..., La 5-11-66
Noise in Newboro, A 4-19-23
Noisy Neighbors 7-24-29
Noite Vazia 5-19-65
Noix de Coco 3-22-29
Nojo Aos Caes 12-09-70
Nokaut 9-01-71
Nokea Ja Kultaa 5-08-46
Nomads of the North 10-01-20
Nomugi Pass (See: Ah! Nomugi Toge)
Non C'è Pace Tra Gli Ulivi 1-10-51
Non Contate Su Di Noi 8-23-78
Non Coupable 10-22-47
Non-Matrimonial Story, A (See: Dulscy)
Non-Scheduled Train, A 11-25-59
Non Scherzare Con le Donne 7-24-57
Non-Stop Flight 7-07-26
Non-Stop New York 9-29-37
Non Ti Conosco Piu 2-26-36
Nona, La 5-23-79
None but the Brave 9-05-28
None but the Brave 2-10-65
None but the Lonely Heart 10-04-44
None Shall Escape 4-12-44
Nonexistent Knight, The (See: Cavaliere Inesistente, Il)
Nonna Sabella, La 9-11-57
Noodle (See: Csipetke)
Noon (See: Podne)
Noose 10-06-48
Noose, The 3-21-28
Noose, The (See: I'd Give My Life)
Noose for a Gunman 5-18-60
Noose Hangs High, The 4-07-48
Nor the Moon by Night 7-30-58
Nora Inu 8-19-59
Nora Prentiss 2-05-47
Nora, the Contraband's Daughter 2-19-10
Norah O'Neale 10-30-34
Nordsee Ist Mordsee 6-16-76

Norma Rae 2-28-79
Normal Life (See: Vie Normale, La)
Normal Young Man (See: Giovane Normale, Il)
Norman ... Is That You? 9-29-76
Normandie Nieman 4-20-60
Normannerne 4-07-76
Normans, The (See: Normannerne)
Norng Mia 5-24-78
Noroit 9-21-77
Norseman, The 7-05-78
North Avenue Irregulars, The 1-17-79
North by Northwest 7-01-59
North China Commune 3-12-80
North Dallas Forty 7-25-79
North from Lone Star 6-25-41
North Hotel (See: Hotel du Nord)
North of Hudson Bay 3-12-24
North of Nevada 4-02-24
North of Nome 1-20-37
North of Shanghai 3-08-39
North of the Great Divide 11-22-50
North of the Rio Grande 5-19-22
North of the Yukon 6-14-39
North of 36 12-10-24
North Sea Is Dead Sea (See: Nordsee Ist Mordsee)
North Sea Patrol 1-03-40
North Star 3-31-26
North Star, The 10-13-43
North to Alaska 11-09-60
North to the Klondike 1-21-42
North West Frontier 10-14-59
North Wind's Malice 10-22-20
Northern Courier (See: Correo Del Norte, El)
Northern Frontier 2-27-35
Northern Lights 11-15-78
Northern Patrol 7-15-53
Northern Pursuit 10-20-43
Northern Safari 6-05-68
Northwest Mounted Police 10-23-40
Northwest Outpost 5-14-47
Northwest Passage 2-14-40
Northwest Rangers 10-28-42
Northwest Stampede 6-30-48
Northwest Territory 2-13-52
Northwest Wind (See: Noroit)
Norwood 4-29-70
Nos Maitres les Domestiques 11-26-30
Nosferatu: Phantom der Nacht 1-24-79
Nosferatu the Vampire 12-25-29
Nosferatu: The Vampire (See: Nosferatu: Phantom der Nacht)
Nosotros Dos 10-02-57
Nosotros Los Muchachos 12-25-40
Nostra Signora Dei Turchi 9-11-68
Not a Drum Was Heard 3-19-24
Not a Word to Morgenstein (See: Af Mila le Morgenstein)
Not as a Stranger 6-15-55
Not as Wicked as All That ... (See: Pas Si Mechant Que Ca ...)
Not Built for Runnin' 10-29-24
Not Damaged 6-11-30
Not Delivered (See: Echec au Porteur)
Not Dumb, the Bird (See: Pas Folle la Guepe)
Not Everything That Flies Is a Bird 3-21-79 (Also see: Nicht
    Alles Was Fliegt Ist Ein Vogel)
Not for Children (See: Barnfoerbjudet)
Not for Publication 7-13-27
Not Guilty (See: Non Coupable)
Not Guilty 11-26-15
Not Guilty 8-05-21
Not Just Another Woman 1-30-74
Not Much on the Mouth (See: Pas Sur la Bouche)
Not My Sister 5-12-16
Not of This Earth 3-27-57
Not Quite a Lady 9-05-28
Not Quite Decent 5-08-29
Not So Bad As It Seemed 12-03-10
Not So Dumb 2-12-30
Not So Long Ago 7-29-25
Not Tonight Henry 1-18-61
Not Wanted 6-22-49
Not Wanted on Voyage 2-23-38
Not Wanted on Voyage 11-13-57
Not with My Wife, You Don't 9-21-66
Notebooks of Major Thompson (See: Carnets du Major Thompson, Les)
Nothing but a Man 9-09-64
Nothing but Broken Dishes (See: Kirik Canaklar)
Nothing But Lies (See: Rien Que Des Mensonges)
Nothing but Lies 9-03-20
Nothing but the Best 3-18-64

Nothing but the Truth (See: Kun Sanheden or Rien Que la Verite)
Nothing but the Truth 1-23-20
Nothing but the Truth 4-24-29
Nothing but the Truth 7-30-41
Nothing but Trouble 11-29-44
Nothing but Trouble with Love (See: Nichts Als Aerger Mit der Liebe)
Nothing by Chance 1-29-75
Nothing Ever Happens (See: Nunca Pasa Nada)
Nothing Personal 3-12-80
Nothing Sacred 12-01-37
Nothing to Report (See: R.A.S.)
Nothing to Wear 1-16-29
Notoriety 10-20-22
Notorious 7-24-46
Notorious Affair, A 4-30-30
Notorious but Nice 3-06-34
Notorious Gentleman, A 2-20-35
Notorious Lady, The 4-13-27
Notorious Landlady, The 6-27-62
Notorious Lone Wolf, The 3-13-46
Notorious Miss Lisle, The 8-20-20
Notorious Mrs. Sands, The 5-14-20
Notre-Dame de Paris 1-16-57
Notte, La 3-29-61
Notte Brava, La 1-27-60
Notte Che Evelyn Usca Dalla Tomba, La (See: Night Evelyn Came Out of the Grave, The)
Notte di San Juan, La 11-17-71
Notti Bianche 9-25-57
Nouba (See: Nouba Des Femmes du Mont Chenoua, La)
Nouba Des Femmes du Mont Chenoua, La 9-19-79
Nous Etions Un Seul Homme 12-24-80
Nous Irons a Monte Carlo 2-27-52
Nous Irons a Paris 3-29-50
Nous Irons Tous au Paradis 11-23-77
Nous Maigrirons Ensemble 9-05-79
Nous N'irons Plus au Bois 4-16-69
Nous Ne Viellirons Pas Ensemble 5-10-72
Nous Sommes des Juifs Arabes En Israel 11-23-77
Nous Sommes Tous les Assassins 5-28-52
Nouveau Journal d'une Femme en Blanc 4-20-66
Nouveau Testament 3-04-36
Nouveau Venu, Le 8-22-79
Nouveaux Aristocrats, Les 1-17-62
Novel of a Poor Young Man, The (See: Novela de un Joven Pobre, La)
Novela de un Joven Pobre 5-27-42
Novela de un Joven Pobre, La 5-08-68
November 1828 7-25-79
November Night (See: Noc Listopadowa)
Novia de Primavera, La 1-13-43
Novia En Apuros, Una 4-29-42
Novice, The (See: Suora Giovane, La)
Novices, Les 11-18-70
Novinar 8-29-79
Novios Para las Muchachas 2-26-41
Now and Forever 10-16-34
Now and Forever 2-29-56
Now Barabbas Was a Robber 6-01-49
Now I'll Tell 5-29-34
Now or Never 8-15-79
Now That April's Here 7-09-58
Now, Voyager 8-19-42
Now We'll Be Happy (See: Ahora Seremos Felices)
Now We're in the Air 12-14-27
Now Where Did the 7th Company Get To? (See: Mais Ou Est Donc Passe la 7eme Compagnie?)
Now You See Him, Now You Don't 7-05-72
Nowhere to Go 12-03-58
Noz W Wodzie 9-12-62
'Nth Commandment 4-12-23
Nu Borjar Livet 9-15-48
Nu Comme un Ver 6-06-33
Nu Gaar Den Paa Dagmar 11-01-72
Nuage Entre les Dents, Un 5-15-74
Nuchia de Piatra 5-16-73
Nude Bomb, The 5-07-80
Nude Childhood (See: Enfance Nue, L')
Nude General, The (See: Hadaka No Taisho)
Nude Odyssey (See: Odissea Nuda)
Nude Restaurant, The 11-22-67
Nudist Paradise 2-25-59
Nudity (See: Nagota)
Nuernberger Prozess, Der 12-10-58
Nues vom Raeuber Hotzenplotz 5-23-79
Nuestra Cosa (See: Our Latin Thing)
Nuestros Odiosos Maridos 5-30-62

Nueve Cartas a Berta 8-02-67
Nuevo Amanecer, Un 1-06-43
Nuevos, Los 11-28-73
Nuevos Espanoles, Los 1-15-75
Nugel Bujan 7-29-64
Nugget Nell 8-01-19
Nuisance, The 5-30-33
Nuit a l'Hotel, La 5-31-32
Nuit Americaine, La 5-23-73
Nuit d'Or 12-15-76
Nuit de Noces, Une 6-28-50
Nuit de Saint-Germain des Pres, La 5-18-77
Nuit des Adieux, La 11-30-66
Nuit des Bulgares, La 4-21-71
Nuit des Espions, La 8-19-59
Nuit du Carrefour, La 5-10-32
Nuit Est a Nous, La 3-18-31
Nuit Est Mon Royaume, La 9-19-51
Nuit et Brouillard 7-11-56
Nuit Infidele, La 10-02-68
Nuit Moscovites 12-11-34
Nuit Tous les Chats Sont Gris, La 11-16-77
No. 96 5-22-74
Number One 8-06-69
Number One 6-13-73
No. 111 11-17-37
Number 111 4-06-38
Number, Please 7-14-31
Number 17 2-04-21
Number Seventeen 8-02-32
Number Two (See: Numero Deux)
Numbered Men 6-11-30
Numero Deux 10-08-75
Nun, The (See: Religieuse, La)
Nun and the Sergeant, The 7-11-62
Nun at the Crossroads, A 3-25-70
Nunca Es Tarde 10-26-77
Nunca Pasa Nada 9-04-63
Nuns of Sant' Arcangelo, The (See: Monache di Sant'Archangelo, Le)
Nun's Story, The 5-06-59
Nunzio 4-26-78
Nuoruns Sumussa 7-24-46
Nuovi Angeli, I 2-28-62
Nur Am Rhein 9-29-31
Nur Du 1-12-32
Nuremberg 12-13-61
Nuremberg Trial, The (See: Nuernberger Prozess, Der)
Nuremberg Trials, The 5-28-47
Nurse Edith Cavell 8-23-39
Nurse from Brooklyn, The 4-13-38
Nurse Marjorie 5-28-20
Nurse on Wheels 2-05-64
Nurses, The (See: Dadathes, I)
Nurse's Secret, The 6-11-41
Nursing a Viper 11-13-09
Nut, The 3-11-21
Nut Farm, The 4-17-35
Nutcracker Fantasy 8-08-79
Nutty Professor, The 5-22-63
Nyar a Hegyen 11-15-67 and 1-31-68
Nybyggarna 3-22-72
Nyckeln Och Ringen 12-10-47
Nymphettes, Les 2-22-61
Nyt Legetoej 5-18-77

O Alienista 5-27-70
O Amuleto de Ogum 5-28-75
O Anthropos Me To Garyfallo 12-24-80
O Asymvivastos 10-31-79
O Bandido da Luz Vermelha 3-26-69
O Beautiful Istanbul 8-02-67
O Beijo 8-04-65
O Bravo Guerreiro 6-25-69
O Cangaceiros 4-29-53
O Casamento 5-19-76
O Caso Claudia 10-17-79
O Caso Dos Irmaos Naves 7-19-67
O Cerco 5-06-70
O Cidade Do Nome De Deus 10-29-69
O Coronele e Lobisomem 5-30-79

O Corpo Ardente 7-13-66
O Desafio 5-11-66
O Desterrado 12-14-49
O Destino em Apuros 1-20-54
08/15 12-15-54
08/15 at Home (See: 08/15 in der Heimat)
08/15 in der Heimat 4-18-56
08/15--Part II (See: 08/15--Zweiter Teil)
08/15--Zweiter Teil 10-05-55
O Estranho Mundo de Ze do Caixao 5-14-69
O Femeie Pentru Un Anotimp 7-23-69
O Fovos 7-06-66
O Homem Que Comprou O Mundo 7-09-69
O Impossivel Acontece 4-22-70
O.K. 7-08-70
O.K. Nero (See: O.K. Nerone)
O.K. Nerone 3-26-52
O.K. Patron 3-06-74
O Kakos Dromos 10-28-36
O Lucky Man! 4-18-73
O, Madda 5-18-77
O Megalexandros 9-17-80
O Moravske Zemi 8-16-78
O, My Darling Clementine 12-01-43
O Necem Jinem 10-30-63
O Neos Parthenonas 11-05-75
O Padre e a Moca 7-06-66
O Pagador de Promess 5-30-62
O Palacio Dos Anjos 5-13-70
O Passado e o Presente 10-15-80
O Profeta da Fome 7-15-70
O Psarovannos 10-26-66
O Quarto 4-30-69
O Recado 10-27-71
O.S.S. 5-15-46
O Salto 9-06-67
O Slavnosti a Hostech 8-10-66
O Sobrado 9-11-57
O Sole Mio 2-08-50
O Tesouro de Zapata 3-26-69
O Thanatos Tou Alexandrou 11-23-66
O Thekatos Tritos 11-15-67
O Thiassos 6-04-75
O.U. West 7-29-25
O Vecoch Nadprirozonych 7-29-59
O, What a Beard 9-25-09
O Zestos Minas Augoustos 11-09-66
Oakdale Affair, The 11-07-19
Oase 4-20-55
Oasis (See: Oase or Oaza)
Oath, The 3-11-21
Oath and the Man, The 10-01-10
Oath of a Viking, The 6-18-15
Oath of Obedience (See: Bushido)
Oathbound 8-04-22
Oaths (See: Serments)
Oaza 8-16-72
Obchod Na Korze 5-26-65
Obedience to Her Mother 9-04-08
Obey the Law 12-29-26
Obey the Law 3-14-33
Obey Your Husband 8-15-28
Objasnenie w Lubwi 2-07-79
Object--Matrimony 3-20-29
Objectif 500 Millions 8-03-66
Objective, Burma! 1-31-45
Objective 500 Million (See: Objectif 500 Millions)
Obliging Young Lady 11-05-41
Oblong Box, The 6-11-69
Obratinaya Sviaz 9-06-78
Obsessed 8-29-51
Obsessed of Catule, The (See: Vereda da Salvacao)
Obsessed Ones, The (See: Megszallottak)
Obsession (See: Ossessione or Junoon)
Obsession 8-17-49
Obsession 12-15-54
Obsession 7-07-76
Obsessions 6-04-69
Obzalovany 7-29-64
Ocalenie 5-23-73
Ocalic Miasto 8-03-77
Ocana, an Intermittent Portrait (See: Ocana, Retrat Intermitent)
Ocana, Retrat Intermitent 5-24-78
Occasional Work of a Slave (See: Gelegenhietsarbeit Einer
    Sklavin)
Occasionally Yours 10-22-20
Occhio Selvaggio, L' 7-26-67
Occupation in 26 Pictures (See: Okupacija U 26 Slika)

Occupe-Toi d'Amelie 12-20-32
Occupe-Toi d'Amelie 10-19-49
Oceano 8-04-71
Ocean's Eleven 8-10-60
Ochazuke No Aji (See: Flavor of Green Tea over Rice, The)
Octagon, The 8-13-80
October Man, The 9-10-47
October Revolution, The (See: Revolution D'Octobre)
Octopus, The 7-23-15
Odd Angry Shot, The 4-25-79
Odd Couple, The 5-01-68
Odd Job, The 11-01-78
Odd Man Out 2-12-47
Odd Mr. Victor, The (See: Etrange Monsieur Victor, L')
Odd Number (See: Cifra Impar)
Odd Pair of Limbs 5-23-08
Oddballs, The (See: Czudaki)
Odds Against Tomorrow 10-07-59
Odds On 10-17-28
Ode to Billy Joe 6-09-76
Odemarksprasten 1-01-47
Oder Keine, Die 10-18-32
Odessa File, The 10-08-74
Odette 3-21-28
Odette 6-14-50
Odio a Mi Cuerpo 6-05-74
Odisea de los Andes, La 10-27-76
Odissea Nuda 5-10-61
Odongo 7-11-56
Odwiedziny Prezydenta 9-13-61
Odyssey 2-16-77
Odyssey of the North 9-19-14
Oedipus Rex 1-02-57
Oedipus Rex (See: Edipo Re)
Oedipus the King 7-03-68
Oeil du Maitre, L' 4-23-80
Oeil du Malin, L' 3-28-62
Oeil du Monocle, L' 11-28-62
Oeil Pour Oeil 9-25-57
Oejeblikket 10-15-80
Oelprinz, Der 11-10-65
O'er Crag and Torrent 4-09-10
Oese, Die 2-19-64
Oeuf, L' 4-26-72
Oeufs Brouilles, Les 4-07-76
Oeufs de l'Autruche, Les 10-23-57
Of Death and Deads (See: Des Morts)
Of Gods and the Dead (See: Os Deuses e Os Mortos)
Of Human Bondage 7-03-34
Of Human Bondage 7-03-46
Of Human Bondage 7-01-64
Of Human Hearts 2-09-38
Of Love and Desire 8-28-63
Of Love and Lust 11-30-60
Of Men and Money (See: I-Ro-Ha-Ni-Ho-He-To)
Of Men and Music 11-29-50
Of Mice and Men 1-03-40
Of Stars and Men 8-30-61
Of These Thousand Pleasures (See: Vaghe Stelle Dell'Orsa)
Off Bedside Limits (See: Maa Vaere En Sengekant, Der)
Off Limits 2-04-53
Off Season (See: Fuori Stagione)
Off the Edge 3-16-77
Off the Highway 9-23-25
Off the Path of Virtue (See: Kleine Seitensprung, Der)
Off the Record 2-22-39
Off the Wall 4-06-77
Off to the Races 2-03-37
Offbeat 3-01-61
Offender, The 11-12-24
Offense, The 5-16-73
Offering, The 12-07-66
Office Girl 6-28-32
Office Manager, The (See: Herr Buerovorsteher, Der)
Office Party, The (See: Julefrokosten)
Office Picnic, The 8-21-74
Office Scandal, The 7-24-29
Office Wife, The 10-01-30
Officer and the Lady, The 7-16-41
Officer Jim 6-19-14
Officer O'Brien 2-26-30
Officer 666 12-18-14
Officer 666 11-05-20
Officer 13 1-31-33
Officier de Police Sans Importance, Un 5-02-73
Offshore Pirate 3-04-21
Oficio de Pinieblas 10-29-80
O'Garry of the Mounted 3-13-15

Og Sa er der Bal Bagefter 12-30-70
Oggetti Smarriti 5-14-80
Oggi, Domani e Dopodomani 3-30-66
Ogheya Ala el Mamar 8-09-72
Oginsaga 4-18-79
Ogniomistrez Kalen (See: Artillery Sergeant Kalen)
Ogon No Paatonaa 12-26-79
Ogro 9-19-79
O.H.M.S. 2-03-37
O. Henry's Full House 8-20-52
O'Henry's Stories 3-23-17
Oh, America 11-05-75
Oh Baby 8-11-26
Oh, Boy! 6-13-19
Oh Dad, Poor Dad, Mama's Hung You in the Closet and I'm Feeling
    So Sad 2-15-67
Oh Daddy! 4-03-35
Oh, Doctor 10-05-17
Oh, Doctor! 2-25-25
Oh Doctor 6-23-37
Oh Dolci Baci e Languide Carezze 2-04-70
Oh, For a Man 12-03-30
Oh, God 10-05-77
Oh, God! Book II 10-01-80
Oh Heavenly Dog 7-16-80
Oh, Johnny! 1-25-19
Oh Johnny, How You Can Love 2-14-40
Oh Jonathan Oh Jonathan 5-30-73
Oh Kay 8-29-28
Oh, Lady, Lady! 12-24-20
Oh, Men! Oh, Women! 2-20-57
Oh, Mr. Porter! 10-20-37
Oh, Old Student Happiness (See: Alte Burscherherlichkeit)
Oh, Pain, Little Pain, Pain (See: Ay, Pena, Penita, Pena)
Oh Pop! 7-06-17
Oh Rosalinda 11-30-55
Oh! Que Mambo 6-10-59
Oh, Sun (See: Soleil O)
Oh, Susanna 3-24-37
Oh! Susanna 3-14-51
Oh! That Wife of Mine! (See: Ah! Afti I Guineka Mou)
Oh the Days (See: Alyam Alyam)
Oh, To Be on the Band Wagon (See: Man Sku Vaere Noget Ved
    Musikken)
Oh, Uncle 9-04-09
Oh! What a Lovely War 4-16-69
Oh, What a Night 12-01-26
Oh, What a Night 9-06-44
Oh! What a Nurse 2-24-26
Oh, What Lungs! 8-22-08
Oh Yeah! 12-25-29
Oh, You Beautiful Doll 9-21-49
Oh, You Doggie 1-08-10
Oh, You Skeleton 10-29-10
Oh, You Women! 6-20-19
Ohlednuti 10-01-69
Ohne Datum 7-11-62
Oil for the Lamps of China 6-12-35
Oil Girls, The (See: Petroleuses, Les)
Oil Prince, The (See: Oelprinz, Der)
Oily Maniac 10-20-76
Oily Scoundrel, An 5-05-16
Oiseau de Paradis, L' 11-14-62
Oiseau Rare, L' 9-05-73
Oiseau Rare, Un 6-12-35
Oiseaux Vont Mourir Au Peru, Les 7-24-68
Ojciec Krolowej 10-01-80
Ojo de la Cerradura, El (See: Eavesdropper, The)
Ojos Mas Lindosdel Mundo, Los 9-08-43
Ojos Tapatios 4-19-61
Ojos Vendados, Los 5-31-78
Ok Ketten 11-16-77
Oka Oorie Katha 5-31-78
Okasan 1-26-55
Okasareta Byakui 7-14-71
Okay America 9-13-32
Okay Bill 2-24-71
Okay for Sound 5-12-37
Okinawa 2-27-52
Oklahoma 10-12-55
Oklahoma Annie 4-09-52
Oklahoma Badlands 3-03-48
Oklahoma Crude 6-06-73
Oklahoma Frontier 12-06-39
Oklahoma Jim 12-29-31
Oklahoma Kid, The 3-15-39
Oklahoma Sheriff, The 7-16-30
Oklahoma Territory 2-10-60

Oklahoma Terror 9-06-39
Oklahoma Woman 7-04-56
Oklahoman, The 5-01-57
Okraina 5-16-33
Oksigen 8-12-70
Oktoberi Vasarnap 2-27-80
Okupacija U 26 Slika 8-09-78
Ola & Julia 9-13-67
Old Acquaintance 11-03-43
Old Actor, The 7-25-08
Old Age Handicap 5-23-28
Old and New 5-14-30
Old Barn Dance 1-12-38
Old Bill 3-28-28
Old Bill and Son 12-25-40
Old Bill Through the Ages 4-16-24
Old Boyfriends 3-21-79
Old Chaps, The (See: Vieux de la Vieille, Les)
Old Chisholm Trail 1-20-43
Old Clock at Roenneberga, The (See: Klockan Pa Ronneberga)
Old Clothes 11-11-25
Old Code 12-05-28
Old Comedy, The (See: Staromodnaia Komedia)
Old Corral, The 8-04-37
Old Country Where Rimbaud Died, The (See: Vieux Pays Ou Rimbaud)
    Est Mort, Le)
Old Curiosity Shop, The 1-01-35 and 12-25-35
Old Dad 5-27-21
Old Dark House, The 11-01-32
Old Dark House, The 10-23-63
Old Dracula 11-12-75
Old English 8-27-30
Old Fashioned Boy 11-05-20
Old-Fashioned Girl, An 12-08-48
Old-Fashioned Way, The 7-17-34
Old Fashioned Woman 1-01-75
Old Fashioned Young Man, An 4-13-17
Old Folks at Home, The 10-06-16
Old Fritz, The (See: Alte Fritz, Der)
Old Frontier 8-09-50
Old Hartwell's Cub 5-24-18
Old Heidelberg 10-08-15
Old Home Week 5-27-25
Old Homestead, The 2-11-16
Old Homestead, The 10-13-22
Old Homestead, The 10-09-35
Old Homestead, The 8-26-42
Old House, The 12-14-77
Old Hutch 12-09-36
Old Ironsides 12-08-26
Old Jar Craftsman, The (See: Dok Jinnung Nurguni)
Old Lady, The (See: Vecchia Signora, La)
Old Lady 31 5-28-20
Old Longshoreman, The 11-26-10
Old Lord of Ventor, The 10-30-09
Old Los Angeles 4-07-48
Old Louisiana 7-13-38
Old Loves and New 4-21-26
Old Maid 8-20-39
Old Maid, The (See: Vieille Fille, La)
Old Maid's Baby, The 2-14-19
Old Maid's Parrot 8-29-08
Old Man, The 1-19-32
Old Man and the Boy, The (See: Vieil Homme et l'Enfant, Le)
Old Man and the Sea, The 5-21-58
Old Man Rhythm 9-25-35
Old Memory, The (See: Vieja Memoria, La)
Old Mother Riley 6-25-52
Old Nest, The 7-01-21
Old Oklahoma Plains 8-20-52
Old Overland Trail 2-25-53
Old Rifle, The (See: Vieux Fusil, Le)
Old San Francisco 6-29-27
Old Scoundrel, The (See: A Ven Gazember)
Old Shatterhand 7-22-64
Old Shoes 4-08-25
Old Skinflint, The (See: Viejo Hucha, El)
Old Soak, The 10-20-26
Old Soldiers Never Die 3-18-31
Old Song, The (See: Alte Lied, Das)
Old Sweetheart of Mine 5-30-23
Old Swimmin' Hole 2-25-21
Old Swimming Hole, The 10-01-10
Old Swimming Hole, The 1-08-41
Old Titans Are Still Here (See: Leva de Gamla Gudar, An)
Old West, The 1-09-52
Old Wives for New 5-24-18
Old Woman, An (See: Wai Tok Kra)

Old Wyoming Trail 11-24-37
Old Yeller 11-20-57
Old Young People, The 4-11-62
Oldas es Kotes 4-15-64
Oldest Law, The 5-17-18
Oldest Profession in the World (See: Plus Vieux Metier du Monde,
    Le)
Ole Brandis' Eyes 10-02-14
Ole Dole Doff 7-03-68
Ole Kreivitar, En 5-08-46
Olimpia 10-22-30
Olimpia Agli Amici 10-28-70
Olimpia To Her Friends (See: Olimpia Agli Amici)
Olimpiada 40 7-30-80
Olive Trees of Justice, The (See: Oliviers de la Justice, Les)
Oliver 10-02-68
Oliver Twist 12-15-16
Oliver Twist 11-10-22
Oliver Twist 4-18-33
Oliver Twist 6-30-48
Oliver Twist, Jr. 5-06-21
Oliver's Story 12-20-78
Olivia 5-16-51
Oliviers de la Justice, Les 5-16-62
Olla-Podrida 4-18-08
Olly, Olly, Oxen Free 8-16-78
Olovna Brigada 8-13-80
Olsen-Banden Deruda 10-19-77
Olsen-Banden Gaar Amok 10-24-73
Olsen-Banden Gaar I Krig 11-22-78
Olsen-Banden I Jylland 10-13-71
Olsen-Banden Overgiver Sig Aldrig 12-26-79
Olsen-Banden Paa Spanden 10-15-69
Olsen-Banden Paa Sporet 10-01-75
Olsen-Banden Ser Roedt 10-13-76
Olsen Bandens Sidste Bedrifter 10-23-74
Olsen-Bandens Store Kup 10-18-72
Olsen Gang Goes to War, The (See: Olsen-Banden Gaar I Krig)
Olsen Gang in a Fix, The (See: Olsen-Banden Paa Spanden)
Olsen Gang in Jutland, The (See: Olsen-Banden I Jylland)
Olsen Gang Never Surrenders, The (See: Olsen-Banden Overgiver
    Sig Aldrig)
Olsen Gang on the Track, The (See: Olsen-Banden Paa Sporet)
Olsen Gang Outta Sight, The (See: Olsen-Banden Deruda)
Olsen Gang Runs Amok, The (See: Olsen-Banden Gaar Amok)
Olsen Gang Sees Red, The (See: Olsen-Banden Ser Roedt)
Olsen Gang's Big Score, The (See: Olsen-Bandens Store Kup)
Olsen's Night Out 1-09-34
Oltre Il Bene e Il Male 10-12-77
Olvidados, Los 5-16-51
Olyan Mint Otthon 5-24-78
Olympia 11-26-30
Olympia-Olympia 7-12-72
Olympiad I Vitt 5-12-48
Olympic Elk, The 1-09-52
Olympic Games in White (See: Olympiad I Vitt)
Olympic Hero, The 9-26-28
Olympic Winter Games at Innsbruck (See: Olympische Winterspiele
    in Innsbruck)
Olympics 40 (See: Olimpiada 40)
Olympics in Mexico 7-22-70
Olympische Winterspiele in Innsbruck 7-08-64
Om Kjaerligheten Synger De 1-08-47
Om 7 Flickor 1-30-74
Omaha Trail, The 9-16-42
O'Malley of the Mounted 2-11-21
O'Malley of the Mounted 4-08-36
O'Malley Rides Alone 2-05-30
Omar Gatlato 3-18-77 and 8-03-77
Omar Khayyam 8-07-57
Omar the Tent Maker 1-25-23
Ombre des Chatreaux, L' 12-01-76
Ombre d'une Chance, L' 1-30-74
Ombre et Lumiere 7-11-51
Ombrellone, L' 3-30-66
Ombres et Mirages 8-09-67
Ombres Fuyantes 7-12-32
Omega Man, The 8-04-71
Omen, The 6-09-76
Omicron 9-11-63
Ominous House, The (See: Suria Dighal Bari)
Omnia Vincit Amor 10-28-70
Omniscient, The (See: Sarvasakshi)
Omoo-Omoo 6-22-49
On 5-25-66
On a Clear Day You Can See Forever 6-17-70
On a Nice Summer Day (See: Par un Beau Matin D'Ete)
On a Racket 1-22-10

On a Retrouve la 7e Compagnie 12-24-75
On a Small Island (See: Na Malenkom Ostrove)
On a Vole la Cuisse de Jupiter 2-27-80
On a Vole la Joconde 6-08-66
On a Vole un Homme 4-03-34
On Again--Off Again 8-11-37
On Aime Qu'une Fois 6-28-50
On an Empty Balcony (See: En El Balcon Vacio)
On an Island with You 4-28-48
On Another Man's Pass 8-28-09
On Any Sunday 7-21-71
On Approval 9-17-30
On Approval 3-22-44
On Aura Tout Vu 7-21-76
On Borrowed Time 7-05-39
On Both Sides of Roll Way (See: Beiderseits Der Rollbahn)
On Company Business 3-12-80
On Dangerous Ground 12-29-16
On Dangerous Ground 12-05-51
On Dangerous Paths 7-30-15
On Demande Compagnon 6-06-33
On Desert Sands 1-15-15
On Dress Parade 11-01-39
On Efface Tout! 8-23-78
On Est Toujours Trop Bon Avec les Femmes 7-07-71
On Fortune's Wheel 3-28-13
On Friday at Eleven 10-25-61
On Her Doorsteps 10-22-10
On Her Majesty's Secret Service 12-17-69
On Her Wedding Night 7-30-15
On His Own 9-27-39
On His Wedding Day 3-28-13
On Moonlight Bay 7-11-51
On N'Arrete Pas le Printemps 9-22-71
On N'Enterre Pas le Dimanche 5-11-60
On N'Est Pas Serieux Quand On a 17 Ans 11-20-74
On Ne Meurt Pas Comme Ca 7-24-46
On Ne Roule Pas Antoinette 6-10-36
On Our Selection 8-02-32
On Paper Planes (See: Na Avionima Od Papira)
On Peut le Dire Sans Se Facher 1-18-78
On Probation 5-27-25
On Record 4-06-17
On S'Est Trompe D'Histoire D'Amour 5-15-74
On Stage Everybody 7-11-45
On Such a Night 8-18-37
On the Air 2-13-34
On the Avenue 2-10-37
On the Bank of the River 1-15-10
On the Battle Line 10-31-14
On the Beach 12-02-59
On the Beat 12-19-62
On the Border 11-27-09
On the Border 2-05-30
On the Bowery 9-12-56
On the Comet (See: Na Komete)
On the Divide 1-09-29 and 2-13-29
On the Double 5-17-61
On the Fertile Land (See: Bereketli Topraklar Uzerinde)
On the Fiddle 10-18-61
On the Great White Trail 8-10-38
On the High Seas 10-06-22
On the Island (See: Auf Der Insel)
On the Isle of Samoa 7-26-50
On the Jump 11-08-18
On the Lam (See: Cavale, La)
On the Level 7-09-30
On the Loose 7-25-51
On the Move (See: Abfahrer, Die or Utkozben)
On the Nickel 3-26-80
On the Night of the Fire 11-22-39
On the Old Spanish Trail 10-22-47
On the Other Side of the Street 11-13-29
On the Point of Death (See: In Punto Di Morte)
On the Quiet 8-30-18
On the Reef 1-22-10
On the Repperbahn At Half Past Midnight (See: Auf der Repperbahn
    Nachts Um Halb Eins)
On the Riviera 4-25-51
On the Road to Cairo (See: Rumbo al Cairo)
On the Russian Frontier 10-08-15
On the Side-Line (See: Szepek Es Bolondok)
On the Spot 6-26-40
On the Steps of the Throne 8-21-14
On the Stroke of Three 1-21-25
On the Stroke of 12 1-25-28
On the Sunny Side 2-04-42

On the Sunnyside (See: Pa Solsidan)
On the Tagus Border (See: Ribatejo)
On the Threshold of Space 3-07-56
On the Tiger's Back (See: A Cavallo Della Tigre)
On the Tip of the Tongue (See: Du Bout Des Levres)
On the Town 12-07-49
On the Tracks of the Missing (See: Po Diryata Na Bezsledno
    Izcheznalite)
On the U.P. Trail 7-20-27
On the Waterfront 7-14-54
On the White Trails (See: Na Bialym Szlaku)
On the Yard 11-15-78
On Their Own 6-12-40
On Thin Ice 3-11-25
On Those Shoulders (See: Pa Dessa Skuldror)
On Time 6-15-27
On to Reno 7-25-28
On Top of All (See: Sa Ibabaw Ng Lahat)
On Top of Old Smokey 3-04-53
On Trial 6-15-17
On Trial 11-21-28
On Trial 3-29-39
On Tuesdays, Orchids (See: Martes, Orquideas, Los)
On with the Dance 2-20-20
On with the Show 6-05-29
On Your Back 9-17-30
On Your Toes 1-18-28
On Your Toes 10-25-39
On ze Boulevard 7-13-27
Onawanda 10-02-09
Once 10-03-73 and 12-18-74
Once a Crook 7-09-41
Once a Doctor 2-03-37
Once a Gentleman 10-08-30
Once a Greek (See: Griesche Sucht Griechin)
Once a Jolly Swagman 1-12-49
Once a Lady 11-10-31
Once a Mason 3-14-19
Once a Plumber 9-24-20
Once a Sinner 1-21-31
Once a Sinner 2-20-52
Once a Thief 6-28-50
Once a Thief 8-25-65
Once in a Blue Moon 12-09-36
Once in a Lifetime (See: Una Vez en la Vida)
Once in a Lifetime 11-01-32
Once in a Million 4-01-36
Once in Paris 11-08-78
Once Is Enough (See: Il Suffit d'une Fois)
Once Is Not Enough 6-18-75
Once More, My Darling 7-27-49
Once More with Feeling 2-10-60
Once There Was a Girl 12-26-45
Once to Every Bachelor 9-25-34
Once to Every Man 11-29-18
Once to Every Woman 12-17-20
Once to Every Woman 3-27-34
Once Upon a Dream 2-09-49
Once Upon a Honeymoon 11-04-42
Once Upon a Horse 8-06-58
Once Upon a Scoundrel 11-28-73
Once Upon a Thursday 5-20-42
Once Upon a Time (See: Ondanondu Kaladalli)
Once Upon a Time 4-26-44
Once Upon a Time 5-05-76
Once Upon a Time in the East (See: Il Etait Une Fois Dans L'Est)
Once Upon a Time in the West 5-28-69
Once Upon a War 11-30-66
Once Upon Andrea (See: Tous A Poil Et Qu'on En Finisse!)
Once You Kiss a Stranger 9-03-69
Onda Cirkeln, Den 7-12-67
Onda Ogon 4-02-47
Ondanondu Kaladalli 1-31-79
Ondata di Calore 4-01-70
One (See: Eins)
One A.M. 8-04-16
One a Minute 6-10-21
One and Only, The 1-25-78
One and Only, Genuine, Original Family Band, The 3-20-68
1 April 2000 2-18-53
One Arabian Night 10-07-21
One Arabian Night 12-20-23
One-Armed Boxer vs. the Flying Guillotine 11-26-75
One Between, The 7-09-15
One Big Affair 3-05-52
One Body Too Many 10-18-44
One Brief Summer 3-10-71
One Bullet Is Enough (See: Une Balle Suffit ...)

One by One 1-01-75
One Can Say It Without Getting Angry (See: On Peut Le Dire Sans
    Se Facher)
One Can't Forget Such a Girl (See: So Ein Maedel)
1¢ 7-11-56
One Chance in a Million 5-18-27
One Clear Call 6-23-22
One Crowded Night 8-21-40
One Dark Night 12-06-39
One Day 2-11-16
One Day--A Cat (See: Az Prijde Kocour)
One Day in December (See: Un Dia De Diciembre)
One Day in the Life of Ivan Denisovich 5-19-71
One Day Is More Beautiful Than the Others (See: Tag Ist Schoener
    Als Der Andere, Ein)
One Day Joy (See: Un Jour La Fete)
One Day More, One Day Less (See: Plusz-Minusz Egy Nap)
One Desire 7-06-55
One Does Not Bury Sunday (See: On N'Enterre Pas Le Dimanche)
One Does Not Die That Way (See: On Ne Meurt Pas Comme Ca)
One Dollar Bid 7-05-18
$1-a-Year Man 3-25-21
One-Eighth Apache 2-15-23
One Embarrassing Night 8-20-30
One Equals Two? 4-23-75
One Exciting Adventure 1-01-35
One Exciting Night 10-13-22 and 10-27-22
One Exciting Night 6-13-45
One Exciting Week 6-12-46
One-Eyed Jacks 3-15-61
One Family 7-23-30
One Fine Day (See: Certo Giorno, Un)
One Flew over the Cuckoo's Nest 11-19-75
One Foot in Heaven 10-01-41
One Foot in Hell 8-03-60
One Fourth of Humanity: The China Story 10-09-68
One Frightened Night 10-09-35
One Girl's Confession 3-11-53
One Glorious Day 2-03-22
One Glorious Scrap 12-14-27
One Good Turn 1-12-55
One Hamlet Less (See: Un Amleto Di Meno)
One Heavenly Night 1-14-31
One Hour Late 2-05-35
One Hour of Love 1-05-27
One Hour to Live 11-08-39
One Hour with You 3-29-32 (Also see: Une Heure Pres de Toi)
141 Days, The (See: De 141 Dage)
141 Perc a Befejezetlen Mondatbol 3-12-75
109 in the Shade 1-25-08
One Hundred and One Dalmatians 1-18-61
120-As Tempo 10-27-37
125 Rooms of Comfort 11-20-74
100 Briques et des Tuiles 5-05-65
100 Days of Napoleon (See: Campo di Maggio)
100 Little Mothers (See: Cento Piccoloe Mamme)
100 Men and a Girl 9-08-37
100 Million and Trouble (See: 100 Briques et des Tuiles)
100 Rifles 3-12-69
100,000 Dollars au Soleil 5-06-64
100,000 Dollars in the Sun (See: 100,000 Dollars au Soleil)
One in a Million 3-27-35
One in a Million 1-06-37
One Inch from Victory 5-10-44
One Increasing Purpose 1-12-27
One Is a Lonely Number 3-22-72
One Is Always Too Good to Women (See: On Est Toujours Trop Bon
    Avec les Femmes)
One Is Guilty 5-29-34
One Is Not Serious at 17 (See: On N'Est Pas Serieux Quand On
    a 17 Ans)
One Last Fling 7-06-49
One Law for Both 5-04-17
One-Legged Acrobats 4-23-10
One-Legged Man 11-21-08
One Life for Another (See: Una Vida por Otra)
One Little Indian 6-13-73
One Mad Kiss 7-23-30
One Man 5-25-77
One-Man Band, The (See: Homme Orchestre, L')
One Man Dog 3-20-29
One Man Game, A 12-29-26
One Man Justice 10-13-37
One Man Law 2-16-32
One Man Too Many (See: Homme De Trop, Un)
One-Man Trail, The 5-13-21
One-Man Trail, The 5-11-27

One Man's Journey 9-05-33
One Man's Law 7-10-40
One Man's Loss (See: Den Enes Doed ...)
One Man's War (See: Yheden Miehen Sota)
One Man's Way 2-05-64
One Mile from Heaven 7-21-37
One Million B.C. 5-01-40
One Million Dollars (See: Congiuntura, La)
One Million Dollars 11-12-15
1,000,000 Eyes of Su-Muru, The 6-14-67
One Million Years B.C. 12-28-66
One Minute to Play 9-01-26
One Minute to Zero 7-16-52
One More American 2-22-18
One More River 8-14-34
One More Spring 2-27-35
One More Time 6-03-70
One More Tomorrow 5-15-46
One More Train to Rob 4-21-71
One Must Live Dangerously (See: Il Faut Vivre Dangereusement)
One Mysterious Night 10-25-44
One New York Night 5-08-35
One Night 7-23-24
One Night ... A Train (See: Un Soir ... Un Train)
One Night Affair, A (See: Affaire D'Une Nuit, L')
One Night and Then 2-19-10
One Night, at Dinner (See: Metti, Una Sera a Cena)
One Night at Susie's 11-26-30
One Night in Life with One Woman (See: Isang Gabi Sa Buhay Ng
   Isang Babae)
One Night in Lisbon 5-14-41
One Night in Paris 4-05-23
One Night in Paris 7-24-40
One Night in the Tropics 11-06-40
One Night of Fame (See: Al Diavolo con Celebrita)
One Night of Love 9-11-34
One Night on the Beach (See: Un Soir Sur la Plage)
One Night Stand 8-25-76
One Night, Three Women (See: Isang Gabi, Tatlong Babae)
One Night with You 4-28-48
One of a Kind 5-26-76
One of Many 2-16-17
One of Our Aircraft Is Missing 4-29-42
One of Our Dinosaurs Is Missing 6-18-75
One of Our Girls 6-12-14
One of the Bravest 3-03-26
One of the Finest 6-06-19
One of the Millions 11-07-14
One of Those (See: Una di Quelle)
One of Those Things (See: Haendeligt Uheld)
One of Us (See: Eine Von Uns)
One on Max 10-22-10
One on One 6-15-77
One on Top of the Other 1-19-72
One Only Loves Once (See: On Aime Qu'Une Fois)
One or the Other (See: Einer Von Uns Beiden)
One People (See: Wan Pipel)
One Plus One (See: En Och En)
One Plus One 12-11-68
1 + 1 = 3 11-07-79
One Plus One (Exploring the Kinsey Reports) 8-23-61
One Potato, Two Potato 5-06-64
One Rainy Afternoon 5-20-36
One Romantic Night 6-04-30
One Round Hogan 10-26-27
One Shot Ross 10-12-17
One Silver Dollar 6-18-75
One Silver Piece (See: Jeden Stribrny)
One Sings, the Other Doesn't (See: Une Chante, L'Autre Pas, L')
One Splendid Hour 5-29-29
One Spy Too Many 9-28-66
One Step Away 10-02-68
One Stolen Night 2-01-23
One Stolen Night 5-08-29
One Summer of Happiness (See: Hon Dansade En Sommar)
One Sunday Afternoon 9-05-33
One Sunday Afternoon 12-08-48
One Swallow Does Not Make a Summer (See: Fluga Ger Ingen
   Sommar, En)
One That Got Away, The 10-23-57
One Third of a Nation 2-15-39
1,000 Convicts and a Woman 10-27-71
1001 Arabian Nights 12-09-59
1,002d Night, The (See: Mille et Deuxieme Nuit)
One Thousand Dollars 7-05-18
$1,000 a Minute 12-25-35
$1,000 a Touchdown 9-27-39

One Thrilling Night 7-01-42
One Too Many 11-22-50
One Touch of Venus 8-25-48
One-Trick Pony 10-01-80
One, Two, Three 11-29-61
1 2 3 Duan Mahaphai 6-22-77
One, Two, Three, Four! (See: Un, Deux, Trois, Quatre!)
123 Monster Express (See: 123 Duan Mahaphai)
One Two Two (See: 122 Rue De Provence)
One Way Boogie Woogie 4-26-78
One Way Passage 10-18-32
One Way Pendulum 1-27-65
One Way Street 4-12-50
One-Way Ticket (See: Aller Simple, Un)
One-Way Ticket 1-08-36
One Way to Love 1-02-46
One Way Trail 5-14-20
One Way Trail 12-22-31
One Way Wahini 9-29-65
One Week of Life 5-23-19
One Week of Love 11-17-22
One Who Came from Heaven, The (See: Auandar Anapu)
One Wild Night 5-11-38
One Wild Oat 5-30-51
One Wild Week 8-26-21
One Wish Too Many 4-28-65
One Woman, The 9-20-18
One-Woman Idea 6-12-29
One Woman Is Not Enough? (See: Frau Genuegt Nicht?, Eine)
One Woman to Another 9-21-27
One Wonderful Night 8-14-14
One Wonderful Night 1-05-23
One Year (See: Ein Jahr)
One Year Later 11-21-33
One Year to Live 7-08-25
Ongewijde Aarde (See: Unconsecrated Earth)
Oni Srajalis Za Rodinou 5-28-75
Onibaba 2-10-65
Onion Chase, The (See: Course a L'Echalote, La)
Onion Field, The 5-23-79
Onionhead 9-24-58
Onkel Aus Amerika, Der 2-18-53
Onkel Toms Huette 5-19-65
Onkraj 8-12-70
Only a Mother (See: Bara en Mor)
Only a Shop Girl 12-22-22
Only Angels Have Wings 5-17-39
Only 15 (See: 15 Yok Yok)
Only for You (See: Vain Sinulle)
Only Game in Town, The 1-28-70
Only Girl, The 7-04-33
Only God Knows 10-16-74
Only on the Rhine (See: Nur Am Rhein)
Only Once in a Lifetime 9-26-79
Only One, The (See: Edinstvennaja)
Only Saps Work 12-17-30
Only Sixteen Part 2 (See: Rak Otaroot)
Only Son, An (See: Fils Unique, Un)
Only Son, The 6-19-14
Only the Brave 3-12-30
Only the Valiant 3-07-51
Only the Wind Knows the Answer (See: Antwort Kennt Nur Der
   Wind, Die)
Only Their Clothes Are Old (See: Velhos Sao Os Trapos)
Only Thing, The 11-25-25
Only Thing You Know, The 9-08-71
Only 38 6-14-23
Only Two Can Play 1-24-62
Only Way, The 9-23-25
Only Way, The 5-13-70
Only Way Home, The 9-27-72
Only Way Out, The 4-02-15
Only When I Larf 7-03-68
Only Woman, The 11-05-24
Only Yesterday 11-14-33
Only You (See: Nur Du)
Only You Know and I Know 4-28-71
Onna Ga Kaidan O Agaru Yoki 9-14-60
Onna No Rekishi 7-29-64
Onore Della Figlia Del Popola, L' 1-13-37
Onore e Sacrificio (See: Dishonored)
Onze Mille Verges, Les 11-05-75
Opa Schulz 5-18-77
Open All Night 9-10-24
Open All Night 11-06-34
Open City 2-27-46
Open Door to the Sea (See: Porte du Large, La)
Open Letter 10-23-68

Oscar Wilde 5-25-60
Osennie Svadjby 10-30-68
Osenny Maraphon 9-12-79
O'Shaughnessy's Boy 10-09-35
Osinda 7-27-77
Osma Vrata 8-19-59
Osmiat 10-07-70
Ospite, L' 9-22-71
Oss Emellan 4-08-70
Oss 117 Prend des Vacances 2-25-70
Oss 117 Takes a Holiday (See: Oss 117 Prend des Vacances)
Ossa Krivi I Nichta 10-14-64
Ossessione 11-04-59
Ossudeni Doushi 1-14-76
Ostia 10-28-70
Ostre Sledovane Vlaky 10-26-66
Ostrich Eggs, The (See: Oeufs de l'Autruche, Les)
Ostrov Stribrnych Volavek 3-09-77
Osvajanje Slobode 9-05-79
Oswalt Kolle: Dein Mann, Das Unbekannte Wesen 4-08-70
Oswalt Kolle--Pay Example: Adultery (See: Oswalt Kolle--Zum
    Beispiel: Ehebruch)
Oswalt Kolle: Your Husband, the Unknown Creature (See: Oswalt
    Kolle: Dein Mann, Das Unbekannte Wesen)
Oswalt Kolle--Zum Beispiel: Ehebruch 8-27-69
Ot Nishto-Neshto 6-11-80
Ot Ora Negyven 12-27-39
Otages, Les 5-03-39
Otalia de Bahia (See: Os Pastores da Noite)
Otalia de Bahia 9-29-76
Otarova Vdova 9-10-58
Otar's Widow (See: Otarova Vdova)
Otchi Dom 5-20-59
Othchi Tchornia (See: Dark Eyes)
Othello 4-30-10
Othello 10-23-14
Othello 8-06-15
Othello 6-02-22 and 2-22-23
Othello 5-21-52
Othello 5-16-56 and 3-16-60
Othello 12-15-65
Other, The 9-10-30 (Also see: Andere, Der)
Other, The 5-24-72
Other Christopher, The (See: Otro Cristobal, El)
Other Francisco, The (See: Otro Francisco, El)
Other Half of the Note, The 5-15-14
Other Half of the Sky: A China Memoir, The 2-19-75
Other Kind of Love 8-20-24
Other Letter, The (See: To Allo Gramma)
Other Love, The 4-02-47
Other Man, The 2-01-18
Other Man's Wife, The 6-13-19
Other Men's Daughters 7-26-18
Other Men's Women 4-22-31
Other One, The (See: Otra, La)
Other One, The 10-04-67
Other One's Mug, The (See: Gueule de l'Autre, La)
Other One's Son, The (See: Fils de l'Autre, Le)
Other People's Children 3-07-13
Other People's Money (See: Argent des Autres, L')
Other Side of Joey, The 8-16-72
Other Side of Life (See: Vie a L'Envers, La)
Other Side of Midnight, The 6-08-77
Other Side of Paradise (See: Envers du Paradis, L')
Other Side of the Door, The 1-07-16
Other Side of the Mountain, The 3-19-75
Other Side of the Mountain, Part 2, The 2-08-78
Other Side of the Underneath, The 12-06-72
Other Smile, The (See: Andere Laechein, Das)
Other Truth, The (See: Seconde Verite, La)
Other Voices 3-26-69
Other Way, The 11-26-10
Other Woman, The 4-22-21
Other Woman, The 12-15-54
Other Woman's Story, The 3-31-26
Other Women's Husbands, The 4-28-26
Other World of Winston Churchill 4-19-67
Others, The (See: Autres, Les)
Otietz Sergii 10-25-78
Otley 1-22-69
Ototo 5-17-61
Otra, La 1-01-47
Otro Cristobal, El 5-29-63
Otro Francisco, El 8-06-75
Otter, The (See: Loutre, La)
Ottokar Der Weltverbesserer 6-28-78
Ottokar, The World Reformer (See: Ottokar Der Weltverbesserer)
Ou Est Passe Tom? 10-27-71

Ou Etes-Vous Donc...? 10-29-69
Ouchard 3-05-10
Our Betters 2-28-33
Our Boy (See: Varan Pojke)
Our Bridge of Ships 8-23-18
Our Daily Bread (See: Uski Roti)
Our Daily Bread 10-09-34
Our Daily Bread 10-18-50
Our Dancing Daughters 10-10-28
Our Fighting Forces 4-13-17
Our Fighting Navy 5-12-37
Our Flags Lead Us Forward (See: Hitlerjunge Quex)
Our Girl Friday 12-30-53
Our Hateful Husbands (See: Nuestros Odiosos Maridos)
Our Hearts Were Growing Up 3-13-46
Our Hearts Were Young and Gay 9-06-44
Our Hospitality 12-13-23
Our Incredible World 10-26-66
Our Johnny (See: Johnny Unser)
Our Lady of Compassion (See: A Compadecida)
Our Lady of the Turks (See: Nostra Signora Dei Turchi)
Our Land (See: Ma Bhoomi)
Our Last Spring 7-06-60
Our Latin Thing 7-26-72
Our Leading Citizen 6-16-22
Our Leading Citizen 8-02-39
Our Little Girl 6-12-35
Our Little Wife 2-15-18
Our Lord's Vineyard (See: Vignes du Seigneur, Les)
Our Man Flint 1-12-66
Our Man in Havana 1-13-60
Our Masters, the Servants (See: Nos Maitres les Domestiques)
Our Miss Brooks 2-15-56
Our Modern Maidens 9-11-29
Our Mother's House 9-06-67
Our Mrs. McChesney 8-23-18
Our Mutual Friend 12-09-21
Our Mutual Girl 2-13-14
Our Neighbors--The Carters 11-08-39
Our Own Little Flat 11-28-08
Our Relations 11-18-36
Our Russian Front 2-18-42
Our Time 4-03-74
Our Town 5-15-40
Our Very Own 3-22-50
Our Vines Have Tender Grapes 7-18-45
Our Wife 8-20-41
Our Willi Is the Best (See: Unser Willi Ist der Beste)
Our Winning Season 5-17-78
Ouranos 5-29-63
Ours, L' 2-22-61
Ours et la Poupee, L' 2-04-70
Ourselves Alone 5-13-36
Ourselves Alone 8-11-37
Oursin Dans la Poche, Un 12-28-77
Out All Night 10-12-27
Out All Night 4-11-33
Out California Way 12-11-46
Out for a Day 10-16-09
Out for Mischief 10-22-10
Out of a Clear Sky 9-27-18
Out of an Old Man's Head (See: I Huvet Paa En Gammal Gubbe)
Out of Breath (See: A Bout de Souffle)
Out of Darkness 10-29-15
Out of Frame (See: Fuori Campo)
Out of It (See: Carapate, La)
Out of It 10-22-69
Out of Luck 7-26-23
Out of Season 7-16-75
Out of Sight 5-18-66
Out of Sight; Out of Mind 4-09-10
Out of the Blue 8-27-47
Out of the Blue 5-28-80
Out of the Chorus 4-01-21
Out of the Clouds 2-23-55
Out of the Depths 9-16-21
Out of the Depths 3-20-46
Out of the Drifts 3-10-16
Out of the Dust 1-31-20
Out of the Fog 2-21-19
Out of the Fog 6-11-41
Out of the Past 12-18-14
Out of the Past 11-30-27
Out of the Past 11-19-47
Out of the Ruins 8-22-28
Out of the Shadow 1-17-19
Out of the Silent North 6-16-22
Out of the Snows 11-26-20

Out of the Storm 6-18-20
Out of the Storm 9-01-48
Out of the Tiger's Mouth 7-11-62
Out of the West 11-24-26
Out of the Wreck 4-20-17
Out of This World 6-06-45
Out of This World 4-21-54
Out of Touch 9-01-71
Out-of-Towners, The 3-25-70
Out of Whack (See: Rien Ne Va Plus)
Out on Parole (See: Libertad Provisional)
Out One Spectre 8-21-74
Out to Win 9-13-23
Out West 1-25-18
Out West with the Hardys 11-23-38
Out West with the Peppers 7-10-40
Out Yonder 1-16-20
Outback 5-26-71
Outcast 12-08-22
Outcast 11-28-28
Outcast 3-10-37
Outcast, The 6-23-54
Outcast Lady 11-06-34
Outcast of Black Mesa 5-10-50
Outcast of the Islands 1-23-52
Outcast Souls 2-08-28
Outcasts of Poker Flat, The 7-11-19
Outcasts of Poker Flat, The 5-07-52
Outcasts of the Trail 9-21-49
Outcry 3-23-49
Outdoorsman, The 2-12-69
Outer Edge, The 11-05-15
Outer Gate, The 11-24-31
Outfit, The 10-24-73
Outing-Chester Pictures 4-05-18
Outlaw, The 2-10-43
Outlaw Blues 7-06-77
Outlaw Country 5-11-49
Outlaw Deputy 12-04-35
Outlaw Dog, The 6-08-27
Outlaw Express 7-20-38
Outlaw Gold 3-07-51
Outlaw Josey Wales, The 6-30-76
Outlaw Justice 2-28-33
Outlaw Morality (See: Moral Der Banditen, Die)
Outlaw Reforms, The 4-17-14
Outlaw Stallion, The 6-23-54
Outlaw Trail, The 5-10-44
Outlaw Treasure 10-19-55
Outlaw Women 4-16-52
Outlawed 2-13-29
Outlawed Guns 10-16-35
Outlaws, The (See: Buraikan)
Outlaw's Daughter, The 9-23-25
Outlaw's Daughter, The 11-17-54
Outlaws Is Coming, The 1-13-65
Outlaws of Pine Ridge 11-25-42
Outlaws of Red River 5-11-27 and 5-18-27
Outlaws of Sante Fe 7-19-44
Outlaws of Sonora 4-20-38
Outlaws of Texas 5-30-51
Outlaws of the Desert 9-24-41
Outlaws of the Orient 9-08-37
Outlaws of the Panhandle 3-26-41
Outlaws of the Prairie 1-26-38
Outlaws of the Rio Grande 2-26-41
Outlaws of the Rockies 11-14-45
Outlaw's Paradise 4-26-39
Outlaw's Son, The 7-10-57
Outpost in Morocco 3-23-49
Outpost of Hell (See: Dokuritsu Kikanjutai Imada Shagekichu)
Outpost of the Mounties 11-29-39
Outrage 8-23-50
Outrage, The 9-30-64
Outrageous 6-01-77
Outriders 3-08-50
Outside Chance 9-20-78
Outside In 9-20-72
Outside of Paradise 2-16-38
Outside the Law 1-21-21
Outside the Law 9-03-30
Outside the Law 4-18-56
Outside the Three-Mile Limit 3-13-40
Outside the Wall 2-01-50
Outside These Walls 7-12-39
Outside Woman, The 4-08-21
Outsider, The (See: Berlinger)
Outsider, The 2-24-26

Outsider, The 4-29-31 and 4-04-33
Outsider, The 2-15-39
Outsider, The 12-20-61
Outsider, The 12-05-79
Outsiders (See: Ceddo)
Outsiders, The (See: Caifanes, Los or Os Marginais)
Outskirts (See: Okraina)
Outward Bound 9-24-30
Outwitted 10-22-10
Outwitted 1-21-25
Outwitted 11-23-17
Ouvert Contre X 7-30-52
Oval Diamond, The 3-03-16
Ovcar 8-18-71
Over and Under (See: Drunter und Drieber)
Over-Exposed 2-29-56
Over Here 11-30-17
Over Mountain Passes 10-01-10
Over My Dead Body 12-09-42
Over Night 12-31-15
Over She Goes 9-01-37
Over the Border 6-09-22
Over the Border 5-31-50
Over the Edge 5-23-79
Over the Goal 10-06-37
Over the Hill 11-23-17
Over the Hill 11-24-31
Over the Hill to the Poorhouse 9-24-20
Over the Moon 11-08-39
Over the Odds 11-22-61
Over the Seven Seas 12-20-32
Over the Top 4-05-18
Over the Wall 3-16-38
Over the Wire 1-15-10
Over the Wire 8-05-21
Over There 10-19-17
Over There 5-23-28
Over 21 7-25-45
Over-Under, Sideways-Down 11-16-77
Overalls 3-24-16
Overcoat, The (See: Cappotto, Il or Shinel)
Overdoing It (See: Se le Fue la Mano)
Overland Bound 4-23-30 and 6-11-30
Overland Express 5-11-38
Overland Limited 7-22-25
Overland Mail 12-06-39
Overland Mail Robbery 12-22-43
Overland Pacific 2-10-54
Overland Red 3-05-20
Overland Stage, The 2-02-27
Overland Stage Raiders 9-28-28
Overland Telegraph 12-05-51
Overland Telegraph, The 4-03-29
Overland with Kit Carson 10-11-39
Overlanders, The 9-25-46
Overlord 7-09-75
Overtaxed, The (See: Tartassati, I)
Overture to Glory 2-14-40
Overval (See: Resistance)
Ovoce Stromj Rajskych Jime 5-13-70
Owd Bob 2-02-38
Owl and the Pussycat, The 11-11-70
Ox-Bow Incident, The 5-12-43
Oxala 9-10-80
Oxygen (See: Oksigen)
Oysterman's Gold 7-03-09
Oz 8-11-76

P

P.J. 2-14-68
PT 109 3-20-63
Pa Dessa Skuldror 11-24-48
Pa Solsidan 3-04-36 and 9-16-36
Paa'n Igen, Amalie 3-07-73
Paarunger 5-15-68
Pablo 3-10-78
Pace That Thrills, The 11-11-25
Pace That Thrills, The 3-12-52
Pacha, Le 4-03-68
Pacific Adventure 12-03-47
Pacific Challenge 1-29-75

Pacific Destiny 6-13-56
Pacific High 2-13-80
Pacific Liner 12-28-38
Pacific Rendezvous 5-20-42
Pacific Vibrations 11-11-70
Pacifist, The (See: Pacifista, La)
Pacifista, La 12-08-71
Paciorki Jednego Rozanca 7-30-80
Pack, The 8-24-77
Pack Train 7-01-53
Pack Up Your Troubles 10-04-32
Pack Up Your Troubles 11-01-39
Paco 10-08-75
Paco L'Infallible (See: Paco the Infallible)
Paco the Infallible 3-12-80
Pacsirta 5-13-64
Pact with the Devil (See: Patto Col Diavolo)
Pad (and How to Use It), The 8-17-66
Padatik 5-29-74
Paddy 3-18-70
Paddy, Next Best Thing 2-22-23
Paddy, Next Best Thing 8-29-33
Paddy O'Day 2-12-36
Paddy O'Hara 4-13-17
Padlocked 8-04-26
Padre di Famiglia, Il (See: Head of the Family)
Padre, Padrone 5-25-77
Padri e Figli 4-03-57
Padrone e L'Operaio, Il 12-31-75
Padurea Spinzuratilor 6-02-65
Pae Kao 1-25-78
Pafnucio Santo 10-05-77
Pagan, The 5-15-29
Pagan Lady 9-22-31
Pagan Love Song 12-20-50
Page d'Amour, Une 12-28-77
Page Miss Glory 9-04-35
Page Mystery, The 4-20-17
Page of Love, A (See: Page d'Amour, Une)
Page of Madness, A (See: Kurutta Ippeiji)
Pageant of Russia 8-13-47
Pagine Chiuse 5-24-69
Pagliacci 2-25-31
Pagliacci 12-30-36
Paid 1-07-31
Paid in Advance 12-05-19
Paid in Full 2-26-10
Paid in Full 2-28-19
Paid in Full 12-21-49
Paid to Dance 11-10-37
Paid to Love 7-27-27
Pain des Jules, Le 7-06-60
Pain in the Neck, The (See: Emmerdeur, L')
Pain Vivant, Le 3-16-55
Paint Your Wagon 10-15-69
Painted Angel, The 1-08-30
Painted Desert 3-18-31
Painted Desert 9-21-38
Painted Flapper, The 1-21-25
Painted Hills, The 3-28-51
Painted Lie, The 4-13-17
Painted Lily, The 7-05-18
Painted Lips (See: Boquitas Pintadas)
Painted Lips 2-01-18
Painted People 1-31-24
Painted Ponies 9-21-27
Painted Soul, The 12-31-15
Painted Stallion, The 2-16-38
Painted Trail 5-18-38
Painted Veil, The 12-11-34
Painted Woman 9-20-32
Painted World, The 8-14-14
Painted Youth 5-08-29
Painters Painting 3-07-73
Painting the Clouds with Sunshine 9-05-51
Painting the Town 8-03-27
Pair of Cupids, A 8-09-18
Pair of Kings, A 6-16-22
Pair of Silk Stockings, A 7-19-18
Pair of Sixes, A 6-07-18
Pais, Lo 5-30-73
Pais Llamado Chile, Un 7-19-61
Pais Portatil 10-10-79
Pais S.A. 10-01-75
Paix Sur les Champs 4-21-71
Paisan 2-11-48
Pajama Game, The 8-07-57
Pajama Party 11-18-64

Pajamas 11-09-27
Pajarito Gomez 7-07-65
Pajaros de Baden-Baden, Los 2-25-76
Pal Joey 9-11-57
Pal o' Mine 6-04-24
Palabras de Max, Las 3-15-78
Palac 10-15-80
Palace, The (See: Palac)
Palace Hotel 5-14-52
Palace of Angels, The (See: O Palacio Dos Anjos)
Palace of Flame 5-29-14
Palace of the King 12-06-23
Palace Scandal 6-08-49
Palaces of a Queen 12-07-66
Palais de Danse 9-05-28
Palaver 7-23-69
Pale Face's Wooing 11-27-09
Pale Horseman, The 5-15-46
Palec Bozy 8-28-74
Paleface, The 7-21-22
Paleface, The 10-20-48
Palermo-Wolfsburg 2-13-80
Palestine 5-28-47
Paliser Case, The 2-20-20
Pallieter 12-24-75
Palm Beach 5-23-79
Palm Beach Girl 6-23-26
Palm Beach Story, The 11-04-42
Palm Springs 6-24-36
Palm Springs Weekend 11-06-63
Palm Sunday (See: Viragvasarnap)
Palmy Days 9-29-31
Paloma, La 10-28-36
Paloma, La 5-15-74
Paloma Brava 3-01-61
Palomino 2-01-50
Palooka 3-06-34
Pals, The (See: Drugarcine)
Pals First 10-04-18
Pals First 8-25-26
Pals in Blue 6-18-15
Pals in Paradise 11-24-26
Pals of the Golden West 1-16-52
Pals of the Pecos 6-04-41
Pals of the Prairie 7-31-29
Pals of the Saddle 9-14-38
Pals of the Silver Sage 5-29-40
Pamela, Pamela You Are ... 12-18-68
Pampa Salvaje 7-27-66
Pampered Youth 3-04-25
Pan-American 2-21-45
Pan Redaktor Szaleje 6-29-38
Pan Twardowski 9-29-37
Pan Wolodyjowski (See: Colonel Wolodyjowski)
Panagoulis Lives (See: Panagulis Zei)
Panagulis Zei 10-15-80
Panama Flo 1-26-32
Panama Hattie 7-22-42
Panama Lady 6-07-39
Panama Patrol 8-16-39
Panama Picture Shows 1-03-13
Panama Sal 12-25-57
Paname 3-21-28
Panamericana 1-15-69
Panamint's Bad Man 8-10-38
Pancho Villa and Valentina (See: Pancho Villa y la Valentina)
Pancho Villa Returns 10-25-50
Pancho Villa y la Valentina 9-14-60
Pandemonium (See: Langit, Lupa)
Pandillero, El 5-10-61
Pandora and the Flying Dutchman 10-10-51
Pandora's Box (See: Buechse der Pandora)
Pandora's Box 12-11-29
Pane, Amore, e.... 3-28-56
Pane, Amore, e Fantasia 1-20-54
Pane, Amore, e Gelosia 1-26-55
Pane e Cioccolata 2-27-74
Panel Story 6-11-80
Panhandle 1-28-48
Panic Button 4-15-64
Panic in Chicago 7-14-31
Panic in Needle Park 5-26-71
Panic in the City 11-06-68
Panic in the Streets 6-14-50
Panic in the Year Zero 7-04-62
Panic Is Over (See: Crise Est Finie, La)
Panic on the Air 4-22-36
Panic on the Train (See: Ludzie Z Pociagu)

Paris, My Love (See: Parigi O Cara)
Paris N'Existe Pas 3-12-69
Paris--New York 5-15-40
Paris 1900 2-16-49 and 5-24-50
Paris Nous Appartenir 6-28-60
Paris Palace Hotel 11-07-56
Paris Playboys 3-10-54
Paris Secret 6-16-65
Paris Seen By ... (See: Paris Vu Par ...)
Paris Still Sings (See: Paris Chante Toujours)
Paris Sweetheart (See: Paris-Beguin)
Paris Underground 8-22-45
Paris Urchin (See: Gamin de Paris)
Paris Vu Par ... 5-26-65
Paris Waltz, The (See: Valse de Paris, La)
Paris When It Sizzles 3-18-64
Parisian, The 8-25-31
Parisian Life, The (See: Vie Parisienne, La)
Parisian Nights 6-03-25
Parisian Romance, A 1-14-16
Parisian Romance, A 12-16-21
Parisian Romance, A 10-18-32
Parisian Tigress, The 4-04-19
Parisienne, Une 1-22-58
Parisiennes 4-11-28
Parisiennes, Les 1-31-62
Park Avenue Lodger 4-07-37
Park of Caserta, The 1-08-10
Park Row 8-06-52
Parlez-Moi d'Amour 10-22-75
Parliamo di Donne 4-15-64
Parlor, Bedroom and Bath 7-30-20
Parlor, Bedroom and Bath 4-08-31
Parmi les Decombres 8-12-59
Parmigiana, La 4-17-63
Parnell 6-09-37
Parola di Ladro 4-03-57
Parole 7-01-36
Parole Fixer 2-07-40
Parole Girl 4-11-33
Parole, Inc. 1-05-49
Parole Racket 3-10-37
Paroled from the Big House 10-12-38
Paroled-to-Die 1-12-38
Parque de Madrid 6-03-59
Parranda 3-23-77
Parrish 3-22-61
Parson and the Outlaw 9-04-57
Parson of Kirchfield, The (See: Pfarrer Von Kirchfeld, Der)
Parson of Panamint, The 9-15-16
Parson of Panamint, The 6-25-41
Parson's Prayer, The 12-04-09
Parson's Umbrella, The 1-22-10
Part de l'Ombre, La (See: Blind Desire)
Part des Lions, La 9-29-71
Part du Feu, La 1-11-78
Part of the Family 9-15-71
Part Time Wife, The 3-24-26
Parted Curtains 10-07-21
Particular Friendships (See: Amities Particulieres, Les)
Partie du Plaisir, La 1-01-75
Parting of the Trails, The 4-02-30
Partir 9-29-31
Partire 10-26-38
Partisan Mission (See: Zamach)
Partisan Stories (See: Partizanske Price)
Partisani 8-21-74
Partisans (See: Partisani)
Partizanske Price 8-10-60
Partner 9-18-68
Partners 3-01-32
Partners 10-06-76
Partners Again 2-17-26
Partners in Crime 5-02-28
Partners in Crime 10-20-37
Partners in Time 4-24-46
Partners of Adventure (See: Parceiros de Aventura)
Partners of the Night 3-05-20
Partners of the Plains 2-16-38
Partners of the Sunset 4-21-22
Partners of the Tide 4-08-21
Partners of the Trail 9-01-31
Partners of the Trail 3-29-44
Partners Three 4-11-19
Parts the Clonus Horror (Clonus Horror, The) 11-14-79
Party, The 3-20-68

Party Crashers, The 9-17-58
Party Doesn't Answer (See: Teilnehmer Antwortet Nicht)
Party Girl 1-08-30
Party Girl 10-22-58
Party Husband 5-20-31
Party Wire 5-22-35
Party's Over, The 10-16-34
Party's Over, The 5-19-65
Parvi Urok 5-25-60
Pas de Pitie Pour les Femmes 5-02-51
Pas de Probleme! 7-23-75
Pas de Roses Pour OSS 117 8-21-68
Pas Folle la Guepe 12-13-72
Pas Koji Je Voleo Vozove 2-22-78
Pas Paa Ryggen, Professor 8-31-77
Pas Perdus, Les 6-17-64
Pas Question le Samedi 2-24-65
Pas Si Mechant que Ca ... 2-05-75
Pas Sur la Bouche 10-20-31
Pasazerka 12-25-63
Pascual Duarte 5-19-76
Pasi 4-23-80
Pasion Desnuda, La 7-08-53
Pasja 8-02-78
Paskutine Atostogu Diena 8-04-65
Pasos 9-11-57
Pasquale 5-26-16
Pasqualino: Settebellezze 1-14-76
Pasqualino: Seven Beauties (See: Pasqualino: Settebellezze)
Pass, The (See: Permission, La)
Passage, The 2-28-79
Passage du Rhin, Le 9-14-60
Passage to Marseilles 2-16-44
Passage West 5-30-51
Passager Clandestin, Le 9-03-58
Passager de la Pluie, Le 1-28-70
Passagers, Les 3-09-77
Passante, La 7-18-51
Passaporto Rosso 9-09-36
Passaros de Asas Cartadas 7-31-63
Passatore, Il (See: Bullet for Stefano, A)
Passe du Diable, La 11-11-59
Passe Montagne 7-26-78
Passe Simple, Le 7-27-77
Passe Ton Bac d'Abord 10-03-79
Passeggiata, La 1-27-54
Passenger, The (See: Pasazerka)
Passenger, The 3-19-75
Passenger of the Rain (See: Passager de la Pluie, Le)
Passengers (See: Ghorba, El)
Passengers, The (See: Passagers, Les)
Passeport Pour le Monde 11-18-59
Passeport 13,444 7-21-31
Passerby, The (See: Passante, La)
Passers By 3-31-16
Passers-By 6-25-20
Passing Days (See: Idu Dani)
Passing of Mr. Quinn 8-29-28
Passing of the Third Floor Back, The 9-25-35 and 5-06-36
Passing Shadow, The 2-12-10
Passing Through 8-31-77
Passing Thru 9-09-21
Passion (See: Pasja)
Passion, A (See: Passion, En)
Passion 12-17-20
Passion 10-24-51
Passion 10-06-54
Passion, En 5-06-70
Passion According to Matthew (See: Muke Po Mati)
Passion According to St. Matthew, The (See: Passione Secondo San
    Matteo, La)
Passion Flower, The 4-08-21
Passion Flower, The 12-24-30
Passion Flower Hotel (See: Leidenschaftliche Bluemchen)
Passion Island 12-21-27
Passion Island 5-12-43
Passion of Joan of Arc, The 4-10-29
Passion of St. Francis, The 12-20-32
Passion Song 3-20-29
Passionate Adventure, The 6-17-25
Passionate Friends 12-06-23
Passionate Friends, The 2-09-49
Passionate Life of Clemenceau (See: Vie Passionnee De Clemenceau,
    La)
Passionate Pilgrim 1-07-21
Passionate Plumber, The 3-15-32
Passionate Stranger, The 3-06-57
Passionate Strangers 7-06-66

Passionate Summer, The 10-01-58
Passionate Youth 7-08-25
Passione Secondo San Matteo, La 9-07-49
Passionnelle 2-04-48
Passionnement 10-18-32
Passions (See: Leidenschaften)
Passions of Carol, The 3-19-75
Passion's Pathway 9-17-24
Passion's Playground 6-11-20
Passkey to Danger 8-14-46
Passover Plot, The 11-03-76
Passport for the World (See: Passeport Pour Le Monde)
Passport Husband 7-27-38
Passport to Adventure 2-02-44
Passport to Alcatraz 6-19-40
Passport to Hell 8-30-32
Passport to Pimlico 5-18-49
Passport to Shame 11-26-58
Passport to Suez 8-18-43
Passport to Treason 9-19-56
Password: Heron (See: Kennwort: Reiher)
Password Is Courage, The 10-17-62
Past, The (See: Czas Przeszly)
Past and the Present, The (See: O Passado e o Presente)
Past of Mary Holmes 5-02-33
Pasteboard Crown 5-19-22
Pasteur 11-13-35 and 2-12-36
Pastor Hall 6-12-40 and 7-31-40
Pastoral Hide and Seek (See: Den'en Ni Shisu)
Pastorale 6-28-78
Pastures of Disorder (See: Patres du Disordre, Les)
Pat and Mike 5-14-52   .
Pat and Patachon 3-20-29
Pat Garrett and Billy the Kid 5-30-73
Patagonia Rebelde, La 7-10-74
Patata Bollente, La 2-20-80
Patate 11-18-64
Patate 10-29-69
Patates, Les 12-10-69
Patayin Mo Sa Sindak Si Barbara 9-25-74
Patch of Blue, A 12-08-65
Patchwork Girl of Oz 9-26-14
Patent Leather Kid, The 8-17-27
Path of Happiness, The 2-11-16
Path to the Kingdom (See: Sor Intrepida)
Pather Panchali 6-06-56
Pathetic Symphony 12-19-28
Pathfinder, The 12-17-52
Paths of Enemies 11-06-35
Paths of Glory 11-20-57
Paths of Paradise 7-01-25
Paths of War (See: Shtigje Te Luftes)
Patient from Punkville, The 11-27-09
Patient in Room 18, The 1-26-38
Patient Vanishes, The 5-28-47
Patres du Disordre, Les 9-20-67
Patria 11-24-16
Patria, Amore e Dovere 4-14-37
Patrick 7-26-78
Patrick the Great 4-18-45
Patrie 12-04-46
Patriot 4-03-29
Patriot, The (See: Patriote, Le or Patriotin, Die)
Patriot, The 8-18-16
Patriot, The 8-22-28
Patriot and the Spy, The 6-18-15
Patriot Game--A Decade Long Battle for the North of Ireland, The
    6-18-80
Patriote, Le 7-20-28
Patrioten 9-22-37
Patriotin, Die 10-31-79
Patrol, The (See: Sayarim)
Patsy 2-22-23
Patsy, The 4-25-28
Patsy, The 7-01-64
Patterns 3-21-56
Patterson-Harris Fight 8-27-58
Patterson-Johansson 6-29-60
Patterson-Liston Fight 10-03-62
Pattes Blanches 9-28-49
Patto Col Diavolo 9-28-49
Patton 1-21-70
Patty 2-18-76
Pauker, Der 1-14-59
Paul 7-16-69
Paul and Michelle 4-24-74
Paul and Virginia 2-22-28

Paul, Lisa and Caroline 2-16-77
Paul Street Boys, The 7-17-29
Paula 5-14-52
Paula Cautiva 11-13-63
Paulina 1880 6-07-72
Paulina Is Leaving (See: Paulina S'en Va)
Paulina S'en Va 9-17-69
Pauper Millionaire 6-16-22
Paura, La 3-02-55
Pavilion VI 10-31-79
Pavle Pavlovic 8-20-75
Pavlinka 9-04-74
Paw 5-18-60
Paw, The (See: Pranke, Die)
Pawn, The (See: Pion, Le)
Pawn of Fate, The 2-25-16
Pawn Ticket 210 1-25-23
Pawnbroker, The 7-08-64
Pawned 12-15-22
Pawnee 7-17-57
Pawns of Passion 6-19-29
Pawnshop, The 10-06-16
Paws of the Bear 6-22-17
Pax? 5-23-73
Pay As You Enter 8-29-28
Pay Car 9-04-09
Pay Day 5-31-18
Pay Day 4-07-22
Pay Me 8-17-17
Pay Off, The 11-12-30
Pay or Die 4-27-60
Pay Up, Madam! (See: Fizessen Nagysad)
Payak Rai Thaiteep 8-20-75
Payday 1-17-73
Paying His Debt 5-03-18
Paying the Limit 4-16-24 and 9-03-24
Paying the Piper 1-21-21
Paying the Price 7-14-16
Paying the Price 6-01-27
Payment, The 7-21-16
Payment Deferred 11-15-32
Payment in Blood 12-11-68
Payment on Demand 2-21-51
Payoff, The (See: Mazzetta, La)
Payoff, The 11-13-35
Payoff, The 4-14-43
Payroll 4-26-61
Pays Bleu, Le 2-23-77
Pays de Cocagne 3-24-71
Pays d'Ou Je Viens, Le 12-19-56
Pays Sans Etoiles, Le 4-24-46
Pazzi di Giola (See: Two on a Vacation)
Pe Aici Nu Se Trece 6-21-78
Peace (See: Hoa-Binh)
Peace? (See: Pax?)
Peace and Quiet 8-30-23
"Peace at Any Price" Man, The 6-25-15
Peace Killers, The 10-20-71
Peace of the Roaring River, The 8-15-19
Peace Over the Fields (See: Paix Sur Les Champs)
Peace to Who Enters (See: Myr Vodjaschemu)
Peaceful Age, The (See: Eta Della Pace, L')
Peaceful Peters 10-27-22
Peaceful Valley 10-15-20
Peaceful Valley, The (See: Dolyna Miru)
Peaceful Years, The 12-22-48
Peacemaker, The 11-21-56
Peach Blossom (See: Flor de Durazno)
Peach o' Reno, The 12-29-31
Peach Skin 2-20-29
Peacock Alley 11-18-21
Peacock Fan, The 5-22-29
Peacock Feathers 1-13-26
Peak of Fate, The 6-17-25
Peaks of Destiny 11-30-27
Peaks of Zelengore, The (See: Vrhovi Zelengore)
Pearl, The (See: Perle, La)
Pearl, The 2-11-48
Pearl Fisher, The 12-21-07
Pearl in the Crown (See: Perla W Koronie)
Pearl of Death, The 8-30-44
Pearl of Paradise, The 11-10-16
Pearl of the Punjab, A 7-10-14
Pearl of the South Pacific 7-13-55
Pearls Down Below (See: Perlicky Na Dne)
Pearls of the Crown 4-13-38 (Also see: Perles de la Couronne,
    Les)

Perfect "36," The 12-11-14
Perfect Understanding 2-28-33
Perfect Woman, The 7-30-20
Perfect Woman, The 6-01-49
Perfectionist, The 4-30-52
Performance 8-05-70
Performance Will Be Followed with a Dance, The (See: Og Sa Er Der Bal Bagefter)
Perfume of the Lady in Black (See: Parfum de la Dame en Noir)
Perfumed Nightmare, The (See: Mababangong Bangungot)
Perhaps a Gentleman (See: Kanske en Gentlemen)
Perilous Holiday 6-05-46
Perilous Journey, A 5-13-53
Perilous Waters 1-21-48
Perils of Divorce, The 6-16-16
Perils of Pauline, The 4-10-14
Perils of Pauline, The 5-28-47
Perils of Pauline, The 5-10-67
Perils of the Jungle 7-27-27
Period of Adjustment 10-31-62
Periodista Turner, El 10-30-68
Periplanissis 10-31-79
Perjury 8-19-21
Perjury 5-22-29
Perla W Koronie 5-17-72
Perlas Ng Silangan 8-27-69
Perle, La 8-09-32
Perles de la Couronne, Les 5-26-37 (Also see: Pearls of the Crown)
Perlicky Na Dne 8-04-65
Permanent Wave, The 8-03-27
Permette? Rocco Papaleo 12-01-71
Permission, La 11-08-67
Permission to Kill 12-03-75
Pero No Vas a Cambiar Nunca Margarita? 11-22-78
Perrak 5-27-70
Perri 8-21-57
Perro, El 8-17-77
Perro de Alambre 11-19-80
Persecution 11-13-74
Persecution and Assassination of Jean-Paul Marat As Performed by the Inmates of the Asylum of Charenton Under the Direction of the Marquis De Sade, The 2-08-67
Persecution Hasta Valencia (See: Narco Men, The)
Perseguidor, El 4-03-63
Pershing's Crusaders 5-31-18
Persian Lamb Coat, The (See: Cappotto Di Astrakan, Il)
Persiane Chiuse (See: Behind Closed Shutters)
Persona 11-30-66
Persona Honrada Se Necesita 9-03-41
Personal Affair 10-28-53
Personal Affairs (See: Licne Stvari)
Personal Conduct of Henry, The 11-20-09
Personal Maid 9-08-31
Personal Maid's Secret 12-11-35
Personal Opinion, A (See: Sobstvennoie Minienie)
Personal Property 4-21-37
Personal Secretary 9-28-38
Personality 2-26-30
Personality Kid, The 8-07-34
Personality Kid, The 8-14-46
Personals 5-10-72
Personel 4-21-76
Persons in Hiding 1-25-39
Persuader, The 11-13-57
Persuasive Peggy 11-09-17
Peruvaziambalan 2-13-80
Perverse Tales (See: Contes Pervers)
Pervy Den Mira 9-09-59
Pesma 8-23-61
Pest, The 4-25-19
Pesti Mese 6-16-37
Pesti Szerelem 5-15-34
Pet Holek Na Krku 7-24-68
Pet Minuta Raja 8-19-59
Pet of the Big Horn Ranch 10-16-09
Pet Z Milionu 9-23-59
Petal on the Current, The 8-08-19
Pete Kelly's Blues 8-03-55
Pete 'n' Tillie 12-13-72
Pete Seeger ... A Song and a Stone 2-02-72
Pete the Tender (See: Pierrot La Tendresse)
Peter 2-05-35
Peter Ibbetson 10-21-21
Peter Ibbetson 11-13-35
Peter im Schnee 8-04-37
Peter in the Snow (See: Peter im Schnee)

Peter Pan 12-31-24
Peter Pan 1-14-53
Peter the First 12-22-37
Peter the Great 6-28-23
Peter Vinogradov 5-08-35
Peter Voss, der Held des Tages 4-13-60
Peter Voss, Hero of the Day (See: Peter Voss, der Held des Tages)
Petersen 8-28-74
Peterson and Bendel 9-26-33
Pete's Dragon 11-09-77
Petete and Trapito (See: Petete y Trapito)
Petete y Trapito 8-20-75
Petey Wheatstraw 5-03-78
Peticion, La 8-25-76
Petit a Petit 9-02-70
Petit Baigneur, Le 6-12-68
Petit Cafe, Le 5-27-31
Petit Chose, Le 6-29-38
Petit Etranger, Le 5-23-62
Petit Marcel, Le 3-17-76
Petit Matin, Le 9-22-71
Petit Poucet, Le 12-27-72
Petit Prof, Le 8-19-59
Petit Soldat, Le 2-20-63
Petit Theatre de Jean Renoir, Le 7-14-71
Petite, La 8-12-59
Petite Cafe, La 1-28-31
Petite Chocolatiere, La 3-15-32
Petite de Montparnasse 4-12-32
Petite Fille en Velours Bleu, La 9-06-78
Petite Sirene, La 8-20-80
Petite Vertu, La 3-06-68
Petites Fugues, Les 5-23-79
Petition for Pardon (See: Recours en Grace)
Petits, Les 1-06-37
Petits Calins, Les 2-08-78
Petits Matins, Les 4-25-62
Petoff '73 5-30-73
Petrified Forest, The 2-12-36
Petrija's Wreath (See: Petrijin Venac)
Petrijin Venac 8-13-80
Petrolejove Lampy 5-17-72
Petroleuses, Les 12-29-71
Petrus 10-09-46
Petschki-Lawotschki 12-08-76
Petticoat Fever 3-25-36
Petticoat Larceny 7-14-43
Petticoat Pilot 3-01-18
Petticoat Pirates 12-27-61
Petticoat Politics 2-12-41
Pettigrew's Girl 4-18-19
Petty Girl 8-23-50
Petty Thieves (See: Eierdiebe)
Petualang Cinta 4-25-79
Petulia 5-01-68
Peu, Beaucoup, Passionnement, Un 3-24-71
Peu de Soleil dans l'Eau Froide, Un 11-17-71
Peur Sur la Ville 4-23-75
Peyton Place 12-18-57
Pez Que Fuma, El 12-21-77
Pezzo, Capopezzo, e Capitano 10-01-58
Pfarrer von Kirchfield, Der 8-24-55
Pfarrer von St. Pauli, Der 9-30-70
Pfingstausflug, Der 4-18-79
Phaedra 6-06-62
Phai Kam Plerng 2-23-77
Phairak Soom Suang 6-18-75
Phantasm 3-07-79
Phantastic Idea, A (See: Toller Einfall, Ein)
Phantastic World of Matthew Madson, The 4-17-74
Phantom 1-05-23
Phantom, The 6-23-16
Phantom Broadcast, The 8-01-33
Phantom Cart, The (See: Charrette Fantome, La)
Phantom City 1-16-29
Phantom Cowboy 4-02-41
Phantom Creeps, The 8-09-39
Phantom Express 2-03-26
Phantom Express 9-27-32
Phantom Fiend, The 4-24-35
Phantom Flyer, The 5-02-28
Phantom Fortune, The 2-10-15
Phantom Fortunes, The 9-15-16
Phantom from Space, The 5-20-53
Phantom from 10,000 Leagues, The 1-11-56
Phantom Gold 9-28-38
Phantom Honeymoon, The 11-21-19
Phantom Horse, The (See: Mabaroshi Nouma)

Phantom Killer 12-09-42
Phantom Lady 1-26-44
Phantom Light, The 7-17-35
Phantom Love (See: Ai No Borei)
Phantom Melody 1-23-20
Phantom of Chinatown 1-01-41
Phantom of Crestwood 10-18-32
Phantom of 42nd Street 6-06-45
Phantom of Freedom, The (See: Fantome de la Liberte, Le)
Phantom of Paris, The 11-17-31
Phantom of Soho, The 8-02-67
Phantom of the Desert 2-18-31
Phantom of the North 6-05-29
Phantom of the Opera, The 9-09-25 and 2-12-30
Phantom of the Opera, The 8-18-43
Phantom of the Opera, The 6-13-62
Phantom of the Operetta, The (See: Fantasma de la Opereta, El)
Phantom of the Paradise 10-30-74
Phantom of the Range 2-08-28 and 5-02-28
Phantom of the Range 6-15-38
Phantom of the Rue Morgue 3-03-54
Phantom of the Turf 5-09-28
Phantom on Horseback, The (See: Kisertet Lublon)
Phantom Patrol 7-28-37
Phantom Plainsmen, The 10-21-42
Phantom President, The 10-04-32
Phantom Raiders 5-29-40
Phantom Rancher 3-13-40
Phantom Ranger 3-21-28
Phantom Ranger 6-22-38
Phantom Ride from Aix-les-Bains 10-22-10
Phantom Rider, The 10-02-29
Phantom Speaks, The 6-06-45
Phantom Stage, The 12-06-39
Phantom Stagecoach, The 4-03-57
Phantom Stockman, The 8-12-52
Phantom Strikes, The 11-15-39
Phantom Submarine 2-19-41
Phantom Thunderbolt 6-27-33
Phantom Tollbooth, The 10-14-70
Phantom Valley 8-11-48
Phantom von Soho, Das (See: Phantom of Soho, The)
Phantom Witness, The 1-21-16
Pharaoh (See: Faroan)
Pharaoh; or, Israel in Egypt 11-12-10
Pharaoh's Curse, The 1-30-57
Pharaoh's Woman, The 4-26-61
Phase IV 10-09-74
Phedre 11-06-68
Phenix City Story, The 7-20-55
Phffft 10-20-54
Phil-for-Short 5-30-19
Philadelphia Story, The 11-27-40
Phillip Holden--Waster 10-13-16
Philo Vance Returns 4-30-47
Philo Vance's Gamble 4-30-47
Philo Vance's Secret Mission 11-26-47
Philosopher's Stone, The (See: Parash Pathar)
Philosophie Dans le Boudoir, La (See: Beyond Love and Evil)
Phobia 9-10-80
Phone Call from a Stranger 1-09-52
Phoney, The (See: Faux-Cul, Le)
Phooying 7-09-80
Phooying Yay Chai Daeng 7-06-77
Photo Souvenir 2-01-78
Photography (See: Fotografia)
Phuen Rak 3-09-77
Phyllis of the Follies 12-05-28
Phynx, The 5-13-70
Physical Culture Fields 10-23-09
Physician, The 6-13-28
Pi Hua Kad 4-09-80
Piacieri Del Sabato Notte, I 11-16-60
Piaf 4-10-74
Pianeta Venere 9-13-72
Piano in Mid-Air, A (See: Zongora a Levegoben)
Pianos Mechaniques, Les 5-26-65
Piatto Piange, Il 2-12-75
Piazza Vuota, La 9-08-71
Pibe Cabeza, El 7-30-75
Pic et Pic et Colegram 7-12-72
Picasso 12-28-55
Picasso, l'Homme et Son Oeuvre 6-12-74
Picasso Look, The (See: Regard Picasso, Le)
Picasso, Painter of the Century (See: Picasso, Peintre du Siecle)
Picasso, Peintre du Siecle 5-30-73
Picasso, the Man and His Work (See: Picasso, l'Homme et Son Oeuvre)

Picasso, un Portrait 11-18-70
Picassos Aeventyr 6-21-78
Piccadilly 4-03-29 and 7-24-29
Piccadilly Incident 8-28-46
Piccadilly Jim 2-06-20
Piccadilly Jim 9-02-36
Piccadilly Third Stop 9-14-60
Piccolo Archimede, Il 10-03-79
Piccolo Hotel 11-01-39
Piccolo Martire, Il (See: Little Martyr, The)
Pick a Star 6-02-37
Pick Up 3-28-33
Pickpocket 1-20-60
Pickup 7-18-51
Pickup on South Street 5-13-53
Pickwick Papers, The 11-26-52
Picnic 12-07-55
Picnic at Hanging Rock 11-05-75
Pictura 4-02-52
Picture Brides 5-29-34
Picture Mommy Dead 9-07-66
Picture of Dorian Gray, The 3-07-45
Picture Show Man, The 4-13-77
Picture Snatcher, The 5-23-33
Pictures from a Strange Land (See: Bilder Aus Einem Fremden Land)
Pidgin Island 1-05-17
Pie in the Sky 1-01-64
Piece of Blue Sky, A (See: Parce Plavog Neba)
Piece of the Action, A 10-05-77
Pieces of China 7-07-26
Pieces of Dreams 8-26-70
Pieces of Silver 3-05-15
Pied, A Cheval et en Voiture 10-23-57
Pied Piper, The 7-08-42
Pied Piper, The 5-10-72
Pied Piper Malone 1-31-24
Piedra Libre 5-05-76
Piege, Le 9-03-58
Piege Pour Cendrillon 11-10-65
Pieges 2-07-40
Piel de Verano 9-06-61
Piel de Zapa, La 12-15-43
Pier, The (See: Molo)
Pier 5, Havana 6-24-59
Pier 13 8-14-40
Pier 23 5-16-51
Pierre and Paul (See: Pierre et Paul)
Pierre et Paul 6-11-69
Pierre of the Plains 4-24-14
Pierre of the Plains 6-17-42
Pierrot La Tendresse 12-28-60
Pierrot Le Fou 9-08-65
Pierrot, the Prodigal 6-12-14
Piervij Utchitelh 9-14-66
Pierwszy Dzieri Wolnosci 6-23-65
Piesen O Sivom Holubovi 5-17-61
Pigen Fra Egborg 9-24-69
Pigen Og Droemmeslottet 10-02-74
Pigen Og Millionaeren 11-10-65
Pigen Og Pressefotografen 10-14-64
Pigeon Shoot (See: Tiro al Piccione)
Pigeon That Took Rome, The 7-04-62
Piger I Troejen 8-27-75
Piger I Troejen 2 10-27-76
Piger Til Soes 9-28-77
Piggies 5-20-70
Pigmy World, The 11-13-09
Pig's War, The (See: Guerra del Cerdo, La)
Pigskin Parade 11-18-36
Pigsty (See: Porcile)
Piker's Dream 2-01-08
Pikku Pietarin Piha 7-04-62
Pile Ou Face 6-09-71
Pile ou Face 9-10-80
Pilgrim, The 3-01-23
Pilgrim, Farewell 9-17-80
Pilgrim Lady 1-22-47
Pilgrimage 7-18-33
Pilgrimage 5-10-72
Pilgrimage to the Virgin (See: Procesi K Panence)
Pilgrims of the Night 10-07-21
Pillaged (See: Mise a Sac)
Pillagers, The 4-23-10
Pillar of Fire 4-17-63
Pillar of Salt (See: Sobalvany)
Pillars of Society, The 8-04-16

Pillars of Society (See: Stutzen der Gesellschaft)
Pillars of the Sky 8-08-56
Pillole di Ercole, Le 11-09-60
Pillory, The 11-10-16
Pillow of Death 12-12-45
Pillow Talk 8-12-59
Pillow to Post 5-16-45
Pilot No. 5 4-07-43
Pim Pam Pum ... Fire (See: Pim, Pam, Pum ... Fuego!)
Pim, Pam, Pum ... Fuego! 9-17-75
Pimeanpirtin Havitys 7-02-47
Pimienta 6-08-66
Pimienta y Pimenton 8-19-70
Pimpernel Smith 7-09-41
Pimpernel Svensson 2-11-53
Pin Up Girl 4-19-44
Pinch Hitter, The 4-27-17
Pindorama 6-02-17
Pingwin 8-10-66
Pink Flamingos 12-11-74
Pink Gods 9-29-22
Pink Jungle, The 7-24-68
Pink Narcissus 5-26-71
Pink Panther, The 1-15-64
Pink Panther Strikes Again, The 12-15-76
Pink String and Sealing Wax 12-12-45
Pink Tights 10-08-20
Pink Zone (See: Zona Roja)
Pinky 10-05-49
Pinocchio 1-31-40
Pinocchio 1-13-71
Pinocchio in Outer Space 10-20-65
Pinto Kid, The 4-11-28
Pinto Kid, The 2-05-41
Pinto Rustlers 1-27-37
Pion, Le 11-22-78
Pioneer Days 6-01-07
Pioneer Days 2-07-40
Pioneer Justice 7-02-47
Pioneer Marshall 1-11-50
Pioneer Scout, The 4-11-28
Pioneer Trail, The 9-21-38
Pioneers, The (See: Os Bandeirantes)
Pioneers, The 6-25-41
Pioneers, The 3-16-77
Pioneers, The 11-05-80
Pioneers of the Frontier 2-14-40
Pioneers of the West 1-29-30
Pioneers of the West 3-13-40
Pioniere von Ingolstadt, Die (See: Recruits in Ingolstadt)
Pipe Dreams 11-03-76
Pipes, The (See: Dymky)
Pipes of Pan 3-08-23
Pippa Passes 10-09-09
Pippi in the South Seas 7-17-74
Pippi Langstrump Pa De Sju Haven (See: Pippi in the South Seas)
Pique Dame 10-25-44
Piranas, Las 11-08-67
Piranha 8-09-78
Piranhas, The (See: Piranas, Las)
Pirate, The 5-28-24
Pirate, The 3-31-48
Pirate of the Seven Seas, The 4-16-41
Pirates, The 11-21-08
Pirate's Fiancee, The (See: Fiancee du Pirate, La)
Pirates of Blood River, The 7-25-62 and 8-08-62
Pirates of Capri, The 12-07-49
Pirates of Monterey 11-12-47
Pirates of the Bois De Boulogne (See: Corsaires Du Bois De
    Boulogne, Les)
Pirates of the Skies 4-12-39
Pirates of the Sky 5-11-27
Pirates of Tortuga 10-04-61
Pirates of Tripoli 1-26-55
Pirates on Horseback 5-21-41
Pirate's Treasure, The 5-11-07
Piri Knows All (See: Piri Mindent Tud)
Piri Mindent Tud 5-21-32 and 1-31-33
Pirosmani 6-12-74
Piscine, La 2-19-69
Pistol, The (See: Pistolen)
Pistol for Ringo, A (See: Pistola Per Ringo, Una)
Pistol Harvest 7-25-51
Pistol Packin' Mama 12-15-43
Pistol Shot, A 10-11-67
Pistola Per Ringo, Una 6-23-65
Pistolen 11-28-73
Pistoleros de Casa Grande, Los (See: Gunfighters of Casa Grande)

Pistonne, Le 3-11-70
Pit and the Pendulum, The 4-02-15
Pit and the Pendulum, The 8-09-61
Pit Stop 5-21-69
Pitfall 8-04-48
Pitfall, The (See: Kashi To Kodomo)
Pitfalls of a Big City 4-18-19
Pitfalls of Passion 11-16-27
Pitie Pour les Vamps 12-05-56
Pittsburgh 12-02-42
Pittsburgh Kid, The 9-03-41
Pity for the Vamps (See: Pitie Pour les Vamps)
Piu Bella Donna Del Mondo, La 11-16-55
Piu Bella Serata Della Mia Vita, La 12-27-72
Piu Comico Spettacolo Del Mondo, Il 3-17-54
Pixie at the Wheel 9-03-24
Piyama de Adan, El 7-29-42
Place Called Glory, A 8-10-66
Place Called Today, A 6-21-72
Place for Lovers, A 6-18-69
Place in the Sun, A 7-18-51
Place of Honeymoons, A 10-29-20
Place of One's Own, A 5-23-45
Place to Go, A 4-29-64
Place Without Limits, The (See: Lugar Sin Limites, El)
Placeres Conyugales 4-15-64
Placido 1-17-62
Plague of the Zombies, The 1-26-66
Plain Clothes Man, A 7-11-08
Plain Girl (See: A Csunya Lany)
Plain Jane 9-01-16
Plainsman, The 1-20-37
Plainsman and the Lady, The 11-06-46
Plaisir, Le 3-26-52
Plaisirs de Paris 1-28-53
Plan of His 19 Years, The (See: Jukyu-Sai No Chizu)
Planet of the Apes 2-07-68
Planet of the Vampires 12-01-65
Planete Sauvage, La 5-16-73
Plank, The 5-10-67
Planque, La 10-10-62
Planter's Wife, The 11-07-08
Planter's Wife, The 10-01-52
Plastered in Paris 9-26-28
Plastic Age, The 7-21-26
Plastic Dome of Norma Jean, The 11-02-66
Platanov 1-19-77
Platinum Blonde 11-03-31
Platinum High School 5-11-60
Platoon 317 (See: 317 Section, La)
Play Dirty 1-15-69
Play Girl 3-22-32
Play Girl 12-18-40
Play Girl, The 4-25-28
Play It Again, Sam 4-19-72
Play It As It Lays 9-13-72
Play Misty for Me 9-15-71
Play on the Tenne, The (See: Spiel auf der Tenne)
Play Safe 4-20-27
Playboy, The (See: Petualang Cinta)
Playboy of Paris, The 11-15-30 (Also see: Petite Cafe, La)
Player Pianos, The (See: Pianos Mechaniques, Les)
Players 6-13-79
Players, The 8-06-75
Playful Tenant 2-01-08
Playgirl 4-21-54
Playgirls and the Vampire, The 5-06-64
Playing Around 4-02-30
Playing Double 3-08-23
Playing It Wild 5-30-23
Playing Soldiers (See: Mali Vojnici)
Playing Square 8-12-21
Playing the Game 4-19-18
Playing with Fire (See: Jeu Avec le Feu, Le)
Playing with Fire 4-28-16
Playing with Souls 5-06-25
Playmates 11-12-41
Plaything of Broadway 3-18-21
Playthings of Desire 5-13-25
Playthings of Destiny 11-18-21
Playthings of Passion 5-30-19
Playtime 12-27-67
Plaza Suite 5-12-71
Pleasant August, The (See: Stiliga Augusta)
Pleasant Young Gentleman, A 11-20-63
Pleasantville 8-25-76
Please Believe Me 3-15-50
Please Don't Eat the Daisies 3-23-60

Please Get Married 11-07-19
Please Help Emily 11-30-17
Please Murder Me 2-08-56
Please Teacher 3-03-37
Please Turn Over 1-20-60
Pleasure (See: Plaisir, Le)
Pleasure 3-15-32
Pleasure at Her Majesty's, The 11-24-76
Pleasure Before Business 5-04-27
Pleasure Buyers 2-17-26
Pleasure Crazed 7-17-29
Pleasure Cruise 4-04-33
Pleasure Game, The 3-04-70
Pleasure Garden, The 11-03-26
Pleasure Girls, The 6-02-25
Pleasure Mad 1-10-24
Pleasure of His Company, The 5-10-61
Pleasure Palace 5-23-73
Pleasure Seekers, The 12-30-64
Pleasure Way, The (See: Partie du Plaisir, La)
Pleasures of Paris (See: Plaisirs de Paris)
Pleasures of Saturday Night, The (See: Piacieri Del Sabato
    Notte, I)
Pleasures of the Rich 4-14-26
Pledge, The (See: Serment, Le)
Pledgemasters, The 9-01-71
Plein de Super, Le 4-07-76
Plein Soleil 3-23-60
Pleins Feux Sur l'Assassin 4-19-61
Pleins Feux Sur Stanislas 10-13-65
Pleneno Yato 5-30-62
Plern 5-30-79
Ples U Kisi 8-09-61
Pleure Pas la Bouche Pleine 11-28-73
Ploetzliche Einsamkeit Des Konrad Steiner, Die 7-07-76
Plokhoy Khoroshyi Chelovek 6-26-74
Plomienne Serca 10-13-37
Plot, The (See: Complot, Le)
Plot Thickens, The 12-16-36
Plot to Kill Roosevelt, The 11-03-48
Plotters, The (See: Intrigantes, Les)
Plotzliche Reichtun der Armen Leute von Kombach, Der 7-28-71
Plough and the Stars, The 2-03-37
Plumber, The 3-26-80
Plunder 1-28-31
Plunder of the Sun 8-12-53
Plunder Road 12-04-57
Plunderer, The 5-28-15
Plunderers, The 11-03-48
Plunderers, The 11-09-60
Plunger, The 12-17-20
Plunging Hoofs 4-17-29
Plurals (See: Plurielles)
Plurielles 3-14-79
Plus Belle Fille du Monde, La 1-02-52
Plus Belles des Vies, Les 12-05-56
Plus Belles Escroqueries du Monde, Les (See: Beautiful Swindlers,
    The)
Plus Ca Va, Moins Ca Va 8-31-77
Plus des Vacances Pour le Bon Dieu 5-24-50
Plus Heureux des Hommes, Le 2-18-53
Plus Vieux Metier du Monde, Le 5-24-67
Plusz-Minusz Egy Nap 10-03-73
Plutonium 8-15-79
Plymouth Adventure, The 10-22-52
Po Diryata Na Bezsledno Izcheznalite 7-25-79
Po Mai Tidet 1-25-78
Poachers (See: Furtivos)
Pocahontas 10-03-08
Pocatello Kid, The 2-02-32
Pocharde, La 7-08-53
Pochti Lyubovna Istorya 6-11-80
Pocket Lover, The (See: Amant de Poche, L')
Pocket Money 2-16-72
Pocketful of Chestnuts (See: Castagne Sone Buone, Le)
Pocketful of Miracles 11-01-61
Podne 8-14-68
Podranki 5-18-77
Poedino 2-03-60
Poem, The (See: Pesma)
Poem of the Sea (See: Poima O More)
Poems in Pictures 9-24-10
Poet and Muse (See: Runoilija Ja Muusa)
Poet and the Little Mother, The (See: Poeten Og Lillemor)
Poet and Tsar 9-07-38

Poeten Og Lillemor 7-22-59
Poet's Pub 7-13-49
Pofon 1-20-37
Pogled U Zjenicu Sunca 5-25-66
Pogon B 8-12-59
Pohod 8-21-68
Poil de Carotte 12-20-32 and 5-30-33
Poil de Carotte 6-18-52
Poil de Carotte 9-12-73
Poima O More 10-12-60
Point Blank 9-06-67
Point de Chute 9-30-70
Point de Mire, Le 10-26-77
Point du Jour, Le 6-15-49
Point 905 (See: Kota 905)
Point of Order 9-18-63
Point of View 8-06-20
Pointe Courtel, La 7-11-56
Pointed Heels 1-01-30
Pointing Finger, The 12-19-19
Points West 9-18-29
Poison 9-10-24
Poison, Le 1-02-52
Poison at 2:30 (See: Dos y Media ... Veneno, Las)
Poison Pen 7-12-39 and 7-02-41
Poitin 3-21-79
Pojken I Tradet 7-04-62
Pokelanie 2-14-62
Poker Faces 9-15-26
Pokfoci 3-02-77
Pokoj Z Widkiem Na Morze 8-23-78
Pokriv 5-31-78
Polare 4-07-76
Polemonta 11-05-75
Polenov Prah 8-21-74
Polenta 8-20-80
Policarpo 4-15-49
Police, The 5-26-16
Police Call 8-29-33
Police Car 17 11-07-33
Police Chief Pepe (See: Commissario Pepe, Il)
Police Commissioner, The (See: Commissario, Il)
Police Dog Story, The 3-08-61
Police Inspector Accuses, A (See: Comisar Acuza, Un)
Police Mondaine 5-05-37
Police Officer Without Importance, A (See: Officier De Police
    Sans Importance, Un)
Police Patrol, The 9-02-25
Police Python 357 4-07-76
Police Raid (See: Razzia)
Police Station Davidswache (See: Polizeirevier Davidswache)
Police War, The (See: Guerre des Policiers, La)
Policeman Waeckerli in Danger (See: Polizist Waeckerli In Gefahr)
Policeman's Revolver, A 1-08-10
Policemen's Little Run 2-16-07
Policewoman (See: Poliziotta, La)
Policing the Plains 12-28-27
Polish Jew, The (See: Juif Polonais, Le)
Polish Passion (See: Polnische Passion)
Politeness Pays 3-03-16
Political Asylum 12-24-75
Politicians, The 3-04-70
Politics 2-12-10
Politics 8-04-31
Polizeirevier Davidswache 12-30-64
Polizia Ringrazia, La 6-28-72
Poliziotta, La 1-22-75
Polizist Waeckerli In Gefahr 1-18-67
Pollen Dust (See: Polenov Prah)
Polly Ann 9-14-17
Polly of the Circus 9-14-17
Polly of the Circus 3-22-32
Polly of the Storm Country 9-17-20
Polly Put the Kettle On 12-29-16
Polly Redhead 2-09-17
Polly with a Past 1-14-21
Pollyanna 1-23-20
Pollyanna 4-13-60
Polnische Passion 7-15-64
Polnocna Omsa 7-18-62
Polo Joe 11-11-36
Poloh 1-19-77
Polawanie Na Muchy 5-28-69 and 2-18-70
Polvere Di Stelle 1-30-74
Pom Pom Girls, The 9-15-76
Pomme, La 10-22-69
Pomme, la Queue et les Pepins, La 10-23-74
Pompeii 10-03-13

Pompieri di Viggiu, I 6-01-49
Pondeljak Ili Utorak 12-07-66
Pont de Singe, Le 4-28-76
Pony Express 3-04-53
Pony Express, The 9-16-25
Pony Express Rider, The 10-22-10
Pony Post 12-24-40
Pony Soldier 11-05-52
Poo Lom 1-19-77
Poodle (See: Caniche)
Pool of Flame, The 3-10-16
Pool of London 2-28-51
Poor but Handsome (See: Poveri Ma Belli)
Poor Cow 12-13-67
Poor Girl Pretty Girl (See: Belle Ma Povere)
Poor Girls 7-27-27
Poor Girl's Honor, The (See: Onore della Figlia del Popolo, L')
Poor in Paradise (See: Gueux au Paradis, Les)
Poor Little Maria (See: Marja Pieni)
Poor Little Peppina 2-25-16
Poor Little Rich Girl 7-01-36
Poor Little Rich Girl, A 3-09-17
Poor Little Sven (See: Stackars Lille Sven)
Poor Lucas (See: Bedniyat Louka)
Poor Man's Romance, A 4-25-08
Poor Men's Wives 2-01-23
Poor Millionaire, The 5-14-30
Poor Nut, The 7-20-27
Poor Old Bill 7-14-31
Poor Relation, A 4-14-22
Poor Relations 10-31-19
Poor Rich, The (See: Szegeny Gazdagok)
Poor Rich, The 5-15-34
Poor Rich Man, The 12-27-18
Pop Always Pays 6-19-40
Pop Game 11-22-67
Popcorn 10-29-69
Pope Joan 8-23-72
Pope Pius X and the Vatican 10-31-14
Popeye 12-10-80
Popi 4-16-69
Popiol I Diament 9-16-59
Popioly 3-23-66
Popovich Brothers of South Chicago, The 4-12-78
Poppy 6-08-17
Poppy 6-24-36
Poppy Girl's Husband, The 3-28-19
Poppy Is Also a Flower, The 11-23-66 (Also see: Mohn Ist Auch eine Blume)
Popsy Pop 3-24-71
Popular Sin, The 12-22-26
Popular Train (See: Lacrimme e Sorrisi)
Popular Tune, A 11-26-10
Poquianchis, Las 2-09-77
Por Mis Pistolas 1-01-69
Por Que Te Engana Tu Marido? 4-09-69
Porcelain Anniversary, The (See: Noces de Porcelaine, Les)
Porci Con le Ali 7-13-77
Porcile 9-17-69
Porgey's Bouquet 11-07-13
Porgi L'Altra Guancia 1-15-75
Porgy and Bess 7-01-59
Pori 4-10-29
Pork Chop Hill 5-06-59
Porn Flakes 3-23-77
Porno at the School of Scandal (See: Porr I Skandalskolan)
Porno Pop 6-23-71
Pornografi--En Musical 8-18-71
Pornography--A Musical (See: Pornografi--En Musical)
Pornography Copenhagen 1970 4-29-70
Pornography in Denmark 4-15-70
Porr I Skandalskolan 8-14-74
Porridge 7-25-79
Port Afrique 5-23-56
Port Arthur 10-15-41
Port de Desir, Le 6-29-55
Port of Desire (See: Port de Desir, Le)
Port of 40 Thieves 9-06-44
Port of Hate 8-16-39
Port of Hell 1-19-55
Port of Lost Dreams, The 4-03-35
Port of Missing Girls 8-01-28
Port of Missing Girls 4-06-38
Port of Missing Men 5-15-14
Port of Missing Men 10-29-30
Port of New York 11-23-49
Port of Seven Seas 6-29-38

Port Said 5-12-48
Port Sinister 2-18-53
Portable Country (See: Pais Portatil)
Porte des Lilas 10-23-57
Porte du Large, La 11-25-36
Portentosa Vida Del Padre Vincent, La 9-13-78
Porter, The (See: Baara)
Portes de Feu, Les 5-03-72
Portes de la Nuit, Les 12-18-46
Portia on Trial 11-10-37
Portland Expose 8-14-57
Portnoy's Complaint 6-21-72
Porto Das Caixas 5-15-63
Portrait d'un Assassin, Le 1-18-50
Portrait de Marianne, Le 10-14-70
Portrait de Son Pere, Le 2-24-54
Portrait from Life 12-22-48
Portrait in Black 6-08-60
Portrait in the Rain (See: Portret S Dojdem)
Portrait of a Champion (See: Kuldetes)
Portrait of a Female Drunkard (See: Bildnis einer Trinkerin)
Portrait of a Mobster 3-29-61
Portrait of a 60% Perfect Man 5-28-80
Portrait of a Woman 5-01-46
Portrait of an Assassin (See: Portrait d'un Assassin, Le)
Portrait of Chieko 3-20-68
Portrait of Clare 8-02-50
Portrait of Fidel Castro 7-09-75
Portrait of Innocence 6-16-48
Portrait of Jason 10-04-67
Portrait of Jennie 12-29-48
Portrait of Shunkin, A (See: Shunkin Sho)
Portrait of Teresa (See: Retrato de Teresa)
Portrait of the Artist As a Young Man, A 4-25-79
Portrait Robot 11-21-62
Portraits of Women (See: Naisenkuvia)
Portret S Dojdem 7-12-78
Ports of Call 3-25-25 and 5-06-25
Portuguese Rhapsody (See: Rhapsodia Portuguesa)
Portuguese Vacation (See: Vacances Portugaises)
Poseban Tretman 5-14-80 and 5-21-80
Poseidon Adventure, The 12-13-72
Poslednata Douma 5-22-74
Posledni Ruze Od Casanovi 7-20-66
Posledno Liato 7-24-74
Poslizg 8-16-72
Posljednji Podvig Diverzanta Oblaka 8-09-78
Posowi Mnja W Dal Swjet Luju 7-05-78
Posse 5-28-75
Posse from Hell 3-15-61
Possedees, Les 5-16-56
Possessed 12-01-31
Possessed 6-04-47
Possessed, The (See: Possedees, Les)
Possession 2-10-22
Possession of Joel Delaney, The 5-17-72
Post Office Investigator 9-28-49
Postal Inspector 9-09-36
Postav Dom, Zasad Strca 3-05-80
Postava K Podpirani 5-06-64
Postgraduate, The 9-09-70
Postillon von Lonjumeau, Der (See: King Smiles--Paris Laughs)
Postman, The (See: Al Boustagui or Postschi)
Postman Always Rings Twice, The 3-20-46
Postman Didn't Ring, The 6-03-42
Postman Goes to War, The (See: Facteur S'En Va-T-En Guerre, Le)
Postman's Knock 4-04-62
Postmark for Danger 1-25-56
Postmaster's Daughter, The 8-21-46
Postmeisterin, Die 10-21-25
Postmistress, The (See: Postmeisterin, Die)
Posto, Il 9-06-61
Postschi 7-12-72
Pot, The (See: Maenak America)
Pot-Bouille 12-04-57
Pot Carriers, The 5-30-62
Pot Luck 4-22-36
Pot O'Gold 4-09-41
Potash and Perlmutter 9-13-23
Potato (See: Patate)
Potato Fritz 5-26-76
Potatoes, The (See: Patates, Les)
Potemkin (See: Cruiser Potemkin and Potemkin, The)
Potemkin, The 12-08-26
Potere, Il 9-22-71
Poto and Cabengo 12-12-79
Potop 9-25-74
Potota, La 7-12-61

Pots, Pans and Poetry 3-04-11
Potters, The 1-19-27
Pouce 1-12-72
Poudre d'Escampette, La 9-22-71
Poule, La 6-06-33
Pound 8-19-70
Poupee, La 1-28-21
Poupee, La 5-09-62
Pour Clemence 8-31-77
Pour la Suite de Monde 5-15-63
Pour le Meilleur et Pour le Pire 10-01-75
Pour un Sou d'Amour 3-15-32
Pourquoi Israel? 6-20-73
Pourquoi l'Amerique 11-05-69
Pourquoi Pas? 12-14-77
Pourquoi Viens-Tu Si Tard? 8-19-59
Pourvu Qu'On Ait l'Ivresse 10-16-74
Poussiere Sur la Ville 7-10-68
Poveri Ma Belli 2-27-57
Poverty of Riches, A 11-25-21
Povestj Plamenykh Let 5-17-61
Povra Tak Otpisanih 8-17-77
Povratak 8-15-79
Powder Burns 4-07-71
Powder My Back 8-08-28
Powder River 5-13-53
Powder River Rustlers 2-08-50
Powder Town 5-13-42
Powdersmoke Range 3-11-36
Power (See: Potere, Il)
Power 10-25-18
Power 7-18-28
Power 11-28-28
Power 10-09-34
Power, The 1-24-68
Power and the Glory, The 8-23-18
Power and the Glory, The 8-22-33
Power and the Land 10-02-40
Power and the Prize, The 9-12-56
Power and the Truth, The (See: Puterea Si Adevarul)
Power Behind the Nation, The 9-17-47
Power Dive 4-09-41
Power Divine, The 9-27-23
Power of a Lie 1-05-23
Power of Darkness 10-31-28
Power of Decision, The 4-13-17
Power of Evil, The 9-29-16
Power of Evil, The 8-14-29
Power of Labor, The 9-26-08
Power of Life, The (See: Dee Kraft Phun Leben)
Power of Men Is the Patience of Women, The (See: Macht der
    Maenner Ist die Geduld der Frauen, Die)
Power of Silence, The 10-24-28
Power of the Press, The 12-05-28
Power of the Press, The 2-24-43
Power of the Weak, The 6-16-26
Power of the Whistler, The 3-28-45
Power of Wong Fai-Hung Shakes the City of Five Goats, The
    2-21-68
Power Play 8-30-78
Power Within, The 2-10-22
Powers Girl, The 12-23-42
Powers That Prey 3-15-18
Pozdravi Mariju, Sedmina 8-20-69
Pozegnania 7-29-59
Poznajete Li Pavla Plesa 8-25-76
Pozo, El (See: Well, The)
Pozor 3-14-33
Practically Yours 12-20-44
Praeriens Skrappe Drenge 9-30-70
Praesten I Vejlby 9-20-72
Praetorius (See: Dr. Med. Hiob Praetorius)
Prairie, The 8-25-48
Prairie Badmen 7-24-46
Prairie Chickens 7-14-43
Prairie Express 12-03-47
Prairie Justice 11-30-38
Prairie King, The 5-25-27
Prairie Law 6-26-40
Prairie Moon 10-19-38
Prairie Pioneers 2-26-41
Prairie Roundup 1-24-51
Prairie Rustlers 1-23-46
Prairie Schooners 11-13-40
Prairie Stranger 9-03-41
Prairie Thunder 12-01-37
Prairie Wife, The 5-13-25
Praise Agent, The 8-08-19

Praise Marx and Pass the Ammunition 9-23-70
Praised Be What Hardens You (See: Gelobt Sei Was Hart Macht)
Pranke, Die 12-01-31
Prapanch 8-15-62
Prasad 12-31-75
Prata Palomares 5-10-72
Praterbuben 2-26-47
Pratidwandi 9-08-71
Prato, Il 9-05-79
Pratyusha 2-27-80
Prawo I Piese 7-29-64
Praznovanje Pomladi 8-16-78
Pre Istine 8-14-68
Prea Mic Pentru Um Razboi Atit De Mare 10-14-70
Prebroiavane Na Divite Zaitsi 8-21-74
Precarious Bank Teller, The (See: Rag, Arturo De Fanti, Bancario-
    Precario)
Precipice, The 11-19-58
Predator, The (See: Alpagueur, L')
Predstava Hamlet U Mrdusi Donjoj 8-22-73
Prefab Story (See: Panel Story)
Prefetto Di Ferro, Il 11-16-77
Pregnant by a Ghost (See: Kun Pi)
Prehistoric Women 1-03-51
Prehistoric Women 1-25-67
Preis Fuers Ueberleben, Der 2-13-80
Prejudice 2-23-49
Preliminary Trial (See: Vorumntersuchung)
Prelude a la Gloire 7-12-50
Prelude to Fame 5-10-50
Prelude to Glory (See: Prelude a la Gloire)
Prelude to Madness 11-02-49
Prelude to Spain (See: Preludio a Espana)
Prelude to War 5-12-43
Preludio a Espana 5-10-72
Preludio d'Amore 2-11-48
Premature Burial 3-14-62
Premia 12-03-75
Premier Rendezvous (See: Her First Affair)
Premier Voyage 7-02-80
Premiere 2-24-37
Premiere Fois, La 12-01-76
Premieres Armes, Les 9-06-50
Premonition, The 11-26-75
Prenez Garde a la Peinture 5-16-33
Prep and Pep 12-26-28
Preparation for the Festival (See: Matsuri No Junbi)
Prepared to Die 12-27-23
Preparez Vos Mouchoirs 1-11-78
Presage (See: Presagio)
Presagio 10-09-74
Prescott Kid, The 10-21-36
Prescription for Romance 12-22-37
Present Times (See: Jelenido)
Presenting Lily Mars 4-28-43
President, Le 3-15-61
President, The 1-23-29
President Haudecoeur, Le 5-08-40
President Vanishes, The 12-11-34
Presidentessa 12-10-52
President's Analyst, The 12-20-67
President's Lady, The 3-11-53
President's Mystery, The 10-21-36
President's Special, The 2-19-10
Press for Time 12-14-66
Pressure 12-01-76
Pressure of Guilt 2-05-64
Pressure Point 9-12-62
Prestige 2-09-32
Prestuplenie I Nakazanie 9-02-70
Presuda 8-17-77
Prete Sposato, Il 1-20-71
Pretender, The 10-18-18
Pretender, The 8-20-47
Pretenders, The 8-25-16
Pretres Interdits 1-02-74
Pretty Baby 7-26-50
Pretty Baby 4-05-78
Pretty-Boy and Rosa (See: Smukke-Arne and Rosa)
Pretty Boy Floyd 1-20-60
Pretty Clothes 1-18-28
Pretty Girl of Nice 9-18-09
Pretty Good for a Human (See: Aika Hyva Ihmiseksi)
Pretty Ladies 7-15-25
Pretty Little Beach, A (See: Si Jolie Petite Plage, Une)
Pretty Maids All in a Row 3-03-71
Pretty May (See: Joli Mai, Le)
Pretty Miller Girl, The (See: Belle Meuniere, La)
Pretty Mrs. Smith 4-23-15

Promise Me Nothing (See: Versprich Mir Nichts)
Promised Land, The (See: Tierra Prometida, La or Ziemia Obiecana)
Promised Lands 7-10-74
Promises in the Dark 10-31-79
Promises, Promises 8-07-63
Promitheas Se Theftero Prosopo 11-05-75
Prong Nee Chan Ja Rak Koon 5-21-80
Proof of the Wild (See: Yasei No Shomei)
Proper Time, The 11-25-59
Proper Way, The (See: Kosadate Gokko)
Property Is No Longer a Theft (See: Proprieta' Non E Piu' Un Furto, La)
Prophecy 6-13-79
Prophet of Hunger, The (See: O Profeta Da Fome)
Prophet's Paradise 3-10-22
Propre de l'Homme, Le 10-26-60
Proprieta' Non E Piu' Un Furto, La 7-11-73
Prosfygopoula 9-28-38
Proshaite Golubi 8-02-61
Proshu Slova 7-28-76
Prosperity 11-29-32
Prossopo Me Prossopo 1-23-66
Prostitute 6-04-80
Prostitution 6-16-76
Prostitution, La 4-17-63
Prostitution File (See: Dossier Prostitution)
Protagonisti, I 5-22-68
Protagonists, The (See: Protagonisti, I)
Protect Us 5-15-14
Protecteur, Le 7-03-74
Protection 9-11-29
Protector, The (See: Protecteur, Le)
Protest 8-16-67
Protevousianikes Peripeties 7-31-57
Proud and the Profane, The 5-30-56
Proud, Damned and Dead 5-07-69
Proud Flesh 4-15-25
Proud Heart 11-04-25
Proud Ones, The (See: Orgueilleux, Les)
Proud Ones, The 5-30-56
Proud Rebel, The 4-02-58
Proud Rider, The 10-06-71
Proud Twins, The 8-22-79
Proud Valley, The 1-31-40
Prova d'Orchestra 3-07-79
Providence 1-12-77
Provincial, The (See: Provinciale, La)
Provincial Actors (See: Aktorzy Prowincjonalni)
Provinciale, La 4-29-53
Provinciale, La 12-10-80
Provisional Liberty (See: Liberte Sureveille)
Provocation (See: Du Gamia, Du Fria)
Prowler, The 4-25-51
Prowlers of the Night 12-01-26
Prowlers of the Sea 7-25-28
Proxies 4-15-21
Prozess, Der 3-17-48
Prudence and the Pill 5-15-68
Prudence on Broadway 7-18-19
Prune des Bois 2-06-80
Prunella 6-07-18
Przed Odlotem 10-15-80
Przepraszam, Czy Tu Bija? 2-09-77 and 6-01-77
P.S. 6-11-80
Psex-Analysis (See: Psexonalisis)
Psexanalysed or The Neurotics, The (See: Psexonalizados O Los Neuroticos, Los)
Psexoanalisis 7-24-68
Psexonalizados O Los Neuroticos, Los 10-29-69
Psyche 59 4-29-64
Psychic, The 5-16-79
Psychic Killer 11-05-75
Psycho 6-22-60
Psycho-Circus 5-24-67
Psychologie des Orgasmus 9-02-70
Psychology of the Orgasm (See: Psychologie des Orgasmus)
Psychomania 2-19-64 and 12-16-64
Psychopath, The 5-11-66
Psychotronic Man, The 5-07-80
Psych-Out 3-13-68
Psychout for Murder 1-27-71
P'tit Vient Vite, Le 11-01-72
Ptizi I Hrutki 10-29-69
Public Affair, A 3-28-62
Public Be Damned, The 6-29-17
Public Cowboy No. 1 9-22-37
Public Deb. No. 1 8-28-40

Public Defender 8-04-31
Public Defender, The 10-05-17
Public Enemies 1-28-42
Public Enemy, The 4-29-31
Public Enemy No. 1 (See: Ennemi Public No. 1, L')
Public Enemy's Wife, The 7-15-36
Public Eye, The 7-12-72
Public Hero No. 1 6-12-35
Public Menace 9-25-35
Public Nuisance No. 1 3-11-36
Public Opinion 8-18-16
Public Opinion 10-30-35
Public Pigeon No. 1 1-16-57
Public Rumor (See: Rumeur Publique)
Public School, The (See: Communale, La)
Public Stenographer 1-30-34
Public Wedding 9-15-37
Publicity Madness 10-19-27
Puccini 5-20-53
Puddin'head 7-02-41
Pudd'nhead Wilson 2-04-16
Pueblerina 8-10-49
Pueblito 7-11-62
Puente, La 8-10-77
Pufnstuf 6-03-70
Pugachev 7-13-38
Pugni In Tasca, I 8-25-65
Puits Aux Trois Verites, Le 9-27-61
Pukotina Raja 8-12-59
Pulgarcito (See: Tom Thumb)
Pull-Over Rouge, Le 12-12-79
Pullman Train 13 Late (See: D-Zug 13 Hat Verspaetung)
Pulp 8-30-72
Pulsation, A (See: Pulsation, Une)
Pulsation, Une 2-25-70
Pulse of Life, The 3-23-17
Pumping Iron 1-19-77
Pumpkin Eater, The 5-20-64
Punatukka 7-08-70
Punch and Judy Man, The 4-17-63
Punishment, The (See: Punition, La)
Punishment Island (See: Shokei No Shima)
Punishment Park 6-30-71
Punishment to the Traitor (See: Castigo Al Traidor)
Punition, La 5-08-63
Punition, La 7-18-73
Punk in London 3-28-79
Punk Rock Movie, The 6-21-78
Punktchen Und Anton 1-20-54
Pupa, La 1-22-64
Puppe Kaputt 10-12-77
Puppet, The (See: Hampelmann, Der)
Puppet Crown, The 8-06-15
Puppet on a Chain 8-11-71
Puppets 9-22-16
Puppets 6-23-26
Puppets of Fate 4-22-21
Puppets Under Starry Skies (See: Hoshizora No Marionette)
Puppy Love 3-28-19
Purchase Price, The 7-19-32
Pure Grit 1-10-24
Pure Hell of St. Trinian's, The 12-28-60
Pure S 5-26-76
Purgatory (See: Fegefeuer or Skaerseldan)
Purgatory Eroica (See: Rengoku Eroica)
Purimspieler, Der 12-08-37
Puritain, Le 3-23-38
Puritan, The (See: Puritain, Le)
Purity 7-07-16
Purity of Heart (See: Reinheit des Herzens, Die)
Purple Accacias (See: Lila Akac, A)
Purple and Wash-blue (See: Purpur und Waschblau)
Purple Cipher, The 10-29-20
Purple Dawn 5-17-23
Purple Gang, The 1-13-60
Purple Heart, The 2-23-44
Purple Heart Diary 11-07-51
Purple Highway 7-26-23
Purple Hills, The 10-25-61
Purple Lady, The 6-16-16
Purple Lily, The 4-12-18
Purple Mask, The 6-01-55
Purple Night, The 10-01-15
Purple Plain 9-22-54
Purple Taxi, The (See: Taxi Mauve, Un)
Purple V, The 3-24-43
Purple Vigilantes 2-02-38
Purpur und Waschblau 10-13-31 and 7-12-32
Pursued 11-27-34

Pursued 2-19-47
Pursuer, The (See: Perseguidor, El)
Pursuing Shadow, The 8-06-15
Pursuing Vengeance, The 6-02-16
Pursuit 10-09-35
Pursuit in the Steppe 6-25-80
Pursuit of Happiness, The 10-30-34
Pursuit of Happiness, The 2-24-71
Pursuit of the Graff Spee (See: Battle of River Plate)
Pursuit of the Phantom 1-08-15
Pursuit to Algiers 10-31-45
Push Cart Race, A 11-14-08
Pusher, The 1-20-60
Pushover 7-28-54
Puss & Kram 9-27-67
Puss in Boots (See: Gato Con Botas, El)
Pussy Talk 11-19-75
Pussycat, Pussycat, I Love You 3-25-70
Pustolov Pred Vratima 8-30-61
Puszta Princess 2-15-39
Pusztai Szel 12-15-37
Put 'Em Up 5-02-28
Put On Ice (See: Kaltgestellt)
Put on the Spot 9-16-36
Put U Raj 8-18-71
Put Up Your Hands 2-28-19
Putain Respectueuse, La 9-17-52
Puterea Si Adevarul 9-13-72
Putik Ka Man ... Sa Alabok Magbabalik 9-29-76
Putney Swope 7-09-69
Putovanje Na Mjesto Nesrece 8-18-71
Puttin' On the Ritz 2-19-30
Putting It Over 7-04-19
Putting It Over 8-25-22
Putting One Over 7-04-19
Puzzle of a Downfall Child 11-04-70
Puzzle of the Silver Half-Moon, The (See: Raetsel des Silbernen
    Halbmonds, Das)
Pyat' Vecherov 2-28-79
Pygmalion 9-07-38
Pygmies 10-17-73
Pygmy Island 11-22-50
Pyramid of the Sun-God, The (See: Pyramide Des Sonnengottes, Die)
Pyramide Des Sonnengottes, Die 11-24-65
Pyramide Humaine, La 1-18-61
Pyretos Stin Asphalto 11-08-67
Pyro 4-29-64
Pyx, The 10-03-73

Q

Q Planes 3-15-39
Q-Ships 7-11-28 and 9-26-28
Qanas, El 4-09-80
Qivitoq 5-22-57
Qua La Mano 8-13-80
Quackser Fortune Has a Cousin in the Bronx 7-15-70
Quadrille 2-23-38
Quadroon 5-10-72
Quadrophenia 5-02-79
Quai de Grenelle (See: Danger Is a Woman)
Quai des Blondes 5-26-54
Quai des Brumes, Le 6-15-38
Quai des Orfevres 10-22-47
Quai Notre-Dame 7-05-61
Quality Films 8-11-22
Quality Street 11-09-27
Quality Street 4-14-37
Quand la Femme S'en Mele 1-22-58
Quand la Ville S'Eveille 12-17-75
Quand Nous Etions Petits Enfants 8-02-61
Quand On Est Belle 4-12-32
Quand Passent les Faisans 10-13-65
Quand Tu Liras Cette Lettre 1-20-54
Quando le Donne Avevano la Coda 12-23-70
Quantez 8-28-57
Quanto e'Bello Lu Murire Accisco 12-03-75
Quantrill's Raiders 5-07-58
Quarante-Huit Heures d'Amour 7-02-69
Quarantined Rivals 3-30-27
Quare Fellow, The 10-17-62
Quarrel, The 10-01-10
Quarterback, The 10-13-26

Quarterback, The 10-02-40
Quarterly Balance-Taking (See: Bilans Kwartalny)
Quartet 11-03-48
Quartier Interdit 2-06-52
Quatermass Conclusion 2-13-80
Quatermass Experiment, The 9-07-55
Quatre Cents Coups, Les 4-29-59
Quatre de l'Infanterie 1-07-31
Quatre d'Entre Elles 10-30-68
Quatre du Moana, Les 7-29-59
Quatre Nuits d'un Reveur 7-07-71
Quatres Verites, Les 1-02-63
Quattro Giornate di Napoli, Le (See: Four Days of Naples, The)
Quattro Mosche di Velluto Grigio 1-19-72
Que Bonito Amor 10-12-60
Que Dios Me Perdone 5-12-48
Que Es El Otono? 6-01-77
Que Hacer? 5-17-72
Que Hombre Tan Simpatico! 2-23-44
Que la Bete Meure 9-17-69
Que la Fete Commence 3-05-75
Que Lindo es Michoacan 5-10-44
Que Viva Mexico 9-05-79
Quebec 2-28-51
Quebec-My-Love 5-20-70
Quebracho 7-31-74
Queen, The 5-15-68
Queen Bee, The (See: Jo-Bachi or Ape Regina, L')
Queen Bee, The 10-19-55
Queen Christina 1-02-34
Queen for a Day 3-21-51
Queen for a Night 1-01-47
Queen High 8-13-30
Queen in Australia 5-26-54
Queen Louise 5-02-28
Queen Luise (See: Koenigin Luise)
Queen Margaret 10-03-14
Queen o' Diamonds 4-21-26
Queen o' the Turf 5-12-22
Queen of a Night, The (See: Koenigin einer Nacht, Die)
Queen of Babylon 8-15-56
Queen of Blood 3-26-69
Queen of Burlesque 2-19-10
Queen of Burlesque 7-03-46
Queen of Clubs, The (See: Dama Spathi)
Queen of Hearts, The 12-03-10
Queen of Hearts, The 3-25-36
Queen of Love (See: Koenigin Der Liebe)
Queen of Outer Space 8-13-58
Queen of Sheba 4-15-21
Queen of Sheba 11-11-53
Queen of Sin 3-29-23
Queen of Spades (See: Dame de Pique, La)
Queen of Spades, The 3-30-49
Queen of Spades, The 12-20-61
Queen of Sparta (See: Regina di Sparta, La)
Queen of the Chorus 6-06-28
Queen of the Mob 7-03-40
Queen of the Moulin Rouge 11-03-22
Queen of the Night Clubs 3-20-29
Queen of the Quarry 8-28-09
Queen of the Ranch 4-24-09
Queen of the Roses 7-21-16
Queen of the Scala (See: Regina Della Scala)
Queen of the Skull Clan 10-03-14
Queen of the Yukon 10-16-40
Queenie 12-09-21
Queens, The 4-03-68
Queen's Father, The (See: Ojciec Krolowej)
Queen's Favorite 5-17-23
Queen's Guards, The 10-25-61
Queen's Hussar, The (See: A Kiralyno Huszarja)
Queen's Necklace, The (See: Collier de la Reine, Le)
Queen's Ransom, A 10-13-76
Queen's World Tour, A 3-10-54
Queer Assignment, The (See: Extravagante Mission, L')
Queer Cargo 8-17-38
Queimada (See: Burn)
Quele Do Pajeu 12-03-69
Quella Piccola Differenza 1-28-70
Quelle Strane Occasioni 3-09-77
Quelq'un Derrier la Porte 9-01-71
Quelque Part, Quelqu'un 11-15-72
Quelques Arpents de Neige ... 3-07-73
Quelques Messieurs Trop Tranquilles 2-21-73
Quem e Beta? 6-27-73

Quentin Durward   10-19-55
Querida, La   5-26-76
Queridas Amigas   7-09-80
Queridisimos Verdugos   5-04-77
Queridos Companeros   3-22-78
Query   10-03-45
Qu'est Ce Que Tu Veux Julie?   3-23-77
Quest for Love   9-29-71
Quest for the Lost City   12-22-54
Quest of Life, The   9-29-16
Questa Specie d'Amore   2-07-73
Questa Volta Parliamo Di Uomini   4-28-65
Questi Ragazzi   3-24-37
Question, La   4-27-77
Question, The (See: Question, La)
Question, The   2-25-16
Question de Vie   5-19-71
Question Mark   11-21-73
Question of Adultery, A   7-23-58
Question of Honor, A   3-17-22 and 8-11-22
Question of Life, A (See: Question de Vie)
Question of Today   5-02-28
Question 7   7-05-61
Questione d'Onore, Una   2-23-66
Questo Amore Ai Confini Del Mondo   8-10-60
Questo Si Che E'Amore   3-01-78
Qui?   10-14-70
Qui Etes-Vous Mr. Sorge?   4-19-61
Qui Etes-Vous Polly Magoo?   11-02-66
Qui Veut Tuer Carlos? (See: Dead Run)
Quick   9-13-32
Quick and the Dead, The   3-06-63
Quick, Before It Melts   12-16-64
Quick Gun, The   4-15-64
Quick Millions   4-22-31
Quick Millions   8-16-39
Quick Money   2-16-38
Quick on the Trigger   5-25-49
Quick Triggers   7-18-28
Quicksand   12-20-18
Quicksand   3-01-50
Quicksands   3-29-23
Quien Puede Matar a un Nino?   5-05-76
Quien Sabe   7-19-67
Quiere Casarse Conmigo?   3-22-67
Quiet American, The   1-22-58
Quiet Daddy, The (See: Pere Tranquille, Le)
Quiet Day in Belfast, A   2-20-74
Quiet Days in Clichy   5-13-70
Quiet Flows the Don (See: Tichy Don)
Quiet Gun, The   3-27-57
Quiet Is the Night (See: Wsrod Nocnej Ciszy)
Quiet Man, The   5-14-52
Quiet One, The   2-16-49
Quiet Place in the Country, A (See: Tranquillo Posto di
    Campagna, Un)
Quiet Please, Murder   12-16-42
Quiet Summer, A (See: Mirno Leto)
Quiet Wedding, A   3-05-41
Quiet Week-end   5-15-46
Quijote Sin Mancha, Un   2-25-70
Quiller Memorandum, The   11-16-66
Quincannon, Frontier Scout   4-18-56
Quincy Adams Sawyer   12-01-22
Quinney's   12-28-27
Quinta Calumnia, La   2-05-41
Quintet   2-07-79
Quite Good Chaps (See: Dost Dobri Chlai)
Quite Ordinary Life, A (See: Ket Elhatarozas)
Quitter, The   4-24-29
Quitters, The   3-20-34
Quixote Without La Mancha, A (See: Quijote Sin Mancha, Un)
Quo Vadis   4-25-13
Quo Vadis?   2-18-25 and 7-31-29
Quo Vadis   11-14-51

R

R.A.F.   7-03-35
R.A.S.   8-29-73
R.P.M.   9-16-70
R.S.V.P.   12-16-21
Ra Expeditions, The   1-12-72
Ra-mu   2-13-29
Raba Lubvi   6-14-78
Rabbi and the Shikse, The   6-30-76
Rabbit Case, The (See: Causa Kralik)
Rabbit in the Pit (See: Haeschen In der Grube)
Rabbit, Run   11-04-70
Rabbit Test   2-22-78
Rabbit Trap, The   7-08-59
Rabble, The   4-10-68
Rabia, La   5-16-79
Rabid   6-29-77
Rabindranath Tagore   8-02-61
Racconti Romani   3-28-56
Race, The   4-07-16
Race d'Ep   3-05-80
Race des "Seigneurs," La   4-24-74
Race for Life, A   2-01-28
Race for Life, A   2-09-55
Race for Your Life, Charlie Brown   6-29-77
Race in the Head, The (See: Course En Tete, La)
Race Street   6-23-48
Race, the Spirit of Franco (See: Raza, El Espiritu De Franco)
Race Track   3-07-33
Race with the Devil   6-11-75
Racers, The   2-02-55
Racetrack Winners (See: As Du Turf, Les)
Rachel and the Stranger   8-04-48
Rachel, Rachel   8-21-68
Rachinee Fin   10-08-75
Racing Blood   8-25-26
Racing Blood   4-06-38
Racing Blood   3-24-54
Racing Fool, The   10-05-27
Racing for Life   8-20-24
Racing Hearts   2-22-23
Racing Lady   1-20-37
Racing Luck   11-10-48
Racing Romance   5-12-26
Racing Romeo   10-26-27
Racing Strain, The   1-24-33
Racing Youth   4-19-32
Rack, The   4-18-56
Racket, The   7-11-28
Racket, The   10-17-51
Racket Busters   8-17-38
Racketeer, The   1-08-30
Racketeers in Exile   4-14-37
Racketeers of the Range   5-31-39
Rackety Rax   11-08-32
Rad Bizom a Felesegem   5-12-37
Radar Secret Service   1-18-50
Radio Bar   1-27-37
Radio Bug, The   9-15-26
Radio City Revels   2-02-38
Radio On   9-12-79
Radio Parade of 1935   1-01-35
Radio Patrol   7-19-32
Radio Patrol   9-15-37
Radio Stars on Parade   8-08-45
Radio Surprises (See: Surprises Radio)
Raetsel des Silbernen Halbmonds, Das   8-23-72
Rafal U Nebo   8-20-58
Rafferty and the Gold Dust Twins   1-15-75
Raffles   12-07-17
Raffles   4-29-25
Raffles   7-30-30
Raffles   12-20-39
Rafles Sur la Ville   3-19-58
Rafter Romance   1-16-34
Rag, Arturo De Fanti, Bancario-Precario   4-23-80
Rag Man, The   3-04-25
Raga   12-01-71
Ragamuffin, The   1-28-16
Ragamuffin of Tormes, The (See: Lazarillo de Tormes, El)
Ragazza Con la Pistola, La   7-24-68
Ragazza Con la Valigia, La   3-29-61

Ragazza de Latte, La 11-25-70
Ragazza Del Palio, La 3-26-58
Ragazza Delle Saline, La 7-24-57
Ragazza di Bube, La 1-15-64
Ragazza di Passaggio, La 9-06-72
Ragazza di Via Millelire, La 9-10-80
Ragazza e il Generale, La 6-28-67
Ragazza in Pigiama Giallo, La 2-08-78
Ragazza in Vetrina, La 5-03-61
Ragazza Piuttosto Complicata, Una 1-22-69
Ragazze di Piazza di Spagna 4-02-52
Ragazze de Sanfrediano, Le 4-15-55
Ragazzi del Massacro, I (See: Woman On Fire, A)
Ragazzo di Borgata 6-16-76
Rage (See: Rabia, La)
Rage 11-30-66
Rage 11-08-72
Rage at Dawn 3-09-55
Rage au Corps, La 3-31-54
Rage au Poign, La 2-26-75
Rage in Heaven 3-05-41
Rage of Paris, The 10-07-21
Rage of Paris, The 6-15-38
Rage to Live, A 9-15-65
Ragged Earl, The 10-10-14
Ragged Edge, The 6-07-23
Ragged Football (See: Pelota de Trapo)
Ragged Heiress 4-07-22
Ragged Princess, The 10-20-16
Raggedy Ann and Andy 3-16-77
Raggen 5-27-36
Raggen, That's Me (See: Raggen)
Raging Bull 11-12-80
Raging Fists (See: Rage au Poign, La)
Raging Moon, The 2-03-71
Raging Tide, The 10-17-51
Ragione Per Morire, Una (See: Reason to Live, A Reason to Die, A)
Ragman's Daughter, The 5-24-72
Ragpickers' Angel (See: Ari No Machi No Maria)
Ragpickers of Emmaus, The (See: Chiffonniers d'Emmaus, Les)
Rags 8-06-15
Rags, Old Iron 3-12-10
Rags to Riches 9-29-22
Rags to Riches 8-13-41
Ragtime 12-28-27
Ragtime Cowboy Joe 10-02-40
Rai Saneh Ha 7-11-79
Raices de Piedra 8-07-63
Raices de Sangre 6-20-79
Raid, The 6-02-54
Raid in St. Pauli (See: Razzia in St. Pauli)
Raid on Rommel 2-24-71
Raid on the Drug Ring (See: Razzia Sur la Chnouf)
Raider Emden, The 5-02-28
Raiders, The 3-03-16
Raiders, The 7-08-21
Raiders, The 10-08-52
Raiders of Leyte Gulf 8-28-63
Raiders of Red Gap 5-03-44
Raiders of San Joaquin 6-02-43
Raiders of the Border 2-16-44
Raiders of the Range 4-01-42
Raiders of the Seven Seas 5-29-53
Raiders of Tomahawk Creek 11-08-50
Raids on the City (See: Rafles Sur la Ville)
Rail Rider, The 8-18-16
Railroad Fight (See: Bataille du Rail)
Railroad Man, The (See: Ferroviere, Il)
Railroad Workers (See: Rallare)
Railroaded 6-14-23
Railroaded 10-08-47
Rails into Laramie 3-24-54
Railway Children, The 12-30-70
Railway on the Ice Sea 1-22-10
Rain 10-18-32
Rain for a Dusty Summer 9-15-71
Rain or Shine 7-23-30
Rain People, The 6-25-69
Rainbow 12-16-21
Rainbow, The 1-12-17
Rainbow, The 11-01-44
Rainbow Boys, The 4-11-73
Rainbow Bridge 3-29-72
Rainbow Dilemma, The (See: Lek Pa Regnbagen)
Rainbow Island 9-06-44
Rainbow Jacket 6-09-54
Rainbow Man 4-24-29
Rainbow on the River 12-23-36

Rainbow over Broadway 12-26-33
Rainbow over Texas 5-08-46
Rainbow over the Range 11-06-40
Rainbow Princess, The 10-27-16
Rainbow Ranch 10-24-33
Rainbow Rangers 8-20-24
Rainbow 'Round My Shoulder 8-06-52
Rainbow Trail, The 10-18-18
Rainbow Trail, The 6-03-25
Rainbow Trail, The 2-02-32
Rainbow Valley 5-15-35
Rainbow's End 7-17-35
Rainey African Hunt 6-26-14
Rainha Diaba, A 10-01-75
Raining in the Mountain 7-18-79
Rainmaker, The 5-19-26
Rainmaker, The 12-12-56
Rainmakers, The 11-06-35
Rains Came, The 9-13-39
Rains of Ranchipur, The 12-14-55
Raintree County 10-09-57
Rainy Love, A (See: Amour de Pluie, Un)
Raisces 6-01-55
Raise Ravens (See: Cria Cuervos)
Raise the Titanic 8-06-80
Raisin in the Sun, A 3-29-61
Raising a Riot 3-16-55
Raising the Wind 9-27-61
Raison d'Etat, La 5-24-78
Raison du Plus Fou, La 4-04-73
Rak 4-26-72
Rak Kam Lok 5-24-78
Rak Otaroot 7-06-77
Rak Ri Sayar 6-20-79
Rakas 9-12-62
Rake's Progress, The 12-05-45
Rakoczi Indulo 10-28-36
Rakoczi March (See: Rakoczi Indulo)
Rallarblod 8-22-79
Rallare 2-18-48
Rally Round the Flag 12-18-09
Rally 'Round the Flag, Boys 12-24-58
Ralph Benefits by Others' Curiosity 9-04-09
Ramble in Erin 11-21-51
Ramble Through Ceylon, A 12-03-10
Rambles in Paris 3-07-13
Ramblin' Kid, The 9-13-23
Rambling Ranger 8-03-27
Ramona 2-25-16 and 4-07-16
Ramona 5-16-28
Ramona 10-14-36
Rampage 8-14-63
Rampant Age, The 1-15-30
Rampart of Desire (See: Rempart Des Beguines, Le)
Ramparts of Age (See: Remparts d'Argile)
Ramparts We Watch, The 7-24-40
Ramper 12-21-27
Ramrod 2-26-47
Ramshackle House 1-07-25
Ramuntcho 3-23-38
Ran & Ran 6-11-80
Ran Salu (See: Yellow Robes, The)
Ranch King's Daughter, The 1-29-10
Ranch Riders 12-14-27
Rancho Deluxe 3-26-75
Rancho Grande 12-07-38
Rancho Grande 3-27-40
Rancho Notorious 2-06-52
Rancor of the Soil (See: Rencor de la Tierra, El)
Randolph Family, The 3-14-45
Random Harvest 11-25-42
Range Beyond the Blue 3-12-47
Range Busters, The 11-20-40
Range Courage 7-20-27
Range Defenders 7-14-37
Range Justice 11-23-49
Range Land 3-01-50
Range Law 12-08-31
Range Law 8-16-44
Range War 8-30-39
Ranger, The 5-31-18
Ranger and the Lady, The 7-24-40
Ranger Courage 7-28-37
Ranger of Cherokee Strip, The 11-09-49
Ranger of the Big Pines 7-29-25
Ranger of the North 12-28-27
Ranger's Code 9-26-33

Rangers of Fortune 9-11-40
Ranger's Roundup 9-21-38
Rangers Step In 11-03-37
Rangers Take Over, The 3-31-43
Rangle River 1-20-37
Rango 2-25-31
Rani Radovi 7-16-69
Rank Outsider, A 12-17-20
Rannstensungar 10-08-75
Ransom 8-15-28
Ransom! 1-11-56
Ransom 4-24-74 and 3-26-75
Ransom, The 1-14-16
Ransomed; or, A Prisoner of War 10-08-10
Ransom's Folly 9-24-15
Ranson's Folly 6-02-14 and 6-09-26
Raoni 3-08-78
Rapace, Le 4-24-68
Rape, The (See: Viol, Le)
Rape of a Sweet Young Girl (See: Viol D'Une Jeunne Fille Douce,
    Le)
Rape of the Sabines, The (See: Enlevement des Sabines, L')
Rape--The Anders Case (See: Voldtekt (Tilfellet Anders))
Raphael, or the Debauched One (See: Raphael, ou le Debauche)
Raphael, ou le Debauche 4-14-71
Rapids, The 7-04-23
Rappel Immediat 7-12-39
Rapportpigen 2-27-74
Rapture (See: Arrebato)
Rapture 3-09-49
Rapture 8-25-65
Rare Breed, The 2-02-66
Rare Bird (See: Oiseau Rare, Un)
Ras le Bol 9-05-73
Rascal 6-11-69
Rascals (See: Turlupins, Les)
Rascals 5-25-38
Rascel-Fifi 3-19-58
Rascoala 5-18-66
Rash One, The (See: Espontaneo, El)
Rasho Mon 9-19-51
Raspoutine 10-06-54
Rasputin 9-14-17
Rasputin 1-23-29
Rasputin 3-08-32
Rasputin 10-18-39
Rasputin and the Empress 12-27-32
Rasputin--The Mad Monk 4-27-66
Rasskaz Moei Materi 9-17-58
Rasskaz O Neisvestnom Celoveke 9-17-80
Rat 8-10-60
Rat, The 8-21-14
Rat, The 9-23-25
Rat, The 11-24-37
Rat d'Amerique, Le 5-29-63
Rat Fink 1-12-66
Rat Pfink and Boo Boo 9-14-66
Rat Race, The (See: Je Vais Craquer)
Rat Race, The 5-04-60
Ratai 2-19-64
Ratas, Las 4-03-63
Ratataplan 9-05-79
Rather Complicated Girl, A (See: Ragazza Piuttosto Complicata,
    Una)
Rationing 1-26-44
Raton Pass 2-28-51
Rats 10-29-10
Rats, The (See: Ratten, Die or Ratas, Las)
Rats of Tobruk, The 2-07-45
Rats Wake Up, The (See: Budjenje Pacova)
Ratsel Um Beate 3-23-38
Ratten, Die 7-13-55
Rattle of a Simple Man 9-16-64
Rattlesnake, The (See: Cascabel)
Raub der Mona Lisa 9-15-31 and 4-05-32
Raub der Sabinerinnen 2-10-37
Raubfischer In Hellas 11-25-59
Raulito, La 9-03-75
Rauschgift 12-20-32
Ravagers 5-30-79
Ravagers, The 12-08-65
Raven, The 11-12-15
Raven, The 7-10-35
Raven, The 2-25-48
Raven, The 2-06-63
Raven Street (See: Kvarteret Korpen)
Raven's Dance, The (See: Korpinpolska)

Ravished Armenia 2-28-19
Ravishing (See: Ravissante)
Ravishing Idiot, A (See: Ravissante Idiote, Une)
Ravissante 2-01-61
Ravissante Idiote, Une 4-01-64
Raw Deal 5-19-48
Raw Deal 2-09-77
Raw Edge 7-25-56
Raw Timber 11-09-38
Raw Wind in Eden 7-23-58
Rawhide 4-06-38
Rawhide 3-07-51
Rawhide Kid, The 1-18-28
Rawhide Rangers 8-20-41
Rawhide Years, The 6-06-56
Ray of Sunlight, A (See: Kratko Sluntze)
Raya and Sekina 7-29-53
Raymie 5-04-60
Raymond (See: Ramuntcho)
Raza, El Espiritu de Franco 11-23-77
Razlom 12-03-30
Razor in the Flesh (See: A Navalha Na Carne)
Razor's Edge, The 11-20-46
Razumov 3-17-37
Razza Selvaggia 10-15-80
Razzia 6-16-48
Razzia in St. Pauli 6-07-32
Razzia Sur la Chnouf 6-08-55
Re Burlone, Il 4-08-36
Re: Lucky Luciano 11-14-73
Reach for Glory 8-08-62 and 11-14-62
Reach for the Sky 7-18-56
Reaching for the Moon 11-23-17
Reaching for the Moon 1-07-31
Reaching for the Sun 4-09-41
Ready for Action (See: Klart Till Drabbning)
Ready for Love 12-04-34
Ready for the People 10-21-64
Ready in a Minute 4-30-10
Ready Money 11-14-14
Ready, Willing and Able 3-17-37
Real Adventure, The 6-30-22
Real Bargain, The (See: Bonne Occase, La)
Real Folks 2-08-18
Real Game, The (See: Hamiskhak Ha'Amiti)
Real Glory, The 9-13-39
Real Guilty, The (See: Vrai Coupable, Le)
Real Life 3-07-79
Realengo 18 7-04-62
Really Big Family, The 3-08-67
Reap the Wild Wind 3-25-42
Reapers, The 3-31-16
Rear Window 7-14-54
Reason to Live, a Reason to Die, A 2-27-74
Reason Why, The 5-03-18
Rebecca 3-27-40
Rebecca of Sunnybrook Farm 9-07-17
Rebecca of Sunnybrook Farm 8-02-32
Rebecca of Sunnybrook Farm 3-09-38
Rebel, The (See: Revolte, Le; Al Moutmarred; Rebelle, Le; or
    Rebelde, El)
Rebel, The 8-01-33
Rebel, The 3-15-61
Rebel City 5-13-53
Rebel in Town 6-27-56
Rebel Intruders, The 10-29-80
Rebel Patagonia, The (See: Patagonia Rebelde, La)
Rebel Set, The 7-15-59
Rebel Without a Cause 10-26-55
Rebelde, El 3-14-45
Rebelion de los Colgados, La 9-08-54
Rebelle, Le 9-01-31
Rebelle, Le 12-03-80
Rebellion (See: Jiouchi)
Rebellion 5-04-38
Rebellion of the Hanged, The (See: Rebelion de los Colgados, La)
Rebellious Bride, The 4-11-19
Rebellious Daughters 9-21-38
Rebels Against the Light 11-18-64
Rebels of Lomanach, The (See: Revoltes de Lomanach, Les)
Rebound 9-01-31
Rebozo De Soledad, El 10-01-52
Recaptured Love 8-13-30
Recess 7-02-69
Recif de Corail 5-03-39
Reckless 4-24-35
Reckless, The (See: Bella Grinta, Una)
Reckless Age, The 6-11-24

Red Wheat (See: Crveno Klasje)
Red, White and Black, The 12-23-70
Red, White and Blue 3-03-71
Red, White and Blue Blood 1-04-18
Red Widow, The 4-28-16
Red Wine 3-20-29
Red Wing's Gratitude 10-16-09
Red Woman, The 2-02-17
Redeemed Criminal, The 1-07-11
Redeemer, The (See: Izbavitelj)
Redeeming Sin, The 1-21-25
Redeeming Sin, The 2-20-29
Redemption 10-03-14
Redemption 5-04-17
Redemption 5-07-30
Redemption of David Corson, The 4-17-14
Redes (See: Wave, The)
Redhead 5-23-19
Redhead 7-02-41
Redhead, The (See: Rote, Die or Punatukka)
Redhead, The 4-24-14
Redhead and the Cowboy, The 12-13-50
Redhead from Manhattan, The 6-16-43
Redhead from Wyoming, The 12-24-52
Redheads on Parade 9-04-35
Redheads Preferred 12-29-26
Redman and the Child, The 8-01-08
Redskin 1-30-29
Reducing 1-21-31
Redwood Forest Trail 9-20-50
Reed Case, The 7-20-17
Reedham's Orphanage Festival 1910 10-01-10
Reef of Stars 9-27-23
Reenactment, The (See: Reconstitiurea)
Referee, The 5-26-22
Refinements in Love 8-04-71
Reflection (See: Reflexion)
Reflection of Fear, A 3-14-73
Reflections (See: Tukerkepek or Zrcadleni)
Reflections in a Golden Eye 10-11-67
Reflexion 4-22-70
Reform Candidate, The 12-31-15
Reform Girl 12-12-33
Reform School 5-03-39
Reform School Girl 8-28-57
Reformatory 6-29-38
Reformer and the Redhead, The 3-08-50
Refuge (See: Zuflucht)
Refuge 8-09-23
Refugee, The 6-19-40
Refugees in Madrid (See: Refugiados en Madrid)
Refugiados en Madrid 6-22-38
Refusal, The (See: Verweigerung, Der)
Regard Picasso, Le 9-06-67
Regates de San Francisco, Les 5-04-60
Regattas of San Francisco, The (See: Regates de San Francisco,
   Les)
Regenerates, The 11-23-17
Regeneration, The 9-24-15
Regeneration of Love, The 3-12-15
Regenta, La 1-22-75
Regent's Wife, The (See: Regenta, La)
Reggae 10-06-71
Reggae Sunsplash 10-01-80
Reggie Mixes In 6-02-16
Regiment's Champion, The (See: Champion du Regiment)
Regina Della Scala 11-03-37
Regina di Sparta, La 3-04-31
Regina Maris 7-02-69
Registered Nurse 6-05-34
Reg'lar Fellers 12-10-41
Regle du Jeu, La 8-30-39
Regne du Jour, Le 5-03-67
Regno di Napoli, Il 6-28-78
Regreso Al Silencio 3-08-67
Regular Fellow, A 4-25-19
Regular Fellow, A 10-14-25
Regular Fellow, A (See: Ganzer Kerl, Ein)
Regular Girl, A 11-14-19
Regular Scout, A 12-01-26
Rehearsal Goes On, The 9-14-60
Reifende Jugend 10-17-33 and 1-08-36
Reifezeit 4-21-76
Reign of Terror 5-18-49
Reina Zanahoria 1-25-78
Reincarnate, The 5-05-71
Reincarnation of Peter Proud, The 4-02-75
Reinheit Des Herzens, Die 5-14-80

Reivers, The 11-26-69
Rejanne Padovani 6-13-73
Rejected Woman, The 5-07-24
Rejs 3-05-80
Rejuvenation of Aunt Mary 7-27-27
Rekava 7-24-57
Rekolekcje 10-04-78
Rekopis Znaleziony W Saragossie 9-15-65
Rektor Paa Sengekanten 3-22-72
Relax, Freddie 10-19-66
Relay Race (See: Stafeta)
Release the Prisoners, It's Spring (See: Slapp Fangarne Loss, Det
   Ar Var)
Relentless 1-14-48
Religieuse, La 3-30-66
Reluctant Astronaut, The 1-18-67
Reluctant Debutante, The 8-06-58
Reluctant Dragon, The 6-11-41
Reluctant Gunfighter, The (See: Mue Peun Khia)
Reluctant Saint, The 8-08-62
Reluctant Widow, The 9-05-51
Remains of the Shipwreck, The (See: Restos del Naufragio, Los)
Remains To Be Seen 4-22-53
Remarkable Andrew, The 1-21-42
Remarkable Mr. Kipps, The 3-11-42
Remarkable Mr. Pennypacker, The 2-11-59
Rembrandt 11-18-36 and 12-09-36
Rembrandt--Fecit 1669 5-10-78
Rembrandt--1669 (See: Rembrandt--Fecit 1669)
Remedy for Riches 3-12-41
Remember 2-09-27
Remember? 11-08-39
Remember Last Night 11-27-35
Remember My Name 10-11-78
Remember Pearl Harbor 5-13-42
Remember the Day 12-24-41
Remember the Night 1-10-40
Remembering (See: Recordando)
Remembrance 10-13-22
Reminiscences of a Journey to Lithuania 10-11-72
Remodeling Her Husband 6-11-20
Remontons les Champs-Elysees 12-21-38
Remorque (See: Stormy Waters)
Remote Control 12-10-30
Remounting the Champs-Elysees (See: Remontons les Champs-
   Elysees)
Remous 4-03-35
Removalists, The 10-08-75
Rempart des Beguines, Le 10-11-72
Remparts d'Argile 5-06-70
Remureru Bijo (See: House of the Sleeping Virgins, The)
Renaldo and Clara 2-01-78
Rencontre a Paris 7-11-56
Rencontres 3-07-62
Rencor de la Tierra, El 11-30-49
Rend Mig I Revolutionen! 10-21-70
Rend Mig I Traditionerne 10-03-79
Rendez-Moi Ma Peau 11-19-80
Rendez-vous, Le 11-01-61
Rendez-Vous a Bray 7-14-71
Rendez-Vous a Melbourne 4-17-57
Rendez-Vous d'Anna, Les 10-25-78
Rendez-Vous de Juillet 10-19-49
Rendez-Vous de Minuit, Le 6-13-62
Rendez-Vous du Diable, Les 8-26-59
Rendez-Vous en Foret, Les 1-26-72
Rendezvous 5-03-32
Rendezvous 10-30-35
Rendezvous, The (See: Yakusoku)
Rendezvous, The 1-03-24
Rendezvous a Grenade 7-30-52
Rendezvous at Midnight 4-24-35
Rendezvous in Black Forest (See: Stelldichein im Schwarzald,
   Ein)
Rendezvous in Salzkammergut 4-14-48
Rendezvous in Vienna (See: Rendezvous in Wien)
Rendezvous in Wien 2-23-38
Rendezvous 24 5-01-46
Rendezvous with Forgotten Years (See: Stevnemoete Met Giemte Ar)
Rene la Canne 3-09-77
Rene the Cane (See: Rene la Canne)
Renegade Ranger 10-05-38
Renegade Trail 7-26-39
Renegades 11-12-30
Renegades 5-15-46
Renegades of the Sage 9-20-50
Renegade's Sister, The 7-17-14

Riders of the Deadline 1-05-44 and 1-19-44
Riders of the Desert 7-12-32
Riders of the Dusk 1-11-50
Riders of the Frontier 8-23-39
Riders of the Night 5-10-18
Riders of the North 4-22-31
Riders of the Northland 9-09-42
Riders of the Purple Sage 10-04-18
Riders of the Purple Sage 4-15-25
Riders of the Purple Sage 9-29-31
Riders of the Purple Sage 9-17-41
Riders of the Range 10-26-49
Riders of the Rio Grande 10-02-29
Riders of the Rio Grande 10-13-43
Riders of the Rockies 9-08-37
Riders of the Timberline 9-24-41
Riders of the West 12-21-27
Riders of the West 9-30-42
Riders of the Whistling Pines 3-23-49
Riders of Vengeance 6-13-19
Riders of Whistling Skull 4-21-37
Riders to the Stars 1-20-54
Ridgeway of Montana 6-25-24
Ridin' Down the Canyon 12-09-42 and 3-10-43
Ridin' for Justice 1-05-32
Ridin' Law 7-09-30
Ridin' Mad 1-28-25
Ridin' on a Rainbow 1-29-41
Ridin' Romeo 7-15-21
Ridin' the Lone Trail 11-03-37
Ridin' the Outlaw Trail 2-14-51
Ridin' the Wind 11-18-25
Ridin' Through 3-25-25
Ridin' Wild 11-24-22
Riding Avenger, The 7-15-36
Riding for Fame 6-06-28
Riding for Life 9-21-27
Riding High 11-10-43
Riding High 1-11-50
Riding On 6-16-37
Riding on Air 6-30-37
Riding Rascal, The 12-08-26
Riding School, The (See: Maneges)
Riding Shotgun 3-10-54
Riding the Cherokee Trail 3-26-41
Riding the Sunset Trail 11-26-41
Riding the Wind 9-10-41
Riding to Fame 7-06-27
Riding Tornado, The 7-12-32
Riding West 9-20-44
Riding with Death 12-16-21
Rien Ne Va Plus 1-16-80
Rien Que Des Mensonges 6-06-33
Rien Que la Verite 9-29-31
Riff-Raff 1-15-36
Riffraff 6-11-47
Rififi Among the Women (See: Du Rififi Chez les Femmes)
Rififi in Amsterdam 10-24-62
Rififi in Tokyo 3-20-63
Riflemen, The (See: Carabiniers, Les)
Rig Mand, En 2-21-79
Right Approach, The 5-10-61
Right Cross 8-16-50
Right Direction, The 2-02-17
Right Hand of the Devil, The 8-07-63
Right of Man, The (See: Propre de L'Homme, Le)
Right of the Maddest, The (See: Raison du Plus Fou, La)
Right of Way, The 7-09-15
Right of Way, The 3-05-20
Right of Way, The 3-25-31
Right Off the Bat 10-01-15
Right On! 10-21-70
Right Out of History--The Making of Judy Chicago's Dinner Party
    9-03-80
Right That Failed 3-24-22
Right to Be Born, The (See: Derecho de Nacer, El)
Right to Happiness 9-05-19
Right to Lie, The 11-14-19
Right to Live, The 2-20-35
Right to Love, The (See: Droit D'Aimer, Le)
Right to Love, The 8-27-20
Right to Love, The 1-07-31
Right to Romance, The 12-19-33
Right to the Heart (See: Jusqu'au Coeur)
Right to the Heart 1-21-42
Right Way, The 11-04-21
Rights of Man, The 10-29-15
Rigolbouche 11-11-36

Rigoletto 11-16-49
Rikugun Nakano Gakko 6-22-66
Riley the Cop 12-05-28
Rim of the Canyon 9-07-49
Rimfire 3-30-49
Rimpatriata, La 7-03-63
Rimrock Jones 1-25-18
Rimsky-Korsakov 3-17-54
Rincon de las Virgenes, El 7-17-74
Ring, The 10-19-27
Ring, The 8-20-52
Ring and the Man, The 6-12-14
Ring Around the Clock 5-13-53
Ring Around the Moon 2-19-36
Ring of Bright Water 4-16-69
Ring of Fear 7-07-54
Ring of Fire 4-26-61
Ring of Spies 4-01-64
Ringards, Les 10-11-78
Ringer, The 9-12-28
Ringer, The 6-07-32
Rings Around the World 9-28-66
Rings on Her Fingers 3-11-42
Ringside 7-20-49
Ringside Maisie 7-30-41
Rinty of the Desert 6-06-28
Rio 10-04-39
Rio Bravo 2-18-59
Rio Conchos 10-07-64
Rio Grande 5-07-20
Rio Grande 1-11-39
Rio Grande 11-08-50
Rio Grande Patrol 11-08-50
Rio Grande Ranger 2-03-37
Rio Grande Romance 5-12-37
Rio Lobo 12-02-70
Rio Negro 8-03-77
Rio Rita 10-09-29
Rio Rita 3-18-42
Rio Zone Norte 8-27-58
Riot 12-11-68
Riot in Cell Block 11 2-10-54
Riot in Juvenile Prison 4-15-59
Riot on Sunset Strip 3-08-67
Riot Squad 1-07-42
Rip-Off 10-13-71
Rip Roaring Riley 10-30-35
Rip Tide 4-03-34
Rip-Tide, The 9-13-23
Rip Van Winkle 11-28-14
Rip Van Winkle 9-23-21
Ripe for Killing (See: Bonnes A Tuer)
Ripening Wheat (See: Erik a Buzakalasz)
Risa de la Ciudad, La 11-21-62
Risaia, La 7-25-56
Rise and Fall of Legs Diamond, The 1-27-60
Rise and Fall of the World As Seen from a Sexual Position, The
    6-28-72
Rise and Rise of Michael Rimmer, The 11-25-70
Rise and Shine 11-19-41
Rise, Fair Sun (See: Asayake No Uta)
Rise of Jennie Cushing, The 11-16-17
Rise of Susan, The 12-08-16
Rising Damp 3-12-80
Rising of the Moon, The 6-12-57
Rising Storm (See: Noi Gio)
Rising Sun 4-09-80
Risk of Living, The (See: Risque de Vivre, Le)
Riskiton Varjossa 5-15-46
Risks of Profession (See: Risques du Metier, Les)
Risky Business 12-10-20
Risky Business 9-08-26
Risky Business 3-29-39
Risky Road, The 4-12-18
Riso Amaro 11-16-49
Risque de Vivre, Le 5-28-80
Risques du Metier, Les 1-24-68
Rita 2-22-50
Rita 8-27-58
Rite, The (See: Ritorna)
Rite of Spring (See: Acto da Primavera)
Rites of May, The (See: Itim)
Ritorna 5-21-69
Ritorno 10-03-73
Ritorno di Casanova, Il 10-04-78
Ritorno di Ringo, Il 2-02-66
Ritratto di Borghesia in Nero (See: Nest of Vipers)
Ritter der Nacht 11-14-28

Rock Island Trail 5-03-50
Rock 'n' Roll 1-10-79
Rock 'n' Roll High School 4-25-79
Rock 'n' Roll Wolf 6-14-78
Rock of Souls, The (See: Penon de las Animas, El)
Rock, Pretty Baby 11-21-56
Rock, Rock, Rock! 12-12-56
Rockabilly Baby 10-23-57
Rockabye 12-06-32
Rockers 10-18-78
Rocket, The (See: Fusee, La)
Rocket Man 5-05-54
Rockets Galore 9-24-58
Rocketship X-M 5-03-50
Rockin' the Blues 10-03-56
Rocking Horse Winner, The 12-21-49
Rockinghorse (See: Susetz)
Rockshow 12-10-80
Rocky 11-10-76
Rocky Horror Picture Show, The 9-24-75
Rocky Mountain 10-04-50
Rocky Mountain Mystery 4-03-35
Rocky Mountain Rangers 7-03-40
Rocky Rhodes 1-01-35
Rocky Road, The 1-08-10
Rocky Road to Dublin, The 5-15-68
Rocky II 6-13-79
Rod Stewart and Faces and Keith Richard 8-27-75
Roda Dagen 5-31-32
Rodeo 3-05-52
Rodeo King and the Senorita 7-25-51
Rodeo Rhythm 12-17-41
Rodney Steps In 7-14-31
Roede Kappe, Den 1-25-67
Roede Rubin, Den 3-11-70
Roger Corman: Hollywood's "Wild Angel" 6-28-78
Roger la Honte 4-17-46
Roger Touhy, Gangster 5-24-44
Rogopag 9-25-63
Rogue Cop 9-01-54
Rogue in Love, A 10-27-22
Rogue of the Range 4-28-37
Rogue of the Rio Grande 12-17-30
Rogue River 2-21-51
Rogue Song, The 2-05-30 (Also see: Chant du Bandit, Le)
Rogues and Romance 1-28-21
Rogues Gallery 2-21-45
Rogue's March 12-31-52
Rogues of Sherwood Forest 6-21-50
Rogue's Regiment 10-06-48
Rogue's Tavern, The 7-15-36
Roguish Stories (See: Storie Scellerate)
Roi, Le (See: King, The)
Roi, Le 1-11-50
Roi de Coeur, Le 12-28-66
Roi des Champs Elysees, Le 1-22-35
Roi des Palaces, Le 10-18-32
Roi des Resquilleurs, Le 12-17-30 and 6-14-32
Roi du Cirage 12-01-31
Roi et l'Oiseau, Le 4-23-80
Roi Sans Divertissement, Un 10-02-63
Rolande, or Chronicle of a Passion 3-15-72
Rolando Rivas, Cabdriver (See: Rolando Rivas, Taxista)
Rolando Rivas, Taxista 10-30-74
Role, The (See: Bhumika)
Role of My Family in the Revolution, The (See: Uloga Moje
    Porodice U Svetskoj Revolluciji)
Roll Along, Cowboy 6-01-38
Roll On Texas Moon 9-18-46
Roll, Thunder, Roll! 5-11-49
Roll Wagons Roll 12-20-39
Rolled Stockings 7-20-27
Roller Boogie 12-12-79
Rollerball 6-25-75
Rollercoaster 4-27-77
Rollin' Home to Texas 2-26-41
Rollin' Plains 8-31-38
Rollin' Westward 8-23-39
Rolling Caravans 8-17-38
Rolling Home 6-09-26
Rolling Home 4-02-75
Rolling Stones 8-25-16
Rolling Terror, The (See: Neal of the Navy: Part X)
Rolling Thunder 10-05-77
Roma 3-29-72
Roma a Mano Armata 4-14-76
Roma, Ore 11 5-28-52
Roma Rivuole Cesare 10-02-74

Roman, The 2-19-10
Roman d'un Tricheur, Le 10-14-36
Roman Holiday 7-01-53
Roman Rhythm (See: Tempo Di Roma)
Roman Scandals 12-26-33
Roman Spring of Mrs. Stone, The 12-06-61
Roman Tales (See: Racconti Romani)
Romana, La 9-22-54
Romance 8-27-30
Romance (See: Romanze)
Romance a l'Inconnue 13-18-31
Romance and Arabella 2-07-19
Romance and Riches 5-19-37
Romance and Rings 1-17-19
Romance at the Danube (See: Dunaparti Randevu)
Romance de Medio Siglo 10-25-44
Romance During Office Hours (See: Sluzhebni Roman)
Romance for Bugle (See: Romance Por Kridlovku)
Romance in Budapest (See: Pesti Szerelem)
Romance in Flanders 9-22-37
Romance in House of Hapsburg (See: Liebesroman im Hause Habsburg,
    Ein)
Romance in Manhattan 1-22-35
Romance in the Andes 10-30-09
Romance in the Dark 2-16-38
Romance in the Rain 3-15-23
Romance Land 3-15-23
Romance of a Gypsy Camp 8-29-08
Romance of a Horse Thief 7-21-71
Romance of a Million 12-29-26
Romance of a Necklace, The 10-22-10
Romance of a Poor Girl 10-23-09
Romance of a Rogue 8-29-28
Romance of Aniceto & Francesca 11-02-66
Romance of Billy Goat Hill 9-29-16
Romance of Christine, The 11-18-21
Romance of Half a Century (See: Romance de Medio Siglo)
Romance of Happy Valley, A 1-31-19
Romance of Hefty Burke, The 1-07-11
Romance of Hine Moa 10-02-29
Romance of Lovers (See: Romans O Vljublennych)
Romance of Promoters, The 12-03-20
Romance of Rosy Ridge, The 7-02-47
Romance of Tarzan, The 10-18-18
Romance of the Air, A 11-15-18
Romance of the Limberlost 7-20-38
Romance of the Redwoods, A 5-18-17
Romance of the Redwoods, A 4-19-39
Romance of the Rio Grande 11-13-29
Romance of the Rio Grande 1-01-41
Romance of the Rockies 2-16-38
Romance of the Underworld 1-09-29
Romance of the Underworld, A 4-05-18
Romance of the West 2-13-46
Romance on the High Seas 6-09-48
Romance on the Range 7-29-42
Romance on the Run 5-11-38
Romance Por Kridlovku 7-26-67
Romance Ranch 7-16-24
Romance Rides the Range 12-23-36
Romance Road 10-21-25
Romanoff and Juliet 5-10-61
Romans O Vljublennych 7-31-74
Romantic Adventuress, The 2-11-21
Romantic Age, The 12-21-27
Romantic Age, The 12-14-49
Romantic Englishwoman, The 5-28-75
Romantic Italy 9-11-09
Romantic Journey, The 12-01-16
Romantic Rogue, The 11-02-27
Romanticism (See: Romantika)
Romantik Paa Sengekanten 10-17-73
Romantika 8-22-73
Romany Rye, The 7-31-14 and 4-23-15
Romanze 12-30-36
Romanzo Popolare 12-11-74
Rome Adventure 3-21-62
Rome: Armed to the Teeth (See: Roma a Mano Armata)
Rome Express 12-06-32 and 2-28-33
Rome, Open City 12-24-45
Rome-Paris-Rome (See: Signori in Carrozza)
Rome Wants Another Caesar (See: Roma Rivuole Cesare)
Romeo and Juliet 10-27-16
Romeo and Juliet 8-26-36
Romeo and Juliet 9-08-54
Romeo and Juliet 5-18-55
Romeo and Juliet 10-05-66

Romeo and Juliet 3-13-68
Romeo and Juliet 9-04-68
Romeo, Julie a Tma 9-14-60
Romeo, Juliet and Shadows (See: Romeo, Julie a Tma)
Romona's Father 1-14-11
Ronde, La 7-12-50
Ronde, La 10-28-64
Ronde des Heures 3-11-31 and 2-09-32
Rondo 5-10-67
Ronny 1-12-32 and 4-19-32
Roof, A (See: Pokriv)
Roof, The (See: Tetto, Il)
Roof Garden, The (See: Terraza, La)
Roof of Japan, The (See: Shiros Sammyahu)
Roof of the World, The 7-23-30
Roof Over Your Head, A (See: Es Dach Ueberem Chopf)
Roof Tree 1-27-22
Rooftree (See: Tvarbalk)
Roogie's Bump 9-22-54
Rooie Sien 5-14-75
Rookery Nook 2-26-30
Rookie, The 11-25-59
Rookie Cop, The 5-10-39
Rookie Fireman 9-06-50
Rookies 4-27-27
Rookies in Burma 12-08-43
Rookies on Parade 4-30-41
Rookie's Return, The 1-28-21
Rookies Run Amok (See: Bidasses En Folie, Les)
Room and Board 9-09-21
Room at the Top 1-28-59
Room for One More 1-16-52
Room for the Aged (See: Helyet az Oregeknek)
Room Service 9-14-38
Room 13 (See: Zimmer 13)
Room with a View on the Sea, A (See: Pokoj Z Widkiem Na Morze)
Rommmates 2-17-71
Rooney 4-09-58
Roosevelt in Africa 4-23-10
Roosevelt Reviewing the French Troops 11-05-10
Roosevelt Story, The 7-02-47
Rooster, The (See: Hatarnegol)
Rooster Cogburn 10-15-75
Roosters of Dawn, The (See: Gallos de la Madrugada, Los)
Root, The (See: Ugat)
Root of All Evil 2-19-47
Rootin' Tootin' Rhythm 8-04-37
Roots (See: Raisces)
Roots of Blood (See: Raices de Sangre)
Roots of Heaven 10-22-58
Roots of Stone (See: Raices de Piedra)
Rope 9-01-48
Rope of Flesh 8-18-65
Rope of Sand 6-29-49
Roped 1-31-19
Ropin' Fool 11-11-21
Rosa and Lin (See: Rosa und Lin)
Rosa Blanca, La 9-06-72
Rosa de America 6-19-46
Rosa de Francia 2-26-36
Rosa di Bagdad, La 9-28-49
Rosa Per Tutti, Una (See: Rose for Everyone, A)
Rosa Rossa, La 5-23-73
Rosa und Lin 12-06-72
Rosal Bendito, El 2-10-37
Rosalie 12-22-37
Rosary, The 3-31-22
Rosary, The 7-14-31
Rosas Del Milagro, Las 4-27-60
Rosaura a Las Diez 5-21-58
Rosaura at 10 o'clock (See: Rosaura a Las Diez)
Rose, The 10-10-79
Rose Bernd 5-22-57 and 7-24-57
Rose Bowl 12-09-36
Rose Bowl Story, The 8-27-52
Rose-Colored Telephone, The (See: Telephone Rose, Le)
Rose de la Mer, La 3-19-47
Rose di Danzica, Le 10-03-79
Rose for Everyone, A 7-12-67
Rose-Marie 2-15-28
Rose Marie 2-05-36
Rose Marie 3-03-54
Rose o' Salem Town 10-01-10
Rose of America (See: Rosa de America)
Rose of Bagdad, The (See: Rosa di Bagdad, La)
Rose of Cimarron 3-12-52
Rose of France (See: Rosa de Francia)

Rose of Kildare, The 11-23-27
Rose of Nome, The 9-03-20
Rose of Paris, The 10-15-24
Rose of Stambul, The (See: Rose Von Stambul, Die)
Rose of the Bower 8-31-27
Rose of the Golden West 9-28-27
Rose of the Rancho, The 11-21-14
Rose of the Rancho, The 1-15-36
Rose of the Rio Grande 7-13-38
Rose of the Sea 6-16-22
Rose of the South 11-24-16
Rose of the Tenderloin, A 11-27-09
Rose of the Tenements 4-13-27
Rose of the West 7-25-19
Rose of the World 1-11-18
Rose of the World 11-11-25
Rose of the Yukon 1-26-49
Rose of Tralee 10-26-38
Rose of Washington Square 5-10-39
Rose Spot (See: Macchia Rosa)
Rose Tattoo, The 11-02-55
Rose-Tinted Dreams (See: Ruzove Sny)
Rose von Stambul, Die 7-08-53
Roseanna McCoy 8-17-49
Rosebud 3-26-75
Roseland 10-05-77
Rosemarie 9-17-58
Rosemary 12-10-15
Rosemary Climbs the Heights 11-01-18
Rosemary's Baby 5-29-68
Rosen fuer den Staatsanwalt 5-18-60
Rosenkavalier, Der 7-25-62
Rosenmontag 4-01-31
Roses Are Red 11-05-47
Roses for the Prosecutor (See: Rosen Fuer Den Staatsanwalt)
Roses of Danzig, The (See: Rose di Danzica, Le)
Roses of Picardy 5-02-28 and 12-11-29
Rosie 11-01-67
Rosie O'Grady 2-09-17
Rosie O'Grady 9-22-36
Rosie the Riveter 4-05-44
Rosier de Mme. Husson, Le 3-01-32 (Also see: He)
Rosiere de Pessac, La 5-14-69
Rosita 9-06-23
Ross-Armstrong Fight 6-08-38
Ross-Canzoneri Fight 9-19-33
Rossetto, Il 4-27-60
Rossini 2-04-48
Rosszemberek 2-28-79
Roswolsky's Sweetheart 10-14-21
Rotagg 11-27-46
Rote, Die 7-11-62
Rote Strumpf, Der 12-31-80
Rothchild 10-19-38
Rotten to the Core 7-21-65
Roue, La 1-19-47
Rouge and Riches 2-13-20
Rouge Est Mis, Le 7-24-57
Rouge et le Noir, Le 12-01-54
Rouged Lips 8-30-23
Rough and Ready 4-19-18
Rough and the Smooth 10-14-59
Rough Cut 6-18-80
Rough Day for the Queen (See: Rude Journee Pour la Reine)
Rough Diamond (See: Diamante Bruto)
Rough Diamond 11-25-21
Rough House Rosie 5-25-27
Rough Lover, The 3-01-18
Rough Neck, The 1-25-19
Rough Night in Jericho 8-09-67
Rough Riders, The 3-30-27
Rough Riders of Durango 2-07-51
Rough Riders' Roundup 4-12-39
Rough Ridin' Rhythm 1-26-38
Rough Riding Red 11-14-28
Rough Romance 6-18-30
Rough Shod 6-30-22
Rough Shoot 2-25-53
Rough, Tough and Ready 3-28-45
Rough, Tough West, The 6-25-52
Rough Waters 7-30-30
Rough Weather Courtship, A 9-10-10
Roughly Speaking 1-31-45
Roughneck, The 12-03-24
Roughshod 5-11-49
Roulette 2-28-24
Round, The (See: Ronde, La)
Round of Hours (See: Ronde des Heures)

Round the Clock (See: Ronde des Heures)
Round Trip (See: Aller Retour)
Round Trip 7-12-67
Rounders, The 1-13-65
Round-Up, The 9-10-20
Roundup, The (See: Bloko)
Roundup, The 3-19-41
Roundup Time in Texas 7-07-37 (Also see: Round-Up Time in Texas)
Round-Up Time in Texas 8-04-37 (Also see: Roundup Time in Texas)
Rousalochka 7-28-76
Roustabout 11-11-64
Route de Corinthe, La 10-25-67
Route de Salina, La 11-18-70
Route Napoleon, La 11-25-53
Route Sans Issue 3-24-48
Routes du Sud, Les 5-03-78
Routine Has to Be Broken (See: Hay Que Romper La Rutina)
Roveh Huliot 3-21-79
Rover Turns Santa Claus 8-28-09
Rovin' Tumbleweeds 1-10-40
Rowdy, The 9-23-21
Rowdyman, The 6-07-72
Roxie Hart 2-04-42
Roy Likit 9-26-79
Royal African Rifles, The 9-30-53
Royal American, A 8-10-27
Royal Ark 11-15-23
Royal Ballet 1-20-60
Royal Ballet Girl, The (See: K. und K. Ballettmaedel, Das)
Royal Bed, The 2-04-31
Royal Box, The 5-22-14
Royal Box, The 1-01-30
Royal Cavalcade 4-17-35
Royal Children (See: Konigskinder)
Royal Divorce, A 10-12-38
Royal Family, A 8-20-15
Royal Family, The 12-24-30
Royal Flash 10-01-75
Royal Hunt, The (See: Mrigayaa)
Royal Hunt of the Sun 10-01-69
Royal Imposter, A 1-01-15
Royal Journey 1-23-52
Royal Mounted Patrol 12-31-41
Royal Oak, The 11-15-23
Royal Rider, The 12-04-29
Royal Romance, A 4-23-30
Royal Scandal, A 3-21-45
Royal Scandal, The 9-25-29
Royal Symphony 3-10-54
Royal Vacation (See: Vacances Royales)
Royal Waltz, The (See: Koenigswalzer)
Royal Waltz, The 4-15-36
Royal Wedding 2-07-51
Royalists, The (See: Chouans, Les)
Royalut 7-25-79
Rozina the Love-Child 3-02-49
Rozmarne Leto 6-19-68
Rubacuori 4-22-31 and 3-15-32
Rubber 4-01-36
Rubber Gun, The 8-31-77
Rubber Heels 6-29-27
Rubber Racketeers 7-01-42
Rubber Tires 3-09-27
Rube and the Baron, The 3-14-13
Rubens 7-13-49
Rubia's Jungle 3-17-71
Rubicon 9-22-31
Ruby 5-18-77
Ruby Gentry 12-24-52
Ruchome Piaski 4-09-69
Rude Boy 2-27-80
Rude Journee Pour la Reine 12-12-73
Rue de l'Estrapade 5-20-53
Rue des Prairies 12-16-59
Rue du Pied-de-Grue 12-19-79
Rue Haute 4-28-76
Rue Sans Joie, La 6-01-38
Rue Sans Nom, La 1-23-34
Ruf der Goetter 7-24-57
Rufus 5-14-75
Rug Maker's Daughter, The 7-09-15
Rugged O'Riordans, The 12-14-49
Rugged Water 6-22-25
Ruggles of Red Gap 3-15-18
Ruggles of Red Gap 9-13-23
Ruggles of Red Gap 3-13-35
Ruisseau, Le 11-30-38
Ruiter in die Nag, Die (See: Rider in the Night, The)

Rule G. 2-05-15
Ruler of the Road 4-12-18
Rulers of the Sea 9-20-39
Rules of the Game (See: Regle du Jeu, La)
Ruling Class, The 4-19-72
Ruling Passion, The 2-04-16
Ruling Passion, The 1-27-22
Ruling Passions 10-04-18
Ruling Voice, The 11-10-31
Rum Boulevard (See: Boulevard Du Rhum)
Rumba 2-27-35
Rumble on the Docks 11-28-56
Rumbo Al Cairo 11-06-35
Rumeur Publique 8-11-54
Rumeurs 1-08-47
Rummy, The 9-29-16
Run After Me Until I Catch You (See: Cours Apres Moi Que Je T'Attrape)
Run & Run (See: Ran & Ran)
Run, Angel, Run 4-23-69
Run Away, I Love You (See: Byugai, Obicham Te)
Run for Cover 3-23-55
Run for the Hills 7-08-53
Run for the Money 1-28-70
Run for the Roses 11-15-78
Run for the Sun 7-25-56
Run for Your Money, A 12-07-49
Run Like a Thief 1-17-68
Run of the Arrow 5-29-57
Run Silent, Run Deep 3-26-58
Run the Wild River 6-16-71
Run Wild, Run Free 4-02-69
Runaround, The 8-11-31
Runaround, The 6-05-46
Runaway 11-18-64
Runaway, The (See: Atithi)
Runaway, The 4-28-26
Runaway Boy, The (See: Bari Trekey Paliye)
Runaway Bride 5-21-30
Runaway Bus, The 3-03-54
Runaway Daughters 1-16-57
Runaway Freight, The 11-14-13
Runaway Girls 11-07-28
Runaway Wife, The 8-27-15
Runner Stumbles, The 4-11-79
Running 6-06-79
Running Away from a Fortune 1-07-11
Running Empty 8-07-63
Running Fence 1-25-78
Running Fight, The 7-09-15
Running Man, The 8-07-63
Running Target 11-28-56
Running Water 10-27-22
Running Wild 6-15-27
Running Wild 11-02-55
Runoilija Ja Muusa 9-05-79
Rupert of Hentzau 7-12-23
Rupture, La 9-30-70
Rural Teacher, The (See: Kru Ban Nok)
Rush Hour (See: Stosszeit)
Rush Hour, The 2-08-28
Rush to Judgment 6-07-67
Ruslan and Ludmila (See: Ruslan i Ludmila)
Ruslan i Ludmila 4-17-74
Russia 1-09-29
Russia 3-15-72
Russia Marches On 2-23-38
Russia on Parade 9-11-46
Russian Ballerina 9-17-47
Russian Heroine, A 1-29-10
Russian Holiday 10-05-55
Russian Revolution, The 8-24-17
Russian Roulette 7-16-75
Russian Story, The 6-02-43
Russians Are Coming, the Russians Are Coming, The 5-25-66
Rust Never Sleeps 7-25-79
Rustic Chivalry (See: Cavalleria Rusticana)
Rustlers 3-23-49
Rustler's Hideout 11-08-44
Rustlers of Devil's Canyon 7-09-47
Rustlers on Horseback 11-15-50
Rustler's Paradise 7-10-35
Rustler's Ranch 4-14-26
Rustler's Valley 7-07-37
Rustlin' for Cupid 6-23-26
Rustling a Bride 5-23-19
Rusty Leads the Way 7-28-48
Rusty Rides Alone 11-07-33

S

St. Elmo 11-29-23
Saint from Krejcarek, The (See: Svatej z Krejcareku)
St. Hans Celebration (See: Sankt Hans Fest)
Saint in London, The 7-12-39
Saint in New York, The 5-25-38
Saint in Palm Springs, The 1-08-41
St. Ives 7-21-76
Saint Jack 5-02-79
Saint Joan 5-08-57
Saint Lies in Wait, The (See: Saint Prend L'Affut, Le)
St. Louis Blues 2-08-39
St. Louis Blues 4-09-58
St. Louis Kid, The 11-06-34
St. Matthews Passion 11-30-49
Saint Meets the Tiger, The 8-04-43
Saint Michael Had a Rooster (See: San Michele Aveva Un Gallo)
St. Pauli Report 3-22-72
Saint Prend L'Affut, Le 11-23-66
St. Simeon of the Desert (See: San Simeon Del Desierto)
Saint Strikes Back, The 3-01-39
Saint Takes Over, The 4-24-40
Saint That Forged a Country (See: Virgen Que Forjo una Patria,
  La)
Saint Therese of Lisieux (See: Little Flower of Jesus)
Saint Tropez Blues 3-08-61
St. Valentine's Day (See: Dia de Los Enamorados, El)
St. Valentine's Day Massacre, The 7-05-67
St. Val's Mystery (See: Mystere de Saint-Val, Le)
Sainte Famille, La 4-25-73
Sainted Devil, A 11-26-24
"Sainted" Sisters, The 3-10-48
Saintes Nitouches, Les 8-28-63
Saintly Sinner, The 2-16-17
Saintly Sinners 1-24-62
Saint's Adventure, The 7-13-17
Saints and Sinners 6-16-16
Saints and Sinners 7-06-49
Saints and Their Sorrows 12-25-14
Saint's Double Trouble, The 2-14-40
Saint's Girl Friday, The 3-17-54
Saint's Vacation, The 6-18-41
Sait-On Jamais 7-24-57
Sajenko--the Soviet 1-16-29
Sakada 4-07-76
Sakka Mat, El 10-26-77
Sal of Singapore 1-30-29
Sala de Guardia 5-28-52
Salach Shabati 6-24-64
Salad by the Roots, The (See: Des Pissenlits Par la Racine)
Salad-Days (See: Zielone Lata)
Saladin 7-24-63
Salaire de la Peur, Le 4-29-53
Salak Jitr 6-13-79
Salamander, The 12-17-15
Salamandre, La 7-07-71
Salammbo 4-16-15
Salamoniko 12-27-72
Salangit Mesra 4-25-79
Salary 200 Monthly (See: Pofon)
Salauds Vont en Enfer, Les 3-28-56
Sale Histoire, Une 11-16-77
Sale Reveur 4-05-78
Sales Temps Pour les Mouches 3-22-67
Salesgirls' Idol, The 6-05-09
Saleslady 1-26-38
Saleslady, The 3-31-16
Salesman 2-26-69
Sally 3-18-25
Sally 12-25-29
Sally and Saint Anne 6-25-52
Sally Bishop 12-27-23
Sally Bishop 11-08-32
Sally Fieldgood & Co. 2-26-75
Sally in Our Alley 7-28-16
Sally in Our Alley 7-21-31
Sally, Irene and Mary 12-09-25
Sally, Irene and Mary 3-02-38
Sally of Our Alley 11-02-27
Sally of the Sawdust 8-05-25
Sally of the Scandals 7-04-28
Sally of the Subway 2-23-32
Sally's Hounds 10-02-68
Sally's Irish Rose 11-26-58
Sally's Shoulders 12-26-28
Salo O la Centiventi Giornate Di Sodoma 12-03-75
Salo or The 120 Days of Sodom (See: Salo O la Centiventi Giornate
  Di Sodoma)
Salome 2-28-13
Salome 10-11-18

Salome 1-05-23
Salome 3-18-53
Salome 9-13-72
Salome of the Tenements 2-25-25
Salome, Where She Danced 4-11-45
Salomy Jane 10-31-14
Salomy Jane 8-09-23
Salon Kitty 1-19-77
Salonika Terrorists, The (See: Solunski Atentatori)
Saloon Bar 7-10-40
Salsa 4-07-76
Salt and Pepper 7-31-68
Salt Lake Raiders 5-17-50
Salt of the Earth 3-17-54
Salto 9-08-65
Salto a la Gloria 8-12-59
Salto Mortale (See: Trapeze)
Salto Mortale 9-01-31
Salto Nel Vuoto 3-26-80
Saltstaenk Och Krutgubbar 1-01-47
Salty O'Rourke 2-21-45
Saludos 12-09-42
Saludos Amigos (See: Saludos)
Salut en De Kost 10-30-74
Salut I Forca Al Canut 2-27-80
Salut, Jerusalem 7-12-72
Salut l'Artiste 12-26-73
Salut, Voleurs 7-04-73
Salute 8-21-29 and 10-09-29
Salute for Three 6-16-43
Salute John Citizen 9-02-42
Salute to Courage 1-21-42
Salute to the Marines 7-28-43
Salvage 6-17-21
Salvation (See: Ocalenie)
Salvation Hunters, The 2-04-25
Salvation Jane 5-11-27
Salvation Joan 4-07-16
Salvation Nell 8-20-15
Salvation Nell 7-01-21
Salvation Nell 7-07-31
Salvator Stabel, The (See: Stajnia Na Salwatorze)
Salvatore Giuliano 12-27-61
Salvo d'Acquisto 7-28-76
Salzburg Connection, The 8-02-72
Sam 8-12-59
Sam Langford and Jim Flynn Fight 4-23-10
Sam Whiskey 2-05-69
Samar 4-11-62
Samarang 7-04-33
Samaritan's Courtship, The 2-12-10
Samba Da Criacao Do Munco 2-21-79
Samba of the Creation of the World (See: Samba Da Criacao Do
  Munco)
Sambizanga 4-25-73
Same Jakki 5-22-57
Same Time, Next Year 11-22-78
Samma No Aji 9-18-63
Sammy Going South 3-27-63
Sammy Stops the World 12-27-78
Samo Ljudi 9-11-57
Samodivsko Horo 11-17-76
Samorastniki 10-28-64
Samourai, Le 11-08-67
Sampan (See: San Ban)
Sampson (See: Samson)
Sampson 3-25-36
Samskara 9-06-72
Samson 3-20-14
Samson 1-08-15
Samson 8-30-61
Samson and Delilah 10-26-49
Samson and the Slave Queen 9-09-64
Samson's Betrayal 12-03-10
Samuel Fuller and the Big Red One 5-16-79
Samurai, Part I 11-16-55
Samurai, Part II 11-01-67
Samurai, Part III 11-15-67
Samurai, The (See: Samourai, Le)
Samurai Assassin 3-17-65
Samurai Banners (See: Furin Kazan)
Samurai from Nowhere 6-03-64
Samvetsomma Adolf 3-04-36 and 2-24-37
Samyong 9-08-65
San 12-07-66
San Antone 3-04-53
San Antone Ambush 10-12-49

San Antonio 11-21-45
San Antonio Rose 6-25-41
San Babila: 8 P.M. (See: San Babila: 20 H)
San Babila: 20 H 8-10-77
San Ban 9-18-68
San Demetrio--London 1-19-44
San Diego, I Love You 9-06-44
San Domingo 12-09-70
San Fernando Valley 8-30-44
San Francisco 7-01-36
San Francisco Docks 1-01-41
San Francisco Nights 12-28-27
San Francisco Story, The 4-09-52
San Gottardo 8-31-77
San Michele Aveva Un Gallo 11-17-71
San Quentin 7-28-37
San Quentin 12-04-46
San Simeon Del Desierto 6-16-65
Sanatorium Pod Klepsydra 6-06-73
Sanctuary 2-22-61
Sand 6-25-20
Sand 5-04-49
Sand 11-03-71
Sand Castle, The 9-13-61
Sand Pebbles, The 12-21-66
Sandakan 8 (See: Bokyo)
Sanders of the River 4-17-35 and 7-03-35
Sandflow 3-24-37
Sandpiper, The 6-30-63
Sandra 12-24-24
Sandra, the Making of a Woman 5-20-70
Sands of Iwo Jima 12-14-49
Sands of the Desert 10-10-14
Sands of the Desert 9-14-60
Sands of the Kalahari 10-27-65
Sandstone 2-23-77
Sandwich Man, The 8-17-66
Sandy 7-19-18
Sandy 5-12-26
Sandy Burke of U-Bar-U 1-31-19
Sandy Gets Her Man 11-13-40
Sandy Is a Lady 5-22-40
Sandy, the Poacher 10-23-09
Sanfte Lauf, Der 6-28-67
Sang a la Tete, Le 11-07-56
Sang d'un Poete 11-07-33
Sang et Lumieres 5-05-54
Sang Nok Soo 11-14-62
Sangaree 5-27-53
Sangen Om Stockholm 4-02-47
Sangre Negra (See: Native Son)
Sanitarium, The 10-15-10
Sanjuro 6-20-62
Sankt Hans Fest 5-21-47
Sannikov's Land 8-01-73
Sans Famille 7-09-58
Sand Lendemain 4-17-40
Sans Mobile Apparent 9-29-71
Sans Sommation 3-21-73
Sans Tambour Ni Trompette 6-15-60
Sansho Dayu 10-06-54
Santa 5-31-32 and 9-13-32
Santa and the Three Bears 12-16-70
Santa Claus 9-28-60
Santa Claus and the Miner's Child 12-18-09
Santa Claus Has Blue Eyes (See: Pere Noel A Les Yeux Bleus, Le)
Santa Esperanza 10-29-80
Sante Fe 4-25-51
Santa Fe Bound 5-12-37
Santa Fe Marshal 1-17-40
Santa Fe Passage 5-11-55
Santa Fe Scouts 6-30-43
Santa Fe Stampede 12-07-38
Santa Fe Trail 12-18-40
Santa Fe Trail, The 10-22-30
Santa's Christmas Circus 11-02-66
Santee 10-03-73
Santi and Veena (See: Santi Veena)
Santi Veena 12-29-76
Santiago 6-20-56
Santo de la Espada, El 4-22-70
Santo Oficio, El 5-29-74
Sao 5 9-22-76
Sao Jom Tu 4-16-75
Sao Jomken 8-31-77
Sao Rang Sung 10-08-75

Sao Thang Tam 7-27-77
Sap, The 3-05-30
Sap from Syracuse 7-30-30
Saphead, The 2-18-21
Sapho 3-16-17
Sapho 12-30-70
Sapphire 4-29-59
Sappho 5-09-08
Sappho 10-14-21
Sappho, Darling 3-12-69
Sapporo Winter Olympics 9-13-72
Saprofita, Il 10-30-74
Saps at Sea 5-01-40
Sara Akash 10-14-70
Sara Lar Sig Folkvett 2-23-38
Sara Learns Manners (See: Sara Lar Sig Folkvett)
Saraba Eiga No Tomo Yo 11-07-79
Saraband Dance, The 3-19-10
Saraband for Dead Lovers 9-15-48
Sarabe Mosukowa Gurentai 5-22-68
Saracen Blade 5-19-54
Saragossa Manuscript, The (See: Rekopis Zanelziony W Saragossie)
Sarah and Son 3-19-30 (Also see: Wiegenlied)
Sarah's Last Man (See: Ultimo Uomo Di Sara, L')
Sarang Bang Sonnim Omoni 9-05-62
Sarati le Terrible 9-29-37
Sarati the Terrible (See: Sarati le Terrible)
Saratoga 7-14-37
Saratoga Trunk 11-21-45
Sardinia: Ransom (See: Sequestro Di Persona)
Sarga Csiko 2-03-37
Sarge Goes to College 5-07-47
Sarie Marais 7-28-31
Sarong Girl 6-23-43
Sarten Por el Mango, La 3-21-73
Sartre by Himself (See: Sartre Par Lui-Meme)
Sartre Par Lui-Meme 12-15-76
Sarumba 3-22-50
Sarvasakshi 2-20-80
Sasaki Kojiro 5-10-67
Sasayaki No Joe (See: Whispering Joe)
Saskatchewan 2-24-54
Sasom I en Spegel 1-03-62
Sasquatch 1-18-78
Satan and the Woman 3-21-28
Satan Bug, The 3-10-65
Satan in Sables 10-14-25
Satan Junior 3-07-19
Satan Met a Lady 7-29-36
Satan Never Sleeps 2-21-62
Satan Town 8-25-26
Satanis, the Devil's Mass 3-11-70
Satan's Brew (See: Satansbraten)
Satan's Cradle 11-09-49
Satan's Paradise (See: Paradis de Satan, Le)
Satan's Private Door 3-23-17
Satan's Sadists 1-14-70
Satan's Sister 6-17-25
Satansbraten 11-24-76
Satchmo the Great 9-11-57
Satellite in the Sky 7-11-56
Satin Girl 12-06-23
Satin Woman, The 7-20-27
Satogashi Ga Kawereru Toki 7-12-67
Satori 1-02-74
Satri Ti Lok Leum 3-26-75
Satsujinkyo Jidai 3-29-67
Saturday Island 3-26-52
Saturday Morning 5-05-71
Saturday Night (See: Noche Del Sabado, La or Subotom Uvece)
Saturday Night 1-27-22
Saturday Night and Sunday Morning 11-09-60
Saturday Night at the Baths 4-16-75
Saturday Night Dance, The (See: Bal de Samedi Soir, Le)
Saturday Night Fever 12-14-77
Saturday Night in Apple Valley 11-17-65
Saturday Night Kid, The 11-20-29
Saturday Night Out 3-18-64
Saturday's Children 5-01-29
Saturday's Children 4-10-40
Saturday's Hero 8-22-51
Saturday's Heroes 9-29-37
Saturday's Millions 10-17-33
Saturn 3 2-20-80
Satyricon 9-17-69
Sauce for the Goose 8-30-18
Saucy Sue 6-12-09
Sauerbruch 11-10-54

Saul and David (See: Saul e David)
Saul e David 6-23-65
Saut de l'Ange, Le 10-20-71
Sauvage, Le 12-10-75
Sauve Qui Peut la Vie 5-28-80
Sauveur, Le 8-25-71
Savage, The (See: Sauvage, Le)
Savage, The 10-26-17
Savage, The 8-04-26
Savage, The 1-14-53
Savage Boy, The (See: Garcon Sauvage, Le)
Savage Breed (See: Razza Selvaggia)
Savage Brigade 12-15-48
Savage Child, The (See: Enfant Sauvage, L')
Savage Drums 7-11-51
Savage Eye, The (See: Occhio Selvaggio, L')
Savage Eye, The 9-16-59
Savage Frontier 5-27-53
Savage Girl 5-02-33
Savage Gold 8-01-33
Savage Guns, The 12-19-62
Savage Horde 7-05-50
Savage Innocents, The 6-29-60
Savage Is Loose, The 10-16-74
Savage Messiah 9-13-72
Savage Mutiny 1-21-53
Savage Pampas (See: Pampa Salvaje)
Savage Party, The (See: Fete Sauvage, La)
Savage Passions 6-08-27
Savage Planet, The (See: Planete Sauvage, La)
Savage Sam 5-22-63
Savage Seven, The 5-15-68
Savage Shadows 6-11-69
Savage Splendor 7-27-49
Savage State, The (See: Etat Sauvage, L')
Savage Summer, A (See: Ete Sauvage, Un)
Savage Wild, The 1-28-70
Savage Woman, The 8-16-18
Savages 5-17-72
Save the Children 9-19-73
Save the City (See: Ocalic Miasto)
Save the Tiger 2-07-73
Saved by Her Prayers 1-21-11
Saved by Wireless 11-05-15
Saved from the Quicksand 9-25-09
Saved from the Tide 2-26-10
Saved in Mid-Air 6-25-15
Saving the Family Name 9-01-16
Savior, The (See: Sauveur, Le)
Saviour, The 8-13-80
Savithri 2-13-80
Savoy Lancers (See: Lancieri di Savoia)
Sawdust 7-26-23
Sawdust Paradise 8-29-28
Sawdust Ring, The 7-20-17
Sawdust Trail, The 7-30-24
Saxofone 11-22-78
Saxon Charm, The 9-08-48
Saxophone (See: Saxofone)
Say Hello to Yesterday 2-03-71
Say It Again 6-09-26
Say It in French 11-30-38
Say It with Diamonds 6-08-27
Say It with Flowers (See: Dites-Le Avec Des Fleurs)
Say It with Songs 8-14-29
Say One for Me 6-10-59
Say, Young Fellow 6-21-18
Sayama No Kuroi Ame 1-06-74
Sayarim 11-01-67
Sayat Nova 6-21-78
Sayonara 11-13-57
Says O'Reilly to McNab 2-02-38
Sbandati 9-28-55
Sbatti Il Mostro In Primo Pagina 11-15-72
Scalawag 10-24-73
Scales of Justice 10-09-09
Scales of Justice 7-31-14
Scalphunters, The 3-06-68
Scamp, The 10-16-57
Scandal 7-16-15
Scandal 11-02-17
Scandal 4-24-29
Scandal 10-30-29
Scandal 8-20-80
Scandal, The (See: Scandale, Le)
Scandal About Eve (See: Skandal Um Eva)
Scandal at Scourie 4-29-53
Scandal du Grand Hotel 4-25-33

Scandal for Sale 4-12-32
Scandal in Bad Ischl 2-12-58
Scandal in Grand Hotel (See: Scandale du Grand Hotel)
Scandal in Paris, A 6-12-29 and 8-14-29
Scandal in Paris, A 7-10-46
Scandal in Sorrento (See: Pane, Amore, E ...)
Scandal in the Family (See: Escandalo en la Familia)
Scandal, Inc. 8-08-56
Scandal Proof 7-08-25
Scandal Sheet 2-11-31
Scandal Sheet 1-10-40
Scandal Sheet 1-09-52
Scandal Street 7-28-26
Scandal Street 2-09-38
Scandale, Le 3-15-67
Scandale du Grand Hotel 4-25-33
Scandalo (See: Submission)
Scandalous John 6-23-71
Scandals 3-20-34
Scandals of Clochemerle 3-22-50
Scano Boa 8-02-61
Scapegoat, The 7-22-59
Scapegrace (See: Balarrasa)
Scapolo, Lo 7-18-56
Scar, The (See: Blizna or Pae Kao)
Scar, The 4-04-19
Scar of the Century (See: Seiki No Tsume Ato)
Scarab Ring 7-22-21
Scaramouche 9-20-23 and 10-04-23
Scaramouche 5-14-52
Scarecrow 4-11-73
Scarecrow in a Garden of Cucumbers 2-23-72
Scared Stiff 4-11-45
Scared Stiff 4-15-53
Scared to Death 7-16-47
Scareheads 10-27-31
Scarf, The 3-21-51
Scarface 5-24-32
Scarlet Angel 5-28-52
Scarlet Bazaar, The (See: Kermesse Rouge, La)
Scarlet Brand 8-09-32
Scarlet Car, The 11-30-17
Scarlet Car, The 1-19-23
Scarlet Claw, The 5-24-44
Scarlet Clue, The 5-16-45
Scarlet Coat, The 6-22-55
Scarlet Dawn 11-08-32
Scarlet Days 11-14-19
Scarlet Dove, The 6-13-28
Scarlet Drop, The 4-19-18
Scarlet Empress, The 9-18-34
Scarlet Hour, The 4-18-56
Scarlet Lady, The 8-22-28
Scarlet Letter, The (See: Scharlachrote Buchstabe, Der)
Scarlet Letter, The 2-16-17
Scarlet Letter, The 8-11-26
Scarlet Letter, The 9-25-34
Scarlet Lily 7-12-23
Scarlet Oath, The 10-13-16
Scarlet Pages 12-10-30
Scarlet Pimpernel, The 7-17-29
Scarlet Pimpernel, The 2-12-35
Scarlet River 5-30-33
Scarlet Road, The 2-18-16
Scarlet Runner, The 9-22-16
Scarlet Sails 10-11-61
Scarlet Seas 1-09-29
Scarlet Shadow, The 3-14-19
Scarlet Sin, The 8-20-15
Scarlet Sinner, The 1-20-26
Scarlet Spear, The 3-17-54
Scarlet Street 1-02-46
Scarlet Trail, The 1-03-19
Scarlet Week End 11-01-32
Scarlet West, The 9-16-25
Scarlet Woman, The (See: Femme Ecarlate, La)
Scarlet Woman, The 6-16-16
Scarpo Al Sole, Le 6-10-36
Scars of Dracula, The 10-28-70
Scars of Jealousy 5-10-23
Scatenato, Lo (See: Catch As Catch Can)
Scatterbrain 7-10-40
Scattered Clouds (See: Midaregumo)
Scattered Pages (See: Brokiga Blad)
Scattergood Baines 2-12-41
Scattergood Meets Broadway 8-27-41
Scattergood Pulls the Strings 5-14-41
Scattergood Rides High 3-18-42
Scattergood Survives a Murder 10-14-42

Seven Golden Men (See: Sette Uomini D'Oro)
Seven Golden Men Strike Again (See: Grande Colpo Dei Sette Uomini D'Oro, Il)
Seven Guns for the MacGregors 12-04-68
Seven Guys and a Gal (See: Sept Hommes et une Garce)
7 Hills of Rome, The 1-08-58
Seven Journeys 3-21-51
Seven Keys to Baldpate 8-31-17
Seven Keys to Baldpate 10-21-25 and 11-04-25
Seven Keys to Baldpate 1-01-30
7 Keys to Baldpate 12-18-35
Seven Keys to Baldpate 6-04-47
Seven Little Foys, The 6-01-55
Seven-Man Army 4-28-76
Seven Men from Now 7-11-56
Seven Men, One Woman (See: Sept Hommes, Une Femme)
Seven Miles from Alcatraz 11-11-42
Seven Minutes, The 7-07-71
Seven Nights in Japan 9-22-76
Seven of the Big Bear (See: I Sette Dell' Orsa Maggiore)
Seven Pearls, The 9-14-17
Seven Per-Cent Solution, The 10-06-76
Seven Ravens, The 4-15-53
Seven Samurai, The (See: Shichinin No Samurai)
Seven Seas to Calais 3-06-63
Seven Sinners 12-09-25
Seven Sinners 8-26-36
Seven Sinners 10-30-40
Seven Sins, The (See: Siete Pecados, Los)
Seven Sisters 7-30-15
Seven Swans, The 1-04-18
Seven Sweethearts 8-12-42
Seven Thieves 1-20-60
Seven Thunders 9-11-57
Seven Times a Day (See: 7 Fois ... (Par Jour))
Seven-Ups, The 12-26-73
Seven Waves Away 3-13-57
Seven Ways from Sundown 9-15-60
Seven Were Saved 2-19-47
Seven Women 12-08-65
Seven Women from Hell 10-18-61
Seven Wonders of the World 4-11-56
Seven Year Itch, The 6-08-55
Seven Years Hard Luck (See: Sieben Jahre Pech)
Seventeen (See: Sytten)
Seventeen 2-21-40
1789 6-26-74
1776 11-08-72
1776, or Hessian Renegades 9-11-09
Seventeenth Heaven (See: 17eme Ciel, Le)
17th Parallel: Vietnam at War (See: 17e Parallele le Vietnam en Guerre)
Seventh Bandit, The 7-21-26
Seventh Cavalry 10-24-56
Seventh Commandment, The (See: Septieme Commandment, Le)
Seventh Company Has Been Found, The (See: On A Retrouve La 7e Compagnie)
Seventh Company Outdoors, The (See: Septieme Compagnie Au Clair Du Lune, La)
Seventh Continent, The (See: Sedmi Kontinent)
Seventh Cross, The 7-19-44
Seventh Dawn, The 6-24-64
Seventh Day, The 3-17-22
Seventh Heaven (See: Septieme Ciel, Le)
Seventh Heaven 5-11-27
Seventh Heaven 3-31-37
Seventh Jurist, The (See: Septieme Jure, Le)
Seventh Noon, The 10-29-15
Seventh Seal, The (See: Sjunde Inseglet, Der)
Seventh Sheriff 12-20-23
Seventh Sin, The 5-15-57
Seventh Veil, The 10-31-45
Seventh Victim, The 8-18-43
Seventh Voyage of Sinbad, The 11-26-58
75 Years of a Cinema Museum 12-06-72
79 av Stodinni (See: Gogo)
77 Park Lane 7-14-31
77 Rue Chagrin 12-01-31
70,000 Witnesses 9-06-32
Seventy Times Seven (See: Setenta Veces Siete)
Severed Head, A 2-03-71
Sevres Porcelain 8-28-09
Sewers of Paradise, The (See: Egouts du Paradis, Les)
Sex 4-02-20
Sex and Astrology 1-20-71
Sex and the Single Gay 6-17-70
Sex and the Single Girl 12-23-64
Sex Crazy (See: Sessomatto)

Sex Criminal, The 5-22-63
Sex Demon 7-23-75
Sex En Gros 6-23-71
Sex Freaks 3-13-74
Sex Galore (See: Sex En Gros)
Sex-Jack 7-14-71
Sex Lure, The 11-10-16
Sex O'Clock U.S.A. 8-04-76
Sex of the Angels, The (See: Sesso Degli Angeli, Il)
Sex Perverse 9-30-70
Sex Power 7-08-70
Sex Qui Parlez, Le (See: Pussy Talk)
Sex Shop, Le 10-18-72
Sex Thief, The 3-13-74
Sextanerin, Die 9-14-38
Sextet (See: Sekstet)
Sextette 3-08-78
Sextool 3-12-75
Sexual Customs in Scandinavia 3-01-72
Sexual Encounter Group 12-02-70
Sexual Freedom in Denmark 3-18-70
Sexual Liberty Now 6-28-72
Sexual Practices in Sweden 11-18-70
Sexy Smugglers, The (See: Contrabandieres, Les)
Sey Seyeti 8-20-80
Sfida, La 9-17-58
Sh! The Octopus 12-08-37
Sha-Nu 5-28-75
Shabe Quzi 5-06-64
Shack Out On 101 11-30-55
Shackelton 8-08-28
Shackled 6-28-18
Shackles of Gold 5-12-22
Shades of Gray 2-04-48
Shades of Silk 12-12-79
Shadow, The 7-01-36
Shadow, The 12-22-37
Shadow and Light (See: Ombre et Lumiere)
Shadow Army, The (See: Armee Des Ombres, L')
Shadow Between, The 9-29-31
Shadow from the Past, The (See: Mennelsyden Varjo)
Shadow in the Sky 12-19-51
Shadow Line (See: Linea D'Ombra)
Shadow Man 12-09-53
Shadow of a Chance (See: Ombre d'une Chance, L')
Shadow of a Doubt 2-27-35
Shadow of a Doubt 1-13-43
Shadow of a Flying Bird (See: Stin Letajiciho Ptacka)
Shadow of a Woman 8-14-46
Shadow of Doubt, The 4-07-16
Shadow of Fear 6-06-56
Shadow of Her Past, The 7-21-16
Shadow of Rosalie Byrnes, The 5-28-20
Shadow of Terror 11-21-45
Shadow of the Castles (See: Ombre des Chateaux, L')
Shadow of the Cat 5-03-61
Shadow of the Desert 3-26-24
Shadow of the Eagle 9-06-50
Shadow of the Hawk 7-14-76
Shadow of the Law 6-11-30
Shadow of the Past, A 11-19-10
Shadow of the Thin Man 10-22-41
Shadow on the Wall 12-08-26
Shadow on the Wall 3-15-50
Shadow on the Window, The 2-27-57
Shadow over Angkor 7-30-69
Shadow Returns, The 8-28-46
Shadow Valley 12-03-47
Shadowed into the Underworld 9-03-15
Shadows 6-25-15
Shadows 2-14-19
Shadows 11-03-22
Shadows 8-31-60 and 2-15-61
Shadows and Mirages (See: Ombres et Mirages)
Shadows and Sunshine 11-03-16
Shadows Are Getting Longer, The (See: Schatten Werden Laenger, Die)
Shadows in the Night 8-02-44
Shadows of a Hot Summer (See: Stiny Horkeho Leta)
Shadows of Angels (See: Schatten der Engel)
Shadows of Conscience 3-17-22
Shadows of Fear 11-07-28
Shadows of Night 9-26-28
Shadows of Sing Sing 2-27-34
Shadows of Suspicion 5-09-19
Shadows of Suspicion 10-18-44
Shadows of the Law 4-21-26
Shadows of the Night (See: Nachgestalten)

Shadows of the Orient 10-13-37
Shadows of the Past (See: Parmi les Decombres or Schatten der
    Vergangenheit)
Shadows of the Past 1-14-11
Shadows of the Past 6-10-14
Shadows of the Past 8-27-15
Shadows of the Sea 1-06-22
Shadows of the Underworld (See: Schatten der Unterwelt)
Shadows of the West 9-28-49
Shadows of Tombstone 10-07-53
Shadows on the Sage 12-30-42
'Shadows on the Stairs 4-16-41
Shadows over Chinatown 9-18-46
Shadows over Shanghai 12-07-38
Shady Lady 3-27-29
Shady Lady 9-05-45
Shaft 6-16-71
Shaft in Africa 6-20-73
Shaft's Big Score 6-21-72
Shaggy 4-14-48
Shaggy D.A., The 12-15-76
Shaggy Dog, The 2-25-59
Shah of Iran, The 1-16-80
Shake Hands with Murder 6-14-44
Shake Hands with the Devil 5-13-59
Shake, Rattle and Rock! 1-16-57
Shakedown 8-19-36
Shakedown 8-23-50
Shakedown, The 4-10-29
Shakedown, The 2-13-34
Shakedown, The 1-27-60
Shakespeare-Wallah 7-14-65
Shakiest Gun in the West, The 3-27-68
Shakuntala 1-07-48
Shalako 9-25-68
Shall We Dance 5-12-37
Shall We Dance, Mr. Teacher? (See: Far Jag Lov, Magistern!)
Shall We Forgive Her? 10-05-17
Sham 5-20-21
Shame (See: Skammen; Stud; or Pozor)
Shame 11-16-17
Shame 8-05-21
Shame, Shame, Everybody Knows Her Name 8-19-70
Shameful Behavior? 10-20-26
Shameless (See: Schamlos)
Shampoo 2-12-75
Shamrock and the Rose 7-06-27
Shamrock Handicap, The 7-07-26
Shamrock Hill 4-20-49
Shams of Society 12-02-21
Shamus 1-31-73
Shane 4-15-53
Shanghai 7-24-35
Shanghai Bound 11-09-27
Shanghai Chest 9-08-48
Shanghai Cobra, The 8-08-45
Shanghai Drama, The 1-17-45
Shanghai Express 2-23-32
Shanghai Gesture 12-24-41
Shanghai Lady 11-13-29
Shanghai Madness 9-26-33
Shanghai Rose 5-22-29
Shanghai Story 9-29-54
Shanghaied (See: Chaplin in "Shanghaied")
Shanghaied 9-14-27
Shanghaied Baby, The 1-29-15
Shanghaied Love 11-10-31
Shanks 10-09-74
Shannons of Broadway 12-25-29
Shantata! Court Chaloo Aahey 9-20-72
Shanty Town (See: Soderkakar)
Shantytown 4-21-43
Shaolin Abbot 11-21-79
Shaolin Avengers 7-21-76
Shaolin Rescuers 7-25-79
Shape of Things to Come, The 12-19-79
Sharen Sviat (Izpit & Gola Savest) 8-30-72
Shark God, The (See: Omoo-Omoo)
Shark Hunters, The (See: Tiburoneros)
Shark Master, The 9-09-21
Shark Monroe 7-12-18
Shark River 11-11-53
Shark Woman, The 6-04-41
Sharkey-Schmeling 6-28-32
Sharkfighters, The 10-31-56
Shark's Treasure 5-07-75
Sharp Shooters 1-25-28

Sharply Watched Trains (See: Ostre Sledovane Vlaky)
Sharpshooter Bruggler (See: Standschuetze Bruggler)
Sharpshooters 9-21-38
Shatranj Ke Khilari 12-14-77
Shattered 7-13-27
Shattered Idols 6-16-22
Shattered Lives 7-08-25
Shattered Reputations 8-30-23
Shavlool 11-04-70
Shazdeh Ehtejab 12-18-74
She 4-27-17
She 7-14-26
She 7-31-35
She 4-21-65
She and He (See: Kanajox To Kare)
She and He 12-31-69
She and the Three (See: Sie Und Die Drei)
She Asked for It 9-01-37
She Couldn't Help It 2-25-21
She Couldn't Say No 2-19-30
She Couldn't Say No 1-22-41
She Couldn't Say No 1-13-54
She Couldn't Take It 11-13-35
She-Creature, The 9-05-56
She Defends Her Country 6-09-43
She Demons 3-19-58
She Devil 4-10-57
She Devil, The 12-06-18
She-Devil, The 9-23-25
She-Devil Island 9-16-36
She Didn't Say No! 10-08-58
She Does Not Drink, Smoke or Flirt, But ... She Talks! (See:
    Elle Boit Pas, Elle Fume Pas, Elle Drague Pas, Mais ...
    Elle Cause!)
She Done Him Wrong 2-14-33
She Gets Her Man 9-11-35
She Gets Her Man 1-10-45
She-Gods of Shark Reef 12-10-58
She Goes to War 6-12-29
She Had to Choose 9-25-34
She Had to Eat 7-14-37
She Has What It Takes 6-02-43
She Is Grown Up Now 8-06-75
She Knew All the Answers 5-21-41
She Loved a Fireman 11-17-37
She Loves and Lies 1-09-20
She Loves Me Not 9-11-34
She Made Her Bed 5-01-34
She Married a Cop 7-05-39
She Married an Artist 1-05-38
She Married Her Boss 10-02-35
She No Longer Talks ... She Shoots (See: Elle Ne Cause Plus Elle
    Flingue)
She Shall Have Music 12-18-35
She Steps Out 3-19-30
She Wanted a Bow Wow 4-30-10
She Wanted a Millionaire 2-23-32
She Was a Lady 8-28-34
She-Wolf, The (See: Lupa, La)
She Wolf, The 7-11-19
She-Wolf, The 6-02-31
She-Wolf of London 4-10-46
She Wolves 8-19-25
She Wolves, The (See: Louves, Les)
She Wore a Yellow Ribbon 7-27-49
She Wrote the Book 5-15-46
Sheba Baby 4-23-75
Shed No Tears 7-14-48
Sheepman 4-23-58
Sheer Luck 6-02-31
Shehar Aur Sapna 8-12-64
Sheherazade 5-29-63
Sheik, The 11-11-21
Sheik Steps Out, The 7-28-37
Sheik's Wife, The 3-10-22
Sheila Levine Is Dead and Living in New York 2-05-75
Shell 43 7-28-16
Shell Game, The 3-08-18
She'll Have To Go 5-09-62
Sheltered Daughters 5-20-21
Shenandoah 4-14-65
Shenanigans 9-21-77
Shep Comes Home 1-12-49
Shepherd (See: Ovcar)
Shepherd Girl, The 9-08-65
Shepherd King 12-13-23
Shepherd of Kingdom Come 2-02-20
Shepherd of Seven Hills 8-15-33
Shepherd of the Hills, The 2-22-38

Shepherd of the Hills, The   6-18-41
Shepherd of the Ozarks   4-08-42
Shepherdess and Chimneysweep (See: Bergere et le Ramoneur, La)
Shepper-Newfounder   12-31-30
Sheriff, The   11-29-18
Sheriff of Fractured Jaw, The   11-05-58
Sheriff of Sage Valley, The   12-09-42
Sheriff of Tombstone, The   5-21-41
Sheriff of Wichita   3-02-49
Sheriff's Son, The   4-04-19
"Sherlock" Brown   8-11-22
Sherlock Holmes   5-19-16
Sherlock Holmes   1-27-22 and 5-12-22
Sherlock Holmes   11-15-32
Sherlock Holmes and the Secret Weapon   12-30-42
Sherlock Holmes and the Spider Woman   1-12-44
Sherlock Holmes and the Voice of Terror   9-09-42
Sherlock Holmes Faces Death   9-08-43
Sherlock Holmes' Fatal Hour   7-14-31
Sherlock Holmes in Washington   3-31-43
Sherlock Jr.   5-28-24
Sherry   6-11-20
She's a Sheik   11-23-27
She's a Sweetheart   1-10-45
She's Back on Broadway   1-28-53
She's Dangerous   3-24-37
She's for Me   12-08-43
She's Got Everything   12-29-37
She's in the Army   6-24-42
She's My Baby   6-08-27
She's My Weakness   6-25-30
She's No Lady   8-18-37
She's Working Her Way Through College   6-11-52
Sheshet Hayamim   4-10-68
Shichinin No Samurai   9-08-54
Shield for Murder   9-01-54
Shield of Honor   12-14-27
Shifting Sands (See: Ruchome Piaski)
Shifting Sands   8-30-18
Shigaon Shel Moledeth   5-21-80
Shijin No Ai   9-06-67
Shillingbury Blowers, The   3-26-80
Shin Heike Monogatari   8-09-61
Shinbone Alley   3-31-71
Shine Brightly, My Star (See: Gori, Gori, Moja Zvezda)
Shine On, Harvest Moon   3-15-39
Shine On Harvest Moon   3-15-44
Shinel   9-02-59
Shining, The   5-28-80
Shining Hour, The   11-16-38
Shining Victory   5-28-41
Shinju Ten No Amijima   9-10-69
Shinjuku Dorobo Nikki   6-11-69
Shinken Shobu   6-28-72
Ship Ahoy   4-22-42
Ship Cafe   11-27-35
Ship Comes In, A   9-05-28
Ship Dae Eui Ban Hang   11-09-60
Ship from Shanghai, The   4-30-30
Ship of Damned Women, The (See: Nave Delle Donne Maledette, La)
Ship of Doom, The   11-30-17
Ship of Fools   5-05-65
Ship of Lost Men   10-16-29
Ship of Wanted Men   11-21-33
Ship That Died of Shame, The   5-11-55
Ship to India-Land, A (See: Skepp Till India-Land)
Shipbuilders, The   1-19-44
Shipmates   5-27-31
Shipmates Forever   10-23-35
Ship's Husband, The   11-12-10
Ships of Hate   7-28-31
Ships of the Night   3-27-29
Ships with Wings   1-07-42
Shipwrecked   7-07-26
Shipwrecked Among Cannibals   7-09-20
Shipyard Sally   8-16-39
Shir Hashirim   10-23-35
Shiralee, The   7-24-57
Shirasagui   5-20-59
Shiraz   10-10-28 and 3-20-29
Shirley Kaye   12-14-17
Shirley of the Circus   1-05-23
Shirley Thompson Versus the Aliens   6-28-72
Shiroi Kyoto   11-02-66
Shiros Sammyahu   5-22-57
Shiwjot Takoj Paren   7-05-78
Shmonah Be'ikvot Ekhad   12-16-64
Sho O Suteyo, Machi E Deyo   10-27-71

Shock   11-20-34
Shock   1-16-46
Shock, The   5-30-23
Shock Corridor   7-10-63
Shock Punch, The   5-13-25
Shock Treatment (See: Traitement De Choc)
Shock Treatment   2-26-64
Shock Waves   10-08-80
Shocking Miss Pilgrim, The   1-01-47
Shocking Night, A   1-21-21
Shockproof   1-26-49
Shoe-Shine   8-13-47
Shoes   6-16-16
Shoes of the Fisherman, The   11-20-68
Shoes That Danced, The   3-01-18
Shoeshine Boys (See: Sciuscia)
Shogun Assassin   11-19-80
Shokei No Shima   7-27-66
Sholay   2-09-77
Shonen   6-25-69
Shoosh   5-11-27
Shoot   6-02-76
Shoot First   6-17-53
Shoot It: Black, Shoot It: Blue   12-04-74
Shoot Loud, Louder ... I Don't Understand   1-11-67
Shoot Out   5-26-71
Shoot-Out at Medicine Bend   4-10-57
Shoot the Piano Player (See: Tirez Sur le Pianiste)
Shoot the Works   7-10-34
Shoot to Kill   4-09-47
Shootin' for Love   7-04-23
Shootin' Irons   4-25-28
Shootin' Mad   10-25-18
Shootin' Romance   2-10-26
Shooting High   3-06-40
Shooting in the Haunted Woods   1-15-10
Shooting of Dan McGrew, The   5-14-15
Shooting of Dan McGrew, The   6-11-24
Shooting Stars   2-29-28 (2 reviews) and 6-13-28
Shooting Straight   7-30-30
Shootist, The   7-28-76
Shop Angel   5-03-32
Shop Around the Corner, The   1-10-40
Shop at Sly Corner, The   1-29-47
Shop Girl, The   6-23-16
Shop Girls of Paris   6-25-47
Shopworn   4-05-32
Shopworn Angel   1-09-29
Shopworn Angel   7-13-38
Shore Acres   10-23-14
Shore Acres   5-21-20
Shore Leave   9-16-25
Shore of Waiting   7-24-63
Shors   12-13-39
Short and Sweet (See: Grands Moyens, Les)
Short Cut to Hell   9-25-57
Short Eyes   10-05-77
Short Grass   12-06-50
Short Is the Summer   8-20-69
Short Letter to Mother, A (See: A Brivele der Mamen)
Short Memory, The (See: Memoire Courte, La)
Short-Sighted Mary   9-04-09
Shot at Dawn, The (See: Schuss im Morgengrauen or Coup de Feu
   a L'Aube)
Shot in the Dark, A   5-22-35
Shot in the Dark, A   5-21-41
Shot in the Dark, A   6-24-64
Shot in the Talker Studio, The   8-13-30
Shotgun   3-30-55
Shotgun Pass   3-15-32
Shots in the Sky (See: Rafal U Nebo)
Shots in 3/4 Time (See: Schuesse im 3/4 Takt)
Should a Baby Die?   3-03-16
Should a Doctor Tell?   10-08-30 and 8-25-31
Should a Girl Marry?   9-18-29
Should a Girl Marry?   7-19-39
Should a Husband Forgive?   10-31-19
Should a Mother Tell?   7-16-15
Should a Wife Forgive?   11-05-15
Should a Wife Work?   2-03-22
Should a Woman Divorce?   1-01-15
Should a Woman Tell?   5-01-14
Should a Woman Tell?   1-23-20
Should Husbands Work?   7-26-39
Should Ladies Behave?   12-19-33
Should She Obey?   9-07-17
Should We Wed Them? (See: Faut-il les Marier?)
Shoulder Arms (See: Chaplin's "Shoulder Arms")

Shout, The 5-24-78
Shout at the Devil 4-14-76
Shout It from Housetops (See: Criez-Le Sur Les Toits)
Show, The 3-16-27
Show Boat 4-24-29
Show Boat 5-20-36
Show Boat 6-06-51
Show Business (See: Chobizenesse)
Show Business 4-19-44
Show Down, The 8-10-17
Show Folks 12-12-28
Show Girl 11-07-28
Show Girl in Hollywood 5-14-30
Show Goes On, The 8-17-38
Show of Shows 11-27-29
Show Off, The 8-25-26
Show Off, The 3-20-34
Show People 11-14-28
Show Them No Mercy 12-11-35
Show Your License 9-11-09
Showboat 1988 4-26-78
Showdown 4-03-63
Showdown 5-23-73
Showdown, The 3-07-28
Showdown, The 4-03-40
Showdown, The 8-30-50
Showdown at Abilene 8-15-56
Showdown at Boot Hill 6-11-58
Showdown for Zatoichi 10-09-68
Showoff, The 8-14-46
Shraga Katan 9-27-78
Shriek in the Night 7-25-33
Shriek of Araby 6-14-23
Shrike, The 5-04-55
Shrine of Happiness, The 2-25-16
Shrine of Victory, The 8-25-43
Shtigje Te Luftes 6-13-79
Shtourets v Ouhoto 11-17-76
Shuban (See: Scandal)
Shuetzen Koenig, Der 5-09-33
Shunkin Sho 5-25-77
Shunko 1-25-61
Shura 5-10-72
Shussho Iwai (See: Wolves, The)
Shut My Big Mouth 2-25-42
Shut Up Gulls! (See: Vos Gueules, Les Mouettes!)
Shuttered Room, The 7-05-67
Shuttle, The 3-01-18
Shuzenji Monogatari 9-07-55
Shvedski Krale 11-06-68
Si C'Etait a Refaire 11-10-76
Si J'Avais Quatre Dromadaires 12-14-66
Si J'Etais un Espion (ou Breakdown) 10-04-67
Si Joli Village, Un 3-28-79
Si Jolie Petite Plage, Une 2-23-49 and 7-06-49
Si Le Vent Te Fait Peur 5-25-60
Si l'Empereur Savait Ca 11-19-30 and 2-18-31
Si Paris Nous Etait Conte 2-29-56
Si Simple Histoire, Une 5-20-70
Si Tous les Gars Du Monde ... 3-14-56
Si Tu Veux 9-27-32
Si Versailles M'Etait Conte 3-17-54
Si Volvemos a Vernos 4-10-68
Si Yo Fuera Millonario 11-21-62
Si Yo Fuera Rica 5-07-41
Siamo Italiani 7-07-65
Siavash in Persepolis 8-04-65
Siawase No Cakusoku Hankeci 8-09-78
Sib Tamruat Toh Buntung 6-20-79
Siberia 6-02-26
Siberiade 6-06-79
Siberian Lady Macbeth (See: Siberska Ledi Magbet)
Siberian Patrol 5-31-32
Siberska Ledi Magbet 5-20-64
Sicilian Uprising (See: Vespro Siciliano)
Sicilians, The (See: Clan des Siciliens, Le)
Siddhartha 9-13-72
Side Show 9-22-31
Side Show of Life 7-23-24
Side Street 12-28-49
Side Streets 8-21-34
Sidecar Racers 8-20-75
Sidelong Glances of a Pigeon Kicker, The 10-28-70
Sideshow 6-14-50
Sideshow, The 2-20-29
Sidewalks of London 1-24-40
Sidewalks of New York 8-09-23
Sidewalks of New York 11-17-31

Sidewinder 1 7-27-77
Sie Und Die Drei 7-21-22
Sieben Jahre Pech 10-23-57
Sieben Ohrfeigen 10-27-37
Sieben Sommersprossen 6-28-78
Sieben Tage Frist 5-14-69
Sieg Im Westen 5-14-41
Siege 6-17-25
Siege at Red River 3-24-54
Siege of Fort Bismarck 3-20-68
Siege of Leningrad 2-10-43
Siege of Pinchgut, The 7-08-59
Siege of Sidney Street, The 10-19-60
Siege of Syracuse, The 1-24-62
Siege of the Alcazar (See: Sin Novedad en el Alcazar)
Siege of the Saxons 8-21-63
Siegel Gottes, Das 2-23-49
Sieger, Der 4-12-32
Siegerin, Die 3-06-29
Siegfried 12-23-25
Sierra 4-26-50
Sierra Baron 7-02-58
Sierra Maestra 9-17-69
Sierra Maldita 9-08-54
Sierra Passage 12-13-50
Sierra Stranger 5-01-57
Sierra Sue 11-12-41
Siete Dias de Enero 5-02-79
Siete Locos, Los 7-11-73
Siete Pecados, Los 8-26-59
Sigfried 4-09-15
Sign Invisible, The 3-01-18
Sign of Four 5-17-23
Sign of the Cactus 3-04-25
Sign of the Cross 12-06-32
Sign of the Cross, The 12-25-14
Sign of the Four, The 8-30-32
Sign of the Gladiator 10-28-59
Sign of the Jack O'Lantern 2-10-22
Sign of the Lion, The (See: Signe du Lion, Le)
Sign of the Pagan 11-10-54
Sign of the Poppy, The 12-01-16
Sign of the Ram, The 2-04-48
Sign of the Rose 3-10-22
Sign of the Wolf 9-03-41
Sign of Venus (See: Segno di Venere, Il)
Sign on the Door 7-22-21
Signal, The (See: Lassatok Felein)
Signal over the City (See: Signali Nad Gradom)
Signal Tower, The 6-04-24 and 7-23-24
Signali Nad Gradom 8-09-61
Signe Arsene Lupin 2-03-60
Signe du Lion, Le 7-13-60
Signed Arsene Lupin (See: Signe Arsene Lupin)
Signet Ring, The 10-29-10
Signor Max, Il 12-15-37
Signora di Montecarlo, La 1-04-39
Signora di Tutta 1-08-35
Signora di Tutti, La 1-08-35 and 4-01-36
Signora Senza Camelie 7-29-53
Signore e Signori 3-09-66
Signore e Signori, Buonanotte 1-19-77
Signori in Carrozza 12-05-51
Signpost to Murder 12-23-64
Signs of Life (See: Leibenszeichen)
Signs of the Zodiac 7-24-63
Signum Laudis 7-30-80
Sikator 9-13-67
Silas Marner 2-25-16
Silas Marner 5-26-22
Silence (See: Milczenie)
Silence 5-26-26
Silence 8-18-31
Silence 5-01-74
Silence, A (See: Chinmoku)
Silence, The 10-02-63
Silence de la Mer, Le 5-18-49
Silence Est d'Or, Le (See: Man About Town)
Silence Has No Wings 11-09-66
Silence of Dean Maitland 6-26-34
Silence of Dean Maitland, The 8-27-15
Silence of the Heart (See: Golu Hadawatha)
Silence of the Sea (See: Silence de la Mer, Le)
Silence ... On Tourne 5-05-76
Silence! The Court Is in Session (See: Shantata! Court Chaloo Aahey)
Silence ... We're Shooting (See: Silence ... On Tourne)
Silencers, The 2-09-66
Silencieux, Le 3-14-73

Silent Accuser, The 11-26-24
Silent Avenger, The 8-17-27
Silent Barriers 3-31-37
Silent Battle, The 7-21-16
Silent Call 11-18-21
Silent Call, The 6-21-61
Silent Command 9-06-23
Silent Conflict 4-07-48
Silent Cry, The 11-30-77
Silent Dust 2-09-49
Silent Enemy, The 5-21-30
Silent Enemy, The 3-12-58
Silent Friends (See: Deux Amis Silencieux)
Silent Hero, The 8-10-27
Silent Lady, The 11-23-17
Silent Lover, The 11-17-26
Silent Man, The 11-30-17
Silent Master, The 6-02-17
Silent Movie 6-23-76
Silent Mystery, The 11-29-18
Silent Nephew, The (See: Neveu Silencieux, Un)
Silent One, The (See: Silencieux, Le)
Silent Partner, The 5-11-17
Silent Partner, The 8-23-23
Silent Partner, The 6-07-44
Silent Partner, The 4-04-79
Silent Playground, The 4-22-64
Silent Plea, The 3-12-15
Silent Power 11-17-26
Silent Rider, The 12-20-18
Silent Running 3-08-72
Silent Sanderson 6-10-25
Silent Scream 1-30-80
Silent Sentinel 7-24-29
Silent Strength 2-07-19
Silent Trail, The 3-20-29
Silent Village, The 7-14-43
Silent Voice, The 8-27-15
Silent Vow 5-12-22
Silent Watcher, The 10-22-24
Silent Witness, The 2-09-32
Silent Witness, The 9-27-78
Silent Woman, The 9-13-18
Silhouettes (See: Silouettes)
Silk Express, The 6-27-33
Silk Hat Harry 7-18-19
Silk Hat Kid 8-14-35
Silk Hose and High Pressure 11-05-15
Silk Legs 12-28-27
Silk-Lined Burglar, The 4-04-19
Silk Stockings 2-11-21
Silk Stockings 5-22-57
Silk, Sunshine, and Blood (See: Seda, Sangre y Sol)
Silk Worms (See: Gusanos De Sada)
Silken Affair, The 10-17-56
Silken Chinese Dress, The (See: China Poblana)
Silken Shackles 5-26-26
Silks and Saddles 12-05-28
Silks and Satins 6-16-16
Sillon y la Gran Duquesa, El 9-29-43
Silly Billies 4-08-36
Silna Voda 6-16-76
Silom Otac 8-19-70
Silouettes 11-08-67
Siluri Umani 4-27-55
Silver Bandit, The 3-29-50
Silver Bears, The 11-23-77
Silver Bullet, The 8-05-42
Silver Canyon 6-13-51
Silver Car, The 7-22-21
Silver Chalice, The 12-22-54
Silver City 10-03-51
Silver City Bonanza 3-21-51
Silver City Raiders 11-24-43
Silver Comes Through 5-25-27 and 6-29-27
Silver Cord 5-09-33
Silver Darlings, The 9-10-47
Silver Dollar, The 12-27-32
Silver Dream Racer 4-02-80
Silver Fleet, The 3-24-43
Silver Horde 10-29-30
Silver Horde, The 5-14-20
Silver King, The 1-10-19
Silver King, The 9-04-29
Silver Lining, The 1-28-21
Silver Lining, The 11-16-27
Silver Lining, The 5-31-32
Silver Lode 5-12-54

Silver Queen 1-13-43
Silver Raiders 12-27-50
Silver River 5-05-48
Silver Skates 1-20-43
Silver Slave, The 1-18-28
Silver Spurs 7-21-43
Silver Stallion 6-18-41
Silver Star 3-02-55
Silver Streak, The 1-22-35
Silver Streak 12-01-76
Silver Threads Among the Gold 6-11-15
Silver Trail, The 1-05-38
Silver Trails 3-16-49
Silver Treasure 7-28-26
Silver Valley 11-02-27
Silver Whip, The 2-04-53
Silver Wings 5-26-22
Silverspurs 4-01-36
Simba 1-25-28
Simba 2-02-55
Simbaddha 7-12-72
Simchon Family, The (See: Mishpahat Simchon)
Simitrio 10-18-61
Simon 2-27-80
Simon and Laura 12-28-55
Simon, King of the Witches 4-07-71
Simon the Jester 10-01-15
Simon the Jester 11-25-25
Simone 4-23-10
Simone Barbes, or Virtue (See: Simone Barbes ou la Vertu)
Simone Barbes ou la Vertu 5-07-80
Simple Case of Money, A 2-06-52
Simple Charity 11-19-10
Simple Event, A 12-26-73
Simple Heart, A (See: Cuore Semplice, Un)
Simple Histoire, Une 9-30-70
Simple Melody, A (See: Enkel Melodi, En)
Simple Mistake, A 10-01-10
Simple Past, The (See: Passe Simple, Le)
Simple Rustic Tale, A 1-21-11
Simple Sis 6-08-27
Simple Souls 5-28-20
Simple Story, A (See: Histoire Simple, Une; or Si Simple Histoire
    Une; or Simple Histoire, Une)
Simple Tailor 2-27-34
Simplemente Maria 10-07-70
Simply, Maria (See: Simplemente Maria)
Sin 8-08-13
Sin 10-08-15
Sin, The (See: El Haram)
Sin Cargo 12-08-26
Sin Flood 11-03-22
Sin Novedad En El Alcazar 1-22-41
Sin of Anna Lans 5-24-50
Sin of Harold Diddlebock, The 2-19-47
Sin of Madelon Claudet, The 11-03-31
Sin of Martha Queed, The 11-25-21
Sin of Nora Moran 12-19-33
Sin Ship 5-27-31
Sin Sister 3-27-29
Sin Takes a Holiday 12-03-30
Sin That Was His, The 12-10-20
Sin Town 9-30-42
Sin Woman, The 4-13-17
Sin Ye Do, The 11-24-16
Sinai Commando-S 12-04-68
Sinaia 6-13-62
Sinbad and the Eye of the Tiger 5-25-77
Sinbad the Sailor 1-15-47
Since You Went Away 7-19-44
Sincerely Yours 11-02-55
Sinderella and the Golden Bra 12-23-64
Sindoor 6-18-80
Sinews of Steel 6-08-27
Sinews of War, The 3-21-13
Sinfonia Amazonica 9-30-53
Sinfonia Argentina 11-25-42
Sinfonia de Una Vida 5-08-46
Sinful and Sweet 9-18-29
Sinful Davey 2-26-69
Sinful Dwarf, The 12-12-73
Sinful Life of Franciszek Bula, The (See: Grzeszny Zywot
    Franciszka Buly)
Sing a Jingle 12-29-43
Sing and Be Happy 6-23-37
Sing and Like It 4-17-34
Sing and Swing 8-05-64

Sing Another Chorus 9-10-41
Sing, Baby, Sing 9-16-36
Sing, Boy, Sing 1-15-58
Sing, Cowboy, Sing 7-21-37
Sing, Dance, Plenty Hot 8-07-40
Sing for Your Supper 12-03-41
Sing Me a Love Song 12-30-36
Sing, Neighbor, Sing 8-16-44
Sing Sam Oy 4-06-77
Sing Sing Nights 1-29-35
Sing Sing Thanksgiving 4-17-74
Sing, Sinner, Sing 8-15-33
Sing While You're Able 4-14-37
Sing You Sinners 8-17-38
Sing Your Way Home 11-14-45
Sing Your Worries Away 1-07-42
Singapore 8-06-47
Singapore Mutiny 10-17-28
Singapore Woman 5-14-41
Singe en Hiver, Un 5-16-62
Singed 7-13-27
Singed Wings 12-01-22
Singende Engel (See: Singing Angels)
Singende Haus, Das (See: Singing House, The)
Singende Jugend 9-15-37
Singende Stadt, Die 11-19-30 and 5-31-32
Singer, The (See: Cantor, El)
Singer and the Dancer, The 4-27-77
Singer Jim McKee 3-26-24
Singer Not the Song, The 1-18-61
Singin' in the Corn 11-20-46
Singin' in the Rain 3-12-52
Singing Angels 2-04-48
Singing Blacksmith, The 11-09-38
Singing Buckaroo 3-24-37
Singing Cowboy, The 11-25-36
Singing Cowgirl, The 5-31-39
Singing During the Occupation (See: Chantons Sous L'Occupation)
Singing Fool, The 9-26-28
Singing Guns 3-15-50
Singing House, The 8-13-47
Singing in the Dark 3-14-56
Singing Kid, The 4-08-36
Singing Marine, The 7-07-37
Singing Nun, The 3-09-66
Singing Outlaw, The 12-29-37
Singing River, The 10-28-21
Singing Sheriff, The 9-13-44
Singing Taxi Driver 5-20-53
Singing Town, The (See: Singende Stadt, Die)
Singing Vagabond 7-29-36
Single-Handed 6-24-53
Single Man 1-16-29
Single Standard, The 7-31-29
Single Track 12-02-21
Single Wives 7-30-24
Singlehanded Sanders 4-19-32
Singoalla 3-08-50
Sinha Moca 9-09-53
Sinister Hands 8-16-32
Sinister Journey 9-22-48
Sink or Swim 7-30-20
Sink the Bismarck 2-24-60
Sinner, The (See: Tang Fu Yu Sheng Nu)
Sinner, The 2-21-51
Sinner of Magdala 4-26-50
Sinner Take All 2-10-37
Sinners 4-30-20
Sinner's Holiday 10-15-30
Sinners in Heaven 9-10-24
Sinners in Love 11-21-28
Sinners in Paradise 5-04-38
Sinners in Silk 9-10-24
Sinners in the Sun 5-17-32
Sinners of Paris (See: Rafles sur la Ville)
Sinners Parade 11-14-28
Sins in the Family (See: Peccati In Famiglia)
Sins of Her Parent 11-10-16
Sins of Jezebel, The 11-18-53
Sins of Man 6-24-36
Sins of Men, The 5-19-16
Sins of Rachel Cade, The 9-14-60
Sins of Rome 6-30-54
Sins of Rosanne 10-15-20
Sins of Society, The 1-14-16
Sins of the Children 7-30-30
Sins of the Fathers 1-30-29

Sins of the Fathers 4-28-48
Sins of the Fathers, The 11-27-09
Sins of the Mothers 1-01-15
Sin's Payday 5-10-32
Sioux Blood 5-22-29
Sioux City Sue 11-27-46
Sir Arne's Treasure 12-02-25
Sir Henry at Rawlinson End 7-16-80
Sir-Loin 12-06-23
Siren, The 12-11-14
Siren, The 6-29-17
Siren, The 2-22-28
Siren Call 9-15-22
Siren of Atlantis 12-15-48
Siren of Bagdad 5-20-53
Siren of Corsica, A 4-02-15
Siren of Seville 11-19-24
Siren of the Tropics 1-18-28
Sirene du Mississipi 7-02-69
Siren's Necklace 9-25-09
Sirens of the Sea 8-31-17
Siripala and Ranmenika 1-26-77
Sirius 7-14-76
Sirocco 6-06-51
Sirocco Blow, The (See: Coup de Sirocco, Le)
Sirocco d'Hiver 6-18-69
Siroco 12-01-31
Siroma Sam Al'sam Besan 8-12-70
Sis Hopkins 3-07-19
Sis Hopkins 4-09-41
Sissi 5-15-57
Sissignore 1-15-69
Sistemo L'America e Torno 2-27-74
Sister Against Sister 3-09-17
Sister Angelica 10-16-09
Sister-in-Law, The (See: Norng Mia)
Sister Kenny 7-17-46
Sister Lieutenant, The 5-09-45
Sister Maria (See: Maria Nover)
Sister of Mercy 3-20-29
Sister of Six, A 10-13-16
Sister to Assist 'Er, A 9-01-22
Sister to Assist 'Er, A 10-12-27
Sister to Assist 'Er, A 3-26-30
Sister to Salome, A 7-23-20
Sisters 4-07-22
Sisters 3-21-73
Sisters, The (See: Hermanas, Las)
Sisters, The 10-05-38
Sisters of Eve 11-28-28
Sisters of the Golden Circle 6-28-18
Sisters, or the Balance of Happiness (See: Schwestern, oder
    die Balance des Gluecks)
Sister's Sacrifice, A 1-22-10
Sisters Under the Skin 6-12-34
Sit Tight 2-25-31
Sita's Wedding (See: Seetha Kalyanam)
Sitting Bull 9-15-54
Sitting Ducks 11-21-79
Sitting on the Edge of Tomorrow with the Feet Hanging (See:
    Sentados Al Borde Del La Manana Con Los Pies Colgando)
Sitting on the Moon 9-30-36
Sitting Pretty 12-05-33
Sitting Pretty 2-25-48
Sitting Target 2-23-72
Situation Hopeless--But Not Serious 10-06-65
Six Bears and a Clown 7-14-76
Six Best Cellars 3-12-20
Six Black Horses 3-14-62
Six Bridges to Cross 1-19-55
Six Card Stud 9-03-75
Six Cylinder Love 12-13-23
Six Cylinder Love 5-20-31
Six-Day Bike Rider 11-06-34
Six Days 9-20-23
Six Days, The (See: Sheshet Hayamim)
Six Fifty, The 9-27-23
Six-Gun Gold 8-27-41
Six-Gun Law 2-25-48
Six Gun Man 1-23-46
Six-Gun Rhythm 6-21-39
Six Hours to Live 10-25-32
Six Lessons from Mme. La Zonga 2-26-41
Six of a Kind 3-13-34
Six P.M. 2-06-46
Six Pack Annie 12-17-75
6.5 Special 4-09-58
Six-Shooter Andy 3-15-18
Six Shootin' Sheriff 8-17-38

Sogni Muono All'Alba, I 1-17-62
Sogni nel Cassetto, I 10-09-57
Sogno Di Butterfly, Il 11-15-39 and 2-26-41
Soho Gorilla, The (See: Gorilla Von Soho, Der)
Soif des Hommes, La 5-24-50
Soil 10-22-30
Soil Is Thirsty 5-10-32
Soiled Hands (See: Mains Sales, Les)
Soir de Rafle, Un 7-21-31 and 10-20-31
Sois Belle et Tais Toi 7-09-58
Sol En El Espejo, El 7-11-62
Sol En Llamas 3-21-62
Sol Madrid 1-24-68
Sol Over Klara 5-10-44
Sola 3-04-31
Sola 9-29-76
Solange du Lebst 11-30-55
Solaris 5-24-72
Sold 8-13-15
Sold at Auction 1-26-17
Sold for Marriage 4-07-16
Soldadera, La 9-07-66
Soldados 1-17-79
Soldat Bom 2-02-49
Soldat Laforet, Le 3-17-71
Soldaten Kameraden 10-07-36
Soldatesse, Le 8-04-65
Soldaty Svobody 7-27-77
Soldier and the Lady, The 4-14-37
Soldier Blue 8-12-70
Soldier Comrades (See: Soldaten Kameraden)
Soldier in the Rain 11-20-63
Soldier Martin (See: Martin Soldat)
Soldier of Fortune 5-25-55
Soldier of Orange 1-17-79
Soldiers (See: Soldados)
Soldiers and Women 5-14-30
Soldiers Never Cry 2-28-79
Soldier's Oath, A 12-31-15
Soldiers of Fortune 3-27-14
Soldiers of Fortune 11-14-19
Soldiers of Freedom (See: Soldaty Svobody)
Soldiers of the King 3-28-33
Soldiers of the Storm 5-23-33
Soldier's Prayer, A 4-18-62
Soldiers Reminder (See: Krigsmans Erinran)
Soldier's Tale, The 10-28-64
Soldiers Three 3-14-51
Soldier's Wife, A 7-17-29
Soledad 10-01-58
Soledade 7-28-76
Soledad's Shawl (See: Rebozo de Soledad, El)
Soleil Dans l'Oeil, Le 7-11-62
Soleil de Printemps 10-22-69
Soleil des Hyenes 5-25-77
Soleil des Voyous, Le 6-14-67
Soleil En Face, Le 2-27-80
Soleil Noir 12-21-66
Soleil O 5-06-70
Soleil Qui Rit Rouge, Le 4-17-74
Soleil Rouge 9-29-71
Soleil Se Leve en Retard, Le 7-27-77
Soleils de l'Ile de Paques, Les 6-28-72
Solemn Communion (See: Communion Solennelle, La)
Solid Gold Cadillac, The 8-15-56
Soliga Solberg 9-23-42
Solitaire, Le 11-28-73
Solitaire Man, The 9-26-33
Solitary Child 12-17-58
Solitary Conquerors, The (See: Conquerants Solitaires, Les)
Solo 2-18-70
Solo 3-08-78
Solo Flight 10-29-75
Solo Per Te 9-14-38
Solo Sunny 3-05-80
Solomon and Sheba 11-04-59
Solomon in Society 1-05-23
Solomon King 10-02-74
Solos En la Madrugada 4-26-78
Solstik Pa Badehotellet 9-05-73
Soltero Dificil, Un 6-28-50
Soluna 10-16-68
Solunski Atentatori 8-23-61
Som Havets Nakna Vind 11-27-68
Sombra Verde 3-16-55
Sombras de Gloria 2-19-30

Sombrero 2-25-53
Sombrero de Tres Picos 8-16-44
Some Arpents of Snow (See: Quelques Arpents de Neige ...)
Some Bride 6-13-19
Some Call It Loving 10-24-73
Some Came Running 12-24-58
Some Girls Do 2-05-69
Some Interviews on Personal Questions (See: Neskolko Interwju Po
    Litschnym Woprosam)
Some Kind of a Nut 9-24-69
Some Kind of Saint (See: Komischer Heiliger, Ein)
Some Liar 5-09-19
Some Like It Hot 5-10-39
Some Like It Hot 2-25-59
Some Mother's Boy 6-05-29
Some of My Best Friends Are ... 9-08-71
Some One in the House 1-28-21
Some People 7-25-62
Some Pun'kins 10-07-25
Some Too Quiet Gentlemen (See: Quelques Messieurs Trop
    Tranquilles)
Some Won't Go 10-08-69
Somebody Killed Her Husband 9-27-78
Somebody Loves Me 8-20-52
Somebody Up There Likes Me 7-04-56
Somebody's Darling 12-23-25
Somebody's Mother 5-19-26
Somebody's Stolen the Thigh of Jupiter (See: On A Vole la Cuisse
    de Jupiter)
Someone 12-11-68
Someone Behind the Door (See: Quelq'un Derrier La Porte)
Someone to Love 12-05-28
Someone to Remember 8-04-43
Something Always Happens 5-23-28
Something Beautiful (See: Sesuatau Yang Indah)
Something Big 11-10-71
Something Different 1-21-21
Something Floats on the Water (See: Algo Flota Sobre El Agua)
Something for Everyone 7-22-70
Something for the Birds 10-08-52
Something for the Boys 11-01-44
Something in the Wind 7-23-47
Something Like Love (See: Come L'Amore)
Something Money Can't Buy 7-16-52
Something of Value 5-01-57
Something Out of Nothing (See: Ot Nishto-Neshto)
Something Short of Paradise 9-26-79
Something to Do 5-09-19
Something to Hide 7-26-72
Something to Live For 1-30-52
Something to Shout About 2-10-43
Something to Sing About 9-01-37
Something to Think About 10-22-20
Something Wild 12-27-61
Something's Rotten 5-16-79
Sometime Sweet Susan 12-18-74
Sometimes a Great Notion 11-17-71
Sometimes I Even Like Me 10-02-68
Somewhat Like This (See: Kapos Etsi)
Somewhere Beyond Love (See: Delitto D'Amore)
Somewhere I'll Find You 8-05-42
Somewhere in Berlin 8-17-49
Somewhere in Europe (See: Valahol Europaban)
Somewhere in France 10-06-16
Somewhere in Georgia 6-08-17
Somewhere in Sonora 3-30-27
Somewhere in Sonora 6-27-33
Somewhere in the Night 5-08-46
Somewhere in Time 9-24-80
Somewhere, Someone (See: Quelque Part, Quelqu'un)
Sommaren Med Monika 7-07-54
Sommarlek 11-28-51
Sommarnattens Leende 5-16-56
Somme, The 12-21-27
Sommer I Tyrol 3-24-65
Sommergaeste 2-11-76
Sommersprossen 10-16-68
Somnambul 3-06-29
Somnambulist (See: Somnambul)
Somnambulists (See: Sonambulos)
Son, The (See: Fils, Le)
Son Altesse l'Amour 11-10-31
Son Comes Home, A 9-09-36
Son Copain 1-10-51
Son-Daughter, The 1-03-33
Son Dernier Role 10-02-46

Son from America, A (See: Fils d'Amerique, Un)
Son from Vingaarden, The (See: Soennen Fra Vingaarden)
Son Is Born, A 11-06-46
Son of a Badman 11-30-49
Son of a Gunfighter 4-27-66
Son of a Sailor 12-05-33
Son of a Witch (See: Wajan)
Son of Ali Baba 8-13-52
Son of Amr Is Dead, The (See: Fils D'Amr Est Mort, Le)
Son of Belle Starr 7-08-53
Son of Billy the Kid 9-14-49
Son of Captain Blood, The 3-18-64
Son of Caroline Cherie, The (See: Fils de Caroline Cherie, Le)
Son of Chao Phya (See: Look Chao Phya)
Son of D'Artagnan, The (See: Figlio di D'Artagnan, Il)
Son of Davy Crockett, The 7-09-41
Son of Destiny, A 6-25-15
Son of Dr. Jekyll, The 10-03-51
Son of Dracula 11-03-43
Son of Erin, A 12-15-16
Son of Flubber 1-16-63
Son of Frankenstein 1-18-39
Son of Fury 1-07-42
Son of God's Country 9-22-48
Son of His Father 10-19-17
Son of His Father 9-30-25
Son of India 7-28-31
Son of Kong 1-02-34
Son of Lassie 4-25-45
Son of Mongolia 11-25-36
Son of Monte Cristo 12-04-40
Son of Oklahoma 11-01-32
Son of Paleface 7-16-52
Son of Roaring Dan 8-14-40
Son of Robin Hood 6-24-59
Son of Sinbad 6-01-55
Son of the Gods 2-05-30
Son of the Gods, A 8-11-22
Son of the Golden West 12-05-28
Son of the Immortals, A 5-12-16
Son of the Land 5-27-31
Son of the Navy 4-10-40
Son of the Plains 8-11-31
Son of the Pusta (See: Sarga Csiko)
Son of the Regiment 4-21-48
Son of the Renegade 3-25-53
Son of the Sheik 7-14-26
Son of the Wolf 7-14-22
Sonambulos 10-11-78
Sonar Kella 11-19-75
Sonar, No Cuesta Nada 11-19-41
Sonata Nad Ozerom 1-19-77
Sonata Over the Lake (See: Sonata Nad Ozerom)
Sonatas 9-16-59
Soncni Krik 8-14-68
Sondag I Septembre, En 9-04-63
Song 11-14-28
Song, a Kiss, a Girl, A (See: Lied, ein Kuss, ein Maedel, Ein)
Song and Dance Man 2-03-26
Song and Dance Man 3-18-36
Song and the Silence, The 2-05-69
Song for Miss Julie, A 2-21-45
Song for You, A (See: Lied Fuer Dich, Ein)
Song Goes Round the World (See: Lied Geht Um die Welt, Ein)
Song Is Born, A 8-25-48
Song Is Ended, The 10-29-30 (Also see: Lied Ist Aus, Das)
Song o' My Heart 3-19-30
Song of Arizona 3-13-46
Song of Bernadette, The 12-22-43
Song of Ceylon 8-18-37
Song of China 11-11-36
Song of Freedom 9-09-36
Song of Happiness 12-11-34
Song of Hate, The 9-17-15
Song of Idaho 3-31-48
Song of India 2-16-49
Song of Life 8-04-22
Song of Life, The (See: Lied vom Leben, Das)
Song of Life, The 10-20-31
Song of Love 11-20-29
Song of Love 7-23-47
Song of Love, The (See: Om Kjaerligheten Synger De)
Song of Love, The 2-28-24
Song of My Heart 11-05-47
Song of My Heart 1-10-51
Song of Nevada 6-14-44
Song of Night, The (See: Lied Einer Nacht, Das)
Song of Norway 11-04-70

Song of Old Wyoming 9-05-45 and 4-10-46
Song of Paris 2-27-52
Song of Roland, The (See: Chanson de Roland, La)
Song of Russia 12-29-43
Song of Scheherazade 1-29-47
Song of Sixpence, A 6-08-17
Song of Songs 7-25-33
Song of Songs, The 2-22-18
Song of Stockholm (See: Sangen Om Stockholm)
Song of Surrender 9-14-49
Song of Texas 6-02-43
Song of the Balalaika, The (See: Lied der Balalaik, Das)
Song of the Buckaroo 1-18-39
Song of the Butterfly (See: Sogno di Butterfly, Il)
Song of the Caballero 7-09-30
Song of the Canary 3-28-79
Song of the City 5-05-37
Song of the Cradle, The 11-06-09
Song of the Eagle 5-02-33
Song of the Firemen (See: Hori, Ma Panenko)
Song of the Flame 5-14-30
Song of the Gray Pigeon (See: Piesen O Sivom Holubovi)
Song of the Islands 2-04-42
Song of the Land 11-25-53
Song of the Little Road (See: Pather Panchali)
Song of the Marimba (See: Al Son de la Marimba)
Song of the Open Road 5-03-44
Song of the Pass (See: Ogheya Ala El Mamar)
Song of the Road 5-08-40
Song of the Saddle 3-25-36
Song of the Sarong 4-25-45
Song of the Siren, The 1-07-16
Song of the Soul 10-15-20
Song of the Soul 6-03-21
Song of the Soul, The 3-01-18
Song of the South 11-06-46
Song of the Street (See: Cantiga Da Rua)
Song of the Streets (See: Dans les Rues)
Song of the Sun (See: Canzone del Sole, La)
Song of the Thin Man 7-23-47
Song of the Trail 12-23-36
Song of the Wage Slave, The 9-24-15
Song of the Wards (See: Cancion de los Barrios)
Song of the West 3-05-30
Song of the Wildwood Flute, The 12-03-10
Song of the Woods 9-13-61
Song of the World (See: Chant du Monde, Le)
Song Remains the Same, The 10-20-76
Song That Reached His Heart, The 10-15-10
Song to Remember, A (See: Cancion Para Recordar, Una)
Song to Remember, A 1-24-45
Song Without End 6-22-60
Song You Gave Me 8-15-33
Songs and Bullets 5-18-38
Songs for After a War (See: Canciones Para Despues De Una Guerra)
Songstress, The (See: Maja de los Cantares, La)
Sonne von St. Moritz, Die 9-01-54
Sonntag Des Lebens 4-29-31
Sonntagskinder 5-21-80
Sonny 6-02-22
Sonny & Jed 2-27-74
Sonny Boy 3-06-29
Sono Fotogenico 5-28-80
Sono Stato Io 5-23-73
Sono Stato Un Agente Cia 8-23-78
Sonora Kid 3-02-27
Sonora Stagecoach 8-23-44
Sons and Daughters 5-10-67
Sons and Lovers 5-25-60
Sons for the Return Home 10-31-79
Sons o' Guns 5-20-36
Sons of Adventure 9-29-48
Sons of Fire (See: Szarvassa Valt Fiuk)
Sons of Katie Elder, The 6-30-65
Sons of New Mexico 12-28-49
Sons of Silence, The (See: Abnae el Samte)
Sons of Steel 4-17-35
Sons of the Desert 1-09-34
Sons of the Earth (See: Afincaos, Los)
Sons of the Gods 2-05-30
Sons of the Legion 10-05-38
Sons of the Pioneers 9-02-42
Sons of the Saddle 8-20-30
Sons of the Sea 11-29-39
Sons of Water, The (See: Fils de l'Eau, Les)
Sonya and the Madman 8-03-77
Sooky 12-22-31

Sooner or Later 3-19-20
Soot and Gold (See: Nokea Ja Kultaa)
Sooterang 10-20-65
Sophia (See: Zofia)
Sophie Lang 7-24-34
Sophie Lang Goes West 9-08-37
Sophie's Ways (See: Stances a Sophie, Les)
Sophomore, The 8-28-29
Sor Intrepida 1-20-54
Sorcerer 6-29-77
Sorcerer, The (See: Hexer, Der)
Sorcerers, The 6-28-67
Sorceress, The (See: Sorciere, La)
Sorciere, La 12-26-56
Sorcieres de Salem, Les 6-12-57
Sorok Pervyi 5-22-57
Sorority Girl 12-04-57
Sorority House 5-10-39
Sorpasso, Il 12-26-62
Sorrell and Son 11-16-27
Sorrell and Son 6-05-34
Sorrell Flower (See: Fleur D'Oseille)
Sorrow of the Gentry 5-28-75
Sorrowful Jones 4-13-49
Sorrows of Lenka, The 4-11-62
Sorrows of Love, The 6-02-16
Sorrows of Satan, The 10-20-26
Sorrows of Young Werther, The (See: Leiden des Jungen Werther,
   Die)
Sorry, Wrong Number 7-28-48
Sortie de Secours 10-21-70
So's Your Old Man 11-03-26
So's Your Uncle 11-24-43
Sospetto, Il 8-27-75
Sotto il Segno Dello Scorpione 9-03-69
Souffle au Coeur, Le 4-14-71
Souhvezdi Panny 8-03-66
Soukroma Vichrice 7-24-68
Soul Fire 5-06-25
Soul for Sale, A 5-24-18
Soul in Trust, A 3-08-18
Soul Market, A 3-10-16
Soul Mates 5-19-16
Soul Mates 1-06-26
Soul of a Magdalene, The 5-25-17
Soul of a Monster, The 9-13-44
Soul of a Woman, The 9-03-15
Soul of Broadway, The 10-22-15
Soul of Buddha, The 5-17-18
Soul of France, The 10-16-29
Soul of Kura San, The 11-03-16
Soul of Nigger Charley, The 5-16-73
Soul of Rafael, The 5-28-20
Soul of the Beast 5-24-23
Soul of the Slums 12-29-31
Soul of Youth 8-20-20
Soul Sister (See: Soulsister)
Soul to Devils, A (See: Chimimorya)
Soul to Soul 8-25-71
Soul Without Windows, A 9-20-18
Souls Adrift 8-03-17
Souls Aflame 7-18-28
Souls at Sea 8-11-37
Soul's Awakening 9-01-22
Souls for Sables 9-16-25
Souls for Sale 3-29-23
Souls in Bondage 2-18-16
Souls in Pawn 10-08-15
Souls of Men 6-17-21
Souls Triumphant 6-02-17
Soulsister 9-03-80
Sound and the Fury, The 3-04-59
Sound Barrier 7-30-52
Sound of Fury, The 12-06-50
Sound of Life, The 2-28-62
Sound of Music, The 3-03-65
Sound Off 4-09-52
Sounder 8-16-72
Sounder, Part 2 10-13-76
Soup du Jour 9-24-75
Soup to Nuts 10-29-30
Soupe Froide, La 1-22-75
Soupirant, Le 2-27-63
Source, The 8-16-18
Sourdough 3-02-77
Souriciere, La 4-26-50
Sourire dans la Tempete, Un 5-02-51
Sourire Vertical, Le 7-04-73

Sous-Doues, Les 7-02-80
Sous la Lune du Maroc 1-24-33
Sous le Casque de Cuir 5-10-32
Sous le Ciel de Paris 5-16-51
Sous le Ciel de Provence 5-01-57
Sous le Signe de Monte-Cristo 1-15-69
Sous le Signe du Taureau 4-16-69
Sous les Toits de Paris 5-14-30 and 12-24-30
Sous les Yeux d'Occident 5-06-36
South of Algiers 3-25-53
South of Arizona 10-05-38
South of Caliente 10-31-51
South of Death Valley 7-12-50
South of Dixie 5-24-44
South of Pago Pago 7-17-40
South of Panama 6-18-41
South of Rio 8-10-49
South of St. Louis 2-16-49
South of Santa Fe 4-29-42
South of Suez 12-25-40
South of Suva 6-23-22
South of Tahiti 10-22-41
South of Tana River (See: Syd For Tana River)
South of the Border 12-13-39
South of the Equator 1-07-25
South of the Highway (See: Soder om Landsvagen)
South of the Northern Lights 2-08-23
South of the Rio Grande 5-10-32
South of the Rio Grande 12-12-45
South Pacific 3-26-58
South Pacific Trail 11-12-52
South Riding 1-19-38 and 7-27-38
South Sea Adventures 4-05-32
South Sea Bubble, A 8-22-28
South Sea Love 1-17-24
South Sea Love 2-08-28
South Sea Rose 12-11-29
South Sea Sinner 1-04-50
South Sea Woman 6-03-53
South Seas 5-28-30
South Seas Adventure 7-16-58
South to Karanga 8-14-40
South Wind (See: Vento Del Sud)
Southern Bar (See: Bar du Sud)
Southern Carrier (See: Courrier Sud)
Southern Cross (See: Croix Du Sud)
Southern Justice 5-25-17
Southern Love 2-21-24
Southern Roses 10-21-36
Southern Star, The (See: Etoile du Sud, L')
Southern Tunis 10-08-10
Southern Yankee, A 8-11-48
Southerner, The 5-02-45
Southerners, The 5-29-14
Southside 1-1000 10-11-50
Southward Ho 6-07-39
Southwest Passage 4-14-54
Souvenir d'Italie 6-12-57
Souvenir of Gibraltar 5-07-75
Souvenirs d'En France 8-20-75
Souvenirs Perdus 1-10-51
Sovereign, The (See: Herrscher, Der)
Soviet Border, The 3-01-39
Soviet Frontiers on the Danube 7-02-41
Soviet Power 9-10-41
Soviet Russia Today 9-27-39
Soviets on Parade 3-07-33
Sovsem Propashtshiy 5-22-74
Sovversivo, I (See: Subversives, The)
Sowers, The 3-31-16
Sowers and Reapers 5-18-17
Sowing the Wind 6-24-21
Sowing the Wind 3-20-29
Soy Mexica 9-18-67
Soy Puro Mexicano 6-09-43
Soy Un Delincuente 9-07-77
Soylent Green 4-18-73
Space Children 6-18-58
Space Coast 5-23-79
Space Cruiser Yamato 12-21-77
Space Master X-7 7-23-58
Space Mission: Zero Hour (See: Zero)
Space Movie, The 3-05-80
Spaceflight IC-1 10-06-65
Spaceways 7-08-53
Spain Again (See: Espana Otra Vez)
Spain Fights On (See: Will of a People, The)
Spain in Flames 2-03-37

Spalovac Mrtvol 7-16-69
Spangles 1-19-27
Spanische Fliege, Die 1-12-32
Spanish Affair 2-05-58
Spanish Cape Mystery 11-20-35
Spanish Dancer 10-11-23
Spanish Fiesta, The (See: Fete Espagnole, La)
Spanish Fury (See: Furia Espanola)
Spanish Gardener, The 1-02-57
Spanish Jade, The 3-05-15
Spanish Loyalty 11-26-10
Spanish Main, The 10-03-45
Spanish Romance, A 10-17-08
Spanking at School (See: Klassenkeile)
Spara Forte, Piu Forte, Non Capisco (See: Shoot Loud, Louder ...
    I Don't Understand)
Spare the Rod 5-31-61
Sparkle 4-07-76
Sparkling Winds (See: Fenyes Szelek)
Sparrows 9-22-26
Sparrows Are Birds Too (See: A Vereb Is Madar)
Sparrows Can't Sing 4-03-63
Spartacus 10-12-60
Spartakiada 7-10-29
Spartan Girl, The 3-27-14
Spasatel 9-10-80
Spat, The (See: Zizanie, La)
Spawn of the Desert 5-10-23
Spawn of the North 8-24-38
Speak Easily 8-23-32
Speak to Me of Love (See: Parlez-Moi D'Amour)
Speakeasy 3-13-29
Special Agent 9-25-35
Special Agent 4-27-49
Special Agent K-7 9-08-37
Special Delivery (See: Entrega Immediata or Von Himmel Gefallen)
Special Delivery 4-27-27
Special Delivery 7-07-76
Special Edition (See: Editie Speciala)
Special Education (See: Specijalno Vaspitanje)
Special Inspector 4-19-39
Special Investigator 4-29-36
Special Servicer 5-10-67
Special Therapy (See: Poseban Tretman)
Special Treatment (See: Poseban Tretman)
Specijalno Vaspitanje 5-25-77
Speckled Band, The 3-25-31 and 11-10-31
Specter of the Rose 5-22-46
Spectre of Edgar Allan Poe, The 5-08-74
Spectre Vert, Le 5-21-30
Spectro at the Hour of Midnight 4-02-15
Speed 4-22-25
Speed 5-20-36
Speed Classic 12-26-28
Speed Cop 2-09-27
Speed Crazed 5-25-27
Speed Crazy 5-20-59
Speed Demon, The 8-12-35
Speed Devils 7-10-35
Speed Fever 9-20-78
Speed Girl, The 11-18-21
Speed King, The 2-15-23
Speed Limit, The 5-19-26
Speed Limited 12-25-40
Speed Mad 12-09-25 and 5-05-26
Speed Madness 12-02-25
Speed Madness 10-11-32
Speed Maniac, The 9-26-19
Speed Reporter 4-06-38
Speed Spook, The 10-22-24
Speed to Burn 6-08-38
Speed to Spare 6-09-37
Speed to Spare 2-18-48
Speed Wings 4-03-34
Speeding Thru 10-27-26
Speeding Venus, The 10-06-26
Speedway 9-25-29
Speedway 5-22-68
Speedy 4-11-28
Speedy Smith 12-14-27
Spell of the Looking Glass (See: Im Bann des Eulenspiegels)
Spell of the Yukon, The 5-12-16
Spellbinder 7-26-39
Spellbound 1-29-41
Spellbound 10-31-45
Spencer's Mountain 2-27-63
Spender, The 10-15-15

Spenders, The 1-28-21
Spending Money (See: Argent De Poche, L')
Spendthrift 7-29-36
Spendthrift, The 6-11-15
Sperduti Nel Buio 5-18-49
Spermula 6-23-76
Spessart Inn, The (See: Wirthaus im Spessart, Das)
Spetters 4-02-80
Sphinx, The 2-18-16
Sphinx, The 7-11-33
Spice of Life 1-13-54
Spider, The 2-11-16
Spider, The 9-08-31
Spider, The 2-07-40
Spider, The 10-10-45
Spider, The 11-05-58
Spider and the Fly, The 6-02-16
Spider and the Fly, The 12-07-49
Spider and the Rose, The 7-26-23
Spider Football (See: Pokfoci)
Spider Webs 5-18-27
Spider Woman Strikes Back, The 3-20-46
Spider's Strategy, The (See: Strategia Del Ragno)
Spider's Web 1-11-39
Spiel Auf der Tenne 11-03-37
Spieler, The 2-27-29
Spielst Du mit Schraegen Voegeln 5-21-69
Spies 3-06-29 (Also see: Spione)
Spies, The (See: Espions, Les)
Spies at Work (See: Spione am Werk)
Spies' Night (See: Nuit des Espions, La)
Spies of the Air 4-26-39
Spijun X-25 Javlja 8-10-60
Spike's Gang, The 4-10-74
Spin a Dark Web 9-26-56
Spindle of Life, The 9-28-17
Spinout 10-19-66
Spione 5-02-28
Spione am Werk 4-25-33
Spione von Odessa, Der (See: Spy of Odessa, The)
Spiral (See: Spirala)
Spiral of Mist, A (See: Spirale di Nebbia, Una)
Spiral Road, The 5-30-62
Spiral Staircase, The 1-09-46
Spirala 5-31-78
Spirale, La 4-14-76
Spirale Di Nebbia, Una 10-12-77
Spirit and the Flesh, The 8-25-48
Spirit Is Willing, The 7-19-67
Spirit Lake Massacre 8-03-27
Spirit of Culver 3-01-39
Spirit of Devilry (See: Diable au Corps, Le)
Spirit of Good, The 7-16-20
Spirit of Notre Dame 10-06-31
Spirit of Romance, The 5-04-17
Spirit of St. Louis, The 2-20-57
Spirit of '17, The 1-25-18
Spirit of Stanford 10-07-42
Spirit of the Beehive (See: Espiritu de la Colmena, El)
Spirit of the Poppy 10-17-14
Spirit of the West 5-31-32
Spirit of the Wind 5-23-79
Spirit of West Point, The 10-08-47
Spirit of Youth 3-20-29
Spirit of Youth 1-05-38
Spiritual Boxer, The 12-31-75
Spiritualist, The 8-04-48
Spite Bride, The 9-26-19
Spite Marriage 3-27-29
Spitfire 3-13-34
Spitfire, The 7-03-14
Spitfire, The 6-25-24
Spitfire of Seville, The 7-18-19
Splav Meduze 8-13-80
Splendid Crime, The 12-16-25
Splendid Fellows 12-25-34
Splendid Hazard, A 9-24-20 and 12-17-20
Splendid Lie, The 3-10-22
Splendid Road, The 1-20-26
Splendid Sin, The 10-03-19
Splendid Sinner, The 4-05-18
Splendor 11-27-35
Splendor in the Grass 8-30-61
Splinters 2-05-30
Split, The 10-02-68
Split Second 3-18-53
Splitting the Breeze 9-07-27
Spodelena Lyubov 7-18-79

Steel Preferred 12-23-25
Steel Town 3-05-52
Steel Trap, The 10-22-52
Steele of the Royal Mounted 6-17-25
Steelheart 11-18-21
Steelyard Blues 1-31-73
Stefania 12-11-68
Stehaufmaedchen 6-03-70
Steinach Film 2-08-23
Steinreicher Mann, Ein 3-01-32
Stella 12-15-43
Stella 7-19-50
Stella 5-11-55 and 5-01-57
Stella Da Falla 8-30-72
Stella Dallas 11-18-25
Stella Dallas 7-28-37
Stella Maris 1-25-18
Stella Maris 3-17-26
Stella Parish 11-06-35
Stelldichein im Schwarzwald, Ein 2-24-37
Step by Step 7-17-46
Step Down to Terror 9-17-58
Step Lively 6-21-44
Step Lively, Jeeves 4-07-37
Step-Mother, The 2-12-10
Step On It 5-26-22
Stepbrothers (See: Ibo Kyodai)
Stepchild 6-11-47
Stepford Wives, The 2-12-75
Stephen Steps Out 11-22-23
Stepmother, The (See: Madrasta, La)
Steppa, La 7-18-62
Steppe, The 8-30-78
Steppenwolf 10-23-74
Steppin' Fast 7-12-23
Steppin' in Society 6-06-45
Stepping Along 12-08-26
Stepping Lively 10-29-24
Stepping Out 9-26-19
Stepping Sisters 1-12-32
Stepping Stone, The 3-31-16 and 9-27-18
Steps, The (See: Steppa, La)
Sterile Cuckoo, The 10-08-69
Stern von Afrika, Der 12-04-57
Sterne 5-13-59
Sternstein Manor, The (See: Sternsteinhof)
Sternsteinhof 7-14-76
Stevie 9-06-78
Stevnemoete Met Giemte Ar 9-11-57
Stew in the Caribbean (See: Estouffade a la Caraibe)
Stewardesses, The 9-16-70
Sticenik 9-28-66
Stici Pre Svitanja 8-09-78
Stick Around 4-30-20
Stick to Your Guns 9-24-41
Stick Up, The 5-24-78
Sticks and Stones 1-28-70
Stigma 8-16-72
Stigma, The 10-15-10
Stiletto 7-30-69
Stiliga Augusta 1-22-47
Still Alarm, The 8-23-18
Still Alarm, The 6-30-26
Still Life (See: Tabiate Bijan or Stilleben)
Still Waters 11-12-15
Stilleben 10-24-79
Stimme des Blutes 1-12-38
Stimme des Herzens, Die 5-26-37
Stin Letajiciho Ptacka 6-21-78
Stine and the Boys (See: Stine Og Drengene)
Stine Og Drengene 3-26-69
Sting, The 12-12-73
Sting of the Lash 10-21-21
Sting of the Scorpion 1-17-24
Stingaree 5-22-34
Stiny Horkeho Leta 8-02-78
Stir 7-26-80
Stir Crazy 12-03-80
Stirring Days in Old Virginia 3-06-09
Stitch in Time, A 12-25-63
Stjernerne Og Vandbaererne (See: Stars and the Water Carriers, The)
Sto Dnej Possle Detstwa 7-16-75
Stocks and Blondes 10-24-28
Stoerfried, Der 12-04-35
Stoff Aus Dem Die Traeume Sind, Der 10-04-72
Stoker, The 7-19-32

Stolen Air-ship, The (See: Ukradena Vzducholod)
Stolen Bride, The 8-10-27
Stolen Claim, The 11-19-10
Stolen Face 5-28-52
Stolen Face, The (See: Gestohlene Gesicht, Das)
Stolen Father, The 10-22-10
Stolen Gems 9-11-09
Stolen Harmony 4-24-35
Stolen Heaven 2-18-31
Stolen Heaven 4-27-38
Stolen Holiday 2-03-37
Stolen Hours 10-02-63
Stolen Identity 4-08-53
Stolen Kiss 4-09-20
Stolen Kisses (See: Baisers Voles)
Stolen Kisses 5-08-29
Stolen Life 2-01-39
Stolen Life, A 5-01-46
Stolen Love 1-16-29
Stolen Magic 10-08-15
Stolen Orders 6-07-18
Stolen Paradise, The 6-08-17
Stolen Pleasures 2-02-27
Stolen Rembrandt, The 5-08-14
Stolen Siege Gun Plans, The 5-14-15
Stolen Sweets 9-25-34
Stolen Voice, The 8-20-15
Stolen Wireless, The 10-16-09
Stolz der 3. Kompagnie, Der 1-26-32
Stomach In, Chest Out! 9-02-59
Stone 7-24-74
Stone Cold Dead 2-27-80
Stone in Heaven (See: Batu-Bato Sa Langit)
Stone Killer, The 8-22-73
Stone of Silver Creek 4-10-35
Stone Wedding (See: Nuchia De Piatra)
Stony Island 11-15-78
Stooge, The 10-08-52
Stool Pigeon 10-24-28
Stoolie, The (See: Doulos, Le)
Stoolie, The 11-22-72
Stop 6-09-71
Stop Calling Me Baby! (See: Moi, Fleur Bleue)
Stop Flirting 6-17-25
Stop It! (See: At Dere Tor)
Stop! Look! and Laugh! 6-29-60
Stop, Look and Listen 5-12-26
Stop, Look and Love 8-30-39
Stop Press Girl, The 6-08-49
Stop That Man 4-18-28
Stop the Drums (See: Arretez les Tambours)
Stop the World--I Want to Get Off 4-06-66
Stop, Thief 2-12-15
Stop, Thief 8-20-20
Stop, You're Killing Me 12-17-52
Stopar 2-28-79
Stopover Tokyo 10-30-57
Storch Streikt, Der 9-15-31 and 5-03-32
Storia de Confine 8-16-72
Storia Di Una Monaca Di Clausura 12-05-73
Storia Milanese, Una 9-12-62
Storie Scellerate 8-29-73
Storie Sulla Sabbia 9-04-63
Stories About Lenin 8-06-58
Stories from a Flying Trunk 11-21-79
Stories of My Mother (See: Rasskaz Moei Materi)
Stories on a Train 7-24-63
Stories on the Sand (See: Storie Sulla Sabbia)
Stork 12-29-71
Stork Bites Man 8-13-47
Stork Club, The 10-10-45
Stork Pays Off 11-12-41
Stork Said Yes, The (See: Ciguena Dijo Si, La)
Stork Strikes, The (See: Storch Streikt, Der)
Stork Talk 4-11-62
Storm (See: Orage)
Storm, The (See: Jhor)
Storm, The 9-08-16
Storm, The 6-23-22
Storm, The 8-27-30
Storm, The 11-02-38
Storm at Daybreak 7-25-33
Storm Boy 12-29-76
Storm Center 8-01-56
Storm Daughter 4-16-24
Storm Fear 12-28-55
Storm Girl 4-26-23
Storm in a Teacup 6-09-37

Storm of the Plains (See: Pusztai Szel)
Storm of the Wild Kaiser 7-14-65
Storm over Asia (See: Tempete Sur l'Asie)
Storm over Asia 3-06-29 and 9-10-30
Storm over Bengal 12-14-38
Storm over Lisbon 8-30-44
Storm over the Andes 10-02-35
Storm over the Nile 11-23-55
Storm over Tibet 12-19-51
Storm over Wyoming 2-08-50
Storm Rider 3-20-57
Storm Swept 3-15-23
Storm Warning (See: Stormvarsel)
Storm Warning 12-06-50
Stormbound 1-23-52
Stormo Atlantico, Lo 7-28-31
Storms in May (See: Gewitter im Mai)
Storms of Passion (See: Stuerme der Leidenschaft)
Storms of the Heart 7-31-14
Stormtroopers (See: Sturmtruppen)
Stormvarsel 1-22-69
Stormy 12-11-35
Stormy Crossing 8-27-58
Stormy Knight, A 9-14-17
Stormy Seas 7-19-23
Stormy the Thoroughbred 3-10-54
Stormy Trails 12-23-36 and 2-02-38
Stormy Waters 6-27-28
Stormy Waters 6-19-46
Stormy Weather 6-02-43
Stormy Wine (See: Bourlive Vino)
Story of a Bad Woman, The (See: Historia de una Mala Mujer)
Story of a Bank Note 10-09-09
Story of a Citizen Above All Suspicion (See: Indagine su un
    Cittadino Al Di Sopra di Ogni Sospetto)
Story of a Girl Alone (See: Historia de una Chica Sola)
Story of a Goldfish (See: Histoire d'un Poisson Rouge)
Story of a Good Guy, The (See: Bushkhugin Ulger)
Story of a Mother, The (See: Historien om en Moder)
Story of a Night (See: Historia de una Noche)
Story of a Rose 9-25-09
Story of a Sin (See: Dzieje Grzechu)
Story of a Trickster, The (See: Roman d'un Tricheur, Le)
Story of a Woman 2-04-70
Story of Adele H., The (See: Histoire d'Adele H., L')
Story of an Unknown Man (See: Rasskaz O Neisvestnom Celoveke)
Story of Barbara (See: Historien om Barbara)
Story of Chikmatsu, The 2-05-58
Story of Chinese Gods, The 5-19-76
Story of Choonhyang (See: Sung Choonhyang)
Story of Cinderella, The (See: Slipper and the Rose, The)
Story of Dr. Wassell, The 4-26-44
Story of Esther Costello, The 8-21-57
Story of F, The 2-10-71
Story of G.I. Joe, The 6-20-45
Story of Genji, The (See: Genji Monogatari)
Story of Gilbert and Sullivan, The 5-13-53
Story of Joanna, The 10-29-75
Story of Love and Anarchy (See: Film d'Amore e d'Anarchia)
Story of Mankind, The 10-23-57
Story of Michelangelo (See: Titan, The)
Story of Molly X, The 11-09-49
Story of My Foolishness (See: Butasagom Tortenete)
Story of O., The (See: Histoire d'O., L')
Story of Paul (See: Histoire de Paul)
Story of Pure Love 7-16-58
Story of Ruth, The 6-08-60
Story of Seabiscuit, The 11-02-49
Story of Susan, The 5-11-77
Story of the Burning Years (See: Povestj Plamennykh Let)
Story of the Count of Monte Cristo, The 6-13-62
Story of the Dragon, The 10-27-76
Story of the Nineties, A (See: Historia Del 900)
Story of the Pope, The 12-25-46
Story of the Vatican, The 8-13-41
Story of Three Loves, The 3-04-53
Story of Tosca, The 12-17-47
Story of Vernon and Irene Castle, The 4-05-39
Story of Vickie, The 1-22-58
Story of Will Rogers, The 7-16-52
Story on Page One, The 12-30-59
Story Without a Name 10-08-24
Stosszeit 5-13-70
Stowaway 12-23-36
Stowaways (See: Blinde Passagiere)
Strada, La 9-22-54
Stradivarius 11-06-35

Strafbataillon 999 4-13-60
Strah 8-20-75
Straight from Paris 7-22-21
Straight from the Heart 3-27-35
Straight from the Shoulder 11-18-36
Straight Is the Way 2-25-21
Straight Is the Way 9-04-34
Straight, Place and Show 9-28-38
Straight Road, The 11-14-14
Straight Shooter 1-31-40 and 5-15-40
Straight Shootin' 3-07-28
Straight Time 3-22-78
Straight Way, The 10-06-16
Straightaway 1-23-34
Strainul 7-29-64
Strait-Jacket 1-15-64
Strait-Laced Girl, A (See: Fille Cousue De Fil Blanc, Une)
Stranded 7-28-16
Stranded 9-21-27
Stranded 6-26-35
Stranded 5-26-65
Stranded in Paris 12-15-26
Strange Adventure 2-14-33
Strange Affair 11-29-44
Strange Affair, The 7-24-68
Strange Alibi 4-30-41
Strange Bargain 9-21-49
Strange Bedfellows 12-16-64
Strange Boarder, The 4-23-20
Strange Boarders 6-01-38
Strange Cargo 2-20-29
Strange Cargo 3-06-40
Strange Case of Captain Ramper, The 6-06-28
Strange Case of Dr. Meade, The 2-01-39
Strange Case of Dr. RX, The 4-01-42
Strange Case of Mary Page, The (serial), Part I: 1-28-16;
    Part II: 2-04-16; Part III: 2-11-16; Part IV: 2-18-16
Strange City (See: Fremde Stadt)
Strange Confession 11-14-45
Strange Conquest 4-17-46
Strange Day, The (See: Giornata Balorda, La)
Strange Death of Adolf Hitler, The 10-13-43
Strange Deception 5-20-53
Strange Desire of Mr. Bard (See: Etrange Desir de Monsieur
    Bard, L')
Strange Door, The 10-31-51
Strange Events (See: Quelle Strane Occasioni)
Strange Faces 12-14-38
Strange Fascination 10-01-52
Strange Fate (See: Etrange Destin)
Strange Game (See: Drole De Jeu)
Strange Girl (See: Cudna Devojka)
Strange Gods 7-09-58
Strange Guest, A (See: Seltsamer Gast, Ein)
Strange Guests (See: Caida, La)
Strange Harbor (See: Fremmande Hamn)
Strange Holiday 10-24-45 and 11-06-46
Strange Interlude 9-06-32
Strange Intruder 9-05-56
Strange Justice 11-01-32
Strange Kind of Colonel, A (See: Drole de Colonel, Un)
Strange Lady in Town 4-13-55
Strange Letters (See: Tschushije Pissma)
Strange Lie of Nina Petrowna, The 5-08-29
Strange Love of Martha Ivers, The 3-13-46
Strange Lovers 7-10-63
Strange Madame X, The (See: Etrange Madame X, L')
Strange Mr. Gregory, The 12-19-45
Strange Mr. Stevens, The (See: Etrange Monsieur Steve, L')
Strange Mrs. Crane, The 10-13-48
Strange Night, The (See: Conigliaccio, Il)
Strange One, The 4-03-57
Strange People (See: Strannye Ljudi)
Strange People 6-20-33
Strange Resemblance, A 5-15-09
Strange Role, A (See: Herkulesfurdoi Emlek)
Strange Shadows in an Empty Room 2-16-77
Strange Story, A 7-30-15
Strange Story of Sylvia Gray, The (See: Sylvia Gray)
Strange Transgressor, A 6-29-17
Strange Triangle 5-08-46
Strange Vengeance of Rosalie, The 6-28-72
Strange Voyage 12-19-45
Strange Wives 2-05-35
Strange Woman, A (See: Strannaya Zhenshina)
Strange Woman, The 12-27-18
Strange Woman, The 10-30-46
Strange World 4-09-52

Strange World of Planet X, The 3-12-58
Strange World of Ze do Caixao, The (See: O Estranho Mundo De Ze Do Caixao)
Stranger, The (See: Vieras Mies; Strainul; or Straniera, La)
Stranger, The 2-07-24
Stranger, The 5-22-46
Stranger, The 9-20-67
Stranger and the Fog, The (See: Gharibeh-Va-Meh)
Stranger at My Door 4-18-56
Stranger from Arizona, The 9-21-38
Stranger from Pecos, The 7-28-43
Stranger from Somewhere, A 11-17-16
Stranger from Texas, The 1-10-40
Stranger in My Arms 3-11-59
Stranger in the City, A 7-24-63
Stranger in the House 5-31-67
Stranger in Town, A 7-12-32
Stranger in Town, A 2-10-43
Stranger in Town, A 3-27-68
Stranger Knocks, A (See: Fremmed Banker Paa, En)
Stranger of the Hills 6-07-23
Stranger of the North 2-07-24
Stranger on Horseback 3-02-55
Stranger on the Third Floor 9-04-40
Stranger Returns, The 8-28-68
Stranger Than Fiction 12-16-21
Stranger Wore a Gun, The 8-05-53
Strangers 9-28-55
Strangers 8-09-72
Strangers, The (See: Etrangers, Les)
Strangers All 6-26-35
Strangers' Banquet 1-05-23
Stranger's Gundown, The 4-17-74
Stranger's Hand, The (See: Mano Dello Strangiero)
Stranger's Hand, The 7-14-54
Strangers Honeymoon 3-17-37
Strangers in Love 3-08-32
Strangers in the City 5-09-62
Strangers in the House 10-19-49
Strangers May Kiss 4-15-31
Stranger's Melody (See: Dendang Perantau)
Strangers of the Evening 6-07-32
Strangers of the Night 10-11-23
Strangers on a Train 6-20-51
Strangers on Honeymoon 12-16-36
Stranger's Return, The 8-01-33
Strangers--The Road to Liberty (See: Gaijin--Caminos da Liberdade)
Strangers When We Meet 5-25-60
Strangler, The (See: Etrangleur, L')
Strangler, The 4-08-64
Stranglers of Bombay, The 12-23-59
Stranglers of Paris, The 3-05-15
Straniera, La 4-15-31
Straniero, Il (See: Stranger, The)
Strannaya Zhenshina 9-12-79
Strannye Ljudi 12-01-76
Strano Vizio Della Signora Ward, Lo (See: Next)
Strassemusik 9-02-36
Strategia Del Ragno 9-02-70
Strategic Air Command 3-30-55
Strategy (See: Harcmodor)
Strategy of Terror 1-15-69
Stratford Adventure 5-05-54
Stratton Story, The 4-20-49
Strauberg Is Here (See: Strauberg Ist Da)
Strauberg Ist Da 3-29-78
Strauss' Great Waltz 4-17-35
Strauss' Salome 3-22-23
Stravinsky Portrait, A 2-07-68
Straw Dogs 12-01-70
Strawberry Blonde, The 2-19-41
Strawberry, Lemon and Mint (See: De Fresa, Limon y Menta)
Strawberry Roan, The 12-13-33
Strawberry Roan, The 1-17-45
Strawberry Roan, The 4-28-48
Strawberry Statement, The 5-13-70
Stray Dog (See: Nora Inu)
Straying Rooster (See: Gallo en Corral Ajeno, Un)
Straziami Ma Di Baci Saziami 11-13-68
Stream, The (See: Ruisseau, Le)
Streamline Express 9-25-35
Street, The (See: Gatan or Ulica)
Street, The 9-07-27
Street Angel 4-11-28
Street Bandits 11-21-51
Street Calls, The 10-27-48
Street Corner 12-01-48

Street Corner 3-25-53
Street Corners 9-11-29
Street Gangs of Hong Kong 3-20-74
Street Girl 8-07-29
Street Is My Beat, The 8-31-66
Street Music (See: Strassemusik)
Street of Chance 2-05-30
Street of Chance 9-30-42
Street of Forgotten Men 7-22-25
Street of Illusion 10-31-28
Street of Joy (See: Akasen Tamanoi Nekeraremasu)
Street of Memories 7-03-40
Street of Missing Men 4-26-39 and 11-15-39
Street of Seven Stars, The 5-25-18
Street of Sin 5-30-78
Street of the Crane's Foot (See: Rue du Pied-De-Grue)
Street of Women 5-31-32
Street People 9-29-76
Street Scene 9-01-31
Street Scenes 1970 9-23-70
Street Singer (See: Goualeuse, La)
Street Singer, The 3-24-37
Street Thieves, The (See: Atracadores, Los)
Street with No Name, The 6-23-48
Street Without a Name (See: Rue Sans Nom, La)
Street Without End (See: Gade Uden Ende)
Street Without Joy (See: Rue Sans Joie, La)
Streetcar Named Desire, A 6-20-51
Streetfighter, The 2-05-75
Streets of Algiers, The 6-13-28
Streets of Ghost Town, The 8-16-50
Streets of Laredo 2-09-49
Streets of New York, The 7-25-13
Streets of New York, The 12-08-22 and 12-22-22
Streets of New York, The 4-19-39
Streets of San Francisco, The 4-27-49
Streets of Shanghai 2-22-28
Streets of Sinners 9-04-57
Streets of Sorrow 7-06-27
Streghe, Le (See: Witches, The)
Stregoni Di Citta' 8-29-73
Strength of Donald McKenzie, The 8-11-16
Strength of the Weak, The 3-03-16
Stress Es Tres, Tres 9-18-68
Stress Is Three, Three (See: Stress Es Tres, Tres)
Strich Durch die Rechnung 11-22-32
Strictly Business 1-19-32
Strictly Confidential 10-10-19
Strictly Confidential 11-11-59
Strictly Dishonorable 11-17-31
Strictly Dishonorable 7-04-51
Strictly Dynamite 7-10-34
Strictly in the Groove 11-11-42
Strictly Modern 5-07-30
Strictly Personal 3-21-33
Strictly Unconventional 7-16-30
Strife Eternal, The 12-10-15
Strike at the Steel Works, The 6-25-15
Strike It Rich 12-01-48
Strike Me Pink 1-22-36
Strike Up the Band 9-18-40
Strikers, The (See: Compagni, I)
Strikers, The 1-15-15
String Beans 12-20-18
Strip, The 8-08-51
Striporama 10-28-53
Stripper, The 4-24-63
Striving for Fortune 1-05-27
Stroemer 11-17-16
Strogoff 11-18-70
Strohfeuer 9-13-72
Stroke of Midnight, The 6-09-22
Stromboli 2-15-50
Strong Arm, The (See: Brazo Fuerte, El)
Strong Boy 4-03-29
Strong Ferdinand (See: Starke Ferdinand, Der)
Strong Man, The 9-08-26
Strong Revenge, A 3-07-13
Strong Water (See: Silna Voda)
Strong Way, The 1-04-18
Strong Woman, Weak Man (See: Tsuyomushi Onna To Yowamushi Otoko)
Stronger Love, The 8-18-16
Stronger Than Death 1-23-20
Stronger Than Desire 6-28-39
Stronger Than Paragraphs (See: Staerker Als Paragraphen)
Stronger Than the Sun 3-12-80
Stronger Vow, The 5-02-19
Stronger Will, The 4-11-28

Strongest Karate, The 5-12-76
Strongest Man in the World, The 2-05-75
Strongheart 4-17-14
Stronghold 2-06-52
Stronghold of Toughs (See: Grajski Biki)
Strongroom 6-06-62
Stroszek 7-20-77
Structure of Crystal, The (See: Struktura Krysztalu)
Struggle (See: Agonas)
Struggle, The 4-07-16
Struggle, The 5-06-21
Struggle, The 12-15-31
Struggle Everlasting, The 12-21-17
Struggle for Eagle Park (See: Venner)
Struggle for Life 6-26-35
Struktura Krysztalu 10-29-69
Stuckey's Last Stand 5-07-80
Stud 6-19-68
Stud, The (See: Etalon, L')
Stud, The 3-29-78
Stud Farm, The (See: Manesgazda)
Stud Farm, The 6-25-69
Student Nurses, The 9-23-70
Student of Prague, The 11-24-26
Student Prince, The 9-28-27
Student Prince, The 5-26-54
Student Romance 10-21-36
Student Sein 5-06-31
Student Song, A 9-17-30
Student Tour 10-16-34
Studenten auf Schafott 9-06-72
Studentenlied aus Heidelburg (See: Student Song, A)
Student's Hotel (See: Hotel des Etudiants)
Students of Iglo (See: Igloi Diakok)
Students on the Gallows (See: Studenten auf Schafott)
Students' Road (See: Chemin des Ecoliers, Le)
Student's Romance, A 8-07-35
Student's Song of Heidelberg, A (See: Burschenlied Aus
    Heidelberg, Ein)
Studio Girl, The 2-01-18
Studio Murder Mystery, The 6-12-29
Studs Lonigan 7-27-60
Study in Scarlet, A 6-06-33
Study of Love (See: Comizi d'Amore)
Study of Susanne, A (See: Susanne Im Bade)
Stuerme der Leidenschaft 2-16-32
Stuff That Dreams Are Made Of, The (See: Stoff Aus Dem Die
    Traeume Sind, Der)
Stukas 8-25-43
Stumme, Der 8-25-76
Stunde Null 4-27-77
Stunt Man, The 6-11-80
Stunt Pilot 7-26-39
Stunts 6-08-77
Stupende Le Mie Amiche 10-08-80
Stupid Boy Friend, The (See: Ang Boyfriend Kung Badoy)
Stupid Life (See: Chiwit Batsop)
Stupid Prince, The 1-19-27
Sturme der Leidenschaft (See: Tempest)
Sturmtruppen 1-25-77
Sturz, Der 2-07-79
Stutzen der Gesellschaft 11-18-36
Styridsatstyri 8-27-58
Su e Giu 5-26-65
Su Hermana Menor 6-09-43
Su Mejor Alumno 7-12-44
Su Primer Baile 7-22-42
Sua Giornata di Gloria, La 7-02-69
Sub Rosa Rising 6-23-71
Sube y Baja 5-20-59
Subject Was Roses, The 9-25-68
Sublokator 11-02-66
Submarine 9-05-28
Submarine Alert 6-23-43
Submarine Base 9-08-43
Submarine Command 8-29-51
Submarine D-1 11-17-37
Submarine Eye, The 6-08-17
Submarine Patrol 11-02-38
Submarine Pirate, A 11-19-15
Submarine Raider 6-24-42
Submarine Seahawk 1-28-59
Submarine X-1 8-27-69
Submarines Heading Westward (See: Submarinos Rumbo Al Oeste)
Submarinos Rumbo Al Oeste 9-30-42
Submersion of Japan, The (See: Nippon Chinbotsu)

Submission 7-20-77
Subotom Uvece 7-02-58
Substitute Wife, The 10-14-25
Subteranul 7-26-67
Subterfuge 6-18-69
Subterranean, The (See: Subteranul)
Subterraneans, The 6-22-60
Suburban, The 9-24-15
Suburban Romance, A (See: Zizkowska Romance)
Suburban Roulette 6-12-68
Suburban Wives 5-17-72
Suburbanite's Ingenious Alarm, A 5-16-08
Suburbs Are Everywhere, The (See: Elle Court, Elle Court La
    Banlieu)
Subversives, The 10-04-67
Subway Express 5-06-31
Subway Sadie 9-15-26
Success (See: Successo, Il)
Success 7-12-23
Success at Any Price 5-08-34
Successful Calamity, A 9-27-32
Successive Slidings of Pleasure (See: Glissements Progressifs
    du Plaisir)
Successo, Il 10-23-63
Sucedio en la Habana 7-20-38
Such a Little Pirate 10-11-18
Such a Little Queen 9-26-14
Such a Little Queen 7-08-21
Such a Long Absence (See: Aussi Longue Absence, Une)
Such a Lovely Kid Like Me (See: Belle Fille Comme Moi, Une)
Such a Lovely Town (See: Si Joli Village, Un)
Such a Pretty Little Beach (See: Si Jolie Petite Plage, Une)
Such a Young Girl 7-14-65
Such Good Friends 12-22-71
Such Men Are Dangerous 3-12-30
Such Women Are Dangerous 6-12-34
Suckalo 11-17-76
Sucker Money 4-11-33
Sucre, Le 11-08-78
Sudan 3-07-45
Sudba Czelovieka 5-13-59
Sudbine 8-16-78
Sudden Bill Dorn 1-12-38
Sudden Danger 12-28-55
Sudden Fear 7-23-52
Sudden Fury 6-04-75
Sudden Gentleman, The 11-30-17
Sudden Jim 8-10-17
Sudden Loneliness of Konrad Steiner, The (See: Ploetzliche
    Einsamkeit des Konrad Steiner, Die)
Sudden Money 3-22-39
Sudden Riches 5-12-16
Sudden Wealth of the Poor People of Kombach, The (See: Plotzliche
    Reichtun Der Armen Leute Von Kombach, Der)
Suddenly 9-08-54
Suddenly It's Spring 2-12-47
Suddenly, Last Summer 12-16-59
Suds 7-02-20
Sue Ultime 12 Ore (See: His Last 12 Hours)
Sued for Libel 10-18-39
Suehne 12-21-27
Suendige Grenze, Die 12-05-51 and 7-02-52
Suerte Llama Tres Veces, La 8-04-43
Suez 10-19-38
Suffer Little Children--For Such Is the Kingdom of Labor
    9-04-09
Sufferloh 10-31-79
Sugar, The (See: Sucre, Le)
Sugar Harvest (See: Zafra)
Sugar Hill 2-06-74
Sugar, Honey and Pepper (See: Zucchero, Miele e Peperoncino)
Sugarfoot 1-31-51
Sugarland Express, The 3-20-74
Suicidate, Mi Amor 10-18-61
Suicide Attack 4-04-51
Suicide Battalion 3-26-58
Suicide Club, The 9-26-14
Suicide Fleet 12-01-31
Suicide Legion 7-24-40
Suicide Mission 11-07-56
Suicide of a Hollywood Extra 6-20-28
Suit Case Mystery, The 4-02-10
Suitcase, The (See: Valise, La)
Suite California, Stops and Passes 4-11-79
Suitor, The (See: Bejleren or Soupirant, Le)

Suitor's Competition 10-02-09
Suivez Cet Homme 5-20-53
Sujata 5-26-60
Sullivans, The 2-09-44
Sullivan's Empire 6-07-67
Suliivan's Travels 12-10-41
Sult 5-18-66
Sultans, Les 6-01-66
Sultan's Daughter, The 1-12-44
Sum Gaegooli Manse! 7-11-73
Summer and Smoke 9-06-61
Summer Bachelors 12-22-26
Summer Boarding 8-17-17
Summer Camp 6-06-79
Summer Chronicle (See: Chronique D'Un Ete)
Summer Flirtation, A 10-15-10
Summer Frenzy (See: Frenesia d'Estate)
Summer Fruit (See: Fruits de l'Ete, Les)
Summer Girl, The 8-18-16
Summer Guests (See: Sommergaeste)
Summer Holiday 3-17-48
Summer Holiday 1-23-63
Summer Hotel (See: Hotel de Verano)
Summer Idyl, A 9-10-10
Summer in Tyrol (See: Sommer I Tyrol)
Summer Lighting (See: Strohfeuer)
Summer Lightning 7-25-33
Summer Love 2-05-58
Summer Magic 6-26-63
Summer of '42 4-21-71
Summer of Love, A (See: Kaerleks Sommar, En)
Summer of Secrets 12-29-76
Summer of the 17th Doll 3-30-60
Summer on Mountain (See: Nyar A Hegyen)
Summer on the Hill (See: Nyar A Hegyen)
Summer Place, A 10-07-59
Summer Rain, A 3-26-80
Summer Revolt (See: Kesakapina)
Summer Run 8-21-74
Summer Soldiers 10-04-72
Summer Stock 8-09-50
Summer Storm (See: Orage d'Ete)
Summer Storm 5-24-44
Summer Sunday, A (See: Domenica d'Estate, Una)
Summer Swim (See: Piel de Verano)
Summer Tragedy, A 9-24-10
Summer Trail (See: Muurahaispolku)
Summer Wishes, Winter Dreams 10-24-73
Summer with Monica (See: Sommaren Med Monika)
Summerfield 9-07-77
Summerplay (See: Sommarlek)
Summer's Children 5-16-79
Summertime 6-08-55
Summertime Killer, The 7-12-72
Summertree 6-16-71
Summit 9-11-68
Sun Also Rises, The 8-28-57
Sun and Shadow (See: Slnceto I Sjankata)
Sun and Showers (See: Meg-O-Ruerda)
Sun Comes Up, The 1-05-49
Sun from Another Sky (See: Sunce Tudeg Neba)
Sun in the Mirror, The (See: Sol En El Espejo, El)
Sun in the Net, The (See: Slunce V Siti)
Sun in Your Eyes (See: Soleil Dans L'Oeil, Le)
Sun Never Sets, The 6-07-39
Sun of St. Moritz, The (See: Sonne Von St. Moritz, Die)
Sun of the Hyenes (See: Soleil des Hyenes)
Sun over Klara (See: Sol Over Klara)
Sun over Sweden 4-13-38
Sun over the Swamp (See: Gunesli Bataklik)
Sun Sets at Dawn, The 11-08-50
Sun Shines, The 3-15-39
Sun Shines Bright, The 5-06-53
Sun Tai Sil Yen Yin (See: Between Tears and Smiles)
Sun That Smiles Red, The (See: Soleil Qui Rit Rouge, Le)
Sun-Up 8-19-25
Sun Valley Serenade 7-23-41
Sun Worshippers, The (See: Neal of the Navy: Part VIII)
Sun Worshippers, The 11-01-23
Suna No Kaori (See: Night of the Seagull, The)
Suna No Onna 5-06-64
Sunbeam, The 11-17-16
Sunbonnet Sue 10-10-45
Sunburn 8-08-79
Sunce Tudeg Neba 8-21-68
Sunday (See: Nedelja)
Sunday Afternoon (See: Domingo A Tarde)
Sunday at Six O'Clock (See: Duminica La Ora 6)

Sunday, Bloody Sunday 7-07-71
Sunday Children (See: Niedzielne Dzieci or Sonntagskinder)
Sunday Dinner for a Soldier 12-06-44
Sunday Games (See: Nedeini Matchove)
Sunday in New York 12-18-63
Sunday in October, A (See: Oktoberi Vasarnap)
Sunday in September, A (See: Sondag I Septembre, En)
Sunday in the Country 4-09-75
Sunday Is Always Sunday (See: Domenica e Sempre Domenica)
Sunday Lovers 12-17-80
Sunday of Life, The (See: Dimanche de la Vie, Le or Sonntag Des
   Lebens)
Sunday Parents (See: Vasarnapi Szulok)
Sunday Punch 4-15-42
Sunday Too Far Away 5-28-75
Sunday Woman (See: Donna Della Domenica, La)
Sundays at Ville d'Avary (See: Dimanches de Ville D'Avary, Les)
Sunday's Chronicle, A (See: To Chroniko Mias Kyriakas)
Sunday's Killers (See: Dimanche)
Sunderin, Die (See: Sinner, The)
Sundown 12-03-24
Sundown 10-15-41
Sundown Jim 3-11-42
Sundown Kid, The 1-13-43
Sundown on the Prairie 3-15-39
Sundown Rider, The 11-18-36
Sundown Riders 10-11-44
Sundown Saunders 8-18-37
Sundown Slim 10-15-20
Sundown Trail, The 11-10-31
Sundown Valley 7-26-44
Sundowners 1-11-50
Sundowners, The 11-02-60
Sunflower, The 3-25-70
Sung Choonhyang 8-30-61
Sunken Submarine, The 10-01-10
Sunny 12-31-30
Sunny 5-21-41
Sunny Beach Revolution (See: Revolution I Vandkanten)
Sunny Side (See: Pa Solsidan)
Sunny Side of the Street 8-29-51
Sunny Side Up 10-09-29
Sunny Skies 5-21-30
Sunny Sunberg (See: Soliga Solberg)
Sunny Whirlpool (See: Soncni Krik)
Sunny Youth 8-21-35
Sunnyside 6-20-19
Sunnyside 6-06-79
Sunrise 9-28-27
Sunrise at Campobello 9-21-60
Sunrise Trail 4-01-31
Sun's Burial, The (See: Taiyo No Hakaba)
Suns of Easter Island, The (See: Soleils de l'Ile de Paques, Les)
Sunseed 5-23-73
Sunset 9-24-10
Sunset Boulevard 4-19-50
Sunset Clouds (See: Akamegumo)
Sunset Derby, The 6-15-27
Sunset in El Dorado 9-26-45
Sunset in the West 9-27-50
Sunset in Vienna 7-07-37
Sunset in Wyoming 8-13-41
Sunset Legion 5-23-28
Sunset Murder Case, The 9-03-41
Sunset of Power 2-19-36
Sunset on the Desert 6-17-42
Sunset Pass 2-20-29
Sunset Pass 7-17-46
Sunset Range 5-15-35
Sunset Serenade 9-09-42
Sunset Sprague 12-17-20
Sunset Trail, The 9-28-17
Sunset Trail, The 11-12-24
Sunset Trail, The 5-17-32
Sunset Trail, The 10-26-38
Sunshine 1-16-29
Sunshine Ahead 2-12-36
Sunshine Alley 11-09-17
Sunshine and Gold 4-13-17
Sunshine Boys, The 10-29-75
Sunshine Dad 4-21-16
Sunshine Molly 3-12-15
Sunshine Nan 4-19-18
Sunshine of Paradise Alley 1-12-27
Sunshine Sue 11-26-10
Sunshine Susie 12-29-31
Sunshine Trail, The 8-30-23
Sunstroke (See: Slnchev Udar)

Sunstroke at the Beach Resort (See: Solstik Pa Badehotellet)
Sunstruck 1-24-73
Suntanned Ones, The (See: Bronzes, Les)
Sunugin Ang Samar! 9-25-74
Suor Letizia 9-19-56
Suora Giovane, La 9-16-64
Sup Sap Bup Dap 10-15-75
Supe For Tva 4-23-47
Super, El 3-28-79
Super Cops, The 3-20-74
Super Fight, The 12-31-69
Super Fly T.N.T. 6-20-73
Super He-Man, The (See: Supermacho, El)
Super Sex 12-08-22
Super Sleuth 7-14-37
Super Speed 4-08-25
Super Super Adventure, The (See: Super Super Aventura, La)
Super Super Aventura, La 6-18-75
Super Van 4-13-77
Super Vixens 3-12-75
Superb Trip, The (See: Viree Superbe, La)
Superbeast 10-04-72
Superdad 1-16-74
Superfly 8-02-72
Supergirl 3-31-71
Supermacho, El 3-30-60
Superman 12-13-78
Superman and the Mole Men 12-12-51
Superman II 12-03-80
Supermarket 8-28-74
Supernatural 4-25-33
Supersonic Man 8-29-79
Superspeed 12-04-35
Superstars in Film Concert 8-18-71
Supper for Two (See: Supe For Tva)
Supply and Demand 6-02-22
Supply Column Soldier, The (See: Voinikat Ot Oboza)
Support Your Local Gunfighter 5-12-71
Support Your Local Sheriff 2-26-69
Suppose They Gave a War and Nobody Came 5-27-70
Supreme Kid, The 8-04-76
Supreme Passion, The 3-15-23
Supreme Sacrifice, The 3-17-16
Supreme Temptation, The 3-24-16
Supreme Tests 12-20-23
Sur le Pave de Berlin 5-16-33
Sur un Arbre Perche 5-05-71
Surcouf, le Tigre des Sept Mers (See: Sea Pirate, The)
Sure Fire Flint 1-05-23
Surf, The 12-21-49
Surf Girl, The 8-11-16
Surfari 7-19-67
Surgeons (See: Hirourzi)
Surging Seas 6-18-24
Suria Dighal Bari 7-30-80
Surprise Hour (See: Hora de Las Sorpresas, La)
Surprise Package 10-12-60
Surprise Party (See: I Like Mike)
Surprise Sock (See: Chaussette Surprise)
Surprises du Divorce 5-09-33
Surprises Radio 6-05-40
Surrender 11-09-27
Surrender 12-01-31
Surrender 10-11-50
Surrender, The 9-24-15
Surrender--Hell! 8-05-59
Surrounded, The (See: Encercles, Les)
Suru 4-25-79
Surveyors, The (See: Arpenteurs, Les)
Survival 1-22-30
Survival 1967 6-05-68
Survival Run 3-05-80
Survivors (See: Sobrevivientes, Los)
Sus Anos Dorados 11-05-80
Susan and God 6-05-40
Susan Lenox 10-20-31
Susan Rocks the Boat 5-05-16
Susan Slade 10-04-61
Susan Slept Here 6-23-54
Susana y Yo 4-10-57
Susanna and Me (See: Susana y Yo)
Susanna Pass 5-04-49
Susannah of the Mounties 6-21-39
Susanne Cleans Up (See: Susanne Macht Ordnung)
Susanne im Bade 9-22-37
Susanne Macht Ordnung 10-13-31
Susan's Gentleman 3-16-17
Susetz 8-23-78

Susie Snowflake 6-30-16
Susie Steps Out 11-20-46
Suspect 11-23-60
Suspect, The (See: Sospetto, Il)
Suspect, The 5-19-16
Suspect, The 12-27-44
Suspected Person 12-29-43
Suspects, Les 10-23-57
Suspects, Les 12-18-74
Suspense 7-23-30 and 11-12-30
Suspense 3-27-46
Suspicion 12-03-10
Suspicion 11-15-18
Suspicion 9-24-41
Suspicious Wife, The 8-21-14
Suspiria 3-09-77
Susuz Yaz 7-08-64
Sutedelan 12-14-77
Sutjeska 8-15-73
Sutter's Gold 4-01-36
Sutyi a Szerencsegyerek 1-26-38
Sutyi, the Lucky Child (See: Sutyi a Szerencsegyerek)
Suzanna 3-29-23
Suzanne 9-17-80
Suzy 7-29-36
Suzy Saxophone 8-22-28
Svadba 7-17-74
Svanger Pa Slottet, Det 8-19-59
Svarta Palmkronor 10-16-68
Svatba Bez Prstynku 7-26-72
Svatej z Krejcareku 10-28-70
Svegliati e Uccidi Lutring 4-20-66
Sven Dufva, the Hero (See: Sven Tuuava)
Sven Klang Quintet, The (See: Sven Klangs Kvintett)
Sven Klangs Kvintett 12-29-76
Sven Tuuava 7-15-59
Svengali 5-06-31
Svengali 1-12-55
Svensk Tiger, En 8-11-48
Svenska Bilder 11-18-64
Svenske Ryttaren 3-29-50
Sverige at Svenskarna 9-17-80
Svet Patri Nam 8-30-39
Svetozar Markovic 8-13-80
Svezia, Inferno e Paradiso 1-29-69
Svoi Sriedi Chougikh 7-31-74
Svtackovia Siroty a Blazni 6-03-70
Swallowed by the Deep 1-29-10
Swallows and Amazons 10-16-74
Swami 12-14-77
Swamp, The 11-04-21
Swamp Fire 5-15-46
Swamp Fox, The 5-08-14 and 6-19-14
Swamp Water 10-22-41
Swamp Woman 12-31-41
Swamp Women 10-31-56
Swan, The 3-04-25
Swan, The 4-11-56
Swan Lake 1-20-60
Swan Lake 9-29-71
Swan Lake, The 7-26-67
Swan Song (See: Canto Del Cisne, El)
Swanee River 4-15-31
Swanee River 12-27-39
Swansong Days (See: Giorni Contati, I)
Swap (See: Trampa)
Swap Meet 9-19-79
Swarm, The 7-19-78
Swashbuckler 7-28-76
Swastika 5-23-73
Swat the Spy 11-01-18
Sweater Girl 5-06-42
Swede Larsen 6-12-14
Sweden for the Swedes (See: Sverige at Svenskarna)
Sweden, Heaven and Hell (See: Svezia, Inferno e Paradiso)
Sweden Hielm Family (See: Familien Swedenhielm)
Sweden (the Gota Canal) 9-11-09
Swedenhielms 9-11-35
Swedish Horseman (See: Svenske Ryttaren)
Swedish Love Story, A (See: Karlekshistoria, En)
Swedish Minx 7-06-77
Swedish Portraits (See: Svenska Bilder)
Swedish Tiger, A (See: Svensk Tiger, En)
Sweeney 1-19-77
Sweeney 2 5-03-78
Sweepings 3-28-33
Sweepstake Annie 2-27-35

Sweepstakes 6-30-31
Sweepstakes Winner 6-28-39
Sweet Adeline 1-20-26
Sweet Adeline 1-08-35
Sweet Agony 4-03-74
Sweet and Lowdown 8-02-44
Sweet and Sour (See: Dragees au Poivre)
Sweet Anna (See: Edes Anna)
Sweet Bird of Youth 2-28-62
Sweet Body of Deborah, The 2-26-69
Sweet Charity 1-29-69
Sweet Creek County War, The 1-24-79
Sweet Deception (See: Mandarine, La)
Sweet Hunters 9-17-69
Sweet Jesus, Preacher Man 5-30-73
Sweet Kisses and Languid Caresses (See: Oh Dolci Baci E Languide
   Carezze)
Sweet Kitty Bellairs 5-19-16
Sweet Kitty Bellairs 9-10-30
Sweet Lavender 10-08-20
Sweet Life, The (See: Dolce Vita, La)
Sweet, Like Berries, My Love (See: Habibeti--Ya Habba Atoot)
Sweet Love, Bitter 2-01-67
Sweet Mamma 7-16-30
Sweet Movie 5-22-74
Sweet Music 2-27-35
Sweet Nights, The (See: Dolci Notti, Le)
Sweet November 2-07-68
Sweet Punkin' 4-07-76
Sweet Revenge (See: Kiri-No-Hata)
Sweet Ride, The 5-08-68
Sweet Rosie O'Grady 9-22-43
Sweet Saviour 9-01-71
Sweet Sins of Sexy Susan (See: Wirtin von der Lahn, Die)
Sweet Sixteen 10-03-28
Sweet Smell of Success 6-19-57
Sweet Stepmother (See: Edes Mostoha)
Sweet Substitute 11-11-64
Sweet Surrender 12-18-35
Sweet Suzy 7-11-73
Sweet Sweetback's Baadasssss Song 4-21-71
Sweet Thieves (See: Ladroes de Cinema)
Sweet Toronto 1-19-72
Sweet Violence 4-25-62 (Also see: Douce Violence)
Sweet William 4-02-80
Sweet Woman (See: Sladkaia Jentchina)
Sweetheart (See: Fen)
Sweetheart of Sigma Chi 11-14-33
Sweetheart of Sigma Chi 11-27-46
Sweetheart of the Campus 6-25-41
Sweetheart of the Fleet 8-12-42
Sweetheart of the Navy 7-07-37
Sweethearts 12-21-38
Sweethearts and Wives 7-02-30
Sweethearts of the U.S.A. 3-01-44
Sweethearts qn Parade 10-01-30
Sweethearts on Parade 7-29-53
Sweetie 10-30-29
Sweetness of Love (See: Douceur d'Aimer, La)
Sweetness of Loving, The (See: Douceur d'Aimer, La)
Swell Guy 12-11-46
Swell-Head 5-08-35
Swelled Head, A (See: Grosse Tete, Une)
Swelled Head, The 10-26-27
Swift Shadow, The 11-23-27
Swifty 1-29-36
Swilin' Racket, The 5-02-28
Swim, Girl, Swim 9-07-27
Swimmer, The 5-15-68
Swimming Pool, The (See: Piscine, La or Basseinut)
Swindle, The (See: Entourloupe, L')
Swindler, The (See: Bidone, Il)
Swindler and the Lord, The (See: Gauner Und Der Liebe Gott, Der)
Swing Fever 2-02-44
Swing High 7-02-30
Swing High, Swing Low 4-21-37
Swing It, Professor 1-12-38
Swing It, Sailor 11-10-37
Swing It, Soldier 10-29-41
Swing Out, Sister 5-02-45
Swing Out the Blues 1-26-44
Swing Shift Maisie 5-05-43
Swing, Sister, Swing 12-14-38
Swing That Cheer 11-16-38
Swing Time 9-02-36
Swing Your Lady 1-26-38
Swing Your Partner 5-05-43
Swinger, The (See: Michetonneuse, La)

Swinger, The 11-02-66
Swingin' Along 7-11-62
Swingin' on a Rainbow 8-29-45
Swingin' Summer, A 3-03-65
Swinging Cheerleaders, The 6-26-74
Swingtime Johnny 12-22-43
Swiss Affair, The (See: Affaire Suisse, L')
Swiss Family Robinson 2-07-40
Swiss Family Robinson 11-09-60
Swiss Guide, The 11-05-10
Swiss Made 10-22-69
Swiss Miss 5-11-38
Swiss Tour 12-28-49
Swissmakers, The (See: Schweizermacher, Die)
Switch in Time, A 12-25-63
Sword, The (See: Kard, A)
Sword and the Balance, The (See: Glaive et la Balance, La)
Sword and the Rose, The 7-01-53
Sword in the Desert 8-24-49
Sword in the Stone, The 10-02-63
Sword of Ali Baba, The 3-31-65
Sword of Doom, The 4-12-67
Sword of Monte Cristo, The 3-14-51
Sword of Sherwood Forest 1-11-61
Sword of the Avenger 5-12-48
Sword of the Conqueror 9-19-62
Sword of Valor 5-14-24
Sword of Venus 1-21-53
Swords of Death (See: Shinken Shobu)
Swordsman, The 10-22-47
Swordsman of Siena, The 11-14-62
Sworn Enemy, The 9-16-36
Syd For Tana River 2-12-64
Sylvia 2-03-65
Sylvia Gray 10-31-14
Sylvia of the Secret Service 11-09-17
Sylvia Scarlett 1-15-36
Sylvie and the Phantom 10-18-50
Symphonie d'Amour 3-20-46
Symphonie Fantastique 12-10-47
Symphonie Pastorale, La 11-06-46 and 9-15-48
Symphonie Pour un Messacre 8-14-63
Symphony for a Massacre (See: Symphonie Pour un Messacre)
Symphony in Two Flats 7-30-30
Symphony of Life (See: Sinfonia de una Vida)
Symphony of Life 1-12-49
Symphony of Living 7-03-35
Symphony of Six Million 4-19-32
Symptoms 5-22-74
Synanon 5-05-65
Syncopating Sue 11-03-26
Syncopation 4-10-29
Syncopation 5-06-42
Synnin Jaljet 7-02-47
Synnove Solbakken 8-27-58
Synthetic Film, or How the King Kong Monster Was Testified To by
   Fantasy and Precision (See: Synthetischer Film oder Wie das
   Monster King Kong von Fantasie & Praezision Gezeugt Wurde)
Synthetic Sin 1-09-29
Synthetischer Film oder Wie das Monster King Kong von Fantasie
   & Praezision Gezeugt Wurde 9-03-75
Syntomo Dialima 11-09-66
Syskonbadd 1-18-67
System, The 3-25-53
System, The 8-12-64
System, The 5-07-80
Sytten 9-15-65
Szabadits Meg a Gonosztol 2-28-79
Szansa 6-11-80
Szarvassa Valt Fiuk 3-19-75
Szegeny Gazdagok 3-15-39
Szemuvegesek 10-22-69
Szenzacio 3-03-37
Szepek Es Bolondok 3-02-77
Szerelem 5-26-71
Szerelem Elektra 3-05-75
Szerelembol Nosultem 1-19-38 and 2-23-38
Szerelmesfilm 9-16-70
Szerelmi Almok 9-11-35 and 1-13-37
Szeressetek Odor Emiliat! 3-11-70
Szevasz; Vera 6-28-67
Sziget a Szarasfoldon 2-26-69
Szindbad 9-06-72
Szkice Warszaskie 10-14-70
Szpital Przemienienia 2-28-79
Szyfry 8-16-67

T

THT Range Feud 11-24-31
THX 1138 3-17-71
T-Men 12-17-47
TNT Jackson 2-19-75
T.R. Baskin 10-13-71
Ta Chi (See: Last Woman of Shang)
Ta Chromata Tis Iridos 11-06-74
Ta'Det Som En Mand, Frue 4-09-75
Ta Kourelia Tragoudoun Akoma 11-28-79
Ta Lidt Solskin 11-05-69
Taala Pohjantahden Alla 7-30-69
Taalat Blamilch 4-09-69
Tabarin 7-09-58
Tabernac 2-12-75
Tabiate Bijan 7-10-74
Table Aux-Creves, La 4-02-52
Table Top Ranch 11-17-22
Taboo (See: Tabu)
Taboos of the World 5-26-65
Tabor Ollhodit Webo 12-01-76
Tabu 3-25-31
Tabu 2-23-77
Tabu No. 2 5-26-65
Tachi and Her Fathers 6-13-79
Tactics of Cupid, The 9-24-10
Taenk Paa Et Tal 4-09-69
Taenzerin von Sanssouci 10-18-32
Taetowierung 7-05-67
Taft in Chicago 9-25-09
Tag, An Dem Elvis Nach Bremerhaven Kam, Der 9-17-80
Tag Day at Silver Gulch 1-21-11
Tag Ist Schoener Als der Andere, Ein 4-01-70
Tagebuch 4-21-76
Tagebuch einer Kokette (See: Diary of a Cocotte)
Tagebuch eines Liebenden 1-19-77
Taggart 12-09-64
Tagged Atoms (See: Belyazani Atomi)
Tahati 7-24-57
Tahiti Honey 3-31-43
Tahiti Nights 1-31-45
Tahitian, The 10-17-56
Tai Woman Doctor, The 8-02-61
Taiga 11-19-58
Tail Spin 2-01-39
Tailor from Ulm, The (See: Schneider Vom Ulm, Der)
Tailor Made Man, A 10-20-22
Tailor Made Man, A 4-29-31
Tainted Money 4-01-25
Taiyo No Hakaba 8-29-62
Taiyo o Nusunda Otoko 10-29-80
Tajna Nikole Tesle 8-13-80
Take, The 5-15-74
Take a Chance 11-28-33
Take a Giant Step 12-09-59
Take a Girl Like You 10-14-70
Take a Hard Ride 7-09-75
Take a Letter, Darling 5-06-42
Take a Little Sunshine (See: Ta Lidt Solskin)
Take All of Me 3-08-78
Take Care of Amelie (See: Occupe-Toi d'Amelie)
Take Care of My Little Girl 6-13-51
Take Care When She Gets Started (See: Wehe Wenn Sie Losgelassen)
Take Down 1-24-79
Take Her, She's Mine 10-16-63
Take It Big 6-07-44
Take It Easy (See: Nie Ma Mocnych)
Take It Easy, It's a Waltz (See: Laisse Aller, C'Est Une Valse)
Take It from Me 11-03-26
Take It Like a Man, Ma'm (See: Ta'Det Som En Mand, Frue)
Take It or Leave It 7-12-44
Take It to the Limit 3-26-80
Take Me Home 10-24-28
Take Me Out to the Ball Game 3-09-49
Take Me to the Ritz (See: Emmenez-Moi au Ritz)
Take Me to Town 5-20-53
Take My Life 7-08-42
Take My Life 5-14-47
Take My Tip 5-26-37
Take Off (See: Hit' Romemont)
Take One 8-17-77
Take One False Step 6-01-49

Take the Heir 1-29-30
Take the High Ground 9-23-53
Take the Money and Run 8-20-69
Take the Stand 9-11-34
Take 2 9-06-72
Takeoff, The (See: Bzlet)
Takiji Kobayashi 7-31-74
Taking a Chance 2-20-29
Taking Chances 3-17-22
Taking of Christina, The 3-17-76
Taking of Pelham 1-2-3, The 10-02-74
Taking of Power by Louis XIV, The (See: Prise de Pouvoir Par Louis XIV, La)
Taking Off 3-17-71
Takt Og Tone i Himmselsengen 2-16-72
Tale of a Leg, The 1-22-10
Tale of Crimes (See: Historia de Crimenes)
Tale of Five Cities 5-23-51
Tale of Peonies and Lanterns, A (See: Kaidan Botan Doro)
Tale of the Backwoods, A 1-15-10
Tale of the Fiddle, The 11-06-09
Tale of the Navajos 3-02-49
Tale of the Sea 12-28-07
Tale of the West, A 4-24-09
Tale of Two Cities, A 3-16-17
Tale of Two Cities, A 1-01-36
Tale of Two Cities, A 2-12-58
Tale of Two Worlds, A 4-22-21
Talent Scout 8-25-37
Tales after the Rain (See: Ugetsu Monogatari)
Tales from the Crypt 3-08-72
Tales from the Vienna Woods (See: Geschichten Aus Dem Weinerwald)
Tales of a Young Scamp (See: Lausbubenges Chichten)
Tales of Beatrix Potter, The 4-14-71
Tales of Blood (See: Krvava Bajka)
Tales of Chikamatsu (See: Chikamatsu Monogatari)
Tales of Hoffmann 4-04-51
Tales of Manhattan 8-05-42
Tales of Mystery and Imagination (See: Histoires Extraordinaires)
Tales of Palestine 3-12-47
Tales of Robin Hood 1-09-52
Tales of Terror 5-30-62
Tales That Witness Madness 10-31-73
Talisman 5-31-78
Talisman, The 10-09-68
Talk About a Lady 5-22-46
Talk About a Stranger 2-27-52
Talk About Jacqueline 10-07-42
Talk of Hollywood 1-01-30
Talk of the Devil 12-23-26 and 5-19-37
Talk of the Town 7-29-42
Talk of the Town, The 9-20-18
Talker, The 5-13-25
Talking About Jacqueline (See: Man Spricht Ueber Jacqueline)
Tall, Dark and Handsome 1-22-41
Tall Fishing Tales 3-06-74
Tall Headlines 4-23-52
Tall in the Saddle 9-27-44
Tall Man Riding 5-11-55
Tall Men, The 9-28-55
Tall Shadows of the Wind (See: Saiehaieh Bolan de Bad)
Tall Story 2-10-60
Tall Stranger, The 11-06-57
Tall T, The 4-03-57
Tall Target, The 8-01-51
Tall Texan, The 2-11-53
Tall Timbers 10-27-37
Tally Brown, N.Y. 4-18-79
Talpa 1-16-57
Talpuk Alatt Futyul a Szel 9-29-76
Tam Lin 11-24-71
Tam Na Konecne 5-31-61
Tam O'Shanter 9-10-15
Tama Na Erap 8-07-74
Tamahine 8-07-63 and 4-01-64
Tamango 2-12-58
Tamarind Seed, The 7-10-74
Tambor de Tacuari, El 9-01-48
T-A-M-I Show, The 11-18-64
Taming 11-13-68
Taming a Husband 3-05-10
Taming of Dorothy, The 11-15-50
Taming of the Shrew, The 12-04-29 and 11-02-66
Taming of the Shrew, The 3-01-67
Taming of the West, The 7-08-25
Taming of the West, The 10-11-39
Taming of Wild Bill, The 11-19-10
Taming Sutton's Gal 10-16-57

Tchien Gnu You Houn 5-18-60
Te Csak Pipalj, Ladanyi 3-23-38
Te Necesito Tanto, Amor 3-24-76
Te Quiero Para Mi 4-25-45
Tea and Sympathy 9-26-56
Tea for Three 11-02-27
Tea for Two 8-16-50
Tea with a Kick 10-11-23
Teacher, The (See: Brigadista, El)
Teacher from Vigevano, The (See: Maestro di Vigevano, Il)
Teacher's Pet 3-19-58
Teahouse of the August Moon 10-17-56
Tear Gas Squad 5-15-40
Tear in the Ocean, A (See: Larme Dans L'Ocean, Une)
Tears of Happiness 2-27-50
Tears on the Lion's Mane (See: Namido o Shishi No Tategami)
Teaser, The 6-17-25
Teaserama 1-19-55
Techo de Cristal, El 5-12-71
Teci, Teci, Kuza Moj 12-15-76
Teckman Mystery 8-24-55
Teddy Bear, The (See: Bamse)
Teddy Bears, The 3-09-07
Teddy Girl (See: Fai Lui Ching Chuen)
Teen Age 6-21-44
Teen-Age Crime Wave 10-12-55
Teen Age Thunder 10-02-57
Teen Kanya 8-15-62
Teenage Caveman 9-17-58
Teenage Cowgirls 2-21-73
Teenage Doll 10-16-57
Teenage Millionaire 8-23-61
Teenage Monster 1-08-58
Teenage Mother 10-02-68
Teenage Rebel 10-24-56
Teenage Rebellion 5-24-67
Teenagers 7-05-61
Teenagers, Les 5-15-68
Teenagers from Outer Space 6-03-59
Teeth 3-11-25
Teeth of the Tiger, The 12-05-19
Tegnup 8-19-59
Teilnehmer Antwortet Nicht 12-13-32
Tel Aviv Taxi 1-02-57
Telefon 12-14-77
Teleften Apostoli (See: Last Mission, The)
Telegramele 6-01-60
Telegramme Pour M. Herriot (See: Paris Incident)
Telegrams (See: Telegramele)
Telegraph Trail 4-04-33
Telephone Bar, The (See: Bar du Telephone, Le)
Telephone Book, The 9-29-71
Telephone Call, The 10-23-09
Telephone Girl, The 5-18-27
Telephone Operator 2-16-38
Telephone Public 7-16-80
Telephone Rose, Le 9-24-75
Telesme Schekaste 7-22-59
Teleview, The 1-05-23
Television Spy 11-22-39
Tell England 3-18-31
Tell Him I Love Him (See: Dites Lui Que Je L'Aime)
Tell It to a Star 8-15-45
Tell It to Sweeny 10-19-27
Tell It to the Judge 11-16-49
Tell It to the Marines 12-06-18
Tell It to the Marines 12-29-26
Tell Me a Riddle 12-10-80
Tell Me in the Sunlight 4-12-67
Tell Me Lies 2-14-68
Tell Me That You Love Me Junie Moon 5-20-70
Tell Me Who to Kill (See: Dis-Moi Qui Tuer)
Tell Me, Who You Are (See: Sag Mir, Wer Du Bist)
Tell Me You Love Me (See: Dis-Moi Que Tu M'Aimes)
Tell No Tales 5-17-39
Tell Tale Heart, The 6-19-34
Tell Them Willie Boy Is Here 10-22-69
Tell Your Children 10-06-22
Telling the World 7-18-28
Telltale Reflections 11-13-09
Telltale Step, The 6-02-17
Tema di Marco 9-06-72
Tembo 12-19-51
Temne Slunce 7-30-80
Temoin, Le 10-11-78
Temoin Dans la Ville, Un 8-19-59
Temperamental Wife, A 9-19-19

Temperate Zone (See: Mersekelt Egov)
Tempered Steel 6-28-18
Tempest 5-23-28
Tempest 3-22-32
Tempest, The (See: Tempete, La)
Tempest, The 12-10-58
Tempest, The 9-12-79
Tempest in the Flesh (See: Rage au Corps, La)
Tempete, La 5-15-40
Tempete Sur l'Asie 6-01-38
Temple Drake 5-09-33
Temple of Dusk, The 11-01-18
Temple of Venus 11-01-23
Temple Tower 5-14-30
Tempo Di Roma 2-20-63
Tempo S E Fermato, Il 11-04-64
Temporary Marriage 9-13-23
Temporary Sheriff 4-04-28
Temporary Widow 11-12-30
Temporary Wife, A 1-23-20
Temps de l'Avant, Le 5-19-76
Temps de Mourir, Le 3-18-70
Temps de Vivre, Le 3-26-69
Temps des Doryphores 1-17-68
Temps des Oeufs Durs, Les 7-02-58
Temps du Ghetto, Le 9-27-61 (Also see: Witnesses, The)
Temps d'une Chasse, Le 9-06-72 and 11-01-72
Temps Morts 9-17-80
Temptation 12-31-15
Temptation 5-30-23
Temptation 7-24-29
Temptation 3-06-35
Temptation 12-11-46
Temptation, The 9-11-09
Temptation Harbor 3-05-47
Temptation in the Summer Wind (See: Versuchung im Sommerwind)
Temptations 6-16-76
Temptations of a Shop Girl 12-07-27
Tempter, The 2-27-74
Tempter, The 11-01-78
Temptress, The 10-13-26
Temptress, The 2-05-58 and 7-09-58
10 9-26-79
Ten Cents a Dance 3-11-31
Ten Cents a Dance 6-13-45
Ten Commandments, The 12-27-23
Ten Commandments, The 10-10-56
Ten Days That Shook the World 11-07-28
Ten Days to Tulara 10-29-58
Ten Days Wonder (See: Decade Prodigieuse, La)
Ten Dollar Raise, The 5-13-21
Ten Dollar Raise, The 5-08-35
Ten from Your Show of Shows 3-07-73
Ten Gentlemen from West Point 6-03-42
Ten Laps to Go 6-15-38
Ten Little Indians 12-29-65
Ten Little Indians 2-26-75
10. Mai, Der 12-11-57
Ten Minute Alibi 2-12-35
Ten Nights in a Barroom 6-19-09
Ten Nights in a Barroom 5-12-22
Ten Nights in a Barroom 3-04-31
Ten North Frederick 4-30-58
Ten of Diamonds 8-31-17
10% Nadeja 1-26-77
Ten Percent of Hope (See: 10% Nadeja)
10 Ready Rifles (See: Diez Fusiles Esperan)
Ten Rifles Wait (See: Diez Fusiles Esperan)
10 Rillington Place 2-10-71
Ten Seconds to Hell 7-15-59
Ten Tall Men 10-24-51
10:30 P.M. Summer 10-19-66
10:32 in the Morning 2-23-66
Ten Thousand Bedrooms 2-20-57
Ten Thousand Suns, The (See: Tizezer Nap)
Ten Wanted Men 2-09-55
Ten Who Dared 9-28-60
Ten Years 5-27-25
Tenant, The (See: Inquilino or Locotaire, Le)
Tenants, The (See: Sakada)
Tenda Dos Milagres 7-13-77
Tender and Violent Elizabeth (See: Tendre et Violente Elisabeth)
Tender Comrade 12-29-43
Tender Cop (See: Tendre Poulet)
Tender Cousins (See: Tendres Cousines)
Tender Enemy, The (See: Tendre Ennemie, La)

Tender Hearts 1-26-55
Tender Hoodlum (See: Tendre Voyou)
Tender Hour, The 6-08-27
Tender Is the Night 1-17-62
Tender Trap, The 10-26-55
Tender Warrior, The 4-14-71
Tender Years, The 12-03-47
Tenderfoot 5-24-32
Tenderfoot Goes West 6-23-37
Tenderloin 3-21-28 (2 reviews)
Tenderly 1-15-69
Tenderness (See: Tendresse, La; Niejnosti; or Zaertlichkeit)
Tenderness, My Fanny! (See: Et La Tendresse? ... Bordel!)
Tenderness of Wolves, The (See: Zaertlichkeit der Woelfe)
Tendre Ennemie, La 4-06-38
Tendre et Violente Elisabeth 6-15-60
Tendre Poulet 12-21-77
Tendre Voyou 10-12-66
Tendres Cousines 12-03-80
Tendresse, La 6-18-30
Tendresse Ordinaire 4-25-73
Tengamos la Guerra en Paz 8-24-77
Tengo Fe En Ti 7-17-40
Tengoku To-Jigoku 9-04-63
Teni Zabytykh Predkov 9-08-65
Tennessee Champ 2-17-54
Tennessee Johnson 12-16-42
Tennessee's Pardner 2-11-16
Tennessee's Partner 9-28-55
Tense Moments from Opera 7-14-22
Tense Moments from Plays 7-21-22
Tension 11-23-49
Tension at Table Rock 10-03-56
Tent of Miracles, The (See: Tenda Dos Milagres)
Tentacion Desnuda, La (See: Woman and Temptation)
Tentacles 6-15-77
Tentacles of the North 1-26-27
Tentation de Barbizon, La 4-17-46
Tenth Avenue 10-10-28
Tenth Avenue Angel 1-21-48
Tenth Avenue Kid 8-31-38
Tenth Case, The 12-07-17
Tenth Man, The 9-02-36
Tenth of May, The (See: 10. Mai, Der)
10th Symphony, The (See: Dixieme Symphonie, La)
Tenth Victim, The 12-22-65
Tenth Woman, The 10-22-24
Tenting Tonight on the Old Camp Ground 3-03-43
Tents of Allah, The 4-05-23
Tentativo Sentimentale, Un 9-04-63
Teorema 9-18-68
Tercera Palabra, La 12-05-56
Tercera Puerta, La 9-29-76
Teresa 2-28-51
Teresa 12-16-70
Teresa la Ladra 10-24-73
Teresa the Thief (See: Teresa la Ladra)
Term of Trial 8-29-62
Terminal Man, The 5-29-74
Tero Nodim Parey 8-10-66
Terra Em Transe 5-10-67
Terra Madre 11-10-31
Terra Trema, La 4-26-50
Terrace, The (See: Terraza, La)
Terrain Vague 11-23-60
Terraza, La 7-03-63
Terrazza, La 3-05-80
Terre Qui Meurt, La 6-24-36
Terreur des Dames, La 12-19-56
Terrible Beauty, A 5-18-60
Terrible Lovers, The (See: Amants Terribles, Les)
Terrible Night, The (See: Noche Terrible, La)
Terrible Parents, The (See: Parents Terribles, Les)
Terrible Quarrel 3-20-09
Terrific Scent of Fresh Hay, A (See: Irrer Duft Von Frischem
     Heu, Ein)
Territorial Militia (See: Milizia Territoriale)
Territorie des Autres, Le 5-13-70
Territory of Others, The (See: Territorie des Autres, Le)
Terror 3-16-77
Terror 12-19-79
Terror, The 2-09-17
Terror, The 5-21-20
Terror, The 8-22-28
Terror, The 8-06-41
Terror at Midnight 4-18-56
Terror by Night 1-30-46
Terror from the Year 5,000 11-05-58

Terror House 6-09-43
Terror in a Texas Town 8-20-58
Terror in the Jungle 11-20-68
Terror in the Wax Museum 5-23-73
Terror Island 4-30-20
Terror Mountain 10-17-28
Terror of Bar X, The 6-01-27
Terror of Cavite (See: Bergado)
Terror of the Garrison (See: Schrecken der Garnison, Der)
Terror Street 12-02-53
Terror Trail 2-14-33
Terror Train 10-01-80
Terror with Women, The (See: Terreur des Dames, La)
Terrorist, The (See: Terrorista, Il)
Terrorista, Il 9-04-63
Terrorists, The (See: Ransom)
Terrornauts, The 10-18-67
Terrors on Horseback 4-17-46
Terry Whitmore, For Example 11-05-69
Tesha 9-12-28
Tesoro de la Isla Maciel, El 8-13-41
Tess 11-07-79
Tess of the d'Urbervilles 7-30-24
Tess of the Storm Country 4-03-14
Tess of the Storm Country 11-17-22
Tess of the Storm Country 11-22-32
Tess of the Storm Country 2-01-61
Tessie 9-23-25
Test of Honor, The 4-11-19
Test of Manhood, The 10-31-14
Test Pilot 4-20-38
Test Pilot Pirx 8-15-79
Testament 8-20-75
Testament d'Orphee, Le 3-02-60
Testament du Docteur Cordelier, Le 9-16-59
Testament du Dr. Mabuse 4-25-33 and 5-09-33
Testigos, Los 7-07-71
Testing Block, The 12-10-20
Testing Their Love 1-22-10
Tete Contre les Murs, La 12-24-58
Tete de Normande St.-Onge, La 5-19-76
Tetes Brulees, Les 12-20-67
Tetetoria 3-02-77
Tetto, Il 2-06-57
Teufel Hat Gut Lachen, Der 12-28-60
Teufel in Seide 4-11-56
Teufel Spielte Balalaika, Der 7-19-61
Teufels General, Des 7-06-55
Teufelsinsel, Die 9-22-76
Tevya 12-27-39
Tex 12-10-20
Tex Rides with the Boy Scouts 11-03-37
Tex Takes a Holiday 12-13-32
Texan, The 5-21-30
Texan Meets Calamity Jane, The 10-18-50
Texans, The 8-03-38
Texans Never Cry 3-07-51
Texas 10-08-41
Texas Across the River 9-14-66
Texas Bad Man 9-27-32
Texas Bad Man 2-24-54
Texas, Brooklyn and Heaven 7-14-48
Texas Buddies 11-15-32
Texas Carnival 9-12-51
Texas Chain Saw Massacre, The 11-06-74
Texas City 3-26-52
Texas Dynamo 6-14-50
Texas Gunfighter 5-31-32
Texas Kid, The 1-19-44
Texas Lady 11-30-55
Texas Lawmen 2-20-52
Texas Marshal 6-18-41
Texas Masquerade 1-26-44
Texas Pioneers 6-14-32
Texas Ranger, The 5-06-31
Texas Rangers, The 9-30-36
Texas Rangers, The 6-06-51
Texas Rangers Ride Again, The 11-06-40
Texas Stagecoach 3-27-40
Texas Stampede 6-07-39
Texas Steer, A 8-06-15
Texas Steer, A 1-11-28
Texas Terror 4-03-35
Texas Terrors 11-20-40
Texas to Bataan 10-14-42
Texas Tommy 8-14-29
Texas Tornado 3-06-34
Texas Trail, The 7-08-25

Texas Trail, The 12-22-37
Texas Wildcats, The 10-25-39
Thai Tiger's Roar (See: Payak Rai Thaiteep)
Thais 3-19-15
Thais 1-04-18
Thampu 1-31-79
Thanassi Get Your Gun (See: Thanassi Pare To Opio Sou)
Thanassi Pare To Opio Sou 11-15-72
Thank God It's Friday 5-17-78
Thank You 10-07-25
Thank You, Aunt (See: Grazie, Tia)
Thank You, Jeeves 9-23-36
Thank You, Mr. Moto 1-12-38
Thank You Very Much (See: Fumo Di Londra)
Thank Your Lucky Stars 8-18-43
Thanks a Million 11-20-35
Thanks for Everything 12-07-38
Thanks for Listening 10-27-37
Thanks for the Buggy Ride 1-25-28
Thanks for the Memory 11-09-38
Thark 8-09-32
That Brennan Girl 11-20-46
That Brief Summer (See: Korte Sommer, Den)
That Certain Age 10-05-38
That Certain Feeling 6-06-56
That Certain Something 6-18-41
That Certain Thing 5-02-28
That Certain Urge (See: Voglia Matta, La)
That Certain Woman 8-04-37
That Chink at Golden Gulch 10-15-10
That Cold Day in the Park 5-28-69
That Dangerous Age 4-20-49
That Darn Cat 9-22-65
That Darned Grandfather (See: Ce Sacre Grand-Pere)
That Darned Kid (See: Cette Sacree Gamine)
That Dawn Should Be Peaceful (See: A Sori Sdesi Tihje)
That Dear Victor (See: Ce Cher Victor)
That Devil Quemado 7-08-25
That Dirty Dog Morris 6-11-24
That Forsyte Woman 10-26-49
That French Lady 10-08-24
That Funny Feeling 6-23-65
That Gang of Mine 1-01-41
That Girl of Dixon's 3-05-10
That Hagen Girl 10-22-47
That Hamilton Woman! 3-26-41
That House in the Outskirts (See: Aquella Casa en las Afueras)
That I May Live 5-12-37
That Is the Dawn (See: Cela S'Appelle L'Aurore)
That Kind of Woman 8-12-59
That Lady 3-30-55
That Lady in Ermine 7-14-48
That Little Difference (See: Quella Piccola Differenza)
That Long Night (See: Aquella Larga Noche)
That Long Night in 1943 (See: Lunga Notte Del '43, La)
That Lucky Touch 8-20-75
That Man Bolt 12-26-73
That Man from Tangier 4-15-53
That Man's Here Again 4-21-37
That Midnight Kiss 8-24-49
That Model from Paris 10-27-26
That Murder in Berlin 3-20-29
That Nazty Nuisance 6-02-43
That Night (See: Cette Nuit La)
That Night 7-24-57
That Night in Rio 3-12-41
That Night with You 9-19-45
That Obscure Object of Desire (See: Cet Obscure Objet du Desir)
That Old Bum (See: Cette Vielle Canaille)
That Only Happened Once (See: Gab's Nur Einmal, Das)
That Other Woman 10-21-42
That Riviera Touch 4-06-66
That Royale Girl 1-13-26
That Sinking Feeling 9-19-79
That Something 4-08-21
That Splendid November 6-23-71
That Summer (See: Ete, L' or Ekino To Kalokeri)
That Summer 7-04-79
That Tender Age (See: Age Ingrat, L')
That Tender Age or The Adolescents (See: Fleur de l'Age
    ou Les Adolescentes, La)
That Tender Touch 11-26-69
That Touch of Mink 5-09-62
That Uncertain Feeling 3-19-41
That Was Our Rommel (See: War Unser Rommel, Das)
That Way with Women 2-19-47
That Wild West 12-10-24
That Woman Opposite 6-05-57

That Wonderful Urge 11-24-48
That'll Be the Day 11-28-73
That's a Good Girl 10-17-33
That's Adultery 11-26-75
That's Enough, Man (See: Tama Na Erap)
That's Entertainment! 4-17-74
That's Entertainment, Part 2 5-05-76
That's Good 3-28-19
That's Gratitude 11-06-34
That's Life (See: C'est la Vie!)
That's Me, Too (See: Sadan Er Jeg Ogsaa)
That's My Baby 4-14-26
That's My Baby 2-15-28
That's My Baby 10-25-44
That's My Boy 11-22-32
That's My Boy 6-13-51
That's My Gal 6-04-47
That's My Man 4-09-47
That's My Story 12-01-37
That's Right--You're Wrong 11-22-39
That's the Spirit 5-16-45
That's the Ticket 5-08-40
That's the Way It Is 10-28-70
That's the Way of the World 8-06-75
That's the Way the Cookie Crumbles (See: Zivi Bili Pa Vidjeli)
That's What They All Say 2-26-10
Thaw (See: Tauwetter)
Thea, Femme Moderne 4-11-33
Thea, the Modern Woman (See: Thea, Femme Moderne)
Theatre de M. et Mme. Kabal 5-03-67
Theatre Girls 3-21-79
Theatre of Blood 4-25-73
Theft in the Dark, A 5-14-15
Theft of the Mona Lisa (See: Raub der Mona Lisa)
Their Big Moment 9-11-34
Their Chaperoned Honeymoon 1-08-10
Their Day of Rest 6-13-19
Their Golden Years (See: Sus Anos Dorados)
Their Hour 4-11-28
Their Last Night (See: Leur Derniere Nuit)
Their Mutual Child 1-21-21
Their Own Desire 1-29-30
Theirs Is the Glory 8-28-46
Thelma 12-01-22
Thelma Jordan 11-02-49
Them (See: Ils)
Them 4-14-54
Themroc 2-21-73
Then and Now 12-04-09
Then Came Bronson 11-25-70
Then Came the Legend (See: Apoi S-A Nascut Legenda)
Then Came the Woman 11-24-26
Then I'll Come Back to You 3-31-16
Then There Were Three 12-13-61
Theo Against the Rest of the World (See: Theo Gegen Den Rest
    Der Welt)
Theo Gegen Den Rest Der Welt 6-04-80
Theodor Koerner 5-16-33
Theodora 10-21-21
Theodora Goes Wild 11-18-36
Theodora, Imperatrice Byzantine 7-28-54
Theodora, Slave Empress (See: Theodora, Imperatrice Byzantine)
Theodore and Co. (See: Theodore et Cie)
Theodore et Cie 4-25-33
Theorem (See: Teorema)
There Ain't No Justice 6-28-39
There Are No Thieves in This Village (See: En Este Pueblo No Hay
    Ladrones)
There Burns a Fire (See: Det Brinner En Eld)
There Goes Kelly 2-28-45
There Goes My Girl 6-16-37
There Goes My Heart 9-28-38
There Goes Susie 9-25-34
There Goes the Bride 11-15-32 and 3-07-33
There Goes the Bride 12-24-80
There Goes the Groom 10-13-37
There Grows a Green Pine in the Woods (See: U Gori Raste Zelen
    Bor)
There Is Another Sun 6-20-51
There Is No Forgetting (See: Il N'Y A Pas D'Oubli)
There Is No Smoke (See: Il N'Y A Pas De Fumee)
There Is No 13 7-01-74
There Is Only One Love (See: Es Gibt Nur Eine Liebe)
There Is Such a Guy (See: Zhivyot Takoy Paren)
There Is the Brunet (See: Brune Que Voila, La)
There on the Great Ranch (See: Alla en el Rancho Grande)
There Was a Crooked Man 9-14-60
There Was a Crooked Man 11-04-70

There Was a Lad (See: Shiwjot Takoj Paren)
There Was Once a Cop (See: Il Etait Une Fois Un Flic)
There Was Once a Guy 11-04-64
There Was Once an Old Couple (See: Gili-Bili Starik So
    Staroukhoi)
There Were Nine Bachelors (See: Ils Etaient Neuf Celibataires)
There's a Girl in My Heart 11-23-49
There's a Girl in My Soup 12-16-70
There's a Train Every Hour (See: Il y a un Train Toutes les
    Heures)
There's Always a Way to Find a Way (See: Y'A Toujours Moyen de
    Moyenner)
There's Always a Woman 5-04-38
There's Always Tomorrow 1-18-56
There's Always Vanilla 1-12-72
There's But One Love (See: Es Gibt Nur Eine Liebe)
There's No Business Like Show Business 12-08-54
There's No Place Like Home 11-26-10
There's Something About a Soldier 1-12-44
There's That Woman Again 1-11-39
Therese and Isabelle 5-15-68
Therese Desqueyroux 9-12-62
Therese Raquin 6-13-28
Therese Raquin 10-07-53
These Are the Damned 7-14-65
These Charming People 8-11-31
These Children (See: Questi Ragazzi)
These Dangerous Years 7-24-57
These Glamour Girls 9-06-39
These Kids Are Grown-Ups (See: Ils Sont Grands Ces Petits)
These Men (See: Esos Hombres)
These Sorcerers Are Mad (See: Ils Sont Fous Ces Sorciers)
These 30 Years 5-29-34
These Thousand Hills 1-21-59
These Three 3-25-36
These Wilder Years 7-25-56
They All Come Out 7-05-39
They All Kissed the Bride 6-03-42
They Are All Like That (See: Saadan Er De Alle)
They Are Not Angels 6-02-48
They Are Not Oranges, They Are Horses (See: Det Er Ikke
    Appelsiner, Det Er Heste)
They Are Their Own Gifts 3-14-79
They Asked for It 7-05-39
They Call Her One Eye 6-26-74
They Call It Sin 10-25-32
They Call Me Mister Tibbs 7-08-70
They Call Me Trinity 11-03-71
They Call Us Misfits (See: Dom Kallar Oss Mods)
They Came by Night 3-13-40
They Came from Beyond Space 10-11-67
They Came from Within 3-24-76
They Came to a City 9-13-44
They Came to Blow Up America 4-21-43
They Came to Cordura 9-23-59
They Came to Rob Las Vegas (See: Las Vegas 500 Milliones)
They Dare Not Love 4-30-41
They Died with Their Boots On 11-19-41
They Drive by Night 7-10-40
They Flew Alone 5-13-42
They Fought for Their Country (See: Oni Srajalis Za Rodinou)
They Gave Him a Gun 5-19-37
They Got Me Covered 12-30-42
They Had to See Paris 10-16-29
They Just Had to Get Married 2-14-33
They Knew Mr. Knight 8-29-45
They Knew What They Wanted 10-09-40
They Like 'em Rough 8-04-22
They Live by Night (See: Twisted Road, The)
They Loved Life (See: Kanal)
They Made Her a Spy 4-05-39
They Made Me a Criminal 1-25-39
They Made Me a Fugitive 7-02-47
They Made Me a Killer 1-30-46
They Met in a Taxi 9-16-36
They Met in Argentina 5-14-41
They Met in Bombay 6-25-41
They Met in Moscow 6-14-44
They Met in the Dark 5-23-45
They Met on Skis 12-25-40
They Might Be Giants 3-03-71
They Never Come Back 6-07-32
They Only Kill Their Masters 11-15-72
They Raid by Night 9-02-42
They Rode West 10-20-54
They Shall Have Music 7-12-39
They Shall Overcome 1-01-75
They Shall Pay 8-26-21
They Shoot Horses, Don't They? 11-26-69

They Wanted Peace 1-17-40
They Wanted to Marry 2-24-37
They Went That-a-Way and That-a-Way 12-06-78
They Were Expendable 11-21-45
They Were Not Divided 4-05-50
They Were Sisters 5-30-45
They Were So Young 1-26-55
They Were Ten (See: Hem Hayu Asara)
They Were Ten 11-09-60 and 4-26-61
They Were 12 Women (See: Elles Etaient Douze Femmes)
They Who Dare 2-24-54
They Won't Believe Me 7-23-47
They Won't Forget 6-30-37
They're a Weird Mob 9-14-66
They're Off 9-07-17
They're Off 8-08-19
They've Changed Faces (See: Hanno Cambiato Faccia)
Thi Asimanton Aformin 11-06-74
Thief, The (See: Voleur, Le)
Thief, The 12-25-14
Thief, The 9-24-52
Thief in Paradise 1-28-25
Thief in the Bedroom 7-13-60
Thief in the Dark 6-13-28
Thief of Bagdad, The 3-26-24
Thief of Bagdad, The 10-16-40
Thief of Baghdad, The 7-05-61
Thief of Damascus 3-26-52
Thief of Tibidabo, The (See: Voleur de Tibidabo, Le)
Thief of Venice, The 11-12-52
Thief Who Came to Dinner, The 2-28-73
Thieves 11-14-13
Thieves 11-07-19 and 12-19-19
Thieves 2-16-77
Thieves, The (See: Truands, Les)
Thieves Fall Out 6-04-41
Thieves Gold 3-22-18
Thieves' Highway 9-07-49
Thieves Like Us 2-20-74
Thin Ice 7-04-19
Thin Ice 8-25-37
Thin Line, The 12-03-80
Thin Man, The 7-03-34
Thin Man Goes Home, The 11-22-44
Thin Red Line, The 4-22-64
Thing, The 4-04-51
Thing That Couldn't Die, The 5-07-58
Thing We Love, The 3-15-18
Thing with Two Heads, The 7-19-72
Things of Life, The (See: Choses de la Vie, Les)
Things That Don't Pass By (See: Dingen Die Niet Voorbijgaan)
Things to Come 3-04-36 and 4-22-36
Things Will Jump (See: Ca Va Barder)
Think Fast, Mr. Moto 8-18-37
Think of a Number (See: Taenk Paa Et Tal)
Think of It, Jack (See: Pensaci Giacomino)
Thinker, The 8-18-22
Third, The (See: Dritte, Der)
Third After the Sun, The 7-25-73
Third Alarm 1-12-23
Third Alarm 12-24-30
Third Base (See: Sado)
Third Cry, The (See: Troisieme Cri, Le)
Third Day, The 7-14-65
Third Degree 1-05-27 and 2-16-27
Third Degree, The 5-23-19
Third Door, The (See: Tercera Puerta, La)
Third Finger, Left Hand 10-16-40
Third Generation, The (See: Dritte Generation, Die)
Third Kiss, The 9-19-19
Third Man, The 9-07-49
Third Man on the Mountain 9-16-59
Third of a Man 9-05-62
3rd of November 1918 (See: 3 November 1918)
Third Part of the Night, The (See: Trzeciej Czesci Nocy)
Third Secret, The 4-22-64
Third Sex, The (See: Dritte Geschiecht, Das)
Third Time Lucky 1-19-49
Third Voice, The 1-27-60
Third Walker, The 9-20-78
Third Woman, The 3-19-20
Third Word, The (See: Tercera Palabra, La)
Third World, Prisoner in the Street 8-13-80
Thirst (See: Torst)
Thirst 12-26-79
Thirst for Love (See: Sed d' Amor or Ai No Kawaki)
Thirteen, The 5-26-37 and 6-23-37

Thirteen at the Table (See: Treize a Table)
13 Days in France (See: 13 Jours en France)
Thirteen Fighting Men   3-23-60
13 Frightened Girls   6-19-63
13 Ghosts   6-29-60
Thirteen Girls Smile at the Sky (See: 13 Kislany Mosolyog Az
    Egre)
Thirteen Hours by Air   5-06-36
13 Jours en France   7-10-68
13 Kislany Mosolyog Az Egre   11-09-38
13 Lead Soldiers   5-05-48
13 Men and a Girl   8-18-31
13 Rue Madeleine   12-18-46
13 Washington Square   2-01-28
13 West Street   5-09-62
13 Women   10-18-32
Thirteenth Chair, The   10-30-19
Thirteenth Chair, The   1-22-30
Thirteenth Chair, The   6-02-37
13th Commandment, The   2-13-20
13th Girl, The   12-31-15
Thirteenth Guest, The   9-06-32
13th Hour, The   11-30-27
13th Juror, The   11-23-27
13th Labor of Hercules, The   6-08-17
13th Letter, The   1-24-51
Thirteenth Man, The (See: O Thekatos Tritos)
13th Man, The   8-04-37
30th Piece of Silver, The   5-14-20
Thirty a Week   10-18-18
30-Day Princess, The   5-15-34
Thirty Days   12-01-22 and 12-15-22
30 Foot Bride of Candy Rock, The   8-12-59
30 Is a Dangerous Age, Cynthia   3-06-68
Thirty Seconds of Love (See: Trenta Secondi d'Amore)
30 Seconds over Tokyo   11-15-44
$30,000   4-02-20
30 Years of Fun   2-13-63
39 East   9-17-20
39 Steps, The   6-19-35 and 9-18-35
39 Steps, The   3-18-59
39 Steps, The   11-29-78
36 Hours   12-16-64
36 Hours to Kill   8-19-36
36 Le Grand Tournant   2-18-70
36 the Turning Point (See: 36 Le Grand Tournant)
This Above All   5-13-42
This Age Without Pity (See: Cet Age Sans Pitie)
This Angry Age   4-30-58
This Answering Service Takes No Messages (See: Ce Repondeur
    Ne Prend Pas De Message)
This Could Be the Night   4-10-57
This Crazy World of Ours (See: Bube U Glavi)
This Day and Age   8-29-33
This Desired Body (See: Ce Corps Tant Desire)
This Earth Is Mine   4-22-59
This England   3-12-41
This Freedom   11-22-23 and 11-29-23
This Girl Irene (See: Maedchen Irene, Das)
This Gun for Hire   3-18-42
This Happy Breed   6-07-44 and 4-16-47
This Happy Feeling   3-19-58
This Hero Stuff   7-25-19
This Human Child (See: Ditte Menneskebarn)
This Is a Hijack   6-13-73
This Is America   8-01-33
This Is China   10-06-37
This Is Heaven   4-03-29
This Is Joy (See: Esto es Alegria)
This Is Korea!   8-22-51
This Is Love, Isn't It? (See: Was Heisst'n Hier Liebe)
This Is My Affair   6-02-37
This Is My Alaska   2-12-69
This Is My Love   9-29-54
This Is My Street   1-22-64
This Is Russia   12-11-57
This Is Simonal (See: E Simonal)
This Is the Army   8-04-43
This Is the Enemy   7-08-42
This Is the Half Century (See: Ce Siecle a 50 Ans)
This Is the Land   7-15-36
This Is the Life   7-17-14
This Is the Life   11-19-15
This Is the Life   9-19-33
This Is the Life   10-09-35
This Is the Life   5-03-44
This Is the Night   4-19-32
This Is What Biafra Is   10-08-69
This Is Your Army   6-09-54 and 12-15-54

This Island Earth   3-30-55
This Kind of Love (See: Questa Specie d'Amore)
This Land Is Mine   3-17-43
This Love at the End of the World (See: Questo Amore Ai Confini
    Del Mondo)
This Love of Ours   10-24-45
This Man In Paris   7-05-39
This Man Is Dangerous (See: Cet Homme Est Dangereux)
This Man Is Mine   4-17-34
This Man Is Mine   9-25-46
This Man Is News   7-26-39
This Man's Navy   1-10-45
This Marriage Business   6-08-38
This Modern Age   9-08-31
This Nude World   7-11-33
This One or None (See: Oder Keine, Die)
This Pretty World (See: Ce Joli Monde)
This Property Is Condemned   6-15-66
This Rebel Breed   2-10-60
This Reckless Age   1-12-32
This Rockin' Globe (See: Kloden Rokker)
This Savage Land   8-27-69
This Side of Heaven   2-13-34
This Side of the Law   6-07-50
This Sporting Age   10-04-32
This Sporting Life   2-13-63
This Summer at Five (See: Kesalla Kello Viisi)
This Thing Called Love   12-18-29
This Thing Called Love   12-25-40
This Time for Keeps   2-11-42
This Time for Keeps   10-08-47
This Time Let's Talk About Men (See: Questa Volta Parliamo di
    Uomini)
This Transient Life (See: Mujo)
This Was a Woman   2-11-48
This Was My Path (See: Igy Joettem)
This Was Pancho Villa (See: Asi Era Pancho Villa)
This Was Paris   2-18-42
This Way Please   9-15-37
This Wine of Love   1-28-48
This Woman   10-22-24
This Woman Is Dangerous   1-30-52
This Woman Is Mine   9-11-35
This Woman Is Mine   8-27-41
This Year Jerusalem   4-02-69
This'll Make You Whistle   11-25-36
Thomas   2-19-75
Thomas and the Bewitched (See: Thomas e ... Gli Indemoniati)
Thomas Crown Affair, The   6-19-68
Thomas e ... Gli Indemoniati   10-14-70
Thomas er Fredloes   10-16-68
Thomas l'Imposteur   4-28-65
Thomas, the Imposter (See: Thomas l'Imposteur)
Thomas, the Restless One (See: Thomas er Fredloes)
Thomasine and Bushrod   4-10-74
Thompson's Night with the Police   12-05-08
Thorns and Orange Blossoms   1-05-23
Thorobred, The   8-26-25
Thoroughbred   6-03-36
Thoroughbred, The   8-15-16
Thoroughbreds   1-24-45
Thoroughbreds Don't Cry   11-17-37
Thoroughly Modern Millie   3-29-67
Those Calloways   11-18-64
Those Crazy Years (See: Aquellos Anos Locos)
Those Damned Savages (See: Maudits Sauvages, Les)
Those Daring Young Men in Their Jaunty Jalopies   5-28-69
Those Dirty Dogs   5-29-74
Those Endearing Young Charms   6-20-45
Those Fantastic Flying Fools   6-28-67
Those High Grey Walls   10-25-39
Those Lips Those Eyes   8-13-80
Those Magnificent Men in Their Flying Machines (or How I Flew
    from London to Paris in 25 Hours and 11 Minutes)   6-02-65
Those of the Side Show (See: Vom Rummelplatz, Die)
Those of the 'Viking' (See: Ceux du 'Viking')
Those Quiet Japanese (See: Yasashi Nipponjin)
Those Redheads from Seattle   9-23-53
Those Three About Christine (See: Drei Um Christine, Die)
Those Three French Girls   10-15-30
Those We Love   9-20-32
Those Were the Days   5-22-40
Those Were the Years (See: C'Eravama Tanti Amati)
Those Who Dance   7-02-24
Those Who Dance   7-09-30
Those Who Dare   3-11-25
Those Who Pay   12-14-17
Those Who Take Risks   7-24-63

Those Who Toil 6-23-16
Those Who Wear Glasses (See: Szemuvegesek)
Those Without Sin 4-13-17
Those Wonderful Men with a Crank (See: Bajecni Muzi S Klikou)
Tho'tléss Women 11-19-20
Thou Art Peace (See: Tu Eres la Paz)
Thou Art the Man 1-07-14
Thou Art the Man 6-04-20
Thou Shall Not Kill ... But Once 7-02-75
Thou Shalt Not 5-29-14
Thou Shalt Not Kill (See: Tu Ne Tueras Point or No Mataras)
Thou Shalt Not Kill 12-13-39
Thou Shalt Not Steal 6-25-15
Thou Shalt Not Steal 10-20-65
Thou Shalt Remember (See: Yiskor)
Thousand and One Hands, A (See: Mille et Une Mains)
Thousand and One Nights, A 6-13-45
Thousand Clowns, A 12-01-65
Thousand Dollar Husband, The 5-26-16
Thousand Plane Raid, The 7-23-69
Thousand to One, A 12-17-20
Thousands Cheer 9-15-43
Thousandth Window, The (See: Millieme Fenetre, La)
Threads of Destiny 10-23-14
Threads of Fate 1-26-17
Threat, The (See: Menace, La)
Threat, The 6-20-28
Threat, The 10-26-49
Threat, The 2-24-60
Threats (See: Menaces)
Three (See: Tri)
Three 6-04-69
Three Ages, The 10-04-23
Three Argentines in Paris (See: Tres Argentinos en Paris)
Three Bad Men 8-18-26
Three Bad Sisters 1-11-56
Three Bites of the Apple 2-22-67
Three Blind Mice 6-08-38
Three Blondes in His Life 1-25-61
Three Boys, One Girl (See: Trois Garcons, Une Fille)
Three Brave Men 1-16-57
Three Buckaroos 7-21-22
Three Caballeros, The 12-13-44
Three Came Home 2-15-50
Three Came to Kill 4-06-60
Three Card Monte 9-20-78
Three Cases of Murder 3-16-55
Three Cheers for Love 8-05-36
Three Cheers for the Irish 3-13-40
Three Coins in the Fountain 5-12-54
Three Comrades 5-25-38
Three Comrades and One Invention 10-17-28
Three-Cornered Hat (See: Cappello a Tre Punte, Il or Sombrero
    de Tres Picos)
Three Cornered Moon 8-15-33
Three Daring Daughters 2-11-48
Three Daughters (See: Tri Dcery)
Three Days After Immortality 12-11-63
Three Days and a Child 2-01-67
Three Days in Jail (See: Drei Tage Mitelarest)
Three Days Love (See: Drei Tage Liebe)
Three Days of the Condor 9-17-75
Three Days of Viktor Tschernikoff, The 10-23-68
Three Days to Live (See: Trois Jours a Vivre)
Three Days to Live 4-30-24
3 Desperate Men 1-17-51
Three Disordered Children (See: Trois Enfants Dans le Desordre)
Three Dragons (See: Harom Sarkany)
Three Faces East 2-10-26
Three Faces East 9-10-30
Three Faces of a Woman (See: Tre Volti, I)
Three Faces of Eve, The 8-21-57
Three Fingered Jack 1-08-10
3 for Bedroom C 6-04-52
3 for Jamie Dawn 7-11-56
Three for the Show 2-16-55
Three Forbidden Stories (See: Tre Storie Proibite)
Three Friends, The 10-22-10
Three Girls About Town 10-22-41
Three Girls and Schubert (See: Drei Maederl Um Schubert)
Three Girls Lost 5-06-31
Three Girls Named Anna (See: Tri Ane)
Three Godfathers 3-11-36
Three Godfathers 12-01-48
Three Godfathers, The 6-16-16
Three Gold Coins 7-09-20
Three Green Eyes 4-25-19
Three Guns for Texas 5-22-68

Three Guys Named Mike 2-14-51
Three Hats for Lisa 5-26-65
Three Hearts for Julia 1-06-43
Three Henchmen of Lampaio (See: Tres Cabras de Lampaio)
Three Hours 3-09-27
Three Hours 11-22-44
Three Hours for Love (See: Tri Sata Zsa Ljuhav)
Three Hours to Kill 9-08-54
365 Nights in Hollywood 11-13-34
322 10-29-69
300 Spartans, The 8-22-62
300 Year Weekend, The 3-03-71
Three Husbands 11-08-50
Three in Exile 11-04-25
Three in One 8-01-56
Three in the Attic 12-25-68
3 into 2 Won't Go 6-25-69
Three Is a Family 11-22-44
Three Jumps Ahead 5-30-23
3 Kids and a Queen 11-13-35
Three Legionnaires 7-14-37
Three Little Girls in Blue 9-04-46
Three Little Sisters 8-02-44
Three Little Words 7-12-50
Three Live Ghosts 1-06-22
Three Live Ghosts 10-02-29
Three Lives 10-20-71
Three Lives of Thomasina 12-18-63
Three Loves 6-02-31
Three Loves Has Nancy 9-07-38
Three Loves in Rio (See: Meus Amores No Rio)
Three Make a Pair (See: Trois Font la Paire, Les)
Three Married Men 9-30-36
Three Maxims 7-15-36
Three Men and a Girl 4-04-19
Three Men from Texas 1-15-41
Three Men in a Boat 6-06-33
Three Men in a Boat 1-02-57
Three Men in Search of a Troll (See: Tre Mand Frem For En Trold)
Three Men in the Snow (See: Drei Maenner im Schnee)
Three Men in White 5-03-44
Three Men of the River (See: Tres Hombres del Rio)
Three Men on a Horse (See: Trois Hommes Sur un Cheval)
Three Men on a Horse 12-02-36
Three Men to Destroy (See: Trois Hommes a Abattre)
Three Mesquiteers, The 4-07-37
Three Miles Up 9-28-27
Three Mounted Men 11-01-18
Three Moves to Freedom 9-21-60
Three Musketeers, The (See: Tres Mosqueteros or Trois
    Mousquetaires, Les)
Three Musketeers, The 1-16-14
Three Musketeers, The 3-06-14
Three Musketeers, The 9-02-21
Three Musketeers, The 9-16-21
Three Musketeers, The 11-06-35
Three Musketeers, The 2-08-39
Three Musketeers, The 10-20-48
Three Musketeers, The 12-26-73
Three Must-Get-Theres, The 9-01-22
Three Naked Flappers 1-16-29
Three Nights of Love (See: Egy Szerelem Harom Ejszakaja or
    3 Notti d'Amore)
3 Notti d'Amore 12-30-64
3 November 1918 4-07-65
Three Nuts in Search of a Bolt 6-17-64
3 O'Clock in the Morning 2-28-24
Three of a Kind 7-01-36
Three of Many 12-08-16
Three of Them, The 9-17-10
Three of Us, The 12-25-14
Three on a Couch 6-08-66
Three on a Honeymoon (See: Hochzeitsreise Zu Dritt)
Three on a Honeymoon 5-08-34
Three on a Match 11-01-32
Three on a Ticket 4-09-47
Three on a Week End 6-15-38
Three on the Trail 5-06-36
Three Pals 9-22-16
Three Passions 5-08-29
Three Penny Opera 5-20-31 and 7-13-60
Three Penny Opera 3-13-63
Three + Two 10-16-63
Three Quarters of a Sun (See: Tri Cetvrtine Sunca)
Three Queens and a Jack 2-26-10
Three Rascals in Hidden Fortress (See: Kakushitoride No
    Sanakunin)
Three Rats, The (See: Tres Ratas, Las)
Three Reasons for Haste 9-18-09

Three Ring Circus 10-27-54
Three-Ring Marriage 10-03-28
Three Rings and a Goat (See: J. Rufus Wallingford)
Three Rogues 4-08-31
Three Romeos and a Juliet (See: Tres Romeos y Una Julieta)
Three Rooms in Manhattan (See: Trois Chambres a Manhattan)
Three Russian Girls 1-05-44
Three Sad Tigers (See: Tres Tristes Tigres)
Three Sailors and a Blonde (See: Drei Blaue Jungs und ein
    Blondes Maedel)
Three Sailors and a Girl 11-25-53
Three Scenes with Ingmar Bergman (See: Tre Scener Med Ingmar
    Bergman)
Three Secrets 8-30-50
317 Section, La 3-10-65
Three Shadows, The 3-27-14
Three Sinners 4-25-28
3 Sinners 7-16-52
Three Sisters, The 4-23-30
Three Sisters, The 9-09-70
Three Smart Girls 1-27-37
Three Smart Girls Grow Up 3-22-39
Three Sons 10-04-39
Three Sons O'Guns 9-10-41
Three Spinsters (See: Harom Sarkany)
Three Steps in Life 7-21-65
Three Steps into the Emptiness (See: Tri Koraka U Prazno)
Three Steps North 6-13-51
3 Stooges Go Around the World in a Daze, The 8-28-63
3 Stooges in Orbit, The 7-11-62
3 Stooges Meet Hercules, The 1-24-62
3 Stooges vs. The Wonder Women 5-21-75
Three Strangers 1-30-46
Three Stripes in the Sun 10-26-55
Three Succeed 9-18-29
Three Tales of Chekhov 10-11-61
3:10 to Yuma 8-14-57
Three Texas Steers 8-02-39
Three Thanksgivings 11-27-09
Three the Hard Way 6-26-74
Three Thousand Million Without an Elevator (See: Trois Milliards
    Sans Ascenseur)
Three Tigers Against Three Tigers (See: Tre Tigri Contro Tre
    Tigri)
Three Times Anna (See: Tres Veces Ana)
3 x Gordon 10-25-18
Three to Go 4-07-71
Three Tough Guys 3-20-74
Three Treasures, The 12-28-60
Three Two One (See: Tatlo, Dalawa, Isa)
Three Violent People 12-26-56
Three Waltzes (See: Trois Valses)
Three Warriors 11-09-77
Three Wax Men 2-06-29
Three Week Ends 12-12-28
Three Weeks 10-17-14
Three Weeks 4-02-24
Three Weeks in Paris 5-19-26
Three Weeks of Love 10-27-65
Three Weird Sisters, The 3-10-48
Three Who Loved 8-11-31
Three Wise Fools 7-26-23
Three Wise Fools 6-12-46
Three Wise Girls 2-09-32
Three Wise Guys 5-27-36
Three Wise Men, The (See: Tres Reyes Magos, Los)
Three Wishes (See: Drei Wenschen)
Three Women (See: Trois Femmes)
Three Women 10-08-24
Three Women 4-13-77
Three Word Brand 9-30-21
Three Worlds of Gulliver, The 12-07-60
Three Young Texans 1-13-54
Three's a Crowd 10-05-27
Three's a Crowd 9-12-45
Threesome 9-24-69
Threshold 9 Illusions 10-11-72
Threshold of Spring 6-06-79
Threshold of the Void, The (See: Seuil Du Vide, Le)
Thrill Chaser, The 1-17-24
Thrill Hunter, The 6-16-26
Thrill Hunter, The 10-17-33
Thrill Killers, The 6-16-65
Thrill of a Lifetime 11-10-37
Thrill of a Romance 5-23-45
Thrill of Brazil, The 9-11-46
Thrill of It All, The 6-12-63
Thrill of Youth, The 11-01-32

Thrill Seekers, The 2-01-28
Thrillarama Adventure 8-15-56
Thriller Story (See: Serie Noire)
Thriller-en Grym Film (See: They Call Her One Eye)
Throne of Blood 1-24-62
Throne of the Gods 12-26-33
Through a Glass Window 4-28-22
Through and Through (See: Na Wylot)
Through Central Africa 3-12-15
Through Fire to Fame 5-08-14
Through Snow to Sunshine 2-26-10
Through the Ashes of the Empire (See: Prin Cenusa Imperiului)
Through the Clouds 12-03-10
Through the Dark 1-10-24
Through the Looking Glass 9-15-76
Through the Shadows 4-23-24
Through the Storm 9-01-22
Through the Toils 6-13-19
Through the Wall 10-06-16
Through the Wrong Door 7-25-19
Through Thick and Thin 9-08-26
Through Turbulent Waters 7-02-15
Throw Away Your Books, Rally in the Streets (See: Sho O Suteyo,
    Machi E Deyo)
Throw of the Dice, A 1-22-30 and 5-28-30
Throwback, The 11-06-35
Thru Darkest Africa 3-30-27
Thru Different Eyes 4-17-29
Thru Different Eyes 6-03-42
Thru the Back Door 5-20-21
Thrushes Are Still Singing, The (See: Ta Kourelia Tragoudoun
    Akoma)
Thruster, The (See: Arriviste, L')
Thumb Tripping 10-04-72
Thumbs Down 7-13-27
Thumbs Up! (See: Pouce)
Thumbs Up 6-16-43
Thunder 7-10-29
Thunder Afloat 9-20-39
Thunder Alley 3-29-67
Thunder Among the Leaves (See: Trueno Entre Las Hojas, El)
Thunder and Lightning 6-29-77
Thunder Bay 5-06-53
Thunder Below 6-21-32
Thunder Birds 10-21-42
Thunder God, The 9-12-28
Thunder in Carolina 7-06-60
Thunder in God's Country 4-18-51
Thunder in the City 1-27-37 and 4-28-37
Thunder in the Desert 5-18-38
Thunder in the East 10-29-52
Thunder in the Hills 5-28-47
Thunder in the Night 9-18-35
Thunder in the Pines 4-06-49
Thunder in the Sun 3-25-59
Thunder Island 6-17-21
Thunder Island 10-02-63
Thunder Mountain 10-02-35
Thunder Mountain 5-14-47
Thunder of Drums, A 8-30-61
Thunder of God, The (See: Tonnerre de Dieu, Le)
Thunder on the Hill 8-08-51
Thunder over Arizona 10-24-56
Thunder over Mexico 9-26-33
Thunder over Texas 10-23-34
Thunder over the Plains 11-11-53
Thunder over the Prairie 7-30-41
Thunder Riders 5-02-28
Thunder River Feud 3-04-42
Thunder Road 4-23-58
Thunder Rock 12-30-42
Thunder Town 3-27-46
Thunder Trail 9-29-37
Thunderball 12-22-65
Thunderbird 6 7-24-68
Thunderbirds 11-26-52
Thunderbirds Are Go 12-28-66
Thunderbolt 6-26-29
Thunderbolt 9-09-36
Thunderbolt 10-31-45
Thunderbolt, The 11-14-19
Thunderbolt and Lightfoot 5-29-74
Thunderclap 8-05-21
Thundercrack 4-07-76
Thundergate 1-10-24
Thunderhead--Son of Flicka 1-31-45
Thunderhoof 7-07-48

Thundering Caravans 8-06-52
Thundering Dawn 11-29-23
Thundering Fatty (See: Dunderklumpen)
Thundering Frontier 9-18-40
Thundering Gun Slingers 9-27-44
Thundering Herd, The 11-14-14 and 8-06-15
Thundering Herd, The 2-25-25
Thundering Herd, The 6-05-34
Thundering Hoofs 1-14-25
Thundering Hoofs 12-31-41
Thundering Jets 4-16-58
Thundering Mountains (See: Nevesinjska Puska)
Thundering Thompson 10-16-29
Thundering Trail, The 12-12-51
Thundering West 3-08-39
Thunderstorm 10-02-34
Thunderstorm 6-20-56
Thursday We Shall Sing Like Sunday (See: Jeudi On Chantera
    Comme Dimanche)
Thursdays Never Again 7-05-78
Thus Finishes the Night (See: Ainsi Finit La Nuit)
Thy Name Is Woman 3-05-24
Thy Neighbor's Wife 9-16-53
Thy Soul Shall Bear Witness (See: Korkarlen)
Ti-Cul Tougas 5-18-77
Ti Ekanes Ston Polemo Thanass I 11-03-71
Ti i J 9-06-72
Ti-Koyo and His Shark 12-19-62
Ti-Koyo e il Suo Pescecane (See: Ti-Koyo and His Shark)
Ti Ritrovera 6-22-49
Tia Tula, La 4-28-65
Tiao Medonho 9-19-62
Tiara Tahiti 7-18-62
Tiburoneros 7-31-63
Tic-Tac-Toe (See: Tres En Raya)
Tichy Don 8-06-58
... tick ... tick ... tick ... 1-28-70
Ticket-of-Leave Man, The 11-28-14
Ticket to Crime 12-25-34
Ticket to Paradise 7-15-36
Ticket to Tomahawk, A 4-19-50
Tickle Me 6-16-65
Tickled to Death 10-30-09
Ticklish Affair, A 7-03-63
Tidal Wave and West Wind (See: Daluyong At Habagat)
Tides of Barnegat, The 5-25-17
Tides of Fate 8-24-17
Tides of Passion 4-22-25
Tidikawa and Friends 6-19-74
Tie That Binds, The 6-07-23
Tiempo d'Amore 8-12-64
Tiempo de Morir 8-10-66
Tiempos de Constitucion 10-18-78
Tieng Goi, Phiatruoc 9-05-79
Tieplo Tvoio Ruk 8-16-72
Tiergarten 3-05-80
Tierra Del Fuego 1-26-49
Tierra Magica 7-22-59
Tierra Prometida, La 4-24-74
Tierra Quemada 9-18-68
Tierra y el Cielo, La 3-15-78
Ties for the Olympics (See: Krawatten Fuer Olympia)
Tigar 8-16-78
Tiger, Der (See: Tiger, The)
Tiger, The (See: Tigar)
Tiger, The 5-14-30
Tiger and Crane Fists 9-22-76
Tiger and the Flame 5-11-55
Tiger and the Pussycat, The 7-05-67
Tiger Bay 4-08-59
Tiger Fangs 12-01-43
Tiger Girl 2-20-20
Tiger Girl 9-07-55
Tiger in the Smoke 12-05-56
Tiger Likes Fresh Flesh, The (See: Tigre Aime la Chair Fraiche,
    Le)
Tiger Love 6-18-24
Tiger Makes Out, The 9-20-67
Tiger Man, The 4-26-18
Tiger Murder Case, The (See: Tiger von Berlin, Der)
Tiger of Eschnapur, The (See: Tiger von Eschnapur, Der)
Tiger Rose 11-29-23 and 12-06-23
Tiger Rose 1-01-30
Tiger Shark 9-27-32
Tiger Sprays Himself with Dynamite, The (See: Tigre Se Parfume
    a la Dynamite, Le)
Tiger Thompson 8-20-24

Tiger True 2-04-21
Tiger von Berlin, Der 9-17-30
Tiger von Eschnapur, Der 3-09-38
Tiger von Eschnapur, Der 5-20-59
Tiger Walks, A 3-18-64
Tiger Woman, The 2-23-17
Tiger Woman, The 12-26-45
Tiger's Claw, The 4-05-23
Tiger's Coat, The 12-03-20
Tiger's Way, The (See: Tang Sua Phan)
Tight Rope, The (See: Corde Raide, La)
Tight Shoes 6-11-41
Tight Spot 5-04-55
Tigre, Il (See: Tiger and the Pussycat, The)
Tigre Aime la Chair Fraiche, Le 12-02-64
Tigre de Chamberi 3-12-58
Tigre Se Parfume a la Dynamite, Le 12-22-65
Tigres Del Desierto, Los 2-10-60
Tigress, The 12-25-14
Tigress, The 8-20-15
Tigress, The 11-30-27
Tiina 9-14-77
Tijuana Story, The 10-09-57
Tiki Tiki 10-06-71
'Til We Meet Again 4-24-40
Till Death Us Do Part 12-18-68
Till Divorce Us Do Part (See: Hasta Que El Matrimonio Nos
    Separe)
Till Five Minutes Past Twelve (See: Bis Funf Minuten Nach
    Zwolf)
Till Gladje 10-06-71
Till the Clouds Roll By 11-13-46
Till the Doors of Hell (See: Intill Helvetets Portar)
Till the End of the World (See: Jusqu'au Bout du Monde)
Till the End of Time 6-12-46
Till the Happy End (See: Bis Zum Happy End)
Till We Meet Again 10-20-22
Till We Meet Again 5-13-36
Till We Meet Again 8-30-44
Tillie 2-17-22
Tillie and Gus 11-14-33
Tillie the Toiler 6-08-27
Tillie the Toiler 8-13-41
Tillie Wakes Up 1-19-17
Tillie's Punctured Romance 1-01-15
Tillie's Punctured Romance 6-20-28
Tillie's Tomato Surprise 10-01-15
Tillsammans Med Gunilla Mondag Kvall Och Tisdag (See: Guilt)
Tilly of Bloomsbury 5-13-31
Tilt 4-11-79
Tiltott Terulet 2-26-69
Tim 5-23-79
Tim Tyler's Luck 1-12-38
Timber 8-12-42
Timber Fury 9-06-50
Timber Queen 1-05-44
Timber Stampede 10-25-39
Timber Trail, The 6-30-48
Timber War, The 3-04-36
Timber Wolf, The 12-02-25
Timberjack 2-09-55
Timbuktu 10-14-59
Time After Time 9-05-79
Time and Hour of Augusto Matraga, The (See: A Hora et Vez de
    Augusto Matraga)
Time and the Touch, The 9-05-62
Time Bomb 2-18-53
Time for Dying, A 10-06-71
Time for Killing, A 7-03-68
Time Gentlemen Please! 9-23-53
Time in the Sun, A 10-09-40
Time Limit 9-18-57
Time Lock 9-04-57
Time Locks and Diamonds 7-13-17
Time Machine, The 7-20-60
Time of a Hunt, The (See: Temps d'une Chasse, Le)
Time of Before, The (See: Temps De L'Avant, Le)
Time of Desire, The 8-21-57
Time of Indifference, A (See: Indifferenti, Gli)
Time of Love (See: Tiempo D'Amore)
Time of Maturity (See: Reifezeit)
Time of Roses (See: Ruusujen Aika)
Time of the Ghetto, The (See: Temps du Ghetto, Le)
Time of the Heathen 7-11-62
Time of the Innocent (See: Zeit der Schuldlosen)
Time of the Potato Blight (See: Temps des Doryphores)
Time of the Storks (See: Zeit der Storche)
Time of the Wolves 2-25-70

Time of Their Lives, The 8-14-46
Time of Your Life, The 5-26-48
Time on Her Hands (See: Dani)
Time Out for Murder 9-07-38
Time Out for Rhythm 5-28-41
Time Out for Romance 3-17-37
Time Out of Mind 3-19-47
Time, Place and Girl 7-10-29
Time Stood Still (See: Tempo S E Fermato, Il)
Time, the Comedian 12-16-25
Time, the Place and the Girl, The 12-11-46
Time to Die (See: Tiempo de Morir or Temps de Mourir, Le)
Time to Get Married 11-07-08
Time to Kill 12-09-42
Time to Live (See: Temps de Vivre, Le or Zeit Zu Leben)
Time to Love 6-22-27
Time to Love and a Time to Die, A 4-02-58
Time to Sing, A 8-14-68
Time Travelers, The 11-25-64
Time Within Memory (See: Seigenki)
Time Without Pity 4-17-57
Times Are Out of Joint, The 10-01-10
Times For 10-28-70
Times Have Changed 1-17-24
Times of the Constitution (See: Tiempos de Constitucion)
Times Square 9-10-80
Times Square Lady 3-20-35
Times Square Playboy 5-06-36
Times Without War (See: Vreme Bez Rata)
Timetable 2-08-56
Timid Terror, The 12-22-26
Timothy's Quest 9-15-22
Timothy's Quest 3-04-36
Tin Drum, The (See: Blechtrommel, Die)
Tin Gods 9-22-26
Tin Hats 12-08-26
Tin Pan Alley 11-27-40
Tin Star, The 10-16-57
Tine 7-21-65
Tingler, The 8-05-59
Tinimbang Ka Nguni't Kulang 7-17-74
Tinsel 6-28-18
Tintin and the Lake of Sharks (See: Tintin et le Lac Aux
    Requins)
Tintin and the Mystery of the Golden Fleece (See: Tintin et
    le Mystere de la Toison d'Or)
Tintin and the Sun Temple (See: Tintin et le Temple du Soleil)
Tintin et le Lac Aux Requins 1-10-73
Tintin et le Mystere de la Toison d'Or 1-17-62
Tintin et le Temple du Soleil 2-11-70
Tiny Lund: Hard Charger 6-11-69
Tioga Kid, The 3-10-48
Tip-Off, The 6-12-29
Tip-Off, The 10-27-31
Tip-Off Girls, The 3-23-38
Tip on a Dead Jockey 8-14-57
Tipchang 12-18-74
Tipped Off 8-16-23
Tiptoes 6-08-27
Tirak Cong Norng Noo 8-15-79
Tire au Flanc 9-12-28
Tire-au-Flanc 8-09-61
Tired Business Man, The 11-30-27
Tired Death, The 11-18-21
Tired Theodore (See: Trotte Teodor)
Tirez Sur le Pianiste 8-31-60
Tiro Al Aire 11-05-80
Tiro Al Piccione 9-13-61
Tiro de Gracia 7-09-69
'Tis Now the Very Witching Hour of Night 9-25-09
Tis Pity She's a Whore (See: Addio, Fratello Crudele)
Tish 7-22-42
Tisztelet a Kivetelnek 2-24-37
Tit Coq 3-11-53
Tit for Tat (See: Nije Nego)
Tit for Tat 9-01-22
Titan, The 12-28-49
Titanic 4-15-53
Titfield Thunderbolt 3-25-53
Titicut Follies, The 10-04-67
Title Shot 9-26-79
Tizezer Nap 5-03-67
Tizoc 9-11-57
Tjaerehandleren 8-25-71
Tjorven, Batsman Och Moses 8-18-65
Tkies Khaf 9-21-38
Tko Pjeva Zlo Ne Misli 8-11-71

Tlayucan 7-04-62
To 7-07-65
To a Finish 10-28-21
To Allo Gramma 10-27-76
To an Unknown God (See: A Un Dios Desconocido)
To Be a Student (See: Student Sein)
To Be Afraid and Make Others Afraid (See: Angst Haben Und Angst
    Machen)
To Be Free (See: Etre Libre)
To Be Free 10-25-72
To Be or Not to Be 2-18-42
To Be 20 in the Aures (See: Avoir 20 Ans Dans les Aures)
To Beat the Band 11-27-35
To Catch a Thief 7-20-55
To Cherish and Protect 8-27-15
To Chroniko Mias Kyriakis 11-05-75
To Defend My Love (See: Difendo Il Mio Amore)
To Die for Nothing (See: Morire Gratis)
To Each His Hell (See: A Chacun Son Enfer)
To Each His Life (See: Cada Quien Su Vida)
To Each His Own (See: A Ciascuno Il Suo)
To Each His Own 3-13-46
To Find a Man 1-26-72
To Forget Venice 1-23-80
To Grab the Ring 7-17-68
To Have and Have Not 10-11-44
To Have and Hold 11-10-22
To Have and to Hold 3-03-16
To Hell and Back 7-20-55
To Hell with School (See: Zum Teufel Mit Der Penne)
To Hell with the Kaiser 7-05-18
To Hell with This Priest (See: Al Diablo con Este Cura)
To Him That Hath 9-13-18
To Homa Vaftike Kokkino 7-20-66
To Ingrid My Love, Lisa 3-26-69
To Kelli Miden 11-05-75
To Kill a Mockingbird 12-12-62
To Kill in Silence 6-28-72
To Kill This Love (See: Trzeba Zabic Te Milosc)
To Koritsi Me Ta Mara 5-16-56
To Leave (See: Partir)
To Liv 1-22-47
To Live (See: Vivere or Ikaru)
To Live a Long Life 6-25-80
To Live in Peace 11-26-47
To Love (See: Att Alska)
To Love Again 7-14-71
To Love Ophelia (See: Per Amare Ofelia)
To Love the Damned (See: Maledetti Vi Amero')
To Mary--With Love 9-02-36
To Mega Docoumento 10-31-79
To New Shores (See: Zu Neuen Ufern)
To Nhei the Equeh 9-10-58
To Oblige a Lady 3-04-31
To Paris with Love 1-19-55
To Please a Lady 10-04-50
To Please One Woman 12-24-20
To Proxenio Tis Annas 11-15-72
To Return (See: Volver)
To Search for a Golden Earth (See: Kdo Hleda Zlate Dno)
To Sir, With Love 6-14-67
To Squeal (See: Zinker, Der)
To Telefteo Psemma 5-21-58
To the Ballot Boxes, Citizens (See: Aux Urnes, Citoyens)
To the Devil a Daughter 3-10-76
To the Ends of the Earth (See: In Capo al Mondo)
To the Ends of the Earth 1-21-48
To the Eyes of Memory (See: Aux Yeux du Souvenir)
To the Four Winds (See: A Los Cuatro Vientos)
To the Highest Bidder 7-19-18
To the Ladies 11-29-23
To the Last Drop (See: Ate a Ultima Gota)
To the Last Man 8-30-23
To the Last Man 10-31-33
To the Point, Darling (See: Zur Sache, Schatzchen)
To the Polls, Citizens (See: Aux Urnes, Citoyens)
To the Shores of Tripoli 3-11-42
To the Victor 3-31-48
To Trap a Spy 2-16-66
To Woody Allen, from Europe with Love 12-17-80
Toa 11-30-49
Toast of New Orleans, The 8-30-50
Toast of New York 7-14-37
Toast to Love 11-21-51
Tobacco (See: Tutune)
Tobacco Road 2-26-41
Tobi 1-17-79
Toboggan 4-17-34

Tobogganing in Switzerland 3-14-13
Tobor the Great 9-01-54
Tobruk 12-21-66
Toby Tyler 1-13-60
Toccata and Fugue in D Minor 10-16-46
Tod des Fischers Marc Leblanc, Der 4-27-77
Tod des Flohzirkusdirektors Oder Ottocaro Weiss Reformiert Seine
    Firma, Der 8-22-73
Tod oder Freiheit 3-29-78
Toda Nudez Sera Castigada 5-30-73 and 7-11-73
Today 6-15-17
Today 11-19-30
Today I Hang 3-11-42
Today Is for the Championship 7-23-80
Today We Live 4-18-33
Todd Killings, The 8-18-71
Todd of the Times 1-25-19
Todesmagazin Oder Wie Werde Ich ein Blumentopf? 12-05-79
Todesschuesse am Broadway 6-11-69
Todo Modo 3-26-80
Todo un Caballero 8-13-47
Todo un Hombre 11-17-43
Together 10-11-18
Together 6-06-56
Together 1-12-72
Together Again 11-08-44
Together Brothers 8-14-74
Together for Days 12-06-72
Together We Live 10-23-35
Toha--Hero of Southern Bandung 7-24-63
Toi Ashita 4-23-80
Toi Ippon No Michi 2-22-78
Toi Le Venom 11-19-58
Toilers, The 10-31-28
Toilers of the Sea 11-22-23
Tokaji Rapszodia 2-16-38
Tokay Rhapsody (See: Tokaji Rapszodia)
Tokio Siren, A 6-18-20
Toklat 12-29-71
Tokoloshe 10-27-71
Tokyo After Dark 2-04-59
Tokyo File 212 4-25-51
Tokyo Joe 10-12-49
Tokyo Olympiad 5-26-65
Tokyo Rose 12-05-45
Tokyo Senso Sengo Hiwa 7-21-71
Tol'able David 1-06-22
Tol'able David 11-19-30
Told at Twilight 3-09-17
Told in the Hills 9-12-19
Toll Gate 4-23-20
Toll of Mammon 6-26-14
Toll of the Desert 1-15-36
Toll of the Sea 12-01-22
Tolldreisten Frauen des Honore de Balzac, Die (See: Brazen
    Women of Balzac, The)
Tolle Lola, Die 12-21-27
Toller Einfall, Ein 5-31-32
Toller Hecht auf Krummer Tour 2-21-62
Tom 10-03-73
Tom and His Pals 1-19-27
Tom Brown of Culver 8-02-32
Tom Brown's School Days 6-26-40
Tom Brown's Schooldays 5-02-51
Tom, Dick and Harry 7-16-41
Tom Horn 4-02-80
Tom Jones 7-31-63
Tom Sawyer 12-07-17
Tom Sawyer 12-24-30
Tom Sawyer 2-16-38
Tom Sawyer 3-14-73
Tom Sawyer, Detective 2-15-39
Tom Thumb (See: Petit Poucet, Le)
Tom Thumb 12-03-58
Tom Thumb 10-25-67
Tomahawk 1-10-51
Tomahawk Trail, The 1-02-57
Tomas--A Child You Cannot Reach (See: Tomas--et Barn, du Ikke
    Kan naa)
Tomas--et Barn, du Ikke Kan naa 12-03-80
Tomasa 10-01-69
Tomb of Ligeia 1-20-65
Tomb of the Angels (See: Fossa Degli Angeli, La)
Tombe du Ciel 9-04-46
Tombolo 12-28-49
Tomboy 5-15-40
Tomboy, The (See: Sao Jomken)
Tombstone 6-17-42

Tombstone Canyon 4-11-33
Tomi (See: A Megfagyott Gyermek)
Tommy 2-03-37
Tommy 3-12-75
Tommy the Toreador 1-13-60
Tomorrow 9-16-70
Tomorrow 2-02-72
Tomorrow and Tomorrow 2-02-32
Tomorrow at Seven 7-04-33
Tomorrow, China (See: Demain, La Chine)
Tomorrow, I'll Commit Suicide (See: Manana Me Suicido)
Tomorrow Is Another Day (See: Domani e Un Altro Giorno)
Tomorrow Is Another Day 8-15-51
Tomorrow Is Forever 1-16-46
Tomorrow Is Too Late (See: Domani e Troppo Tardi)
Tomorrow It Will Be Better (See: Morgen Gaat Het Beter)
Tomorrow, My Love (See: I Morgen, Min Elskede)
Tomorrow Never Comes 3-01-78
Tomorrow, Pheasant (See: Holnap Lesz Facan)
Tomorrow the World 12-20-44
Tomorrow We Live 3-17-43
Tomorrow's a Wonderful Day 4-13-49
Tomorrow's Another Day (See: Manana Sera Otro Dia)
Tomorrow's Children (See: Demain les Momes)
Tomorrow's Love 1-07-25
Tomorrow's Yesterday 4-15-64
Tomoyuki Yamashita 7-08-53
Tong Man, The 12-19-19
Tongue of Scandal, The 4-09-10
Tongues of Flame 12-20-18
Tongues of Flame 12-17-24
Tongues of Men, The 1-28-16
Tongues of Scandal 6-29-27
Toni 6-20-28
Toni 3-19-35
Tonight a Town Dies 8-02-61
Tonight and Every Night 1-31-45
Tonight at 11 (See: Stanotte All Undici)
Tonight at Twelve 9-25-29
Tonight Is Ours 1-24-33
Tonight or Never (See: Ce Soir Ou Jamais or Heute Nacht Oder Nie)
Tonight or Never 12-22-31
Tonight the Skirts Fly (See: Ce Soir les Jupons Volent)
Tonight We Raid Calais 3-31-43
Tonight We Sing 1-28-53
Tonight's the Night (See: Notte Brava, La)
Tonio Kroeger 9-16-64
Tonite Let's All Make Love in London 10-04-67
Tonka 12-17-58
Tonka Sibenice 3-19-30
Tonnerre de Dieu, Le 10-06-65
Tonny on the Wrong Road 7-04-62
Tons of Money 1-14-31
Tonto Basin Outlaws 11-26-41
Tontons Flingueurs, Les 12-25-63 and 4-15-64
Tony America 10-11-18
Tony Draws a Horse 5-23-51
Tony Rome 11-08-67
Too Bad She's Bad (See: Peccato Che Sia Una Canaglia)
Too Busy to Work 12-06-32
Too Busy to Work 11-01-39
Too Dangerous to Live 4-19-39
Too Fat to Fight 12-06-18
Too Hot to Handle 9-21-38
Too Hot to Handle 9-28-60
Too Late Blues 11-08-61
Too Late for Tears 4-13-49
Too Late the Hero 5-06-70
Too Lean for Love? (See: Fuer Die Liebe Nach Zu Mager?)
Too Little for Such a Big War (See: Prea Mic Pentru Um Razboi
    Atit De Mare)
Too Many Blondes 5-21-41
Too Many Cooks 8-18-31
Too Many Crooks 7-04-19
Too Many Crooks 2-18-59
Too Many Girls 10-09-40
Too Many Husbands 3-06-40
Too Many Kisses 3-04-25
Too Many Millions 12-13-18
Too Many on the Job 10-16-09
Too Many Parents 4-22-36
Too Many Winners 6-04-47
Too Many Wives 4-28-37
Too Much Business 5-05-22
Too Much Champagne 3-14-08
Too Much Harmony 9-26-33
Too Much Is Too Much (See: Trop C'Est Trop)
Too Much Money 3-24-26
Too Much Speed 6-10-21

Toward the Unknown 9-26-56
Towards Ecstasy (See: Vers L'Extase)
Towards Joy (See: Till Gladje)
Tower of Lies, The 9-30-25
Tower of London 11-22-39
Tower of Nesle, The (See: Tour de Nesle, La)
Tower of Terror 4-24-14
Tower of Terror 7-01-42
Towering Inferno, The 12-18-74
Towing 5-24-78
Town Bloody Hall 3-19-80
Town Called Hell, A 10-20-71
Town Is All Upset, A (See: Stadt Steht Kopf)
Town Is Full of Secrets, The (See: Stadt Ist Voller Geheimnisse,
    Die)
Town Like Alice, A 3-14-56
Town on Trial 2-06-57
Town Scandal, The 4-26-23
Town Tale (See: Pueblerina)
Town Tamer 8-04-65
Town That Dreaded Sundown, The 1-26-77
Town That Forgot God, The 11-03-22
Town Went Wild, The 4-11-45
Town Without Pity 10-11-61
Toxi 9-17-52
Toy, The (See: Jouet, Le)
Toy Tiger 4-18-56
Toy Wife, The 6-08-56
Toymaker, the Doll, and the Devil, The 12-03-10
Toymaker's Secret, The 1-22-10
Toys Are Not for Children 6-21-72
Toys in the Attic 6-26-63
Toys on a Field of Blue 10-18-61
Tozi Istinski Musch 9-24-75
Tracassin, Le 1-31-62
Trace of a Girl (See: Spur Eines Madchens)
Traces (See: Wechma)
Traces of a Black-Haired Girl (See: Tragovi Crne Devojke)
Track of the Cat 11-10-54
Track of Thunder 2-14-68
Trackdown 3-31-76
Tracked 11-14-28
Tracked by the Police 6-15-27
Tracked in the Snow Country 7-22-25
Tracked to Earth 3-31-22
Tracks 5-19-76
Tracy's G-Men 8-16-39
Trade Winds 12-21-38
Trader Horn 2-11-31
Trader Horn 6-13-73
Trader Hornee 6-17-70
Tradition 7-08-21
Tradition de Minuit, La 5-24-39
Traditions, My Behind (See: Rend Mig I Traditionerne)
Traellenes Oproer 10-17-79
Traemunde Mund, Der 10-18-32
Traffic (See: Trafic)
Traffic Cop, The 4-07-16
Traffic in Crime 10-09-46
Traffic in Hearts 6-25-24
Traffic in Souls 11-28-13
Trafic 5-05-71
Tragedies of Crystal Globe 7-09-15
Tragedy at Midnight, A 3-04-42
Tragedy in the Career of General Villa, The 5-15-14
Tragedy of Love 7-25-79
Tragedy of the Mill, The 1-15-10
Tragedy of Youth 3-21-28
Tragic Adventure, A 3-19-10
Tragic Chase (See: Caccia Tragica)
Tragic Spell (See: Incantesimo Tragico)
Tragodie Tou Aegaeou 11-21-62
Tragovi Crne Devojke 7-26-72
Traidor, El 4-13-38
Traidores, Los 6-19-74
Traidores de San Angel, Los 11-08-67
Trail Blazers, The 10-30-40
Trail Drive 2-03-37
Trail Guide 1-23-52
Trail of a Cigarette, The 7-23-20
Trail of Horse Thieves 2-13-29
Trail of '98, The 3-28-28
Trail of Robin Hood, The 12-20-50
Trail of Terror 3-08-44
Trail of the Axe 10-06-22
Trail of the Golden West 2-18-31
Trail of the Law 1-31-24
Trail of the Lonesome Pine 2-11-16

Trail of the Lonesome Pine 3-22-23
Trail of the Lonesome Pine 2-26-36
Trail of the Mounties 7-20-49
Trail of the Octopus 10-24-19
Trail of the Shadow, The 7-13-17
Trail of the Silver Spurs 1-22-41
Trail of the Vigilantes 12-11-40
Trail of the Yukon 8-03-49 and 10-12-49
Trail of Vengeance 6-23-37
Trail Riders, The 5-06-25
Trail Street 2-26-47
Trail to San Antone 1-29-47
Trail to Yesterday, The 5-10-18
Trailin' 1-06-22
Trailin' West 10-21-36
Trailing African Wilds 4-19-23
Trailing Double Trouble 12-04-40
Trailing North 6-06-33
Trailing the Killer 12-06-32
Trailing Trouble 4-02-30
Trailing Trouble 12-29-37
Trail's End, The 8-11-22
Trail's End, The 7-06-49
Trails of Danger 1-21-31
Trails of the Wild 12-04-35 and 12-16-36
Train, Le 11-28-73
Train, The (See: Train, Le)
Train, The 9-30-64
Train for Venice, The (See: Train Pour Venise, Le)
Train Goes East, The 9-07-49
Train in the Snow (See: Vlak U Snijegu)
Train of Events 8-24-49
Train Pour Venise, Le 10-05-38
Train Ride to Hollywood 11-05-75
Train Robbers, The 1-31-73
Train Rouge, Le 8-29-73
Train to Alcatraz 7-14-48
Train to Tombstone 9-06-50
Train Without a Timetable (See: Vlak Bez Vosnog Reda)
Trained Birds 10-02-09
Training Bulls for the Fight 9-11-09
Traitement de Choc 2-14-73
Traitor, The (See: Verraeter or Traidor, El)
Traitor, The 11-04-36
Traitor Within, The 12-02-42
Traitors (See: Verraeter or Traidores, Los)
Traitors 1-30-57
Traitors of San Angel, The (See: Traidores de San Angel, Los)
Tramp, The 6-19-14
Tramp Dog, The 2-09-07
Tramp, Tramp, Tramp 5-26-26
Tramp, Tramp, Tramp 4-01-42
Trampa 2-28-79
Tramplers, The 7-06-66
Tranquillo Posto di Campagna, Un 7-09-69
Trans-Europe-Express 1-18-67
Transatlantic 8-04-31
Transatlantic Merry-Go-Round 11-06-34
Transatlantic Tunnel 10-30-35
Transatlantiques, Les 3-21-28
Transgression 6-16-31
Transient Lady 3-13-35
Transit 2-20-80
Transmigration of Souls (See: Seelenwanderung)
Transport from Paradise (See: Transport z Raje)
Transport of Fire 4-01-31
Transport z Raje 2-13-63
Trap, The (See: Piege, Le)
Trap, The 4-05-18
Trap, The 5-05-22
Trap, The 2-04-59
Trap, The 9-21-66
Trap, The 6-18-80
Trap for Cinderella (See: Piege Pour Cendrillon)
Trapeni (See: Sorrows of Lenka, The)
Trapeze 5-10-32 and 2-20-34
Trapeze 5-30-56
Trapp Familie, Die 6-12-57
Trapp Familie in Amerika, Die 4-08-59
Trapp Family, The 3-08-61 (Also see: Trapp Familie, Die)
Trapp Family in America, The (See: Trapp Familie in Amerika, Die)
Trapped 5-13-31
Trapped 4-28-37
Trapped 9-28-49
Trapped by Boston Blackie 4-28-48
Trapped by Camera 12-11-14
Trapped by G-Men 11-10-37

Trapped by Television 6-17-36
Trapped in a Submarine 2-09-32
Trapped in Tangiers 7-06-60
Trapped in the Sky 5-03-39
Trapper and the Redskins, The 2-26-10
Trappers, The 10-16-09
Traque, La 5-21-75
Trara um Liebe 9-22-31
Trash 9-30-70
Trastevere 1-19-72
Trastienda, La 7-21-76
Tratta Delle Bianche, La 11-12-52 (Also see: Girls Marked
    Danger)
Traum vom Rhein, Der 12-11-35
Traum von Lieschen Mueller, Der 1-17-62
Traum von Schonbrunn 6-06-33
Trauma 10-30-63
Traumende Mund, Der (See: Melo)
Traumstadt 10-09-74
Traumstrasse der Welt 7-09-58
Traumulus 2-26-36 and 9-23-36
Travail C'Est la Liberte, Le 2-10-60
Travelin' On 3-17-22
Traveling Companion (See: Companero de Viaje)
Traveling Companions (See: Petschki-Lawotschki)
Traveling Executioner, The 10-07-70
Traveling Husbands 8-11-31
Traveling Saleslady, The 4-03-35
Traveling Salesman, The 12-29-16
Traveling Salesman, The 4-29-21
Traveling Saleswoman, The 12-28-49
Traveller's Joy 4-18-51
Travels of a Flea 4-18-08
Travels on the Sly (See: Voyage en Douce, Le)
Travels with Anita 2-14-79
Travels with My Aunt 12-06-72
Traversee de Paris, La 9-19-56
Traviata, La (See: Lost One, The)
Traviata, La 2-28-68
Traviesa Molinera, La 11-06-34
Travolti Da Un Insolito Destino Nell'Azzurro Mare d'Agosto
    1-01-75
Trawler Fishing in a Hurricane 4-30-10
Tre Mand Frem For En Trold 3-22-67
Tre Scener Med Ingmar Bergman 11-12-75
Tre Storie Proibite 12-10-52
Tre Tigri Contro Tre Tigri 11-23-77
Tre Volti, I 2-24-65
Treachery Rides the Range 6-03-36
Treadowata 2-02-77
Treason (See: Prodossia)
Treason 5-04-17
Treason Trial 3-11-31
Treasure, The (See: Nidhanaya or Schatz, Der)
Treasure, The 11-27-29
Treasure, The 4-18-51
Treasure Island 1-18-18
Treasure Island 4-16-20
Treasure Island 8-21-34
Treasure Island 6-21-50
Treasure Island 11-01-72
Treasure of Cantenac, The (See: Tresor de Cantenac, Le)
Treasure of Lost Canyon 2-13-52
Treasure of Maciel Island, The (See: Tesoro de la Isla Maciel,
    El)
Treasure of Matecumbe 7-07-76
Treasure of Monte Cristo 9-21-49
Treasure of Pancho Villa, The 9-28-55
Treasure of Ruby Hills, The 3-16-55
Treasure of San Teresa 12-23-59
Treasure of Silver Lake (See: Schatz im Silbersee, Der)
Treasure of the Golden Condor 1-21-53
Treasure of the Sierra Madre, The 1-07-48
Treasure of the Wrecked Vessel 1-01-36
Treasure of Zapata, The (See: O Tesouro De Zapata)
Treasured Earth 1-10-51
Treat 'Em Rough 1-17-19
Treat 'Em Rough 1-21-42
Tredowata 1-06-37
Tredowata 2-02-77
Tree, The 6-11-69
Tree Grows in Brooklyn, A 1-24-45
Tree of Guernica, The (See: Arbre de Guernica, L')
Tree of Knowledge 1-16-20
Tree of Wooden Clogs, The (See: Albero Degli Zoccoli, L')
Tree Without Fruit (See: Hedelmaton Puu)
Tree Without Roots, A (See: Drvo Bez Koren)
Trees Are Blooming in Vienna (See: im Prater Blueh'n Wieder die
    Baeume)

Trefle a Cinq Feuilles, Le 9-20-72
Tregua, La 9-04-74
Treichville 3-11-59
Treize a Table 4-11-56
Trek, The (See: Pohod)
Trembling Hour, The 11-21-19
Tremendously Rich Man, A (See: Steinreicher Mann, Ein)
Tren 9-05-79
Tren Internacional 12-15-54
Trenck 11-22-32
Trener 8-16-78
Trenta Secondi d'Amore 4-07-37
Trent's Last Case 11-05-52
Tres Argentinos en Paris 2-02-38
Tres Cabras de Lampaio 9-12-62
Tres En Raya 9-12-79
Tres Hombres del Rio 5-19-43
Tres Mosqueteros, Las 10-28-42
Tres Ratas, Las 9-11-46
Tres Reyes Magos, Los 7-14-76
Tres Romeos y Una Julieta 5-31-61
Tres Tristes Tigres 9-06-61
Tres Tristes Tigres 1-15-69
Tres Veces Ana 4-11-62 and 7-04-62
Tresor de Cantenac, Le 3-15-50
Trespasser, The 9-18-29 and 10-02-29
Trespasser, The 7-09-47
Trespassers, The 6-09-76
Treve, La 3-26-69
Trey O'Hearts, The 8-07-14
Tri 7-20-66
Tri Ane 8-10-60
Tri Cetvrtine Sunca 8-12-59
Tri Dcery 6-26-68
Tri Koraka U Prazno 8-20-58
Tri Sata Zsa Ljuhav 8-21-68
Tri Topolia Na Pliushiche 7-02-69
Trial 8-03-55
Trial, The (See: Strange Case of Mary Page, The: Part II or
    Prozess, Der)
Trial, The 1-02-63
Trial Marriage 4-17-29
Trial of Billy Jack, The 11-13-74
Trial of Daniel Westhof, The 2-22-28
Trial of Joan of Arc, The (See: Proces de Jeanne d'Arc)
Trial of Mary Dugan, The 4-03-29 (Also see: Mordprozess Mary
    Dugan)
Trial of Mary Dugan, The 2-12-41
Trial of Sergeant Rutledge, The 4-13-60
Trial of the Catonsville Nine, The 5-10-72
Trial of the Judges, The (See: I Diki Ton Dikaston)
Trial of Vivienne Ware, The 5-03-32
Trial Without Jury 7-19-50
Trials of Alger Hiss, The 3-12-80
Trials of Oscar Wilde, The 6-01-60
Triangle (See: Triangulo)
Triangle Ecorche, Le 4-09-75
Triangle of Four (See: Triangle de Cuatro)
Triangulo 9-06-72
Triangulo de Cuatro 7-30-75
Tribulations d'Un Chinois en Chine, Les 10-27-65
Tribute 12-03-80
Tribute to a Bad Man 3-21-56
Tricheurs, Les 12-03-58
Trick Baby 1-10-73
Trick for Trick 6-13-33
Trick of Fate, A 2-14-19
Trick of Hearts, A 3-21-28
Tricky Dummies 9-18-09
Tricky Game of Love, The (See: Hry Lasky Salive)
Tricky Twins 8-08-08
Tricyclist, The (See: Triporteur, Le)
Triflers 1-09-20
Trifling with Honor 5-30-23
Trifling Women 10-06-22
Trigger Fingers 1-21-25
Trigger Fingers 12-20-39
Trigger, Jr. 7-05-50
Trigger Pals 1-11-39
Trigger Smith 4-05-39
Trigger Tricks 6-25-30
Trigger Trio 12-15-37
Trilby 9-10-15
Trilby 7-26-23
Trilogie des Wiedersehens 5-23-79
Trilogy of Wiedersehens (See: Trilogie des Wiedersehens)
Trimmed in Scarlet 4-19-23
Trinity Is Still My Name (See: Continuavano a Chiamarlo Trinita)

258

Trio 8-09-50
Trio 5-03-67
Trio Infernal, Le 5-15-74
Triomphe de Michel Strogoff, Le 1-17-62
Trionfo Dell'Amore, Il 4-06-38
Triorama 2-18-53
Trip, The (See: Viaggio, Il)
Trip, The 8-16-67
Trip Across Paris, The (See: Traversee de Paris, La)
Trip Along the Rhine, A 3-26-10
Trip Around My Cranium (See: Utazas A Koponyam Korul)
Trip Through China (See: Promenade en Chine)
Trip Through Purgatory (See: Voyage en Grande Tartarie)
Trip Through Scotland, A 11-12-10
Trip Through the Rocky and Selkirk Mountains in Canada, A
    11-19-10
Trip Thru China, A 5-18-17
Trip to America, A 10-29-52
Trip to Biarritz, The (See: Voyage a Biarritz, Le)
Trip to Mars, A 2-26-10
Trip to Mars, A 7-18-19
Trip to Paradise, A 10-07-21
Trip to Paramountown, A 7-07-22
Trip to Paris, A 6-15-38
Trip to the Argentine, A 12-03-15
Trip to the Centre of the Earth (See: Viaje Al Centro de la
    Tierra)
Trip to the Isle of Jersey 9-24-10
Trip to Yosemite, A 10-09-09
Tripes au Soleil, Les 3-18-59
Triple Cross 12-21-66
Triple Death of the Third Character, The (See: Triple Mort du
    Troisieme Personnage, La)
Triple Death of the Third Personage, The (See: Triple Mort du
    Troisieme Personnage)
Triple Echo, The 5-23-73
Triple Irons 10-17-73
Triple Justice 10-09-40
Triple Mort du Troisieme Personnage, La 10-03-79 and 7-30-80
Triple Threat 9-29-48
Triple Trouble 9-13-50
Tripoli 10-11-50
Triporteur, Le 3-12-58
Tristan and Isolde (See: Tristan et Iseult)
Tristan et Iseult 7-18-73
Tristana 4-08-70
Triumph 9-07-17
Triumph 4-23-24
Triumph of Love (See: Trionfo Dell'Amore, Il)
Triumph of Love 4-23-47
Triumph of Michael Strogoff, The (See: Triomphe de Michael
    Strogoff, Le)
Triumph of Right 4-03-14
Triumph of Sherlock Holmes, The 5-29-35
Triumph of the Scarlet Pimpernel 12-05-28
Triumph of the Weak, The 5-10-18
Triumph of Venus, The 3-01-18
Trixie from Broadway 6-06-19
Trocadero 4-26-44
Trocadero Bleu Citron 9-27-78
Trocadero Blue and Yellow (See: Trocadero Bleu Citron)
Troe Sutok Posle Bessmertiya (See: Three Days After Immortality)
Trofej 8-15-79
Trog 9-30-70
Troika 12-10-69
Trois Chambres a Manhattan 9-15-65
Trois Enfants Dans le Desordre 6-15-66
Trois Femmes 5-14-52
Trois Femmes 8-12-64
Trois Font la Paire, Les 7-10-57
Trois Garcons, Une Fille 1-26-49
Trois Hommes a Abattre 11-12-80
Trois Hommes Sur un Cheval 1-14-70
Trois Jours a Vivre 5-07-58
Trois Masques, Les 11-20-29
Trois Milliards Sans Ascenseur 11-01-72
Trois Mousquetaires, Les (See: Three Musketeers, The)
Trois Mousquetaires, Les 5-09-33
Trois Mousquetaires, Les 11-25-53
Trois Mousquetaires, Les 11-01-61
Trois Valses 1-25-39
Troisieme Cri, Le 8-28-74
Trojan Brothers 1-02-46
Trojan Women, The 6-02-71
Troll 5-23-73
Trollenberg Terror, The 10-15-58
Tromba, the Tiger Man 11-19-52
Trompe l'Oeil 3-19-75

Troop B, 16th Cavalry in Maneuvers 1-22-10
Trooper Hook 6-26-57
Trooper O'Neil 7-28-22
Troopers Three 2-19-30
Troopship 4-27-38
Trop C'Est Trop 6-18-75
Trop Jolies Pour Etre Honnetes 12-20-72
Trop Petit Mon Ami 10-21-70
Tropen Nachte 5-27-31
Trophy (See: Trofej)
Tropic Fury 9-13-39
Tropic Holiday 7-06-38
Tropic of Cancer 2-18-70
Tropic Zone 12-17-52
Tropical Ecstasy 10-07-70
Tropical Heat Wave 10-01-52
Tropical Nights (See: Tropen Nachte)
Tropical Nights 2-20-29
Tropici 10-02-68
Tropics (See: Tropici)
Trotta 12-08-71 and 5-24-72
Trotte Teodor 1-26-32
Trottie True 8-17-49
Trou, Le 4-13-60
Trou Dans le Mur, Un 6-18-30
Trou Normand, Le 2-18-53
Troubador, The 3-26-10
Troubib, Le 12-12-79
Trouble 5-26-22
Trouble Ahead 10-21-36
Trouble Along the Way 3-18-53
Trouble Among Widows (See: Du Grabuge Chez Les Veuves)
Trouble at Midnight 11-10-37
Trouble Buster, The 10-12-17
Trouble-Fesses, Le 10-13-76
Trouble-Fete 5-20-64
Trouble for Two 6-03-36
Trouble in Bahia for O.S.S. 117 (See: Furia a Bahia Pour O.S.S.
    117)
Trouble in Morocco 3-17-37
Trouble in Paradise 11-15-32
Trouble in Store 12-30-53
Trouble in Sundown 7-05-39
Trouble in Texas 7-07-37
Trouble in the Glen 6-30-54
Trouble-maker, The (See: Stoerfried, Der)
Trouble Makers 12-22-48
Trouble Man 11-08-72
Trouble Preferred 1-19-49
Trouble with Angels, The 3-30-66
Trouble with Girls, The 5-14-69
Trouble with Harry, The 10-12-55
Trouble with Wives, The 8-05-25
Trouble with Women, The 7-16-47
Troubled Heart (See: Coeur Ebloui, Le)
Troublemaker, The 7-01-64
Troubles of a Bride 5-06-25
Troubles of Alfred, The (See: Malheurs d'Alfred, Les)
Troublesome Wives 9-12-28
Trouper, The 7-21-22
Trouping with Ellen 12-03-24
Trout (See: Truchas, Las)
Trovatore, Il 8-24-49
Truands, Les 6-13-56
Truant Husband, The 1-28-21
Truce, The (See: Treve, La or Tregua, La)
Truchas, Las 3-15-78
Truck, The (See: Camion, Le)
Truck Busters 1-20-43
Truck It 2-21-73
Truck Stop Women 11-13-74
Truck Turner 6-26-74
True and the False, The 1-19-55
True As a Turtle 6-18-24
True As Steel 6-18-24
True Blue 6-07-18
True Confession 11-24-37
True Friends 12-22-54
True Gang Murders 12-06-61
True Grit 5-21-69
True Heart Susie 6-06-19
True Heaven 2-13-29
True Jacob, The (See: Wahre Jacob, Der)
True Life of Dracula, The (See: Vlad Tepes)
True Love 10-23-68
True Nature of Bernadette, The (See: Vraie Nature de Bernadette,
    La)
True Nobility 3-24-16

True Story of Eskimo Nell, The 4-09-75
True Story of Jesse James, The 2-20-57
True Story of Lynn Stuart, The 2-19-58
True to His Oath 1-22-10
True to Life 8-11-43
True to the Army 3-18-42
True to the Navy 5-28-30
Trueno Entre Las Hojas, El 9-04-57
Trufflers, The 3-30-17
Truman Capote's Trilogy 11-05-69
Trumpet Blows, The 4-17-34
Trumpet Call, The 5-21-15
Trumpet Call of Love (See: Trara Um Liebe)
Trumpet Island 10-22-20
Trumpeter, The (See: A Trombitas)
Trunk to Cairo 1-11-67
Trust (See: Doverie)
Trust Your Wife 2-17-22
Trusted Outlaw 4-14-37
Truth, The (See: Verite, La)
Truth, The 9-03-20
Truth About Africa, The 4-18-33
Truth About Bebe Donge, The (See: Verite Sur Bebe Donge, La)
Truth About Husbands, The 12-17-20
Truth About Murder, The 4-24-46
Truth About Rosemarie, The (See: Wahrheit Ueber Rosemarie, Die)
Truth About Spring, The 3-24-65
Truth About Women, The 10-15-24
Truth About Women, The 2-12-58
Truth About Youth, The 12-17-30
Truth on the Savolta Affair, The (See: Verdad Sobre El Caso Savolta, La)
Truth Wagon, The 4-23-15
Truthful Liar, The 4-28-22
Truthful Sex, The 2-02-27
Truthful Tulliver 12-29-15
Truxa 2-24-37
Truxton King 4-05-23
Try and Get It 4-02-24
Trygon Factor, The 1-01-69
Tryptych 6-18-80
Trzeba Zabic Te Milosc 6-01-77
Trzeciej Czesci Nocy 9-22-71
Tsar to Lenin 3-10-37
Tschetan, Der Indianerjunge 4-18-73
Tschushije Pissma 3-09-77
Tsekloput (See: Cyclops)
Tsenu Smerti Sprosi u Miortvykh 8-29-79
Tsuyomushi Onna To Yowamushi Otoko 7-24-68
Tu Eres la Paz 9-23-42
Tu M'ami--To T'amo 3-31-43
Tu Me Enloqueces 9-22-76
Tu Moisonnera la Tempete 6-25-69
Tu Ne Tueras Point 8-30-61
Tu Seras Duchesse 3-08-32 and 5-17-32
Tu Seras Terriblement Gentille 4-10-68
Tucker's Top Hand 7-16-24
Tucson 5-04-49
Tudor 4-15-64
Tudor Rose (See: Lady Jane Grey)
Tuer Geht Auf, Eine 2-07-33
Tuesday's Guest (See: Invite du Mardi, L')
Tueur, Le 3-15-72
Tugboat Annie 8-15-33
Tugboat Annie Sails Again 10-23-40
Tuhottu Nuoruns 5-05-48
Tukerkepek 2-09-77
Tulipani di Haarlem, I 5-27-70
Tulipe Noire, La 3-18-64
Tulips of Harlem, The (See: Tulipani di Haarlem, I)
Tulipunainen Kyykkynee 7-12-61
Tulsa 3-23-49
Tulsa Kid, The 7-31-40
Tumbledown Ranch in Arizona 5-21-41
Tumbleweed 11-18-53
Tumbleweed Trail, The 11-06-46
Tumbleweeds 12-23-25
Tumbling River 8-17-27
Tumbling Tumbleweeds 2-05-36
Tumult 10-01-69
Tumult of Sentiments (See: Flor de Mayo)
Tumult-Sonja, Age 16 (See: Tumult)
Tumultuous Honeymoon, A 11-13-09
Tuna Clipper 3-16-49
Tundra 12-09-36
Tunel, El 5-28-52
Tunes of Glory 9-14-60
Tunisian Victory 3-08-44

Tunnel, Der 12-05-33
Tunnel, The (See: Tunel, El or Tunnel, Der)
Tunnel, The 1-09-34
Tunnel of Love 10-15-58
Tunnel Warfare (See: Di Dao Chan)
Tunnelvision 4-07-76
Tunney-Dempsey Fight 9-28-27
Tunney-Heeney Fight 8-01-28
Tuntematon Sotilas 7-25-56
Turco Napoletano, Il 12-16-53
Turkey, The (See: Dindon, Le)
Turkish Delight (See: Turks Fruit)
Turks Fruit 3-21-73
Turksib 5-28-30
Turlupins, Les 3-05-80
Turmoil, The 12-31-24
Turn Back the Clock 8-29-33
Turn Back the Hours 5-02-28 and 5-09-28
Turn of a Card, The 3-15-18
Turn of the Handle, The (See: Retour de Manivelle)
Turn of the Road, The 3-21-19
Turn of the Tide, The 10-30-35
Turn of the Wheel, The 9-06-18
Turn Off the Moon 5-26-37
Turn On to Love 9-24-69
Turn the Key Softly 5-13-53
Turn the Other Cheek (See: Porgi L'Altra Guancia)
Turn to the Right 1-27-22
Turnabout 5-08-40
Turned Up 11-12-24
Turner the Journalist (See: Periodista Turner, El)
Turners of Prospect Road, The 3-26-47
Turning Point, The 3-12-24
Turning Point, The 10-30-46
Turning Point, The 9-17-52
Turning Point, The 10-19-77
Turning the Tables 11-07-19
Turning Wind, The (See: Barravento)
Tusk 3-26-80
Tute Cabrero 10-23-68
Tutte le Altre Ragazze Lo Fanno (See: All the Other Girls Do)
Tutte le Domeniche Mattina 9-13-72
Tutti a Casa (See: Everybody Go Home)
Tutti Figli di 'Mammasantissima' (See: Italian Graffiti)
Tutti Innamorati 5-13-59
Tuttles of Tahiti 3-18-42
Tutto a Posto e Niente in Ordine 8-14-74
Tutune 5-22-63
Tuulinen Paiva 7-31-63
Tuvia Vesheva Benotav 4-17-68
Tuxedo Junction 12-03-41
Tuzolto Utca 25 7-24-74
Tva Kvinnor 2-04-48
Tvaa Kvinnor 4-16-75
Tvarbalk 5-17-67
Tvoy Sovremenik 6-19-68
Twee Vrouwen 5-16-79
Twelfth Night, The 2-12-10
Twelfth Night, The 3-14-56
12 Angry Men 2-27-57
Twelve Chairs 7-24-63
Twelve Chairs, The (See: Dvenatets)
12 Chairs, The 10-28-70
12 Crowded Hours 3-01-39
12 Girls and One Man (See: 12 Maedchen und 1 Mann)
Twelve Hours by the Clock (See: Douze Heures D'Horloge)
Twelve Hours to Kill 5-04-60
12 Labors of Asterix, The (See: 12 Travaux d'Asterix, Les)
Twelve Miles Out 7-27-27
Twelve Months 6-25-80
12 O'Clock High 12-21-49
12 + 1 5-20-70
Twelve to the Moon 6-22-60
20th Century 5-08-34
$20 a Week 6-11-24
25th Hour, The 2-08-67
25 Fireman's Street (See: Tuzolto Utca 25)
25 Years a King 4-03-35
25 Years--Impressions 2-23-77
24 Eyes (See: Nijushi No Hitomi)
24 Hours 10-06-31
24 Hours in the Life of a Woman (See: Vingt Quatre Heures de la Vie d'une Femme)
24 Hours of a Woman's Life 9-17-52
24 Hours Out of the Life of a Woman (See: 24 Stunden Aus Dem Leben Einer Frau)
24 Hours with Ilse--Private Party (See: Et Doegn Med Ilse)

Twenty Girls and the Teachers (See: Zwanzig Maedchen und die Pauker)
20 Hours 7-21-65
20 Million Miles to Earth 6-12-57
20 Million Sweethearts 5-01-34
20 Mule Team 5-01-40
Twenty-One 4-05-18
Twenty-One 2-21-24
21 Days 5-03-39
21 Days in Europe 11-10-71
Twenty Plus Two 1-31-62
22nd Day, The (See: Baishey Stravana)
22nd June, 1897 2-13-80
27A 6-19-74
27 Down Bombay-Varanasi Express 8-28-74
27th Day, The 5-22-57
20,000 Eyes 7-05-61
20,000 Leagues Across Earth (See: 20,000 Lieues Sur la Terre)
20,000 Leagues Under the Sea 12-29-16
20,000 Leagues Under the Sea 12-15-54
20,000 Lieues Sur la Terre 3-08-61
20,000 Men a Year 10-25-39
20,000 Years in Sing-Sing 1-17-33
23 1/2 Hours Leave 10-13-19
23 1/2 Hours Leave 5-12-37
23 Paces to Baker Street 5-16-56
20 Years and One Night (See: Veinte Anos y Una Noche)
20 Years of the Academy Awards 3-31-48
Twice a Man 2-26-64
Twice a Woman (See: Twee Vrouwen)
Twice Blessed 5-30-45
Twice Born Woman, The 7-01-21
Twice Round the Daffodils 4-11-62
Twice Told Tales 9-25-63
Twice Wedding 9-03-30
Twilight 12-24-69
Twilight for the Gods 7-09-58
Twilight in the Sierras 4-05-50
Twilight of Honor 9-18-63
Twilight on the Rio Grande 4-16-47
Twilight on the Trail 10-01-41
Twilight Sleep, The 8-27-15 and 11-05-15
Twilight Story, The 10-18-61
Twilight's Last Gleaming 2-02-77
Twin Beds 11-05-20
Twin Beds 7-17-29
Twin Beds 4-22-42
Twin Husbands 5-29-34 and 7-17-34
Twin Maneuver (See: Manoever Zwilling)
Twin Pawns 10-03-19
Twin Sisters of Kyoto 12-11-63
Twinkle in God's Eye 10-12-55
Twinkletoes 12-29-26
Twinky 1-28-70
Twins 8-06-47
Twins of Evil 10-20-71
Twins of Suffering Creek 7-09-20
Twist, The (See: Folies Bourgeoises)
Twist Around the Clock 12-27-61
Twist of Sand, A 9-04-68
Twisted Nerve, The 12-11-68
Twisted Road, The 6-30-48
Two 7-31-74
Two a Penny 7-03-68
Two Against the World 8-23-32
Two Against the World 7-15-36
Two Alone 4-10-34
Two and Two Make Six 6-06-62
Two Angels and a Sinner (See: Dos Angeles y un Pecador)
Two Anonymous Letters 5-21-47
Two Arabian Nights 10-26-27
Two Before Zero 10-24-62
Two Blondes and a Redhead 12-03-47
Two Boys in Blue 10-29-10
Two Brides, The 4-25-19
Two Bright Boys 9-20-39
Two Brothers 8-22-28
Two Can Play 6-16-26
Two Careful Fellows (See: Dos Tipos de Cuidado)
Two Champions of Shaolin 7-02-80
Two Chums Looking for a Wife 11-20-09
Two Colonels, The (See: Due Colonelli, I)
Two Crowded Hours 7-21-31
Two Daughters (See: Teen Kanya)
Two Days 2-06-29
Two Days for Life (See: Zwei Tage Fuers Leben)
Two Disobedient Sons (See: Dos Hijos Desobedientes)
Two Dollar Bettor 9-26-51

$2 Haircut, The (See: Coupe a Dix Francs, La)
Two Edged Sword, The 4-07-16
Two English Girls and the Continent (See: Deux Anglaises et le Continent, Les)
Two Eyes--Twelve Hands (See: Do Ankhen Barah Haath)
Two Eyes, Twelve Hands 11-19-58
Two-Faced Woman 10-22-41
Two Faces of Dr. Jekyll, The 10-19-60
Two Fisted 10-09-35
Two-Fisted Gentleman 8-26-36
Two Fisted Justice 2-16-32
Two Fisted Justice 2-10-43
Two-Fisted Law 9-20-32
Two-Fisted Rangers 1-10-40
Two-Fisted Sheriff 8-25-37
Two Flags West 10-11-50
Two Flaming Youths 1-11-28
Two for Danger 4-03-40
Two for the Road 5-03-67
Two for the Seesaw 10-24-62
Two for Tonight 9-04-35
Two Gals and a Guy 6-06-51
Two Gentlemen Sharing 9-10-69
Two Girls and a Sailor 4-26-44
Two Girls on Broadway 4-24-40
Two Girls Wanted 9-21-27
Two Grooms for a Bride 6-19-57
Two-Gun Betty 1-10-19
Two Gun Justice 6-08-38
Two-Gun Lady 1-18-56
Two Gun Law 6-09-37
Two Gun Man 7-14-26
Two Gun Man 6-16-31
Two-Gun of Tumblewood 7-27-27
Two-Gun Sheriff 4-23-41
Two Gun Troubador 7-12-39
Two Guns and a Badge 9-15-54
Two Guys from Milwaukee 7-31-46
Two Guys from Texas 8-04-48
Two Half Times in Hell (See: Ket Felido A Pokolban)
Two-Headed Spy, The 11-26-58
Two Heads on a Pillow 10-09-34
Two Heartbeats 12-20-72
Two Hearts and One Heaven (See: Dos Corazones y un Cielo)
Two Hearts in Harmony 11-20-35
Two Hearts in One Beat (See: Zwei Herzen in Ein Schlag)
Two Hearts in 3/4 Time 4-02-30
Two Hearts in Waltz Time (See: Zwei Herzen im 3-4 Takt)
Two Hearts That Beat As One (See: Zwei Herzen in Ein Schlag)
Two Hours to Kill (See: Deux Heures a Tuer)
Two Humans (See: Zwei Menschen)
Two Hundred a Month (See: Havi 200 Fix)
200 Motels 11-03-71
Two in a Car (See: Zwei in einem Auto)
Two in a Crowd 10-07-36
Two in a Crowd 10-07-72
Two in a Taxi 9-17-41
Two in Revolt 4-29-36
Two in the Dark 2-05-36
Two in the Steppes 11-04-64
Two Kennedys, The (See: Due Kennedy, I)
Two Kinds of Women 2-03-22
Two Kinds of Women 1-19-32
Two Kouney Lemels 8-24-66
Two Ladies and a Beggar 5-08-09
Two-Lane Blacktop 6-23-71
Two Latins from Manhattan 10-01-41
Two Left Feet 5-19-65
Two Like Us (See: Zwei Wie Wir)
Two Lions in the Sun (See: Deux Lions au Soleil)
Two Little Bears, The 12-20-61
Two Little Imps 7-13-17
Two Little Vagabonds 2-04-25
Two Little Waifs 11-12-10
Two Lives (See: To Liv)
Two Lost Worlds 1-31-51
Two Love Crimes (See: Deux Crimes D'Amour)
Two Lovers 3-28-28
Two Lovers and a Coquette 8-28-09
Two Loves 5-03-61
Two-Man Submarine 3-29-43
Two Memories, The (See: Deux Memoires, Les)
Two Men and a Woman 2-23-17
Two Men in Manhattan (See: Deux Hommes Dans Manhattan)
Two Men in Town (See: Llegaron Dos Hombres or Deux Hommes Dans La Ville)
Two Men of Karamoja 5-08-74
Two-Minute Warning 11-03-76

Two Minutes to Go 10-28-21
Two Minutes to Play 10-13-37
Two Misanthropists, The (See: Due Misantropi, I)
Two Mr. Whites, The 10-30-09
Two Moons 1-28-21
Two Mothers, The (See: Due Madri, Le)
Two Mrs. Carrolls, The 4-02-47
Two Mules for Sister Sara 4-15-70
Two Natures Within Him, The 5-28-15
Two O'Clock Courage 4-18-45
Two of a Kind 6-13-51
Two of Them, The (See: Ok Ketten)
Two of Us, The 2-16-38
Two on a Guillotine 1-13-65
Two on a Vacation 12-10-47
Two or Three Things I Know About Her (See: Deux ou Trois Choses
    Que Je Sais D'Elle)
Two Orphans, The (See: Deux Orphelins, Les or Dos Huerianas, Las)
Two Orphans, The 9-10-15
Two Orphans, The 10-25-50
Two Outlaws 10-31-28
Two Paths, The 1-14-11
Two Pennies of Hope (See: Due Soldi di Speranza)
Two Pennies' Worth of Violets (See: Deux Sous de Violettes)
Two People (See: To)
Two People 3-14-73
Two Pieces of Bread (See: Due Pezzi di Pane)
Two Prisoners (See: Ket Fogoly)
Two Raffles 2-12-10
Two Rivals, The (See: Dos Rivales, Los)
Two Roads (See: Duvidha)
Two Rode Together 6-21-61
Two Seasons of Life (See: Deux Saisons de la Vie, Les)
Two Seconds 5-24-32
Two Senoritas from Chicago 6-23-43
Two Sides to a Story 12-04-09
Two Sinners 9-18-35
Two Sisters 7-03-29
Two Sisters 12-14-38
Two Sisters, The 9-17-10
Two Sisters from Boston 3-06-46
Two Smart People 6-05-46
Two Soldiers 8-02-44
Two Solitudes 8-23-78
Two Soul Woman, The 5-03-18
Two Super Cops (See: Deux Super Flics)
2001: A Space Odyssey 4-03-68
2076 Olympiad 6-22-77
2,000 Weeks 4-02-69
2,000 Women 9-13-44
2000 Years Later 2-26-69
Two Tickets to Broadway 10-10-51
Two Tickets to London 6-16-43
Two Tickets to Paris 9-26-62
Two Ties (See: Zwei Kravaten)
2 x 2 3-27-46
Two Truths, The (See: Deux Verites, Les)
Two Waifs and a Stray 9-24-10
Two-Way Stretch 2-03-60
Two Weeks 2-06-20
Two Weeks in Another Town 8-08-62
Two Weeks Off 6-26-29
Two Weeks to Live 2-03-43
Two Weeks--With Love 10-11-50
Two Weeks with Pay 5-27-21
Two Who Dared 6-16-37
Two Wise Maids 3-10-37
Two Wishes (See: Ket Vallomas)
Two Women (See: Tvaa Kvinnor or Tva Kvinnor)
Two Women 11-07-14 and 1-22-15
Two Women 11-06-40
Two Women 5-10-61
Two Women and a Man 11-20-09
Two Women in Gold (See: Deux Femmes en Or)
Two Worlds 8-13-30 and 10-15-30
2 Yanks in Trinidad 3-25-42
Two Years Before the Mast 8-28-46
Twonky, The 6-17-53
Two's Company 5-13-36
Tycoon 12-17-47
Tyomichen Paivakirja 7-19-67
Type Comme Moi Ne Devrait Jamais Mourir, Un 9-01-76
Typhon a Nagsaki 6-19-57
Typhoon 5-01-40
Typhoon, The 11-28-14
Typhoon No. 13 9-11-57
Typhoon on Nagasaki (See: Typhon a Nagsaki)
Typhoon Treasure 6-28-39

Tyrant of Florence, The 12-24-10
Tyrant of Red Gulch 12-12-28
Tyrant of the Sea 3-01-50
Tytto Onnen Ohjaksissa 3-19-47

U

U-Boat Prisoner 8-16-44
U-Boat 29 10-11-39
U Gori Raste Zelen Bor 9-01-71
U Ozera 8-05-70
U.P. Trail, The 11-12-20
U Raskoraku 7-17-68
U.S. Smith 7-25-28
U.S.C. vs. Tulane 1-26-32
U.S.S. Teakettle 2-28-51
U.S.S.R. Newsreel 7-08-36
USSR on the Screen (See: Soviet Russia Today)
U.S.S.R. Today 4-22-53
U Toszezon 9-06-67
U-Turn 7-04-73
U Tvoyego Poroga (See: At Your Doorstep)
Ubagaruma 9-11-57
Ubangi 6-02-31
Ubistvo Na Svirep i Podmukao Nacin i Iz Nishkih Pobudaj 8-26-70
Ubranie Prawie Nowe 10-07-64
Uccellacci e Uccellini 5-26-66
Uccidere In Silenzio (See: To Kill in Silence)
Uchujin Tokyo Ni Arawaru 12-25-57
Uden en Traevl 9-18-68
Udhetim Ne Pranvere 1-10-79
Udienza, L' 7-12-72
Udoli Vcel 7-24-68
Uebergang, Der 7-25-79
Ugat 3-05-75
Ugetsu Monogatari 9-09-53
Ugly American, The 4-03-63
Ugly Dachshund, The 12-22-65
Ugly, Dirty and Bad (See: Brutti, Sporchi E Cattivi)
Ugly Mess, An (See: Maledetto Imbroglio, Un)
Ugly Ones, The 9-11-68
Uj Gilgames 7-15-64
Ukamau 8-03-66
Ukradena Vzducholod 10-01-69
Ukraine in Flames 4-19-44
Ukroschenie Ognia 8-16-72
Ukryty w Sloncu 10-15-80
Uli der Knecht 1-19-55
Uli der Paechter 2-01-56
Uli the Servant (See: Uli der Knecht)
Uli the Tenant (See: Uli der Paechter)
Ulica 1-31-33
Ulli und Marei 10-12-49
Uloga Moje Porodice U Svetskoj Revolluciji 8-18-71
Ultima Cena, La 5-03-78
Ultima Noapte a Copilarie 11-26-69
Ultima Notte d'Amore, L' 10-23-57
Ultimatum 11-30-38
Ultimi Cinque Minuti, Gli 11-16-55
Ultimi Tre Giorni, Gli 8-31-77
Ultimo Cuple, El 6-19-57
Ultimo Encuentro 5-17-67
Ultimo Incontro 1-09-52
Ultimo Paradiso, L' 7-24-57
Ultimo Refugio 9-17-41
Ultimo Tango A Parigi (See: Last Tango in Paris)
Ultimo Uomo di Sara, L' 3-06-74
Ulysses 12-08-54
Ulysses 3-15-67
Ulzana's Raid 10-18-72
Um Eine Nasenlaenge 9-15-31
Um Freiheit und Liebe 2-23-38
Um Sonho de Vampiros 10-14-70
Uma Abelha Na Chuva 8-02-72
Umberto D. 6-04-52
Umbrella, The 8-01-33
Umbrella Coup, The (See: Coup du Parapluie, Le)
Umbrellas of Cherbourg, The (See: Parapluies de Cherbourg, Les)
Umsetzer, Der 5-11-77
Umut 8-02-78
Un Amleto di Meno 5-30-73
Un de la Montagne 12-18-34
Un, Deux, Trois, Quatre! 8-31-60

Un Dia De Diciembre 10-31-62
Un et l'Autre, L' (See: Other One, The)
Un Jour la Fete 3-05-75
Un Soir sur la Plage 7-05-61
Un Soir ... un Train 10-16-68
Una di Quelle 12-30-53
Una Vez en la Vida 8-27-41
Una Vida Por Otra 7-10-34
Unanstaendige Profit, Der 4-27-77
Unappreciated Genius 4-10-09
Unashamed 7-19-32
Unashamed 8-10-38
Unattainable, The 8-25-16
Unbekannte, Die 12-16-36
Unbeliever, The 2-15-18 and 5-03-18
Unblazed Trail 9-20-23
Unborn, The 6-23-16
Unbroken Promise, The 8-01-19
Uncatchable Frederic, The (See: Insaisissable Frederic, L')
Uncensored 1-19-44
Uncertain Glory 4-05-44
Uncertain Lady 8-07-34
Unchained 1-26-55
Uncharted Seas 6-03-21
Unchastened Woman, The 4-26-18
Uncivilized 10-21-36
Unclaimed Goods 4-19-18
Uncle, The 7-20-66
Uncle Bernac 7-22-21
Uncle Bill 7-17-14
Uncle Bill's Bull 5-02-08
Uncle from America (See: Onkel aus Amerika, Der)
Uncle Harry 8-08-45
Uncle Joe Shannon 11-29-78
Uncle Sam of Freedom Ridge 10-01-20
Uncle Silas 10-22-47
Uncle Tom's Cabin (See: Onkel Toms Huette)
Uncle Tom's Cabin 9-05-13
Uncle Tom's Cabin 9-04-14
Uncle Tom's Cabin 8-09-18
Uncle Tom's Cabin 11-09-27 and 12-10-58
Uncle Vanya 4-23-58
Uncle Vanya 7-28-71
Uncommon Thief, An 10-25-67
Uncompromising Man, A (See: O Asymvivastos)
Unconquered 9-24-47
Unconquered, The 6-23-54
Unconquered People 1-11-50
Unconquered Woman 9-01-22
Unconscious Heroism 9-24-10
Unconsecrated Earth 10-18-67
Und das Am Montagmorgen 7-08-59
Und der Regen Verwischt Jede Spur 1-10-73
Und die Liebe Lacht Dazu 7-24-57
Und Es Leuchtet die Pussta 3-14-33
Und Jimmy Ging Zum Regenbogen 4-14-71
... Und Noch Frech Dazu! 3-02-60
Und Wer Kuesst Mich? 4-25-33
Undead, The 2-27-57
Undefeated, The 10-01-69
Under a False Flag (See: Under Fals Flagg)
Under a Texas Moon 4-09-30
Under Age (See: Unter Achtzehn)
Under Age 5-21-41
Under Black Eagle 5-09-28
Under California Stars 5-12-48
Under Capricorn 9-14-49
Under Colorado Skies 12-17-47
Under Cover 8-04-16
Under-Cover Man 12-06-32
Under Cover of Night (See: Jagte Raho)
Under Cover of Night 1-27-37
Under Crimson Skies 8-06-20
Under 18 12-29-31
Under Fals Flagg 2-03-37
Under False Colors 10-12-17
Under False Flag (See: Unter Falscher Flagge)
Under Fire 9-25-57
Under Four Flags 11-22-18
Under-Gifted, The (See: Sous-Doues, Les)
Under Greenwood Tree 9-18-29
Under Handicap 9-07-17
Under Lock and Key (See: Unter Verschluss)
Under Mexicali Stars 11-29-50
Under Milk Wood 9-08-71
Under Montana Skies 10-22-30
Under My Skin 3-15-50
Under Nevada Skies 8-28-46
Under Oath 8-25-22
Under Parisian Roofs (See: Sous les Toits de Paris)

Under Pressure 2-05-35
Under-Pup, The 8-30-39
Under Secret Orders 12-12-33
Under Secret Orders 7-07-43
Under Skies of Provence (See: Sous Le Ciel De Provence)
Under Strange Flags 8-25-37
Under Suspicion 2-08-18
Under Suspicion 1-07-31
Under Suspicion 12-22-37
Under Ten Flags 9-07-60
Under Texas Skies 1-21-31
Under Texas Skies 9-18-40
Under the Big Top 9-14-38
Under the Black Robe 10-31-14
Under the Bridges (See: Unter den Bruecken)
Under the Flag of the Rising Sun (See: Gunki Hatameku Motoni)
Under the Gaslight 8-13-15
Under the Greenwood Tree 12-13-18
Under the Gun 12-20-50
Under the Lantern (See: Unter der Laterne)
Under the Lash 10-21-21
Under the Leather Helmet (See: Sous le Casque de Cuir)
Under the Pampas Moon 6-05-35
Under the Paris Sky (See: Sous le Ciel de Paris)
Under the Pavement Lies the Strand (See: Unterm Pflaster Ist der Strand)
Under the Red Robe 6-02-37
Under the Red Sea 10-01-52
Under the Roofs of Paris (See: Sous les Toits de Paris)
Under the Rouge 7-22-25
Under the Sea 10-10-14
Under the Sign of Monte-Cristo (See: Sous le Signe de Monte-Cristo)
Under the Sign of the Bull (See: Sous le Signe du Taureau)
Under the Sign of the Scorpion (See: Sotto il Segno Dello Scorpione)
Under the Star Spangled Banner 2-08-08
Under the Sun of Rome 10-12-49
Under the Tonto Rim 6-04-47
Under the Top 1-10-19
Under the Yoke 6-21-18
Under the Yum Yum Tree 10-09-63
Under Tonto Rim 4-04-28
Under Two Flags 8-04-16
Under Two Flags 9-29-22
Under Two Flags 5-06-36
Under Western Eyes (See: Sous les Yeux d'Occident)
Under Western Skies 3-03-26
Under Western Skies 1-03-45
Under Western Stars 4-20-38
Under Your Hat 10-23-40
Under Your Spell 11-18-36
Undercover 8-18-43
Undercover Agent 4-19-39
Undercover Agent 11-25-53
Undercover Doctor 6-07-39
Undercover Girl 11-01-50
Undercover Maisie 3-05-47
Undercover Man 5-06-42 and 1-06-43
Undercover Man, The 3-23-49
Undercover Woman, The 7-03-46
Undercovers Hero 8-20-75
Undercurrent 10-02-46
Undercurrent 1-30-57
Undercurrent, The 11-21-19
Underdog, The 11-24-43
Underground 8-22-28 and 2-27-29
Underground 6-25-41
Underground 10-14-70
Underground 5-12-76
Underground, The (See: Clandestins, Les)
Underground and Emigrants 9-29-76
Underground Guerrillas 9-27-44
Underground Rustlers 1-21-42
Underground U.S.A. 6-25-80
Underneath the Paint 12-18-14
Undersea Girl 11-13-57
Understanding Heart 5-11-27
Understudy, The 7-14-22
Undertaker and His Pals 10-18-67
Undertaker Parlor Computer, The (See: Ordinateur Des Pompes Funebres, L')
Undertow 3-05-30
Undertow 11-30-49
Underwater! 1-12-55
Underwater City, The 2-07-62
Underwater Warrior 2-26-58
Underwear, The (See: Hose, Die)
Underworld 8-24-27

V

VD 5-23-73
V Enfrenta Blitzkrieg 12-31-41
V Faces the Blitzkrieg, The (See: V Enfrenta Blitzkrieg)
V.I.P.s, The 8-14-63
V Tvoi Rukah Jizn 9-02-59
Va Voir Maman ... Papa Travaille 3-15-78
Vacaciones en Acapulco 5-17-61
Vacaciones en el Otro Mundo 6-24-42
Vacances a la Mer 11-13-63
Vacances de Monsieur Hulot, Les 4-29-53
Vacances en Enfer 6-21-61
Vacances Portugaises 11-06-63
Vacances Royales 5-14-80
Vacanza, La 9-15-71
Vacanza del Diavolo, La 3-25-31
Vacanze Col Gangster 7-30-52
Vacanze In Val Trebbia 10-08-80
Vacation, The (See: Vacanza, La)
Vacation by the Sea (See: Vacances a la Mer)
Vacation from Love 10-05-38
Vacation from Marriage 11-28-45
Vacation in Hell (See: Vacances en Enfer)
Vacation in Reno 10-16-46
Vacation with a Gangster (See: Vacanze Col Gangster)
Vacations in Acapulco (See: Vacaciones en Acapulco)
Vacations in the Other World (See: Vacaciones en el Otro
   Mundo)
Vacations in Val Trebbia (See: Vacanze In Val Trebbia)
Vache et le Prisonnier, La 3-02-60
Vadertje Langbeen 10-26-38
Vado, L'Ammazzo, e Torno (See: Any Gun Can Play)
Vagabond, The 7-14-16
Vagabond Cub, The 2-20-29
Vagabond Humor (See: Humeur Vagabonde, L')
Vagabond King, The 2-26-30
Vagabond King, The 9-05-56
Vagabond Lady 6-19-35
Vagabond Lover 12-04-29
Vagabond Luck 12-19-19
Vagabond of France, A 1-10-19
Vagabond Prince, The 9-22-16
Vagabond Queen, The 9-03-30
Vagabond Trail 6-11-24
Vagabonds (See: Vagabunden)
Vagabond's Ball (See: Lumpenbal)
Vagabunden 11-16-49
Vagaries of Love, The 9-24-10
Vaghe Stelle Dell'Orsa 9-15-65
Vagon Li 8-25-76
Vain Sinulle 5-08-46
Vainqueurs et Vaincus 8-22-62
Valachi Papers, The 10-25-72
Valahol Europaban 2-04-48
Valborgsmassoafton 11-20-35
Valdez Is Coming 3-10-71
Vale of Aude, The 3-05-10
Valencia 12-29-26
Valentine Girl, The 4-27-17
Valentino 2-21-51
Valentino 9-21-77
Valerie 7-24-57
Valerie 6-04-69
Valerie a Tyden Divu 8-19-70
Valerie and the Week of Wonders (See: Valerie a Tyden Divu)
Valet of Tormes, The (See: Lazarillo de Tormes, El)
Valet's Wife, The 12-05-08
Valfangare (See: Whalers, The)
Vali 6-14-67
Valiant, The 5-15-29
Valiant, The 1-24-62
Valiant Hombre, The 12-15-48
Valiant Is the Word for Carrie 10-14-36
Valiant Ones, The 10-16-74
Valiants of Virginia, The 6-30-16
Valientes No Mueren, Los 11-21-62
Valise, La 11-21-73
Valkoinen Peura 5-13-53
Valle Negro 11-17-43
Vallee, La 8-30-72
Valley, The (See: Vallee, La)
Valley of Decision, The 4-11-45

Valley of Doubt 7-30-20
Valley of Eagles 10-10-51
Valley of Fire 11-07-51
Valley of Gwangi, The 4-30-69
Valley of Hate, The 7-09-24
Valley of Head Hunters 7-29-53
Valley of Hell, The 8-17-27
Valley of Hunted Men, The 5-02-28
Valley of Lost Hope, The 10-08-15
Valley of Lost Souls 7-31-57
Valley of Mystery 4-26-67
Valley of Silent Men 9-01-22
Valley of Song 6-24-53
Valley of the Bees (See: Udoli Vcel)
Valley of the Dolls 12-20-67
Valley of the Dragons 11-22-61
Valley of the Giants 12-07-27
Valley of the Giants 8-17-38
Valley of the Giants, The 9-05-19
Valley of the Kings 7-07-54
Valley of the Moon, The 8-14-14
Valley of the Redwoods 4-20-60
Valley of the Sun 1-14-42
Valley of the Zombies 5-29-46
Valley of Tomorrow 2-13-20
Valley of Vengeance 8-30-44
Valparaiso Express (See: Tren Internacional)
Valparaiso Mi Amor 5-13-70
Valparaiso My Love (See: Valparaiso Mi Amor)
Valparaiso, Valparaiso! 2-17-71
Valse de Paris, La 5-24-50
Valse du Gorille, La 10-21-59
Valseuses, Les 3-27-74
Value for Money 8-17-55
Valurile Dunarii 7-20-66
Vamonos, Barbara 10-11-78
Vamp, The 7-19-18
Vamping Venus 6-27-28
Vampire, The 8-13-15
Vampire Bat 1-24-33
Vampire de Dusseldorf, Le 3-24-65
Vampire Lovers, The 9-16-70
Vampire of Dusseldorf, The (See: Vampire de Dusseldorf, Le)
Vampires, The (See: Vampiri, I)
Vampire's Dream, A (See: Um Sonho De Vampiros)
Vampire's Ghost, The 6-06-45
Vampires of the Night 3-13-14
Vampiri, I 6-12-57
Vampyres 11-20-74
Van Gogh 7-13-49
Van Nuys Blvd. 5-19-79
Vanda Teres 3-05-75
Vanderbilt Cup Race 11-07-08
Vandring i Solen, En 1-10-79
Vanessa 5-04-77
Vanessa, Her Love Story 4-17-35
Vangelo Secondo Matteo, Il 9-16-64
Vanina Vanini 9-06-61
Vanishing American, The 10-21-25
Vanishing American, The 11-23-55
Vanishing Frontier, The 9-30-32
Vanishing Outpost, The 1-09-52
Vanishing Pioneer, The 8-22-28
Vanishing Point 2-03-71
Vanishing Prairie, The 8-04-54
Vanishing Virginian, The 12-03-41
Vanishing Westerner, The 5-03-50
Vanishing Wilderness, The 1-30-74
Vanity 12-29-16
Vanity 6-15-27
Vanity Fair 10-29-15
Vanity Fair 5-10-23
Vanity Fair 5-10-32
Vanity Pool 12-06-18
Vanity Street 10-11-32
Vanity's Price 10-15-24
Vanquished, The 5-13-53
Var Engang en Krig, Der (See: Once Upon a War)
Var Herr Luggar Johansson 12-12-45
Var Sin Vag 6-16-48
Varan Pojke 10-21-36
Varan the Unbelievable 12-19-62
Vargas Inn (See: Venta de Vargas)
Variete Csillagai 5-17-39
Varietease 8-04-54
Varietee 1-20-26
Varietes 11-10-71
Varieties 10-30-35

Variety 6-30-26
Variety Girls 7-16-47
Variety Stars 3-02-55
Variety Time 8-04-48
Various Facts About Paris (See: Faits Divers A Paris)
Varmint, The 8-10-17
Varmlanders, The (See: Varmlanningarna)
Varmlanningarna 11-22-32
Varsity 10-31-28
Varsity Show 8-11-37
Vas y Maman 8-30-78
Vasarnapi Szulok 2-27-80
Vase de Noces 1-15-75
Vasember 3-17-37
Vasili's Return 9-30-53
Vaso de Whisky, Un 8-05-59
Vast Sudan, The 6-25-24
Vasvirag 5-21-58
Vatican, The 10-11-50
Vatsa Sisaan, Rinta Ulos! (See: Stomach In, Chest Out!)
Vaude Ziji Lide 7-26-61
Vault of Horror, The 3-21-73
Vautours, Les 6-28-78
Vautrin, the Thief 11-16-49
Vaxdockan 8-08-62
Vdovstvo Karoline Zasler 12-29-76
Vecchia Signora, La 12-13-32
Veertig Jaren 9-21-38
Vegul 3-12-75
Veil of Happiness 5-02-28
Veiled Adventure, The 5-16-19
Veiled Marriage 3-26-20
Veiled Woman, The 9-08-22
Veiled Woman, The 6-26-29
Veille d'Armes 1-08-36
Veils of Bagdad, The 9-30-53
Veinte Anos y Una Noche 8-06-41
Velhos Sao Os Trapos 10-15-80
Veliki i Mali 9-17-58
Velvet Hands (See: Mani Di Velluto)
Velvet Paw, The 9-01-16
Velvet Touch, The 7-21-48
Velvet Vampire, The 8-18-71
Ven, Mi Corazon Te Llama 10-28-42
Vendemaire 5-15-68
Vendetta 10-09-09
Vendetta 12-23-21
Vendetta 11-22-50
Vendetta, The 10-03-14
Venerable Ones, The (See: Venerables Todos, Los)
Venerables Todos, Los 5-22-63
Venere di Cheronea, La 3-19-58
Venere Imperiale 1-30-63
Venetian Affair, The 1-11-67
Venetian Anonymous, The (See: Anonimo Veneziano)
Venetian Bird 10-29-52
Venetian Honeymoon (See: Noces Venetiennes, Les)
Venetian Night, A 9-26-14
Venezia, Ultima Serata di Carnevale 9-17-80
Venga a Prendero Il Caffe Da Noi 10-28-70
Venganza, La 5-21-58
Vengeance 5-10-18
Vengeance 3-05-30
Vengeance, The (See: Venganza, La)
Vengeance Is Mine 2-04-16
Vengeance Is Mine 3-26-80
Vengeance of Durand, The 11-14-19
Vengeance of Fu Manchu, The 1-17-68
Vengeance of She, The 4-10-68
Vengeance of the Deep 4-19-23
Vengeance of the Deep 2-28-40
Vengeance of the Wilds, The 6-18-15
Vengeance Trail, The 11-04-21
Vengeance Valley 2-07-51
Venial Sin (See: Peccato Veniale)
Venice: Last Night of Carnival (See: Venezia, Ultima Serata di
    Carnevale)
Venner 7-06-60
Venom (See: Gift)
Vent de l'Est, Le 5-20-70
Vent des Aures, Le 5-10-67
Vent Se Leve, Le 3-04-59
Venta de Vargas 10-07-59
Vento Del Sud 9-14-60
Venus 6-26-29 and 10-16-29
Venus de l'Or, La 6-01-38
Venus in Furs 5-06-70
Venus in Peltz (See: Venus in Furs)

Venus in the East 1-31-19
Venus Makes Trouble 5-19-37
Venus Model, The 6-14-18
Venus of Cheronea, The (See: Venere di Cheronea, La)
Venus of the South Seas 6-11-24
Venus of Venice 5-04-27
Venusberg 5-15-63
Vera 10-03-73
Vera and Daughters (See: Vera Holgk et Ses Filles)
Vera Cruz 12-22-54
Vera Holgk et Ses Filles 6-06-33
Vera Romeyke Is Not Acceptable (See: Vera Romeyke Ist Nicht
    Tragbar)
Vera Romeyke Ist Nicht Tragbar 7-14-76
Vera, the Medium 1-05-17
Vera's Training (See: Angi Vera)
Verbena de la Paloma, La 1-15-36
Verboten 3-25-59
Verbrande Brug 10-08-75
Verdad Sobre El Caso Savolta, La 5-28-80
Verdammt Gutes Leben, Ein 3-29-78
Verdammt Zur Suende 12-02-64
Verden er Fuld af Boern 2-13-80
Verdes Praderas, Las 7-04-79
Verdict 9-18-74
Verdict, The (See: Presuda; Sentence, La; or Wyrok)
Verdict, The 6-10-25
Verdict, The 11-06-46
Verdugo, El 9-11-63
Vereda Da Salvacao 7-14-65
Vereingetorix, Gaul's Hero 4-10-09
Vererbte Triebe (See: Inherited Passions)
Vergine Per Il Principe, Una 3-16-66
Verginita 4-22-53
Vergtimmen 2-28-68
Veri Az Ordog A Feleseget 11-16-77
Verirrte Jugend 4-03-29
Verite, La 11-23-60
Verite Sur Bebe Donge, La 3-12-52
Verkaufte Braut 5-01-34
Verklungene Traeume 12-10-30
Verklungenes Wien 12-05-51
Verliebte Firma, Die 3-22-32
Verliebte Leute 3-09-55
Verlobte, Die 7-23-80
Verloren Maandag 11-21-73
Verlorene, Der 9-05-51
Verlorene Ehre der Katharina Blum, Die 10-01-75
Verlorene Engel, Der 10-01-80
Verlorene Schuh 1-10-24
Verlorene Sohn 1-22-35
Verlorene Tal, Das 7-01-36
Verlorenes Leben 4-14-76
Vermilion Door 10-20-65
Vermillion Pencil 3-17-22
Vernost Materi 12-27-67
Verona Trial (See: Processo di Verona, Il)
Veronicas Svededug 11-30-77
Veronica's Veil (See: Veronicas Svededug)
Veronique or the Summer of My 13th Year (See: Veronique Ou L'Ete
    de Mes 13 Ans)
Veronique Ou l'Ete de Mes 13 Ans 4-09-75
Verraeter 10-07-36 and 1-27-37
Verrohung Des Franz Blum, Der 3-26-75
Vers l'Extase 8-31-60
Versailles 9-11-09
Versprich Mir Nichts 10-13-37
Versteck, Das 3-12-80
Versuchen Sie Meine Schwester 6-23-31
Versuchung im Sommerwind 6-13-73
Verte Moisson, La 2-03-60
Vertical Smile, The (See: Sourire Vertical, Le)
Vertige Pour un Tueur 9-30-70
Vertigine Bianca 4-18-56
Vertigo 7-03-46
Vertigo 5-14-58
Vertigo for a Killer (See: Vertige Pour un Tueur)
Vertreibung aus dem Paradies, Die 4-20-77
Veruntreute Himmel, Der 12-17-58
Verwehte Spuren 11-02-38
Verweigerung, Der 9-20-72
Verworking Van Herman Durer (See: Demise of Herman Durer, The)
Very Big Withdrawal, A 5-23-79
Very Confidential 11-30-27
Very Edge, The 5-08-63
Very Good Young Man, A 8-08-19

Very Handy Man, A 12-14-66
Very Honorable Guy, A 5-22-34
Very Idea, The 8-06-20
Very Idea, The 8-28-29
Very Important Person 4-26-61
Very Moral Night, A (See: Egy Erkolcsos Ejszaka)
Very Natural Thing, A 5-29-74
Very Special Favor, A 7-07-65
Very Thought of You, The 10-18-44
Very Young Lady, A 4-30-41
Vespro Siciliano 1-18-50
Vessel of Wrath 3-16-38
Vest Pocket Love (See: Amour de Poche)
Vetar Je Stao Pred Zoru 8-12-59
Vetchni Vremena 8-27-75
Veterinarian's Adopted Children, The (See: Dyrlaegens Plejeboern)
Veuve Couderc, La 10-27-71
Veuve en Or, Une 11-05-69
Vi Hemslavinor 6-07-44
Vi Som Gar Koksvagen 1-24-33
Via Margutta 11-09-60
Via Pony Express 5-09-33
Via Wireless 9-24-15
Viaccia, La 5-10-61
Viagem Ai Fim Do Mundo 10-30-68
Viager, Le 1-26-72
Viaggio, Il 9-25-74
Viaggio in Italia (See: Journey to Italy)
Viaje, El 11-11-42
Viaje Al Centro de la Tierra 9-28-77
Viaje Fantastico en Globo 7-14-76
Vic Dyson Pays 7-22-25
Vica a Vadevezos 6-27-33
Vica, the Canoeist (See: Vica a Vadevezos)
Vicar of Bray, The 5-26-37
Vicar of Vejlby, The (See: Praesten I Vejlby)
Vicar of Wakefield, The 3-02-17
Vice and Virtue (See: Nugel Bujan)
Vice and Virtue 5-14-15
Vice and Virtue 3-13-63
Vice et la Vertu, Le (See: Vice and Virtue)
Vice of Fools, The 12-03-20
Vice Racket 5-19-37
Vice Raid 12-16-59
Vice Squad (See: Brigade Mondaine)
Vice Squad 7-08-53
Vice Squad, The 6-09-31
Vichingo Venuto Dal Sud, Il 9-22-71
Vicious Breed, The 6-18-58
Vicious Circle, The (See: Onda Cirkeln, Den)
Vicious Circle, The 5-26-48
Vicious Years, The 2-22-50
Vicki 9-09-53
Vicomte de Bragelonne, Le 1-26-55
Vicomte Regle Ses Comptes, Le 4-19-67
Victim 9-06-61
Victim, The 12-29-16
Victim of Circumstances, A 1-08-10
Victim of His Honesty, A 6-27-08
Victim of Passion (See: Jua Arom)
Victim of Sin 11-28-13
Victim of War, A 2-26-15
Victim Strikes Back, The (See: Cave Se Rebiffe, Le)
Victims of Persecution 6-20-33
Victoire en Chantant, La 10-13-76
Victor 7-04-51
Victor, The 7-26-23
Victor Frankenstein 5-25-77
Victor of Hampton Roads (See: Great John Ericsson, The)
Victoria 6-06-79
Victoria and Her Hussar (See: Viktoria und Ihr Husar)
Victoria Cross, The 3-05-15
Victoria the Great 8-25-37
Victors, The 10-30-63
Victors and Vanquished (See: Vainqueurs et Vaincus)
Victors and Vanquished 5-03-50
Victory 11-28-19
Victory 3-28-28
Victory 12-18-40
Victory 3-17-76
Victory at Sea 5-19-54
Victory March (See: Marcia Trionfale)
Victory of Conscience, The 9-01-16
Victory of Love (See: Kerleken Segrar)
Victory Thru Air Power 7-07-43
Vida Alrededor, La 11-11-59
Vida Cambia, La 11-03-76
Vidas Secas 12-25-63

Vie, Une 9-17-58
Vie a Deux, La 11-05-58
Vie a l'Envers, La 5-06-64
Vie Chantee, La 11-21-51
Vie Commence Demain, La (See: Life Begins Tomorrow)
Vie de Boheme, La 6-16-16
Vie de Boheme, La 11-12-47
Vie de Chateau, La 2-09-66
Vie Devant Soi, La 10-26-77
Vie d'un Honnete Homme, La 3-25-53
Vie en Rose, La 5-05-48
Vie Est a Nous, La 11-26-69
Vie Est Belle, La 12-05-56
Vie Facile, La 10-20-71
Vie Heureuse de Leopold Z, La 8-18-65
Vie, l'Amour, la Mort, La 2-12-69
Vie Normale, La 8-02-67
Vie Parisienne, La 2-12-36
Vie Parisienne, La 1-18-78
Vie Passionnee de Clemenceau, La 7-08-53
Vie Privee, La 2-14-62
Vie Revee, La 11-01-72
Vieil Homme et l'Enfant, La 2-22-67
Vieille Dame Indigne, La 3-31-65
Vieille Fille, La 1-12-72
Vieja Memoria, La 10-04-78
Viejo Hucha, El 6-03-42
Viele Kamen Vorbei 7-25-56
Vien, Du Stadt der Lieder 5-07-30 and 3-25-31
Vienna, As It Was (See: Verklungenes Wien)
Vienna, City of My Dreams (See: Wien, Du Stadt Meiner Traeume)
Vienna, City of Song (See: Vien, Du Stadt der Lieder)
Vienna Dances (See: Wien Tanzt)
Vienna Maidens (See: Wiener Madeln)
Vienna Melodies 8-13-47
Vienna Philharmonic 12-01-48
Viennese Nights 12-03-30
Vient de Paraitre 11-30-49
Viente Distante, El 8-04-65
Viento Negro 9-08-65
24 Stunden aus dem Leben einer Frau 10-27-31
Vieras Mies 8-06-58
Vierge du Rhin, La 12-30-53
Vierge Folle 12-21-38
Vierges, Les 6-19-63
Vierte von Rechts, Die 3-06-29
Vietnam 2-23-72
Vieux de la Vielle, Les 9-28-60
Vieux Fusil, Le 9-03-75
Vieux Pays Ou Rimbaud Est Mort, Le 5-25-77
View from Pompey's Head, The 10-26-55
View from the Bridge, A 10-18-61
Vigil in the Night 2-07-40
Vigilante Force 4-14-76
Vigilante Hideout 8-09-50
Vigilantes, The 9-06-18
Vigilantes of Boomtown 2-12-47
Vigilantes Return, The 7-09-47
Vignes du Seigneur, Les 10-18-32
Vignes du Seigneur, Les 1-28-59
Vihreae Leski 10-16-68
Viki 12-15-37
Viking, The 12-05-28
Viking, The 6-23-31
Viking Queen, The 8-30-67
Viking Who Came from the South, The (See: Vichingo Venuto Dal Sud, Il)
Vikings, The 5-21-58
Viktor und Viktoria 3-06-34
Viktoria und Ihr Husar 1-05-32 and 4-11-33
Vilaines Manieres, Les 8-29-73
Vildfaglar 6-15-60
Villa! 9-10-58
Villa Borghese 2-03-54
Villa for Sale (See: Ez a Villa Elado)
Villa Rides 6-12-68
Villa Zone 1-14-76
Village, The 9-30-53
Village Barn Dance 1-31-40
Village Blacksmith 11-10-22
Village Blacksmith, The 3-17-16
Village Chestnut, The 12-20-18
Village de la Colere, Le 1-22-47
Village Head at the Border, The (See: Phooying Yay Chai Daeng)
Village Marathon Race 12-05-08
Village of Daughters 3-21-62

Village of Sin, The 11-14-28 and 5-22-29
Village of the Damned 6-29-60
Village of the Eight Tombs (See: Yatsu Hakamura)
Village of the Giants 10-06-65
Village of Wrath, The (See: Village de la Colere, Le)
Village on the River 7-22-59 and 12-09-59
Village Performance of Hamlet, A (See: Predstava Hamleta U Mrdusi
    Donjoj)
Village Sleuth 9-17-20
Village Sweetness (See: Douceur Du Village, La)
Village Tale 6-26-35
Village Teacher 7-07-48
Village Vampire, A 3-17-16
Villain 6-02-71
Villain, The 7-18-79
Villain Still Pursued Her, The 7-24-40
Villeggiatura, La 5-30-73
Vilna Legend, A 9-28-49
Vincent, Francois, Paul and the Others (See: Vincent, Francois,
    Paul et les Autres)
Vincent, Francois, Paul et les Autres 9-25-74
Vincent Mit l'Ane Dans un Pre 12-03-75
Vincent Puts the Ass in a Field (See: Vincent Mit l'Ane Dans un
    Pre)
Vines of the Lord, The (See: Vignes du Seigneur, Les)
28 Jours de Clairette 5-30-33
Vingt Quatre Heures de la Vie d'une Femme 5-15-68
Vintage, The 3-20-57
Vintage Wine 7-03-35
Vinterboern 9-20-78
Viol, Le 12-27-67
Viol d'une Jeunne Fille Douce, Le 9-18-68
Viola and Sebastian 5-23-73
Violanta 9-28-77
Violated! 12-16-53
Violated Angels (See: Okasareta Byakui)
Violated Love (See: Amour Viole, L')
Violation of Claudia, The 6-15-77
Violators, The 11-20-57
Violence 4-09-47
Violence at the Square (See: Nasilje Na Trgu)
Violent City (See: Citta Violenta)
Violent Fate (See: Hecho Violento, Un)
Violent Men, The 12-22-54
Violent Ones, The 10-11-67
Violent Playground 1-22-58
Violent Road 4-23-58
Violent Saturday 4-13-55
Violent Summer (See: Estate Violenta)
Violents, Les 3-26-58
Violenza Segreta 5-15-63
Violer Er Blaa 5-21-75
Violet (See: Ljubica)
Violets Are Blue (See: Violer Er Blaa)
Violette et Francois 3-30-77
Violette Imperiale 6-20-28
Violette Noziere 5-24-78
Violettes Imperiales 2-28-24
Violin Maker of Cremona, The 3-12-10
Violin of M'sieur, The 6-19-14
Violins at the Ball (See: Violons du Bal, Les)
Violons du Bal, Les 2-27-74
Viragvasarnap 3-11-70
Viree Superbe, La 6-26-74
Virgen Morena, La (See: Virgin of Guadalupe)
Virgen Que Forjo Una Patria, La 6-07-44
Virgin, The 10-22-24
Virgin and the Gypsy, The 6-17-70
Virgin Cocotte, The 4-10-29
Virgin for the Prince, A (See: Vergine Per Il Principe, Una)
Virgin Island 11-05-58
Virgin Named Mary, A 10-29-75
Virgin of Guadalupe 5-19-43
Virgin of Pessac, The (See: Rosiere de Pessac, La)
Virgin of Stamboul 3-26-20
Virgin Paradise 8-12-21
Virgin Queen, The 2-08-23
Virgin Queen, The 7-27-55
Virgin Soldiers, The 10-22-69
Virgin Spring, The (See: Jungfrukallan)
Virgin Witch, The 6-21-78
Virginia 1-15-41
Virginia City 3-20-40
Virginia Judge, The 10-23-35
Virginian, The 9-11-14
Virginian, The 11-29-23
Virginian, The 12-25-29

Virginian, The 1-30-46
Virginie 11-14-62
Virgins, The (See: Vierges, Les)
Virgins of Bali, The 12-13-32
Virgin's Sacrifice, A 6-16-22
Viridiana 5-24-61
Virilita 2-18-76
Virility (See: Virilita)
Virtually Married (See: Casi Casados)
Virtue 11-01-32
Virtue's Revolt 5-27-25
Virtuous Husband 5-13-31
Virtuous Liars 4-02-24
Virtuous Men 4-11-19
Virtuous Model, The 9-19-19
Virtuous Sin, The 10-29-30
Virtuous Sinners 5-16-19
Virtuous Vamp, A 11-21-19
Virtuous Wives 1-03-19
Virus 5-28-80
Visages de France, Les 2-03-37
Viscount Settles Accounts, The (See: Vicomte Regle Ses Comptes,
    Le)
Visionari, I 10-23-68
Visionaries, The (See: Visionari, I)
Visions of a Nag 11-27-09
Visions of Eight 5-30-73
Visit, The (See: Visita, La)
Visit, The 5-13-64
Visit from the President, A (See: Odwiedziny Prezydenta)
Visit to a Chief's Son 3-20-74
Visit to a Small Planet 2-03-60
Visit to Biskra, A 9-11-09
Visit to the Nursery, A 4-25-08
Visit to Uncle, A 10-30-09
Visita, La 2-12-64
Visitatore, Il (See: Visitor, The)
Visiteur, Le 1-15-47
Visiteurs du Soir, Les (See: Devil's Envoys, The)
Visitor, The 11-21-73
Visitor, The 3-26-80
Visitors, The 2-02-72
Viskingar Och Rop (See: Cries and Whispers)
Visnja Na Tasmajdanu 8-20-69
Vita, a Volte e Molto Dura, Vero Provvidenza?, La 11-15-72
Vita di Donizetti, La (See: Life of Donizetti, The)
Vita Difficile, Una 2-28-62
Vita Sporten, Den 10-15-69
Vital Question, The 3-31-16
Vitelloni, I 10-14-53 and 11-14-56
Viuda de Montiel, La 3-05-80
Viva Cisco Kid 3-20-40
Viva Italia 7-12-78
Viva Jalisco Que Es Mi Tierra 4-26-61
Viva Knievel! 6-08-77
Viva La Clase Media 5-07-80
Viva la Muerte 3-17-71
Viva la Muerte ... Tua (See: Don't Turn the Other Cheek)
Viva la Vida! 10-22-69
Viva Las Vegas 5-20-64
Viva Lo Imposible 9-17-58
Viva Maria 12-08-65
Viva Max 12-17-69
Viva Villa 4-17-34
Viva Zapata! 2-06-52
Vivacious Lady 5-04-38
Vivan Los Novios 5-06-70
Vive Henri IV, Vive l'Amour 4-26-61
Vive la France 9-27-18
Vive la France 10-09-74
Vive la Liberte 6-26-46
Vive la Mort 10-22-69
Vive la Nation 2-14-40
Vivere 1-20-37
Vivette 7-12-18
Vivir Del Cuento 3-09-60
Vivre Ensemble 5-16-73
Vivre la Nuit 6-12-68
Vivre Pour Vivre (See: Live for Life)
Vivre Sa Vie 8-29-62
Vixen 10-30-68
Vixen, The 12-08-16
Vixens, The 1-29-69
Viza Zla 8-12-59
Vizi Privati, Pubbliche Virtu 5-26-76
Vlad Tepes 5-30-79
Vladimir and Rosa 4-28-71
Vlak Bez Vosnog Reda 5-13-59

269

W

Wages of Fear, The (See: Salaire de la Peur, Le)
Wages of Virtue 11-26-24
Wagon Master 10-02-29
Wagon Show 5-02-28
Wagon Tracks 8-15-19
Wagon Tracks West 10-27-43
Wagon Trail 5-29-35
Wagon Train 1-08-41
Wagon Train 9-10-52
Wagon Wheels 10-09-34
Wagonmaster 4-12-50
Wagons Roll at Night, The 4-30-41
Wagons West 6-18-52
Wagons Westward 6-26-40 and 7-24-40
Wahlverwandschaften, Die 4-02-75
Wahnsinn, Das Ganze Leven Ist Wahnsinn 9-03-80
Wahre Jacob, Der 8-11-31
Wahrheit Ueber Rosemarie, Die 3-09-60
Wai Tok Kra 10-25-78
Waif (See: Gamin)
Waif, The 12-19-08
Waif, The 5-22-14
Waif, The 12-10-15
Waifs 8-02-18
Waifs, The 3-24-16
Waikiki Wedding 3-31-37
Wait a Minute! (See: Alljon Meg A Menet!)
Wait for Me 3-21-45
Wait 'Til the Sun Shines, Nellie 5-28-52
Wait Until Dark 10-25-67
Waiter No. 5 11-12-10
Waiting for Daddy (See: Esperando a Papa)
Waiting for Fidel 2-04-76
Waiting Room for Death (See: I Dodens Vantrum)
Waiting Soul, The 3-30-17
Wajan 4-29-38
Wakamba! 6-29-55
Wake Island 8-12-42
Wake Me When It's Over 3-30-60
Wake of the Red Witch 1-05-49
Wake Up and Dream 10-16-34
Wake Up and Dream 11-27-46
Wake Up and Live 4-28-37
Wake Up Dear (See: Reveille-Toi Cherie)
Wakefield Case, The 4-08-21
Waking Up the Town 4-01-25
Waldwinter 11-18-36
Walk, The (See: Passeggiata, La)
Walk a Crooked Mile 9-08-48
Walk a Crooked Path 11-26-69
Walk, Don't Run 6-29-66
Walk East on Beacon 4-30-52
Walk Fory, The (See: Bastyasetany)
Walk in the Shadow 2-02-66
Walk in the Spring Rain, A 4-15-70
Walk in the Sun, A (See: Vandring I Solen, En)
Walk in the Sun, A 11-28-45
Walk into Hell 7-31-57
Walk Like a Dragon 6-08-60
Walk on the Wild Side 1-31-62
Walk on Water if You Can (See: Ga Pa Vattnet Om Du Kan)
Walk Proud 5-16-79
Walk Softly, Stranger 8-23-50
Walk Tall 10-26-60
Walk the Angry Beach 3-08-61
Walk the Proud Land 7-11-56
Walk with Love and Death, A 9-10-69
Walkabout 5-19-71
Walkers on the Tiger's Tale (See: Torano O)
Walking Back 6-13-28
Walking Dead, The 3-04-36
Walking Down Broadway 2-02-38
Walking Hills, The 3-02-49
Walking My Baby Back Home 11-11-53
Walking on Air 9-16-36
Walking Stick, The 3-18-70
Walking Tall 2-28-73
Walking Tall, Part 2 7-16-75
Walking Upright (See: Aufrechte Gang, Der)
Walkover (See: Walkower)
Walkower 5-19-65
Wall, The (See: Mur, Le; Deewar; or Zidul)
Wall Between, The 4-07-16
Wall Engravings (See: Au Pan Coupe)
Wall Flower 7-07-22
Wall in Jerusalem, A (See: Mur a Jerusalem, Un)
Wall of Noise 8-14-63
Wall Street 11-27-29

Wall Street Cowboy 9-06-39
Wall Street Mystery, The 5-28-20
Wall Street Tragedy, A 8-18-16
Walled In, The (See: Zazidani)
Wallflower 5-19-48
Wallflowers 4-04-28
Wallingford 12-09-21
Wallingford 10-13-31
Walls (See: Falak)
Walls, The (See: Al Aswar)
Walls Came Tumbling Down, The 5-22-46
Walls of Fire 1-20-71
Walls of Freedom, The (See: Frihetens Murar)
Walls of Gold 10-24-33
Walls of Hell, The (See: Intramuros)
Walls of Jericho, The 12-11-14
Walls of Jericho, The 7-04-48
Walls of Malapaga, The 3-29-50
Walpurgis Night (See: Valborgsmassoafton)
Waltz Around the Stefanstower (See: Walzer um den Stefansturm, Ein)
Waltz by Strauss, A (See: Walzer vom Strauss)
Waltz Dream, The 7-28-26
Waltz for You, A (See: Walzer Fuer Dich, Ein)
Waltz of Love (See: Liebeswalzer)
Waltz of the Toreadors 4-18-62
Waltz Paradise (See: Walzerparadies)
Waltz Time 6-27-33 and 10-03-33
Waltz Time 7-04-45
Waltzers, The (See: Valseuses, Les)
Waltzes from Vienna 3-06-34
Walzer fuer Dich, Ein 10-07-36
Walzer um den Stefansturm, Ein 2-10-37
Walzer vom Strauss 2-16-32
Walzerkrug 11-20-34
Walzerparadies 3-07-33
Walzertraum, Ein 1-27-26
Wan Pipel 10-13-76
Wanda 9-02-70
Wanda Nevada 5-30-79
Wanda's Affair 11-12-20
Wanderer of the Wasteland, The 5-21-24
Wanderer of the Wasteland, The 10-16-35
Wanderer of the Wasteland, The 9-26-45
Wanderers, The (See: Girovaghi, I or Matatabi)
Wanderers, The 1-07-16
Wanderers, The 7-11-79
Wanderers of the West 9-24-41
Wandering (See: Bloudeni or Periplanissis)
Wandering Beast, The (See: Bete Errante, La)
Wandering Daughters 7-04-23
Wandering Fires 12-16-25
Wandering Footsteps 10-28-25 and 6-16-26
Wandering Girls 2-23-27
Wandering Husband, The 6-11-24
Wandering Jew, The (See: Ebreo Errante, L')
Wandering Jew, The 4-22-21
Wandering Jew, The 6-21-23
Wandering Jew, The 12-05-33 and 1-15-35
Wandering Jew, The 10-24-33
Waning Sex, The 9-01-26
Wanted 3-03-37
Wanted, a Child 10-09-09
Wanted--a Home 9-22-16
Wanted--a Husband 12-19-19
Wanted at Headquarters 10-22-20
Wanted by Scotland Yard 7-12-39
Wanted by the Law 5-07-24
Wanted by the Police 9-28-28
Wanted for Murder 12-13-18
Wanted for Murder 9-22-37
Wanted for Murder 4-03-46
Wanted: Jane Turner 12-02-36
Wanted Men 7-15-36
Wanters, The 3-12-24
Wanting Weight, The (See: Falsche Gewicht, Das)
War (See: Rat)
War After the War, The (See: Ha'mil'hama Le'ahar Ha'mil'hama)
War Against Mrs. Hadley, The 8-05-42
War and Peace 8-22-56
War and Peace Parts I & II: 7-28-65; Part III: 5-10-67; Entire version: 5-01-68
War and Peace--Part IV (See: Voina I Mir)
War and the Woman 9-28-17
War Arrow 12-09-53
War at Home, The 12-05-79
War Between Men and Women, The 5-17-72
War Between the Planets 2-10-71

War Brides 11-17-16
War Bride's Secret, The 10-13-16
War Correspondent 8-16-32
War Correspondents 8-29-13
War Drums 4-03-57
War Game, The 9-07-66
War-Gods of the Deep 6-16-65
War Horse 2-09-27
War Hunt 3-14-62
War in Europe, The 10-31-14
War Is a Racket 12-11-34
War Is Over, The (See: Guerre Est Finie, La)
War Is War (See: A La Guerre Comme A La Guerre)
War Italian Style 2-08-67
War Lord 7-07-37
War Lord, The 10-06-65
War Lover, The 10-24-62
War Nurse 10-29-30
War o' Dreams 7-09-15
War of the Buttons (See: Guerre des Boutons, La)
War of the Colossal Beast 8-20-58
War of the Pastries, The (See: Guerra de los Pasteles, La)
War of the Range 12-12-33
War of the Satellites 5-14-58
War of the Worlds 3-04-53
War of the Zombies, The 9-22-65
War of Wars, The 10-03-14
War on Three Fronts, The 4-06-17
War Paint 10-20-26
War Paint 7-08-53
War Starts in Cuba (See: Guerra Empieza En Cuba, La)
War Time Sweetheart, A 6-05-09
War Unser Rommel, Das 8-12-53
War Wagon, The 5-24-67
Ware Case, The 1-16-29
Ware Case, The 12-14-38
Warfare in the Flesh, The 4-27-17
Warfare in the Skies 8-07-14
Warkill 6-28-67
Warlock 4-01-59
Warlords of Atlantis 7-26-78
Warm December, A 4-18-73
Warm in the Bud 2-04-70
Warm Life, The (See: Calda Vita, La)
Warm Wind (See: Garm Hava)
Warming Up 6-27-28
Warmth (See: Toplo)
Warmth of Your Hands, The (See: Tieplo Tvoio Ruk)
Warn London 5-29-34
Warning, The 1-18-28
Warning of a Holy Prostitute (See: Warnung vor einer Heiligen
    Nutte)
Warning Shadows 12-03-24
Warning Shot (See: Riasztoloves)
Warning Shot 1-11-67
Warning to Wantons 1-12-49
Warnung vor einer Heiligen Nutte 9-22-71 and 7-12-72
Warpath 6-06-51
Warrendale 5-03-67
Warrens of Virginia, The 2-19-15
Warrens of Virginia, The 10-08-24
Warring Clans (See: Sengoku Yaro)
Warrior, The 7-20-17
Warrior and the Slave Girl, The 10-28-59
Warrior Empress, The 5-17-61
Warrior Within, The 6-29-77
Warriors, The 2-14-79
Warrior's Husband, The 5-16-33
Warrior's Rest (See: Repos du Guerrier, Le)
War's End 5-29-34
Wartezimmer zum Jenseits 5-13-64
Warui Yatsura 7-30-80
Warum Laeuft Herr R. Amok? 7-08-70
Was Bin Ich Ohne Dich? 12-18-35
Was Frauen Traeumen 4-18-33 and 5-09-33
Was He Guilty? 12-28-27
Was Heisst'n Hier Liebe 5-23-79
Was Ich Bin, Sind Meine Filme 1-24-79
Was Ist denn Bloss mit Willi Los? 8-19-70
Was It Bigamy? 9-02-25
Was Kostet Liebe (See: What Price Love)
Was Oshidajet Grashdanka Nikanorova 2-28-79
Was She Guilty 9-01-22
Was Soll'n Wir Denn Machen Ohne Den Tod? 9-17-80
Wasch Syn i Brat 12-01-76
Wash Out My Faults (See: Hugasan Mo Ang Aking Kasalaman)
Washington at Valley Forge 3-06-14
Washington Masquerade 7-26-32

Washington Melodrama 4-23-41
Washington Merry-Go-Round 10-25-32
Washington Story 7-02-52
Wasp, The 3-01-18
Wasp Woman, The 3-23-60
Waste-Land, The (See: Terrain Vague)
Wasted Love 1-01-30
Wasted Years, The 6-23-16
Wastrel, The 5-17-61
Wastrels, The (See: Vitelloni, I)
Wat Zien Ik 10-13-71
Watan 11-09-60
Watashi Ga Suteta Onna 7-23-69
Watch Him Step 5-12-22
Watch My Smoke 1-25-23
Watch on the Rhine 7-28-43
Watch Out for Love (See: Cuidado Con El Amor)
Watch Out for the Eyes (See: Attention Les Yeux)
Watch Out, La Tour (See: Tour, Prends Barde!, La)
Watch the Birdie 11-29-50
Watch Your Step 5-19-22
Watch Your Steps 8-09-23
Watch Your Stern 9-28-60
Watch Your Wife 4-14-26
Watched 9-18-74
Watcher in the Woods, The 4-23-80
Watchmaker of Saint-Paul, The (See: Horloger de Saint-Paul, L')
Watchtower of Tomorrow 4-04-45
Water Babies, The 4-25-79
Water Birds 6-11-52
Water-Carrier Is Dead, The (See: Sakka Mat, El)
Water Cars (See: Voitures d'Eau, Les)
Water Flyer, The 3-19-10
Water Gypsies, The 4-19-32
Water Hole, The 9-05-28
Water It and Dew for the Thirsty Soil (See: Diligin Mo Ng Hamog
    Ang Uhaw Na Lupa)
Water Like a Black Buffalo (See: Apa Ca Un Bivol Negru)
Water on the Ground (See: Agua en el Suelo, El)
Water Rustlers 3-15-39
Water Spider, The (See: Araignee D'Eau, L')
Water Was So Clear, The (See: Gaki Zoshi)
Water, Water, Everywhere 2-06-20
Waterfront 10-24-28
Waterfront 7-19-39
Waterfront 8-02-44
Waterfront 8-09-50
Waterfront at Midnight 5-05-48
Waterfront Lady 11-06-35
Waterfront Wolves 2-28-24
Waterhole #3 10-04-67
Waterless Summer (See: Susuz Yaz)
Waterloo 11-04-70
Waterloo Bridge 5-15-40
Waterloo Road 2-07-45
Watermelon Man 6-03-70
Watership Down 10-18-78
Watts Monster, The 10-24-79
Wattstax 2-07-73
Watusi 4-15-59
Wave, The 4-28-37
WAVE, a WAC, and a Marine, A 8-16-44
Waves After Waves (See: Dheuer Pare Dheu)
Waves of Change 8-12-70
Wax Model, The 3-02-17
Way, The (See: Voie, La)
Way Ahead, The 6-21-44
Way Back, The 9-10-15
Way Back Home 1-19-32
Way Down East 9-10-20 and 3-18-31
Way Down East 11-06-35
Way Down on El Rancho Grande (See: Alla En El Rancho Grande)
Way Down South 8-23-39
Way for a Sailor 12-17-30
Way Into Life, The (See: Weg Ins Leben, Der)
Way of a Gaucho 10-08-52
Way of a Girl, The 4-01-25
Way of a Maid 11-11-21
Way of a Man, The 1-31-24
Way of a Man with a Maid, The 1-25-19
Way of a Woman, The 8-01-19
Way of All Flesh, The 6-29-27
Way of All Flesh, The 4-29-40
Way of All Men, The 9-24-30
Way of the Wind, The 12-22-76
Way of the World, The 6-16-16
Way of the Wrong Road, The (See: Chemin de la Mauvaise Route, Le)

Way Out (See: Verloren Maandag)
Way Out 1-11-67
Way Out, The 3-15-18
Way Out, The 4-11-56
Way Out West 8-20-30
Way Out West 5-05-37
Way to Love, The 11-14-33
Way to Paradise, The (See: Put U Raj)
Way to Strength and Beauty, The 8-03-27
Way to the Gold, The 5-08-57
Way to the Stars, The 6-20-45
Way ... Way Out 10-19-66
Way We Live Now, The 6-03-70
Way We Were, The 9-26-73
Way West, The 5-17-67
Way Women Love, The 2-11-21
Ways of Love 12-20-50
Ways of Love Are Strange (See: Liebe Geht Seltsame Wege)
Ways of Sin, The (See: Synnin Jaljet)
Wayside Pebble, The 9-13-61
Wayward 2-16-32
Wayward Bus, The 5-29-57
Wayward Girl, The 9-25-57
We Accuse 5-30-45
We Americans 4-04-28
We Are All Demons (See: Klabautermanden)
We Are All Murderers (See: Nous Sommes Tous les Assassins)
We Are All Naked 2-04-70
We Are Arab Jews in Israel (See: Nous Sommes Des Juifs Arabes
    en Israel)
We Are from Kronstadt 5-06-36
We Are Not Alone 11-15-39
We Are the Guinea Pigs 5-07-80
We Are the Marines 12-09-42
We Can't All Be Angels (See: Wenn Wir Alle Engel Waeren)
We Can't Have Everything 7-12-18
We Cellar Children (See: Wir Kellerkinder)
We Chop the Teachers into Mince-Meat (See: Wir Hau'n die Pauker
    in die Pfanne)
We Dive at Dawn 6-02-43
We Forget Everything! (See: On Efface Tout!)
We Go Fast 9-10-41
We Have Our Moments 5-05-37
We Home Toilers (See: Vi Hemslavinor)
We Italians (See: Siamo Italiani)
We Joined the Navy 12-05-62
We Live Again 11-06-34
We Live Again 9-15-48
We Lived Through Buchenwald 2-19-47
We Meet at Toves (See: Saa Modes Vi Hos Tove)
We Moderns 12-09-25
We Shall Go to Paris (See: Nous Irons a Paris)
We Should Worry 7-05-18
We Two (See: Hum Dono or Nosotros Dos)
We--Two (See: Wir--Zwei)
We Two France (See: A Nous Deux La France)
We Want the Colonels (See: Vogliamo I Colonnelli)
We Went to College 7-29-36
We Were Dancing 1-21-42
We Were Mistaken About a Love Story (See: On S'Est Trompe
    D'Histoire D'Amour)
We Were One Man (See: Nous Etions Un Seul Homme)
We Were Seven Sisters (See: Eravamo Sette Sorelle)
We Were Strangers 4-27-49
We Who Are About to Die 1-06-37
We Who Are Young 7-17-40
We Will All Go to Heaven (See: Nous Irons Tous Au Paradis)
We Will Come Back 10-20-43
We Will Go to Monte Carlo (See: Nous Irons a Monte Carlo)
We Will Not Grow Old Together (See: Nous Ne Vieillirons Pas
    Ensemble)
We Will Remember (See: Senjo Ni Nagareru Uta)
We Won't Go to the Woods Any More (See: Nous N'Irons Plus Au
    Bois)
Weak and the Wicked, The 2-17-54
Weak Spot, The (See: Faille, La)
Weak Woman, A (See: Faible Femme, Une)
Weak Women (See: Faibles Femmes)
Weaker Sex, The 12-29-16
Weaker Sex, The 10-06-48
Weaker Vessel, The 7-25-19
Weakness of Man, The 7-07-16
Wealth 7-01-21
Weapon, The 6-12-57
Weapons, The (See: As Armas)
Weapons of Destruction (See: Vynalez Zkazy)
Weary River 1-30-29

Weary Theodor (See: Muede Theodor, Der)
Weaver of Dreams, A 2-22-18
Weaver of Miracles, The 7-04-62
Weavers, The 10-09-29
Weavers of Life 12-03-20
Web, The (See: Strange Case of Mary Page, The: Part III)
Web, The 5-28-47
Web of Chance 1-31-20
Web of Danger 6-18-47
Web of Deceit 1-23-20
Web of Desire, The 2-23-17
Web of Evidence 9-09-59
Web of Fate 8-28-09
Web of Fate 2-01-28
Web of Intrigue, A 11-08-18
Web of Life, The 4-06-17
Webb's Electrical Pictures 5-08-14
Webster Boy, The 6-27-62
Wechma 11-29-72
Wedding, A 9-06-78
Wedding, The (See: Wesele; Svadba; or Dugun)
Wedding at Sun Island (See: Brollopet Pa Solo)
Wedding Bells 8-19-21
Wedding Bells 6-29-27
Wedding Certificate 7-14-65
Wedding Day (See: Evordulo)
Wedding Day, The 7-31-57
Wedding Dream, A (See: Hochzeitstraum, Ein)
Wedding in Monaco, The 5-16-56
Wedding in White 10-18-72
Wedding March, The (See: Marcia Nuziale, La)
Wedding March, The 10-17-28
Wedding March, The 2-06-29
Wedding Night (See: Brollopsnatten or Noche de Bodas)
Wedding Night, The 3-20-35
Wedding of Palt, The 3-03-37
Wedding of the Fairy Princess 8-01-56
Wedding of Zein, The 7-05-78
Wedding Party, The 4-09-69
Wedding Present 11-25-36
Wedding Rehearsal 10-18-32
Wedding Ring, The (See: Alliance, L')
Wedding Rings 5-14-30
Wedding Song, The 1-13-26
Wedding--Swedish Style (See: Brollopsbesvar)
Wedding-Trip, The (See: Hochzeitsreise, Die)
Wedding Trough (See: Vase De Noces)
Wedding Without Rings (See: Svatba Bez Prstynku)
Weddings and Babies 9-17-58
Wedlock 7-19-18
Wednesday Children, The 6-20-73
Wednesday's Child 12-18-34
Wee Lady Betty 8-31-17
Wee MacGregor's Sweetheart 8-11-22
Wee Willie Winkie 6-30-37
Weed 5-17-72
Week-End 11-13-63
Week End, The 7-30-20
Week-End im Paradies 10-27-31 (See also: Weekend im Paradies)
Week-End Marriage 6-07-32
Week End Millionaire 4-07-37
Week-End Wives 12-12-28
Week-Ends Only 6-21-32
Week In, Week Out (See: Settimana Come Un'Altra, Una)
Weekend, Le 1-10-68
Weekend a Zuydcoote 12-30-64
Weekend at the Waldorf 7-25-45
Weekend for Three 10-29-41
Weekend im Paradies 11-01-32
Weekend in Havana 9-17-41
Weekend in Paradise (See: Week-End im Paradies or Weekend im
    Paradies)
Weekend Murders, The 5-10-72
Weekend of a Champion 7-12-72
Weekend of Fear 2-16-66
Weekend of Shadows 5-10-78
Weekend Pass 2-02-44
Weekend Pass 10-18-61
Weekend with Father 11-28-51
Weekend with Lulu 5-16-62
Weekend Wives 7-03-29
Week's Leave, A 1-09-46
Week's Vacation, A (See: Semaine de Vacances, Une)
Weeping for a Bandit (See: Llanto Por Un Bandido)
Weg ins Leben, Der 10-13-31
Weg Ohne Umkehr 6-30-54 (Also see: No Way Back)
Wege in Der Nacht 9-19-79

Wehe Wenn Sie Losgelassen 6-30-26
Weib im Dschungel 4-08-31
Weiberregiment 8-05-36 and 9-16-36
Weibsteufel, Der 7-06-66
Weird Woman 4-05-44
Weisse Daemon, Der 12-20-32
Weisse Rausch, Der 12-29-31 and 3-30-38
Weissen Rosen von Ravensberg, Die (See: White Roses of
     Ravensberg, The)
Welcome (See: Dobro Poshalovat)
Welcome Children 6-10-21
Welcome Danger 10-23-29
Welcome Home 5-20-25
Welcome Home 8-28-35
Welcome Home, Soldier Boys 2-16-72
Welcome Mr. Marshall (See: Bienvenido Mr. Marshall)
Welcome, Mr. Washington 6-28-44
Welcome Reverend! (See: Benvenuto, Reverendo!)
Welcome Stranger 10-15-24
Welcome Stranger 4-30-47
Welcome the Queen! 5-26-54
Welcome to Arrow Beach 5-15-74
Welcome to Blood City 10-26-77
Welcome to Britain 11-10-76
Welcome to Hard Times 3-29-67
Welcome to L.A. 12-01-76
Welcome to My Nightmare 1-21-76
Welcome to the Club 8-11-71
Welikatara 8-30-72
Well, The 9-05-51
Well, The 11-04-64
We'll Bury You 10-10-62
We'll Call Him Andrea (See: Chiameremo Andrea, Lo)
Well-Digger's Daughter (See: Fille du Puisatier, La)
Well Earned Medal, A 1-08-10
We'll Eat the Fruit of Paradise (See: Ovoce Stromj Rajskych
     Jime)
Well-Filled Day, A (See: Journee Bien Remplie, Une)
Well-Groomed Bride, The 1-30-46
We'll Grow Thin Together (See: Nous Maigriirons Ensemble)
We'll Live Till Monday (See: Dozhivem do Polnidelnika)
Well of Three Truths, The (See: Puits aux Trois Verites, Le)
We'll Smile Again 10-21-42
Wells Fargo 12-08-37
Wells Fargo Gunmaster 5-16-51
Wellsprings of My World, The (See: Herfra Min Verden Gaar)
Welsh Singer, A 8-25-16
Welt Dreht Sich Verkehrt, Die (See: World Turns Backward, The)
Welte Weg, Der 9-11-46
Wench, The 3-09-49
Wenn die Glocken Hell Erklingen 3-02-60
Wenn die Liebe Mode Macht 1-17-33
Wenn die Musik Nicht Waer 4-07-37
Wenn die Tollen Tanten Kommen 11-18-70
Wenn Suess das Mondlicht auf den Huegeln Schlaeft 11-26-69
Wenn Wir Alle Engel Waeren 10-28-36 and 10-13-37
Went the Day Well? 11-11-42
Wer im Glashaus Liebt (Der Graben) 7-14-71
Wer Nimmt Liebe Ernst 10-13-31
We're All Gamblers 10-12-27
We're Going To Be Rich 7-06-38
We're Going to Eat You 5-07-80
We're in the Legion Now 6-09-37
We're in the Money 8-28-35
We're in the Navy Now 11-10-26
We're No Angels 6-15-55
We're Not Dressing 5-01-34
We're Not Made of Stone (See: No Somos De Piedra)
We're Not Married 6-25-52
We're on the Jury 2-17-37
We're Only Human 1-22-36
We're Rich Again 9-04-34
Were We All Angels (See: Wenn Wir Alle Engel Waeren)
Werewolf, The 6-13-56
Werewolf in a Girl's Dormitory 6-19-63
Werewolf of London 5-15-35
Werewolf of Washington 10-10-73
Werewolves on Wheels 10-13-71
Werther 10-22-10
Wesele 10-03-73
West, The 10-31-28
West 11 10-16-63
West End Jungle 11-01-61
West Is East 11-24-22
West of Abilene 7-17-40
West of Broadway 2-02-32
West of Carson City 5-08-40

West of Cheyenne 3-04-31
West of Cheyenne 8-24-38
West of Chicago 8-25-22
West of El Dorado 10-12-49
West of Nevada 7-22-36
West of Pinto Basin 12-11-40
West of Rainbow's End 8-25-26 and 11-17-26
West of Rainbow's End 3-09-38
West of Sante Fe 12-14-38
West of Shanghai 11-03-37
West of Singapore 4-04-33
West of Sonora 11-10-48
West of Texas 5-05-43
West of the Alamo 7-03-46
West of the Brazos 4-26-50
West of the Divide 5-15-34
West of the Pecos 1-01-35
West of the Pecos 6-06-45
West of the Rockies 8-06-30 and 7-14-31
West of Tombstone 4-08-42
West of Wyoming 4-12-50
West of Zanzibar 1-09-29
West of Zanzibar 4-07-54
West Point 1-11-28
West Point of the Air 4-10-35
West Point Story, The 11-15-50
West Point Widow 6-11-41
West Side Kid 8-18-43
West Side Story 9-27-61
West to Glory 4-30-47
West Wind 9-17-15
Westbound 3-25-59
Westbound Limited 11-17-37
Westbound Mail 4-07-37
Westbound Stage 3-06-40
Western Approaches 1-03-45
Western Caravans 6-28-39
Western Code 2-21-33
Western Courage 3-18-36
Western Cyclone 6-16-43
Western Electric Films 1-25-19
Western Firebrands 1-27-22
Western Frontier 12-25-35
Western Gold 11-03-37
Western Hearts 9-23-21
Western Heritage 2-04-48
Western Honor 7-02-30
Western Jamboree 12-21-38
Western Limited 10-18-32
Western Luck 7-09-24
Western Mail 3-04-42
Western Musketeer, A 2-01-23
Western Night, A 1-14-11
Western Pacific Agent 3-22-50
Western Renegades 1-04-50
Western Rover, The 6-15-27
Western Speed 5-19-22
Western Trails 6-29-38
Western Union 2-05-41
Western Vengeance 7-30-24
Western Wallop 10-15-24
Western Whirlwind, The 4-27-27
Westerner, The 12-16-36
Westerner, The 9-25-40
Westerners, The 8-08-19
Westerplatte Resists 7-26-67
Westland Case, The 10-06-37
Westward Bound 3-18-31
Westward Bound 3-22-44
Westward Ho 2-19-36
Westward Ho 4-29-42
Westward Ho the Wagons 12-19-56
Westward Passage 6-07-32
Westward the Women 11-21-51
Westward Trail, The 2-25-48
Westworld 8-15-73
Weswanie 7-28-71
Wet Gold 9-09-21
Wet Paint 5-19-26
Wet Parade, The 4-26-32
Wet Rainbow 10-30-74
Wetbacks 3-07-56
We've Come a Long, Long Way 6-28-44
We've Never Been Licked 8-04-43
We've Seen Everything (See: On Aura Tout Vu)
Whale That Had a Toothache, A (See: Baleine Qui Avait Mal Aux
     Dents, Une)
Whalers, The 10-28-42

When Love Is Over (See: Apres L'Amour)
When Love Is Young 4-21-37
When Love Was Blind 3-30-17
When Lovers Part 1-07-11
When Men Are Tempted 1-04-18
When Moscow Laughs 9-18-29
When Mother Is Out (See: Me Vang Nha)
When Mother Returns (See: Cuando Regree Mama)
When My Baby Smiles at Me 11-10-48
When My Heart Calls (See: Ven, Mi Corazon Te Llama)
When My Lady Smiles 8-27-15
When Odds Are Even 4-30-24
When Peace Breaks Out (See: Cuando Estallo la Paz)
When Romance Rides 4-14-22
When Rome Ruled 8-21-14
When Seconds Count 6-01-27
When She's Pretty (See: Quand On Est Belle)
When Strangers Marry 5-30-33
When Strangers Marry 11-22-44
When Strangers Meet 11-20-34
When Svante Disappeared (See: Da Svante Forsvandt)
When Sweet the Moonlight Is Sleeping on the Hills (See: Wenn
    Suess das Mondlicht auf den Huegeln Schlaeft)
When the Bells Sound Clearly (See: Wenn die Glocken Hell
    Erklingen)
When the Bough Breaks 11-26-47
When the Boys Meet the Girls 12-01-65
When the Child Appears (See: Lorsque l'Enfant Parait)
When the City Awakes (See: Quand la Ville S'Eveille)
When the Clock Strikes 5-31-61
When the Clouds Roll By 1-03-20
When the Cookie Crumbles (See: Satogashi Ga Kawareru Toki)
When the Daltons Ride 7-31-40
When the Desert Smiles 10-31-19
When the Devil Came by Night (See: Nachts, Wenn der Teufel Kam)
When the Door Opened 12-23-25
When the Fires Started (See: Uzavreli Grad)
When the Heart Sings (See: Cuando Canta El Corazon)
When the Heavens Fall (See: Kun Taivas Putoaa)
When the Law Rides 7-18-28
When the Legends Die 8-09-72
When the Lights Go On Again 12-13-44
When the Mad Aunts Are Coming (See: Wenn die Tollen Tanten
    Kommen)
When the Orange Tree Flowers (See: Cuando Florezca El Naranjo)
When the Pheasants Pass (See: Quand Passent les Faisans)
When the Poppies Bloom Again (See: Dokter Pulder Zaait
    Papavers)
When the Rain Is Falling (See: Driver Dagg Faller Regn)
When the Redskins Rode 5-09-51
When the Sun Rises (See: Hababam Sinifi Tatilde)
When the Trees Were Big (See: Koda Derevia Byli Bolchini)
When the Wife's Away 12-22-26
When the Woman Butts In (See: Quand la Femme S'En Mele or
    Kam Cert Nemuze)
When Thief Meets Thief 6-16-37
When Time Ran Out 4-02-80
When Tomorrow Comes 8-16-39
When Tomorrow Dies 1-26-66
When True Love Dawns 7-06-17
When We Are Married 3-31-43
When We Were Boys 2-09-07
When We Were Children (See: Quand Nous Etions Petits Enfants)
When We Were 21 4-02-15
When We Were Young 10-31-14
When Were You Born? 6-15-38
When Willie Comes Marching Home 1-04-50
When Women Had Tails (See: Quando Le Donne Avevano La Coda)
When Women Win 11-27-09
When Worlds Collide 8-29-51
When You Can't Believe Anyone (See: Fushin No Toki)
When You Come Home 4-02-47
When You Comin' Back, Red Ryder? 2-07-79
When You Hear the Bells (See: Kad Cujes Zvona)
When You Read This Letter (See: Quand Tu Liras Cette Lettre)
When You're in Love 2-24-37
When You're Smiling 8-23-50
When's Your Birthday? 3-24-37
Where Angels Go, Trouble Follows 4-03-68
Where Are My Children? 4-14-16
Where Are You from Johnny? (See: D'Ou Viens-Tu Johnny?)
Where Are You Going? (See: Saan Ka Papunta)
Where Are You Going On Holiday? (See: Dove Vai In Vacanza?)
Where Are You Heart? (See: Donde Estas Corazon?)
Where Are You Then...? (See: Ou Etes-Vous Donc...?)
Where Are Your Children? 12-01-43
Where Bonds Are Loosed 10-03-19 and 11-07-19
Where Cowboy Is King 5-28-15

Where Danger Lives 6-21-50
Where Did Tom Go? (See: Ou Est Passe Tom?)
Where Did You Get That Girl? 3-26-41
Where Do We Go from Here? 5-23-45
Where Does It Hurt? 8-16-72
Where Eagles Dare 12-11-68
Where East Is East 5-29-29
Where Has Poor Mickey Gone 4-22-64
Where Is Beta? (See: Quem E Beta?)
Where Is Colleti? 4-24-14
Where Is My Child? 12-01-37
Where Is My Wandering Boy Tonight? 2-10-22
Where Is the Body, Moeller? (See: Hvor Er Liget, Moeller?)
Where Is This Girl? 12-06-32
Where Is This West? 12-06-23
Where It's At 4-23-69
Where Lights Are Low 8-05-21
Where Love Has Gone 10-14-64
Where Love Leads 9-22-16
Where Men Are Men 9-23-21
Where No Vultures Fly 11-21-51
Where Sinners Meet 5-29-34
Where the Boys Are 11-30-60
Where the Buffalo Roam 11-02-38
Where the Buffalo Roam 4-02-80
Where the Bullets Fly 11-09-66
Where the Hot Wind Blows 9-21-60
Where the Lilies Bloom 2-06-74
Where the North Begins 9-27-23
Where the Pavement Ends 4-05-23
Where the Red Fern Grows 5-29-74
Where the Sidewalk Ends 6-28-50
Where the Spies Are 12-08-65
Where the Trail Begins 7-13-27
Where the Trail Divides 10-17-14
Where the West Begins 2-14-19
Where the West Begins 3-23-38
Where the Wind Blows (See: Dit Vindarna Bar)
Where There's Life 10-08-47
Where To After the Rain? (See: Kuda Posle Kise)
Where Trails Divide 10-20-37
Where Was I? 8-26-25
Where Was Your Majesty Between 3 & 5? 3-24-65
Where Were You When the Lights Went Out? 6-12-68
Where Words Fail 8-11-48 (Also see: Donde Mueren las Palabras)
Where's Charley? 7-02-52
Where's George 8-21-35
Where's Jack? 4-09-69
Where's Mary? 10-10-19
Where's Poppa? 11-11-70
Wherever She Goes 2-04-53
Wherever You Are, Mr. President (See: Gziekolwiek Jestes, Panie
    Prezydencie)
Which Shall It Be? 4-09-24
Which Way Is Up? 11-02-77
Which Way to the Front? 7-29-70
Which Woman? 6-14-18
Whiffs 10-01-75
While I Love 10-22-47
While Justice Waits 1-12-23
While London Sleeps 12-22-26
While New York Sleeps 9-03-20
While New York Sleeps 12-21-38
While Paris Sleeps 1-19-23
While Paris Sleeps 6-14-32
While Plucking the Daisies (See: En Effeuillant la Marguerite)
While Satan Sleeps 6-30-22
While the City Sleeps 10-24-28
While the City Sleeps 5-02-56
While the Doors Were Closed (See: Medan Porten Var Stangd)
While the Patient Slept 3-06-35
While the Sun Shines 2-19-47
While There's War There's Hope (See: Finche C'e Guerra C'e
    Speranza)
Whims of Society 2-08-18
Whip, The (See: Cravache, La)
Whip, The 3-30-17
Whip, The 9-19-28
Whip Hand, The 10-24-51
Whip Woman, The 2-15-28
Whiplash 12-22-48
Whipped 2-15-50
Whipping Cream Hero, The (See: De Verloedering Van de Swieps)
Whipsaw 1-29-36
Whirl of Life, The 10-22-15
Whirl of Life, The 3-27-29 and 7-03-29
Whirl of Paris, The 6-20-28
Whirlpool, The 6-28-18

276

Whirlpool 5-08-34
Whirlpool 11-23-49
Whirlpool 3-25-59
Whirlpool 9-02-70
Whirlwind 4-04-51
Whirlwind 7-31-68
Whirlwind Horseman 7-06-38
Whirlwind of Paris 2-13-46
Whirlwind of Youth, The 6-08-27
Whirlwind Raiders 5-12-48
Whiskey Galore 6-22-49
Whisper Market 9-03-20
Whispered Name 2-14-24
Whisperers, The 7-12-67
Whispering Chorus, The 3-29-18
Whispering City 5-07-47 and 11-12-47
Whispering Death 4-21-76
Whispering Devils 11-26-20
Whispering Enemies 3-01-39
Whispering Ghosts 4-22-42
Whispering Joe 5-08-68
Whispering Sage 4-06-27
Whispering Smith 6-16-16
Whispering Smith 5-12-26
Whispering Smith 2-19-36
Whispering Smith 12-08-48
Whispering Smith Vs. Scotland Yard 3-12-52
Whispering Winds 10-02-29
Whispers 7-02-20
Whist 9-17-10
Whistle, The 4-01-21
Whistle at Eaton Falls 8-01-51
Whistle Down the Wind 8-02-61
Whistle Stop 1-09-46
Whistler, The 5-03-44
Whistlin' Dan 6-28-32
Whistling Bullets 10-06-37
Whistling Hills 12-26-51
Whistling in Brooklyn 9-29-43
Whistling in Dixie 10-28-42
Whistling in the Dark 1-31-33
Whistling in the Dark 8-06-41
White and Unmarried 6-03-21
White Angel, The 7-01-36
White Banners 5-25-38
White Barbarian, A 2-22-23
White Bear, The 5-09-62
White Beret (See: Boina Blanca)
White Bim with Black Ear (See: Beli Bim--Chornoye Ukho)
White Bird Marked with Black, The (See: Bielaya Ptitsa S
    Tchornem Piatnom)
White Black Sheep, The 12-22-26
White Bondage 7-21-37
White Buffalo, The 9-21-77
White Caravan 5-20-64
White Cargo (See: Cargaison Blanche)
White Cargo 2-26-30
White Cargo 9-16-42
White Christmas 9-01-54
White Circle 9-03-20
White Cliffs of Dover, The 3-15-44
White Cockatoo 1-15-35
White Collar Blues (See: Fantozzi)
White Corridors 6-27-51
White Cradle Inn 4-02-47
White Dawn, The 7-17-74
White Death 12-09-36
White Demon, The (See: Weisse Daemon, Der)
White Desert, The 7-08-25
White Devil, The (See: Diavolo Bianco, Il)
White Devil, The 9-01-31
White Dove, The (See: Holubice)
White Eagle (See: Aguila Blanca)
White Eagle 9-27-32
White Face 12-05-33
White Fang 7-22-36
White Feather 2-09-55
White Fire 2-10-54
White Flannels 3-23-27
White Flower, The 3-08-23
White Fury 3-26-69
White Game, The (See: Vita Sporten, Den)
White Gloves of the Devil, The (See: Gants Blancs du Diable, Les)
White Goddess, The 3-19-15
White Gold 3-02-27
White Grass (See: Belle Trave)
White-Haired Girl, The 9-06-72

White Hands 2-03-22
White Heat 6-19-34
White Heat 8-31-49
White Heather, The 5-09-19
White Hell 11-17-22
White Hell of Pitz-Palu, The 1-02-52
White Hell of Piz Palu, The 12-11-29
White Heron, The (See: Shirasagui)
White Hope 11-03-22
White Horse, The (See: Caballo Blanco, El)
White Horse Inn (See: Hosteria del Caballito Blanco, La)
White Hunter 12-02-36
White Hunter 12-25-63
White in Bad Light 1-15-75
White Intoxication, The (See: Weisse Rausch, Der)
White Legion 12-23-36
White Legs (See: Pattes Blanches)
White Lie, The 5-22-14
White Lie, The 9-27-18
White Lies 6-25-20
White Lies 1-01-35
White Lightning 3-04-53
White Lightning 6-06-73
White Line, The 12-10-52
White Line Fever 7-16-75
White Love (See: Hoito Rabu)
White Mane 12-23-53
White Man's Chance, A 8-15-19
White Man's Law, The 4-26-18
White Moll, The 7-23-20
White Monkey, The 6-10-25
White Moor, The 7-21-65
White Moth 6-18-24
White Nights (See: Beliye Nochi or Notti Bianche)
White Oak 11-04-21
White Orchid 12-01-54
White Outlaw 9-16-25
White Panther 1-31-24
White Pants Willie 7-27-27
White Parade, The 11-13-34
White Pongo 12-05-45
White Rat 7-12-72
White Raven, The 1-19-17
White, Red, Yellow, Pink 11-30-66
White Reindeer, The (See: Valkoinen Peura)
White Rock 2-02-77
White Room, The (See: Bialata Staia)
White Rose, The (See: Rosa Blanca, La)
White Rose, The 5-24-23
White Rose of Hong Kong 12-29-65
White Roses of Ravensberg, The 5-22-29
White Savage 4-14-43
White Shadows in the South Seas 8-08-28
White Sheik, The (See: Sceicco Bianco, Lo)
White Sheik, The 2-08-28 and 12-11-29
White Ship, The (See: Belyi Parohod)
White Shoulders 6-09-31
White Sin, The 5-07-24
White Sister 3-14-73
White Sister, The (See: Hermana Blanca, La)
White Sister, The 7-30-15
White Sister, The 9-13-23
White Sister, The 3-21-33
White Slave (See: Esclave Blanche, L' or De Blanke Slavin)
White Slave Trade, The (See: Tratta Delle Bianche, La)
White Slave Traffic 12-12-13
White Slaver 1-02-14
White Squadron (See: Squadrone Bianco)
White Squaw, The 10-03-56
White Stallion, The 10-08-47
White Terror, The 7-23-15
White Tie and Tails 11-13-46
White Tiger, The 11-22-23
White Tower, The 6-14-50
White Trial (See: Procesul Alb)
White Unicorn, The 11-12-47
White Vertigo (See: Vertigine Bianca)
White Warrior, The 2-01-61
White Wilderness, The 6-25-58
White Witch Doctor 6-17-53
White Woman 11-21-33
White, Yellow, Black (See: Bianco, Il Giallo, Il Nero, Il)
White Youth 12-17-20
White Zombie 8-02-32
Whitewashed Walls 4-25-19
Whitey (See: De Witte Van Sichem)
Whither Germany? 4-25-33

Whity 7-14-71
Whizzer (See: Schluchtenflitzer)
Who? (See: Qui?)
Who Am I? 7-22-21
Who Are the DeBolts? (And Where Did They Get 19 Kids?)
    10-12-77
Who Are You Mr. Sorge? (See: Qui Etes-Vous Mr. Sorge?)
Who Are You Polly Magoo? (See: Qui Etes-Vous Polly Magoo?)
Who Can Kill a Child? (See: Quien Puede Matar A Un Nino?)
Who Cares? 1-17-19
Who Cares ... Anatomy of a Delivery Boy (See: Bof ... Anatomie
    D'Un Livreur)
Who Does What to Whom? (See: Hvem Ska' Med Hvem?)
Who Done It? 11-04-42
Who Done It? 3-28-56
Who Fears the Devil? 11-01-72
Who Goes There 11-23-17
Who Goes There! 6-25-52
Who Has Seen the Wind 11-16-77
Who Is Boss 9-10-10
Who Is Happier Than I? (See: Chi E' Piu Felice Di Me?)
Who Is Harry Kellerman and Why Is He Saying All Those Terrible
    Things About Me? 6-16-71
Who Is Hope Schuyler? 3-11-42
Who Is Killing the Great Chefs of Europe? 9-20-78
Who Is "Number One"? 10-26-17
Who Is to Blame 5-24-18
Who Is Your Servant? 2-27-20
Who Killed Aunt Maggie 11-06-40
Who Killed "Doc" Robbin 5-05-48
Who Killed Gail Preston? 3-09-38
Who Killed Jessie? (See: Kdo Chce Zabot Jessii?)
Who Killed John Savage 12-01-37
Who Killed Mary Whats'ername? 11-10-71
Who Killed Max? 3-04-11
Who Killed Santa Claus? 4-28-48
Who Killed Teddy Bear 10-06-65
Who Killed Walton? 4-19-18
Who Knows? (See: Quien Sabe)
Who Knows? 11-29-18
Who Leaves in the Rain (See: Kto Odchadza v Dazdi)
Who Loved Him Best 2-15-18
Who Owns the Rug? 10-08-10
Who Says I Can't Ride a Rainbow? 12-01-71
Who Shall Take My Life? 9-13-18
Who Slew Auntie Roo? 12-22-71
Who Takes Love Seriously (See: Wer Nimmt Liebe Ernst)
Who Was She? (See: Woh Kaun Thi?)
Who Was That Lady? 1-13-60
Who Will Marry Me? 1-25-19
Whole Town Accuses, The (See: Toute la Ville Accuse)
Whole Town's Talking, The 3-06-35
Whole Truth, The 8-06-58
Who'll Stop the Rain? 5-24-78
Wholly Moses 6-18-80
Whom God Forgives (See: Amanecer en Puerta Oscura)
Whom the Gods Destroy 12-08-16
Whom the Gods Destroy 7-17-34
Whoopee 10-08-30
Who's Afraid of Virginia Woolf? 6-22-66
Who's Been Sleeping in My Bed? 12-04-63
Who's Cheating? 7-09-24
Who's Crazy? 8-04-65
Who's Got the Action? 12-12-62
Who's Minding the Mint? 9-27-67
Who's Minding the Store? 11-20-63
Who's That Knocking at My Door? 9-11-68
Who's That Singing Over There? (See: Ko To Tamo Peva)
Who's Your Neighbor? 6-22-17
Why America (See: Pourquoi L'Amerique)
Why Announce Your Marriage? 2-03-22
Why Be Good? 5-08-29
Why Blame Me? 2-08-18
Why Bring That Up? 10-09-29
Why Change Your Wife? 4-30-20
Why Cry at Parting? 2-12-30
Why Do They Do It? (See: Hvorfor Goer De Det?)
Why Do You Come So Late? (See: Pourquoi Viens-Tu Si Tard?)
Why Does Mr. R. Run Amok? (See: Warum Laeuft Herr R. Amok?)
Why Does One Kill a Magistrate (See: Perche si Uccide Un
    Magistrato)
Why Does Your Husband Deceive You? (See: Por Que Te Engana Tu
    Marido?)
Why Get Married? 8-06-24
Why Girls Go Back Home 5-19-26
Why Girls Leave Home 10-02-09
Why Girls Leave Home 8-08-45
Why Hungarian Films Are Bad (See: Miert Rosszak a Magyar Filmek)

Why Israel? (See: Pourquoi Israel?)
Why Korea? 1-24-51
Why Leave Home? 9-18-29
Why Men Forget 1-27-22
Why Men Leave Home 10-13-22
Why Men Leave Home 5-14-24
Why Not? (See: Pourquoi Pas)
Why Rock the Boat? 10-09-74
Why Russians Are Revolting 6-03-70
Why Sailors Go Wrong 4-11-28
Why Shoot the Teacher 7-13-77
Why Smith Left Home 10-17-19
Why They Married 11-27-09
Why This War? 10-11-39
Why Weep at Parting? 10-30-29
Why Women Love 12-16-25
Why Women Remarry 11-01-23
Why Worry 9-06-23
Why Would I Lie? 8-06-80
Wiano 10-28-64
Wichita 6-29-55
Wicked 9-22-31
Wicked As They Come 5-30-56
Wicked Darling, The 2-07-19
Wicked Dreams of Paula Schultz, The 1-10-68
Wicked Lady, The 11-28-45
Wicked, Wicked 4-18-73
Wicked Woman 11-25-53
Wicked Woman, A 12-18-34
Wickedness Preferred 2-22-28
Wicker Man, The 5-15-74
Wicket Gate, The (See: Drzwi W Murze)
Wide Open 1-19-27
Wide Open 3-26-30
Wide Open Faces 4-20-38
Wide Open Marriage 12-25-74
Wide Open Town 7-30-41
Wide Open Town, A 3-03-22
Wide Point 2-26-69
Widecombe Fair 10-30-29
Widow, The 10-23-09
Widow by Proxy 9-26-19
Widow Couderc (See: Veuve Couderc, La)
Widow from Chicago 12-24-30
Widow from Monte Carlo 1-29-36
Widow Montiel, The (See: Viuda de Montiel, La)
Widower, The (See: Po Mai Tidet)
Widowhood of Karolina Zasler, The (See: Vdovstvo Karoline
    Zasler)
Widow's Choice, The 1-21-11
Widow's Might, The 1-25-18
Widow's Nest 12-14-77
... Wie Einst Lili Marleen 11-14-56
Wie Ich ein Neger Wurde 7-15-70
Wie Kommt Ein so Reizendes Maedchen zu Diesem Gewerbe?
    9-30-70
Wie Kurz Ist die Zeit zum Lieben 5-20-70
Wie Werde Ich Reich und Gluecklich? (See: How Do I Become
    Rich and Happy?)
Wie Zwei Froehliche Luftschiffer 10-29-69
Wiegenlied 7-23-30
Wien, du Stadt der Lieder 5-07-30 and 3-25-31
Wien, Du Stadt Meiner Traeume 2-12-58
Wien Tanzt 10-10-51
Wiener Madeln 2-08-50
Wife, The (See: Savithri)
Wife Against Wife 6-30-22
Wife and Motor Trouble 3-10-16
Wife by Proxy, A 1-12-17
Wife, Doctor and Nurse 9-08-37
Wife, Husband and Friend 2-15-39
Wife in Name Only 10-18-23
Wife No. 13 (See: Al Zouga Talattshar)
Wife Number 2 8-03-17
Wife of Cain, The 11-07-14
Wife of General Ling, The 4-21-37 and 2-23-38
Wife of Monte Cristo, The 3-27-46
Wife of the Centaur 1-07-25
Wife or Child 10-02-09
Wife or Country 12-27-18 and 1-10-19
Wife Savers 1-18-28
Wife Swappers, The 8-12-70
Wife Takes a Flyer, The 4-22-42
Wife That Wasn't Wanted, The 9-16-25
Wife Trap 5-12-22
Wife vs. Secretary 3-04-36
Wife Wanted, A 3-14-13
Wife's Awakening, A 9-09-21
Wife's Family, The 6-16-31

With Hoops of Steel 5-10-18
With Joyous Heart (See: A Coeur Joie)
With Lee in Virginia 3-21-14
With Lots of Love (See: Con Mucho Carino)
With Love and Kisses (See: Med Kaerlig Hilsen)
With Love and Kisses 1-20-37
With Love and Tenderness (See: S Lyubov I Nezhnost)
With Max Linder (See: En Compagnie de Max Linder)
With Neatness and Dispatch 4-19-18
With Nobody (See: Pri Nikogo)
With Oak-Leaves and Fig-Leaf (See: Mit Eichenlaub und
   Feigenblatt)
With Shared Love (See: Spodelena Lyubov)
With Six You Get Eggroll 8-07-68
With Sven Hedin Through Asia's Deserts (See: Asia's Desert)
With Taft in Panama 3-06-09
With the Allies at Salonica 4-21-16
With the Blood of Others (See: Par Le Sang Des Autres)
With the Lives of Others (See: Avec le Peau des Autres)
With These Hands 6-21-50
With This Ring 9-23-25 and 6-23-26
With You and Without You (See: S Toboi Y Bes Tebia)
Within Man's Power 6-09-54
Within Prison Walls 9-26-28
Within the Cup 3-22-18
Within the Gates 6-18-15
Within the Law 5-04-17
Within the Law 5-03-23
Within the Law 4-12-39
Within These Walls 6-06-45
Without a Flag (See: Senza Bandiera)
Without a Home 4-19-39
Without a Soul 11-10-16
Without a Stitch of Clothing (See: Uden en Travel)
Without Anaesthetic (See: Bez Znieczulenia)
Without Apparent Motive (See: Sans Mobile Apparent)
Without Appeal (See: Sans Sommation)
Without Benefit of Clergy 6-24-21
Without Date (See: Ohne Datum)
Without Dowry 4-17-46
Without Each Other 5-23-62
Without Family (See: Senza Famiglia Nullatenenti Cercano
   Affetto)
Without Fear 5-12-22
Without Honor 12-21-17
Without Honor 11-09-49
Without Honors 4-05-32
Without Hope 1-08-15
Without Limit 3-25-21
Without Love (See: Bez Milosci)
Without Love 3-21-45
Without Mercy 9-30-25
Without Orders 11-11-36
Without Pity 12-14-49
Without Prejudice 10-13-48
Without Reservations 5-08-46
Without Tomorrow (See: Sans Lendemain)
Without Trumpet or Drum (See: Sans Tambour Ni Trompette)
Without Warning 4-02-52
Without Warning 9-24-80
Witness, The (See: Temoin, Le)
Witness Chair, The 4-22-36
Witness for the Defense 9-19-19
Witness for the Prosecution 12-04-57
Witness in the City (See: Temoin Dans la Ville, Un)
Witness to Murder 4-21-54
Witness Vanishes, The 10-25-39
Witnesses, The (See: Testigos, Los)
Witnesses, The 11-15-67
Wits vs. Wits 6-11-20
Wives (See: Hustruer)
Wives 2-27-14
Wives and Lovers 7-31-63
Wives and Obscurities (See: Moglie E Buoi ...)
Wives and Other Wives 12-06-18
Wives Beware 5-30-33
Wives Never Know 11-04-36
Wives Under Suspicion 6-08-38
Wiz, The 10-04-78
Wizard, The 11-30-27
Wizard of Baghdad, The 12-14-60
Wizard of Oz, The 4-22-25
Wizard of Oz, The 8-16-39
Wizard of Waukesha, The 3-12-80
Wizards 2-02-77
Wizia Lokalna 1901 9-24-80
Wobblies, The 10-24-79

Wodzirej 10-25-78
Woe to the Conqueror 2-05-15
Wognie Broda Nyet 10-29-69
Woh Kaun Thi? 10-20-65
Wolf, The 9-26-19
Wolf and His Mate, The 11-30-17
Wolf and the Dove, The (See: Loba y la Paloma, La)
Wolf Call 5-24-39
Wolf-Cubs of Niquoluna, The (See: Prune des Bois)
Wolf Fangs 12-14-27
Wolf Hunt, The 12-04-09
Wolf Hunters, The 7-28-26
Wolf Hunters, The 2-08-50
Wolf Larsen 10-15-58
Wolf Law 10-27-22
Wolf Lowry 6-02-17
Wolf Man, The 9-17-15
Wolf Man, The 4-16-24
Wolf Man, The 12-17-41
Wolf of Debt, The 10-08-15
Wolf of New York 1-24-40
Wolf of Prokletija (See: Vuk Sa Prokletija)
Wolf of Wall Street, The 1-30-29
Wolf Pack 4-07-22
Wolf Song 2-27-29
Wolf Trap, The (See: Vlci Jama or Vrci Jana)
Wolf Woman, The 9-01-16
Wolfpen Principle, The 3-20-74
Wolf's Clothing 3-30-27
Wolf's Clothing 4-01-36
Wolf's Prey, The 1-01-15
Wolf's Trail 1-18-28
Wolverine 8-26-21
Wolves (See: Wanted Men)
Wolves, The 6-28-72
Wolves Hunt at Night (See: Loups Chassent la Nuit, Les)
Wolves in the Depth (See: Lupi Nell'Abisso)
Wolves in the Sheepfold, The (See: Loups Dans la Bergerie, Les)
Wolves of Kultur No. 4 10-25-18
Wolves of the Air 5-04-27
Wolves of the Border 5-17-18
Wolves of the City 2-20-29
Wolves of the North 5-20-21
Wolves of the Rail 1-18-18
Wolves of the Range 6-14-44
Wolves of the Sea 2-02-38
Wolves of the Underworld 1-15-36
Wolz: Leben und Verklaerung eines Deutschen Anarchisten 6-02-76
Wolz: Life and Illusion of a German Anarchist (See: Wolz: Leben
   und Verklaerung eines Deutschen Anarchisten)
Woman 11-01-18
Woman 2-08-50
Woman, A (See: Mujer, Una or Phooying)
Woman, The 5-07-15
Woman Accused 3-14-33
Woman Across the Way, The (See: Frau Gegenuber, Die)
Woman Against the World 3-28-28
Woman Against the World 5-11-38
Woman Against Woman 4-03-14 and 5-08-14
Woman Against Woman 6-22-38
Woman Alone, A 1-05-17
Woman Alone, A 6-24-36
Woman Alone, The 3-03-37
Woman and a Woman, A (See: Kobieta I Kobieta)
Woman and Lover (See: Donna E Bello)
Woman and Temptation 11-29-67
Woman and the Beast 12-21-17
Woman and the Jungle, The (See: Mujer y la Selva, La)
Woman and the Law 3-15-18
Woman and the Puppet, The (See: Femme et le Pantin, La)
Woman and Wife 1-18-18
Woman and Wine 4-23-15
Woman at Her Window (See: Femme a Sa Fenetre, Une)
Woman Banker, The (See: Banquiere, La)
Woman Beneath, The 9-14-17
Woman Between, The 2-11-31
Woman Between, The 10-27-31
Woman Between Dog and Wolf, A (See: Een Vrouw Tussen Hond En
   Wolf)
Woman Between Friends, The 2-22-18
Woman Branded, A 5-02-33
Woman Chases Man 6-16-37
Woman Commands, A 2-02-32
Woman Conquers, A 2-22-23
Woman Cop, The (See: Femme Flic, La)
Woman Disputed 11-14-28
Woman Doctor 2-15-39
Woman Dressed as a Man, The (See: Femme en Homme, La)

Woman for a Season, A (See: O Femeie Pentru Un Anotimp)
Woman for Joe 9-07-55
Woman from Beirut (See: Dama de Beirut, La)
Woman from Hell, The 7-31-29
Woman from Monte Carlo, The 1-05-32
Woman from Moscow, The 11-07-28
Woman from Tangier, The 2-04-48
Woman from the Torrid Land (See: Mujer de La Tierra Caliente, La)
Woman Gives, The 4-16-20
Woman God Changed, The 5-27-21
Woman God Forgot, The 11-02-17
Woman Hater, The 9-11-09
Woman Hater, The 9-03-15
Woman Hater, The 7-15-25
Woman Hater, The 10-27-48
Woman He Chose, The 11-14-19
Woman He Loved, The 9-08-22
Woman He Married, The 11-22-18
Woman He Married, The 4-14-22
Woman He Scorned, The 5-14-30
Woman He Wronged, The 12-18-14
Woman Hungry 3-25-31
Woman I Abandoned, The (See: Watashi Ga Suteta Onna)
Woman I Love, The 5-08-29
Woman I Love, The 4-21-37
Woman I Stole, The 7-04-33
Woman in a Dressing Gown 7-24-57
Woman in Black, The 8-20-15
Woman in Blue, The (See: Femme En Bleu, La)
Woman in Chains 2-22-23
Woman in Chains 11-22-32
Woman in Command 6-05-34
Woman in Distress 1-20-37
Woman in 47, The 2-04-16
Woman in Fur Coat (See: Kvinna I Leopard)
Woman in Green, The 6-20-45
Woman in Hiding 12-14-49
Woman in His House 3-04-21
Woman in Politics, The 1-28-16
Woman in Question 10-18-50
Woman in Red, The 3-27-35
Woman in Room 13, The 4-09-20
Woman in Room 13, The 5-24-32
Woman in Scarlet 8-02-32
Woman in the Dark 5-22-35
Woman in the Dark 1-16-52
Woman in the Dunes (See: Suna No Onna)
Woman in the Hall, The 11-12-47
Woman in the Jungle (See: Weib im Dschungel)
Woman in the Moon, The 11-13-29
Woman in the Night, A 3-20-29
Woman in the Resistance, A (See: Mia Gyneka Stin Antistassi)
Woman in the Suit Case 1-16-20
Woman in the Window, The 10-11-44
Woman in White (See: Kvinna I Vitt)
Woman in White 6-05-29 and 7-24-29
Woman in White, The 4-21-48
Woman Is a Stranger, The (See: Etrangere, L')
Woman Is a Wonderful Thing (See: Donna E una Cosa Meravigliosa, La)
Woman Is Always a Woman, A (See: Femme Est une Femme, Une)
Woman Is the Judge, A 10-04-39
Woman Knows What She Wants, A (See: Frau, Die Weiss, Was Sie Will, Eine)
Woman Laughs Last (See: Femina Ridens)
Woman Like Eve, A 3-26-80
Woman Longed For 5-22-29
Woman, Man, City (See: Mujer, Un Hombre, Une Ciudad, Una)
Woman Next Door, The 9-10-15
Woman Next Door, The 5-23-19
Woman Obsessed 5-27-59
Woman of Affairs, A 1-23-29
Woman of Distinction, A 3-08-50
Woman of Everyone, The (See: A Mulher de Todos)
Woman of Evil 1-26-49
Woman of Experience, A 7-14-31
Woman of Impulse, A 9-27-18
Woman of Lies, The 10-24-19
Woman of Mystery 5-29-14
Woman of No Importance 6-30-22
Woman of No Importance, A (See: Mujer Sin Importancia, Una)
Woman of Paris, A 9-27-23
Woman of Pleasure, A 11-21-19
Woman of Redemption, A 6-14-18
Woman of Rome (See: Romana, La)
Woman of Samaria, The 11-12-10
Woman of Straw 5-06-64
Woman of the River 8-07-57

Woman of the Town, The 12-15-43
Woman of the World, A 12-16-25
Woman of the Year 1-14-42
Woman on Fire, A 5-06-70
Woman on Jury, The 5-28-24
Woman on the Beach, The 4-23-47
Woman on the Index, The 3-28-19
Woman on the Run 10-04-50
Woman on Trial 9-28-27
Woman, One Day, A (See: Femme, Un Jour, Une)
Woman One Longs For, The (See: Woman Longed For)
Woman Pays, The 11-19-15
Woman Power 10-20-26
Woman Proof 11-01-23
Woman Racket, The 3-05-30
Woman Rebels, A 11-04-36
Woman Rhymes with Human (See: Menschenfrauen)
Woman Tempted, The 5-02-28
Woman the Germans Shot, The 11-01-18
Woman There Was, A 6-13-19
Woman They Almost Lynched, The 4-01-53
Woman They Talk About, The (See: Frau Von Der Man Spricht)
Woman Thief (See: Voleur de Femmes)
Woman Thou Gavest Me, The 6-13-19
Woman Times Seven 6-21-67
Woman to Woman 4-02-24
Woman to Woman 11-13-29
Woman to Woman 10-30-46
Woman to Woman 3-12-75
Woman Trap 9-04-29
Woman Trap 3-11-36
Woman Trouble 6-01-49
Woman Unafraid 4-24-34
Woman Under Cover, The 10-24-19
Woman Under Oath, The 6-20-19
Woman Under the Influence, A 10-16-74
Woman Untamed 10-29-20
Woman, Wake Up 3-31-22
Woman Wanted 8-14-35
Woman Who Came Back 12-19-45
Woman Who Came Back, The 10-04-18
Woman Who Dared, The 3-12-15
Woman Who Dared, The 7-07-16
Woman Who Dared, The 3-23-49
Woman Who Did Not Care, The 8-10-27
Woman Who Fooled Herself, The 11-17-22
Woman Who Gave, The 11-01-18
Woman Who Obeyed, The 10-11-23
Woman Who Sinned, The 7-09-24
Woman Who Understood, The 3-26-20
Woman Who Walked Alone, The 6-09-22
Woman Who Wouldn't Die, The 5-05-65
Woman Wills, A 5-05-16
Woman Wise 2-29-28; 3-21-28; and 4-18-28
Woman-Wise 1-20-37
Woman with Four Faces, The 6-21-23
Woman with Red Boots, The (See: Femme Aux Bottes Rouges, La)
Woman with Responsibilities, A (See: Frau Mit Verantwortung, Eine)
Woman with the Dog, The (See: Dama S Sobatchkoi)
Woman with the Knife, The (See: Femme Au Couteau, La)
Woman without a Face 10-15-47
Woman Without a Soul (See: Mujer Sin Alma, La)
Woman Without Camelias, The (See: Signora Senza Camelie)
Woman Without Importance, A (See: Frau Ohne Bedeutung, Eine)
Woman, Woman 1-31-19
Woman, You Should Not Have Been Created (See: Babae, Hindi Ka Dapat Nilalang)
Womaneater, The 6-10-59
Womanhandled 1-13-26
Womanhood 4-06-17
Womanlight (See: Clair de Femme)
Woman's Awakening, A 3-30-17
Woman's Business, A 7-30-20
Woman's Caprice, A 4-09-10
Woman's Case, A 9-10-69
Woman's Conquest, A 8-20-15
Woman's Daring, A 10-13-16
Woman's Devotion, A 11-28-56
Woman's Experience, A 9-20-18
Woman's Face, A (See: Kvinnas Ansikte, En)
Woman's Face, A 5-07-41
Woman's Faith, A 7-29-25
Woman's Fight, A 8-25-16
Woman's Heart, A 9-08-26
Woman's Kingdom, The 7-17-68
Woman's Law 12-07-27
Woman's Law, The 4-07-16

Woman's Life, A (See: Onna No Rekishi)
Woman's Man, A 7-16-20 and 10-29-20
Woman's Past, A 11-19-15
Woman's Place, A 10-21-21
Woman's Power, A 2-18-16
Woman's Resurrection, A 5-21-15
Woman's Secret, A 4-16-24
Woman's Secret, A 2-09-49
Woman's Side, The 1-06-22
Woman's Strategy, A 1-29-10
Woman's Testament (See: Jokyo)
Woman's Treachery, A 4-24-14
Woman's Vanity, A 10-15-10
Woman's Vengeance, A 12-24-47
Woman's Way, A 8-11-16
Woman's Way, A 4-18-28
Woman's Wit, A 10-23-09
Woman's Woman, A 10-13-22
Woman's World 9-29-54
Women, The (See: Femmes, Les)
Women, The 9-06-39
Women Alone (See: Donne Sole)
Women and Bandits (See: Donne e Briganti)
Women and Gold 1-21-25
Women Are Like That 4-13-38
Women Are My Weakness 7-17-29
Women Are Trouble 9-02-36
Women Disappear (See: Des Femmes Disparaissent)
Women Duelling (See: Duelle)
Women Everywhere 6-25-30
Women First 12-10-24
Women from Headquarters 5-17-50
Women Go On Forever 10-20-31
Women in Bondage 11-24-43
Women in Cell Block 7 9-11-74
Women in His Life 1-30-34
Women in Love 11-19-69
Women in Prison 2-09-38
Women in Prison 1-30-57
Women in the Night 1-14-48
Women in the Sun (See: Femmes Au Soleil)
Women in the Wind 2-01-39 and 4-19-39
Women in War 5-29-40
Women Love Once 6-30-31
Women Men Forget 7-21-22
Women Men Marry 1-05-23
Women Men Marry 7-14-31
Women Men Marry 9-22-37
Women Must Dress 4-17-35
Women of All Nations 6-02-31
Women of Doom (See: Melancolicas, Las)
Women of Glamour 3-10-37
Women of Niskavuori (See: Niskavuoren Naiset)
Women of Paris (See: Femmes de Paris)
Women of Pitcairn Island, The 2-06-57
Women of the Bois du Boulogne (See: Dames du Bois du Boulogne,
   Les)
Women of the Night (See: Yoru No Onnatachi)
Women of the North Country 7-30-52
Women of the Prehistoric Planet 11-23-66
Women of the World (See: Donna Nel Mondo, La)
Women of Twilight 1-28-53
Women They Talk About 10-17-28
Women Waiting (See: Kvinnors Vantan)
Women Want Diamonds 4-27-27
Women Who Dare 5-09-28
Women Who Give 6-04-24
Women Who Wait 8-19-21
Women Without Names (See: Femmes Sans Nom)
Women Without Names 2-21-40
Women Women (See: Femmes, Femmes)
Women Won't Tell 1-17-33
Women's Clothes 3-17-22
Women's Club (See: Club de Femmes)
Women's Confidant, The (See: Confident de Ces Dames, Le)
Women's Dreams (See: Kvinna Drom or Was Frauen Traeumen)
Women's Games (See: Jeux de Femmes)
Women's Paradise (See: Frauenparadies, Das)
Women's Prison 1-26-55
Women's Prisons (See: Prisons de Femmes)
Women's Regiment (See: Weiberregiment)
Women's Wares 11-23-27
Won by a Holdup 1-29-10
Won in the Clouds 5-02-28
Won in the Desert 7-17-09
Won Ton Ton, the Dog Who Saved Hollywood 5-05-76
Wonder Bar 3-06-34
Wonder Boy 12-26-51

Wonder Child (See: Entfuehrung ins Gluck)
Wonder Man, The 6-04-20
Wonder Man, The 4-25-45
Wonder of It All, The 1-02-74
Wonder of Women 7-24-29
Wonderful Adventure, The 10-08-15
Wonderful Age, The (See: Bel Age, Le)
Wonderful Chance 7-21-22
Wonderful Country, The 9-30-59
Wonderful Day, The (See: Merveilleuse Journee, La)
Wonderful Day, The 7-04-28
Wonderful Lie, The 7-03-29 and 7-31-29
Wonderful Lies of Nina Petrova, The 6-04-30
Wonderful Life 7-08-64
Wonderful Mentality (See: Belle Mentalite)
Wonderful Night, A 6-13-19
Wonderful Plates 12-03-10
Wonderful Thing 11-11-21
Wonderful Things 6-18-58
Wonderful Times 5-02-51
Wonderful Wife, A 4-28-22
Wonderful World of the Brothers Grimm, The 7-18-62
Wonderful Year 6-02-22
Wonderful Years, The (See: Wunderbaren Jahre, Die)
Wonderland of Big Game 4-26-23
Wonderland of Love (See: Wunderland der Liebe)
Wonders of Aladdin, The 11-01-61
Wonders of Nature 8-28-09
Wonders of the Sea 3-22-23
Wonders of the Wilds 4-01-25
Wonderwall 1-15-69
Wood Chopping in Canada 3-28-08
Wood Nymph, The 1-07-16
Wooden Crosses (See: Croix de Bois, Les)
Wooden Gun, The (See: Roveh Huliot)
Wooden Horse, The 8-02-50
Wooden Shoes 8-24-17
Woodpeckers Don't Get Headaches (See: Ne Bolit Golowa U Djatla)
Woodstock 4-01-70
Wooing of Princess Pat, The 2-22-18
Woolen Stocking Peddlar, The (See: Hosekraemmeren)
Word, The (See: Ordet)
Word Is Out 3-08-78
Words and Music 10-02-29
Words and Music 12-08-48
Words and Music By 5-23-19
Work (See: Charlie Chaplin in "Work" or Avodah)
Work Is A Four-Letter Word 6-12-68
Work Is Freedom (See: Travail C'Est La Liberte, Le)
Working Class Goes to Heaven, The (See: Classe Operaia Va In
   Paradiso, La)
Working Man, The 4-25-33
Working Woman (See: Mujeres Que Trabajan)
World Accuses, The 3-27-35
World Aflame, The 8-01-19
World Against Him, The 12-15-16
World and His Wife, The 7-23-20
World and Its Woman, The 9-12-19
World and the Flesh 5-10-32
World and Woman 9-23-21
World at Her Feet, The 7-20-27
World at Night, The (See: Mondo di Notte, Il)
World at Night No. 3 (See: Mondo di Notte No. 3, Il)
World at War, The 9-02-42
World by Night 8-16-61
World by Night No. 2 7-11-62
World Changes, The 10-31-33
World Dances 11-10-54
World, Flesh and the Devil, The (See: Mundo, Demonio y Carne)
World for Ransom 2-03-54
World Gone Mad 4-18-33
World in Flames 10-16-40
World in His Arms, The 6-18-52
World in My Corner 2-01-56
World in My Pocket, The 3-08-61
World in Revolt 6-12-34
World Is Full of Married Men, The 6-06-79
World Is Just a "B" Movie, The 3-17-71
World Is Ours, The (See: Svet Patri Nam)
World Moves On 7-03-34
World of Abbott and Costello, The 4-07-65
World of Apu, The (See: Apur Sanshar)
World of Folly, A 7-02-20
World of Henry Orient, The 3-18-64
World of Love, A (See: Mundo de Amor, Un)
World of Plenty 7-14-43
World of Silence, The (See: Monde du Silence, Le)
World of Suzie Wong, The 11-16-60

X

Y

Yasashi Nipponjin 9-06-72
Yasei No Shomei 11-15-78
Yashaga Ike (See: Demon Pond)
Yassa Mossa 3-25-53
Yatsu Hakamura 12-14-77
Yawar Mallku 9-24-69 and 4-29-70
Yawmun Akher 2-20-80
Year Long Road, The (See: Cesta Duga Godinu Dana)
Year of School, A (See: Anno di Scuola, Un)
Year of the Caribou 10-30-74
Year of the Hare, The (See: Janiksen Vuosi)
Year of the Horse, The 3-30-66
Year of the Woman, The 8-22-73
Year 01, The (See: An 01, L')
Year One (See: Anno Uno)
Yearling, The 11-27-46
Yearning (See: Midareru)
Years Between, The 4-10-46
Years of Youth 9-14-60
Yeh Nuat Sua 6-08-77
Yehudi Menuhin--Chemin de Lumiere 9-01-71
Yehudi Menuhin--Road of Light (See: Yehudi Menuhin--Chemin de
    Lumiere)
Yellow Back, The 10-20-26
Yellow Balloon, The 2-18-53
Yellow Bullet, The 3-30-17
Yellow Cab Man 2-22-50
Yellow Canary 11-10-43
Yellow Canary, The 4-17-63
Yellow Cargo 11-18-36
Yellow Claw, The 2-04-21
Yellow Cruise 11-25-36
Yellow Devil, The (See: Schut, Der)
Yellow Dog, The (See: Chien Jaune, Le)
Yellow Dog, The 10-18-18
Yellow Dust 2-26-36
Yellow Fin 10-24-51
Yellow Fingers 5-19-26
Yellow Flag, The (See: Gelbe Flagge, Die)
Yellow Flower, The (See: Dao Ruang)
Yellow Handkerchief of Happiness, A (See: Siawase No Cakusoku
    Hankeci)
Yellow House at Pinnasberg, The (See: Gelbe Haus am Pinnasberg,
    Das)
Yellow House of King Fu, The (See: Gelbe Haus des King Fu, Das)
Yellow Jack 5-25-38
Yellow Lily, The 5-23-28
Yellow Mask, The 8-13-30 and 12-10-30
Yellow Men and Gold 6-02-22
Yellow Menace, The 8-11-16 and 9-01-16
Yellow Mountain, The 11-24-54
Yellow Packet, The (See: Neal of the Navy: Part II)
Yellow Pass, The 8-29-28 and 12-19-28
Yellow Passport, The 2-04-16
Yellow Peril, The (See: Neal of the Navy: Part IX)
Yellow Robes, The 10-18-67
Yellow Rolls-Royce, The 1-13-65
Yellow Rose of Texas, The 5-17-44
Yellow Sands 7-20-38
Yellow Sky 11-24-48
Yellow Slippers, The (See: Historia Zoltej Cizemki)
Yellow Stain 5-19-22
Yellow Star, The (See: Gelbe Stern, Der)
Yellow Streak, A 12-17-15
Yellow Submarine 7-24-68
Yellow Teddybears, The 8-14-63
Yellow Ticket, The 5-24-18
Yellow Ticket, The 11-03-31
Yellow Tomahawk, The 5-19-54
Yellow Typhoon, The 5-14-20
Yellowback 4-17-29
Yellowneck 3-09-55
Yellowstone 9-23-36
Yellowstone Kelly 8-12-59
Yes (See: Igen)
Yes ... But ... (See: Ne Men ... Alla)
Yes, Madam 11-23-38
Yes, Mr. Brown 2-07-33
Yes, My Darling Daughter 2-08-39
Yes or No? 7-09-20
Yes Sir, Mr. Bones 8-01-51
Yes Sir, That's My Baby 8-10-49
Yesterday (See: Tegnup)
Yesterday 4-16-80
Yesterday and Today 3-03-54
Yesterday in Fact 11-04-64
Yesterday, Today and Tomorrow 4-01-64

Yesterday's Boys Didn't Use Hair-Fixers (See: Muchachos de Antes
    No Usaban Gomina, Los)
Yesterday's Enemy 9-23-59
Yesterday's Hero 11-28-79
Yesterday's Heroes 10-09-40
Yesterday's Tomorrow (See: Zwischengleis)
Yesterday's Wife 11-29-23
Yeti 1-18-78
Yeux Cernes, Les 9-30-64
Yeux de l'Amour, Les 2-03-60
Yeux Fermes, Les 4-26-72
Yeux Ne Veulent Pas en Tout Temps Se Fermer ou Peut-Etre Qu'un
    Jour Rome Se Permettra de Choisir a Son Tour 9-16-70
Yeux Noirs, Les 7-17-35
Yeux Sans Visage, Les 8-26-59
Yheden Miehen Sota 7-24-74
Yiddisher Boy, A 4-24-09
Yiddle with His Fiddle 1-06-37
Yidishe Tochter 5-23-33
Yield to the Night 6-27-56
Yim Sawasdi 11-29-78
Yiskor 6-06-33
Yksityisalue 5-15-63 and 10-14-64
Yo Baile Con Don Porfirio (See: I Danced with Don Porfirio)
Yo Conoci Esa Mujer 1-28-42
Yo la Primero 2-12-75
Yo Mate a Facundo 8-20-75
Yo No Soy la Mata Hari 11-01-50
Yo, Pecador 2-03-60
Yo Quiero Morir Contigo 8-20-41
Yo Quiero Ser Bataclana 5-28-41
Yod Manoot Computer 5-11-77
Yodelin' Kid from Pine Ridge 10-13-37
Yoga--A Road to Happiness (See: Yoga--En Vej Til Lykee)
Yoga--En Vej Til Lykee 4-30-75
Yoho 2-24-65
Yojimbo 8-30-61
Yojohan Fusuma No Shitabari 1-02-74
Yokel, The (See: Capitan, Le)
Yokel Boy 3-25-42
Yokihi 6-15-55
Yoko Ono Film No. 4 8-30-67
Yolanda 2-21-24
Yolanda 1-20-43
Yolanda and the Thief 10-17-45
Yolanta 12-30-64
Yollymoon 7-10-63
Yomegaeru Kinro 1-23-80
Yompaban Cha 2-01-78
Yorck 11-29-32
York 1-12-32
York State Folks 9-17-15
Yoru No Onnatachi 9-11-57
Yoru No Tsuzani 6-25-58
Yosemite Trail 11-17-22
Yoshiwara 9-08-37
Yotsuya Kwaidan 8-10-66 (Also see: Illusion of Blood)
Yotz' Im Kavua 5-30-79
You (See: Du)
You and Me (See: Ti i J)
You and Me 6-08-38
You Are Guilty 10-25-23
You Are in Danger 11-08-23
You Are Like a Wild Chrysanthemum (See: Nogiku no Gotoki Kimi
    Nariki)
You Are My Joy (See: Du Bist Mein Glueck)
You Are My Love (See: Mi Amor Eres Tu)
You Are Not Alone (See: Du Er Ikke Alene)
You Are the Venom (See: Toi le Venom)
You Are the Woman That Everybody Loves 4-24-29
You Are the World for Me (See: Du Bist die Welt Fuer Mich)
You Are Weighed But Found Lacking (See: Tinimbang Ka Nguni't
    Kulang)
You Are What You Eat 9-04-68
You Belong to Me 9-18-34
You Belong to Me 10-29-41
You Better Watch Out 12-03-80
You Came Along 7-04-45
You Can Talk Now (See: Ustedes Tienen La Palabra)
You Can't Beat Love 7-07-37
You Can't Beat the Irish 5-07-52
You Can't Beat the Law 4-04-28 and 5-09-28
You Can't Believe Everything 7-12-18
You Can't Buy Everything 2-06-34
You Can't Buy Luck 5-19-37
You Can't Cheat an Honest Man 2-22-39
You Can't Escape Forever 9-23-42
You Can't Fool an Irishman 12-13-50

You Can't Fool Antoinette (See: On Ne Roule Pas Antoinette)
You Can't Fool Your Wife 4-26-23
You Can't Fool Your Wife 5-29-40
You Can't Get Away with Murder 1-25-39
You Can't Have Everything 7-28-37
You Can't Hold Back Spring (See: On N'Arrete Pas Le Printemps)
You Can't Ration Love 3-01-44
You Can't Run Away from It 10-03-56
You Can't See 'Round Corners 2-26-69
You Can't Take It with You 9-07-38
You Can't Win 'Em All 7-22-70
You Do It Cutie (See: A Toi De Faire Mignonne)
You for Me 7-23-52
You Get It! (See: Vous Pigez!)
You Gotta Stay Happy 11-03-48
You Have to Run Fast 8-23-61
You Know What Sailors Are 2-17-54
You Light Up My Life 8-10-77
You Live and Learn 9-08-37
You Made Me Love You 8-15-33; 6-05-34; and 7-24-34
You Make Me Crazy (See: Tu Me Enloqueces)
You May Be Next 3-04-36
You Must Be Joking 8-11-65
You Must Choose Life (See: Waehle das Leben)
You Never Can Tell 10-08-20
You Never Can Tell 8-29-51
You Never Know Women 7-28-26
You Never Know Your Luck 11-14-19
You Never Saw Such a Girl 3-14-19
You Only Live Once 2-03-37
You Only Live Twice 6-14-67
You Said a Mouthful 11-22-32
You Were a Prophet, My Dear (See: Profeta Voltal Szivem)
You Were Meant for Me 1-21-48
You Were Never Lovelier 10-07-42
You Will Be a Duchess (See: Tu Seras Duchesse)
You Will Be My Husband (See: Maga Lesz a Ferjem)
You Will Be My Wife (See: Vous Serez Ma Femme)
You Will Be Terribly Nice (See: Tu Seras Terriblement Gentille)
You Will Reap the Tempest (See: Tu Moisonnera la Tempete)
You Will Remember 1-01-41
You Won't Have Alsace-Lorraine (See: Vous N'Aurez Pas L'Alsace
    et La Lorraine)
You'd Be Surprised 9-29-26
You'd Be Surprised 5-14-30
You'll Find Out 11-20-40
You'll Like My Mother 10-11-72
You'll Never Get Rich 9-24-41
Young America 7-07-22
Young America 5-10-32
Young America 1-07-42
Young Americans 9-06-67
Young and Beautiful 9-25-34
Young and Beautiful Ones, The (See: Jovenes y Bellas)
Young and Dangerous 10-16-57
Young and Healthy As a Rose (See: Mlad I Zdrav Kao Ruza)
Young and Innocent 12-08-37
Young and the Brave, The 5-15-63
Young and the Guilty, The 3-26-58
Young and Wild 3-26-58
Young and Willing 2-10-43
Young Animals, The 9-25-68
Young Aphrodites 7-03-63
Young As You Feel 8-11-31
Young As You Feel 3-06-40
Young at Heart 12-15-64
Young Attila (See: Giovane Attila, Il)
Young Bess 4-29-53
Young Bill Hickok 10-02-40
Young Billy Young 9-10-69
Young Blood 1-24-33
Young Bride 4-19-32
Young Buffalo Bill 5-01-40
Young Captives 2-11-59
Young Cassidy 3-03-65
Young Chopin 12-31-52
Young Couple, A (See: Jeune Couple, Un)
Young Cycle Girls, The 1-24-79
Young Daniel Boone 3-01-50
Young Desire 7-30-30
Young Diana 9-01-22
Young Dillinger 6-16-65
Young Dr. Kildare 10-19-38
Young Doctors, The 8-23-61
Young Donovan's Kid 5-27-31
Young Don't Cry, The 7-24-57
Young Dynamite 12-15-37
Young Eagles 3-26-30

Young Forest 12-04-35
Young Frankenstein 12-18-74
Young Fugitives 7-20-38
Young Fury 2-03-65
Young Girls of Rochefort, The (See: Demoiselles de Rochefort,
    Les)
Young Girl's Troubles, A (See: Kris)
Young Guard, The 12-28-49
Young Guns, The 8-22-56
Young Guns of Texas 11-07-62
Young Husbands (See: Giovani Mariti)
Young Ideas 7-23-24
Young Ideas 8-04-43
Young in Heart, The 11-02-38
Young Jesse James 8-10-60
Young Ladies of Wilko, The (See: Panny Z Wilka)
Young Lady Chatterley 5-18-77
Young Lady's Fool, The 9-13-61
Young Land, The 4-22-59
Young Lions, The 3-19-58
Young Lochinvar 11-01-23
Young Lord, The (See: Junge Lord, Der)
Young Love (See: Junge Liebe or Liebelei)
Young Love 3-11-36
Young Lovers 9-01-54
Young Lovers, The 10-14-64
Young Man and Moby Dick, The (See: Mlady Muz A Bila Velryba)
Young Man of Manhattan 4-23-30
Young Man with a Horn 2-08-50
Young Man with Ideas 2-27-52
Young Master, The 2-27-80
Young Men's Fancy 8-16-39
Young Mr. Lincoln 6-07-39
Young Mr. Pitt, The 7-01-42
Young Monk, The (See: Junge Moench, Der)
Young Mrs. Winthrop 3-26-20
Young Nowheres 10-09-29
Young One, The 5-18-60 and 2-01-61
Young Ones (See: Jovenes, Los)
Young Ones, The 12-20-61
Young Ones Are Even Cold in the Summer (See: Kleine Frieren
    Auch Im Sommer)
Young People (See: Jovenes, Los)
Young People 7-17-40
Young People, The 7-21-71
Young Philadelphians, The 4-29-59
Young Pushkin 12-22-37
Young Racers, The 6-12-63
Young Rajah, The 11-10-22
Young Rebel, The (See: Joven Rebelde, El)
Young Romance 2-05-15
Young Runaways, The 9-11-68
Young Sanchez 4-15-64
Young Savages, The 4-26-61
Young Sinner, The (See: Junge Suenderin, Die)
Young Sinner, The 6-09-65
Young Sinners 5-13-31
Young Soldier, The 7-21-65
Young Stranger, The 3-20-57
Young, the Evil and the Savage, The 8-21-68
Young Tigers, The (See: Giovani Tigri, I)
Young Toerless, The (See: Junge Toerless, Der)
Young Tom Edison 2-14-40
Young Want to Live, The 7-14-65
Young Warriors, The 4-12-67
Young Whirlwind, The 10-17-28
Young Widow 2-20-46
Young Winston 7-26-72
Young Wives' Tale 6-23-54
Young Wolves, The (See: Jeunes Loups, Les)
Young Woman of Bai-Sao, The 7-24-63
Young Woodley 7-16-30 and 10-01-30
Youngblood 5-10-78
Youngblood Hawke 11-04-64
Younger Brothers, The 6-20-08
Younger Brothers, The 5-04-49
Younger Generation, The 3-20-29
Youngest Profession, The 3-03-43
Youngsters (See: Petits, Les)
Your Best Friend 4-07-22
Your Cheatin' Heart 11-04-64
Your Child, That Unknown Creature (See: Dein Kind, Das Unbekannte
    Wesen)
Your Contemporary (See: Tvoy Sovremenik)
Your Friend and Mine 5-17-23
Your Girl and Mine 12-18-14
Your Husband Is My Lover (See: Mister Mo, Lover Boy Ko)

Z